CALIFORNIA

AND NEVADA

MACMILLAN • USA

Macmillan Travel
A Simon & Schuster Macmillan Company
15 Columbus Circle
New York, NY 10023

MACMILLAN is a registered trademark of Macmillan, Inc.

Manufactured in the United States of America

10 9 8 7 6 5 4 3 2 1

ISSN: 1079-3577
ISBN: 0-02-860146-7

SPECIAL SALES

Bulk purchases (10+ copies) of Frommer's travel guides are available to corporations at special discounts. The Special Sales Department can produce custom editions to be used as premiums and/or for sales promotion to suit individual needs. Existing editions can be produced with custom cover imprints such as corporate logos. For more information, write to: Special Sales, Simon & Schuster, 1230 Avenue of the Americas, New York, NY 10020.

CONTENTS

INTRODUCTION

America on Wheels introduces a brand-new lodgings rating system—one that factors in the latest trends in travel preferences, technologies, and amenities and is based on thorough inspections by experienced travel professionals. We rate establishments from 1 to 5 flags, plus a unique rating we call Ultra, a special award reserved for only a handful of outstanding properties in each category. Our restaurant selections represent the ethnic diversity of today's dining scene and are categorized with symbols according to their special features, ambience, and services available. In addition, the series provides in-depth sightseeing information, including driving tours and best-of-the-state highlights.

STATE INTRODUCTIONS

Our coverage of each state in the *America on Wheels* series begins with background information that will help familiarize you with your destination. Included is a summary of the state's history and an overview of its geography, followed by practical tips that we hope you will find useful in planning your trip—what kind of weather to expect, what to pack, sources of information within the state, driving rules and regulations, and other essentials.

The "Best of the State" section provides you with a rundown of the top sights and attractions and the most popular festivals and special events around the state. It also includes infomation on spectator sports and an "A to Z" list of recreational activities available to you.

DRIVING TOURS

The scenic driving tours guide you along some of the most popular sightseeing routes. Every tour is keyed to a map and includes mileage information and precise directions, refreshment stops, and, for longer tours, recommended places to stay.

THE LISTINGS

The cities are organized alphabetically within each state. Below each city name, you'll find a map page number and map location. These refer to the color maps at the back of the book.

Types of Lodgings

Here's how we define the lodging categories used in *America on Wheels.*

Motel

A motel usually has 1 to 3 floors, and many of the guest rooms have doors facing the parking lot or outdoor corridors. A motel may only have a small, serviceable lobby and usually offers only limited services; the nearest restaurant may be down the street. A motel is most likely to be located alongside a highway or in a resort area.

Hotel

A hotel usually has 3 or more floors with elevators. It may or may not have parking, but if it does, entry to the guest rooms is likely to be through the lobby rather than directly from the parking lot. A range of lodgings is available (such as standard rooms, deluxe rooms, and suites), and a range of services is available (such as bellhops, room service, and a concierge). Many hotels have a restaurant or coffee shop open for breakfast, lunch, and dinner; they may have a cocktail lounge/bar. Recreational facilities may be available (such as a swimming pool, fitness center, and tennis courts).

Resort

A resort usually has more extensive facilities and recreational activities than a hotel, and offers 3 meals a day. The atmosphere is generally more informal than at comparable hotels.

Lodge

A lodge is essentially a small hotel in a rural, remote, or mountainous location. The atmosphere, service, and furniture may be more casual than you'd find in a regular hotel, and there may not be televisions or telephones in every guest room. The facilities usually include a coffee shop or restaurant, bar or cocktail lounge, game room, and indoor or outdoor swimming pool or hot tub. In ski areas, the lounge usually has a fireplace and facilities for storing ski gear.

Inn

An inn is a small-scale hotel or lodge, usually in an older building that may or may not have been designed for lodgings, and it is often located in interesting surroundings. An inn should have a warm, welcoming atmosphere, with a more homelike quality to its furnishings and facilities. The guest rooms may be individually decorated in a style appropriate to the inn's age and location, and the rooms may or may not have telephones, televisions, or private bathrooms. An inn usually has a lounge or sitting room for guests (with parlor games and perhaps a television) and a small dining room that may or may not be open to the public. Breakfast, however, is almost always served.

How the Lodgings Are Rated

Every hotel, motel, resort, inn, and lodge rated in this series has been subjected to a thorough hands-on inspection by our team of accomplished travel professionals. We ask the kinds of questions that readers would ask if they could inspect the rooms in advance for themselves (How good is the soundproofing? How firm is the bed? What condition are the room furnishings in?). Then all of the inspection reports are reviewed by regional editors who are experts on their territories. The top-rated properties are then rechecked by a special consultant who has been reviewing and critiquing luxury hotels around the world for almost 25 years. *Establishments are not charged to be included in our series.*

Our ratings are based on *average* guest rooms—not lavish suites or concierge floors—so they're not artificially high. Therefore, in some cases a hotel rated 4 flags may indeed have individual rooms or suites that might fall into the 5-flag category; conversely, a 4-flag

hotel may have a few rooms in its lowest price range that might otherwise warrant 3 flags.

The detailed ratings vary by category of lodgings—for example, the criteria imposed on a hotel are more rigorous than those for a motel—and some features that are considered essential in, for example, a 4-flag city hotel are relaxed for a resort that offers alternative attractions, sporting facilities, and/or beautiful and spacious grounds. Likewise, amenities such as telephones and televisions—essential in hotels and motels—are not required in inns, often the destination for lovers of peace and quiet. Instead, the criteria take into account such features as individually decorated rooms and complimentary afternoon tea.

There are, of course, several basic attributes that apply to all lodgings across the board: the cleanliness and maintenance of the building as a whole; the housekeeping in individual rooms; safety, both indoors and out; the quality and practicality of the furnishings; the quality and availability of the amenities; the caliber of the facilities; the extent and/or condition of the grounds; the ambience and cleanliness in the dining rooms; and the caliber and professionalism of the service in relation to the rates and types of lodging. Since the *America on Wheels* rating system is highly rigorous, just because a property has garnered only 1 flag does not mean it is inadequate or substandard.

WHAT THE INDIVIDUAL RATINGS MEAN

≋ 1 Flag

These properties have surpassed the minimum requirements of cleanliness, safety, convenience, and amenities; the staff may be limited, but guests can generally expect a friendly, hospitable greeting. They will have basic amenities, such as air conditioning or heating where appropriate, telephones, and televisions. The bathrooms may have only showers rather than tubs, and just 1 towel for each guest, but showers and towels must be clean. The 1-flag properties are by no means places to avoid, since they can represent exceptional value.

≋ ≋ 2 Flags

In addition to having all of the basic attributes of 1-flag lodgings, these properties will have some extra amenities, such as bellhops to help with the luggage, ice buckets in each room, and better quality furnishings. Some extra services may include availability of cribs and irons, and wake-up service.

☰ ☰ ☰ 3 Flags

These properties have all the basics noted above but also offer a more generous complement of amenities, such as firmer beds, larger desks, more drawer space, extra blankets and pillows, cable or satellite TV, alarm clock/radios, room service (although hours may be limited), and dry cleaning and/or laundry services.

☰ ☰ ☰ ☰ 4 Flags

This is the realm of luxury, with refinements in amenities, furnishings, and service—such as larger rooms, more dependable soundproofing, 2 telephones per room, in-room movies, in-room safes, thick towels, hair dryers, twice-daily maid service, turndown service, concierge service, and 24-hour room service.

☰ ☰ ☰ ☰ ☰ 5 Flags

These properties have everything the 4-flag properties have, plus a more personal level of service and more sumptuous amenities, among them bathrobes, superior linens, and blackout drapes for lightproofing. Facilities normally include a business center and fitness center. Generally speaking, guests pay handsomely to stay in these properties.

ᗣ Ultra

This crème-de-la-crème rating is reserved for those rare hotels and resorts, possibly also motels and inns, that are truly outstanding in every or almost every department—places with a "Grand Hotel" presence, an almost flawless level of service, and a standard of dining equal to that of the finest restaurants.

Unrated

In the few cases where an inspector was not able to make a detailed inspection, the property is listed as "Unrated." Also, in some cases where a property was in the process of changing owners or managers, or if the property was undergoing the kind of major renovations that made formal evaluation impossible, then, again, the inspectors have listed it as "Unrated."

Types of Dining

Restaurant

A restaurant serves complete meals.

Refreshment Stop

A refreshment stop serves drinks and/or snacks only (such as an ice cream parlor, bakery, or coffee bar).

How the Restaurants Were Evaluated

All of the restaurants reviewed in this series have been through the kind of thorough inspection described for accommodations, above. Our inspectors have evaluated everything from freshness of ingredients to noise level and spacing of tables.

Unique to the *America on Wheels* series are the easy-to-read symbols that identify for you a restaurant's special features, ambience, and services. With them you can determine at a glance whether a place is a local favorite, offers exceptional value, or is "worth a splurge."

How to Read the Listings

LODGINGS

Introductory Information

The rating is followed by the establishment's name, address, neighborhood (if located in a major city), telephone numbers, and fax number (if there is one). When appropriate, you'll also find the location of the establishment, highway information with exit number, and/or more specific directions. In the resort listings, the number of acres is indicated. Also included are our inspectors' comments, which provide some description and discuss any outstanding features or special information about the establishment. If the lodging is not rated, it will be noted at the end of this section.

Rooms

The number and type of accommodations available is followed by the information on check-in/check-out times. If there is anything worth noting about rooms, whether the size or decor or furnishings, inspectors' comments will follow.

Amenities

The amenities available in the majority of the guest rooms are indicated by symbols and then a list. Because travelers usually expect air conditioning, telephones, and televisions in their guest rooms, we specifically note when those amenities are not available. If the accommodations have minibars, terraces, fireplaces, or Jacuzzis, we indicate that here.

Services

The services available are indicated by symbols and then a list. There may be a fee for some of the services. "Babysitting available" means the establishment can put you in touch with local babysitters and/or agencies. An establishment that accepts pets may nevertheless place restrictions on the types or size of pets allowed.

Facilities

The facilities available are indicated by symbols followed by a list; all are on the premises, except for cross-country and downhill skiing, which are within 10 miles. The lifeguard listed refers to a beach lifeguard, not a pool lifeguard. Our "Accessible for People With Disabilities" symbol appears where establishments claim to have guest rooms with such accessibility.

Rates

If the establishment's rates vary throughout the year, then the rates given are for the high season. The rates listed are EP (no meals included), unless otherwise noted. We'll tell you if there is a charge for an extra person to stay in a room; if children stay free, and if so, up to what age; if there are minimum stay requirements; if the rates are ever higher for special events or holidays; if AP (3 meals) or MAP (breakfast and dinner) rates are also available; and/or if special packages are available. The parking rates (if the establishment has parking) are followed by the credit card information.

Always confirm the rates when you are making your reservations, and ask about taxes and other charges, which are not included in our rates.

RESTAURANTS

Introductory Information

If a restaurant is a local favorite, an exceptional value, or "worth a splurge," this will be noted by a special symbol at the beginning of the listing. Then the establishment's name, address, neighborhood (if located in a major city), and telephone number are listed. Next comes the location of the establishment, highway information with exit number, and/or more specific directions, as appropriate. The types of cuisine are followed by our inspectors' comments on everything from decor to menu highlights.

The "FYI" Heading

After the reservations policy, we tell you if there is live entertainment, a children's menu, a dress code, and a no-smoking policy for the entire restaurant. If the restaurant does not offer a full bar, we tell you what the liquor policy is.

Hours of Operation

Under the "Open" heading, "HS" indicates that the hours listed are for the high season only; otherwise, the hours listed are year-round. It's a good idea to call ahead to confirm the hours of operation, especially in the off-season.

Prices

Prices given are for the dinner main courses (unless otherwise noted). If a prix-fixe dinner is offered during all of the dinner hours, that price is listed here, too. This section ends with credit card information, followed by any appropriate symbol(s).

Accessibility for People With Disabilities

The accessibility symbol appears in listings where the restaurant has a level entrance or an access ramp, a doorway at least 36 inches wide, and restrooms that are on the same floor as the dining room, with doorways at least 32 inches wide and properly outfitted stalls.

ATTRACTIONS

Introductory Information

The name, street address, neighborhood (if located in a major city), and telephone number are followed by a brief rundown of the attraction's high points and key attributes—so you can quickly determine if it's worth a full day of exploration or just a brief detour.

Hours of Operation & Admission

Service information includes hours of operation and the cost of admission. The cost is indicated by 1 to 4 dollar signs ($, $$, $$$, or $$$$) or by "Free," if no fee is charged. It's a good idea to call ahead to confirm the hours.

DISABLED TRAVELER INFORMATION

The Americans with Disabilities Act (ADA) of 1990 required that all public facilities and commercial establishments be made accessible to disabled persons by January 26, 1992. Any property opened after January 26, 1993, must be built in accordance with the ADA Accessible Guidelines. Note, however, that not all establishments have completed their renovations to conform with the law; be sure to call ahead to determine if your specific needs can be met.

TAXES

State and city taxes vary widely and are not included in the prices in this book. Always ask about the taxes when you are making your reservations. State sales tax is given under "Essentials" in the introduction to each state.

A DISCLAIMER

Readers are advised that prices fluctuate in the course of time and travel information changes under the impact of the varied and volatile factors that affect the travel industry. The publisher cannot be held responsible for the experiences of readers while traveling. Readers are invited to send ideas, comments, and suggestions for future editions to: *America on Wheels,* Macmillan Travel, 15 Columbus Circle, New York, NY 10023.

ABBREVIATIONS

A/C	air conditioning
AP	American Plan (rates include breakfast, lunch, and dinner)
avail	available
BB	Bed-and-Breakfast Plan (rates include full breakfast)
bldg	building
CC	credit cards
CI	check-in time
CO	check-out time
CP	Continental Plan (rates include continental breakfast)
ctges	cottages
ctr	center
D	double
effic	efficiencies
evnts	events
HS	high season
info	information
int'l	international
ltd	limited
maj	major
MAP	Modified American Plan (rates include breakfast and dinner)
Mem Day	Memorial Day
mi	miles
min	minimum
MM	mile marker
PF	prix fixe (a fixed-price meal)
pking	parking
refrig	refrigerator
rms	rooms
rsts	restaurants
S	single
satel	satellite
spec	special
stes	suites
svce	service
tel	telephone
univ	university
w/	with
wknds	weekends

TOLL-FREE NUMBERS

The following toll-free telephone numbers were accurate at press time; *America on Wheels* cannot be held responsible for any number that has changed. The "TDD" numbers are answered by a telecommunications service for the deaf and hard-of-hearing. Be sure to dial "1" before each number.

Lodgings

Best Western International, Inc
(800) 528-1234 Continental USA and Canada
(800) 528-2222 TDD

Budgetel Inns
(800) 4-BUDGET Continental USA and Canada

Budget Host
(800) BUD-HOST Continental USA

Clarion Hotels
(800) CLARION Continental USA and Canada
(800) 228-3323 TDD

Comfort Inns
(800) 228-5150 Continental USA and Canada
(800) 228-3323 TDD

Courtyard by Marriott
(800) 321-2211 Continental USA and Canada
(800) 228-7014 TDD

Days Inn
(800) 325-2525 Continental USA and Canada
(800) 325-3297 TDD

Doubletree Hotels
(800) 222-TREE Continental USA

Drury Inn
(800) 325-8300 Continental USA and Canada
(800) 325-0583 TDD

Econo Lodges
(800) 446-6900 Continental USA and Canada
(800) 228-3323 TDD

Embassy Suites
(800) 362-2779 Continental USA and Canada

Exel Inns of America
(800) 356-8013 Continental USA and Canada

Fairfield Inn by Marriott
(800) 228-2800 Continental USA and Canada
(800) 228-7014 TDD

Fairmont Hotels
(800) 527-4727 Continental USA

Forte Hotels
(800) 225-5843 Continental USA and Canada

Four Seasons Hotels
(800) 332-3442 Continental USA
(800) 268-6282 Canada

Friendship Inns
(800) 453-4511 Continental USA
(800) 228-3323 TDD

Guest Quarters Suites
(800) 424-2900 Continental USA

Hampton Inn
(800) HAMPTON Continental USA and Canada

Hilton Hotels Corporation
(800) HILTONS Continental USA and Canada
(800) 368-1133 TDD

Holiday Inn
(800) HOLIDAY Continental USA and Canada
(800) 238-5544 TDD

Howard Johnson
(800) 654-2000 Continental USA and Canada
(800) 654-8442 TDD

Hyatt Hotels and Resorts
(800) 228-9000 Continental USA and Canada
(800) 228-9548 TDD

Inns of America
(800) 826-0778 Continental USA and Canada

Intercontinental Hotels
(800) 327-0200 Continental USA and Canada

ITT Sheraton
(800) 325-3535 Continental USA and Canada
(800) 325-1717 TDD

La Quinta Motor Inns, Inc
(800) 531-5900 Continental USA and Canada
(800) 426-3101 TDD

Loews Hotels
(800) 223-0888 Continental USA and Canada

Marriott Hotels
(800) 228-9290 Continental USA and Canada
(800) 228-7014 TDD

Master Hosts Inns
(800) 251-1962 Continental USA and Canada

Meridien
(800) 543-4300 Continental USA and Canada

Omni Hotels
(800) 843-6664 Continental USA and Canada

Park Inns International
(800) 437-PARK Continental USA and Canada

Quality Inns
(800) 228-5151 Continental USA and Canada
(800) 228-3323 TDD

Radisson Hotels International
(800) 333-3333 Continental USA and Canada

Ramada
(800) 2-RAMADA Continental USA and Canada
(800) 228-3232 TDD

Red Carpet Inns
(800) 251-1962 Continental USA and Canada

Red Lion Hotels and Inns
(800) 547-8010 Continental USA and Canada

Red Roof Inns
(800) 843-7663 Continental USA and Canada
(800) 843-9999

Residence Inn by Marriott
(800) 331-3131 Continental USA and Canada
(800) 228-7014 TDD

Resinter
(800) 221-4542 Continental USA and Canada

Ritz-Carlton
(800) 241-3333 Continental USA and Canada

Rodeway Inns
(800) 228-2000 Continental USA and Canada
(800) 228-3323 TDD

Scottish Inns
(800) 251-1962 Continental USA and Canada

Shilo Inns
(800) 222-2244 Continental USA and Canada

Signature Inns
(800) 822-5252 Continental USA and Canada

Stouffer Renaissance Hotels International
(800) HOTELS-1 Continental USA and Canada
(800) 833-4747 TDD

Super 8 Motels
(800) 800-8000 Continental USA and Canada
(800) 533-6634 TDD

Susse Chalet Motor Lodges & Inns
(800) 258-1980 Continental USA and Canada

Travelodge
(800) 255-3050 Continental USA and Canada

Vagabond Hotels Inc.
(800) 522-1555 Continental USA and Canada

Westin Hotels and Resorts
(800) 228-3000 Continental USA and Canada
(800) 254-5440 TDD

Wyndham Hotels and Resorts
(800) 822-4200 Continental USA and Canada

Car Rental Agencies

Advantage Rent-A-Car
(800) 777-5500 Continental USA and Canada

Airways Rent A Car
(800) 952-9200 Continental USA

Alamo Rent A Car
(800) 327-9633 Continental USA and Canada

Allstate Car Rental
(800) 634-6186 Continental USA and Canada

Avis
(800) 331-1212 Continental USA and Canada

Budget Rent A Car
(800) 527-0700 Continental USA and Canada

Dollar Rent A Car
(800) 800-4000 Continental USA and Canada

Enterprise Rent-A-Car
(800) 325-8007 Continental USA and Canada

Hertz
(800) 654-3131 Continental USA

National Car Rental
(800) CAR-RENT Continental USA and Canada

Payless Car Rental
(800) PAYLESS Continental USA and Canada

Rent-A-Wreck
(800) 535-1391 Continental USA

Sears Rent A Car
(800) 527-0770 Continental USA and Canada

Thrifty Rent-A-Car
(800) 367-2277 Continental USA

U-Save Auto Rental of America
(800) 272-USAV Continental USA and Canada

Value Rent-A-Car
(800) 327-2501 Continental USA and Canada

Airlines

American Airlines
(800) 433-7300 Continental USA and Canada

Canadian Airlines International
(800) 426-7000 Continental USA
(800) 665-1177 Canada

Continental Airlines
(800) 525-0280 Continental USA
(800) 421-2456 Canada

Delta Air Lines
(800) 221-1212 Continental USA

Northwest Airlines
(800) 225-2525 Continental USA and Canada

Southwest Airlines
(800) 435-9792 Continental USA and Canada

Trans World Airlines
(800) 221-2000 Continental USA

United Airlines
(800) 241-6522 Continental USA and Canada

USAir
(800) 428-4322 Continental USA and Canada

Train

Amtrak
(800) USA-RAIL Continental USA

Bus

Greyhound
(800) 231-2222 Continental USA

THE TOP-RATED LODGINGS

Ultra

Hotel Bel-Air, Los Angeles
Regent Beverly Wilshire, Beverly Hills
The Sherman House, San Francisco

5 Flags

The Peninsula Beverly Hills
Ritz-Carlton Laguna Niguel, Dana Point

4 Flags

CALIFORNIA

Albion River Inn, Albion
Auberge du Soleil, Rutherford
Bel Age Hotel, West Hollywood
Beverly Hilton, Beverly Hills
Beverly Prescott Hotel, Beverly Hills
Blue Lantern Inn, Dana Point
Bodega Bay Lodge Best Western
Campton Place Hotel, San Francisco
Casa Madrona Hotel, Sausalito
Century Plaza Hotel & Tower, Los Angeles
Chateau du Sureau, Oakhurst
Claremont Resort, Spa & Tennis Club, Oakland
The Cliffs at Shell Beach–Oceanfront Resort Hotel,
    Shell Beach
Country Side Suites, Ontario
Crown Sterling Suites, El Segundo
Dana Point Resort, Dana Point
The Donatello, San Francisco
Doubletree Hotel Pasadena at Plaza las Fuentes
Eiler's Inn, Laguna Beach
El Enchanto Hotel & Garden Villas, Santa Barbara
Fairmont Hotel, San Jose
Fountain Grove Inn, Santa Rosa
Four Seasons Biltmore, Santa Barbara
Four Seasons Clift San Francisco
Four Seasons Hotel, Los Angeles
Four Seasons Hotel, Newport Beach
Furnace Creek Inn Resort, Death Valley
Galleria Park Hotel, San Francisco
Grant Hyatt San Francisco on Union Square

Green Gables Inn, Pacific Grove
Harbor House, Elk
Heritage House, Little River
Hotel Carter and Carter House, Eureka
Hotel De Anza, San Jose
Hotel del Coronado, Coronado
Hotel Inter-Continental Los Angeles at
    California Plaza
Hotel Majestic, San Francisco
Hotel Nikko San Francisco
Hotel Sainte Claire, San Jose
Hotel Sofitel, Redwood City
Huntington Hotel, San Francisco
Hyatt Grand Champions, Indian Wells
Hyatt Regency La Jolla
Hyatt Regency Los Angeles
Hyatt Regency Sacramento
Hyatt Regency San Diego
Hyatt Regency Suites Palm Springs
Inn at Depot Hill, Capitola-by-the-Sea
Inn at Rancho Santa Fe, Rancho Santa Fe
The Inn at Saratoga
Inn at Spanish Bay, Pebble Beach
Inn at the Opera, San Francisco
Janet Kay's, Big Bear Lake
JW Marriott Hotel at Century City, Los Angeles
La Casa del Zorro, Borrego Springs
La Costa Resort and Spa, Carlsbad
La Maida House, North Hollywood
La Quinta Resort & Club, La Quinta

La Residence Country Inn, Napa
La Valencia Hotel, La Jolla
Lafayette Park Hotel, Lafayette
Le Meridien San Diego at Coronado
Lodge at Pebble Beach
Loews Coronado Bay Resort, Coronado
Los Angeles Renaissance Hotel
Los Olivos Grand Hotel
Madrona Manor, Healdsburg
Malibu Beach Inn, Malibu
Mandarin Oriental, San Francisco
Mark Hopkins Inter-Continental San Francisco
Marriott's Desert Springs, Palm Desert
Marriott's Rancho Las Palmas Resort & Country
   Club, Rancho Mirage
Martine Inn, Pacific Grove
Meadowood Resort Hotel, St Helena
New Otani Hotel and Garden, Los Angeles
Newport Beach Marriott Hotel & Tennis Club
Noyo River Lodge, Fort Bragg
Ojai Valley Inn, Ojai
Old Monterey Inn, Monterey
The Pan Pacific Hotel-San Francisco
Park Hyatt San Francisco
Pelican Cove Inn, Carlsbad
Post Ranch Inn, Big Sur
Prescott Hotel, San Francisco
Quail Lodge Resort & Golf Club, Carmel Valley
Radisson Hotel Sacramento
Rancho Caymus, Rutherford
Rancho Valencia Resort, Rancho Santa Fe
Red Lion Hotel-Glendale
Resort at Squaw Creek, Olympic Valley
Ritz-Carlton Huntington Hotel, Pasadena
Ritz-Carlton Marina del Ray
Ritz-Carlton Rancho Mirage
Ritz-Carlton San Francisco

San Ysidro Ranch, Montecito
Santa Clara Marriott
Seacliff, Gualala
Seal Beach Inn & Gardens, Seal Beach
Seal Cove Inn, Moss Beach
Seven Gables Inn, Pacific Grove
Sheraton Grande Torrey Pines, La Jolla
Sheraton Grande, Los Angeles
Sheraton Los Angeles Airport
Sheraton Miramar Hotel, Santa Monica
Sheraton Universal, Universal City
Shutters on the Beach, Santa Monica
Simpson House Inn, Santa Barbara
Sonoma Mission Inn & Spa
Stanford Inn by the Sea-Big River Lodge,
   Mendocino
Stanford Park Hotel, Menlo Park
Sterling Hotel, Sacramento
Stevenswood Lodge, Little River
Stouffer Esmeralda Resort, Indian Wells
Stouffer Stanford Court Hotel, San Francisco
Sundance Villas, Palm Springs
Sunset Marquis Hotel & Villas, West Hollywood
Surf and Sand Hotel, Laguna Beach
Timberhill Ranch, Cazadero
Universal City Hilton
Ventana, Big Sur
Vintners Inn, Santa Rosa
Waterfront Plaza Hotel, Oakland
Westgate Hotel, San Diego
Westin Hotel, Millbrae
Westin Mission Hills Resort, Rancho Mirage
Westin South Coast Plaza, Costa Mesa
Westwood Marquis Hotel and Gardens,
   Los Angeles
Whale Watch Inn, Gualala
Wyndham Checkers Hotel Los Angeles

NEVADA
Bally's Las Vegas
Caesars Palace, Las Vegas
Harrah's Casino Hotel Lake Tahoe, Stateline
Harvey's Resort Hotel & Casino, Stateline
Las Vegas Hilton

CALIFORNIA

A WORLD IN ONE STATE

The "promised land" is how generations have viewed California. Its great natural beauty, enviable climate, promise of boundless wealth, and carefree, can-do mentality have lured millions west in pursuit of the American dream, if only for a few days' or weeks' vacation. No one goes home disappointed, though many people are surprised to find that there's far more to California than they thought there was.

The state is large enough and diverse enough that half the vacationers in California are Californians seeing a California other than their own. The state's dozen separate regions are as distinct one from the other as the nations of Europe—with equally distinctive scenery.

Within the state's borders are the Lower 48's lowest point—Death Valley—and its highest point—Mt Whitney, which anchors America's longest mountain chain, wherein you'll find the nation's tallest waterfall (Yosemite Falls). California's native giant sequoia is the world's largest tree; its coast redwood is the tallest. The state even has the world's oldest living thing—the bristlecone pine tree, which lives more than 5,000 years at a crisp altitude of 11,000 feet. In California, snowcapped mountains loom over parched deserts. Lava landscapes border lush valleys. Even the 1,245-mile coastline baffles with its changing moods: While the southern quarter has golden beaches of Hollywood lore, farther north breakers crash ashore and tear at windswept headlands.

California is also a convergence of climatic extremes, a fact that takes many visitors to San Francisco by surprise (they're the ones shivering in shorts in summer, when the cool fogs roll in). In winter you can sunbathe in San Diego while skiers are making the most of fresh snow in the mountains.

The state, with the largest population in the United States, is an economic powerhouse; if cast adrift, it would have the world's 7th largest economy. It leads the nation, for example, in the bounty of its agricultural products. And high-tech Silicon Valley is aptly named: The birthplace of microcomputers still leads the way into the future.

Californians like to flaunt their wealth—not ostentatiously, but in a casual, cosmopolitan lifestyle that makes the most of the pleasures the state has to offer. California is a haven for boaters, surfers, hikers, bikers, horseback riders, and other lovers of sport and the great outdoors. And Californians have parlayed their love of the good life into a sophisticated style—even a "state of mind"—that is reflected in everything from fashion and architecture to California nouvelle cuisine.

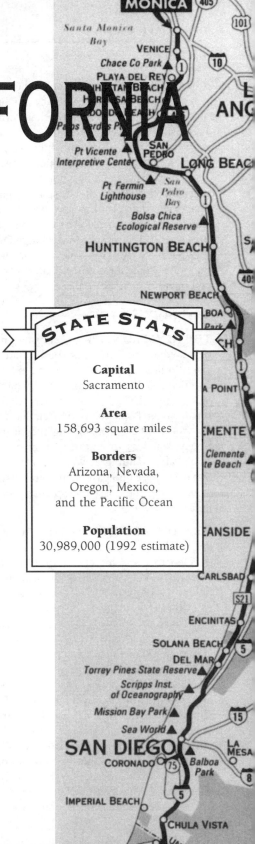

STATE STATS

Capital
Sacramento

Area
158,693 square miles

Borders
Arizona, Nevada,
Oregon, Mexico,
and the Pacific Ocean

Population
30,989,000 (1992 estimate)

Even the people revel in being different, whether it's a matter of personal idiosyncrasy or ethnic and cultural diversity. The cities, too, have their own character. San Francisco, for example, compact and stylish, bounded by water and bristling with hills, is not cut from the same cloth as Los Angeles, which sprawls nondescriptly, its parts connected by a network of freeways. Add to these facets the fact that despite its glitzy, up-to-date image, the state also has a historic dimension—everything from prehistoric fossils to movie-star footprints is preserved here, from the Wells Fargo Overland Stage to the Queen Mary. The state may not have everything, but one thing is sure. When you've seen one California, you haven't seen them all.

A Brief History

THE NEW FRONTIER   California's recorded history began when the Portuguese-born sailor Juan Rodríguez Cabrillo landed at San Diego on September 24, 1542, and planted the flag of Spain. No "white" face was seen again until 1579, when Francis Drake stopped for repairs near Point Reyes and claimed "Nova Albion" for Queen Elizabeth I of England. It was the Spanish legacy that was to endure, however, and fittingly, in 1602, after landing at what he christened Monterey, Sebastian Vizcaino gave many other bays and promontories along the coast the Spanish names we still use today.

MISSION ACCOMPLISHED   The area languished for another 140 years before King Charles of Spain decided to press his claim. In 1742, he ordered the construction of a chain of Franciscan missions, ostensibly for the purpose of converting the Native Americans to Catholicism. The 21 missions, which stretch from San Diego to Sonoma, were completed in 1823 and connected by a dirt road—El Camino Real—that closely parallels today's US 101.

Many missions brutally exploited the Native American labor and grew into vast, wealthy estates. Perhaps 500,000 Indians lived widely scattered throughout the region when the Spanish arrived; within 2 centuries they were almost extinct, decimated by European diseases, the whip, and the musket ball.

Remarkably, in all this time no European sailors had come upon San Francisco Bay—it was a Spanish expedition seeking an overland route to Monterey that first saw the magnificent natural harbor, in 1769. That

same year, Gaspar de Portola founded San Diego, the first permanent settlement in California and one of four military *presidios* built to deter the intrusion of rival colonial powers. Small towns, or *pueblos,* followed: San Jose in 1777; Los Angeles in 1781.

THE RUSSIANS ARE COMING   Although the region was neglected by colonial Spain for the first half of the 19th century, colonists were arriving from other quarters. In 1812, Russian fur trappers had descended from Alaska and established Fort Ross, north of San Francisco. French trappers, too, made incursions, as did the English, emboldened in their weakened claims on North America by the Vancouver-based Hudson Bay Company.

In 1821, when Mexico gained independence from Spain, California declared its allegiance to Mexico. The region quickly fell under the influence of a few *Californios,* Mexican ranchers who grew immensely rich rearing cattle on vast land grants. When Mexico secularized the missions in 1834, the *rancheros* seized these lands, too, and established near-feudal fiefdoms over the Indians.

UP WITH THE STARS 'N' STRIPES   The Mexicans forbid US citizens from settling in California. The early 1800s, however, saw many Americans arrive, some after a 3-month journey by sea, others after having

---

❦ *Fun Facts* ❧

• *One of every 7 Americans lives in California.*

• *The grizzly bear, the official state animal, is actually extinct in California.*

• *The 275-foot-tall General Sherman giant sequoia tree in Sequoia National Park adds enough wood growth annually to make a 60-foot-tall tree of average proportions.*

• *At any given time, there are more cars on southern California's highways than in any other area of the country.*

• *Nearly every salad eaten in the United States contains at least one thing grown in California.*

• *San Francisco's cable cars are the country's only moving National Landmark.*

blazed overland trails in wagon trains. The US government fostered the migration, inspired by the expansionist doctrine of Manifest Destiny—a belief that the United States was almost duty-bound to acquire the West.

The United States attempted to purchase California from Mexico in 1846, prompting a band of zealous American settlers to hoist the Bear Flag standard in Sonoma and to declare California an independent republic. The standard, carrying the words "California Republic," is today the official state flag. The outbreak of the Mexican-American War ended the republic 23 days later when Commodore John Sloat raised the US standard in Monterey. America's acquisition of California was ratified on February 2, 1848.

GOLD!   Only 9 days before that, a more momentous event had occurred. On January 24, James Marshall, a sawmill foreman, had found flakes of gold on the banks of the South Fork of the American River. The leaked word led to a flood of would-be millionaires, and California became truly an El Dorado in December, when President Polk exhibited 230 ounces of gold to Congress. The news reverberated around the world, sparking the California Gold Rush. Within 3 years, California's population soared from fewer than 10,000 people to more than 100,000. San Francisco Bay was choked by sailing vessels that dropped anchor and were promptly abandoned by gold-hungry crews. Lands lay idle as farmers and laborers took to the Sierra foothills.

Prices soared and many farmers and merchants—and even a few miners—grew fabulously rich on the trade that transformed inland river ports such as Sacramento and Stockton into major cities. Many of the new arrivals even brought a degree of culture to the frontier: Operatic and literary societies sprouted alongside gambling halls and bordellos.

Money means might; the gold boom hastened statehood in 1850, and lit the development fuse. The wineries of the Napa and Sonoma Valleys, for example, were established in the late 1850s. And many towns in northern California are still wedded to the logging industry that grew up to supply lumber to the mines.

BOOM & BUST   Within 15 years the gold boom was over. While Civil War battles raged to the east, Californians busied themselves completing the transcontinental railroad, finished in 1869 with the help of large numbers of Irish and Chinese laborers. Mexican labor-ers helped turn the northern Central Valley into a breadbasket. And industries began to flourish in the cities.

By 1874, when the State Capitol building—a copy of the one in Washington, DC—was completed in Sacramento, California had come of age as a self-reliant, dynamic entity.

COMING ON STRONG   Southern California had lagged behind until now: Its population was no more than 10,000 in 1875, the year the Santa Fe railroad reached Los Angeles. Settlers taking advantage of $1 fares from Kansas City soon became the first wave in a migratory trend that has barely faltered. The railroad opened southern California to trade. Oranges were planted and quickly took to the sunshine and fertile soil, launching San Diego and Los Angeles to prominence as shipping ports.

The oil discovered beneath Los Angeles in 1892 helped to fuel the automobile and, later, the aeronautical industries, which grew rapidly after the turn of the century. When the motion picture industry moved here in the first decade of the 20th century (after William Selig filmed *The Count of Monte Cristo* in Los Angeles in 1907), the glamorous lifestyle of the movie stars and the all-year pleasant climate that served as their backdrop boosted southern California's popularity even further. In response, a whole generation packed its bags, said goodbye to the snow storms and dust bowls, and headed west in search of the good life of the Golden State.

A CLOSER LOOK
Geography

California is the 3rd-largest state (only Alaska and Texas are bigger). Pushed up against the **Pacific Ocean,** its coast extends north in a series of sweeping beaches, bays, and soaring headlands for over 1,200 miles from Mexico to the Oregon border. A series of mountain chains—the forested **Coast Ranges**—lie just inland, paralleling almost the entire coastline. Most of the state's population lives on the relatively narrow strip of land between these mountains and the ocean—a questionable location, since it is subject to the ever-present jerks and upheavals of a thousand seismic fault lines.

At the southwestern corner of the state sits **San**

DRIVING DISTANCES:

Los Angeles

96 miles SW of Santa Barbara
103 miles W of Palm Springs
120 miles NW of San Diego
265 miles SW of Las Vegas, NV
332 miles SE of Monterey
379 miles SE of San Francisco
383 miles SE of Sacramento
659 miles SE of Eureka

San Francisco

87 miles SW of Sacramento
115 miles NW of Monterey
227 miles SW of Reno, NV
278 miles SE of Eureka
321 miles NW of Santa Barbara
379 miles NW of Los Angeles
548 miles NW of San Diego
577 miles NW of Las Vegas, NV

Sacramento

87 miles NE of San Francisco
134 miles SW of Reno, NV
185 miles NE of Monterey
304 miles SW of Eureka
383 miles NW of Los Angeles
391 miles NE of Santa Barbara
484 miles NW of Palm Springs
557 miles NW of Las Vegas, NV

Diego. This pretty naval town with a vital Mexican community has Spanish roots dating back to 1769, when a mission, which still stands, was built. From here, you can make a pilgrimage north along El Camino Real, the mission trail stretching from San Diego to Sonoma. **Los Angeles,** the nation's 2nd-largest city, dominates southern California beneath its pall of smog. Much of the city sprawls across miles of flat, uneventful terrain, marked by monotonous housing developments and unending strip malls and crisscrossed by an amazing number of freeways. Of course, Los Angeles is also a magnetic and fashionable city that is home to the world's most important film industry, world-class restaurants, high-class shopping, beaches, and a variety of attractions.

The **Central Coast** displays California's natural drama at its best. North of the seaside resort of Santa Barbara, Calif 1 dips and careens along Big Sur, with the sea a thousand feet below. Inland, grapes and other fruits and vegetables grow sheltered from seasonal fogs. Here you'll find **Monterey,** with its venerable fishing wharfs and superb aquarium; and **Carmel,** with historic charm and art galleries.

San Francisco anchors the Bay Area and combines the best qualities of the world's great cities. "The City" can boast of its Chinatown, Golden Gate Park, sky-high financial district, Union Square for shopping, Alcatraz, and gabled, bay-windowed Victorian houses that survived the 1906 quake. It even has the nation's only moving National Landmark—its historic cable cars—museums galore, and more restaurants per capita than any other city on earth. Across the Bay, **Berkeley** is famed for its university and zany living; **Oakland** has a fabulous museum and an inner-city tidal lake that is the world's largest and was also America's first nature reserve.

Cross the Golden Gate Bridge and you'll be surrounded by the extraordinary calm of California's romantic **North Coast.** Inland, beyond the artist colony–resort of Sausalito, are the Napa and Sonoma Valleys—wine regions par excellence. Along the coast are Point Reyes National Seashore, Bodega Bay, delicately beautiful beaches, and rugged promontories that lead the way to **Mendocino,** one of several New England–style villages where writers and artists rub shoulders with fishermen, ranchers, and lumberjacks. Farther north, Eureka and Ferndale are repositories of Victorian grandeur, and pockets of coast redwood spiral above the fogbound landscape.

Northeast California is a rugged, less-traveled region unfamiliar to most Californians. Two active volcanoes—snow-capped Mt Lassen (10,457 feet) and Mt Shasta (14,162 feet)—reign over a wilderness favored by hardy backpackers. Here, real cowboys still travel to the biggest rodeo in the West, and Native Americans still net leaping salmon. Lakes and hot springs provide for relaxation. Naturalist John Muir exhorted: "Climb the mountains and get their good tidings." The Pacific Crest Trail, which passes through here and ultimately reaches the Mexican border, lets you do just that.

To the south, flanking the Nevada border, are the mighty **Sierra Nevada** with, to their east, the White Mountains separated by a thin depression called the

Owens Valley. The Sierras—a massive block of granite that continues to rise 3 inches a year—run 400 miles north-to-south and soar to over 14,000 feet at Sequoia, Kings Canyon, and Yosemite National Parks. They are sheathed in the remnants of glaciers that gouged massive valleys, with resplendent waterfalls that cascade from their flanks.

Gold Country, in the Sierra Nevada foothills, rings with the echoes of the Gold Rush era. When gold was discovered in 1848, 100,000 adventurers rushed in to pan the rivers and tear down the hillsides. The only gold you're likely to see is on the autumn leaves, but the region is liberally sprinkled with quaint bed-and-breakfast inns, historic mining museums, and many of the original settlements, such as Placerville, Sutter Creek, Sonora, and colorful Nevada City.

Between the Sierra Nevada and the Coast Ranges is the **Central Valley,** a 400-mile long, 100-mile wide stretch of the richest soil on earth. **Sacramento,** the state capital, anchors the valley, which extends down the center of California. Farther south, towns such as Fresno are booming from cotton, rice, grapes, and other agricultural products of the valley.

Southeast California is the state's dry corner, sizzling hot in summer, when temperatures in **Death Valley** can top 130°F. Death Valley's 3,000 square miles encompass wind-blown sand, dry salt flats, and sere mountains. Joshua Tree National Monument and Anza-Borrego Desert State Park embody a different aspect—a living desert, palette-bright in spring. Lush **Palm Springs** boasts the largest desert palm oasis in the world. Golf courses and upscale resorts complete the picture.

Climate

The common perception that California has a Mediterranean climate characterized by sun and warmth, with rain mainly in winter, holds true for much, but not all, of the state. Climatic extremes based on elevation and distance from the ocean are dramatic.

San Diego, in the south, is generally warm and dry year-round; Los Angeles' pleasingly warm (and occasionally rainy) winters tempt sun-lovers to the beach, as do summers, which are hot and often humid. The great desert areas east of Los Angeles invite exploration November through April, when days are dry and warm but not searing as they are in summer, when 120° temperatures discourage probing.

San Francisco's maritime climate is temperate: cool to mild in winter, though never freezing, and rarely topping 70°F in summer, when fogs often roll in to keep things cool. Indeed, San Francisco can be chilly in summer (other Bay Area cities escape the fog and are correspondingly warmer). The Central Coast shares San Francisco's climate, though warming farther south. North along the coast, the fogs and rain increase and winds can be forceful.

Farther inland, the mercury soars in summer and many folks leave town for the milder temperatures of the mountains. In winter, snow settles over the Sierras and Shasta-Cascades, drawing skiers to the downhill slopes. Winter storms often lash the mountains.

AVERAGE MONTHLY TEMPERATURES (°F) & INCHES OF RAINFALL			
	Los Angeles	**San Francisco**	**San Diego**
Jan	64/2.8	56/4.0	56/1.9
Feb	64/3.0	60/3.6	57/1.5
Mar	66/1.5	64/2.6	58/1.6
Apr	69/1.0	67/1.7	61/0.8
May	72/0.2	70/0.6	64/0.2
June	75/0.1	72/0.2	66/0.1
July	80/0.0	74/0.0	70/0.0
Aug	78/0.0	74/0.0	72/0.1
Sept	80/0.2	77/0.2	70/0.1
Oct	77/0.4	71/0.6	66/0.3
Nov	74/1.5	64/2.0	61/1.3
Dec	68/2.5	58/3.7	57/1.2

Rainfall varies from 80 inches in Del Norte County in the state's northwestern corner to as low as 3 inches in Imperial County in the southeastern corner.

What to Pack

Where and when you go dictates what to pack. If traveling widely throughout the state, pack with varying climates in mind, though there's no need to overload.

Cool, cotton clothes will suffice for most of the year, though adequately warm clothing for San Francisco, the North Coast, and nights in the mountains may be required even in summer (San Francisco is often much cooler than first-time visitors expect).

Californians tend to dress casually, though upscale restaurants may have a dress code. San Francisco is more elegant by both day and night.

Pack sturdy footwear for exploring state and national parks. Bring sunscreen, too, especially if heading to the deserts or mountains (even in winter) or beaches. Don't forget your sunglasses!

Tourist Information

For a free state map and *Discover the Californias* visitors guide listing attractions, events, and accommodations, call 800/862-2543. Additional information on the state can be obtained from the **California Office of Tourism,** 801 K St, Suite 1600, Sacramento, CA 95814 (tel 916/322-2881).

Almost every town and region has its own visitors bureau or chamber of commerce, listed in the *Discover the Californias* guide. For information on northern California, contact the **San Francisco Convention and Visitors Bureau,** 201 3rd St, Suite 900, San Francisco, CA 94103 (tel 415/974-6900); or the Redwood Empire Association, 785 Market St, San Francisco, CA 94103 (tel 415/543-8334). For southern California, contact the **Greater Los Angeles Visitors and Convention Bureau,** 515 S Figueroa St, Los Angeles, CA 90071 (tel 213/624-7300); or the **San Diego Convention and Visitors Bureau,** 11 Horton Plaza, San Diego, CA 92101 (tel 619/236-1212).

For camping reservations and information on state parks, contact the **Department of Parks and Recreation,** Box 2390, Sacramento, CA 95811 (tel 916/653-6995).

Driving Rules & Regulations

Minimum age for drivers is 16 with driver's training, 18 without. Unless otherwise noted, the speed limit on California highways is 55 mph, although on many sections motorists drive well in excess of the limit. The California Highway Patrol is extremely efficient and uses aircraft to help enforce speed limits. Use of seat belts is mandatory for all passengers, and children under 4 years or under 40 pounds must be secured in an approved child safety seat. Motorcyclists must wear a helmet. Auto insurance is also mandatory; the car's registration and proof of insurance must be carried in the car. Right turns are allowed after stops at a red light.

Drunk driving laws are restrictive and strictly enforced. Note that it is illegal to carry an open container of alcohol in your car. A zero tolerance law is in effect—anyone under 21 with a measurable amount of alcohol loses his or her driver's license for a year.

Other Driving Tips: If heading into the Sierras or Shasta-Cascades for a winter ski trip, top up on antifreeze and carry snow chains for your tires; chains are mandatory in certain areas. For road conditions, call 916/445-7623 in northern California; 213/628-7623 in southern California.

Renting a Car

All of the major car rental firms have offices throughout the state. Minimum age requirements range from 19 to 25. Collision damage waiver (CDW) protection is sold separately (check with your credit card or insurance company to see if you are already covered).

- **Alamo** (tel toll free 800/327-9633)
- **Avis** (tel 800/331-1212)
- **Budget** (tel 800/527-0700)
- **Dollar** (tel 800/421-6868)
- **General** (tel 800/327-7607)
- **Hertz** (tel 800/654-3131)
- **National** (tel 800/328-4567)
- **Thrifty** (tel 800/367-2277)

Many local companies also offer car rentals at lower rates.

Essentials

Area Code: California has 13 area codes. **Southern California:** The area code for Los Angeles is 213; for the Pasadena area, 818; for Long Beach, Beverly Hills, Santa Monica, and environs, 310; for Orange County, 714; for the Riverside region, 909; for San Diego and the deserts, 619; for Bakersfield, Santa Barbara, and the south Central Coast, 805. **Central California:** for Fresno, the south Central Valley, and Yosemite, the area code is 209; for San Jose, Monterey, and the north Central Coast, 408. **Northern California:** for San Francisco, the area code is 415; for Oakland and the East Bay, 510; for Napa Valley and the North Coast, 707; for Sacramento, the north Central Valley, Lake Tahoe, and Shasta-Cascade, 916.

Emergencies: Call 911 from anywhere in the state to summon emergency police, fire, or ambulance services.

Liquor Laws: Alcoholic beverages may be purchased by anyone 21 years or older, with proof of age. Licensing hours are 6am to 2am.

Smoking: California is aggressively anti-smoking, though local ordinances vary widely. Smoking is not allowed on public transportation or in public buildings. Many restaurants maintain a small smoking section, though even many bars are nonsmoking. Many car rental companies have smoke-free cars and hotels offer smoke-free rooms.

Taxes: California's base statewide sales tax is 7.25%. Most cities and counties impose an additional tax of 0.25 to 1.25%.

Time Zone: California is in the Pacific time zone (GMT minus 8 hours), 3 hours behind New York.

BEST OF THE STATE
What to See & Do

NATIONAL PARKS California boasts 17 national parks, including national monuments, historic sites, and recreational areas totaling 4.1 million acres. In addition, 18 state forests offer recreation such as backpacking, trailbiking, and downhill skiing, as well as picnic areas and marinas. **Yosemite** is the crowning glory of California's extensive park system. Rounded granite domes, spectacular waterfalls, alpine meadows, groves of giant sequoias—all accessed by miles of hiking trails that crisscross the valley and mountainous backcountry. Yet you don't need to hike, if you don't want to—it's all visible from the car window.

Two parks side by side and administered as one, **Sequoia/Kings Canyon** challenges Yosemite with more of the same high-mountain splendor. Jewel-like lakes, high-country wilderness, and the state's largest concentration of giant sequoias, including the General Sherman Tree, the largest of *all* living things, are topped off by the Palisades Glacier, North America's most southerly.

The sear, wind-scoured landscapes of **Death Valley National Monument** feature salt lake beds and sand dunes nestled at 282 feet below sea level in the hollow of purple-tinged mountains. **Point Reyes National Seashore** has widely varied, but always dramatically wild, coastal landscapes, as well as the historic Point Reyes lighthouse, a Miwok Indian village replica, and miles of trails. And in **Redwoods National Park,** visitors can drive through a redwood tree and see the thousands of other soaring redwoods that loom over a matrix of parks preserving 113,200 acres of these 350-foot-tall giants.

STATE PARKS If you thought deserts were stark, visit **Anza-Borrego Desert State Park** in spring, when the cactus and wildflowers bloom. Hiking and biking trails lead through 1,000 square miles of spectacular beauty. **Humboldt Redwoods State Park** is a driver's delight. Scenic Calif 254 winds 33 miles along the Avenue of the Giants, and there are also hiking and riding trails leading through the 51,000-acre park. **Julian Pfeiffer Burns State Park** may be a small package, but it delivers Big Sur's spectacular coastal scenery of plunging cliffs and crashing breakers backed by mountains sheltering majestic redwoods. And for a change of pace there's **Marshall Gold Discovery Site,** at Coloma in the Gold Country, a re-created Gold Rush town at the site where it all began. The museum tells the tale.

NATURAL WONDERS Tallest, oldest, deepest, highest—the state is full of natural wonders, many of them enshrined in national or state parks. For one there's **Yosemite Valley,** a 7-mile-long, glacier-carved nave with granite walls rising almost a mile straight up, giant sequoias, and plunging waterfalls, including Yosemite Falls—the 5th-highest and, possibly, the most beautiful in the world. **Lake Tahoe,** the largest alpine lake in North America (12 miles wide and 22 miles long), plummets to depths of 1,645 feet. Hiking, biking, boating, and winter skiing make this a year-round favorite. **Mono Lake,** 5 miles south of Lee Vining, hosts the state's largest nesting colony of California gulls. Exotic tufa flowers formed by mineral deposits rise up eerily from the briny waters of this shrimp-filled lake. Off the beaten track and overlooked by tourists, the deep **underground caverns** of the Sierra foothills feature fabulous crystalline formations and lakes you can paddle across. The largest are Moaning Cavern and California Caverns, near the towns of San Andreas and Angels Camp.

FAMILY FAVORITES   Some people say California itself is a theme park. Families are offered a multitude of attractions—most concentrated in southern California. **Disneyland** bills itself as the "Happiest Place on Earth," and 12 million visitors a year seem to think so. Mickey and Minnie and other Disney characters can show you around 7 theme lands where family fun blends with fantasy and some genuinely scary rides. The newest attraction is Mickey's Toontown. **Universal Studios,** America's 3rd-largest manmade attraction, hosts 5 million visitors a year. Simulated earthquakes, the Wild West with gunfights and nose-diving stunt men, *Jaws* lunging menacingly, the *E.T.* adventure into another world, and dozens of other attractions give Disneyland a run for its money. **Knott's Berry Farm** offers 150 landscaped acres of family entertainment, including rides and specialty shops. San Diego's **Sea World** is the world's largest marine park, where you can feed the dolphins, stingrays, walruses, seals, and sea lions and watch killer whales perform. And then there's **Marine World Africa/USA** in Vallejo, northern California's answer to the San Diego Zoo and Sea World. Kids and parents and more than 2,000 animals enjoy the oceanarium and wildlife park.

BEACHES   A whole lifestyle has evolved around southern California's beaches—the inspiration of legend and song. Swimmers should respect warnings

posted by lifeguards. Farther north, where the beaches are for wading and strolling, leave the ocean to surfers.

The beach at **Oceanside,** north of San Diego, offers shallow water for swimming and waves that lure surfers for the annual World Body Surfing Championships. **Huntington Beach** is the self-proclaimed "Surfing Capital of the World." Sunbathe, play volleyball, and when the sun goes down light a barbecue in a beachside fire-ring. In **Venice** the beach is outshone by its boardwalk: a stage for bikini-clad rollerbladers, jugglers, and muscular beefcakes showing their bodies beautiful. **Stinson Beach,** north of San Francisco, is 2 golden miles long, perfect for strolling, and popular with surf fishers.

HISTORIC BUILDINGS   Contrary to popular opinion, California does have a past, and important and intriguing buildings illustrate it. Some of the best include **Hearst San Simeon,** better known as Hearst Castle, which fulfilled tycoon William Randolph Hearst's neoclassic dream. The sprawling mansion contains more than 100 rooms filled with priceless art and antiques. **Carmel Mission,** dating from 1770, represents a unique style of early Spanish architecture, while **Scotty's Castle,** a mansion built in the 1920s by desert rat "Death Valley Scotty" (Walter Scott), shows off its Spanish-Moorish style.

ARCHITECTURE   At one time or another, the Japanese, Spanish, Chinese, English, and many others have settled in California, so take your pick of architectural styles. **Chinatown,** San Francisco, whisks you to the Orient with its 24 square blocks of red-and-green pagoda roofs festooned with dragons, while **Eureka** boasts more gingerbread Victorian houses than anywhere in America; the gothic Carson Mansion lords over them all. **Solvang** has been called cute and kitschy, but everyone agrees it has charm. It was founded by Danes who erected their half-timbered houses and even a windmill in hommage to the style they'd left behind.

GARDENS   If you tire of the wilds, nature's beauty can be found growing at parks and gardens around the state. **Golden Gate Park,** in San Francisco, showcases over 1,000 acres of meadows, lakes, and flowers, including the Japanese Tea Garden, Strybing Arboretum, and the Conservatory of Flowers, the oldest botanical garden west of the Mississippi. **Mendocino**

Coast Botanical Gardens competes with the spectacular coast with almost 50 acres of colorful flowers and shrubs accessible by nature trails, while the **Los Angeles State and County Arboretum,** in Arcadia, features 130 acres of showy plants from around the globe.

WILDLIFE California boasts an amazing array of plant and animal life and offers an abundance of places to view the variety. At the **San Diego Zoo,** one of the world's finest zoos, you'll find aardvarks, zebras, and everything in between; happily, birds and beasts live in replicated natural environments, sort of a "home away from home." The **Monterey Bay Aquarium,** on historic Cannery Row, has over 6,500 creatures in various aquariums, including a 3-story, 335,000-gallon tank that provides an unmatched look at local sea life.

The largest marine preserve in the North America, the **National Marine Sanctuary** extends along California's coast from just north of the Golden Gate Bridge south past Big Sur to San Simeon in Monterey County. Humpback whales and sea otters are commonly seen, and blue whales, one of the largest creatures on earth, have even made a reappearance. The **Tule Elk State Reserve,** near Stockdale, protects this endangered native species, which was once as common throughout the Central Valley as bison were on the central plains. And **Año Nuevo State Park,** 20 miles north of Santa Cruz, protects a rookery of elephant seals. Don't get too close—the ill-tempered bulls can weigh 2,000 pounds.

Events/Festivals

Los Angeles & Southern California

- **Tournament of Roses Parade,** Pasadena. Colorful festival of flowers, music, and equestrian splendor. New Year's Day. For tickets, contact Pasadena Tournament of Roses, 391 S Orange Grove Blvd, Pasadena, CA 91184 (tel 818/449-ROSE).
- **Rose Bowl,** Pasadena. One of the country's most prestigious college football showdowns. New Year's Day. Call 818/449-ROSE for tickets.
- **Los Angeles Marathon,** Los Angeles. Mid-March. Call 310/444-5544 for information.
- **Renaissance Pleasure Faire,** San Bernadino. A re-created Elizabethan marketplace with over 2,000 costumed performers and living history displays. April–June. Call 800-52-FAIRE.
- **Cherry Festival,** Beaumont. Contact the Cherry

Festival Association, PO Box 216, Beaumont, CA 92223 (tel 714/845-9541).
- **Festival of Arts and Pageant of the Masters,** Laguna Beach. Arts and crafts fair and a pageant re-creating great works of art with live models and music. Mid-July through August. Call 714/494-1145.
- **Parade of Lights,** Long Beach. A parade of boats illuminates the Long Beach harbor. December. Call 310/435-4093.

Central California

- **Whale Watch,** Big Sur. Guided whale-watching as gray whales migrate to and from their Mexican breeding grounds. Saturdays throughout January. Call 408/667-2315.
- **Annual Dixieland Festival,** Monterey. Mid-March. Call 408/443-5260.
- **Big Sur Marathon,** Big Sur. A 26-mile marathon run on scenic Calif 1 along the Big Sur coast. April. Call 408/625-6226.
- **Calaveras County Fair and Jumping Frog Jubilee,** Angels Camp. World-famous jumping frog competition, plus professional rodeo, music, dancing. Mid-May. Call the 39th District Agricultural Association at 209/736-2561.
- **Gilroy Garlic Festival,** Gilroy. Late July. Call 408/842-1625.
- **San Luis Obispo Mozart Festival,** San Luis Obispo. Orchestra, chamber, solo, choral, and opera performances. Late July. Call 916/543-4580 for information and tickets.
- **Monterey Jazz Festival,** Monterey. Jazz greats gather for the oldest jazz festival in the United States. September. Call 408/373-3366.
- **Annual Clam Festival,** Pismo Beach. Lively family festival with clam dig. Mid-October. Call 805/773-3113.
- **Butterfly Parade,** Pacific Grove. Costumed schoolchildren welcome returning monarch butterflies. October. Call 408/646-6520.
- **Monterey Grand Prix,** Monterey. One of the oldest continuously held race events in the United States. September 8, 9, 10. Contact SCRAMP, PO Box 2078, Monterey, CA 98940 (tel 408/648-5111).

San Francisco & Northern California

- **Chinese New Year Festival and Parade,** San Francisco. Annual celebration of the Chinese lunar New Year, with colorful parade and Miss China-town USA pageant. Early Februrary. Call 415/982-3000.
- **Snowfest,** Tahoe City. The largest winter festival in the West, including fireworks, ski races, polar bear swim, and torchlight ski parade. Mid-March. Call 916/583-7625.
- **San Francisco International Film Festival,** San Francisco. Acclaimed as the most eclectic and adventurous film festival in the United States. April–May. Call 415/567-4641.
- **Carnaval,** San Francisco. Salsa, samba, and reggae. Late May. Call 415/826-1401.
- **Lesbian/Gay Freedom Day Parade and Celebration,** San Francisco. Late June. Call 415/864-FREE.
- **Western States 100-Mile Run,** Foresthill. 100-mile run in 24 hours begins in Squaw Valley and ends in Auburn. June. Contact Western States Foundation, 701 High St, Auburn, CA 95603 (tel 916/823-7282).
- **California State Fair,** Sacramento. One of the largest agricultural fairs in the country, with carnival exhibitions, horse racing, and top-name entertainment. Late August. Call 916/541-5458.
- **Sausalito Art Festival,** Sausalito. One of the West's finest outdoor art exhibitions. Early September. Call 415/332-0505.
- **Russian River Jazz Festival,** Guerneville. American and international jazz greats play beneath the redwoods. Early September. Call 707/869-3940.
- **Fleet Week,** San Francisco. Gathering of ships ranging from aircraft carriers to sailing vessels. Mid-October. Call 415/395-3923.

Spectator Sports

AUTO RACING   In northern California, auto-racing fans gather at **Sears Point** (tel 707/938-8448), in the heart of wine country, from February through September. Farther south, the Sports Car Racing Association of Monterery Peninsula sponsors a wide roster of events, including motorcycle races, at **Laguna Seca** (tel 408/373-1811), off Calif 68, near Monterey. In southern California, the choices are **Riverside International**

Raceway; San Diego's **Del Mar** racetrack; or **Long Beach,** whose streets echo with the roar of Formula One cars during the Toyota Grand Prix, held in April (tel 310/981-2600).

BASEBALL   Take your pick of no less than 5 major league teams. The **San Francisco Giants** of the National League and the **Oakland Athletics** of the American League, the Bay Area's contingent, play at Candlestick Park (tel 415/467-8000) and the Oakland Coliseum (tel 510/638-0500), respectively. Dodger Stadium (tel 213/224-1400) hosts the **Los Angeles Dodgers,** the Giants' archrivals, while in Orange County the **California Angels,** the A's divisional rival, swing their bats at Anaheim Stadium (tel 714/634-2000). Farther south, the **San Diego Padres,** the third National League team in California, play at Jack Murphy Stadium (tel 619/283-4494).

BASKETBALL   Californians are enthusiastic basketball fans during the National Basketball Association season, November through May. Undisputed best of the state, at least in past years, have been the **Los Angeles Lakers,** who play at the Great Western Forum (tel 310/673-1300). If you can't get tickets, try the **LA Clippers,** who appear at the Sports Arena (tel 213/748-8000). In northern California, the **Golden State Warriors** keep the fans on their toes at Oakland's Coliseum Arena (tel 510/638-6000).

COLLEGE FOOTBALL   California has produced some of America's finest college football teams, whose clashes culminate in the **Rose Bowl,** held each New Year's Day between the champions of the West and Midwest divisions, and in the battle between Stanford University and the Bears of UC Berkeley. A lottery is held for the Rose Bowl—send a postcard (postmarked between September 15 and October 15) to Rose Bowl Ticket Drawing, PO Box 7122, Pasadena, CA 91109 (tel 213/793-7193).

PRO FOOTBALL   Four professional football teams take to the gridiron September through late December. Northern California's sole contribution, the **San Francisco 49ers,** kick off their games at Candlestick Park (tel 415/468-2249). The **Los Angeles Rams** play at Anaheim Stadium (tel 310/277-4748); the hard-hitting **Los Angeles Raiders** are based at Memorial Coliseum (tel 310/322-5901). Farther south, the **San Diego**

Chargers take to the gridiron at Jack Murphy Stadium (tel 619/280-2111).

HOCKEY   California is home to 3 NHL teams, which play regular season games from October to April. For game information contact the **Los Angeles Kings** at the Great Western Forum (tel 310/673-6003), the **San Jose Sharks** at the San Jose Arena (tel 408/287-9200), and the **Anaheim Mighty Ducks** at Arrowhead Pond (tel 714/704-2700).

HORSE RACING   There are several horse racing venues within the compass of both Los Angeles and San Francisco. Southern Californians go to **Hollywood Park Racetrack** in Inglewood (tel 310/419-1500), home of the $1 million Hollywood Gold Cup Race, where thoroughbred races are held April to June and November to December. **Santa Anita Park** in Arcadia (tel 818/574-7223) also offers thoroughbred racing, with a season stretching from October to April. In northern California, **Golden Gate Fields** (tel 510/526-3020) has thoroughbred racing January to June, and **Bay Meadows** in San Mateo (tel 415/574-RACE) has a schedule of both thoroughbred and quarterhorse races September to January. Head for Bay Meadows (tel 415/574-RACE) in **San Mateo.**

Activities A to Z

BICYCLING   California is tailor-made for bicycle touring. The state is laced with bicycle lanes and off-road trails, and many locally based tour companies specialize in group bicycle tours designed for everyone from beginners to competitive cyclers. Popular routes include the Pacific coast, the redwood forests, Napa Valley, and Gold Country. CALTRANS, the state highway department, publishes a *Bikecentennial Tour Guide* that includes detailed route maps, typical weather conditions, grades, and safety tips. Contact CALTRANS, 6002 Folsom Blvd, Sacramento, CA 95819.

Among operators of organized tours, **Backroads** of Berkeley (tel 510/527-1555) offers a wide range of weekend and week-long guided trips with overnights in deluxe country inns and/or campgrounds. The **American Youth Hostels** also offers organized bicycle tours for all age groups. Their programs cover a wide span of regions and are generally less expensive than trips run by commercial tour companies. Contact AYH, Central California Council, PO Box 28148, San Jose, CA 95159

(tel 408/298-0670). Mammoth Mountain, on the Sierra Nevada's eastern slope, and the Tahoe region offer miles of ski runs "groomed" in summer for mountain biking. For information on guided bike tours, contact **Mammoth Mountain Bike Park** at 619/934-0606. Sports shops around Lake Tahoe and Mammoth rent mountain bikes for around $20 a day.

CAMPING   California's vast state park system has more than 17,500 campsites; most are open year-round. Many have walk-in environmental campsites. Reservations are recommended for summer, holidays, and weekends, and can be made up to 8 weeks in advance by contacting MISTIX, PO Box 85705, San Diego, CA 92138 (tel 800/444-7275). The California Travel Parks Association can provide an *RV & Camping Guide* listing locations and facilities of private campgrounds; write to ESG Mail Service, PO Box 5648, Auburn, CA 95604 (tel 916/885-1624).

CLIMBING   The Sierra Nevada have countless near-vertical granite rock faces, of which Yosemite's Half Dome and El Capitan are best known. Several top-quality climbing schools, including the Yosemite Mountaineering School (tel 209/372-1244), teach beginners the rudiments of rock climbing.

FISHING   This is the state's most popular participatory sport. A fishing license is required of all persons 16 or over for both ocean and inland waters (some public piers allow ocean fishing without a license). For information contact the California Department of Fish and Game, License and Revenue Branch, 3211 S St, Sacramento, CA 95815 (tel 916/739-3380). Public fishing piers are legion along the coast, and rock cod, salmon, and albacore are all prized catches. Rivers throughout the state—especially those in Trinity and Shasta counties—prove happy hunting grounds, particularly when the salmon and steelhead head upstream. Lakes such as Clear Lake and Lake Almanor are stocked with a wide variety of species. Guided sportfishing trips are offered from most major coastal ports.

GOLF   Hundreds of public and private golf courses throughout the state cater to golfers. San Diego, with 82 courses, is billed as "Golfland USA." Likewise, Palm Springs enjoys its moniker as "Winter Golf Capital of the World," with 85 courses and 1,435 holes. Although the Monterey Peninsula has "only" 17 courses, it claims to be *the* "Golf Capital of the World"—Pebble Beach Golf Course leads the way, with rippling oceanside fairways that challenge the world's finest players (alas, green fees here are $200 per person). Local telephone directories provide listings of golf courses.

HIKING   Hiking opportunities abound in the state and national parks. The trails system is well developed and maintained. Trail maps for individual parks are available at the ranger stations upon entry. Hardy backpackers may wish to hike the magnificent **John Muir Trail,** which follows the crest of the Sierra Nevada for 212 miles from the summit of Mt Whitney to Yosemite National Park. The **Sierra Club** offers dozens of guided backpacking trips in the Sierra Nevada, as well as in Anza-Borrego Desert State Park and the Mojave Desert. Contact the Outings Department, Sierra Club, 730 Polk St, San Francisco, CA 94109 (tel 415/923-5630).

PACK TRIPS   These offer a premier way to explore the Sierra Nevada and the remote, starkly beautiful northeastern corner of California. On some, mules or llamas carry your gear (you hike unhindered); on others, you ride horseback. For information on the Eastern Sierra High Packers Association and a list of members, contact the Bishop Chamber of Commerce, 690 N Main St, Bishop, CA 93514 (tel 619/873-8405). Rock Creek Pack Station, PO Box 248, Bishop, CA 93514 (tel 619/935-4493), welcomes participants on mustang-tracking trips into the Inyo National Forest.

SAILING   Sailing clubs and yacht charter companies line the coast from San Diego to San Francisco Bay, and both San Diego and San Francisco enjoy conditions—and settings—that are the envy of sailors worldwide. The **Olympic Circle Sailing Club** (tel 510/843-4200) in Berkeley, and the **California Sailing Academy** (tel 310/821-3433) in Marina del Rey are both recommended for certification courses and yacht rentals. Boaters also have access to more than 420 recreational lakes.

SKIING   With 15 alpine and 9 cross-country areas, Lake Tahoe offers the greatest concentration of skiing in North America; it blossomed on the world scene in 1960 when the Winter Olympics were held at Squaw Valley. Resorts here cover 19 mountains, with 400 runs. For brochures, contact Ski Lake Tahoe, PO Box 1654, Zephyr Cove, NV 89448 (tel 702/588-8598). Ski season normally runs November through May. Most popular downhill areas are:

- **Squaw Valley,** 6 miles northwest of the town of Tahoe City, on Calif 89, with 4,000 acres of slopes and 32 lifts, including a 150-passenger cable car.
- **Alpine Meadows,** 6 miles west of the town of Tahoe City, on Calif 89, with over 100 runs, and 13 lifts.
- **Heavenly,** 2 miles southeast of the town of South Lake Tahoe, with more than 85 runs and 23 lifts.
- **Kirkwood,** 30 miles S of the town of South Lake Tahoe, off Calif 88 with over 70 runs, 11 lifts, and an extensive Nordic ski center.
- **Northstar,** 12 miles northeast of the town of Tahoe City, off Calif 267, with 55 runs and 11 lifts.

Farther south, **Mammoth Lakes** (tel 619/934-2571) is equally popular and boasts miles of outstanding runs. Here, too, an expansive web of cross-country trails lure Nordic skiers into the wilderness. Cross-country skiers are also drawn to **Mt Shasta Ski Park** (tel 916/926-8600) and **Lassen Ski Park** (tel 916/529-1512) in northern California; and to Yosemite National Park, at the **Tamarack Cross-Country Ski Center** (tel 619/934-2442) and **Yosemite Cross-Country Ski School** (tel 209/372-1244).

TENNIS   One look at a roll-call of Grand Slam champions can prove that California produces its share of tennis stars. The state's idyllic climate makes tennis one of its most popular sports. Virtually every hotel worth its salt has courts, and public courts are found all over the state. Almost every city has a parks and recreation department, which you'll find listed under "Government" in local telephone directories. The following can provide information: Northern California Tennis Association (tel 510/748-7373) and Southern California Tennis Association (tel 310/208-3838).

WHALE-WATCHING   The annual December-through-April migration of the beloved California gray whale can be viewed from promontories all along the coast. Good spots are **Whale Point** in La Jolla, **Cabrillo National Monument** at Point Loma, **Chimney Rock** at Point Reyes National Seashore, **Mendocino**

Headlands State Park, and **Trinidad Head** in Humboldt County. For an eyeball-to-eyeball encounter take a guided cruise. Dolphin Charters, 1007 Leneve Place, El Cerrito, CA 94530 (tel 510/527-9622) offers half-day and longer whale-watching cruises from San Francisco Bay. In southern California, contact Pacific Sea-Fari Tours, 2803 Emerson St, San Diego, CA 92106 (tel 619/222-1414).

WHITE-WATER RAFTING   The Sierra foothills and Trinity Alps of northern California are drained by effervescent rivers that offer superb white-water rafting. The Kern River, deep in Sequoia National Park, is closest to southern California. The American, Tuolumne, Merced, and Stanislaus Rivers all plunge from the Sierras and tumble through historic Gold Country. Farther north, the Klamath is popular, and wilder runs are available on the Burnt Gorge of the Trinity River. Echo: The Wilderness Company, 6529 Telegraph Ave, Oakland, CA 94609 (tel 510/652-1600) and Whitewater Voyages, PO Box 20400, El Sobrante, CA 94820 (tel 510/222-5994) provide brochures describing professionally guided raft trips throughout the state.

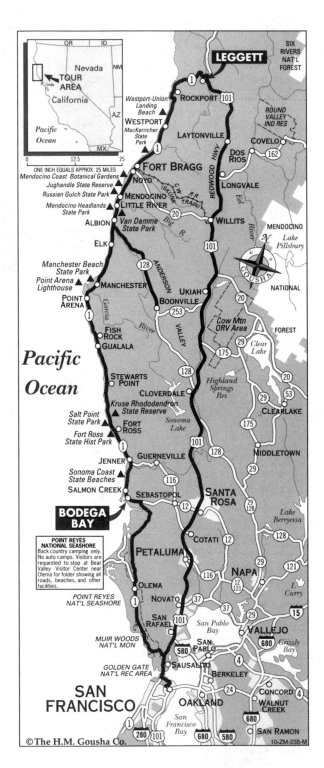

SCENIC DRIVING TOUR #1

THE NORTH COAST

Start: Bodega Bay
Finish: Leggett
Distance: 155 miles
Time: 3–4 days
Highlights: Stunning coastal vistas, a 19th-century fort, New England–style villages, a scenic train ride, redwood forests for hiking, and small, quiet beaches

This tour follows California's North Coast, a rugged region of plunging shorelines and pounding surf that reaches nearly 400 miles north from San Francisco to the Oregon border. You'll be following Calif 1 (the State Coast Highway), a sinuous, thin line of 2-lane asphalt just north of the Golden Gate Bridge. Calif 1 takes you away from big-city skyscrapers as it hugs steep cliffs and wraps around hairpin turns, rarely moving from the sight, sound, and smell of the Pacific Ocean. The further north you drive, the more rugged the scenery. Starting your tour from Bodega Bay, you'll encounter an ever-changing landscape of windswept headlands, long, lonesome stretches of sand, and windswept moors. In places, the recently uplifted Coastal Range Mountains come close to shore. Groves of tall redwoods, reaching heights in excess of 300 feet, lie tucked in the cool, fern-choked riverbottoms. Much of the coast is preserved in state parks and beaches perfect for fishing, hiking, horseback riding, collecting shells, and picnicking. Swimming, however, is not recommended, due to dangerous riptides, treacherous undertows, and offshore eddies.

Along the way, you'll drive through villages packed with well-preserved Victorian homes, many of them resurrected as cozy bed-and-breakfasts, often on the very edge of the cliffs. You'll find numerous art galleries, gift shops, and seafood restaurants. Sometimes the highway descends to cross at the rivermouths where giant sand bars form warm gathering places for crowds of seals. Great blue herons, coots, ducks, and egrets also wade in the rivermouth waters and lagoons. From November through April, gray whales make their annual 6,000-mile migrations between Alaska and Baja California; they come close to the North Coast shore, where they are easily spotted from high vantage points.

There are few boat tours, however, because the cold and stormy waters discourage them.

Yellow road signs warn of road hazards—cows or deer, which are commonly seen grazing the margins. Keep your speed down, for logging trucks, too, careen around the blind curves north of Fort Bragg. A dozen or so gas stations are spaced well-apart in the 100 miles between Jenner and Fort Bragg.

Allow 4 days for dawdling. Summer is high season; mid-week travel is best, as inns are often fully booked well in advance on weekends. Spring and autumn are best. Note that some inns and restaurants close in off-season, and many do not accept credit cards. For additional information on accommodations, restaurants, and attractions in the region covered by this tour, look under specific cities in the listings portion of this book.

Calif 1 is reached from San Francisco across the Golden Gate Bridge by traveling north on US 101 to the Mill Valley (Calif 1) exit. The road climbs over the coastal mountains and drops to Stinson Beach; follow Calif 1 north past the shores of pencil-thin Tomales Bay to Bodega Bay. An alternate route follows US 101 to San Rafael. Take the 4th St (Sir Francis Drake Hwy) exit and continue west to Calif 1 at Point Reyes Station; turn right. Alternately, continue north on US 101 to Santa Rosa; take Calif 12 (Bodega Hwy) west via Sebastopol to Calif 1. Begin at the **Bodega Bay Area Visitors Center** (tel 707/875-3422) at 850 Calif 1, where you can pick up maps and brochures.

1. **Bodega Bay** is a relaxed fishing village that was named by Spanish explorer Juan Fransisco de la Bodega, who anchored the *Sonora* here in 1775. The Russians established a sea otter hunting base here in 1808 but left in 1841. They were replaced by Yankees who built a steam-operated sawmill in 1843. Today the community is a popular weekend vacation spot for San Franciscans; trendy bed-and-breakfast inns and boutiques are multiplying while the local fishing fleet—the largest between San Francisco and Eureka—dwindles. The broad bay itself supports gulls, egrets, herons, pelicans, and other bird species. California gray whales also come close to shore in winter. Catch the town's tranquil mood at **The Tides,** at Lucas Wharf, a dockside tackle shop that doubles as fish market, bar, and restaurant. It's a great place to enjoy breakfast as fishing boats unload their catches of salmon or Dungeness crab.

Drive north 1 mile on Calif 1 to East Shore Rd and turn left. After less than ½ mile, turn right onto Bay Flat Rd and follow it about 3 ½ miles to Bodega Head, from where you have a spectacular view of:

2. **Sonoma Coast state beaches** (tel 707/875-3483), which protect 13 miles of coast north of Bodega Bay. Craggy headlands separate tiny coves (many renowned for their tidepools) and wide beaches backed by sweeping dunes. Bodega Head, to the south, is a popular whale-watching spot. Footpaths lead from the Head to Bodega Dunes, while trails lead down to the many other beaches from Calif 1; the beaches and their access points are clearly signposted. Shell Beach is favored by beachcombers seeking a treasure chest of shells. Surf anglers favor Portuguese Beach. Goat Rock, to the north, at the mouth of the Russian River, is popular with seals. The park headquarters and information center is on Salmon Creek Beach.

Follow Calif 1 north as it turns briefly inland and crosses the Russian River to the junction with Calif 116. Guerneville is 13 miles to the right. Turn left and proceed on Calif 1 heading west towards the Pacific and Jenner, which perches on the steep bluff on the north bank of the Russian River. As you continue north on Calif 1, several pull-offs provide superb views south to Goat Rock and the Sonoma Coast beaches. After 12 miles you reach:

3. **Fort Ross State Historic Park** (tel 707/847-3286). The Russian-American Company founded Fort Ross in 1812 as imperial Russia's furthermost permanent protective outpost against the Spanish. The Russians hunted the local sea otter population to near extinction before departing in 1852. The weathered redwood stockade with octagonal turrets, officers' quarters, barracks, and a Russian Orthodox chapel have been meticulously reconstructed to look as they did when occupied. The commandant's house is the original. The visitor center in this 1,160-acre park features fascinating displays about Native American, Russian, and Yankee logging communities, as well as historic artifacts.

Continue north on Calif 1. After 2.3 miles you will pass the Benjamin Bufano *Peace* sculpture that looms over Timber Cove. Proceed north 3 miles through cypress forest until you reach:

4. **Salt Point State Park** (tel 707/847-3221), with 6 miles of rugged coastline and neighboring inland mountains. Miles of trails tempt hikers and horse-back riders for forays through forests of stunted pines, cypress, and mature redwoods that attain only a few feet in height. Dozens of snug coves hidden along the shore feature *tafoni,* strange formations sculpted from the soft sandstone cliffs by wind and wave. Several old Pomo Indian village sites are scattered throughout the 6,000-acre park.

   As you head north 4 miles on Calif 1 you will pass several beaches before turning right to follow the hard-packed dirt road uphill for ½ mile to:

5. **Kruse Rhododendron State Reserve** (tel 707/847-3221), where you can experience the contrast between the intimate (rhododendrons) and the spectacular (redwoods) on a loop trail that leads through 317 acres of coastal vegetation. Clusters of pink and cream-colored rhododendrons blaze gloriously April through June; they grow more than 15 feet tall. Ferns, violets, orchids, and other plants linger year-round.

   Back on Calif 1, head north 5 miles to Stewarts Point. Proceed through Sea Ranch, a residential community of 1,200 or so houses that stretch for 7 miles along the coast. You will have ample access to Sea Ranch's many beaches, indicated by signs reading "Coastal Access." Ten miles north of Stewarts Point you reach:

6. **Gualala Regional Park,** a coastal reserve enveloping redwoods and secluded beaches. A trail leads to Del Mar Landing, a perfect spot for watching seals, which bask on the rocks offshore. The waters are popular with abalone divers, and fishermen cast for silver salmon and steelhead trout.

   As you continue north on Calif 1 you will cross the Gualala River into Mendocino County, and after 1 mile enter:

7. **Gualala,** which nestles atop the northern coastal bluffs overlooking the pretty rivermouth of the Gualala River. Once a logging settlement and now

a budding art center, sleepy Gualala (pronounced wah-LA-la; from the Pomos Indians' *wala'li* or "meeting place of the waters") comes alive each August when it hosts the Arts in the Redwoods Festival, with local artists' displays. Many artists also show their works year-round at the Gallery.

☕

REFRESHMENT STOP

Try **Captain's Quarters,** 39350 Shoreline Hwy (tel 707/884-9511), a weathered timber oasis with fabulous ocean vistas; on the outdoor terrace, you can dine on Sonoma grilled chicken, ham-and-cheese melts, prawn salad, or fresh fish.

Exit Gualala heading north on Calif 1 and proceed 13 miles to Iversen Lane, on your left. Follow Iversen for 1.2 miles to Arena Cove Wharf, a large public pier. Back on Calif 1, continue north 100 yards into:

8. **Point Arena,** a peaceful hamlet with venerable timber-framed facades facing the street. In the 1870s, the now-shrunken town was the busiest port between San Francisco and Eureka. Today the seasonal sea urchin harvest to serve Japanese tastebuds is revitalizing Point Arena. A restored 1927 vauderville theater (The Arena) still functions as concert hall, movie house, and playhouse.

   Two miles north of Point Arena on Calif 1 you will pass an interesting cemetery on the left, immediately beyond which is Lighthouse Rd. Turn left and follow the paved but bumpy road about 2 miles through windswept meadows to:

9. **Point Arena Lighthouse** (tel 707/882-2777). This historic 115-feet-tall lighthouse was built in 1908 of steel-reinforced concrete. Climb to the top for the fabulous view and superb whale-watching; gray whales often pause in the cove near the lighthouse during their annual migrations. Then, tour the adjacent maritime museum in the Fog Signal Building.

   Continue north through pastureland along Calif 1. After almost 2½ miles you will reach Stoneboro

Rd on your left. Stoneboro and Kinney Rd, about 1½ miles further north in the tiny village of Manchester, both lead to:

10. **Manchester State Beach** (tel 707/937-5804) a 5-mile-long sandy strip, windswept and strewn with driftwood, and backed by tall dunes with heaps of wildflowers. The **Arena Rock Underwater Preserve,** 2 miles offshore, is a favorite of divers. The San Andreas fault, which runs along the North Coast for many miles, threatens this area. Winter steelhead run in the Garcia River, whose bottomlands are a favored winter habitat for whistling swans that migrate from the Arctic Circle.

    As you continue north on Calif 1 via the lovely clifftop village of Irish Beach, you may stop after 4 miles at a vista point to enjoy the sweeping coastal views. After 5 miles, the road makes a 2-mile-long snaking descent and ascent of the Elk River valley to the quaint village of Elk. Proceed north 7 miles to the junction of Calif 128. Calif 1 continues to the left, westward to Fort Bragg. To the right, Calif 128 leads 20 miles to the:

11. **Anderson Valley,** a thriving farming and apple-growing region well worth the short detour. At its center is **Boonville,** where friendly locals may "harp Boont" for you. The local dialect called Bootling dates back to isolated pioneer days and can be sampled, along with robust local ales, at the **Buckhorn Saloon** brewpub (tel 707/895-BEER).

    Return to Calif 1. Back at the junction with Calif 128, follow Calif 1 west, heading toward the Pacific. Continue 3 miles via the hamlet of Albion. After another 4 miles you will pass through the former-lumber-port-turned-hostelry-hub of Little River, on the northern edge of which on the right is the entry to:

12. **Van Damme State Park** (tel 707/937-5804), which has a tiny beach safe for swimming (1 of the few along the North Coast) and alluring forests. A visitor center and museum made of handsplit timbers provide exhibits on the area's natural history. The Bog Trail leads to a marsh of foul-smelling skunk-cabbage. An additional 10 miles of trails (including a wheelchair-accessible trail) penetrate the 5-mile-long, 2,160-acre preserve, fol-

lowing the Little River from its mouth through a ravine of ferns and redwoods to a bonsai-like pygmy forest. Rhododendrons also grow in profusion.

REFRESHMENT STOP

For superb service and a romantic ambience, dine at **Little River Inn,** 7751 N Calif 1 (tel 707/937-5942), where California nouvelle finds its way into such tasty entrees as spring rack of lamb, herb roasted chicken, fresh margarita swordfish, and grilled polenta with porcini mushroom sauce.

Back on Calif 1 continue north almost 2½ miles and cross the bridge over the Big River to Main St. Turn left and enter the town of:

13. **Mendocino,** an impressive showcase of Cape Cod–style architecture that is included in its entirety on the National Register of Historic Places. It often stars as a New England stand-in for films and television shows. Mendocino's name was bestowed as early as 1542 by a Spanish expedition in honor of Antonio de Mendoza, Viceroy of New Spain. In 1852, Yankee loggers established a sawmill on the beach and built their handsome redwood homes and prim churches on the bluffs overlooking the rivermouth. In the 1960s, Mendocino was discovered by hippies and artists, lured by the town's irrepressible beauty and the opening of the **Mendocino Art Center,** at 45200 Little Lake Rd (tel 707/937-5818), which displays the work of local and national artists. Ranchers, artists, loggers, and marijuana farmers still make up the core of the populace.

    Mendocino is small enough to be easily explored on a 2-hour walking tour, yet deserves a 2-day stay. Your tour should begin at **Ford House** (tel 707/937-5804), on the south side of Main St, an immaculately restored 1854 structure that is Mendocino's oldest existing residence; it now functions as the **Visitor Information Bureau.** Across the road is the **Kelley House Museum,**

45007 Albion St (tel 707/937-5791), in a pretty 1861 gingerbread-trim home that is furnished with Victoriana and local memorabilia. Also on Main St is the landmark Gothic-style **Presbyterian Church,** built in 1868. **Blair House,** at the junction of Ford and Little Lake Sts, is the setting for the television series *Murder, She Wrote.* Note the old Masonic Temple—now the **Savings Bank of Mendocino**—topped by an allegorical statue of Father Time and The Maiden carved from a single redwood. Another local curiosity is the **Kwan Ti Temple,** on Albion St between Kasten and Osborne Sts (by appointment only; (tel 707/937-4506).

When you're sated with architectural delights, there are countless antique stores, art galleries, and chic restaurants to enthrall you. Feeling romantic? Then take a horse-drawn carriage ride offered by **Mendocino Carriage Company** (tel 800/399-1454), May to December.

A trail from the corner of Hesser and Main Sts leads to the meadow-topped:

14. **Mendocino Headlands State Park** (tel 707/937-5804), immediately north and west of town. The 347-acre park provides tidepools, wave tunnels, and tiny coves for exploring; 2 beaches for bronzing and bathing; and clifftop trails. The headlands form vantage points for mid-winter whale-watching. Sea otters can often be seen amid the kelp beds.

Back on Coast Calif 1, continue north 3½ miles to Point Cabrillo Dr and turn left to enter:

15. **Russian Gulch State Park** (tel 707/937-5804), combining a canyon thick with redwoods and rhododendrons, a sweeping bay with sandy beach and well-protected tidepools, and coastal headlands splashed with wildflowers. Hiking and cycling trails braid the park. Separate trails lead up the canyon to Russian Gulch Falls.

Continue north on Calif 1 for a little over 1 mile to:

16. **Jughandle State Reserve** (tel 707/937-5804), where cliffs offer the 2.5-mile "Ecological Staircase" nature trail that leads from sea level through 5 terraces uplifted from the sea approximately 100,000 years apart. Each of the terraces is covered with a unique vegetation: The lowermost, youngest step has been colonized by salt-resistant wildflowers; fir, pine, spruce, and hemlock dominate the 2nd terrace; the uppermost features a rare example of Mendocino pygmy forest of gnarled, stunted cypress trees and pine. At the south end of the 769-acre park is **Casper Headlands State Beach,** which protects a ½-mile of sand bordered by seasonal wildflowers.

Proceed 2½ miles north on Calif 1, and on your left you will pass the entrance to:

17. **Mendocino Coast Botanical Garden** (tel 707/965-4352), fronted by a nursery. Two miles of trails lead through 47 acres of splashy shrubs and wildflowers. A self-guided tour leads through native plant communities and coastal pine forest complemented by rhododendrons, azaleas, and fuschias planted by human hand.

Continue north along Calif 1 for 2 miles to N Harbor Dr, on your right. Follow N Harbor Dr as it snakes down into the Noyo River canyon and the wharfs of:

18. **Noyo,** a tiny fishing port sheltered in the river mouth at the southern end of Fort Bragg. The fishing fleet that harbors here supplies local restaurants with fresh seafood daily. Noyo is a good place for whale-watching and fishing forays.

🍵

REFRESHMENT STOP

At 780 N Harbor Dr is the unpretentious **Wharf Restaurant** (tel 707/964-4283), which combines harborside views with reasonably priced steaks, salads, and seafood specialties—grilled halibut and salmon, crabs, and shellfish stews—fresh from the wharfs.

Back on Calif 1, continue north ½ mile past the:

19. **Georgia-Pacific Sawmill,** the world's largest redwood sawmill, stretching 6 kilometers from just north of the Noyo River. More than 3½ million

redwood and Douglas fir seedlings are raised annually in a miniature forest at the **Georgia Pacific Tree Nursery** (tel 707/964-5651), on Main St (Calif 1). A nature trail leads through the nursery, which is open to the public.

As you drive past the lumber yards, you will enter:

20. **Fort Bragg,** the largest town on the North Coast between San Francisco and Eureka. The robust, no-nonsense logging community retains a strong Finnish and Portuguese heritage. A large Native American population also remains. Fort Bragg began as a fort, built in 1857 to oversee the Mendocino Indian Reservation, and is named for Confederate hero General Braxton Bragg; it was abandoned in 1867 when the reservation was moved. Stop by the **Guest House Museum,** Main St, (tel 707/961-2825), next to the Laurel Street Train Depot, for a history of logging. It's housed in a 1892 Victorian home built for the Union Lumber Company's founder. The town also has a thriving artists community.

You should park your car next to the Guest House Museum and Skunk Depot at the foot of Laurel St and take a journey on the:

21. **California Western Railroad's *Skunk* Train** (tel 707/964-6371), which offers a cliff-hanging ride up Noyo River Gulch and over the rugged coastal mountains to Willits. Disembark midway at Northspur for a snack before returning to Fort Bragg, or continue to Willits. The scenic excursion follows a 40-mile route, crisscrossing the river on wooden trestles as it ascends from 80-feet elevation to 1,365 feet at Willits. In sleepy Willits, call in at the **Mendocino County Museum,** 400 E Commercial St (tel 707/459-2736), where Native American basketry and pioneer-period artifacts are displayed, along with contemporary and traditional art. *Skunk* schedules vary between a choice of 4 venerable engines, including the "Ole No 45" Baldwin Steam Engine.

Exit Fort Bragg continuing north on Calif 1 with an old trestle railway bridge on the left. On the left, after 3 miles, is the entrance to:

22. **MacKerricher State Park** (tel 707/937-5804), 1,600 acres and 10 miles of dark sand beach favored by hikers, bikers, and fishermen. Harbor seals gather at Seal Rock. The park's headland, Laguna Point, is a favored spot, too, for viewing migrating whales November through April. Lake Cleone is a fancied rest spot for migratory waterfowl.

Back on Calif 1, you will cut temporarily inland through forests encroached upon by massive sand dunes that come right up to the road. After 9 miles, a vista point on the left allows you to savor views along 10 Mile Dunes beach. Another 3 miles brings you to:

23. **Westport,** the last village on the coast. This remote and pretty New England–style coastal mill "town" is popular with abalone divers and for surf fishing. From here, you can have intoxicating views north towards the Lost Coast.

One mile north of Westport on Calif 1, you will pass the first of several turn-offs on your left for:

24. **Westport-Union Landing State Beach** (tel 707/937-5804), a slender 41-acre park that attracts tidepoolers, surf fishermen, and abalone divers.

As you continue north on Calif 1 you will pass a sign on the right that reads NARROW WINDING ROAD FOR NEXT 22 MILES. WATCH FOR BICYCLES. Five miles north of Westport, Calif 1 suddenly swings inland and follows a tortuous route through the mountains to Leggett, where a sign announces END HIGHWAY 1. Drive carefully. The narrow road snakes steeply, and giant logging trucks thunder downhill through the gloomy forest en route to the Georgia-Pacific coast sawmill. About 21 miles after leaving the coast, you reach Leggett Drive-Thru Tree Rd on your right. Turn right and follow the road ½ mile through the homespun hamlet of Leggett to:

25. **Drive-Thru Tree Park** (tel 707/925-6363), a privately-owned 200-acre virgin redwood grove dominated by the renowned Chandelier Drive-Thru Tree (315-feet-tall with a 21-foot base).

Return to Calif 1, turn right and proceed to the junction with US 101 (the Redwood Hwy). Turn right to return to San Francisco on US 101. Turn left for the great redwood parks and Oregon.

SCENIC DRIVING TOUR #2

HIGHWAY 1: MONTEREY TO SANTA BARBARA

Start: Monterey
Finish: Santa Barbara
Distance: Approximately 275 miles
Time: 2–3 days
Highlights: Phenomenal scenery, seaside towns, redwood forests, Spanish missions, factory outlets, America's most outrageous castle

One minute, you're driving at sea level; less than a mile later, the road skedaddles up to 1,000 feet and your eardrums are popping. Welcome to one of the most famous roadways in the world—California's Highway 1, also known as the Cabrillo Highway (and referred to in this tour as Calif 1). The road skims the California coast from Mendocino to south of Los Angeles, but during this tour, you'll explore its most celebrated stretch, running from the Monterey Peninsula to Santa Barbara. Located 120 miles south of San Francisco and 330 miles north of Los Angeles, the Monterey Peninsula forms the southernmost nub of Monterey Bay and encompasses 4 distinct communities: Monterey, Pacific Grove, Pebble Beach, and Carmel-by-the-Sea. It's easy to travel from one town to the next, since only 3 miles separate Carmel from Monterey.

Because the peninsula offers so many attractions, you'll probably want to stay overnight in the area. The top address is **The Lodge at Pebble Beach,** on 17 Mile Dr (tel 408/624-3811 or toll free 800/654-9300), where most rooms have fireplaces and an ocean view. If you're looking for the quintessential B&B, head for **Seven Gables Inn** (tel 408/372-4341), overlooking Lover's Point in Pacific Grove. A good choice for bargain hunters is the **Best Western Inn–Town House Lodge** in Carmel—homely, but right near the center of town.

For additional information on accommodations, restaurants, and attractions in the region covered by the tour, look under specific cities in the listings portion of this book.

To reach the peninsula from San Francisco, take I-280 south to San Jose, then pick up US 101 S. At Prunedale, take Calif 156 W, which merges into Calif 1, and proceed south to:

1. **Monterey.** Try to spend a day exploring this town before embarking on the rest of your journey. Monterey owes its prominence to its immense bay, measuring almost 60 miles long and 13 miles wide. First settled in 1770, Monterey served as the capital of Alta (Upper) California originally for the Spanish and later for the Mexicans. Step back into the past along Monterey's "Path of History," a self-guided walking tour past about a dozen well-preserved 18th- and 19th-century adobe structures. You can visit some of the buildings, including the Spanish colonial–style **Larkin House,** 510 Calle Principal, and **Colton Hall,** 522 Pacific St between Madison and Jefferson Sts, where California's first constitution was written in 1849. You can obtain a free walking-tour map from **Monterey State Historic Park,** Cooper-Molera Adobe, Polk and Alvarado Sts (tel 408/649-7118).

Next head for the waterfront and **Fisherman's Wharf.** Although the pier is lined with T-shirt and souvenir shops, it still retains a seafaring spirit, amplified by the gulls' squawks and briny aromas from the boiling crab pots. Pick up a "walkaway" shrimp or crab cocktail from a food stall, or enjoy a seafood dinner at **Abalonetti** or **Domenico's.**

From the 1920s to the 1940s, Monterey was the sardine-packing capital of the world. John Steinbeck vividly captured this raucous era of factory workers, fishermen, and hustlers in his novel *Cannery Row*. Today, **Cannery Row,** on Monterey Bay between David and Drake Aves, has been reborn, with souvenir shops and restaurants occupying former bars and bordellos. The biggest attraction here is the **Monterey Bay Aquarium,** 886 Cannery Row (tel 408/648-4888), located in the former Hovden sardine cannery. The star exhibit is the 3-story kelp forest aquarium, where leopard sharks and schools of silver sardines cruise. Visitors can also watch the captivating sea otters, aquatic clowns who float on their backs and whack open clams with small stones.

From Cannery Row, drive southwest (inland) on David Ave, then turn right on Lighthouse Ave. Proceed through the town of **Pacific Grove,** which was founded at the turn of the century as a strict Methodist summer community; several of the ornate Victorian houses have been converted into bed-and-breakfast inns. Turn left at:

2. **17 Mile Drive.** At the Pacific Grove Gate entrance to this scenic drive, you must pay a toll of $6.50 per car. Set your odometer to "zero"; mileages given in the following section are calculated from the entrance gate. The route runs through privately owned, 5,000-acre Del Monte Forest and Pebble Beach, twining its way past wave-lashed seacoast and through pine groves shrouded in mist. Much of the vegetation you see is unique to this region, and some plant species are endangered. The **Coastal Bluff Walking Trail** (mile 2.2) offers a good opportunity to stretch your legs and observe the scenery. At mile 3.4, you'll come to **Bird and Seal Rocks,** offshore outcrops where sea lions and harbor seals ("downstairs") and thousands of cormorants and sea gulls ("upstairs") share their rocky roost in cacophonous harmony; you can gaze at the scene through fuzzy-quality telescopes for 25 cents. The symbol of the Monterey Peninsula, the famous **Lone Cypress** stands grandly on a nearly barren rock facing the sea (mile 6). Experts estimate the tree is between 200 and 300 years old.

The next section of roadway is flanked by some spectacular homes—minicastles, really, in styles ranging from Mediterranean to Norman to Cape Cod. Zip code 93953 for Pebble Beach vanquishes Beverly Hills in terms of exclusivity. A prime oceanfront estate recently sold for $12 million; vacant lots can run $1 million to $6 million. At mile 8, you'll pass the elegant **Lodge at Pebble Beach,** known for its top-ranked Pebble Beach Golf Links. Since 1919, this beautiful course designed by Jack Neville and Douglas Grant has been home to some of golf's most prestigious tournaments, including the annual AT&T Pebble Beach National ProAm, plus several US Open Championships.

While 17-Mile Drive swings back north and inland through Del Monte Forest, the driving tour bears south into Carmel-by-the-Sea. Exit 17 Mile Drive through Carmel Gate onto North San Antonio. Turn right (west) onto Ocean Ave. Continue to:

3. **Carmel Beach,** a mile-long sweep of sand edged by Monterey pines and steep sand dunes. Sunsets here are usually marvelous, with vistas stretching from Point Lobos to Pebble Beach. Drive back east on Ocean Ave to explore the town of Carmel itself, which centers on Ocean Ave between Monte Verde and Mission Sts. Park where you can—traffic is a jungle, especially on summer weekends. Your best bet might be the free parking lot at Vista Lobos Park (on 3rd Ave and Junipero St).

Carmel can best be described by what it lacks. The community has no neon signs, courthouse, or jail, and few sidewalks. Instead of street addresses, houses are identified by locale (such as ''on Lincoln between 7th and 8th) or melodic names, such as ''Merry Oaks'' or ''Sea Nymph.'' The town has an abundance of art galleries and gourmet restaurants that give it the panache of the south of France.

Shopping and browsing are preferred pastimes here. Art lovers will want to check out galleries such as **Simic,** San Carlos St between 5th and 6th Aves, and **Hanson,** Ocean Ave and San Carlos St. **Weston Gallery,** 6th Ave between Dolores and Lincoln Sts, displays works by major 19th- and 20th-century photographers. For antiques, top stores include **Luciano Antiques,** San Carlos St between 5th and 6th Aves, and **Great Things Antiques,** Ocean Ave between Lincoln and Dolores Sts.

Other favorite shops include **Walter White Gallery,** San Carlos St between 5th and 6th Aves, for art glass; **Ladyfingers,** Dolores St between Ocean and 7th Aves, for designer jewelry; **Pierre Deux,** Ocean Ave at Monte Verde St, with Country French furnishings; and **Conway of Asia,** Dolores St between Ocean and 7th Aves, displaying fantastic Asian art objects, from bronze Buddhas to gilded sword hilts.

Reclaim your car and go east on Ocean Ave, then south (right) on Junipero St, which turns into Rio Rd. Drive to:

4. **Carmel Mission,** 3080 Rio Rd at Lausen Dr (tel 408/624-3600), officially known as the Basilica of Mission San Carlos Borromeo del Rio Carmelo. Built in 1793 of local sandstone, this lovely structure has a star window over the rough-hewn

---

☕

REFRESHMENT STOP

At **Casanova,** 5th Ave between San Carlos and Mission Sts (tel 408/625-0501), you can sit at a table in the garden courtyard while enjoying excellent Northern Italian and French country cuisine. **The Grill,** Ocean Ave between Dolores and Lincoln Sts (tel 408/624-2569), is garnering local raves for its modern, art-filled interior and creative cuisine, such as oak-grilled salmon with okra and sweet-potato tempura.

---

doorway and 2 uneven towers, 1 of them capped by a Moorish dome. In addition, the mission is known for its attractive gardens and fountains. It is most closely associated with Father Junipero Serra, the Franciscan friar who oversaw the establishment of 21 different California missions; he is buried at the foot of the church altar.

Leaving the mission, turn right (east) on Rio Rd, and continue about ½ mile to Calif 1. Turn right (south). In just over 2 miles, you come to:

5. **Point Lobos State Reserve** (tel 408/624-4909), which Robert Louis Stevenson called ''the most beautiful meeting of land and sea on earth.'' At this preserve just south of Carmel Bay, you can hike past stands of cypress twisted by the ocean winds and stroll along hidden coves and lagoons, perhaps spying some sea otters floating in the kelp beds. Park rangers often lead guided nature walks. This is a wonderful spot for a picnic.

Retrace your route back to Calif 1 and turn south. The roadway sidewinds the cliffs, with nothing between you and the blue Pacific but a sheer 1,000-foot drop. There are plenty of scenic overlooks, so you can pull over to photograph the views. About 11 miles after Point Lobos, you'll come to a Calif 1 landmark:

6. **Bixby Creek Bridge,** which looks as if it were spun by a drunken spider. Measuring 260 feet high and 700 feet long, it was the highest single-arch bridge in the world when constructed in 1932.

Roughly 9 miles after the bridge, your next stop is:

7. **Point Sur Lighthouse** (tel 408/625-4419), a State Historic Park and the only intact 19th-century lighthouse open to the public in California. The beacon stands 361 feet above the surf at what was once a notorious ships' graveyard. Three-hour tours of the area are offered Wednesday, Saturday, and Sunday, weather permitting.

The landscape changes dramatically in about 9 miles, heading inland from sun-bleached coastal grasslands to cool green redwoods and oaks. You are now entering famous:

8. **Big Sur,** one of the last American frontiers, a place where the highway first came through in the 1930s, and phone service began in the 1950s. Residents still have to drive 30 miles to Carmel to pick up their dry cleaning or a new oil filter for the pickup. The name comes from the Spanish, who referred to the entire unexplored region south of their settlement in Monterey as El Sur Grande. Vistas offer contrasts: jagged cliffs and smooth white beaches, towering redwoods and scruffy

---

🍵

REFRESHMENT STOP

Time your drive so you can ogle the views from one of Big Sur's clifftop restaurants, all 2 to 3 miles south of Molera State Park. Under chef David Daniels, major gourmet American food is happening at **Ventana** (tel 408/667-2331), where you can dine on a deck beneath trees, under white umbrellas, or in a ridgetop pergola woven with vines. Perched at the very brink of the cliffs, **Sierra Mar at Post Ranch Inn** (tel 408/667-2200) offers views heretofore known only by seagulls, and excellent contemporary Californian cuisine. Or slip into a 1960s hippie time warp at **Nepenthe** (tel 408/667-2345), serving basic burgers, sandwiches, chicken, and fish in a casual atmosphere.

---

chaparral. For years, the region has been a haven for avant-garde writers such as Henry Miller and Jack Kerouac. You can hike through the forests at **Pfeiffer Big Sur State Park** (tel 408/667-2315), where the Waterfall Trail climbs through a redwood canyon to 40-foot falls. **Molera State Park** (tel 408/667-2315) covers 9,000 acres and has a variety of hiking trails along the river, cliffs, and beach.

Once again, head south on Calif 1, which continues its scenic crescendos with the unusual boulder formations at **Pacific Valley** (23 miles south of Nepenthe) and the vista point at **Willow Creek** in **Los Padres National Forest** (34 miles south of Nepenthe), commanding spectacular views of sentinel-like rocks and pounding surf. About 60 miles south of Nepenthe, the road suddenly levels off into undulating green cow country. About 70 years ago, everything you can see around you—about 50 miles of prime coastline—belonged to William Randolph Hearst. Your next stop is his most outrageous and most lasting achievement:

9. **Hearst Castle (San Simeon).** Some 130 rooms; art treasures ranging from tapestries by Rubens to a wine bucket made from 30 pounds of pure silver; a dining room lined with a 13th-century Italian choir stall. This is the larger-than-life world of La Cuesta Encantada—the Enchanted Hill—the estate built by tycoon William Randolph Hearst. In 1935, Hearst, the newspaper publisher who perfected yellow journalism and the Hollywood producer who made movies like *Young Mr. Lincoln*, was worth $220 million—the equivalent of $2 billion today. Working with architect Julia Morgan, he spent $3 million and almost 30 years crafting this extravagant Mediterranean revival mansion, which in fact was never completed. Hearst heirs donated the castle to the state of California in 1958, and the California Park Service now runs several different tours of the grounds.

On the tour, you experience the castle as guests would have, sauntering past the magnificent white Carrera marble Neptune Pool, walking through a guest "cottage" with its plaster ceiling leafed in 22-karat gold, and entering the castle itself, known as La Casa Grande. In its heyday, guests included luminaries from the world of politics (Winston Churchill, Calvin Coolidge); royalty (the Duke and Duchess of Windsor); and Hollywood (Cary Grant, Vivien Leigh, Rudolph Valentino).

Because of the tremendous popularity of Hearst Castle, it is absolutely essential that you purchase your tickets in advance. To make reservations, call 800/444-4445.

Leaving Hearst Castle, turn left (south) on Calif 1. From here to Santa Barbara, you'll be driving along both good roads and highways, with none of the vertiginous curves found between Carmel and Hearst Castle. Continue another 5 miles to:

10. **Morro Strand State Park.** At this 2-mile-long beach, you might see surfers shredding the waves against the backdrop of Morro Rock, a 576-foot outcrop attached to the mainland by a skinny sand isthmus. Unfortunately, the vistas are marred by a trio of smoke stacks from Pacific Gas & Electric. Swimming is usually safe at Morro Strand, although no lifeguards are on duty.

Continue south on Calif 1. On the outskirts of San Luis Obispo, Calif 1 joins up with US 101, a main north-south route through California. You can continue south on US 101, or, if you are interested in California missions, continue straight on Calif 1, which becomes Santa Rosa St in town. Go right on Monterey St, which dead-ends at:

11. **Mission San Luis Obispo de Tolosa,** 782 Monterey (tel 805/543-6850), with its shady plaza and thick walls. Founded in 1772, it has 3 bells hanging from an opening above the entrance and was one of the first buildings in California to have a red clay-tile roof—now a fixture of West Coast architecture. In addition to early photos, artifacts on view include a re-creation of a friar's bedroom.

If you've visited the mission, retrace your route and pick up US 101 south. In a little over 8 miles, you'll reach Pismo Beach, where you should continue south on US 101 to Buellton; then take Calif 246 west 15 miles to Purisima Rd. After 2 miles, you'll arrive at:

12. **La Purisima Mission State Historic Park,** 2295 Purisima Rd (tel 805/733-3713). Dating to 1787, the enclave is the most completely restored of California's 21 missions. It's one of the best places to get a sense of early mission life, with re-created workshops including a soap factory and tannery, and real cattle, sheep, and horses grazing in the corrals.

Leaving the mission, turn east (left) on Calif 246. Continue approximately 18 miles to:

13. **Solvang.** Founded in 1911 by Danish-American educators, most of the town features old world architecture. The result is Scandinavia as it might have been rendered by Walt Disney, with half-timbered and thatched storefronts, cobblestone walks, and a few windmills. There is a good selection of shops selling such Danish treats as *ableskivers,* a round pancake drizzled with jam and powdered sugar, and *medisterpole,* a locally made sausage. But the main draw here is the factory outlets for brands like Izod, Dansk, and Oneida.

A slice of old-time California lies just up the road in the rolling hills of Santa Ynez Valley. Resume your route east on Calif 246. At the last light leaving Solvang, turn left on Alamo Pintado Rd. Continue about 5 miles, then turn right at the only stop sign for miles onto an unmarked road. A hundred yards later, turn left at the next stop sign onto Grand Ave. Drive about ½ mile and you're in:

14. **Los Olivos,** formerly a stagecoach stop at a narrow-gauge railroad. This quintessential small town—all 2 blocks of it—has 1- and 2-story wood-frame buildings, and a flagpole plunked in the middle of the main street, Grand Ave. Men ride fine Arabian horses through the center of town, and kids wander barefoot into the grocery store.

There are also some fine shops for browsing. **Gallery Liz Montana** (2890 Grand Ave) carries some intriguing western art. **Los Olivos Tasting Room & Wine Shop** (2905 Grand Ave) offers samples of mostly Santa Barbara County wines, from vintners who do not have their own tasting rooms. **Donlee Gallery** (2933 Grand Ave) features paintings and sculpture, and **White Oak Gallery** (2920 Grand Ave) has paintings and hand-crafted furniture.

From Los Olivos, retrace your route back on Grand Ave and Alamo Pintado Rd. Turn left (east) on Calif 246. If you've got more wine-tasting on your mind, stop at:

15. **The Gainey Vineyard,** 3950 E Hwy 246, Santa Ynez (tel 805/688-0558), part of 1,800-acre Gainey Ranch in the Santa Ynez Valley. The Spanish-style winery opened in 1984 and soon achieved a reputation for its premium varietals, including cabernet sauvignon, pinot noir, and chardonnay. In addition to winery tours and tastings, there's a vineyard garden with picnic tables.

Leaving Gainey, turn right (east) on Calif 246. Proceed ½ mile to Calif 154 and turn right (south). Designated a California Scenic Highway, Calif 154 lives up to its appellation as you leave Santa Ynez, curving through a lovely valley backed by the crumpled green face of the Santa Ynez Mountains. Shortly, on the left, you'll pass Lake Cachuma, a shimmering blue mirror washing into the receding lines of ridges. Watch for the Vista Point on your left.

🍵

REFRESHMENT STOP

About 8 miles after you merge onto Calif 154 from Calif 246, look for the Stagecoach Rd exit on your right. Turn right and head for a drink at **Cold Spring Tavern,** 5995 Stagecoach Rd (tel 805/967-0066), a 126-year-old former stagecoach stop. There's great live music Wednesday through Sunday nights, featuring anything from country-and-western to jazz.

About 30 miles from Los Olivos, Calif 154 shimmies its way down through narrow mountain passes to Santa Barbara. Turn left on State St, then left on Constance and left on Los Olivos to:

16. **Mission Santa Barbara,** 2201 Laguna St (tel 805/682-4713). Established in 1786 and called the "Queen of the Missions," it commands a beautiful view of the Pacific, with twin bell towers set against a backdrop of eucalyptus-clad foothills. Its unusual design blends classical and colonial styles: The padres adapted a design from a Roman temple. Today, the former living quarters house an excellent museum tracing mission history.

After leaving the mission, turn right on Los Olivos, then left on State St to downtown Santa Barbara. Snuggled between the Santa Ynez Mountains and the Pacific about 90 miles north of Los Angeles, the city's setting equals that of any village along the Côte d'Azur. Santa Barbara has always appealed to major power brokers from business (the Armours and Firestones), movies and television (Michael Douglas, Jonathan Winters, Jane Seymour), and politics (Ronald Reagan established his "White House West" here).

Santa Barbara's finest accommodations match the scenic setting. Queen of the city is the **Four Seasons Biltmore** (tel 805/969-2261 or 800/332-3442), built Spanish-style with tranquil courtyards and located right across from the beach. Located in the Santa Ynez foothills, the individual cottages at **San Ysidro Ranch** (tel 805/969-5046 or 800/868-6788) offer hideaway seclusion on 540 acres. **Harbor View Inn** (tel 805/963-0780 or 800/755-0222) is located directly across from Stearns Wharf and the Pacific Ocean.

With the improvement of US 101 so that it no longer slices downtown Santa Barbara in half, State St is booming with recently opened shops and restaurants. State St ends at the oceanfront and:

17. **Stearns Wharf,** which extends a half-mile over the Pacific. The wharf, which was owned by actor Jimmy Cagney and his brother in the 1940s, offers a picture-postcard California view—sailboats heeling with the wind, sunbathers strolling along the shore, and a chorus line of swaying palm trees along the esplanade.

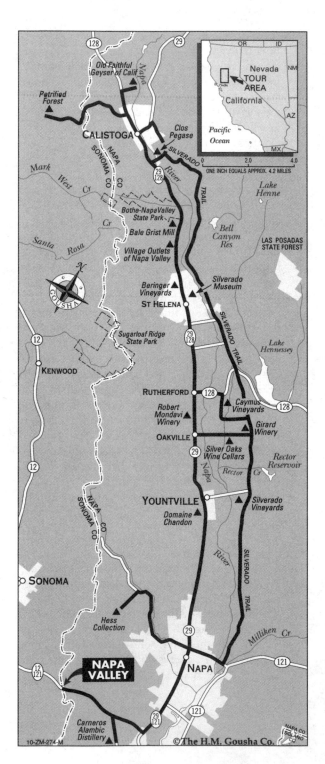

SCENIC DRIVING TOUR #3

NAPA VALLEY

Start: Carneros Alambic Distillery, Napa
Finish: Silverado Trail
Distance: Approximately 65 miles
Time: 5–8 hours
Highlights: Wining and dining at America's best wineries and restaurants, a museum dedicated to Robert Louis Stevenson, a geyser, a petrified forest, shopping

Flanked by the Mayacamas and Vacaville mountain ranges, the peaceful, green Napa Valley, America's foremost wine-growing region, is dotted with wood-frame houses, stone wineries, and ordered rows of vineyards. The region stretches about 30 miles from Carneros to Calistoga. In between, road signs identify towns whose names grace many a wine label: Oakville, Yountville, Rutherford, St Helena. This tour loops through the valley, stopping at several wineries renowned for not only their wines but their settings and architecture. You'll also have time to explore the historic towns of St Helena and Calistoga, and lunch or dine at one of the valley's superb restaurants.

Should you want to stay overnight in Napa Valley, you have many excellent choices. With individual villas snuggled in an olive grove in the Rutherford foothills, luxurious **Auberge du Soleil** (tel 707/963-1211 or toll free 800/348-5406) feels like an inn in Provence. **Vintage Inn** (tel 707/944-1112 or 800/351-1133) offers a lot of charm for the price, with 2-story units surrounded by lovely manicured grounds.

For additional information on accommodations, restaurants, and attractions in the region covered by the tour, look under specific cities in the listings portion of this book.

Napa Valley is located 45 miles north of San Francisco, about an hour's drive from the city. Take the Golden Gate Bridge from San Francisco, which puts you on US 101 N. Drive approximately 20 miles and exit at Calif 37/Napa-Vallejo, which goes east. Continue 7.7 miles and turn left (north) on Calif 121. After a little more than 6½ miles, Calif 121 veers off sharply to the right (east) just before a red blinking traffic light—stay on Calif 121, which in a few miles runs together with Calif 12. About 5 miles from the traffic light, you reach the **Napa-Sonoma County Line,** where Napa Valley suddenly makes a grand appearance, laid out like an intricate tapestry of trellised greenery. Continue on Calif 12/121. About 3 miles from the Napa county line, turn right (south) on Cuttings Wharf Rd. Proceed 1 mile to:

1. **Carneros Alambic Distillery,** 1250 Cuttings Wharf Rd (tel 707/253-9055), the first alambic brandy distillery in the United States. Depending on the time of year you visit, you might be able to sample ugni blanc or French colombard grapes in the field, or watch the stills in action. Although there's no sampling, you do get to sniff and identify the different spirits that go into the final blend. You'll enjoy a look at the stills, copper pots that look like giant Aladdin's lamps, and a visit to the barrel room.

Retrace your route to Calif 12/121 and turn right (east), rejoining the main tour route. At the intersection of Calif 12/121 and Calif 29, turn left (north) on Calif 29, the main north/south route through Napa Valley, also called St Helena Hwy between Yountville and St Helena. In 3 miles, you'll see **Napa Factory Stores,** name-brand outlets that just recently opened.

Many prominent vineyards are located directly on Calif 29. But to get a real sense of Napa, explore some of the side roads, such as the byway suggested for the next stop. From the intersection of Calif 12/121 with Calif 29, proceed north to the 1st stoplight and the Redwood Rd/Trancas intersection. Turn left on Redwood Rd. Drive 4.3 miles; watch for the marked turnoff on the left for:

2. **The Hess Collection,** 4411 Redwood Rd (tel 707/255-1144), set in 2 historic stone buildings built in 1903 on the slopes of Mt Veeder. This elegant Napa winery has tastings ($2.50 per person), video screenings about wine making, and spacious galleries displaying paintings and sculptures by contemporary American and European artists, including Morris Louis, Robert Motherwell, Frank Stella, and Francis Bacon. Both the winery and the art collection are owned by Donald Hess, Swiss-American scion of a beer and beverage fortune.

Return to Calif 29 and turn left (north). The landscape remains busily suburban for about 5½ miles until you reach the small town of Yountville, named after the area's first permanent settler and grape planter, George Yount, who arrived in 1831. Take the Yountville–Veterans Home exit, turn left (west). After crossing the railroad tracks, turn right into:

3. **Domaine Chandon,** California Dr (tel 707/944-2280). Lakes, fountains, and spreading oak trees enhance the grounds at this stone-faced winery built into the hillside. Founded in 1743 by Claude Moet, Moet-Hennessy was the first respected French wine producer to begin operations in Napa Valley in 1973. Domaine Chandon's product is called sparkling wine, not champagne—The name champagne is properly limited to wines produced in the designated region of France. Domaine Chandon wines are produced by the classic French *méthode champenoise* and undergo 2 fermentations: the first in open tanks, the second in the bottle. On the tour given here, you'll find out how both white and red grapes go into champagne, and walk through the huge tank room where each 14,100-gallon steel container holds enough liquid to supply you with the equivalent of a bottle of wine a day for 200 years. At the end of the 1-hour tour, you can sample the winery's 5 different *cuvées* (blends) for $3 to $5 a glass, or eat at the fine restaurant.

Ｕ

REFRESHMENT STOP

The best restaurant in the valley is also the loveliest—**The French Laundry,** 6629 Jefferson St, Yountville (tel 707/944-2380), set in an enchanting stone cottage. Opened in 1994, the restaurant under chef/owner Thomas Keller is deftly turning out contemporary French-influenced cuisine that rivals France's finest.

Return to Calif 29 and go north. You are now driving through one of Napa's most illustrious wine growing regions, encompassing the towns of

Oakville, Rutherford, and St Helena. This is the district of the "Rutherford Bench," a gravelly soil said to impart a unique flavor to wines produced here. The next stop in Oakville visits the operations of the grower and vintner regarded as the leading force in California wine making today, the:

4. **Robert Mondavi Winery,** 7801 St Helena Hwy in Oakville (tel 707/226-1335). Housed in serene, Spanish-style buildings, this winery, founded in 1966, is today run by Robert Mondavi along with his 2 sons and a daughter. They provide the most comprehensive winery-tour program in Napa Valley. The basic 1-hour complimentary tour and tasting (no reservations required) covers grape growing, wine making, and the sensory appreciation of wine. Other sessions (reservations required) delve more deeply into viticulture and wine making, wine and food pairings, and "essence" tasting. The winery is also a setting for art shows, literary presentations, concerts, and the annual Summer Music Festival.

Leaving Mondavi, turn left (north) on Calif 29. This area has scenic back roads such as the following circular route, which winds past some of the valley's top small vineyards. Turn right on Calif 128 (also called Rutherford Cross Rd) and almost immediately you are surrounded by vineyards. The road crosses the Napa River, which flows through the valley. Turn right on Conn Creek Rd; at the intersection is **Caymus Vineyards** (tel 707/963-4204), a good choice for wine tasting ($2). Continue south on Conn Creek Rd and turn left on Skellenger Lane to the Silverado Trail, where you turn right. Just before Oakville Cross Rd is **Girard Winery** (tel 707/944-8577) on your right. Girard produces some notable wines, including cabernet sauvignon, chardonnay, and a Benton Lane pinot noir (from Oregon); tastings are complimentary. Turn right (west) on Oakville Cross Rd, where you'll pass **Silver Oaks Wine Cellars** (tel 707/944-8808) on the left, with some wonderful cabernets from both Napa and Alexander Valleys. Tastings cost $5. You'll also see one of the boldest examples of the different architectural styles that have flourished in the valley: the pink Moorish towers of **Groth,** 750 Oakville Crossroad (open for tours and tast-

ings by appointment only; tel 707/944-0290). Tastings cost $3 and are refundable against wine purchases. Continue back to Calif 29, having completed the scenic loop.

Continue about 5 miles north on Calif 29 to:

5. **St Helena.** This enclave is Napa Valley's answer to Carmel, with many splendid 19th-century stone and brick buildings renovated into boutiques and galleries. Park your car and stroll down Main St (Calif 29). Interesting stores include **Reeds,** 1302 Main St, for women's clothing and accessories, and **Napa Valley Olive Oil Manufacturing,** 835 Charter Oak Ave, which has produced California regular and extra-virgin olive oil for 70 years. Nearby, Dansk and Gorham factory outlets are located at 801 Main St.

Literary buffs should visit the **Silverado Museum,** 1492 Library Lane (tel 707/963-3757). The small museum packs in an enormous variety of Robert Louis Stevenson's manuscripts and personal belongings; when the writer was broke and unable to afford $10 a week for room and board in Calistoga, he stayed in an abandoned bunkhouse at the Old Silverado Mine on Mt St Helena. The book he wrote about his experiences, *The Silverado Squatters,* provides a fascinating glimpse of late 1800s Napa Valley life and of Stevenson's prescience in praising early valley wines: "The smack of Californian earth shall linger on the palate of your grandson."

🍺

REFRESHMENT STOP

At **Tra Vigne** (1050 Charter Oak Ave, St Helena (tel 707/963-4444), chef/part owner Michael Chiarello's Italian dishes showcase fresh-garnered produce in dishes like ripe figs grilled in a band of prosciutto, and tender raviolis stuffed with sweet crab and whipped potatoes, napped in a saffron-butter sauce.

Once again, point your wheels "up valley," to the north. The landscape starts to change here as the valley narrows and becomes more lush. Temperatures will also be considerably warmer than in Carneros or Napa—often 10°F hotter—since the coolness and fog of San Francisco Bay do not penetrate this far north.

Less than ½ mile north of the town of St Helena, you'll come to:

6. **Beringer Vineyards,** 2000 Main St (tel 707/963-7115). Built in 1883, the turreted mansion on the grounds, called Rhine House, is a copy of the Beringer family's ancestral home in Germany, complete with inlaid wood floors, handcrafted wainscoting, and stained-glass windows. Today, the mansion serves as a hospitality center and tasting room for visitors to the award-winning winery, which produces such classics as the Beringer Private Reserve cabernet sauvignons. Complimentary tours are held every half hour.

Just north of Beringer, the **Culinary Institute of America** has taken over the century-old Greystone building as its West Coast campus. Back east, the school is considered the most important training ground for new chefs in the country. In addition to classrooms, kitchens, and bakeshops, the structure will house a public restaurant, where students will be able to hone their skills. At this writing, the school was scheduled to open in spring 1995.

About 1½ miles north of the Culinary Institute, you'll arrive at:

7. **Village Outlets of Napa Valley,** 3111 North St Helena Hwy. This small, select factory outlet is beautified by olive trees in the parking lot. It includes boutiques for Joan & David, Brooks Brothers, London Fog, and Donna Karan.

Continue north on Calif 29 for almost 1 mile to:

8. **Bale Grist Mill,** a former flour mill founded by an early Napa Valley pioneer, Dr Edward Bale. Today, the mill is a state historic park; fully restored, it has the largest working water wheel in America. You can enjoy several cool and shady walking trails here, plus picnic areas at **Bothe-Napa Valley State Park** (tel 707/942-4575), just to the north.

Drive about 3½ miles north on Calif 29 to Dunaweal Lane and turn right (east). Go east ½ mile on Dunaweal Lane to:

9. **Clos Pegase,** 1060 Dunaweal Lane, Calistoga (tel 707/942-4981). With larger-than-life portals and columns, this monumental, neoclassical structure reflects architect Michael Graves's goal to build "a temple to wine." In the early 1980s, owner Jan Shrem worked with legendary winemaker Andre Tchelistcheff (the Russian émigré who first brought fine French wine-making techniques to the valley) to create the elegant wines produced here. Tastings ($3) showcase the best of the winery's varietals; the merlots are especially round and juicy. Guided tours are held daily.

Return to Calif 29 and turn right (north). In 2 miles, Calif 29 veers off to the right and becomes known as Lincoln Ave as it enters downtown:

10. **Calistoga.** The town was founded in the mid–19th century as a health spa, thanks to its mineral-rich underground hot springs. The main promoter behind the town was flamboyant newspaperman Sam Brannan, who had scooped reports about the discovery at Sutter's Fort that sparked the California Gold Rush. He dubbed the burg Calistoga, "The Saratoga of California," linking its waters to the most famous spa resort back east.

Lincoln Ave, the town's principal thoroughfare, is lined by a mix of turn-of-the-century stone, stucco, and brick-front buildings. Compared with the groomed gentrification of St Helena, Calistoga has a slower pace and a small-town sweetness. There are a few interesting stores to browse. **Donlee Fine Arts,** 1316 Lincoln Ave, has a fine selection of paintings and sculpture, especially western art. For book lovers, **The Calistoga Bookstore,** 1343 Lincoln Ave, carries a wide range of titles, including works on Napa Valley. Located just south of town on Calif 29 is the **Calistoga Pottery,** 1001 Foothill Blvd. Owner Jeff Manfredi crafts some appealing mugs, plates, and vinegar pots, among other pieces.

Next, in contrast to the ancient art of wine making, turn your attention to a natural wonder. From Calistoga, go north 1.2 miles on Calif 128 and turn right on Tubbs Lane. Drive ½ mile to:

11. **Old Faithful Geyser,** 1299 Tubbs Lane (tel 707/942-6463). Like its namesake in Yellowstone National Park, this geyser is one of the few in the world to erupt on a regular schedule—every 40

minutes or so. Starting with a few wisps of steam, the geyser suddenly blows 350° water some 60 to 100 feet in the air.

At the small front counter, you may meet Olga Kolbek, the retired university professor who has owned the geyser since 1973. After logging eruptions for several years, she noticed that the geyser acts erratically before major earthquakes, stretching intervals between performances. Scientists have verified her observations, and researchers are now tracking the geyser's behavior to help predict earthquakes. Call ahead to get some idea what time eruptions are expected that day.

Return south on Calif 128 towards Calistoga. At Petrified Forest Rd, you can turn right to:

12. **The Petrified Forest** (tel 707/942-6667). The same volcanic activity that fuels Old Faithful Geyser caused a huge eruption of lava and ash some 3 million years ago, burying a redwood forest. Over the years, wood cells in the fallen trees were replaced with crystallized silica until the trees turned completely to stone. You can walk a trail past petrified wood specimens, many of which were already 2,000 years old when they were covered over.

From Calistoga town, continue northeast on Lincoln Ave/Calif 29 to the **Silverado Trail,** and turn right (south). During the 19th century, the route was used to carry cinnabar from mines at Mt St Helena to the river docks in Napa. Aside from its wineries (prestigious names such as Stag's Leap, Clos du Val, and more), the Silverado Trail is almost totally noncommercial and far less trafficked than Calif 29. If you'd like to sample more wines, try **Silverado Vineyards,** 6121 Silverado Trail, Napa (tel 707/944-1770), owned by the family of the late Walt Disney. Wines are good and very reasonably priced, and there's no charge to taste current releases; sampling of reserves and library wines runs from $2 to $5 per glass.

At Trancas Street in Napa (the only traffic light), turn right (west) to Calif 29.

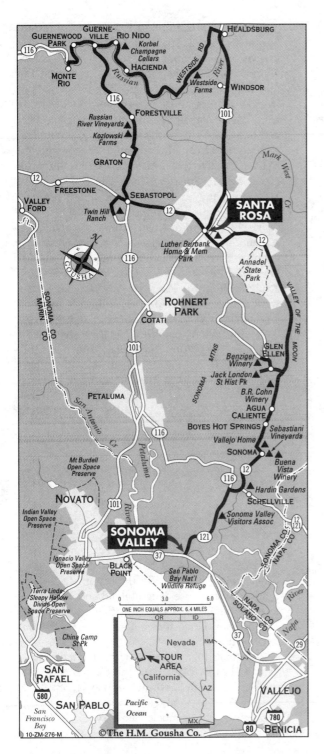

SCENIC DRIVING TOUR #4

SONOMA COUNTY

Start: Sonoma Valley Visitors Association
Finish: Twin Hill Ranch, Sebastopol
Distance: Approximately 95 miles
Time: 5–8 hours
Highlights: Sonoma town and its Mission, wine tasting, Jack London's former ranch, quaint towns, farm stands, and the Russian River Valley

While outsiders often group Sonoma together with Napa as "California Wine Country," the 2 adjoining countries north of San Francisco are as different as chardonnay and cabernet sauvignon. In practically every way, Sonoma is more laid-back than its counterpart to the east. Sonoma landscapes are gentler, with green-velvet hills manicured by contented Holsteins. Fog tendrils linger among redwood groves, and rivers meander gently from mountains to the sea. The whole Sonoma lifestyle seems more rural, a sweet throwback to vintage Americana. This driving tour concentrates on the southern portion of the county.

Sonoma's 1,600 square miles take in about 120 wineries and 10 different appellations (wine growing regions), each with unique soil conditions and microclimates. But in contrast to Napa, where wine is the "raisin d'être," Sonoma remains more agrarianly diversified. On 100-acre farms and in tiny backyard plots, over 170 specialty food growers produce edibles so impeccable that their specialties are airlifted to such elite restaurants as Spago in Los Angeles and Paul Prudhomme's in New Orleans.

The Sonoma County line is roughly 25 miles (a 45-minute drive) from San Francisco. From the city, take the Golden Gate Bridge, which puts you on US 101 N. Drive approximately 20 miles and exit at Calif 37/Napa-Vallejo, which goes east. Continue 7.7 miles and turn left (north) on Calif 121, where the tour begins. As you drive north on Calif 121, you'll soon see vineyards. This is the Carneros region, the southernmost wine-growing appellation in Sonoma. Fog and wind from San Pablo Bay cool this region, making it ideal for growing chardonnay and pinot noir. In about 5 miles, you'll come to:

1. **Sonoma Valley Visitors Association,** 25200 Arnold Dr (Calif 121), Sonoma (tel 707/996-1090), the perfect place to pick up brochures and maps about area attractions and obtain information about the area. The office is located at the same turn-off as Viansa Winery.

☕

REFRESHMENT STOP

If you plan to picnic, get your provisions at **Angelo's Wine Country Deli,** 23400 Arnold Dr (Calif 121) (tel 707/938-3688). Angelo Ibleto smokes all his own meats, fish, and turkey, and one of his oversize sandwiches is big enough to feed two.

Approximately 2 miles later, Calif 121 veers off sharply to the right (east) just before a red blinking traffic light—stay on Calif 121. In less than a mile, turn left on Calif 12, towards Sonoma town. Drive approximately ¼ mile to:

2. **Hardin Gardens,** 22660 Broadway (tel 707/935-7466). Owned by Dennis and Maria Hardin, this is the best little farm stand in southern Sonoma. On their 3 acres, the Hardins grow impeccable produce: sweet cucumbers, glossy purple eggplants, ripe, red tomatoes. Open June–October.

Leaving the farm, resume your northerly route on Calif 12 as you drive through the southernmost nub of Sonoma Valley, a crescent-shaped dale measuring 17 miles long and 7 miles wide. Its environs take in 35 wineries and 6,000 acres of vineyards, as well as one of the most historic towns in California:

3. **Sonoma.** The community quickly captivates visitors with its lovely green plaza, laid out in 1835 and now a National Historic Landmark. If City Hall looks familiar, that's because it doubled for the Tuscany County Courthouse on the TV series *Falcon Crest.* The **Sonoma Valley Visitors Center** is located here at 453 1st St E.

Several Spanish and Mexican colonial–era structures remain along the Plaza on Spain St,

including the **Mission San Francisco Solano de Sonoma,** 114 E Spain St (tel 707/938-9560), known more commonly as the Sonoma Mission. Founded in 1823, the adobe church is the last and northernmost of the 21 California missions built by the Franciscan friars. Although extensively restored, the mission still conveys the simplicity and isolation of life at the end of the Camino Real with its austere padre's quarters and courtyard shaded by olive trees. Also stop at the **Barracks** (1st St E and E Spain St), erected in 1836 to house Mexican army troops; exhibits here chronicle early 19th-century California history.

The century-old adobe and stone buildings surrounding Sonoma Plaza now house fashionable shops and restaurants. Interesting stores include **Legends,** 483 1st St W, for crafts and jewelry; **Zambezi Trading Co,** 107 W Napa St, with a wonderful selection of African furnishings and artifacts; and **Vine Arts Gallery,** 107 E Napa St, with wine country paintings and prints by Claudia Wagner. The **Wine Exchange,** 452 1st St E, carries many West Coast labels and offers beer and wine tastings. Just a few blocks from the Plaza, cheese lovers should head for the **Vella Cheese Company,** 315 2nd St E, run by the Vella family for over 60 years.

Two historic wineries are located just short drives from the center of town. The California wine industry literally began at **Buena Vista,** 18000 Old Winery Rd (tel 707/938-1266), founded in 1857 by Colonel Agoston Haraszthy, a Hungarian count. In the early 1860s, California's governor commissioned Haraszthy to go to Europe and bring back hundreds of the best grape varieties, which became the foundation stock for California's wine industry. On the self-guided winery tour, you can peruse delightful old photos, visit the tasting room, and view the cellars, which were chipped out of limestone cliffs by Chinese laborers with pick-axes.

Sonoma's first vineyards were planted by Mission friars in 1825. Those same lands now produce grapes for **Sebastiani Vineyards,** 389 4th St E (tel 707/938-5532), established at the turn of the century by Samuele Sebastiani. A complete tour explains the wine-making process and showcases the winery's beautiful collection of hand-carved casks.

🍵

REFRESHMENT STOP

For innovative and delicious cuisine, try the **East Side Oyster Bar & Grill,** 133 E Napa St, Sonoma (tel 707/939-1266), under owner/chef Charles Saunders. Packed with "multicultural" ingredients, the dishes taste as good as they sound. A typical dish: clam linguine soused with garlic, smoked chile peppers, chorizo sausage, oregano, and a splash of tequila.

Because there is so much to see and do in Sonoma town, you can easily spend your entire day here. But should you want to explore the county further, resume your drive by heading west from the Plaza on W Spain St. Drive 2 blocks from the Plaza, then turn right into the:

4. **Vallejo Home,** W Spain St near 3rd St E (tel 707/938-9559), built by General Mariano Guadalupe Vallejo, the Mexican commandante who supported the American takeover of the territory. He served as a state senator and mayor of Sonoma after California became a US state in 1850, and was also California's first commercial wine maker. In contrast to the adobe-and-red-tile style of Sonoma, the house Vallejo chose for himself reflects a New England Gothic style architecture. Most of the furniture in the house, including a rosewood concert grand piano, belonged to the Vallejo family.

Leaving the Vallejo home, turn right (west) on W Spain St, continue several blocks, then turn right (north) on Calif 12, also called Sonoma Hwy. The names of towns you'll pass—Boyes Hot Springs, Agua Caliente—clue you in that this is thermal territory. About 1½ miles from where you turned onto Calif 12, you'll pass one of California's finest resort spas, the **Sonoma Mission Inn,** Calif 12 and Boyes Blvd (tel 707/938-9000). Spa facilities are superb, and recently the resort began filling its pools and whirlpools with water from natural hot springs, which had been dormant for many years.

This is also one of Sonoma's premier wine-growing regions. One of the best wineries in the area open to the public is:

5. **BR Cohn,** 15140 Sonoma Hwy (tel 707/938-4064), set in an gnarled olive grove nearly a century old (the former dairy now serves as the aging room). The winery is owned by the former manager of the rock group the Doobie Brothers. Nearby hot springs create a "banana belt" warm climate, enabling the winery to produce some especially good cabernets. During the summer, Shakespeare plays are performed in the outdoor amphitheater.

A little over 1 mile from BR Cohn, turn left on Arnold Dr, which heads into the petitely picturesque town of Glen Ellen. Go straight onto London Ranch Rd and continue 1 mile to:

6. **Jack London State Historic Park,** 2400 London Ranch Rd (tel 707/938-5216). "When I first came here, tired of cities and people, I settled down on 130 acres of the most beautiful land to be found in California," Jack London wrote, speaking about the tract that he named Beauty Ranch. Today the former ranch is part of this park, where you can visit **The House of Happy Walls,** filled with London memorabilia, from rejection slips to the old-fashioned dictaphone and typewriter on which the writer created such American classics as *The Call of the Wild* and *The Sea Wolf.* Another exhibit features a silent newsreel showing a vibrant London on his farm, driving a team of Shire horses and balancing an armful of squirming piglets. Six days after the footage was shot, London committed suicide.

The 800 acres included in the park today are laced with excellent trails where you can hike or horseback-ride through woods of oaks and madrona (call 707/996-8566 for information about horseback riding). And, if you've brought lunch, picnic tables are available.

Leaving Jack London State Historic Park, retrace your route back to Calif 12. Just down from the park on London Ranch Rd, you can also stop at:

7. **Benziger Family Winery,** 1883 London Ranch Rd (tel 707/935-4046). Although the winery is a major operation, you'll be struck by the low-key facilities, set in a series of white, wood-frame buildings modeled after the 1868 ranch house that is the property's centerpiece. In addition to free tours and tastings, the winery has an excellent "wine discovery center," a walk-through vineyard where exhibits explain rootstocks, grafting and trellising techniques, and different varietals.

Back at Calif 12, resume your route north. Soon you'll pass some of Sonoma's best-known vineyards, many of which offer complimentary tastings, including **Chateau St Jean,** 8555 Sonoma Hwy, Kenwood (tel 707/833-4134); **St Francis,** 8450 Sonoma Hwy, Kenwood (tel 707/833-4666); and **Kenwood,** 9592 Sonoma Hwy, Kenwood (tel 707/833-5891).

🍺 REFRESHMENT STOP

In Sonoma Valley, the dining highlight is **Kenwood,** 9900 Calif 12, Kenwood (tel 707/833-6326), a small restaurant serving French country fare, with only 15 tables inside, plus seating on the terrace surrounded by vineyards.

Calif 12 continues to the northwest and then melds into:

8. **Santa Rosa,** the urban hub of Sonoma and the county seat. Among the car dealerships and fast food joints, you'll locate some special places, if you want to stop. Visit the **Luther Burbank Home and Gardens,** Santa Rosa Ave at Sonoma Ave (tel 707/524-5445) where the famous horticulturist worked from 1875 to 1926. Another famous Santa Rosa resident is cartoonist Charles Schulz. You can buy Charlie Brown, Lucy, and Linus paraphernalia at **Snoopy's Gallery and Gift Shop** at the Redwood Empire Ice Arena, 1667 W Steele Lane (tel 707/546-3385).

In Santa Rosa, Calif 12 makes a sharp left onto Farmers Lane, then resumes its westerly route—

keep following the signs for Calif 12. At the junction with US 101, take US 101 north (towards Eureka) approximately 12 miles to the Central Healdsburg exit. Go straight ½ mile to the town of:

9. **Healdsburg.** Located in the heart of Russian River country, the tiny burg enchants visitors with its tree-shaded plaza surrounded by lively shops and restaurants. Browse through the excellent selection of boutiques. **Irish Cottage,** 112 Matheson St, carries fine antiques, while **Innpressions Gallery,** 110 Matheson St, features paintings and handmade jewelry, and **Robinson & Co,** 108 Matheson St, offers neat kitchen wares. **RS Basso,** 115 Plaza, has decorative objects for the home, and **Options,** 126 Plaza, displays international crafts.

From the plaza, take Healdsburg Ave to Mill St and turn right. Mill St soon becomes Westside Rd—one of the most beautiful drives in Sonoma. The road passes through acres of vineyards along the banks of the Russian River, which stretches 70 miles from Ukiah to its juncture with the Pacific Ocean at Jenner. There are several small swimming beaches along its winding route, including **Memorial Beach** in Healdsburg, **Monte Rio Beach** in Monte Rio, and **Johnson's Beach** in Guerneville.

Cool redwood scenery and an interesting history come together here. The area draws its name from Russian fur traders who settled along the coast during the 1800s, moving from their territory in Alaska. Interestingly, the Russians are credited with planting the first grapevines in northern California, importing them from Peru as early as 1817. Heavy rainfall in winter and frequent fog on summer mornings make the region suited to the pinot noir and chardonnay grapes used in sparkling wines.

Drive 7 miles to:

10. **Westside Farms,** 7097 Westside Rd (tel 707/431-1432). If you've ever pondered changing your life, chat with Ron and Pam Kaiser, who own Westside Farms, set right on the Russian River. In the late 1980s, the Kaisers quit their fast-paced careers in investment banking to become farmers and wine growers. In addition to 40 acres of pinot noir and chardonnay, they plant over 20 acres of

---

REFRESHMENT STOP

A "must" for visitors is **the Downtown Bakery & Creamery,** 308-A Center St, Healdsburg (tel 707/431-2719), partly owned by Lindsey Shere, pastry chef at the celebrated Chez Panisse restaurant in Berkeley. You'll quickly be seduced by the thick milkshakes and the delectable baked goods.

produce. The fruits (and vegetables) of their labors are on sale at their old-time farm stand (open May to December), displaying basket after basket of just-harvested produce.

After 5 miles, Westside Rd ends at River Rd; turn right (west). Continue on River Rd 2½ miles to:

11. **Korbel Champagne Cellars,** 13250 River Rd, Guerneville (tel 707/887-2294). The brick and redwood timber winery was built in 1886 by the 3 Korbel brothers, Czech immigrants. On the tour, you can learn all about champagne-making, viewing production from the press to the corking machines. Tours and tastings are free. Outdoors, don't miss the lovely gardens, with over 250 varieties of antique roses in bloom during the summer.

Leaving Korbel, turn right (west) back onto River Rd. After about 3 miles, you'll come to:

12. **Guerneville.** This former logging town is now a hippie community, where you'll encounter plenty of tie-dye T-shirts and posters about meditation therapy; it's also a popular gay getaway.

At junction of River Rd with Calif 116, proceed southeast on Calif 116, almost immediately crossing the Russian River. In 6 miles, you'll reach:

13. **Russian River Vineyards,** 5700 Gravenstein Hwy N, Forestville (tel 707/887-1575). This small, family-owned winery has earned top reviews with its organically grown grapes, especially for the Rossi Ranch zinfandel, intensely flavored with grapes harvested from dry-farmed vines planted in 1910. In addition to the winery, the property also has a good Greek restaurant, **Topolos**.

Resume your route southeast on Calif 116 and drive for ¼ mile to:

14. **Kozlowski Farms,** 5566 Gravenstein Hwy (Calif 116), Forestville (tel 707/887-1587). Over 40 years ago, the Kozlowski family decided to plant a few raspberry bushes among their apple orchards. Soon, Mrs. Kozlowski was wondering what to do with all those berries, so she made a pot of raspberry jam, gluing paper labels on a few jars to sell. The product of her home kitchen became the precursor for the 67 items produced by Kozlowski Farms. The shop sparkles like a Tiffany showcase, with rows of jewel-tone preserves, all made on the premises.

Continue along Calif 116 to **Sebastopol.** Turn right (west) on Bodega Ave and go about 1 mile before turning left immediately after the cemetery onto Pleasant Hill Rd. Proceed approximately 1½ miles to:

15. **Twin Hill Ranch,** 1689 Pleasant Hill Rd (tel 707/823-2815), farmed by Darrel Hurst and his family for over 50 years. You can choose from 40 varieties of flavorful apples, plus luscious homemade pies.

Return down Pleasant Hill Rd and turn right (east) on Bodega Ave, which becomes Calif 12. Continue about 8 miles to US 101 S; it is about a 45-mile drive from the Golden Gate Bridge and San Francisco.

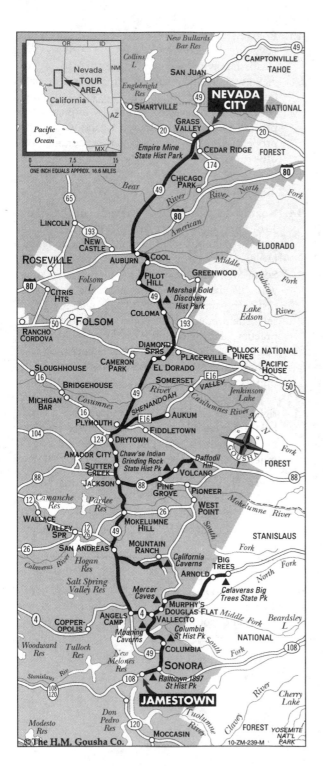

SCENIC DRIVING TOUR #5

HIGHWAY 49 & GOLD COUNTRY

Start: Nevada City
Finish: Jamestown
Distance: 230 miles, including sidetrips
Time: 3–4 days
Highlights: Columbia State Historical Park, Railtown 1897, gold rush-era mine towns, natural caverns, white-water rafting

California State Highway 49—the Golden Chain Highway—slices a nearly 300-mile route through Gold Country, linking the main towns and villages created in the Sierra foothills by the Gold Rush of 1848-59. The region, about 150 miles east of San Francisco, is awash in history, and following this former stagecoach and supply route is tantamount to a historic adventure. This tour covers sights between Nevada City, in the north, and Jamestown, in the south.

Beginning in the spring of 1848, the cry of "Gold!" brought tens of thousands of settlers to the western foothills of the Sierras. The peak mining years lasted a decade, during which over $600 million in gold was plucked from the hills. The flood of wanna-be-millionaires ended with the last of the gold, and left behind were some 500 towns; more than half disappeared as quickly as the miners, who migrated to San Francisco and other cities. Today, many communities in the region pride themselves on their well-preserved Gold Rush–era buildings, with main streets straight out of old western movies. The rustic mining towns have antique shops, pioneer cemeteries, and general stores, while ubiquitous museums tell the history of Gold Country. Peaceful backroads lead to boutique wineries in sheltered valleys.

The gently sloping terrain is cut through by fast-flowing rivers—the American, Stanislaus, Mokelumne, and Tuolumne—that offer white-water thrills for kayakers, canoers, and rafters. Active visitors can also take advantage of rock climbing, caving, and hiking. The region is full of natural splendors: rolling whalebacked foothills and dramatic canyons; woodlands of blue oak, incense cedar, and ponderosa pine dominating the hills; poplar, alder, and willow lining the riverbanks; and groves of giant sequoia sequestered in cooler hollows. With luck, you may sight black bears, raccoons, skunks, and deer, which are abundant throughout the foothills. Be wary, however, of poison oak, which is also common.

Calif 49 can be reached from San Francisco or Sacramento by traveling east on I-80 to exit 14, at Auburn. Alternately, take I-580 to I-205 to I-5 to Manteca to Calif 120, which meets Calif 49 at Chinese Camp, near Jamestown. A longer but prettier route follows Calif 24 from Oakland to I-680 to Calif 4, a 2-lane road that snakes through farmland to Calif 49 at Angels camp. From the Lake Tahoe area, head north on Calif 89 to I-80 and west to Calif 20 to Nevada City. Located at the junction of Calif 49 and Calif 20 is the heart of:

1. **Nevada City,** a pretty town where at one point during the gold rush, 10,000 miners were working every foot of ground within a radius of 3 miles. Later, Nevada City became the inland retreat of wealthy San Francisco families, whose carefully preserved Victorian houses still hug the hillsides. The town is a happy blend of Old West and art deco, exemplified by the Nevada County Courthouse. Take a carriage ride through the narrow, historic streets, or opt for a self-guided walking tour. The **Chamber of Commerce** (tel 916/265-2692), in the old Assay Office at 132 Main St, has free guides and maps. The slender 1861 Firehouse Number 1 (214 Main St) is festooned with gingerbread trim and houses the **Nevada County Historical Society Museum** (tel 916/265-5468), with its collection of gold rush relics. Dominating the gaslamp-lit town center is the handsome, 3-story, green-and-white 1856 **National Hotel,** 211 Broad St (tel 916/265-4551). The **Miners Foundry and Cultural Center,** in the old foundry building at 325 Spring St (tel 916/265-5804) is a showplace of Victorian arts and crafts. Linger overnight to take in a performance of the **Nevada Theater,** 401 Broad St (tel 916/265-8587); built in 1865, it hosted Mark Twain's first-ever lecture. Friday and Saturday afternoon, tours are offered at the **Nevada City Brewing Company,** 75 Bost Ave (tel 916/265-2446). **The Nevada City Winery,** 321 Spring St (tel 916/265-9463), also offers tastings and tours.

At the junction of Broad and Union Sts is the ramp onto Calif 49. Follow the "Golden Chain

---

Freeway" south 3.3 miles to E Main St and turn left into:

2. **Grass Valley,** the former hard-rock capital of the Northern Mines that yielded $14 million in the first year of the Gold Rush. Today it lures tourists with its balconied Victorian-era buildings and gas lamps along Main and Mill Sts; its Cornish heritage (many Cornish hard-rock miners once settled here); and the colorful saga of Irish-born Lola Montez, paramour of European royals and notables, who scandalized Europe with her racy "spider dance" before making her way across America to settle in Grass Valley in 1852. Lola passed her skills on to a young local lass, Lotta Crabtree, who captivated the miners and the rest of America and eventually amassed a fortune. The **Lola Montez Home,** a replica of the original, at 248 Mill St (tel 916/273-4667), is now the local tourist office. The **Grass Valley Museum,** corner of Church and Chapel Sts (tel 916/272-8188), boasts historical displays and a collection of 10,000 antiquarian books in the town's former (1865) schoolhouse.

Exit North Star and turn left on McCourtney Rd. Turn right on Calif 20 (Empire St), cross over Calif 49, and head east uphill 1½ miles to:

3. **Empire Mine State Historic Park,** 10791 E Empire St (tel 916/273-8522), where you can tour what once was the deepest, richest, and largest hard-rock gold mine in California. Its owner, William Bourne, became one of the wealthiest men in California. A shaft leads more than a mile down to 367 miles of underground mines. A model of the tunnel complex can be viewed near the park entrance. Some 10 miles of hiking trails

lead past mining relics, old shafts, and forest. Bourn's baronial cottage, replete with original furnishings, overlooks the site amid imposing formal gardens.

Return via E Empire St to Calif 49 and continue south. The route narrows down to a single lane; you will have plenty of opportunity to pass slower vehicles using passing lanes spaced at regular intervals. After 2 miles, a sign advises you to "Turn on headlights for the next 14 miles." Proceed south to Lincoln Way. Turn right and enter historic:

4. **Auburn,** whose 5-square-block, perfectly preserved "old town" is steeped in gold rush flavor. A walk along Lincoln Way, and Commercial, Court, and Sacramento Sts takes you back into the past; the **Chamber of Commerce,** 601 Lincoln Way (tel 916/885-5616), has a walking tour brochure. Begin at the base of Washington St and the massive statue of Claude Chana making his historic find of gold in Auburn Creek in 1848. Nearby is the 1893 **Hook and Ladder Company Firehouse,** still home to California's first motorized fire engine. The **post office** at the corner of Lincoln and Sacramento Sts is the oldest continuously used post office in California, opened in 1851. The stately, neoclassical structure clinging to the hill above Old Town is the 1894 **Placer County Courthouse,** featuring an impressive dome. Downtown Auburn, centered on Lincoln Way, is a piece of homey 1950s Americana. At 1273 High St, a log-and-stone building (a 1940s WPA project) houses the **Placer County Museum** (tel 916/889-4156), home to a walk-through mining tunnel and historical items telling the tale of Placer County.

Exit Auburn along Lincoln Way, which merges with Calif 49 (High St). Continue south as Calif 49 scales the flanks of the American River ravine. After 16 miles enter **Coloma** and the:

5. **Marshall Gold Discovery Site,** 310 Back St (tel 916/622-3470), site of the discovery that changed the history of the West. The 240-acre historic park contains a functioning full-size replica of John Sutter's sawmill where, in 1848, overseer James Marshall found flecks of gold on the banks of the American River. Within a year, 10,000 miners

---

REFRESHMENT STOP

For a taste of the Gold Country's Chinese connection, try **Shanghai Restaurant,** 289 Washington St (tel 916/823-2613), which dishes out standard but flavorful Cantonese fare at budget prices.

---

poured in. Sutter lost most of his land with the invasion and died impoverished in 1880. Marshall was tricked out of his claim, and died in poverty in 1879. He lies buried on the hillside, where his massive effigy (reached via One Way Rd) overlooks the site of his momentous find. A nature trail begins here and is particularly pleasing in fall when the leaves turn gold. Demonstrations of panning for gold are given at Sutter's Mill each afternoon. Most of Coloma lies within the Historic Park, and includes a working smithy, Chinese stores, a theater, and a pioneer cemetery. In summer, Columa is also a mecca for whitewater enthusiasts who push off here to run the American River's south fork.

Continue 7 miles south through pine and oak forest to the junction with I-50. Cross, staying on Calif 49, and enter:

6. **Placerville,** where you can take a sidewalk stroll that brings you back to the '50s—of this century and last. Placerville was formerly known as Hangtown, named for the "necktie party" by which 3 desperadoes met their demise in 1849. A dummy strung up outside the **Hangman's Tree Bar,** 905 Main St (tel 707/622-3878), reminds tourists to

---

REFRESHMENT STOP

When locals hanker for "hangtown fry" they head for the **Miner's Cafe,** 480 Main St, Placerville (tel 916/622-6018). The hometown creation is an omelette stuffed with oysters and bacon.

---

behave. Many of California's richest men grew wealthy in Placerville catering to the mining stampede. Mark Hopkins, who rose to become a railroad magnate, began his steam-powered ascent selling groceries on Main St, where Leland Stanford (later founder of Stanford University) also had a store; and John Studebaker launched his success with wheeled vehicles by building wheelbarrows. You can see one of his barrows at the **El Dorado County Historical Museum,** 100 Pacerville Dr (tel 916/621-5865), 2 miles west of town, which also displays Native American baskets and arts, mining equipment, plus an old stagecoach and steam locomotive. Northwest of town is the **Gold Bug Mine,** Bedford Ave (tel 916/622-0832), America's only city-owned gold mine and one of the few where the public can descend narrow, well-lit, but chilly mine tunnels (bring a jacket).

Turn left onto Calif 49 (Pacific St) at the base of Main St (a Shell gas station is on your right) and continue south, noticing the cottonwoods as the 2-lane road winds through rolling foothills then dips into oak woodland as you ascend a steep-sided canyon to Plymouth. Turn left on Plymouth-Shenandoah Rd (County Rd E-16) and proceed east 7 miles through the:

7. **Shenandoah Valley,** where wine grapes were first planted during the gold rush, when the valley was named for the Virginians who settled here. The original California wine region dwindled to just 1 winery before a recent blossoming revived the Amador County region. Tours and tastings are offered by most of the 18 wineries clustered throughout the valley. The **Sobon Estate,** 14430 Shenadoah Rd (tel 209/245-6555), was founded in 1856. California's 4th oldest winery (formerly D'Agostini Winery) is now a state historic landmark, with a free museum in a fieldstone building displaying early agricultural and winemaking techniques. For a map listing wineries, contact the **Amador County Chamber of Commerce,** 125 Peek St, Ste B, in Jackson (tel 209/223-0350).

Back on Calif 49, continue south 6 miles through Amador City, whose buildings cluster around a sharp bend in the road; it's California's smallest incorporated city—just 1 block long. Proceed 2 miles south to:

8. **Sutter Creek,** a real charmer with its high sidewalks and balconied facades along spiffed-up Main St, full of false-front brick-and-timber art galleries, gift stores, and dusty antique stores. At the end of Eureka St, on the creek east of Main St, is the 1873 **Knights Foundry** (tel 209/267-5543), the only existing water-powered foundry in the United States.

🍺

REFRESHMENT STOP

In the heart of Sutter Creek is the fancifully named **Ron and Nancy's Palace Restaurant & Saloon,** 76 Main St (tel 209/267-1355). Classic Italian favorites like linguine with clam sauce, veal scaloppine, and chicken marsala are served amid historic surroundings highlighted by lace tableclothes and period furnishings.

Continue south on Calif 49 for 4 miles to the Jackson Fire Station and turn left onto Main St in:

9. **Jackson,** the region's largest town (pop. 3,800). The **Amador County Museum,** 225 Church St (tel 209/223-6386), parlays Jackson's mining history with working scale models and a stamp mill with piston-like crushers that pulverized rock. The museum's mementos also commemorate the Chinese who worked as indentured laborers in the area. **Kennedy Tailing Wheels Park,** on Jackson Gate Rd, preserves 2 soaring 58-foot wheels that once lifted mine waste to an impounding dam. A walk along the well-worn wooden sidewalks of crooked Main St leads past brick buildings with iron doors and shutters to guard against fire. Jackson's renowned bordellos and gambling halls didn't close until the late 1950s, and even today there are card parlors on Main St.

Continue south on Calif 49 ½ mile to Calif 88. A Chevron gas station and the Chamber of Commerce will be on the right, at the junction. Turn left and follow the snaking road east to Pine Grove. After 10 miles, turn left on Pine Grove–Volcano Rd and continue north 1½ miles to:

10. **Chaw'se Indian Grinding Rock State Historic Park,** 14881 Pine Grove–Volcano Rd (tel 209/ 296-7488), a 136-acre preserve of grassy meadows, black oaks, and pine that was once home to the Miwok tribe. Gold miners brutally chased out and decimated the largely peaceable Native American populations who inhabited the Sierra foothills. The **Chaw'se Regional Indian Museum** profiles their vibrant culture and features a reconstructed native village replete with bark tepees, a granary, roundhouse (or *hun'ge*), and a Miwok ball field.

Continue north on Pine Grove–Volcano Rd to the Y-junction with Pioneer-Volcano Rd (be wary of merging traffic). Proceed into:

11. **Volcano,** a remote hamlet nestled in a deep, crater-like setting. Little remains to remind visitors that Volcano was once sinfully sybaritic, or that in its gold rush heyday it boasted the state's first observatory, lending library, literary and debating societies, and community theater. Performances by Volcano Pioneers Community Theater Group at the **Cobblestone Theater** (tel 209/296-4696), a former assay office on Main St, are a far cry from Volcano's once bawdy nightlife.

☕

REFRESHMENT STOP

The place to eat hereabouts is the **St George Hotel,** 16104 Pine Grove–Volcano Rd (tel 209/296-4458), an 1864 structure on the National Register of Historic Places, with maple vines clambering up the outside walls. Inexpensive American fare, including a special Sunday chicken lunch, are served in the genteel dining room.

In Volcano, Pioneer-Volcano Rd swings right and becomes Ram's Horn Grade. In springtime, follow Ram's Horn north 3 miles to the junction of Shake Ridge Rd and:

12. **Daffodil Hill,** where the McLaughlin family has been planting daffodils—over 300,000 at current count—for over 140 years. Mid-March to mid-April, the forested hillside explodes in a stunning floral display.

Return via Volcano and Pine Grove to Jackson. Turn left on Calif 49 and proceed south on the meandering road for 16 miles to:

13. **Mokelumne Hill,** another once-bawdy town where gold claims were limited to 16 square feet because the local hills were so rich. Fires ravaged Mokelumne in 1854, 1864, and 1874, but the now sleepy village still has several venerable Victorian structures.

Back on Calif 49, the road straightens out for most of the 7 miles south to the T-junction with Calif 12. Turn left and continue on Calif 49 1 mile to:

14. **San Andreas,** named for the mission church that served the Mexicans who founded the town in 1848. The charming classical revival buildings date from 1858, after a fire destroyed the town; the Queen Anne homes sprang up during the 1893–1905 boom, when San Andreas thrived as a copper-producing town. The handsome brick **County Courthouse,** 30 N Main St, has been immaculately restored and now houses the **Calaveras County Museum** (tel 209/754-6513), which provides a pamphlet that describes a self-guided historic walking tour of the town. The museum pays deference to the Miwok Indians. It also features re-creations of a miner's cabin and general store. The gentleman bandit Black Bart (alias Charles Bolton) was tried and sentenced here in 1883; he robbed gold from 28 Wells Fargo stagecoaches between 1875 and 1883.

Continue south on Calif 49 and turn left after 1 mile onto Mountain Ranch Rd (opposite the law offices of Airola & Airola). After 8 miles, turn right onto Michel Rd to Cave City Rd. Turn left and continue as the road descends to:

15. **California Caverns** (tel 209/736-2708), within whose bowels noted 19th-century naturalist John Muir recorded "chamber after chamber more and more magnificent, all a-glitter like a glacier cave with icicle-like stalactites and stalagmites combining in forms of indescribable beauty." The caverns

first opened to the public in 1850 and a small resort town, Cave City, grew around the small inconspicuous entrance, which gives no hint of the grandeur of the many crystal chambers within. The 1-hour "Trail of Lights" tour gives no indication, either, of the size of the caverns, which have not yet been fully explored. Adventurous souls can take a Wild Expedition tour to reach underground lakes.

Return to Calif 49 and continue south 11 miles to:

16. **Angels Camp,** whose name is derived from commercial, not spiritual, reasons—Henry Angel was the first storekeeper. The town began life in 1849 as a gold rush boomtown and later became a hardrock gold mining capital. Mark Twain worked the diggings briefly from 1864 to 1865 and heard the tale that inspired his first successful short story, "The Celebrated Jumping Frog of Calaveras County." The annual Jumping Frog Jubilee—in which frogs compete over 3 measured hops for a $1,500 purse for the winner's owner—is held the 3rd weekend in May in the Frogtown fairgrounds south of town. A short hop west of town is the **Angels Camp Museum,** 753 S Main St (tel 209/736-2963), displaying gold rush artifacts and horse-drawn wagons.

Turn left onto Calif 4 (Vallecito Rd) at the south end of town, head east 10 miles, and take the "Business District" turn-off to the left into historic:

17. **Murphys,** an attractive 1-street former gold rush town shaded by cottonwoods, sycamores, and elms, and known to locals as "Queen of the Sierras." Murphys is named for 2 Irish brothers who founded the town in 1848. On Main St, the iron-shuttered **Old Timers Museum** (tel 209/728-3679) houses such curiosities as a smithy that still clangs out showers of sparks. The **Black Bart Playhouse** (tel 209/728-3675) has weekend performances in April and November. Black Bart, Ulysses S Grant, Mark Twain, and William Randholph Hearst were among the famous lodgers at the 1856 **Murphys Hotel.** The hostelry once had a reputation for Wild West violence. Its atmospheric bar has many tales to tell—the bullet holes in the doors are real—and is *the* place to enjoy a

---

🍶

REFRESHMENT STOP

The historic **Murphys Hotel Restaurant,** Main St (tel 209/728-3444), serves liver and onions and other steadfast meat-based American fare, alongside pastas, cioppino, pork dijonnaise, and seafood fettuccine.

---

cool beer from the Murphy Creek Brewing Company.

Opposite the Murphys Hotel is the narrow entrance to Sheep Ranch Rd. Turn right and follow the bumpy road uphill 1 mile to:

18. **Mercer Caves,** 1665 Sheep Ranch Rd (tel 209/728-2101), exhibiting an enormous variety of bizarre and exotic limestone formations within its 10 subterranean caverns. Miwok Indians used to bury their dead inside the chilly caves, which Mother Nature maintains at a steady 55 degrees.

Back in Murphys, return to Calif 4 and continue east, following the snaking road uphill for 14 miles through stately pine to:

19. **Calaveras Big Tree State Park** (tel 209/795-2334), at an elevation of between 4,000 and 5,000 feet, and well worth the detour. The park protects 2 magnificent groves of giant sequoias, which grow only on the western slopes of the Sierra Nevada. The North Grove offers an easy mile-long loop trail; the larger South Grove, 9 miles south, is easily seen on the Big Trees Creek self-guided loop. A longer Lava Bluffs Trail leads to ancient lava formations. There are also deep canyons for exploring, riverside beaches for picnicking, guided hikes, fishing, and winter snow-shoeing and cross-country skiing.

Return via Murphys on Calif 4 to Parrotts Ferry Rd (County Rd E-18). Turn left and proceed south 1½ miles to:

20. **Moaning Caverns,** 5350 Moaning Cave Rd (209/736-2708), where a 100-foot spiral staircase leads down to the floor of a natural limestone cavern, the deepest in the state and large enough to hold

the Statue of Liberty. Native Americans held the caves in awe because of the moans that emanated from the entrance. Alas, the staircase altered the acoustics, and the caves no longer moan. The oldest human remains ever found in America were discovered here, preserved in the mineral deposits (they date back more than 13,000 years).

Continue on Parrotts Ferry Rd as it winds south through the ravine of the Stanislaus River to:

21. **Columbia State Historic Park** (tel 209/532-4301), where you recall a time when the "Gem of the Southern Mines" was the state's 2nd-largest city. Gone are the bordellos and 159 gambling halls where dirty, bearded miners rubbed shoulders with bankers and ladies of the night. But the whole 12-square-block "downtown" has been restored as an outdoor living-history museum where shop clerks wear period costumes, a blacksmith forges tools, and a saloon with swing doors still serves sarsaparilla. You can also take a bumpy, 15-minute ride in an authentic stagecoach.

"Talking buttons" on building exteriors provide taped information for a self-guided tour. Highlights include California's oldest barbershop (dating back to 1865), an early dentist's office, and the **Livery Stable,** at Fulton St and Broadway, with displays of old-time wagons. Engine Co No 1 firehouse, on State St, houses the restored, fancifully decorated *Papeete* fire pumper acquired in 1859. The **Columbia Gazette & Printing Museum,** housed in a replica of the original 1855 building, has exhibits on printing and newspaper life in early California. The **Miwok Heritage**

☕

REFRESHMENT STOP

Crisp linens, high-back chairs, and period decor add to the pleasure of eating at the **City Hotel Dining Room,** Main St (tel 209/532-1479). The moderately priced French cuisine is delicious—typical treats include angel-hair pasta, roast leg of lamb, and duck breast with black fig and apple-raisin sauce.

Museum, 11175 Damin Rd (tel 209/533-8660), displays artifacts in a cedar bark lodge. "Mellerdramers" by the Columbia Actors' Repertory are still offered at the **Fallon House Theatre** (tel 209/532-4644) in the restored **Fallon Hotel** on Washington St. Finally, don't leave town before visiting the **Nelson Candy Kitchen,** on Main St, to purchase hand-dipped chocolates made using gold rush–era recipes. The town is open daily 9am–5pm.

Continue south on Parrott's Ferry Rd until reaching the T-junction with Calif 49. Turn left and proceed 2 miles to:

22. **Sonora,** founded by Mexican miners who were soon driven out by greedy gringo miners. Sonora's Big Bonanza was the richest pocket mine in the Mother Lode, and the town was known as "Queen of the Southern Mines." The town continues to prosper thanks to its impressive, well-preserved Victorian homes and a tranquility that attracts tourists and retirees, young and old. Washington St, the main street, has 19th-century mansions as well as the 1859 **St James Episcopal Church.** Old West paintings and local history exhibits are on display at the **Tuolumne County Museum & History Center,** 158 W Bradford Ave (tel 209/532-1317), housed in the town's 1857 jail. The **Tuolumne County Courthouse,** on W Yaney St, is an intriguing amalgam of marble, green sandstone, and yellow brick; it has a copper door and a Byzantine clock tower.

Turn right at the Bank of America in downtown Sonora to continue on Calif 49, which after 2 miles merges with Calif 108. Turn left at the T-junction and continue 1½ miles south to 5th Ave. Turn left and after ½ mile enter:

23. **Railtown 1897 State Historic Park** (tel 209/984-3953), which preserves the locomotives and carriages of the Sierra Railway Company in the old Sierra Railway Depot. Trains began operating from Jamestown in 1897, hauling passengers and freight through the Mother Lode. The 23-acre, open-air museum includes the West's only operating steam roundhouse. During summer weekends, board the 80-year-old steam-powered *Mother Lode Cannon* for excursions through the Sierra foothills.

Return along 5th Ave to Willow St. Turn left and follow Willow to Main St, in the heart of downtown:

24. **Jamestown,** which, beloved by Hollywood, has starred in such films and TV shows as *High Noon, Lassie, The Lone Ranger, Butch Cassidy and the Sundance Kid,* and *Little House on the Prairie.* The ¼-mile-long Main St features shops, galleries, and Gold Rush buildings turned into cozy bed-and-breakfast inns. Kids can pan for fake gold in the horse trough outside the livery stable at 18170 Main St; adults can sign up with **Gold Prospecting Expeditions** (tel 209/984-4653) and go panning for the real thing.

The end of Main St merges with Calif 49 announcing the end of your tour.

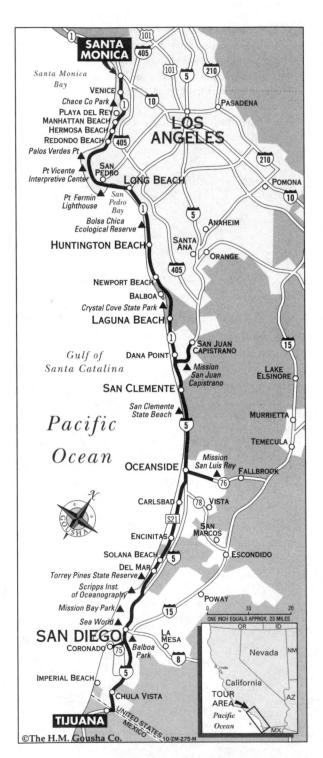

SCENIC DRIVING TOUR #6

SANTA MONICA TO THE MEXICAN BORDER

Start:	Santa Monica
Finish:	Tijuana
Distance:	Approximately 190 miles
Time:	2–3 days
Highlights:	Little beach towns, sophisticated seaside resorts, sea life parks and museums, historic buildings, yacht marinas, trend-setting restaurants and luxurious hotels

This meandering route winds through some of southern California's most well-known towns and cities, with the Pacific Ocean serving as a backdrop. Although the area certainly has its share of museums, nature is the main highlight of this scenic drive, which focuses on seaside communities with wide sandy beaches, where you'll find tanned, buffed bodies engaged in volleyball games and wet-suited surfers poised to catch that perfect wave. In certain places, restrictions of nature or development take the tour a mile or more away from the surging surf, but it always manages to wander back toward the ocean.

For additional information on accommodations, restaurants, and attractions in the region covered by the tour, look under specific cities in the listings portion of this book.

Santa Monica may be reached from the Los Angeles area by traveling west on US 10 (the Santa Monica Fwy) to the Main St exit. If at any time on this trip you zigzag off the prescribed route, it's easy to find your way back if you remember that as you go south the ocean will always be on your right.

1. **Santa Monica** is worth a stop even before you begin your drive. As you exit US 10 onto Main St, turn right and proceed 1 block to Colorado Ave, then turn left and the famed **Santa Monica Pier** is directly in front of you. At the pier, you can take a look at the beautifully restored carousel with its 46 galloping horses. Some come here to fish or for the bumper cars, shooting gallery, and arcade games. Back on Main St, proceed south and turn right on Beach St, continuing 2 blocks to Ocean Ave, a palm-lined thoroughfare along the beach.

   At Hollister Ave, Ocean Ave changes its name to Barnard, which curves to the right, bringing you back to Main St.

REFRESHMENT STOP

On the corner of Main and Marine Sts is **Schatzi on Main** (tel 310/399-4800), an appealing, casual restaurant owned by Arnold Schwarzenegger and Maria Shriver, with an imaginative menu of light entrees. "The Terminator" himself often stops by.

From Schatzi on Main, continue south on Main St 1 block to:

2. **Venice,** a funky beach town with ramshackle buildings (many being restored) supported by grandiose Doric columns. These are remnants of a turn-of-the-century city with canals, meant to mimic its Italian namesake. Today Venice is a web of little one-way streets, hardly more than alleys. From Main St, turn right on Windward Ave, find a place to park, and you'll be set for a stroll on the **Venice Boardwalk** with **Muscle Beach** and its sidewalk musicians, bikini-clad rollerbladers, and bodybuilders.

    Leave the Venice area on any small street heading away from the ocean, turn right on to Pacific Ave, and you're headed for:

3. **Marina del Rey,** the world's largest manmade small craft harbor. Turn left onto Washington St, proceed 3 blocks, then go right on Via Marina one short block, then left on Admiralty Way. This takes you through the heart of the marina area, full of trendy restaurants, ritzy hotels, and gorgeous yachts.

    For a stop, turn right on Mindanao Way 1 block to:

4. **Burton W Chace County Park,** a pleasant grassy area for boat watching. Backtrack to Admiralty Way, turn right 1 block, and you'll find that Admiralty dead-ends into Fiji Way.

    Turn left onto Fiji Way and proceed ½ block to Lincoln Blvd. Follow Lincoln for ½ mile to Jefferson Blvd, turn right onto Jefferson, then angle left onto Culver Blvd and you'll be in Playa del Rey, yet another funky little beach town. At Vista del Mar, angle left 2 blocks through town to parallel

Dockweiler State Beach. Within 3 miles you'll come to:

5. **Manhattan Beach,** where Vista del Mar changes names to Highland Ave, which soon becomes Manhattan Beach Blvd. Narrow streets near the ocean provide limited parking, and if you're here on a sunny summer weekend, count on creeping along at about 5 miles an hour. Look to the right as you cross Manhattan Beach Blvd to see the **Manhattan Beach Pier,** where you can stroll and catch the breezes.

    Take Manhattan Beach Blvd a mile or so until it becomes Hermosa Ave, and you're in Hermosa Beach, following a wide boulevard with typical beach houses. Crossing Herondo St, Hermosa Ave becomes Harbor Dr, and you're now in:

6. **Redondo Beach,** where, at the corner of Harbor Dr and Marina Way, the Southern California Edison building is decorated with a marvelous whale mural. On the right, luxury yachts snuggle into King Harbor, an upscale private marina. Within blocks Harbor Dr almost turns back on itself, and becomes Pacific Ave for 1 short block. At Catalina Ave, turn right and follow Catalina to Torrance Ave. You can park in the area and explore the shops and restaurants on the **Redondo Pier.** For dramatic views of wave-washed beaches and the ocean, angle left off of Torrance onto Esplanade. This cliffside road winds past beautiful upscale homes, leads into Paseo de la Playa, then connects with Palos Verdes Blvd S, taking you out onto the:

7. **Palos Verdes Peninsula,** one of Southern California's loveliest residential areas, strikingly different from the crowded little beach towns you've just inched through. The Peninsula affords sweeping ocean vistas and estate-like homes with red Spanish-tile roofs.

    Palos Verdes Blvd becomes Palos Verdes Dr, which takes you for about 4 miles along the bluffs. On the right, just past Hawthorne Blvd you come to the:

8. **Point Vicente Interpretive Center,** where you can park in the lot to enjoy coastline views, and look at exhibits on the area's geology and videos on Pacific Gray whales. Behind the center, a little

trail lined with cypress and palos verdes trees has scattered picnic tables where you can scan the sea for a glimpse of the area's famous sea mammals. Whale-watching season extends from December 1 to April 30.

Return to Palos Verdes Dr. About 2 miles south of Point Vicente you come to:

9. **Wayfarer's Chapel,** designed by Lloyd Wright, son of Frank Lloyd Wright. The chapel is dramatically constructed of stone and glass, with the same plants flourishing inside that grow beyond the transparent walls.

Back on Palos Verdes Dr, through an area called Portuguese Bend, signs warn of "earth movement." The roller-coaster road verifies that the terrain is subject to occasional landslides triggered by the infamous earthquake faults in most of Southern California.

Continue south on Palos Verdes Dr 1½ miles where the road splits, and veer right on 25th St. Proceed 1 mile to Western Ave, turn right onto Western, then left onto Paseo Del Mar within 1 mile. This brings you to:

10. **Point Fermin Lighthouse and the Cabrillo Marine Museum** in San Pedro. This 1800s clapboard structure topped with a beacon is now a great place for whale-watching. The **Cabrillo Marine Museum,** 3720 Stephen White Dr, has a shark tank and 3 dozen huge aquariums housing denizens of the deep.

Leaving the Marine Museum, turn right onto Pacific Ave, and you'll have the opportunity to turn right onto any number of small side streets that will take you to:

11. **The Los Angeles Harbor,** the busiest commercial port on the West Coast. Before getting on the bridge, you can detour to any close-to-the water streets to take a look at the container ships, tankers, and luxury liners. As you explore, at the bottom of 6th St, you'll come to:

12. **Ports O'Call Village,** a little enclave of boutiques and restaurants that looks like an 1800s port town.

This can be a confusing area, so your best bet is to watch for signs for the Vincent Thomas Bridge, and green signs that indicate Calif 47 and Terminal Island, which take you directly onto the:

13. **Vincent Thomas Bridge,** a graceful 6,060-foot-long suspension structure 185 feet above the shipping channel and built in 1963. There is no toll as you proceed toward Long Beach. Once you've crossed the bridge, you can start looking for signs that say:

14. **Queen Mary, Long Beach Harbor** (tel 310/435-3511), which direct you to the famous liner that became permanently moored here at Pier J in 1964. The elegant Queen is a fascinating remnant of the golden age of cruising when well-to-do families often traveled with maids. Take a guided tour to see how the ship looked during World War II when it became a troop transport. The liner is now a first-class hotel.

Leave the Queen Mary the way you entered, cross the Queensway Bridge, and you'll be on Shoreline Dr entering:

15. **Long Beach,** once a rowdy navy town with a slightly unsavory image. As you drive along Ocean Ave you'll find that it's now a pleasant place with landmark historic buildings amicably co-existing with sleek skyscrapers and modern edifices. As you follow along Ocean Ave, take the time to admire the whale mural by the famous artist Weiland on the **Convention Center's** walls. **Bluff Park,** along Ocean Blvd, has benches for views of passing ships. Four-mile-long **Belmont Shore** is the city's most attractive beach area with boutiques, bookstores, and restaurants.

Within about 3 miles you'll come to:

16. **Naples,** a canal-crossed section in south Long Beach, best seen via **Gondola Getaway,** 5437 E Ocean Blvd. Gondoliers in stripe shirts serenade you while they pole authentic Italian gondolas past expensive homes.

Leaving Gondola Getaway, backtrack about 6 blocks on Ocean Blvd to Livingston, and bear right onto Livingston. Within about 2 miles, turn right (south) onto Calif 1 (Pacific Coast Hwy). You'll stay on Calif 1 past the marshy Bolsa Chica Ecological Reserve on the right. You'll have sight of an unbroken expanse of silvery sand for about 8 miles, until you come to:

17. **Huntington Beach,** one of the largest beach towns in the area, and Huntington State Beach,

famed for its reliable waves and considered by many to be the surfing capital of the world.

If you're ready for a meal, continue on to the Huntington Beach Pier.

🍺 REFRESHMENT STOP

Seafood's the specialty at **Maxwell's**, 317 Pacific Coast Hwy (tel 714/536-2555), at Huntington Beach pier. A 1921 dance hall-cum-roller rink, it is now a prime place to munch a flaky popover and watch a lively beach volleyball game. Ask for a table on the sunny deck.

Back on Calif 1, head south and in 5 minutes you'll be in:

18. **Newport Beach,** a series of manmade islands and attractive neighborhoods. As you enter town you can stop at **Balboa Marina** to hop aboard the *Isla Mujeres* for a close-up look at gorgeous waterside homes.

Follow the signs on Calif 1 to **Balboa Island,** the most famous of the little islands that dot a large small-craft harbor. You'll see small, expensive cottages with private boats moored at their front doors. Take the 3-car ferry to the **Balboa Peninsula** and the "Fun Zone," a carnival-like strip along the bay with a ferris wheel and arcade games. It surrounds the landmark Victorian **Pavilion** (tel 714/675-9444), built in 1906 as a bathhouse and now the terminal for Catalina Island Passenger Service boats, harbor cruises, and whale-watching trips.

Back on Calif 1 heading south, follow **Crystal Cove State Park** on your right for about 8 miles to:

19. **Laguna Beach,** a renowned art colony. Get off traffic-clogged Calif 1 as soon as possible, park your car, and then explore the community's wonderful galleries and shops, such as **Pottery Shack,** 1212 S Coast Hwy (Calif 1), an open-air market with gourmet foods and tableware for sale, and **Fahrenheit 451,** 540 S Coast Hwy, an intellectu-

ally stimulating bookstore with unusual titles. (Note that in Laguna Beach, Calif 1 is called "Coast Highway" on signs). At **Heisler Park,** take a pleasant stroll among fragrant roses along bluffs overlooking the ocean.

Exceptional hotels and inns make this area an ideal first-night stop. By continuing on Calif 1 a couple of miles south to Ritz-Carlton Dr, then turning right, you can follow signs to the luxurious:

20. **Ritz-Carlton Laguna Niguel,** 33533 Ritz-Carlton Dr (tel 714/240-2000), which is actually in the town of Dana Point. This hotel exudes elegance, although it's perfectly all right to check in wearing shorts and T-shirts. Like a classic Mediterranean villa, it sits on a 150-foot bluff with a 180-degree view of the sea. If you wander down the hill to the hotel's lovely beach, a tram will be waiting so you don't have to endure the uphill climb. Even if you're not staying here, time your visit for afternoon tea, a civilized custom executed to perfection at this famous hostelry.

Leave the Ritz-Carlton and head back to Calif 1 going south where within 2 miles you'll come to:

21. **Dana Point,** named for author Richard Henry Dana, who visited the area in 1835 and wrote the novel *Two Years Before the Mast*. The town recalls his trip with a full-size replica of his schooner, *The Pilgrim,* at anchor in Dana Cove. **Dana Island** has picnic tables, walking paths, shops, and fishing at Dana Wharf.

Get back on Calif 1 and continue south about 3 miles to Del Obispo St. Turn left, proceed about 4 miles, turn left on Camino Capistrano St and within 2 blocks you'll reach:

22. **Mission San Juan Capistrano** (tel 714/248-2049), in the town the swallows flock back to each March. Although the 1812 earthquake destroyed much of this magnificent mission, its restoration is in progress. Its Serra Chapel (1777) and exhibits representing 18th-century mission life are part of a self-guided tour.

Backtrack to Calif 1 which becomes Camino Real, and continue south about 5 miles to:

23. **San Clemente,** famous as Richard Nixon's Western White House, although the town today bears little trace of the controversial president. You can

take a look at **Casa Romantica,** the first home built in the area, overlooking the **San Clemente Pier.** At **San Clemente State Beach,** for $6 per car, you can drive to a pleasant wooded area, opening onto the sand, for a picnic and a swim.

In San Clemente, Calif 1 and Camino Real pretty much disappear, and your only option is to join up with US 5 (San Diego Fwy) for the first freeway driving on this trip. The yellow "fleeing family" signs you see note the state's illegal immigrant situation, warning motorists that Mexican nationals who may have come this far by vehicle, may now jump out and run through traffic as they try to evade Immigration and Naturalization officers at the checkpoint ahead.

The 2 huge mounds on the right along the ocean are part of the San Onofre Nuclear Power Plant. About 5 miles down the freeway, exit on Mission Ave (Calif 76) and turn left (inland) about 4½ miles to:

24. **Mission San Luis Rey de Francia** (tel 916/757-3651), one of the best-preserved missions established by Father Serra along the coast. There's a shady picnic area and a small museum.

Retrace your steps on Mission Ave, cross over US 5 and where Mission dead-ends into the beach you'll find yourself at Oceanside Pier, where the waves will be dotted with surfers if the surf's up.

Backtrack to Mission Ave, and turn right (south) onto Hill St (S21) to:

25. **Carlsbad,** where S21 becomes a wide 4-lane road next to a great beach for swimming. Snack stands are conveniently available. Follow S21 about 5 miles south to:

26. **Encinitas,** where the golden Middle-Eastern-looking domes you see on the right belong to the **Self Realization Fellowship.** This monastic retreat belonging to an East Indian religious sect was built in the 1920s. Continue south on S21 another mile or so to:

27. **San Elijo Lagoon,** which provides a safe, marshy habitat for dozens of species of migrating birds, some of which you can glimpse from on-site walking trails.

Follow S21 along the ocean to:

28. **Solana Beach,** with numerous restaurants and fuel stations. At the seaside end of Lomas Santa Fe Dr, **Fletcher Cove** shelters a good, accessible swimming beach beneath towering cliffs.

Continue south on S21 about 2 miles to:

29. **Del Mar** and its famous race track, which you can see on the left from S21. The track was a hangout for the cream of Hollywood glitterati during the 1930s. Today Del Mar has luxury hotels, upscale boutiques, and a delightful beach. You can park your car at the old Del Mar train station (where surfers with boards are regular passengers) and take a walk along breezy ocean bluffs.

Back on S21, within 4 miles you'll find you're in the middle of:

30. **Torrey Pines State Reserve,** which protects the world's rarest pine, the gnarled, knotted Torrey Pine. You may want to allow a morning or afternoon to explore the trails in this wild, lovely place with stunning ocean views.

From here on into **San Diego** you can follow any of the roads marked "Scenic Drive," and enjoy what you see. As you leave the reserve, S21 veers to the left, and North Torrey Pines Rd angles to the right. Follow North Torrey Pines Rd for about a mile until you come to La Jolla Shores Dr (not La Jolla Village Dr) on the right. Follow La Jolla Shores Dr and in about a mile signs will direct you to the:

31. **Steven Birch Aquarium-Museum** (tel 619/534-3474), part of the Scripps Institution of Oceanography. Mammoth wall-size aquariums house such favorites as the giant octopus and toothy moray eels. Outside, a man-made tidepool hides spiny sea urchins, starfish, anemones, and sea cucumbers. You can take a simulated submersible ride in the DSV Deep Diver to see strange creatures of the ocean's abysses.

Continue on La Jolla Shores Dr which connects back up with Torrey Pines Rd within about a mile and a half. Follow Torrey Pines Rd to Prospect Place and turn right about 6 blocks to:

32. **La Jolla Village,** a special shopping-dining area of La Jolla. Park wherever you can as walking is the only way to see this charming little area success-

fully. Stop at **John Cole's Book Shop** with its rare, out-of-print collection and current titles. Everyone spends time at **The Cove,** popular since pirates used it to hide their stash. The small, sandy crescent is ringed with cliffs that continue under water, forming the nooks and crannies of the **San Diego–La Jolla Underwater Park,** a favorite of snorkelers and scuba divers. The grassy park above The Cove is a scenic spot for picnics.

When you're ready to leave, inch through the traffic on Prospect Place for less than a mile where it connects with La Jolla Blvd. Continue through Pacific Beach where you turn left on Garnet Ave and proceed about 8 blocks to Ingraham St. Go right onto Ingraham and within minutes you'll be in:

33. **Mission Bay Park,** San Diego's great aquatic playground. Once an odoriferous tidal basin, it now has almost 30 miles of beaches and quiet lagoons that attract swimmers, windsurfers, water skiers, cyclists, and other sports-minded sorts. Explore at your leisure, being sure not to miss:

34. **Sea World,** 1720 S Shores Rd (tel 619/226-3901), accessible by following signs directing you from Ingraham St. It is home to the world-famous killer whale, Shamu, and baby Shamu, whose aquatic antics are broadcast onto a giant screen in Shamu Stadium. Bottlenose dolphins, pilot whales, otters, and others perform in regularly scheduled shows. The aquariums and animal exhibits are always open for between-show visits.

Leave Sea World via Mission Bay Dr, cross the San Diego River and you see freeway entrance signs for US 8 E. Stay on US 8 E for just over a mile, then proceed to US 5 S. In about 2½ miles, exit at Front St/2nd Ave, continue straight onto 2nd Ave, turn right on 4th St, and continue 7 blocks to:

35. **Horton Plaza** (tel 619/238-1596), a mega-shopping center with classy boutiques and 4 major department stores. It is part of a recently-renewed downtown San Diego, and features entertainment and cultural exhibits. Adjacent is the **Gaslamp Quarter,** bounded by Broadway and Waterfront, and 4th and 5th Sts. This historic area encompasses 16 blocks of 19th-century buildings, now restored to house offices, restaurants, and shops.

You can leave downtown via 5th St (it's one-way in the direction you want to go), and proceed to Broadway where you'll turn left onto 12th Ave which becomes Park Blvd, taking you directly to:

36. **Balboa Park** (tel 619/235-1100), San Diego's crown jewel, with one of the greatest collections of galleries and museums in the state. The **San Diego Museum of Art,** 1450 El Prado (tel 619/232-7931), has French Impressionist paintings, Italian Renaissance art, and Asian works among its permanent collections. American and European paintings are represented at the **Timken Gallery,** 1500 El Prado (tel 619/239-5548). **Reuben H Fleet Space Theater and Science Center,** 1875 El Prado (tel 619/238-1233), has an Omnimax film theater, a Laserium, and a science center with hands-on learning exhibits. Half a dozen other museums make Balboa Park definitely worth a day's visit. Also within Balboa Park is the:

37. **San Diego Zoo,** 2920 Zoo Dr (tel 619/234-3153), considered one of the finest zoos in the world. San Diego's climate makes it possible to keep an enormous variety of animals—including rare and exotic species—outdoors all year long; they're housed in barless enclosures resembling their natural habitats.

The San Diego area is a wonderful spot for an overnight stop because it has so much to offer. Hotels range from sleek high-rises and luxury resorts to historic dowagers to small budget inns.

To reach an area of very special hotels and resorts, backtrack to US 5 S, and follow signs to Calif 75 and:

38. **Coronado,** a peninsula reached via a graceful bridge across San Diego Bay. On its southern end, Coronado is attached to the mainland by a narrow strip of sand called the Silver Strand, an exclusive enclave since the late 1800s. The elegant Victorian **Hotel Del Coronado,** 1500 Orange Ave (tel 619/522-8000), built in 1888, has tall cupolas, turrets, and gingerbread trim.

Leaving the hotel, turn left onto Orange Ave, which becomes Silver Strand Blvd in less than a mile, and continue past the US Naval Amphibious Base, a total of about 7 miles to:

39. **Loews Coronado Bay Resort,** 4000 Coronado Bay Rd (tel 619/424-4000), a sleek, new recreational accommodation that offers posh, casual elegance and views of Pacific sunsets on one side and the sparkling lights of San Diego on the other. It has its own 80-slip yacht marina.

    If you can bear to leave, exit the resort onto Silver Strand Blvd (Calif 75), turn left, and within 10 minutes you'll hook up with US 5 (San Diego Fwy). Follow it for another 10 minutes and you're at the Mexican border.

40. **Tijuana** is far from the drowsy, dusty little border town it once was, when all you could do was buy trinkets and liquor, and bargain for leather goods and ladies of the evening. The town has cleaned up its act and now has first-class hotels, restaurants, and attractions. It's best to park your car on the American side and walk across the border, avoiding the necessity to buy Mexican auto insurance. Within walking distance is **Mexitlan,** with scale models of Mexican sculptures, temples, monuments, and other architectural works. You'll also see handiwork of some of Mexico's master craftsmen. You'll need a taxi to get over to the **Tijuana Cultural Center, Paseo de los Héroes,** unmistakable on the city's low-rise skyline because of the globular shape of its Omnimax film theater. Fast-paced jai alai is played nightly in the **Caliente Fronton Palacio,** 1578 Avenida Revolucion at Calle 7. Traditional bullfights are held in 2 local rings each Sunday from May to September.

    An alternative to driving to Tijuana is the Tijuana Trolley, a light-rail system with frequent daily runs from downtown San Diego to the border.

    You can be back in the Los Angeles area within 2½ hours if you pick your times carefully, avoiding a drive between 7 and 9:30am and between 3:30 and 7pm. Just hop back on US 5 and head north.

ALBION

Map page M-2, C1 (S of Mendocino)

Inn 🏨

≣≣≣≣ **Albion River Inn**, 3790 Calif 1, PO Box 100, Albion, CA 95410; tel 707/937-1919 or toll free 800/479-7944. 7 mi S of Mendocino. 10 acres. Perched on bluffs above the Mendocino coast, with dramatic views from a large deck overlooking Albion Cove. **Rooms:** 14 rms; 6 ctges/villas. CI 3pm/CO noon. No smoking. Rooms have classy decor, huge bathrooms, stone fireplaces, and fabulous wooden furniture. **Amenities:** 🛁 👤 📺 Refrig, bathrobes. No A/C or TV. All units w/terraces, all w/fireplaces, some w/Jacuzzis. Complimentary wine in room. **Services:** ✗ 🍽 Masseur. **Facilities:** 🍴 ⅗ 1 rst (see also "Restaurants" below), 1 bar. Great restaurant. Good walking trails to beaches and bluffs. **Rates (CP):** HS June–Oct from $180 ctge/villa. Extra person $20. Children under 5 stay free. Min stay wknds. Lower rates off-season. Pking: Outdoor, free. Ltd CC.

Restaurant 🍽

Albion River Inn, 3790 Calif 1, Albion; tel 707/937-1919. 7 mi S of Mendocino. **Californian/Southwestern.** Offers one of the best ocean views on the Pacific coast and overlooks a manicured, flower-fringed lawn that leads to Albion Cove. Work of famous photographers is displayed on walls. Menu includes Pacific Rim bouillabaisse, roasted garlic, caesar salad, breast of Muscovy duck, pasta. Bar offers over 250 wines and 24 scotch whiskies. **FYI:** Reservations recommended. Piano. **Open:** HS spring–fall dinner Sun–Thurs 5:30–10pm, Fri–Sat 5–10pm. Reduced hours off-season. **Prices:** Main courses $11–$19. Maj CC. ♥ 📷 🏔 ⅗

ALTURAS

Map page M-2, A3

Attraction 🏛

Modoc National Wildlife Refuge; tel 916/233-3572. Located 2 miles south of town on County Rd 115. A primary nesting site for the Canada goose, as well as many other species of birds, this refuge provides great opportunities for birdwatchers. Public fishing only at Dorris Reservoir Recreation area (except during waterfowl hunting season). **Open:** Refuge, daily dawn–dusk; office, Mon–Fri 8am–4:30pm. Free.

ANAHEIM

Map page M-3, D2

See also **Buena Park, Garden Grove, Orange**

Hotels 🏨

≣≣ **Anaheim Conestoga Hotel**, 1240 S Walnut St, Anaheim, CA 92802; tel 714/535-0300 or toll free 800/824-5459; fax 714/491-8953. Harbor Blvd exit off I-5. **Rooms:** 252 rms and stes. Exec-level rms avail. CI 3pm/CO noon. Express checkout avail. Nonsmoking rms avail. Ask for one of the larger rooms. **Amenities:** 🛁 📺 A/C, cable TV w/movies, refrig, VCR. **Services:** 🍽 🔑 🚗 📠 ♻ ✈ Car-rental desk, children's program, babysitting. Shuttle to Disneyland. **Facilities:** 🏋 🎾 🏊 ⅗ 2 rsts, 2 bars, games rm, whirlpool. Use of 8 lighted tennis courts next door for a fee. **Rates:** HS May 30–Sept 5 $89–$109 S or D; from $125 ste. Children under 18 stay free. Lower rates off-season. Spec packages avail. Pking: Outdoor, free. Maj CC.

≣≣≣ **Anaheim Hilton & Towers**, 777 Convention Way, Anaheim, CA 92802; tel 714/740-4321 or toll free 800/HIL-TONS, 800/233-6904 in the US, 800/433-9923 in Canada; fax 714/740-4252. Harbor Blvd S exit off I-5. 5 acres. Conveniently located 2 blocks from Disneyland and within walking distance to the Convention Center. The hotel's extensive facilities make it almost a mini city. Dramatic lobby with pool and fountain. **Rooms:** 1,600 rms and stes. Exec-level rms avail. CI 3pm/CO noon. Express checkout avail. Nonsmoking rms avail. Recently redecorated. Tower rooms are suites. **Amenities:** 🛁 👤 🧊 A/C, cable TV w/movies, refrig, VCR, voice mail, in-rm safe, shoe polisher. Some units w/minibars, some w/terraces. **Services:** ✗ 🔑 📹 🚗 📠 ♻ ✈ Twice-daily maid svce, car-rental desk, masseur, children's program, babysitting. Shuttle to Disneyland. **Facilities:** 🏋 🎾 🏊 💻 ⅗ 4 rsts (see also "Restaurants" below), 2 bars (1 w/entertainment), games rm, spa, sauna, steam rm, whirlpool, beauty salon, day-care ctr, washer/dryer. Basketball courts. **Rates:** $89–$150 S; $99–$170 D; from $225 ste. Extra person $20. Children under 18 stay free. Higher rates for spec evnts/hols. Spec packages avail. Pking: Indoor/outdoor, $6. Maj CC.

≣≣≣ **Anaheim Marriott Hotel**, 700 W Convention Way, Anaheim, CA 92802; tel 714/750-8000 or toll free 800/228-9290; fax 714/748-2449. Katella Ave exit off I-5. Standard hotel adjacent to the Anaheim Convention Center. **Rooms:** 1,033 rms and stes. Exec-level rms avail. CI 4pm/CO noon. Express checkout avail. Nonsmoking rms avail. Nice, clean, and roomy. **Amenities:** 🛁 🧊 A/C, cable TV w/movies, voice mail. Some units w/terraces. Iron and ironing boards in room.

Services: X ▭ VP 🚐 △ ↩ ◁ Car-rental desk, babysitting. **Facilities:** 🏋 🚿 🍴 💻 🛁 ⛓ 3 rsts (see also "Restaurants" below), 1 bar, games rm, spa, sauna, steam rm, whirlpool, beauty salon, washer/dryer. Business center offers teleconferencing. **Rates:** $160–$180 S or D; from $250 ste. Children under 18 stay free. Spec packages avail. Pking: Indoor/outdoor, $6–$12. Maj CC.

≣ **Anaheim Plaza Hotel**, 1700 S Harbor Blvd, Anaheim, CA 92802; tel 714/772-5900 or toll free 800/228-1357; fax 714/772-8386. Harbor Blvd exit off I-5. A 30-year-old property that could use some cleaning up and landscaping. Lobby furniture is damaged. **Rooms:** 300 rms and stes. CI 3pm/CO noon. Nonsmoking rms avail. Renovations made rooms only average. Very nice large counter in the bathroom. **Amenities:** 📺 ⚙ 🖃 A/C, cable TV. Some units w/terraces. **Services:** X 🚐 △ ↩ Car-rental desk, babysitting. Complimentary shuttle to Disneyland. **Facilities:** 🏋 🏊 ⛓ 1 rst, 1 bar, games rm, whirlpool, washer/dryer. Very large pool; meeting rooms overlook the pool. **Rates:** HS June–Aug $95–$110 S or D; from $175 ste. Extra person $10. Children under 17 stay free. Lower rates off-season. Spec packages avail. Pking: Outdoor, free. Maj CC.

≣≣≣ **Crown Sterling Suites**, 3100 E Frontera, Anaheim, CA 92806; tel 714/632-1221 or toll free 800/433-4600; fax 714/632-9963. 8 mi NE of Disneyland. Glassell exit off Calif 91; south to Frontera. A bit off the beaten path, this lovely all-suites hotel is decorated like the old South, with a pretty atrium, koi pond, and bridges. **Rooms:** 222 stes. CI 3pm/CO noon. Express checkout avail. Nonsmoking rms avail. All suites have a sofa sleeper in the living room, 2 TVs, microwave, and iron with ironing board. **Amenities:** 📺 ⚙ 🖃 A/C, cable TV w/movies, refrig, voice mail. All units w/minibars, all w/terraces. **Services:** X 🚐 △ ↩ ◁ Car-rental desk, babysitting. Free shuttle to Disneyland and Knott's berry farm. **Facilities:** 🏋 🏊 ⛓ 2 rsts, 2 bars (w/entertainment), sauna, steam rm, whirlpool, washer/dryer. New indoor pool. **Rates (BB):** HS June–Aug from $135 ste. Extra person $10. Children under 12 stay free. Lower rates off-season. Higher rates for spec evnts/hols. Spec packages avail. Pking: Outdoor, free. Maj CC.

≣≣ **Hampton Inn**, 300 E Katella Way, Anaheim, CA 92802; tel 714/772-8713 or toll free 800/HAMPTON; fax 714/778-1235. Katella Way exit off I-5; left turn on Katella Way. Fairly new 5-story building, very clean and well kept. About 1 mile from Disneyland and Anaheim Convention Center. **Rooms:** 136 rms and stes. CI 3pm/CO noon. Nonsmoking rms avail. Furniture, wall coverings, and carpet are very clean and fresh-looking. Average-size rooms. **Amenities:** 📺 ⚙ A/C, cable TV w/movies. **Services:** 🚐 △ ↩ ◁ Car-rental desk, babysitting. Continental breakfast in lobby. Coffee and tea available 24 hours. Bell cart available. Shuttle to Disneyland. **Facilities:** 🏋

🏊 ⛓ Lifeguard. **Rates (CP):** HS June–Aug $55–$59 S; $65–$69 D; from $100 ste. Children under 18 stay free. Lower rates off-season. Spec packages avail. Pking: Outdoor, free. Maj CC.

≣≣ **Holiday Inn Maingate**, 1850 S Harbor Blvd, Anaheim, CA 92802; tel 714/750-2801 or toll free 800/624-6855; fax 714/971-4754. Harbor Blvd exit off I-5; 3 blocks W of freeway. Conveniently located 2-building hotel. **Rooms:** 312 rms and stes. CI 3pm/CO noon. Nonsmoking rms avail. Average, with old-fashioned furniture. Small bathrooms with no counter space. **Amenities:** 📺 ⚙ 🖃 A/C, cable TV w/movies. **Services:** X ▭ 🚐 △ ↩ Car-rental desk, babysitting. Children under 12 eat free at the hotel restaurant. Complimentary shuttle service to Knott's Berry Farm and Disneyland. **Facilities:** 🏋 🏊 ⛓ 1 rst, 1 bar (w/entertainment), lifeguard, games rm, washer/dryer. Children's pool. **Rates:** $89 S or D; from $175 ste. Children under 19 stay free. Spec packages avail. Pking: Outdoor, free. Maj CC.

≣≣ **Howard Johnson Hotel**, 1380 S Harbor Blvd, Anaheim, CA 92802; tel 714/776-6120 or toll free 800/422-4228; fax 714/533-3578. Harbor Blvd exit off I-5. Nice hotel right across the street from Disneyland. **Rooms:** 320 rms and stes. CI 4pm/CO noon. Nonsmoking rms avail. Small- to average-size rooms are very clean; those close to freeway are noisy. **Amenities:** 📺 ⚙ 🖃 A/C, cable TV w/movies, refrig. 1 unit w/minibar, all w/terraces. **Services:** X 🚐 △ Car-rental desk, babysitting. Shuttle to Disneyland. Tour desk in lobby. **Facilities:** 🏋 🏊 1 rst, lifeguard, games rm, whirlpool, washer/dryer. **Rates:** HS June–Aug $70–$78 S or D; from $88 ste. Extra person $10. Children under 18 stay free. Lower rates off-season. Spec packages avail. Pking: Outdoor, free. Maj CC.

≣≣≣ **Pan Pacific Hotel Anaheim**, 1717 S West St, Anaheim, CA 92802; tel 714/999-0990 or toll free 800/821-8976; fax 714/999-0745. Ball Rd exit off I-5; turn right on Ball, left on West St. Next door to the Disneyland Hotel, with easy access to the Disneyland tram and monorail. Undergoing complete renovation with new furniture, fixtures, art, and carpeting in rooms and lobby. **Rooms:** 502 rms and stes. CI 3pm/CO noon. Express checkout avail. Nonsmoking rms avail. All rooms have 2 double beds. **Amenities:** 📺 ⚙ 🖗 A/C, cable TV w/movies, voice mail. Some units w/terraces. **Services:** X ▭ VP 🚐 △ ↩ ◁ Social director, children's program, babysitting. Electric cart to Disneyland Hotel. Great kids' club is in a large room with lots of activities plus an outside play area. **Facilities:** 🏋 🏊 ⛓ 2 rsts, 2 bars, games rm, whirlpool, playground. Nice pool area with shuffleboard, table tennis, large Jacuzzi, snack bar. Grassy area with gazebo available for weddings. Japanese restaurant with sushi bar. **Rates:** HS June–Aug $145–$155 S; $155–$165 D;

from $300 ste. Children under 18 stay free. Lower rates off-season. Higher rates for spec evnts/hols. Spec packages avail. Pking: Indoor/outdoor, $7. Maj CC.

≣≣ **Peacock Suites**, 1745 S Haster St, Anaheim, CA 92802; tel 714/535-8255 or toll free 800/522-6401; fax 714/535-8914. Katella exit off I-5. Attractive, new suites. **Rooms:** 140 stes. CI 3pm/CO 11am. Nonsmoking rms avail. **Amenities:** 🛅 🗐 ☜ A/C, cable TV w/movies, refrig, VCR, in-rm safe. Some units w/Jacuzzis. Microwave. **Services:** ☛ 🚗 🖥 ☜ Babysitting. Shuttle to Disneyland. **Facilities:** 🔲 ⚑ ♿ Games rm, whirlpool, washer/dryer. **Rates:** HS June–Sept from $69 ste. Children under 16 stay free. Lower rates off-season. Higher rates for spec evnts/hols. Spec packages avail. Pking: Indoor/outdoor, free. Maj CC.

≣≣ **Quality Hotel & Conference Center**, 616 Convention Way, Anaheim, CA 92802; tel 714/750-3131 or toll free 800/231-6215; fax 714/750-9027. Harbor Blvd exit off I-5; drive south; turn left on Convention Way. One block from Disneyland, ½ block from Anaheim Convention Center. **Rooms:** 284 rms and stes. CI 4pm/CO noon. Nonsmoking rms avail. Newly renovated rooms are pleasantly decorated and fairly large. **Amenities:** 🛅 ⚐ 🗐 A/C, cable TV w/movies, refrig, in-rm safe. Some units w/terraces. Studio suites have refrigerators, microwaves, sofa beds. **Services:** ✕ ☛ 🚗 🖥 ☜ 🍽 Car-rental desk, babysitting. Free shuttle bus to Disneyland. **Facilities:** 🔲 🚍 ♿ 2 rsts, 1 bar (w/entertainment), games rm, beauty salon, washer/dryer. Pool has new bar and snack cabana. **Rates:** HS June–Aug $85–$100 S; $95–$110 D; from $275 ste. Extra person $10. Children under 17 stay free. Lower rates off-season. Spec packages avail. Pking: Outdoor, $4. Maj CC.

≣≣≣ **Residence Inn by Marriott**, 1700 S Clementine St, Anaheim, CA 92802; tel 714/533-3555 or toll free 800/331-3100; fax 714/535-7626. Katella Ave exit off I-5. Apartment-style accommodations within walking distance of Disneyland. **Rooms:** 200 stes and effic. CI 4pm/CO noon. Nonsmoking rms avail. **Amenities:** 🛅 ⚐ 🗐 A/C, cable TV, refrig. Some units w/terraces, some w/fireplaces, some w/Jacuzzis. **Services:** ✕ 🚗 🖥 ☜ 🍽 Car-rental desk, babysitting. Hospitality hour. Shuttle to Disneyland and Convention Center. Local restaurants will deliver. **Facilities:** 🔲 🏐 🎱 ♿ Whirlpool, playground, washer/dryer. Basketball and volleyball areas. **Rates (CP):** HS June 15–Aug 25 from $165 ste; from $165 effic. Extra person $10. Children under 12 stay free. Lower rates off-season. Spec packages avail. Pking: Outdoor, free. Maj CC.

≣≣≣ **Sheraton-Anaheim Hotel**, 1015 W Ball Rd, Anaheim, CA 92802; tel 714/778-1700 or toll free 800/325-3535; fax 714/535-3889. Ball Rd exit off I-5 S; Harbor exit off I-5 N. Newly renovated, the hotel is quite plush with a new lobby, 4

courtyards, and lovely landscaping. **Rooms:** 491 rms and stes. Exec-level rms avail. CI 3pm/CO noon. Express checkout avail. Nonsmoking rms avail. Large, attractive rooms with new furnishings and carpets. Very upscale. **Amenities:** 🛅 ⚐ ☜ A/C, cable TV w/movies, voice mail, in-rm safe. Some units w/terraces. **Services:** ✕ ☛ 🚗 🖥 ☜ Babysitting. Shuttle to Disneyland. **Facilities:** 🔲 ⚑ 🔲 ♿ 2 rsts, 1 bar, games rm, washer/dryer. Gourmet deli on premises. Lovely gardens for parties and wedding receptions. **Rates:** HS June–Aug $110–$130 S or D; from $150 ste. Extra person $15. Children under 18 stay free. Lower rates off-season. Higher rates for spec evnts/hols. Spec packages avail. Pking: Outdoor, free. Maj CC.

Motels

≣≣ **Anaheim Desert Palm Inn & Suites**, 631 W Katella Ave, Anaheim, CA 92802; tel 714/535-1133 or toll free 800/635-5423; fax 714/491-7409. Harbor Blvd exit off I-5; west on Katella. **Rooms:** 103 rms and stes. CI 2pm/CO 11am. Nonsmoking rms avail. **Amenities:** 🛅 A/C, cable TV w/movies, refrig, VCR. Some units w/terraces, some w/Jacuzzis. Microwave. **Services:** 🚗 🖥 ☜ Car-rental desk, babysitting. Shuttle to Disneyland. Continental breakfast. **Facilities:** 🔲 ⚑ ♿ Games rm, sauna, whirlpool, washer/dryer. **Rates (CP):** HS June–Sept 15 $59–$89 S; $69–$99 D; from $89 ste. Extra person $4. Children under 18 stay free. Min stay spec evnts. Lower rates off-season. Higher rates for spec evnts/hols. Pking: Indoor/outdoor, free. Maj CC.

≣≣≣ **Anaheim International Inn & Suites**, 2060 S Harbor Blvd, Anaheim, CA 92802; tel 714/971-9393 or toll free 800/251-2345; fax 714/971-2706. Harbor Blvd exit off I-5. Motel-style property, clean and well maintained. **Rooms:** 119 rms and stes. CI 3pm/CO 11am. Nonsmoking rms avail. In good condition. **Amenities:** 🛅 ⚐ 🗐 A/C, cable TV w/movies, refrig, in-rm safe. Some units w/minibars. Microwave. **Services:** 🚗 🖥 ☜ Car-rental desk, babysitting. Complimentary shuttle service to Disneyland. **Facilities:** 🔲 ♿ Lifeguard, games rm, whirlpool, washer/dryer. **Rates (CP):** HS June–Aug $49–$69 S or D; from $78 ste. Children under 18 stay free. Lower rates off-season. Higher rates for spec evnts/hols. Spec packages avail. Pking: Indoor, free. Maj CC.

≣ **Anaheim Stadium Travelodge**, 1700 E Katella Ave, Anaheim, CA 92805; tel 714/634-1920 or toll free 800/634-1920; fax 714/634-0366. Katella exit off I-5. Clean but plain property needs some work. Nice location close to both Disneyland and Anaheim Stadium. **Rooms:** 72 rms. CI 3pm/CO 11am. Nonsmoking rms avail. Average in size, with dark furniture in bad repair. **Amenities:** 🛅 ⚐ A/C, cable TV. Some rooms have coffeemaker and refrigerator. **Services:** 🚗 🖥 ☜ Car-rental desk, babysitting. **Facilities:** ⛓ 🔟 ♿ Whirlpool, washer/dryer. **Rates:** HS June–Aug $49–$52 S; $52–$60 D. Children under 12 stay free. Lower rates off-season. Higher rates for spec evnts/hols. Pking: Outdoor, free. Maj CC.

≡≡≡ **Best Western Stardust Inn**, 1057 W Ball Rd, Anaheim, CA 92802; tel 714/774-7600 or toll free 800/222-3639; fax 714/535-6953. Ball Rd exit off I-5. Older property, located on the back side of Disneyland. **Rooms:** 103 rms and stes. CI 3pm/CO 11am. Express checkout avail. Nonsmoking rms avail. Large rooms, clean and adequate. **Amenities:** 🔟 ⓒ A/C, cable TV, refrig. Some units w/minibars, some w/terraces. **Services:** ✗ 🚐 🖼 ⌂ ⌂ Babysitting. **Facilities:** ⛓ 🔟 ♿ 1 rst, 1 bar, sauna, whirlpool, washer/dryer. **Rates (BB):** HS June–Sept $48–$68 S; $54–$92 D; from $100 ste. Extra person $6. Children under 17 stay free. Lower rates off-season. Higher rates for spec evnts/hols. Pking: Outdoor, free. Maj CC.

≡ **Brookhurst Plaza Inn**, 711 S Brookhurst St, Anaheim, CA 92804; tel 714/999-1220 or toll free 800/266-9555; fax 714/758-1047. Brookhurst exit off I-5. Located a bit far from major attractions. **Rooms:** 91 rms and stes. CI 2pm/CO 11am. Nonsmoking rms avail. **Amenities:** 🔟 ⓒ A/C, cable TV, refrig. Some units w/Jacuzzis. **Services:** 🚐 🖼 ⌂ Car-rental desk, babysitting. Shuttle available to Knott's berry farm. **Facilities:** ⛓ 🔟 ♿ 1 rst, 1 bar, sauna, whirlpool, washer/dryer. Restaurant and lounge have recently been remodeled. **Rates (CP):** HS June–Aug $50–$60 S; $60–$80 D; from $75 ste. Extra person $6. Children under 11 stay free. Lower rates off-season. Higher rates for spec evnts/hols. Spec packages avail. Pking: Outdoor, free. Maj CC.

≡≡ **Candy Cane Inn**, 1747 S Harbor Blvd, Anaheim, CA 92802; tel 714/774-5284 or toll free 800/345-7057; fax 714/772-5462. Harbor Blvd exit off I-5; go south. Really a motel, this is located within walking distance of the Magic Kingdom and close to a dozen more attractions. **Rooms:** 172 rms. CI 3pm/CO 11am. Nonsmoking rms avail. Decorated in bright floral motifs with comfortable furnishings, including queen-size beds and a separate dressing and vanity area. **Amenities:** 🔟 ⓒ A/C, cable TV w/movies. **Services:** 🚐 🖼 ⌂ Complimentary breakfast in courtyard. Shuttle to Disneyland. 24-hour switchboard for business travelers. **Facilities:** ⛓ ♿ Whirlpool, washer/dryer. **Rates (CP):** HS Dec 21–Jan 1/Mar 18–Apr 9/June 16–Sept 5 $79–$84 S or D. Children under 17 stay free. Lower rates off-season. Spec packages avail. Pking: Outdoor, free. Maj CC.

≡≡ **Cavalier Inn & Suites**, 11811 Harbor Blvd, Anaheim, CA 92802; tel 714/750-1000 or toll free 800/821-2768; fax 714/971-3839. Harbor Blvd S exit off I-5 S. A very clean small property, enhanced by plants and flowers. **Rooms:** 100 rms and stes. CI 3pm/CO 11am. Nonsmoking rms avail. Nice furniture for a motel. Some rooms are being upgraded with new mattresses

and furnishings. **Amenities:** 🔟 ⓒ A/C, cable TV w/movies, refrig. Microwave. **Services:** 🚐 ⌂ ⌂ Car-rental desk, babysitting. Complimentary shuttle to Disneyland. **Facilities:** ⛓ ♿ Whirlpool, washer/dryer. Very nice pool and hot tub area. **Rates (CP):** HS Jun–Aug $79 S or D; from $99 ste. Children under 16 stay free. Min stay HS. Lower rates off-season. Spec packages avail. Pking: Outdoor, free. Maj CC.

≡≡ **Comfort Inn Maingate**, 2200 S Harbor Blvd, Anaheim, CA 92802; tel 714/750-5211 or toll free 800/479-5210; fax 714/750-2226. Harbor Blvd exit off I-5 S. Clean, neat, small, with plenty of parking. Located 6 blocks from Disneyland. **Rooms:** 69 rms. CI 3pm/CO 11am. Nonsmoking rms avail. Average accommodations, remodeled in late 1993. **Amenities:** 🔟 ⓒ 🖼 A/C, cable TV w/movies. Some units w/minibars. Some rooms have refrigerators. **Services:** 🚐 🖼 ⌂ Car-rental desk, babysitting. Free shuttle to Disneyland. Complimentary afternoon tea. **Facilities:** ⛓ Whirlpool, washer/dryer. **Rates (CP):** HS June–Aug $44–$64 S; $49–$69 D. Extra person $5. Children under 18 stay free. Lower rates off-season. Higher rates for spec evnts/hols. Spec packages avail. Pking: Outdoor, free. Maj CC.

≡≡ **Comfort Suites Anaheim Hills**, 201 N Via Cortez St, Anaheim, CA 92807; tel 714/637-8790 or toll free 800/221-2221; fax 714/637-8790. Imperial Blvd exit S off Calif 91; left on Santa Ana Canyon Rd; left on Via Cortez. Commercial property with mostly corporate business clientele during the week. Four stories in a southwestern theme. Fairly well maintained; landscaping needs attention. **Rooms:** 160 stes. Exec-level rms avail. CI 3pm/CO noon. Nonsmoking rms avail. Average to fairly large accommodations. Rooms with 1 king bed have space for a couch and seem spacious; rooms with 2 queen beds feel a lot smaller. **Amenities:** 🔟 ⓒ 🖼 ⌖ A/C, cable TV w/movies, refrig. Some units w/Jacuzzis. VCR upon request. The larger king suites have a full kitchen and Jacuzzi. **Services:** 🚐 🖼 ⌂ Car-rental desk, babysitting. Free shuttle service to Disneyland (10 miles away). Afternoon happy hour. **Facilities:** ⛓ 🏋 🔟 ♿ Whirlpool, washer/dryer. **Rates (CP):** HS June–Aug from $64 ste. Children under 18 stay free. Lower rates off-season. Spec packages avail. Pking: Outdoor, free. Maj CC.

≡≡≡ **Days Inn Suites**, 1111 S Harbor Blvd, Anaheim, CA 92805; tel 800/654-7503 or toll free 800/654-7503; fax 714/758-0573. Harbor Blvd N off I-5. An average motel-style place. Despite the "suites" in the name, rooms are the standard motel size. **Rooms:** 80 rms and stes. CI 3pm/CO noon. Nonsmoking rms avail. Recently remodeled. **Amenities:** 🔟 ⓒ 🖼 A/C, cable TV w/movies, refrig. Microwaves. **Services:** 🚐 🖼 ⌂ Car-rental desk, babysitting. Free shuttle to Disneyland. Fax and copying available at front desk. **Facilities:** ⛓ Whirlpool, washer/dryer.

Rates (CP): HS June–Aug $55 S or D; from $79 ste. Children under 18 stay free. Lower rates off-season. Higher rates for spec evnts/hols. Spec packages avail. Pking: Outdoor, free. Maj CC.

▤▤ **Ramada Inn–Disneyland**, 1331 E Katella Ave, Anaheim, CA 92805; tel 714/978-8088 or toll free 800/228-0586; fax 714/937-5622. Exit I-5 at Katella; go E. Motel-style property is undergoing renovation and landscaping. Remodeled lobby is very attractive. 1 block from Anaheim Stadium, 1 mile from Disneyland and convention center. **Rooms:** 240 rms and stes. CI 3pm/CO noon. Nonsmoking rms avail. **Amenities:** 🛁 ♨ 🖭 A/C, cable TV w/movies, in-rm safe. **Services:** ✕ 🖛 🚗 🛆 ⎕ Car-rental desk, babysitting. Free shuttle to Disneyland, Knott's berry farm, and convention center. **Facilities:** 🛐 📷 300 ♿ 1 rst, 1 bar, games rm, sauna, whirlpool, playground, washer/dryer. **Rates:** HS June–Aug $55 S or D; from $65 ste. Extra person $10. Children under 13 stay free. Lower rates off-season. Spec packages avail. Pking: Outdoor, free. Maj CC.

▤ **Travelodge Apollo Inn**, 1741 S West St, Anaheim, CA 92802; tel 714/772-9750 or toll free 800/826-1616; fax 714/635-1502. Ball Rd exit off I-5; west on Ball to West St. Great location across from Disneyland. **Rooms:** 136 rms. CI 3pm/CO noon. Nonsmoking rms avail. **Amenities:** 🛁 ♨ 🖭 A/C, TV w/movies, refrig. **Services:** 🚗 🛆 ⎕ Car-rental desk. Shuttle to Disneyland. **Facilities:** 🛐 ♿ 1 rst, games rm, sauna, steam rm, whirlpool, washer/dryer. **Rates:** HS June–Aug $60 S; $65 D. Children under 18 stay free. Min stay spec evnts. Lower rates off-season. Spec packages avail. Pking: Outdoor, free. Maj CC.

▤▤▤ **Travelodge Maingate**, 1717 S Harbor Blvd, Anaheim, CA 92802; tel 800/826-1616 or toll free 800/826-1616; fax 714/635-1502. Harbor Blvd exit off I-5; go south. Ten-story building within walking distance of Disneyland. **Rooms:** 254 rms and stes. CI 3pm/CO noon. Nonsmoking rms avail. Some family suites and oversized rooms. **Amenities:** 🛁 ♨ 🖭 A/C, cable TV. **Services:** 🚗 🛆 ⎕ Car-rental desk. Front desk will help arrange tours and shopping shuttles. **Facilities:** 🛐 1 rst, sauna, whirlpool, washer/dryer. Large heated pools. Children's wading pool. **Rates:** HS June–Aug $65–$70 S or D; from $85 ste. Children under 18 stay free. Min stay spec evnts. Lower rates off-season. Spec packages avail. Pking: Outdoor, free. Maj CC. Senior, corporate, and military discounts.

Resort

▤▤▤ **Disneyland Hotel**, 1150 W Cerritos Ave, Anaheim, CA 92802; tel 714/778-6600; fax 714/956-6582. Ball Rd exit off I-5; to West St. 60 acres. Disneyland monorail stops here. Hotel has beautiful grounds, with koi ponds, waterfalls, marina, beach area, and more. Great for families. **Rooms:** 1,136 rms and stes.

Exec-level rms avail. CI 3pm/CO 11am. Express checkout avail. Nonsmoking rms avail. Spotless rooms are large with nice linens, artwork, and views. All have unique Disney touches. Imperial suites are very impressive, with grand pianos. **Amenities:** 🛁 ♨ 🍽 A/C, cable TV w/movies, stereo/tape player, voice mail, in-rm safe. All units w/minibars, all w/terraces, 1 w/Jacuzzi. Wet bars and refrigerators in some rooms. Soaps, robes, and towels with Disney themes. Mickey Mouse cookies, milk, and plush animals at front door. **Services:** ✕ 🖛 VP 🚗 🛆 ⎕ Twice-daily maid svce, car-rental desk, babysitting. Shuttle services available. **Facilities:** 🛐 △ 🏊10 📷 6K ⎕ ♿ 6 rsts, 5 bars (2 w/entertainment), lifeguard, games rm, whirlpool, playground. Large exhibit hall and grand ballroom for large conventions. Shops. Paddle boats in marina. Large games room. Facilities for weddings. **Rates:** HS June–Aug/Christmas $150–$230 S or D; from $300 ste. Children under 18 stay free. Lower rates off-season. Spec packages avail. Pking: Indoor/outdoor, $10. Maj CC.

Restaurants ▯▯▯

Foxfire Restaurant, in Canyon Plaza Shopping Center, 5717 E Santa Ana Canyon Rd, Anaheim (Anaheim Hills); tel 714/974-5400. Imperial Blvd exit off Calif 91. **Continental.** A large restaurant with several dining rooms decorated in a variety of styles. Specialties include Louisiana jambalaya with Cajun spices, rack of lamb bouquetière carved at your table, and a mixed grill of top sirloin, fresh fish, and mild sausage. **FYI:** Reservations recommended. Band/country music/rock. Children's menu. **Open:** Lunch daily 11am–3pm; dinner daily 5–10pm; brunch Sun 10am–2pm. **Prices:** Main courses $9.95–$22.95. Maj CC. ♥ ♿

Hastings Grill, in Anaheim Hilton & Towers, 777 Convention Way, Anaheim; tel 714/740-4422. S Harbor Blvd exit off I-5. **Californian.** Elegant decor features polished teak, mahogany, and lots of etched glass. Modern California cuisine includes everything from lamb carpaccio with baby greens and couscous to saffron linguini with shrimp, scallops, mussels, and chardonnay sauce. There are also more traditional offerings such as poached salmon, Dover sole, duck à l'orange, and filet mignon. **FYI:** Reservations recommended. Dress code. **Open:** Lunch Mon–Fri 11:30am–2pm; dinner Mon–Sat 6–11pm. **Prices:** Main courses $14.50–$24.50. Maj CC. ♿

JW's, in the Anaheim Marriott Hotel, 700 W Convention Way, Anaheim; tel 714/750-0900. Harbor Blvd exit off I-5. **Continental.** Fancy yet comfortable. The menu features many hors d'oeuvres, including tuna tartare with wasabi, venison kidneys with polenta and wild mushrooms, and escargots. Entrees include a variety of seafood choices, all cooked creatively, and meat courses like filet mignon, roast saddle of wild boar, and veal loin. **FYI:** Reservations recommended. Harp. **Open:** Mon–Sat 6–10pm. Closed some hols. **Prices:** Main courses $18–$30. Maj CC. ● VP ⅃

Mr Stox, 1105 E Katella Ave, Anaheim; tel 714/634-2994. Katella Ave exit off I-5; located near Anaheim Stadium. **Californian.** Charming decor, with excellent choice of seafood, meat, and game. Bake own breads and desserts. Good wine cellar. **FYI:** Reservations recommended. Piano. Children's menu. Dress code. **Open:** Lunch Mon–Fri 11:30am–2:30pm; dinner Mon–Sun 5:30–10pm. **Prices:** Main courses $12–$25. Maj CC. ● VP

♥ **Pavia**, in Anaheim Hilton & Towers, 777 Convention Way, Anaheim; tel 714/750-4419. Harbor Blvd exit off I-5. **Italian.** A Roman archway and marble columns lend an elegant atmosphere to this hotel restaurant, which specializes in pasta and seafood. Dishes include tortellini with pesto and spaghetti all'aragosta, which blends cognac with lobster sauce and lobster medallions. **FYI:** Reservations recommended. Combo. Dress code. **Open:** Tues–Sun 6–11pm. **Prices:** Main courses $16.50–$30. Maj CC. ● ⅃

★ **Thee White House**, 887 S Anaheim Blvd, Anaheim; tel 714/772-1381. Ball Rd exit off I-5; east 1 mi to Anaheim Blvd, north 3 blocks. **Italian.** A restaurant in a large 1909 house, with decorations of the period. Northern Italian specialties include pan-seared ahi with pinot grigio sauce, medallions of pork with pink peppercorn-Cointreau sauce, and grilled swordfish with citrus beurre blanc. Alfresco dining when weather permits. Complimentary limo service from local hotels and businesses. **FYI:** Reservations recommended. Children's menu. Dress code. **Open:** Lunch daily 11:30am–2pm; dinner daily 5–10pm. Closed some hols. **Prices:** Main courses $14–$24; PF dinner $25. Maj CC. ● VP ⅃

Attractions ▥

DISNEYLAND ATTRACTIONS

Disneyland. Conceived by Walt Disney as a theme park that adults could enjoy along with their kids, Disneyland debuted in 1955. Located at 1313 Harbor Blvd (tel 714/999-4565), the park is divided into 8 sections, each with rides, shows, and attractions that coincide with that area's particular theme. These areas are:

Main Street, USA, recalling the aura of American small town life around the turn of the century. A steam-powered train that circles the entire park departs from the Main Street Depot, and amid the penny arcades and novelty shops are the Audio-Animatronic show, "Great Moments with Mr Lincoln," and an old-time cinema featuring "The Walt Disney Story." The Main Street Electrical Parade route runs through here nightly in the summer.

Adventureland is inspired by exotic regions of Asia, Africa, and the South Pacific. Audio-Animatronic flowers, birds, and talking tiki statues present a musical comedy in the Enchanted Tiki Room. On the Jungle Cruise, riders encounter wild animals and hostile natives. Also here are Pirates of the Caribbean, a hydroflume ride down a plunging waterfall and through pirate caves; and Splash Mountain, one of the largest towering log-flume attractions in the world.

Frontierland, depicting the pioneer spirit of America's westward expansion, includes Tom Sawyer's Island, Gold Rush-era entertainment at the Golden Horseshoe Jamboree, and a ride aboard a runaway mine train on the Big Thunder Mountain Railroad.

Fantasyland has rides based on famous children's books, including Disney movie favorites like Pinocchio, Snow White, and Dumbo. Featured attractions here are It's a Small World, and the Matterhorn Bobsleds, a fog-shrouded rollercoaster trip through chilling caverns and cloud banks.

Tomorrowland envisions the world of the future. Two of the most popular rides in Disneyland are here: Space Mountain, an indoor rollercoaster ride through the void of interstellar space; and Star Tours, a flight simulator-based excursion to the Moon of Endor.

New Orleans Square, set in the roisterous atmosphere of colonial New Orleans, features the eerie Haunted Mansion and the extremely popular Audio-Animatronic escapades of the Pirates of the Caribbean.

Critter Country is the Old South, but populated by the likes of Audio-Animatronic bears, who perform at the Country Bear Playhouse. Also here is the log flume ride, Splash Mountain, based on a scene from the classic Disney film *Song of the South*.

Mickey's Toontown is a brightly colored, out-of-scale animated cartoon town brought to life, where guests can visit the home of Mickey Mouse. Also featured are Chip 'n Dale's Tree Slide and Acorn Crawl, and Roger Rabbit's Car Toon Spin. **Open:** Mid-Sept–May, Mon–Fri 10am–6pm, Sat–Sun 9am–midnight; June–mid-Sept plus Thanksgiving, Christmas, and Easter, daily 8am–1am. $$$$

ANOTHER ATTRACTION

Anaheim Stadium, 2000 Gene Autrey Way; tel 714/254-3120. Behind-the-scenes guided tours of "the Big A" (home of the LA Rams and California Angels) visit the players' locker rooms, press areas, private suites, and other working areas of the stadium (all subject to availability). **Open:** Daily, phone for schedule. $

APTOS

Map page M-2, D2 (E of Santa Cruz)

Hotel 🛏

≡≡ **Best Western Seacliff Inn**, 7500 Old Dominion Court, Aptos, CA 95003; tel 408/688-7300 or toll free 800/528-1234, 800/367-2003 in CA; fax 408/685-3003. 5 mi E of Santa Cruz. Seacliff Blvd exit off Calif 1. This property is very nice and well kept. Beautifully tended grounds. **Rooms:** 140 rms and stes. CI 3pm/CO noon. Express checkout avail. Nonsmoking rms avail. In size and decor, superior to the average hotel/motel accommodations. **Amenities:** 🛏 ⚙ 🖬 A/C, cable TV w/movies. All units w/terraces, some w/Jacuzzis. **Services:** ✕ 🚐 ⛱ 🛎 Babysitting. **Facilities:** 🖼 200 ⅄ 1 rst, 1 bar, whirlpool. **Rates:** HS July–Sept $59–$180 S; $59–$180 D; from $165 ste. Extra person $10. Children under 12 stay free. Min stay HS. Lower rates off-season. Pking: Outdoor, free. Maj CC.

ARCADIA

Map page M-3, D2 (E of Pasadena)

Hotels 🛏

≡≡≡ **Embassy Suites Hotel**, 211 E Huntington Dr, Arcadia, CA 91106; tel 818/445-8545 or toll free 800/EMBASSY; fax 818/445-8548. 7 mi E of Pasadena. Huntington Dr exit off I-210. Lovely atrium and courtyard entrance. Near Santa Anita Racetrack, and a short ride from the Rose Bowl. Good for families. **Rooms:** 194 stes. CI 1pm/CO 1pm. Express checkout avail. Nonsmoking rms avail. **Amenities:** 🛏 ⚙ 🖬 🍴 A/C, cable TV w/movies, refrig. All units w/minibars, some w/terraces. 2 TVs. **Services:** ✕ 🚐 ⛱ 🛎 🌨 Car-rental desk, babysitting. Complimentary happy hour. Meeting planning services. **Facilities:** 🖼 ⛏ ⅄ 1 rst, 2 bars (1 w/entertainment), sauna, steam rm, whirlpool, washer/dryer. **Rates (MAP):** From $125 ste. Extra person $10. Children under 12 stay free. Higher rates for spec evnts/hols. Spec packages avail. Pking: Outdoor, free. Maj CC. Senior discounts.

≡≡≡ **Hampton Inn**, 311 E Huntington Dr, Arcadia, CA 91106; tel 818/574-5600 or toll free 800/HAMPTON; fax 818/446-2748. 6 mi E of Pasadena. Huntington Dr exit off I-210. Nice hotel 5 minutes from Santa Anita Racetrack. **Rooms:** 131 rms. CI 3pm/CO noon. Nonsmoking rms avail. Pleasant, clean accommodations. **Amenities:** 🛏 ⚙ A/C, cable TV w/movies. Free local telephone calls. **Services:** ⛱ 🛎 🌨 Babysitting. Free coffee in lobby 24 hours. **Facilities:** 🖼 35 ⅄ **Rates:** $57–$65 S; $67–$75 D. Extra person $10. Children under 18 stay free. Min stay spec evnts. Higher rates for spec evnts/hols. Pking: Outdoor, free. Maj CC. Good value.

≡≡≡ **Residence Inn by Marriott**, 321 E Huntington Dr, Arcadia, CA 91105; tel 818/446-6500 or toll free 800/331-3131; fax 818/446-5824. Huntington Dr exit off I-210. Like a home away from home; lovely gardens. **Rooms:** 120 rms, stes, and effic. CI 3pm/CO noon. Nonsmoking rms avail. Rooms have full kitchens. **Amenities:** 🛏 ⚙ 🖬 🍴 A/C, cable TV w/movies, refrig, VCR. Some units w/terraces, some w/fireplaces. **Services:** ✕ 🚐 ⛱ 🛎 🌨 Children's program, babysitting. **Facilities:** 🖼 ⅄1 30 ⅄ Whirlpool, day-care ctr, playground, washer/dryer. Use of barbecue. Sport court for baseball, volleyball, or tennis. **Rates:** $112 S or D; from $142 ste; from $112 effic. Children under 18 stay free. Higher rates for spec evnts/hols. Spec packages avail. Pking: Outdoor, free. Maj CC. Honeymoon packages.

Restaurants 🍽

♥★ **Chez Sateau**, 850 S Baldwin Ave, Arcadia; tel 818/446-8806. Baldwin Ave exit off I-210. **French.** Chef/owner Ryo Sato was on the US Culinary Olympic Team and has a very loyal following. His menu features roast sea bass, grilled swordfish, festival of lobster, roast duck with mango chutney, marinated pork tenderloin, and grilled filet mignon. **FYI:** Reservations recommended. Guitar. Jacket required. **Open:** Lunch Tues–Fri 11:30am–2:30pm; dinner Tues–Thurs 5:30–9pm, Fri–Sat 5:30–10pm, Sun 5:30–9pm; brunch Sun 10:30am–2:30pm. Closed some hols. **Prices:** Main courses $9.50–$21; PF dinner $17.50. Maj CC. ♥ 🍺 📷 🚗 💳 VP ⅄

★ **Reuben's**, 1150 W Colorado Blvd, Arcadia; tel 818/446-5551. Michillinda exit off I-210. **Diner.** This neighborhood restaurant, popular with families and seniors, is decorated in aqua and peach in a southwestern motif and offers fresh fish, steaks, and barbecued ribs. **FYI:** Reservations recommended. Country music. Children's menu. **Open:** Dinner Mon–Thurs 4–9pm, Fri–Sat 4–10pm, Sun 4–9pm; brunch Sun 10am–2pm. Closed Dec 25. **Prices:** Main courses $10.95–$27.95; PF dinner $9.95. Maj CC. 📷 💳 ⅄

Attraction 📷

Santa Anita Park, 285 W Huntington Dr; tel 818/574-RACE. Thoroughbred racing facility offers parimutuel betting; grandstand and clubhouse seating. Dining facilities; children's playground. Free behind-the-scenes guided tours weekend mornings. **Open:** Racing early Oct–early Nov and late Dec–late Apr Wed–Sun; phone for schedule. $$$

AUBURN

Map page M-2, C2

Motels 🏨

≣≣ Auburn Inn, 1875 Auburn Ravine Rd, Auburn, CA 95603; tel 916/885-1800 or toll free 800/272-1444; fax 916/888-6424. 35 mi N of Sacramento. Auburn Ravine Rd exit off I-80. Clean, moderately priced highway motel with interior corridors and neatly landscaped pool area. **Rooms:** 81 rms and stes. CI 4pm/CO noon. Nonsmoking rms avail. Quiet. **Amenities:** 🛋 🅰 🖥 A/C, cable TV, shoe polisher. 1 unit w/terrace. **Services:** 🍽 Coffee 24 hours. **Facilities:** 🏋 120 🚹 Whirlpool, washer/dryer. Kitchen adjacent to conference room allows catering for small groups. **Rates (CP):** $54–$60 S; $60–$66 D; from $100 ste. Extra person $6. Children under 12 stay free. Min stay spec evnts. Higher rates for spec evnts/hols. Spec packages avail. Pking: Outdoor, free. Maj CC.

≣≣ Best Western Golden Key Motel, 13450 Lincoln Way, Auburn, CA 95603; tel 916/885-8611 or toll free 800/201-0121; fax 916/885-0319. Lincoln Way exit off I-80. Good bet for a comfortable stay, with tidy landscaped grounds, fine furniture, and superior bedding and linens. **Rooms:** 68 rms. CI 2pm/CO noon. Nonsmoking rms avail. Upholstered chairs, desk, country pine furniture—a step up from most motels. **Amenities:** 🛋 🅰 🖥 A/C, cable TV, shoe polisher. **Services:** 🍽 🛎 Complimentary doughnuts and coffee in morning; 24-hour staff; fax services; hearing-assist devices. **Facilities:** 🏋 15 Whirlpool, washer/dryer. Pool heated all year. **Rates (CP):** HS Apr–Labor Day $52–$62 S; $58–$68 D. Extra person $4. Children under 12 stay free. Min stay spec evnts. Lower rates off-season. Higher rates for spec evnts/hols. Spec packages avail. Pking: Outdoor, free. Maj CC.

Restaurants ⅋

The Headquarter House at Raspberry Hill, in Raspberry Hill Golf Course, 14500 Musso Rd, Auburn; tel 916/878-1906. Bell Rd exit off I-80; drive southeast on Bell Rd to end and turn left on Musso Rd to golf course entrance. **American.** Old-fashioned decor with high-backed chairs in a large dining room decorated with lots of greens and brown. Outdoor dining also available. Meat is popular here, including ribs, porterhouse, and filet. Prawns, cioppino, trout, and duck are also served. **FYI:** Reservations recommended. Piano. Children's menu. Dress code. **Open:** Lunch Mon–Sat 11:30am–2:30pm; dinner Mon–Sat 5–10pm, Sun 4:30–9:30pm; brunch Sun 10am–2pm. **Prices:** Main courses $7.95–$21.95. Maj CC. 🍽 🖼 🚹

Latitudes, 130 Maple St, Auburn (Historic Auburn); tel 916/885-9535. Maple or Nevada exit off I-80. **International.** A light and airy country garden setting overlooking the old courthouse. Patio dining available. Unusual dishes include African peanut stew, curried tofu, and poulet fromage; at lunch, there are spinach-chicken crêpes and tempeh burgers. Vegetarian dishes and microbrewery beers are available. **FYI:** Reservations recommended. Guitar. Beer and wine only. **Open:** Lunch Mon–Fri 11am–2:30pm; dinner Wed–Sun 5–9pm, Fri–Sat 5–10pm; brunch Sun 10am–3pm. Closed Dec 25. **Prices:** Main courses $7.95–$16.95. Maj CC. 🍽 🍽 🖼

AVALON

Map page M-3, E2

Hotels 🏨

≣≣ Catalina Canyon Hotel, 888 Country Club Dr, PO Box 736, Avalon, CA 90704; tel 310/510-0325 or toll free 800/253-9361; fax 310/510-0900. Located in a canyon above Avalon, with beautiful grounds and a lovely swimming pool. **Rooms:** 75 rms and stes. Exec-level rms avail. CI 2pm/CO 11am. Nonsmoking rms avail. Large, somewhat sparse rooms. **Amenities:** 🛋 🅰 🖥 A/C, cable TV. 1 unit w/minibar, all w/terraces, 1 w/Jacuzzi. **Services:** 🚐 🍽 Social director, babysitting. **Facilities:** 🏋 150 🚹 1 rst, 1 bar, sauna, steam rm, whirlpool, washer/dryer. Golf and tennis nearby. **Rates:** HS May–Oct $125–$135 S or D; from $300 ste. Extra person $20. Min stay wknds. Lower rates off-season. Spec packages avail. Pking: Outdoor, free. Maj CC.

≣≣ Glenmore Plaza Hotel, 120 Sumner Ave, PO Box 155, Avalon, CA 90704; tel 310/510-0017 or toll free 800/748-5660, 800/422-8254 in CA; fax 310/510-2833. A bit off the beaten path, a hotel in an old Victorian house. **Rooms:** 45 rms and stes. CI 1pm/CO 10:30am. Rooms are small and decorated with wicker furniture. **Amenities:** 🛋 Cable TV, stereo/tape player. No A/C. 1 unit w/terrace, some w/Jacuzzis. **Services:** 🍽 Continental breakfast. **Rates (CP):** HS June–Oct $125–$225 S or D; from $265 ste. Extra person $15. Lower rates off-season. Spec packages avail. Maj CC. Not the best value in town.

≣≣ Hotel Macrae, 409 Crescent Ave, PO Box 1517, Avalon, CA 90704; tel 310/510-0246 or toll free 800/698-2266; fax 310/510-9632. On the promenade, just steps from the beach; a real California feeling with Mediterranean decor. **Rooms:** 24 rms. CI 2pm/CO 11am. Nonsmoking rms avail. Rooms are small; some have views of the harbor. **Amenities:** 🅰 Cable TV, VCR. No A/C or phone. **Services:** 🍽 Free use of beach towels and chairs. **Facilities:** 1 beach (bay), lifeguard. **Rates (CP):** HS May–Oct $90–$170 S or D. Lower rates off-season. Spec packages avail. Ltd CC.

≣≣≣ **Hotel Metropole**, 205 Crescent Ave, PO Box 1900, Avalon, CA 90704; tel 310/510-1884 or toll free 800/541-8528, 800/300-8528 in CA; fax 310/510-2534. One of the nicest hotels on the island, located in the Metropole Marketplace. Relaxing and lovely. **Rooms:** 48 rms and stes. Exec-level rms avail. CI 3pm/CO 11am. Nonsmoking rms avail. Rooms are tastefully decorated; smoking is allowed only on balconies. **Amenities:** 🛏 🕭 A/C, cable TV w/movies, refrig, bathrobes. All units w/minibars, some w/terraces, some w/fireplaces, some w/Jacuzzis. HBO, Movie Channel. **Services:** ⥁ Twice-daily maid svce, babysitting. Staff is very helpful and courteous. Free use of beach towels. **Facilities:** 🗖 🖳 🕭 2 rsts (see also "Restaurants" below), 2 bars (1 w/entertainment), 1 beach (bay), lifeguard, games rm, whirlpool, beauty salon, washer/dryer. **Rates (CP):** HS May–Oct $110–$179 S or D; from $225 ste. Extra person $15. Children under 12 stay free. Min stay wknds. Lower rates off-season. Spec packages avail. Maj CC.

≣≣ **Hotel St Lauren**, 231 Beacon St, PO Box 497, Avalon, CA 90704; tel 310/510-2299 or toll free 800/400-0744; fax 310/510-1369. Great old-style hotel with incredible views, built in the late 1980s to re-create the Victorian era. Lovely rooftop patio. **Rooms:** 42 rms and stes. CI 2pm/CO 11am. Rooms are spacious and tastefully decorated in dark woods, with ceiling fans and Victorian-era armchairs. **Amenities:** 🛏 Cable TV. No A/C. Some units w/terraces, some w/Jacuzzis. **Services:** ⥁ Babysitting. **Facilities:** 🗖 🖳 🕭 Whirlpool. **Rates (CP):** HS June–Sept 15 $85–$180 S or D; from $200 ste. Extra person $20. Children under 12 stay free. Min stay wknds. Lower rates off-season. Higher rates for spec evnts/hols. Spec packages avail. Maj CC.

≣≣ **Hotel Villa Portofino**, 111 Crescent Ave, Avalon, CA 90704; tel 310/510-0555 or toll free 800/34-OCEAN; fax 310/510-0839. With its inviting facade, this hotel looks like a California garden apartment building. **Rooms:** 34 rms and stes. CI 1pm/CO 11am. Light, airy rooms. **Amenities:** 🕭 🖪 Cable TV. No A/C or phone. Some units w/terraces, 1 w/fireplace. **Services:** ⥁ Babysitting. **Facilities:** 🗖 🕭 1 rst, 1 bar. **Rates (CP):** HS June–Oct $86–$200 S or D; from $150 ste. Extra person $10. Min stay wknds. Lower rates off-season. Higher rates for spec evnts/hols. Spec packages avail. Maj CC.

≣≣≣ **Hotel Vista Del Mar**, 417 Crescent Ave, PO Box 1979, Avalon, CA 90704; tel 310/510-1452; fax 310/510-2917. One of the most pleasant hotels on the island, on the main promenade across from the beach. The lobby is airy and inviting with palm trees, orchids, wicker rocking chairs, and fountains.

Rooms: 15 rms. CI 11am/CO 2pm. Nonsmoking rms avail. Rooms, decorated in soothing pastel colors, are extremely spacious with great views. Smoking allowed only on balconies. **Amenities:** 🛏 🕭 🖪 🍹 A/C, cable TV w/movies, refrig, VCR, bathrobes. Some units w/minibars, all w/terraces, some w/fireplaces, some w/Jacuzzis. Showtime, Movie Channel. **Services:** ⥁ Free use of beach towels. **Facilities:** 1 beach (bay), lifeguard. **Rates (CP):** HS May–Oct $95–$275 S or D. Extra person $15. Children under 2 stay free. Lower rates off-season. Spec packages avail. Maj CC. Reservations recommended 1–2 months in advance in summer.

≣≣ **Zane Grey Pueblo Hotel**, Off Chimes Tower Rd, PO Box 216, Avalon, CA 90704; tel 310/510-0966 or toll free 800/378-3256. Rustic, pueblo-style hotel decorated with Indian art and earth tones. Like being in a cabin in the hills overlooking Avalon Bay. **Rooms:** 18 rms. CI 11am/CO 10am. Rooms are named after Zane Grey's books. Some have decorative fireplaces. **Amenities:** No A/C, phone, or TV. Some units w/terraces. **Services:** 🚐 **Facilities:** 🖪 **Rates (CP):** HS May 31–Oct $75–$125 S or D. Extra person $35. Min stay wknds. Lower rates off-season. Maj CC.

Inn

≣≣ **Catalina Island Inn**, 125 Metropole, PO Box 467, Avalon, CA 90704; tel 310/510-1623; fax 310/510-7218. Lovely Victorian-style hotel, 1 block from the beach. **Rooms:** 36 rms and stes. CI 1pm/CO 11am. Top-floor rooms are the best, with high ceilings and 1920s decor. Many accommodations have ocean views. **Amenities:** 🛏 Cable TV. No A/C. Some units w/terraces. **Services:** ⥁ Babysitting. **Facilities:** 🖳 Beauty salon. **Rates (CP):** HS May–Oct $110–$160 D; from $185 ste. Extra person $10. Min stay wknds. Lower rates off-season. Spec packages avail. Ltd CC.

Restaurants 🍴

★ **The Busy Bee**, 306 Crescent Ave, Avalon; tel 310/510-1983. **Continental.** A very beachy place, with a patio bar on stilts over the water. Very popular on nice days for large salads, deli-style sandwiches, health-food sandwiches, buffalo burgers, pork chops, and prime steaks. Closed in bad weather. **FYI:** Reservations not accepted. **Open:** Daily 8am–10pm. Closed some hols; Thanksgiving–Dec 26. **Prices:** Main courses $5.95–$15.95. Maj CC. 🍷 🖼 🎭 🕭

The Channel House, in the Hotel Metropole, 205 Crescent Ave, Avalon; tel 310/510-1617. **Continental.** With white wood furniture and green umbrellas, it evokes the feeling of a country club. Inside are white wicker chairs and plants hanging from the rafters. Pepper steak flambé, New Zealand green-lip mussels, duck à l'orange with Grand Marnier. The calamari steak and the caesar salad are highly recommended. **FYI:** Reservations recommended. Piano. Children's menu. **Open:** HS July–Oct lunch daily 11am–2pm; dinner daily 5–10pm. Reduced hours off-season. Closed Feb. **Prices:** Main courses $15.95–$23.95. Maj CC. 🚢 🏞

El Galleon, 411 Crescent Ave, Avalon; tel 310/510-1188. **New American/Seafood.** Pirate-ship decor, complete with portholes on the walls, heavy wrought-iron chandeliers, and wooden captain's chairs. Seafood, hamburgers with shoestring fries. **FYI:** Reservations accepted. Guitar. Children's menu. **Open:** Lunch daily 11am–2:30pm; dinner daily 5–10pm. **Prices:** Main courses $11.95–$24.95. Maj CC. 🏞 🍴

Sand Trap, Avalon Canyon Rd, Avalon; tel 310/510-1349. **Mexican.** Good value and an inviting Mexican ambience. Outdoor dining available on a large brick patio. Dishes include fish tacos, fresh guacamole, several types of burrito, and a myriad of breakfast omelettes. Just a short walk out of town next to the golf course. **FYI:** Reservations accepted. Beer and wine only. **Open:** HS June–Aug daily 7:30am–3:30pm. Reduced hours off-season. Closed Dec 25; Dec 15–31. **Prices:** Lunch main courses $3–$6.75. No CC. 🚢 🍴

Attractions 💼

Avalon Casino Building, Crescent Ave; tel toll free 800/428-2566. The most famous structure on Catalina Island is also one of the oldest. The casino was the first resort building erected to attract vacationers from the mainland. Built in 1929, the massive circular rotunda, topped by a red tile roof, appears on posters and postcards in shops all around town. The casino is best known for its beautiful art deco ballroom that once hosted top big bands like the Tommy Dorsey and the Glen Miller orchestras. You can see the inside of the building by attending a ballroom event or a film (the Casino is Avalon's primary movie theater). Otherwise, admission is by guided tour only, operated daily by the Santa Catalina Island Company (tel 310/510-2500 or toll free 800/4-AVALON).

Catalina Island Museum, Crescent Ave; tel 310/510-2414. Located on the ground floor of the Avalon Casino, the museum features exhibits on island history, archeology, and natural history as well as an excellent relief map that details the island's interior. **Open:** Daily 10:30am–4pm. $

Wrigley Memorial and Botanical Garden; tel 310/510-2288. The Wrigley Memorial honors William Wrigley, Jr, and his contributions to the development of Catalina Island. Built from 1933 to 1934, as many Catalina materials as possible were used

in its construction. The red roof tiles and the colorful, handmade glazed tile used for finishing came from the Catalina Pottery plant, which operated from 1927 to 1937.

In 1969 the garden was expanded and revitalized. Special emphasis is given to California island endemic plants (plants that are native to one or more California islands, but grow nowhere else). Eight of these are found only on Catalina Island itself. **Open:** Daily 8am–5pm. $

Avalon Pleasure Pier, Crescent Ave and Catalina St. Jutting out into Crescent Cove, the wood plank pier affords excellent views of the town and surrounding mountains. Food stands and bait-and-tackle shops line the pier.

BAKERSFIELD
Map page M-3, C2

Hotels 🏨

▬▬▬ **Best Western Hill House**, 700 Truxtun Ave, Bakersfield, CA 93301 (Downtown); tel 805/327-4064 or toll free 800/528-1234; fax 805/327-1247. The best hotel in central downtown Bakersfield, located across from the Convention Center. Pleasant building with white columns and worn brick facade. **Rooms:** 99 rms. CI 3pm/CO noon. Nonsmoking rms avail. Clean and simple. **Amenities:** 🛁 A/C, cable TV. Some units w/terraces. **Services:** 🛎 🍴 **Facilities:** 🏋 🍴 🛗 2 rsts, 1 bar. **Rates (CP):** $55–$60 S or D. Extra person $5. Children under 12 stay free. Higher rates for spec evnts/hols. Spec packages avail. Pking: Outdoor, free. Maj CC.

▬▬▬ **Courtyard by Marriott**, 3601 Marriott Dr, Bakersfield, CA 93308 (Downtown); tel 805/324-6660 or toll free 800/321-2211; fax 805/324-1185. Fastidiously clean property, reliable and quiet despite location. Filled mostly with business travelers on weekdays, and leisure travelers on weekends. **Rooms:** 146 rms and stes. Exec-level rms avail. CI 3pm/CO 1pm. Express checkout avail. Nonsmoking rms avail. Rooms for travelers with disabilities connect to other rooms. Entire wings are nonsmoking. **Amenities:** 🛁 🍴 🖥 A/C, cable TV w/movies. All units w/terraces. **Services:** 🛗 🍴 Children's program, babysitting. **Facilities:** 🏋 🍴 🛗 👤 1 rst, 1 bar, games rm, whirlpool, washer/dryer. **Rates:** $74–$84 S; $85–$95 D; from $95 ste. Children under 18 stay free. Pking: Outdoor, free. Maj CC.

▬▬ **Radisson Suites Inn**, 828 Real Rd, Bakersfield, CA 93309; tel 805/322-9988 or toll free 800/333-3333; fax 805/322-3668. California Ave exit off Calif 99; turn south on Real Rd. Property opened in October 1993. Near busy highway, but rooms are quiet. **Rooms:** 80 stes. CI 3pm/CO noon. Nonsmoking rms avail. Accommodations can be small, but are clean and bright. **Amenities:** 🔒 🅰 🖭 🍴 A/C, cable TV, refrig, voice mail. Some units w/terraces, some w/Jacuzzis. Wet bar. **Services:** 🛆 ➔ Babysitting. **Facilities:** 🔗 🖳 ⬛ ᵹ Sauna, whirlpool, washer/dryer. **Rates (CP):** From $89 ste. Extra person $6. Children under 16 stay free. Spec packages avail. Pking: Outdoor, free. Maj CC.

🟰🟰🟰 Red Lion Hotel, 3100 Camino del Rio Court, Bakersfield, CA 93308; tel 805/323-7111 or toll free 800/547-8010; fax 805/323-0331. Calif 58 E exit off Calif 99. The most elegant hotel in Bakersfield; as quiet as a library, despite busy freeway nearby. **Rooms:** 262 rms and stes. CI 3pm/CO 1pm. Express checkout avail. Nonsmoking rms avail. Light sleepers should ask for a room on the quieter side of the hotel. Only 1 room (with 2 beds) for guests with disabilities. **Amenities:** 🔒 🅰 A/C, satel TV w/movies, shoe polisher. All units w/terraces, some w/Jacuzzis. **Services:** ✗ 🚗 🛆 ➔ ⬅ **Facilities:** 🔗 🖳 ᵹ 2 rsts (*see also* "Restaurants" below), 1 bar (w/entertainment), whirlpool. **Rates:** HS Sept 1–Dec 31/Apr 1–June 15 $109–$139 S; $124–$154 D; from $300 ste. Extra person $15. Children under 18 stay free. Lower rates off-season. Spec packages avail. Pking: Outdoor, free. Maj CC.

🟰🟰🟰 Residence Inn by Marriott, 4241 Chester Lane, Bakersfield, CA 93309; tel 805/321-9800 or toll free 800/331-3131; fax 805/321-0721. California Ave exit off Calif 99; go west 1 block; turn right on Chester. Very homey and comfortable. **Rooms:** 114 effic. CI 3pm/CO 1pm. Nonsmoking rms avail. All rooms have full kitchens and breakfast bars equipped with utensils. Special smoke alarm for handicapped-accessible suite. **Amenities:** 🔒 🅰 🖭 A/C, satel TV, refrig, voice mail. Some units w/fireplaces. **Services:** ✗ 🚗 🛆 ➔ ⬅ Social director, babysitting. Social hour in lounge Monday–Friday 5–7pm. Videos available in lobby. **Facilities:** 🔗 🖳 🖳 ᵹ Whirlpool, playground, washer/dryer. **Rates (BB):** From $85 effic. Children under 18 stay free. Min stay spec evnts. Spec packages avail. Pking: Outdoor, free. Maj CC.

🟰🟰🟰 Sheraton Inn Bakersfield, 5101 California Ave, Bakersfield, CA 93309; tel 805/325-9700 or toll free 800/500-5399; fax 805/323-3508. California Ave exit off Calif 99; go ¾ mile west. Exceptionally quiet, upscale property catering to business travelers. Spacious, comfortable lobby. **Rooms:** 197 rms and stes. Exec-level rms avail. CI 3pm/CO 1pm. Express checkout avail. Nonsmoking rms avail. Rooms have electronic key entry system. **Amenities:** 🔒 🅰 🖭 A/C, cable TV w/movies, voice mail, shoe polisher. Some units w/terraces. **Services:** ✗ 🚗 🛆 ➔ ⬅ Social director, babysitting. **Facilities:** 🔗 🖳 🖳 ⬛ ᵹ 2 rsts (*see also* "Restaurants" below), 2 bars, spa, whirlpool.

Beautiful pool area in central courtyard shaded by trellises and plants. Free use of nearby Family Fitness Center. **Rates (CP):** HS Spring–Fall $120 S; $129 D; from $175 ste. Extra person $10. Children under 18 stay free. Lower rates off-season. Spec packages avail. Pking: Outdoor, free. Maj CC.

Motels

🟰🟰 California Inn, 1030 Wible Rd, Bakersfield, CA 93304; tel 805/834-3377 or toll free 800/707-8000; fax 805/834-4439. Ming Ave exit off Calif 99. Newer property; a good budget choice. **Rooms:** 61 rms. CI 2pm/CO noon. Nonsmoking rms avail. Simple but clean rooms. **Amenities:** 🔒 🖭 A/C, cable TV, refrig. 1 unit w/terrace. **Services:** ➔ **Facilities:** 🔗 🖳 ᵹ Sauna, whirlpool, washer/dryer. **Rates (CP):** $36–$45 S; $39–$49 D. Extra person $4. Children under 18 stay free. Pking: Outdoor, free. Maj CC.

🟰 Econo Lodge–Bakersfield, 2700 White Lane, Bakersfield, CA 93304; tel 805/832-3111; fax 805/832-4591. White Lane exit off Calif 99. A very basic property. **Rooms:** 152 rms. CI 1pm/CO 11am. Nonsmoking rms avail. **Amenities:** 🔒 A/C, TV, in-rm safe. **Services:** 🚗 ⬅ Car-rental desk, babysitting. **Facilities:** 🔗 🖳 ᵹ 1 bar, washer/dryer. **Rates:** $30 S or D. Children under 18 stay free. Pking: Outdoor, free. Maj CC.

🟰🟰 La Quinta Motor Inn, 3232 Riverside Dr, Bakersfield, CA 93308 (Downtown); tel 805/325-7400 or toll free 800/531-5900; fax 805/324-6032. Clean, newish property with a comfortable lobby and a convenient location. Good value. **Rooms:** 129 rms and stes. Exec-level rms avail. CI open/CO noon. Express checkout avail. Nonsmoking rms avail. Smallish rooms, newly painted; fine for a short stay. **Amenities:** 🔒 🅰 A/C, satel TV w/movies. **Services:** 🚗 🛆 ➔ ⬅ **Facilities:** 🔗 🖳 ᵹ Washer/dryer. **Rates (CP):** $52–$59 S; $60–$67 D; from $65 ste. Children under 18 stay free. Higher rates for spec evnts/hols. Spec packages avail. Pking: Outdoor, free. Maj CC.

🟰🟰 Ramada Inn, 3535 Rosedale Hwy, Bakersfield, CA 93308 (Downtown); tel 805/327-0681 or toll free 800/228-2828; fax 805/324-1648. Rosedale exit off Calif 99. Convenient to freeways. Looks deluxe because of recent upgrading, but basically a standard chain hotel. **Rooms:** 197 rms. CI 4pm/CO noon. Nonsmoking rms avail. **Amenities:** 🔒 🅰 A/C, cable TV. Some units w/terraces. **Services:** ✗ 🚗 🛆 ➔ **Facilities:** 🔗 🖳 ᵹ 1 rst, 1 bar (w/entertainment), whirlpool, washer/dryer. **Rates:** $62 S; $67 D. Extra person $5. Children under 18 stay free. Pking: Outdoor, free. Maj CC.

🟰🟰 Skyway Inn, 1305 Skyway Dr, Bakersfield, CA 93308 (Oildale); tel 805/399-9321; fax 805/399-2615. Airport Dr exit off Calif 99; go north to Skyway Dr, turn left at entrance to

Meadows Field. Convenient location for air travelers. **Rooms:** 63 rms, stes, and effic. CI 7am/CO noon. Nonsmoking rms avail. Rooms are light, airy, and unique, each with a name and theme, such as "Modern Romance" or "Ocean View." Adorned with bric-a-brac and creative lighting in an attempt to add personality to otherwise ordinary rooms. **Amenities:** 🖥 👁 🖭 A/C, cable TV. Some units w/terraces. **Services:** ✗ ⊠ 🛏 Car-rental desk. **Facilities:** 🖪 🔟 2 rsts (*see also* "Restaurants" below), 1 bar (w/entertainment), whirlpool. **Rates:** HS May–Aug $45–$51 D; from $69 ste; from $50 effic. Extra person $6. Children under 18 stay free. Lower rates off-season. Spec packages avail. Pking: Outdoor, free. Maj CC.

Restaurants 🍴

Anton's Airport Bar & Grill, in the Skyway Inn, 1229 Skyway Dr, Bakersfield (Oildale); tel 805/399-3300. Airport Dr exit off Calif 99. **Californian.** Quiet and elegant with comfortable booths and plush chairs. Large windows face airport runways. The house specialty is salmon baked on a cedar plank served with a lemon beurre blanc sauce. **FYI:** Reservations recommended. Piano. **Open:** Breakfast Mon–Fri 5:30am–noon, Sat–Sun 5:30am–3pm; lunch daily 11am–4pm; dinner Mon–Sat 5–10pm, Sun 5–9pm. **Prices:** Main courses $12.95–$18.95. Maj CC. ⦿ 🖼 &

♟ The Bistro, in the Sheraton Bakersfield Inn, 5105 California Ave, Bakersfield; tel 805/323-3905. Stockdale Hwy exit off Calif 99. **Californian/Continental.** Southwestern Indian artifacts displays, plush booths, wooden shutters on windows. Cuisine is a mixture of ethnic and California dishes— pastas, seafood, salads, and poultry, prepared imaginatively. Selection of cognacs. **FYI:** Reservations recommended. Guitar. Dress code. **Open:** Breakfast Mon–Fri 6:30–10am, Sat 7:30–11am; lunch Mon–Fri 11am–2pm, Sat 11:30am–2pm; dinner daily 6–10pm; brunch Sun 10am–2pm. **Prices:** Main courses $13.95–$24.95. Maj CC. ⦿ &

Cafe Med, in Northridge Plaza, 5600 Auburn St, Bakersfield; tel 805/873-8106. Fairfax exit off Calif 178. **Mediterranean/ Middle Eastern.** Small storefront restaurant with cramped elegance. Bright, tasteful, clean. Eclectic menu features Italian, Greek, Spanish, French, Egyptian, and Moroccan foods. Also at: 5486 California Ave, Bakersfield (805/327-3544). **FYI:** Reservations recommended. Dancing. Beer and wine only. **Open:** Sun–Thurs 11am–9pm, Fri–Sat 11am–10pm. Closed some hols. **Prices:** Main courses $7.95–$17.95. Maj CC. &

★ Frugatti's Wood-Fired Pizza, in Fountain Plaza Shopping Center, 600 Coffee Rd, Bakersfield; tel 805/836-2000. 2 mi W of downtown. At Truxtun Ave. **Italian.** Eclectic mix of old produce labels, nostalgic soda signs, old lights, and old pictures. Brick wood-burning oven in center of the room for making pizzas and baking pastas. Low-fat and vegetarian choices. Great cheesecakes. **FYI:** Reservations not accepted. Children's menu. Beer and wine only. **Open:** Lunch Mon–Sat 11am–2pm; dinner Sun–Thurs 4:30–10pm, Fri–Sat 4:30–11pm. Closed some hols. **Prices:** Main courses $5.25–$10.95. Maj CC. 👥 &

♟★ Mama Tosca's Ristorante Italiano, in Laurelglen Plaza, 6631 Ming Ave, Bakersfield; tel 805/831-1242. Ming Ave exit off Calif 99; go west 3 miles to corner of Ashe Rd. **Italian.** A small room with white stucco walls and green carpeting. Among the Italian specialties, osso bucco is popular. Steaks and seafood also available. Marinated carrots with garlic and olive oil come with the bread. **FYI:** Reservations recommended. Blues/jazz. Dress code. **Open:** Lunch Mon–Fri 11:30am–2pm; dinner Mon–Sat 5:30–10pm. Closed some hols. **Prices:** Main courses $9.95–$27.50. Maj CC. ⦿ &

♟ Misty's, in the Red Lion Hotel, 3100 Camino del Rio Court, Bakersfield; tel 805/323-7111. Rosedale Hwy exit off Calif 99. **Californian/Continental.** A high-beamed ceiling gives the impression of a ski lodge, but the decor is subdued and elegant. Booths are plush and inviting. Grilled shrimp, tomatillo corn chowder, and red onion–cider soup are some of the varied dishes served. Excellent wine list. **FYI:** Reservations recommended. Dress code. **Open:** Lunch Mon–Fri 11:30am–1:30pm; dinner Sun–Thurs 5:30–9:30pm, Fri–Sat 5:30–10pm; brunch Sun 9am–2pm. Closed some hols. **Prices:** Main courses $9.50–$16.95. Maj CC. ⦿ &

★ The Noriega Hotel, 525 Sumner St, Bakersfield; tel 805/322-8419. **Basque.** This Basque bar-restaurant is difficult to find, but worth the effort. Specialties include pickled tongue, oxtail soup, lamb stew, and spare ribs. Everything is served family-style at a fixed price that includes wine and dessert. More food than you can eat. **FYI:** Reservations accepted. **Open:** Breakfast Tues–Sun 7am–9pm; lunch Tues–Sun noon; dinner Tues–Sun 7pm. Closed some hols; Aug 1–15. **Prices:** PF dinner $15. No CC. ▪

Attractions 🖼

Kern County Museum, 3801 Chester Ave; tel 805/323-8368. More than 50 buildings depicting the natural and human history of Kern County are spread over 14 shaded acres here. Structures include an 1868 log cabin, a general store, schoolhouse, church, oil rig, and a 1891 Queen Anne-style Victorian mansion. The main museum building houses a variety of permanent and changing exhibitions. **Open:** Mon–Fri 8am–5pm, Sat and hols 10am–5pm, Sun noon–5pm. Closed some hols. $$

Tule Elk State Reserve, 8653 Station Rd; tel 805/765-5004. Located 20 miles west of town via Stockdale Hwy. From the mid-1800s, Tule elk, native to California, gradually lost their habitat to agricultural development. By 1895, only 28 animals survived. The elk have been given protection on this 950-acre preserve. Viewing platform, binoculars available for rent; exhibits of local wildlife at headquarters. **Open:** Daily 8am–sunset. $$

BARSTOW

Map page M-3, D3

See also Yermo

Motels 🛏

▤▤ **Holiday Inn Express**, 1861 West Main St, Barstow, CA 92311; tel 619/256-1300 or toll free 800/HOLIDAY; fax 619/256-6807. E Main St exit off I-15; ¾ mi W. Built in 1992, the property still feels brand new. **Rooms:** 65 rms. CI 11am/CO 11am. Nonsmoking rms avail. **Amenities:** 🛏 A/C, cable TV w/movies, VCR. **Services:** ⟲ ⟳ **Facilities:** 🔧 🔟 ⅀ Pets allowed at an additional charge. **Rates (CP):** $50 S; $55 D. Extra person $6. Children under 12 stay free. Pking: Outdoor, free. Maj CC. Discount for government employees.

▤▤ **Quality Inn**, 1520 E Main St, Barstow, CA 92311; tel 619/256-6891 or toll free 800/221-2222. E Main St exit off I-15; ¼ mi W. Nice lobby and interior courtyard. **Rooms:** 100 rms. CI 1pm/CO noon. Nonsmoking rms avail. **Amenities:** 🛏 A/C, cable TV w/movies. **Services:** ✕ ⟲ ⟳ **Facilities:** 🔧 🔢 ⅀ 1 rst, 1 bar, washer/dryer. **Rates:** $49 S; $55 D. Extra person $6. Children under 18 stay free. Pking: Outdoor, free. Maj CC.

Attractions 🏛

California Desert Information Center, 831 Barstow Rd; tel 619/256-8313. The center provides regional visitor services, including current local road information, campground and recreation area information, and California campfire permits. Exhibits include desert plants and animals, an outdoor desert plant exhibit, a pond containing desert fish, and a bookstore. **Open:** Daily 9am–5pm. Closed some hols. Free.

Rainbow Basin Natural Area; tel 619/256-8313. Located 8 miles north of Barstow via Fort Irwin Rd, Rainbow Basin is a visual treat. Millions of years worth of sediment have piled up to form a basin with an amazing array of colors. There are 3 hiking trails of moderate difficulty through the area. Unimproved

camping facilities are available at Owl Creek Campground; visitors should bring water. Best time to visit is late fall–early spring. **Open:** Daily 24 hours. Free.

Calico Early Man Archaeological Site; tel 619/256-3591. Located 15 miles northeast of Barstow via I-15; take the Mineola exit and follow signs north 2½ miles along graded dirt roads. Begun in 1964, this site has been classified as a stone tool workshop, quarry, and campsite used by early nomadic hunter-gatherers about 200,000 years ago. It is the oldest evidence of human activity in the Americas. The Calico project was the only New World project undertaken by the archeologist/paleontologist Dr Louis S B Leakey, who was director of the project until his death in 1972.

On guided tours through 2 of the master pits, chipped-stone tools fashioned by the earliest Americans are still visible in the walls and floors. A small museum displays examples of recovered artifacts. For further information contact the Bureau of Land Management, Barstow Resource Area, 150 Coolwater Lane, Barstow, CA 92311. **Open:** Tours, Thurs–Sun 9:30 and 11:30am, 1:30 and 3:30pm. Closed some hols. Free.

Afton Canyon. Located 40 miles east of Barstow via I-15. Afton Canyon, the "Grand Canyon of the Mojave," was created about 19,000 years ago when Lake Manix drained. The canyon walls tower 300 feet above the Mojave River, their multicolored stratigraphy and varied textures providing a unique scenic experience. Hiking is possible along the river and through numerous side canyons, but trails are unmarked and rough, and a flashlight is essential when exploring some of the side canyons. Afton Canyon Campground provides restrooms, grills, picnic tables, water, and shade ramadas. More information can be provided by the California Desert Information Center (see above). **Open:** Daily sunrise–sunset. Free.

BEAUMONT

Map page M-3, D3

Motel 🛏

▤ **Best Western El Rancho Motel**, 550 Beaumont Ave, Beaumont, CA 92223; tel 909/845-2176; fax 909/845-7559. Beaumont Ave exit off I-10. Contemporary motel lacking character and landscaping. Restaurant is located nearby. **Rooms:** 52 rms and stes. CI 2pm/CO noon. Nonsmoking rms avail. **Amenities:** 🛏 A/C, cable TV w/movies. **Services:** ⟲ **Facilities:** 🔧 🔢 1 rst, 1 bar. Pool area needs work. **Rates (CP):** $40–$43 S or D; from $56 ste. Extra person $3. Pking: Outdoor, free. Maj CC.

BERKELEY

Map page M-2, D2 (S of Richmond)

Hotels 🛏

≣≣≣ **Berkeley Marina Marriott**, 200 Marina Blvd, Berkeley, CA 94710 (Berkeley Marina); tel 510/548-7920 or toll free 800/243-0625; fax 510/548-7944. University Ave exit off I-80. Very well kept, with new furnishings. Extensive recent interior renovations. **Rooms:** 373 rms and stes. Exec-level rms avail. CI 3pm/CO noon. Express checkout avail. Nonsmoking rms avail. Many rooms face the marina with views of San Francisco. **Amenities:** 🛏 ⚙ A/C, cable TV w/movies. All units w/terraces. Iron and ironing board in rooms. **Services:** ✗ ⊷ ⚑ ⚘ Car-rental desk, babysitting. Hotel can arrange for windsurfing, waterskiing, or sailing excursions. **Facilities:** ⚑ ⚑ ⚑ 700 ⚙ 1 rst, 1 bar (w/entertainment), sauna, whirlpool, washer/dryer. Pool with fitness center is for adults only. Volleyball court. **Rates:** $129–$139 S or D; from $500 ste. Children under 18 stay free. Spec packages avail. Pking: Outdoor, free. Maj CC.

≣ **The French Hotel**, 1538 Shattuck Ave, Berkeley, CA 94709 (North Berkeley); tel 510/548-9930; fax 510/649-0982. Excellent location in an upscale Berkeley neighborhood near shops and fine restaurants. **Rooms:** 18 rms. CI 3pm/CO 11am. Nonsmoking rms avail. Decidedly basic, with wire-basket drawers, wire closet racks. Carpets, while clean, are very worn. **Amenities:** 🛏 ⚙ TV. No A/C. Some units w/terraces. **Services:** ⊚ ⚘ **Facilities:** 1 rst. Popular ground-level cafe is pleasant if noisy, with some sidewalk tables in the French tradition. **Rates:** $68–$125 S or D. Children under 18 stay free. Pking: Indoor/outdoor, free. Maj CC.

≣≣≣ **Gramma's Rose Garden Inn**, 2740 Telegraph Ave, Berkeley, CA 94705; tel 510/549-2145; fax 510/549-1085. Charming, with 3 cottages and 2 Victorian houses clustered around a landscaped courtyard. **Rooms:** 40 rms. CI 2pm/CO noon. Nonsmoking rms avail. Nice decor in keeping with turn-of-the-century theme. Some cottages have leaded-glass windows. **Amenities:** 🛏 ⚙ Cable TV w/movies. No A/C. Some units w/terraces, some w/fireplaces. **Services:** ⚘ Babysitting. Complimentary wine and cheese from 5–8pm daily. **Rates (BB):** $85–$145 S or D. Extra person $10. Children under 12 stay free. Spec packages avail. Pking: Outdoor, free. Maj CC. Some lower rates Sunday–Thursday.

≣≣≣ **Hotel Durant**, 2600 Durant Ave, Berkeley, CA 94704; tel 510/845-8981 or toll free 800/238-7268; fax 510/486-8336. Best location in Berkeley, close to Telegraph Ave and the University of California. **Rooms:** 140 rms and stes. CI 2pm/CO noon. Nonsmoking rms avail. Tastefully decorated in a traditional homey style. **Amenities:** 🛏 ⚙ Cable TV w/movies. No A/C. **Services:** ✗ VP ⚑ ⚑ ⚘ **Facilities:** 75 ⚙ 2 rsts, 1 bar. Guests may purchase discounted day passes for university sports facilities, such as a pool and tennis and racquetball courts. **Rates (CP):** $107–$127 S or D; from $140 ste. Extra person $15. Children under 12 stay free. Min stay HS. Higher rates for spec evnts/hols. Pking: Outdoor, $5. Maj CC.

≣≣ **Hotel Shattuck**, 2086 Allston Way, at Shattuck Ave, Berkeley, CA 94704 (Downtown); tel 510/845-7300 or toll free 800/237-5359, 800/742-8825 in CA; fax 510/644-2088. In downtown Berkeley, yet within walking distance of the University of California. Older building nicely updated. Outside street noise fairly bad during the day. **Rooms:** 175 rms and stes. CI 3pm/CO noon. Nonsmoking rms avail. Older, traditional style, but neat and clean. **Amenities:** 🛏 TV w/movies. No A/C. 1 unit w/fireplace. **Services:** ⚑ ⚑ ⚘ Babysitting. **Facilities:** 20 ⚙ Washer/dryer. **Rates (CP):** HS May, June, Aug, Nov $69–$90 S; $79–$99 D; from $99 ste. Extra person $15. Children under 12 stay free. Lower rates off-season. Higher rates for spec evnts/hols. Spec packages avail. Maj CC.

≣≣ **Ramada Inn**, 920 University Ave, Berkeley, CA 94710; tel 510/849-1121 or·toll free 800/954-7575; fax 510/845-4397. University exit off I-80. Spacious lobby, recently redecorated. **Rooms:** 110 rms and stes. Exec-level rms avail. CI 3pm/CO noon. Nonsmoking rms avail. **Amenities:** 🛏 ⚙ A/C, TV w/movies. Some units w/terraces. **Services:** ✗ ⚑ ⚘ ⚑ Car-rental desk. **Facilities:** ⚑ 350 ⚙ 1 rst, 1 bar (w/entertainment). Nice pool, a rarity in Berkeley. Restaurant has giant-screen TV. **Rates:** HS May–Sept $53–$57 S; $55–$59 D; from $89 ste. Extra person $6. Children under 18 stay free. Lower rates off-season. Spec packages avail. Pking: Indoor/outdoor, free. Maj CC.

Restaurants 🍽

♣★ **Chez Panisse**, 1517 Shattuck Ave, Berkeley; tel 510/548-5525. At Cedar St. **Californian.** The birthplace of California cuisine, this warm and cozy spot, owned by acclaimed chef Alice Waters, offers perfectly prepared and wonderfully fresh dishes, using only the finest ingredients. The ambience is quiet and a bit formal, but not stuffy. Fixed-price menu changes daily and may include grilled quail, salmon, and eggplant ravioli. **FYI:** Reservations recommended. Dress code. Beer and wine only. **Open:** Mon–Sat 5–10pm. Closed some hols. **Prices:** PF dinner $35–$65. Maj CC. ⚙

★ **Chez Panisse Cafe**, 1517 Shattuck Ave, Berkeley; tel 510/548-5525. At Cedar St. **Californian.** Upstairs from the original

Chez Panisse, a perfect opportunity to try renowned chef Alice Waters's innovative California cuisine at a much lower price than the more formal restaurant downstairs. Especially nice for lunch. **FYI:** Reservations accepted. Children's menu. Dress code. Beer and wine only. **Open:** Lunch Mon–Sat 11:30am–3pm; dinner Mon–Sat 5–11:30pm. Closed some hols. **Prices:** Main courses $13.50–$16.50; PF dinner $24.50. Maj CC.

Ginger Island, 1820 4th St, Berkeley; tel 510/644-0444. At Hearse St. **Asian.** Open, airy, and cozy, this relatively new restaurant features chef Bruce Cost, formerly of the well-regarded Monsoon. The highly stylized cuisine is inspired by the cooking of Thailand and China. Ginger is used throughout the menu on specialties like tea-smoked duck, red-curry noodles, fresh sea scallops, and hamburger with Asian salsa. **FYI:** Reservations accepted. Dress code. **Open:** Mon–Thurs 11:30am–9:30pm, Fri–Sat 11:30am–11pm, Sun 10:30am–9:30pm. Closed some hols. **Prices:** Main courses $7.50–$17.50. Maj CC. &

Lalime's, 1329 Gilman St, Berkeley; tel 510/527-9838. **Mediterranean.** This roomy, split-level dining room is decorated in pink with modern touches and is a perfect setting to enjoy the highly stylized cooking. Dishes inspired by the south of France and northern Italy. Frequently changing menu; extensive wine list. **FYI:** Reservations recommended. Dress code. Beer and wine only. **Open:** Mon–Thurs 5:30–9:30pm, Fri–Sat 5:30–10:30pm, Sun 5–9pm. Closed some hols. **Prices:** Main courses $10–$16; PF dinner $15–$30. Ltd CC. &

Larry Blake's, 2367 Telegraph Ave, Berkeley; tel 510/848-0886. **American.** Three floors of eating, drinking, and dancing: Upstairs is a cocktail lounge. On the ground floor, sandwiches, salads, steaks, stir fry, and burritos are served. In the basement is a blues bar complete with dance floor—big names in blues often play here. **FYI:** Reservations accepted. Blues. **Open:** Mon–Fri 11:30am–10pm, Sat–Sun 10am–10pm. Closed Dec 25. **Prices:** Main courses $4.65–$10.95. Maj CC.

Mermaid, 824 University Ave, Berkeley; tel 510/843-1189. University Ave exit off I-880/80. **Cambodian.** Split-level dining room with pastel shades of blue and green and Cambodian artwork. Aromatic salads and appetizers and unique curries using lemongrass, garlic, and other piquant spices. **FYI:** Reservations accepted. Beer and wine only. **Open:** Lunch Mon–Sat 11:30am–2:30pm; dinner Sun–Thurs 5–10pm, Fri–Sat 5–11pm. **Prices:** Main courses $6.25–$9.95. Maj CC.

Nakapan, 1921 Martin Luther King Jr Way, Berkeley; tel 510/548-3050. University Ave exit off I-880/80; go 1½ miles west and turn left on Martin Luther King Jr Way. **Thai.** Tucked away from the main street, this is one of the best-kept secrets in town.

The hardwood floors and open-beamed ceiling create a warm and cozy ambience in which to enjoy the wide variety of curries and other Thai specialties. Daily specials typically include seafood. **FYI:** Reservations accepted. Beer and wine only. **Open:** Lunch Mon–Fri 11:30am–3pm; dinner daily 5–10pm. Closed some hols. **Prices:** Main courses $6.95–$9.50. Maj CC.

Santa Fe Bar & Grill, 1310 University Ave, Berkeley; tel 510/841-4740. **Southwestern.** A popular restaurant in a remodeled Santa Fe Railway station. The mission-revival building has a whitewashed exterior and interior done in earth tones, with a tiled-floor entryway. The chef prepares grilled and smoked meat, seafood, and pasta dishes. A pianist specializes in popular tunes of the '30s and '40s. **FYI:** Reservations recommended. Piano. Dress code. **Open:** Lunch Mon–Fri 11:30am–3pm; dinner Sun–Thurs 5–10pm, Fri–Sat 5–11pm. Closed some hols. **Prices:** Main courses $13.50–$16.95. Maj CC.

★ **Smokey Joe's Cafe**, 1620 Shattuck Ave, Berkeley; tel 510/548-4616. At Cedar St. **Cafe/Vegetarian.** A Berkeley institution. Nothing fancy, just hearty breakfasts and truck stop–style vegetarian fare. "Where the elite meet to eat no meat." **FYI:** Reservations not accepted. Beer and wine only. **Open:** Sun–Thurs 8am–3pm, Fri–Sat 6am–9pm. **Prices:** Main courses $4.35–$6.95. No CC.

Venezia Caffe & Ristorante, 1799 University Ave, Berkeley; tel 510/849-4681. University Ave exit off I-880/80. **Italian.** Attractively designed to resemble an Italian piazza, featuring a fountain in the center and wrought-iron balconies hanging from the walls. Serves up classic Italian food with an emphasis on the freshest California produce. Diners can watch the chef at work through a large picture window. **FYI:** Reservations accepted. Children's menu. Beer and wine only. **Open:** Lunch Mon–Fri 11:30am–2:30pm; dinner Mon–Thurs 5:30–10pm, Fri–Sat 5–10pm, Sun 5–9:30pm. Closed some hols. **Prices:** Main courses $9.95–$13.95. Maj CC. &

Attractions

UNIVERSITY OF CALIFORNIA

University of California Visitor Center, 2200 University Ave; tel 510/642-5215. Tours of the Berkeley campus, the oldest of the 9 University of California campuses, begin at the Visitor Center and are offered during the school year on Monday, Wednesday, and Friday, with some pre-scheduled tours on Saturday (call ahead for details). Included on the tour is the campus's signature feature, a 300-foot **Campanile**, officially known as the Jane K Sather Memorial Tower. The granite tower houses a clock with 4 faces measuring 17 feet in diameter along with a 61-bell carillon that is played several times daily. **Open:** Mon–Fri 8:30am–4:30pm. Closed some hols. Free.

Phoebe A Hearst Museum of Anthropology, 103 Kroeber Hall; tel 510/643-7648. Contains permanent and changing exhibitions dealing with all aspects of human culture. **Open:** Mon–Wed and Fri 10am–4:30pm, Thurs 10am–9pm, Sat–Sun noon–4:30pm. $

University Art Museum and Pacific Film Archive, 2626 Bancroft Way; tel 510/642-0808 (galleries) or 642-1124 (film). Founded in the 1960 as UC–Berkeley's principal visual arts center, the UAM/PFA has become one of the largest university art museums in the United States. Its collections emphasize 20th-century painting, sculpture, photography, and conceptual art, and it has significant holdings in Asian art. The Pacific Film Archive maintains a collection of 6,000 film titles, with strengths in Soviet, American avante-garde, and Japanese cinema. A complementary program of guided tours, lectures, and special events is offered; 650 films and videos are screened each year. **Open:** Wed and Fri–Sun 11am–5pm, Thurs 11am–9pm. Closed some hols. $$$

University of California Botanical Garden, Centennial Dr; tel 510/642-3343. Established in 1890, the Botanical Garden was moved to this site in Strawberry Canyon in the 1920s. More than 10,000 species of plants are spread over 33 acres, all arranged by region; one-third of the area is devoted to plants native to California. Some of the other 19 areas include the 5-acre **Mather Redwood Grove,** a re-created coastal redwood forest; the **Southern African region,** with lilies, iceplants, and aloes; and the **Mesoamerican region,** featuring a large Mexican handflower tree.

Shuttlebuses run from the campus at half-hour intervals on weekdays only. Free guided tours are offered on weekends only (contact the Visitor Center for more information). **Open:** Daily 9am–4:45pm. Closed Dec 25. Free.

OTHER ATTRACTIONS
Judah L Magnes Museum (Jewish Museum of the West), 2911 Russell St; tel 510/549-6950. Permanent collection of over 10,000 Jewish ceremonial objects, folk, and fine art, including works by Marc Chagall, Max Liebermann, and many others. Changing exhibits feature shows from around the world. Also Western Jewish History Center, with the world's largest archive of records of Jews in the 13 original states; Blumenthal Library with rare books, manuscripts, and photographs. Museum shop. **Open:** Sun–Thurs 10am–4pm. Closed some hols. Free.

Tilden Regional Park; tel 510/635-0135. Accessible via Cañon Dr, Shasta Rd, or South Park Dr, all off Grizzly Peak Blvd. Tilden is one of the 3 oldest parks in the East Bay District. The park includes Lake Anza, with a sandy beach for swimming (generally May–October; fee charged); the Brazil Building, with interiors from the Brazilian exhibit at the 1939 World's Fair; a splendid antique carousel with hand-carved animals and a calliope; and the Little Train, a scaled-down steam train offering rides along a scenic ridge. An 18-hole golf course with clubhouse and pro shop; hiking and bridle trails; pony rides.

Within the park is the **Tilden Nature Study Area,** offering nature study programs in a 70-acre setting that includes a wide variety of plant and animal life; Little Farm and Environmental Education Center; 10 miles of hiking trails; several ponds; and a creek. **Open:** Daily 8am–10pm. Free.

BEVERLY HILLS
Map page M-3, D2 (NE of Santa Monica)

Hotels 🛏

📊📊📊 **Beverly Hilton**, 9876 Wilshire Blvd, Beverly Hills, CA 90210; tel 310/274-7777 or toll free 800/445-8667; fax 310/285-1313. Located at the west end of Beverly Hills, en route to UCLA. Although the atmosphere is almost sterile, this large, well-staffed hotel serves guests well. Owner Merv Griffin resides on the premises. **Rooms:** 581 rms and stes. CI 2pm/CO noon. Express checkout avail. Nonsmoking rms avail. Rooms are attractive, with nice appointments. **Amenities:** 📱 ⚓ 🎛 🗑 A/C, cable TV w/movies, refrig, VCR, voice mail, in-rm safe, shoe polisher, bathrobes. All units w/minibars, some w/terraces. **Services:** 🍽 ⭏ 🅿 🚗 🖼 🛎 ⟨♦⟩ Twice-daily maid svce, car-rental desk, masseur, children's program, babysitting. **Facilities:** 🛝 🛟 [1.5] 🖥 ᒼ 4 rsts, 4 bars (2 w/entertainment), lifeguard, beauty salon. Gift shops on premises. Close to shopping and restaurants. **Rates:** $145–$220 S; $170–$245 D; from $300 ste. Extra person $30. Children under 18 stay free. Spec packages avail. Pking: Indoor/outdoor, $15. Maj CC.

📊📊📊 **Beverly Prescott Hotel**, 1224 S Beverwil Dr, Beverly Hills, CA 90035; tel 310/277-2800 or toll free 800/421-3212; fax 310/203-9537. A very attractive, boutique-style hotel with an inviting lobby and comfortable atmosphere. However, it is located away from points of interest and main business district. Part of well-regarded Kimpton hotel group. Excellent views of city. **Rooms:** 139 rms and stes. Exec-level rms avail. CI 3pm/CO noon. Express checkout avail. Nonsmoking rms avail. Light and airy; superb accommodations. **Amenities:** 📱 ⚓ 🗑 A/C, cable TV w/movies, refrig, VCR, stereo/tape player, voice mail, in-rm safe, bathrobes. All units w/minibars, all w/terraces, some w/Jacuzzis. Business rooms equipped with computers and laser printers. **Services:** 🍽️ 🔑 VP 🚗 🛄 ⤴️ Twice-daily maid svce, car-rental desk, masseur, babysitting. **Facilities:** 🏋️ 🛎️ 📶 🖥️ & 1 rst, 1 bar, whirlpool. **Rates:** $150 S or D; from $300 ste. Extra person $20. Children under 16 stay free. Spec packages avail. Pking: Outdoor, $12. Maj CC.

≣≣≣ **Hotel Rodeo**, 360 N Rodeo Dr, Beverly Hills, CA 90210; tel 310/273-0300 or toll free 800/356-7575; fax 310/859-8730. Boutique hotel catering to Europeans and corporate travelers. Not particularly posh. Close to Beverly Hills shops. **Rooms:** 86 rms and stes. Exec-level rms avail. CI 2pm/CO noon. Nonsmoking rms avail. Rooms are small but passable, some with king-size beds. Should have rooms for guests with disabilities by press time. **Amenities:** 🛁 🍷 🖥️ 🍽️ A/C, cable TV w/movies. Some units w/minibars, some w/terraces. **Services:** ✗ 🔑 VP 🚗 🛄 ⤴️ Twice-daily maid svce, car-rental desk, babysitting. **Facilities:** 🏋️ 🖥️ 1 rst, 1 bar, washer/dryer. Indoor/outdoor restaurant in front of the hotel. **Rates:** HS Late May–late Aug $120–$160 S or D; from $200 ste. Extra person $20. Children under 17 stay free. Lower rates off-season. AP and MAP rates avail. Pking: Indoor/outdoor, $9. Maj CC.

≣≣≣≣≣ **The Peninsula Beverly Hills**, 9882 Little Santa Monica Blvd, Beverly Hills, CA 90212; tel 310/551-2888 or toll free 800/462-7899; fax 310/788-2319. 2½ acres. Shoe-horned into a tiny spot just a corner too far from the shops, but the curved driveway with fountains and flowers makes an appropriately posh entrance. Superior rooms, elegant service. **Rooms:** 195 rms and stes. CI 2pm/CO noon. Express checkout avail. Nonsmoking rms avail. Meticulous appointments. French doors open inward from wrought iron balustrade to form a pseudo-balcony. Ultra-luxurious suites in "garden villas" (2-story town-houses in a courtyard with planters) are elegant and quiet but don't get much daylight. **Amenities:** 🛁 🍷 🍽️ A/C, cable TV w/movies, refrig, VCR, voice mail, in-rm safe, shoe polisher, bathrobes. All units w/minibars, some w/terraces, some w/fire-places, some w/Jacuzzis. Bedside panel summons maid and valet and activates "Do Not Disturb" sign. Reading pillows. **Services:** 🍽️ 🔑 VP 🚗 🛄 ⤴️ ⤵️ Twice-daily maid svce, masseur, babysitting. Tea and cookies on arrival. Courtesy Rolls-Royce for trips to Century City and Rodeo Drive. 24-hour concierge. The hotel comes close to the style of service offered by its pacesetter namesake in Hong Kong—white-gloved page boys open doors and valets are made available for each floor around the clock. **Facilities:** 🏋️ 🛎️ 📶 🖥️ & 2 rsts (*see also* "Restaurants" below), 2 bars (1 w/entertainment), lifeguard, spa, sauna, steam rm, whirlpool, beauty salon. 60-foot lap-pool, 12 poolside cabanas with phones. Fitness center offers personal trainers. Business center services include personalized stationery and resumes.

Outstanding dining room, mansion-like sitting room for after-noon tea, clubby wood-paneled bar. **Rates:** $280–$425 S or D; from $500 ste. Extra person $35. Children under 18 stay free. Spec packages avail. Pking: Indoor, $14. Maj CC.

◖◗ **Regent Beverly Wilshire**, 9500 Wilshire Blvd, Beverly Hills, CA 90212; tel 310/275-5200 or toll free 800/545-4000; fax 510/274-2851. This old-time favorite in a prime location is looking better than ever under its new Regent ownership. It is perhaps the only hotel in LA that comes close in appearance and style to its grand European peers. The elegance of the marble and wood-paneled lobby can at times be marred by batches of tourists taking each other's picture in the place where Julia Roberts and Richard Gere cavorted in *Pretty Woman*. **Rooms:** 290 rms and stes. CI 3pm/CO noon. Express checkout avail. Nonsmoking rms avail. Spacious and stylish, yet very efficient. **Amenities:** 🛁 🍷 🍽️ A/C, cable TV, refrig, shoe polisher, bathrobes. All units w/minibars, some w/terraces, some w/Jacuzzis. Extra-large shower stalls with twin adjustable shower heads; 60-channel TV, plus 8-inch TV in bathroom; VCRs on request, free of charge; bathroom scale and heat lamp, leather-and-teak clothes brush. "Welcome" snack—strawberries, crème fraîche, and brown sugar. Special "pet amenity" kit. **Services:** 🍽️ 🔑 VP 🚗 🛄 ⤴️ ⤵️ Twice-daily maid svce, car-rental desk, masseur, children's program, babysitting. Overnight laundry service. Guests are escorted to rooms by reception staff. **Facilities:** 🏋️ 🛎️ 📶 🖥️ & 3 rsts (*see also* "Restaurants" below), 1 bar (w/entertainment), lifeguard, spa, sauna, steam rm, whirlpool, beauty salon. Elegant art deco dining room, perky streetside cafe, sumptuous lounge for light snacks and afternoon tea. Rooftop pool (open 24 hours) with cabanas. Fitness center with personal trainers. Spacious, well-equipped business center (including laptop, cellular phone, and fax machine rentals). **Rates:** $255–$365 S; $275–$385 D; from $425 ste. Extra person $30. Children under 14 stay free. Spec packages avail. Pking: Indoor, $14.50. Maj CC. A few dollars less than its cousin, the Four Seasons, but offers more.

Restaurants 🍴

The Belvedere, in the Peninsula Beverly Hills, 9882 Little Santa Monica Blvd, Beverly Hills; tel 310/788-2306. At Wilshire Blvd. **Californian.** Overlooking a blooming garden, this opulently appointed restaurant was designed like a lush summer villa. Chef Bill Bracken's contemporary dishes with subtle ethnic influences include house-smoked salmon on potato cakes with marinated onions, breaded rare ahi tuna with mango and mizuna salad, and an exotic California fruit plate. Outrageous desserts, served on gold-painted Japanese glassware, include white chocolate pea-nut-butter crunch, and hot chocolate and sorbet. **FYI:** Reservations recommended. **Open:** Breakfast daily 6:30–10am; lunch daily 11:30am–2:30pm; dinner daily 6:30–10:30pm; brunch Sun 11:30am–2:30pm. **Prices:** Main courses $18–$25. Ltd CC. ♥ ⚓ VP ⚹

Bombay Palace, 8690 Wilshire Blvd, Beverly Hills; tel 310/659-9944. **Indian.** Nestled behind arched, 16-foot windows, this candlelit restaurant honoring the city of Bombay is filled with art objects and miniature Indian paintings. Around the upper walls are 200 individually illuminated wall pockets filled with gold-plated Indian gods. Large variety of regional favorites from the tandoor ovens, as well as vegetarian dishes, including homemade cottage cheese stewed in tomato gravy and sautéed okra fingers. **FYI:** Reservations recommended. **Open:** Lunch Mon–Fri 11:30am–2:30pm; dinner daily 5:30–11pm; brunch Sat–Sun noon–3pm. **Prices:** Main courses $15–$20; PF dinner $25–$30. Maj CC. 🄫 🚗 VP ⚹

Celestino, 236 S Beverly Dr, Beverly Hills; tel 310/859-8601. **Italian.** Large and airy, with huge windows open to the street. The risottos are marvelous; so are lamb chops with fennel and red-wine sauce, and the eggplant soufflé. Attentive, old-world service from the young staff. **FYI:** Reservations accepted. **Open:** Lunch Mon–Fri 11:30am–3:30pm; dinner daily 5:30–10pm. Closed some hols. **Prices:** Main courses $10–$22. Maj CC. VP ⚹

Chez Hélène, 267 S Beverly Dr, Beverly Hills; tel 310/276-1558. Between Wilshire and Olympic Blvds at corner of Gregory Way. **French.** Housed in a charming chalet with outdoor dining in the middle of busy Beverly Hills, this is the only French-Canadian restaurant in LA. Uncomplicated preparations by chef-owner Mimi Hebert include chilled cucumber soup and poached chicken with Dijon mustard and béchamel. Homemade pies and tortes, plus specialties like pear Belle Hélène and strawberries Romanoff, for dessert. **FYI:** Reservations recommended. Beer and wine only. **Open:** HS June–Aug/Dec lunch Mon–Sat 11:30am–3pm; dinner daily 5:30–10:30pm. Reduced hours off-season. Closed some hols. **Prices:** Main courses $12.50–$23.50. Maj CC. ♥ ⚓ 🖼 🄫

Club Room, in Neiman Marcus, 9700 Wilshire Blvd, Beverly Hills; tel 310/550-5900. Corner of Wilshire Blvd and Roxbury. 4th level. **Eclectic.** Stellar food together with extraordinary service make this a "find" for lunch. Views of nearby houses and fine paintings of floral subjects. Specialties include crabmeat cakes with sweet-corn purée, lobster salad, and popovers; for dessert, toasted pecan ball and cappuccino ice cream pie. Afternoon tea is elegantly served. **FYI:** Reservations recommended. Children's menu. Dress code. **Open:** Daily 11am–3pm. Closed some hols. **Prices:** Lunch main courses $12–$20. Ltd CC. VP ⚹

★ **David Slay's La Veranda**, 225 S Beverly Dr, Beverly Hills; tel 310/274-7246. **New American.** No-nonsense, debonair midwestern decor in this powerhouse dining room matches the hearty American cuisine by owner-chef David Slay of St Louis restaurant fame. The chef prepares a tempting, original grazing menu on Sunday nights. Specialties include grilled veal chop with garlic sauce, salmon with horseradish and chili-mint sauce, smoked salmon quesadilla, and homemade desserts like almond tuille with banana ice cream and caramel sauce. **FYI:** Reservations recommended. **Open:** Lunch Tues–Sun 11:30am–2:30pm; dinner daily 5–10:30pm. Closed some hols. **Prices:** Main courses $18–$24. Maj CC. 🄫 VP ⚹

♣ **The Dining Room**, in the Regent Beverly Wilshire, 9500 Wilshire Blvd, Beverly Hills; tel 310/275-5200. At Rodeo Dr. **Eclectic.** Renovated and refined, filled with Biedermeir and Regency furnishings, silk curtains, and oil paintings. Specialties include hand-carved smoked Scottish salmon, oven-roasted Maine lobster and cauliflower-fennel puree, and Russian caviars. Lavish Sunday brunch (prix fixe at $38) may include butterflied fillet of beef or grilled swordfish. **FYI:** Reservations recommended. Combo/piano. Children's menu. Jacket required. **Open:** Breakfast Mon–Fri 7–10:30am, Sat 8–10:30am; lunch Mon–Sat 11:30am–3pm; dinner Mon–Sat 6–10pm, Sun 5–9pm; brunch Sun 10:30am–3pm. **Prices:** Main courses $23–$35; PF dinner $35–$98. Maj CC. ♥ VP ⚹

Ⓢ★ **Ed Debevic's**, 134 N La Cienega Blvd, Beverly Hills; tel 310/659-1952. La Cienega Blvd exit off I-10. **Burgers/American.** Friendly, frenzied, spacious '50s-themed restaurant. Comfort food includes meatloaf, freshly baked bread, chili, and burgers. A tiny hot fudge sundae is available for 59¢. **FYI:** Reservations recommended. Children's menu. **Open:** Sun–Thurs 11:30am–11pm, Fri–Sat 11:30am–1am. Closed some hols. **Prices:** Main courses $2.95–$6.95. Maj CC. 🄫 VP ⚹

Emporio Armani Express, 9533 Brighton Way, Beverly Hills; tel 310/271-9940. **Italian.** Owned by designer Giorgio Armani, this luxurious, intimate hideaway is located on the 2nd floor of his Armani boutique. Decor is subtle and sophisticated; the staff is attentive, attractive, and thoroughly Italian. The menu features a range of regional Italian dishes, including lasagne with mousse of lobster and ricotta; and penne with cauliflower, raisins, and pine nuts. Special requests are welcomed by the chef. **FYI:** Reservations recommended. **Open:** Mon–Thurs 11:30am–11pm, Fri–Sat 11:30am–midnight, Sun noon–10pm. Closed some hols. **Prices:** Main courses $10–$24. Maj CC. ♥ VP ⚹

The Grill on the Alley, 9560 Dayton Way, Beverly Hills; tel 310/276-0615. **American Grill.** A handsome turn-of-the-century-style grill featuring a massive mahogany bar, wooden booths, and a black-and-white tiled floor. The front door is located in an alleyway off Wilshire. Specialties are charcoal-broiled swordfish and calf's liver with bacon and onions. **FYI:** Reservations recommended. Dress code. **Open:** Mon–Sat 11:30am–11pm. Closed some hols. **Prices:** Main courses $15–$30. Maj CC. 🏺 VP ⅏

Il Pastaio, 400 N Canon Dr, Beverly Hills; tel 310/205-5444. **Italian.** Recently opened, this tiny, casual restaurant is decorated with burnished wood, floor-to-ceiling windows, and artwork. Menu includes several variations of carpaccio (venison, swordfish, ahi tuna), pasta, and risotto. Try the tagliolini with Sicilian-style pesto or risotto with saffron and Parmesan cheese. **FYI:** Reservations not accepted. **Open:** Daily 11:30am–11pm. Closed some hols. **Prices:** Main courses $7.50–$12. Maj CC. VP

Kate Mantilini, 9101 Wilshire Blvd, Beverly Hills; tel 310/278-3699. **American.** Dedicated to a hard-boiled female fight promoter, this restaurant features dramatic, stylish concrete and glass architecture and serves generous portions to both celebrities and insomniacs all day and late into the night. The upscale diner-style menu includes rotisserie chicken, white chili, meatloaf, and garlic spinach. **FYI:** Reservations accepted. **Open:** Mon–Thurs 7:30am–1am, Fri 7:30am–3am, Sat noon–3am, Sun noon–midnight. Closed some hols. **Prices:** Main courses $8.95–$26. Maj CC. 🏺 🚗 VP ⅏

Ⓢ **Lawry's The Prime Rib**, 100 N La Cienega Blvd, Beverly Hills; tel 310/652-2827. **American.** Lawry's was founded in 1938 as a mecca for lovers of aged prime rib. Today it also attracts diners who seek a good value. The cavernous main dining room has a dignified air and is filled with oil portraits and a fresco of Versailles. Service is ceremonial, yet friendly. The menu has expanded in recent years to include fish dishes. Among the favorites of regulars are creamed spinach, huge baked potatoes, and pecan praline tart. **FYI:** Reservations recommended. Children's menu. Dress code. **Open:** Mon–Thurs 5–10pm, Fri 5–11pm, Sat 4:30–11pm, Sun 4–10pm. Closed Dec 25. **Prices:** Main courses $18.95–$24.95. Maj CC. 🏺 🏺 ♥ VP ⅏

♥★ **L'Escoffier**, in the Beverly Hilton, 9876 Wilshire Blvd, Beverly Hills; tel 310/274-7777. **French.** 1950s dining room with penthouse view of the city and a sunken circular dance floor. The food straddles the line between classical and bistro cuisine. Specialties include a variety of soups and terrines like cold avocado soup; smoked salmon quenelles; and lamb prepared 3 ways. Lush desserts. **FYI:** Reservations recommended. Combo. Jacket required. **Open:** Tues–Sat 6:30–10pm. Closed some hols; Aug 10–31. **Prices:** Main courses $19–$29; PF dinner $39–$47. Maj CC. ♥ 🏔 VP ⅏

★ **The Mandarin**, 430 N Camden Dr, Beverly Hills; tel 310/859-0926. **Chinese.** The mother of all Chinese restaurants in Los Angeles, the Mandarin offers both Szechuan and Mandarin fare. The restaurant is decorated with lacquered woods and bamboo, with long windows overlooking a plant-filled brick walkway. Specialties include sautéed lobster in a noodle basket, curried vegetable fried rice, and glazed walnuts on fried spinach leaves. **FYI:** Reservations recommended. **Open:** Mon–Thurs 11:30am–10pm, Fri 11:30am–10:30pm, Sat–Sun 5–10pm. Closed some hols. **Prices:** Main courses $25–$75. Maj CC. 🏺 🚗 VP

★ **Maple Drive**, in Maple Plaza Office Building, 345 N Maple Dr, Beverly Hills; tel 310/274-9800. 2 blocks N of Burton Way. **New American.** A spacious, multi-level wood-and-concrete structure, with wraparound windows looking out to the tree-lined neighborhood. A creation of owner Tony Bill and chef Leonard Schwarz, it's a favorite with art and entertainment luminaries, who come for original, American-style comfort food with international touches, such as meatloaf with spinach and mashed potatoes. Other treats include leg of lamb with calamata and olives, and sautéed Dover sole with remoulade sauce. **FYI:** Reservations recommended. Combo/jazz. **Open:** Lunch Mon–Fri 11:30am–2:30pm; dinner Mon–Thurs 6–10pm, Fri–Sat 6–11pm. Closed some hols. **Prices:** Main courses $17–$29. Maj CC. VP ⅏

♥★ **Matsuhisa**, 129 N La Cienega Blvd, Beverly Hills; tel 310/659-9639. **Japanese.** Owner/chef Nobu Matsuhisa is the most popular and well-known sushi chef in Los Angeles. Sample the tempura and sushi bar, or opt for an entree such as squid "pasta" with garlic sauce, halibut cheek with pepper sauce, or baked black cod and tiger shrimp in pepper sauce. **FYI:** Reservations recommended. Beer and wine only. **Open:** Lunch Mon–Fri 11:45am–2:15pm; dinner daily 5:45–10:15pm. Closed some hols. **Prices:** PF dinner $23–$26. Maj CC. VP ⅏

McCormick & Schmick's, in Two Rodeo, 206 N Rodeo Dr, Beverly Hills; tel 310/859-0434. **Seafood.** Completely gutted and redesigned 2-story space located in the Two Rodeo complex on some of the most expensive real estate in the world. Luxurious and comfortable, with dark wood and beveled glass and an open kitchen. Daily seafood specials may include cedar-planked salmon cooked American Indian style, rare oysters, or Pacific halibut. **FYI:** Reservations accepted. **Open:** Daily 11:30am–11:30pm. **Prices:** Main courses $10–$25. Maj CC. ♥ 🏺 VP ⅏

★ **Mr Chow's**, 433 N Camden Dr, Beverly Hills; tel 310/278-9911. **Chinese.** Portraits of Michael Chow by Keith Haring and Andy Warhol dominate the room, which is often packed with celebrities. Specialties include Mr Chow's classic noodles; other choices include marinated gambler's duck, chicken satay, gambei (mushrooms, chicken, seaweed, and walnuts), squab rolled in lettuce, and sweet-and-sour soup. A bargain for lunch. **FYI:** Reservations recommended. **Open:** Lunch daily noon–2:30pm; dinner daily 6–11:30pm. Closed some hols. **Prices:** Main courses $8.50–$25. Maj CC. VP &

(S) ✱ **The Players Restaurant and Bar**, 9513 Santa Monica Blvd, Beverly Hills; tel 310/278-6669. **Hungarian/International.** Located in a charming country-style house complete with wicker, chintz, and a dark wood sideboard for serving desserts. This second-generation restaurant begun by Mama Weiss draws tourists and local celebrities alike for such Hungarian specialties as veal goulash and paprika chicken, as well as more contemporary California-style fare. **FYI:** Reservations recommended. **Open:** Lunch daily 11:30am–4pm; dinner daily 4–11pm. Closed some hols. **Prices:** Main courses $8.75–$21.95. Maj CC. ♥ 🍽 🖼 VP &

✱ **RJ's The Rib Joint**, 252 N Beverly Dr, Beverly Hills; tel 310/274-7427. **Regional American.** A rollicking, old-fashioned, country-style, cavernous party center in the heart of the Beverly Hills shopping district. Created by Bob Morris of Gladstone fame, the restaurant is known for generously portioned baby-back ribs, firehouse chili, hickory-smoked baked potatoes, and the Rib Joint Sampler with armadillo eggs (actually a nest of mild jalapeños stuffed with cream cheese, then fried). **FYI:** Reservations recommended. Children's menu. **Open:** Fri–Sat 11:30am–11pm, Sun 10:30am–10pm, Mon–Thurs 11:30am–10pm. **Prices:** Main courses $11.95–$25. Maj CC. 🖼 VP

♣ **Ruth's Chris Steakhouse**, 224 S Beverly Dr, Beverly Hills; tel 310/859-8744. **American.** Upscale yet low-key, with an open kitchen and elevated leather booths. The restaurant's trademark is aged, corn-fed beef, broiled at very high temperatures to seal in the flavor. Seven potato preparations to choose from. **FYI:** Reservations recommended. **Open:** Sun–Thurs 5–9:30pm, Fri–Sat 5–10:30pm. Closed some hols. **Prices:** Main courses $17–$45. Maj CC. 🖼 VP &

Trader Vic's, in the Beverly Hilton, 9876 Wilshire Blvd, Beverly Hills (Century City); tel 310/274-7777. **International.** Polynesian-themed restaurant with a nostalgic feel. Although it attracts some older couples, Trader Vic's is also the newest "in" spot for UCLA students, who pack the bar on Friday nights for tropical drinks and pu pu platters. **FYI:** Reservations recommended. **Open:** Daily 5am–midnight. Closed some hols. **Prices:** Main courses $8–$30. Maj CC. VP &

BIG BEAR CITY
Map page M-3, D3 (E of Big Bear Lake)

Restaurant 🍽

(S) **Landings–The Cafe**, in the airport terminal, 501 W Valley Blvd, Big Bear City; tel 909/585-3762. **Californian.** A fine restaurant at a tiny airport. The larger dining room faces the runway but is not too close. Good for breakfast, lunch, and dinner, with dishes like pecan pancakes and cedar-planked salmon. The now-famous special is Dom Perignon champagne and 2 peanut butter sandwiches for $99.99. **FYI:** Reservations recommended. Children's menu. Beer and wine only. **Open:** HS July–Sept breakfast Wed–Mon 8am–3pm; lunch Wed–Mon 8am–3pm; dinner Wed–Sun 5–8pm. Reduced hours off-season. Closed some hols. **Prices:** Main courses $8.50–$17.95. Ltd CC. &

BIG BEAR LAKE
Map page M-3, D3

See also Big Bear City, Big Bear Lake Village

Hotel 🏨

≣≣≣ **Forest Shores Inn**, 40670 Lakeview Dr, PO Box 946, Big Bear Lake, CA 92315; tel 909/866-6551. ¼ mi W of downtown on Calif 18. Located on the lakeshore, a complex of 3-story condo units. Guest can rent a ground-floor fully-equipped studio apartment, one of the 2-bedroom apartments on the top 2 floors, or an entire unit. **Rooms:** 23 effic. CI 3pm/CO noon. Nonsmoking rms avail. **Amenities:** 📺 ♨ 🎬 Cable TV, refrig, VCR. No A/C. All units w/terraces, all w/fireplaces. **Services:** 🛎 Babysitting. **Facilities:** 🏊 🏋 🎮 Games rm, sauna, whirlpool. **Rates:** HS June–Sept/Nov–Apr from $120 effic. Children under 18 stay free. Min stay wknds. Lower rates off-season. Higher rates for spec evnts/hols. Spec packages avail. Pking: Indoor/outdoor, free. Maj CC.

Motels

≣≣ **Frontier Lodge & Motel**, 40472 Big Bear Blvd, PO Box 687, Big Bear Lake, CA 92315; tel 909/866-5888 or toll free 800/451-6401, 800/457-6401 in CA; fax 909/866-4372. ¼ mi W of Big Bear Lake Village on Calif 18. An interesting mix of cabins and motel rooms. Some need renovation. **Rooms:** 18 rms; 25 ctges/villas. CI 2pm/CO 11am. Quality varies widely. Cabin 30 is splendid with 2 bedrooms, Jacuzzi, and stone fireplace. **Amenities:** 🛏 🔲 Cable TV w/movies, refrig. No A/C. Some units w/terraces, some w/fireplaces, some w/Jacuzzis. **Services:** 🛎 🍽 Babysitting. VCR and movie rentals. **Facilities:** 🏕 🖤 🏊 🐟 & 1 beach (lake shore), games rm, playground. Ping-Pong, volleyball, basketball, boat slips. **Rates:** HS July–Sept/Nov 15–Apr 15 $73 S or D; from $65 ctge/villa. Extra person $10. Min stay wknds. Lower rates off-season. Higher rates for spec evnts/hols. Spec packages avail. Pking: Outdoor, free. Maj CC.

≡≡ **Goldmine Lodge**, 42268 Moonridge Rd, PO Box 198, Big Bear Lake, CA 92315; tel 909/866-8786 or toll free 800/487-3168; fax 909/866-1592. On Calif 18 1½ mi E of Big Bear Lake Village. Nestled in a grove of large pine trees, this property is rustic but comfortable. **Rooms:** 11 rms and stes. CI 2pm/CO 11am. **Amenities:** 🛏 🐾 🔲 Cable TV w/movies, refrig. No A/C. Some units w/fireplaces. **Services:** 🛎 **Facilities:** 🏊 🐟 Whirlpool, playground. Nice picnic and barbecue area. **Rates (CP):** HS Nov–Apr $69 S or D; from $105 ste. Extra person $10. Children under 12 stay free. Min stay spec evnts. Lower rates off-season. Higher rates for spec evnts/hols. Spec packages avail. Pking: Outdoor, free. Maj CC.

≡≡≡ **Grey Squirrel Resort**, 39372 Big Bear Blvd, PO Box 5404, Big Bear Lake, CA 92315; tel 909/866-4335; fax 909/866-6271. 2 mi W of Big Bear Lake Village, on Calif 18. Nicely furnished cabins with fully equipped kitchens. **Rooms:** 17 ctges/villas. CI 2pm/CO 11am. Nonsmoking rms avail. The quality of cabins varies considerably. 'Doe' is one of the most charming, with an upscale country motif and in-room Jacuzzi. **Amenities:** 🛏 🐾 🔲 Cable TV, refrig, stereo/tape player. No A/C. All units w/terraces, all w/fireplaces, 1 w/Jacuzzi. **Services:** 🛎 🍽 Babysitting. **Facilities:** 🏕 🏊 🐟 Lawn games, whirlpool, playground, washer/dryer. Barbecue grills, volleyball court, shuffleboard, horseshoes, basketball court. Pool is enclosed in fall and winter. Plans to add fishing pond and ice rink. **Rates:** HS June–Oct/Nov–Apr from $75 ctge/villa. Extra person $10. Min stay wknds. Lower rates off-season. Higher rates for spec evnts/hols. Spec packages avail. Pking: Outdoor, free. Maj CC.

≡≡≡ **Sleepy Forest Cottages**, 426 Eureka Dr, Big Bear Lake, CA 92315; tel 909/866-7567 or toll free 800/544-7454. 1 mi E of Big Bear Lake Village. Very nice cottages decorated in an upscale country motif and set amid tree-shaded grounds. **Rooms:** 17 ctges/villas. CI 4pm/CO 11am. Nonsmoking rms avail. **Amenities:** 🛏 🐾 🔲 TV, refrig. No A/C. Some units w/terraces, all w/fireplaces, some w/Jacuzzis. **Services:** 🛎 **Facilities:** 🏊 🐟 🖳 Washer/dryer. **Rates (CP):** From $74 ctge/villa. Extra person $10. Children under 5 stay free. Min stay wknds. Higher rates for spec evnts/hols. Spec packages avail. Pking: Outdoor, free. Maj CC.

≡≡ **Wishing Well Motel**, 540 Pine Knot Blvd, PO Box 577, Big Bear Lake, CA 92315; tel 909/866-3505 or toll free 800/541-3505; fax 909/866-6821. ½ block from Calif 18 on Calif 18 Business Rte. Right in the village, among lovely pine trees. **Rooms:** 15 rms. CI 1pm/CO 11am. **Amenities:** 🛏 🐾 Cable TV. No A/C. **Services:** 🚗 🛎 🍽 **Facilities:** 🏊 🐟 **Rates (CP):** HS July–Sept/Nov–Apr $79–$89 S or D. Min stay HS. Lower rates off-season. Higher rates for spec evnts/hols. Spec packages avail. Pking: Outdoor, free. Maj CC.

Inn

≡≡≡≡ **Janet Kay's**, 695 Paine Rd, PO Box 3874, Big Bear Lake, CA 92315; tel 909/866-6800 or toll free 800/243-7031. 2 blocks W of Big Bear Lake Village; 1 block S of Calif 18. Beautiful colonial-style bed-and-breakfast. **Rooms:** 18 rms and stes (2 w/shared bath). CI 3pm/CO noon. No smoking. Rooms are large, luxuriously appointed, and all unique in their decor. **Amenities:** 🛏 🐾 Cable TV. No A/C. Some units w/terraces, some w/fireplaces, all w/Jacuzzis. **Services:** Afternoon tea and wine/sherry served. Full breakfast. **Facilities:** 🏊 🐟 🍴 & Guest lounge. **Rates (BB):** HS Nov–Apr $69–$129 S or D w/shared bath, $79–$149 S or D w/private bath; from $119 ste. Lower rates off-season. Higher rates for spec evnts/hols. Spec packages avail. Pking: Outdoor, free. Ltd CC. Ski packages available.

Resort

≡≡≡ **Marina Riviera Resort**, 40770 Lakeview Dr, PO Box 979, Big Bear Lake, CA 92315; tel 909/866-7545; fax 714/866-6705. On Calif 18, 1 block W of Pine Knot Blvd. A well-maintained family resort with lots of recreational facilities. **Rooms:** 42 rms and stes. CI 3pm/CO 11am. Nonsmoking rms avail. **Amenities:** 🛏 🐾 🔲 Cable TV w/movies, refrig. No A/C. All units w/terraces, some w/fireplaces, some w/Jacuzzis. **Services:** 🛎 Babysitting. **Facilities:** 🏕 🖤 🏊 🐟 ⚓ 🚤 1 beach (lake shore), lawn games, snorkeling, whirlpool, playground. Private boat dock; putting green and driving cage; barbecue facilities; horseshoes, volleyball, table tennis, and billiards. **Rates (CP):** $90–$110 S or D; from $135 ste. Min stay wknds. Higher rates for spec evnts/hols. Spec packages avail. Pking: Outdoor, free. Maj CC.

Restaurant 🍽

Blue Whale Lakeside, 350 Alden Rd, Big Bear Lake; tel 909/866-5514. N of Calif 18; 2 blocks E of Pine Knot Blvd. **Seafood/Steak.** Nautical decor, and great views of Big Bear Lake from every table. Fresh fish and lobsters are delivered three times each week. Broiled and roasted meats and poultry are imaginatively prepared. The Tail of the Whale lounge becomes an oyster bar on weekend summer afternoons. **FYI:** Reservations recommended. Combo/guitar/piano. Children's menu. **Open:** Lunch Fri–Sun noon–3pm; dinner daily 4–10pm; brunch Sun 9am–2pm. **Prices:** Main courses $10.95–$29.95. Maj CC. 📷

Attraction 💼

Alpine Slide and Recreation Area; tel 909/866-4626. Located in Big Bear Lake Village, about ¼ mile west on Calif 18. This amusement park features an alpine sled–type ride that operates year-round (call ahead in winter; additional fee charged), plus a water slide in the summer and a man-made snow hill with inner tube rentals in winter. Also miniature golf, horseback riding. **Open:** Mid-June–mid-Sept, daily 10am–6pm; Easter–mid-June and mid-Sept–Oct, Sat–Sun 10am–dusk; Nov–Easter, daily 10am–dusk. $$$$

BIG BEAR LAKE VILLAGE
Map page M-3, D3

Restaurant 🍴

★ **The Iron Squirrel**, 646 Pine Knot Blvd, Big Bear Lake Village; tel 909/866-9121. 1 block S of Calif 18. **French.** A restaurant that transports you to the French countryside. The dining room has tapestry-covered booths, French antiques, and gentle lighting. Cuisine is traditional French with a contemporary lightness; duck in orange and Grand Marnier sauce is a house favorite. **FYI:** Reservations recommended. **Open:** Lunch Mon–Sat 11:30am–1:45pm; dinner Mon–Thurs 5:30–8:30pm, Fri–Sun 5:30–9pm. Closed Dec 25. **Prices:** Main courses $15.95–$21.95. Maj CC. ♥

BIG SUR
Map page M-2, E3

Hotels 🏨

▤▤▤▤ **Post Ranch Inn**, Calif 1, PO Box 291, Big Sur, CA 93920; tel 408/667-2200 or toll free 800/527-2200; fax 408/667-2824. 28 mi S of Carmel. Opened in 1992, amid the seaside cliffs of Big Sur. Redwood villas are built into the hillsides (deer sometimes graze on the roofs) or among the trees. Ambience is very modern, yet rustic. **Rooms:** 30 ctges/villas. CI 4pm/CO

1pm. Nonsmoking rms avail. Coast House villas occupy round "towers," with a curvilinear sofa in front of the fireplace. Top-of-the-line Ocean Houses, with cliff-edge perches and private slate terraces, book up fast. **Amenities:** 🛅 📟 🍽 A/C, refrig, stereo/tape player, in-rm safe, bathrobes. All units w/minibars, all w/terraces, all w/fireplaces, all w/Jacuzzis. All accommodations have spa tables for in-room treatments. **Services:** ✕ ☎ 🆅🅿 🚗 🛄 🛎 Twice-daily maid svce, social director, masseur, babysitting. Guided nature hikes, pioneer history walks, wine tastings, astronomy sessions. Many different massages and treatments are offered, and there's a tarot reader on staff. **Facilities:** 🛅📺🛄 👤 1 rst (see also "Restaurants" below), 1 bar. No health club yet, but yoga and aerobics classes are held by the stunning lap-length pool. **Rates (CP):** From $265 ctge/villa. Extra person $50. Children under 2 stay free. Min stay wknds. Lower rates off-season. Spec packages avail. Pking: Outdoor, free. Maj CC. Midweek, midwinter package includes 2 nights' accommodations and 2 massages for $595 per couple.

▤▤▤▤ **Ventana**, Calif 1, Big Sur, CA 93920; tel 408/667-2331 or toll free 800/628-6500; fax 408/667-2419. 28 mi S of Carmel. 243 acres. Located among redwoods and bay trees on a ridge 1,200 feet above the Pacific, Ventana's low cedar buildings harmonize with the golden Santa Lucia foothills. **Rooms:** 59 rms, stes, and effic; 3 ctges/villas. CI 4:30/CO 1pm. Nonsmoking rms avail. Rooms have the feel of a sumptuous wilderness lodge, with rough-hewn plank walls and tiled floors. Even standard rooms have ocean views and lattice-shaded balconies. **Amenities:** 🛅🕹📟 🍽 A/C, satel TV w/movies, refrig, VCR, in-rm safe, bathrobes. All units w/minibars, all w/terraces, some w/fireplaces, some w/Jacuzzis. Almost every room has a fireplace, with logs already stacked. **Services:** ✕ 🛄 Twice-daily maid svce, masseur. Continental breakfast, with fresh-squeezed juice, granola, yogurt, and more. Complimentary wine and cheese each afternoon. Video rentals available from front desk. **Facilities:** 🛅🍴🎱🖥👤 1 rst (see also "Restaurants" below), 1 bar (w/entertainment), spa, sauna, steam rm, whirlpool. Japanese-style bathhouse has hot tubs and saunas tactfully divided into areas for men, women, and couples. Brand-new fitness center. **Rates (CP):** HS June–Oct $195–$485 S or D; from $890 ste; from $495 effic; from $295 ctge/villa. Extra person $50. Min stay wknds and spec evnts. Lower rates off-season. Pking: Outdoor, free. Maj CC.

Lodge

▤▤ **Big Sur Lodge**, Pfeiffer Big Sur State Park, PO Box 190, Big Sur, CA 93920; tel 408/667-3100 or toll free 800/424-4787; fax 408/667-3110. 26 mi S of Carmel. Pfeiffer Big Sur State Pk exit off Calif 1. A reasonably priced alternative to camping. There's tourist hubbub around the lobby and restaurant, but rooms are set away beyond a stand of redwoods. Grounds are extremely well kept, and you'll often see deer nibbling on the grass. **Rooms:** 61 rms, stes, and effic. CI 4pm/CO 11am. Nonsmoking rms avail. Standard motel-quality rooms clustered in 1-story buildings with 2 to 6 units in each, surrounded by broad green lawns. All are slated for recarpeting and painting by 1995. **Amenities:** No A/C, phone, or TV. All units w/terraces, some w/fireplaces. **Services:** Masseur, babysitting. **Facilities:** ⛴ 💯 1 rst. The pool is especially attractive, set off by a wrought-iron fence. Restaurant serves beer and wine. **Rates:** HS June–Labor Day $109–$159 S or D; from $129 ste; from $99 effic. Children under 18 stay free. Min stay wknds. Lower rates off-season. Spec packages avail. Pking: Outdoor, free. Ltd CC. You must pay for your room before you stay. Rates include admission to Pfeiffer Big Sur State Park.

Restaurants 🍴

★ **Nepenthe**, Calif 1, Big Sur; tel 408/667-2345. 30 mi S of Carmel. **Californian.** A '60s counterculture holdout, complete with piped-in sitar music. Climb the zigzagging stairway to dine on decks with Pacific views. Burgers and sandwiches for lunch; fish, steaks, or chicken for dinner. **FYI:** Reservations accepted. **Open:** Lunch daily 11:30am–4:30pm; dinner daily 5–10pm. Closed Thanksgiving. **Prices:** Main courses $10–$23.50. Maj CC. 🟢 ⛴ 🏞 👪 ⚕

Sierra Mar, in Post Ranch Inn, Calif 1, PO Box 291, Big Sur; tel 408/667-2200. 28 mi S of Carmel. **Californian.** Ocean-view dining beside floor-to-ceiling windows at cliff's edge. Decor is minimalist, with slate floors and simple wood chairs. The 4-course prix-fixe menu changes daily; it might include sole with lemon grass, papaya, and chile, or guinea hen with truffle risotto. Very large wine list. Be sure to make reservations. **FYI:** Reservations recommended. Dress code. **Open:** Lunch Sat–Sun noon–2:15pm; dinner daily 5:30–10pm. **Prices:** PF dinner $55. Maj CC. 🟢 ⛴ 🏞 VP ⚕

♣ **Ventana**, Calif 1, Big Sur; tel 408/667-2331. 28 mi S of Carmel. Look for Ventana sign on east side of road. **Californian/French.** Panoramic seacoast views and superb cuisine. Noted chef David Daniels offers preparations such as baby salad greens under a crown of fennel shavings, or a roast chicken with crisp skin headily infused with garlic, accompanied by delicious carrot ravioli. **FYI:** Reservations recommended. Guitar. Dress code. **Open:** Lunch Mon–Fri noon–3pm, Sat–Sun 11am–3pm; dinner daily 6–9:30pm. **Prices:** Main courses $21.50–$27.50; PF dinner $35–$45. Maj CC. 🟢 ⛴ 🖼 🏞 ⚕

Attractions 💼

Bixby Bridge, Calif 1 (Cabrillo Hwy). Perhaps the most photographed structure on the Big Sur coast, this vertigo-inducing bridge, towering nearly 260 feet above Bixby Creek Canyon, was said to be the longest concrete arch span in the world when it was constructed in 1932. Several observation alcoves are located at regular intervals along the bridge. Free.

Andrew Molera State Park, Calif 1 (Cabrillo Hwy); tel 408/667-2315. Enter the park via a short driveway off Calif 1 that leads to the parking lot; the park is ¼-mile walk from there. Here you will find a beach and walk-in campground as well as equestrian trails and hiking and nature trails. Hikes include the Bluffs Trail, an easy 2-mile trail that winds along the ocean to the bluff; the Headlands Trail, a 1-mile hike that leads to the Headlands above the mouth of Big Sur River as it flows into the ocean; and the Bobcat Trail, about 2 miles long, which passes through the redwoods along the Big Sur River. **Open:** Daily sunrise–sunset. $$$

Julia Pfeiffer Burns State Park, Calif 1 (Cabrillo Hwy); tel 408/667-2315. This 1,800-acre wooded day-use park offers several trails, including one geared to novice hikers (⅓-mile long) that ends with a view of McWay Falls, which drop 50 feet into the ocean. Picnic area. **Open:** Daily sunrise–sunset. $$$

Pfeiffer–Big Sur State Park, Sycamore Canyon Rd off Calif 1 (Cabrillo Hwy); tel 408/667-2315. The Big Sur River runs through the center of this thickly wooded 810-acre park. An information booth at the park entrance can provide detailed maps of the well-tended nature trails that criss-cross through the redwoods. Nature center has displays on the natural and cultural history of the area. Popular hikes include an easy ½-mile trek to Pfeiffer Falls; the ¼-mile-long Oak Grove Trail, which takes off from the Pfeiffer Falls trailhead; and the Valley View Trail, which begins at the falls and climbs 400 feet in a distance of a ½-mile. The trail ends in a high point that provides a view of the entire Big Sur Valley and Point Sur. **Open:** Daily sunrise–sunset. $$$

BISHOP

Map page M-3, B2

Motels 🛏

🏨🏨 **Best Western Holiday Spa Lodge**, 1025 North Main St, Bishop, CA 93514; tel 619/873-3543 or toll free 800/576-3543; fax 619/872-4777. On US 395. Clean, pleasant property with beautiful landscaping. **Rooms:** 89 rms and stes. CI 3pm/CO 11am. Nonsmoking rms avail. Deluxe rooms are much nicer than standard ones, which are small and old. **Amenities:** 🔋 🕭 📶 🍴 A/C, cable TV w/movies, refrig. 1 unit w/fireplace. Microwave. VCR for rent. **Services:** 🏧 🏧 **Facilities:** 🔋 🕭 Whirlpool. **Rates:** HS May–Oct $56 S; $64–$78 D; from $87 ste. Extra person $10. Children under 18 stay free. Lower rates off-season. Higher rates for spec evnts/hols. Pking: Outdoor, free. Maj CC.

🍴🍴 **Creekside Inn–Best Western**, 725 N Main Street, Bishop, CA 93514; tel 619/872-3044 or toll free 800/273-3550; fax 619/872-1300. 25 mi S of Mammoth Lakes. Attractive brick facade and beautiful new landscaping. Handsome lobby with fireplace. **Rooms:** 89 rms and stes. CI 1pm/CO 1pm. Nonsmoking rms avail. Nice colonial furniture. Suites have a living room, 2 bedrooms, and kitchen. **Amenities:** 🔋 🕭 A/C, cable TV. **Services:** 🚗 🏧 🏧 🏧 Babysitting. **Facilities:** 🔋 🕭 Whirlpool. Room for cleaning fish. Creekside pool. **Rates (CP):** HS May–Oct $89–$99 S or D; from $180 ste. Extra person $12. Children under 13 stay free. Lower rates off-season. Higher rates for spec evnts/hols. Spec packages avail. Pking: Outdoor, free. Maj CC.

🍴 **Days Inn**, 724 W Line St, Bishop, CA 93514; tel 619/872-1095 or toll free 800/325-2525; fax 619/872-1095. 25 mi S of Mammoth Lakes. 2 blocks off US 395. New property in an attractive southwestern style. **Rooms:** 34 rms and stes. CI 2pm/CO 11am. Nonsmoking rms avail. Clean, simple, well-appointed rooms. **Amenities:** 🔋 📶 A/C, cable TV, refrig. 1 unit w/Jacuzzi. Ceiling fan; microwave. VCRs for rent. **Services:** 🏧 **Facilities:** 🕭 Whirlpool. **Rates:** HS Apr–Oct $55–$69 S; $69–$79 D; from $80 ste. Extra person $6. Children under 12 stay free. Lower rates off-season. Higher rates for spec evnts/hols. Spec packages avail. Pking: Outdoor, free. Maj CC.

Attractions 🗝

Paiute Shoshone Indian Cultural Center, 2300 W Line St (Calif 168); tel 619/873-4478. More than 1,000 years ago, the Owens Valley, bordered by the Sierra Nevada Mountains to the west and the White and Inyo ranges on the east, was the territory of the Shoshone and the Paiute. Hunters and gatherers, these people lived in harmony with nature; all of their needs—food, clothing, housing, medicine, arts, and entertainment—were satisfied by the land. Museum exhibits display food preparation methods, basketry, flinting, artwork, and other "life ways" of the the Paiute and Shoshone people. **Open:** Mon–Fri 9am–5pm, Sat–Sun 10am–4pm. Closed some hols. Free.

Laws Railroad Museum and Historical Site, Silver Canyon Rd; tel 619/873-5950. The legacy of the last narrow-gauge railroad west of the Rockies is preserved at this site. Visitors can see the original 1883 Laws Depot, Laws Post Office, and Agent's

House, as well as the locomotive, string of cars, and exhibits of railroad memorabilia. Museum buildings house fascinating collections from Owens Valley pioneer days. Reception center with gifts, books, and souvenirs. **Open:** Daily 10am–4pm, weather permitting. Closed some hols. Free.

Ancient Bristlecone Pine Forest, Calif 168; tel 619/873-2500. The oldest known continuously growing organism in the world is a 4,700-year-old bristlecone pine named **Methuselah** in the Schulman Grove of the Ancient Bristlecone Pine Forest. Sculpted over centuries by wind, blowing ice, and sand, bristlecones develop unique and exquisite shapes of golden-hued wood. The visitor center offers interpretive talks, self-guided trails, displays, books and maps, and a picnic area (no drinking water available). **Open:** Mem Day–Columbus Day, daily 24 hours. Free.

BLUE JAY

Map page M-3, D3

Restaurant 🍴

The Royal Oak, 27187 Calif 189, Blue Jay; tel 909/337-6018. 1½ mi SW of Lake Arrowhead Village. **Continental.** The ambience melds English Tudor style with a country-club atmosphere. Cuisine is rich and hearty, featuring steaks, chops, seafood, and pasta. Reduced prices are offered for Wednesday and Thursday romantic dinners. **FYI:** Reservations recommended. Piano. Children's menu. Dress code. **Open:** Dinner Sun–Thurs 5–9pm, Fri–Sat 5–11pm; brunch Sun 10:30am–3pm. Closed some hols. **Prices:** Main courses $12.95–$29.95. Maj CC. 💗 🔋

BODEGA BAY

Map page M-2, C1 (S of Jenner)

Hotels 🏨

🍴🍴 **Holiday Inn Bodega Bay**, 521 Calif 1 N, Bodega Bay, CA 94923; tel 707/875-2217 or toll free 800/346-6999; fax 707/875-2964. Located near a golf course and right on the bay, a very well-maintained property. **Rooms:** 44 rms and stes. CI 3pm/CO noon. Express checkout avail. Nonsmoking rms avail. Dull standard rooms have good views but don't smell fresh. Some rooms have a Roman spa. **Amenities:** 🔋 🕭 🍴 Cable TV, refrig, VCR. No A/C. All units w/minibars, all w/terraces, some w/fireplaces, some w/Jacuzzis. **Services:** 🏧 **Facilities:** 📶 🕭 Whirlpool, washer/dryer. **Rates:** HS Apr–Nov $89–$180 S or D; from

$175 ste. Extra person $10. Children under 12 stay free. Min stay HS. Lower rates off-season. Higher rates for spec evnts/hols. Pking: Outdoor, free. Maj CC. Rates go up on weekends.

≣≣≣ **Inn at the Tides**, 800 Calif 1, PO Box 640, Bodega Bay, CA 94923; tel 707/875-2751 or toll free 800/541-7788; fax 707/875-3023. Attractive hotel overlooking Bodega Bay; located near several state beaches and a golf course. **Rooms:** 86 rms. CI 3pm/CO noon. Nonsmoking rms avail. Spacious rooms with views of bay and highway, but some smelled a bit smoky. **Amenities:** 🛏 ⚟ ▣ 🍽 A/C, cable TV w/movies, refrig, bathrobes. Some units w/terraces, some w/fireplaces. **Services:** ✕ 🛎 Masseur. Firewood supplied. Daily newspaper delivered to room. **Facilities:** 🛆 🛥 🌊 100 ⚐ 1 rst, 1 bar, sauna, whirlpool, washer/dryer. Large pool area is glassed in to protect from wind. **Rates (CP):** $120–$230 S or D. Extra person $20. Children under 12 stay free. Min stay spec evnts. Lower rates off-season. Spec packages avail. Pking: Outdoor, free. Maj CC. Golf packages available.

Lodge

≣≣≣≣ **Bodega Bay Lodge Best Western**, 103 Calif 1, Bodega Bay, CA 94923; tel 707/875-3525 or toll free 800/368-2468. 4 acres. A quiet, peaceful place ¼ mile from the beach, with beautiful grounds and expansive views of the bay, ocean, and marshes. Lobby has fish tanks with local marine life. **Rooms:** 74 rms and stes. CI 3pm/CO 11:30am. Nonsmoking rms avail. Rooms are very cozy, clean, and comfortable and have views of the bay and marshlands. **Amenities:** 🛏 ⚟ ▣ 🍽 Cable TV, refrig, bathrobes. No A/C. All units w/minibars, all w/terraces, some w/fireplaces, some w/Jacuzzis. **Services:** ✕ 🛎 Masseur. Complimentary afternoon wine in lobby. Gourmet picnic lunch for excursions available. **Facilities:** 🛆 🚴 🌊 100 ⚐ 1 rst, sauna, whirlpool, washer/dryer. Dining room offers seafood and pasta. Good California cuisine restaurant on premises. An 18-hole golf course is next door. **Rates:** HS June–Oct $125–$210 S or D; from $210 ste. Extra person $10. Children under 12 stay free. Min stay HS. Lower rates off-season. Spec packages avail. Pking: Outdoor, free. Maj CC. Golf packages available. Rates $20 less Sunday–Thursday.

Restaurant 🍴

Lucas Wharf, 595 Calif 1, Bodega Bay; tel 707/875-3522. **Seafood.** The best seafood spot in Bodega, right on a fishing wharf. It serves good local seafood: calamari, steamed mussels and clams, salmon, crab Louis; also tasty appetizers, chowder, and fish and chips. **FYI:** Reservations accepted. **Open:** HS Oct–

May Sun–Thurs 11:30am–9pm, Fri–Sat 11:30am–9:30pm. Reduced hours off-season. Closed some hols. **Prices:** Main courses $13–$16. Ltd CC. ♿

BOONEVILLE
Map page M-2, C1

Restaurant 🍴

★ **The Boonville Hotel**, Calif 128 at Lambert Lane, Booneville; tel 707/895-2210. **Californian.** A charming restaurant set in a historic hotel surrounded by beautiful gardens. The atmosphere is fresh and clean, refined yet casual. The menu changes daily; typical offerings include delicious pizza, ahi tuna with mango-and-lime salsa, superb caesar salad, and lamb chops. Local wines and beers served. **FYI:** Reservations recommended. Beer and wine only. **Open:** Wed–Sun 6–9pm. Closed January. **Prices:** Main courses $10–$17. Maj CC. 🍷 ♿

BORREGO SPRINGS
Map page M-3, E3 (NW of Ocotillo Wells)

Resort 🏨

≣≣≣≣ **La Casa del Zorro**, 3845 Yaqui Pass Rd, PO Box 127, Borrego Springs, CA 92004; tel 619/767-5323 or toll free 800/824-1884; fax 619/767-4782. 34 acres. A beautiful oasis in the desert, surrounded by over 500,000 acres of unforgettable natural scenery of Anza-Borrego Desert State Park. **Rooms:** 79 rms and stes; 19 ctges/villas. CI 4pm/CO noon. Express checkout avail. Nonsmoking rms avail. Each room is decorated with artifacts of the early California heritage of Borrego Springs. **Amenities:** 🛏 ⚟ ▣ 🍽 A/C, cable TV w/movies, shoe polisher, bathrobes. Some units w/minibars, some w/terraces, some w/fireplaces, some w/Jacuzzis. **Services:** ✕ 🛎 🚗 🛎 🐕 Twice-daily maid svce, babysitting. **Facilities:** 🛆 🚴 ⚟🌊 🌊 100 ♿ 1 rst, 1 bar (w/entertainment), lawn games, whirlpool, beauty salon, playground. **Rates:** HS Nov–May 18 $80–$98 S or D; from $125 ste; from $150 ctge/villa. Extra person $10. Children under 12 stay free. Min stay wknds and spec evnts. Lower rates off-season. Spec packages avail. Pking: Outdoor, free. Maj CC.

Attraction 🏛

Anza-Borrego Desert State Park; tel 619/767-4205 (Visitor Center) or 767-5311 (Park). The nation's largest state park,

Anza-Borrego encompasses over 500,000 acres of desert wilderness just 40 miles east of Temecula. The best time to visit is mid-March through early April when wildflowers and cactus bloom throughout the park. The Visitor Center, located just north of Borrego Springs, can provide maps, books, and cards, and screens an audiovisual presentation on the changing faces of the desert. Self-guided hikes of the Borrego Palm Canyon lead to an oasis of fan palms with a spring and waterfall. **Open:** Oct–May, daily 9am–5pm; June–Sept, Sat–Sun 9am–5pm. $$

BOULDER CREEK

Map page M-2, D2 (N of Santa Cruz)

Attraction 🖼

Big Basin Redwoods State Park, 21600 Big Basin Way; tel 408/338-6132. Located 23 miles north of Santa Cruz via Calif 9 and Calif 236. California's oldest state park, Big Basin Redwoods was California's second state park, created in 1902. (The state's first park, also created as a redwood preserve, was redesignated Yosemite National Park in 1890.) Comprising nearly 19,000 acres, the park contains redwood groves, 80 miles of hiking trails, and 150 campsites (no hookups). A small museum has displays of the area's abundant plant and animal life. **Open:** Daily 6am–10pm. $$

BREA

Map page M-3, D2 (S of Pomona)

Hotel 🏨

☰☰☰ Embassy Suites, 900 E Birch St, Brea, CA 92621; tel 714/990-6000 or toll free 800/EMBASSY; fax 714/990-1653. 10 mi NE of Disneyland. Imperial Highway exit off Calif 57. All-suites hotel decorated in an Egyptian motif. Well-suited for business travelers and families; located between the Brea Civic Center and the Brea Mall. **Rooms:** 229 stes. Exec-level rms avail. CI 3pm/CO 1pm. Express checkout avail. Nonsmoking rms avail. All suites have queen-size beds and are beautifully decorated. **Amenities:** 🛅 ⚗ 🖭 ❦ A/C, cable TV w/movies, refrig, voice mail. Some units w/terraces. Iron and ironing board in each room. **Services:** ✗ ⬛ 🛆 ⏎ Twice-daily maid svce, babysitting. Complimentary breakfast and afternoon snacks. Free shuttle to Disneyland and Knott's Berry Farm. **Facilities:** 🗗 ⛟ 500 ⅃ 1 rst, 1 bar, spa, sauna, whirlpool, washer/dryer. Gift shop. **Rates (BB):** From $155 ste. Extra person $10. Children under 12 stay free. Higher rates for spec evnts/hols. AP rates avail. Spec packages avail. Pking: Indoor, free. Maj CC.

BUENA PARK

Map page M-3, D2 (W of Anaheim)

For Disneyland, see Anaheim

Hotels 🖼

☰☰☰ Buena Park Hotel, 7675 Crescent Ave, Buena Park, CA 90620; tel 714/995-1111 or toll free 800/422-4444 in the US, 800/325-8734 in Canada; fax 714/828-8590. Beach Blvd exit off Calif 91. A great location—guests can walk to Knott's Berry Farm or take a shuttle to Disneyland, just 10 minutes away. **Rooms:** 350 rms and stes. Exec-level rms avail. CI 3pm/CO noon. Nonsmoking rms avail. Rooms are large. **Amenities:** 🛅 ⚗ 🖭 A/C, satel TV w/movies. 1 unit w/terrace, 1 w/Jacuzzi. **Services:** ✗ ⬛ 🚗 🛆 ⏎ Car-rental desk, babysitting. **Facilities:** 🗗 🗒 2 rsts, 1 bar (w/entertainment), games rm, whirlpool, washer/dryer. **Rates:** HS June–Aug $64–$85 S; $74–$95 D; from $125 ste. Children under 18 stay free. Lower rates off-season. Higher rates for spec evnts/hols. Spec packages avail. Pking: Outdoor, free. Maj CC.

☰☰☰ Embassy Suites, 7762 Beach Blvd, Buena Park, CA 90620; tel 714/739-5600 or toll free 800/362-2779; fax 714/521-9650. Beach Blvd exit off Calif 91. This all-suites property has a nice courtyard and open lobby. **Rooms:** 202 rms and stes. CI 3pm/CO noon. Express checkout avail. Nonsmoking rms avail. **Amenities:** 🛅 ⚗ 🖭 A/C, cable TV w/movies, refrig, voice mail. All units w/minibars, some w/terraces. Microwaves. **Services:** ✗ 🛆 ⏎ Babysitting. Complimentary breakfast buffet and morning newspaper. **Facilities:** 🗗 250 ⅃ 1 rst, 1 bar, games rm, whirlpool, washer/dryer. Gas BBQ grills. **Rates (BB):** HS June 6–Aug 27 $144–$154 S or D; from $144 ste. Extra person $15. Children under 12 stay free. Lower rates off-season. Spec packages avail. Pking: Outdoor, free. Maj CC.

☰☰☰ Holiday Inn Buena Park, 7000 Beach Blvd, Buena Park, CA 90620; tel 714/522-7000 or toll free 800/522-7006; fax 714/522-7020. Beach Blvd exit off Calif 91. Close to the freeway, but well-soundproofed. **Rooms:** 246 rms and stes. Exec-level rms avail. CI 3pm/CO noon. Express checkout avail. Nonsmoking rms avail. Nicely decorated with a fresh, contemporary look. **Amenities:** 🛅 ⚗ 🖭 A/C, cable TV w/movies. Some units w/minibars, some w/terraces. **Services:** ✗ ⬛ 🚗 🛆 ⏎ ⏏ Twice-daily maid svce, car-rental desk, babysitting. **Facilities:** 🗗 600 ⅃ 1 rst, 1 bar (w/entertainment), games rm, whirlpool, playground, washer/dryer. **Rates:** HS June–Aug $89–$129 S or D; from $150 ste. Extra person $10. Children under 11 stay free. Lower rates off-season. Spec packages avail. Pking: Outdoor, free. Maj CC.

Motels

☰☰☰ Courtyard by Marriott, 7621 Beach Blvd, Buena Park, CA 90620; tel 714/670-6600 or toll free 800/321-2211; fax 714/670-0360. Beach Blvd exit off Calif 91. Looks like new, although it opened in 1986. Just what travelers want to see when they are tired and ready to check into a nice room. **Rooms:** 145 rms and stes. CI 3pm/CO 1pm. Express checkout avail. **Amenities:** 🛜 🛎 A/C, cable TV w/movies. Some units w/mini-bars, some w/terraces. **Services:** ✗ ☒ ⊃ Babysitting. **Facilities:** 🛱 🛳 🔲 ᕫ 1 rst, spa, whirlpool, washer/dryer. Gazebo. **Rates:** HS May–Sept 15 $64–$69 S; $74–$79 D; from $84 ste. Extra person $10. Children under 17 stay free. Lower rates off-season. Pking: Outdoor, free. Maj CC.

☰☰☰ Fairfield Inn by Marriott, 7032 Orangethorpe Ave, Buena Park, CA 90621; tel 714/523-1488 or toll free 800/228-2800; fax 714/523-1488. Beach Blvd exit off Calif 91. Very clean hotel that is kept up to Marriott standards. **Rooms:** 133 rms. CI 3pm/CO noon. Nonsmoking rms avail. Rooms are basic, but great for the price. **Amenities:** 🛜 🛎 A/C, cable TV w/movies. **Services:** ☒ ⊃ **Facilities:** 🛱 🔟 ᕫ **Rates (CP):** HS June–Aug $35–$38 S; $42 D. Children under 17 stay free. Lower rates off-season. Higher rates for spec evnts/hols. Spec packages avail. Pking: Outdoor, free. Maj CC.

☰☰ Farm De Ville, 7800 Crescent Ave, Buena Park, CA 90620; tel 714/527-2201 or toll free 800/982-7800; fax 714/826-3826. Beach Blvd exit off Calif 91. New management. A major renovation is slated to begin by 1995. Close to Disneyland; right across from Knott's Berry Farm. **Rooms:** 130 rms and stes. CI 3pm/CO noon. Nonsmoking rms avail. Rooms are a bit small. **Amenities:** 🛜 A/C, cable TV. **Services:** ⊃ Babysitting. **Facilities:** 🛱 🔟 Steam rm, washer/dryer. **Rates:** HS June–Aug $32–$36 S or D; from $48 ste. Children under 12 stay free. Lower rates off-season. Higher rates for spec evnts/hols. Spec packages avail. Pking: Outdoor, free. Maj CC.

☰☰ Hampton Inn Buena Park, 7828 Orangethorpe Ave, Buena Park, CA 90620; tel 714/670-7200 or toll free 800/727-7205; fax 714/522-3319. Beach Blvd exit off Calif 91. Clean and well-kept. 7 miles from Disneyland and minutes from Knott's Berry Farm. **Rooms:** 175 rms. CI 2pm/CO noon. Nonsmoking rms avail. Choice of 1 king-size or 2 double beds. **Amenities:** 🛜 🛎 A/C, cable TV w/movies. **Services:** 🚗 ☒ ⊃ Car-rental desk, babysitting. Complimentary snacks and beverages. Free local calls. Free shuttle to Disneyland and Knott's Berry Farm. **Facilities:** 🛱 🔟 ᕫ Whirlpool, washer/dryer. Pool heated. **Rates (CP):** HS June–Aug $64–$69 S; $69–$74 D. Extra person $5. Children under 18 stay free. Min stay spec evnts. Lower rates off-season. Higher rates for spec evnts/hols. Spec packages avail. Pking: Outdoor, free. Maj CC.

Restaurant 🍴

Marie Callender Restaurant, 5960 Orangethorpe Ave, Buena Park; tel 714/522-0170. Orangethorpe/Valley View exit off Calif 91. **American.** Homey restaurant known for its extensive salad bar and homemade soups. Part of a chain that began as a pie shop, it's a great place for family dining. **FYI:** Reservations accepted. Children's menu. **Open:** Mon–Thurs 11am–10pm, Fri–Sat 11am–11pm, Sun 9am–10pm. Closed Dec 25. **Prices:** Main courses $7.95–$13.95. Maj CC. 🅿️ ᕫ

Attractions 📷

Knott's Berry Farm, 8039 Beach Blvd; tel 714/827-1776 or 220-5200 (recorded info). Knott's Berry Farm grew out of the enormous popularity of the roadside stand operated by Walter and Cordelia Knott during the Great Depression. The Knotts sold pies, preserves, and homemade chicken dinners from their 10-acre farm, and lines became so long that they decided to create an Old West Ghost Town to amuse waiting customers. The famous Chicken Dinner Restaurant now serves more than a million meals a year, and the park maintains the Old West motif throughout 5 themed adventure areas, each with rides, shows, and other attractions:

Old West Ghost Town, the original attraction, is a collection of authentic buildings that have been relocated from actual western ghost towns and refurbished; **Fiesta Village** has a south-of-the-border theme and features a rollercoaster that runs backward; **Roaring '20s** contains the Sky Tower, a thrilling parachute ride; **Wild Water Wilderness** features a whitewater ride called Bigfoot Rapids; and **Camp Snoopy** is a 6-acre play area where members of the Peanuts gang greet guests and pose for pictures. **Open:** Summer, Mon–Thurs 9am–11pm, Fri–Sun 9am–midnight; fall–spring, Mon–Thurs 10am–6pm, Fri–Sun 10am–10pm. Opening times vary; call for latest information. $$$$

Movieland Wax Museum, 7711 Beach Blvd (Calif 39); tel 714/522-1155. Memorable motion picture scenes are painstakingly re-created here in wax. Tableaux depicting stars and famous films include Humphrey Bogart and Katherine Hepburn in *The African Queen,* Laurel and Hardy in *The Perfect Day,* and such newer stars as *Superman* and the crew of *Star Trek.* New personalities are added yearly. **Open:** Daily 9am–7pm. $$$$

BURBANK

Map page M-3, D2 (NW of Glendale)

Hotels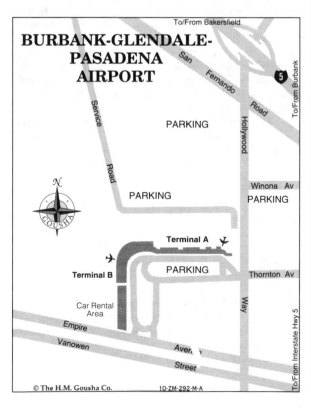

≡≡≡ **Burbank Airport Hilton & Convention Center**, 2500 Hollywood Way, Burbank, CA 91505; tel 818/843-6000 or toll free 800/468-3576, 800/643-7400 in CA; fax 818/842-9720. Well kept, and although at entrance to Burbank Airport, there's no airplane noise. **Rooms:** 500 rms and stes. CI 3pm/CO noon. Express checkout avail. Nonsmoking rms avail. Adequate, middle-of-the-road decor. **Amenities:** A/C, cable TV w/movies, refrig, voice mail, shoe polisher, bathrobes. Some units w/minibars, some w/terraces, some w/Jacuzzis. **Services:** Car-rental desk. Complimentary transportation to Universal Studios Tour. **Facilities:** 1 rst, 1 bar (w/entertainment), spa, sauna, whirlpool, washer/dryer. Passes available to neighboring World's Gym. **Rates:** $106–$176 S; $121–$176 D; from $146 ste. Extra person $15. Children under 18 stay free. Higher rates for spec evnts/hols. Spec packages avail. Pking: Outdoor, $3. Maj CC.

To/From Bakersfield

BURBANK-GLENDALE-PASADENA AIRPORT

PARKING

PARKING

Terminal A

Terminal B

PARKING

Car Rental Area

Empire

Vanowen

Avenue

Street

Winona Av
PARKING

Thornton Av

Way

San Fernando Road

Hollywood Road

Service Road

5 To/From Burbank

To/From Interstate Hwy 5

N GOUSHA

© The H.M. Gousha Co.   10-ZM-292-M-A

≡≡≡ **Ramada Inn Burbank Airport**, 2900 N San Fernando Blvd, Burbank, CA 91504; tel 818/843-5955 or toll free 800/228-2828; fax 818/845-9030. Very nice hotel for the neighborhood; located close to the studios. Great pool area and attractive garden. **Rooms:** 144 rms and stes. CI 2pm/CO noon. Nonsmoking rms avail. Large rooms with little or no freeway or airport noise. **Amenities:** A/C, cable TV w/movies, refrig. Some units w/Jacuzzis. **Services:** Car-rental desk, babysitting. **Facilities:** 1 rst, 1 bar, games rm. **Rates:** HS June 15–Sept 1 $85 S; $95 D; from $130 ste. Extra person $10. Children under 18 stay free. Lower rates off-season. Higher rates for spec evnts/hols. Spec packages avail. Pking: Outdoor, free. Maj CC.

BURLINGAME

Map page M-2, D2 (N of San Mateo)

Hotels

≡≡≡ **Crown Sterling Suites**, 150 Anza Blvd, Burlingame, CA 94010; tel 415/342-4600 or toll free 800/433-4600; fax 415/343-8137. Broadway/Burlingame exit off US 101 S; N Anza exit off US 101 N. Elaborate lobby combines neoclassical and Victorian furnishings and woodwork with an atrium housing cages of parrots, a koi pond, and waterfalls. Ongoing renovations. **Rooms:** 338 stes. CI 3pm/CO noon. Express checkout avail. Nonsmoking rms avail. Some rooms have fantastic water views. Nice appointments with new, fine linens. **Amenities:** A/C, satel TV w/movies, refrig, voice mail. All units w/minibars, all w/terraces. **Services:** Car-rental desk, babysitting. Full breakfast included. Complimentary cocktails in lobby. **Facilities:** 1 rst, 1 bar (w/entertainment), sauna, steam rm, whirlpool, washer/dryer. Beautiful pool area. **Rates (BB):** From $119 ste. Extra person $10. Children under 12 stay free. Spec packages avail. Pking: Outdoor, free. Maj CC.

≡≡ **Doubletree Hotel**, 835 Airport Blvd, Burlingame, CA 94010; tel 415/344-5500 or toll free 800/222-TREE; fax 415/340-8851. 15 mi S of San Francisco. Broadway E exit off US 101 S; Anza Blvd exit off US 101 N. Across the street from San Francisco Bay, the hotel offers lovely views from top floors and a restaurant with an extensive menu. **Rooms:** 291 rms and stes. CI 3pm/CO noon. Express checkout avail. Nonsmoking rms avail. **Amenities:** A/C, TV w/movies. **Services:** Babysitting. **Facilities:** 1 rst, 1 bar. Excellent waterfront jogging path. **Rates (CP):** HS June–Sept $109–$139 S; $109–$139 D; from $150 ste. Extra person $10. Children under 18 stay free. Lower rates off-season. Higher rates for spec evnts/hols. AP and MAP rates avail. Spec packages avail. Pking: Outdoor, free. Maj CC.

≣≣≣ **Holiday Inn Crowne Plaza**, 600 Airport Blvd, Burlingame, CA 94010; tel 415/340-8500 or toll free 800/827-0880; fax 415/343-1546. 15 mi S of San Francisco. Broadway-Burlingame exit off US 101. A luxurious hotel located on San Francisco Bay near the airport. **Rooms:** 405 rms and stes. Exec-level rms avail. CI 3pm/CO noon. Express checkout avail. Nonsmoking rms avail. **Amenities:** 🛏️ 🅰️ 🍽️ A/C, cable TV w/movies, refrig. Some units w/minibars. **Services:** ✕ 🗝️ 🚗 🛄 🍽️ Car-rental desk, babysitting. Excellent service. Continental breakfast in lounge. Hot and cold hors d'oeuvres and cocktails in the evening. **Facilities:** 🛎️ 🏊 🏋️ 🖥️ 🛗 🖥️ 🚿 1 rst, 1 bar (w/entertainment), spa, sauna, steam rm, whirlpool, washer/dryer. Executive floor has private access. Meandering jogging path hugs the bay. **Rates:** HS Mar–Oct $119 S or D; from $119 ste. Extra person $10. Children under 18 stay free. Lower rates off-season. Spec packages avail. Pking: Outdoor, free. Maj CC.

≣≣≣ **Hyatt Regency–San Francisco Airport**, 1333 Bayshore Hwy, Burlingame, CA 94010; tel 415/347-1234 or toll free 800/233-1234; fax 415/347-5948. 15 mi S of San Francisco. Broadway exit off US 101; go east over freeway overpass, follow signs to Bayshore Hwy. A busy hotel that anticipates guests' needs. Popular among leisure travelers, corporate travelers, and conventioneers. **Rooms:** 793 rms and stes. Exec-level rms avail. CI 3pm/CO noon. Express checkout avail. Nonsmoking rms avail. Some rooms have views of hills or of San Francisco Bay. **Amenities:** 🛏️ 🅰️ 📺 🍽️ A/C, cable TV w/movies, refrig, VCR, stereo/tape player, voice mail. Some units w/terraces, some w/Jacuzzis. Intercom in every room for emergency information. **Services:** 🍴 🗝️ 🆅🅿️ 🚗 🛄 🍽️ Car-rental desk, babysitting. **Facilities:** 🛎️ 🏊 🏋️ 🖥️ 🛗 🖥️ 🚿 3 rsts, 2 bars (1 w/entertainment), spa, sauna, whirlpool. Largest hotel and meeting facilities between South San Francisco and Los Angeles. Deli open 24 hours. **Rates:** $155–$200 S; $180–$225 D; from $199 ste. Extra person $25. Children under 18 stay free. AP rates avail. Spec packages avail. Pking: Indoor/outdoor, free. Maj CC. Business Plan (add $15) includes breakfast, fax machines in room, and use of business center.

≣≣ **Radisson Hotel San Francisco Airport**, 1177 Airport Blvd, Burlingame, CA 94010; tel 415/342-9200 or toll free 800/333-3333; fax 415/342-1655. Broadway exit off US 101; right at Airport Blvd. Changed from a Sheraton to a Radisson property in 1993. **Rooms:** 301 rms and stes. CI 3pm/CO noon. Nonsmoking rms avail. Most of the guest rooms have new beds, mattresses, furniture, and flooring. **Amenities:** 🛏️ 🅰️ 📺 🍽️ A/C, cable TV w/movies, bathrobes. **Services:** ✕ 🚗 🛄 🍽️ Free newspapers.

Late (4pm) checkout available upon request. **Facilities:** 🛎️ 🚴 🏋️ 🛗 🏊 1 rst, 1 bar, whirlpool, beauty salon, playground, washer/dryer. An indoor/outdoor pool and glassed-in fitness center were slated to be added during renovation. **Rates (CP):** $100–$110 S; $130–$140 D; from $250 ste. Extra person $10. Children under 16 stay free. Higher rates for spec evnts/hols. Spec packages avail. Pking: Indoor/outdoor, free. Maj CC.

≣≣≣ **Ramada San Francisco Airport**, 1250 Old Bayshore, Burlingame, CA 94010; tel 415/347-2381 or toll free 800/227-2381; fax 415/348-8838. Broadway/Airport Blvd exit off US 101. Light-filled 2-story lobby with open staircase and lots of brass, glass, and potted plants. Furniture looks a bit shabby. **Rooms:** 145 rms and stes. CI 2pm/CO noon. Express checkout avail. Nonsmoking rms avail. **Amenities:** 🛏️ 🅰️ A/C, cable TV w/movies. **Services:** ✕ 🚗 🛄 🍽️ Babysitting. Wheelchair-accessible van available. **Facilities:** 🛎️ 🛗 🏊 1 rst, 1 bar (w/entertainment). **Rates (BB):** HS Apr–Sept $88 S; $98 D; from $120 ste. Extra person $10. Children under 18 stay free. Lower rates off-season. Spec packages avail. Pking: Outdoor, free. Maj CC.

≣≣≣ **San Francisco Airport Marriot**, 1800 Old Bayshore Hwy, Burlingame, CA 94010; tel 415/692-9100 or toll free 800/228-9290; fax 415/692-8016. Millbrae Ave E exit off US 101; right onto Old Bayshore Hwy. Convenient location for travelers with an atrium-style lobby and views of San Francisco Bay. **Rooms:** 684 rms and stes. Exec-level rms avail. CI 3pm/CO noon. Express checkout avail. Nonsmoking rms avail. Noise varies according to flight patterns. **Amenities:** 🛏️ 🅰️ A/C, cable TV w/movies, voice mail. **Services:** 🍴 🗝️ 🆅🅿️ 🚗 🛄 🍽️ Car-rental desk, babysitting. Daily newspapers. **Facilities:** 🛎️ 🚴 🏋️ 🛗 🖥️ 🏊 1 rst, 2 bars, spa, sauna, whirlpool, washer/dryer. **Rates:** $89–$145 S or D; from $195 ste. Children under 18 stay free. MAP rates avail. Spec packages avail. Pking: Outdoor, free. Maj CC. Lower rates on weekends and holidays.

Motel

≣ **Days Inn–San Francisco Airport**, 777 Airport Blvd, Burlingame, CA 94010; tel 415/342-7772 or toll free 800/DAYS INN; fax 415/342-2035. 15 mi S of San Francisco. Broadway-Burlingame exit off US 101. This property borders on a lagoon and is surrounded by upscale hotels. **Rooms:** 200 rms. CI 2pm/CO noon. Nonsmoking rms avail. **Amenities:** 🛏️ 🅰️ 📺 🍽️ A/C, satel TV w/movies, in-rm safe. **Services:** 🚗 🛄 🍽️ 🍽️ Babysitting. **Facilities:** 🛎️ 🏋️ 🛗 🏊 1 rst. **Rates:** HS July–Sept $72–$89 S; $82–$110 D. Extra person $10. Children under 12 stay free. Lower rates off-season. Higher rates for spec evnts/hols. Spec packages avail. Pking: Outdoor, free. Maj CC. "Park and fly" packages available.

CALEXICO

Map page M-3, E4

Motel 🏨

🛏 **Hollie's Fiesta Motel**, 801 Imperial Ave, Calexico, CA 92231; tel 619/357-3271; fax 619/357-7975. Imperial Ave exit off Calif 98. Only minutes from Mexico; popular with business travelers. **Rooms:** 60 rms. CI noon/CO noon. Nonsmoking rms avail. **Amenities:** 🛏 A/C, cable TV w/movies. Some rooms have refrigerators. **Services:** ✕ 🛎 **Facilities:** 🛗 🏊 ₺ 2 rsts, 1 bar (w/entertainment). **Rates:** $41 S; $47 D. Extra person $6. Children under 13 stay free. Higher rates for spec evnts/hols. Pking: Outdoor, free. Maj CC.

CALISTOGA

Map page M-2, C1

Motels 🏨

🛏🛏 **Comfort Inn**, 1865 Lincoln Ave, Calistoga, CA 94515; tel 707/942-9400 or toll free 800/221-2222; fax 707/942-5262. E on Lincoln off Calif 128. Reasonably attractive, comfortable motel, well-located for exploring Calistoga and the rest of the Napa Valley. **Rooms:** 55 rms. CI 3pm/CO 11am. Nonsmoking rms avail. **Amenities:** 🛏 🖥 A/C, cable TV, refrig. Some units w/terraces. **Services:** 🛎 Babysitting. **Facilities:** 🛗 🏊 ₺ 1 rst, spa, sauna, steam rm, whirlpool. Nearly completed conference room will accommodate up to 100. Breakfast room is under construction. **Rates:** HS Apr–Nov $55–$125 S or D. Extra person $7. Children under 18 stay free. Lower rates off-season. Spec packages avail. Pking: Outdoor, free. Maj CC. Spa packages include room, spa visit, and dinner for 2.

🛏🛏 **Dr Wilkinson's Hot Springs**, 1507 Lincoln Ave, Calistoga, CA 94515; tel 707/942-4102. E on Lincoln off Calif 128. Family-owned and -operated motel with a full-service spa. **Rooms:** 42 rms and effic; 4 ctges/villas. CI 3pm/CO noon. Nonsmoking rms avail. Average motel-style rooms. **Amenities:** 🛏 🖥 A/C, satel TV, refrig. All units w/minibars. **Services:** 🛎 Masseur, babysitting. **Facilities:** 🛗 🏊 Spa, steam rm, whirlpool. Separate spa facilities for men and women. Volcanic-ash mud baths, as well as mineral pools and baths. Facial salon. Exercise class offered once a week. **Rates:** HS May 1–Oct 1 $69–$88 S; $74–$99 D; from $84 effic; from $89 ctge/villa. Extra person $8. Min stay wknds. Lower rates off-season. Higher rates for spec evnts/hols. Spec packages avail. Pking: Outdoor, free. Maj CC. Special spa and salon packages available.

Restaurants 🍽

★ **All Seasons Cafe & Wine Shop**, 1400 Lincoln Ave, Calistoga; tel 707/942-9111. E on Lincoln off Calif 128. **New American.** Located on the ground floor of the old Mayflower Hotel (built in 1912), the café has a comfortable, old-fashioned interior with ceiling fans, a checkerboard floor, and marble-topped tables. Atmosphere is casual and personal. Food is California-American with various ethnic influences. Menu offers imaginative pizzas and pastas based on seasonal ingredients. **FYI:** Reservations recommended. Beer and wine only. **Open:** Lunch Thurs–Tues 11am–4pm; dinner Thurs–Tues 5–10pm; brunch Fri–Sun 9am–12pm. Closed Dec 25. **Prices:** Main courses $8.95–$18.95. Ltd CC. ❤ 🖼 ₺

🍷 **Catahoula**, in Mount View Hotel, 1457 Lincoln Ave, Calistoga (Downtown); tel 707/942-2275. Between Washington St and Fairway. **Regional American.** Launched in 1994, this new restaurant quickly became a mega-hit. The decor is a pastiche of objects rescued from salvage yards and marinas. The wonderful food is spiced with accents from noted chef Jan Birnbaum's southern heritage. Top choices include griddled hominy cakes or the lavender pork loin with gingered figs. **FYI:** Reservations recommended. Jazz. **Open:** HS June–Sept lunch Mon noon–2:30pm, Wed–Fri noon–2:30pm, Sat–Sun noon–3:30pm; dinner Mon 5:30–10pm, Wed–Fri 5:30–10pm, Sat–Sun 5:30–10:30pm. Reduced hours off-season. Closed Jan. **Prices:** Main courses $13.50–$21. Ltd CC. ₺

Attractions 💼

Calistoga Depot, 1458 Lincoln Ave; tel 707/942-5556. The tiny town's former railroad station now houses a variety of shops, a restaurant, and the Calistoga Chamber of Commerce. Alongside the building are 6 restored passenger cars dating from 1916 to the early 1920s, each of which houses enticing shops.

Old Faithful Geyser of California, 1299 Tubbs Lane; tel 707/942-6463. Situated between Calif 29 and Calif 128; follow signs from downtown Calistoga. One of 3 Old Faithful geysers in the world, this one normally erupts at intervals of about 40 minutes. The display lasts about 3 minutes, and you'll learn a lot about the origins of geothermal steam. There are picnic facilities and a gift and snack shop. **Open:** Summer, daily 9am–6pm; fall–spring, daily 9am–5pm. $$

CAMARILLO

Map page M-3, D2 (W of Thousand Oaks)

Hotels 🛏

≣≣ **Camarillo Courtyard by Marriott**, 4994 Verdugo Way, Camarillo, CA 93012; tel 805/388-1020 or toll free 800/321-2211; fax 805/987-6274. Pleasant Valley Rd exit off US 101. Excellent location, surrounded by restaurants and shops. **Rooms:** 130 rms and stes. CI 3pm/CO 1pm. Express checkout avail. Nonsmoking rms avail. **Amenities:** 🛢 🛗 🖥 A/C, cable TV w/movies. Some units w/terraces. **Services:** 🖥 🐾 Twice-daily maid svce. Lounge open only 4–9pm Monday through Saturday; restaurant serves only a breakfast buffet. **Facilities:** 🖼 🏓 🗔 🛂 1 rst, 1 bar, whirlpool, washer/dryer. **Rates:** $49–$82 S or D; from $66 ste. Extra person $10. Children under 12 stay free. Min stay spec evnts. Higher rates for spec evnts/hols. Spec packages avail. Pking: Outdoor, free. Maj CC.

≣≣ **Country Inn at Camarillo**, 1405 Del Norte Rd, Camarillo, CA 93010; tel 805/983-7171 or toll free 800/44-RELAX; fax 805/988-1838. 10 mi S of Ventura. Del Norte Rd exit off US 101. Visible from freeway but still hard to find on access road. Very quiet. **Rooms:** 100 rms and stes. CI 3pm/CO noon. Nonsmoking rms avail. **Amenities:** 🛢 🛗 🐾 A/C, cable TV, refrig, VCR. Some units w/fireplaces, some w/Jacuzzis. Microwave. **Services:** 🖥 🐾 Complimentary breakfast and 2-hour evening cocktail party. **Facilities:** 🖼 🛂 Whirlpool, washer/dryer. **Rates (BB):** $74–$89 S; $84–$99 D; from $125 ste. Extra person $10. Children under 12 stay free. Min stay. Higher rates for spec evnts/hols. Spec packages avail. Pking: Outdoor, free. Maj CC.

≣≣ **Del Norte Inn**, 4444 Central Ave, Camarillo, CA 93010; tel 805/485-3999 or toll free 800/44-RELAX; fax 805/485-1820. 10 mi S of Ventura. Del Norte Rd exit off US 101. Recently renovated, with basic but acceptable rooms. **Rooms:** 111 rms and stes. CI 3pm/CO noon. Nonsmoking rms avail. **Amenities:** 🛢 🛗 🐾 A/C, cable TV, refrig, VCR. Some units w/fireplaces. **Services:** 🚐 🖥 🐾 **Facilities:** 🖼 🛂 Whirlpool, washer/dryer. **Rates (CP):** $69–$74 S; $79–$84 D; from $100 ste. Extra person $10. Children under 12 stay free. Min stay. Spec packages avail. Pking: Outdoor, free. Maj CC.

Restaurant 🍴

★ **Giovanni's**, in Mission Oaks Shopping Center, 5227 Mission Oaks Blvd, Camarillo; tel 805/484-4376. Pleasant Valley exit off US 101. **Italian.** One of the best Italian restaurants in the area. Decor is simple, and tables are spaced far enough apart to ensure privacy. Homemade pasta specialties are featured; fruit-flavored gelati is prepared daily. Monthly fixed-price wine dinners. Banquet rooms for private parties. **FYI:** Reservations recommended. Children's menu. **Open:** Lunch Tues–Fri 11:30am–2:30pm; dinner Tues–Sun 5–10pm. Closed some hols. **Prices:** Main courses $9.95–$21.95; PF dinner $32. Maj CC. ♥ ☑ 🛂

CAMBRIA

Map page M-2, E2 (N of Morro Bay)

See also **San Simeon**

Motels 🛏

≣≣ **Best Western Fireside Inn**, 6700 Moonstone Beach Dr, Cambria, CA 93428; tel 805/927-8661 or toll free 800/528-1234; fax 805/927-8584. Moonstone Beach Dr exit off Calif 1. Property shows signs of age, but is undergoing renovation. **Rooms:** 46 rms. CI 3pm/CO 11am. Nonsmoking rms avail. Decor changes from building to building. **Amenities:** 🛢 🛗 🖥 🐾 Cable TV w/movies, refrig. No A/C. Some units w/terraces, all w/fireplaces, some w/Jacuzzis. **Services:** 🐾 **Facilities:** 🖼 🗔 🛂 1 beach (ocean), whirlpool. Fireside breakfast room. **Rates (CP):** HS July–mid-Sept $85–$130 S or D. Extra person $10. Children under 18 stay free. Min stay wknds. Lower rates off-season. Higher rates for spec evnts/hols. Spec packages avail. Pking: Outdoor, free. Maj CC.

≣≣≣ **Blue Dolphin Inn**, 6470 Moonstone Beach Dr, Cambria, CA 93428; tel 805/927-3300. Moonstone Beach Dr exit off Calif 1. A thoroughly and thoughtfully decorated modern property that looks like a cross between a little bed-and-breakfast and a country inn. Romantic and feminine. **Rooms:** 18 rms. CI 3pm/CO 11am. Nonsmoking rms avail. Print wallpaper, pine desk, iron and brass bedsteads. **Amenities:** 🛢 🛗 🐾 Cable TV w/movies, refrig, VCR. No A/C. Some units w/terraces, all w/fireplaces, some w/Jacuzzis. **Services:** 🐾 Breakfast, afternoon tea and cookies. **Facilities:** 🛂 Tea room. **Rates (CP):** HS Easter–Oct $95–$185 S or D. Extra person $5. Lower rates off-season. Pking: Outdoor, free. Maj CC.

≣≣≣ **Cambria Landing on Moonstone Beach**, 6530 Moonstone Beach Dr, Cambria, CA 93428; tel 805/927-1619. Moonstone Beach Dr exit off Calif 1. The inside is much nicer than the exterior. **Rooms:** 21 rms. CI 3pm/CO 11am. Nonsmoking rms avail. Spacious ocean-view rooms. Nice prints accent the walls, and beds are either cherry-wood sleigh style or early American oak. **Amenities:** 🛢 🐾 A/C, cable TV w/movies. Some units w/terraces, all w/fireplaces. Champagne or wine in room upon arrival. Gas fireplaces. **Services:** Front desk open until 10pm. Continental breakfast in bed, with homemade coffee cake.

Facilities: ⚲ 1 beach (ocean), whirlpool. **Rates (BB):** HS July–Sept $75–$170 S or D. Children under 5 stay free. Min stay spec evnts. Lower rates off-season. Higher rates for spec evnts/hols. Spec packages avail. Pking: Outdoor, free. Ltd CC.

≡≡≡ **Fog Catcher Inn**, 6400 Moonstone Beach Dr, Cambria, CA 93428; tel 805/927-1400 or toll free 800/425-4121. 6 mi S of Hearst Castle. Newer but quaint property; looks like something from an English village. **Rooms:** 60 rms, stes, and effic. CI 3pm/CO 11am. Nonsmoking rms avail. Country decor. Many rooms have ocean views. **Amenities:** 🛏 📺 🕐 Cable TV, refrig. No A/C. All units w/minibars, 1 w/terrace, all w/fireplaces. Microwave. **Services:** ⊂⊃ Complimentary full breakfast. **Facilities:** 🏊 & Whirlpool. **Rates (BB):** HS Mem Day–Labor Day $90–$165 S or D; from $205 effic. Extra person $5. Children under 2 stay free. Min stay HS and spec evnts. Lower rates off-season. Pking: Outdoor, free. Maj CC.

≡≡ **Mariners Inn**, 6180 Moonstone Beach Dr, Cambria, CA 93428; tel 805/927-4624 or toll free 800/344-0407; fax 805/927-3425. ¼ mi W of Cambria. Moonstone Beach Dr exit off Calif 1. Old-style motel; acceptable if not romantic. **Rooms:** 26 rms. CI 3pm/CO 11am. Nonsmoking rms avail. **Amenities:** 🛏 Cable TV w/movies. No A/C. Some units w/minibars, some w/fireplaces. **Services:** ⊂⊃ ⊲⊳ **Facilities:** & 1 beach (ocean), whirlpool. **Rates (CP):** HS July–Aug $69–$109 S; $79–$109 D. Extra person $10. Children under 10 stay free. Lower rates off-season. Higher rates for spec evnts/hols. Spec packages avail. Pking: Outdoor, free. Maj CC. Lower than for other nearby lodging.

≡≡≡ **Sand Pebbles Inn**, 6252 Moonstone Beach Dr, Cambria, CA 93428; tel 805/927-5600. Moonstone Beach Dr exit off Calif 1. A newer property decorated like a bed-and-breakfast but with all the comforts of a modern hotel. Spotless. **Rooms:** 23 rms. CI 3pm/CO 11am. Nonsmoking rms avail. Rooms are decorated with personal touches: original art, books, fresh flowers. **Amenities:** 🛏 ⊙ 🕐 Cable TV w/movies, refrig, VCR. No A/C. Some units w/terraces, all w/fireplaces, some w/Jacuzzis. **Services:** ⊂⊃ Afternoon tea and cookies. **Facilities:** & **Rates (CP):** HS May–Oct $85–$185 S or D. Extra person $5. Lower rates off-season. Spec packages avail. Pking: Outdoor, free. Maj CC.

≡≡≡ **Sea Otter Inn**, 6656 Moonstone Beach Dr, Cambria, CA 93428; tel 805/927-5888. Moonstone Beach Dr exit off Calif 1. Across from the beach, a gray wooden Victorian-style low-rise trimmed with pink and maroon. Clean and thoughtfully appointed. **Rooms:** 25 rms and stes. CI 3pm/CO 11am. Nicely decorated rooms with bleached pine furniture. Some have four-poster beds and patchwork quilts; some ocean views. **Amenities:** 🛏 ⊙ 📺 Cable TV, refrig, VCR. No A/C. All units

w/fireplaces, some w/Jacuzzis. Gas fireplaces. **Services:** ⊂⊃ **Facilities:** 🏊 & Whirlpool. Well-landscaped pool and hot-tub area. **Rates (BB):** HS Mem Day–Labor Day $65–$90 S; $70–$95 D; from $110 ste. Extra person $5. Children under 8 stay free. Min stay wknds. Lower rates off-season. Spec packages avail. Pking: Outdoor, free. Ltd CC.

Lodge

≡≡≡ **Cambria Pines Lodge**, 2905 Burton Dr, Cambria, CA 93428; tel 805/927-4200 or toll free 800/445-6868; fax 805/927-4016. Burton Dr exit off Calif 1. 25 acres. Set amid lovely wooded grounds—there's even a resident peacock. New lodge building is done in a mountain style; attractive lounge has a large stone fireplace. **Rooms:** 100 rms and stes; 25 ctges/villas. CI 3pm/CO 11am. Nonsmoking rms avail. Range from funky cabins to large, tastefully furnished suites with original artwork, pleasant views, and a peaceful atmosphere. **Amenities:** 🛏 📺 Cable TV, refrig, VCR. No A/C. Some units w/terraces, some w/fireplaces. **Services:** 🚐 ⊂⊃ ⊲⊳ Masseur. **Facilities:** 🏊 ⚑ 🔲 & 1 rst, 1 bar (w/entertainment), sauna, steam rm, whirlpool, beauty salon. Indoor pool. **Rates:** HS Mem Day–Labor Day $65–$115 S or D; from $95 ste; from $60 ctge/villa. Extra person $5. Children under 12 stay free. Min stay spec evnts. Lower rates off-season. Pking: Outdoor, free. Maj CC. Special packages for Hearst Castle 8 miles to the north.

Restaurants 🍴

★ **The Brambles Dinner House**, 4005 Burton Dr, Cambria; tel 805/927-4716. **Seafood/Steak.** This English-style cottage has several rooms decorated with antiques. The menu is traditional: prime rib with Yorkshire pudding, rack of lamb, chicken Cordon Bleu, steak, lobster tail, crab legs, and other seafood. **FYI:** Reservations recommended. Children's menu. Dress code. **Open:** Dinner Mon–Fri 4–9:30pm, Sat 4–10pm; brunch Sun 9:30am–2pm. **Prices:** Main courses $10.95–$18.91. Maj CC. ■ 👥 💟 &

The Hamlet Restaurant at Moonstone Gardens, Calif 1, Cambria; tel 805/927-3535. Exotic Garden Dr exit off Calif 1. **Continental.** Lovely 2-story wood-and-glass building offering a casual dining atmosphere with exquisite coastal views. Lunch is offered on a wonderful outdoor patio, with dinner served downstairs. Menu specialties include poached salmon, grilled swordfish, rack of lamb, and Alaskan king crab. The wine list is extensive, and there's a wine-tasting bar and wine shop at the facility. Leave time to stroll around the Moonstone Gardens. **FYI:** Reservations accepted. Jazz/piano. **Open:** Lunch daily

11:30am–4pm; dinner daily 5–9pm. Closed Sun after Thanksgiving–Dec 26. **Prices:** Main courses $12.95–$24.95. Ltd CC. ▲▲ &

Moonstone Beach Bar & Grill, 6550 Moonstone Beach Dr, Cambria; tel 805/927-3859. **New American/Seafood.** Casual indoor and outdoor dining with ocean views. Menu items include seafood pastas, many fish specials, grilled meats, and chicken. **FYI:** Reservations not accepted. Children's menu. Beer and wine only. **Open:** Lunch Mon–Sat 11am–3pm; dinner daily 5:30–9pm; brunch Sun 10am–2pm. Closed Dec 25. **Prices:** Main courses $11.95–$22.95. Ltd CC. ▲ ▲▲ ▪▪

★ **Mustache Pete's Italian-American Eatery**, in the Corner Store, 4090 Burton Dr, Cambria; tel 805/927-8589. Main St exit off Calif 1. **Italian.** Something for everyone, with an upstairs antique-filled dining room, a sidewalk cafe downstairs, and a lovely patio outside. Pizza, pasta, cioppino, veal and chicken dishes, espresso bar. 15 beers on tap, Sunday champagne brunch. **FYI:** Reservations recommended. Children's menu. **Open:** Lunch Mon–Sat 11am–4pm, Sun 1–4pm; dinner Mon–Thurs 4–9pm, Fri–Sun 4am–10pm; brunch Sun 10am–1pm. Closed Dec 25. **Prices:** Main courses $12–$22. Maj CC. ▲ 🚗 ▣

CAMPBELL

Map page M-2, D2 (S of Santa Clara)

Hotels 🏨

▤▤ **Campbell Inn**, 675 E Campbell Ave, Campbell, CA 95008; tel 408/374-4300 or toll free 800/582-4449; fax 408/379-0695. 6 mi SW of San Jose. Hamilton Ave exit off Hwy 17 S. Centrally located. Sports-minded guests like this property. **Rooms:** 99 rms and stes. CI 2pm/CO noon. Nonsmoking rms avail. **Amenities:** 🛏 & A/C, cable TV w/movies, refrig, VCR, stereo/tape player. Some units w/terraces, some w/fireplaces, some w/Jacuzzis. **Services:** 🚗 △ ⬧ ❖ Car-rental desk. Free movies for VCR. Complimentary shuttle transports guests up to 10 miles. **Facilities:** ▣ 🚲 🏋 🕿 ⛳ & Spa, whirlpool, washer/dryer. **Rates (CP):** $138–$175 S or D; from $185 ste. Extra person $10. Children under 12 stay free. Higher rates for spec evnts/hols. Pking: Outdoor, free. Maj CC.

▤▤▤ **Pruneyard Inn**, 1995 S Bascom Ave, Campbell, CA 95008; tel 408/559-4300 or toll free 800/822-4200 in the US, 800/631-4200 in Canada; fax 408/559-9919. 5 mi SW of San Jose. Hamilton Ave exit off Hwy 17 S. Next to a shopping center, a pleasant surprise, with large, cheery rooms. **Rooms:** 118 rms and stes. CI 2pm/CO noon. Nonsmoking rms avail. Studio units

have kitchenette with stove, microwave, toaster, and extra storage space; 60% of rooms are nonsmoking. **Amenities:** 🛏 & ▣ A/C, cable TV w/movies, refrig, VCR. All units w/minibars, some w/terraces, some w/fireplaces, some w/Jacuzzis. European-style breakfast with cheese, ham, turkey, croissants, and fruits. Coffee available 24 hours. **Services:** ✕ 🚗 △ ⬧ Car-rental desk, babysitting. **Facilities:** ▣ 🚲 🏋 & Whirlpool. **Rates (CP):** HS June–Sept $109–$129 S; $119–$139 D; from $175 ste. Extra person $10. Children under 12 stay free. Min stay spec evnts. Lower rates off-season. Spec packages avail. Pking: Outdoor, free. Maj CC. For an additional $10, you can upgrade to a room with fireplace or spa tub.

▤▤▤ **Residence Inn by Marriott**, 2761 S Bascom Ave, Campbell, CA 95008; tel 408/559-1551 or toll free 800/331-3131; fax 408/371-9808. 5 mi W of San Jose. Camden Ave exit off Calif 17; left on Bascom. Like living in a condo complex; popular with corporate clients and leisure travelers who stay for long periods. **Rooms:** 80 stes. CI 3pm/CO noon. Nonsmoking rms avail. All have full kitchen. Up to 3 people can stay in a studio suite; up to 5 in a penthouse suite. **Amenities:** 🛏 & ▣ A/C, cable TV w/movies, refrig. Some units w/terraces, some w/fireplaces. **Services:** 🚗 △ ⬧ ❖ Babysitting. Complimentary breakfast, newspapers, and evening beverages and hors d'oeuvres; full barbecue Thursdays in summer. **Facilities:** ▣ 🏋 & Whirlpool, washer/dryer. **Rates (BB):** From $109 ste. Children under 18 stay free. Pking: Outdoor, free. Maj CC. Rates fluctuate according to availability. Lower rates for longer stays, and for stays reserved further in advance.

CAPITOLA-BY-THE-SEA

Map page M-2, D5 (S of Santa Cruz)

Inn 🗝

▤▤▤▤ **Inn at Depot Hill**, 250 Monterey Ave, Capitola-by-the-Sea, CA 95010; tel 408/462-3376 or toll free 800/572-2632; fax 408/462-3697. Capitola/Soquel exit off Calif 1; take Bay Ave/Monterey Ave toward ocean. An exquisite inn in a vintage 1901 railroad terminal, combining turn-of-the-century flair with modern comforts. Serene garden courtyard features a lily pond with goldfish. **Rooms:** 8 rms and stes. CI 3pm/CO 11:30am. No smoking. Each room is unique. Delft Room has featherbed swathed in linen and lace, and private patio with Jacuzzi. Capitola Beach Room is done in modulations of beige. Opulent marble bathrooms. **Amenities:** 🛏 & ▣ 🍽 Cable TV, VCR, stereo/tape player, bathrobes. No A/C. Some units w/terraces, all w/fireplaces, some w/Jacuzzis. **Services:** ✗ 🛏 Twice-daily maid svce, masseur, afternoon tea and wine/sherry served. Breakfast can be served in guest rooms, the dining room, or gardens. Extensive library of videotapes and cassettes available. **Facilities:** [70] ♿ Guest lounge. The courtyard is popular for weddings. **Rates (BB):** HS July–Sept $165–$195 S or D; from $195 ste. Extra person $20. Min stay wknds. Lower rates off-season. Pking: Outdoor, free. Ltd CC.

CARLSBAD

Map page M-3, E2 (S of Oceanside)

Motels 🏨

≡≡ **Best Western Beach Terrace Inn**, 2775 Ocean St, Carlsbad, CA 92008; tel 619/729-5951 or toll free 800/433-5415; fax 619/729-1078. 35 mi N of San Diego. Carlsbad Village Dr exit off I-5. One of few motels in the area located right on the beach; no frills but great location. **Rooms:** 49 rms, stes, and effic. Exec-level rms avail. CI 2pm/CO 11am. Nonsmoking rms avail. Many rooms have excellent ocean views. **Amenities:** 🛎🍸📺🎧 A/C, cable TV w/movies, refrig, VCR, in-rm safe, shoe polisher, bathrobes. Some units w/terraces, some w/fireplaces, 1 w/Jacuzzi. **Services:** 📠🛎 Telephone services for the hearing-impaired. **Facilities:** 🏊 [65] ♿ 1 beach (ocean), whirlpool, washer/dryer. Even meeting rooms have ocean vistas. **Rates (CP):** HS June 16–Sept 15 $99–$168 S or D; from $270 ste; from $99 effic. Extra person $10. Min stay spec evnts. Lower rates off-season. Spec packages avail. Pking: Outdoor, free. Maj CC.

≡≡≡ **Tamarack Beach Resort**, 3200 Carlsbad Blvd, Carlsbad, CA 92008; tel 619/729-3500 or toll free 800/334-2199; fax 619/434-5942. 30 mi N of San Diego. Tamarack exit off I-5. Across the road from a beautiful white-sand beach, and close to the shops and restaurants at Carlsbad Village. **Rooms:** 77 rms, stes, and effic. CI 3pm/CO noon. Tasteful, modern decor. Rooms that face west have great ocean views. **Amenities:** 🛎🍸📺 A/C, cable TV w/movies, refrig, VCR. Some units w/terraces. VCRs are built into entertainment centers. **Services:** 📠🛎🛏 Car-rental desk, social director, children's program. **Facilities:** 🏊 ⛱[50]♿ 1 rst, 1 bar (w/entertainment), games rm, whirlpool, playground, washer/dryer. Free film library, barbecues, pool tables, video games, table tennis. **Rates:** HS June 15–Sept 15 $100–$120 S; $110–$130 D; from $135 ste; from $135 effic. Extra person $10. Children under 12 stay free. Min stay HS. Lower rates off-season. Spec packages avail. Pking: Indoor, free. Maj CC.

Inn

≡≡≡≡ **Pelican Cove Inn**, 320 Walnut Ave, Carlsbad, CA 92008; tel 619/434-5995. 30 mi N of San Diego. Carlsbad Village Dr exit off I-5. A gem located close to the beach and Carlsbad Village. Guests immediately feel at home at this peaceful, romantic, cozy bed-and-breakfast. **Rooms:** 8 rms. CI 3pm/CO 11am. No smoking. Exceptional rooms, well decorated with antique and contemporary furnishings. **Amenities:** 🍸 Cable TV. No A/C or phone. All units w/fireplaces, some w/Jacuzzis. **Services:** ✗ Babysitting, afternoon tea served. Management will help with touring needs, and for an extra charge will prepare a picnic basket. **Facilities:** ♿ Guest lounge. Romantic garden area for breakfast or a chat before dinner. **Rates (BB):** HS June–Sept $85–$175 S or D. Extra person $15. Min stay wknds. Lower rates off-season. Spec packages avail. Pking: Indoor/outdoor, free. Ltd CC.

Resorts

≡≡≡ **Carlsbad Inn Beach Resort**, 3075 Carlsbad Blvd, Carlsbad, CA 92008; tel 619/434-7020 or toll free 800/235-3939; fax 619/729-4853. 35 mi N of San Diego. Carlsbad Village W exit off I-5; left on Carlsbad Blvd. 4 acres. Overlooking the ocean, convenient to shops and restaurants, this European-style inn has all the modern comforts amid well-kept grounds. **Rooms:** 60 rms and stes. Exec-level rms avail. CI 4pm/CO 11am. Nonsmoking rms avail. **Amenities:** 🛎🍸📺 A/C, cable TV, refrig, VCR. Some units w/terraces, some w/fireplaces, some w/Jacuzzis. **Services:** 📠🛎🛏 Car-rental desk, social director, children's program, babysitting. Free walking tours of historic Carlsbad. **Facilities:** 🏊⛱[80]♿ 1 rst, 1 bar, 1 beach (ocean), board surfing, lawn games, spa, sauna, whirlpool, playground, washer/dryer. Guest also have access to hotel's beach cabana and surfboards and boogie boards. **Rates:** HS June–Aug $105–$115 S; $115–$145 D; from $145 ste. Extra person $10. Children under 12 stay free. Min stay HS. Lower rates off-season. Spec packages avail. Pking: Indoor/outdoor, free. Maj CC.

≡≡≡≡ **La Costa Resort and Spa**, Costa del Mar Rd, Carlsbad, CA 92009; tel 619/438-9111 or toll free 800/854-5000; fax 619/931-7585. 30 mi N of San Diego. La Costa exit off I-5. 400 acres. One of the finest spa resorts in the country, this place has something for everyone, from children to seniors. Attention to detail is apparent throughout the property. **Rooms:** 478 rms and stes. CI 4pm/CO noon. Express checkout avail. Nonsmoking rms avail. Rooms are elegantly appointed. Deluxe rooms overlooking the golf course; 1- and 2-bedroom suites and 3- and 4-bedroom executive homes available. **Amenities:** 🛎🍸📺 A/C, cable TV w/movies, in-rm safe, bathrobes. Some units w/minibars, some w/terraces, some w/Jacuzzis. **Services:** ✗ 🔑 VP 🚐 🖼 ☊ Twice-daily maid svce, car-rental desk, social director, masseur, children's program, babysitting. Excellent staff. Nutrition programs and spa cuisine. **Facilities:** 🏊 🚴 ▶36 🎾 🎣14 ⛳ 🏋️ 🎱 💻 ♿ 5 rsts, 2 bars (1 w/entertainment), games rm, spa, sauna, steam rm, whirlpool, beauty salon, day-care ctr, playground. **Rates:** $215–$400 S or D; from $375 ste. Extra person $35. Children under 18 stay free. MAP rates avail. Spec packages avail. Pking: Outdoor, free. Maj CC. Golf, tennis, and spa packages.

🏨🏨 **Olympic Resort Hotel & Spa**, 6111 El Camino Real, Carlsbad, CA 92009; tel 619/438-8330 or toll free 800/522-8330; fax 619/431-0838. 35 mi N of San Diego. Palomar Airport Rd exit off I-5. 11 acres. Close to the small Palomar Airport, this is a good deal for the active traveler. **Rooms:** 78 rms and stes. CI 3pm/CO noon. Nonsmoking rms avail. Below average rooms. **Amenities:** 🏠 🍷 📺 A/C, cable TV w/movies. All units w/terraces. **Services:** 🖼 ☊ Car-rental desk, masseur, babysitting. Spa services such as facials and herbal wraps. **Facilities:** 🏊 🎾 🎣 🏋️ 🏊225 ♿ 2 rsts, 1 bar, spa, sauna, steam rm, whirlpool, beauty salon, day-care ctr. Good-size meeting and banquet rooms; 4 putting greens, 53 driving stations; lap pool in addition to the main pool. **Rates:** HS June 15–Sept 15 $75 S; $85 D; from $135 ste. Extra person $10. Children under 5 stay free. Lower rates off-season. Spec packages avail. Pking: Outdoor, free. Maj CC.

Restaurants 🍴

⑤ **Branci's Caldo Pomodoro**, 2907 State St, Carlsbad; tel 619/720-9998. Carlsbad Village Dr exit off I-5. **Italian.** A quaint corner cafe with lots of natural light, brick floors, and an outdoor patio. Known for superb sauces over pasta, particularly the chicken caldo pomodoro made with a spicy marinara sauce, and the fresh clams and mussels sautéed in a spicy red sauce. **FYI:** Reservations recommended. Guitar. Children's menu. Beer and wine only. **Open:** Lunch daily 11am–4pm; dinner daily 4–10pm. Closed some hols. **Prices:** Main courses $7.95–$18.95. Maj CC. ♿

Neimans, 2978 Carlsbad Blvd, Carlsbad; tel 619/729-4131. Carlsbad Village Dr exit off I-5. **Californian.** A town landmark in a turn-of-the-century Victorian mansion. In addition to the casual bar area with hardwood floors and wooden stools, there's a more formal rotunda for dining, with large picture windows. Known for Cajun chicken with pasta, prime rib, fresh sourdough bread, and Snickers pie for dessert. **FYI:** Reservations not accepted. Dress code. **Open:** HS Memorial Day–Oct lunch Mon–Sat 11:30am–5pm; dinner Mon–Sun 5–10pm; brunch Sun 9:30am–2pm. Reduced hours off-season. **Prices:** Main courses $9.95–$14.95. Maj CC. 🍖 🍽 💟 ♿

⑤ **Tip Top Meats**, 6118 Paseo del Norte, Carlsbad; tel 619/438-2620. Palomar Airport Rd exit off I-5; E to Paseo del Norte. **Deli.** A European deli with a western flair. The specialty is meats in massive portions, including prime rib roast with mashed potatoes, sausages of all kinds, sauerbraten, country-style pork ribs, steaks, and meatloaf. **FYI:** Reservations not accepted. Beer and wine only. **Open:** Daily 7am–8pm. Closed some hols. **Prices:** Main courses $2.25–$4.98. Ltd CC. ♿

CARMEL-BY-THE-SEA

Map page M-2, E1

Hotels 🏨

🏨🏨🏨 **Best Western Carmel Bay View Inn**, Junipero St, between 5th and 6th Aves, PO Box 3715, Carmel-by-the-Sea, CA 93921; tel 408/624-1831 or toll free 800/343-1831; fax 408/625-2336. Ocean Ave exit off Calif 1. Well maintained, with flower borders everywhere. **Rooms:** 58 rms and stes. CI 2pm/CO 11am. Nonsmoking rms avail. Clean, cozy, and comfortable. Each individually decorated. **Amenities:** 🏠 🍷 📺 Cable TV. No A/C. Some units w/terraces, some w/fireplaces. **Services:** Masseur, babysitting. **Facilities:** 🏊 🏊20 ♿ **Rates (CP):** HS July–Sept $110–$180 S or D; from $180 ste. Extra person $10. Children under 12 stay free. Min stay HS, wknds, and spec evnts. Lower rates off-season. Higher rates for spec evnts/hols. Pking: Indoor/outdoor, free. Maj CC.

🏨🏨 **Carmel Mission Inn–Best Western**, 3665 Rio Rd, Carmel-by-the-Sea, CA 93922; tel 408/624-1841 or toll free 800/384-9090; fax 408/624-8684. Rio Rd east of Calif 1. Located near The Barnyard and the Crossroads Shopping Center, this property has a little too much asphalt despite lots of flowers. Very well maintained. **Rooms:** 165 rms and stes. CI 4pm/CO noon. Nonsmoking rms avail. Rooms are clean, spacious, and pleasant. **Amenities:** 🏠 🍷 Cable TV, refrig. No A/C. Some units w/minibars, some w/terraces. **Services:** ✗ 🖼 ☊ 🍷 Masseur, babysitting. **Facilities:** 🏊 🏊500 ♿ 1 rst, 1 bar, whirlpool. **Rates:** HS June–Oct $99–$129 S; $109–$139 D; from $189 ste. Extra person $10. Children under 15 stay free. Min stay wknds and spec evnts. Lower rates off-season. Spec packages avail. Pking: Outdoor, free. Maj CC.

🏨 **Carmel's Best Western Town House Lodge**, San Carlos, at 5th, PO Box 3574, Carmel-by-the-Sea, CA 93921; tel 408/624-1261. Located close to shops, galleries, and restaurants. Nice interior. **Rooms:** 28 rms. CI 2pm/CO 11am. Nonsmoking rms avail. Decorated in earth tones, the rooms are large, clean, and airy. **Amenities:** 🛅 🖭 ☏ Cable TV. No A/C. **Services:** Babysitting. **Facilities:** 🛅 **Rates:** HS Apr–Oct $84–$145 S or D. Extra person $6. Min stay HS and wknds. Lower rates off-season. Higher rates for spec evnts/hols. Pking: Outdoor, free. Maj CC.

≡≡≡ **Dolphin Inn**, San Carlos St and 4th Ave, PO Box 1900, Carmel-by-the-Sea, CA 93921; tel 408/624-2745; fax 408/ 624-2967. N on San Carlos off Ocean Ave. Spacious grounds are full of flowers. **Rooms:** 27 rms, stes, and effic. CI 3pm/CO noon. Nonsmoking rms avail. **Amenities:** 🛅 & 🖭 ☏ Cable TV, refrig, bathrobes. No A/C. Some units w/terraces, some w/fireplaces. **Services:** 🖾 🗇 **Facilities:** 🛅 **Rates (CP):** HS July–Aug $99–$143 S or D; from $195 ste; from $195 effic. Extra person $15. Children under 12 stay free. Min stay wknds. Lower rates off-season. Spec packages avail. Pking: Outdoor, free. Maj CC.

≡≡≡ **Highlands Inn**, Carmel Highlands, PO Box 1700, Carmel-by-the-Sea, CA 93921; tel 408/624-3801 or toll free 800/682-4811; fax 408/626-1574. 4 mi S of Carmel on Calif 1. Just a stone's throw from Carmel proper, Carmel Highlands counterpoints cliffs and wind-bowed Monterey cypresses with the Pacific Ocean. The inn feels like a sophisticated mountain lodge, with 2-story, cedar-shingled villas and lovely grounds. **Rooms:** 140 rms and stes; 2 ctges/villas. CI 4pm/CO noon. Light earth tones and contemporary furnishings complement the seaside locale. Some rooms have views of the water. Extensive renovations slated over the next 2 years. **Amenities:** 🛅 & 🖭 ☏ Cable TV w/movies, refrig, VCR, bathrobes. No A/C. Some units w/minibars, all w/terraces, some w/fireplaces, some w/Jacuzzis. **Services:** ✕ 🖙 🖤 🚗 🖾 🗇 ⛐ Twice-daily maid svce, car-rental desk, masseur, children's program, babysitting. Very service-oriented, especially helpful for guests with disabilities. **Facilities:** 🛅 🔢 & 2 rsts (*see also* ''Restaurants'' below), 2 bars (1 w/entertainment), whirlpool. Attractive kidney-shaped pool surrounded by decks and ferns. **Rates (CP):** HS July 15–Oct $225–$550 S or D; from $325 ste; from $265 ctge/villa. Children under 16 stay free. Min stay wknds and spec evnts. Lower rates off-season. Higher rates for spec evnts/hols. Spec packages avail. Pking: Indoor/outdoor, free. Maj CC.

≡≡≡ **Horizon Inn**, Junipero St and 3rd Ave, PO Box 1693, Carmel-by-the-Sea, CA 93921; tel 408/624-5327 or toll free 800/350-7723; fax 408/626-8253. Ocean Ave exit off Calif 1. Lovely hotel with lots of flower-filled gardens and excellent views of the bay. **Rooms:** 26 rms, stes, and effic. CI 3pm/CO noon. Nonsmoking rms avail. Rooms are large, well-maintained, and comfortably furnished. Some have kitchens. **Amenities:** 🛅 🖭 ☏ Cable TV, refrig. No A/C. Some units w/terraces, some w/fireplaces, some w/Jacuzzis. **Services:** 🖾 🗇 Babysitting. **Facilities:** 🛅 & **Rates (CP):** HS May–Oct $99–$149 S or D;

from $140 ste; from $179 effic. Extra person $15. Children under 12 stay free. Min stay wknds. Lower rates off-season. Spec packages avail. Pking: Indoor, free. Maj CC.

≡≡≡ **La Playa Hotel**, Camino Real at 8th St, PO Box 900, Carmel-by-the-Sea, CA 93921; tel 408/624-6476 or toll free 800/582-8900; fax 408/624-7966. A Mediterranean-style resort with brick patios and a red-tile roof, located close to town and Carmel Beach. The lobby creates a grand first impression, with Mexican-tile floors, antiques, and a fireplace flanked by 2 statues from Hearst Castle. **Rooms:** 80 rms and stes; 5 ctges/villas. CI 3pm/CO noon. In keeping with the architecture, rooms have Mediterranean-style furnishings (curlicued chairs, low chests); many pieces are carved with the hotel's mermaid logo. Accommodations face the ocean, gardens, patio, or Carmel residences. **Amenities:** 🛅 & ☏ Cable TV, refrig. No A/C. All units w/mini-bars, some w/terraces, some w/fireplaces. **Services:** ✕ 🖙 🖤 🖾 🗇 Twice-daily maid svce, babysitting. Concierge can assist with restaurant reservations, golf or tennis times, and sightseeing excursions. **Facilities:** 🛅 🔢 & 1 rst, 1 bar. Award-winning formal gardens. **Rates:** $110–$210 S or D; from $210 ste; from $210 ctge/villa. Extra person $15. Children under 12 stay free. Min stay wknds and spec evnts. Maj CC.

≡≡ **Mission Ranch**, 26270 Dolores, Carmel-by-the-Sea, CA 93923; tel 408/624-6436 or toll free 800/538-8221; fax 408/ 626-4163. Rio Rd exit off Calif 1; head west; turn left on Lasuen (after Carmel Mission). 22 acres. Clint Eastwood not only has a restaurant in town, but also owns this 1857 farmhouse, once home to the Marin family. Cottages and bunkhouses are scattered around this large property, in a setting of cypress and eucalyptus trees near the sea. **Rooms:** 31 rms and stes; 29 ctges/villas. CI 3pm/CO 11am. Nonsmoking rms avail. 6 rooms in the farmhouse, surrounding a Victorian parlor. The Bunkhouse is a restored cottage with living, dining, and bedrooms plus a full kitchen. Best values are the Main rooms. Meadow View rooms offer ocean views. **Amenities:** 🛅 & 🖭 Cable TV, bathrobes. No A/C. Some units w/terraces, some w/fireplaces, some w/Jacuzzis. **Services:** 🗇 Twice-daily maid svce, masseur, babysitting. Continental breakfast in the clubhouse. **Facilities:** 🍷6 🏌 🎾 & 1 rst, 1 bar (w/entertainment). 2 party barns for special events for up to 50 people. Pro shop. **Rates (CP):** HS Aug–Oct $95–$225 S or D; from $195 ste; from $95 ctge/villa. Extra person $15. Min stay wknds and spec evnts. Lower rates off-season. Pking: Outdoor, Maj CC.

≡≡≡ **Sundial Lodge**, Monte Verde at 7th St, PO Box J, Carmel-by-the-Sea, CA 93921; tel 408/624-8578; fax 408/ 626-1018. Pleasant 100-year-old garden apartments converted into a hotel, with lots of flowers and ocean views. Not recommended for children; children under 5 not permitted. **Rooms:**

19 rms, stes, and effic. CI 2pm/CO 11:30am. Nonsmoking rms avail. Quaint rooms with unique furnishings, from antiques to thrift-store castoffs. Some rooms are small with outdated kitchens, but everything is immaculate. **Amenities:** 🛁 🕭 📺 Cable TV, refrig. No A/C. **Services:** ☞ Babysitting. **Rates (CP):** $105–$140 S or D; from $140 ste; from $115 effic. Extra person $15. Min stay wknds and spec evnts. Higher rates for spec evnts/hols. Maj CC.

Motels

📺📺📺 **Adobe Inn–Carmel**, Dolores St and 8th Ave, PO Box 4115, Carmel-by-the-Sea, CA 93921; tel 408/624-3933 or toll free 800/388-3933; fax 408/624-8636. Comparatively reasonable rates make this one of the best places to stay in Carmel. Very attractive grounds with lots of flowers. **Rooms:** 20 rms and stes. CI 3pm/CO noon. Nonsmoking rms avail. Rooms are attractive and spacious. Some have views. **Amenities:** 🛁 🕭 📺 ☎ Cable TV, refrig. No A/C. Some units w/terraces, all w/fireplaces. **Services:** ✗ 🖾 Masseur, babysitting. Continental breakfast delivered to room. Staff is extremely professional. **Facilities:** 🔄 🔥 1 rst (see also "Restaurants" below), 1 bar, sauna. **Rates (CP):** HS June–Oct $120–$200 S or D; from $240 ste. Extra person $20. Children under 16 stay free. Min stay HS, wknds, and spec evnts. Lower rates off-season. Pking: Indoor, free. Maj CC.

📺📺 **Candlelight Inn**, San Carlos St between 4th and 5th Aves, PO Box 1900, Carmel-by-the-Sea, CA 93921; tel 408/624-6451 or toll free 800/433-4732; fax 408/624-2967. Charming, with a shingled roof, brick chimneys, and wood-trimmed exterior. **Rooms:** 20 rms, stes, and effic. CI 3pm/CO noon. Nonsmoking rms avail. Decorated in country French style. Many accommodations have kitchens. **Amenities:** 🛁 📺 Cable TV. No A/C. Some units w/fireplaces. **Services:** 🖾 🛋 **Facilities:** 🔄 **Rates (CP):** HS May–Oct $129–$149 S or D; from $135 ste; from $149 effic. Extra person $15. Children under 12 stay free. Min stay wknds. Lower rates off-season. Spec packages avail. Pking: Outdoor, free. Maj CC.

📺 **Carmel Wayfarer Inn**, 4th Ave and Mission St, PO Box 1896, Carmel-by-the-Sea, CA 93921; tel 408/624-2711 or toll free 800/533-2711. Colorful Carmel stone steps lead up to this 1910 building. It's nicer outside than inside, but still functional. **Rooms:** 15 rms and stes. CI 3pm/CO noon. Nonsmoking rms avail. Rooms have aging decor, but are clean. **Amenities:** 🛁 🕭 📺 Cable TV, refrig, VCR. No A/C. Some units w/terraces, some w/fireplaces. **Services:** 🛋 Babysitting. **Rates (CP):** HS July–Sept $70–$142 S or D; from $138 ste. Extra person $16. Lower rates off-season. Pking: Outdoor, free. Maj CC.

📺📺 **Comfort Inn Carmel**, Carpenter and 2nd, Carmel-by-the-Sea, CA 93921; tel 408/624-3113 or toll free 800/228-5160; fax 408/624-5456. Cottages and bungalows interspersed with fountains, flowers, tables, and umbrellas. **Rooms:** 31 rms and stes; 6 ctges/villas. CI 2pm/CO 11am. Nonsmoking rms avail. The Honeymoon Suite is quaint and nice. **Amenities:** 🛁 🕭 📺 Cable TV, refrig. No A/C. Some units w/terraces, some w/fireplaces. Microwaves, popcorn poppers in all rooms. **Services:** 🛋 Babysitting. Complimentary weekday newspapers. **Facilities:** Sauna, whirlpool. Barbecue pit. Oriental gardens with waterfalls. **Rates (CP):** HS May–Oct $80–$200 S or D; from $125 ste; from $150 ctge/villa. Children under 18 stay free. Min stay HS, wknds, and spec evnts. Lower rates off-season. Spec packages avail. Pking: Outdoor, free. Maj CC.

📺📺📺 **Hofsas House**, San Carlos and 4th, PO Box 1195, Carmel-by-the-Sea, CA 93921; tel 408/624-2745 or toll free 800/421-4000, 800/252-0211 in CA. Looks like a Scandinavian cottage, with lots of flowers and some ocean views. **Rooms:** 38 rms, stes, and effic. CI 3pm/CO noon. Nonsmoking rms avail. Individually decorated rooms are spacious and comfortable with lots of bright colors. **Amenities:** 🛁 📺 ☎ Cable TV, refrig. No A/C. Some units w/terraces, some w/fireplaces. **Services:** 🖾 🛋 Babysitting. Continental breakfast brought to your room. **Facilities:** 🔄 Sauna. **Rates (CP):** HS July–Sept $80–$198 S; $110–$198 D; from $198 ste; from $143 effic. Lower rates off-season. Higher rates for spec evnts/hols. Spec packages avail. Pking: Outdoor, free. Maj CC.

📺📺 **Lobos Lodge**, Monte Verde at Ocean Ave, PO Box L-1, Carmel-by-the-Sea, CA 93921; tel 408/624-3874; fax 408/624-0135. Sculpted hedges edge the paths to the rooms at this colorful inn, located on a corner near the beach and downtown Carmel. The grounds are minimal, but well maintained and very beautiful. **Rooms:** 30 rms, stes, and effic. CI 2pm/CO noon. Some have ocean views; all are lovely and comfortable. Dressing rooms off the bathroom are very nice. **Amenities:** 🛁 Cable TV, refrig, bathrobes. No A/C. Some units w/terraces, all w/fireplaces. **Services:** Continental breakfast delivered to room. **Facilities:** 🔥 **Rates (CP):** HS May–Oct $93–$125 S or D; from $140 ste; from $140 effic. Extra person $25. Children under 3 stay free. Min stay wknds. Lower rates off-season. Pking: Outdoor, free. Maj CC.

📺📺 **Tickle Pink Inn at Carmel Highlands**, 55 Highland Dr, Carmel-by-the-Sea, CA 93923; tel 408/624-1244 or toll free 800/635-4774; fax 408/626-9516. Surrounded by overgrown foliage, this property is hidden away in the lovely Carmel Highlands above the ocean. **Rooms:** 35 rms, stes, and effic; 1 ctge/villa. CI noon/CO noon. Soft colors, such as sea-foam green and pink, decorate each room. Standard rooms are average but roomy. **Amenities:** 🛏 📠 Cable TV, refrig, VCR, bathrobes. No A/C. Some units w/terraces, some w/fireplaces, some w/Jacuzzis. Wine and cheese in the afternoon. **Services:** ✕ 🍷 **Facilities:** 🔟 **Rates (CP):** $145–$289 S or D; from $229 ste; from $172 effic; from $172 ctge/villa. Extra person $25. Min stay wknds and spec evnts. Higher rates for spec evnts/hols. Pking: Outdoor, free. Maj CC.

▤▤ **Wayside Inn**, 7th and Mission, Carmel-by-the-Sea, CA 93921; tel 408/624-5336 or toll free 800/433-4732; fax 408/624-2967. Small, but very cozy and quiet. Carmel rustic decor with lots of pine. Close to everything. **Rooms:** 22 rms and stes. CI 3pm/CO noon. Nonsmoking rms avail. Clean and comfortable. **Amenities:** 🛏 ⏰ 📠 Cable TV, refrig. No A/C. Some units w/terraces, some w/fireplaces. **Services:** ✕ 🛄 🍷 🐕 Babysitting. Continental breakfast and morning newspaper delivered to your door. **Rates (CP):** $99–$199 S or D; from $135 ste. Extra person $15. Children under 12 stay free. Min stay wknds. Spec packages avail. Pking: Outdoor, free. Maj CC.

Inns

▤▤▤ **Carriage House Inn**, Junipero St, Carmel-by-the-Sea, CA 93921; tel 408/625-2585 or toll free 800/433-4732; fax 408/626-6974. Between 7th and 8th Aves. Looks like a large wood-shingled apartment complex in a charming home away from home. Unsuitable for children under 12. **Rooms:** 13 rms and stes. CI 3pm/CO noon. Rooms are lush and homey, with king-size beds, down comforters, and sunken tubs. **Amenities:** 🛏 ⏰ Cable TV, VCR, bathrobes. No A/C. All units w/fireplaces, all w/Jacuzzis. Breakfast served in the lounge or in your room. **Services:** ✕ 🛄 Babysitting, wine/sherry served. **Facilities:** Guest lounge. **Rates (CP):** HS May–Oct $175–$250 S or D; from $250 ste. Extra person $15. Lower rates off-season. Spec packages avail. Pking: Outdoor, free. Ltd CC.

▤▤▤ **Cobblestone Inn**, Junipero between 7th and 8th, PO Box 3185, Carmel-by-the-Sea, CA 93921; tel 408/625-5222; fax 408/625-0478. Located in a quiet neighborhood, this stone-covered inn is managed by a family that owns several others in northern California. Guest rooms wrap around a slate courtyard and gardens, while French doors lead to a lobby with a stone fireplace. **Rooms:** 24 rms and stes. CI 2pm/CO noon. No smoking. Individually decorated in tasteful English decor, with a stone fireplace, sitting chair, and queen or king bed. **Amenities:** 🛏 ⏰ Cable TV, refrig, bathrobes. No A/C. All units w/fireplaces. **Services:** ✕ 🛄 🍷 Afternoon tea and wine/sherry served. Full breakfast in bed or on the stone patio. Cookies as well as hot and cold beverages always available. **Facilities:** Guest lounge. **Rates (BB):** $95–$175 D; from $145 ste. Children under 3 stay free. Pking: Outdoor, free. Ltd CC.

▤▤▤ **Cypress Inn**, Lincoln, at 7th, PO Box Y, Carmel-by-the-Sea, CA 93921; tel 408/624-3871 or toll free 800/443-7443 in CA; fax 408/624-8216. A warm, comfortable place with lovely gardens; resembles a striking Moorish Mediterranean palace with a red tile roof. One of the most formal places in town. **Rooms:** 33 rms. CI 3pm/CO noon. Rooms are elegantly furnished and comfortable. **Amenities:** 🛏 Cable TV. No A/C. Some units w/terraces, some w/fireplaces. **Services:** ✕ 🔑 🛄 🍷 🐕 Twice-daily maid svce, wine/sherry served. Continental breakfast in sunny breakfast room; complimentary fruit basket, daily newspaper. **Facilities:** 🦽 1 bar, guest lounge. **Rates (CP):** HS May–Oct $98–$246 D. Extra person $15. Children under 5 stay free. Min stay wknds. Lower rates off-season. Ltd CC.

▤▤ **Green Lantern Inn**, 7th and Casanova, PO Box 1114, Carmel-by-the-Sea, CA 93921; tel 408/624-4392; fax 408/624-9591. This large, turn-of-the-century gabled house occupies a spacious corner location. Surrounded by flowers, plants, statuettes and little walkways. **Rooms:** 19 rms and stes. CI 2pm/CO 11am. No smoking. Each room is different and very unusual; all are within earshot of the ocean. **Amenities:** 🛏 Cable TV. No A/C. 1 unit w/minibar, some w/terraces, some w/fireplaces. **Services:** 🍷 Afternoon tea and wine/sherry served. Wine, tea, cookies and cheese offered in the early evenings. Innkeeper will help book reservations for restaurants and attractions. **Facilities:** 🔟 Guest lounge. **Rates (CP):** HS May–Oct $82–$110 S or D; from $179 ste. Extra person $10. Children under 18 stay free. Min stay wknds and spec evnts. Lower rates off-season. Higher rates for spec evnts/hols. Maj CC.

▤▤ **Svendsgaard's**, San Carlos St at 4th Ave, PO Box 1900, Carmel-by-the-Sea, CA 93921; tel 408/624-1511 or toll free 800/433-4732; fax 408/624-2969. This well-maintained 2-story inn has extensive gardens flanking a courtyard and swimming pool. **Rooms:** 34 rms and stes. CI 3pm/CO noon. Nonsmoking rms avail. All are tastefully decorated. **Amenities:** 🛏 ⏰ 📠 Cable TV, refrig. No A/C. Some units w/fireplaces. Coffee in each room. Many have kitchenettes. **Services:** 🛄 🍷 Babysitting. Excellent staff. **Facilities:** 🏋 🛢 Guest lounge. **Rates (CP):** HS May–Oct $99–$143 S or D; from $179 ste. Extra person $15. Children under 12 stay free. Min stay wknds and spec evnts. Lower rates off-season. Spec packages avail. Pking: Outdoor, free. Maj CC.

▤▤ **Village Inn**, Ocean Ave and Junipero St, PO Box 5275, Carmel-by-the-Sea, CA 93921; tel 408/624-3864 or toll free 800/346-3864; fax 408/626-6763. On Junipero N of Ocean Ave. Winner of the 1994 Carmel Flower Fair. The gardens are lovely, but a large asphalt parking lot and steady traffic detract from the inn's charm. **Rooms:** 34 rms and stes. CI 2pm/CO 11am. Nonsmoking rms avail. **Amenities:** 🛏 ⏰ Cable TV, refrig. No

A/C. Some units w/fireplaces. **Services:** ♫ Masseur, babysitting. **Rates (CP):** HS July–Aug $98–$135 S or D; from $149 ste. Extra person $10. Min stay wknds and spec evnts. Lower rates off-season. Pking: Outdoor, free. Maj CC.

Restaurants 🍴

Ⓢ **Adobe Inn Bully III**, Dolores St, Carmel-by-the-Sea; tel 408/625-1750. At 8th Ave. **Pub.** Carmel's answer to an authentic English pub, with a cozy fireplace and a friendly staff. Serves classic British fare, like bangers and mash, and shepherd's pie. Two large-screen TVs, and a private room that accommodates 30. **FYI:** Reservations recommended. **Open:** Lunch daily 11:30am–5pm; dinner daily 5:30–9:30pm. Closed some hols. **Prices:** Main courses $12.95–$22.95. Maj CC. 🔲🔲👍

♥ **Anton & Michel**, Mission St, Carmel-by-the-Sea; tel 408/624-2406. Between Ocean and 7th Aves. **Continental.** Lovely ambience, with a flower-filled courtyard and one of the prettiest bars in Carmel. This local favorite serves rack of lamb, crabmeat ravioli, chicken Jerusalem, and several varieties of seafood. Wine list has over 450 offerings. **FYI:** Reservations recommended. **Open:** Lunch daily 11:30am–3pm; dinner daily 5:30–9:30pm. Closed some hols. **Prices:** Main courses $16–$26. Maj CC. 👁 🏞👍

♥★ **Casanova**, 5th Ave, Carmel-by-the-Sea; tel 408/625-0501. Between San Carlos and Mission Sts. **French/Italian.** One of the most romantic restaurants around; winner of numerous awards for ambience and cuisine. Decor gives the feel of a fine European home. Specialties include rabbit in a wild mushroom broth, fresh swordfish, and suckling pig. **FYI:** Reservations recommended. Beer and wine only. **Open:** Breakfast daily 8–11:30am; lunch daily noon–3pm; dinner daily 5–10pm; brunch Sun 9:30am–3pm. **Prices:** Main courses $19.75–$29.75. Ltd CC. 👁👍

Chez Felix Restaurant Français, Monte Verde & 7th Street, Carmel-by-the-Sea; tel 408/624-4707. **French.** Intimate European-style restaurant is a favorite of locals. Try the chicken with 5 different types of mushrooms. **FYI:** Reservations recommended. Beer and wine only. **Open:** Mon–Sat 6–9. Closed Jan 1–21. **Prices:** Main courses $14.75–$19.50. Maj CC. 👁

Clam Box, Mission St, Carmel-by-the-Sea; tel 408/624-8597. Between 5th and 6th Aves. **Seafood.** Cozy and intimate, comfortable without being fancy. Seating is at an outdoor glass-roofed patio. A separate lounge has paintings of sports figures and is popular with locals. The emphasis here is on fresh fish, such as a baked salmon Breval, with mushrooms, tomatoes, shrimp, and white wine sauce, topped with Parmesan. There are also casseroles and a daily pasta, as well as chicken, pot roast,

steak, and many seafood appetizers. **FYI:** Reservations accepted. Children's menu. **Open:** Lunch Tues–Sat 11:30am–2:30pm; dinner Tues–Sun 4:30–9pm. Closed some hols; 3 weeks before Christmas. **Prices:** Main courses $6.50–$25.50. Maj CC. 👍

The General Store & Forge in the Forest, Junipero and 5th Aves, Carmel-by-the-Sea; tel 408/624-2233. **New American.** Casual indoor and outdoor dining make the General Store popular with tourists and locals alike. Patio features a cozy fireplace. Choose from a wide variety of appetizers, soups and salads, burgers, pasta, pizzas, and grilled specialties including steaks, fish, chicken, or pork chops. The Forge in the Forest offers more formal dining. **FYI:** Reservations accepted. **Open:** Lunch daily 11:30am–3pm; dinner daily 5–10pm; brunch Sun 11:30am–3pm. **Prices:** Main courses $7.50–$17.50. Maj CC. 🔲🔲🔲👍

★ **The Grill**, Ocean Ave, Carmel-by-the-Sea; tel 408/624-2569. Between Delores St and Lincoln Ave. **New American.** Decorated with Eyvind Earle paintings and exotic bromeliads, this new restaurant is run by the owners of the highly regarded Anton & Michel's. Menu includes rack of lamb in herb mustard with tarragon, duck ravioli, and changing daily specials. **FYI:** Reservations accepted. Beer and wine only. **Open:** Lunch daily 11:30am–3pm; dinner daily 5–10pm. **Prices:** Main courses $12.25–$19.50. Maj CC.

The Hog's Breath Inn, San Carlos St, Carmel-by-the-Sea; tel 408/625-1044. Between 5th and 6th Aves. **American.** Everyone who comes here hopes to spy co-owner Clint Eastwood, former mayor of Carmel. The rustic setting features a boar's head, bed warmers on the walls, and movie posters for Clint's films. Specials include the High Plains prime rib with vegetables, the Dirty Harry burger with cheese, and the Sudden Impact, broiled Polish sausage with jack cheese and jalapeños. **FYI:** Reservations not accepted. **Open:** Lunch daily 11:30am–3pm; dinner daily 5–10pm; brunch Sun 11am–3pm. Closed Dec 25. **Prices:** Main courses $9.25–$19.95. Maj CC. 🔲🔲👍

Ⓢ★ **La Bohème**, Dolores St, Carmel-by-the-Sea; tel 408/624-7500. At 7th St. **European Country.** Romantic European atmosphere. All dinners are prix-fixe, and only 1 menu (which varies) is served each night. Menu changes daily. Vegetarian meal also available. **FYI:** Reservations not accepted. Beer and wine only. **Open:** Daily 5:30–10pm. Closed Dec 4–26. **Prices:** PF dinner $19.75. Ltd CC. 👁

♥ **L'escargot**, Mission St, Carmel-by-the-Sea; tel 408/624-4914. Between 4th and 5th Aves. **French.** A romantic country-French-style restaurant with an antique plate collection. Specialties include chicken in cream sauce with mushrooms, Madeira, and truffles, as well as veal, steak, and duck dishes. A private dining room accommodates groups of up to 20. **FYI:** Reservations recommended. **Open:** Mon–Sat 5:30–9:30pm. Closed some hols; Dec 1–Dec 14. **Prices:** Main courses $17.95–$23.95; PF dinner $15.95. Maj CC. ♥ ▼

Mondo's Trattoria, Dolores St, Carmel-by-the-Sea; tel 408/624-8977. Between Ocean and 7th Aves. **Italian.** Charmingly decorated with Italian accents, this attractive, cozy restaurant has won lots of local awards. The menu features roast chicken with herbs served with polenta and vegetables, as well as fish and many pasta dishes. **FYI:** Reservations recommended. Beer and wine only. **Open:** Lunch daily 11:30am–3pm; dinner daily 5:30–10pm. Closed some hols. **Prices:** Main courses $8.25–$16.25. Maj CC. ♥

♥ **Pacific's Edge**, in the Highlands Inn, Calif 1, Carmel-by-the-Sea; tel 408/624-0471. **Regional American.** The best ocean views from the Monterey Peninsula are visible from almost every table in this spacious, romantic room. This is the place to splurge on a romantic sunset dinner, or enjoy cocktails in the lounge. The award-winning chef turns out delights such as crab cakes with artichoke-tomato relish, potato-wrapped halibut on a roasted shallot confit, and a wide assortment of vegetable dishes starring produce from the Central Valley. **FYI:** Reservations recommended. Piano. Children's menu. Jacket required. **Open:** Lunch daily 11am–2pm; dinner daily 6–10pm; brunch Sun 10am–2pm. **Prices:** Main courses $22–$29; PF dinner $40. Maj CC. ♥ ▲▲ VP ⅃

Patisserie Boissiere, in Carmel Plaza, Mission St, Carmel-by-the-Sea; tel 408/624-5008. Between Ocean and 7th Aves. **French.** Refined but not fancy, with lovely art. A bakery on the premises makes the place smell wonderful, both at small glass tables and outside on the little terrace. A specialty is half a duck, oven-roasted and served with apricot-orange brandy sauce. **FYI:** Reservations recommended. Beer and wine only. **Open:** Breakfast Mon–Fri 9–11:30am, Sat–Sun 9:30–11:30am; lunch daily 11:30am–4:30pm; dinner Wed–Sun 5:30–9pm. Closed some hols. **Prices:** Main courses $8.95–$12.95. Maj CC.

♥ **Rafaello**, Mission St, Carmel-by-the-Sea; tel 408/624-1541. Between Ocean and 7th Aves. **Italian/Mediterranean.** Intimate and beautiful. Settings are formal, the cooking exquisite, and service experienced. Veal scaloppine Toscana with wine sauce, mushrooms, and tomatoes, lamb dishes, chicken cacciatore, and many pastas. **FYI:** Reservations recommended. Jacket required. Beer and wine only. **Open:** Wed–Mon 6–10pm. Closed hols; Jan 1–10. **Prices:** Main courses $16–$21. Maj CC. ♥

★ **Rio Grill**, in the Crossroads Center, 101 Crossroads Blvd, Carmel-by-the-Sea; tel 408/625-5436. **Californian/Southwestern.** Consistently rated by locals as the best restaurant in town. Decorated in a colorful southwestern motif, with butcher paper and crayons on each table and tasteful artwork lining the walls. Specialties include rack of lamb, smoked baby back ribs, smoked chicken, and oak-grilled fresh fish. **FYI:** Reservations recommended. **Open:** Lunch daily 11:30am–5pm; dinner daily 5–10pm. Closed some hols. **Prices:** Main courses $8.65–$21. Maj CC. ▦ ▅ ⅃

Sans Souci, Lincoln St, Carmel-by-the-Sea; tel 408/624-6220. Between 5th and 6th Aves. **French.** This restaurant, composed of 3 rooms, manages to seem genteel and elegant without being intimidatingly formal. The award-winning menu features abalone, guinea fowl stuffed with apricots and pecans, and veal with morels and cream. **FYI:** Reservations recommended. Jacket required. Beer and wine only. **Open:** Thurs–Tues 5:30–11pm. **Prices:** Main courses $18.50–$28. Maj CC. ♥

⑤ **Silver Jones**, 3690 The Barnyard, Carmel-by-the-Sea; tel 408/624-5200. **Regional American.** A casual and inviting setting, with sculpture by local artist Nick Lulitch and year-round outdoor dining. One specialty is Greek lamb fillet, cooked in red wine with eggplant and olives and served with spinach polenta. **FYI:** Reservations accepted. Children's menu. **Open:** Lunch Mon–Sat 11:30am–3pm, Sun 11am–3pm; dinner Sun–Thurs 5:30–9pm, Fri–Sat 5:30–9:30pm; brunch Sun 11am–3pm. Closed Dec 25. **Prices:** Main courses $7.95–$16.95. Maj CC. ▰ ▨ ▦ ⅃

★ **Sobo's**, San Carlos St, Carmel-by-the-Sea; tel 408/624-2888. Between Ocean and 7th Aves. **Continental.** A hidden jewel frequented by artists and writers since it opened in 1993. Comfortable and cozy dining room with a large, lovely bar. Nice bistro-style menu featuring soups, salads, and sandwiches. **FYI:** Reservations not accepted. **Open:** Daily 11am–9pm. **Prices:** Main courses $6.50–$9. Ltd CC. ♥ ⅃

Tuck Box English Room, Dolores St, Carmel-by-the-Sea; tel 408/624-6365. At 7th Ave. **British.** Cozy and charmingly decorated. Simple fare is prepared well in this often-crowded English tea room. Specials include scones and homemade jams. **FYI:** Reservations not accepted. No liquor license. **Open:** Breakfast daily 8–11:30am; lunch daily noon–3:45pm. Closed some hols; Dec 1–29. **Prices:** Lunch main courses $5–$8. No CC. ▰

CARMEL VALLEY

Map page M-2, E2 (E of Carmel-by-the-Sea)

Hotel 🖼

≣≣ **Country Garden Inns**, 102 W Carmel Valley Rd, PO Box 504, Carmel Valley, CA 93924; tel 408/659-5361; fax 408/ 659-2392. 12 mi E of Carmel. Calif 68 W exit off US 101; left on Los Laureles Grade; left on Carmel Valley Rd. Located in lovely, sunny Carmel Valley, surrounded by hilly, tree-covered countryside and beautiful gardens. **Rooms:** 46 rms, stes, and effic. CI 2pm/CO noon. Nonsmoking rms avail. Country French decor; tasteful and very individual with lots of wicker. **Amenities:** 🛅 Cable TV. No A/C. All units w/terraces, some w/fireplaces. **Services:** ✗ 🛎 Babysitting. **Facilities:** 🔲 🔲 🛆 **Rates (BB):** HS May–Oct $79–$129 S; $89–$159 D; from $159 ste; from $129 effic. Extra person $20. Children under 3 stay free. Min stay spec evnts. Lower rates off-season. Spec packages avail. Pking: Outdoor, free. Maj CC.

Resorts

≣≣≣ **Carmel Valley Ranch Resort**, 1 Old Ranch Rd, Carmel Valley, CA 93923; tel 408/625-9500 or toll free 800/4-CARMEL; fax 408/624-2858. Carmel Valley Rd exit off Calif 1; continue 6.5 mi, then right on Robinson Cyn Rd. 1,700 acres. Located in a serene valley that's often sunny when the coast is fogged in. New ownership plans $5.5 million in much-needed improvements. **Rooms:** 100 stes. CI 4pm/CO noon. Express checkout avail. Nonsmoking rms avail. Spacious (800 to 1,200 square-foot) accommodations in low gray buildings surrounded by oaks. Carpets and upholsteries look noticeably fatigued. Deluxe rooms are nicer than standard ones, which seem dark. **Amenities:** 🛅 ৬ 🔳 🖐 A/C, cable TV w/movies, refrig, stereo/ tape player, bathrobes. All units w/minibars, all w/terraces, all w/fireplaces, some w/Jacuzzis. Some rooms feature private hot tubs. **Services:** ✗ 🔑 VP 🚐 🛆 🛎 Twice-daily maid svce, carrental desk, masseur, babysitting. A host greets guests at the front entrance and personally escorts them to their rooms. **Facilities:** 🔲 🚴 ▶₁₈ 🏂 🏊₁₂ 🎱 💻 ৬ 3 rsts, 3 bars (1 w/entertainment), sauna, whirlpool, playground. Pete Dye–designed championship golf course. Pool is splendid, banked with colorful planters and flowerbeds. Otherwise, the grounds could use more spit and polish. **Rates:** From $260 ste. Extra person $20. Children under 16 stay free. Min stay wknds and spec evnts. AP and MAP rates avail. Spec packages avail. Pking: Outdoor, free. Maj CC. Golf, tennis, romance, and adventure packages available.

≣≣≣≣ **Quail Lodge Resort & Golf Club**, 8205 Valley Greens Dr, Carmel Valley, CA 93923; tel 408/624-1581 or toll free 800/538-9516; fax 408/624-3726. 5 mi E of Carmel-by-the-Sea. Carmel Valley Rd exit off US 1, then 3½ miles east. 800 acres. A longtime favorite and an alternative to the millionaire-priced golf resorts in nearby Pebble Beach. Serene, hilly setting, tucked into the corner of an 800-acre preserve, with ponds and well-tended gardens and walkways shaded by trumpet vine. **Rooms:** 100 rms, stes. CI 4pm/CO 1pm. Nonsmoking rms avail. 1- and 2-story motel-like wings, fashioned from pine in contemporary rustic style, with patios or balconies. Bathrooms have separate dressing areas. Doorside parking for most rooms. Recent rehab has brightened the decor but deep-pile wall-to-wall carpeting conjures up memories of early Howard Johnsons. Rooms 171 through 185 are too close to main road traffic. **Amenities:** 🛅 ৬ 🔳 🖐 A/C, cable TV w/movies, refrig, bathrobes. All units w/minibars, all w/terraces, some w/fireplaces, some w/Jacuzzis. Newer Executive Villas with fireplaces and hardwood hot tubs in walled patios. Complimentary half-bottle of California wine in rooms. Krups coffeemakers and 6 types of tea; minibars come with enough glasses for entertaining. Fleet of minivans and Mercedes sedans for airport transfers (by reservation, for a fee). VCRs and 100 cassettes for rent. **Services:** ✗ 🚐 🛆 🛎 🖐 Twice-daily maid svce, babysitting. Complimentary afternoon tea and cookies in the lounge library. Friendly, polite, country-clubby service. **Facilities:** 🔲 ▶₁₈ 🏂 🏊₄ 🎱₂₂₀ ৬ 2 rsts (see also "Restaurants" below), 2 bars (1 w/entertainment), lawn games, whirlpool. Lots of nature trails, biking, and jogging paths. Ideal venue for golfers: challenging, rarely crowded course; moderate green fees; optional carts; starting times 8 minutes apart. **Rates:** HS June–Oct $195–$245 S or D; from $285 ste. Extra person $25. Children under 12 stay free. Min stay spec evnts. Lower rates off-season. Spec packages avail. Pking: Outdoor, free. Maj CC.

Restaurants 🍽

★ **The Covey**, in Quail Lodge Resort & Golf Club, 8205 Valley Greens Dr, Carmel Valley; tel 408/624-1581. 5 mi E of Carmel. From US 1, take Carmel Valley Rd exit, then drive 3½ miles east. **Refined European.** Comfortable atmosphere and commendable cuisine. The decor is contemporary rustic, with dark pine walls, roof beams, and large windows overlooking a pond. Tables are on 2 levels. Specialties include artichoke hollandaise, rack of lamb, Santa Barbara abalone with lemon butter, vacherin au chocolat. Outstanding wine list. **FYI:** Reservations recommended. Piano. Jacket required. **Open:** Daily 6–10pm. **Prices:** Main courses $19–$49. Maj CC. ♥ 🏷 ৬

Lone Wolf Grill, in Carmel Valley Inn, Los Laurels Grade, Carmel Valley; tel 408/659-WOLF. **Regional American.** Rustic, southwestern atmosphere with custom wood furniture and period photographs. Where else can you dine on emu, elk, buffalo, or rattlesnake? Less adventurous diners can opt for other specialties, such as enchiladas or calamari. There's also dining around the pool area. **FYI:** Reservations recommended. **Open:** Lunch Mon–Sat 11am–4pm; dinner daily 5–10pm; brunch Sun 10:30am–3:30pm. **Prices:** Main courses $5–$20. Maj CC.

Will's Fargo Restaurant in the Village, W Carmel Valley Road, Carmel Valley; tel 408/659-2774. At El Caminito Chambers Lane. **Seafood/Steak.** Sometimes noisy steakhouse built of brick and Carmel stone and filled with antiques. Meals include a relish tray, soup, and salad. Steaks can be cut to size. **FYI:** Reservations recommended. **Open:** Mon–Sat 5:30–10pm, Sun 5–10pm. Closed some hols. **Prices:** Main courses $13.95–$24.95. Maj CC.

CATHEDRAL CITY

Map page M-3, D3 (SW of Thousand Palms)

Motel

Days Inn Suites, 69-151 E Palm Canyon Dr, Cathedral City, CA 92234; tel 619/324-5939 or toll free 800/325-2525; fax 619/324-3034. Located just minutes from Restaurant Row in Rancho Mirage. **Rooms:** 97 rms and stes. CI 3pm/CO noon. Nonsmoking rms avail. Ideal for families; the 1- and 2-bedroom suites have kitchens. **Amenities:** A/C, cable TV w/movies, refrig. 1 unit w/terrace. **Services:** **Facilities:** Whirlpool. **Rates (CP):** HS Jan 11–May $89–$104 S or D; from $104 ste. Extra person $10. Children under 16 stay free. Lower rates off-season. Pking: Outdoor, free. Maj CC.

Resort

Doubletree Resort at Desert Princess Country Club, 67-967 Vista Chino, Cathedral City, CA 92234; tel 619/322-7000 or toll free 800/637-0577; fax 619/322-6853. At Landau. 400 acres. This resort offers spectacular views of the surrounding mountains. **Rooms:** 349 rms, stes, and effic. CI 3pm/CO noon. Express checkout avail. Nonsmoking rms avail. Spacious rooms. **Amenities:** A/C, cable TV w/movies, refrig, in-rm safe. All units w/terraces, some w/fireplaces. A box of Doubletree chocolate chip cookies is given to guests upon arrival. **Services:** Car-rental desk, masseur, babysitting. **Facilities:** 27 5 1 rst, 2 bars (1 w/entertainment), lifeguard, games rm, lawn games, racquetball, squash, spa, sauna, whirlpool, beauty salon. Access to health club at Desert Princess Country Club. **Rates:** HS Jan–

Apr $205–$235 S or D; from $275 ste; from $225 effic. Extra person $15. Children under 18 stay free. Lower rates off-season. Spec packages avail. Pking: Outdoor, free. Maj CC.

Restaurant

The Red Bird Diner, in Mission Plaza-Lucky Center, 35-955 Date Palm Dr, Cathedral City; tel 619/324-7707. Date Palm Dr exit off I-10. **American.** Transports you back to the 1950s, complete with old-fashioned jukebox, soda fountain, and murals depicting Jimmy Dean and Elvis. Lipstick-red vinyl banquettes and chrome-backed chairs complete this time-capsule. Milkshakes, giant hamburgers, banana splits. **FYI:** Reservations accepted. Children's menu. Beer and wine only. **Open:** Daily 7am–8:30pm. Closed some hols; Aug 15–31. **Prices:** Main courses $6.95–$12.95. Maj CC.

CAZADERO

Map page M-2, C1 (SW of Healdsburg)

Lodge

Timberhill Ranch, 35755 Hauser Bridge Rd, Cazadero, CA 95421; tel 707/847-3258; fax 707/847-3258. 18.7 mi N of Jenner. Meyers Grade Rd exit off Calif 1. A narrow country road twines through redwood groves to this country retreat hidden away on 80 acres. It's a paradise for couples who want to get away from it all, located near some spectacular hiking trails to the Pacific. Fifty percent of guests are returnees. **Rooms:** 15 ctges/villas. CI 4pm/CO noon. Nonsmoking rms avail. Decorated country style, with patchwork quilts and armoires. Sitting on the large deck, you'll be astounded by the utter silence of the woodlands. **Amenities:** Refrig, stereo/tape player, bathrobes. No A/C, phone, or TV. All units w/minibars, all w/terraces, all w/fireplaces. At these prices, you would expect more than a bathroom with a prefab plastic shower (no tub) and fake flowers folded into the towels. **Services:** Twice-daily maid svce. Personalized service. Rates include 6-course dinner for two, served on exquisite china, with cut-crystal and sterling silver. **Facilities:** 2 1 rst, whirlpool. TV in main lodge. The resident menagerie includes miniature horses, pot-bellied goats, llamas, ducks pond, and dogs. Fitness center was expected for 1995. **Rates (MAP):** From $325 ctge/villa. Min stay wknds and spec evnts. Higher rates for spec evnts/hols. Pking: Outdoor, free. Ltd CC.

CERRITOS

Map page M-3, D2 (W of Anaheim)

Hotel ⌂

≡≡≡ **Sheraton Cerritos Towne Center**, 12725 Center Court Dr, Cerritos, CA 90701; tel 310/809-1500 or toll free 800/325-3535; fax 310/403-2080. Bloomfield exit off Calif 91. A new hotel, part of the new 125-acre Towne Center Project. Clean and quiet accommodations in the heart of a rapidly growing area. **Rooms:** 203 rms and stes. CI 3pm/CO noon. Express checkout avail. Nonsmoking rms avail. **Amenities:** ⌂ ⌂ ⌂ A/C, cable TV w/movies, voice mail. Some units w/minibars. **Services:** ✗ ☞ VP 🚐 ⌂ ⌂ ⌂ Twice-daily maid svce, babysitting. **Facilities:** ⌂ ⌂ 500 ⌂ ⌂ 1 rst, 1 bar, whirlpool. **Rates:** $110–$150 S; from $160 ste. Extra person $15. Children under 17 stay free. Spec packages avail. Pking: Outdoor, free. Maj CC. Several packages are available, including one that includes tickets to cultural performances.

CHICO

Map page M-2, B2

Hotels ⌂

≡≡ **Best Western Heritage Inn**, 25 Heritage Lane, Chico, CA 95926; tel 916/894-8600 or toll free 800/446-4291; fax 916/894-8600 ext 142. Cohassett Rd exit off Calif 99 N; immediate left into K-mart lot; immediate left on Heritage Lane. Nicely run establishment. **Rooms:** 101 rms. CI noon/CO 11am. Nonsmoking rms avail. **Amenities:** ⌂ ⌂ ⌂ A/C, cable TV, refrig. **Services:** ⌂ ⌂ **Facilities:** ⌂ 135 Whirlpool. **Rates (CP):** $55–$67 S; $59–$75 D. Extra person $5. Children under 12 stay free. Pking: Outdoor, free. Maj CC. Various discounts available.

≡≡≡ **Holiday Inn**, 685 Manzanita Court, Chico, CA 95926; tel 916/345-2491 or toll free 800/HOLIDAY; fax 916/893-3040. Cohassett Rd exit off Calif 99; left onto Mangrove Ave; left onto Manzanita Court. A full-service hotel. **Rooms:** 171 rms and stes. CI 4pm/CO noon. Nonsmoking rms avail. **Amenities:** ⌂ ⌂ A/C, satel TV w/movies. **Services:** ✗ 🚐 ⌂ ⌂ ⌂ **Facilities:** ⌂ ⌂ 380 ⌂ ⌂ 1 rst, 1 bar (w/entertainment), whirlpool, washer/dryer. Good facilities for business meetings. **Rates:** HS Sept–May $72 S or D; from $95 ste. Extra person $6. Children under 12 stay free. Lower rates off-season. Higher rates for spec evnts/hols. Spec packages avail. Pking: Outdoor, free. Maj CC.

≡≡≡ **Oxford Suites**, 2035 Business Lane, Chico, CA 95928; tel 916/899-9090 or toll free 800/870-SUITE; fax 916/899-9476. 20th St E exit off Calif 99; ¼ mi to Business Lane; turn right. Superb lodging at a reasonable price for business or pleasure travelers. **Rooms:** 97 stes. CI 2pm/CO 1pm. Nonsmoking rms avail. Options range from simple rooms to grand suites. **Amenities:** ⌂ ⌂ A/C, cable TV w/movies, refrig, VCR. Suites have microwaves. **Services:** 🚐 ⌂ ⌂ ⌂ Complimentary full breakfast and evening reception with drinks and hors d'oeuvres. Fax and copying services available. **Facilities:** ⌂ 125 ⌂ Whirlpool, washer/dryer. **Rates (BB):** From $62 ste. Extra person $6. Children under 10 stay free. Spec packages avail. Pking: Outdoor, free. Maj CC. Discounts for qualified business travelers and government-agency personnel. Add 10% for pets.

Motel

≡ **Safari Motel**, 2352 The Esplanade, Chico, CA 95926; tel 916/343-3201. 2 mi N of downtown; Main St becomes The Esplanade. Major upgrade of rooms in progress. **Rooms:** 50 rms. CI noon/CO 11am. Nonsmoking rms avail. **Amenities:** ⌂ ⌂ ⌂ ⌂ A/C, cable TV w/movies. **Services:** ⌂ ⌂ **Facilities:** ⌂ Lovely swimming pool. **Rates:** $37–$40 S; $39–$42 D. Extra person $4. Children under 12 stay free. Pking: Outdoor, free. Maj CC.

Restaurant ⍾

$ ★ **Sierra Nevada Brewing Co Taproom & Restaurant**, 1075 E 20th St, Chico; tel 916/345-2739. **Pub.** This highly acclaimed microbrewery is nirvana for the aficionado of finely crafted beer, ale, porter, and stout. It has a joyfully boisterous pub with good food. The pub fare at lunch focuses on a selection of sandwiches, while the dinner menu includes pasta, seafood, steaks, and chicken dishes. Enormous, gleaming copper brewing vessels are visible from the copper-covered bar. Families with small kids will feel comfortable here. **FYI:** Reservations accepted. Children's menu. Beer and wine only. **Open:** Lunch Tues–Sat 11am–3pm; dinner Tues–Sat 5–9pm; brunch Sun 10am–2pm. Closed some hols. **Prices:** Main courses $6.95–$18.95. Ltd CC. ⌂

Attractions ⌂

Chico Museum, 141 Salem St; tel 916/891-4336. A museum of regional history, the Chico Museum features permanent and changing exhibits housed in the 1907 Carnegie Library. Featured in 1995 will be an exhibit on the Diamond Match Company and the Gum San exhibit, chronicling the Chinese experience in America. **Open:** Wed–Sun noon–4pm. Closed some hols. Free.

Bidwell Mansion State Historic Park, 525 Esplanade; tel 916/895-6144. This 26-room mansion was the home of Gen John Bidwell, Chico founding father and US presidential candidate in 1892. Guests who were once entertained in the house included such notables as President and Mrs Rutherford B Hayes, Gen William T Sherman, Susan B Anthony, and naturalist John Muir. Acquired by the State of California in 1964, the mansion has been restored and furnished in period style. **Open:** Daily 10am–5pm. Closed some hols. $

CHIRIACO SUMMIT
Map page M-3, D3 (E of Indio)

Attraction 🖼

General Patton Memorial Museum, 2 Chiriaco Rd; tel 619/227-3483. Established to honor the flamboyant, colorful, and controversial general, this museum is on a site selected and developed by Patton in 1942 as a desert training center to prepare troops for US involvement in North Africa. Known as Camp Young, the area once covered 18,000 square miles, making it the largest military installation and maneuver area in the world.

Exhibits display memorabilia from General Patton's life and career as well as displays on southern California water development and regional geology and plant and animal life of the desert and mountains. **Open:** Daily 9am–5pm. Closed some hols. $

CHULA VISTA
Map page M-3, E3 (E of Imperial Beach)

Motels 🛏

Days Inn of San Diego Bay, 225 Bay Blvd, Chula Vista, CA 91910; tel 619/425-8200 or toll free 800/453-3297; fax 619/426-7411. 8 mi S of San Diego. E St exit off I-5. Exterior needs some attention and landscaping. Across from Ecology Center and close to trolley. **Rooms:** 118 rms. CI 2pm/CO noon. Nonsmoking rms avail. Rooms are nice and are undergoing renovation, with new wallpaper and TVs. **Amenities:** 🛁 A/C, satel TV w/movies, in-rm safe. **Services:** 🛆 ⅃ Small charge for local phone calls. Photocopy and fax services available. **Facilities:** 🛗 ᘒ 1 rst, washer/dryer. Restaurant adjacent. **Rates:** HS July–Aug $39–$69 S or D. Children under 18 stay free. Lower rates off-season. Spec packages avail. Pking: Outdoor, free. Maj CC. No personal checks; $20 telephone deposit required.

La Quinta Motor Inn, 150 Bonita Rd, Chula Vista, CA 91910; tel 619/691-1211 or toll free 800/531-5900; fax 619/427-0135. 8 mi S of San Diego. E St/Bonita Rd exit off I-805. Newly renovated, with a clean and nicely decorated lobby. **Rooms:** 141 rms. CI 3pm/CO noon. Nonsmoking rms avail. Rooms are attractive; king rooms have recliners. Redecoration scheduled. **Amenities:** 🛁 ᘒ A/C, satel TV w/movies. Free toiletries available in lobby. **Services:** 🛆 ⅃ ⅏ Fax available; 24-hour coffee service in lobby. Arrangements can be made for group check-in and check-out. **Facilities:** 🛗 ᘒ Spa. Free use of nearby health club. Restaurant next door. **Rates (CP):** $56–$62 S; $62–$68 D. Extra person $6. Children under 18 stay free. Higher rates for spec evnts/hols. Pking: Outdoor, free. Maj CC. Special commercial rates and AARP rates.

Vagabond Inn, 230 Broadway, Chula Vista, CA 91910; tel 619/422-8305 or toll free 800/522-1555; fax 619/425-3645. 8 mi S of San Diego. E St (Chula Vista) exit off I-5; 2 blocks east on E St, right on Broadway. Nice grounds but inconsistent maintenance in the pool area. Parking is handy and plentiful. **Rooms:** 91 rms and effic. CI 2pm/CO noon. Express checkout avail. Nonsmoking rms avail. Rooms are pleasantly coordinated and clean, but bathrooms need updating. Family suites and kitchenettes are convenient for groups. **Amenities:** 🛁 ᘒ A/C, cable TV w/movies. **Services:** 🛆 ⅃ ⅏ Babysitting. **Facilities:** 🛗 ᘒ Playground. Pools and playground are to undergo renovation. **Rates (CP):** HS May 16–Sept 15 $42 S or D; from $42 effic. Extra person $5. Children under 16 stay free. Lower rates off-season. Higher rates for spec evnts/hols. Spec packages avail. Pking: Outdoor, free. Maj CC.

Restaurant 🍽

Jakes–South Bay, in Chula Vista Marina, 570 Marina Pkwy, Chula Vista; tel 619/476-0400. 8 mi S of San Diego. J St exit off I-5. **Seafood.** Nautical-themed restaurant decorated with polished wood, brass, and historical photos of San Diego, with large windows overlooking the marina. Specialties of the house include cioppino, shrimp scampi, and pasta. Also at: 15th and Coast, Del Mar (619/755-2002). **FYI:** Reservations recommended. Children's menu. **Open:** Lunch Mon–Fri 11:15am–2:30pm; dinner Mon–Sat 5–10pm, Sun 4:30–9:30pm; brunch Sun 10am–2:30pm. Closed some hols. **Prices:** Main courses $11.95–$27.95. Maj CC. 🟦 🟦 ᘒ

Attraction 🖼

Chula Vista Nature Center, 1000 Gunpowder Point Dr; tel 619/422-2473. Located within the Sweetwater Marsh National Wildlife Center. Visitors must take a shuttle bus from the parking area, just off I-5 at the E St exit. The nature center offers a rare view into the natural history and ecology of California wetlands. A variety of exhibits provide an experiential tour through the different ecological zones of the marsh. A number of wildlife specimens from the refuge are on display, including leopard sharks and burrowing owls. Observation tower and deck (binoculars available for rent). Special programs; bookstore and gift shop. **Open:** Tues–Sun, and Mon hols, 10am–5pm; also open every Mon in summer. Closed some hols. $$

CLAREMONT

Map page M-3, D2 (N of Pomona)

Hotel 🖥

≣≣ **Griswold's Hotel & Entertainment Center**, 555 W Foothill Blvd, Claremont, CA 91711; tel 909/626-2411 or toll free 800/854-5733; fax 909/624-0756. Indian Hill Blvd exit off I-10; N 1¾ mi to Calif 66 (Foothill Blvd); 1 block W. This well-established complex of hotel, restaurants, theater, and shops is undergoing a total renovation and upgrade. **Rooms:** 270 rms and stes. CI 3pm/CO noon. Nonsmoking rms avail. **Amenities:** 🔒🐾 A/C, TV w/movies. Some units w/terraces. **Services:** ✗ 🚙 🖳 🖵 Car-rental desk. **Facilities:** 🔟 500 ዼ 3 rsts, 1 bar, whirlpool. **Rates:** $55 S; $62 D; from $85 ste. Extra person $10. Children under 12 stay free. Min stay spec evnts. Higher rates for spec evnts/hols. Spec packages avail. Pking: Outdoor, free. Maj CC.

Motel

≣≣ **Ramada Inn & Tennis Club**, 840 S Indian Hill Blvd, Claremont, CA 91711; tel 909/621-4831 or toll free 800/322-6559; fax 909/626-8452. S Indian Hill Blvd exit off I-10. Average motel with first-class tennis facilities and a Japanese restaurant. **Rooms:** 125 rms. CI 3pm/CO noon. Nonsmoking rms avail. Simply decorated rooms. **Amenities:** 🔒 🐾 A/C, cable TV w/movies, refrig. **Services:** ✗ 🚙 🖳 🖵 🐾 **Facilities:** 🔟 🐾 60 ዼ 1 rst, 1 bar, sauna, whirlpool, washer/dryer. Rusty Miller's Tennis Academy on premises offers classes from beginner to advanced. **Rates (CP):** $54–$59 S; $60–$67 D. Extra person $8. Children under 12 stay free. Higher rates for spec evnts/hols. Spec packages avail. Pking: Outdoor, free. Maj CC.

Attraction 📷

Rancho Santa Ana Botanic Garden, 1500 N College Ave; tel 909/625-8767. This 86-acre garden at the base of the San Gabriel Mountains displays a rich collection of California's diverse native plants. The 2½-acre California Cultivar Garden exhibits cultivated plant varieties selected or hybridized from native plants, with cedar pavilions and interpretive panels discussing the origin of cultivated varieties. Gift shop. **Open:** Daily 8am–5pm. Closed some hols. Free.

CLEARLAKE

Map page M-2, C1

See also **Kelseyville**

Motels 🖥

≣≣ **Best Western El Grande Inn**, 15135 Lakeshore Dr, PO Box 4598, Clearlake, CA 95422; tel 707/994-2000 or toll free 800/528-1234; fax 707/994-2042. 3 mi NW of jct Calif 53/Calif 29 via 40th Ave. Dramatic 45-foot-tall atrium lobby with fountain is very inviting. **Rooms:** 67 rms and stes. CI 3pm/CO 11am. Nonsmoking rms avail. **Amenities:** 🔒 🐾 🖳 A/C, cable TV w/movies, refrig. Some units w/minibars. **Services:** 🖳 🖵 **Facilities:** 🔟 150 ዼ 1 rst, 1 bar, steam rm, whirlpool. Coffee shop open 24 hours. **Rates:** HS Apr–Oct 15 $67 S; $73 D; from $72 ste. Extra person $6. Children under 5 stay free. Min stay HS and wknds. Lower rates off-season. Pking: Outdoor, free. Maj CC.

≣≣ **Highlands Inn**, 13865 Lakeshore Dr, Clearlake, CA 95422; tel 707/994-8982 or toll free 800/300-8982; fax 707/994-0613. 4 mi NW of jct Calif 53/Calif 29 via 40th Ave. Built in 1992. Sparkling clean. Stark exterior but attractive rooms. **Rooms:** 20 rms and stes. CI noon/CO 11am. Nonsmoking rms avail. **Amenities:** 🔒 🐾 🖳 A/C, cable TV. **Services:** 🖳 🖵 **Facilities:** 🔟 🐾 ዼ 1 beach (lake shore), washer/dryer. **Rates:** HS June–Sept $55–$75 S or D; from $80 ste. Extra person $5. Children under 5 stay free. Min stay HS and wknds. Lower rates off-season. Spec packages avail. Pking: Outdoor, free. Maj CC.

CONCORD

Map page M-2, D2 (W of Stockton)

See also **Pleasant Hill**

Hotels 🖥

≣≣≣ **Concord Hilton**, 1970 Diamond Blvd, Concord, CA 94520; tel 510/827-2000 or toll free 800/826-2644; fax 510/827-2113. Willow Pass Road exit off I-68. Attractive hotel with rather luxurious interiors. **Rooms:** 328 rms and stes. CI 3pm/CO noon. Express checkout avail. Nonsmoking rms avail. Rooms are slightly larger than average and tastefully decorated. **Amenities:** 🔒 🐾 A/C, cable TV w/movies, voice mail. Some units w/Jacuzzis.

Services: ✕ ▣ ⌐ Twice-daily maid svce, babysitting. Free shuttle to shopping and rapid-transit station. **Facilities:** ⌂ ☒ ⏻ ⏹ ⅙ 2 rsts, 2 bars (1 w/entertainment), whirlpool, washer/dryer. **Rates:** $89–$138 S; $99–$148 D; from $225 ste. Extra person $10. Children under 18 stay free. Spec packages avail. Pking: Outdoor, free. Maj CC.

☰☰ Sheraton Hotel & Conference Center, 45 John Glenn Dr, Concord, CA 94520; tel 510/825-7700 or toll free 800/325-3535; fax 510/825-9567. Concord Ave exit off I-680; left onto Diamond Rd; right onto Concord. Lowrise hotel built around a large, beautifully landscaped central atrium covered with a large skylight. There is even a koi pond. Private airport across the street. **Rooms:** 323 rms and stes. Exec-level rms avail. CI 2pm/CO noon. Nonsmoking rms avail. **Amenities:** ⛁ ⓐ ☎ A/C, cable TV w/movies, voice mail. Some units w/terraces. **Services:** ✕ ▣ ⌐ Babysitting. **Facilities:** ⌂ ⏻ ⏹ 💻 ⅙ 1 rst, 1 bar (w/entertainment), whirlpool. Pool is small for number of guests. Indoor putting green. 18-hole golf course adjacent to property. **Rates:** $110 S; $120 D; from $145 ste. Extra person $15. Children under 18 stay free. Spec packages avail. Pking: Outdoor, free. Maj CC.

Restaurant ▯

China Pavilion, 2050 Diamond Blvd, Concord; tel 510/827-2212. At Willow Pass Rd. **Chinese.** Decorated with the regal icons of China, red wall hangings, carved wood, and mystic lion and dragon figures, this large family restaurant offers traditional Chinese fare. **FYI:** Reservations accepted. Dress code. **Open:** Lunch daily 11:30am–2:30pm; dinner daily 4–10pm. **Prices:** Main courses $5.50–$14.95. Maj CC. ▦ ⅙

CORONA

Map page M-3, D3 (S of San Bernardino)

Motels ▤

☰☰ Best Western Kings Inn, 1084 Pomona Rd, Corona, CA 91720; tel 909/734-4241 or toll free 800/892-5464; fax 909/279-5371. Lincoln Ave exit off Calif 91; 1 block N. Quiet, nicely kept property with easy highway access. Close to Glen Ivy Hot Springs Spa. **Rooms:** 88 rms. CI 2pm/CO noon. Nonsmoking rms avail. **Amenities:** ⛁ ⓐ 🍴 A/C, cable TV w/movies, refrig. **Services:** ⛟ ▣ ⌐ **Facilities:** ⌂ ⏹ ⅙ Whirlpool. **Rates (CP):** $49 S; $54 D. Extra person $5. Children under 12 stay free. Spec packages avail. Pking: Outdoor, free. Maj CC.

☰ Corona Travelodge, 1701 W 6th St, Corona, CA 91720; tel 909/735-5500 or toll free 800/578-7878. 6th St exit off Calif 91.

Not fancy, but nicely kept. **Rooms:** 45 rms. CI noon/CO 11am. Nonsmoking rms avail. Extremely large rooms. **Amenities:** ⛁ A/C, TV, refrig. Some units w/Jacuzzis. **Services:** ⌐ ⬀ **Facilities:** ⌂ **Rates:** $33 S; $35 D. Extra person $5. Pking: Outdoor, free. Maj CC.

☰☰☰ Country Side Inn, 2260 Griffin Way, Corona, CA 91719; tel 909/734-2140 or toll free 800/448-8810. McKinley exit off Calif 91; 1 block N. This well-maintained property is part of a southern California chain. **Rooms:** 100 rms. CI 3pm/CO noon. Nonsmoking rms avail. **Amenities:** ⛁ ⓐ A/C, cable TV w/movies, refrig. **Services:** ▣ ⌐ Complimentary full breakfast buffet, evening refreshments, morning newspaper, and fresh fruit in the lobby. **Facilities:** ⌂ ⏹ 💻 ⅙ Whirlpool. Free passes to a local health club. **Rates (BB):** $59 S; $69 D. Extra person $10. Children under 12 stay free. Spec packages avail. Pking: Outdoor, free. Maj CC.

CORONA DEL MAR

Map page M-3, E2 (N of Laguna Beach)

Restaurants ▯

★ Mayur, 2931 East Coast Hwy, Corona del Mar; tel 714/675-6622. **Indian.** Considered one of the best places in California for Indian food. Mayur means "peacock," and the interior colors here reflect this. Cuisine features chicken cooked in a clay oven, nan, and fresh vegetables in spicy curries. Many vegetarian dishes. **FYI:** Reservations recommended. Dress code. Beer and wine only. **Open:** Lunch Mon–Fri 11:30am–2:30pm; dinner daily 5–10:30pm; brunch Sun 11:30am–2:30pm. **Prices:** Main courses $15–$20; PF dinner $20–$25. Maj CC. ♥ ⅙

Trees, 440 Heliotrope Ave, Corona del Mar; tel 714/673-0910. ¼ block S of Pacific Coast Hwy; behind the Port Theatre. **New American.** A lovely, romantic setting in what was once a private home. Three small dining rooms with soothing decor, a fireplace, soft lighting, and picture windows facing a garden courtyard. Contemporary American bistro food with oriental touches includes meatloaf, Thai fried chicken, stir fry, Maryland crabcakes, and smoked trout ravioli. **FYI:** Reservations recommended. Piano. Children's menu. **Open:** Mon–Fri 5–10pm, Sat 5:30–10:30pm, Sun 5:30–9:30pm. Closed Dec 25. **Prices:** Main courses $9.95–$18.95. Maj CC. ♥ ⅙

Attraction ▬

Sherman Library and Gardens, 2647 E Pacific Coast Hwy; tel 714/673-2261. Begun in 1966, the Sherman Library and Gardens now occupy a full city block along the Pacific Coast Hwy

(Calif 1). They are named after Moses H Sherman (1853–1932), educator and California pioneer. The library provides a historical research center devoted to the study of the Pacific Southwest. It contains 15,000 books and pamphlets, large collections of maps and photographs, and about 2,000 papers and documents.

The botanical collections range from rare cacti and succulents of desert regions to exotic vegetation of tropical climates. In effect, the gardens are a museum of living plants, displayed in an attractive setting of fountains, sculpture, and well-tended shrubs and lawns. The Discovery Garden is designed especially (but not exclusively) for the visually impaired, with an emphasis on plants whose essential appeal is to the sense of touch or smell. **Open:** Daily 10:30am–4pm. Closed some hols. $

CORONADO

Map page M-3, E3

Hotels 🛏

≡≡ **El Cordova Hotel**, 1351 Orange Ave, Coronado, CA 92118; tel 619/435-4131 or toll free 800/229-2032; fax 619/435-0632. 4 mi SW of San Diego. Coronado Bridge exit off I-5; left on Orange Ave. A historic country mansion built in 1902 and converted to a hotel in the 1930s. Rooms are approached by stairways from the central courtyard. **Rooms:** 40 rms, stes, and effic. CI 2pm/CO noon. Express checkout avail. Nonsmoking rms avail. Furnishings are color-coordinated and in fair condition. **Amenities:** 🛏 🕭 Cable TV w/movies, shoe polisher. No A/C. Some units w/terraces. **Services:** 🔁 Babysitting. Secretarial service. Security desk open until 11pm. **Facilities:** 🛋 🚲 🖥 1 rst, 1 bar, beauty salon, washer/dryer. Florist, travel agency, deli, gift shop, sport shop. Charcoal grills available for use by guests. **Rates:** HS June 16–Sept 15 $80–$85 S or D; from $125 ste; from $125 effic. Extra person $10. Children under 12 stay free. Min stay wknds. Lower rates off-season. Maj CC.

≡≡≡ **Le Meridien San Diego at Coronado**, 2000 2nd St, Coronado, CA 92118; tel 619/435-3000 or toll free 800/543-4300; fax 619/435-3032. Calif 75/San Diego–Coronado Bay Br exit off I-5; right on Glorieta Blvd. The French Riviera on San Diego Bay, with potted palms in the lobby, plus koi ponds, waterfalls, and an aviary in the courtyard. The sounds of rushing water and cooing birds create a tranquil mood. Major faux pas is the soiled, worn-out carpeting in corridors. **Rooms:** 272 rms and stes; 28 ctges/villas. CI 3pm/CO noon. Express checkout avail. Nonsmoking rms avail. All accommodations measure over 500 square feet and reflect plenty of style, especially the large blue-and-white-tiled bathrooms with marble counters and huge mirrors. **Amenities:** 🛏 🕭 🍴 A/C, cable TV w/movies, refrig, shoe

polisher, bathrobes. All units w/minibars, all w/terraces, some w/Jacuzzis. Standard rooms offer deep soaking tubs, while executive suites and villas feature Jacuzzis. All have European-style shower heads and outdated hairdryers. **Services:** 🍴 🔑 🚐 🧳 🔁 🏊 Twice-daily maid svce, car-rental desk, masseur, children's program, babysitting. **Facilities:** 🛋 🚲 🏓 🏊 📺 📶 🖥 🕭 2 rsts (see also "Restaurants" below), 2 bars (1 w/entertainment), lifeguard, games rm, spa, sauna, whirlpool, beauty salon. Edged by palm trees, the large, free-form main pool enjoys great views. The spa is associated with Clarins Institut de Beauté, which offers a range of services from massages and herbal body wraps to personal fitness training. **Rates:** $165–$255 S or D; from $475 ste; from $205 ctge/villa. Extra person $15. Children under 12 stay free. Spec packages avail. Pking: Indoor/outdoor, $7–$8. Maj CC.

Motel

≡≡≡ **Glorietta Bay Inn**, 1630 Glorietta Blvd, Coronado, CA 92118; tel 619/435-3101 or toll free 800/283-9383; fax 619/435-6182. 4 mi SW of San Diego. Coronado Bridge exit off I-5; left on Orange Ave, go 1 mi, turn left on Glorietta Blvd. Formerly the Spreckels Mansion (built circa 1908), this Edwardian-style hotel is a historic landmark. Just 2 blocks from the beach. **Rooms:** 98 rms and stes. CI 4pm/CO noon. Nonsmoking rms avail. Rooms are nicely appointed. **Amenities:** 🛏 🕭 🍴 A/C, cable TV, refrig. Some units w/terraces, 1 w/Jacuzzi. Phone equipment for hearing-impaired guests. **Services:** 🧳 🔁 Babysitting. **Facilities:** 🛋 🚲 🏊 🕭 Whirlpool, washer/dryer. Close to shops, restaurants, golf, jogging trails, and surfing area. **Rates:** HS June 18–Sept 8 $89–$130 S; $99–$130 D; from $170 ste. Extra person $10. Min stay wknds. Lower rates off-season. Spec packages avail. Pking: Outdoor, free. Maj CC.

Resorts

≡≡≡≡ **Hotel del Coronado**, 1500 Orange Ave, Coronado, CA 92118; tel 619/522-8000 or toll free 800/HOTEL-DEL; fax 619/522-8262. Calif 75/San Diego–Coronado Bay Br exit off I-5; over bridge, left on Orange Ave. An extravagant, red-turreted seaside palace, opened in 1888, that shimmers with Gilded Age romance. Here, the duke of Windsor met his duchess, and Marilyn Monroe frolicked in *Some Like It Hot*. A National Historic Landmark. **Rooms:** 691 rms and stes. CI 4pm/CO noon. Express checkout avail. Nonsmoking rms avail. Rooms in the vintage main building offer old-time charm, with high ceilings, creaky floors, and period fixtures. (The resident ghost—a young lady of tragic past—is said to haunt room 3312.) The newer Ocean Tower accommodations are bland but up to date, and air-conditioned. **Amenities:** 🛏 🕭 A/C, cable TV w/movies, shoe polisher. All units w/minibars, some w/terraces. **Services:** 🍴

🔑 VP 🚐 ⛵ ♫ Car-rental desk, masseur, children's program, babysitting. Summer activities for kids include day camps, tennis programs, supervised evening programs, and more. **Facilities:** 🔥 🚴 🎾 🏌 🔟 💻 ♿ 4 rsts (*see also* "Restaurants" below), 3 bars (2 w/entertainment), 1 beach (ocean), lifeguard, board surfing, games rm, lawn games, spa, sauna, steam rm, whirlpool, beauty salon. The history gallery showcases old photos of the hotel's construction and visiting celebrities. The Galleria features stores selling everything from fudge to precious jewels. **Rates:** $154–$359 S or D; from $399 ste. Extra person $25. Children under 15 stay free. Min stay wknds. AP and MAP rates avail. Spec packages avail. Pking: Outdoor, $10. Maj CC.

≣≣≣≣ **Loews Coronado Bay Resort**, 4000 Coronado Bay Rd, Coronado, CA 92118; tel 619/424-4000 or toll free 800/81-LOEWS; fax 619/424-4400. Calif 75/San Diego–Coronado Bay Br exit off I-5; over bridge, left on Orange Ave/Silver Strand Blvd about 4 mi, then left on Coronado Bay Rd. 15 acres. Set on a private peninsula, this hotel is beachy and businesslike at the same time. Views range from downtown San Diego to the Mexican border. Open, airy lobby is embellished with a grand double stairway of polished brass. **Rooms:** 440 rms and stes. CI 4pm/CO noon. Express checkout avail. Nonsmoking rms avail. Rooms are nicely if not lavishly decorated with floral-print bedspreads. Large bathrooms with deep "steeping" tubs. **Amenities:** 📺 🅰 ☎ A/C, cable TV w/movies, refrig, in-rm safe, bathrobes. All units w/minibars, all w/terraces. **Services:** 🍽 🔑 VP 🚐 ⛵ ♫ ⚓ Twice-daily maid svce, car-rental desk, masseur, children's program, babysitting. Year-round Commodore Kids Club program includes arts and crafts projects, nature hikes, beach games, plus evening events. **Facilities:** 🔥 🚴 ⚓ 🛥 🎾 🚣 ⚓ 🏌 🔟 💻 ♿ 3 rsts (*see also* "Restaurants" below), 4 bars (1 w/entertainment), lifeguard, games rm, spa, sauna, steam rm, whirlpool, beauty salon, washer/dryer. For sailing enthusiasts, there's an 80-slip marina, sailboat instruction and rental, powerboats, and lots more. Beautiful Silver Strand State Beach is a short stroll away. **Rates:** $165 S or D; from $495 ste. Children under 12 stay free. Min stay wknds and spec evnts. Spec packages avail. Pking: Indoor/outdoor, $8–$11. Maj CC.

Restaurants 🍴

Azzura Point, in Loews Coronado Bay Resort, 4000 Coronado Bay Rd, Coronado; tel 619/424-4000. 8 mi SW of San Diego. Coronado Bay Br exit off I-5. **Californian/Asian.** Palladian windows set in white walls, teal and ivory stenciled flooring, and rattan chairs create a lovely foreground for the bay views here. California seafood dishes predominate; also available are seared sea scallops with pasta, Chinese smoked lobster, and a changing

wine list. **FYI:** Reservations recommended. **Open:** Dinner Sun–Thurs 6–10pm, Fri–Sat 6–11pm. **Prices:** Main courses $17.25–$22.95; PF dinner $30. Maj CC. 📶 VP ♿

The Brigantine, 1333 Orange Ave, Coronado; tel 619/435-4166. 4 mi SW of San Diego. Coronado Bay Br exit off I-5. **Seafood.** Polished wood and brass coordinate nicely with the nautical motif. The specialty is fresh seafood, as well as corn-fed beef and free-range chicken. The wine list is extensive. Also at: 2725 Shelter Island Dr, Point Loma (619/224-2871); 3263 Camino del Mar, Del Mar (619/481-1166); 2444 San Diego Ave, San Diego (619/298-9840). **FYI:** Reservations accepted. **Open:** Lunch Mon–Fri 11:30am–2:30pm; dinner Sun–Thurs 5–10:30pm, Fri–Sat 5–11:30pm. Closed some hols. **Prices:** Main courses $7.95–$42.50. Maj CC. 💟 ♿

Chart House, 1701 Strand Way, Coronado; tel 619/435-0155. 4 mi SW of San Diego. Coronado Bay Br exit off I-5. Across from Hotel del Coronado. **Seafood.** Built in 1887, this restaurant was first a boat house for the Hotel Coronado. Decor is nautical Victorian, with tiffany lamps in the dining room and leaded glass in the back bar. Fresh fish, including sea bass and mahi mahi, predominates, but prime rib and mud pie are also popular. **FYI:** Reservations recommended. Children's menu. **Open:** Sun–Thurs 5–10pm, Fri 5–10:30pm, Sat 5–11pm. **Prices:** Main courses $15.50–$45.95. Maj CC. 🍺 🍷 💟 ♿

Crown-Coronet Room, in Hotel Del Coronado, 1500 Orange Ave, Coronado; tel 619/522-8496. 4 mi SW of San Diego. Coronado Bay Br exit off I-5. **Californian/French.** A Victorian setting, with a soaring ceiling, damask fabric walls above wainscoting, and tapestry chairs. The chandeliers were designed by *Wizard of Oz* author Frank Baum. Sunday brunch is a tradition here; at other meals, seafood is a good choice. **FYI:** Reservations recommended. Dancing. Children's menu. **Open:** Breakfast Mon–Sat 7–11:15am; lunch Mon–Sat 11:30am–3pm; dinner Mon–Sat 5–9:30pm, Sun 5–9pm; brunch Sun 9am–2pm. **Prices:** Main courses $11.95–$24.95. Maj CC. ♥ 🍺 💟 VP ♿

Mandarin Cafe, in Coronado Plaza, 1330 Orange Ave, Coronado; tel 619/435-2771. 4 mi SW of San Diego. Coronado Bay Br exit off I-5; just north of Hotel del Coronado. **Chinese.** Offers a wide range of Mandarin and Szechaun cuisine in a charming setting with skylights, windows looking out to a garden, and some ocean views. **FYI:** Reservations recommended. Beer and wine only. **Open:** Mon–Thurs 11am–10pm, Fri–Sat 11am–11pm, Sun 1–10pm. Closed Thanksgiving. **Prices:** Main courses $6.50–$12.50. Maj CC. 🍷 📶 💟 ♿

Marius, in Le Meridien San Diego at Coronado, 2000 2nd St, Coronado; tel 619/435-3000. Calif 75/San Diego–Coronado Bay Br exit off I-5; go over bridge; right onto Glorieta Blvd. **French.**

Elegant but not stuffy, adorned with crystal sconces, mirrors, and oil paintings. The Provençale cuisine features such entrees as duck breast encrusted with rosemary in a lavender-honey sauce, or lobster galettes. Prix-fixe dinners are offered in 3, 4, or 5 courses. **FYI:** Reservations recommended. Jacket required. **Open:** Tues–Sat 6–10pm. **Prices:** PF dinner $39–$75. Maj CC. 🆅&

McP's Irish Pub, 1107 Orange Ave, Coronado; tel 619/435-5280. 4 mi SW of San Diego. Coronado Bay Br exit off I-5. **American/Irish.** A classic pub with green accents and lots of wood. The patio with 20 tables is a good place to people-watch. Specialties include corned beef with cabbage and Mulligan stew. **FYI:** Reservations recommended. Combo. Children's menu. **Open:** HS June–Sept Mon–Fri 11am–9pm, Sat–Sun 9am–9pm. Reduced hours off-season. Closed Dec 25. **Prices:** Main courses $4.95–$17.95. Maj CC. 🍽&

♦ **Primavera Ristorante**, 932 Orange Ave, Coronado; tel 619/435-0454. 4 mi SW of San Diego. Coronado Bay Br exit off I-5 to Orange Ave and turn left. **Italian.** An elegant dining room and bar decorated in muted mauve tones, with cream linens and polished wood. The upstairs room has an adjoining patio for private parties. Entrees include veal chops, osso buco, and fresh fish. For dessert, homemade tiramisù. **FYI:** Reservations recommended. Dress code. **Open:** Lunch Mon–Fri 11am–2:30pm; dinner daily 5–10:30pm. Closed some hols. **Prices:** Main courses $11.95–$19.95. Maj CC. ♥&

CORTE MADERA

Map page M-2, D1 (S of San Rafael)

Motel 🏨

≣≣≣ **Corte Madera Inn–Best Western**, 1815 Redwood Hwy, Corte Madera, CA 94925; tel 415/924-1502 or toll free 800/777-9670; fax 415/924-5419. From US 101 S: Madera Blvd exit; from US 101 N: Mt Tamalpais/Paradise Dr exit; left over freeway, right on Madera Blvd. A typical motel exterior surrounded by beautifully landscaped grounds with rolling lawns. Large lobby has a massive stone fireplace. **Rooms:** 110 rms and stes. CI 3pm/CO noon. Nonsmoking rms avail. Some rooms have showers only, no tub. Solarium rooms have large skylights, while deluxe courtyard accommodations are larger and have wet bars. Live plants in many rooms. **Amenities:** 🛗&A/C, cable TV w/movies, refrig, VCR. Some units w/minibars, all w/terraces, some w/fireplaces, some w/Jacuzzis. **Services:** ✕🛎🗄🛏 Car-rental desk, babysitting. Complimentary van service to local shops, restaurants, and to airport bus. "Dining passport" allows guests to eat at selected local restaurants and charge meals to

their rooms. **Facilities:** 🛗🏊🎱& 1 rst, 1 bar, games rm, whirlpool, playground, washer/dryer. Spectacular junior olympic-size pool with lap lanes, heated all year. Compact but complete workout room with Lifecycles, rowing machine, and more. **Rates (CP):** HS May–Sept $80–$98 S; $88–$106 D; from $135 ste. Extra person $8. Children under 18 stay free. Min stay HS and spec evnts. Lower rates off-season. Higher rates for spec evnts/hols. Spec packages avail. Pking: Outdoor, free. Maj CC.

COSTA MESA

Map page M-3, E2 (S of Santa Ana)

Hotels 🏨

≣ **Best Western Newport Mesa Inn**, 2642 Newport Blvd, Costa Mesa, CA 92627; tel 800/554-2378 or toll free 800/554-2378; fax 714/642-1220. 2 mi S of Newport. Fair Del Mar exit off Calif 55. Clean and efficient. In a good, if slightly noisy, location. **Rooms:** 98 rms and stes. CI 2pm/CO noon. Nonsmoking rms avail. Basic but adequate. **Amenities:** 🛗&A/C, cable TV. Some units w/Jacuzzis. **Services:** 🛎🗄🛏🍴 Children's program, babysitting. **Facilities:** 🛗🏊&Sauna, whirlpool, washer/dryer. **Rates:** HS June–Aug $56–$75 S; $58–$80 D; from $99 ste. Extra person $6. Children under 12 stay free. Lower rates off-season. Spec packages avail. Pking: Indoor/outdoor, free. Maj CC.

≣≣≣ **Costa Mesa Marriott Suites**, 500 Anton Blvd, Costa Mesa, CA 92626; tel 714/957-1100 or toll free 800/228-9290; fax 714/966-8495. Bristol N exit off I-405; right on Anton. Excellent hotel close to airports, business parks, and shopping center. Especially attractive for the business traveler. **Rooms:** 253 rms and stes. CI 4pm/CO noon. Express checkout avail. Nonsmoking rms avail. Large, spacious, and airy. **Amenities:** 🛗&🗄🍴A/C, cable TV w/movies, refrig, voice mail, shoe polisher. Some units w/terraces. **Services:** ✕🛎🛎🗄🛏🍴 Car-rental desk, babysitting. **Facilities:** 🛗🏊🏋🎱& 1 rst, 1 bar, whirlpool, washer/dryer. **Rates:** $59–$139 S or D; from $99 ste. Extra person $10. Children under 16 stay free. Higher rates for spec evnts/hols. Spec packages avail. Pking: Indoor/outdoor, free. Maj CC.

≣≣ **Country Side Inn & Suites**, 325 Bristol St, Costa Mesa, CA 92626; tel 714/549-0300 or toll free 800/322-9992; fax 714/662-0828. Bristol St S exit off I-405 S; at Red Hill. Quiet area, yet close to business parks, major shopping centers, and Orange County Airport. **Rooms:** 290 rms and stes. CI 3pm/CO noon. Express checkout avail. Nonsmoking rms avail. **Amenities:** 🛗&A/C, cable TV w/movies, VCR, shoe polisher. Some units w/Jacuzzis. **Services:** ✕🛎🆅🗄🛏 Babysitting. **Facilities:** 🏊 🛂 📶 ♿ 1 rst, 1 bar (w/entertainment), whirlpool, washer/dryer. **Rates (BB):** $77–$120 S; $87–$130 D; from $87 ste. Extra person $10. Children under 12 stay free. Higher rates for spec evnts/hols. Spec packages avail. Pking: Outdoor, free. Maj CC.

≣≣ Holiday Inn–Costa Mesa/Orange County Airport, 3131 Bristol St, Costa Mesa, CA 92626; tel 714/557-3000 or toll free 800/221-7220; fax 714/957-8185. Bristol S exit off I-405. Clean, efficient hotel adjacent to the airport. **Rooms:** 197 rms and stes. Exec-level rms avail. CI 3pm/CO noon. Express checkout avail. Nonsmoking rms avail. Comfortable and clean. **Amenities:** 🛁 🕐 A/C, cable TV. All units w/terraces. **Services:** ✕ 🕏 🚗 🖥 🐾 **Facilities:** 🏊 🛂 📶 ♿ 1 rst, 1 bar, sauna, washer/dryer. **Rates:** $52–$59 S or D; from $175 ste. Children under 12 stay free. Spec packages avail. Pking: Indoor/outdoor, free. Maj CC.

≣≣≣≣ Westin South Coast Plaza, 686 Anton Blvd, Costa Mesa, CA 92626; tel 714/540-2500 or toll free 800/228-3000; fax 714/662-6695. Bristol St exit off I-405; go right on Anton Blvd. Located in the middle of a business park next to a major shopping center. A sleekly sophisticated beige marble lobby opens onto a center courtyard with a huge waterfall, and the pool deck is very attractive. **Rooms:** 390 rms and stes. CI 3pm/CO 1pm. Express checkout avail. Rooms are large—almost 300 square feet—and decorated in a medley of beiges. All have oversize work desks. Nonsmoking regulations are lax here, and the lobby and hallways reek from cigarettes; however, nonsmoking floors are available. **Amenities:** 🛁 🕐 🖥 🍷 A/C, cable TV w/movies, refrig, voice mail, shoe polisher. All units w/minibars. Fax machines in 15th-floor rooms. **Services:** 🍽 🕏 VP 🚗 🖥 🐾 🐾 Twice-daily maid svce, car-rental desk, babysitting. Complimentary evening hors d'oeuvres served in the lobby lounge. Transportation available to Disneyland and Newport Beach. **Facilities:** 🏊 🛂 📶 🖥 ♿ 1 rst, 1 bar (w/entertainment). In addition to the workout facilities on the pool deck (with cardio machines and free weights), guests have privileges ($20) at a nearby health club. **Rates:** $159 S or D; from $200 ste. Extra person $20. Children under 18 stay free. Spec packages avail. Pking: Indoor, free. Maj CC.

Motels

≣ Comfort Inn, 2430 Newport Blvd, Costa Mesa, CA 92626; tel 714/631-7840 or toll free 800/221-2222; fax 714/548-3720. Del Mar exit off Calif 55. Clean and adequate. Public areas could use upgrades. **Rooms:** 58 rms. CI 1pm/CO 11am. Nonsmoking rms avail. Drapes, carpets, and bedspreads look worn. **Amenities:** 🛁 A/C, cable TV. **Facilities:** 🏊 ♿ Whirlpool.

Rates: HS May 15–Sept 15 $40–$45 S; $58 D. Extra person $3. Children under 18 stay free. Lower rates off-season. Spec packages avail. Pking: Outdoor, free. Maj CC.

≣≣ Inn at Costa Mesa, 3151 Harbor Blvd, Costa Mesa, CA 92626; tel 714/540-8571; fax 714/979-9647. Harbor Blvd S exit off I-405. Clean, comfortable accommodations adjacent to highway; a bit noisy. **Rooms:** 50 rms and stes. CI 3pm/CO 11am. Nonsmoking rms avail. **Amenities:** 🛁 🕐 A/C, cable TV, refrig. **Facilities:** 🏊 **Rates:** HS May–Sept $38–$42 S; $44–$46 D; from $60 ste. Children under 18 stay free. Lower rates off-season. Pking: Outdoor, free. Maj CC.

≣≣ La Quinta Inn, 1515 S Coast Dr, Costa Mesa, CA 92626; tel 714/957-5841 or toll free 800/531-5900; fax 714/432-7159. Harbor Blvd exit off I-405; go north on Harbor to S Coast Dr; turn left into parking lot. Clean and conveniently located near the airport, with a new, upgraded lobby. **Rooms:** 162 rms. CI 3pm/CO noon. Nonsmoking rms avail. Clean, light, and airy. **Amenities:** 🛁 🕐 A/C, cable TV w/movies. **Services:** 🚗 🖥 🐾 🐾 **Facilities:** 🏊 📶 ♿ **Rates (CP):** $45–$57 S; $50–$62 D. Extra person $5. Children under 18 stay free. Higher rates for spec evnts/hols. Spec packages avail. Pking: Outdoor, free. Maj CC.

≣≣ Newport Beach Days Inn, 2100 Newport Blvd, Costa Mesa, CA 92627; tel 714/642-2670; fax 714/642-2677. 22nd St–Victoria exit off Calif 55 S; left onto Bay; left onto Newport. A family-oriented property in a noisy location. Convenient to freeways. **Rooms:** 31 rms and stes. CI 11am/CO 11am. Nonsmoking rms avail. **Amenities:** 🛁 🕐 🍷 A/C, cable TV, refrig. All units w/minibars, some w/terraces. **Services:** 🐾 Children's program. **Facilities:** 🏊 Washer/dryer. **Rates:** HS May–Sept $42–$50 S; $48–$65 D; from $58 ste. Extra person $4. Children under 18 stay free. Lower rates off-season. Higher rates for spec evnts/hols. Spec packages avail. Pking: Outdoor, free. Maj CC.

Restaurants 🍴

Bangkok IV, in Crystal Court, 3333 Bear St, Costa Mesa; tel 714/540-7661. Bristol St exit off I-405. **Thai.** Simple, black-and-white decor, accented with single pink anthuriums at the tables. Thai menu emphasizes fresh ingredients, lots of spices, and attractive arrangements. Customers can choose degree of hotness in dishes from a scale of 1 to 10. **FYI:** Reservations recommended. Beer and wine only. **Open:** Mon–Sat 11am–10pm, Sun 11am–9pm. Closed some hols. **Prices:** Main courses $9.95–$17.95. Maj CC. 🅿 VP ♿

Diva, in Plaza Tower, 600 Anton Blvd, Ste 100, Costa Mesa; tel 714/754-0600. Bristol St N exit off I-405 S. **Californian.** Great for business entertaining. Yellow walls, black drapes, and purple light fixtures create a New York bistro–style atmosphere. Imaginative dishes include lobster and shrimp cakes on a bed of asparagus with tarragon sauce, chicken and beef satay with spicy peanut sauce and cucumber relish, and grilled seafood cassoulet on a bed of corn chowder. **FYI:** Reservations recommended. Guitar/piano/singer. **Open:** Lunch Mon–Fri 11:30am–3pm; dinner Sun–Mon 4:30–9pm, Tues–Wed 5–10pm, Thurs 5–11pm, Fri–Sat 5pm–midnight. Closed some hols. **Prices:** Main courses $8.75–$18. Maj CC. 🚢 VP &

The Golden Truffle, 1767 Newport Blvd, Costa Mesa; tel 714/645-9858. Calif 55 S exit off I-405; continue on Newport Blvd to 17th St and turn right. **Caribbean/French.** Colorful flower boxes invite diners into this restaurant in the heart of Costa Mesa. Menu ranges from spa-type dishes to more traditional offerings; among the specialties are spicy Thai chicken with samba noodles, pot roast á la Mom, and Maine lobster ravioli with artichoke cream. Daily specials feature fresh fish. Location makes this a good takeoff spot for an after-dinner stroll. **FYI:** Reservations recommended. Beer and wine only. **Open:** Lunch Tues–Fri 11:30am–2:30pm; dinner Tues–Sat 6–10pm. Closed some hols; Dec 24–Jan 3. **Prices:** Main courses $12.95–$24.95; PF dinner $38. Maj CC. 🌑 &

★ **Il Fornaio**, 650 Anton, Costa Mesa; tel 714/668-0880. Bristol St N exit off I-405. **Italian.** Italian-style bistro with tile floors and dark wood accents. Wide variety of Italian specialties includes antipasti, pizza, and pasta, as well as chicken, veal, fish, beef, and pork dishes. Wood-burning rotisserie chicken is a specialty, as is the Parmesan ciabatta, an Italian bread served with all meals. **FYI:** Reservations recommended. **Open:** Sun–Mon 11:30am–9pm, Tues–Thurs 11:30am–10pm, Fri–Sat 11:30am–11pm. Closed some hols. **Prices:** Main courses $7–$15. Maj CC. 🚢 📷 VP &

CRESCENT CITY

Map page M-2, A1

Motel 🎞

≣ **Curly Redwood Lodge**, 701 Redwood Hwy S, Crescent City, CA 95531; tel 707/464-2137; fax 707/464-1655. US 101 to S end of Crescent City. Built from a single redwood tree; the wood exhibits an extremely rare curly grain. Across the highway from beach and harbor. **Rooms:** 36 rms. CI noon/CO 11am. Nonsmoking rms avail. **Amenities:** 🎀 Cable TV. No A/C. **Services:** 🛎 Outgoing telephone calls anytime, but incoming calls can be received only until 11pm. **Rates:** HS July–Aug $59–$64 S or D. Extra person $5. Children under 5 stay free. Lower rates off-season. Pking: Outdoor, free. Maj CC.

Attractions 💼

Battery Point Lighthouse; tel 707/464-3089. At Battery Point, foot of A St. Accessible only at low tide, this is one of the tallest lighthouses in the United States. Completed in 1892, it was considered the worst duty in the Lighthouse Station Service (later the US Coast Guard); between 1892 and 1937, there were 37 resignations and 26 transfer requests made from the lighthouse. During a storm in 1952, waves broke windows in the lantern room, 146 feet above sea level. The lighthouse was automated in 1953, and abandoned in 1975.

Now maintained as a museum, the lighthouse contains the restored keeper's room, an 1856 Lighthouse Service banjo clock, and items from the *Emidio,* the first commercial vessel torpedoed off the Pacific coast in World War II. **Open:** Apr–Sept, Wed–Sun 10am–4pm (tides permitting). $

Del Norte County Historical Society Museum, 577 H St; tel 707/464-3922. Local history exhibits contained in the former county jail building include the Fourth Order Fresnel Lens from the lighthouse at Battery Point (18 feet tall and weighing 5,000 pounds), as well as Native American and pioneer artifacts and displays. **Open:** Hours vary; phone ahead. $

Undersea World, 304 US 101S; tel 707/464-3522. Featured here is a 500,000-gallon tank containing a reef exhibit and a variety of undersea creatures; large shark exhibit; sea lion shows; tide pool. **Open:** May–Sept, daily 8am–8pm; Oct–Apr, daily 9am–5pm. Closed some hols. $$$

Lake Earl State Park, Old Mill Rd; tel 707/464/9533 or 445-6547. Located just north of town, Lake Earl is surrounded by 5,000 acres of wetlands, wooded hillsides, grassy meadows, sand dunes, and beaches. Numerous species of birds, including the Peregrine falcon and the rare Canada Aleutian goose, may be seen in the forests and wetlands. Coyotes, deer, and raccoons may be observed along the trails, while sea lions and harbor seals can be found along the coast. Spring and early summer bring spectacular displays of blooming wildflowers.

About 20 miles of hiking and bridle trails wind through a variety of landscapes. Fishing for salmon and steelhead is good in the Smith River; Cutthroat trout can be found in Lake Earl; and bass and crappie abound in Dead Lake.

Two primitive camping areas are available in the park. One is a horse camp with corrals (also available to hikers); the other includes 6 secluded walk-in sites near the parking lot. (**Note:** Potable water is *not* provided at these sites.) Camping fees are collected at Jedediah Smith and Del Norte campgrounds (see both). **Open:** Daily sunrise–sunset. Free.

Redwood National Park, 1111 2nd St; tel 707/464-6101 or toll free 800/423-6101. Established in 1968, Redwood National

Park comprises 113,000 acres of diverse topography, including 30 miles of coastline that are the domain of the towering coast redwood tree *Sequoia sempervirens*. The worlds tallest tree (367.8 feet), and the second, third, and sixth tallest trees are all within a mile of each other on Redwood Creek.

The park is made up of 5 separate areas: Hiouchi, Crescent City, Klamath, Prairie Creek, and Orick, each with its own distinctive trails, overlooks, and picnicking areas. Jedediah Smith Redwoods, Del Norte Coast Redwoods (see both), and Prairie Creek Redwoods state parks, each providing camping facilities, are located within the boundaries of the national park. The Crescent City and Redwood visitor centers are open year-round; Hioucho Information Center is open spring–fall. For detailed information contact the Superintendent at the above address. **Open:** Daily 24 hours. Free.

Del Norte Coast Redwoods State Park, 4241 Kings Valley Rd; tel 707/464-9533 or 458-3310. Located 7 miles south of town via US 101, this park is in the heart of California's rain forest, with an average annual rainfall of 100 inches. Nine hiking trails of varying difficulty traverse the park, leading through fields of wildflowers and stands of redwoods covering the slopes leading up from the rocky coastline.

Mill Creek Campground, situated in a lush, second-growth forest, contains 145 campsites, most able to accommodate trailers and RVs. A logging company occupied the site in the 1920s and 1930s; remants of the operation can be seen along some of the trails. **Open:** Daily 24 hours. $$

Jedediah Smith Redwoods State Park, 1375 Elk Valley Rd; tel 707/464-9533 or 445-6547. Named for famous mountain man Jedediah Strong Smith, this 10,000-acre park is reached by US 199 off of US 101. It consists mainly of old-growth coast redwood forest, and is bisected by the Smith River, one of the cleanest in the nation. Fishing, canoeing, and other water sports are popular in summer, and there are trails suited to hiking, cycling, and horseback riding.

There are more than 100 campsites, many along the river. Reservations are recommended Memorial Day weekend–Labor Day. There is a beautiful riverside picnic area as well. **Open:** Daily 24 hours. $$

CULVER CITY

Map page M-3, D2 (E of Santa Monica)

Hotels ⬛

Culver Hotel, 9400 Culver Blvd, Culver City, CA 90232; tel 310/838-3547; fax 310/836-7105. Historic hotel across from MGM Studios, built and once owned by John Wayne. Unrated.

Rooms: 48 rms and stes. Exec-level rms avail. CI 2pm/CO noon. Nonsmoking rms avail. **Amenities:** 🛁 ⬚ 🖥 📶 A/C, cable TV, refrig. Some units w/minibars, some w/terraces, some w/fireplaces, some w/Jacuzzis. **Services:** ✕ ☛ ⬜ ↵ Car-rental desk, babysitting. Complimentary continental breakfast. **Facilities:** 🔲100 🖳 🔥 2 rsts, 1 bar (w/entertainment), spa, beauty salon, washer/dryer. **Rates:** $69 S; $79 D; from $100 ste. Children under 12 stay free. Pking: Outdoor, free. Maj CC.

🚩🚩🚩 **Howard Johnson Plaza Hotel**, 5990 Green Valley Circle, Culver City, CA 90230 (Los Angeles Int'l Airport); tel 310/641-7740 or toll free 800/700-4656; fax 310/645-7045. Sepulveda exit off I-405. Small lobby and average rooms. **Rooms:** 200 rms. Exec-level rms avail. CI 3pm/CO noon. Express checkout avail. Nonsmoking rms avail. **Amenities:** 🛁 ⬚ A/C, cable TV w/movies. **Services:** ✕ 🖼 ⬜ ↵ ⬗ Car-rental desk, babysitting. **Facilities:** 🔥 🍴 🔲300 🖳 🔥 1 rst, 1 bar, spa, sauna, steam rm, whirlpool. **Rates:** $65 S or D. Extra person $10. Children under 18 stay free. Spec packages avail. Pking: Outdoor, free. Maj CC.

🚩🚩🚩 **Ramada Park International Airport**, 6333 Bristol Pkwy, Culver City, CA 90230 (Los Angeles Int'l Airport); tel 310/670-3200 or toll free 800/321-5575; fax 310/641-8925. Small business hotel near airport. Features expansive, marble-floored lobby and numerous comfortable sitting areas. **Rooms:** 260 rms and stes. CI 1pm/CO noon. Nonsmoking rms avail. **Amenities:** 🛁 A/C, cable TV, refrig. **Services:** 🍽 ☛ 🖼 ⬜ ↵ Car-rental desk, babysitting. **Facilities:** 🔥 🍴 🔲250 1 rst, 1 bar (w/entertainment), whirlpool, washer/dryer. **Rates:** HS May–Oct $85–$99 S; $95–$109 D; from $250 ste. Extra person $10. Children under 18 stay free. Lower rates off-season. Spec packages avail. Pking: Outdoor, free. Maj CC.

🚩🚩🚩 **Red Lion**, 6161 Centinela Ave, Culver City, CA 90230 (Los Angeles Int'l Airport); tel 310/649-1776 or toll free 800/547-8010; fax 310/547-8010. Well-kept commercial airport hotel with large, impressive lobby. **Rooms:** 368 rms, stes, and effic. Exec-level rms avail. CI 3pm/CO noon. Express checkout avail. Nonsmoking rms avail. **Amenities:** 🛁 ⬚ 📶 A/C, cable TV w/movies, refrig. 1 unit w/Jacuzzi. **Services:** ✕ ☛ 🖼 ⬜ ↵ Car-rental desk, social director, masseur, children's program. Free shopping shuttle to nearby mall. **Facilities:** 🔥 🍴 🔲600 🖳 🔥 2 rsts, 1 bar (w/entertainment), whirlpool, washer/dryer. **Rates:** $99 S or D; from $350 ste; from $325 effic. Children under 18 stay free. Spec packages avail. Pking: Indoor, free. Pking: Outdoor, free. Maj CC.

CUPERTINO

Map page M-2, D2 (S of Santa Clara)

Hotels 🛏

▦▦▦ **Courtyard by Marriott**, 10605 N Wolfe Rd, Cupertino, CA 95014; tel 408/252-9100 or toll free 800/321-2211; fax 408/252-0632. 10 mi N of San Jose. Wolfe Rd N exit off I-280; left at Pruneridge Rd; left to Courtyard. Located near major Silicon Valley companies; a popular hotel for businesspeople. **Rooms:** 149 rms and stes. Exec-level rms avail. CI 3pm/CO 1pm. Express checkout avail. Nonsmoking rms avail. **Amenities:** 🎞☕ A/C, satel TV w/movies. Some units w/terraces. Hot water dispenser in room for tea and coffee. **Services:** 🖈↺ Free hors d'oeuvres Monday–Thursday. "Courtyard Club" guests receive free weekday newspapers, local calls, and domestic faxes. **Facilities:** 🏋🏊♨ 1 rst, 1 bar, whirlpool, washer/dryer. Exercise room with Nautilus equipment in separate building. **Rates:** $95 S; $105 D; from $109 ste. Extra person $10. Higher rates for spec evnts/hols. Pking: Outdoor, free. Maj CC. Lower weekend rates.

▦▦▦ **Cupertino Inn**, 10889 N DeAnza Blvd, Cupertino, CA 95014; tel 408/996-7700 or toll free 800/222-4828; fax 408/257-0578. 6 mi N of San Jose. Cupertino/Sunny Ave exit off I-280 N; go right, make U-turn. Located near major Silicon Valley companies; a good choice for bargain weekends. Although right next to I-280, it somehow seems to be in its own world, thanks to a pleasant courtyard. **Rooms:** 125 rms and stes. CI 2pm/CO noon. Express checkout avail. Nonsmoking rms avail. **Amenities:** 🎞☕ A/C, satel TV w/movies, refrig, VCR, bathrobes. All units w/minibars, some w/fireplaces, some w/Jacuzzis. **Services:** 🍴 VP 🚗🖈↺ Twice-daily maid svce. Portable bar serves complimentary drinks and hors d'oeuvres from 5pm. **Facilities:** 🏋♨ Whirlpool. **Rates (BB):** $115–$126 S; $130–$141 D; from $135 ste. Extra person $15. Children under 18 stay free. Spec packages avail. Pking: Outdoor, free. Maj CC. Weekend discounts.

Restaurant 🍴

Ⓢ ★ **Armadillo Willy's**, 10235 S De Anza Blvd, Cupertino; tel 408/252-7427. Calif 9 exit off I-280. **Barbecue/Burgers.** Popular eatery known for its barbecued ribs. Chili, Cajun hot links, and charbroiled chicken served. Country-western music plays in background. Also at: 1031 N San Antonio Rd, Los Altos (415/941-2922); 2624 Homestead Rd, Santa Clara (408/247-1100); 995 Saratoga Ave, San Jose (408/255-RIBS); 878 Blossom Hill Rd, San Jose (408/244-RIBS). **FYI:** Reservations not accepted.

Beer and wine only. **Open:** Mon–Fri 11am–10pm, Sat noon–10pm, Sun noon–9pm. Closed some hols. **Prices:** Main courses $7.50–$13.95. Maj CC. 🍽 📺 ♿

DANA POINT

Map page M-3, E2 (S of Laguna Beach)

Hotel 🛏

▦▦▦ **Dana Point Hilton—All-Suite Inn**, 34402 Pacific Coast Hwy, Dana Point, CA 92629; tel 714/661-1100 or toll free 800/634-4586; fax 714/489-0628. Great location across the street from the beach. Convenient access to marina, shopping center, and beach parks. **Rooms:** 197 stes. Exec-level rms avail. CI 4pm/CO noon. Express checkout avail. Nonsmoking rms avail. Spacious rooms with views of the ocean. **Amenities:** 🎞☕ A/C, cable TV w/movies, refrig, VCR, shoe polisher. All units w/minibars, all w/terraces, some w/fireplaces, some w/Jacuzzis. **Services:** ✕🔑 VP 🖈↺ Social director, masseur, children's program. **Facilities:** 🏋🚴♨ 📻 💻♿ 1 rst, 2 bars (1 w/entertainment), board surfing, games rm, sauna, whirlpool. **Rates (CP):** HS June 16–Sept 15 from $135 ste. Extra person $15. Children under 18 stay free. Min stay spec evnts. Lower rates off-season. Spec packages avail. Pking: Indoor, $3. Maj CC.

Inn

▦▦▦ **Blue Lantern Inn**, 34343 St of the Blue Lantern, Dana Point, CA 92629; tel 714/661-1304; fax 714/496-1483. Pacific Coast Hwy N exit off I-5. With ocean views from its promontory perch, the inn looks as if it were on Cape Cod. **Rooms:** 29 rms and stes. CI 3pm/CO noon. Beautifully decorated—cute and cozy. **Amenities:** 🎞☕ A/C, cable TV, refrig, shoe polisher, bathrobes. Some units w/terraces, all w/fireplaces, all w/Jacuzzis. **Services:** ✕🔑 VP🖈↺ Twice-daily maid svce, car-rental desk, masseur. Personalized service. **Facilities:** 🚴 🏋♨ ♿ Washer/dryer. **Rates:** $135–$350 S or D; from $350 ste. Extra person $15. Children under 5 stay free. Spec packages avail. Pking: Outdoor, free. Ltd CC.

Resorts

▦▦▦ **Dana Point Resort**, 25135 Park Lantern, Dana Point, CA 92629; tel 714/661-5000 or toll free 800/533-9748; fax 714/661-5358. 70 mi S of Los Angeles. Pacific Coast Hwy N exit off I-5 (San Diego); left at Dana Harbor Dr; right onto Park Lantern. 42 acres. Lovely, picturesque property with stunning ocean views beyond well-maintained lawns. Perched on a precipice, within walking distance of the harbor, beach, and shops. Spacious and colorful, with red roof and white clapboard. **Rooms:** 348 rms and stes. Exec-level rms avail. CI 3pm/CO noon. Express checkout avail. Nonsmoking rms avail. New, clean and spacious, decorated with the colors of a California sunset. Large bathrooms and nice balconies. **Amenities:** 🛗 🌡 🍴 A/C, cable TV w/movies, bathrobes. All units w/minibars, some w/terraces, 1 w/Jacuzzi. **Services:** ✕ 🗝 VP 🖥 🛎 Twice-daily maid svce, car-rental desk, social director, masseur, children's program, babysitting. Very service-oriented staff. **Facilities:** 🛗 🚲 📺 🏌 🏊 🖥 ⚐ 1 rst, 2 bars (1 w/entertainment), 1 beach (ocean), lifeguard, games rm, lawn games, spa, sauna, steam rm, whirlpool, playground. Restaurant has ocean views. **Rates:** $170–$280 S or D; from $300 ste. Extra person $20. Children under 16 stay free. Spec packages avail. Pking: Indoor/outdoor, free. Maj CC.

≣≣≣≣ **The Ritz-Carlton Laguna Niguel**, 33533 Ritz-Carlton Dr, Dana Point, CA 92629 (Monarch Beach); tel 714/240-2000 or toll free 800/287-2706; fax 714/240-1061. 17 mi S of Newport Beach. 18 acres. Old World meets Pacific Rim at this majestic setting on a 150-foot-high bluff above a 2-mile-long beach. Glorious gardens, terraces, and fountained patios outdoors; silk-lined lobby, limestone fireplace, vaulted ceilings, and more than a 1,000 potted plants indoors. But some guests may find the palatial airs out of keeping with the location. **Rooms:** 393 rms and stes. Exec-level rms avail. CI 3pm/CO noon. Express checkout avail. Nonsmoking rms avail. Above-average dimensions. Italian marble bathrooms with double vanities. Sumptuous furnishings and fabrics, though in some cases rooms are overfurnished to the point of being cramped. **Amenities:** 🛗 🌡 🍴 A/C, cable TV, refrig, voice mail, in-rm safe, shoe polisher, bathrobes. All units w/minibars, all w/terraces, some w/fireplaces. **Services:** 🍽 🗝 VP 🚐 🖥 ⚐ Twice-daily maid svce, car-rental desk, masseur, children's program, babysitting. Regular shuttle to and from beach and golf course. Room service on Rosenthal china. 2 staffers for every room; generally alert response to requests (and the maids still take time to insert a bookmark at the appropriate place in *TV Guide*). **Facilities:** 🛗 ⛳18 🏊 ⚓4 🏌 600 🖥 🌡 4 rsts (*see also* "Restaurants" below), 5 bars (2 w/entertainment), 1 beach (ocean), lifeguard, games rm, lawn games, sauna, steam rm, whirlpool, beauty salon, day-care ctr. 24-hour business center. First-rate sports facilities; public (not private) golf course designed by Robert Trent Jones II. Smart fitness center with unisex steam rooms. Ritz-Carlton Club in penthouse. Ravishing arched lounge for sunset watching; clubby library lounge for nightcaps. **Rates:** $215–$475 S or D; from $500 ste. Children under 18 stay free. Min stay spec evnts. Spec packages avail. Pking: Indoor/outdoor, $15. Maj CC. Lower rates for rooms facing courtyards, not coastline.

Restaurant 🍴

The Dining Room, in the Ritz-Carlton Laguna Niguel, 33533 Ritz-Carlton Dr, Dana Point (Monarch Beach); tel 714/240-2000. 2 mi N of Dana Point. Take Crown Valley Pkwy exit from San Diego Fwy west to Pacific Coast Hwy. **Continental/French.** Serious dining and knowledgeable waiters, with dishes that generally live up to their lofty titles. The gracious setting features French provincial chandeliers and European genre paintings. Specialties include seared ahi tuna, pyramid of salmon with truffles and golden tomato emulsion, breast of Petaluma chicken with couscous and curry sauce, and orange chocolate fondant with blood orange sauce. Excellent wine list. **FYI:** Reservations recommended. Jacket required. **Open:** Tues–Sun 6–10pm. **Prices:** PF dinner $35–$65. Maj CC. ♥ VP 🌡

DAVIS
Map page M-2, C2

Hotel 🏨

≣≣ **Ramada Inn–Davis**, 110 F St, Davis, CA 95616; tel 916/753-3600 or toll free 800/753-0035. Richards Blvd exit off I-80. Only hotel in university town. Pleasant town atmosphere, safe neighborhood. **Rooms:** 135 rms and stes. CI 3pm/CO noon. Nonsmoking rms avail. Rather basic. **Amenities:** 🛗 🌡 A/C, cable TV w/movies. Some units w/terraces, 1 w/Jacuzzi. VCR and refrigerator available for rent. **Services:** 🖥 ⚐ Car-rental desk. Group check-in available. **Facilities:** 🛗 130 🌡 1 rst, 1 bar. Pool heated April–November. Use of Davis Athletic Club. **Rates:** HS Mar–Oct $59–$85 S; $69–$95 D; from $85 ste. Extra person $10. Children under 16 stay free. Min stay spec evnts. Lower rates off-season. Higher rates for spec evnts/hols. MAP rates avail. Spec packages avail. Pking: Outdoor, free. Maj CC. Business rate includes voucher for free complete breakfast at adjacent restaurant.

DEATH VALLEY
Map page M-3, C3

Hotel 🏨

≣≣≣≣ **Furnace Creek Inn Resort**, Calif 190, PO Box 187, Death Valley, CA 92328; tel 619/786-2345; fax 619/786-2307. 140 mi W of Las Vegas. Beautiful Spanish-Moorish hotel built of stone and adobe, with arched entries, abundant Spanish tile and beamed ceilings. Surrounded by flower gardens, palm trees, and a stream that feeds 3 koi ponds. **Rooms:** 70 rms and stes. CI

4pm/CO noon. Express checkout avail. Nonsmoking rms avail. Elegantly appointed, with adobe walls, tiled fireplaces, and overstuffed furniture. **Amenities:** 🔒 💧 A/C, cable TV w/movies. Some units w/minibars, some w/terraces, some w/fireplaces, some w/Jacuzzis. **Services:** VP 🚐 🛍 ↺ **Facilities:** 🏊 🏌 ⛳ ♿ 2 rsts, 2 bars (1 w/entertainment), lifeguard, games rm, spa. Tranquil sitting room off lobby has clubby atmosphere with couches, a grand piano, book-filled shelves, and floral arrangements. Inn dining room has formal atmosphere with views of Death Valley. L'Ottimos Italian Restaurant has an extensive wine list. Horseback riding stables and golf located nearby. **Rates (MAP):** $225 S; $275 D; from $375 ste. Extra person $30. Children under 5 stay free. Pking: Outdoor, free. Maj CC.

Motels

≣≣ Furnace Creek Ranch Resort, Calif 190, PO Box 187, Death Valley, CA 92328; tel 619/786-2345; fax 619/786-2514. 140 mi W of Las Vegas. Weathered buildings, corrals, stables, and western artifacts form the backdrop for this rambling ranch, set in a lush oasis. **Rooms:** 224 rms. CI 4pm/CO noon. Express checkout avail. Nonsmoking rms avail. Older rooms in duplex cabins have wood paneling, brown carpeting, wooden tables, and chairs. The more modern "deluxe" and "park view" rooms in motel have comfortable furnishings, patios, and balconies. **Amenities:** 🔒 A/C, satel TV, refrig. Some units w/terraces. **Services:** 🚐 ↺ ⛷ **Facilities:** 🏊 ▶18 🏌 ♿ 3 rsts, 3 bars (1 w/entertainment), washer/dryer. Steakhouse serves up huge portions of mostly American fare. Saloon has western atmosphere, with Stetsons and spurs on the walls and Randy Travis on the jukebox. **Rates:** $70–$120 S or D. Extra person $14. Children under 18 stay free. Pking: Outdoor, free. Maj CC.

≣≣ Stove Pipe Wells Village, Calif 190, Death Valley, CA 92328; tel 619/786-2387; fax 619/786-2389. 23 miles from Furnace Creek. Lobby overlooks pool and is decorated with wooden tables and chairs, and a handmade Indian rug. The wall-sized map of Death Valley is handy for travelers. **Rooms:** 83 rms. CI 3pm/CO 11am. Nonsmoking rms avail. Older, motel-style rooms have a rustic feel, with brown carpeting and bedspreads, and wooden armchairs. Western landscapes adorn the walls. **Amenities:** A/C. No phone or TV. **Services:** 🚐 ↺ ⛷ Children's program. **Facilities:** 🏊 ♿ 1 rst, 1 bar, washer/dryer. Bar is a western-style saloon. **Rates:** $58–$75 S or D. Extra person $11. Children under 12 stay free. Pking: Outdoor, free. Ltd CC.

DEATH VALLEY NATIONAL PARK

Map page M-3, B3 to C3

Long the unchallenged domain of the Panamint tribe, an offshoot of the Shoshone, Death Valley is one of the most enthralling natural wonders in the United States. From atop the rocky platform symbolically named **Dante's View,** at the edge of a dizzying sheer drop of 5,120 feet, sprawls in blinding clarity the vast expanse of the salt flats and the lowest point on the continent, 282 feet below sea level. On the other side of the **Devil's Golf Course** and its weird salt formations, the eternal snows of Mt Whitney rise in contrast with sun-blasted rocks and sand dunes.

The 2-billion-year-old valley, once the bed of an Ice Age sea, is home to a surprising array of animal life. More than 30 species of mammal, including coyote, porcupine, and kangaroo rat, survive here, along with dozens of insects, reptile species, and birds, most notably vultures and crows. Certain kinds of small fish can be found nowhere on earth except in the scanty waters of Salt Creek or the palm groves of Furnace Creek.

A national monument since 1933, the region was upgraded in 1994 to national park status and expanded to 3.3 million acres, making it the largest national park outside Alaska. Death Valley was named when a group of pioneers died of thirst and exhaustion while attempting to cross it on Christmas Day, 1849. (When visiting Death Valley it is extremely important to carry plenty of water—an untrained person could die of dehydration in 3 hours in this climate.)

Two excellent highways run north–south and east–west through the park. Only the main roads are patrolled regularly; it can be very dangerous to venture off of them in summer. The **visitor center** at Furnace Creek provides information, directions, and presents an orientation film (tel 619/786-2331). Following are some highlights of the monument.

Scotty's Castle, 52 miles NW of Furnace Creek on Calif 190 and Grapevine Rd. Wealthy Chicago businessman Albert Johnson and his friend, Walter Scotty, a professional cowboy from the Buffalo Bill troupe, built this sumptuously decorated and improbable castle in the Hollywood Hispano-Moorish style between 1922 and 1931. Guided tours daily, on the hour.

Artists Drive, 11 miles S of Furnace Creek. A narrow, one-way road amid splendid gorges and multicolored landscapes. A treat for color photographers.

Devil's Golf Course, 8 miles S of Furnace Creek. A vast salt flat studded with 20-inch-high salt rocks that lives up to its name.

Golden Canyon, 4 miles S of Furnace Creek. This half-mile path cuts through splendid rock formations of gold, bright red, ochre, and bronze. A photographer's dream.

DEL MAR

Map page M-3, E3

Hotels 🛏

☰☰☰ Del Mar Hilton, 15575 Jimmy Durante Blvd, Del Mar, CA 92014; tel 619/792-5200 or toll free 800/345-6565; fax 619/792-0353. 17 mi N of San Diego. Via de la Valle exit off I-5; go west. Located across from the Del Mar Race Track and a mile from the beach, this is an elegant hotel in every respect. Grounds and restrooms are sparkling clean. **Rooms:** 245 rms and stes. CI 4pm/CO noon. Express checkout avail. Nonsmoking rms avail. **Amenities:** 🛏 🕭 🍴 A/C, cable TV w/movies, shoe polisher. All units w/minibars, all w/terraces, some w/Jacuzzis. **Services:** ✗ ☎ VP 🚗 🖂 🛎 Car-rental desk, children's program, babysitting. **Facilities:** 🔥 🖼 ♿ 2 rsts, 2 bars (1 w/entertainment), whirlpool. Next door is a 59-tee driving range and tennis courts, all lighted, as well as a miniature golf course and arcade. **Rates:** HS July 25–Sept 15 $105–$150 S; $120–$165 D; from $225 ste. Extra person $15. Children under 18 stay free. Min stay spec evnts. Lower rates off-season. Spec packages avail. Pking: Outdoor, free. Maj CC.

L'Auberge Del Mar, 1540 Camino del Mar, Del Mar, CA 92014; tel 619/259-1515 or toll free 800/553-1336; fax 619/755-4940. 15 mi N of San Diego. Del Mar Heights Rd exit off I-5; go west, then right on Camino del Mar. This hotel has a jewel of a setting, located on a hill just above a popular swimming and surfing beach. Also convenient to shops and restaurants downtown. Architecture features a shingled roof with gables. Slated for much-needed refurbishment. Unrated. **Rooms:** 123 rms and stes. CI 4pm/CO noon. Nonsmoking rms avail. Rooms are large; top-floor rooms have high ceilings. **Amenities:** 🛏 🕭 🍴 A/C, cable TV w/movies, refrig, shoe polisher. All units w/minibars, all w/terraces, some w/Jacuzzis. **Services:** ✗ ☎ VP 🚗 🖂 🛎 Car-rental desk, masseur, babysitting. **Facilities:** 🔥 🚴 📷 🎾 🖼 🎱 ♿ 1 rst, 1 bar (w/entertainment), spa, sauna, steam rm, whirlpool, beauty salon. The Jimmy Durante pub is a popular hangout after the races at nearby Del Mar Racetrack. Exercise bikes, stair machines, and free weights are available at the outdoor sports pavilion; personal trainer available by appointment. **Rates:** HS June–Sept $179–$249 S or D; from $400 ste. Extra person $10. Children under 18 stay free. Lower rates off-season. Spec packages avail. Pking: Indoor/outdoor, $5–$8. Maj CC.

Inns

☰☰☰ Del Mar Inn, 720 Camino del Mar, Del Mar, CA 92014; tel 619/755-9765 or toll free 800/451-4515; fax 619/792-8196. 17 mi N of San Diego. Del Mar Heights Rd exit off I-5; west on Del Mar Heights Rd, north on Camino del Mar, U-turn at 9th St. 1.5 acres. A Charming, cozy inn located near the ocean and Del Mar Village. An exceptional flower garden and grounds add the elegance of old England. **Rooms:** 80 rms and stes. CI 2pm/CO 2pm. **Amenities:** 🛏 A/C, TV w/movies. Some units w/terraces. **Services:** ✗ 🚗 🖂 🛎 Babysitting, afternoon tea served. **Facilities:** 🔥 🖼 ♿ Whirlpool, washer/dryer, guest lounge. **Rates (CP):** HS June 15–Labor Day $85–$115 S or D; from $90 ste. Extra person $4. Children under 16 stay free. Lower rates off-season. Higher rates for spec evnts/hols. Spec packages avail. Pking: Outdoor, free. Ltd CC.

☰☰☰ Rock Haus Bed & Breakfast Inn, 410 15th St, Del Mar, CA 92014; tel 619/481-3764. 18 mi N of San Diego. Del Mar Heights Rd exit off I-5; west to Camino Del Mar, north to 15th St. Within walking distance of the beach, Del Mar Village, and shops and restaurants; a famous romantic retreat. Unsuitable for children under 13. **Rooms:** 10 rms (6 w/shared bath). CI 2pm/CO 11am. No smoking. Each room is different. Some have ocean views, and the Huntsman room has a fireplace. **Amenities:** 🛏 🕭 No A/C or TV. 1 unit w/fireplace. **Services:** Afternoon tea served. **Facilities:** 🖼 Guest lounge. Breakfast area with stunning view of ocean can be set up for business meetings. **Rates (CP):** HS July–Sept $90–$100 S or D w/shared bath, $120–$150 S or D w/private bath. Min stay HS. Lower rates off-season. Spec packages avail. Pking: Outdoor, free. Ltd CC.

Restaurants 🍴

Cilantros, 3702 Via de la Valle, Del Mar; tel 619/259-8777. 22 mi N of San Diego. Via de la Valle exit off I-5. **Southwestern.** Southwestern decor, with whitewashed tables, wrought-iron accents, etched stone pillars, and cactus centerpieces. Choices include spit-roasted chicken, shark fajitas, and tapas bar. **FYI:** Reservations recommended. Children's menu. Dress code. **Open:** HS May–Sept lunch daily 11:30am–2:30pm; dinner Sun–Thurs 5–10pm, Fri–Sat 5–10:30pm; brunch Sun 11:30am–2:30pm. Reduced hours off-season. Closed some hols. **Prices:** Main courses $12.95–$21.25. Maj CC. VP ♿

⑤ Il Fornaio Cucina Italiana, in Del Mar Plaza, 1555 Camino Del Mar, Del Mar; tel 619/755-8876. 20 mi N of San Diego. Del Mar Heights Rd exit off I-5. **Italian.** With a spectacular ocean view, frescoed walls, and a heated patio where you can watch the sunset, this lovely Italian restaurant has a sophisticated feel. Food choices include grilled eggplant with goat cheese and sun-dried tomatoes; pasta stuffed with lobster, ricotta cheese, leeks, and lemon cream; and for dessert, ricotta cheesecake. **FYI:** Reservations recommended. Dress code. **Open:** Lunch daily 11:30am–3:30pm; dinner daily 5–11pm; brunch Sat 11am–3pm, Sun 10am–3pm. Closed some hols. **Prices:** Main courses $7.95–$18.50. Maj CC. 🍴 🖼 VP 🚹

Pacifica Del Mar, in Del Mar Plaza, 1555 Camino Del Mar, Del Mar; tel 619/792-0476. 20 mi N of San Diego. Del Mar Heights Rd exit off I-5. **Californian/Pacific Rim.** Newly refurbished bar just off the stylish dining room has become a gathering place for Del Mar locals. Cozy restaurant features an aquarium in the main salon, a glass-enclosed patio with heaters, and a lovely ocean view. Menu includes corn chowder with chicken, wok-seared duck salad, and sashimi ahi tempura. **FYI:** Reservations recommended. Dress code. **Open:** Lunch daily 11am–4pm; dinner daily 4–10:30pm; brunch Sun 9am–2pm. **Prices:** Main courses $11.80–$20.60; PF dinner $12.80–$15.80. Maj CC. 🍴 🖼 ❤ VP 🚹

Spices Thai Cafe, in Piazza Carmel, 3810 Carmel Valley Rd, Del Mar; tel 619/259-0891. 19 mi N of San Diego. Carmel Valley Rd exit off I-5. **Thai/Vegetarian.** A modest restaurant located in a shopping center, with quite pleasant ambience. Decorated with pink walls and black lacquer furniture; a nice bar lines one side of the room. Menu highlights include eggplant with chile sauce; spicy duck with ginger, chile, and black bean sauce; and pineapple curry. Many vegetarian dishes available. **FYI:** Reservations not accepted. Beer and wine only. **Open:** Lunch daily 11am–3pm; dinner daily 3–10pm. Closed some hols. **Prices:** Main courses $6.95–$14.95. Maj CC. 🚹

DESERT HOT SPRINGS

Map page M-3, D3 (N of Palm Springs)

Hotel 🏨

🛏 **Desert Hot Springs Spa Hotel**, 10-805 Palm Dr, Desert Hot Springs, CA 92240; tel 619/329-6495 or toll free 800/808-7727, 800/843-6053 in CA; fax 619/329-6915. Palm Dr exit off I-10. The San Jacinto and San Gorgonio peaks provide a dramatic backdrop for the spa's 7 mineral pools. **Rooms:** 50 rms and stes. CI 3pm/CO 11am. Some rooms and corridors are in need of renovation. **Amenities:** 🛠 A/C, cable TV, shoe polisher. All units w/terraces. **Services:** ✗ 🛎 Masseur. **Facilities:** 🏋 1 rst, 1 bar, lifeguard, lawn games, spa, sauna, whirlpool, beauty salon. **Rates:** HS Dec 24–May $79–$99 S or D; from $109 ste. Extra person $10. Children under 12 stay free. Min stay wknds. Lower rates off-season. Higher rates for spec evnts/hols. Spec packages avail. Pking: Outdoor, free. Maj CC.

Resort

🏨🏨🏨 **Two Bunch Palms Resort & Spa**, 67-425 Two Bunch Palms Trail, Desert Hot Springs, CA 92240; tel 619/329-8791 or toll free 800/472-4334; fax 619/329-1317. Palm Dr exit off I-10. 50 acres. This posh yet intimate spa resort, renowned for its mineral waters, is truly an oasis in the desert. Widely considered one of the world's best spas. **Rooms:** 40 rms, stes, and effic; 4 ctges/villas. CI 3pm/CO noon. Nonsmoking rms avail. One- and 2-bedroom villas are decorated with antiques and contemporary touches. **Amenities:** 🛠 🛁 📺 🍷 A/C, cable TV, refrig. All units w/terraces, some w/fireplaces, some w/Jacuzzis. Many cottages have wet bars. **Services:** Masseur. Excellent staff. **Facilities:** 🏋 🚲 ⛳ 🎾 🍴 🚹 1 rst, 1 bar (w/entertainment), spa, sauna, steam rm, whirlpool, washer/dryer. Mud-bath complex, hot mineral pool, 2 lakes. **Rates (CP):** $110–$232 S or D; from $252 ste; from $286 effic; from $360 ctge/villa. Min stay. Pking: Outdoor, free. Maj CC.

Attraction 🏛

Cabot's Old Indian Pueblo Museum, 67616 East Desert View; tel 619/329-7610. A designated California Point of Historic Interest, this 35-room mansion serves as a showcase of Native American culture. Guided tours take in exhibits of Native American history, art, and artifacts, including a 43-foot Indian head carved out of redwood. **Open:** Sept–June, Wed–Sun 10am–4pm; July–Aug phone for hours. $

DIAMOND BAR

Map page M-3, D2 (N of Anaheim)

Hotel 🏨

🏨🏨🏨 **Radisson Inn Diamond Bar**, 21725 E Gateway Dr, Diamond Bar, CA 91765; tel 909/860-5440 or toll free 800/333-3333; fax 909/860-8224. Grand Ave S exit off I-60; 1 block S to Golden Springs; right ½ mi. A full-service hotel especially suited for corporate meetings. **Rooms:** 175 rms and stes. Exec-level rms avail. CI 3pm/CO noon. Express checkout avail. Nonsmoking rms avail. "Green" suites, with filtered air and hypo-allergenic soaps and shampoos, are available. **Amenities:** 🛠 🛁 A/C, cable TV w/movies. Some units w/terraces. **Services:** ✗ 🚐 🛄 🛎 🖐 Car-rental desk, masseur. **Facilities:** 🏋 🏊 🖥 🚹 1 rst, 1 bar, whirlpool. Complimentary access to nearby health club. **Rates:** $69 S; $79 D; from $79 ste. Extra person $10. Children under 17 stay free. Spec packages avail. Pking: Outdoor, free. Maj CC.

DISNEYLAND

See Anaheim

DUNSMUIR

Map page M-2, A2

Motels 🖼

▤ **Cedar Lodge Motel**, 4201 Dunsmuir Ave, Dunsmuir, CA 96025; tel 916/235-4331. Dunsmuir/Siskiyou exit off I-5; go ½ mi west. Guests enjoy the largest exotic aviary in northern California, featuring endangered species of parrots. **Rooms:** 13 rms and stes. CI noon/CO 11am. Nonsmoking rms avail. **Amenities:** 🛗 🖀 A/C, cable TV. Some units w/terraces. **Services:** ⌦ **Facilities:** 🛐 Sport fishing for 17- to 20-inch trout in the Sacramento River, just outside your door. **Rates:** HS May–Nov $33–$36 S; $37–$60 D; from $60 ste. Extra person $4. Lower rates off-season. Pking: Outdoor, free. Maj CC.

▤▤▤ **Railroad Park Resort–Caboose Motel**, 100 Railroad Park Rd, Dunsmuir, CA 96025; tel 916/235-4440 or toll free 800/974-RAIL; fax 916/235-4470. Railroad Park Rd exit off I-5; 1 mi S of Dunsmuir. A unique concept: a motel housed in superbly restored cabooses and a boxcar from famous American railroads, on tracks surrounded by spectacular Castle Crags State Park. **Rooms:** 23 rms; 4 ctges/villas. CI noon/CO 11am. Nonsmoking rms avail. **Amenities:** 🛗 ⚓ 🖀 🍽 A/C, satel TV w/movies, refrig. Some units w/terraces. **Services:** 🚗 ⌦ Wonderful staff. **Facilities:** 🛐 🛗 🛐 & 1 rst, 1 bar (w/entertainment), whirlpool, washer/dryer. Boxcar with lift for travelers with disabilities. **Rates:** HS May–Sept $60–$85 S; $65–$85 D; from $65 ctge/villa. Extra person $5. Lower rates off-season. Spec packages avail. Pking: Outdoor, free. Maj CC.

Resort

▤▤ **Cave Springs**, 4727 Dunsmuir Ave, Dunsmuir, CA 96025; tel 916/235-2721. Dunsmuir-Siskiyou exit off I-5; go west. 15 acres. Affable hosts Louie and Belinda Dewey work hard to ensure that a good time is had by all at this low-key resort, with its forested grounds and 20-inch trout just waiting to be caught in the restored Sacramento River that borders the property. **Rooms:** 10 rms, stes, and effic; 15 ctges/villas. CI 2pm/CO 11am. Nonsmoking rms avail. Intriguing mix of motel rooms, suites, cabins, and stationary mobile homes. Space to park RV. **Amenities:** 🛗 ⚓ 🖀 A/C, cable TV w/movies, refrig, VCR. All units w/terraces. The 1-bedroom cabins each have a 2-burner

stove. The 2-bedroom cabins each have a 3-burner stove with oven. **Services:** 🚗 ⌦ ⌦ Daily maid service is not included in the cabin rates, but fresh linen is furnished. **Facilities:** 🛗 🛐 Whirlpool, playground, washer/dryer. **Rates:** HS May–Sept/ Nov–Apr $33–$49 S; $33–$60 D; from $55 ste; from $33 effic; from $33 ctge/villa. Extra person $3. Children under 2 stay free. Min stay spec evnts. Lower rates off-season. Pking: Outdoor, free. Maj CC. Cabins and mobile homes can be rented by the week. Cabin rates discounted 25% September 21–June 9.

EDWARDS

Map page M-3, D2

Attraction 🖼

NASA Dryden Flight Research Center, Rosamond Blvd exit off Calif 14; tel 805/258-3449. Located at Edwards Air Force Base. NASA's primary institution for flight research, Dryden has been involved in modern flight testing from the days of the *X-1*, the first aircraft to break the sound barrier, to the early developmental research on the space shuttle. Two guided, 90-minute tours begin with a film, after which guests are escorted through a hangar where aircraft can be viewed. The walking portion of the tour is within a controlled-access area. Advance reservations are required. **Open:** Visitor center, Mon–Fri 7:45am–3:45pm; tours Mon–Fri 10:15am and 1:15pm. Closed some hols and shuttle landing days. Free.

EL CAJON

Map page M-3, E3 (E of La Mesa)

Motels 🖼

▤▤▤ **Best Western Continental Inn**, 650 N Mollison Ave, El Cajon, CA 92021; tel 619/442-0601 or toll free 800/88-BEST-1; fax 619/442-0152. 18 mi E of San Diego. Mollison Ave exit off I-8. Very clean, with brand-new 3-story building. **Rooms:** 97 rms, stes, and effic. CI 2pm/CO 11am. Nonsmoking rms avail. Nicely decorated in blue and beige. **Amenities:** 🛗 A/C, cable TV, refrig. Some units w/minibars, some w/terraces, some w/Jacuzzis. Some rooms have wet bars. **Services:** Coffee in lobby. Staff will arrange for airport shuttle. **Facilities:** 🛗 🛐 & Whirlpool, washer/dryer. **Rates (CP):** HS June 15–Sept 12 $46–$90 S; $49–$90 D; from $65 ste; from $55 effic. Extra person $5. Children under 12 stay free. Lower rates off-season. Pking: Outdoor, free. Maj CC.

≣≣ **Plaza International Inn**, 683 N Mollison Ave, El Cajon, CA 92021; tel 619/442-0973. 18 mi NE of San Diego. Mollison Ave exit off I-8. Exterior needs some maintenance, but the pool area is clean and well kept. **Rooms:** 60 rms and effic. CI 3pm/CO 11am. Nonsmoking rms avail. Many rooms have been refurbished and are attractively decorated. **Amenities:** 🛏 🖵 A/C, cable TV, refrig. **Services:** 🔑 ⌧ Exceptionally helpful staff. **Facilities:** 🔒 Sauna, whirlpool. Denny's restaurant next door. **Rates:** $29–$35 S; $35–$39 D. Pking: Outdoor, free. Maj CC. Efficiencies available by the week only, from $195/week.

≣ **Super 8 Motel**, 588 N Mollison Ave, El Cajon, CA 92021; tel 619/579-1144 or toll free 800/800-8000; fax 619/579-1787. 18 mi NE of San Diego, exit Mollison off I-8. South on Mollison ½ block. The lobby (behind a fast-food restaurant) can be difficult to locate, but the staff is welcoming. **Rooms:** 40 rms. CI 11am/CO 11am. Nonsmoking rms avail. Rooms are adequate but need improved security. **Amenities:** 🛏 A/C, cable TV w/movies, refrig. **Services:** ⌧ **Facilities:** 🔒 🏊 Whirlpool. **Rates (CP):** HS June–Nov $30–$35 S; $35–$45 D. Extra person $5. Children under 12 stay free. Lower rates off-season. Higher rates for spec evnts/hols. Pking: Outdoor, free. Maj CC.

Resort

≣≣≣ **Singing Hills Country Club & Lodge**, 3007 Dehesa Rd, El Cajon, CA 92019; tel 619/442-3425 or toll free 800/457-5568; fax 619/442-9574. Exit 2nd Ave off I-8. 720 acres. Peaceful resort with beautiful rustic grounds. **Rooms:** 102 rms and stes. CI 4pm/CO 1:30pm. Rooms are nicely coordinated thanks to ongoing renovation. **Amenities:** 🛏 🖵 A/C, satel TV, refrig. All units w/terraces. Some rooms have coffeemakers and hair dryers. **Services:** 🔑 🚗 ⌧ Use of fax machine available. VCR rentals. **Facilities:** 🔒 ▶ 54 🍴 🏊 🏌 1 rst, 1 bar (w/entertainment), whirlpool, washer/dryer. Golf and tennis and pros available for lessons. **Rates:** $77–$196 S; $82–$196 D; from $104 ste. Extra person $12. Children under 10 stay free. Spec packages avail. Pking: Outdoor, free. Maj CC.

EL CENTRO
Map page M-3, E4

See also **Calexico, Holtville**

Hotels 🛏

≣≣ **Ramada Inn**, 1455 Ocotillo Dr, El Centro, CA 92243; tel 619/352-5152 or toll free 800/272-6232; fax 619/337-1567. Imperial Ave exit off I-8; 1 mi N to Ocotillo Dr. Popular with business travelers. **Rooms:** 147 rms. CI 3pm/CO noon. Non-

smoking rms avail. **Amenities:** 🛏 🖵 A/C, cable TV w/movies. **Services:** 🍴 🚗 ⌧ ⌧ **Facilities:** 🔒 🍴 🖵 🏌 1 rst, 1 bar. **Rates:** $50 S; $56 D; from $75 ste. Extra person $6. Children under 17 stay free. Spec packages avail. Pking: Outdoor, free. Ltd CC.

≣≣ **Vacation Inn**, 2000 Cottonwood Circle, El Centro, CA 92243; tel 619/352-9523 or toll free 800/328-6289; fax 619/353-7620. Imperial Ave exit off I-8. Everything for the corporate and leisure traveler. **Rooms:** 189 rms. CI 3pm/CO noon. Nonsmoking rms avail. Kitchenettes available. **Amenities:** 🛏 🖵 A/C, cable TV w/movies. **Services:** ✗ ⌧ ⌧ **Facilities:** 🔒 🍴 🏌 1 rst, 1 bar, whirlpool, washer/dryer. RV park on-site. **Rates:** $49 S; $51–$54 D. Extra person $5. Children under 17 stay free. Pking: Outdoor, free. Maj CC.

Motels

≣≣ **El Dorado Motel**, 1464 Adams Ave, El Centro, CA 92243 (Downtown); tel 619/352-7333 or toll free 800/874-5532. Imperial Ave exit off I-8; 1 mi N to Adams Ave. Small but friendly motel with lots of extras. **Rooms:** 72 rms and effic. CI noon/CO noon. Nonsmoking rms avail. Many have kitchenettes. **Amenities:** 🛏 A/C, cable TV w/movies. Refrigerators available at no extra charge. Many rooms have VCRs and free HBO. **Services:** 🚗 ⌧ ⌧ Free local phone calls; free videos. Complimentary shuttle to bus station. **Facilities:** 🔒 🖵 🏌 Large parking lot for trucks and RVs. **Rates (CP):** $32 S; $41 D; from $36 effic. Extra person $4. Children under 12 stay free. Pking: Outdoor, free. Maj CC.

≣ **Motel 6**, 395 Smoketree Dr, El Centro, CA 92243; tel 619/353-6766. 4th Ave exit off I-8; N to Smoketree Dr. Good freeway access. Popular with truckers. **Rooms:** 156 rms. CI 3pm/CO noon. Nonsmoking rms avail. Small rooms. **Amenities:** 🛏 A/C, satel TV. **Services:** ⌧ ⌧ **Facilities:** 🔒 🏌 Truck parking available. **Rates:** $26 S; $32 D. Extra person $3. Children under 17 stay free. Pking: Outdoor, free. Maj CC.

EL GRANADA
Map page M-2, D1 (S of Pacifica)

Motel 🛏

≣≣ **Harbor View Inn**, 51 Ave Alhambra, El Granada, CA 94018; tel 415/726-2329. Calif 1 exit off Calif 92. Not fancy, but clean. Small lobby. **Rooms:** 17 rms. CI 1pm/CO 11am. Nonsmoking rms avail. **Amenities:** 🛏 TV w/movies. No A/C.

Services: 🏔 🛏 **Rates (CP):** HS June–Aug $65–$75 S or D. Children under 18 stay free. Lower rates off-season. Pking: Outdoor, free. Maj CC.

ELK

Map page M-2, C1 (S of Mendocino)

Inns 🏨

🏔🏔🏔 **Greenwood Pier Inn**, 5928 Calif 1, PO Box 36, Elk, CA 95432; tel 707/877-9997. 1½ acres. Artist-owners have created a slightly funky inn, perched on the cliffs overlooking the Mendocino coast. Stunning views of bay and rocks from lobby and guestrooms. **Rooms:** 11 rms and stes; 4 ctges/villas. CI 2pm/CO noon. Rooms are cozy and individually furnished, with decks overlooking ocean. **Amenities:** Refrig, stereo/tape player. No A/C, phone, or TV. All units w/terraces, all w/fireplaces, some w/Jacuzzis. **Services:** ✗ 🛎 Masseur. Homebaked breakfast goods are delivered to rooms in morning. **Facilities:** ♿ 1 rst, guest lounge. Hot tub on edge of cliff overlooking ocean. During week, dinners can be delivered to rooms. **Rates (CP):** HS June–Oct $100–$120 D; from $195 ste; from $150 ctge/villa. Extra person $12. Children under 5 stay free. Min stay wknds. Lower rates off-season. Pking: Outdoor, free. Ltd CC.

🏔🏔🏔🏔 **Harbor House**, 5600 Calif 1, PO Box 369, Elk, CA 95432; tel 707/877-3203. A romantic hideaway for couples. Built in 1916 entirely of redwood, from the vaulted ceilings to the hand-rubbed paneling. The grand parlor has lovely ocean views. Beautiful flower gardens; winding path leads down to ocean. Unsuitable for children under 10. **Rooms:** 10 rms; 4 ctges/villas. CI 2pm/CO noon. No smoking. Spacious, with ocean views, antique furnishings, clawfoot tubs, and fireplaces. Velvet love seats give accommodations a romantic touch. **Amenities:** 🅰 No A/C, phone, or TV. Some units w/terraces, some w/fireplaces. Cottages have private decks. **Services:** Masseur. Meals created from local products are excellent. **Facilities:** ⚓ 1 rst, 1 beach (ocean), guest lounge. Private beach not suited for swimming. **Rates (MAP):** HS June–Sept $165–$250 D. Extra person $50. Min stay wknds. Lower rates off-season. Pking: Outdoor, free. Ltd CC. Include full breakfast and a 5-course dinner.

EL PORTAL

Map page M-2, D3

Motel 🏨

🏔🏔 **Yosemite View Lodge**, Calif 140, El Portal, CA 95318; tel 209/379-2681 or toll free 800/321-5261; fax 209/379-2704. 14 mi W of Yosemite Village. 2 mi from El Portal entrance; 12 mi from valley floor. Good location near valley floor. Property undergoing full reconstruction, which should bring it to upscale level. **Rooms:** 70 rms and stes. CI 3pm/CO 11am. Nonsmoking rms avail. Very nicely appointed, spacious new mini-suites. Some bathrooms have huge tiled showers. After reconstruction, 90% of rooms will have full kitchenette, including utensils, pots and pans, toaster. **Amenities:** 🎬 🅰 📺 A/C, cable TV w/movies, refrig. All units w/terraces, some w/Jacuzzis. Microwave. **Services:** 🛏 Minimal services at present. **Facilities:** 🍴 🍽 ♿ 2 rsts, 1 bar, whirlpool, washer/dryer. Restaurant next door. Meeting space under construction. **Rates:** $85–$125 S or D; from $120 ste. Min stay wknds and spec evnts. Pking: Outdoor, free. Ltd CC.

EL SEGUNDO

Map page M-3, D2 (NW of Long Beach)

Hotel 🏨

🏔🏔🏔🏔 **Crown Sterling Suites**, 1440 E Imperial Ave, El Segundo, CA 90245 (Los Angeles Int'l Airport); tel 310/640-3600 or toll free 800/433-4600; fax 310/322-0954. A stunning, postmodern atrium building. Very cheerful and welcoming, with beautiful pink marble lobby, elegant, overstuffed sofas, and a pond with koi fish and ducks. Located next to LAX's Imperial Terminal and runways, but soundproofing is superb. **Rooms:** 350 stes. Exec-level rms avail. CI noon/CO 1pm. Express checkout avail. Nonsmoking rms avail. All accommodations are smartly furnished 2-room suites. **Amenities:** 🎬 🅰 📺 A/C, cable TV w/movies, refrig, voice mail. All units w/minibars. Wet bar, microwave, 2 vanity sinks, 2 phone lines. **Services:** ✗ 🚐 🏔 🛏 🛎 Car-rental desk. Multilingual staff. ITT foreign language service. Coffee available in lobby. **Facilities:** 🍴 🏋 🏊 ♿ 1 rst, 1 bar, spa, whirlpool. **Rates (MAP):** From $111 ste. Extra person $15. Children under 12 stay free. MAP rates avail. Spec packages avail. Pking: Indoor, free. Pking: Outdoor, free. Maj CC.

Motel

☰ **LAX Hotel**, 1804 E Sycamore Ave, El Segundo, CA 90245 (Los Angeles Int'l Airport); tel 310/615-0221 or toll free 800/421-5781, 800/854-1349 in CA; fax 310/322-4475. Old bungalow-style hotel from the 1940s; a bit seedy. **Rooms:** 94 rms, stes, and effic. CI 2pm/CO noon. Nonsmoking rms avail. **Amenities:** 🔒 ☕ A/C, cable TV w/movies, refrig. **Services:** 🚗 🖂 ⌂ Continental breakfast. Complimentary shuttle to shopping. **Facilities:** 🔗 ঎ Washer/dryer. **Rates (CP):** HS June–Aug $59–$69 S; $79–$89 D; from $45 ste; from $45 effic. Children under 18 stay free. Lower rates off-season. Spec packages avail. Pking: Outdoor, free. Maj CC.

EMERYVILLE

Map page M-2, D2 (N of Oakland)

Hotel 🖃

☰☰ **Holiday Inn Bay Bridge**, 1800 Powell St, Emeryville, CA 94608; tel 510/658-9300 or toll free 800/HOLIDAY; fax 510/547-8166. Powell St exit off I-80; west of fwy on San Francisco Bay. Closest hotel to San Francisco–Oakland Bay Bridge. Good freeway access to East Bay events. Renovation in progress. **Rooms:** 280 rms and stes. Exec-level rms avail. CI 3pm/CO noon. Express checkout avail. Nonsmoking rms avail. Comfortable, clean, standard Holiday Inn style. Some rooms have Bay and San Francisco views. **Amenities:** 🔒 ☕ ☕ A/C, cable TV w/movies. **Services:** ✗ 🖂 🚗 🖂 ⌂ 🍽 Children's program, babysitting. **Facilities:** 🏊 🖼 ঎ 1 rst, 1 bar, spa. Slated to add fitness center and health spa. **Rates:** HS June–Aug $105–$145 S; $110–$150 D; from $150 ste. Extra person $5. Children under 19 stay free. Lower rates off-season. Spec packages avail. Pking: Outdoor, free. Maj CC.

ESCONDIDO

Map page M-3, E3

Motel 🖃

☰ **Escondido West Travelodge**, 1290 W Valley Pkwy, Escondido, CA 92029; tel 619/489-1010 or toll free 800/541-6012; fax 619/489-7847. Valley Rd exit off I-15. Pleasantly decorated motel affords easy access to the freeway. Some maintenance problems. **Rooms:** 100 rms and stes. CI 2pm/CO noon. Nonsmoking rms avail. Average-size rooms have a bit too much freeway noise. **Amenities:** 🔒 ☕ 🖥 A/C, cable TV. All units w/terraces, some w/Jacuzzis. Refrigerators, microwaves, and VCRs available on request. **Services:** ✗ 🖂 ⌂ Complimentary coffee and newspapers in lobby. Room service from nearby restaurants. **Facilities:** 🔗 🚻 ঎ Whirlpool. **Rates:** $48 S; $56 D; from $100 ste. Extra person $5. Children under 18 stay free. Pking: Outdoor, free. Maj CC.

Resort

☰☰☰ **Welk Resort Center & the Greens Executive Conference Center**, 8860 Lawrence Welk Dr, Escondido, CA 92026; tel 619/749-3000 or toll free 800/932-9355; fax 619/749-9537. 9 mi N of downtown Escondido. Deer Springs Rd exit off I-15. 1,000 acres. Attractive accommodations in a quiet country setting 9 miles north of the city. Facilities are immaculate and grounds are carefully manicured. **Rooms:** 132 rms and stes. Exec-level rms avail. CI 2pm/CO noon. Express checkout avail. Nonsmoking rms avail. Rooms have pleasant decor with floral bedspreads and light wood furnishings. Most have balconies overlooking the golf course. **Amenities:** 🔒 ☕ 🖥 A/C, cable TV. All units w/terraces. Hairdryers available at the front desk. **Services:** 🖂 🖂 ⌂ 🍽 Car-rental desk, babysitting. **Facilities:** 🔗 ⛳ ⛳₃₆ 🏊 🖼 ঎ 3 rsts, 1 bar (w/entertainment), whirlpool, beauty salon. Eateries include main dining room, pizza restaurant, yogurt shop, snack shop, deli. Welk Theatre offers live entertainment. **Rates:** $95–$120 S or D; from $120 ste. Extra person $10. Children under 12 stay free. Spec packages avail. Pking: Outdoor, free. Maj CC.

Restaurants 🍴

Fireside Restaurant, 439 W Washington Ave, Escondido; tel 619/745-1931. 33 mi N of San Diego. Center City Pkwy exit off I-15. **American.** Dark, pub-style atmosphere with black leather booths, exposed brick walls, and a large brick fireplace. The specialty is beef, including prime rib and steaks. Early-bird dinners are a good value. **FYI:** Reservations accepted. **Open:** Lunch Mon–Fri 11:30am–2:30pm; dinner Sun–Thurs 5–9pm, Fri–Sat 5–10pm. **Prices:** Main courses $12.95–$16.95. Maj CC. 🍷঎

Marie Callender Restaurant, 515 W 13th St, Escondido; tel 619/741-3636. 30 mi N of San Diego. Center City Pkwy exit off I-15. **American.** A great place for families. Famous for pies, also serves traditional American fare—roast turkey, hamburgers, and chicken pot pie—and has a huge salad bar. Also at: Horton Plaza, San Diego (619/231-9090); 5405 Balboa, San Diego (619/279-6604); 1300 Orange Ave, San Diego (619/435-1789). **FYI:** Reservations not accepted. Children's menu. **Open:** Mon–Thurs 11am–10pm, Fri–Sat 11am–11pm, Sun 10am–10pm. Closed Dec 25. **Prices:** Main courses $7.95–$9.95. Maj CC. 👥 ঎

Attractions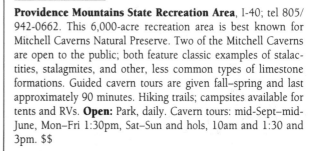

San Diego Wild Animal Park, 15500 San Pasqual Valley Rd; tel 619/747-8702. Located just 30 miles north of San Diego, this park is home to more than 3,000 animals, many of them endangered species, who roam freely over 2,200 acres. Concealed barriers separate the animals into 5 biogeographical areas that simulate the natural environments found in regions of Africa and Asia.

Nairobi Village is a 17-acre area that contains many single-species exhibits, including kangaroos, tigers, cheetahs, lemurs, and gorillas; the Petting Kraal, with young sheep, antelopes, and goats; and the 1¾-mile Kilimanjaro Hiking Trail, with larger animal exhibits and several gardens along the way. Also here are animal shows that feature elephants, free-flying birds, and exotic species.

The rest of the park is accessible only via the **Wgasa Bush Line,** a 5-mile, open-air monorail "safari" (included in price of admission). During the 50-minute ride, guides provide narration as the train travels around the perimeter of each of the African and Asian habitats and the Kilimanjaro Trail. Trains leave every 20–30 minutes; informative videos are presented to those waiting to board.

Most visitor facilities, including shops, food concessions, and a children's playground, are located in Nairobi Village. Wheelchair and stroller rentals are available. Inquire in advance about annual events, special programs, and behind-the-scenes tours. **Open:** June–Aug, daily 9am–5pm; Sept–May, daily 9am–4pm. $$$$

Escondido Historical Society History Museum, 321 N Broadway; tel 619/743-8207. This museum is housed in 5 turn-of-the-century buildings that are known collectively as the "Escondido Heritage Walk." Museum offices are in an 1894 library building; the remaining buildings are furnished with period antiques and reproductions to represent how they were used 100 years ago. The other buildings are: an 1890 Victorian house; a 1900 barn; an 1888 Santa Fe Railroad Depot; a re-created blacksmith shop (where local residents can sign up for blacksmithing classes); and an authentic 1920 Santa Fe Railroad car. **Open:** Thurs–Sat 1–4pm. Closed some hols. Free.

Mount Palomar Observatory; tel 619/742-2119 (recorded info). Located about 35 miles northeast, on County Road S-6. A department of the California Institute of Technology, Palomar Observatory has a 200-inch Hale telescope, the 2nd-largest in the United States, with a visitor gallery in its dome. Exhibits display the workings of the observatory as well as photographs taken by the telescopes. **Open:** Visitors gallery open daily 9am–4pm. Closed some hols. Free.

ESSEX
Map page M-3, D4

Attraction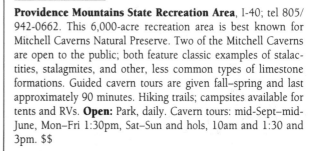

Providence Mountains State Recreation Area, I-40; tel 805/942-0662. This 6,000-acre recreation area is best known for Mitchell Caverns Natural Preserve. Two of the Mitchell Caverns are open to the public; both feature classic examples of stalactities, stalagmites, and other, less common types of limestone formations. Guided cavern tours are given fall–spring and last approximately 90 minutes. Hiking trails; campsites available for tents and RVs. **Open:** Park, daily. Cavern tours: mid-Sept–mid-June, Mon–Fri 1:30pm, Sat–Sun and hols, 10am and 1:30 and 3pm. $$

EUREKA
Map page M-2, A1

Hotel

≡≡≡ **Eureka Inn**, 518-7th St, Eureka, CA 95501 (Downtown); tel 707/442-6441 or toll free 800/862-4906; fax 707/442-1683. US 101 N or S to 7th St; E 2 blocks. A National Historic Landmark built in 1922 in the Tudor style. Huge lobby with potted plants and a view of the lovely swimming pool. **Rooms:** 105 rms and stes. CI 4pm/CO noon. Express checkout avail. Nonsmoking rms avail. **Amenities:** 🛏 👤 Cable TV. No A/C. Some units w/minibars, 1 w/terrace, 1 w/fireplace, 1 w/Jacuzzi. **Services:** 🍴 VP 🚗 ⌂ ↵ ⋈ Masseur, babysitting. **Facilities:** 🛗 ⛳ 300 🖥 👤 2 rsts (*see also* "Restaurants" below), 2 bars (1 w/entertainment), sauna, whirlpool. **Rates:** HS June–Sept 15 $95–$265 S; $130–$290 D; from $150 ste. Extra person $10. Children under 14 stay free. Lower rates off-season. Spec packages avail. Pking: Outdoor, free. Maj CC.

Motels

≡≡ **Best Western Thunderbird Inn**, 5th and Broadway, Eureka, CA 95501; tel 707/443-2234 or toll free 800/521-6996; fax 707/443-3489. At US 101, 4 blocks S of downtown. A very agreeable place for business and vacation travelers. **Rooms:** 115 rms and stes. CI 7am/CO noon. Nonsmoking rms avail. **Amenities:** 🛏 👤 📺 Cable TV w/movies. No A/C. 1 unit w/Jacuzzi. **Services:** ✕ ⌂ ↵ Linens changed daily on request. Room service from adjacent coffee shop noon–10pm. **Facilities:** 🛗 20 👤 Games rm, whirlpool, washer/dryer. Beautiful new pool. **Rates:** HS July–Sept $78–$93 S; $83–$98 D; from $98 ste. Extra person $5. Children under 18 stay free. Lower rates off-season. Spec packages avail. Pking: Outdoor, free. Maj CC.

≣≣ **Carson House Inn**, 1209 4th St, Eureka, CA 95501; tel 707/443-1601 or toll free 800/772-1622; fax 707/444-8365. Centrally located near old town and Eureka's attractions. Family-run. **Rooms:** 60 rms; 1 ctge/villa. CI 2pm/CO noon. Non-smoking rms avail. **Amenities:** 🛅 ♨ 🖵 Cable TV w/movies. No A/C. Some units w/Jacuzzis. **Services:** ⊋ ⊲ Babysitting. **Facilities:** ⛹ 🎱 ⅃ Sauna, whirlpool. Conference facilities in nearby Campton House, owned by same family. **Rates:** $55–$65 S or D; from $75 ctge/villa. Extra person $5. Higher rates for spec evnts/hols. Spec packages avail. Pking: Outdoor, free. Maj CC.

≣ **Comfort Inn**, 2014 4th St, Eureka, CA 95501; tel 707/444-0401 or toll free 800/221-2222; fax 707/442-8145. US 101 at V St. Basic lodging. **Rooms:** 30 rms. CI 11am/CO 11am. Nonsmoking rms avail. **Amenities:** 🛅 ♨ Cable TV w/movies, refrig. No A/C. Some units w/Jacuzzis. **Services:** 🚐 ⊋ **Facilities:** ⅃ **Rates:** HS May–Oct $45–$60 S; $49–$70 D. Extra person $6. Children under 16 stay free. Lower rates off-season. Spec packages avail. Pking: Outdoor, free. Maj CC.

≣ **Eureka Super 8 Motel**, 1304 4th St, Eureka, CA 95501 (Downtown); tel 707/443-3193 or toll free 800/235-3232. On US 101 S. Comfortable place convenient to downtown. **Rooms:** 50 rms and stes. CI noon/CO 11am. Nonsmoking rms avail. **Amenities:** 🛅 Cable TV w/movies. No A/C. Some units w/terraces. **Services:** ⊋ **Facilities:** ⅃ Sauna, steam rm, whirlpool. **Rates:** HS June–Aug $69 S or D; from $74 ste. Extra person $6. Lower rates off-season. Higher rates for spec evnts/hols. Spec packages avail. Pking: Outdoor, free. Maj CC.

≣≣≣ **Red Lion Inn**, 1929 4th St, Eureka, CA 95501; tel 707/445-0844 or toll free 800/547-8010; fax 707/445-2752. US 101 to V St. Well run, newly modernized, regularly upgraded. **Rooms:** 178 rms and stes. Exec-level rms avail. CI 2pm/CO noon. Express checkout avail. Nonsmoking rms avail. **Amenities:** 🛅 ♨ A/C, satel TV w/movies. Some units w/terraces. **Services:** ✗ 🚐 🖼 ⊋ ⊲ **Facilities:** ⅃ 🅿 ⊔ ⅃ 1 rst, 1 bar (w/entertainment), whirlpool. **Rates:** $110–$125 S or D; from $150 ste. Extra person $10. Children under 5 stay free. Spec packages avail. Pking: Outdoor, free. Maj CC. Frequent guest program. Weekend packages available with 2 weeks' notice.

Inn

≣≣≣≣ **Hotel Carter and Carter House**, 301 L St, Eureka, CA 95501 (Old Town); tel 707/444-8062; fax 707/444-8062. L St W exit off US 101. Perfectly proportioned, seamless blend of old-world refinement and California informality. The decor combines fine European antique furnishings with contemporary American art. Very restful. **Rooms:** 33 rms and stes. CI 3pm/CO 11am. No smoking. Guest rooms are beautifully appointed and very comfortable. Choose between the Inn (23 rooms and suites), the Cottage (3 rooms), or the Original House (7 rooms and suites). **Amenities:** 🛅 ♨ ♨ Cable TV w/movies, refrig, VCR, stereo/tape player, bathrobes. No A/C. Some units w/minibars, some w/fireplaces, some w/Jacuzzis. **Services:** ✗ 🖼 ⊋ Babysitting, afternoon tea and wine/sherry served. Included is an exquisite breakfast, late afternoon hors d'oeuvres with wine, and late evening tea with cookies and cordials. **Facilities:** 🍴 ⅃ 1 rst (see also "Restaurants" below). **Rates (BB):** HS Apr–Oct $95–$185 S or D; from $185 ste. Extra person $15. Lower rates off-season. Spec packages avail. Pking: Outdoor, free. Ltd CC.

Restaurants 🍴

★ **Cafe Marina and Woodley's Bar**, Startare Dr, Eureka; tel 707/443-2233. Calif 255 W exit off US 101; follow signs to Marina. **Seafood.** Popular, informal seafood restaurant with fine view of the docks at Humboldt Bay. Grilled, broiled, or fried fish and shellfish. **FYI:** Reservations accepted. Piano. Children's menu. **Open:** HS Apr–Oct daily 7am–10pm. Reduced hours off-season. Closed some hols. **Prices:** Main courses $9.95–$16.95. Maj CC. ⛰

⑤★ **Hotel Carter Dining Room**, in Hotel Carter, 301 L St, Eureka (Old Town); tel 707/444-8062. L St exit off US 101. **New American.** Elegantly presented, creative cuisine from well-known resident chef Jean-Louis Hamiche. Wine list includes more than 150 selections (some rare). **FYI:** Reservations recommended. Guitar. Beer and wine only. **Open:** Breakfast daily 7:30–10am; dinner Thurs–Mon 6–9pm. **Prices:** Main courses $9.95–$17.95. Maj CC. ♥ 🍴 ⅃

The Rib Room, in the Eureka Inn, 7th and F Sts, Eureka; tel 707/442-6441. Take US 101 to 7th St and go east for 2 blocks. **American.** Enhanced by nice lighting, a fireplace, and fresh flowers. Features grilled or roasted meats and poultry, grilled or poached fish—finely prepared and presented. Try grilled medallions of chicken Helena or roast rack of garlic-rosemary lamb. Extensive wine list. **FYI:** Reservations recommended. Piano. **Open:** Daily 6–10pm. **Prices:** Main courses $17.95–$24.95. Maj CC. ♥ 🍴 🖼 VP

Attractions 🖼

Clarke Memorial Museum, 240 E St; tel 707/443-1947. The main attraction of this museum is its world-class collection of Native American basketry and artifacts, including works of the

Hoopa, Yurok, and Karuk people. Humboldt County history is also covered, with collections of pioneer artifacts, 19th- and 20th-century firearms, oil paintings, Victorian furnishings and decorative arts, and examples of early commercial enterprise. **Open:** Tues–Sat noon–4pm. Closed some hols. Free.

Sequoia Park Zoo, 3414 W St; tel 707/442-6552 or 441-4203. This small zoo is surrounded by a 46-acre redwood grove. Among the numerous animal exhibits are a children's playground, picnic areas, and a duck pond. **Open:** Mem Day–Labor Day, Tues–Sun 10am–7pm; rest of the year, Tues–Sun 10am–5pm. Open on Mon hols. Free.

Blue Ox Millworks, at foot of X St; tel 707/444-3437. A working full-production millworks, this facility is also a living museum. It uses machinery from 1852 to 1940 to produce custom and reproduction materials for construction and restoration projects across the country. Visitors are welcome to tour the shop, via elevated walkways and platforms, to see how intricate items of wood, plaster, and metal were fabricated during the Victorian era; workers on hand answer questions about the machinery or their current projects. Also part of the facility are a small sawmill and a blacksmith shop; displays of old-time logging machinery; and a re-created logging "skid" camp. Tours take about 1 hour; casual dress and low-heeled shoes advised. **Open:** Mon–Sat 9am–5pm, Sun 11am–4pm. Closed some hols. $$

FAIRFIELD
Map page M-2, C2

See also Suisun City

Attraction 📷

Anheuser-Busch Fairfield Brewery, 3101 Busch Dr; tel 707/429-7595. Guided, 1½-hour tours offer a live demonstration of the brewing process and relate the history of one of the world's largest producers of beer. No open-toed shoes permitted; children under age 5 are not allowed on the production floor. Tours begin on the hour. **Open:** Tues–Sat 9am–4pm. Closed some hols. Free.

FALLBROOK
Map page M-3, E3 (N of Escondido)

Motels 🛏

Fallbrook Travelodge, 1608 S Mission Rd, Fallbrook, CA 92028; tel 619/723-1127 or toll free 800/578-7878; fax 619/723-2917. Pala Rd/Calif 76 exit off I-15; take Pala Rd west to Mission Rd and turn north. Located on a main street, with some traffic noise during the day. **Rooms:** 36 rms, stes, and effic. CI 2pm/CO 11am. Nonsmoking rms avail. Rooms have large bathrooms but require improved maintenance. Efficiencies have 2-burner stoves and small refrigerators. **Amenities:** 🛏 ⚱ A/C, satel TV. Some units w/terraces. **Services:** 🍽 🛎 Free coffee in lobby. **Facilities:** ⚕ Whirlpool. **Rates:** $45 S; $50–$55 D; from $75 ste; from $55 effic. Extra person $5. Children under 18 stay free. Pking: Outdoor, free. Maj CC.

La Estanica Inn, 3135 S Old Hwy 395, Fallbrook, CA 92028; tel 619/723-2888. Calif 176/Pala Rd exit off I-15. Looks like a Mexican hacienda, with cream-colored stucco walls and a red tile roof, against the backdrop of the unspoiled countryside. The entire property is clean, attractive, and well maintained. **Rooms:** 41 rms and effic. CI noon/CO noon. Decor is southwestern-style. Some rooms have spa baths, 2 sinks, and large showers. **Amenities:** 🛏 ⚱ A/C, cable TV, in-rm safe. Some units w/terraces, some w/Jacuzzis. Hair dryers available on request. **Services:** ✗ 🍽 🛎 Car-rental desk, babysitting. **Facilities:** 🍴 1 rst, 1 bar, whirlpool, washer/dryer. Very attractive restaurant. Nearby are golf courses, hot-air ballooning, and wineries. **Rates:** $68–$78 S or D; from $78 effic. Extra person $10. Children under 12 stay free. Min stay spec evnts. Spec packages avail. Pking: Indoor/outdoor, free. Maj CC. Rates often lower than published.

Resort

Pala Mesa Resort, 2001 Old Hwy 395, Fallbrook, CA 92054; tel 619/728-5881 or toll free 800/722-4700; fax 619/723-8292. Calif 76/Pala Rd exit off I-15. 205 acres. This "golfer's heaven" is a lovely place with well-kept grounds and plenty of activities for the entire family. Good value. **Rooms:** 133 rms and stes. CI 3pm/CO noon. Nonsmoking rms avail. Rooms are spacious. Attractive decor features marble-countered bathrooms and upholstered easy chairs. **Amenities:** 🛏 ⚱ 📺 A/C, cable TV. All units w/minibars, some w/terraces. **Services:** ✗ 🔑 🛄 🍽 Social director, babysitting. Very hospitable staff. Room-service menu also served poolside. Will arrange tours to wineries and other area attractions. **Facilities:** 🍴 🚲 ▶18 ⛳ 🏊 🎾 🏓 ⚕ 2 rsts (*see also* "Restaurants" below), 1 bar (w/entertainment), lawn games, whirlpool. Driving range, putting green, and pro shop. Golf and tennis lessons available. **Rates:** $110–$135 S or D; from $220 ste. Min stay spec evnts. Higher rates for spec evnts/hols. Spec packages avail. Pking: Outdoor, free. Maj CC.

Restaurants ||||

Alexander's, in Pala Mesa Resort, 2001 Old Hwy 395, Fallbrook; tel 619/728-5881. Pala Rd/Calif 76 exit off I-15. **Californian.** Alexander's offers indoor and outdoor dining with a golf-course view. Dining room is very attractive, spacious and gracious, with a country-club feel. Large tables are topped with white tablecloths and fresh flowers. Emphasis is on fresh local produce, especially avocado and citrus. **FYI:** Reservations recommended. Dress code. **Open:** Breakfast Mon–Sat 6–11am, Sun 6–10am; lunch Mon–Sat 11:30am–2pm; dinner Mon–Sat 5:30–9pm, Sun 5–9pm; brunch Sun 10:30am–2pm. **Prices:** Main courses $9.95–$17.95. Maj CC. ♥ ▲ ☑ ᴕ

★ **Garden Center Cafe**, 1625 S Mission Rd, Fallbrook; tel 619/728-4147. Pala Rd/Calif 76 exit off I-15. **Californian.** This building formerly housed a garden nursery, which explains the inspiration for the decor. It's charming: flowers galore, floral-print chairs, impressionist-style paintings, ceiling fans, and floor-to-ceiling windows. The house specialty is southwest chicken salad. Raspberry muffins, cinnamon rolls, scones, and desserts are all made on the premises. **FYI:** Reservations not accepted. Beer and wine only. **Open:** Breakfast Mon–Fri 7:30–10:45am; lunch Mon–Fri 11:15am–2:30pm; dinner Fri 5–8pm; brunch Sat 7:30am–2:30pm, Sun 8am–2pm. Closed some hols. **Prices:** Main courses $10.95–$15.95. Ltd CC. ▲ ᴕ

FERN VALLEY

Map page M-3, D3 (SW of Palm Springs)

Motel ▣

≣ **Woodland Park Manor**, 55350 S Circle Dr, Fern Valley, CA 92549; tel 909/659-2657. Calif 243 exit off I-10. 5 acres. Set amid Ponderosa and Jeffrey pines, cedars, and oak trees. Floor-to-ceiling windows showcase the forest; property could use some updating. **Rooms:** 11 ctges/villas. CI 2pm/CO 11am. Nonsmoking rms avail. Rustic. **Amenities:** Cable TV, refrig. No A/C or phone. All units w/terraces, all w/fireplaces. **Services:** ᴕ **Facilities:** ⚞ ᴕ Lawn games, playground. Picnic tables, Ping-Pong, horseshoes in wooded park. Heated pool open in summer.

Rates: From $69 ste; from $89 effic; from $69 ctge/villa. Children under 18 stay free. Min stay wknds. Pking: Outdoor, free. Ltd CC.

FISH CAMP

Map page M-3, B1

Hotel ▣

≣≣≣ **Marriott Tenaya Lodge at Yosemite**, 1122 Calif 41, PO Box 159, Fish Camp, CA 93623; tel 209/683-6555 or toll free 800/635-5807; fax 209/683-8684. 45 mi N of Fresno. Yosemite's newest luxury hotel. The impressive lobby has soaring, open-beamed ceilings and stone pillars and is accented with Native American art. Located about an hour's drive from the valley floor. **Rooms:** 242 rms and stes. CI 3pm/CO noon. Nonsmoking rms avail. Large and extremely cozy, with separate sitting area. Native American motifs are incorporated into the decor. **Amenities:** ⚞ ᴕ ▦ A/C, cable TV w/movies, in-rm safe. All units w/minibars, all w/terraces. Iron and ironing board in each room. **Services:** ✕ ☞ ▣ ▲ ᴕ Car-rental desk, social director, masseur, babysitting. Event desk plans guest activities. **Facilities:** ⚞ ⚞ ▣ ▲ ▣ ᴕ ▦ ▦ ᴕ 2 rsts, 1 bar (w/entertainment), games rm, lawn games, sauna, steam rm, whirlpool, washer/dryer. Both indoor and outdoor swimming pools. The Sierra Restaurant features local wines from Mariposa and Madera counties, as well as excellent pastas. **Rates:** HS June–Labor Day $189–$209 S or D; from $259 ste. Children under 18 stay free. Lower rates off-season. Higher rates for spec evnts/hols. Spec packages avail. Pking: Outdoor, free. Maj CC.

FOLSOM

Map page M-2, C2

Hotel ▣

≣≣≣ **Radisson Inn at Lake Natoma**, 702 Gold Lake Dr, Folsom, CA 95630; tel 916/351-1500 or toll free 800/333-3333; fax 916/351-1511. 20 mi E of Sacramento. Folsom Blvd exit off US 50; follow signs to Old Folsom. New, quiet property adjacent to American River Parkway, with plush amenities and park surroundings. **Rooms:** 132 rms and stes. CI 3pm/CO noon. Express checkout avail. Nonsmoking rms avail. Ask for room with view. **Amenities:** ⚞ ᴕ ▣ ▦ A/C, cable TV w/movies, refrig. Some units w/minibars, some w/fireplaces, some w/Jacuzzis. **Services:** ✕ ☞ ▦ ▲ ᴕ ᴕ Car-rental desk, masseur, babysitting. **Facilities:** ⚞ ▦ ▦ ▣ ᴕ 1 rst, 1 bar, lawn games, spa, sauna, whirlpool. Small pool amid lovely grounds; 9-hole putting green; volleyball. Cafe/bar has outdoor tables. **Rates:** HS Sept–May $89 S; $99 D; from $210 ste. Extra person $10. Children under 16 stay free. Lower rates off-season. Spec packages avail. Pking: Outdoor, free. Ltd CC. "Romance" package for $149 includes room, massage for 2, champagne on arrival, cheese and fruit platter.

FORESTVILLE
Map page M-2, C1 (E of Jenner)

Restaurant 🍽

Topolos, in Russian River Vineyards, 5700 Gravenstein Hwy N (Calif 116), Forestville; tel 707/887-1562. 1 mi S of Forestville. **Continental/Greek.** The only family-owned and -operated winery/restaurant combination in California. Best for a summery outdoor lunch (the inside dining room is decidedly ordinary). Many Greek specialties on the menu, such as spanakopita (spinach and cheese in filo pastry). Many herbs and vegetables come from the family gardens. **FYI:** Reservations recommended. Combo/guitar/jazz. **Open:** HS May–Oct lunch daily 11:30am–2:30pm; dinner daily 5:30–9:30pm; brunch Sun 10:30am–2:30pm. Reduced hours off-season. Closed some hols. **Prices:** Main courses $14–$20. Maj CC. 🍰

FORT BRAGG
Map page M-2, B1

Motels 🛏

🛏 **Seabird Lodge**, 191 South St, Fort Bragg, CA 95437 (Downtown); tel 707/964-4731 or toll free 800/345-0022 in CA. Ordinary motel on highway downtown. **Rooms:** 65 rms. CI 2pm/CO 11am. Nonsmoking rms avail. Standard decor, but clean. **Amenities:** 🛁 🅿 📺 Cable TV w/movies, refrig. No A/C. **Services:** 🍴 **Facilities:** 🗠 🏊 ⅋ Whirlpool, washer/dryer. **Rates:** HS Apr–Sept $80–$95 S or D. Extra person $5. Children under 12 stay free. Min stay wknds. Lower rates off-season. Spec packages avail. Pking: Outdoor, free. Maj CC.

🛏🛏 **Vista Manor Lodge/Best Western**, 1100 W Main St, Fort Bragg, CA 95437; tel 707/964-4776 or toll free 800/821-9498. Located across from a white-sand beach, reachable via an access tunnel. Extensive grounds not landscaped. **Rooms:** 55 rms and stes; 4 ctges/villas. CI 3pm/CO 11am. Nonsmoking rms avail. Bare and basic. **Amenities:** 🛁 Cable TV. No A/C. Some units w/terraces, some w/fireplaces. **Services:** 🍴 Free morning coffee

and doughnuts. **Facilities:** 🗠 Volleyball net. **Rates:** HS June–Oct $40–$125 S or D; from $75 ste; from $100 ctge/villa. Extra person $5. Lower rates off-season. Pking: Outdoor, free. Maj CC.

Inns

🛏🛏🛏 **The Grey Whale Inn**, 615 N Main, Fort Bragg, CA 95437; tel 707/964-0640 or toll free 800/382-7244; fax 707/964-4408. Stately 1915 hospital building, well decorated but too close to highway traffic. **Rooms:** 14 rms and stes. CI noon/CO noon. No smoking. Huge rooms. 'Albion Terrace' is cozy, with lovely antiques. Unique 'Navarro Ridge' is very big. **Amenities:** 🛁 🅿 No A/C or TV. Some units w/terraces, some w/fireplaces, 1 w/Jacuzzi. **Services:** Afternoon tea served. Breakfast menu changes daily. **Facilities:** 🏓 ⅋ Games rm, guest lounge w/TV. Pool table room, gardens. **Rates (CP):** HS June–Sept $60–$132 S or D; from $132 ste. Extra person $22. Lower rates off-season. Pking: Outdoor, free. Ltd CC. Lower in winter.

🛏🛏🛏🛏 **Noyo River Lodge**, 500 Casa Del Noyo, Fort Bragg, CA 95437; tel 707/964-8045 or toll free 800/628-1126. 5 acres. A large breakfast and lounging deck overlooking harbor and river affords a picturesque view of fishing boats and sea lions. Wonderful gardens surround the inn. **Rooms:** 17 rms and stes. CI 3pm/CO 11am. No smoking. Suites in main building have sitting areas with harbor views, fabulous antiques, and spacious dimensions. **Amenities:** 🅿 📺 Cable TV, bathrobes. No A/C or phone. Some units w/terraces, some w/fireplaces. **Services:** Afternoon tea and wine/sherry served. Coffee and fruit always available in the lobby. Nice breakfasts. **Facilities:** ⅋ Guest lounge w/TV. **Rates (CP):** HS June–Sept $90–$125 D; from $140 ste. Extra person $15. Children under 2 stay free. Min stay wknds. Lower rates off-season. Spec packages avail. Pking: Outdoor, free. Ltd CC.

Restaurants 🍽

The Cliff House, 1011 S Main St, Fort Bragg; tel 707/961-0255. **Californian/Seafood.** Pleasant dining room with floor-to-ceiling windows; all tables enjoy view of the Noyo River and the harbor. The creative menu offers seafood appetizers, smoked duck pasta, chicken in béarnaise sauce, and daily specials. **FYI:** Reservations recommended. Piano. **Open:** Dinner daily 4–10pm. Closed Dec 25. **Prices:** Main courses $12–$19. Maj CC. ⅋

⑤ ★ **Country Gardens Restaurant and Grill**, in Mendocino Botanical Gardens, 18220 W Calif 1, Fort Bragg; tel 707/964-7474. 1 mi S of downtown Fort Bragg. **Californian/Mediterranean.** Simple floral decor. An outdoor deck has umbrella-topped tables in a garden setting. There are many vegetarian specialties, along with fresh grilled fish sandwiches, mushroom crêpe torte, and Chinese chicken salad at lunch. Heartier dinner fare includes grilled steak, kebabs, and shrimp and scallion fritters. **FYI:** Reservations recommended. Beer and wine only. **Open:** Lunch Tues–Sat 11:30am–2:30pm; dinner Tues–Sat 5:30–9:30pm; brunch Sun 10am–3pm. Closed some hols. **Prices:** Main courses $10–$17. Ltd CC. &

North Coast Brewing Company, 444 Main St, Fort Bragg; tel 707/964-2739. **Cajun/Californian.** This old-time pub, American-style, features a taproom and high ceilings. Besides freshly brewed beer, it offers grilled fish, Cajun lasagne, pasta, and clam chowder. **FYI:** Reservations not accepted. Jazz. Beer and wine only. **Open:** HS July–Sept Tues–Fri 4–11:30pm, Sat 2–11:30pm. Reduced hours off-season. Closed Dec 25. **Prices:** Main courses $7.95–$19.95. Ltd CC. &

Attractions ▣

Mendocino Coast Botanical Gardens, 18220 N Calif 1; tel 707/964-4352. Several thousand varieties of native and cultivated plants grow here, making it a garden for all seasons. Major collections in the 37-acre gardens include heathers, perennials, succulents, ivies, Mediterraneans, dwarf conifers, roses, and camelias; also hybrids and dwarf rhododendrons. Pods of migrating grey whales can be seen passing by in December and March. Picnickers welcome. **Open:** Mar–Oct, daily 9am–5pm; Nov–Feb, daily 9am–4pm. Closed some hols. $$

Skunk Train (California Western Railroad), Fort Bragg Depot; tel 707/964-6371. These trains, which can be boarded at the foot of Laurel Ave, travel 40 miles inland along the Redwood Highway (US 101) to Willits. The serpentine route traverses 31 bridges and trestles and 2 deep tunnels, encompassing scenery from forest to fields of wildflowers, grazing cattle, and apple orchards. The nickname "skunk" came from the trains' original gasoline engines. Today the journey is made by deisel-powered trains and motorcars.

The round trip takes 6–7 hours, with time to lunch in Willits before the return leg of the journey. Half-day trips are offered on weekends throughout the year, and daily from mid-June–early Sept. Call for schedule and fare information. **Open:** Round-trip, daily; phone for schedule. $$$$

Georgia–Pacific Corporation Tree Nursery, 275 N Main St; tel 707/964-5651. Located at the junction of Calif 1 and Walnut St. Visitors are welcome to stop in for a free look at some 3 million small trees and seedlings. Visitor center, self-guided nature trail, picnic area. **Open:** Mon–Fri 8:30am–4:30pm. Closed some hols. Free.

FOSTER CITY
Map page M-2, D2 (S of San Mateo)

Hotels ▣

≣≣≣ **Courtyard by Marriott**, 550 Shell Blvd, Foster City, CA 94404; tel 415/377-0600 or toll free 800/321-2211; fax 415/377-1983. Foster City Blvd exit off Calif 92. Pleasant lounge and lobby with European-style furnishings and a fireplace. A courtyard garden is visible through many windows. Very good values. **Rooms:** 147 rms and stes. CI 3pm/CO 1pm. Express checkout avail. Nonsmoking rms avail. Rooms have good desks for conducting business. **Amenities:** ▣ & A/C, cable TV w/movies. Some units w/minibars, all w/terraces. **Services:** ✗ ▣ ▣ ▣ Babysitting. Breakfast bar and business services. **Facilities:** ▣ ▣ ▣ & 1 rst, whirlpool, washer/dryer. Beautiful indoor pool with a partial glass ceiling in a spacious setting with nice views. **Rates:** HS May–Oct $94–$104 S or D; from $104 ste. Extra person $10. Children under 3 stay free. Lower rates off-season. Spec packages avail. Pking: Outdoor, free. Maj CC.

≣≣≣ **Holiday Inn Foster City**, 1221 Chess Dr, Foster City, CA 94404; tel 415/570-5700 or toll free 800/477-5700; fax 415/570-0540. Foster City Blvd exit off Calif 92; turn left off exit, left on Foster City Blvd, left on Chess Dr. Atrium-style hotel. **Rooms:** 238 rms and stes. Exec-level rms avail. CI 2pm/CO noon. Express checkout avail. Nonsmoking rms avail. Rooms facing atrium are darker and may be noisier. **Amenities:** ▣ ▣ ▣ A/C, cable TV w/movies. Some units w/minibars, some w/terraces. **Services:** ✗ ▣ ▣ ▣ ▣ ▣ Twice-daily maid svce, car-rental desk, children's program, babysitting. **Facilities:** ▣ ▣ ▣ & 2 rsts, 2 bars, sauna, whirlpool, washer/dryer. Indoor pool, exercycles. **Rates (CP):** $89 S or D; from $225 ste. Extra person $10. Children under 18 stay free. Spec packages avail. Pking: Indoor/outdoor, free. Maj CC.

FOUNTAIN VALLEY
Map page M-3, D2 (SW of Santa Ana)

Hotel ▣

≣≣≣ **Courtyard by Marriott**, 9950 Slater Ave, Fountain Valley, CA 92708; tel 714/968-5775 or toll free 800/321-2211; fax 714/968-0112. 30 mi S of Los Angeles. Brookhurst exit off I-405; go north; left at first light onto Slater; hotel on left. Geared toward the leisure traveler. Attractive pool area. **Rooms:** 150 rms and stes. CI 3pm/CO 1pm. Express checkout avail. Nonsmoking rms avail. Clean and adequate. **Amenities:** ▣ & ▣ A/C, cable

TV w/movies, shoe polisher. Some units w/terraces. **Services:** ✗ 🛌 🍽️ Babysitting. **Facilities:** 🏋️ 🍴 🎰 ⚹ 1 rst, 1 bar, whirlpool, washer/dryer. **Rates:** $62–$72 S or D; from $75 ste. Children under 18 stay free. Pking: Outdoor, free. Maj CC.

FREMONT

Map page M-2, D2

Hotels 💼

≣≣ **Best Western Thunderbird Inn**, 5400 Mowry Ave, Fremont, CA 94538; tel 510/792-4300 or toll free 800/541-4909; fax 510/792-2643. Mowry E exit off I-880. Although close to the freeway, this lowrise property has a rural ambience because of its setting on landscaped, tree-studded acres. A good value. **Rooms:** 122 rms and stes. CI 2pm/CO noon. Nonsmoking rms avail. Recent redecoration. **Amenities:** 🏋️ ⚹ A/C, cable TV w/movies. Some units w/terraces. Refrigerators and hair dryers available upon request. VCR rental available. **Services:** 🚐 🛌 🍽️ 🛎️ Children's program, babysitting. Use of computer, fax, and copy machine at front desk. **Facilities:** 🏋️ 🎰 ⚹ 1 rst, 1 bar (w/entertainment), lawn games, sauna, whirlpool. Volleyball court. Complimentary use of nearby fitness center. **Rates (CP):** $69–$89 S; $74–$89 D; from $90 ste. Extra person $5. Children under 12 stay free. Spec packages avail. Pking: Outdoor, free. Maj CC.

≣≣ **Courtyard by Marriott**, 47000 Lakeview Blvd, Fremont, CA 94538 (Bayside Business Park); tel 510/656-1800 or toll free 800/321-2211; fax 510/656-2441. Warren Ave W exit off I-880; left on Bayside, left on Gateway, left on Lakeview. Located in a business park and oriented to the business traveler. **Rooms:** 146 rms and stes. CI 3pm/CO 1pm. Express checkout avail. Nonsmoking rms avail. **Amenities:** 🏋️ ⚹ A/C, cable TV w/movies. Some units w/terraces. Suites have refrigerators. **Services:** ✗ 🛌 🍽️ Babysitting. Room service available only at dinnertime. **Facilities:** 🏋️ 🍴 🎰 ⚹ 1 rst, 1 bar, whirlpool, washer/dryer. Large, well-designed indoor pool and whirlpool. Full-service Club Sport gym charges $4 daily fee to guests and is located within walking distance. **Rates:** $84 S; $94 D. Extra person $10. Children under 18 stay free. Spec packages avail. Pking: Outdoor, free. Maj CC.

≣≣≣ **Residence Inn by Marriott**, 5400 Farwell Place, Fremont, CA 94536; tel 510/794-5900 or toll free 800/331-3131; fax 510/793-6587. Mowry E exit off I-880; left at Farwell Dr, left at Farwell Place. An attractive townhouse-like complex close to restaurants, shopping, and the freeway. **Rooms:** 80 stes. CI 3pm/CO noon. Nonsmoking rms avail. All suites have full kitchens seating from 2 people in the studio to 4

in the other guest rooms. **Amenities:** 🏋️ ⚹ 🖥️ A/C, cable TV w/movies, refrig. All units w/fireplaces. Each room contains an iron and ironing board. Games are available from front desk. **Services:** ✗ 🚐 🛌 🍽️ 🛎️ Complimentary social hour Monday-Thursday. **Facilities:** 🏋️ 🎰 ⚹ Whirlpool, washer/dryer. Sport court for volleyball and paddle tennis. **Rates (CP):** From $129 ste. Children under 18 stay free. Pking: Outdoor, free. Maj CC.

Attractions 🏛️

Mission San Jose Chapel and Museum, 43300 Mission Blvd; tel 510/657-1797. Mission San Jose was founded June 11, 1797, the 14th of the 21 Spanish Missions in Alta California. The adobe church is a 1985 replica of the 1809 original; its interior was extensively decorated by following detailed descriptions made during an 1830s decorating project. A small museum containing mission-era artifacts and exhibits on the Ohlone Indians and the restoration is located in a portion of the padres' original living quarters. **Open:** Daily 10am–5pm. Closed some hols. Free.

San Francisco Bay National Wildlife Refuge, 1 Marshlands Rd; tel 510/792-0222. Created in 1972, this 23,000-acre refuge preserves a variety of natural habitats, protecting a vast array of plant and animal life. In the course of a year, more than 250 species of birds visit San Francisco Bay, which provides food, nesting sites, and resting space for migratory birds on the Pacific flyway.

The visitor center is located a half mile south of the Dumbarton Bridge (eastern side), off Thornton Rd (follow signs). Here visitors will find indoor exhibits and a self-guided trail introducing the bay environment and local wildlife. Schedules of naturalist programs and other events can be found here. Books, posters, and other items are for sale.

Miles of trails crisscross the refuge and offer opportunities to glimpse rabbits, ground squirrels, gopher snakes, and other small animals. Boating is permitted in some areas (canoes or kayaks recommended). Some fishing and hunting is permitted (phone ahead for specifics). Camping is not permitted in the refuge, but sites are available at several nearby parks and beaches. **Open:** Visitor center daily 10am–5pm. Closed some hols. Free.

Central Park, 40000 Paseo Padre Pkwy; tel 510/791-4340. This 450-acre park was created around 83-acre Lake Elizabeth in the 1960s. Located at the south end of the park is a swim lagoon with 2½ acres of swimming area surrounded by a 2½-acre beach (swimming fee charged). Throughout the park are numerous recreational opportunities, including several playgrounds, play fields, drop-in picnic areas, snack bars, fishing areas, boat launching facilities and rentals, a fitness course, 18 tennis courts, and a driving range. **Open:** Daily dawn–10pm. Free.

Coyote Hills Regional Park, 8000 Patterson Ranch Rd; tel 510/795-9385. A 1,000-acre wetlands preserve and wildlife sanctuary, this park contains 4 Native American shell mounds that span a period of 2,200 years. The largest site has been set up for group programs by park naturalists. The Visitor Center contains exhibits and has naturalists on hand to answer questions and distribute information.

Hiking, bridle, and bicycle trails lead through all of the major habitat areas and along the Coyote Hills. A variety of naturalist programs are offered to the public (usually on weekends). **Open:** Park, daily 8am–dusk; Visitor Center, Tues–Sun and hols 9:30am–5pm. $

FRESNO
Map page M-2, D3

Hotels 🏨

≡≡≡ Fresno Hilton Hotel, 1055 Van Ness, Fresno, CA 93721 (Downtown); tel 209/485-9000 or toll free 800/445-8667 in the US, 800/221-2424 in Canada; fax 209/485-7666. Ventura St exit E off Calif 99; left on Van Ness. Located on downtown Fulton Mall, near city's financial and government center, and ½ mile from the Amtrak Station. Scheduled to be completely remodelled. **Rooms:** 197 rms and stes. Exec-level rms avail. CI 3pm/CO noon. Express checkout avail. Nonsmoking rms avail. Spacious and nicely decorated. **Amenities:** A/C, cable TV w/movies. Some units w/terraces. **Services:** X Car-rental desk. **Facilities:** 2 rsts, 1 bar (w/entertainment), spa, whirlpool. Security-patrolled underground parking. Lovely ballroom. **Rates:** $65–$119 S or D; from $150 ste. Children under 18 stay free. Higher rates for spec evnts/hols. Spec packages avail. Pking: Indoor, free. Maj CC.

≡≡≡ Holiday Inn–Airport, 5090 E Clinton Ave, Fresno, CA 93727 (Fresno Airport); tel 209/252-3611 or toll free 800/HOLIDAY; fax 209/456-8243. The rooms are nice, but many parts of this 18-year-old property are a bit rundown, a problem that should be solved by scheduled refurbishment. Located opposite Fresno Air Terminal. **Rooms:** 210 rms. Exec-level rms avail. CI 3pm/CO noon. Nonsmoking rms avail. 4 "green" suites are available for guests with allergies (specially treated linens, air and water filtration systems, hypoallergenic toiletries). **Amenities:** A/C, satel TV w/movies. Some units w/terraces. **Services:** X **Facilities:** 1 rst, 1 bar (w/entertainment), games rm, whirlpool, washer/dryer. Lucy's

Lounge is popular for dancing. **Rates:** $76–$80 S or D. Extra person $10. Children under 18 stay free. Spec packages avail. Pking: Outdoor, free. Maj CC.

≡≡≡ Hotel Inn–Centre Plaza, 2233 Ventura Ave, Fresno, CA 93721 (Downtown); tel 209/268-1000 or toll free 800/HOLIDAY; fax 209/486-6625. Ventura St exit off Calif 99. Part of the downtown Fresno Convention Center complex. Elegant, 10-year-old highrise has attractive atrium lobby with waterfall. Renovation just completed. **Rooms:** 320 rms and stes. CI 3pm/CO noon. Express checkout avail. Nonsmoking rms avail. Comfortable and spacious. **Amenities:** A/C, cable TV w/movies, shoe polisher. Some units w/minibars. **Services:** X Twice-daily maid svce, babysitting. **Facilities:** 2 rsts, 2 bars, sauna, whirlpool, beauty salon. **Rates:** $79 S; $87 D; from $89 ste. Extra person $8. Children under 15 stay free. Min stay spec evnts. Higher rates for spec evnts/hols. Spec packages avail. Pking: Indoor/outdoor, free. Maj CC.

≡≡≡ Piccadilly Inn Airport, 5115 E McKinley Ave, Fresno, CA 93727 (Fresno Airport); tel 209/251-6000 or toll free 800/HOTEL-US, 800/HOTEL-CA in CA; fax 209/251-6956. Comfortable hotel, located across from the Fresno Air Terminal. **Rooms:** 185 rms and stes. Exec-level rms avail. CI 3pm/CO 1pm. Express checkout avail. Nonsmoking rms avail. **Amenities:** A/C, satel TV w/movies. Some units w/terraces. Some rooms have refrigerators. **Services:** X Car-rental desk. **Facilities:** 2 rsts, 1 bar (w/entertainment), whirlpool, washer/dryer. The Steak and Anchor Restaurant and Lounge, which serves award-winning ribs, rates highly with Fresno residents. **Rates:** $88–$94 S; $98–$104 D; from $185 ste. Extra person $10. Children under 18 stay free. AP rates avail. Spec packages avail. Pking: Outdoor, free. Maj CC. Weekend discounts available.

≡≡≡ Piccadilly Inn University, 4961 N Cedar Ave, Fresno, CA 93726; tel 209/224-4200 or toll free 800/HOTEL-US, 800/HOTEL-CA in CA; fax 209/227-2382. Shaw Ave exit off Calif 99 or Calif 44; go east to Cedar Ave. A very nice hotel near Fresno State University and several popular restaurants. **Rooms:** 199 rms and stes. Exec-level rms avail. CI 3pm/CO 1pm. Express checkout avail. Nonsmoking rms avail. Beautifully appointed. **Amenities:** A/C, cable TV w/movies. Some units w/minibars, some w/terraces, some w/Jacuzzis. **Services:** X Car-rental desk, babysitting. **Facilities:** 1 rst, 1 bar, whirlpool, washer/dryer. **Rates (BB):** $88–$94 S; $98–$104 D; from $185 ste. Extra person $10. Children under 18 stay free. Spec packages avail. Pking: Outdoor, free. Maj CC.

≡≡≡ Ramada Inn, 324 E Shaw, Fresno, CA 93710; tel 209/224-4040 or toll free 800/241-0756; fax 209/222-4017. Calif 41 N exit off Calif 99 N; Shaw Ave exit off Calif 99 S. This centrally located hotel is a pleasant place to hang your hat. Within walking distance of Fashion Fair shopping mall. **Rooms:** 167 rms and stes. Exec-level rms avail. CI 3pm/CO noon. Express checkout avail. Nonsmoking rms avail. Nicely appointed, spacious rooms. **Amenities:** ☎ ♨ 🖥 A/C, cable TV w/movies. Some units w/minibars, some w/terraces. Four "green suites" available for those with allergies, with special filtration systems and biodegradable soaps. **Services:** ✕ 🚐 🗺 🕭 Car-rental desk, babysitting. **Facilities:** 🗗 🖼 📶 ♿ 1 rst, 1 bar, whirlpool. Sports bar. **Rates:** $67 S; $73 D; from $85 ste. Extra person $6. Children under 18 stay free. Spec packages avail. Pking: Outdoor, free. Maj CC.

Motels

🏳🏳 **Best Western Village Inn**, 3110 N Blackstone Ave, Fresno, CA 93703; tel 209/226-2110 or toll free 800/722-8878; fax 209/226-0539. Ashlan Ave exit off Calif 99; E on Ashlan to Blackstone. New furnishings and a paint job have freshened the look of this conveniently located older motel, close to a mall and fast-food restaurants. **Rooms:** 153 rms. CI 3pm/CO noon. Nonsmoking rms avail. **Amenities:** ☎ 🖥 A/C, cable TV w/movies. **Services:** 🗺 🕭 **Facilities:** 🗗 Whirlpool. **Rates (CP):** $50 S; $58 D. Extra person $3. Children under 12 stay free. Spec packages avail. Pking: Outdoor, free. Maj CC.

🏳🏳 **Best Western Water Tree Inn**, 4141 N Blackstone Ave, Fresno, CA 93730; tel 209/222-4445 or toll free 800/762-9071; fax 209/226-4589. Ashlan Ave exit off Calif 99; E on Ashlan; right on Blackstone. The '70s-style rock entrance dates this property, but refurbishing has kept the rooms inviting. Convenient to businesses and shopping. **Rooms:** 136 rms and stes. CI 1pm/CO noon. Nonsmoking rms avail. **Amenities:** ☎ ♨ 🖥 A/C, cable TV w/movies, refrig, in-rm safe, shoe polisher. Some units w/terraces. **Services:** 🕭 **Facilities:** 🗗 📶 **Rates:** $52–$58 S; $58–$62 D; from $80 ste. Extra person $4. Children under 13 stay free. Pking: Outdoor, free. Maj CC.

🏳 **Blackstone Plaza Inn**, 4061 N Blackstone Ave, Fresno, CA 93726; tel 209/222-5641; fax 209/225-0144. Ashlan exit off Calif 99; E on Ashlan, right on Blackstone. An older motel in need of refurbishing. A change of ownership and renovation was planned at time of inspection. **Rooms:** 115 rms and stes. CI 3pm/CO noon. Nonsmoking rms avail. Clean and spacious. **Amenities:** ☎ 🖥 A/C, cable TV w/movies. **Services:** 🕭 🍽 **Facilities:** 🗗 George's Shish Kabob, a popular local restaurant and nightclub, is adjacent to the motel. **Rates:** $36 S; $42 D; from $49 ste. Extra person $6. Children under 16 stay free. Higher rates for spec evnts/hols. Spec packages avail. Pking: Outdoor, free. Maj CC.

🏳🏳🏳 **Chateau Inn by Piccadilly Inn**, 5113 E McKinley Ave, Fresno, CA 93727; tel 209/456-1418 or toll free 800/445-2428; fax 209/456-1418 ext 200. Clinton Ave exit off Calif 99 N; Clovis Ave exit off Calif 99 S. Charming inn built in 1989 with convenience, budget, and security in mind. **Rooms:** 78 rms. CI 3pm/CO 1pm. Nonsmoking rms avail. Comforters and bed skirts give rooms a homey feel. Two "green" (environmentally friendly) suites, and 4 rooms for guests with disabilities. **Amenities:** ☎ ♨ 🖥 🍴 A/C, cable TV w/movies, VCR. Rooms in deluxe building have refrigerators. **Services:** 🚐 🗺 🕭 Movies for rent. Free passes to full-service athletic club. Free coffee 24 hours. Breakfast at discount of 20% at Piccadilly Inn next door. **Facilities:** 🗗 ♿ **Rates:** $39–$64 S; $45–$70 D. Extra person $6. Children under 18 stay free. Spec packages avail. Pking: Outdoor, free. Maj CC. Special weekend rates.

🏳🏳🏳 **Courtyard by Marriott**, 1551 N Peach Ave, Fresno, CA 93727 (Fresno Airport); tel 209/251-5200 or toll free 800/321-2211; fax 209/454-0552. Clinton exit off Calif 99 N; Clovis Ave exit off Calif 99 S. Recently renovated with new carpeting, furniture, and accessories. **Rooms:** 116 rms. CI 4pm/CO noon. Express checkout avail. Nonsmoking rms avail. Lovely and inviting. **Amenities:** ☎ ♨ 🖥 🍴 A/C, cable TV w/movies. **Services:** 🚐 🗺 🕭 Car-rental desk, babysitting. **Facilities:** 🗗 📶 📶 ♿ 1 rst, 1 bar, washer/dryer. **Rates:** $49–$74 S; $59–$84 D. Extra person $10. Children under 18 stay free. Spec packages avail. Pking: Outdoor, free. Maj CC. Special rates on weekends.

🏳🏳🏳 **Holiday Inn Express**, 6051 N Thesta, Fresno, CA 93710; tel 209/435-6593 or toll free 800/435-9746; fax 209/435-8694. Bullard exit off Calif 41. This new property, opened in spring of 1994, is located near the Fresno Surgery Center in the northwest area of the city. **Rooms:** 55 rms. CI 3pm/CO 11am. Nonsmoking rms avail. Comfortable and nicely decorated. **Amenities:** ☎ ♨ A/C, cable TV. **Services:** 🗺 🕭 **Facilities:** ♿ **Rates (CP):** $65–$75 S; $75–$85 D. Extra person $10. Children under 18 stay free. Min stay spec evnts. Higher rates for spec evnts/hols. Spec packages avail. Pking: Outdoor, free. Maj CC.

🏳🏳🏳 **La Quinta Inn**, 2926 Tulare Ave, Fresno, CA 93721 (Downtown); tel 209/442-1110 or toll free 800/531-5900; fax 209/237-0415. Tulare Ave exit off Calif 41. Clean, pleasant, friendly ambience in a southwestern-style inn. Exterior and lobby recently upgraded, with more renovations scheduled. **Rooms:** 131 rms and stes. Exec-level rms avail. CI open/CO noon. Express checkout avail. Nonsmoking rms avail. King-plus rooms are extra large. **Amenities:** ☎ ♨ A/C, cable TV w/movies. **Services:** 🗺 🕭 🍽 Car-rental desk. Free local calls. **Facilities:**

🔲 70 ♿ **Rates (CP):** $47–$65 S or D; from $75 ste. Extra person $8. Children under 18 stay free. Spec packages avail. Pking: Outdoor, free. Maj CC.

≣≣≣ **Sheraton Smuggler's Inn**, 3737 N Blackstone Ave, Fresno, CA 93726; tel 209/226-2200 or toll free 800/742-1911; fax 209/222-7147. About as nice as a motel can get, with attractive grounds and many good in-room features. Well-worn hallway carpets are scheduled to be replaced. **Rooms:** 205 rms and stes. Exec-level rms avail. CI 3pm/CO 1pm. Express checkout avail. Nonsmoking rms avail. Large rooms are nicely decorated with English-style furnishings, a small sofa, and garish but comfortable reclining armchair. Bathroom has ample Formica counter; plastic shower stall. Although rooms rate highly in terms of individual features, quality and class are lacking. **Amenities:** 🔲 🕹 🖥 🍷 A/C, cable TV w/movies, refrig, voice mail, shoe polisher. Some units w/terraces. The bathroom hairdryer is ancient. **Services:** ✗ 🚗 🖼 🎵 Twice-daily maid svce, car-rental desk. **Facilities:** 🔲 🛶 🔲 400 🖥 ♿ 1 rst, 1 bar (w/entertainment), whirlpool, washer/dryer. Nicest feature here is the big swimming pool, surrounded by trees, lawns, and pergola. **Rates:** $80 S; $85 D; from $190 ste. Extra person $6. Children under 18 stay free. Spec packages avail. Pking: Outdoor, free. Maj CC.

Restaurants 🍴

Applebee's Neighborhood Grill & Bar, in Fig Garden Village Shopping Center, 5126 N Palm Ave, Fresno; tel 209/244-6904. **New American.** A lively bar and grill with a neighborhood atmosphere and a diverse menu. Oak tables and upholstered booths are surrounded by memorabilia from local celebrities and sports figures. The menu includes Santa Fe chicken salad, ribs, and daily specials. Irish coffee and other specialty drinks are available from the bar. Also at: 98 Shaw Ave, Clovis (209/322-9890). **FYI:** Reservations not accepted. Children's menu. **Open:** Mon–Thurs 11am–midnight, Fri–Sat 11am–1am, Sun 11am–10pm. Closed some hols. **Prices:** Main courses $6.59–$9.69. Maj CC. 🎮 ♿

★ **Butterfield Brewing Company**, 777 E Olive Ave, Fresno (Tower District); tel 209/264-5521. Olive Ave exit off Calif 99. **New American.** A fun hangout with views of the brewery vats from the dining area and bar. Home of award-winning, hand-crafted Butterfield Brewery beers. Eclectic menu offers hearty salads, burgers, pasta, chili, appetizers, smoked meats, and fresh fish. Specialties include stuffed chicken wings. **FYI:** Reservations recommended. Blues/jazz. Children's menu. Dress code. Beer and wine only. **Open:** Mon–Thurs 11am–10pm, Fri–Sat 11am–11pm, Sun 11am–9pm. Closed some hols. **Prices:** Main courses $4.95–$12.95. Maj CC. ♿

Harlands, in Fig Garden Village, 722 W Shaw Ave, Fresno; tel 209/225-7100. **Californian.** Harland's features white columns and tablecloths, black chairs, and romantic booths. The menu changes seasonally but is always an eclectic mix of cuisines: Chinese, Italian, French, and regional American. **FYI:** Reservations recommended. Piano. Dress code. **Open:** Lunch Mon–Fri 11:30am–2:30pm; dinner Mon–Sat 6–10pm. Closed some hols. **Prices:** Main courses $9.50–$19.50. Maj CC. ♥ 🚗 ♿

Sal's Mexican Restaurant, 2839 N Blackstone, Fresno; tel 209/227-1686. **Mexican.** Simple decor, fun atmosphere. This family-run operation offers a large menu of Mexican specialties, including Sal's fancy burrito, baked short ribs, chili rellenos, and seafood. Also at: 434 Clovis Ave, Clovis (209/298-7898); 2163 Park St, Selma (209/896-0412); 3316 W Shaw, Fresno (209/271-0836). **FYI:** Reservations not accepted. Children's menu. **Open:** Daily 10:30am–10pm. Closed some hols. **Prices:** Main courses $4.95–$10.95. Maj CC. 🎮 ♿

Attractions 📷

Fresno Metropolitan Museum of Art, History, and Science, 1555 Van Ness Ave; tel 209/441-1444. Featured at this museum are traveling exhibits ranging from art exhibitions to the history of auto racing, along with a permanent collection that includes the Salzer Collection of American and European still-life paintings. Also here are the Rotary Playland Science Gallery, the Bio-Met-Rics Laboratory, and an exhibit on the life of Fresno native William Saroyan, the Pulitzer prize-winning author. Free admission first Wednesday of each month. **Open:** Daily 11am–5pm. Closed some hols. $$

Kearney Mansion Museum, 7160 W Kearney Blvd; tel 209/441-0862. Guided tours are offered of the residence of pioneer land-developer M Theo Kearney. Known as the "Raisin King of California," Kearney had the house built in the center of his 5,000-acre Fruit Vale Estate. Today the museum is located within the historic 225-acre Kearney Park and contains 50% of the mansion's original furnishings, including European wallpapers and art nouveau light fixtures; a thorough restoration project has duplicated much of the remainder. The adjoining servants' quarters now house the ranch kitchen and museum gift shop. **Open:** Fri–Sun 1–4pm. Closed some hols. $$

Meux Home, 1007 R St; tel 209/233-8007. This elegant Victorian home was one of the most elaborate residences in Fresno. It was built in 1889 for Dr Thomas R Meux, a former Confederate surgeon and pioneer Fresno physician, and is the last remaining example of the Victorian houses of Fresno's early years. The house remained in the Meux family until 1973, when it was puchased by the City of Fresno and faithfully restored to its original charm.

The large, roofed porch features several beautifully turned posts and is accented with gingerbread details. The exterior walls of the house are covered with a variety of textures including clapboards, fishscale shingles, and ornamental floral-like relief decoration. Inside, one of the most interesting features is the octagonal master bedroom, with its steep, turreted roof. **Open:** Fri–Sun noon–3pm or by appointment. Closed some hols. $

Chaffee Zoological Gardens, 894 W Belmont Ave; tel 209/498-2671. Located at Olive and Belmont Sts, at the south end of Roeding Park, this 18-acre zoo features a tropical rain forest exhibit, a reptile house, an elephant enclosure, and a petting zoo. An Australian aviary should be open, too. **Open:** Mar–Oct, daily 9am–5pm; Nov–Feb, daily 10am–4pm. $$

FULLERTON

Map page M-3, D2 (N of Anaheim)

Hotels 🏨

≣≣≣ **Fullerton Marriott**, 2701 E Nutwood Ave, Fullerton, CA 92631; tel 714/738-7800 or toll free 800/228-9290; fax 714/738-0288. 7 mi NE of Anaheim. Nutwood exit off Calif 57. New and attractive property, clean and well maintained. **Rooms:** 224 rms and stes. Exec-level rms avail. CI 4pm/CO noon. Express checkout avail. Nonsmoking rms avail. **Amenities:** 🛅👌 ⛄ A/C, cable TV w/movies. Some units w/terraces. Iron and ironing board in closet. Pay-per-view movies. **Services:** ✕ ⟳ ⟲ ◁ Twice-daily maid svce, car-rental desk, babysitting. Some business services available. **Facilities:** 🖼 🏊 📮 300 👌 1 rst, 1 bar, sauna, whirlpool. **Rates:** $69–$89 S or D; from $250 ste. Children under 18 stay free. Spec packages avail. Pking: Indoor/outdoor, free. Maj CC.

≣≣≣ **Fullerton Suite Hotel**, 2932 E Nutwood Ave, Fullerton, CA 92631; tel 714/579-7400 or toll free 800/79-SUITE; fax 714/528-7945. 7 mi N of Anaheim. Nutwood exit off Calif 57. An all-suites hotel that appeals mostly to corporate travelers. Close to several restaurants. **Rooms:** 96 stes. Exec-level rms avail. CI 3pm/CO noon. Express checkout avail. Nonsmoking rms avail. All accommodations are 1-room 'petite suites.' They have marble baths and sitting areas. **Amenities:** 🛅👌📺 ⛄ A/C, cable TV w/movies, refrig. Some units w/terraces, all w/Jacuzzis. **Services:** ✕ 🚐 ⟳ ◁ Car-rental desk. Continental breakfast in lobby or room. Access to nearby racquet club. Room service from next door restaurant. **Facilities:** 🖼 180 👌 Washer/dryer.

Rates (CP): HS Jan–Feb/June–Aug from $79 ste. Extra person $10. Children under 17 stay free. Lower rates off-season. Spec packages avail. Pking: Indoor/outdoor, free. Maj CC.

Motel

≣≣≣ **Holiday Inn**, 222 W Houston Ave, Fullerton, CA 92632; tel 714/992-1700 or toll free 800/553-3441; fax 714/992-4843. 3 mi N of Anaheim. Harbor Blvd exit off Calif 91. Classic Holiday Inn style of early 1970s, remodeled in 1991. Interior is pleasant, exterior average, landscaping minimal. **Rooms:** 289 rms and stes. Exec-level rms avail. CI 3pm/CO noon. Nonsmoking rms avail. Clean, bright rooms. Furniture is nice but plain. Lots of beige. **Amenities:** 🛅👌📺 ⛄ A/C, cable TV w/movies, in-rm safe. Some units w/terraces. **Services:** ✕ 🚐 ⟳ ◁ Twice-daily maid svce, babysitting. **Facilities:** 🖼 📮 600 👌 1 rst, 1 bar, games rm, washer/dryer. Children's pool. Pool area could be cleaner. **Rates:** HS Apr–Oct $85–$105 S; $95–$110 D; from $125 ste. Extra person $5. Children under 16 stay free. Lower rates off-season. Spec packages avail. Pking: Outdoor, free. Maj CC.

Restaurants 🍴

🍴 **Aurora**, 1341 S Euclid St, Fullerton; tel 714/738-0272. Euclid Ave exit off Calif 91; 2 blocks N. **Continental/Italian.** Chef/owner Leo Holczer, with his old-world Swiss charm, makes diners feel right at home. Lots of flowers and paintings in the restaurant. Award-winning cuisine features many game specialties; more than 800 different wines are offered. **FYI:** Reservations recommended. Dress code. **Open:** Closed some hols. **Prices:** Main courses $9.95–$26. Maj CC. ♥ 👌

🍴 **The Cellar**, in Villa del Sol, 305 N Harbor Blvd, Fullerton (Old Fullerton); tel 714/525-5682. Harbor Blvd exit off I-5; 4 mi N on Harbor. **French.** Intimate, elegant dining in an old-world wine cellar. Warm, romantic atmosphere. Food is a light version of classic French cuisine: specialties include Dover sole meunière, and grilled venison medallions with a cranberry port wine sauce and caramelized apple slices. Terrific desserts. Choice of 1,500 wines. **FYI:** Reservations recommended. Jacket required. **Open:** Tues–Sat 5–10:30pm. Closed some hols. **Prices:** Main courses $17–$28; PF dinner $52.50–$80. Maj CC. ♥ ⬛

Attractions 🎫

Fullerton Arboretum; tel 714/773-3579. Located on the campus of California State University, Fullerton; entrance via Associated Rd. These 26 acres at the northeast corner of the campus were opened to the public in 1979. Some of the themed areas include the Botanical Collection; Palm Garden; Subtropical Fruit Grove; Conifer Area; Historic Area; and the Carnivorous Plant Bog. Guided tours are usually available (additional fee charged).

Also on the grounds is the **Heritage House,** built in 1894 and moved to its present site in 1972. Restored to its original appearance, the house is accessible by guided tour on weekends 11:30am–1:30pm (closed Jan and Aug). **Open:** Daily 8am–4:45pm. Closed some hols. $

Muckenthaler Cultural Center, 1201 W Malvern Ave; tel 714/738-6595. The historic Muckenthaler Mansion, surrounded by 8½ acres of manicured grounds, is now a cultural center offering art exhibitions, children's art activities, performing arts, lectures, films, and workshops; dinner theater performances in summer. **Open:** Tues–Sat 10am–4pm, Sun noon–5pm. Closed some hols. Free.

GARBERVILLE

Map page M-2, B1

Hotel 🛏

▤▤▤ Benbow Inn, 445 Lake Benbow Dr, Garberville, CA 95542; tel 707/923-2124. Benbow exit off US 101. Charming National Historic Landmark inn built in 1926 in a Tudor style. No smoking anywhere inside. **Rooms:** 54 rms; 1 ctge/villa. CI 2pm/CO noon. Nonsmoking rms avail. Many rooms have been beautifully renovated. **Amenities:** 🎛 🕭 📷 A/C, refrig, 1 unit w/minibar, some w/terraces, 1 w/fireplace. Some rooms have TV; all have sherry decanters and nice glassware. **Services:** 🖘 🖘 Babysitting. Complimentary tea and scones served in the lobby 3–4pm, mulled wine from 4–5pm in chilly weather. **Facilities:** 🚲 🏊 1 rst (*see also* "Restaurants" below), 1 bar (w/entertainment). Well-kept mini-beach on river shore (no lifeguard). Beautiful garden terrace for dining in good weather. **Rates:** $110–$190 S or D; from $275 ctge/villa. Extra person $15. Higher rates for spec evnts/hols. Spec packages avail. Pking: Outdoor, free. Maj CC.

Motels

▤▤ Best Western Humboldt House Inn, 701 Redwood Dr, Garberville, CA 95542 (Downtown); tel 707/923-2771 or toll free 800/528-1234; fax 707/923-4259. Garberville exit off US 101. A well-run place where the staff strives to please. **Rooms:** 76 rms and stes. CI 3pm/CO 11am. Nonsmoking rms avail. **Amenities:** 🎛 A/C, cable TV w/movies. Some units w/terraces. **Services:** 🖘 🖘 Babysitting. Pets allowed in smoking rooms only. **Facilities:** 🏊 🏊 👤 Whirlpool, washer/dryer. **Rates (CP):** HS June–Oct 15 $66–$69 S or D; from $86 ste. Extra person $5. Children under 5 stay free. Lower rates off-season. Pking: Outdoor, free. Maj CC.

▤ Motel Garberville, 948 Redwood Dr, Garberville, CA 95542 (Downtown); tel 707/923-2422. Garberville exit off US 101. Convenient to restaurants and highway, although set back from road. **Rooms:** 30 rms and stes. CI noon/CO 11am. Nonsmoking rms avail. **Amenities:** 🎛 📷 A/C, cable TV w/movies. Some units w/terraces. **Services:** 🖘 🖘 Pets allowed in 4 rooms. **Facilities:** 👤 1 rst, washer/dryer. **Rates:** HS May–Oct 14 $46–$52 S; $50–$57 D; from $80 ste. Extra person $6. Children under 5 stay free. Lower rates off-season. Pking: Outdoor, free. Maj CC.

▤ Sherwood Forest Motel, 814 Redwood Dr, Garberville, CA 95542 (Downtown); tel 707/923-2721 or toll free 800/544-5756; fax 707/923-3677. Garberville exit off US 101. Beautiful landscaping and warm hospitality lift the spirits of weary travelers. **Rooms:** 33 rms and stes. CI 2pm/CO 11am. Nonsmoking rms avail. **Amenities:** 🎛 🕭 📷 A/C, cable TV w/movies, refrig. 1 unit w/terrace. **Services:** 🖘 🖘 Babysitting. **Facilities:** 🏊 Whirlpool, washer/dryer. **Rates:** HS May–Oct $54–$64 S or D; from $80 ste. Extra person $5. Children under 5 stay free. Lower rates off-season. Pking: Outdoor, free. Maj CC.

Restaurant 🍴

Benbow Inn Dining Room, in the Benbow Inn, 445 Lake Benbow Dr, Garberville; tel 707/923-2124. Benbow exit off US 101. **New American.** Hearty meat, fish, and vegetarian dishes are prepared in imaginative contemporary style. Extensive selection of California wines, including many available by the glass. **FYI:** Reservations recommended. Piano. Children's menu. Dress code. **Open:** HS June 15–Sept 15 breakfast Mon–Sat 8–11am, Sun 8–10am; lunch daily noon–2pm; dinner daily 6–9pm; brunch Sun 10:30am–12:30pm. Reduced hours off-season. Closed 2 wks after Thanksgiving. **Prices:** Main courses $11.95–$19.95. Maj CC. 🍴

Attractions 💼

Avenue of the Giants; tel 707/923-2265. Located 6 miles north of Garberville on US 101. This scenic 33-mile roadway, which roughly parallels US 101, was left intact for sightseers when the freeway was built. The "giants" are majestic coast redwoods (*Sequoia sempervirens*). Over 500,000 acres of them make up the most outstanding display in the redwood belt, where more than 90% of the world's redwoods grow, and which roughly extends between Garberville and the Oregon state line. Their rough-barked columns climb 100 feet or more without a branch—some predate Christianity and are taller than a football field is long. The oldest dated coast redwood is over 2,200 years old.

The drive can be made either north or south, and will take about 1½ hours. Auto tour signs along the roadway indicate stopping points. A driving tour brochure can be picked up at the Phillipsville exit off Calif 101 (northbound) or the Jordan Creek exit off Calif 101 (southbound). Headquarters for Humboldt Redwoods State Park (see below) is on the Avenue at Burlington, 2 miles south of Weott.

Humboldt Redwoods State Park; tel 707/946-2409. Located 15 miles north of Garberville via US 101. The 3rd-largest California state park, Humboldt Redwoods covers over 50,000 acres. Approximately 17,000 of these acres consist of old growth redwood forests, which are generally defined as containing trees over 200 years old. Both US 101 and the Avenue of the Giants (see above) run through the park, paralleling the south fork of the Eel River.

The **visitor center** has several displays that interpret the redwood environment. Slide shows and videos highlight the natural history of the region; naturalist programs are offered as well. The park has facilities for swimming, fishing, hiking, and camping. **Open:** Daily 24 hours. $

GARDEN GROVE

Map page M-3, D2 (N of Santa Ana)

Restaurant 🍴

★ **Peppers Restaurant**, 12361 Chapman Ave, Garden Grove (Disneyland); tel 714/740-1333. Harbor Blvd exit off I-5; 5 blocks S on Harbor, right on Chapman. **Mexican.** A family-style Mexican restaurant with bright decor. Menu includes salads, tacos, enchiladas, burritos, fajitas, steaks, and seafood. An adjoining bar area features dancing to loud music during the evening. Complimentary bus service to and from local hotels. **FYI:** Reservations recommended. Children's menu. Dress code. **Open:** Lunch daily 11:30am–4pm; dinner daily 4–10pm; brunch Sun 10am–2pm. **Prices:** Main courses $7–$20. Maj CC. 🏷 ♿

GIANT FOREST

Map page M-3, B2

Lodge 🏨

📧 **Giant Forest Lodge**, Calif 198, Giant Forest, CA 93271 (Sequoia Nat'l Park); tel 209/561-3314. On Calif 198. Various facilities: deluxe motel to basic rooms, 1- and 2-room cabins with bath, rustic cabins without electricity or bath. Mailing address: Guest Services, PO Box 789, Three Rivers, CA 93271. **Rooms:** 83 rms; 161 ctges/villas. CI 3pm/CO 11am. Nonsmoking rms avail. **Amenities:** 🛁 No A/C, phone, or TV. Some units w/terraces, 1 w/fireplace. Some cabins have wood-burning cooking and heating stoves. **Services:** 🛎 **Facilities:** 🚶 🏞 2 rsts, 1 bar. Park's largest sequoia grove nearby, as are hiking trails. Ranger programs available. **Rates:** HS May–Oct $71–$90 S or D; from $32 ctge/villa. Children under 13 stay free. Lower rates off-season. Spec packages avail. Pking: Outdoor, free. Ltd CC. Deposit required on advance reservations.

GLENDALE

Map page M-3, D2

Hotels 🏨

📧📧 **Best Western Golden Key Motor Hotel**, 123 W Colorado St, Glendale, CA 91204; tel 818/247-0111 or toll free 800/528-1234; fax 818/545-9393. Basic, decent motel. **Rooms:** 55 rms. CI noon/CO noon. Express checkout avail. Nonsmoking rms avail. **Amenities:** 📺 🛁 🍴 A/C, satel TV w/movies, refrig, VCR, bathrobes. Bottled water included with each room. Microwave. **Services:** 🚗 🛎 Car-rental desk, babysitting. Continental breakfast looked sparse. **Facilities:** 🏋 🏊 Whirlpool. **Rates (CP):** $69–$78 S; $69–$81 D. Extra person $5. Children under 12 stay free. Higher rates for spec evnts/hols. Pking: Outdoor, free. Maj CC.

📧📧📧📧 **Red Lion Hotel–Glendale**, 100 W Glenoaks Blvd, Glendale, CA 91202; tel 818/956-5466 or toll free 800/547-8010; fax 818/956-5490. Gorgeous hotel with futuristic deco design. Great views of city from 19th floor. **Rooms:** 348 rms and stes. Exec-level rms avail. CI 3pm/CO noon. Express checkout avail. Nonsmoking rms avail. Lovely pastel decor, very quiet; comfortable for family or business travelers. Room numbers also in Braille. **Amenities:** 📺 🛁 📠 🍴 A/C, cable TV w/movies, bathrobes. All units w/minibars. **Services:** ✕ 🎫 VP 🚌 🏊 🛎 🤵 Twice-daily maid svce, car-rental desk, babysitting. **Facilities:** 🏋 🏓 🏞 ♿ 2 rsts, 3 bars (2 w/entertainment), games rm, sauna, whirlpool, washer/dryer. Orange and magnolia trees soften pool area. Pool has lift for guests with disabilities. Superb fitness room with stacks of towels, drink machine with juice and mineral water. **Rates:** $148–$173 S; $163–$188 D; from $250 ste. Extra person $10. Children under 18 stay free. Higher rates for spec evnts/hols. Spec packages avail. Pking: Indoor, $5–$8. Maj CC.

Restaurant

$ **Cinnabar**, 933 S Brand Blvd, Glendale; tel 818/551-1155. **Californian/Asian.** Restaurant is the ground floor of historic Bekins Warehouse building. Old safe next to '50s jukebox, cane and bamboo chairs, pillars, ornate bar with Japanese lanterns, a high ceiling. Light California-style cuisine offers lemongrass bouillabaisse, yellowtail mille-feuille, snow crab with rice vinegar and red chili sauce. **FYI:** Reservations recommended. **Open:** Lunch Tues–Fri 11:30am–2:30pm; dinner Tues–Thurs 6–9:30pm, Fri–Sat 6–10:30pm. Closed some hols; 2 weeks in September. **Prices:** Main courses $7.50–$18.50. Ltd CC. ♥ ▪ ⑂

Attraction

Forest Lawn Memorial Park, 1712 S Glendale Ave; tel 213/254-3131. There are 5 Forest Lawns in LA, but this is the one you've heard about. Among those entombed here are Jean Harlow, Clark Gable, Carole Lombard, and W C Fields. The Memorial Court of Honor reserves crypts for those whose service to humanity has been outstanding; Gutzon Borglum, creator of Mount Rushmore, and composer Rudolph Friml rest here. The cemetery's biggest draws are two paintings, *The Crucifixion* and *The Resurrection,* part of a narrated show presented daily every hour from 10am to 4pm. There are also a number of cemetery churches and the **Forest Lawn Museum,** with 14th-century stained-glass cathedral windows from the William Randolph Hearst collection, and reproductions of famous artworks, including Michelangelo's *Sotterraneo* and *David.* **Open:** Daily 9am–6pm. Free.

GLEN ELLEN

Map page M-2, C2 (N of Sonoma)

Inn

Gaige House, 13540 Arnold Dr, Glen Ellen, CA 95442; tel 707/935-0237; fax 707/935-6411. Arnold Dr exit off Calif 12. 3 acres. One of the most attractive inns in the county, in a Queen Anne Victorian house decorated with lavish antiques and artwork. Peaceful setting. Unsuitable for children under 16. **Rooms:** 9 rms and stes. CI 3pm/CO 11am. No smoking. Some rooms have 4-poster beds. **Amenities:** No A/C or TV. **Services:** Afternoon tea and wine/sherry served. Full country-style breakfast; complimentary wine and cheese in the evening. **Facilities:** Guest lounge w/TV. Beautiful pool and grounds with hammocks and picnic tables. **Rates (BB):** HS June–Oct $100–$175 D; from $225 ste. Extra person $25. Min stay wknds. Lower rates off-season. Pking: Outdoor, free. Ltd CC.

Restaurant

Garden Court Cafe & Bakery, 13875 Sonoma Hwy 12, Glen Ellen; tel 707/935-1565. 7 mi N of Sonoma. **Cafe.** A fine lunch spot. This sunny place is set in a lovely part of the Sonoma wine country, amid tall oaks and grassy knolls. Kitchen serves up fresh homemade breads and heart-shaped biscuits, plus sandwiches, soups, and salads. **FYI:** Reservations not accepted. Beer and wine only. **Open:** Wed–Sun 7am–2pm. **Prices:** Lunch main courses $4–$7. Ltd CC. ▪

GOLD COUNTRY

See Auburn, Grass Valley, Jackson, Nevada City, Placerville, Sutter Creek

GOLETA

Map page M-3, D1 (W of Santa Barbara)

Motel

Holiday Inn, 5650 Calle Real, Goleta, CA 93117; tel 805/964-6241 or toll free 800/HOLIDAY; fax 805/964-8467. Fairview exit off US 101. Standard Holiday Inn, close to the university, shopping, and restaurants. **Rooms:** 154 rms. Exec-level rms avail. CI 2pm/CO noon. Express checkout avail. Nonsmoking rms avail. Rooms are basic. **Amenities:** A/C, cable TV w/movies. **Services:** ╳ 🐕 ▪ 🛏 **Facilities:** 🏋 ▪ ⑂ 1 rst, 1 bar, washer/dryer. Kids accompanied by parents eat for free in the restaurant. **Rates:** HS May–Sept $78–$160 S or D. Extra person $10. Children under 19 stay free. Min stay spec evnts. Lower rates off-season. Higher rates for spec evnts/hols. Pking: Outdoor, free. Maj CC.

GRANT GROVE

Map page M-3, B2

Motel 🏨

🏨 **Cedar Grove Lodge**, Calif 180, Grant Grove, CA 93262 (Kings Canyon Nat'l Park); tel 209/561-3314. Cedar Grove Village exit off Calif 180. A motel on the banks of the majestic Kings River, reached by a 32-mile drive along a winding 2-lane road with spectacular vistas. River views from communal decks. Close to hiking trails and fishing. Mailing address: Guest Services, PO Box 789, Three Rivers, CA 93271. **Rooms:** 18 rms. CI 4pm/CO 11am. Nonsmoking rms avail. Comfortable. 1 room for guests with disabilities. **Amenities:** 🛁 A/C. No phone or TV. **Services:** 🍽 **Facilities:** 🛗 1 rst. Meals at snack bar. **Rates:** HS May–Oct $78–$90 S or D. Children under 13 stay free. Lower rates off-season. Higher rates for spec evnts/hols. Spec packages avail. Pking: Outdoor, free. Ltd CC. Senior discounts if requested at time of reservation.

Lodges

🏨 **Grant Grove Lodge**, Calif 180, Grant Grove, CA 93633 (Kings Canyon Nat'l Park); tel 209/335-2314; fax 209/335-2364. 55 mi E of Fresno. Calif I-80 to Kings Canyon National Park. Very rustic cabins set in a beautiful pine forest on the edge of Kings Canyon National Park. Mailing address: Guests Services, PO Box 789, Three Rivers, CA 93271. **Rooms:** 52 ctges/villas. CI 4pm/CO 11am. 9 cabins with baths have electricity and indoor plumbing. Other accommodations in "rustic cabins" that have kerosene lanterns and common bathrooms. Some rustic cabins have outdoor wood-burning stoves for cooking; wood is included. **Amenities:** No A/C, phone, or TV. Some units w/terraces. **Services:** 🍽 🛎 **Facilities:** 🛗 🏕 🏇 1 rst, 1 bar. Visitor center, market, and gas station on premises. Horseback riding at nearby stables. **Rates:** HS Mid-Apr–Oct $71 S or D; from $32 ctge/villa. Children under 13 stay free. Lower rates off-season. Higher rates for spec evnts/hols. Spec packages avail. Pking: Outdoor, free. Ltd CC.

🏨 **Montecito-Sequoia Lodge**, 8000 Generals Hwy, Grant Grove, CA 93633 (Kings Canyon Nat'l Park); tel 209/565-3388 or toll free 800/227-9900; fax 209/568-3223. 65 mi E of Fresno. Calif I-80 E to Kings Canyon National Park entrance; continue to fork; go right 8 mi. A barebones mountain lodge/resort in a spectacular setting 7,500 feet above sea level, with views of the snow-capped peaks of the Great Western Divide. Great for families and singles. For reservations, write to 1485 Redwood Dr, Los Altos, CA 94024, or call the toll free number. **Rooms:** 35 rms; 13 ctges/villas. CI 4pm/CO 11am. Lodge rooms have

private baths. Cabins are spare, with no running water, communal showers, and toilets nearby. **Amenities:** No A/C, phone, or TV. **Services:** 🍽 Social director, children's program, babysitting. Hearty buffet-style breakfast and dinner. **Facilities:** 🛗 ⚠ 🛗 🏕 🏇 📷 ⛵ 🏊 1 rst, 1 bar, whirlpool. Summer family camp. Nordic ski center with ski rentals and ice skating; 22 miles of groomed nordic ski trails, and 50 miles of ungroomed trails offering superb backcountry skiing. **Rates (MAP):** HS June 20–Labor Day $88 S; $86–$138 D; from $60 ctge/villa. Extra person $39–$59. Min stay HS. Lower rates off-season. AP rates avail. Pking: Outdoor, free. Maj CC. Children 5–11, $29 per person; children under 5, $8.

GRASS VALLEY

Map page M-2, C2

Hotel 🏨

🏨🏨🏨 **Holbrooke Hotel**, 212 W Main St, Grass Valley, CA 95945; tel 916/273-1353 or toll free 800/933-7077; fax 916/273-0434. Calif 174 exit off Calif 49. This landmark inn is a gem, with modern conveniences and creature comforts. Quite romantic. **Rooms:** 27 rms and stes. CI 3pm/CO 11am. Nonsmoking rms avail. Each room is unique, with high-quality, comfortable furnishings. Some have verandas overlooking Main Street. **Amenities:** 🛁 🛁 A/C, cable TV w/movies. Some units w/terraces, some w/fireplaces. **Services:** ✕ 🔑 🛎 🍽 Babysitting. Some business services available. Complimentary continental breakfast, except Sunday when brunch is sold in the dining room. **Facilities:** 🛗 🛗 1 rst, 2 bars (1 w/entertainment). Reading room. Checkers in the lobby. **Rates (CP):** HS Apr–Dec $66–$106 S or D; from $120 ste. Extra person $10. Children under 10 stay free. Lower rates off-season. Spec packages avail. Pking: Outdoor, free. Maj CC.

Restaurants 🍴

Main Street Cafe and Bar, 213 W Main St, Grass Valley; tel 916/477-6000. Calif 174 exit off Calif 49/20. **Continental.** A pleasant, quiet setting, with white tablecloths and a small patio outside. Interesting dishes include Tomales Bay oysters, salmon ravioli and other pastas, crêpes, blackened filet, and crawfish. **FYI:** Reservations accepted. Guitar/singer. Children's menu. **Open:** Lunch Mon–Sat 11am–3pm; dinner Sun–Thurs 5–9pm, Fri–Sat 5–10pm. Closed some hols. **Prices:** Main courses $9.95–$19.95. Maj CC. 🍴 🛗

★ **Tofanelli's**, 302 W Main St, Grass Valley; tel 916/272-1468. Calif 174 exit off Calif 49. **Californian/Italian.** This popular restaurant serves pasta and seafood in a 19th-century setting, with tin ceiling and brick walls. **FYI:** Reservations not accepted. Beer and wine only. **Open:** Breakfast Mon–Fri 7–11am; lunch Mon–Fri 11:30am–4:30pm; dinner daily 5–9pm; brunch Sat–Sun 9am–2pm. Closed some hols. **Prices:** Main courses $4.95–$11.95. Ltd CC.

Attraction

Empire Mine State Historic Park, 10791 E Empire St; tel 916/273-8522. This is the site of the oldest and richest hardrock gold mine in California. From its discovery in 1850 until its closure in 1956, an estimated 5.8 million ounces of gold were extracted from its 367 miles of underground passages. The 700-acre property was purchased by the State of California in 1975, and a gradual restoration program has transformed the mine into an educational and recreational resource.

Hiking trails are accesible year-round, as are the formal gardens surrounding the residence of the wealthy Bourn family, who owned the mine from 1877–1929. From April–November, guided tours of the mine, the lovely stone "cottage" of the mine owner, and a scale model of the system of mineshafts are made available to visitors. Call ahead for detailed tour information. **Open:** Schedule varies; phone ahead. $

GROVER BEACH

Map page M-3, C1 (S of Pismo Beach)

Motel

▤ ▤ ▤ **Oak Park Inn**, 775 N Oak Park Blvd, Grover Beach, CA 93443; tel 805/481-4448 or toll free 800/549-4448; fax 805/473-3609. Oak Park Rd exit off US 101. Attractive, well-kept property. **Rooms:** 35 rms and stes. CI 2pm/CO noon. Nonsmoking rms avail. Pleasant rooms, with blond wood furnishings, bleached oak desk, and, in the king rooms, a little dining table. **Amenities:** A/C, cable TV w/movies. All units w/terraces, some w/fireplaces, some w/Jacuzzis. **Services:** **Facilities:** Whirlpool, washer/dryer. Fabulous pool landscaped with a waterfall and a small bridge. **Rates (CP):** HS May–Oct $59–$95 S or D; from $95 ste. Extra person $5. Children under 15 stay free. Min stay HS. Lower rates off-season. Pking: Outdoor, free. Maj CC.

GUALALA

Map page M-2, C1

Motel

▤ ▤ **Gualala Country Inn**, 47955 Center St, PO Box 697, Gualala, CA 95445; tel 707/884-4343 or toll free 800/564-4466. Off Calif 1. Clean motel located in town, across from beach. Pleasant lobby. A bargain for the coast. **Rooms:** 20 rms. CI 3pm/CO 11am. Adequate, clean, basic rooms overlook Calif 1 and ocean. **Amenities:** Cable TV. No A/C. Some units w/fireplaces, some w/Jacuzzis. **Services:** Free morning coffee and tea in lobby. **Facilities:** **Rates:** $71–$145 S or D. Children under 18 stay free. Min stay spec evnts. Pking: Outdoor, free. Ltd CC. Good discounts during mid-week.

Inns

▤ ▤ **St Orres**, 36601 S Calif 1, PO Box 523, Gualala, CA 95445; tel 707/884-3303. Set on a wooded hillside overlooking the ocean. Main building features Russian-style architecture, with copper onion domes and wisteria-covered terraces. Charming lobby and bar. **Rooms:** 8 rms (all w/shared bath); 11 ctges/villas. CI 3pm/CO noon. No smoking. Cottages have kitchens and are a bit bare. Decks have views of ocean and meadows. All rooms in main building share bath. **Amenities:** Refrig. No A/C, phone, or TV. Some units w/minibars, some w/terraces, some w/fireplaces. **Services:** Masseur, afternoon tea and wine/sherry served. Breakfast with homemade breads, hot entrees, and fresh fruit. **Facilities:** 1 rst (see also "Restaurants" below), 1 bar, guest lounge. Excellent massage available. **Rates (BB):** HS June–Oct from $90 ctge/villa. Extra person $15. Children under 2 stay free. Min stay wknds and spec evnts. Lower rates off-season. Pking: Outdoor, free. Ltd CC.

▤ ▤ ▤ ▤ **Seacliff**, 39140 S Calif 1, PO Box 697, Gualala, CA 95445; tel 707/884-1213 or toll free 800/400-5053. Very peaceful and offers the best ocean views in area. Lobby is airy and outfitted with a fireplace and telescope for watching wildlife. Unsuitable for children under 18. **Rooms:** 16 rms. CI 3pm/CO 11am. Nonsmoking rms avail. Rooms on bluff overlook Gualala River and beach and have balconies facing the ocean. Upstairs rooms have vaulted ceilings. **Amenities:** Cable TV, refrig, bathrobes. No A/C. All units w/terraces, all w/fireplaces, all w/Jacuzzis. Complimentary champagne or cider in refrigerator; champagne glasses. Binoculars for watching seals, pelicans, and whales. **Facilities:** **Rates:** HS June–Sept $155–$180 S or D. Min stay spec evnts. Lower rates off-season. Pking: Outdoor, free. Ltd CC. Rates lower Sunday–Thursday.

≣≣≣≣ **Whale Watch Inn**, 35100 Calif 1, Gualala, CA 95445; tel 707/884-3667 or toll free 800/WHALE-42. 2½ acres. A romantic retreat with a private staircase down to Mendocino's most beautiful beach. Many activities nearby. **Rooms:** 18 rms and stes. CI 3pm/CO 11am. No smoking. Rooms have gorgeous views and are beautifully furnished. One has an upstairs fireplace and sitting room. **Amenities:** ⌖ No A/C, phone, or TV. All units w/terraces, all w/fireplaces, some w/Jacuzzis. **Services:** ✗ Masseur. Full, fancy breakfast can be served in room. Wine and cheese on Saturday night. **Facilities:** ⅙ 1 beach (ocean), guest lounge. Separate lounge area with fireplace, library, kitchen, and telescope. **Rates (BB):** HS July–Oct $170–$255 D; from $200 ste. Extra person $20. Children under 5 stay free. Min stay wknds and spec evnts. Lower rates off-season. Pking: Outdoor, free. Ltd CC.

Restaurant 🍴

St Orres, Calif 1, Gualala (Sonoma Coast); tel 707/884-3303. **Californian.** A romantic dining room in a Russian-style copper-domed building. With copper place settings and long-stemmed flowers on the tables. The prix-fixe dinner includes 3 courses, with entrees such as wild boar or quail, and vegetarian selections such as grilled vegetable tart. Menu changes regularly. **FYI:** Reservations recommended. Beer and wine only. **Open:** HS June–Nov dinner Sun–Fri 6–9pm, Sat 5:15–9:45pm. Reduced hours off-season. **Prices:** PF dinner $30. No CC. ♥ ⅙

GUERNEVILLE

Map page M-2, C1 (SW of Healdsburg)

Attraction 🖼

Korbel Champagne Cellars, 13250 River Rd; tel 707/887-2294. Tours of this brick-and-redwood winery, built in 1886, explain the champagne-making process brought to the United States by the 3 Korbel brothers from Czechoslovakia. Free tastings are included in the winery tour; garden tours are offered in summer. **Open:** Oct–Apr, daily 9am–4:30pm; May–Sept, daily 9am–5pm. Free.

HALF MOON BAY

Map page M-2, D1 (S of Pacifica)

***See also* El Granada, Moss Beach, Princeton-by-the-Sea**

Hotel 🏨

≣≣≣ **Half Moon Bay Lodge**, 2400 S Cabrillo Hwy, Half Moon Bay, CA 94019; tel 415/726-9000 or toll free 800/368-2468; fax 415/726-7951. Calif 1 exit off Calif 92. Very clean, neat, and attractive throughout. Several beaches within 5 miles. Good value. **Rooms:** 80 rms and stes. CI 3:30pm/CO 11:30am. Nonsmoking rms avail. Large rooms with queen- or king-size beds. Suites are spacious and well appointed. Many rooms overlook the golf course. **Amenities:** 🔱 ⌖ ☎ Cable TV w/movies. No A/C. All units w/terraces, some w/fireplaces, 1 w/Jacuzzi. **Services:** ☒ ↺ Babysitting. Staff can arrange limos to airport and car rentals. **Facilities:** ⅙ ▶18 🏋 🏊70 ⅙ Whirlpool. 2 restaurants adjacent to lodge, 1 moderate and 1 upscale. Glass-walled poolside gazebo with large whirlpool spa. Beach horseback riding. Hiking on beach trails. **Rates:** $115–$150 S or D; from $150 ste. Extra person $10. Children under 12 stay free. Min stay spec evnts. Pking: Outdoor, free. Maj CC.

Motels

≣≣ **Holiday Inn Express**, 230 Cabrillo Hwy (Calif 1), Half Moon Bay, CA 94019; tel 415/726-3400 or toll free 800/HOLIDAY; fax 415/726-1256. ¼ mi S of Half Moon Bay, exit Calif 1 off Calif 92. Smaller than typical Holiday Inn. Clean and basic, with no facilities or restaurant. **Rooms:** 52 rms. CI 3pm/CO noon. Express checkout avail. Nonsmoking rms avail. **Amenities:** 🔱 Cable TV w/movies, VCR. No A/C. Some units w/terraces. VCRs may be rented at front desk. **Services:** ☒ ↺ 🐾 **Facilities:** ⅙ **Rates (CP):** HS mid May–Sept $85–$95 S or D. Extra person $12. Children under 16 stay free. Lower rates off-season. Higher rates for spec evnts/hols. Spec packages avail. Pking: Outdoor, free. Maj CC.

≣≣ **Ramada Limited**, 3020 Calif 1, Half Moon Bay, CA 94019; tel 415/726-9700 or toll free 800/2-RAMADA; fax 415/726-5269. Calif 1 exit off Calif 92. Property is clean, pleasant, and very basic. **Rooms:** 20 rms. CI 1pm/CO 11am. Nonsmoking rms avail. Small and very plain. **Amenities:** 🔱 ⌖ A/C, cable TV w/movies, VCR. Some units w/Jacuzzis. Microwave and refrigerator in 5 rooms. **Services:** ☒ ↺ 🐾 **Facilities:** ⅙ **Rates:** HS May–Sept $55–$95 S; $75–$125 D. Children under 18 stay free. Lower rates off-season. Higher rates for spec evnts/hols. Pking: Outdoor, free. Maj CC. Rates fluctuate depending on length of stay; $10 charge for pets.

Restaurants 🍴

★ **Papa George's Ristorante & Pub**, 2320 Cabrillo Hwy, Half Moon Bay; tel 415/726-9417. Calif 1 exit off Calif 92. **Italian.** Popular with locals and guests from nearby hotels. Country decor with solid tables and chairs and fresh flowers. Colorful pub. Italian menu features spinach pasta filled with ricotta and Parmesan cheese; linguine with mussels; roast duck with Italian sausage and fresh herbs; and rack of lamb. **FYI:** Reservations recommended. Blues/jazz/singer. **Open:** HS Spring–fall lunch Tues–Sun 11:30am–2:30pm; dinner Tues–Sun 5–10pm; brunch Sun 10am–2:30pm. Reduced hours off-season. Closed some hols. **Prices:** Main courses $11.95–$21.95. 🚢 🅿 👪

Pasta Moon, 315 Main St, Half Moon Bay; tel 415/726-5125. Main St exit off Calif 92. **Italian.** Crowded with small tables packed close to each other. Many pastas to choose from. Also at: 425 Marina Blvd, in Oyster Point Marina, San Francisco (415/876-7090). **FYI:** Reservations accepted. **Open:** Lunch Mon–Fri 11:30am–2:30pm, Sat–Sun noon–3pm; dinner Mon–Thurs 5:30–9pm, Fri 5:30–10pm, Sat–Sun 5:30–9:30pm. Closed Dec 25. **Prices:** Main courses $5.95–$12.95. Maj CC.

HANFORD
Map page M-3, B1

Motel 🛏

📶 **Best Western Hanford Inn**, 755 Cadillac Lane, Hanford, CA 93230; tel 209/583-7300 or toll free 800/528-1234; fax 209/582-8455. 11th St exit off Calif 198. An upcoming restoration is needed. **Rooms:** 40 rms and stes. CI 1pm/CO 11am. Nonsmoking rms avail. Mini-suites are a good buy. **Amenities:** 📶 A/C, cable TV w/movies. **Services:** ⏚ **Facilities:** 🏋 ⎚ Washer/dryer. **Rates:** $42–$55 S; $48–$59 D; from $48 ste. Extra person $6. Children under 12 stay free. Spec packages avail. Pking: Outdoor, free. Maj CC.

Inn

📶 **Irwin St Inn**, 522 N Irwin St, Hanford, CA 93230 (Downtown); tel 209/583-8000; fax 209/583-8793. Exit 198 off Calif 99. A B&B inn made up of 4 late–19th-century Victorian homes moved here and restored in the 1970s. **Rooms:** 30 rms and stes. CI 2pm/CO noon. Each room is large and distinctively decorated. **Amenities:** 📶 A/C, cable TV. All units w/terraces. **Services:** ✕ ⎚ ⏚ 🚐 Babysitting. Continental breakfast with homemade "morning glory" muffins. **Facilities:** 🏋 1 rst. Charming restaurant with patio serves breakfast, lunch, and

dinner. **Rates (CP):** $69–$89 S or D; from $99 ste. Children under 12 stay free. Spec packages avail. Pking: Outdoor, free. Ltd CC.

HAWTHORNE
Map page M-3, D2 (NW of Long Beach)

Hotel 🛏

📶 **Cockatoo Inn**, 4334 W Imperial Hwy, Hawthorne, CA 90250 (Los Angeles Int'l Airport); tel 310/619-2291 or toll free 800/458-2800; fax 310/679-4390. Beautiful red-brick and half-timbered complex with garden patios and formal lobby. **Rooms:** 213 rms and stes. Exec-level rms avail. CI 1pm/CO noon. Nonsmoking rms avail. **Amenities:** 📶 ⎚ 📺 A/C, cable TV w/movies. Some units w/terraces, some w/fireplaces, 1 w/Jacuzzi. **Services:** ✕ 🔑 🚐 ⏚ Free shuttle to shopping centers. **Facilities:** 🏋 1 rst, 1 bar. **Rates:** $54 S; $59 D; from $94 ste. Extra person $5. Children under 12 stay free. Pking: Indoor, free. Pking: Outdoor, free. Maj CC.

HAYWARD
Map page M-2, D2 (S of Oakland)

Hotel 🛏

📶 **Executive Inn–Hayward Airport**, 20777 Hesperian Blvd, Hayward, CA 94541 (Oakland Int'l Airport); tel 510/732-6300 or toll free 800/553-5083; fax 510/783-2265. A St W exit off I-880, to Hesperian Blvd. Very pleasant, fairly new hotel adjacent to private airport. Walking distance to good restaurants, golf course, and tennis courts. **Rooms:** 146 rms and stes. CI 1pm/CO noon. Nonsmoking rms avail. Deluxe king rooms are large, with sofa and coffee table. Bathrooms have separate tub and toilet/sink area. **Amenities:** 📶 ⎚ 📺 A/C, cable TV w/movies. Some units w/terraces. King rooms have wet bars, refrigerators. VCRs for rent; videos are free. **Services:** 🚐 ⎚ ⏚ 🚐 Car-rental desk. Complimentary wine and cheese Tuesday and Wednesday 5–7pm. Free shuttle to rapid transit station. **Facilities:** 🏋 🏊 👥 ⎚ Whirlpool, washer/dryer. **Rates (CP):** $72 S; $76 D; from $84 ste. Extra person $4. Children under 12 stay free. Spec packages avail. Pking: Outdoor, free. Maj CC.

Restaurant 🍴

Rue de Main, 22622 Main St, Hayward; tel 510/537-0812. Between B and C Sts. **French.** Located in a historic building. The dining room is painted with murals depicting Parisian street scenes. Standard French menu features such staples as escargots, onion soup, and many dishes with wine- or cream-based sauces. **FYI:** Reservations recommended. Beer and wine only. **Open:** Lunch Tues–Fri 11:30am–2:15pm; dinner Tues–Sat 5:30–10pm. Closed some hols; June 23–30. **Prices:** Main courses $14–$22. Maj CC. &

Attractions 🎒

Hayward Area Historical Society Museum, 22701 Main St; tel 510/581-0223. Housed in a 1927 brick post office building, the museum features permanent displays of a 1923 fire engine, a 1860s fire pumper, a re-created 1930s post office, and maps and photographs of local history. Changing exhibits; gift shop. **Open:** Mon–Fri 11am–4pm, Sat noon–4pm. Closed some hols. Free.

McConaghy House, 18701 Hesperian Blvd; tel 510/581-0223. Guided tours are offered of this 12-room Victorian farmhouse, which is furnished in the style of 1886, the year of its construction. Also on the tour are the carriage house, containing a buggy and farm equipment, and the tank house. The house sports Victorian Christmas decorations during the holiday season. Gift shop with Victorian-style gifts. **Open:** Thurs–Sun 1–4pm. Closed some hols. $

HEALDSBURG

Map page M-2, C1

Hotels 🏨

≋≋ Best Western Dry Creek Inn, 198 Dry Creek Rd, Healdsburg, CA 95448; tel 707/433-0300 or toll free 800/222-5784. At US 101. Close to area attractions. **Rooms:** 102 rms. CI 3pm/CO noon. Express checkout avail. Nonsmoking rms avail. Rooms are clean but lackluster. **Amenities:** 🛁 🍷 📺 🍴 A/C, cable TV w/movies, refrig. **Services:** 🍴 🍷 Complimentary bottle of wine. **Facilities:** 🗄 🏋️ & Washer/dryer. **Rates (CP):** HS June–Oct $70–$79 S or D. Extra person $10. Children under 18 stay free. Min stay spec evnts. Lower rates off-season. Spec packages avail. Pking: Outdoor, free. Maj CC. Low mid-week rates and special packages.

≋≋ Vineyard Valley Inn, 178 Dry Creek Rd, Healdsburg, CA 95448; tel 707/433-0101 or toll free 800/499-0103; fax 707/433-1466. Dry Creek exit off US 101. Clean economy hotel in the heart of wine country. **Rooms:** 24 rms and stes. CI 2pm/CO 11am. Nonsmoking rms avail. Very plain rooms done in soothing blue tones. **Amenities:** 🛁 Cable TV. No A/C. **Services:** 🍴 🍷 **Facilities:** 🏋️ & Sauna, whirlpool. **Rates (CP):** HS June–

Oct $45–$90 S or D; from $90 ste. Extra person $10. Children under 12 stay free. Lower rates off-season. Pking: Outdoor, free. Maj CC. Low midweek rates.

Inns

≋≋≋ Healdsburg Inn on the Plaza, 110 Matheson St, PO Box 1196, Healdsburg, CA 95448; or toll free 800/431-8663. Cute, historic bed-and-breakfast-style inn right on the plaza, with an art gallery in the lobby. Unsuitable for children under 5. **Rooms:** 9 rms. CI 4pm/CO 11am. No smoking. Each room is unique; most have antique clawfoot tubs and iron beds. **Amenities:** 🍷 Cable TV, VCR. No A/C or phone. Some units w/terraces, some w/fireplaces. **Services:** Afternoon tea and wine/sherry served. Free use of videos. Complimentary full champagne breakfast. **Facilities:** Guest lounge w/TV. Nice breakfast room; dine indoors or in garden. **Rates (BB):** HS July–Oct $135–$175 D. Extra person $30. Min stay wknds. Lower rates off-season. Pking: Outdoor, free. Ltd CC.

≋≋≋≋ Madrona Manor, 1001 Westside Rd, PO Box 818, Healdsburg, CA 95448; tel 707/433-4231 or toll free 800/258-4003; fax 707/433-0703. Central Healdsburg exit off US 101; follow Healdsburg Ave to Mill St and turn left; Mill turns into Westside Rd after you cross US 101. 8 acres. One of the nicest places to stay in Sonoma County. Very romantic Victorian inn with lots of history and quiet setting amid beautiful gardens. **Rooms:** 21 rms and stes; 2 ctges/villas. CI 11am/CO 3pm. High ceilings, restored museum-quality antiques, and cozy sitting areas in each room. **Amenities:** 🛁 🍷 Bathrobes. No A/C or TV. Some units w/fireplaces, 1 w/Jacuzzi. **Services:** 📞 🍴 Masseur, wine/sherry served. Wonderful breakfast served in garden. **Facilities:** 🗄 🖼 & 1 rst (*see also* "Restaurants" below), 1 bar, guest lounge. Excellent restaurant with patio dining; lovely pool area. **Rates (BB):** HS Mar–Oct $135–$180 D; from $200 ste; from $200 ctge/villa. Extra person $30. Children under 12 stay free. Min stay HS and wknds. Lower rates off-season. Pking: Outdoor, free. Ltd CC.

Restaurants 🍽️

Bistro Ralph, 109 Plaza St, Healdsburg; tel 707/433-1380. 17 mi N of Santa Rosa. **Californian.** A culinary gem right on the main plaza. Modern restaurant with bentwood chairs, fine linen, and a huge vase of sunflowers at the entrance. Menu highlights organic ingredients from local farmers: dishes include lamb stew niçoise, Szechuan calamari, and sautéed tuna. Local wines. **FYI:** Reservations recommended. Beer and wine only. **Open:** Mon–Fri 11:30am–10pm, Sat–Sun 5:30–10pm. Closed some hols. **Prices:** Main courses $12–$16. Ltd CC. &

Madrona Manor, in the Madrona Manor, 1001 Westside Rd, Healdsburg; tel 800/258-4003. Central Healdsburg exit off US 101; follow Healdsburg Ave to Mill St and turn left; Mill turns into Westside Rd after you cross US 101. **Californian/French.** Exquisite Victorian retreat in wine country, with romantic ambience and outdoor dining overlooking the gardens. Fine cuisine uses exclusively fresh ingredients; 4-course prix-fixe dinner includes wine. All breads, pastries, ice cream, pasta, and cured meats are prepared on site. **FYI:** Reservations recommended. Dress code. Beer and wine only. **Open:** HS Mar–Oct breakfast daily 8–9:45am; dinner daily 6–9pm; brunch Sun 11am–2pm. Reduced hours off-season. **Prices:** Main courses $21–$24; PF dinner $40–$50. Maj CC. ♥ ■ &

Plaza Street Market, 113 Plaza St, Healdsburg; tel 707/431-2800. Central Healdsburg exit off US 101. **Cafe/Cafeteria/Deli.** Lovely restaurant in a beautifully restored 1883 building, with nice wood bar and marble tables. Pleasant indoor and outdoor dining areas face the plaza. Wide variety of sandwiches includes roast turkey breast, smoked chicken, and roasted eggplant. **FYI:** Reservations not accepted. Beer and wine only. **Open:** Daily 9am–6pm. Closed some hols. **Prices:** Lunch main courses $3–$6. Ltd CC. &

Samba Java, 109 A Plaza St, Healdsburg; tel 707/433-5282. 17 mi N of Santa Rosa. Central Healdsburg exit off US 101; continue to the center of town; restaurant is located on north side of plaza. **Californian.** Colorful and fun Caribbean decor in a narrow space with huge primitive artworks and splashy industrial tables. Focus is on fresh local ingredients and good quality at reasonable prices. Highlights on the ever-changing menu could include adzuki bean soup, duck breast with roasted garlic, filet of beef, or fettuccine with shiitake mushrooms. **FYI:** Reservations accepted. Beer and wine only. **Open:** Closed some hols; first week Jan. **Prices:** Main courses $9–$15. Maj CC. &

Tre Scalini, 24 Healdsburg Ave, Healdsburg; tel 707/433-1772. 70 mi N of San Francisco. Central Healdsburg exit off US 101. **Californian/Italian.** Nice Italian decor in a small dining room. Good nouveau Italian food includes risotto with wild mushrooms, fresh cod, and Sonoma rabbit. **FYI:** Reservations recommended. Beer and wine only. **Open:** Mon–Thurs 5–9pm, Fri–Sat 5–10pm. Closed some hols. **Prices:** Main courses $9–$14. Maj CC. &

Refreshment Stop ☕

Downtown Bakery and Creamery, 308A Center St, Healdsburg; tel 707/431-2719. 20 mi N of Santa Rosa. Central Healdsburg exit off US 101. **Cafe.** Large, open bakery right on the plaza, owned by Lindsey Shere, also pastry chef at Chez Panisse. Specializes in peach-polenta cherry tarts, chocolate macaroons, tiramisù, flaky croissants, and gooey cinnamon rolls. **Open:** Mon–Fri 6am–5:30pm, Sat–Sun 7am–5:30pm. Closed some hols; Jan 1–7. No CC.

Attraction 🖼

Simi Winery, 16275 Healdsburg Ave; tel 707/433-6981. In 1876, brothers Guiseppe and Pietro Simi emigrated to northern California, establishing their own cellars in 1890. These cellars housed the entire winemaking operation for 100 years and are now part of the guided tours of the facility, offered at 11am, 1pm, and 3pm. A fee is charged for tasting of premium wines. **Open:** Daily 10am–4:30pm. Closed some hols. Free.

HEMET

Map page M-3, D3

Motels 🛏

≡≡ **Hemet Inn**, 800 W Florida Ave, Hemet, CA 92543; tel 909/929-6366; fax 909/925-3016. Flowering trees provide a nice welcome to this Spanish-style motel. **Rooms:** 65 rms. CI noon/CO noon. Nonsmoking rms avail. King and queen beds available. **Amenities:** 🛏 📺 A/C, cable TV w/movies, shoe polisher. **Services:** 🛎 ⚑ 🖐 Car-rental desk, babysitting. **Facilities:** 🛁 ⛳ 🏊 & Whirlpool, washer/dryer. **Rates (CP):** HS Jan–Mar $49–$59 S; $54–$65 D. Extra person $6. Children under 17 stay free. Lower rates off-season. Pking: Outdoor, free. Maj CC.

≡≡ **Hemet Travelodge**, 1201 W Florida Ave, Hemet, CA 92543; tel 909/766-1902; fax 909/766-7739. Spanish-style architecture with modern, clean interior. **Rooms:** 46 rms. CI noon/CO noon. Nonsmoking rms avail. Rooms have choice of king-size or queen-size beds. **Amenities:** 🛏 🏊 A/C, cable TV w/movies, refrig, shoe polisher. All units w/minibars, all w/terraces, all w/fireplaces, all w/Jacuzzis. **Services:** 🛎 ⚑ 🖐 **Facilities:** 🛁 🏊 & Whirlpool, washer/dryer. **Rates (CP):** HS Oct–May $46 S or D. Extra person $5. Lower rates off-season. Higher rates for spec evnts/hols. Pking: Outdoor, free. Maj CC.

≡≡ **Ramada Inn**, 3885 W Florida Ave, Hemet, CA 92545; tel 909/929-8900 or toll free 800/272-6232. Hemet/Calif 74 exit off I-215. Conveniently located just minutes from shopping and restaurants. **Rooms:** 99 rms and stes. CI noon/CO noon. Nonsmoking rms avail. **Amenities:** 🛏 A/C, satel TV w/movies, refrig, shoe polisher. **Services:** ✕ 🛎 ⚑ 🖐 **Facilities:** 🛁 🏊 & Whirlpool, washer/dryer. 2 restaurants next door. **Rates (CP):** HS Jan–Apr $57 S; $62 D; from $62 ste. Extra person $5.

Children under 18 stay free. Lower rates off-season. Higher rates for spec evnts/hols. Spec packages avail. Pking: Outdoor, free. Maj CC.

Restaurant 🍴

★ **Alejandro's**, 3909 W Florida Ave, Hemet; tel 909/766-1192. **Mexican.** Features white adobe walls hand-painted with festive scenes, high ceilings dotted with elaborate chandeliers, and a thatched-roof cantina. Menu offers enchiladas and burritos and mesquite-grilled meats and seafood, all served by a friendly staff. **FYI:** Reservations accepted. Guitar. Dress code. **Open:** Lunch daily 11am–3pm; dinner daily 3–10pm. Closed some hols. **Prices:** Main courses $5.50–$10.95. Ltd CC. ♿

Attraction 📷

Ramona Bowl, 27400 Ramona Bowl Rd; tel 909/658-3111. Amphitheater built into the side of a mountain. Seating close to 7,000 people, it is the home of the annual Ramona Pageant held every spring. *Ramona*, based on Helen Hunt Jackson's 1884 love story of old California, has been staged since 1923 and is one of the nation's oldest outdoor dramas. Call in advance for detailed information. $$$$

HOLLYWOOD

Map page M-3, D2 (Los Angeles)

See also **North Hollywood, West Hollywood**

Hotel 🛏

≣≣≣ **Chateau Marmont Hotel and Bungalows**, 8221 Sunset Blvd, Hollywood, CA 90046; tel 213/656-1010 or toll free 800/242-8328; fax 213/655-5311. This hotel, set on a hill above Sunset Blvd, is favored by the European and Hollywood entertainment crowd because of its privacy. The original 1929 structure was an apartment building. Howard Hughes lived here, John Belushi died here. **Rooms:** 50 rms, stes, and effic; 13 ctges/villas. CI 1pm/CO noon. Furniture and decorations are vintage 1930s. Almost all suites have kitchens. Cottages and villas surround swimming pool area. **Amenities:** 🛎 🍷 Cable TV w/movies, refrig, VCR, stereo/tape player, in-rm safe, bathrobes. No A/C. All units w/minibars, some w/terraces, some w/fireplaces. **Services:** 🍽 ☎ 🆚 🚗 🛄 ❄ ⚷ Twice-daily maid svce, car-rental desk, babysitting. **Facilities:** 🛢 🏋 🎱 🖥 1 rst, 1 bar. Only valet parking is available due to the small, 30-car garage. **Rates:** $160–$210 S or D; from $240 ste; from $240 effic; from $230 ctge/villa. Children under 18 stay free. Pking: Indoor, free. Maj CC.

Restaurant 🍴

Dav Maghreb, 7651 Sunset Blvd, Hollywood; tel 213/876-7651. Between Fairfax and La Brea Aves. **Moroccan.** Spacious restaurant with elaborate, authentic appointments. Low seating on couches or pillows around tables. Belly dancing show takes place while you eat. Menu includes specialties such as roast squab with rice, almonds, and raisins; traditional roast lamb flavored with cumin and served with lentils; and Morocco's most famous dish, b'stilla (pastry filled with chicken, almonds, eggs and spices). **FYI:** Reservations recommended. Children's menu. **Open:** Tues–Sat 6–11pm, Sun 5:30–10:30pm. Closed Dec 25. **Prices:** PF dinner $18–$29. Ltd CC. 💙 🍴 🍽 ⬛ 🏔 🛎 🕑 🆚

Attractions 📷

Hollywood Sign. These 50-foot-high, white, sheet-metal letters have become a world-famous symbol of this movie industry town. Erected in 1923 to promote real estate development, the sign originally spelled out "HOLLYWOODLAND." Laws prohibit climbing up to the base.

Walk of Fame, Hollywood Blvd and Vine St; tel 213/469-8311. Nearly 2,000 stars are honored on the world's most famous sidewalk. Bronze medallions set into the center of each star pay tribute to famous personalities of all entertainment media. Some of the most popular include Marilyn Monroe, 6744 Hollywood Blvd; James Dean, 1719 Vine St; John Lennon, 1750 Vine St; and Elvis Presley, 6777 Hollywood Blvd. A new star is added to the walk of fame each month, and the public is invited to attend. For dates and times, call the Hollywood Chamber of Commerce's "Event Info Line," 213/469-8311.

Mann's Chinese Theatre, 6925 Hollywood Blvd; tel 213/461-3331. One of Hollywood's greatest landmarks (famous for its entry court, where movie stars' signatures and hand- and footprints are set in concrete), Grauman's Chinese Theatre was opened in 1927 by Sid Grauman, the impresario credited with originating the idea of the spectacular Hollywood "premiere." Opulent both inside and out, the theater combines authentic and simulated Chinese decor; 2 of the theater's columns actually come from a Ming Dynasty temple. Movie tickets cost about what they do at any other movie house. **Open:** Call for showtimes. $$$

Hollywood Memorial Park Cemetery, 6000 Santa Monica Blvd; tel 213/469-1181. Dedicated movie buffs may visit the graves of such stars as Peter Lorre; Douglas Fairbanks, Sr; Tyrone Power; Norma Talmadge; and Cecil B DeMille. Almost every day a mysterious lady in black pays homage at the crypt of Rudolph Valentino. **Open:** Daily 8am–5pm. Free.

Hollywood Wax Museum, 6767 Hollywood Blvd; tel 213/462-8860. Dozens of lifelike figures of famous movie stars are featured here, including characters from recent films such as *Hook* and *Home Alone*. The Chamber of Horrors includes the coffin used in the filming of *The Raven*, as well as a scene from Vincent Price's old hit, *The House of Wax*. Exhibits usually change every few months. **Open:** Sun–Thurs 10am–midnight, Fri–Sat 10am–2am. $$$

HOLTVILLE

Map page M-3, E4 (E of El Centro)

Resort 🏨

≣≣ Barbara Worth Country Club, 2050 Country Club Dr, Holtville, CA 92250; tel 619/356-2806 or toll free 800/356-3806; fax 619/356-4653. 12 mi E of El Centro. 100 acres. Good for business travelers and golfers. **Rooms:** 103 rms and stes. CI 3pm/CO noon. Nonsmoking rms avail. Most rooms have view of golf course. Some have ceiling fans. **Amenities:** 🛁 👜 A/C, cable TV w/movies. Some units w/terraces, some w/Jacuzzis. **Services:** ✗ 🍴 👝 Restaurant has Friday-night fresh seafood buffet. Champagne brunch buffet offered on Sundays. **Facilities:** 🏊 ▶₁₈ 🏋 🎾 ⚏ 👩 1 rst, 1 bar, whirlpool, playground, washer/dryer. **Rates:** $48–$58 S; $54–$64 D; from $123 ste. Extra person $6. Children under 13 stay free. Higher rates for spec evnts/hols. Spec packages avail. Pking: Outdoor, free. Maj CC.

HOPLAND

Map page M-2, C1

Inn 🏨

≣≣≣ Thatcher Inn, 13401 S US 101, Hopland, CA 95449; tel 707/744-1890 or toll free 800/266-1891; fax 707/744-1219. 14 mi N of Cloverdale. Located in the middle of downtown Hopland. The inn was built in 1890 as a stagecoach stop; it is now a designated historic landmark. **Rooms:** 21 rms. CI 3pm/CO noon. No smoking. Decorated in Victorian-style, with brass beds. **Amenities:** 🛁 👜 No A/C or TV. **Services:** ✗ 🍴 Babysitting. **Facilities:** 🏊 1 rst, 1 bar, guest lounge. Great, old-fashioned library with fireplace is available for guests' use. The bar is fabulous, with a malachite counter, oak, and mirrors on the walls. There is also a nice garden, a patio, and a restaurant open on weekends. **Rates (CP):** HS May–Sept $90–$150 D. Extra person $25. Children under 10 stay free. Lower rates off-season.

Spec packages avail. Pking: Outdoor, free. Ltd CC. Weekday escape package includes room, champagne, dinner, and breakfast for 2 for $125.

Restaurant 🍴

★ **The Hopland Brewery**, 13351 US 101 S, Hopland; tel 707/744-1361. 14 mi N of Cloverdale. **Pub.** Beloved for its Red Tail ale, this microbrewery is also a restaurant, with a beer garden popular with locals. Fifty cents buys a 4-ounce sampler of one of the brews. The menu includes spicy chicken wings, Red Tail beans, hamburgers, bratwurst with German potato salad, and similar pub-style food. Bands perform on weekends. **FYI:** Reservations not accepted. Blues/jazz/rock. Beer and wine only. **Open:** Mon–Sat 11am–2am, Sun 11am–10pm. **Prices:** Main courses $4–$7. Ltd CC. 🍴 👩

HUNTINGTON BEACH

Map page M-3, D2

Hotels 🏨

≣≣ Comfort Suites, 16301 Beach Blvd, Huntington Beach, CA 92647; tel 714/841-1812 or toll free 800/221-2222; fax 714/841-0214. 8 mi S of Huntington Beach. Beach Blvd exit off I-405 S. Good choice for business travelers and families; close to a shopping center. **Rooms:** 100 stes. CI noon/CO 11am. Nonsmoking rms avail. Rooms are comfortable with chairs and couches. Suites are particularly nice, and have sofabeds. **Amenities:** 🛁 🍴 A/C, cable TV w/movies, refrig, in-rm safe. Some units w/terraces, some w/Jacuzzis. Free HBO and ESPN. **Services:** 👝 Twice-daily maid svce, car-rental desk. 24-hour coffee service. **Facilities:** 🏊 🍴 👩 Whirlpool, washer/dryer. **Rates (CP):** From $54 ste. Extra person $5. Children under 18 stay free. Pking: Outdoor, free. Maj CC.

≣≣ Holiday Inn Huntington Beach, 7667 Center Ave, Huntington Beach, CA 92547; tel 714/891-0123 or toll free 800/HOLIDAY; fax 714/895-4591. ½ mi S of Huntington Beach. Beach Blvd exit off I-405; follow Beach Blvd toward Huntington Beach; right on Center Ave. Just minutes from Disneyland; a good choice for families. **Rooms:** 224 rms and stes. CI 2pm/CO noon. Nonsmoking rms avail. Modern, comfortable rooms. **Amenities:** 🛁 👜 A/C, cable TV w/movies. **Services:** ✗ 🍴 🚗 🍴 👝 Twice-daily maid svce, car-rental desk. Coffee and doughnuts in the lobby. **Facilities:** 🏊 🍴 🎰 👩 1 rst, 1 bar, whirlpool, washer/dryer. **Rates:** HS May–Sept $89 S or D; from $185 ste. Children under 19 stay free. Lower rates off-season. Spec packages avail. Pking: Indoor/outdoor, free. Maj CC.

≣≣≣ **Waterfront Hilton Beach Resort**, 21100 Pacific Coast Hwy, Huntington Beach, CA 92648 (Downtown); tel 714/960-7873 or toll free 800/HILTONS; fax 714/960-3791. 45 mi S of Los Angeles. Beach Blvd exit off I-405. Very well situated hotel, just across from an 8½-mile beach—southern California's longest. **Rooms:** 300 rms and stes. Exec-level rms avail. CI 4pm/CO noon. Express checkout avail. Nonsmoking rms avail. Tastefully appointed, each with an ocean view. **Amenities:** 🛁 🕐 📺 A/C, cable TV w/movies, refrig. All units w/minibars, all w/terraces, some w/Jacuzzis. **Services:** ✕ 🔑 VP 🚗 🖼 🛎 Twice-daily maid svce, car-rental desk, social director, children's program, babysitting. Multilingual staff. **Facilities:** 🏋 🚲 ⛳ 🛶 ⛵ 🖥 ♿ 2 rsts, 2 bars (1 w/entertainment), 1 beach (ocean), lifeguard, board surfing, spa, whirlpool, day-care ctr, washer/dryer. 14,000 square feet of meeting facilities; 21 meeting rooms available. **Rates:** $125–$195 S; $180–$260 D; from $225 ste. Children under 18 stay free. Spec packages avail. Pking: Indoor/outdoor, free. Maj CC.

Motel

≣≣ **Best Western Regency Inn**, 19360 Beach Blvd, Huntington Beach, CA 92648; tel 714/962-4244 or toll free 800/528-1234; fax 714/963-4724. No-frills hotel located near the beach and close to town; needs some maintenance. Renovation should be completed. **Rooms:** 63 rms, stes, and effic. CI 2pm/CO noon. Nonsmoking rms avail. Rooms are clean but furniture is old. Not much privacy in ground-floor rooms. **Amenities:** 🛁 📺 A/C, TV w/movies. 1 unit w/fireplace. **Services:** 🛎 Car-rental desk, babysitting. Movie rentals. **Facilities:** 🏋 🛶 ♿ Lifeguard, whirlpool, washer/dryer. **Rates:** HS mid May–Oct $49–$69 S; $59–$89 D; from $129 ste; from $79 effic. Extra person $10. Children under 17 stay free. Lower rates off-season. Higher rates for spec evnts/hols. Spec packages avail. Pking: Outdoor, free.

Restaurants 🍽

Baci, 18748 Beach Blvd, Huntington Beach; tel 714/965-1194. Beach Blvd exit off I-405. Restaurant is between Alice and Garfield Sts. **Italian.** Feels like you've stepped into Venice, with Italian paintings, soft lights, and lots of old-world charm. The cozy atmosphere and attentive service create a nice place to dine on Northern Italian dishes of veal osso buco, penne with beef and red wine, and risotto with fresh seafood. **FYI:** Reservations recommended. Combo/guitar/singer. Children's menu. Beer and wine only. **Open:** Daily 5–10pm. **Prices:** Main courses $7.50–$13. Maj CC. ♿

Palm Court, in the Waterfront Hilton Hotel, 21100 Pacific Coast Hwy, Huntington Beach; tel 714/960-7873. Beach Blvd exit off I-405. **New American.** Small restaurant with a garden atmosphere, frequented by guests of the hotel. Filled with plants and birds of paradise, decorated in soothing pastel colors. Serves brunch, salads, and breakfast. House specialty is Maine lobster at $45. **FYI:** Reservations recommended. Piano. Children's menu. **Open:** Breakfast Mon–Sat 6:30–11:30am, Sun 6:30–11am; lunch daily 11am–3pm; dinner Mon–Thurs 5–10pm, Sat–Sun 5–11pm; brunch Sun 10am–3pm. **Prices:** Main courses $12.95–$45. Maj CC. ❤ 🍴 🏞 🛎 VP ♿

Attractions 🏛

Huntington Beach International Surfing Museum, 411 Olive St; tel 714/960-3483. Featured here are permanent and changing exhibits relating to surfing and surfers. Also here is the Nalu Art Gallery, featurng examples of surf-related artwork. **Open:** Summer, daily noon–5pm; fall–spring, Wed–Sun noon–5pm. Closed some hols. $

Huntington State Beach, Pacific Coast Hwy (Calif 1); tel 714/536-1455. Popular with visitors as well as locals, this 2-mile beach area lies between Brookhurst Ave and Beach Blvd. A bike trail connects to Bolsa Chica State Beach (see below). **Open:** Daily 6am–10pm. Free.

Bolsa Chica State Beach, Pacific Coast Highway (Calif 1); tel 714/536-1455. This 4-mile stretch, roughly between Goldenwest and Warner Aves, is one of southern California's most popular. A bike trail runs to Huntington State Beach (see above). **Open:** Daily 6am–10pm. Free.

IDYLLWILD

Map page M-3, D3 (S of Palm Springs)

Motel 🏨

≣≣ **Quiet Creek Inn**, 26345 Delano Dr, PO Box 240, Idyllwild, CA 92549; tel 909/659-6110 or toll free 800/450-6110. 85-90 mi SE of Los Angeles. Calif 243 exit off I-10. 6.5 acres. Nestled in a heavily forested area of the San Jacinto Mountains; modern versions of the old log cabin. The ambience throughout is warm and comfortable. **Rooms:** 11 ctges/villas. CI 2pm/CO 11am. Cedar cabins (5 duplexes) blend with their surroundings; decks overlook Strawberry Creek. **Amenities:** 🕐 📺 Cable TV, refrig. No A/C or phone. All units w/terraces, all w/fireplaces. Loaf of banana-nut bread upon check-in. **Facilities:** 🛶 🎾 Lawn games. Stone barbecue area for guests to use. Lounge chairs and picnic tables are tucked away in creekside locations. **Rates:** From $71 ctge/villa. Children under 18 stay free. Min stay wknds and spec evnts. Pking: Outdoor, free. Ltd CC.

Restaurant ⑪

Gastrognome Restaurant, 54381 Ridgeview Dr, Idyllwild; tel 909/659-5055. US 243 exit off I-10. **Eclectic.** A stone fireplace, antiques, and stained-glass windows create a charming atmosphere. In addition to regular offerings of meat and seafood, specials may include fiery chicken on pasta, New Zealand rack of lamb, or shrimp cilantro-pesto pasta. **FYI:** Reservations accepted. Dress code. **Open:** Sun–Thurs 5–11pm, Fri–Sat 5–10pm. **Prices:** Main courses $9.95–$29.95. Ltd CC. ♥ ▣

Attraction ▦

Mount San Jacinto State Park; tel 909/659-2607. Idyllwild Campground is on Calif 243 in town. This 13,500-acre park consists mostly of wilderness, and contains 3 mountain peaks over 10,000 feet in elevation. Visitors can hike in from the park's west side or ride the Palm Springs Aerial Tramway (see PALM SPRINGS) up the mountain. Wilderness permits are required for hikers and backpackers. **Open:** Summer, Mon–Fri 8am–5pm, Sat–Sun 8am–10pm; fall–spring, daily 8am–5pm. $$

INDIAN WELLS

Map page M-3, D3 (W of Indio)

Resorts ▤

≣≣≣≣ **Hyatt Grand Champions**, 44-600 Indian Wells Lane, Indian Wells, CA 92210; tel 619/341-1000 or toll free 800/233-1234; fax 619/568-2236. Washington exit off I-10, to Calif 111. This European-style resort sits on 34 acres of manicured fairways and gardens, with the San Jacinto Mountains as a backdrop. **Rooms:** 316 rms and stes; 20 ctges/villas. Exec-level rms avail. CI 3pm/CO 1pm. Express checkout avail. Nonsmoking rms avail. Richly appointed, suite-size rooms, decorated in desert colors. **Amenities:** ▣ ⚫ ▣ ⌕ A/C, cable TV w/movies, bathrobes. All units w/minibars, all w/terraces, some w/fireplaces, some w/Jacuzzis. **Services:** ⍟ ☞ 🆅🅿 ▣ ⌔ Twice-daily maid svce, car-rental desk, social director, masseur, children's program, babysitting. Camp Hyatt and Rock Hyatt programs are available for children and teens ages 3–17 at $21 for up to 4 hours and $35 for a full day. **Facilities:** ▣ 🚲 ▶36 ▣ ⚫5 ◧ ⌗ 1.9K ▣ ⌕ 2 rsts, 2 bars (1 w/entertainment), lawn games, spa, sauna, steam rm, whirlpool, beauty salon, day-care ctr, playground. **Rates:** HS Dec 17–May $240–$325 S or D; from $375 ste; from $725 ctge/villa. Extra person $25. Children under 18 stay free. Min stay spec evnts. Lower rates off-season. Spec packages avail. Pking: Indoor/outdoor, free. Maj CC.

≣≣≣≣ **Stouffer Esmeralda Resort**, 44-400 Indian Wells Lane, Indian Wells, CA 92210; tel 619/773-4444 or toll free 800/552-4386; fax 619/346-9308. Washington exit off I-10, to Calif 111; right on Indian Wells Lane. 19.2 acres. This is a desert oasis, guarded by the peaks of the Santa Rosa Mountains, inspired by resorts on the Mediterranean. The hotel's spectacular entrance/lobby area centers on a beautiful curving staircase and atrium. **Rooms:** 560 rms and stes. CI 3pm/CO noon. Express checkout avail. Nonsmoking rms avail. Tastefully appointed rooms, each with its own private balcony. **Amenities:** ▣ ⚫ ⌕ A/C, cable TV w/movies, bathrobes. All units w/minibars, all w/terraces, some w/fireplaces, some w/Jacuzzis. **Services:** ⍟ ☞ 🆅🅿 🚗 ▣ ⌔ ⌖ Twice-daily maid svce, car-rental desk, masseur, children's program, babysitting. **Facilities:** ▣ 🚲 ▶36 ⚫5 ◧ ⌗ 2.6K ▣ ⌕ 2 rsts (see also "Restaurants" below), 1 bar (w/entertainment), lawn games, spa, sauna, steam rm, whirlpool, washer/dryer. One of the swimming pools has its own small, sandy beach. **Rates:** HS Jan–Apr $275–$375 S or D; from $600 ste. Extra person $25. Children under 18 stay free. Lower rates off-season. Spec packages avail. Pking: Indoor/outdoor, free. Maj CC.

Restaurant ⑪

Sirocco, in the Stouffer Esmeralda Resort, 44-400 Indian Wells Lane, Indian Wells; tel 619/773-4444. Washington exit off I-10. **Mediterranean.** Crisp linen and gleaming silver help create an elegant setting for this intimate restaurant. Specializing in Mediterranean cuisine, it serves a selection of different tapas each day, as well as such classic Mediterranean meals as bouillabaisse of fish and shellfish; and a paella of chicken, spicy sausage, and shellfish. Boasts climate-controlled exhibition wine cellars. **FYI:** Reservations recommended. Combo/piano. Dress code. **Open:** HS Sept–May daily 6–10pm. Reduced hours off-season. **Prices:** Main courses $15.50–$24. Maj CC. 🆅🅿 ⌕

INDIO

Map page M-3, D3

Motels ▤

≣≣≣ **Best Western Date Tree Motor Hotel**, 81-909 Indio Blvd, Indio, CA 92201; tel 619/347-3421 or toll free 800/292-5599; fax 619/347-3421. Landscaped citrus and cactus gardens surround this contemporary hotel with its Olympic-size pool. **Rooms:** 117 rms, stes, and effic. CI 1pm/CO noon. Nonsmoking rms avail. **Amenities:** ▣ ⚫ A/C, cable TV, refrig. Some units w/terraces, 1 w/Jacuzzi. **Services:** ⌔ ⌖ Babysitting. **Facilities:** ▣ ⌕ Games rm, lawn games, whirlpool, playground, washer/dryer. **Rates (CP):** HS Jan–Apr $50–$78 S; $64–$98 D; from $105 ste; from $105 effic. Extra person $5. Children under 18 stay free. Min stay wknds. Lower rates off-season. Higher rates for spec evnts/hols. Spec packages avail. Pking: Outdoor, free. Maj CC.

≡ **Comfort Inn**, 43-505 Monroe St, Indio, CA 92201; tel 619/347-4044 or toll free 800/221-2222; fax 619/347-1287. Just minutes away from the business district and shopping area, and situated close to the Indio Date Festival grounds. **Rooms:** 63 rms. CI 2pm/CO 11am. Nonsmoking rms avail. **Amenities:** 🛋 A/C, cable TV w/movies, refrig. **Services:** 🍴 🛎 **Facilities:** 🏋 Whirlpool. **Rates (CP):** HS Dec–May $49–$64 S; $59–$79 D. Extra person $6. Children under 18 stay free. Lower rates off-season. Higher rates for spec evnts/hols. Pking: Outdoor, free. Maj CC.

Restaurant 🍴

Devane's, 80-755 Calif 111, Indio; tel 619/342-5009. Washington exit off I-10 to Calif 111. **Italian.** Small California mission-style building with adobe walls, brick floors, and huge planters. Italian cuisine is the specialty, including such dishes as chicken marsala, veal piccata, pastas, and pizzas. **FYI:** Reservations accepted. Dress code. **Open:** HS Jan–Apr lunch Tues–Fri 11am–3pm; dinner Tues–Sun 4–9:30pm. Reduced hours off-season. Closed some hols; July–Sept. **Prices:** Main courses $9.95–$18.95. Ltd CC. 🍷

Attraction 🏛

Coachella Valley Museum and Cultural Center, 82616 Miles Ave; tel 619/342-6651. Housed in the former home and medical office of Dr Harry Smiley, this museum features Native American artifacts, memorabilia of early Coachella Valley pioneers, as well as changing art exhibits. **Open:** Oct–May, Wed–Sat 10am–4pm, Sun 1–4pm; June and Sept, Fri–Sun 1–4pm. Closed some hols. $

INGLEWOOD

Map page M-3, D2 (E of Santa Monica)

Hotels 🛏

≡≡ **Hampton Inn**, 10300 La Cienega Blvd, Inglewood, CA 90304 (Los Angeles Int'l Airport); tel 310/337-1000 or toll free 800/HAMPTON; fax 310/645-6925. Small airport hotel, well kept but with minimal decor. Lobby is OK but not inviting. **Rooms:** 148 rms. CI 1pm/CO noon. Nonsmoking rms avail. **Amenities:** 🛋 A/C, cable TV w/movies. **Services:** 🚐 🖨 🍴

🛎 Car-rental desk, social director, masseur, children's program, babysitting. Complimentary continental breakfast, newspaper, coffee. No charge for local calls. **Facilities:** 🏊 📺 & Sauna. **Rates:** $65–$75 S; $75–$85 D. Extra person $10. Children under 18 stay free. Spec packages avail. Pking: Indoor, free. Pking: Outdoor, free. Maj CC.

≡≡≡ **Motel 6**, 5101 Century Blvd, Inglewood, CA 90304 (Los Angeles Int'l Airport); tel 310/419-1234. Recently renovated by new owners, motel is surprisingly good. **Rooms:** 249 rms. CI noon/CO noon. Nonsmoking rms avail. Remarkably well-furnished rooms. **Amenities:** 🛋 A/C, cable TV w/movies. **Services:** 🚐 🍴 🛎 Car-rental desk. **Facilities:** 🏋 📺 1 rst, 1 bar. Pool is situated next to the highway. **Rates:** $40 S; $46 D. Extra person $6. Children under 18 stay free. Pking: Outdoor, free. Maj CC.

IRVINE

Map page M-3, D2 (E of Santa Ana)

See also **East Irvine**

Hotels 🛏

≡≡ **Airporter Garden Hotel**, 18700 MacArthur Blvd, Irvine, CA 92715 (John Wayne Airport); tel 714/833-2770 or toll free 800/854-3012; fax 714/757-1228. MacArthur Blvd exit off I-405, left on MacArthur for 1 mile. Nicely landscaped grounds. Quiet location makes this ideal for the business traveler. **Rooms:** 209 rms and stes. Exec-level rms avail. CI 3pm/CO noon. Express checkout avail. Nonsmoking rms avail. Light and cheerful. **Amenities:** 🛋 🕹 📺 A/C, cable TV, VCR, voice mail, shoe polisher. Some units w/minibars, some w/terraces. **Services:** ✗ 🖨 🚐 🖨 🍴 🛎 Car-rental desk, babysitting. **Facilities:** 🏋 🏊 📺 & 2 rsts, 1 bar (w/entertainment), games rm, beauty salon. **Rates:** $89–$130 S; from $140 ste. Children under 18 stay free. Spec packages avail. Pking: Outdoor, free. Maj CC.

≡≡≡ **Courtyard by Marriott**, 2701 Main St, Irvine, CA 92714 (John Wayne Airport); tel 714/757-1200 or toll free 800/321-2211; fax 714/757-1596. Jamboree exit off I-405; take Jamboree Blvd to Main St; property on corner. Clean and well kept. Convenient location near business parks, shopping centers, and airport. **Rooms:** 153 rms and stes. CI 3pm/CO 1pm. Express checkout avail. Nonsmoking rms avail. Very well maintained. **Amenities:** 🛋 🕹 📺 A/C, cable TV w/movies, voice mail. All units w/terraces. **Services:** ✗ 🚐 🖨 🍴 Babysitting. Friendly, efficient staff. **Facilities:** 🏋 🏊 📺 & 1 rst, 1 bar, whirlpool, washer/dryer. Attractive gazebo and pool in central courtyard.

Rates: $80 S; $90 D; from $95 ste. Extra person $10. Children under 18 stay free. Spec packages avail. Pking: Indoor/outdoor, free. Maj CC.

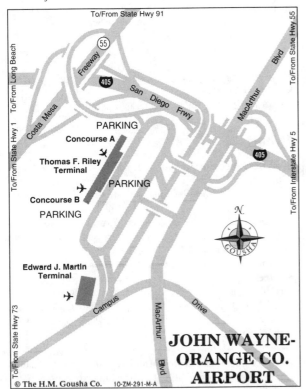

Map: Roads labeled To/From State Hwy 91, To/From Long Beach, To/From State Hwy 55, 55 Freeway, 405, San Diego Frwy, MacArthur Blvd, To/From State Hwy 1, Costa Mesa, To/From Interstate Hwy 5, 405, PARKING, Concourse A, Thomas F. Riley Terminal, PARKING, Concourse B, PARKING, Edward J. Martin Terminal, Campus Drive, MacArthur Blvd, To/From State Hwy 73, N, © The H.M. Gousha Co. 10-ZM-291-M-A, **JOHN WAYNE–ORANGE CO. AIRPORT**

≡≡≡ **Embassy Suites**, 2120 Main St, Irvine, CA 92714 (John Wayne Airport); tel 714/553-8332 or toll free 800/362-2779; fax 714/261-5301. McArthur exit off I-405 S. Close to airport, shopping center, and business parks; suitable for business travelers. Clean. **Rooms:** 293 stes. CI 3pm/CO 1pm. Express checkout avail. Nonsmoking rms avail. Separate living area good for conducting business meetings. **Amenities:** 🛀 🐶 📺 🖐️ A/C, cable TV w/movies, refrig, stereo/tape player, voice mail. **Services:** ✗ 🚐 🛄 🛎️ **Facilities:** 🎱 🏊 🏋️ 1 rst, 1 bar, games rm, spa, sauna. **Rates (BB):** From $159 ste. Children under 12 stay free. Spec packages avail. Pking: Indoor, free. Maj CC. Good value.

≡≡≡ **Hyatt Regency Irvine**, 17900 Jamboree Blvd, Irvine, CA 92714 (John Wayne Airport); tel 714/975-1234 or toll free 800/233-1234; fax 714/863-0531. Jamboree exit off I-405 S. Light and airy atrium-style property. Located in a business park near freeway, airport, and shopping centers. The well-manicured grounds make this the nicest hotel in the area. **Rooms:** 536 rms and stes. Exec-level rms avail. CI 3pm/CO noon. Express checkout avail. Nonsmoking rms avail. Comfortable and newly upgraded. Decorated in creamy colors with pastel accents. **Amenities:** 🛀 🐶 📺 A/C, cable TV w/movies, shoe polisher, bathrobes. Some units w/terraces, some w/Jacuzzis. **Services:** ✗ 🔑 🅿️ 🚐 🛄 🛎️ 🐶 Twice-daily maid svce, car-rental desk, social director, masseur, children's program, babysitting. Shuttle to South Coast Plaza. **Facilities:** 🎱 🚲 🏊 🏋️ 💪 🎾 🖥️ 🛗 2 rsts, 3 bars (1 w/entertainment), games rm, spa, sauna, steam rm, whirlpool. **Rates:** $144–$159 S; $169–$184 D; from $250 ste. Extra person $25. Children under 18 stay free. Higher rates for spec evnts/hols. Spec packages avail. Pking: Outdoor, free. Maj CC.

≡≡≡ **Irvine Marriott at John Wayne Airport**, 18000 Von Karman Ave, Irvine, CA 92715; tel 714/553-0100 or toll free 800/228-9290; fax 714/261-7059. Jamboree exit off I-405 S; right on Michaelson to Von Karman; right into Voll Center Complex. Impressive marble lobby and a uniformed staff set a nice tone. Located in the heart of a business park. **Rooms:** 489 rms and stes. Exec-level rms avail. CI 4pm/CO noon. Express checkout avail. Nonsmoking rms avail. Sophisticated, light, and airy, with a California flair. **Amenities:** 🛀 🐶 📺 A/C, cable TV w/movies, voice mail, shoe polisher. Some units w/terraces. **Services:** ✗ 🔑 🅿️ 🚐 🛄 🛎️ 🐶 Car-rental desk, masseur, babysitting. Special services for business travelers. **Facilities:** 🎱 🚲 🎾 💪 🛗 💪 2 rsts, 2 bars (1 w/entertainment), games rm, whirlpool, playground, washer/dryer. **Rates:** $160 S or D; from $250 ste. Extra person $15. Children under 18 stay free. Spec packages avail. Pking: Outdoor, free. Maj CC.

≡≡≡ **La Quinta Motor Inn**, 14972 Sand Canyon Ave, Irvine, CA 92718 (Old Town Complex); tel 714/551-0909 or toll free 800/531-5900; fax 714/551-2945. 40 mi S of Los Angeles. Sand Canyon exit off I-5. Unique property in a historic landmark, a former grainery. **Rooms:** 148 rms. Exec-level rms avail. CI 3pm/CO noon. Nonsmoking rms avail. Each room is individually decorated. **Amenities:** 🛀 🐶 A/C, cable TV w/movies. **Services:** 🚐 🛄 🛎️ 🐶 Continental breakfast and afternoon hors d'oeuvres. **Facilities:** 🎱 💪 🎾 3 rsts, 2 bars (1 w/entertainment), whirlpool, beauty salon, washer/dryer. **Rates (CP):** $58–$68 S; $63–$73 D. Extra person $5. Children under 18 stay free. Higher rates for spec evnts/hols. Pking: Outdoor, free. Maj CC.

≡≡ **Radisson Plaza Hotel–Orange County Airport**, 18800 MacArthur Blvd, Irvine, CA 92715 (John Wayne Airport); tel 714/833-9999 or toll free 800/333-3333; fax 714/833-3317. MacArthur exit off I-405; turn left at Douglas; then make 2nd left. Older hotel near the airport; site is quite noisy. **Rooms:** 289 rms and stes. Exec-level rms avail. CI 3pm/CO noon. Express checkout avail. Nonsmoking rms avail. Rooms are designed for the business traveler, with large desks and good lighting. **Amenities:** 🔒 🕭 A/C, cable TV w/movies, voice mail, shoe polisher. Some units w/minibars, all w/terraces. Rooms are fully stocked for entertaining. **Services:** ✗ ➤⊟ VP 🚙 ⊠ 🛏 Car-rental desk, babysitting. **Facilities:** 🛗 🏊 🔍 🛺 🔔 800 💻 ⅙ 1 rst, 2 bars, whirlpool. **Rates:** $89–$119 S or D; from $300 ste. Extra person $10. Children under 18 stay free. Spec packages avail. Pking: Outdoor, free. Maj CC.

Restaurants 🍽

Bistro 201, in TransAmerica Building, 18201 Von Karman Ave, Irvine; tel 714/553-9201. ½ mi S of John Wayne Airport. MacArthur Blvd exit off I-405. **International.** Decor features rich colors, white tablecloths, and elegant banquettes; a beautiful bamboo grove is visible from windows. Menu offers an eclectic mix, from carpaccio with arugula, Parmesan, capers, and horse-radish vinaigrette, to grilled shrimp on a bed of polenta with roasted peppers and basil pesto. Desserts include hot Belgian chocolate soufflé and hot apple tart with caramel sauce. **FYI:** Reservations recommended. Jazz/piano. **Open:** Lunch Mon–Fri 11:30am–3:30pm; dinner Mon–Sat 5:30–10:30pm. Closed some hols. **Prices:** Main courses $8.50–$17. Maj CC. ♥ ⚓ VP ⅙

♣ **Chanteclair**, 18912 MacArthur Blvd, Irvine; tel 714/752-8001. MacArthur Blvd exit off I-405. **French.** Like a country château. Each dining room has a fireplace and about 10 diners—very intimate and unusual. The rooms reflect different themes, from pure romance to a French-style study. The menu is high-quality, featuring changing specialties like frogs' legs, fresh tuna, and smoked mackerel with cabbage and Riesling sauce. **FYI:** Reservations recommended. Piano. **Open:** Lunch Sun–Fri 11:30am–2:30pm; dinner daily 6–10pm; brunch Sun 10:30am–2:30pm. Closed some hols. **Prices:** Main courses $14–$25; PF dinner $28–$35. Maj CC. ♥ 🍺 ⚓ 📷 VP ⅙

✹ **Prego**, 18420 Von Karman Ave, Irvine; tel 714/553-1333. Jamboree exit off I-405. **Italian.** A bistro-style restaurant with an extremely attractive and well-trained staff. Glass partitions provide some privacy, yet allow a clear view of the entire restaurant. Lovely flowers accentuate the well-designed space. **FYI:** Reservations recommended. **Open:** Mon–Fri 11:30am–10:30pm, Sat 5–11pm, Sun 5–10pm. Closed some hols. **Prices:** Main courses $5–$18; PF dinner $22.50. Maj CC. ♥ ⚓ VP ⅙

Attraction 🎫

Wild Rivers Waterpark, 8770 Irvine Center Dr; tel 714/768-WILD. Spread over 20 acres, this park offers water rides in 3 main themed sections: Wild Rivers Mountain, with more than 20 thrilling water rides; Thunder Cove, featuring 2 giant wave pools; and Explorer's Island, with child-size water rides, wading and jacuzzi pools. Also several sun decks, sand beaches, arcade, shops, and food concessions. **Open:** Late June–early Sept, daily 10am–8pm; late Apr–late June and early Sept–early Oct, weekends only (hours vary). $$$$

JACKSON

Map page M-2, C2 (SE of Sutter Creek)

Motels 🛏

≣≣ **Best Western Amador Inn**, 200 S Calif 49, Jackson, CA 95642; tel 209/223-0211 or toll free 800/543-5221; fax 209/223-4836. Clean, new buildings have basic amenities with few frills. Convenient to Old Jackson. Lots of parking. **Rooms:** 118 rms and effic. CI 3pm/CO noon. Express checkout avail. Nonsmoking rms avail. Rooms in rear are quieter than those in front. **Amenities:** 🔒 🖭 A/C, cable TV w/movies, voice mail, shoe polisher. Some units w/terraces, some w/fireplaces. **Services:** 🚙 ⊠ 🛏 🔊 Babysitting. **Facilities:** 🛗 800 ⅙ 1 rst, 1 bar. Meeting facilities are in adjacent restaurant. **Rates:** $49–$55 S; $63–$70 D; from $58 effic. Extra person $10. Children under 12 stay free. Higher rates for spec evnts/hols. Spec packages avail. Pking: Outdoor, free. Maj CC.

≣ **El Campo Casa Resort Motel**, 12548 Kennedy Flat Rd, Jackson, CA 95642; tel 209/223-0100. Kennedy Flat Rd exit off Calif 88. Large garden and pool. Hillside views. Great for families. **Rooms:** 15 rms. CI 3pm/CO noon. Express checkout avail. Nonsmoking rms avail. Tile dates from the '40s or '50s. Small showers only. Rooms seen are a bit cramped with 2 queen-size beds. **Amenities:** 🔒 🖭 A/C, TV. **Services:** 🛏 🔊 Babysitting. **Facilities:** 🛗 Playground. Swimming pool has an extra-shallow section for young children. Kids toys, sports equipment: tetherball, horseshoes, badminton. Barbecue pits for guest use. **Rates:** HS May–Oct $37–$56 S; $44–$66 D. Extra person $5. Children under 18 stay free. Lower rates off-season. Spec packages avail. Pking: Outdoor, free. Maj CC.

≣≣ **Jackson Holiday Lodge**, 850 N Calif 49, Jackson, CA 95642; tel 209/223-0486; fax 209/223-2905. Older property. Furnishings are simple, clean, and comfortable. Lobby recently renovated. Rooms are quieter than at many roadside motels. **Rooms:** 28 rms and stes; 8 ctges/villas. CI 3pm/CO noon. Nonsmoking rms avail. Basic. Some roomy cottages with their own patios—great for family. **Amenities:** 🔒 🖭 🍷 A/C, cable TV. Some units w/terraces. **Services:** 🚙 🛏 🔊 Personal requests honored when possible. Can cater to small groups.

Facilities: ⛲ Pool open May–October. **Rates (CP):** $39–$49 S; $44–$57 D; from $63 ste; from $63 ctge/villa. Extra person $5. Children under 2 stay free. Pking: Outdoor, free. Maj CC.

Inn

▄▄▄ **National Hotel**, 2 Water St, Jackson, CA 95642 (Historic Downtown); tel 209/223-0500. Historic brick and timber hotel retains the ambience of the Gold Rush days. **Rooms:** 30 rms (5 w/shared bath). CI 2pm/CO 1pm. Charming rooms, furnished with period antiques, are undergoing renovation; all will be air-conditioned. **Amenities:** No A/C, phone, or TV. Some units w/terraces, some w/fireplaces. Bar/restaurant is rather dour, but springs to life on weekends with honky-tonk and other entertainment. The saloon is the 1862 original. **Facilities:** 1 rst, 1 bar (w/entertainment), games rm. **Rates:** $45–$75 S or D w/shared bath, $45–$105 S or D w/private bath. Extra person $20. Children under 12 stay free. Pking: Outdoor, free. Ltd CC. Rates include a $10 credit toward dinner or 2 $5 credits toward champagne brunch/breakfast.

Attraction 🏛

Amador County Museum, 225 Church St; tel 209/223-6386. Housed in an 1859 building, this museum includes exhibits on the history of the region, especially the Gold Rush. Large-scale working models of the Kennedy Mine make up the museum's featured exhibit. **Open:** Wed–Fri 10am–4pm, Sat–Sun 11am–3pm. Closed some hols. Free.

JAMESTOWN

Map page M-2, D3 (S of Sonora)

Motel 🎬

▄▄ **Sonora Country Inn**, 18755 Chanbroullian Lane, Jamestown, CA 95327; tel 209/984-0315 or toll free 800/847-2211; fax 209/984-4849. 1 mi W of Sonora. Small, adequate roadside hotel near skiing and Gold Country. **Rooms:** 61 rms and stes. CI noon/CO noon. Express checkout avail. Nonsmoking rms avail. **Amenities:** 🛎 A/C, cable TV, refrig. Some units w/terraces. **Services:** 🍴 🛎 Complimentary continental breakfast delivered to room. Pets allowed with prior approval. **Facilities:** ⛲ ♿ Pool heated April–November. **Rates (CP):** HS Apr–Oct $54–$58 S; $64–$69 D; from $125 ste. Extra person $5. Children under 12 stay free. Min stay spec evnts. Lower rates off-season. Pking: Outdoor, free. Maj CC.

Restaurants 🍴

Bella Union Dining Saloon, 18242 Main St, Jamestown; tel 209/984-2421. **Californian/Continental.** This 1888 tin shop has been lovingly converted into a historic treasure, complete with 20-foot high copper ceilings and old brick walls. The turn-of-the-century Victorian bar was brought from San Francisco. Specialties include fresh fish, homemade pasta, and a variety of meats. All soup stocks, sauces, and condiments made fresh. Large selection of imported beers. **FYI:** Reservations recommended. Children's menu. **Open:** Lunch Wed–Sun 11:30am–2:30pm; dinner Tues–Sun 5–10pm. Closed some hols. **Prices:** Main courses $11.50–$27.50; PF dinner $21–$27.50. Maj CC. 🍴 🍷 ♿

$ **Country Kitchen Gourmet Café & Gifts**, 18231 Main St, Jamestown; tel 209/984-3326. **American.** Country-kitchen eatery offering traditional American meals. Try the chicken pot pie, baked breads, pies, or candy. **FYI:** Reservations not accepted. Children's menu. No liquor license. **Open:** Lunch daily 11:30am–5pm. Closed some hols. **Prices:** Lunch main courses $2.80–$4.75. No CC. 🍴 ♿

Kamm's Chinese Restaurant, 18208 Main St, Jamestown; tel 209/984-3105. **Chinese.** A pleasant dining room decorated like a fine tearoom with floral wall coverings; popular with both tourists and locals. Family-run for more than 30 years, they offer a large selection of Chinese specialties, including Kung Pao chicken and shrimp. **FYI:** Reservations recommended. Beer and wine only. **Open:** Lunch Mon–Fri 11:30am–2pm; dinner Mon–Fri 4–9pm, Sat 4–9:30pm. Closed some hols. **Prices:** Main courses $5.50–$10.45. Ltd CC. ♿

Michelangelo Ristorante Italiano, 18128 Main St, Jamestown; tel 209/984-4830. **Italian.** Located in a historic building, with marble tabletops, oak floors, and black vinyl booths. Pasta, plus fresh-made pizza with a variety of toppings. **FYI:** Reservations not accepted. Children's menu. **Open:** Dinner Wed–Mon 5–10pm. Closed some hols. **Prices:** Main courses $7–$14.50. Ltd CC.

★ **The Smoke Cafe**, 18191 Main St, Jamestown; tel 209/984-3733. **Mexican.** Festive southwestern atmosphere and well-prepared food. Tamales, mole poblano and black beans, vegetarian items. Bar offers 15 varieties of tequila. **FYI:** Reservations accepted. Children's menu. **Open:** HS May–Labor Day lunch Sat–Sun 11am–5pm; dinner Tues–Sun 5–10pm. Reduced hours off-season. Closed some hols; Dec 15–31. **Prices:** Main courses $5.75–$10.95. Ltd CC. ♿

JENNER

Map page M-2, C1

Inn 🛏

≡≡≡ Murphy's Jenner Inn, 10400 Calif 1, PO Box 69, Jenner, CA 95450; tel 707/865-2377 or toll free 800/732-2377; fax 707/865-0829. Perched near the mouth of the Russian River in the tiny town of Jenner. Some cabins are right at the water's edge, with spectacular sunset views. **Rooms:** 9 rms and stes; 4 ctges/villas. CI 3pm/CO noon. No smoking. Each cabin is individually decorated; many have kitchens. **Amenities:** 🛋 📺 Refrig. No A/C, phone, or TV. Some units w/terraces, some w/fireplaces, some w/Jacuzzis. **Services:** 🍽 Masseur, afternoon tea and wine/sherry served. Breakfast and afternoon tea served in nice parlor. Staff will make reservations for area attractions, including kayaking, harbor cruises, fishing, etc. **Facilities:** 1 rst, 1 bar, guest lounge. **Rates (CP):** HS Apr–Oct $65–$128 D; from $155 ste; from $118 ctge/villa. Extra person $15. Min stay wknds. Lower rates off-season. Pking: Outdoor, free. Ltd CC. Discount of 15% on weekdays November–April.

Lodge

≡≡≡ Salt Point Lodge, 23255 Calif 1, Jenner, CA 95450; tel 707/847-3234. Picturesque gardens and large sculptures surround this property, 3 miles from Salt Point State Park. **Rooms:** 16 rms. CI 2pm/CO 11am. Nonsmoking rms avail. Rooms are quiet. Ask for an ocean view. **Amenities:** 🛋 📺 🍽 Satel TV, refrig, VCR. No A/C or phone. Some units w/terraces, some w/fireplaces. **Services:** ✕ 🍽 Masseur. **Facilities:** 1 rst, 1 bar, sauna, whirlpool, playground. **Rates:** HS Apr–Nov $47–$127 S or D. Extra person $10. Children under 12 stay free. Min stay wknds. Lower rates off-season. Spec packages avail. Pking: Outdoor, free. Ltd CC.

Restaurant 🍴

River's End, in River's End Resort, US 1, Jenner; tel 707/865-2484. At mouth of Russian River. **Eclectic.** Located at the mouth of the Russian River, overlooking Goat Rock Beach and the Pacific. A great place to watch the sunset from the solarium dining area, or to spy whales through a telescope provided on the deck. Inside, the room is gracious, with wood paneling and salmon-hued tablecloths set with candles. Specialties are coconut-fried shrimp with orange-rum sauce, lobster and beef brochette, medallions of venison with crayfish sauce, and rack of lamb stuffed with oysters. **FYI:** Reservations recommended. **Open:** HS June–Sept Mon–Sat 11am–9:30pm, Sat–Sun 9am–9:30pm. Reduced hours off-season. Closed some hols; Dec 2–Feb 14. **Prices:** Main courses $13–$26; PF dinner $22–$27. Maj CC. ♥ 🏔

JOSHUA TREE NATIONAL PARK

Map page M-3, D3

Located 25 miles east of Indio on I-10. The 558,000-acre national park, newly established with the passage of the California Desert Protection Act of 1994, takes its name from a large yucca belonging to the agave family that in this region grows to between 20 and 30 feet tall. These "trees" were named by early Mormon settlers, who thought the unusual forms looked like Joshua beckoning them farther west. The park connects the Mojave and Colorado Deserts. The Mojave, to the west, is high desert, with an average elevation of 3,000 feet. The eastern low desert is drier and more barren. Five oases scattered around this arid region attract golden eagles, tarantulas, sidewinders, jackrabbits, coyotes, and rattlesnakes.

Over 3,500 established rock climbs make this one of the world's most popular climbing areas. Most visitors, however, come to camp and hike over dozens of marked trails. Most of the western part of the park is relatively flat, so trails are not particularly strenuous. Hikers should carry an ample supply of water at all times, as desert hiking leads quickly to dehydration. Water is available at the visitor centers, Black Rock Canyon campground, and at the Indian Cove Ranger Station.

There are 2 main entrances to Joshua Tree; the most popular approach is via Twentynine Palms, 45 miles northwest of Palm Springs. At this north entrance the **Oasis Visitor Center** offers trail maps, safety information, and advice on visiting the park (open daily 8am–4:30pm; closed Dec 25). The Cottonwood Visitor Center is at the southern entrance to the park, near I-10, 55 miles east of Palm Springs (open daily 8am–4:30pm; closed Dec 25). Call 619/367-7511 for campsite reservations and general information.

JULIAN

Map page M-3, B3

Inns 🛏

≡≡≡ Julian Hotel, 2032 Main St, Julian, CA 92036; tel 619/765-0201. 60 mi NE of San Diego. Calif 79 exit off I-8; N on Calif 79 for 22 miles. Wonderful hotel built in 1897. Victorian decor shows much attention to detail, and there's usually a nice breeze on the veranda. **Rooms:** 15 rms (12 w/shared bath); 2 ctges/villas. CI 2pm/CO noon. No smoking. Each room is individually decorated. Some have clawfoot tubs. **Amenities:** No A/C, phone, or TV. 1 unit w/terrace, 1 w/fireplace. **Services:** ☎ Babysitting, afternoon tea served. **Facilities:** ⊡ Games rm, guest lounge. **Rates (BB):** $38–$82 S or D w/shared bath, $76–$94 D w/private bath; from $95 ctge/villa. Min stay wknds. Spec packages avail. Ltd CC. Only 2 people to a room. Discounts on 2nd rooms are often available midweek.

≣≣ **Julian Lodge**, 4th and C Sts, PO Box 1930, Julian, CA 92036; tel 619/765-1420 or toll free 800/542-1420. 60 mi NE of San Diego. Calif 67 N or Calif 79 N exit off I-8. A cross between a country inn and a motel. Nice rooms and friendly hosts in a charming rural area. **Rooms:** 23 rms. CI 3pm/CO noon. **Amenities:** A/C, cable TV. No phone. Some units w/terraces. 2 rooms have coffeemakers; some have refrigerators. Alarm clocks available from the front desk. **Services:** Breakfast, newspapers, coffee in lobby. **Facilities:** ⊡ & Piano in lobby. **Rates (CP):** $72–$85 D. Extra person $10. Children under 1 stay free. Spec packages avail. Pking: Outdoor, free. Ltd CC.

Restaurants ⑪

Julian Cafe, 2112 Main St, Julian; tel 619/765-2712. Calif 79 exit off I-8. **American.** An Old West theme restaurant in a building constructed in 1872. The cheerful staff serves apple-walnut pancakes, tortilla soup, meatloaf, and apple pie. **FYI:** Reservations not accepted. No liquor license. **Open:** Sat–Sun 7am–8:30pm, Mon–Tues 8am–7:30pm, Thurs–Fri 8am–7:30pm, Wed 8am–5pm. Closed Dec 25. **Prices:** Main courses $7.25–$12.95. Ltd CC. ⬛ 🔳

Julian Grille, 2224 Main St, Julian; tel 619/765-0173. Calif 79 exit off I-8. **American.** Housed in a country Edwardian cottage that was a private residence in the early 1900s. The menu includes prime rib, chicken Jerusalem, Georgia peach chicken, and trout amandine. **FYI:** Reservations recommended. Children's menu. Beer and wine only. **Open:** Lunch Fri–Wed 11:30am–3pm; dinner Tues–Sun 5–9pm. Closed some hols. **Prices:** Main courses $10.95–$19.95. Maj CC. ⬛

Romano's Dodge House, 2718 B St, Julian; tel 619/765-1003. Calif 79 exit off I-8. **Italian.** A good family restaurant, with standard Italian red-and-white decor. Serving pizza, frittatas, braciole (Sicilian rolled and stuffed meat), and homemade breads. **FYI:** Reservations recommended. Beer and wine only. **Open:** Sun–Mon 11am–9pm, Thurs 11am–9pm, Fri–Sat 11am–10pm. Closed some hols. **Prices:** Main courses $8.70–$14.60. No CC. 🔳

Attraction 💼

Eagle Mining Company; tel 619/765-0036. The town of Julian was created in the boom that resulted from the discovery of gold in this area in 1870. The Eagle Mining Company was one of 18 mining operations that produced as much as $13 million worth of gold in their day. Shut down during World War II, the mine was reopened as an attraction in 1967. Guided 1-hour tours through mineshafts bored into the mountain a century ago offer a glimpse into the process of hardrock mining and what life was like for miners of the era. Gold panning demonstration; small museum. **Open:** Daily 10am–3pm. Closed some hols. $$$

KELSEYVILLE

Map page M-2, C1 (S of Lakeport)

Resort 🛎

≣≣ **Konocti Harbor Resort & Spa**, 8727 Soda Bay Rd, Kelseyville, CA 95451; tel 707/279-4281 or toll free 800/862-4930; fax 707/279-9205. Calif 29 N from Lower Lake or S from Kelseyville to Soda Bay Rd; 5 mi to resort. 100 acres. Many resort features, including full spa and golf courses nearby. Popular entertainers perform here on weekends. **Rooms:** 208 rms, stes, and effic; 42 ctges/villas. CI 4pm/CO 11am. Non-smoking rms avail. **Amenities:** 🛢 A/C, cable TV, refrig. Some units w/terraces. **Services:** ♪ Social director, masseur, children's program, babysitting. **Facilities:** ⬜▲⬜◧ 🛴🖥 ⬜ 🖥 & 2 rsts, 5 bars (4 w/entertainment), lifeguard, games rm, spa, sauna, steam rm, whirlpool, beauty salon, playground, washer/dryer. Private heliport. **Rates:** HS May–Oct $59–$85 S or D; from $175 ste; from $140 effic; from $160 ctge/villa. Extra person $10. Children under 12 stay free. Min stay HS. Lower rates off-season. Higher rates for spec evnts/hols. Spec packages avail. Pking: Outdoor, free. Maj CC. Discounts for senior citizens, government employees, and other groups.

KENWOOD

Map page M-2, C1 (E of Santa Rosa)

Restaurant ⑪

Kenwood, 9900 Calif 12, Kenwood; tel 707/833-6326. **French.** Surrounded by pastures and vineyards, this is a tranquil spot for a wine-country meal. Decor is simple, with rattan chairs, wood floors, and contemporary art. There's also a lovely slate patio, with tables sheltered under green umbrellas. The same menu runs all day—from hamburgers to bouillabaisse to a daily pasta special, such as gnocchi with pheasant. Good selection of Sonoma wines by the glass. **FYI:** Reservations recommended. **Open:** Tues–Sun 11:30am–9pm. Closed some hols. **Prices:** Main courses $11.75–$23.50. Ltd CC. ⚓ &

Attraction 📷

Château St Jean, 8555 Sonoma Hwy (Calif 12); tel 707/833-4134. Located at the foot of Sugarloaf Ridge on what was once a private 250-acre country retreat built in 1920. A self-guided tour has detailed photographs and descriptions of the winemaking process. Visitors can sample St Jean's wines, such as Chardonnay, Cabernet Sauvignon, Fume blanc, merlot, Johannisberg Riesling, and Gewuztraminer, at no charge in the tasting room. Picnic grounds. **Open:** Daily 10am–4:30pm. Closed some hols. Free.

KERNVILLE

Map page M-3, C2 (N of Wofford Heights)

Motels 🛏

≣≣ **Kern Lodge Motel**, 67 Valley View, PO Box 66, Kernville, CA 93238; tel 619/376-2223. This charmingly rustic property has wood-paneled walls and a picnic area with barbecue pits. Porch connects the rooms. Humble, but clean. **Rooms:** 15 rms, stes, and effic. CI 2pm/CO 11am. **Amenities:** 📞 📺 Cable TV, refrig. No A/C. Some units w/terraces. **Services:** 🐕 **Facilities:** 🏋 🎱 Games rm. **Rates:** HS May–Oct $50–$95 S; $55–$95 D; from $85 ste; from $60 effic. Extra person $10. Children under 6 stay free. Min stay HS. Lower rates off-season. Higher rates for spec evnts/hols. Pking: Outdoor, free. Maj CC. Rates are reduced on weekdays.

≣≣≣ **Whispering Pines Lodge Bed & Breakfast**, 13745 Sierra Way, Kernville, CA 93238; tel 619/376-3733; fax 619/376-3735. Refurbished cottage-style motel in lovely, rustic country area. Trails lead to the Kern River. **Rooms:** 11 rms, stes, and effic; 11 ctges/villas. CI 3pm/CO 11am. Most rooms have kitchens. **Amenities:** 📞 🍴 📺 A/C, cable TV, refrig, VCR, in-rm safe. Some units w/terraces, some w/fireplaces, some w/Jacuzzis. Gourmet coffee in every room. **Services:** 🍽 🐕 Masseur. **Facilities:** 🏋 🎿 🏊 **Rates (BB):** HS May–Oct from $145 ste; from $109 effic. Extra person $10. Min stay wknds. Lower rates off-season. Spec packages avail. Pking: Outdoor, free. Ltd CC. 2-night minimum on weekends May–October.

Restaurant 🍽

Ewing's on the Kern, 125 Buena Vista, Kernville; tel 619/376-2411. **Continental.** An incredible view of the Kern River and the cliffs surrounding it enhance the rustic country theme. Get there before dusk and you can watch the sun dip beyond the bluffs. Steaks, seafood, chicken, and pastas come in large portions. Sunday brunch is especially popular with children, who can order their french toast filled with peanut butter and jelly. **FYI:** Reservations recommended. Country music. Children's menu. **Open:** HS Mem Day–Labor Day dinner Wed–Mon 4–10pm; brunch Sun 10am–2pm. Reduced hours off-season. **Prices:** Main courses $9.95–$19.95. Maj CC. 🏞 &

KING CITY

Map page M-2, B2

Hotel 🏨

≣ **Keefers**, 615 Canal, King City, CA 93930; tel 408/385-4843; fax 408/385-1254. Canal exit off US 101; exit east. Functional as a travel stop on a long trip. **Rooms:** 47 rms. CI 2pm/CO 11am. Nonsmoking rms avail. **Amenities:** 📞 A/C, cable TV. **Services:** 🛎 🐕 Babysitting. **Facilities:** 🏋 & 1 rst, 1 bar, whirlpool. **Rates (CP):** HS Apr–Oct $45–$48 S; $51–$60 D. Extra person $5. Children under 16 stay free. Min stay spec evnts. Lower rates off-season. Higher rates for spec evnts/hols. Pking: Outdoor, free. Maj CC.

Motel 🛏

≣ **Courtesy Inn**, 4 Broadway, King City, CA 93930; tel 408/385-4646 or toll free 800/350-5616; fax 408/385-6024. Broadway W exit off US 101. Located right off the freeway. Clean and well maintained. Fine as a travel-stop motel. **Rooms:** 64 rms and stes. CI noon/CO noon. Nonsmoking rms avail. **Amenities:** 📞 🍴 📺 A/C, cable TV, refrig. Microwaves. **Services:** ✕ 🛎 🐕 🐶 **Facilities:** 🏋 🎿 & 1 rst, whirlpool, washer/dryer. Barbecue facilities. **Rates (CP):** HS May–Sept $52–$65 S; $57–$69 D; from $65 ste. Extra person $6. Children under 14 stay free. Lower rates off-season. Pking: Outdoor, free. Ltd CC.

Attractions 📷

Monterey County Agricultural and Rural Life Museum; tel 408/385-8020. Located within San Lorenzo Regional Park (see below). The story of Monterey County's agricultural heritage, from mission times to today's advanced agricultural technology, is explored at this museum. The main exhibit barn is filled with artifacts and equipment, and antique farm machinery—some unique to this region—are scattered throughout the site. There is also a working blacksmith shop. A 19th-century schoolhouse, farmhouse, and train depot have been brought to the site and restored; all are open for tours on weekends.

The main exhibit barn also features a Monterey County tourist information center. **Open:** Main exhibit barn, daily 10am–5pm; outbuildings Apr–Oct, Sat–Sun noon–4pm or by appointment. Closed some hols. Free.

San Lorenzo Regional Park, 1160 Broadway; tel 408/385-5964. Located just outside King City, via Broadway exit from US 101. Nestled along the Salinas River, surrounded by the picturesque Salinas Valley, this county park includes the Monterey County Agricultural and Rural Life Museum (see above). The park's day-use amenities include picnic areas, ball fields, and a children's playground. Tent and trailer camp sites. **Open:** Daily sunrise–sunset. $$

KINGS CANYON NATIONAL PARK

Map page M-3, B2

See Sequoia and Kings Canyon National Parks

LAFAYETTE

Map page M-2, D2 (E of San Francisco)

Hotel 🛏

≣≣≣≣ **Lafayette Park Hotel**, 3287 Mt Diablo Blvd, Lafayette, CA 94549; tel 510/283-3700 or toll free 800/368-2468 ext 6; fax 510/284-1621. Pleasant Hills exit off Calif 24; left at ramp; left at stop light. Beautiful Norman French building surrounded by 3 courtyards and lovingly cared for gardens dotted with tables, chairs, and umbrellas. **Rooms:** 139 rms and stes. CI 3pm/CO noon. Express checkout avail. Nonsmoking rms avail. Exquisitely furnished, designer-decorated rooms. Granite countertops in bathrooms. **Amenities:** 🛢 ⚬ 🗍 A/C, cable TV w/movies, bathrobes. All units w/minibars, some w/terraces, some w/fireplaces. Large baker's rack filled with food in each room. VCR available for rent. **Services:** 🍽 ⌧ 𝖵𝖯 ⌧ ⌧ Twice-daily maid svce, social director, children's program, babysitting. Complimentary morning coffee and afternoon wine. Fresh-baked cookies with coffee and tea in the lobby weekday mornings. **Facilities:** 🛢 🏊 🚲 🚹 1 rst, 1 bar, sauna, whirlpool. 3 blocks to jogging path. Tennis courts nearby. **Rates:** HS Apr–

Sept $200–$240 S or D; from $250 ste. Children under 12 stay free. Lower rates off-season. Spec packages avail. Pking: Indoor/outdoor, free. Maj CC.

LAGUNA BEACH

Map page M-3, E2

Hotels 🛏

≣≣ **Capri Laguna Inn on the Beach**, 1441 S Coast Hwy, Laguna Beach, CA 02651; tel 714/494-6533 or toll free 800/225-4551; fax 714/497-6962. Laguna Beach exit off Calif 1. Great location right on the main beach. You can walk down a staircase to the ocean and hear the pounding waves from your room. **Rooms:** 37 rms and stes. CI 3pm/CO noon. Nonsmoking rms avail. Some rooms have kitchenettes. Decor is rather plain, but acceptable. Honeymoon suite is available. **Amenities:** 🛢 ⚬ Cable TV, refrig, stereo/tape player. No A/C. All units w/terraces, some w/fireplaces. **Services:** 🗍 Twice-daily maid svce. Coffee and iced tea in the lobby. **Facilities:** 🛢 🚲 🚹 1 beach (ocean), lifeguard, sauna. Outside picnic area with gas grill. Conveniently located within walking distance of restaurants. **Rates (CP):** HS July–Sept $90–$225 D; from $140 ste. Extra person $10. Children under 12 stay free. Lower rates off-season. Higher rates for spec evnts/hols. Pking: Outdoor, free. Maj CC. Prices are fair when you consider the location.

≣≣≣ **Hotel Laguna Beach Club & Conference Center**, 425 S Coast Hwy, Laguna Beach, CA 92651; tel 714/494-1151 or toll free 800/524-2927; fax 714/497-2163. Historic 1930s hotel, still comfortable and charming, set in a Spanish-style building. With its own beach. Located near shops, restaurants. Popular with the artsy crowd. **Rooms:** 65 rms and stes. CI 2pm/CO noon. Express checkout avail. Nonsmoking rms avail. Most rooms have ocean views. All are large, with walk-in closets. Although hotel is located on the highway in the busiest part of town, the rooms are quiet. **Amenities:** 🛢 ⚬ A/C, cable TV w/movies, voice mail. **Services:** ✕ ⌧ 𝖵𝖯 ⌧ 🗍 Twice-daily maid svce, car-rental desk, babysitting. Boat rentals can be arranged. **Facilities:** 🛢 🚲 🖥 🚹 3 rsts, 1 bar (w/entertainment), 1 beach (ocean), lifeguard, beauty salon, washer/dryer. Rose garden and a gazebo for weddings. **Rates (CP):** HS June–Sept $80–$150 S or D; from $150 ste. Children under 18 stay free. Min stay wknds. Lower rates off-season. Higher rates for spec evnts/hols. Pking: Outdoor, free. Maj CC.

≣≣ **Inn at Laguna Beach**, 211 N Pacific Coast Hwy, Laguna Beach, CA 92651; tel 714/497-9722 or toll free 800/544-4479; fax 714/497-9972. 10 mi S of Newport Beach. Laguna Canyon Rd exit off I-405, toward Laguna Beach; right on Pacific Coast

Hwy. Great location on a cliff overlooking the ocean and the beach; close to shops, galleries, restaurants, and the Laguna scene. **Rooms:** 70 rms and stes. CI 4pm/CO noon. Rooms are undergoing renovation. Some accommodations overlook the highway, but traffic noise is muffled. Other rooms have an ocean view and balcony away from the street. **Amenities:** 🛆 🗘 🗘 A/C, cable TV w/movies, refrig, VCR, bathrobes. All units w/minibars, some w/terraces. Some rooms have microwaves. The only hotel on the beach with air conditioning. **Services:** 🗌 🗘 Masseur, babysitting. **Facilities:** 🗗 🗗 🗗 1 beach (ocean), lifeguard, sauna, whirlpool. **Rates:** HS July–Sept 5 $139–$299 S or D; from $299 ste. Extra person $20. Children under 13 stay free. Min stay HS and wknds. Lower rates off-season. Spec packages avail. Pking: Indoor, free. Maj CC.

≣≣≣≣ Surf & Sand Hotel, 1555 S Coast Hwy, Laguna Beach, CA 92651; tel 714/497-4477 or toll free 800/524-8621; fax 714/494-2897. 20 mi S of John Wayne Airport. Calif 133 exit off I-405; N of downtown Laguna Beach. A lovely, elegant hotel, right on the beach. Very romantic, and close to shops, restaurants, and galleries. **Rooms:** 157 rms and stes. CI 3pm/CO noon. Nonsmoking rms avail. Tasteful rooms invite relaxation. All have great ocean views. **Amenities:** 🛆 🗘 🗘 Cable TV w/movies, refrig, VCR, in-rm safe, bathrobes. No A/C. All units w/minibars, all w/terraces, some w/fireplaces, some w/Jacuzzis. **Services:** ✗ 🗝 🎛 🗌 🗘 Twice-daily maid svce, masseur, children's program, babysitting. Knowledgeable and well-trained staff. **Facilities:** 🗗 🗗 🗗 2 rsts (see also "Restaurants" below), 2 bars (1 w/entertainment), 1 beach (ocean), beauty salon. The pool overlooks the ocean. Restaurants are very good. **Rates:** HS May–Sept $200–$240 D; from $425 ste. Extra person $10. Min stay HS. Lower rates off-season. Spec packages avail. Pking: Indoor, $9. Maj CC.

≣≣≣ Vacation Village, 647 S Coast Hwy, PO Box 66, Laguna Beach, CA 92652; tel 714/494-8566 or toll free 800/843-6895; fax 714/494-1386. Unique hotel in a prime location on the beach, with several buildings and something for everyone; rooms, suites, condos, and a private house used for weddings. Good choice for families. **Rooms:** 130 rms, stes, and effic. CI 3pm/CO 11am. Many rooms and suites have kitchenettes. Rooms are clean and comfortable. Bathrooms are tiny but immaculate. Ocean-view rooms are worth the extra cost. **Amenities:** 🛆 🗘 🎛 🗘 A/C, cable TV. All units w/terraces. **Services:** 🗘 Babysitting. **Facilities:** 🗗 🗗 1 rst, 1 beach (ocean), lifeguard, whirlpool. **Rates:** HS June–Sept $80–$145 S or D; from $95 ste; from $95 effic. Extra person $10. Children under 12 stay free. Min stay HS. Lower rates off-season. Higher rates for spec evnts/hols. Spec packages avail. Pking: Outdoor, free. Maj CC.

Motels

≣≣ Best Western Laguna Reef Inn, 30806 S Coast Hwy, Laguna Beach, CA 92651; tel 714/499-2227 or toll free 800/922-9905; fax 714/499-5575. 3 mi S of Laguna Beach. On Calif 1. Clean, no-nonsense hotel right across from the beach, surrounded by palm trees and flower gardens. A good value. **Rooms:** 43 rms. CI 2pm/CO noon. Nonsmoking rms avail. **Amenities:** 🛆 🗘 A/C, cable TV, refrig. **Services:** 🚐 Twice-daily maid svce. **Facilities:** 🗗 1 beach (ocean), lifeguard, sauna, whirlpool. **Rates (CP):** HS July–Aug $92–$102 S or D. Extra person $10. Lower rates off-season. Spec packages avail. Pking: Outdoor, free. Maj CC.

≣≣ Quality Inn Laguna Beach, 1404 N Coast Hwy, Laguna Beach, CA 92651; tel 714/494-6464 or toll free 800/221-2222; fax 714/494-9776. Laguna Beach exit off Calif 1; exit north. Beach is across the street and down the hill. The hotel is 1 mile from downtown Laguna Beach; out of the congested area, but still convenient for business travelers. **Rooms:** 22 rms and stes. CI 3pm/CO 11am. Nonsmoking rms avail. Good-size rooms feature pink-and-green decor with light wood furniture and large bathrooms. **Amenities:** 🛆 🗘 A/C, cable TV, refrig. Some units w/terraces, some w/Jacuzzis. **Services:** 🗘 Twice-daily maid svce. **Facilities:** 🗗 🗗 🗗 Washer/dryer. **Rates (CP):** HS June–Sept $74–$129 S or D; from $148 ste. Extra person $10. Children under 17 stay free. Min stay HS and wknds. Lower rates off-season. Higher rates for spec evnts/hols. Pking: Indoor, free. Maj CC.

Inn

≣≣≣≣ Eiler's Inn, 741 S Pacific Coast Hwy, Laguna Beach, CA 92651; tel 714/494-3004. The beach is literally in the backyard at this cozy inn with a fountain and romantic courtyard. In the heart of Laguna Beach; splendid atmosphere. Unsuitable for children under 18. **Rooms:** 11 rms and stes. CI 2pm/CO noon. Every room is unique, with furniture of Victorian or early American vintage. **Amenities:** No A/C, phone, or TV. All units w/terraces, some w/fireplaces. Some rooms have refrigerators and microwaves. **Services:** Twice-daily maid svce, babysitting, afternoon tea and wine/sherry served. Breakfast in the courtyard or in your room. **Facilities:** 1 beach (ocean), lifeguard, guest lounge w/TV. **Rates (CP):** $100–$130 S or D; from $175 ste. Extra person $20. Min stay wknds. Pking: Outdoor, free. Ltd CC.

Resorts

≣≣≣ Aliso Creek Inn, 31106 S Coast Hwy, Laguna Beach, CA 92677; tel 714/499-2271 or toll free 800/223-3309; fax

714/499-4601. 83 acres. Big resort nestled in a canyon across the Pacific Coast Highway from the beach—like being in the mountains, with the ocean just a short walk away. Although just off the highway, it feels light years away. **Rooms:** 62 rms and stes. CI 3pm/CO noon. Nonsmoking rms avail. Most units are duplexes with a sitting room and kitchen on the first floor, bedroom upstairs. Most have walk-in closets. **Amenities:** 🛁 ⌚ 📺 Cable TV w/movies, refrig, stereo/tape player. No A/C. All units w/terraces. **Services:** 🛎 Twice-daily maid svce. Sun-deck dining. **Facilities:** 🏊 ▶9 🅿175 ♿ 1 rst, 1 bar (w/entertainment), whirlpool, washer/dryer. Recreation room with Ping Pong and chess. Putting green, driving range, shuffleboard. Bar with wide-screen TV. Ben Brown's, a famous Laguna Beach restaurant, is on the premises. **Rates:** HS July–Aug $74–$128 S or D; from $138 ste. Children under 12 stay free. Lower rates off-season. Higher rates for spec evnts/hols. Spec packages avail. Pking: Outdoor, free. Maj CC.

≡≡≡ **Laguna Riviera Beach Resort & Spa**, 825 S Coast Hwy, Laguna Beach, CA 92651; tel 714/494-1196 or toll free 800/999-2089; fax 714/494-8421. Right on the beach. The hallways are like big decks, and there are lots of palm trees, even on the sun deck in the center of the building. **Rooms:** 41 rms, stes, and effic. CI 3pm/CO noon. Nonsmoking rms avail. Average in size, rooms have green-and-pink flowered bed-spreads. Renovation is ongoing. Some rooms have kitchenettes, some have big balconies. **Amenities:** 🛁 ⌚ 📺 Cable TV w/movies, refrig, stereo/tape player. No A/C. Some units w/ter-races, some w/fireplaces, some w/Jacuzzis. Microwave. **Services:** ✕ 🖼 🛎 Twice-daily maid svce, car-rental desk. Afternoon tea. VCR with classic movies in the lobby. **Facilities:** 🏊 ♿ 1 beach (ocean), sauna, whirlpool. Indoor pool surrounded by glass and a removable roof. **Rates (CP):** HS mid-June–mid-Sept $72–$121 S or D; from $118 ste; from $118 effic. Extra person $10. Children under 5 stay free. Min stay HS. Lower rates off-season. Higher rates for spec evnts/hols. Pking: Outdoor, free. Maj CC.

Restaurants 🍽

★ **Cafe Zinc**, 350 Ocean Ave, Laguna Beach; tel 714/494-6302. **New American.** Good for people-watching, a pleas-ant artsy place with simple decor. Serves popular breakfasts. Innovative vegetarian dishes include black-bean chili, mini-pizza, and roasted eggplant. Tasty desserts. Gourmet shop next door. **FYI:** Reservations not accepted. No liquor license. **Open:** HS July–Aug daily 7am–8pm. Reduced hours off-season. Closed some hols. **Prices:** Main courses $4.95–$6.95. No CC. 🍴

Cafe Zoolu, 860 Glenneyre St, Laguna Beach; tel 714/494-6825. **Californian.** A former antique shop, this cafe has

black straw chairs, 2 tiny fireplaces, and a tiled floor. Varied sophisticated menu features Hawaiian and Chinese dishes as well as old-fashioned meatloaf with mashed potatoes. **FYI:** Reserva-tions recommended. Beer and wine only. **Open:** HS June–Aug daily 5–10pm. Reduced hours off-season. Closed some hols. **Prices:** Main courses $8.50–$17.95. Maj CC. 🍴

Five Feet, 328 Glenneyre St, Laguna Beach; tel 714/497-4955. 1 block E of the Pacific Coast Hwy. **Chinese.** A popular place tucked away under a big tree off the main street. Decor is contemporary Asian, with black and gray chairs, beam ceilings, and flowers on each table. Chinese menu offers braised codfish, the house specialty, as well as striped bass with black beans and ginger, and other seafood dishes. **FYI:** Reservations recommend-ed. Beer and wine only. **Open:** Lunch Fri 11:30am–2:30pm; dinner Sun–Thurs 5–10pm, Fri–Sat 5–11pm. Closed some hols. **Prices:** Main courses $13.95–$23.50. Maj CC. ❤♿

★ **Sorrento Grille**, 370 Glenneyre St, Laguna Beach; tel 714/494-8686. Forest Ave exit off Pacific Coast Hwy (Calif 1); N to Glenneyre. **Italian/Southwestern.** Convenient location in the middle of downtown. Decorated with terra-cotta tiles, cowboy hats, Mexican ponchos, etc. Menu features mesquite-grilled entrees, pasta with chicken and seafood, and organically grown produce. **FYI:** Reservations recommended. Dress code. **Open:** HS July–Sept daily 5:30–10pm. Reduced hours off-season. Closed some hols. **Prices:** Main courses $13.95–$21.95. Maj CC. 🍴

$ 🍷 **Splashes**, in Surf & Sand Hotel, 1555 South Coast Hwy, Laguna Beach; tel 714/497-4477. 12 mi S of John Wayne Airport. **Mediterranean.** Just a few steps from the beach, with simple yet elegant decor. Dine inside by the fireplace, or on the patio, listening to the calming sounds of the ocean. Dishes include salmon, swordfish, Moroccan chicken, osso buco, and other fresh house specialties. **FYI:** Reservations recommended. Children's menu. **Open:** Breakfast daily 7–11am; lunch daily 11:30am–4:30pm; dinner Sun–Thurs 5–10pm, Fri–Sat 5–11pm; brunch Sun 11:30am–4:30pm. **Prices:** Main courses $15–$20. Maj CC. ❤ 🍴 🖼 🏔 🎏 VP ♿

🍷 **The Towers Restaurant**, in Surf and Sand Hotel, 1555 South Coast Hwy, Laguna Beach; tel 714/497-4477. **French/Italian.** As romantic as they come. Art deco motif in a room furnished with soft chairs in beige and green. The bar has a fireplace and a piano player, and picture windows offer spectacular ocean panoramas. Popular is roasted rack of lamb with Dijon crust and garlic pureed potatoes, Maine lobster with pinot noir sauce, tarragon linguini, and crème brûlée for dessert. **FYI:** Reserva-tions recommended. Piano. Children's menu. Dress code. **Open:** Dinner Mon–Thurs 5:30–11pm, Fri–Sun 5:30–10pm. **Prices:** Main courses $16–$28. Maj CC. ❤ 🖼 🏔 VP ♿

★ **242 Cafe**, 242 North Coast Hwy, Laguna Beach; tel 714/494-2444. **Health/Spa.** If you blink, you might pass this cozy place right on the highway, which looks more like a deli than a restaurant. Very popular, there's often a line of locals waiting to get in to sample the offerings on the health-conscious menu of salads, sandwiches, and pastries. **FYI:** Reservations recommended. No liquor license. **Open:** Lunch daily noon–3pm; dinner daily 5–10pm; brunch Sat–Sun 8:30am–noon. Closed some hols. **Prices:** Main courses $2–$8. Ltd CC. [symbol]

Attraction [symbol]

Laguna Art Museum, 307 Cliff Dr; tel 714/494-6531. Ten galleries house exhibitions focusing on American art, with particular emphasis on the art and artists of California. The permanent collection is notable for its collection of Southern California works created between the two World Wars, for early 20th-century photography, and for contemporary art. Lectures, symposia, special events. **Open:** Tues–Sun 11am–5pm. Closed some hols. $$

LA HABRA

Map page M-3, D2 (SW of Pomona)

Attraction [symbol]

Children's Museum at La Habra, 301 S Euclid St; tel 310/905-9793 or 905-9693. Housed in a restored 1923 railroad station, this museum puts children in touch with exhibits dealing with science, history, art, the humanities, and everyday life. Changing exhibits, special events, and programs. **Open:** Mon–Sat 10am–5pm, Sun 1–5pm. Closed some hols. $$

LA JOLLA

Map page M-3, E3

Hotels [symbol]

≣≣ **Best Western Inn by the Sea**, 7830 Fay Ave, La Jolla, CA 92037 (La Jolla Village); tel 619/459-4461 or toll free 800/462-9732; fax 619/456-2578. 12 mi NW of San Diego, exit Ardath Rd off I-5. Ardath Rd exit off I-5 N; La Jolla Village Dr W exit off I-5 S. Well-located property. Adjacent coffee shop. **Rooms:** 133 rms and stes. CI 2pm/CO noon. Nonsmoking rms avail. Pleasant rooms with very attractive decor. All have sliding glass doors that open onto balconies. **Amenities:** [symbol] [symbol] A/C, cable TV w/movies. All units w/terraces, 1 w/fireplace. Refrigera-

tors available by request. **Services:** [symbols] Car-rental desk, babysitting. **Facilities:** [symbols] 1 rst, whirlpool, washer/dryer. **Rates (CP):** HS June–Sept $95–$140 S; $110–$140 D; from $250 ste. Extra person $10. Children under 12 stay free. Min stay spec evnts. Lower rates off-season. Higher rates for spec evnts/hols. Spec packages avail. Pking: Indoor/outdoor, free. Maj CC.

≣≣≣ **Colonial Inn**, 910 Prospect St, La Jolla, CA 92037 (La Jolla Village); tel 619/454-2181 or toll free 800/832-5525, 800/826-1278 in CA; fax 619/454-5679. 12 mi NW of San Diego. Ardath Rd exit off I-5 N; La Jolla Village Dr W exit off I-5 S. Take Torrey Pines Rd to Prospect St and turn right. A 1913 inn with a charming old-world atmosphere, 1 block from the ocean and the park. **Rooms:** 75 rms and stes. CI 3pm/CO noon. Nonsmoking rms avail. Very nice furnishings and fabrics. Every room has a ceiling fan. Some lack air conditioning but have windows that open. **Amenities:** [symbol] Cable TV. No A/C. Some units w/terraces. Refrigerators and terry robes available on request. **Services:** [symbols] Car-rental desk, masseur, babysitting. Afternoon tea in lobby. Turndown service on request. Pianist plays in lobby lounge some afternoons and evenings. Complimentary shoeshine. **Facilities:** [symbols] 1 rst (see also "Restaurants" below), 1 bar. **Rates:** HS July–Sept $135–$200 S or D; from $200 ste. Extra person $10. Children under 18 stay free. Lower rates off-season. Spec packages avail. Maj CC.

≣≣≣ **Embassy Suites San Diego–La Jolla**, 4550 La Jolla Village Dr, La Jolla, CA 92122 (Golden Triangle); tel 619/453-0400 or toll free 800/362-2779; fax 619/453-4226. 14 mi NW of San Diego. La Jolla Village Dr exit off I-5; go east. Very user-friendly hotel. A 12-story atrium is filled with plants, ponds, and waterfalls. Convenient to University Towne Center and Golden Triangle businesses. **Rooms:** 335 rms and stes. CI 4pm/CO noon. Express checkout avail. Nonsmoking rms avail. Sofasleeper in living room, microwave, wet bar. **Amenities:** [symbols] A/C, cable TV w/movies, refrig, voice mail. Some units w/Jacuzzis. Two TVs in every room. Complimentary cooked-to-order breakfast and evening cocktails. **Services:** [symbols] Twice-daily maid svce, car-rental desk, babysitting. **Facilities:** [symbols] 1 rst, 1 bar (w/entertainment), games rm, sauna, whirlpool, washer/dryer. Restaurant has outdoor seating. Avis car rental on premises. **Rates (BB):** HS July–Aug $149 S; $159 D; from $300 ste. Extra person $10. Children under 12 stay free. Min stay spec evnts. Lower rates off-season. Higher rates for spec evnts/hols. Spec packages avail. Pking: Indoor/outdoor, free. Maj CC.

≣≣≣ **Empress Hotel of La Jolla**, 7766 Fay Ave, La Jolla, CA 92037 (La Jolla Village); tel 619/454-3001 or toll free 800/525-6552; fax 619/454-6387. 12 mi NW of San Diego. Ardath

Rd exit off I-5 N; La Jolla Village Dr W exit off I-5 S. Take Torrey Pines Rd to Girard, turn right, then left on Kline St. A small, European-style hotel with a convenient village location. **Rooms:** 73 rms, stes, and effic. CI 3pm/CO noon. Nonsmoking rms avail. Rooms are spacious with high-quality furnishings, marble bathrooms, large mirrors, and soothing decor. **Amenities:** 🛁 ⌚ 🖥 📺 A/C, cable TV, refrig, bathrobes. Some units w/Jacuzzis. **Services:** ✕ VP 🚐 🛎 🐕 Car-rental desk. Continental breakfast served in breakfast room. Shoe polishers on every floor. Room service for lunch and dinner. **Facilities:** 🍴 [65] & 1 rst, 1 bar, sauna, whirlpool. Restaurant on premises is considered one of the best in La Jolla. **Rates (CP):** HS June–Sept $90–$130 S or D; from $250 ste; from $250 effic. Extra person $10. Children under 18 stay free. Min stay spec evnts. Lower rates off-season. Spec packages avail. Maj CC. Good-value packages during low season.

≡≡≡≡ Hyatt Regency La Jolla, 3777 La Jolla Village Dr, La Jolla, CA 92122; tel 619/552-1234 or toll free 800/233-1234; fax 619/552-6066. 15 mi N of San Diego. La Jolla Village Dr exit off I-5; go east. Epic-proportioned elegance, from the massive pillared entrance to the lobby's highly polished brown Italian marble floors. A few Greco-Roman torsos and art deco couches are thrown in for good measure by noted architect Michael Graves. **Rooms:** 400 rms and stes. Exec-level rms avail. CI 3pm/CO noon. Express checkout avail. Nonsmoking rms avail. The signature cherry-wood grid pattern from the lobby shows up on the room furnishings, including the armoire, desk, and nightstand. Very nice bathrooms are tiled in a gray and white, to contrast with a brown marble sink. **Amenities:** 🛁 ⌚ 📺 A/C, cable TV w/movies, shoe polisher. All units w/minibars, some w/Jacuzzis. Irons and ironing boards in all rooms. **Services:** ✕ 🛎 VP 🚐 🛎 🐕 Car-rental desk, masseur, babysitting. Hyatt Business Plan guests receive continental breakfast, free credit card and local calls, 24-hour access to a copier and printer, and more. **Facilities:** 🍴 🚲 ⛳2 🍴 [1.4K] ⛱ & 5 rsts, 2 bars, lifeguard, racquetball, squash, spa, sauna, steam rm, whirlpool. Large pool flanked by Herculean columns. Access to the very exclusive Sporting Club next door, with weight machines, aerobics classes, and spa treatments. Hotel is convenient to other facilities in the Aventine complex, with 5 restaurants including the well-regarded Cafe Japengo (*see also* "Restaurants" below). **Rates:** $124–$210 S or D; from $225 ste. Extra person $25. Children under 18 stay free. Min stay spec evnts. AP and MAP rates avail. Spec packages avail. Pking: Indoor, $7. Maj CC.

≡≡≡≡ La Valencia Hotel, 1132 Prospect St, La Jolla, CA 92037 (La Jolla Village); tel 619/454-0771 or toll free 800/451-0772; fax 619/456-3921. 12 mi NW of San Diego. Ardath Rd exit off I-5 N; La Jolla Village Dr W exit off I-5 S. La Jolla's best accommodations, in a landmark Spanish-colonial hotel with

tiled roof and elegant appointments, and fantastic views of the ocean. **Rooms:** 95 rms, stes, and effic; 5 ctges/villas. CI 3pm/CO noon. Express checkout avail. Elegant rooms have beautiful furnishings, small but lovely marble bathrooms, and excellent ocean views. Two-bedroom bungalows are spacious and good for families. **Amenities:** 🛁 ⌚ 📺 A/C, cable TV w/movies, refrig, voice mail, bathrobes. Some units w/minibars, some w/terraces, some w/Jacuzzis. Fresh fruit basket on arrival. **Services:** 🍽 🛎 VP 🚐 🛎 🐕 👼 Twice-daily maid svce, car-rental desk, babysitting. Complimentary daily newspaper and shoeshine. **Facilities:** 🍴 🍴 [160] 3 rsts (*see also* "Restaurants" below), 1 bar, sauna, whirlpool. Wonderful lounge with ocean view. **Rates:** HS July–Sept $150–$295 S or D; from $325 ste; from $195 effic; from $150 ctge/villa. Extra person $10. Children under 12 stay free. Min stay spec evnts. Lower rates off-season. Pking: Indoor/outdoor, $8. Maj CC.

≡≡ Radisson Hotel La Jolla, 3299 Holiday Ct, La Jolla, CA 92037 (Golden Triangle); tel 619/453-5500 or toll free 800/333-3333; fax 619/453-5550. 13 mi NW of San Diego. La Jolla Village Dr exit off I-5. Lowrise hotel with good proximity to freeway, Golden Triangle businesses, and University of California–San Diego. Bar and dining area are popular with UCSD staff and faculty. **Rooms:** 200 rms, stes, and effic. CI 3pm/CO noon. Express checkout avail. Nonsmoking rms avail. Bright, contemporary decor. **Amenities:** 🛁 ⌚ 📺 A/C, cable TV, VCR. Some units w/terraces. Refrigerators available on request. **Services:** ✕ 🚐 🛎 🐕 Car-rental desk. **Facilities:** 🍴 ⛳2 🍴 [250] & 2 rsts, 1 bar (w/entertainment), whirlpool. Shuffleboard. **Rates:** HS June–Sept $85 S; $95 D; from $150 ste; from $250 effic. Extra person $10. Children under 18 stay free. Min stay spec evnts. Lower rates off-season. Higher rates for spec evnts/hols. Spec packages avail. Pking: Outdoor, free. Maj CC.

≡≡≡ San Diego Marriott–La Jolla, 4240 La Jolla Village Dr, La Jolla, CA 92037 (Golden Triangle); tel 619/587-1414 or toll free 800/228-9290; fax 619/546-8518. 14 mi NW of San Diego. La Jolla Village Dr exit off I-5; go east. A 15-story hotel located in a business park, part of the Golden Triangle. Connected by an elevated walkway to University Towne Center. **Rooms:** 360 rms and stes. Exec-level rms avail. CI 4pm/CO noon. Express checkout avail. Nonsmoking rms avail. **Amenities:** 🛁 ⌚ A/C, cable TV w/movies, voice mail. All units w/terraces. Iron and ironing board in every room. **Services:** ✕ 🛎 VP 🛎 🐕 👼 Car-rental desk, babysitting. Hertz car rental and American Airlines have offices on the premises. **Facilities:** 🍴 🍴 [1.5K] & 2 rsts, 2 bars (1 w/entertainment), games rm, sauna, whirlpool, washer/dryer. Indoor and outdoor pools. **Rates:** HS July–Apr $198–$225 S or D; from $350 ste. Extra person $15. Min stay spec evnts. Lower rates off-season. Higher rates for spec evnts/ hols. Spec packages avail. Pking: Indoor/outdoor, $7–$10. Maj CC.

≣≣ Summer House Inn, 7955 La Jolla Shores Dr, La Jolla, CA 92037 (La Jolla Shores); tel 619/459-0261 or toll free 800/ 666-0261; fax 619/459-7649. 11 mi NW of San Diego. Ardath Rd exit off I-5 N; La Jolla Village Dr W exit off I-5 S. Located just 4 blocks from the beach at a busy intersection. A bit noisy, but rooms on highest floors are acceptably quiet. **Rooms:** 90 rms, stes, and effic. CI 3pm/CO noon. Nonsmoking rms avail. Rooms are in need of renovation. **Amenities:** 🛏 🕭 🎇 A/C, cable TV, refrig, voice mail. All units w/terraces, some w/Jacuzzis. **Services:** ✗ 🚐 🛄 🕭 Car-rental desk, masseur, babysitting. Complimentary continental breakfast. **Facilities:** 🔥 🔟 1 rst (*see also* "Restaurants" below), 1 bar (w/entertainment), sauna, whirlpool, beauty salon, washer/dryer. The inn's restaurant, Elario's, is very good. **Rates (CP):** HS June–Aug $69–$109 S or D; from $125 ste; from $125 effic. Extra person $8. Children under 13 stay free. Min stay HS and wknds. Lower rates off-season. Spec packages avail. Pking: Outdoor, free. Maj CC.

Motels

≣≣ Andrea Villa Inn, 2402 Torrey Pines Rd, La Jolla, CA 92037 (La Jolla Shores); tel 619/459-3311 or toll free 800/LA-JOLLA; fax 619/459-1320. 11 mi NW of San Diego. La Jolla Village Dr W exit off I-55; Ardath Rd exit off I-5 N. Located 5 blocks from the beach on a busy thoroughfare, but set back from the street so it's quiet in most rooms. **Rooms:** 49 rms and effic. CI 3pm/CO noon. Nonsmoking rms avail. Rooms are spacious and attractively decorated, with large closets. Half have full kitchens. **Amenities:** 🛏 A/C, cable TV. 1 unit w/terrace. **Services:** 🚐 🛄 🕭 Continental breakfast buffet. **Facilities:** 🔥 🔟 Whirlpool, washer/dryer. Attractive pool area. Homey breakfast room. **Rates (CP):** HS June–Sept $75 S; $85 D; from $75 effic. Extra person $10. Children under 17 stay free. Min stay spec evnts. Lower rates off-season. Spec packages avail. Pking: Outdoor, free. Maj CC. Higher rates on weekends.

≣≣ La Jolla Cove Suites, 1155 Coast Blvd, PO Box 1067, La Jolla, CA 92038 (La Jolla Village); tel 619/459-2621 or toll free 800/248-2683; fax 619/454-3522. 12 mi NW of San Diego. Ardath Rd exit off I-5 N; La Jolla Village Dr W exit off I-5 S. Take Torrey Pines Rd to Prospect St, turn right. Right across from the La Jolla Cove, with a nice beach and a marine sanctuary popular with divers. Good choice for families. **Rooms:** 116 rms, stes, and effic. CI 3pm/CO 11am. Express checkout avail. Decor is somewhat dated, with old, worn furniture and carpets, but rooms are very spacious and have enormous closets. **Amenities:** 🛏 🕭 Cable TV w/movies, refrig. No A/C. All units w/terraces.

Services: 🛄 🕭 Car-rental desk, masseur, babysitting. Staff is unusually friendly and helpful. Continental breakfast available in the solarium. **Facilities:** 🔥 🏓 🔢 ⅋ Lawn games, racquetball, sauna, steam rm, whirlpool, washer/dryer. Good laundry facilities, nice putting green (putters and balls are provided for free), and lovely pool area. **Rates:** HS June–Sept $65–$120 S or D; from $145 ste; from $115 effic. Extra person $5. Min stay spec evnts. Lower rates off-season. Higher rates for spec evnts/hols. Pking: Indoor/outdoor, free. Maj CC.

≣ La Jolla Travelodge, 1141 Siverado St, La Jolla, CA 92037 (La Jolla Village); tel 619/454-0791 or toll free 800/578-7878; fax 619/459-8534. 12 mi NW of San Diego. La Jolla Village Dr W exit off I-5 S; Ardath Rd exit off I-5 N. Located 3 blocks from the beach in La Jolla Village. **Rooms:** 30 rms and effic. CI 2pm/ CO noon. Nonsmoking rms avail. Rooms are clean and simple. **Amenities:** 🛏 📺 A/C, cable TV. **Services:** 🛄 🕭 Car-rental desk, babysitting. Free newspapers. Check-in often available before 2pm. **Rates:** HS July–Aug $89–$108 S or D; from $94 effic. Extra person $5. Children under 17 stay free. Min stay spec evnts. Lower rates off-season. Higher rates for spec evnts/hols. Spec packages avail. Pking: Outdoor, free. Maj CC.

≣≣ Prospect Park Inn, 1110 Prospect St, La Jolla, CA 92037 (La Jolla Village); tel 619/454-0133 or toll free 800/433-1609; fax 619/454-2056. 12 mi NW of San Diego. Ardath Rd exit off I-5 N; La Jolla Village Dr W exit off I-5 S; Torrey Pines Rd to Prospect St; turn right. A 1947 boarding house for women converted to a charming boutique hotel. Near beach, park, shops, and restaurants. No elevator. **Rooms:** 23 rms, stes, and effic. CI 3pm/CO 11am. Nonsmoking rms avail. Rooms are modern, clean, and attractive. Cove suite is large with lovely ocean view. **Amenities:** 🛏 🕭 📺 🎇 A/C, cable TV. Some units w/terraces. Bottled water provided in every room. **Services:** 🛄 🕭 Car-rental desk, babysitting. Library area offers fruit, cookies, and beverages in the afternoon. Breakfast served in rooms or on sundeck with great ocean view. Beach towels and chairs provided free. Guests may use adjacent indoor parking structure at no charge. **Rates (CP):** $90–$115 S or D; from $200 ste; from $100 effic. Extra person $10. Min stay wknds. Maj CC.

≣≣ Residence Inn by Marriott, 8901 Gilman Dr, La Jolla, CA 92037; tel 619/587-1770 or toll free 800/331-3131; fax 619/552-0387. Gilman Dr exit off I-15. Feels like a condominium complex. Homey ambience. **Rooms:** 287 effic. CI 4pm/CO noon. Nonsmoking rms avail. Suites have complete kitchens and living rooms; 2-bedroom, 2-bath suites available. **Amenities:** 🛏 🕭 📺 A/C, cable TV, refrig. All units w/terraces, some w/fireplaces. Some units have VCRs. **Services:** ✗ 🚐 🛄 🕭 🐾 Car-rental desk, children's program, babysitting. Complimentary fresh fruit and coffee served all day. **Facilities:** 🔥 🔟 ⅋

Whirlpool, washer/dryer. Volleyball, basketball, 5 whirlpools. Use of gas barbecues. Free use of local YMCA. **Rates (CP):** From $139 effic. Extra person $10. Min stay spec evnts. Pking: Outdoor, free. Maj CC.

Scripps Inn, 555 Coast Blvd S, La Jolla, CA 92037 (La Jolla Village); tel 619/454-3391; fax 619/459-6758. 12 mi NW of San Diego. Ardath Rd exit off I-5 N; La Jolla Village Dr W exit off I-5 S; take Torrey Pines Rd to Prospect St; veer right onto Coast Blvd. Charming older motel across the street from a beautiful park and the beach. Small, friendly place to stay. **Rooms:** 13 rms and effic. CI 3pm/CO noon. Quaint furnishings. 5 rooms have cooking facilities. **Amenities:** Cable TV, refrig, in-rm safe. No A/C. Some units w/fireplaces. Shared ocean-view terrace. **Services:** Complimentary continental breakfast is offered in the tiny lobby; guests may take it to their rooms or to the terrace. **Rates (CP):** HS June–Sept $110–$135 S or D; from $130 effic. Extra person $10. Children under 12 stay free. Min stay wknds. Lower rates off-season. Pking: Outdoor, free. Maj CC.

Inn

Bed & Breakfast Inn at La Jolla, 7753 Draper Ave, La Jolla, CA 92037 (La Jolla Village); tel 619/456-2066; fax 619/454-9055. 12 mi NW of San Diego. Ardath Rd exit off I-5 N; La Jolla Village Dr W exit off I-5 S. Historic property built in 1913, then expanded and converted to an inn in 1985. Great location, across from the recreation center and Museum of Contemporary Art. Unsuitable for children under 12. **Rooms:** 16 rms and stes (1 w/shared bath). CI 2pm/CO noon. No smoking. Beautiful decor and fresh flowers in each uniquely decorated room. **Amenities:** A/C, bathrobes. No phone or TV. 1 unit w/terrace, some w/fireplaces. You can request a telephone. **Services:** X Babysitting, wine/sherry served. Complimentary breakfast delivered to room or served in the dining room or garden. **Facilities:** Guest lounge. **Rates (CP):** HS July–Aug $85 S or D w/shared bath, $100–$200 S or D w/private bath; from $225 ste. Extra person $25. Min stay wknds. Lower rates off-season. Higher rates for spec evnts/hols. Spec packages avail. Pking: Outdoor, free. Ltd CC.

Resorts

La Jolla Beach & Tennis Club, 2000 Spindrift Dr, La Jolla, CA 92037 (La Jolla Shores); tel 619/454-7126 or toll free 800/624-2582; fax 619/456-3805. 11 mi NW of San Diego. Ardath Rd exit off I-5 N; La Jolla Village Dr exit off I-5 S. 21 acres. One of the few true beachfront hotels in southern California, formerly an exclusive private club. **Rooms:** 90 rms and effic. CI 4pm/CO noon. Rooms are somewhat dated;

renovation is underway. **Amenities:** Cable TV, refrig. No A/C. Some units w/terraces. **Services:** Car-rental desk, social director, masseur, babysitting. Children's program in summer only. **Facilities:** 2 rsts, 2 bars (1 w/entertainment), 1 beach (ocean), lifeguard, board surfing, lawn games, playground, washer/dryer. Wedding facilities. **Rates:** HS June–Sept $125–$160 S or D; from $140 effic. Extra person $15. Min stay spec evnts. Lower rates off-season. Pking: Outdoor, free. Maj CC.

Sea Lodge, 8110 Camino del Oro, La Jolla, CA 92037 (La Jolla Shores); tel 619/459-8271 or toll free 800/237-5211; fax 619/456-9346. 11 mi NW of San Diego. Ardath Rd exit off I-5 N; La Jolla Village Dr W exit off I-5 S. Take La Jolla Shores Dr to Avenida de la Playa; turn right on Camino del Oro. 2 acres. Ideal location along the boardwalk on the beach. **Rooms:** 128 rms, stes, and effic. CI 4pm/CO noon. Nonsmoking rms avail. **Amenities:** A/C, cable TV, refrig. All units w/terraces. **Services:** X Car-rental desk, babysitting. **Facilities:** 1 rst, 1 bar, 1 beach (ocean), lifeguard, lawn games, sauna, whirlpool, washer/dryer. **Rates:** HS July–Aug $149–$309 S or D; from $379 ste; from $149 effic. Extra person $15. Children under 12 stay free. Min stay HS and wknds. Lower rates off-season. Pking: Indoor, free. Maj CC.

Sheraton Grande Torrey Pines, 10950 N Torrey Pines Rd, La Jolla, CA 92037; tel 619/558-1500 or toll free 800/762-6160; fax 619/450-4584. 15 mi N of San Diego. Genesee Ave exit W off I-5; right on Torrey Pines Rd. A modern, angular hotel with a country-club feel, perched on bluffs above the Pacific. Adjoins Torrey Pines Golf Course. Newly refurbished lobby is austere, verging on the plain. **Rooms:** 393 rms and stes. Exec-level rms avail. CI 3pm/CO noon. Express checkout avail. Nonsmoking rms avail. Very spacious. All accommodations have views of the pool, golf course, or ocean. Mirrored windows provide privacy. **Amenities:** A/C, cable TV w/movies, refrig, voice mail, in-rm safe, shoe polisher, bathrobes. All units w/minibars, all w/terraces, 1 w/Jacuzzi. Valet stand, shoehorn, bathroom scale, and iron and ironing board in each room. **Services:** Twice-daily maid svce, car-rental desk, social director, masseur, babysitting. All rooms are served by a butler, who delivers morning coffee or tea, presses clothes, etc. Complimentary limo service available within the area; free hors d'oeuvres and entertainment nightly. **Facilities:** 1 rst, 2 bars (w/entertainment), lifeguard, lawn games, spa, sauna, whirlpool. Lovely pool area flanked by a balustrade, cypresses, and palms. In addition to the on-premises health club, guests can use the premier facility next door, with weight room, aerobics classes, running track, and basketball courts. **Rates:** $185–$210 S or D; from $300 ste.

Children under 16 stay free. Higher rates for spec evnts/hols. AP and MAP rates avail. Spec packages avail. Pking: Indoor/outdoor, $7–$11. Maj CC.

Restaurants 🍴

Alfonso's of La Jolla, 1251 Prospect St, La Jolla (La Jolla Village); tel 619/454-2232. 12 mi NW of San Diego. Ardath Rd exit off I-5. **Mexican.** A colorful, homey place with brick walls and two fireplaces. Menu lists carne asada burritos, charbroiled steaks in ranchero sauce, large quesadillas, tostadas, tacos, and seafood dishes. Also at: 135 Broadway, San Diego (619/234-7300). **FYI:** Reservations not accepted. **Open:** Mon–Thurs 11am–11pm, Fri–Sat 11am–midnight, Sun 11am–10pm. Closed some hols. **Prices:** Main courses $15–$20. Maj CC. 👥 VP

⑤ Bully's, 5755 La Jolla Blvd, La Jolla (Bird Rock); tel 619/459-2768. 11 mi NW of San Diego. Grand/Garnet exit off I-5. Take either Grand Ave or Garnet Ave W to Mission Blvd and turn north; turn left onto La Jolla Blvd. **American/Steak.** A San Diego watering hole with a dark, publike atmosphere. People come here for the huge portions of prime rib, chicken breast, burgers, and the like. Also at: 2401 Camino del Rio S, San Diego (619/291-2665); 1404 Camino del Mar, Del Mar (619/755-1660). **FYI:** Reservations not accepted. **Open:** Lunch daily 10am–4pm; dinner daily 4:30pm–midnight. Closed some hols. **Prices:** Main courses $5.75–$24.95. Maj CC. ⬤

Cafe Japengo, in the Aventine, 8960 University Center Lane, La Jolla; tel 619/450-3355. La Jolla Village Dr exit off I-5. **Pacific Rim.** The interior designer describes the ultramodern decor as "East meets West," and that sums up the menu as well. In addition to a number of Pacific Rim specialties (10-ingredient fried rice and crisp whole New Zealand snapper Japonaise are 2 favorites), there's a full sushi bar. **FYI:** Reservations accepted. Blues. **Open:** HS June–Sept lunch Mon–Fri 11:30am–2:30pm; dinner Mon–Thurs 6–10:30pm, Fri–Sat 6–11pm, Sun 6–10pm. Reduced hours off-season. Closed some hols. **Prices:** Main courses $15–$22. Maj CC. VP &

♀ Cindy Black's, 5721 La Jolla Blvd, La Jolla; tel 619/456-6299. 11 mi NW of San Diego. Garnet Ave exit off I-5. **French.** A very luxurious setting and a menu to match. Modern art is on display, amid antiques and lovely orchids and roses. Dishes include roasted eggplant soup with tomato-basil relish, pan-broiled Alaskan halibut, and Maryland soft-shell crabs in season. **FYI:** Reservations recommended. **Open:** Lunch Fri 11:30am–2pm; dinner Mon–Sat 5:30–10pm, Sun 5–8pm. Closed Dec 25. **Prices:** Main courses $9.50–$29.95; PF dinner $15.95. Maj CC. ⬤ ⬤

⑤ D'lish Gourmet, 7514 Girard Ave, La Jolla (La Jolla Village); tel 619/459-8118. 12 mi NW of San Diego. Ardath Rd exit off I-5. **Italian/Pizza.** This is a popular place with locals. A lovely restaurant with black-and-white marble floor, black metal chairs with green leather seats, and an art deco ambiance. Wonderful food includes wood-fired pizza, pasta, and Greek grilled chicken. Really amazing value. Also at: 4150 Mission Blvd, Pacific Beach (619/483-4949); 386 E H St, Ste 211, Chula Vista (619/585-1371); 3030 Plaza Bonita Rd, Ste 2180, National City (619/267-4213). **FYI:** Reservations accepted. Beer and wine only. **Open:** Sun–Thurs 11:30am–10pm, Fri–Sat 11:30am–11pm. Closed some hols. **Prices:** Main courses $5.99–$8.99. Maj CC. &

Elario's, in the Summer House Inn, 7955 La Jolla Shores Dr, La Jolla (La Jolla Shores); tel 619/459-0541. 11 mi NW of San Diego. Ardath Rd exit off I-5. **Continental.** A wonderful view, elegant decor, and intimate booths all add up to a romantic dining experience. The menu offers contemporary continental fare such as veal loin medallions with wild mushrooms, seared sea bass with pan-fried potatoes and applewood-smoked bacon, and 5-pepper filet mignon with garlic mashed potatoes and peppery cognac cream. **FYI:** Reservations recommended. Jazz. Dress code. **Open:** Breakfast daily 7–11am; lunch daily 11:30am–2pm; dinner Sun–Thurs 5:30–10pm, Fri–Sat 5:30–10:30pm. **Prices:** Main courses $11–$25. Maj CC. ⬤ 👥 ⬤

♀ George's at the Cove, 1250 Prospect St, La Jolla (La Jolla Village); tel 619/454-4244. 12 mi NW of San Diego. Ardath Rd exit off I-5. **Eclectic.** There are 3 settings to choose from here: a deck with white furnishings and a good view; an upstairs nautical room with ceiling fans; and a downstairs area with wicker furniture and light wood walls. Typical dishes outside are grilled chicken breast, fresh fish, pastas, salads, and some Mexican options; inside, offerings include sea scallops, grilled prawns, and beef tenderloin. **FYI:** Reservations recommended. **Open:** Lunch daily 11:30am–2:30pm; dinner Fri–Sat 5:30–11pm, Sun–Thurs 5:30–10pm. **Prices:** Main courses $16–$25; PF dinner $32. Maj CC. 👥 VP

★ La Jolla Brewing Co, 7536 Fay Ave, La Jolla; tel 619/456-BREW. **New American.** An ultracasual spot that turns out beers named for local surfing spots. Brews can be sampled at 75¢ apiece. The food is good: menu includes oyster "shooters," fish or shrimp tacos, and mahi-mahi sandwiches. **FYI:** Reservations not accepted. Children's menu. Beer and wine only. **Open:** Sun–Thurs 11:30am–11:30pm, Fri–Sat 11:30am–1am. Closed some hols. **Prices:** Main courses $5.45–$9.95. Maj CC. &

Mandarin House, 6765 La Jolla Blvd, La Jolla (Wind n' Sea); tel 619/454-2555. 11 mi NW of San Diego. Ardath Rd exit off I-5. **Chinese.** Most popular Chinese restaurant in San Diego, and winner of many awards. Pretty decor features silk plants, green booths, and peach cloth napkins. Menu specialties include Peking duck, pungent chicken, Mandarin noodles, and cashew chicken. Also at: 1820 Garnet Ave, San Diego (619/273-2288); 2604 5th Ave, San Diego (619/232-1101). **FYI:** Reservations accepted. **Open:** Mon–Thurs 11am–10pm, Fri–Sat 11am–11pm, Sun 2–10pm. Closed Thanksgiving. **Prices:** Main courses $6.25–$14.95; PF dinner $16.75–$65.25. Maj CC.

Pannikin Coffee & Tea, 7467 Girard Ave, La Jolla (La Jolla Village); tel 619/454-5453. 12 mi NW of San Diego. **Cafe.** This cafe serves what may be the best cup of coffee in town. Set in an old home with a patio and little study nooks. Besides an extensive list of teas and coffees, the changing menu includes soups, salads, curries, pastries, fruits, and desserts. Also at: 2636 Via de la Valle, Del Mar (619/481-8007); 3145 Rosecrans St, Point Loma (619/224-2891). **FYI:** Reservations not accepted. No liquor license. **Open:** Mon–Fri 6am–10pm, Sat–Sun 7am–11pm. Closed some hols. **Prices:** Lunch main courses $4–$7. Maj CC.

Pannikin's Brockton Villa Restaurant, 1235 Coast Blvd, La Jolla (La Jolla Village); tel 619/454-7393. 12 mi NW of San Diego. Ardath Rd exit off I-5. **Californian.** Located in a restored, charming, 100-year-old beach cottage. The view of La Jolla Cove is stunning. Among the most popular dishes on the menu are the Greek steamers (3 eggs steam-scrambled, then tossed with feta, tomato, and basil), and the turkey meatloaf sandwich on toasted sourdough with tomato chutney. **FYI:** Reservations accepted. Beer and wine only. **Open:** Mon–Tues 8am–5pm, Wed–Sun 8am–10pm. Closed some hols. **Prices:** Main courses $9.95–$12.95. Maj CC. 🍽 🏔

Piatti, 2182 Avenida de la Playa, La Jolla (La Jolla Shores); tel 619/454-1589. 12 mi NW of San Diego. Ardath Rd exit off I-5. **Italian.** A roomy place with tiled floors and pastel walls painted with larger-than life vegetables and herbs. There is also patio dining. Various pastas, wood-oven pizzas, and seafood dishes are specialties. Italian wines. **FYI:** Reservations recommended. Children's menu. **Open:** Mon–Thurs 11am–10pm, Fri–Sat 11am–11pm, Sun 11am–10pm. Closed some hols. **Prices:** Main courses $6.95–$15. Maj CC. 🍴 ✓ &

Putnam's Restaurant & Bar, in the Colonial Inn, 910 Prospect St, La Jolla (La Jolla Village); tel 619/454-2181. 12 mi NW of San Diego. Ardath Rd exit off I-5. **New American/Californian.** Set in the old Putnam's Drug Store, a slice of La Jolla history. Old-world decor, with polished terrazzo floors, crisp white tablecloths, and fresh flowers, is very appealing. Menu changes seasonally, but could include barbecued chicken, roast duckling, grilled salmon, and roast rack of lamb. **FYI:** Reservations recommended. Piano. Children's menu. Dress code. **Open:**

Breakfast Mon–Fri 7–10am; lunch Mon–Fri 11am–2:30pm; dinner Sun–Thurs 5–10pm, Fri–Sat 5–11pm; brunch Sat–Sun 7am–2:30pm. **Prices:** Main courses $12–$21; PF dinner $19–$22. Maj CC. 🍽 🖼 ✓ VP

Sammy's California Woodfired Pizza, 702 Pearl St, La Jolla (La Jolla Village); tel 619/456-5222. 12 mi NW of San Diego. Ardath Rd exit off I-5. **Californian/Pizza.** Healthy California cuisine at an upscale pizzeria with tiled floors, wood furnishings, and abundant plants. In addition to exotic pizzas, menu includes pastas and many salads. **FYI:** Reservations not accepted. Children's menu. Beer and wine only. **Open:** HS Mem Day–Labor Day daily 11:30am–11pm. Reduced hours off-season. Closed some hols. **Prices:** Main courses $10–$20. Ltd CC. 📷 &

Samson's, in La Jolla Village Square, 8861 Villa La Jolla Dr, La Jolla; tel 619/455-1461. 12 mi NW of San Diego. La Jolla Village Dr exit off I-5. **Jewish.** A lively place, completely renovated in 1994 to evoke the feel of a New York–style deli. One room has walls lined with movie posters; another is decorated with a mural of customers eating at a deli. Menu features corned beef on rye, chicken in a pot, and other classics. Each table is topped with a wooden barrel filled with dill pickles. **FYI:** Reservations accepted. Children's menu. Beer and wine only. **Open:** Mon–Thurs 7am–11pm, Fri–Sat 7am–midnight, Sun 7am–10pm. Closed Dec 25. **Prices:** Main courses $6.99–$14.99. Maj CC. ✓ &

♥ **The Sky Room Restaurant**, in La Valencia Hotel, 1132 Prospect St, La Jolla (La Jolla Village); tel 619/454-0771. 12 mi NW of San Diego. Ardath Rd exit off I-5. **Californian/Mediterranean.** Intimate penthouse room with stunning ocean views from every table. Furnished with wing chairs, fine china, and elegant accoutrements. Known for dishes such as California sea bass with roasted scallops, grilled lobster, free-range chicken, and rack of lamb. **FYI:** Reservations recommended. Jacket required. **Open:** Mon–Sat 6–10pm. **Prices:** Main courses $22–$28; PF dinner $42.50. Maj CC. ♥ 🍽 🏔 VP &

⑤ **Soup Exchange**, 7777 Fay Ave, La Jolla (La Jolla Village); tel 619/459-0212. 12 mi NW of San Diego. Ardath Rd exit off I-5. **Salad/Soup Bar.** An attractive place with comfortable booths, natural light, and lots of plants. The salad bar is extensive and other salads are on the menu. Emphasis on healthy choices from soups to muffins to fresh fruit and yogurt for dessert. Also at: 7095 Clairemont Mesa Blvd, San Diego (619/576-0622); 1840 Garnet Ave, Pacific Beach (619/272-7766); 4282 Esplanade Court, San Diego (619/535-9410). **FYI:** Reservations accepted. Children's menu. Beer and wine only. **Open:** Daily 11am–9pm. Closed some hols. **Prices:** PF dinner $6.85. Ltd CC. 📷 &

♥ **Top O' the Cove**, 1216 Prospect St, La Jolla (La Jolla Village); tel 619/454-7779. 12 mi NW of San Diego. Ardath Rd exit off I-5. **French.** Award-winning restaurant set in a vintage 1893 bungalow. Downstairs, decor is understated and a patio offers garden dining; cuisine includes French classics such as filet mignon in burgundy-wine sauce, or roast rack of lamb. Upstairs are views of La Jolla, and a menu featuring fish and pastas, such as grilled rainbow trout and fusilli with artichoke hearts. **FYI:** Reservations recommended. Piano. **Open:** Lunch Mon–Sat 11:30am–3pm; dinner Sun–Thurs 5:30–10pm, Fri–Sat 5:30–11pm; brunch Sun 10:30am–2:30pm. **Prices:** Main courses $24–$32. Maj CC. ❤ Ⓥ

The Whaling Bar, in La Valencia Hotel, 1132 Prospect St, La Jolla (La Jolla Village); tel 619/454-0771. 12 mi NW of San Diego. Ardath Rd exit off I-5. **Californian/Mediterranean.** Located in a historic 1926 hotel, a restaurant with the look of an elegant club—with brass lamps and black leather upholstery, and whaling memorabilia at the bar. Specials include paella valenciana with sausage; marinated filet mignon; and local lobster salad. **FYI:** Reservations recommended. Dress code. **Open:** Lunch daily 11:30am–5pm; dinner Fri–Sat 6–11pm, Sun–Thurs 6–10pm. **Prices:** Main courses $9–$15. Maj CC. 🍽 Ⓥ

Attraction 💼

Stephen Birch Aquarium-Museum, 2300 Expedition Way; tel 619/534-FISH. A part of the Scripps Institution of Oceanography, University of California, San Diego. Situated on a hillside overlooking the Pacific Ocean, this complex is divided into 3 exhibit areas. The north wing contains the aquarium, which has more than 30 tanks housing over 3,000 fish. A kelp forest 2 stories tall is maintained in a giant tank that can be studied from a specially designed viewing gallery. The south wing contains the Scripps Institute of Oceanography, which features the nation's largest oceanographic exhibition, "Exploring the Blue Planet." Interpretive exhibits here illustrate the history of oceanography, Scripps research, man's relationship with the sea, and include interactive displays on weather, climate, and earthquakes. A simulated submarine ride takes visitors to the ocean floor. Connecting the 2 wings is the Tidepool Plaza, which features an artificial tidal pool where visitors can get a close-up look at the population of sea urchins, sea stars, sea cucumbers, and many other specimens. **Open:** Daily 9am–5pm. Closed some hols. $$$

LAKE ARROWHEAD
Map page M-3, D3

See also Blue Jay

Motel 🏨

☰☰ **Arrowhead Tree Top Lodge**, Calif 173 at Rainbow Dr, PO Box 186, Lake Arrowhead, CA 92352; tel 909/337-2311 or toll free 800/358-TREE. ¼ mi S of Lake Arrowhead Village. Nestled in the pines a few minutes walk from Lake Arrowhead and Lake Arrowhead Village. This place draws many repeat guests. **Rooms:** 20 rms, stes, and effic. CI 2pm/CO 11am. Nonsmoking rms avail. Very simple decor. **Amenities:** Cable TV, refrig. No A/C or phone. Some units w/terraces, some w/fireplaces. **Services:** ⏰ 🛎 Babysitting. **Facilities:** 🎣 🐾 Nice picnic area with barbecue. Nature trail and access to fishing. **Rates:** HS June 15–Jan $68–$130 S or D; from $97 ste; from $84 effic. Children under 18 stay free. Min stay HS. Lower rates off-season. Higher rates for spec evnts/hols. Pking: Outdoor, free. Maj CC.

Resort

☰☰☰ **Lake Arrowhead Resort**, Lake Arrowhead Village, PO Box 1699, Lake Arrowhead, CA 92352; tel 909/336-1511 or toll free 800/800-6791; fax 909/336-3300. This year-round mountain lake resort is great for families as well as for off-site corporate meetings. **Rooms:** 175 rms and stes; 86 ctges/villas. CI 4pm/CO noon. Express checkout avail. Nonsmoking rms avail. **Amenities:** 🎛 🛁 A/C, cable TV w/movies, refrig. All units w/minibars, some w/terraces, some w/fireplaces, some w/Jacuzzis. **Services:** ✕ 🍽 Ⓥ 🖼 ⏰ 🛎 Social director, masseur, children's program, babysitting. **Facilities:** 🎣 🚴 🏊 🍹 ⛷ 🚤 🏐 💻 ⚓ 2 rsts (*see also* "Restaurants" below), 2 bars (1 w/entertainment), 1 beach (lake shore), games rm, lawn games, racquetball, spa, sauna, steam rm, whirlpool, beauty salon, day-care ctr, playground. **Rates:** HS June 13–Oct $119–$219 S or D; from $329 ste; from $259 ctge/villa. Extra person $15. Children under 18 stay free. Lower rates off-season. Spec packages avail. Pking: Outdoor, $5. Maj CC.

Restaurant 🍽

Beau Rivage, in Lake Arrowhead Resort, 27984 Calif 189, Lake Arrowhead; tel 909/336-1511. **New American.** The decor is grand and luxurious, featuring tapestry-covered banquettes and Louis XV–style chairs covered in blue velour. Large windows offer expansive lakeside views from nearly every seat. Dine on chicken in chardonnay cream, pecan-rolled halibut, filet mignon in peppercorn sauce, and medallions of venison. Well-chosen wine list. **FYI:** Reservations recommended. Children's menu. Dress code. **Open:** Dinner Wed–Sun 5–10pm; brunch Sun 10am–2pm. **Prices:** Main courses $14.95–$21.95. Maj CC.

Attraction

Arrowhead Queen; tel 714/866-7574. Located on the waterfront in Lake Arrowhead Village. Narrated, 50-minute cruises depart on the hour to explore the scenic beauty and rich history of the lake and surrounding area. **Open:** Daily 10am–6pm. Closed some hols. $$$

LAKE TAHOE AREA

In California, see **South Lake Tahoe, Tahoe City, Tahoe Vista, Truckee;** *in Nevada, see* **Carson City (NV), Incline Village (NV), Stateline (NV)**

LANCASTER

Map page M-3, D2

See also **Palmdale**

Hotel

≡≡ **Best Western Antelope Valley Inn**, 44055 N Sierra Hwy, Lancaster, CA 93534; tel 805/948-4651 or toll free 800/528-1234; fax 805/948-4651. Ave K exit off US 14. Southwest-themed property has striking pink adobe facade. Large shade trees keep things cool, even in summer. **Rooms:** 148 rms and stes. CI 1pm/CO 1pm. Express checkout avail. Nonsmoking rms avail. **Amenities:** A/C, satel TV w/movies, refrig. **Services:** Babysitting. **Facilities:** 2 rsts (*see also* "Restaurants" below), 1 bar (w/entertainment), whirlpool, beauty salon, playground. Japanese garden in courtyard. **Rates:** $59–$67 S; $63–$73 D; from $95 ste. Extra person $7. Children under 12 stay free. Spec packages avail. Pking: Outdoor, free. Maj CC.

Restaurants

Casa de Miguel, 44245 N Sierra Hwy, Lancaster; tel 805/948-0793. Ave K exit off Calif 14. **Mexican.** Underwent extensive remodeling in 1994. Elevated loft-like dining room is used for banquets. Offers a wide variety of Mexican fare. Try camarones Miguel wrapped in bacon with rice, or chile verde made

with pork. **FYI:** Reservations recommended. Singer. Children's menu. **Open:** Mon–Thurs 11am–10pm, Fri–Sat 11am–11pm, Sun 10am–10pm. Closed some hols. **Prices:** Main courses $6.95–$13.95. Maj CC.

The Desert Rose Bar & Grill, in Best Western Antelope Valley Inn, 44055 N Sierra Hwy, Lancaster; tel 805/948-4651. Ave K exit off Calif 14. Located between Aves J and K. **Southwestern.** A southwestern theme restaurant, complete with a stage and dance floor with live entertainment. Specialties include prime rib, steaks, chicken, and seafood, including trout and catfish. Friday all-you-can-eat buffet. **FYI:** Reservations accepted. Country music/dancing. Children's menu. **Open:** Dinner Mon–Sat 5–10pm. Closed some hols. **Prices:** Main courses $6.38–$17.10. Maj CC.

★ **Downtown Cakes and Company**, 858 W Lancaster Blvd, Lancaster; tel 805/948-2253. Ave K exit off Calif 14. **Californian/French.** A high-ceilinged restaurant with tapestry booths and banquettes, original artwork, and teak floors. The menu includes Italian, French, Thai, and hearty country cuisine. Desserts are excellent; don't miss the pear and walnut salad. **FYI:** Reservations recommended. Children's menu. **Open:** Breakfast Tues–Fri 7:30–11am, Sat–Sun 8:30–11am; lunch Tues–Sun 11am–2:30pm; dinner Tues–Thurs 5–8:30pm, Fri–Sat 5–9:30pm, Sun 5–8:30pm; brunch Sun 8:30am–2:30pm. Closed some hols. **Prices:** Main courses $9.95–$17.95. Maj CC.

LA QUINTA

Map page M-3, D3 (W of Indio)

Resort

≡≡≡≡ **La Quinta Resort & Club**, 49-499 Eisenhower Dr, PO Box 69, La Quinta, CA 92253; tel 619/564-4111 or toll free 800/854-1271, 800/472-4316 in CA; fax 619/564-5758. 125 mi SE of Los Angeles. Washington exit off I-10; right on Eisenhower Dr. 45 acres. The oldest resort in the Palm Springs area. La Quinta is nestled against the Santa Rosa Mountains and surrounded by citrus trees, towering palms, cacti, and flowers. Centerpiece of this Spanish-style resort is the Plaza, with shops and restaurants. **Rooms:** 640 rms and stes. CI 4pm/CO noon. Express checkout avail. Nonsmoking rms avail. Rooms are elegant casitas with refreshment centers and private patios. **Amenities:** A/C, cable TV w/movies, refrig, shoe polisher. All units w/minibars, all w/terraces, some w/fireplaces, some w/Jacuzzis. **Services:** Twice-daily maid svce, car-rental desk, masseur, children's program, babysitting. **Facilities:** 3 rsts (*see also* "Restaurants" below), 3 bars (2 w/entertainment), whirl-

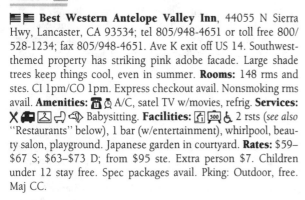

pool, beauty salon. More golf courses (5 championship courses) and tennis courts than any other resort in the region; large main pool, 24 smaller pools, 38 whirlpools. **Rates:** HS Jan–Mar $200–$255 S or D; from $650 ste. Extra person $15. Children under 18 stay free. Min stay spec evnts. Lower rates off-season. Spec packages avail. Pking: Outdoor, free. Maj CC.

Restaurants 🍴

Beachside Cafe, 78-477 Calif 111, La Quinta; tel 619/564-4577. Washington exit off I-10. **American.** Unique cafe decorated with colorful surfboards and other beach paraphernalia. Favorite dishes include barbecued ribs; fish and chips; and the High Tide, a mound of shrimp. **FYI:** Reservations not accepted. Dress code. Beer and wine only. **Open:** Daily 7am–9pm. **Prices:** Main courses $7.95–$12.50. Ltd CC. 🍰 &

🍷 **Dolly Cunard's**, 78-045 Calle Cadiz, La Quinta; tel 619/564-4443. **Eclectic.** A country estate turned into a restaurant. Six distinct dining areas offer views of gardens and rock fountains. The eclectic menu includes rack of lamb with herbs, and charred chiles with 4 cheeses. **FYI:** Reservations recommended. Piano. Jacket required. **Open:** HS Oct–May daily 6–9pm. Reduced hours off-season. Closed some hols; July–Sept. **Prices:** Main courses $16.50–$29. Maj CC. ♥ ▮ 🖼 🏔 VP &

Montañas, in La Quinta Resort & Club, 49-499 Eisenhower Dr, La Quinta; tel 619/564-4111. Washington exit off I-10. **Californian.** Set in what was the original dining room at this posh resort back in 1926. Casual and charming, with works of art from local artists displayed in this Spanish-style hacienda. The robust California cuisine features such items as roast maple chicken and paella. **FYI:** Reservations recommended. Piano. Jacket required. **Open:** HS Sept–May dinner daily 5:30–10pm; brunch Sun 10am–2pm. Reduced hours off-season. Closed mid-June–Aug. **Prices:** Main courses $13–$23. Maj CC. ▮ VP &

LARKSPUR

Map page M-2, D1 (S of San Rafael)

Hotel 🏨

🟰🟰🟰 **Courtyard by Marriott**, 2500 Larkspur Landing Circle, Larkspur, CA 94939; tel 415/925-1800 or toll free 800/321-2211; fax 415/925-1107. Exit off US 101; bear east towards Richmond Bridge, turn left at 1st light onto Larkspur Landing Circle. Extensive landscaping surrounds New England–style, wood-trimmed buildings. Conveniently located near shopping center and ferry to San Francisco. **Rooms:** 146 rms and stes. Exec-level rms avail. CI 3pm/CO noon. Express checkout avail.

Nonsmoking rms avail. Standard rooms are compact but nicely laid out, with all the comforts. All sofas convert into beds—good for families. **Amenities:** 🗄 🕐 🍽 A/C, cable TV w/movies, voice mail. All units w/terraces. **Services:** ✕ 🛎 ⚲ 🔑 Car-rental desk, babysitting. **Facilities:** 🀄 🚣 🏊 & 1 rst, 1 bar, sauna, whirlpool, washer/dryer. The courtyard gardens are lovely and lush, with a nice gazebo for reading and relaxing. **Rates:** HS May–Nov $95–$109 S; $105–$109 D; from $115 ste. Children under 12 stay free. Min stay spec evnts. Lower rates off-season. Higher rates for spec evnts/hols. Pking: Outdoor, free. Maj CC. Suites are an especially good deal—only $20 to $30 more than standard rooms.

Restaurants 🍴

🍷 **Lark Creek Inn**, 234 Magnolia Ave, Larkspur (Downtown); tel 415/924-7766. 10 mi N of San Francisco. Tamalpais Dr/Paradise Dr exit off US 101; West on Tamalpais Dr 1 mi, right on Corte Madera Ave, ½ mi. **New American.** Groves of redwoods, a meandering stream, and a yellow-painted Victorian house create a fairytale setting. Chef Bradley Ogden's philosophy of "Keep it simple; use only the freshest ingredients" shines through. Depending on what's in season, entrees might include grilled quail with tomatillo salsa, or pan-seared local halibut on summer bean and beet salad. **FYI:** Reservations recommended. Children's menu. **Open:** Lunch Mon–Fri 11:30am–2:30pm; dinner Mon–Thurs 5:30–10pm, Fri–Sat 5–10:30pm, Sun 5–10pm; brunch Sun 10am–1:30pm. Closed some hols. **Prices:** Main courses $19–$24.50. Maj CC. ♥ 🍰 &

★ **Left Bank**, 507 Magnolia Ave, Larkspur (Downtown); tel 415/927-3331. **French.** This new and highly successful restaurant—the latest venture of Roland Passot, owner of La Folie in San Francisco—creates a St-Germain-des-Pres ambience with its simple decor of oak floors and alabaster chandeliers. Authentic brassiere fare, from the real cornichons that accompany the rillettes to main courses such as steak with crispy fried potatoes, or whole roasted fish. Wonderful desserts include fresh-fruit tarts. **FYI:** Reservations recommended. Children's menu. **Open:** Mon–Thurs 11:30am–11pm, Fri–Sat 11:30am–midnight, Sun 10am–10pm. Closed some hols. **Prices:** Main courses $9–$19.50. Maj CC. 🍰 🖼 &

LEE VINING
Map page M-3, A2

Motel

▤ **Best Western Lake View Lodge**, 30 Main St, PO Box 345, Lee Vining, CA 93541; tel 619/647-6543 or toll free 800/528-1234. 25 mi N of Mammoth Lakes. 2 mi N of jct Calif 120/US 395 (Main St). The only decent hotel in town. Located 28 miles from the ghost town Bodie, 3 miles from Mono Lake. **Rooms:** 47 rms and stes. CI 4pm/CO 11am. Nonsmoking rms avail. Small but clean. **Amenities:** 🛏 📷 A/C, cable TV w/movies. Special features for hearing/sight-impaired travelers. **Services:** 🔧 🖼 **Facilities:** ⅙ **Rates:** HS June–Oct 1 $50–$83 S or D; from $65 ste. Lower rates off-season. Spec packages avail. Pking: Outdoor, free. Maj CC.

Attraction ▣

Mono Lake; tel 619/647-6595. Located 15 miles east of Yosemite National Park, just east of the town of Lee Vining, Mono Lake is one of the oldest lakes in the Western Hemisphere. An immense inland sea, it covers an area of just over 100 square miles with waters 250 percent more saline than sea water. Lowering of the lake due to diversion of its tributaries has exposed formations of calcium carbonate, which stick out above the waterline. Stratified limestone formations, called tufa, surround the lake. More than a million waterfowl, gulls, and shorebirds populate the surrounding area from April–October.

Mono Basin National Forest Scenic Area Visitor Center, situated on a bluff overlooking the lake, presents an interpretive film on the lake and offers exhibits and interpretive programs led by Forest Service rangers and staff. **Mono Lake Tufa State Reserve,** south on US 395, then east on Calif 120, is the site of several major tufa outcroppings. Interpretive signs along the South Tufa trail explain the origin and formation of tufa. **Mono Lake County Park** offers an idyllic picnicking spot along a small stream shaded by cottonwoods, and a boardwalk trail through delicate tufa formations that leads to the lakeshore. **Open:** Daily 24 hours. Free.

LITTLE RIVER
Map page M-2, C1 (S of Mendocino)

Inn ▣

▤▤▤ **Glendeven**, 8221 N Calif 1, Little River, CA 95456; tel 707/937-0083 or toll free 800/822-4536; fax 707/937-6108. 1½ mi S of Mendocino. 2½ acres. A beautiful, soothing garden setting. **Rooms:** 10 rms and stes. CI 2pm/CO 11am. No smoking. Rooms are spacious and decorated in early American motif, with quilts, pine furniture, 4-poster beds, rag rugs. Some have French doors opening into the gardens. **Amenities:** 🔥 📻 No A/C, phone, or TV. Some units w/terraces, some w/fireplaces. **Services:** ✕ 🍷 Masseur, afternoon tea and wine/sherry served. Coffee and tea are available in the lounge. Breakfast is delivered to your room. **Facilities:** Guest lounge. Pianist in the lounge. **Rates (CP):** HS June–Oct $90–$140 D; from $125 ste. Extra person $20. Children under 1 stay free. Min stay wknds and spec evnts. Lower rates off-season. Spec packages avail. Pking: Outdoor, free. Ltd CC.

Lodges

▤▤▤▤ **Heritage House**, 5200 N Calif 1, Little River, CA 95456; tel 707/937-5885 or toll free 800/235-5885; fax 707/937-0318. Amid gardens, pine forests, and rhododendron dells, overlooking the Mendocino coast. This place has a museumlike quality, with original fixtures and a history display. **Rooms:** 72 rms and stes. CI 2pm/CO noon. Cozy rooms are not luxurious. Each has its own landscaped garden area; most have bay or ocean views. Stay on ocean side of building. Vista 3 and Carousel 4 and 5 are very special rooms. **Amenities:** 📻 No A/C, phone, or TV. Some units w/minibars, some w/terraces, some w/fireplaces, some w/Jacuzzis. Complimentary wine in some rooms. **Services:** 🚙 Masseur, babysitting. Incredible full breakfast and dinner for 2 included in rates. **Facilities:** 🏊 ⅙ 1 rst, 1 bar (w/entertainment), 1 beach (ocean), games rm. Restaurant has French-country feel, and a dining terrace. **Rates (MAP):** HS Apr 15–Oct $170–$350 S or D; from $310 ste. Extra person $65. Children under 6 stay free. Min stay spec evnts. Lower rates off-season. Higher rates for spec evnts/hols. Spec packages avail. Pking: Outdoor, free. Ltd CC.

▤▤▤▤ **Stevenswood Lodge**, 8211 Shoreline Hwy, PO Box 170, Little River, CA 95460; tel 707/937-2810 or toll free 800/421-2810; fax 707/937-1237. 2 mi S of Mendocino. Off Calif 1. Like staying in an art gallery in the woods. This peaceful, contemporary hotel on the inland side of the highway is filled with modern paintings and sculptures in the lobby, halls, and garden. Near Van Damme State Park. Lounge area with fireplace opens to garden. **Rooms:** 10 rms and stes. CI 3pm/CO noon. Nonsmoking rms avail. Modern rooms overlook wooded grounds. **Amenities:** 🛏 🔥 📻 Cable TV w/movies, refrig, bathrobes. No A/C. All units w/minibars, all w/terraces, all w/fireplaces. Down comforters. **Services:** ✕ 🔑 Masseur, babysitting. Complimentary hors d'oeuvres, wine, and full gourmet breakfast. **Facilities:** 🎿 🏊 ⅙ Lawn games. Small business meeting area with fax machines. **Rates (BB):** $95–$195 S or D; from $120 ste. Extra person $25. Children under 2 stay free. Min stay wknds. Spec packages avail. Pking: Outdoor, free. Ltd CC.

Resort

≣≣≣ **Little River Inn**, 7751 N Calif 1, PO Box B, Little River, CA 95456; tel 707/937-5942; fax 707/937-3944. 2 mi S of Mendocino. 225 acres. This charming inn, built in the 1850s and run by the same family for 4 generations, is nestled among the trees next to Van Damme State Park. **Rooms:** 60 rms and stes; 5 ctges/villas. Exec-level rms avail. CI 3pm/CO noon. Nonsmoking rms avail. Rooms are clean, cheerful, and have breathtaking views. Ask for the Van Damme units, which are new, private, have Jacuzzis, and are nearest the ocean. **Amenities:** 🛅 🕭 ☎ Cable TV w/movies, VCR. No A/C. All units w/terraces, some w/fireplaces, some w/Jacuzzis. **Services:** 🖙 🚗 🗗 Babysitting. Free videos. **Facilities:** ▶9 🖾 🖳 🏊 & 1 rst (*see also* "Restaurants" below), 1 bar, 1 beach (ocean). **Rates:** HS Apr–Oct $75–$255 S or D; from $155 ste; from $145 ctge/villa. Extra person $10. Children under 12 stay free. Min stay wknds and spec evnts. Lower rates off-season. Spec packages avail. Pking: Outdoor, free. Maj CC.

Restaurant 🍽️

★ **Little River Inn Restaurant**, 7751 N Calif 1, Little River; tel 707/937-5942. **Californian/Seafood.** Opened in 1939 and run by the same family for 4 generations. Airy and pleasant, with large windows framing a garden montage of flowers and ferns. Try Ole's hotcakes for breakfast. Dinner specialties include pepper steak, lemon prawns, grilled polenta with porcini mushroom sauce, spring rack of lamb. All entrees come with appetizers and caesar salad. **FYI:** Reservations recommended. Guitar. **Open:** HS Apr–Oct breakfast daily 7:30–10:30am; dinner Sun–Thurs 6–9pm, Fri–Sat 6–9:30pm; brunch Sun 7:30am–1pm. Reduced hours off-season. **Prices:** Main courses $14–$21. Maj CC. 🍴 &

LODI

Map page M-2, C2

Motel 🛏️

≣ **Best Western Royal Host Inn**, 710 S Cherokee Lane, Lodi, CA 95240; tel 209/369-8484 or toll free 800/528-1234; fax 209/369-0654. 12 mi N of Stockton. Turner exit off Calif 99. Little ambience, but suitable for an overnight stopover. **Rooms:** 48 rms and stes. CI 2pm/CO 11am. Nonsmoking rms avail.

Slightly worn, but clean. **Amenities:** 🛅 🕭 ☎ A/C, cable TV w/movies. **Services:** 🖾 🗗 🕭 Fax service available through office. **Facilities:** 🖾 🔟 **Rates:** HS Mar–Nov $47 S; $54 D; from $60 ste. Extra person $8. Children under 12 stay free. Lower rates off-season. Pking: Outdoor, free. Maj CC.

LOMPOC

Map page M-3, D1

Hotel 🛏️

≣≣≣ **Embassy Suites**, 1117 N H St, Lompoc, CA 93436; tel 805/735-8311 or toll free 800/433-3182; fax 805/735-8459. Lovely lobby decorated with lots of brick, Spanish tiles, plants, and charming murals. Grounds feature a beautifully landscaped waterfall and pond. Top choice for accommodations in Lompoc. **Rooms:** 156 stes. CI 3pm/CO noon. Express checkout avail. Nonsmoking rms avail. Suites are decorated in French country style. Ladies' executive rooms have more feminine decor with lots of flowers and ruffles. **Amenities:** 🛅 🕭 ☎ A/C, satel TV w/movies, refrig, voice mail. All units w/terraces. Microwaves and wet bars in rooms. **Services:** ✗ 🖾 🗗 Car-rental desk, children's program, babysitting. Complimentary full breakfast served in an attractive room. Adjacent Carrow's restaurant offers room service 11am–11pm. **Facilities:** 🖾 🏋️ 🔟 & 1 rst, 1 bar, whirlpool, washer/dryer. Well-maintained pool and spa. Free use of nearby health club. **Rates (BB):** HS Mar–Oct from $73 ste. Extra person $10. Children under 12 stay free. Min stay spec evnts. Lower rates off-season. Spec packages avail. Pking: Outdoor, free. Maj CC.

Motel 🛏️

≣≣ **Tally Ho Motor Inn**, 1020 E Ocean Ave, Lompoc, CA 93436; tel 805/735-6444 or toll free 800/332-6444; fax 805/735-5558. Calif 246 N exit off US 1. Attractive lobby decorated in hunter green. Near La Purisima Mission. Popular with visitors to Solvang who don't want to pay tourist-town rates. **Rooms:** 53 rms, stes, and effic. CI 3pm/CO noon. Nonsmoking rms avail. Acceptable rooms. **Amenities:** 🛅 🕭 A/C, cable TV. Microwaves in some rooms. **Services:** 🖾 🗗 🕭 Free use of nearby health club. **Facilities:** & Sauna, whirlpool, washer/dryer. **Rates (CP):** $40–$45 S or D; from $55 ste; from $40 effic. Spec packages avail. Pking: Outdoor, free. Maj CC.

Attractions 🧳

Lompoc Museum, 200 South H St; tel 805/736-3888. This museum, housed in a former Carnegie library, focuses on the archeology and history of the Lompoc Valley and Santa Barbara County. The Clarence Ruth Gallery contains ethnographic and archaeological pieces from across the world; the Lompoc Valley Historical Society Gallery has exhibits on the Mission Period, Rancho Period, early Lompoc, and local industries; Gallery III features temporary exhibits and the museum's theater. **Open:** Tues–Fri 1–5pm, Sat–Sun 1–4pm. Closed some hols. Free.

La Purisima Mission State Historic Park, 2295 Purisima Rd; tel 805/733-3713. Of the 21 Franciscan missions in California, 3 are preserved within the state park system. Of these, La Purisima is considered to be the most authentically restored. All major buildings have been rebuilt and furnished as they were around 1820, the grounds have been planted with plants typical of that time, livestock of the correct genetic type have been acquired, and the original aqueduct system is being maintained.

The first mission was destroyed by earthquake in 1812. It was rebuilt the following year, but as the missions gradually came under civil control, the site was abandoned. Beginning in 1934, a combined federal, state, and county effort undertook a complete restoration of La Purisima. It was turned over to the state park system in 1941.

More than 30 rooms are completely restored and furnished, including the church, weaving room, and mission kitchen. Crafts demonstrations, living history programs, and guided tours are offered. There are 12 miles of walking trails on the 900-acre site. **Open:** Daily 8am–5pm. Closed some hols. $$

LONG BEACH

Map page M-3, D2

Hotels 🛎

≋≋≋ **Best Western Golden Sails Hotel**, 6285 E Pacific Coast Hwy, Long Beach, CA 90803; tel 310/596-1631 or toll free 800/762-5333; fax 310/594-0623. 5 mi NE of downtown. 7th St exit off I-405; go west on 7th to Pacific Coast Hwy. Fairly typical Best Western. **Rooms:** 172 rms and stes. Exec-level rms avail. CI 1pm/CO noon. Nonsmoking rms avail. Rooms are tasteful, clean, and comfortable. **Amenities:** 🛗 🕃 A/C, cable TV w/movies, refrig. Some units w/terraces, some w/Jacuzzis. **Services:** ✕ 🖛 🚗 🖾 🕀 Social director, babysitting. **Facilities:** 🔏 [800] 1 rst, 1 bar (w/entertainment), whirlpool, washer/dryer. Reggae music in lounge on weekends. **Rates (BB):** $100–$130 S or D. Extra person $10. Children under 18 stay free. MAP rates avail. Spec packages avail. Pking: Outdoor, free. Maj CC.

≋≋≋ **Long Beach Marriott**, 4700 Airport Plaza Dr, Long Beach, CA 90815 (Long Beach Airport); tel 310/425-5210 or toll free 800/228-9290; fax 310/425-2744. Lakewood Blvd exit off I-405; go north on Lakewood, right on Spring St, right on Airport Plaza Dr. Spacious, well-maintained property. Waterfall in pool area. **Rooms:** 311 rms and stes. Exec-level rms avail. CI 3pm/CO noon. Express checkout avail. Nonsmoking rms avail. Some rooms are noisy. **Amenities:** 🛗 🕃 A/C, cable TV w/movies, stereo/tape player. **Services:** ✕ 🖛 🚗 🖾 🕀 Car-rental desk, social director, babysitting. **Facilities:** 🔏 🖾 🖎 🖳 🕹 2 rsts, 2 bars (1 w/entertainment), spa, sauna, whirlpool. **Rates (BB):** $79–$119 S or D; from $250 ste. Children under 18 stay free. Spec packages avail. Pking: Outdoor, free. Maj CC.

Long Beach Renaissance Hotel, 111 E Ocean Blvd, Long Beach, CA 90802; tel 310/437-5900 or toll free 800/HOTELS1; fax 310/499-2509. Broadway exit off I-710; follow Broadway to Pine, turn right. This 12-story hotel is in the heart of the Long Beach financial district, and within walking distance of shops and restaurants. Beaches and freeways are nearby. Unrated. **Rooms:** 374 rms, stes, and effic. Exec-level rms avail. CI 3pm/CO noon. Express checkout avail. Nonsmoking rms avail. Large, with views of either the city or the ocean. Special Club Rooms available, as well as 3 nonsmoking floors. **Amenities:** 🛗 🕃 🖭 A/C, cable TV w/movies, shoe polisher. All units w/minibars, some w/terraces, some w/Jacuzzis. **Services:** ✕ 🖛 VP 🚗 🖾 🕀 Twice-daily maid svce, car-rental desk, babysitting. Courtesy shuttle to Long Beach, including the Queen Mary. **Facilities:** 🔏 🖾 🖎 🖳 🕃 1 rst, 1 bar (w/entertainment), spa, sauna, steam rm. **Rates:** HS Dec–May $125–$800 S; $145–$800 D; from $195 ste; from $195 effic. Extra person $15. Children under 18 stay free. Lower rates off-season. Higher rates for spec evnts/hols. Spec packages avail. Pking: Indoor, $6–$8. Maj CC. Special honeymoon packages.

Seaport Marina Hotel, 6400 E. Pacific Coast Hwy, Long Beach, CA 90803; tel 310/434-8451 or toll free 800/434-8451; fax 310/598-6028. 2 mi NW of Long Beach City. 7th St exit off I-405; west on 7th to Pacific Coast Hwy. Undergoing major renovation. Unrated. **Rooms:** 242 rms and stes. Exec-level rms avail. CI 3pm/CO 1pm. Nonsmoking rms avail. **Amenities:** 🛗 🖭 🕃 A/C, TV. Some units w/minibars, all w/terraces. **Services:** 🖛 🚗 🕀 🐾 Twice-daily maid svce. **Facilities:** 🔏 [560] 🕃 1 rst, 1 bar (w/entertainment), spa, whirlpool, washer/dryer. **Rates:** HS July–Sept $99 S or D; from $139 ste. Extra person $10. Children under 12 stay free. Lower rates off-season. Higher rates for spec evnts/hols. Pking: Outdoor, free. Maj CC.

≋≋≋ **Sheraton Long Beach**, 333 E Ocean Blvd, Long Beach, CA 90802; tel 310/436-3000 or toll free 800/325-3525; fax 310/499-2096. Broadway exit off I-710 S; right on Elm, right on Ocean. The lobby, airy and filled with greenery, has large windows and skylights; a nice change from similar large hotels.

Rooms: 460 rms and stes. CI 3pm/CO noon. Express checkout avail. Nonsmoking rms avail. **Amenities:** 🛎 🐧 📺 A/C, cable TV w/movies, in-rm safe, shoe polisher. All units w/minibars, some w/Jacuzzis. **Services:** 🍽 🔑 VP 🚗 🅿 🛎 Twice-daily maid svce, babysitting. **Facilities:** 🏊 🎾 🅶🅾🅾 🖥 & 2 rsts, 2 bars (w/entertainment), lifeguard, spa, sauna, whirlpool. The largest ballroom in Long Beach is on the premises. **Rates:** $135–$155 S or D; from $265 ste. Extra person $20. Children under 16 stay free. Spec packages avail. Pking: Indoor, $5–$8. Maj CC.

Motel

🛏 **Vagabond Inn–Long Beach**, 185 Atlantic Ave, Long Beach, CA 90802; tel 310/435-3791 or toll free 800/522-1555; fax 310/436-7510. Atlantic S exit off I-405. A 2-story structure surrounding a pool, this motel is plain, but decent. Management has attempted to beautify the grounds with plantings. **Rooms:** 48 rms and stes. CI 1pm/CO noon. Nonsmoking rms avail. A bit dated and dingy. **Amenities:** 🛎 🐧 A/C, cable TV. Some units w/terraces. **Services:** 🛎 🐕 Continental breakfast includes cereal, yogurt, muffins, danishes and coffee. **Facilities:** 🏊 & **Rates (BB):** HS May–Aug $50 S; $55 D; from $80 ste. Extra person $5. Children under 12 stay free. Min stay spec evnts. Lower rates off-season. Higher rates for spec evnts/hols. Pking: Outdoor, free. Maj CC.

Restaurants 🍴

★ **Dominicks East Village**, 555 E Ocean Blvd, Long Beach; tel 310/437-0626. **American.** Very '40s–New York, with dark wood, black-and-white flooring, brass accents, mirrors, and black-and-white photographs. Specialties are mostly American-style seafood dishes, as well as steak, veal, spaghetti, and macaroni. **FYI:** Reservations recommended. Children's menu. **Open:** Lunch Mon–Fri 11:30am–3pm; dinner Sun–Mon 5:30–9pm, Tues–Thurs 5:30–10pm, Fri–Sat 5:30–11pm. Closed some hols. **Prices:** Main courses $10.95–$26.95; PF dinner $18.95. Maj CC. 🍷 📷 &

♣ **L'Opera Ristorante**, 101 Pine Ave, Long Beach; tel 310/491-0066. Broadway exit off I-710 W; turn right on Pine Ave. **Italian.** This former bank is now an elegant restaurant, with pale-yellow walls offset by faux marble pillars and dark wood accents. Appropriate for people looking for a relaxing, traditional ambience. The large menu has pastas and antipasti; grilled veal lion and osso buco are both popular. The one-time bank vault serves as a wine cellar. **FYI:** Reservations recommended. **Open:** Lunch Mon–Fri 11:30am–5pm; dinner Mon–Thurs 5–11pm, Fri–Sat 5pm–midnight, Sun 5–10pm. Closed Dec 25. **Prices:** Main courses $7.95–$19.95. Maj CC. 📷 VP &

♣ **Mums**, 144 Pine Ave, Long Beach; tel 310/437-7700. Broadway exit off I-710 W; turn right on Pine Ave. **Californian.** Golden wood tones, pillars, palms, exotic flowers, and interesting lighting make this a place for a special occasion. Fresh seafood, pasta, pizza, and unusual choices like Thai chicken linguini and blackened halibut are offered. **FYI:** Reservations recommended. Blues. **Open:** Sun–Mon 11am–10pm, Tues–Wed 11am–11pm, Thurs 11am–midnight, Fri–Sat 11am–1:30am. Closed some hols. **Prices:** Main courses $8–$22. Maj CC. ♥ 🍷 VP &

Attractions 🏛

Queen Mary Seaport, Pier J; tel 310/435-3511. Last of the great super liners, the legendary *Queen Mary* was the largest and most luxurious ocean liner ever built. Catering to the rich and famous of Europe and America, the ship accommodated 2,000 passengers on its maiden voyage to New York City in May, 1936. When it was converted for use as a troop carrier during World War II, the repainted ship became known as the "Gray Ghost" for its ability to avoid German U-boats. It carried a total of 765,429 troops during 6 years of military service and was returned to passenger service in 1947. When the *Queen Mary* was turned over to the city of Long Beach in 1967, it had completed 1,001 crossings of the Atlantic.

Today the ship is a major tourist attraction. Guided and self-guided tours are available that explore various areas of the ship, including the bridge, officers' quarters, engine room, staterooms, and the first-class lounge. Part of the ship contains a 365-room hotel, with rooms that were originally first-class staterooms.

There are numerous restaurants, lounges, and shops aboard the *Queen Mary*. Surrounding the ship is the **Queen's Marketplace**, a 55-acre site featuring still more shops and restaurants, along with strolling musicians and street performers. **Open:** Mid-June–Labor Day, Sun–Thurs, 10am–6pm, Fri–Sat 10am–9pm; after Labor Day–mid-June, daily 10am–6pm. $$

Long Beach Museum of Art, 2300 E Ocean Blvd; tel 310/439-2119. Situated on a bluff overlooking the Pacific ocean, this museum contains a permanent collection spanning 100 years of American and European art, including an internationally renowned collection of video art; also rotating multi-media exhibitions of modern and contemporary art. Sculpture garden; outdoor cafe. Museum shop. **Open:** Wed–Sun 10am–5pm. Closed some hols. $

Rancho Los Alamitos Historic Ranch and Gardens, 6400 Bixby Rd; tel 213/431-3541. The current 7½-acre site is all that remains of what was once a vast land grant that originally comprised 300,000 acres. Rancho Los Alamitos now consists of a 17-room ranch house (circa 1800), 4 acres of graceful gardens, and 6 early-20th-century agricultural outbuildings. Guided tours of the site illustrate ranch life in the 18th and 19th centuries. Special programs throughout the year. **Open:** Wed–Sun 1–5pm. Closed some hols. Free.

LOS ALTOS

Map page M-2, D2 (W of Santa Clara)

Restaurant 🍽️

★ **Chef Chu's**, 1067 N San Antonio Rd, Los Altos; tel 415/948-2696. San Antonio Rd S exit off US 101. **Chinese.** Large floral paintings, etched-glass dividers, and mirrors enhance the simple but tasteful decor. Over 50 beef, lamb, poultry, seafood, pork, and vegetable dishes. Specialties include tangerine beef, candied pecans with prawns, velvet chicken. **FYI:** Reservations recommended. **Open:** Lunch daily 11:30am–4pm; dinner Sun–Thurs 4–9:30pm, Fri–Sat 4–10pm. Closed some hols. **Prices:** Main courses $8–$14; PF dinner $11.95. Maj CC. 🍴 🚗 ♿

LOS ANGELES

Map page M-3, D2

See also **Bel Air, Beverly Hills, Burbank, Cerritos, Culver City, Diamond Beach, Glendale, Hermosa Beach, Hollywood, North Hollywood, West Hollywood, Long Beach, Marina del Rey, Pasadena, Redondo Beach, San Gabriel, San Pedro, Santa Monica, Sherman Oaks, Universal City, Venice, West Los Angeles, Woodland Hills**

TOURIST INFORMATION

Visitors Information Center 685 S Figueroa St, between Wilshire Blvd and 7th St (tel 213/689-8822). Open Mon–Fri 8am–5pm, Sat 8:30am–5pm. For free visitor's kit, write to the Los Angeles Convention and Visitors Bureau, 633 W 5th St, Suite 6000, Los Angeles, CA 90071.

PUBLIC TRANSPORTATION

Southern California Rapid Transit District (RTD) Buses Operate throughout the Los Angeles metropolitan area. Local fare $1.10; fares increase for express and intercounty service. For information call 213/626-4455 or visit RTD's offices at 425 S Main St or in the ARCO Towers at 515 S Flower St.

RTD Blue Line Commuter Rail Operates daily 5:30am–7pm. Runs every 10–20 minutes between 7th and Flower St stations in downtown Los Angeles and 1st St station in Long Beach. 55-minute express trip. Fare $1.10 adults, 55¢ seniors, children under 5 free. For information call 213/626-4455.

Hotels 🛏️

≣≣ **Best Western Executive Motor Inn**, 603 S New Hampshire Ave, Los Angeles, CA 90005; tel 213/385-4444 or toll free 800/528-1234; fax 213/380-5413. Small midtown hotel. Tiny lobby is right off parking area, so security is good at night. **Rooms:** 90 rms and stes. CI noon/CO noon. Nonsmoking rms avail. Plain but comfortable. **Amenities:** 🛏️ A/C, cable TV, refrig. **Services:** 🚐 📷 🍴 Car-rental desk. Complimentary continental breakfast and *LA Times* newspaper daily. **Facilities:** 🏋️ Sauna, whirlpool, washer/dryer. **Rates:** HS July–Aug $59–$62 D; from $65 ste. Extra person $3. Children under 12 stay free. Lower rates off-season. Pking: Indoor, free. Maj CC.

≣≣ **Best Western Mayfair Hotel**, 1256 W 7th St, Los Angeles, CA 90017; tel 213/484-9789 or toll free 800/821-8682; fax 213/484-2769. Lovingly restored grand hotel from the 1920s, in a run-down neighborhood. Lovely lobby with white grand piano, high ceilings, and neoclassical pillars. A frequent backdrop for Hollywood movies. **Rooms:** 294 rms and stes; 294 ctges/villas. CI 4pm/CO noon. Nonsmoking rms avail. Rooms are basic and not as nice as the lobby. **Amenities:** 🛏️ A/C, cable TV w/movies. Nintendo in rooms. **Services:** ✕ 🔑 🚐 📷 🍴 🛎️ Car-rental desk, social director, masseur, children's program, babysitting. Free coffee, newspapers, and happy hour. Free shuttle to downtown and Dodger Stadium. **Facilities:** 🍴 🖼️ ♿ 1 rst, 2 bars (1 w/entertainment), day-care ctr. **Rates:** $75–$115 S; $85–$130 D; from $130 ste. Extra person $15. Children under 18 stay free. Higher rates for spec evnts/hols. Spec packages avail. Pking: Indoor, free. Maj CC.

≣≣≣ **Beverly Hills Ritz Hotel**, 10300 Wilshire Blvd, Los Angeles, CA 90024; tel 310/275-5575 or toll free 800/800-1234; fax 310/278-3325. A very modern setting east of the towers of Wilshire Blvd, near Westwood and Beverly Hills shopping, this property has an inviting environment. **Rooms:** 116 stes and effic. CI 1pm/CO noon. Well-soundproofed rooms are nice and tidy, with contemporary furniture. **Amenities:** 🛏️ 🌀 🍴 A/C, cable TV w/movies, refrig, VCR, in-rm safe. All units w/minibars, some w/terraces. **Services:** ✕ 🔑 🅥🅟 🚐 📷 🍴 🛎️ Twice-daily maid svce, car-rental desk, social director, masseur, babysitting. Good service. **Facilities:** 🏋️ 🍴 🖼️ ♿ 1 rst, 1 bar, games rm, whirlpool, washer/dryer. Tiny bar and restaurant. **Rates:** From $105 ste; from $105 effic. AP and MAP rates avail. Pking: Indoor/outdoor, $8. Maj CC.

≣≣≣ **The Biltmore**, 506 S Grand Ave, Los Angeles, CA 90071 (Downtown); tel 213/612-1575 or toll free 800/245-8673; fax 213/612-1545. The Biltmore has one of LA's most grand, historic lobbies, with lion's-head fountain, parquet floors, and hand-painted ceilings. Furnishings, however, look worn. **Rooms:** 683 rms, stes, and effic. Exec-level rms avail. CI 3pm/CO noon. Express checkout avail. Nonsmoking rms avail. Club and executive suites are attractively done in updated deco style with marble baths. But standard rooms are strictly ordinary, with tired upholstery and small but functional bathrooms. **Amenities:** 🛗 🕭 🗣 A/C, satel TV w/movies, refrig. All units w/minibars, some w/terraces. Business center for club-level guests is equipped with fax, photocopy machines, and IBM-compatible computers. **Services:** 🍽 🖭 🆅🅿 🚐 🛄 🛎 Car-rental desk, masseur, babysitting. **Facilities:** 🏠 🛖 🔢 🖥 🕭 4 rsts, 3 bars, lifeguard, spa, sauna, steam rm, whirlpool, beauty salon. Opulent, art deco indoor swimming pool is inlaid with mosaics. Fitness center has added $30,000 worth of exercise equipment. **Rates:** $185–$225 S; $215–$225 D; from $325 ste; from $1,000 effic. Extra person $30. Children under 18 stay free. Spec packages avail. Pking: Indoor, $16.50. Maj CC.

≣≣≣ **Carlyle Inn**, 1119 S Robertson Blvd, Los Angeles, CA 90035; tel 310/275-4445 or toll free 800/322-7595; fax 310/859-0496. A real find, this charming, modern, European-style hotel is right near Beverly Hills. Rooms are reached by outdoor corridors overlooking a lovely patio. **Rooms:** 32 rms and stes. CI noon/CO 1pm. Nonsmoking rms avail. **Amenities:** 🛗 🕭 🖭 🗣 A/C, cable TV, VCR, bathrobes. All units w/minibars, all w/terraces. Movies are available for rent. **Services:** ✗ 🖭 🆅🅿 🚐 🛄 🛎 Car-rental desk, social director, masseur, children's program, babysitting. Afternoon tea, and apples at front desk. Complimentary shopping shuttle to nearby Beverly Hills. **Facilities:** 🛖 🕭 1 rst, whirlpool. **Rates (MAP):** $105–$120 S; $115–$130 D; from $180 ste. Extra person $10. Children under 10 stay free. Pking: Indoor, $6. Maj CC.

≣≣≣≣ **Century Plaza Hotel & Tower**, 2025 Ave of the Stars, Los Angeles, CA 90067 (Century City); tel 310/551-3300 or toll free 800/228-3000; fax 310/551-3355. Big city, big hotel glamour, with a curvilinear facade and sweeping marble lobby. There are actually 2 hotels; the 322-room tower, and the 750-room main hotel. **Rooms:** 1,072 rms and stes. Exec-level rms avail. CI 3pm/CO 1pm. Express checkout avail. Nonsmoking

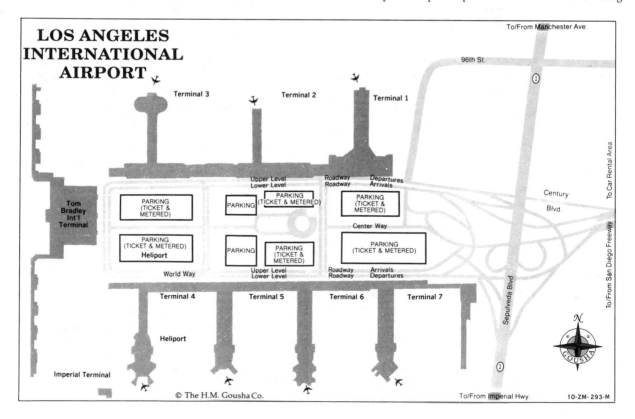

LOS ANGELES INTERNATIONAL AIRPORT

© The H.M. Gousha Co.

10-ZM-293-M

rms avail. Just redone Tower rooms have a sophisticated beige-and-black color scheme, with marble baths. In the main building, west-facing garden rooms are larger. Tiled bathrooms here look a tad outdated. **Amenities:** 🔒 ⚙ 🍷 A/C, cable TV w/movies, refrig, voice mail, in-rm safe, shoe polisher. All units w/minibars, all w/terraces. Tower rooms have fax/modem compatible phones and upgraded toiletries. **Services:** 🍽 🖥 VP 🚗 🛄 ☎ Car-rental desk, masseur, babysitting. In tower rooms: complimentary shoeshine, evening turn-down, and ice service. Children under 12 eat free when accompanied by parents. Ask for details. **Facilities:** 🏋 🏌 3k 💻 ♿ 3 rsts, 3 bars (2 w/entertainment), whirlpool, beauty salon. Both the main building and the Tower have their own health club and swimming pool. The reflecting pool area is popular for weddings. **Rates:** $190–$245 S; $215–$270 D; from $250 ste. Extra person $25. Children under 18 stay free. Spec packages avail. Pking: Indoor/outdoor, $10–$16. Maj CC.

≡≡≡ **Continental Plaza, Los Angeles Airport**, 9750 Airport Blvd, Los Angeles, CA 90045 (Los Angeles Int'l Airport); tel 310/645-4600 or toll free 800/LAX-HOTEL; fax 310/645-7486. High-rise hotel near the airport is very comfortable and well maintained. Complete renovation scheduled. **Rooms:** 570 rms and stes. CI 3pm/CO noon. Express checkout avail. Nonsmoking rms avail. **Amenities:** 🔒 ⚙ A/C, cable TV w/movies. **Services:** 🍽 🖥 VP 🚗 🛄 ☎ Car-rental desk, babysitting. **Facilities:** 🏋 🏌 500 💻 ♿ 1 rst, 1 bar, whirlpool. **Rates:** $79 S; $89 D; from $125 ste. Extra person $10. Children under 18 stay free. Spec packages avail. Pking: Indoor, $5. Pking: Outdoor, $5. Maj CC. Rates will rise after renovation.

≡≡≡ **Embassy Suites LAX/Century Blvd**, 9801 Airport Blvd, Los Angeles, CA 90045 (Los Angeles Int'l Airport); tel 310/215-1000 or toll free 800/EMBASSY; fax 310/215-1952. Typical Embassy Suites atrium design, with glass elevator. Very impressive and upbeat. **Rooms:** 215 stes and effic. CI 1/CO 1pm. Express checkout avail. Nonsmoking rms avail. 2-room suites, nicely furnished with sofa bed in living room. **Amenities:** 🔒 ⚙ 🖥 🍷 A/C, cable TV w/movies, refrig, VCR, voice mail. All units w/terraces. Wet bar, microwave. Nintendo available. **Services:** ✗ 🖥 🚗 🛄 ☎ Car-rental desk, babysitting. Complimentary cocktails and children's drinks, full cooked-to-order breakfast. **Facilities:** 🏋 🏌 370 💻 ♿ 1 rst, 1 bar, sauna, steam rm, whirlpool, day-care ctr, washer/dryer. **Rates:** From $109 ste; from $109 effic. Extra person $15. Children under 17 stay free. AP rates avail. Spec packages avail. Pking: Indoor, $7.70. Maj CC.

≡≡≡≡ **Four Seasons Hotel**, 300 Doheny Dr, Los Angeles, CA 90048; tel 310/273-2222 or toll free 800/332-3442 in the US, 800/268-6282 in Canada; fax 310/859-3824. The exterior of the 16-story structure looks like every other neighborhood condo, but the interior reflects the marbled gleam and refined appointments of a grand manor house. The lobby and living room lead to a small backyard garden with jasmine and magnolia trees. **Rooms:** 285 rms and stes. CI 3pm/CO 1pm. Express checkout avail. Nonsmoking rms avail. Spacious and efficient but uninspired. Specially equipped Executive Suite available for early arrivals/late departures. **Amenities:** 🔒 ⚙ 🍷 A/C, cable TV w/movies, refrig, shoe polisher, bathrobes. All units w/minibars, all w/terraces, some w/fireplaces. **Services:** 🍽 🖥 VP 🚗 🛄 ☎ Twice-daily maid svce, car-rental desk, masseur, children's program, babysitting. Courtesy limos to Rodeo Drive and Century City shops. Car care. Airline ticketing computer. Overnight laundry/dry cleaning; 24-hour seamstresses. Snap-to-it staffers are polite and responsive. **Facilities:** 🏋 🏌 400 ♿ 3 rsts, 2 bars (1 w/entertainment), lifeguard, whirlpool. 2nd-floor pool and sundeck with indoor/outdoor fitness room and refreshment terrace. Despite its top-echelon business clientele, the hotel coddles kids, providing special menus, coloring books, teddy bears, and video games. **Rates:** $300–$330 S; $330–$360 D; from $400 ste. Extra person $15. Children under 18 stay free. Spec packages avail. Pking: Indoor, $15. Maj CC. Rates determined by room size and floor.

≡≡≡ **Holiday Inn**, 1755 N Highland Ave, Los Angeles, CA 90028; tel 213/462-7181; fax 213/466-9072. While the neighborhood may not be the best, the hotel itself is clean and in good condition. **Rooms:** 470 rms, stes, and effic. Exec-level rms avail. CI 3pm/CO noon. Express checkout avail. Nonsmoking rms avail. All rooms measure exactly the same, whether double or suite. Doubles have twin beds, suites have 1 bed and a sofa bed. All bathrooms are narrow. **Amenities:** 🔒 ⚙ A/C, cable TV w/movies, in-rm safe. **Services:** ✗ 🖥 🛄 ☎ Car-rental desk, babysitting. **Facilities:** 🏋 200 ♿ 2 rsts, 2 bars (1 w/entertainment), washer/dryer. **Rates:** HS June–Sept $120–$128 S; $128–$136 D; from $138 ste; from $138 effic. Children under 18 stay free. Lower rates off-season. Higher rates for spec evnts/hols. Spec packages avail. Pking: Indoor, $5.50. Ltd CC.

≡≡≡ **Holiday Inn City Center**, 1020 S Figueroa St, Los Angeles, CA 90015 (Downtown); tel 213/748-1291 or toll free 800/HOLIDAY; fax 213/748-6028. An excellent choice for the business traveler, with a convenient downtown location. **Rooms:** 195 rms and stes. Exec-level rms avail. CI 3pm/CO noon. Nonsmoking rms avail. Rooms are neat, clean, and quite large. **Amenities:** 🔒 ⚙ A/C, cable TV w/movies. **Services:** ✗ 🖥 🚗 🛄 ☎ Car-rental desk, babysitting. **Facilities:** 🏋 🏌 200 💻 ♿ 1 rst, 1 bar, spa, sauna, washer/dryer. **Rates:** $115 S; $125 D; from $150 ste. Extra person $10. Children under 18 stay free. Higher rates for spec evnts/hols. Spec packages avail. Pking: Indoor/outdoor, $8. Maj CC.

≣≣≣ **Holiday Inn Crowne Plaza**, 5985 W Century Blvd, Los Angeles, CA 90045 (Los Angeles Int'l Airport); tel 310/642-7500 or toll free 800/266-7606; fax 310/417-3608. **Rooms:** 615 rms and stes. Exec-level rms avail. CI 3pm/CO noon. Express checkout avail. Nonsmoking rms avail. **Amenities:** 👁 🐕 A/C, cable TV w/movies, refrig. Some units w/minibars. **Services:** 🍴 📟 VP 🚐 🖊 Car-rental desk, social director, masseur, children's program, babysitting. Complimentary newspaper. Free shuttle to beach and shopping. **Facilities:** 500 2 rsts, 2 bars (1 w/entertainment), sauna, steam rm, whirlpool, washer/dryer. **Rates:** $154 S or D; from $350 ste. Extra person $15. Children under 17 stay free. Higher rates for spec evnts/hols. AP and MAP rates avail. Spec packages avail. Pking: Indoor, $7–$10. Maj CC.

≣≣≣ **Holiday Inn Downtown**, 750 Garland Ave, Los Angeles, CA 90017; tel 213/628-5242 or toll free 800/HOLIDAY; fax 213/628-1201. Well-kept and comfortable lodging for the business traveler. Located on a hill on the outskirts of downtown Los Angeles. **Rooms:** 205 rms and stes. CI 1pm/CO noon. Nonsmoking rms avail. **Amenities:** 👁 📺 A/C, cable TV w/movies. **Services:** ✗ 📟 🚐 🖊 Twice-daily maid svce, car-rental desk, babysitting. Complimentary hors d'oeuvres during cocktail hour. Free downtown shopping shuttle. Van service to LA tourist spots for small fee. **Facilities:** 100 🖥 1 rst, 1 bar, washer/dryer. Restaurant offers superb buffet lunch at reasonable price. **Rates:** $99 S; $109 D; from $150 ste. Extra person $10. Children under 17 stay free. Higher rates for spec evnts/hols. AP and MAP rates avail. Spec packages avail. Pking: Indoor/outdoor, free. Maj CC.

≣≣≣ **Holiday Inn–LAX Airport**, 9901 La Cienega Blvd, Los Angeles, CA 90045 (Los Angeles Int'l Airport); tel 310/649-5151 or toll free 800/624-0025; fax 310/670-3619. Immaculate hotel near the airport with a small, well-kept lobby. **Rooms:** 410 rms and stes. Exec-level rms avail. CI 3pm/CO noon. Express checkout avail. Nonsmoking rms avail. **Amenities:** 👁 🐕 A/C, cable TV w/movies. Fax machine in every room. Video games available for extra charge. **Services:** ✗ 📟 🚐 🖊 Twice-daily maid svce, car-rental desk, children's program, babysitting. **Facilities:** 350 1 rst, 1 bar (w/entertainment), spa, washer/dryer. **Rates:** $89 S; $99 D; from $119 ste. Extra person $10. Children under 12 stay free. Higher rates for spec evnts/hols. MAP rates avail. Spec packages avail. Pking: Indoor/outdoor, $5. Maj CC.

🌂 **Hotel Bel-Air**, 701 Stone Canyon Rd, Los Angeles, CA 90077; tel 310/472-1211 or toll free 800/648-4097; fax 310/476-5890. 11 acres. Not so much a hotel as a botanical garden, with a lake for swans and romantic little bungalows for guests, all tucked away in one of the city's most exclusive communities (the Reagans live just up the road). Built in the 1920s in Mediterranean/mission style with red tile roofs, arcades, and fountained courtyards lined with beautiful and unusual flowers. **Rooms:** 92 rms and stes. CI 3pm/CO 1pm. Each room styled individually; most have terra-cotta tiled floors. **Amenities:** 👁 🐕 A/C, cable TV w/movies, refrig, VCR, shoe polisher, bathrobes. All units w/minibars, some w/terraces, some w/fireplaces, some w/Jacuzzis. Some rooms with secluded, flower-perfumed patio. Umbrella in closet; battery-powered emergency lighting; earthquake survival kit. **Services:** 🍴 📟 VP 🚐 🖊 Twice-daily maid svce, car-rental desk, babysitting. Despite the 3-to-1 staff-to-guest ratio and extra touches like setting and lighting guests' fires, the service is not quite as up to snuff as expected, given the tony clientele; however, the sheer seductiveness of the place makes service shortcomings seem much less important than they would be elsewhere. **Facilities:** 200 1 rst (see also "Restaurants" below), 2 bars (1 w/entertainment), lifeguard, beauty salon. New fitness center in the works. Swank dining room, ravishing dining terrace with bougainvillea vines overhead and heated floor. **Rates:** $245–$395 S; $275–$435 D; from $495 ste. Children under 18 stay free. Min stay spec evnts. Pking: Outdoor, $12.50. Maj CC.

≣≣≣ **Hotel Del Capri**, 10587 Wilshire Blvd, Los Angeles, CA 90024; tel 310/474-3511 or toll free 800/444-6835; fax 310/470-9999. Small hotel that shows some wear. Despite the busy street, rooms are quiet. **Rooms:** 80 rms and stes. CI 3pm/CO noon. Nonsmoking rms avail. Suites are small; some have kitchenettes. **Amenities:** 👁 📺 A/C, cable TV w/movies, refrig, VCR. 1 unit w/terrace, some w/Jacuzzis. Adjustable beds. **Services:** ✗ 📟 🚐 🖊 Twice-daily maid svce, car-rental desk. Multilingual staff speaks Italian, French, and German. **Facilities:** 35 Whirlpool, washer/dryer. **Rates (CP):** $85–$105 S; $110–$140 D; from $120 ste. Extra person $10. Children under 12 stay free. Spec packages avail. Pking: Indoor/outdoor, free. Maj CC.

≣≣≣≣ **Hotel Inter-Continental Los Angeles at California Plaza**, 251 S Olive St, Los Angeles, CA 90012 (Downtown); tel 213/617-3300 or toll free 800/442-5251; fax 213/617-3399. Shiny new high-rise in prestigious business plaza, with all kinds of comforts for business travelers. **Rooms:** 433 rms, stes, and effic. Exec-level rms avail. CI 3pm/CO noon. Express checkout avail. Nonsmoking rms avail. **Amenities:** 👁 🐕 A/C, cable TV w/movies, voice mail, bathrobes. All units w/minibars, 1 w/Jacuzzi. **Services:** 🍴 📟 VP 🖊 Car-rental desk, babysitting. Free coffee in lobby. Newspapers delivered to rooms. Special services for Japanese guests, including green tea and Japanese-style robes. **Facilities:** 800 🖥 1 rst, 1 bar (w/entertainment), spa, sauna, steam rm. **Rates:** $170–$230 S;

$200–$260 D; from $350 ste; from $1200 effic. Extra person $30. Children under 14 stay free. Spec packages avail. Pking: Indoor, $18. Maj CC.

Hotel Stillwell, 838 S Grand Ave, Los Angeles, CA 90017 (Downtown); tel 213/627-1151 or toll free 800/553-4774; fax 213/622-8940. Old low-budget hotel in the heart of downtown. **Rooms:** 250 rms. CI 11am/CO 11am. Nonsmoking rms avail. Adequate rooms with walk-in closets. **Amenities:** A/C, cable TV w/movies. **Services:** Car-rental desk, social director, masseur, children's program. Complimentary continental breakfast. Free shuttle to convention center. **Facilities:** 2 rsts, 1 bar, washer/dryer. **Rates:** $45 S or D. Children under 5 stay free. MAP rates avail. Pking: Outdoor, $3. Maj CC.

Hyatt Los Angeles Airport, 6225 W Century Blvd, Los Angeles, CA 90045; tel 310/337-1234 or toll free 800/233-1234; fax 310/641-6924. Large lobby with neoclassical decor, library, and several sitting areas. **Rooms:** 594 rms and stes. Exec-level rms avail. CI 3pm/CO 1pm. Nonsmoking rms avail. Bright, attractive furnishings in rooms. **Amenities:** A/C, cable TV w/movies, voice mail, in-rm safe, bathrobes. All units w/minibars. **Services:** Car-rental desk, babysitting. Free daily newspaper. Airport shuttle with handicapped access. **Facilities:** 2 rsts, 2 bars, spa, sauna, whirlpool, beauty salon. **Rates:** $89–$139 S or D; from $300 ste. Extra person $15. Children under 18 stay free. MAP rates avail. Spec packages avail. Pking: Indoor, $6–$9. Maj CC.

Hyatt Regency Los Angeles, 711 S Hope St, Los Angeles, CA 90017 (Downtown); tel 213/683-1234 or toll free 800/233-1234; fax 213/612-3179. A shining gem of a hotel with a big, beautiful lobby; located at the Broadway Plaza shopping mall. **Rooms:** 485 rms and stes. Exec-level rms avail. CI 3pm/CO 11am. Express checkout avail. Nonsmoking rms avail. **Amenities:** A/C, cable TV w/movies, voice mail. Some units w/minibars. **Services:** Car-rental desk, masseur, children's program, babysitting. Free daily newspaper. Shoe shine service. **Facilities:** 2 rsts, 1 bar (w/entertainment), whirlpool. 2 gift shops. **Rates:** $145–$169 S; $145–$184 D; from $225 ste. Extra person $10. Children under 12 stay free. MAP rates avail. Spec packages avail. Pking: Indoor, $15. Maj CC.

InnTowne Hotel, 925 S Figueroa St, Los Angeles, CA 90015 (Downtown); tel 213/628-2222 or toll free 800/528-1234; fax 213/687-0566. Scruffy but clean motel downtown. **Rooms:** 169 rms and stes. CI noon/CO noon. Nonsmoking rms avail. **Amenities:** A/C, cable TV w/movies, VCR. **Services:** Car-rental desk. **Facilities:** 1 rst, 1 bar. **Rates:** $84 S;

$95 D; from $120 ste. Extra person $12. Children under 12 stay free. Min stay. Higher rates for spec evnts/hols. Pking: Indoor/outdoor, free. Maj CC.

J W Marriott Hotel at Century City, 2151 Ave of the Stars, Los Angeles, CA 90067; tel 310/277-2777 or toll free 800/228-9290; fax 310/785-9240. This hotel shows plenty of panache, especially in the lobby with champagne marble floors, skylight ceiling, crystal chandeliers, and chinoiserie accents. **Rooms:** 367 rms and stes. CI 3pm/CO noon. Express checkout avail. Nonsmoking rms avail. Just refurbished, accommodations and corridors look great, with light furnishings and rich-colored fabrics. Executive rooms have separate living and sleeping areas. **Amenities:** A/C, cable TV w/movies, refrig, shoe polisher, bathrobes. All units w/minibars, all w/terraces, 1 w/fireplace. Toiletries are nicely arranged on a little étagère by the sink. The 27-inch TV provides video messages and checkout. **Services:** Twice-daily maid svce, car-rental desk, masseur, babysitting. Complimentary shoeshine and newspaper, plus free limo service within Century City and to Rodeo Drive. **Facilities:** 1 rst, 1 bar, spa, sauna, steam rm, whirlpool. Although the outdoor pool figured in a scene from *Lethal Weapon 2,* the deck is largely ordinary. **Rates:** $205–$215 S; $225–$235 D; from $275 ste. Extra person $25. Spec packages avail. Pking: Indoor, $14. Maj CC. Executive rooms cost just $10 more than standard ones.

Kawada Hotel, 200 S Hill St, Los Angeles, CA 90012 (Downtown); tel 213/621-4455 or toll free 800/752-9232; fax 213/687-4455. Pleasant, well-kept lobby, furnished in pastels. Caters primarily to Asian business travelers. **Rooms:** 116 rms, stes, and effic. CI 3pm/CO noon. Nonsmoking rms avail. Small but smartly furnished rooms; half have galley kitchens. **Amenities:** A/C, cable TV w/movies, refrig, VCR. **Services:** Car-rental desk, social director, masseur, children's program. Daily newspapers in lobby. Staff speaks Japanese, Tagalog, French, and Spanish, as well as English. **Facilities:** 1 rst, 1 bar (w/entertainment), washer/dryer. **Rates:** $75–$99 S or D; from $125 ste; from $125 effic. Extra person $10. Children under 18 stay free. MAP rates avail. Spec packages avail. Pking: Indoor/outdoor, $6.60. Maj CC. No additional charge for efficiencies.

Los Angeles Airport Marriott, 5855 W Century Blvd, Los Angeles, CA 90045 (Los Angeles Int'l Airport); tel 310/641-5700 or toll free 800/228-9290; fax 310/337-5358. Well-kept, very adequate business hotel. **Rooms:** 1,012 rms and stes. Exec-level rms avail. CI 3pm/CO 1pm. Express checkout avail. Nonsmoking rms avail. **Amenities:** A/C, cable TV w/movies, voice mail, shoe polisher. Some units w/terraces. **Services:** Car-rental desk, babysitting.

Complimentary coffee in lobby in morning, punch in afternoon. ITT language service. Courteous, multilingual staff. **Facilities:** 🔥 ⚽ 📶 💻 ♿ 4 rsts, 2 bars (1 w/entertainment), lifeguard, games rm, spa, sauna, steam rm, whirlpool, beauty salon, washer/dryer. Large, serpentine pool and big lounge area. **Rates:** $79–$139 S or D; from $159 ste. Children under 18 stay free. Spec packages avail. Pking: Indoor/outdoor, $9. Maj CC.

Los Angeles Hilton and Towers, 930 Wilshire Blvd, Los Angeles, CA 90017 (Downtown); tel 213/629-4321 or toll free 800/445-8667; fax 213/612-3977. Big, commercial hotel with good downtown location. **Rooms:** 900 rms and stes. Exec-level rms avail. CI 3pm/CO noon. Express checkout avail. Nonsmoking rms avail. **Amenities:** 🔥 ⚽ A/C, cable TV w/movies, voice mail. **Services:** ✕ 🔌 📺 🚗 📠 🔑 🐕 Twice-daily maid svce, car-rental desk, babysitting. **Facilities:** 🔥 ⚽ 💧 💻 ♿ 3 rsts, 1 bar, sauna, steam rm, whirlpool, beauty salon. Many shops located on 1st level. **Rates:** $139 S; $149 D; from $375 ste. Children under 18 stay free. Higher rates for spec evnts/hols. MAP rates avail. Spec packages avail. Pking: Indoor, $16.50. Maj CC.

Los Angeles Renaissance Hotel, 9620 Airport Blvd, Los Angeles, CA 90045 (Los Angeles Int'l Airport); tel 310/337-2800 or toll free 800/647-6437; fax 310/337-4826. Possibly the finest hotel at the airport, with classic furnishings, superb soundproofing, and dignified service. **Rooms:** 505 rms and stes. Exec-level rms avail. CI 3pm/CO noon. Express checkout avail. Nonsmoking rms avail. Rooms are furnished in dark woods with elegant appointments. **Amenities:** 🔥 ⚽ 📺 🍳 A/C, cable TV w/movies, voice mail, in-rm safe. All units w/minibars. **Services:** 🍽 🔌 📺 🚗 📠 🐕 Car-rental desk, babysitting. Wheelchair-accessible airport shuttle. **Facilities:** 🔥 ⚽ 💧 💻 ♿ 2 rsts, 1 bar (w/entertainment), spa, sauna, steam rm, whirlpool. **Rates:** $145–$195 S; $160–$195 D; from $175 ste. Extra person $20. Children under 18 stay free. Spec packages avail. Pking: Indoor, $8–$9. Maj CC.

Metro Plaza Hotel, 711 N Main St, Los Angeles, CA 90012; tel 213/680-0200 or toll free 800/223-1994. A new hotel on the edge of Chinatown. A small uninviting lobby could be overlooked in light of free parking next door. **Rooms:** 80 rms and stes. CI noon/CO noon. Nonsmoking rms avail. Rooms are small and spare, but imported Chinese furniture adds flair. **Amenities:** 🔥 A/C, cable TV w/movies, in-rm safe. 1 unit w/Jacuzzi. **Services:** 🚗 📠 🐕 Car-rental desk, social director, masseur, children's program. Free coffee in lobby. **Facilities:** 💧 💻 ♿ **Rates:** $59 S; $69–$75 D; from $109 ste. Extra person $6. Children under 12 stay free. Spec packages avail. Pking: Indoor, free. Maj CC.

Miyako Inn, 328 E 1st St, Los Angeles, CA 90012 (Little Tokyo); tel 213/617-2000 or toll free 800/228-6596; fax 213/617-2700. Handy for Japanese visitors, this hotel is in the heart of Little Tokyo and has convenient underground parking nearby. **Rooms:** 174 rms. Exec-level rms avail. CI 2pm/CO noon. Nonsmoking rms avail. Plain but with imported Asian bedspreads. **Amenities:** 🔥 ⚽ A/C, cable TV w/movies, in-rm safe. All units w/minibars. **Services:** ✕ 📺 🚗 📠 🐕 Car-rental desk, masseur. Complimentary Japanese newspaper. Japanese spoken. **Facilities:** 💧 1 rst, 1 bar (w/entertainment), spa, sauna, steam rm, whirlpool, washer/dryer. Gift shop. **Rates:** $89–$102 S; $99–$112 D. Extra person $15. Children under 12 stay free. Spec packages avail. Pking: Indoor, $6.60. Maj CC.

New Otani Hotel and Garden, 120 S Los Angeles St, Los Angeles, CA 90012 (Little Tokyo); tel 213/629-1200 or toll free 800/421-8795; fax 213/622-0980. Located right next to Weller Court and Little Tokyo, this spotless modern high-rise has Japanese decor with simple furnishings, yet it's tasteful and luxurious. **Rooms:** 434 rms and stes. Exec-level rms avail. CI 3pm/CO noon. Express checkout avail. Nonsmoking rms avail. Japanese suites available with tatami-mat floors, futon sleepers, and deep Jacuzzi tubs. **Amenities:** 🔥 ⚽ 🍳 A/C, cable TV w/movies, in-rm safe, shoe polisher. All units w/minibars, some w/terraces, some w/Jacuzzis. Teapots in rooms. **Services:** ✕ 🔌 📺 🚗 📠 🐕 Twice-daily maid svce, car-rental desk, social director, masseur, children's program, babysitting. Free morning coffee. **Facilities:** ⚽ 💧 💻 ♿ 3 rsts, 3 bars (2 w/entertainment), spa, beauty salon, washer/dryer. Japanese restaurant; garden. **Rates:** $155–$275 S; $180–$300 D; from $450 ste. Extra person $25. Children under 12 stay free. Higher rates for spec evnts/hols. Spec packages avail. Pking: Indoor, $13.20–$17.60. Maj CC.

Radisson Wilshire Plaza, 3515 Wilshire Blvd, Los Angeles, CA 90010; tel 213/381-7411 or toll free 800/333-3333; fax 213/386-7379. Elegantly furnished, with a beautiful beige marble floor in lobby. An excellent location, in a mid-Wilshire neighborhood that is supposed to get a subway stop. **Rooms:** 391 rms and stes. Exec-level rms avail. CI 3pm/CO noon. Express checkout avail. Nonsmoking rms avail. **Amenities:** 🔥 ⚽ 📺 A/C, cable TV w/movies, voice mail. All units w/minibars. **Services:** ✕ 🔌 📺 🚗 📠 🐕 Twice-daily maid svce, car-rental desk, social director, masseur, children's program, babysitting. **Facilities:** 🔥 ⚽ 💧 💻 ♿ 2 rsts, 2 bars (1 w/entertainment), beauty salon. **Rates:** $99–$109 S; $109–$129 D; from $200 ste. Extra person $10. Children under 12 stay free. Spec packages avail. Pking: Indoor, $5.50–$7.70. Maj CC.

≣≣≣≣ **Sheraton Grande**, 333 S Figueroa St, Los Angeles, CA 90012 (Downtown); tel 213/617-1133 or toll free 800/LA-GRAND; fax 213/613-0291. An elegant downtown hotel with a beautiful lobby and fine service. **Rooms:** 469 rms and stes. Exec-level rms avail. CI 3pm/CO noon. Express checkout avail. Nonsmoking rms avail. **Amenities:** 🛍 🏧 ⌨ A/C, cable TV w/movies, voice mail, in-rm safe, bathrobes. All units w/minibars, 1 w/fireplace. **Services:** ⫶◎⫶ ⊶ VP 🚗 ⊠ ↩ Twice-daily maid svce, car-rental desk, social director, children's program, babysitting. Free coffee, tea, and newspapers delivered to your room. Free shoeshines and pressing of clothes. **Facilities:** ⌂ ⫼ⁱᴷ⫽ 🖥 ⅙ 3 rsts, 1 bar (w/entertainment). **Rates:** $169 S or D; from $275 ste. Extra person $25. Children under 18 stay free. Spec packages avail. Pking: Indoor, $16.50. Maj CC.

≣≣≣≣ **Sheraton Los Angeles Airport**, 6101 W. Century Blvd, Los Angeles, CA 90045; tel 310/642-1111 or toll free 800/325-3535; fax 310/645-1414. A glamorous big-city business hotel at Los Angeles International Airport. Huge chandeliers decorate an enormous lobby. **Rooms:** 804 rms and stes. Exec-level rms avail. CI 3pm/CO 1pm. Express checkout avail. Nonsmoking rms avail. A wide range of choices of rooms and suites. **Amenities:** 🛍 🏧 📺 A/C, cable TV w/movies, VCR, stereo/tape player, voice mail, bathrobes. All units w/minibars. **Services:** ⫶◎⫶ ⊶ VP 🚗 ⊠ ↩ Car-rental desk, babysitting. Complimentary newspapers. Multilingual staff. **Facilities:** ⌂ ⛲ ⫼ⁱᴷ⫽ 🖥 ⅙ 2 rsts, 2 bars (1 w/entertainment), whirlpool, washer/dryer. More than 100 meeting rooms. **Rates:** $135–$139 S or D; from $125 ste. Extra person $20. Children under 18 stay free. Higher rates for spec evnts/hols. Spec packages avail. Pking: Indoor/outdoor, $8–$9. Maj CC.

≣≣ **Travelodge at LAX**, 5547 W Century Blvd, Los Angeles, CA 90045 (Los Angeles Int'l Airport); tel 310/649-4000 or toll free 800/421-3939; fax 310/649-0311. The hotel lobby is nondescript, but there's a surprisingly beautiful tropical garden surrounding the pool area. **Rooms:** 147 rms. CI open/CO noon. Nonsmoking rms avail. Some rooms have only showers; others have a tub/shower combination. **Amenities:** 🛍 🏧 📺 A/C, cable TV w/movies, VCR. Some units w/terraces. **Services:** ✕ ⊶ 🚗 ⊠ ↩ ⟳ Car-rental desk, babysitting. **Facilities:** ⌂ ⫼³⁰⫽ 🖥 1 rst, 1 bar, washer/dryer. Denny's restaurant attached. **Rates:** HS June 15–Aug $69 S; $74 D. Extra person $8. Children under 18 stay free. Lower rates off-season. Spec packages avail. Pking: Outdoor, free. Ltd CC.

≣≣≣ **Westin Bonaventure**, 404 S Figueroa St, Los Angeles, CA 90071 (Downtown); tel 213/624-1000 or toll free 800/228-3000; fax 213/612-4797. Enormous convention hotel with a huge lobby, outdoor atrium elevators, and numerous areas to drink, dine, and relax. With its mirrored exterior and cylindrical

shape, it's been nicknamed "the LA espresso machine." **Rooms:** 1,368 rms and stes. Exec-level rms avail. CI 3pm/CO 1pm. Express checkout avail. Nonsmoking rms avail. Rooms have contemporary furnishings. Newly refurbished. **Amenities:** 🛍 🏧 ⌨ A/C, cable TV w/movies, stereo/tape player, voice mail, in-rm safe. All units w/minibars. **Services:** ⫶◎⫶ ⊶ VP 🚗 ⊠ ↩ ⟳ Car-rental desk, social director, masseur, children's program, babysitting. **Facilities:** ⌂ ⫼²ᴷ⫽ 🖥 ⅙ 2 rsts, 3 bars, beauty salon. Free use of YMCA across the street. **Rates:** $89–$157 S or D; from $325 ste. Extra person $25. Children under 12 stay free. Higher rates for spec evnts/hols. Spec packages avail. Pking: Indoor, $16.50. Maj CC.

≣≣≣≣ **Westwood Marquis Hotel and Gardens**, 930 Hilgard Ave, Los Angeles, CA 90024 (Westwood Village); tel 310/208-8765 or toll free 800/421-2317; fax 310/824-0355. Located on a quiet residential avenue a few blocks from Westwood and the campus of UCLA, but only 7 minutes from the freeway. The 2 midrise, office-like towers have greenery-swathed facades; the lobby is swank and seems to belong to a different hotel. The gardens of the name refer to a flowery backyard oasis with pool, private cabanas, and patio restaurant. **Rooms:** 258 stes. CI 3pm/CO 1pm. Express checkout avail. Nonsmoking rms avail. Spacious, efficient suites (1, 2, or 3 bedrooms), measuring 550 square feet and up—ideal for longer stays. Some are drab, though currently being upgraded and beautified. **Amenities:** 🛍 🏧 ⌨ A/C, cable TV, refrig, voice mail, shoe polisher, bathrobes. All units w/minibars, 1 w/fireplace. Extra-large minibars. 2 TVs. VCRs and stereos to be added as part of upgrade. **Services:** ⫶◎⫶ ⊶ VP ⊠ ↩ ⟳ Twice-daily maid svce, car-rental desk, babysitting. **Facilities:** ⌂ ⛲ ⫼¹²⁰⫽ ⅙ 3 rsts, 2 bars (1 w/entertainment), lifeguard, spa, sauna, steam rm, whirlpool, beauty salon. 2 popular restaurants: The Dynasty, serving continental cuisine, and the Garden Terrace, particularly popular for breakfast and weekend brunch. **Rates:** From $220 ste. Children under 18 stay free. Spec packages avail. Pking: Indoor, $12. Maj CC.

≣≣≣≣ **Wyndham Checkers Hotel Los Angeles**, 535 S Grand Ave, Los Angeles, CA 90071 (Downtown); tel 213/624-0000 or toll free 800/WYNDHAM; fax 213/624-9906. Between 5th and 6th. An oasis amid the skyscrapers of downtown LA. Small, personalized hotel offers a soothing blond-on-blond color scheme, plus a tranquil library. **Rooms:** 188 rms and stes. CI 3pm/CO noon. Express checkout avail. Nonsmoking rms avail. Beige room decor mingles Louis XV–style furnishings with serene contemporary pieces. Large bathrooms feature coral and white marble, plus big mirrors. **Amenities:** 🛍 🏧 📺 ⌨ A/C, cable TV w/movies, refrig, stereo/tape player, voice mail, shoe polisher, bathrobes. All units w/minibars, some w/terraces, some w/fireplaces. **Services:** ⫶◎⫶ ⊶ VP 🚗 ⊠ ↩ ⟳ Twice-daily maid svce, car-rental desk, masseur, babysitting. Continental breakfast served by the pool. Complimentary limousine service to central downtown area on weekday mornings. Complimentary shoeshine. **Facilities:** 🎣 🎪 📠 🖥 & 1 rst, 1 bar (w/entertainment), spa, sauna, whirlpool. Beautiful rooftop lap pool. **Rates:** $205 S or D; from $350 ste. Extra person $15. Children under 18 stay free. Min stay spec evnts. Spec packages avail. Pking: Indoor, $10–$23. Maj CC.

Restaurants 🍽

Arnie Morton's of Chicago, 435 S La Cienega Blvd, Los Angeles; tel 310/246-1501. **Steak.** This clubby steak house lets you choose your own steak as a cart of meat is rolled past your table. Prime aged beef is expertly prepared, as is Maine lobster. Excellent for business entertaining. **FYI:** Reservations recommended. **Open:** Mon–Sat 5:30–11pm, Sun 5–10pm. Closed some hols. **Prices:** Main courses $15–$29.95. Maj CC. VP &

Authentic Cafe, 7605 Beverly Blvd, Los Angeles; tel 213/939-4626. **Eclectic.** Small, storefront restaurant with southwestern decor and cactus plants on each table. Informal service and good, interesting dishes, including Yucatan marinated chicken breast, Szechuan dumplings, and Argentinean skirt steak. **FYI:** Reservations not accepted. No liquor license. **Open:** Sun 10am–10pm, Mon–Thurs 11:30am–10pm, Fri 11:30am–11pm, Sat 10am–11pm. Closed Dec 25. **Prices:** Main courses $7–$13. Ltd CC. ♥ 🖼 &

★ **Caffe Latte**, 6254 Wilshire Blvd, Los Angeles; tel 213/936-5213. **Regional American/Health/Spa.** Tom Kaplan's storefront-cafe spin-off of Hugo's has the same generously portioned menu with lower prices, a more mellow crowd, plus a coffee roaster and a market for tea and coffee on the premises. Specials include cappuccino pancakes, breakfast classics like Pasta Mama (scrambled with eggs, garlic, and cheese), and an array of sausage dishes. Unusual southwestern-style vegetarian entrees and health-oriented standards like blackened turkey loaf round out the menu. **FYI:** Reservations not accepted. No liquor license. **Open:** Mon–Thurs 7am–9pm, Fri 7am–10pm, Sat–Sun 8am–3pm. Closed some hols. **Prices:** Main courses $4.75–$10. Maj CC. &

Caffe Luna, 7463 Melrose Ave, Los Angeles; tel 213/655-8647. **Italian.** Hip, funky Italian-American cafe spilling out onto the busy street, with an intimate garden patio nestled in the trees out back. Owned and operated by congenial Frenchwoman Corine Lorain and daughter Stephanie, it's crowded from early morning until well past midnight all week. The menu offers wood-burning oven pizzas, regional pastas, panini, homemade desserts, and

baked goods. **FYI:** Reservations accepted. Beer and wine only. **Open:** Sun–Thurs 9am–3am, Fri–Sat 9am–5am. **Prices:** Main courses $9–$12. Maj CC. VP &

Campanile, 624 S La Brea Ave, Los Angeles; tel 213/938-1447. **Italian/Mediterranean.** One of the most popular places in Los Angeles, with a setting reminiscent of an Italian garden. It's always busy and noisy and is a local favorite of those in the entertainment business. The food is excellent and may feature crispy duck, grilled prime rib, and rack of lamb. Fresh breads and desserts made on the premises. **FYI:** Reservations recommended. **Open:** Breakfast Mon–Fri 8–11am, Sat–Sun 8am–1:30pm; lunch Mon–Fri 11:30am–2pm; dinner Mon–Thurs 6–10pm, Fri–Sat 5:30–11pm. Closed some hols. **Prices:** Main courses $15–$26. Maj CC. 🏛 VP &

Cantor's Fairfax Restaurant Delicatessen & Bakery, 419 N Fairfax Ave, Los Angeles (Fairfax District); tel 213/651-2030. **Deli.** A large, somewhat shabby delicatessen, but a Los Angeles institution nonetheless. Known for its excellent bakery goods and Jewish delicacies of corned beef, pastrami, chicken in a pot, and matzo ball soup. **FYI:** Reservations accepted. **Open:** Daily 24 hrs. **Prices:** Main courses $7.95–$12.75. Ltd CC. 🖼 🕐 &

Cava Restaurant and Tapas Bar, in Beverly Plaza Hotel, 8384 W 3rd, Los Angeles; tel 213/658-8898. 2 blocks E of Beverly Center. **Spanish.** Consistently excellent Spanish food served in 2 dining rooms and on an inviting outdoor patio. Tapas include fried calamari with saffron aioli, and fried eggplant stuffed with Spanish ham and Manchego cheese. Among entrees, the paella is a seafood delight. **FYI:** Reservations recommended. Cabaret/dinner theater/island music/jazz. **Open:** Daily 6:30am–midnight. **Prices:** Main courses $8–$16. Maj CC. ♥ 🖼 VP &

Chaya Brasserie, 8741 Alden Dr, Los Angeles; tel 310/859-8833. **French/Italian/Japanese.** Exposed pipes and stands of bamboo create an indoor-outdoor Asian fantasy with a hip Los Angeles feel. Mingle with celebrity agents from nearby Beverly Hills as you feast on Asian- and Italian-inspired cuisine, including salmon, chicken, fresh seaweed salad, and saffron risotto. **FYI:** Reservations recommended. **Open:** Lunch Mon–Fri 11:30am–2:30pm; dinner Mon–Thurs 6–10:30pm, Fri–Sat 6–11pm, Sun 6–10pm. Closed some hols. **Prices:** Main courses $10–$24. Maj CC. VP &

��� **Citrus**, 6703 Melrose Ave, Los Angeles; tel 213/857-0034. **Californian/French.** Chef Michel Richard is regarded as one of the best chefs in Los Angeles, offering superb cuisine at this now famous restaurant. Specialties include salmon Napoleon, lobster and scallop ravioli, osso buco with pasta, and caramelized apple tarts. A large outdoor patio offers fine dining outdoors under Japanese umbrellas. Award-winning wine list. **FYI:** Reservations recommended. **Open:** Lunch Mon–Fri noon–3pm; dinner Mon–Sat 6:15–11pm. Closed some hols. **Prices:** Main courses $20–$28; PF dinner $55. Maj CC. ♥ ⚓ VP ♿

★ **Dive!**, 10250 Santa Monica Blvd, Los Angeles (Century City); tel 310/788-DIVE. Santa Monica Blvd exit off I-405. **Eclectic.** Theme park–style restaurant worthy of co-owners Steven Spielberg and Jeffrey Katzenberg. Monster screens at either end of the "sub" display periscope sightings, and costumed servers communicate with walkie-talkies. Specialties include a vegetarian submarine sandwich with grilled portobello mushrooms, roasted red peppers, and Romano cheese. Desserts include slabs of S'mores and lemon bars with swirls of white chocolate mousse. **FYI:** Reservations not accepted. Children's menu. **Open:** Daily 11:30am–11pm. **Prices:** Main courses $7.95–$14.95. Maj CC. ⚓ 👥 VP ♿

Farmer's Market, Fairfax and 3rd Aves, Los Angeles; tel 213/933-9211. **Food Court.** The granddaddy of the modern food court, and a Los Angeles landmark. An indoor-outdoor complex of over 100 food stalls, offering everything from a corned beef sandwich to Mexican food to Italian pasta. Excellent pastries and a fresh produce market. **FYI:** Reservations not accepted. Beer and wine only. **Open:** Mon–Sat 9am–7pm, Sun 10am–6pm. Closed some hols. **Prices:** Main courses $4–$10. No CC. 🍴 ⚓ ♿

♥ **Four Oaks Restaurant**, 2181 N Beverly Glen Blvd, Los Angeles; tel 310/470-2265. **Californian/French.** Formerly a railway station and a brothel, this century-old country inn surrounded by oak trees is minutes from Beverly Hills. The menu offers house smoked salmon, potato and caramelized onion tart with capers, plum barbequed swordfish, beef tenderloin, and desserts like crème brûlée. Sunday brunch is popular. **FYI:** Reservations recommended. Guitar. **Open:** Lunch Tues–Sun 11:30am–2pm; dinner daily 6–10pm; brunch–Sun 10:30am–2pm. Closed some hols. **Prices:** Main courses $23–$28. Maj CC. ♥🍴⚓🔥👥VP

Grand Star, 943 Sun Mun Way, Los Angeles (New Chinatown); tel 213/626-2285. Between Broadway and Hill St. **Chinese.** Family-owned and -operated for 70 years—and starting to show some wear. Menu specialties feature Cantonese cuisine, including Peking duck. **FYI:** Reservations recommended. **Open:** Daily 5am–10pm. Closed Thanksgiving. **Prices:** Main courses $4.95–$25. Maj CC. 🍴

Horikawa, 111 S San Pedro St, Los Angeles (Little Tokyo); tel 213/680-9355. **Japanese.** Good choice for a business lunch. Japanese-style elegance, with shoji screens, damask fabrics, and soft background music. Offerings include sushi, shrimp tempura, lobster, sukiyaki, and filet mignon. There's a sushi bar and a

teppan room for cooking at your table. **FYI:** Reservations recommended. **Open:** Mon–Fri 6–10pm, Sat 5–10pm. Closed some hols. **Prices:** Main courses $16.50–$22.50; PF dinner $50. Maj CC. ♥ VP ♿

The Ivy, 113 N Robertson Blvd, Los Angeles; tel 310/274-8303. **Eclectic.** Casual decor and beautiful flowers; reminiscent of a country farmhouse. Frequented by Hollywood celebrities. Crab cakes, caesar salad, prime rib, and meat loaf, as well as great desserts. Also at: 1541 Ocean Ave, Santa Monica (310/393-3113). **FYI:** Reservations recommended. **Open:** Mon–Sat 11:30am–11pm, Sun 11:30am–10pm. Closed some hols. **Prices:** Maj CC. ♥ ⚓ VP ♿

La Chaumière, in the Century Plaza Tower, 2055 Ave of the Stars, Los Angeles (Century City); tel 310/551-3360. Santa Monica Blvd exit off I-405; at Olympic Blvd W. **Continental/French.** A pristine, alderwood-paneled country retreat overlooking the bustle of Century City, complete with mural-sized 18th-century-style pastoral paintings and brass chandeliers. Chef Alex Parry's eclectic menu offers sautéed California duckling foie gras; medallions of veal with Madeira-morel cream; crisp Atlantic salmon rolls coated with mushrooms, parsley, and truffles; and dark chocolate or Grand Marnier soufflés. **FYI:** Reservations recommended. Dancing/piano/singer. Dress code. **Open:** Mon–Sat 5:30–10pm. Closed some hols. **Prices:** Main courses $16–$34. Maj CC. ♥ 🖼 📺 VP ♿

Langer's, 704 S Alvarado St, Los Angeles; tel 213/483-8050. **Deli.** This large, typical New York–style deli in a somewhat run-down neighborhood is an old favorite with regulars, who come from all over LA. Phone ahead and a waiter will deliver your order to your car. Lean pastrami sandwich, chopped liver, stuffed cabbage, gefilte fish, chicken in a pot. **FYI:** Reservations accepted. Beer and wine only. **Open:** Daily 6:30am–9pm. Closed some hols. **Prices:** Main courses $2.60–$13.95. Ltd CC. 🍴👥♿

★ **LA Trattoria**, 8022 W 3rd St, Los Angeles; tel 213/658-7607. **Italian.** Clean, minimalist lines, rustic Neapolitan dishes, and chef-owner Peppe Miele's sense of humor make this the place LA's Italian chefs (and tourists) dine. On the upstairs garden terrace, diners enjoy a changing variety of pizzas, grilled sandwiches, and carpaccio, including a version made with lamb and truffle oil. Risotto with porcini mushrooms in herb sauce and penne pasta with vodka in a light pink sauce are other specialties. **FYI:** Reservations recommended. Beer and wine only. **Open:** Lunch Tues–Fri 11:30am–2:30pm; dinner daily 5:30–11pm. Closed some hols. **Prices:** Main courses $18–$23; PF dinner $28–$35. Maj CC. ⚓ 👥 VP ♿

Le Chardonnay, 8284 Melrose Ave, Los Angeles; tel 213/655-8880. **French.** A romantic spot that evokes a Belle Epoque Paris bistro; decorated with dark wood, etched glass, and lots of brass. Goat cheese ravioli, grilled duck sausage, roasted chicken. **FYI:** Reservations recommended. **Open:** Lunch Mon–Fri noon–2pm; dinner Mon–Thurs 6–10pm, Fri–Sat 6–11pm. Closed some hols. **Prices:** Main courses $18.75–$28. Maj CC. ♥ VP &

Little Joe's, 900 N Broadway, Los Angeles (Chinatown); tel 213/489-4900. **Italian/American.** One of the oldest restaurants in Los Angeles, with historic photos lining the wood-paneled walls. Six dining rooms, including a sports bar with giant television. Northern Italian and American cuisine includes veal saltimbocca, homemade ravioli, steaks, chops, and prime rib. **FYI:** Reservations recommended. **Open:** Mon–Fri 11am–9pm, Sat 3–9pm. Closed some hols. **Prices:** Main courses $7.95–$18.50. Maj CC. ■ ▦ VP &

★ **Locanda Veneta**, 8638 W 3rd St, Los Angeles; tel 310/274-1893. Between Robertson and San Vincente Blvds. **Italian.** An intimate, low-key dining room with a high-profile celebrity following. Open kitchen track lighting. The chef has transformed classically hearty Venetian fare into lighter versions. Ravioli filled with lobster in saffron sauce, roasted baby rack of lamb grilled with mustard and walnuts, and a vanilla cream custard with caramel sauce have become trademarks. **FYI:** Reservations recommended. Beer and wine only. **Open:** Lunch Mon–Fri 11:30am–2:30pm; dinner Mon–Thurs 5:30–10:30pm, Fri–Sat 5:30–11pm. Closed some hols. **Prices:** Main courses $9.50–$21. Maj CC. VP

♥ **L'Orangerie Restaurant**, 903 N La Cienega Blvd, Los Angeles (Restaurant Row); tel 310/652-9770. **French.** A romantic spot with old-world charm, designed by noted French architect Valerian S Rybar. Dine on the new front garden terrace among potted orange topiary trees, or in one of the 3 dramatic rooms inside. Fresh Santa Barbara–grown produce, Sonoma County chicken and lamb, fresh fish, Maine lobster. **FYI:** Reservations recommended. Piano. Jacket required. **Open:** Lunch Tues–Fri noon–2pm; dinner Tues–Sun 6:30–11pm. Closed some hols. **Prices:** Main courses $26–$35; PF dinner $60. Maj CC. ♥ ⬥ ▦ VP &

♥ **Lunaria**, 10351 Santa Monica Blvd, Los Angeles (Century City); tel 310/282-8870. At Beverly Glen Blvd. **French.** Summery Mediterranean restaurant, created by legendary owner Bernard Jacoupy, with original impressionist paintings and playfully hand-painted dinner plates. Chef Jean Pierre Bosc's California-French Provençal cuisine uses spectacular sauces and reductions for healthy dishes, like gazpacho and tomato-and-seabass tart. Also on the menu are special steak dishes and a duck confit with cabbage, caramelized apple, and peppercorn sauce. **FYI:** Reservations recommended. Combo/jazz/piano. Dress code. **Open:** Lunch Mon–Fri 11:30am–2:30pm; dinner Tues–Thurs 6:30–10:30pm, Fri–Sat 6pm–midnight. Closed some hols. **Prices:** Main courses $9.50–$21.50. Maj CC. ♥ ▼ VP &

⑤ **Mandarette**, 8386 Beverly Blvd, Los Angeles; tel 213/655-6115. **Chinese.** High ceilings and minimalist, modern decor with subtle lighting. This restaurant introduced the concept of an Asian menu to Los Angeles. Helpful staff presents light, inexpensive gourmet versions of regional dishes, such as Phan rice with smoked chicken or roast duck, eggplant with pork, and green beans with ginger and sesame oil. **FYI:** Reservations recommended. Beer and wine only. **Open:** HS June–Sept lunch Mon–Fri 11am–3pm; dinner Sun–Thurs 5–10:30pm, Fri–Sat 5–11:30pm. Reduced hours off-season. Closed July 4. **Prices:** Main courses $5.25–$9.50. Ltd CC. ▦ 🚗

The Milky Way, 9108 W Pico Blvd, Los Angeles; tel 310/859-0004. **Kosher.** A friendly, cozy place with soothing classical music on tape and Steven Spielberg's poster collection down the back hall. The tiny firecracker hostess, Spielberg's mom Leah Adler, schmoozes with everyone. Kosher specialties (dairy and fish but no meat) include Santa Fe and Pizza de Lox pizzas, salmon roulades, and cabbage rolls. Family-recipe cheesecake for dessert. **FYI:** Reservations recommended. Beer and wine only. **Open:** Lunch Sun–Thurs 11:30am–2:30pm, Fri 11:30am–2pm; dinner Sun–Thurs 5:30–8:30pm. **Prices:** Main courses $9.50–$12.50. Maj CC. &

Mortons, 8764 Melrose Ave, Los Angeles; tel 310/276-5205. **New American.** This is Hard Rock Cafe owner Peter Morton's room for adults. The airy barn of a building is filled with oversized plants, paintings, and power producers. Mortons has more room for non-celebrities since the move across the street, although Monday night is still big-star dinner time. Sweet corn pancakes with grilled lobster, chives and crème fraîche, pear and goat cheese salad with bitter greens, T-bone steak. **FYI:** Reservations recommended. **Open:** Lunch Mon–Fri noon–2:30pm; dinner Mon–Sat 6–11pm. Closed some hols. **Prices:** Main courses $17–$28. Maj CC. VP &

The Original Pantry, 877 S Figuero St, Los Angeles (Downtown); tel 213/972-9279. **American.** A landmark of early Los Angeles, with dark wood panelling and a scruffy Formica counter. Huge portions of meatloaf, steak, corned beef and cabbage, and short ribs. **FYI:** Reservations not accepted. No liquor license. **Open:** Daily 24 hrs. **Prices:** Main courses $4.85–$10.40. No CC. ■ 🕧 &

Otto Rothchilds Bar and Grill, in Los Angeles Music Center, 135 N Grand Ave, Los Angeles (Downtown); tel 213/972-7322.

Continental/American. A convenient place for pre- and post-theater dining, located downtown. Steps lead down from the music center square to the large, clubby, brasserie-style restaurant, where you can get prime rib, grilled fish, pasta, and salads. **FYI:** Reservations recommended. **Open:** Daily 11:30am–midnight. **Prices:** Main courses $14.95–$24.95. Maj CC. ♿

Pacific Dining Car, 1310 W 6th St, Los Angeles; tel 213/483-6000. **Steak/American.** Landmark restaurant since 1921, with a dated but elegant atmosphere reminiscent of an old railroad dining car. Specialties include steaks, chops, rack of lamb, and lobster. Also at: 2700 Wilshire Blvd, Santa Monica (310/453-4000). **FYI:** Reservations recommended. **Open:** HS Sept–May daily 24 hrs. Reduced hours off-season. **Prices:** Main courses $20–$34. Maj CC. 🕙 VP ♿

♣ **Patina**, 5955 Melrose Ave, Los Angeles; tel 213/467-1108. **Californian/French.** Features 3 intimate dining rooms, decorated with understated elegance. Considered one of the best restaurants in the city. Try the Santa Barbara shrimp and the peppered tournedos of tuna with Chinese greens and ponzu sauce. **FYI:** Reservations recommended. **Open:** Lunch Tues–Fri 11:30am–2:30pm; dinner Sun–Thurs 6–9:30pm, Fri 6–10:30pm, Sat 5:30–10:30pm. Closed some hols. **Prices:** Main courses $22–$25. Maj CC. ♥ VP ♿

Philippe the Original, 1001 N Alameda St, Los Angeles; tel 213/628-3781. **Pub/American.** The oldest restaurant in Los Angeles, this landmark still offers coffee at 10¢ a cup. The decor is downright grungy, with sawdust on the floor, long Formica tables, and brown walls. But the food is great and well worth a trip downtown. Known for their french dip sandwich, they also have other sandwiches and potato salad, coleslaw, soups, and pies. **FYI:** Reservations not accepted. Beer and wine only. **Open:** Daily 6am–10pm. Closed some hols. **Prices:** Main courses $3.55–$3.85. No CC. ▆ ♿

The Restaurant, in Hotel Bel-Air, 701 Stone Canyon Rd, Los Angeles; tel 310/472-1211. 1½ mi W of Beverly Hills. Sunset Blvd exit off I-405. **Continental.** Set in a private park bordering Bel-Air estates. There's a cabana-style patio for outdoor dining. Menu features cuisines of the Americas, the Mediterranean, and California—a medley of unusual, seasonal ingredients. The daily menu may include roasted duck breast with creamy citrus polenta or pistachio-crusted striped bass with wild rice, wilted spinach, pancetta, and basil in Dijon sauce. **FYI:** Reservations recommended. Children's menu. Jacket required. **Open:** Breakfast daily 7–10:30am; lunch daily noon–2:30pm; dinner daily 6:30–10:30pm; brunch Sun 11am–2:30pm. **Prices:** Main courses $20–$22. Maj CC. ♥ 🖼 VP ♿

♣ **Rex Il Ristorante**, 617 S Olive St, Los Angeles; tel 213/627-2300. **Italian.** A split-level, art deco–style restaurant reminiscent of a 1930s ocean liner, located in a landmark downtown building. It features elegant, formal service, a piano, and dancing on a black marble floor. Chicken cacciatore, fettuccine, split-pea soup, tiramisù. **FYI:** Reservations recommended. Piano/singer. Jacket required. **Open:** Lunch Thurs–Fri noon–2pm; dinner Mon–Sat 6–10pm. Closed some hols. **Prices:** Main courses $18–$28; PF dinner $55–$70. Maj CC. VP ♿

⑤ **Sonora Cafe**, 180 S La Brea at 2nd St, Los Angeles; tel 213/857-1800. **Southwestern.** Southwestern cuisine with intriguing German and French touches, served amid stucco walls adorned with southwestern art. Specialties include blue-corn chile rellenos, duck tamales with guajillo chile sauce, and crab and wild Oregon mushroom enchilada with smoked chipotle cream sauce. **FYI:** Reservations recommended. Dress code. **Open:** Lunch Mon–Fri 11:30am–2:30pm; dinner Sun 3–9pm, Mon–Thurs 5:30–10pm, Fri–Sat 5:30–11pm; brunch Sat–Sun 10am–3pm. Closed some hols. **Prices:** Main courses $14–$24. Maj CC. ⛴ 🖼 VP ♿

Tokyo Kaikan, 225 S San Pedro St, Los Angeles (Little Tokyo); tel 213/489-1333. **Japanese.** The tropical atmosphere is reminiscent of a country inn, with several intimate dining rooms separated by bamboo and reed walls. Very busy lunch spot in downtown location, with sushi bar, shabu-shabu bar, and cocktail lounge. **FYI:** Reservations recommended. **Open:** Lunch Mon–Fri 11:30am–2pm; dinner Mon–Sat 6–10:30pm. Closed some hols. **Prices:** Main courses $16.90–$40. Maj CC. VP ♿

Water Grill, 544 S Grand Ave, Los Angeles (Downtown); tel 213/891-0900. **Seafood.** Upscale dining room is a good choice for business lunches and dinner, offering lobster, several salmon choices, and a wide variety of other seafood. **FYI:** Reservations recommended. **Open:** Lunch Mon–Fri 11:30am–5pm; dinner Mon–Tues 5–9pm, Wed–Sat 5–10pm, Sun 4:30–9pm. Closed some hols. **Prices:** Main courses $15–$25. Maj CC. VP ♿

Attractions 💼

MUSEUMS

Los Angeles County Museum of Art, 5905 Wilshire Blvd; tel 213/857-6111. The complex consists of 5 modern buildings, all built around a central plaza. The Ahmanson Building houses the permanent collection. Galleries for prints, drawings, and photographs are in the adjacent Hammer Building. The Robert O Anderson Building features mainly 20th-century painting and sculpture, and also houses major special loan exhibitions. The Leo S Bing Center has a 600-seat theater and a 116-seat auditorium. The Pavilion for Japanese Art houses the internationally known Shin'enkan collection of Edo Period (1615–1865), and there are 2 sculpture gardens. Free guided tours daily (phone 213/857-6108 for details). Free admission second Wed of every month. **Open:** Wed–Thurs 10am–5pm, Fri 10am–9pm, Sat–Sun 11am–6pm. Closed some hols. $$$

Natural History Museum of Los Angeles County, 900 Exposition Blvd (Exposition Park); tel 213/744-3466 or 744-3414. The largest natural history museum in the West, this facility houses a seemingly endless array of exhibits chronicling the history of the Earth and its environment from 600 million years ago to the present day. Permanent exhibits include a walk-through vault containing priceless gems, a Children's Discovery Center, insect zoo, and a state-of-the-art Bird Hall. Free guided tours daily at 1pm. **Open:** Tues–Sun 10am–5pm. Closed some hols. $$

Los Angeles Children's Museum, 310 N Main St; tel 213/687-8800. An interactive, fun environment where children learn by doing, the museum is geared toward kids ages 2–10. Areas for exploration include an art studio, a city street scene, TV and recording studios, a water exhibit, and giant foam-filled, Velcro-edged building blocks in Sticky City. In addition, there are all kinds of special activities and workshops, and a theater for children where live performances or special productions are scheduled every weekend. *The museum is closed to the public on weekdays during the school year.* **Open:** Summer, Tues–Fri 11:30am–5pm, Sat–Sun 10am–5pm; fall–spring, Sat–Sun 10am–5pm. Closed some hols. $$

Southwest Museum, 234 Museum Dr; tel 213/221-2164 or 221-2163. Founded in 1907, this is Los Angeles's oldest art museum. It contains one of the finest collections of Native American art and artifacts in the United States, complete with a Cheyenne summer tepee, rare paintings, weapons, moccasins, and other artifacts. Major exhibit spaces are dedicated to the art and culture of Native American groups of the Northwest Coast, the Plains, California, and the Southwest. Three exhibit halls house rotating and traveling exhibits, and an entire wing is devoted to a changing display of more than 400 examples of native North American basketry from the museum's 11,000-piece collection. Guided tours are available on weekends. **Open:** Tues–Sun 11am–5pm. $$

Charles F Lummis Home (*El Alisal*), 200 E Avenue 43; tel 213/222-0546. Charles F Lummis, founder of the Southwest Museum, built this rugged 2-story building himself, using rocks from a nearby arroyo and telegraph poles purchased from the Santa Fe Railroad. Called El Alisal (meaning "place of the sycamores"), Lummis's home became a cultural center for many famous people in the literary, theatrical, political, and arts worlds during the early 1900s.

The house is now occupied by the Historical Society of Southern California, which offers guided tours of the house and garden on request. The attractive, 2-acre gardens surrounding the house were designed to promote water conservation; an experimental yarrow meadow fronting the house's entry court is a substitute for a water-consuming lawn. **Open:** Sat–Sun 1–4pm. Free.

Gene Autry Western Heritage Museum, 4700 Western Heritage Way (Griffith Park); tel 213/667-2000. Fronted by a life-size bronze sculpture of Autry and his horse, Champion, this museum houses one of the most comprehensive collections of Western nostalgia in the world. More than 16,000 artifacts and art pieces, including Gene Autry's personal treasures, illustrate the American West, as well as the romanticism with which it was viewed by artists, authors, and the entertainment industry. Many exhibits were designed by Walt Disney Imagineering. Also included are the *Los Angeles Times* Children's Discovery Gallery, with interactive exhibits, and the Spirit of Community Gallery, which emphasizes the ethnic diversity of the West, including Mormons, Chinese, Germans, and others. **Open:** Tues–Sun 10am–5pm. Closed some hols. $$$

Wells Fargo History Museum, 333 S Grand Ave; tel 213/253-7166. This museum highlights the history of Wells Fargo and its impact on California and the American West. Among the artifacts and exhibits are a 19th-century Concord stagecoach; the Challenge Nugget—a 2-pound lump of 76% pure gold; audiovisual room with films; and mining entrepreneur and Wells Fargo agent Sam Dorsey's gold collection. **Open:** Mon–Fri 9am–5pm. Closed some hols. Free.

OTHER ATTRACTIONS

Warner Brothers Studios, Olive Ave at Hollywood Way (Burbank); tel 818/954-1744. Warner Brothers offers a studio tour that is probably the most comprehensive and intimate around. Called the VIP Tour, it takes only 12 people per group, who look in on actual facilities to watch real actors and technicians at work, whether it is a music score being recorded, a show being edited, or a scene being shot. Because actual production is involved, tours change day to day, and there is no set itinerary. Reservations are recommended; children under 10 are not admitted. **Open:** Mon–Fri 9, 10, and 11am and 1, 2, and 3pm. Closed some hols. $$$$

Descanso Gardens, 1418 Descanso Dr (La Cañada); tel 818/952-4402 or 952-4400 (recorded info). Purchased by Los Angeles County in 1953, Descanso Gardens is famous for the world's largest camelia garden (there are 600 different varieties). The 4-acre rose garden includes some varieties dating back 2,000 years. Each season features different plants. A Japanese-style tea house (open Tuesday–Sunday 11am–4pm) is surrounded by pools, waterfalls, and a rock garden. Free guided walking tours are offered every Sunday at 1pm; guided tram tours (additional fee charged) run Tuesday–Friday at 1, 2, and 3pm, and Saturday–Sunday at 11am. **Open:** Daily 9am–4:30pm. $

Griffith Park; tel 213/665-5188. Accessible via I-5 (Griffith Park or Zoo Dr exits). Home of the Los Angeles Zoo and the Griffith Observatory (see both below), the park's facilities include golf courses, a bird sanctuary, tennis courts, a huge swimming pool, picnic areas, an old-fashioned merry-go-round, and large expanses of wilderness. Free.

Griffith Observatory, 2800 E Observatory Rd (Griffith Park); tel 213/663-8171 (Sky Report) or 664-1181. Located on the south slope of Mt Hollywood, this observatory's 12-inch telescope is one of the largest in California available for use by the public. Before nightfall, guests can enjoy the exhibits in the observatory's Hall of Science or see a planetarium or laser show (phone for schedule; children under 5 admitted only on weekends to the 1:30pm show). **Open:** Summer, daily 12:30–9:45pm; fall–spring, Tues–Fri 2–10pm, Sun 12:30–10pm. $$$

Los Angeles Zoo, 5333 Zoo Dr (Griffith Park); tel 213/666-4090. A zoo with a "cast of thousands," including more than 2,000 mammals, birds, and reptiles. Habitats are divided by continent: North America, South America, Africa, Eurasia, and Australia. The research facility houses more than 50 endangered species. Adventure Island, the children's zoo, looks nothing like a zoo—its 4 distinct habitats are created amid mountains, meadows, deserts, and shorelines. There is an aviary, a tidepool, petting zoo, animal nursery, and outdoor theater for animal performances. **Open:** Daily 10am–5pm. Closed Dec 25. $$$

PROFESSIONAL SPORTS

Dodger Stadium, 1000 Elysian Park Ave; tel 213/224-1500. The LA **Dodgers** major league baseball team plays home games here during the mid-April–early October season. $$$$

Great Western Forum, 3900 W Manchester Ave (Inglewood); tel 213/419-3100. The Forum is the home of the NBA's Los Angeles **Lakers** and the Los Angeles **Kings** of the NHL. Both teams' seasons run from about October–June. $$$$

Los Angeles Memorial Coliseum, 3911 S Figueroa St (Exposition Park); tel 213/747-7111. The Coliseum hosts home games of the NFL's LA **Raiders,** as well as college football games featuring USC, from September–December. $$$$

Sports Arena at Exposition Park, 3911 S Figueroa St; tel 213/748-8000. Part of the same complex as the Coliseum, the Sports Arena is home court for the Los Angeles **Clippers,** also of the NBA. $$$$

LOS ANGELES INTERNATIONAL AIRPORT

See **El Segundo, Hawthorne, Los Angeles**

LOS GATOS

Map page M-2, D2

Hotels 🏨

≣≣≣ **La Hacienda Inn Hotel**, 18840 Saratoga–Los Gatos Rd, Los Gatos, CA 95030; tel 408/354-9230 or toll free 800/235-4570; fax 408/354-7590. A lovely oasis near the Santa Cruz Mountains. Lots of rustic charm. **Rooms:** 21 rms and stes. CI 2pm/CO noon. Cathedral ceilings, redwood walls, skylights, and custom furnishings. **Amenities:** 🛗 🔥 🗑 A/C, TV, refrig. All units w/terraces, some w/fireplaces. **Services:** ✕ 🖾 ↵ Babysitting. **Facilities:** 🗗 🔟 1 rst, 1 bar (w/entertainment), whirlpool, washer/dryer. **Rates (CP):** $78–$105 S; $83–$110 D; from $84 ste. Extra person $10. Children under 6 stay free. Spec packages avail. Pking: Outdoor, free. Maj CC.

≣ **Los Gatos Lodge**, 50 Saratoga Ave, Los Gatos, CA 95032; tel 408/354-3300 or toll free 800/322-8811, 800/231-8676 in CA; fax 408/354-5451. 12 mi SW of San Jose. E Los Gatos exit off Calif 17; go over overpass; right at Alberta. Grounds are spacious and appealing, but the hotel itself needs some renovation. **Rooms:** 120 rms, stes, and effic. CI 3pm/CO noon. Nonsmoking rms avail. **Amenities:** 🛗 🖭 TV. No A/C. Some units w/terraces, 1 w/fireplace. **Services:** ✕ 🖱 🖾 ↵ 🕭 Car-rental desk, masseur, babysitting. **Facilities:** 🗗 🔢 🕭 1 rst, 1 bar (w/entertainment), lawn games, sauna, whirlpool, washer/dryer. **Rates:** HS June–Aug $60–$80 S or D; from $75 ste; from $95 effic. Lower rates off-season. Spec packages avail. Pking: Outdoor, free. Maj CC.

≣≣ **Toll House Hotel**, 140 S Santa Cruz Ave, Los Gatos, CA 95030; tel 408/395-7070 or toll free 800/238-6111, 800/821-5518 in CA; fax 408/395-3730. 12 mi SW of San Jose. Calif

9 exit off Calif 17; right on Calif 9, left on Santa Cruz Ave. Centrally located in the appealing town of Los Gatos; needs some refurbishing. **Rooms:** 98 rms and stes. CI 1pm/CO noon. Express checkout avail. Nonsmoking rms avail. **Amenities:** 🛅 🧊 🛎 A/C, cable TV w/movies. Some units w/terraces. **Services:** 🍽 🚐 🛄 🛎 **Facilities:** 150 🛅 1 rst, 1 bar (w/entertainment), washer/dryer. Large central courtyard is pleasant place to relax. **Rates (CP):** HS Apr–Oct $89 S; $92–$95 D; from $125 ste. Extra person $10. Children under 16 stay free. Min stay HS and wknds. Lower rates off-season. Pking: Outdoor, free. Maj CC.

Lodge

🛏🛏🛏 **Lodge at Villa Felice**, 15350 S Winchester Blvd, Los Gatos, CA 95030; tel 408/395-6710 or toll free 800/662-9229; fax 408/354-1826. 6 mi SW of San Jose. Lark Ave exit off Hwy 17; right on Lark, left on Winchester. Overlooking beautiful Lake Vasona and the Santa Cruz Mountains, this hotel offers fresh air and tranquility in the midst of the bustling Silicon Valley. **Rooms:** 33 rms, stes, and effic. CI 3pm/CO noon. Nonsmoking rms avail. Some rooms have steam saunas. **Amenities:** 🛅🧊 A/C, cable TV, refrig, VCR, shoe polisher. All units w/terraces, some w/fireplaces, some w/Jacuzzis. **Services:** ✗ 🛄 🛎 Babysitting. **Facilities:** 🛅 320 🛅 1 rst, 1 bar (w/entertainment), whirlpool. **Rates (CP):** $98–$119 S or D; from $138 ste; from $220 effic. Extra person $10. Children under 16 stay free. Spec packages avail. Pking: Outdoor, free. Maj CC.

Attractions 📷

Forbes Mill Regional Museum, 75 Church St; tel 408/395-7375. Forbes Mill was an actual flour mill, completed in 1854, and was the first business in Los Gatos. Today it is preserved as a historical landmark. A large photograph on the west interior wall shows the mill site as it appeared in the 1880s. **Open:** Wed–Sun 1–4pm. Closed some hols. $

Tait Avenue Art and Natural History Museum, 4 Tait Ave; tel 408/395-7375. Art on display here includes exhibits by painters, sculptors, designers, photographers, and other talented regional artists. Natural history exhibits include specimens of wildlife, flora and fauna, and gems and minerals of the Los Gatos area and from around the world. Also permanent and changing displays of regional history. **Open:** Wed–Sun 1–4pm. Closed some hols. $

LOS OLIVOS

Map page M-3, D1 (E of Lompoc)

Hotel 🛏

🛏🛏🛏🛏 **Los Olivos Grand Hotel**, 2860 Grand Ave, PO Box 526, Los Olivos, CA 93441; tel 805/688-7788 or toll free 800/446-2455; fax 805/688-1942. Calif 154 exit off US 101; 2 mi to Grand Ave, turn right. A drive through wine country and thoroughbred horse farms leads to this small hotel with turret, dormers, and clapboard siding. Looks venerable, but was actually built in 1984. **Rooms:** 21 rms and stes. CI 3pm/CO noon. Express checkout avail. Nonsmoking rms avail. Extremely welcoming and spacious, with brass faucets, European armoires, eyelet sheets, down comforters. All rooms have a separate sitting area. Tasteful furnishings are somewhat dull. Second-story accommodations have high vaulted ceilings. **Amenities:** 🛅 🧊 🖭 A/C, cable TV, refrig. All units w/fireplaces, some w/Jacuzzis. Upon arrival, guests find a bottle of complimentary local wine waiting. VCRs available upon request. **Services:** ✗ 🚐 🛄 🛎 Twice-daily maid svce, car-rental desk, masseur, babysitting. **Facilities:** 🛅 65 💻 🛅 1 rst, 1 bar, whirlpool. Set in pretty gardens. The pagoda is popular for weddings. **Rates (CP):** $160–$255 S or D; from $300 ste. Children under 18 stay free. Min stay wknds. Spec packages avail. Pking: Indoor/outdoor, free. Maj CC. Rates drop about 20% during the week.

Restaurant 🍽

★ **Side Street Cafe**, 2375 Alamo Pintado, Los Olivos; tel 805/688-8455. **Californian/Coffeehouse.** A bohemian cafe with entertainment ranging from folk singers to string quartets and even political debates. A tea garden out back has tables under the locust trees. Fresh, tasty soups, specials, and coffees change daily; offerings might include pesto pasta, or tomato salad with goat cheese. Great desserts. **FYI:** Reservations recommended. Blues/cabaret/guitar/jazz/piano. Beer and wine only. **Open:** Sun–Thurs 9am–7pm, Sat–Sun 9am–11pm. Closed some hols. **Prices:** Main courses $5–$9. Ltd CC. 🍷 🛅

MADERA

Map page M-2, D3

Motel 🛏

🛏🛏🛏 **Best Western Madera Valley Inn**, 317 N G St, Madera, CA 93637; tel 209/673-5164 or toll free 800/528-1234; fax 209/661-8426. 4th Ave exit off Calif 99 N; Central Madera exit off Calif 99 S. Quiet, pleasant. **Rooms:** 95 rms and stes. Exec-level rms avail. CI noon/CO noon. Nonsmoking rms avail. **Amenities:** 🛏 ♨ 📺 A/C, cable TV w/movies. **Services:** ✗ 🚐 🏊 🔽 🦽 Car-rental desk. **Facilities:** 🏊40 1 rst, 1 bar. Use of nearby athletic club. **Rates:** $53–$56 S; $54–$60 D; from $85 ste. Extra person $4. Children under 12 stay free. Spec packages avail. Pking: Outdoor, free. Maj CC.

Restaurant 🍽

★ **Lucca's**, 325 N Gateway Dr, Madera; tel 209/674-6744. Gateway Dr exit off Calif 99 N. **Italian.** The place to go for lunch or dinner in Madera, owned by the Del Bianco family since they opened it in 1935. Serves old-style hearty Italian cuisine. Famous for its handmade ravioli with special meat sauce; a full range of beef, chicken, lamb, and seafood dishes are also available. Entrees can be ordered à la carte, or, for about $3 more, you get a full dinner, with soup, salad, and a serving of spaghetti or ravioli. **FYI:** Reservations not accepted. Dress code. **Open:** Lunch Tues–Sat 11:30am–3pm; dinner Tues–Sat 3–9:30pm, Sun 2–9:30pm; brunch Sun 11am–2pm. Closed some hols. **Prices:** Main courses $7.80–$18.50. Ltd CC. ♿

MALIBU

Map page M-3, D2 (W of Santa Monica)

Hotel 🏨

▰▰▰▰ **Malibu Beach Inn**, 22878 Pacific Coast Hwy, Malibu, CA 90265; tel 310/456-6444 or toll free 800/4MALIBU; fax 310/456-1499. A gem right on Malibu Beach, with a view of the ocean from every room. Reminiscent of a Mexican hacienda, complete with tiled fountain, wrought iron, and pastel color scheme. **Rooms:** 47 rms and stes. CI 3pm/CO noon. Nonsmoking rms avail. Lavishly decorated. **Amenities:** 🛏 ♨ 📺 🖭 A/C, TV, refrig, VCR, in-rm safe, bathrobes. All units w/minibars, all w/terraces, some w/fireplaces, some w/Jacuzzis. **Services:** 🍽 🔑 🚘 🏊 Twice-daily maid svce, car-rental desk, babysitting. Friendly staff. Complimentary continental breakfast. Room service from neighboring Alice's Restaurant. (*see also* "Restaurants" below). **Facilities:** 🏊30 ♿ 1 beach (ocean). Use of fitness center across the street ($20 fee). **Rates:** HS June–Oct $150–$195 S or D; from $250 ste. Extra person $15. Min stay wknds. Lower rates off-season. Pking: Outdoor, free. Maj CC.

Motels

▰▰ **Casa Malibu**, 22752 Pacific Coast Hwy, Malibu, CA 90265; tel 310/456-2219 or toll free 800/831-0858; fax 310/

456-5418. Located right on the beach, this friendly, family-run motel is comfortable and casual, decorated with pretty furnishings and tropical plants. Spacious deck with great ocean views. **Rooms:** 21 rms and effic. CI 1/CO noon. Nonsmoking rms avail. **Amenities:** 🛏 ♨ 📺 Cable TV, refrig. No A/C. Some units w/terraces, 1 w/fireplace. **Services:** ✗ 🏊 🔽 Babysitting. **Facilities:** 1 beach (ocean). **Rates:** HS June–Sept $90–$150 S or D; from $100 effic. Extra person $10. Min stay spec evnts. Lower rates off-season. Spec packages avail. Pking: Indoor, free. Maj CC.

▰▰ **Malibu Country Inn**, 6506 Westward Beach Rd, Malibu, CA 90265; tel 310/457-9622 or toll free 800/899-9622; fax 310/457-1349. Old California stucco building covered with vines and flowers, set on a hillside overlooking the ocean near Zuma Beach. **Rooms:** 16 rms, stes, and effic. CI 3pm/CO noon. Nonsmoking rms avail. Rooms are pretty and furnished with rattan. **Amenities:** 🛏 📺 Cable TV, refrig. No A/C. All units w/terraces, 1 w/fireplace. Flowers and basket of snacks in rooms. **Services:** ✗ 🔽 🦽 Babysitting. **Facilities:** 🏊80 1 rst. Pretty restaurant at one end of the garden serves poolside breakfast. **Rates:** HS June–Sept $95–$155 S or D; from $135 ste; from $155 effic. Extra person $10. Children under 18 stay free. Lower rates off-season. Spec packages avail. Pking: Outdoor, free. Maj CC. Corporate rates available.

Restaurants 🍽

Alice's Restaurant, 23000 Pacific Coast Hwy, Malibu; tel 213/456-6646. **Californian/Seafood.** In a blue-and-white building on Malibu Pier, this old California beach shack–style restaurant with a funky interior is always crowded. Features barbecued Chilean sea bass, grilled ahi tuna with fresh fruit salsa, broiled mahimahi with soy ginger glaze, grilled chicken adobo. **FYI:** Reservations recommended. **Open:** Daily 11am–10pm. Closed Dec 25. **Prices:** Main courses $13–$19. Ltd CC. ♥ 🍺 🏞 VP

Carlos and Pepe's, 22706 Pacific Coast Hwy, Malibu; tel 310/456-3105. **Mexican/Seafood.** On the beach with a great view of the ocean, this eatery features a big bar with a glass-brick base, glass-topped tables, a juke box, and beer banners hanging from rafters. Menu offers chili relleno, steak and enchiladas, chips and salsa, tequila shooters. Popular with surfers. **FYI:** Reservations recommended. **Open:** Daily 11am–11pm. Closed Dec 25. **Prices:** Main courses $8.95–$16.95. Maj CC. 🍴 🏞 🍱 ♿

♥ **Granita**, in Malibu Colony Plaza, 23725 W Malibu Rd, Malibu; tel 310/456-0488. **Californian/Mediterranean.** A romantic experience with Wolfgang Puck's innovative cooking. Fantasy "underwater" setting—a grotto in pink, aqua, pastel yellow, and greens, with tropical fish tanks sunk into the walls.

Features crisp potato pancake with gravlax, Mediterranean soup with half lobster and couscous, blood-orange granita with brandy-snap tuille. **FYI:** Reservations recommended. **Open:** Lunch Wed–Fri 11:30am–2pm, Sat–Sun 11am–2pm; dinner Mon–Fri 6–10:30pm, Sat–Sun 5:30–10:30pm. Closed some hols. **Prices:** Main courses $19–$26. Ltd CC. 💚 🍴 VP &

Sand Castle, 28128 W Pacific Coast Hwy, Malibu; tel 213/457-2503. At Paradise Cove, 3 mi S of Zuma Beach. **American.** A traditional fish house set in a small cove right on the beach and overlooking the Pacific Ocean. Dine on lobster, steaks, bouillabaisse, and daily fish specials. **FYI:** Reservations recommended. Children's menu. **Open:** Daily 6am–9:30pm. **Prices:** Main courses $8.95–$35. Maj CC. 💚 🖼 💟 &

Attractions 🧳

J Paul Getty Museum, 17985 Pacific Coast Hwy; tel 310/458-2003. A reconstruction of a Roman villa, this magnificent museum is particularly strong in Greek and Roman antiquities and pre-20th-century western European paintings and decorative arts; also medieval and Renaissance manuscripts, drawings, and sculpture, and late 19th- and early 20th-century European and American photography. Two educational interactive videodiscs allow visitors to guide themselves through the rich and complex worlds of Greek vases and illuminated manuscripts with the touch of a finger. *Important:* Parking is free, but visitors are required to phone for a parking reservation 7 to 10 days in advance; walk-in visitors are not permitted. **Open:** Tues–Sun 10am–5pm. Closed some hols. Free.

Adamson House and Malibu Lagoon Museum, 23200 Pacific Coast Hwy; tel 310/456-8432. This restored 1929 Moorish-Spanish Colonial Revival residence incorporates lavish use of the exquisite ceramic tile produced by Malibu Potteries between 1926 and 1932. In addition, the house features hand-carved teakwood doors, hand-painted murals, hand-wrought filigree ironwork, and lead-framed bottled glass windows. The pool and bathhouse, extensively decorated with Malibu tile, several fountains, and winding flagstone pathways, are additional highlights.

The adjoining museum contains artifacts, rare photographs, maps, documents, and other items relating to the history of Malibu. Gift shop. **Open:** Wed–Sat 11am–3pm. Closed some hols. $

MAMMOTH LAKES
Map page M-2, D4 (NW of Tom's Place)

Motels 🛏

≡≡ Quality Inn, Calif 203, PO Box 3507, Mammoth Lakes, CA 93546; tel 619/934-5114 or toll free 800/874-4949; fax 619/934-5165. Calif 203/Main St exit off US 395. New property. Nicely appointed but with minimal public space. **Rooms:** 61 rms and stes. CI 2pm/CO 10am. Nonsmoking rms avail. Spacious and clean with very attractive furniture. **Amenities:** 🛏 📺 Cable TV w/movies. No A/C. Some units w/minibars, some w/Jacuzzis. **Services:** 🍴 **Facilities:** 🏋 🏊 & Whirlpool. **Rates:** HS Nov 25–Mem Day $84–$109 S or D; from $130 ste. Extra person $10. Children under 18 stay free. Min stay wknds. Lower rates off-season. Higher rates for spec evnts/hols. Spec packages avail. Pking: Indoor, free. Maj CC.

≡≡ Shilo Inn, 2963 Main St, PO Box 2179, Mammoth Lakes, CA 93546; tel 619/934-4500 or toll free 800/222-2244 in the US, 800/228-4489 in Canada; fax 619/934-7592. Calif 203/Main St exit off US 395. New property, nicest in Mammoth Lakes. **Rooms:** 70 rms. CI 4pm/CO noon. Nonsmoking rms avail. All rooms are mini-suites, with attractive contemporary furniture. **Amenities:** 🛏 ⚏ 📺 A/C, cable TV w/movies, refrig. All units w/minibars. Microwave in room. **Services:** 🍴 🛎 Complimentary continental breakfast. **Facilities:** 🏠 🏋 🏊 💯 & Spa, sauna, steam rm, whirlpool, washer/dryer. Indoor pool. **Rates:** HS Nov 15–Apr 16 $90–$130 S or D. Extra person $12. Children under 12 stay free. Min stay spec evnts. Lower rates off-season. Higher rates for spec evnts/hols. Spec packages avail. Pking: Indoor, free. Maj CC.

≡≡ Sierra Nevada Inn, 164 Old Mammoth Rd, PO Box 918, Mammoth Lakes, CA 93546; tel 619/934-2515 or toll free 800/824-5132; fax 619/934-7319. 25 mi N of Bishop. Calif 203/Main St exit off US 395; left on Old Mammoth Rd. Big, cozy lobby with a ski-lodge atmosphere; decor is out of date. **Rooms:** 156 rms and stes. CI 3pm/CO 11am. "Suites" are actually connecting rooms. Family rooms with kitchen are rather cold. **Amenities:** 🛏 Cable TV, refrig. No A/C. Some units w/fireplaces. **Services:** 🚐 🍴 Special services for groups. **Facilities:** 🏠 🏋 🏊 🟤 1 rst, 1 bar (w/entertainment), whirlpool, washer/dryer. Pool is small, but whirlpool is large enough for 35 people. **Rates:** HS Nov 15–Apr 15 $64–$86 S or D; from $150 ste. Extra person $6–$10. Children under 12 stay free. Min stay spec evnts. Lower rates off-season. Higher rates for spec evnts/hols. Spec packages avail. Pking: Outdoor, free. Maj CC.

Lodges

≣≣**Alpine Lodge**, 6209 Minaret Rd, PO Box 389, Mammoth Lakes, CA 93546; tel 619/934-8526 or toll free 800/526-0007; fax 619/934-2226. 40 mi N of Bishop. Calif 203/Main St exit off US 395. Typical older ski lodge. **Rooms:** 60 rms; 2 ctges/villas. CI 3pm/CO 10am. Nonsmoking rms avail. **Amenities:** 🛅 📷 Cable TV. No A/C. All units w/terraces. **Services:** 🚐 **Facilities:** 🏌 🏊 🔟 Sauna, whirlpool. Small gift shop. Ski lockers available. **Rates:** HS Nov–Apr 16 $75–$120 S or D; from $150 ctge/villa. Extra person $5. Children under 12 stay free. Lower rates off-season. Higher rates for spec evnts/hols. Spec packages avail. Pking: Outdoor, free. Maj CC.

≣≣**Mammoth Mountain Inn**, 1 Minaret Rd, PO Box 353, Mammoth Lakes, CA 93546; tel 619/934-2581 or toll free 800/228-4947; fax 619/934-0700. Calif 203/Main St exit off US 395; at Mammoth Mt. High-ceilinged lobby with nice carpeting. Good location for winter and summer sports. **Rooms:** 213 rms and stes. CI 4pm/CO 11am. Express checkout avail. Rooms range from small and simple to huge suites that sleep 13. Some are attractive, some look like dorm rooms. **Amenities:** 🛅 📷 Cable TV w/movies, refrig. No A/C. Some units w/terraces. **Services:** ✕ 🍴 🚐 🛎 Car-rental desk, social director, children's program, babysitting. Outdoor adventure-tour service planned. **Facilities:** 🚴 🏂 🎿 🏌 🏊 🔟 3 rsts, 3 bars (1 w/entertainment), games rm, whirlpool, day-care ctr, playground, washer/dryer. Next to ski slope; guests can ski to lift. In summer, near biking, hiking, rock climbing. Flower shop, sport/gift shop on premises. **Rates:** HS Nov–Mar $80–$185 S or D; from $140 ste. Lower rates off-season. Higher rates for spec evnts/hols. Spec packages avail. Pking: Indoor/outdoor, free. Maj CC.

Attractions 🧳

Mammoth Lakes Recreation Area. A 200,000-acre district of Inyo National Forest located off Calif 203, the Mammoth Lakes Recreation Area offers fishing, hiking, boating, snowmobiling, and skiing. It includes many historic and archeological points of interest, and rangers lead interpretive tours in the summer. The visitor center (tel 619/924-5500) conducts evening programs throughout the year.

Dominated by the 11,053-foot peak of Mammoth Mountain, the area is especially centered around **Mammoth Mountain Ski Area** (tel 619/934-2571), with more than 3,500 skiable acres (200 acres with snowmaking facilities), 30 ski lifts, ski instruction, and rentals. Also cross-country trails; sledding and tobogganing; 3 day lodges; day-care facilities; shops, restaurants, and lounges. A scenic gondola ride to the summit operates year-round.

In the summer, **Mammoth Mountain Bike Park** (tel 619/934-0606) offers a variety of trails suited to all levels of expertise. Rentals and equipment shops. Self-guided trail maps available; guided tours. Hiking, picnicking. **Open:** Daily 24 hours. Free.

Devils Postpile National Monument; tel 619/934-2289 or 565-3134 (Oct–mid-June). Located just west of Mammoth Lakes via Calif 203. *Note:* Day-use visitors are *not* allowed to drive into the monument between 7:30am and 5:30pm. During these hours, park at Mammoth Lakes Ski Area and take the shuttle bus to the ranger station (fee charged).

This 800-acre monument was created in 1911 to preserve the Devils Postpile and the spectacular Rainbow Falls, which are located about 2 miles downstream. The picturesque river valley is at 7,600 feet on the western slopes of the Sierra Nevada. An outstanding example of columnar-jointed basalt, Devils Postpile was formed approximately 100,000 years ago by basalt lava erupting from volcanic vents in the earth. As a glacier moved down the Middle Fork of the San Joaquin River about 10,000 years ago, it quarried away one side of the postpile, exposing a 60-foot wall of clearly defined columns; many fallen columns lay in fragments on the talus slope below. A hike to the top of the postpile reveals that the columns have from 3 to 7 sides, their polished tops showing parallel striations where rocks, frozen to the glacial ice, scraped across them. The formation is a half-mile hike from the ranger station.

At **Rainbow Falls** the Middle Fork of the San Joaquin River drops 101 feet over a dark cliff of volcanic lava. The name was inspired by the rainbows that appear at the base of the falls in the afternoon light. Not far from the postpile are the **Soda Springs,** created by gases driven up from areas deep below the surface combining with ground water. The springs consist of cold, highly carbonated, mineralized water. Iron in the water oxidizes upon exposure to the air and stains the surrounding gravel a reddish brown.

The 211-mile **John Muir Trail,** linking Yosemite National Park with Sequoia and Kings Canyon National Parks, passes through Devils Postpile National Monument, with access at Rainbow Falls Trailhead and the ranger station. Hiking is also available along the Rainbow Falls, King Creek, and Pacific Crest trails, and on several short loop trails within the monument.

Camping is usually available at a 21-site area near the ranger station from July to mid-October (fee charged). Fishing is permitted for persons age 16 and over with a California fishing license. Hunting is prohibited. For further information, write to the Superintendent, Devils Postpile National Monument, PO Box 501, Mammoth Lakes, CA 93546. **Open:** Mid-June–Oct, daily 24 hours (weather permitting); call in advance. Free.

MARINA DEL REY

Map page M-3, D2 (SE of Santa Monica)

Hotels

≡≡≡ **Doubletree Marina del Rey Hotel**, 4100 Admiralty Way, Marina del Rey, CA 90292; tel 310/301-3000 or toll free 800/353-6664; fax 310/301-6890. Spacious, charming hotel. **Rooms:** 372 rms and stes. Exec-level rms avail. CI 3pm/CO noon. Nonsmoking rms avail. Rooms have simple, modern furnishings, and are scheduled to be redecorated. **Amenities:** A/C, cable TV w/movies, refrig, in-rm safe. All units w/terraces, 1 w/Jacuzzi. **Services:** Car-rental desk, babysitting. **Facilities:** 1 rst, 1 bar (w/entertainment). Free use of nearby health club; on-site fitness center. **Rates:** $135–$185 S or D; from $270 ste. Extra person $20. Children under 17 stay free. Spec packages avail. Pking: Indoor, $5–$7. Maj CC.

≡≡≡ **Marina del Rey Hotel**, 13534 Bali Way, Marina del Rey, CA 90292; tel 310/301-1000 or toll free 800/882-4000, 800/862-7462 in CA; fax 310/301-8167. 5 mi N of Los Angeles Int'l Airport. Marina Fwy exit off I-405; left onto Lincoln Blvd; right onto Bali Way. The best hotel location in the area, overlooking the boat marina. The lobby is small and modern. **Rooms:** 156 rms and stes. CI 3pm/CO noon. Nonsmoking rms avail. Travertine marble bathrooms have separate dressing area. **Amenities:** A/C, cable TV w/movies, stereo/tape player. All units w/terraces. **Services:** Car-rental desk, babysitting. Complimentary morning coffee. **Facilities:** 1 rst, 1 bar. Free admission at nearby health clubs. Tennis also close by. **Rates:** $130–$150 S; $150–$170 D; from $250 ste. Extra person $20. Children under 18 stay free. Higher rates for spec evnts/hols. Spec packages avail. Pking: Outdoor, free. Maj CC.

≡≡≡ **Marina del Rey Marriott**, 13480 Maxella Ave, Marina del Rey, CA 90292; tel 310/822-8555 or toll free 800/228-9290; fax 310/823-2996. Located a few blocks from the marina, next to a busy shopping center. **Rooms:** 281 rms. Exec-level rms avail. CI 3pm/CO 1pm. Express checkout avail. Nonsmoking rms avail. English-style decor, with mahogany furniture. **Amenities:** A/C, cable TV w/movies. All units w/minibars, some w/terraces. **Services:** Twice-daily maid svce, car-rental desk, babysitting. **Facilities:** 1 rst, 1 bar, spa, sauna, steam rm, whirlpool, washer/dryer. Free use of nearby fitness center. **Rates (MAP):** $79–$129 S or D. Children under 10 stay free. Higher rates for spec evnts/hols. AP rates avail. Spec packages avail. Pking: Outdoor, free. Maj CC.

≡≡≡ **Marina International Hotel & Bungalows**, 4200 Admiralty Way, Marina del rey, CA 90292; tel 310/301-2000 or toll free 800/529-2525; fax 310/301-6687. Charming wood-shingled buildings with patios and decks are arranged among well-tended gardens. Just across the highway from marina and several restaurants. Lobby is pretty and inviting. **Rooms:** 110 rms and stes; 25 ctges/villas. CI 3pm/CO noon. Nonsmoking rms avail. Bright and airy rooms, tastefully decorated in pastels, with views of the marina or the gardens. Some rooms equipped with Braille signs. **Amenities:** A/C, cable TV w/movies. All units w/terraces. **Services:** Car-rental desk, babysitting. Complimentary newspapers in lobby; passes to nearby fitness center. **Facilities:** 1 rst, 1 bar, whirlpool. **Rates:** HS July–Sept $125 S; $140 D; from $155 ste; from $155 ctge/villa. Extra person $15. Children under 12 stay free. Lower rates off-season. Higher rates for spec evnts/hols. Spec packages avail. Pking: Indoor, free. Maj CC.

≡≡≡≡ **Ritz-Carlton Marina del Rey**, 4375 Admiralty Way, Marina del Rey, CA 90292; tel 310/823-1700 or toll free 800/241-3333; fax 310/823-2403. I-90 W exit off I-405; continue on I-90, then exit on Mindanow and go left, then right on Admiralty Way. A waterside setting on the marina promenade, 15 minutes from the LA airport. Crystal chandeliers and oriental-style carpets create a clubby feel. **Rooms:** 306 rms and stes. Exec-level rms avail. CI 3pm/CO noon. Express checkout avail. Nonsmoking rms avail. All rooms have marina vistas, English-style furnishings, and dark wooden armoires accented by Wedgwood and cream fabrics. Gray and white marble baths feature excellent counter space. **Amenities:** A/C, satel TV w/movies, refrig, in-rm safe, shoe polisher, bathrobes. All units w/minibars, all w/terraces, 1 w/fireplace. **Services:** Twice-daily maid svce, car-rental desk, masseur, babysitting. More attention is needed to details; service sometimes slow or shoddy. Complimentary shoeshine available. **Facilities:** 3 rsts, 2 bars (1 w/entertainment), spa, sauna, whirlpool. Promenade is part of the 21-mile coastal path from Malibu to Manhattan Beach—a scenic (and flat) bike ride. Tennis pro on staff. **Rates:** $195–$325 S or D; from $495 ste. Children under 18 stay free. Spec packages avail. Pking: Indoor/outdoor, $15. Maj CC. Many different packages available.

Restaurants

★ **Aunt Kizzy's Back Porch**, in the Villa Marina Shopping Center, 4325 Glencove Ave, Marina del Rey; tel 310/578-1005. **Southern.** Large, barn-like building with a long cafeteria counter with country decor. One of the few southern-style restaurants in Los Angeles, it offers fried chicken, barbecued beef, and catfish, with buffet service at lunch and table service at dinner. **FYI:**

Reservations not accepted. No liquor license. **Open:** Sun–Thurs 11am–10pm, Fri–Sat 11am–11pm. **Prices:** Main courses $7.50–$14. Ltd CC. 🎱 ♿

The Warehouse, 4499 Admiralty Blvd, Marina del Rey; tel 310/823-5451. **International.** Large warehouse with South Seas decor, set right on the water. Very informal atmosphere. Offering seafood, steaks, and pasta. Lively singles scene. **FYI:** Reservations not accepted. Band/combo/harp. **Open:** Lunch Mon–Fri 11:30am–3pm; dinner Mon–Thurs 4–10pm, Fri 4–11pm, Sat 5–11pm, Sun 5–10pm; brunch Sat 11am–3pm, Sun 10am–3pm. Closed Dec 25. **Prices:** Main courses $13.50–$22.95. Maj CC. ♥ 🍴 🖼 🎱 ♿

MARSHALL

Map page M-2, C1 (W of Petaluma)

See also Point Reyes Station

Restaurant 🍴

★ **Tony's**, 18863 Calif 1, Marshall; tel 415/663-1107. 1 mi S of Marshall. **Seafood.** A West Marin tradition since 1948. Decor is negligible, but outrageous views of Tomales Bay make up for it. Tony's is known for its voluptuous barbecued oysters, slathered with tomato sauce or with oil and garlic ($4 for 6). The menu might also feature grilled sole, deep-fried clams, or Dungeness crab. **FYI:** Reservations not accepted. Beer and wine only. **Open:** HS May–Oct Fri–Sun noon–8:30pm. Reduced hours off-season. Closed some hols. **Prices:** Main courses $9.25–$12.75. No CC. 🖼

MENDOCINO

Map page M-2, C1

See also Albion

Hotel 🏨

🔑🔑🔑 **Mendocino Hotel and Garden Suites**, 45080 Main St, PO Box 587, Mendocino, CA 95460; tel 707/937-0511 or toll free 800/548-0513; fax 707/937-0513. Exit 128 W off US 101; N on Calif 1 10 mi. An 1878 hotel decorated with Victorian-era antiques. There's a fun red Victorian plush bar on the ground floor, and loads of historic photos and memorabilia. **Rooms:** 51 rms and stes. CI 4pm/CO noon. Nonsmoking rms avail. Rooms in the main building are small and share baths. Those in the garden are nicer, with fine upholstery and private baths. **Amenities:** 📺 Cable TV, bathrobes. No A/C. Some units w/terraces, some w/fireplaces. **Services:** ✗ 🛎 Twice-daily maid svce, babysitting. **Facilities:** 🛥 ⛳ ♿ 2 rsts, 3 bars, beauty salon. Beach across street. **Rates:** HS July–Oct $50–$180 S or D; from $150 ste. Extra person $20. Min stay wknds. Lower rates off-season. Spec packages avail. Pking: Outdoor, free. Maj CC.

Inns

🔑🔑🔑 **Agate Cove Inn**, 11201 N Lansing St, PO Box 1150, Mendocino, CA 95460; tel 707/937-0551 or toll free 800/527-3111. 1 mi N of downtown Mendocino. 2 acres. A country decor with flowers and quilts—very cute, yet classy at the same time. Lovely seaside setting with beautiful gardens and the sound of waves. **Rooms:** 10 ctges/villas. CI 2pm/CO 11am. No smoking. All cottages are surrounded by gardens; those near the beach are quieter. Ask for Sunshine cottage, which is pretty and has a wood-burning fireplace. **Amenities:** 📺 ⚟ Cable TV. No A/C. Some units w/terraces, some w/fireplaces. All rooms come with sherry decanters and spring water coolers. **Services:** Masseur, wine/sherry served. Breakfast in the lounge might include fresh-baked bread and eggs Benedict. **Facilities:** Guest lounge. **Rates (CP):** HS June–Sept from $79 ctge/villa. Extra person $25. Min stay HS and wknds. Lower rates off-season. Spec packages avail. Pking: Outdoor, free. Ltd CC. Midweek discounts. Add $10 for credit card charges.

🔑🔑🔑 **Joshua Grindle Inn**, 4480 Little Lake Rd, PO Box 647, Mendocino, CA 95460; tel 707/937-4143 or toll free 800/454-6353. At Calif 1. This historic bed-and-breakfast was built in 1879 as the home of banker Joshua Grindle. The innkeepers also own an antique store and have furnished the rooms with period antiques. Main house offers vista views of town and coast. Beautiful grounds and gardens. **Rooms:** 10 rms. CI 1pm/CO 11am. Each room has a unique theme. **Amenities:** No A/C, phone, or TV. Some units w/terraces, some w/fireplaces. **Services:** 🛎 🚐 Social director, wine/sherry served. Sherry and fruit in lounge throughout the day and evening. **Rates (BB):** HS May–Oct $95–$155 S or D. Min stay wknds. Lower rates off-season. Pking: Outdoor, free. Ltd CC.

🔑🔑🔑 **MacCallum House Inn**, Albion St, PO Box 206, Mendocino, CA 95460; tel 707/937-0289. Medocino exit off Calif 1. A bed-and-breakfast in a historic home built in 1882. Each guest room individually decorated with antiques owned by original Mendocino settlers. Wonderful gardens. **Rooms:** 22 rms, stes, and effic (7 w/shared bath). CI 3pm/CO noon. No smoking. Rooms in main building share bath. Upstairs barn guest room has big stone fireplace and vista views over town to ocean. Other rooms located in refurbished water tower, greenhouse, and other buildings. **Amenities:** 🍷 No A/C, phone, or TV. Some units w/terraces, some w/fireplaces. **Services:** 🛏 Masseur, babysitting. **Facilities:** 1 rst, 1 bar, guest lounge. **Rates (CP):** HS May–Dec $75–$90 S or D w/shared bath; $75–$180 S or D w/private bath; from $140 ste; from $130 effic. Extra person $15. Min stay HS, wknds, and spec evnts. Lower rates off-season. Pking: Outdoor, free. Ltd CC.

Lodge

▤▤▤▤ **Stanford Inn by the Sea–Big River Lodge**, 44850 Comptche-Ukiah Rd, PO Box 487, Mendocino, CA 95460; tel 707/937-5615 or toll free 800/331-8884; fax 707/937-0305. On Calif 1. The grounds are beautiful, with an indoor swimming pool in a tropical garden setting, extensive flower and vegetable gardens, a duck pond, and a llama breeding farm. The ivy-covered lodge is warm and cozy, and filled many antique furnishings. **Rooms:** 24 rms, stes, and effic; 2 ctges/villas. CI 4pm/CO noon. Express checkout avail. Nonsmoking rms avail. Many of the rooms have 4-poster beds, artwork from local artists, flower-lined decks overlooking the gardens, down comforters. **Amenities:** 🛏 🕯 🖭 🍷 Cable TV w/movies, refrig, VCR, stereo/tape player, bathrobes. No A/C. All units w/terraces, all w/fireplaces. Complimentary wine and chocolate truffles in rooms. Compact-disc players, free access to a 500-video library. **Services:** 🔧 🍴 🖼 🕬 🕩 Masseur, babysitting. **Facilities:** 🔥 🚲 ⚠ 🏠 🔲 🖥 1 beach (ocean), sauna, whirlpool. The beach and state park are within walking distance. Gift shop in lobby. **Rates (BB):** HS Apr–Oct 15 $160–$190 S or D; from $190 ste; from $200 effic; from $190 ctge/villa. Extra person $20. Children under 2 stay free. Min stay wknds. Lower rates off-season. Pking: Outdoor, free. Maj CC.

Restaurants 🍽

★ **Cafe Beaujolais**, 961 Ukiah St, Mendocino; tel 707/937-5614. 10 mi S of Fort Bragg. **New American.** In a charming old house surrounded by beautiful flower gardens, this is an especially nice spot for a hearty meal. The cafe has its own bakery and vegetable gardens. Menu changes daily, and may list asparagus and mussel soup with saffron, beef-shank stew, or homemade tangerine ice. Weekends are often booked weeks or months in advance. **FYI:** Reservations accepted. Beer and wine only. **Open:** HS Apr–Dec dinner daily 5:45–9pm. Reduced hours off-season. Closed some hols. **Prices:** Main courses $14–$20. No CC.

Mendocino Cafe, 10451 Lansing St, Mendocino; tel 707/937-2422. **Eclectic.** Casual, comfortable dining room, with outdoor tables. Menu is Californian with an Asian twist, featuring hot Thai shrimp, chicken Oaxaca, and many light and healthy dishes. Kitchen will accommodate special dietary needs. **FYI:** Reservations not accepted. Beer and wine only. **Open:** Lunch

Mon–Fri 11am–4pm, Sat 10am–4pm; dinner daily 5–10pm; brunch Sun 10am–4pm. Closed some hols. **Prices:** Main courses $11–$15. Ltd CC. ⚿

Attractions 🏛

Kelley House Museum, 45007 Albion St; tel 707/937-5791. Built in 1861 as the residence of William Henry Kelley and family, this house now contains an extensive library and archives of Mendocino area history. Displays include an outstanding collection of 19th-century photographs of historic Mendocino buildings as well as family portraits. **Open:** Museum: June–Sept, daily 1–4pm; Oct–May, Fri–Mon 1–4pm. Library: Tues–Fri 9am–4pm. Closed some hols. $

Russian Gulch State Park; tel 707/937-5804. Located 2 miles north of town on the west side of Calif 1. The rocky headlands and small, sandy beaches of this park are popular access points for ocean fishing and diving. There are several scenic hiking trails, some also designated for biking and horseback riding. One trail leads to a small but majestic waterfall, and weaves through coastal forests in moderate terrain. A picnic area lies on the headlands portion of the park near a scenic "blowhole," where visitors may enjoy views of misty ocean spray and magnificent sunsets.

The park contains a few fully developed campsites that can accommodate tents, trailers, or motor homes. A little-known horse camp with primitive facilities is located along the boundary of Jackson State Forest. Camping reservations highly recommended in summer; contact MISTIX (tel toll free 800/444-7275). **Open:** Daily 24 hours; may be closed in winter.

Montgomery Woods State Reserve; tel 707/937-5804 (District Office). Remote and beautiful, this reserve is near the hot springs resort of Orrs Springs, on Comptche Rd. These 1,140 acres in the heart of the Coast Range offer picnicking and a 2-mile nature trail through small but impressive old-growth stands of redwoods. **Open:** Daily. Free.

MENLO PARK

Map page M-2, D2 (NW of Palo Alto)

Hotel 🏨

▤▤▤▤ **Stanford Park Hotel**, 100 El Camino Real, Menlo Park, CA 94025; tel 415/322-1234 or toll free 800/368-2468; fax 415/322-0975. With cedar shingles, copper-clad gables, and arched dormers, hotel resembles an over-size California cottage. English-accented lobby features a large brick fireplace. **Rooms:** 162 rms and stes. CI 2pm/CO noon. Express checkout avail.

Nonsmoking rms avail. Good-size rooms feel comfortable and homey. All offer duvet comforters and oversize pillows. Bathrooms feature 2 sinks and red granite counters. Courtyard rooms are quietest. **Amenities:** 🕋 🎨 🍷 A/C, cable TV w/movies, refrig, voice mail. All units w/minibars, some w/terraces, some w/fireplaces. **Services:** 🍴 ⓥⓟ 🚗 📠 🛎 Twice-daily maid svce, car-rental desk, masseur, children's program, babysitting. Complimentary morning coffee or tea in the lobby; fresh-baked cookies and coffee in the evening. Free shuttle within the Menlo Park/Palo Alto area. **Facilities:** 🕋 🛳 ⓵³⁰ ⛳ 1 rst, 1 bar (w/entertainment), spa, sauna, whirlpool. Surrounded by hedges and brick walls, the pool is absolutely lovely, except for the traffic drone. Small workout room with Lifecycle, Lifestep, and treadmill. Piano bar 3 nights a week. **Rates:** $175–$195 S; $190–$210 D; from $210 ste. Extra person $15. Children under 12 stay free. Min stay spec evnts. Spec packages avail. Pking: Outdoor, free. Maj CC.

Restaurants 🍴

Dal Baffo, 878 Santa Cruz Ave, Menlo Park; tel 415/325-1588. Marsh Rd W exit off US 101. **Eclectic.** Dal Baffo (house of the moustache) brings Europe to Santa Cruz. Small dining alcoves, private dining room. Walls are upholstered in Laura Ashley fabrics and watercolors adorn the walls. The Italian dishes are recommended. Extra special is the veal-filled cannelloni with Italian herbs and mozzarella. **FYI:** Reservations recommended. **Open:** Lunch Mon–Fri 11:30am–2pm; dinner Mon–Thurs 5–10pm, Fri–Sat 5–10:30pm. Closed some hols. **Prices:** Main courses $12–$30. Maj CC. ❤ ⛳

Flea St Café, 3607 Alameda de las Pulgas, Menlo Park; tel 415/854-1226. Sand Hill Rd exit off Calif 280; turn east on Sand Hill Rd then north on Alameda de las Pulgas. **Californian.** Chef/owner Jesse Cool is dedicated to organic, chemical-free food. All soup stocks are made from scratch, and salads use locally grown organic lettuces and greens. Many items are available as vegetarian entrees with tofu substitutions. Menu choices not extensive, but carefully chosen and creative. Try blackened catfish with red beans and rice, or smoked chicken. Pastry, biscuits, and breads are all made on-site. **FYI:** Reservations recommended. Beer and wine only. **Open:** Lunch Tues–Fri 11:30am–2pm; dinner Tues–Sun 5:30–9:30pm; brunch Sun 9am–2pm. Closed Dec 25. **Prices:** Main courses $13.50–$17.95. Ltd CC. ⛳

Attraction 🏛

Allied Arts Guild, 75 Arbor Rd; tel 415/325-3259. Located on a small parcel of what was once the vast Rancho de las Pulgas, a land grant from the King of Spain, the Allied Arts Guild is now the site of a European-style crafts guild. Visitors can shop or browse through distinctive shops and studios amid a setting of Spanish colonial architecture and beautiful gardens. Dining at the Allied Arts Guild Restaurant (reservation required). **Open:** Mon–Sat 10am–5pm. Closed some hols. Free.

MERCED
Map page M-2, D3

Motels 🏨

🏨🏨 **Best Western Pine Cone Inn**, 1213 V St, Merced, CA 95340; tel 209/723-3711 or toll free 800/735-3711; fax 209/722-8551. A 30-year-old motel close to area attractions and restaurants. **Rooms:** 98 rms. Exec-level rms avail. CI 2pm/CO noon. Nonsmoking rms avail. Ask for one of the more recently decorated rooms away from Calif 99. One room available for guests with disabilities. **Amenities:** 🔒 🎨 A/C, satel TV w/movies. **Services:** ✗ 📠 🛎 🐾 **Facilities:** 🕋 ⓸⁵ ⛳ 1 rst, 1 bar (w/entertainment). **Rates:** HS May–Aug $52 S; $59 D. Extra person $5. Children under 12 stay free. Lower rates off-season. Higher rates for spec evnts/hols. Spec packages avail. Pking: Outdoor, free. Maj CC. Guests are given a 10% discount at the restaurant.

🏨🏨 **Holiday Inn Express**, 730 Motel Dr, Merced, CA 95340; tel 209/383-0333 or toll free 800/337-0333; fax 209/383-0643. Calif 140 E exit off Calif 99. A 1993 hotel with Spanish-style architecture. Caters to business travelers. Location adjacent to highway is quite noisy; soundproofing is inadequate. **Rooms:** 64 rms and stes. CI 2pm/CO noon. Nonsmoking rms avail. Clean, comfortable rooms, well furnished but small. **Amenities:** 🔒 🎨 A/C, cable TV w/movies. Free Showtime. **Services:** 📠 🛎 Car-rental desk. Free local calls. Complimentary *USA Today.* **Facilities:** 🕋 ⛳ Sauna, whirlpool. **Rates (CP):** $53–$58 S; $58–$63 D; from $84 ste. Extra person $5. Children under 19 stay free. Spec packages avail. Pking: Outdoor, free. Maj CC.

🏨🏨 **Merced Travelodge**, 2000 E Childs Ave, Merced, CA 95340; tel 209/723-3121 or toll free 800/578-7878; fax 209/723-0127. Childs Ave exit off Calif 99. Extensive remodeling of lobby, exterior, and rooms nearing completion. **Rooms:** 110 rms and stes. Exec-level rms avail. CI noon/CO 11am. Nonsmoking rms avail. Junior suites are large with ample seating. Some freeway noise. **Amenities:** 🔒 🎨 🎛 A/C, cable TV w/movies, refrig. All rooms have microwaves. **Services:** ✗ 🚗 📠 🛎 Car-rental desk, babysitting. Full American breakfast at on-premises restaurant. **Facilities:** 🕋 ⓽⁵ ⛳ 1 rst, 1 bar. Eagle's Nest Bar & Grill has patio seating. **Rates (BB):** $51–$65 S or D; from $65 ste. Children under 18 stay free. Higher rates for spec evnts/hols. Spec packages avail. Pking: Outdoor, free. Maj CC.

Attraction 📼

Yosemite Wildlife Museum, 2040 Yosemite Pkwy (Calif 140); tel 209/383-1052. A variety of mounted birds and animals is displayed in natural dioramas depicting their natural habitat, providing up-close views not possible in the wild. **Open:** Mon–Sat 10am–5pm. Closed some hols. $

MILLBRAE

Map page M-2, D2 (NW of San Mateo)

Hotels 🛏

≣≣ **Clarion Hotel**, 401 E Millbrae Ave, Millbrae, CA 94030 (San Francisco Int'l Airport); tel 415/692-6363 or toll free 800/223-7111; fax 415/692-4251. 15 mi S of San Francisco. Millbrae Ave exit off US 101. Very large rooms, a light-filled lobby, and low rates make this an appealing hotel. **Rooms:** 440 rms and stes. CI 3pm/CO 11am. Nonsmoking rms avail. **Amenities:** 🖥 ⚏ A/C, cable TV w/movies. Some units w/Jacuzzis. **Services:** ✗ 🚗 🛁 🍴 🛎 Executive Choice Club, a "frequent stay" program, includes complimentary breakfast, newspaper, welcome drink, and check-cashing privileges. **Facilities:** 🛠 🖥 🗆 🗆 ⚏ 1 rst, 1 bar, whirlpool, washer/dryer. Jogging/walking trail across the street. **Rates:** $79–$89 S; $89–$99 D; from $225 ste. Extra person $10. Higher rates for spec evnts/hols. Spec packages avail. Pking: Outdoor, free. Maj CC.

≣≣≣ **Westin Hotel**, 1 Old Bayshore Hwy, Millbrae, CA 94030 (San Francisco Int'l Airport); tel 415/692-3500 or toll free 800/228-3000; fax 415/872-8104. Millbrae Ave E exit off US 101; make right. Sophisticated lobby with Asian antiques, original art, and the feel of a resort. **Rooms:** 388 rms and stes. Exec-level rms avail. CI 3pm/CO 1pm. Express checkout avail. Nonsmoking rms avail. Good soundproofing. Some rooms have good views of airplanes landing. **Amenities:** 🖥 ⚏ 🍴 A/C, cable TV w/movies, refrig, voice mail. All units w/minibars. Free newspapers. **Services:** 🍽 VP 🚗 🛁 🍴 🛎 Car-rental desk, children's program, babysitting. United Airlines desk, foreign exchange desk. **Facilities:** 🛠 🖥 🗆 🗆 ⚏ 2 rsts, 2 bars (1 w/entertainment), sauna, whirlpool. **Rates:** $155–$180 S; $175–$200 D; from $375 ste. Extra person $20. Children under 17 stay free. Spec packages avail. Pking: Outdoor, free. Maj CC.

Motel

≣≣≣ **Best Western El Rancho Inn & Executive Suites**, 1100 El Camino Real, Millbrae, CA 94030 (San Francisco Int'l Airport); tel 415/588-8500 or toll free 800/826-5500; fax 415/871-7150. Millbrae Ave exit off US 101. This mission-style motel has pink stucco, tile roof, and Spanish arches, with pretty flowerbeds and palm trees. **Rooms:** 300 rms, stes, and effic. CI 3pm/CO 1pm. Express checkout avail. Nonsmoking rms avail. Rooms are nicely furnished with pine and floral fabrics. Sealed windows and central air conditioning. Full facilities for guests with disabilities should be completed. **Amenities:** 🖥 ⚏ 🛒 A/C, cable TV w/movies. Some units w/minibars, some w/terraces, 1 w/Jacuzzi. **Services:** ✗ 🚗 🛁 🍴 🛎 Car-rental desk, babysitting. Family-run with excellent service. **Facilities:** 🛠 🗆 ⚏ 1 rst, 1 bar (w/entertainment), sauna, whirlpool, washer/dryer. Restaurant on premises. **Rates (CP):** HS June–Oct $99 S; $104 D; from $115 ste; from $115 effic. Extra person $5. Children under 18 stay free. Lower rates off-season. Spec packages avail. Pking: Outdoor, free. Maj CC. Stay-and-fly package allows guests to leave car at hotel for up to 3 weeks.

Restaurant 🍴

Hong Kong Flower Lounge Seafood Restaurant, 51 Millbrae Ave, Millbrae; tel 415/878-8108. At El Camino Real. **Chinese.** Imposing 2-tiered restaurant capped by a green-tiled, pagoda-like roof. The bustling 1st floor is outfitted with aquariums, where fish and crustaceans await their fate. The quieter 2nd level offers views of the bay. Fried prawns with walnuts and special sauce, Peking duck, abalone with sea cucumber. Also at: 5322 Geary Blvd, San Francisco (415/668-8998); 1671 El Camino Real, Millbrae (415/588-9972). **FYI:** Reservations recommended. Beer and wine only. **Open:** Lunch Mon–Fri 11am–2:30pm, Sat–Sun 10:30am–2:30pm; dinner Mon–Fri 5:30–10pm, Sat–Sun 5–10:30pm. **Prices:** Main courses $8–$20. Maj CC. 📷 VP ⚏

MILL VALLEY

Map page M-2, D1 (S of San Rafael)

Inn 🛏

Mill Valley Inn, 165 Throckmorton Ave, Mill Valley, CA 94941; tel 415/389-6608 or toll free 800/595-2100; fax 415/389-5051. E Blithedale Ave exit off US 101; go west about 2 mi on E Blithedale, left on Throckmorton. Old-world charm and contemporary whimsy come together in this stylish, brand-new Mediterranean-style hotel. A block from downtown, and next to redwood-shaded Cascade Canyon Creek. Unrated. **Rooms:** 16 rms; 2 ctges/villas. CI 4pm/CO 11am. No smoking. Everything is top-of-the-line, from the Portuguese linens to the cast-stone door frames. **Amenities:** 🖥 A/C, cable TV, shoe polisher. Some units w/terraces, some w/fireplaces. Many rooms have French windows opening onto small balconies; cabins and upper-story rooms feature fireplaces. **Services:** ✗ 🚐 🖼 🎴 Twice-daily maid svce, masseur, wine/sherry served. Continental breakfast and afternoon tea served daily in the open-air espresso bar. Room service by excellent Piazza D'Angelo restaurant next door. **Facilities:** 🔟 ♿ Guest lounge. **Rates (CP):** $110–$135 S or D; from $150 ctge/villa. Extra person $15. Min stay wknds. Higher rates for spec evnts/hols. Spec packages avail. Pking: Indoor, free. Ltd CC. Spa packages available in association with new health club in town.

Restaurants 🍴

★ **Avenue Grill**, 44 E Blithedale Ave, Mill Valley; tel 415/388-6003. **New American/Grill.** Lively and loud—an upscale diner, with chrome bar stools and a funky clock hung over the open-to-view kitchen. Great food comes in large portions, from roasted turkey with all the trimmings to grilled Indonesian glazed chicken with vegetable-fried basmati rice. **FYI:** Reservations recommended. **Open:** Sun–Thurs 5:30–10pm, Fri–Sat 5:30–11pm. Closed July 4. **Prices:** Main courses $8.50–$15. Ltd CC. ♿

Buckeye Roadhouse, 15 Shoreline Hwy, Mill Valley; tel 415/331-2600. **Regional American.** An original, slick wayside tavern, with red-leather banquettes, a high-beamed ceiling, and a big stone fireplace. Prices are reasonable and portions huge. Selections from the grill include ahi tuna, and a skirt steak enlivened by roasted shallots and garlic-mashed potatoes. **FYI:** Reservations recommended. Children's menu. **Open:** Mon–Thurs 11:30am–10:30pm, Fri–Sat 11:30am–11pm, Sun 10:30am–10pm. Closed some hols. **Prices:** Main courses $10.95–$18.95. Ltd CC. 🍷 🍴 VP ♿

♥★ **Piazza D'Angelo**, 22 Miller Ave, Mill Valley; tel 415/388-2000. **Italian.** A favorite with members of the Italian diplomatic community—a slice of Italy in an airy trattoria that's always packed. Dishes include unusual recipes such as home-made bread noodles served with pesto and vegetables, or rack of lamb filled with feta cheese and mint. **FYI:** Reservations recommended. **Open:** Mon–Thurs 11:30am–midnight, Fri–Sat 11:30am–12:30am. Closed some hols. **Prices:** Main courses $7.95–$16.95. Maj CC. 🍷 🍴 VP ♿

Attractions 💼

Mount Tamalpais State Park, 801 Panoramic Hwy; tel 415/388-2070. A favorite retreat of San Franciscans, this park is located 6 miles west of Mill Valley on Panoramic Hwy. The 2,571-foot summit of "Mount Tam" is accessible to cars; bicyclists tackle the slope via the various fire roads up the mountain. The park's numerous trails make it very popular with hikers. Although primarily a day-use park, it offers campsites and several rustic cabins perched on a bluff overlooking the Pacific Ocean. Muir Woods National Monument (see below) is at the foot of the mountain, south of the park. **Open:** Daily; hours vary. $$

Muir Woods National Monument, Calif 1; tel 415/388-2595 or 388-2596. Named in honor of naturalist John Muir, this 550-acre monument is located at the south foot of Mt Tamalpais. The area is maintained much as it was before the arrival of white settlers in the mid-1800s. Picnicking, camping, fishing, and hunting are *not* permitted in the monument. There are 6 miles of trails, including a 1½-mile trail for the disabled. **Open:** Daily 8am–sunset. Free.

MILPITAS
Map page M-2, D2 (N of San Jose)

Hotels 🏨

≣≣≣ **Beverly Heritage Hotel**, 1820 Barber Lane, Milpitas, CA 95035; tel 408/943-9080 or toll free 800/443-4455; fax 408/432-8617. Montague W exit off I-880. Very attractive hotel with the ambience of an English club. The lobby is embellished with antique furniture, silver pots, potted palms, and classical music. Lovely gardens. Located in fairly quiet area. **Rooms:** 196 rms and stes. Exec-level rms avail. CI 3pm/CO noon. Express checkout avail. Nonsmoking rms avail. Suites, which have skylights in living area instead of windows, are a bit odd. Nice furniture with quality upholstery. Bathrooms are in need of upgrading. Lots of seating in king room, with full-size sofa and bench at foot of bed. **Amenities:** 🛁 🔌 🍷 A/C, cable TV w/movies. Some units w/minibars, some w/Jacuzzis. **Services:** ✗ 🍴 🚐 🖼 🎴 Twice-daily maid svce, babysitting. Complimentary continental breakfast in lobby (full breakfast on weekends), and tea in evenings. Complimentary morning newspapers. Business services available. **Facilities:** 🏋 🚲 🏊 🍽 🔟 ♿ 2 rsts, 1 bar (w/entertainment), whirlpool. Free use of bicycles. Attractive fitness center. New bar decorated in English club-style. Lovely restaurant with outdoor seating. Greenhouse. **Rates:** $97–$127 S; $107–$127 D; from $117 ste. Extra person $10. Children under 12 stay free. Spec packages avail. Pking: Outdoor, free. Maj CC.

≣≣≣ **Crown Sterling Suites**, 901 Calaveras Blvd, Milpitas, CA 95035; tel 408/942-0400 or toll free 800/433-4600; fax 408/262-8604. Calaveras exit off I-680 W. Lobby has a tropical feel, with wicker furniture, terra-cotta tile floors, and green and peach carpets. Nine-story enclosed atrium has restaurant, waterfalls, and a rock garden. **Rooms:** 266 stes. CI 3pm/CO 1pm.

Express checkout avail. Nonsmoking rms avail. All suites face the atrium, with good soundproofing sealed windows, and kitchens. **Amenities:** 🎛 ⚿ ☎ A/C, cable TV w/movies, refrig, voice mail. All units w/terraces. Wet bars; 2-line telephones. **Services:** ✗ 🚐 ⊿ ⊱ Car-rental desk, babysitting. Complimentary newspapers and cooked-to-order breakfast. **Facilities:** � 🔲 ⅙ 1 rst, 1 bar, sauna, steam rm, whirlpool, washer/dryer. **Rates (BB):** From $129 ste. Extra person $10. Children under 12 stay free. Higher rates for spec evnts/hols. Spec packages avail. Pking: Outdoor, free. Maj CC.

≣≣≣ **Holiday Inn–San Jose North**, 777 Bellew Dr, Milpitas, CA 95035; tel 408/321-9500 or toll free 800/524-2929; fax 408/321-7443. McCarthy Ave exit off Calif 237; E on McCarthy, left on Bellew Dr. Built in 1986, but still fresh-looking. A nicely run small hotel. Quiet, surrounded by farmland. **Rooms:** 305 rms and stes. Exec-level rms avail. CI 2pm/CO noon. Express checkout avail. Nonsmoking rms avail. Pleasant color scheme with coordinated upholstery, linens, and carpeting. **Amenities:** 🎛 ⚿ A/C, cable TV w/movies. **Services:** ✗ 🚐 ⊿ ⊱ Car-rental desk, babysitting. Luxury level rooms includes continental breakfast. **Facilities:** fi ᵗ🍴 🔲 ⅙ 1 rst, 1 bar (w/entertainment), sauna, whirlpool, washer/dryer. Pool with view of hillsides and farmland. **Rates:** $131 S; $142 D; from $149 ste. Extra person $10. Children under 12 stay free. Spec packages avail. Pking: Outdoor, free. Maj CC.

≣≣≣ **Sheraton San Jose Hotel**, 1801 Barber Lane, Milpitas, CA 95035; tel 408/943-0600 or toll free 800/943-0660; fax 408/943-0484. Montague Expwy exit off I-880; right on McCarthy; right on Barber Lane. Attractive hotel with a lobby overlooking the gardens, pool area, and rock quarry waterfall. **Rooms:** 229 rms. Exec-level rms avail. CI 2pm/CO 1pm. Express checkout avail. Nonsmoking rms avail. Some rooms have views of and access to garden area. **Amenities:** 🎛 ⚿ ☎ A/C, cable TV w/movies, voice mail. Some units w/terraces. **Services:** ✗ 🍽 🚐 ⊿ ⊱ Car-rental desk, babysitting. Cocktail party on Wednesday nights. Computerized driver's guide prints out itineraries. **Facilities:** fi ᵗ🍴 🔲 ☐ ⅙ 2 rsts, 2 bars (1 w/entertainment), whirlpool. Spacious pool area with palms, shrubbery, and waterfall. Guests have access to South Bay Athletic Club for $5 per day. **Rates:** $129 S; $139 D. Extra person $10. Children under 17 stay free. Min stay spec evnts. Higher rates for spec evnts/hols. Spec packages avail. Pking: Outdoor, free. Maj CC.

MISSION HILLS
Map page M-3, D2 (W of San Fernando)

Attraction 🖼

Mission San Fernando, 15151 San Fernando Mission Blvd; tel 818/361-0186. The mission, established in 1747, occupies 7 acres of beautiful grounds. With an arcade of 21 classic arches and adobe walls 4 feet thick, it was a familiar stop for wayfarers along the El Camino Trail. The museum and adjoining cemetery are of particular interest. **Open:** Daily 9am–5pm. $$

MISSION VIEJO
Map page M-3, E2 (N of San Juan Capistrano)

Hotel 🏨

≣ **Fairfield Inn by Marriott**, 26328 Oso Pkwy, Mission Viejo, CA 92691; tel 714/582-7100 or toll free 800/950-1099; fax 714/582-3287. Oso Pkwy exit off I-5; go west. Site is adjacent to freeway and quite noisy. **Rooms:** 158 rms. CI 3pm/CO noon. Nonsmoking rms avail. Clean and adequate. **Amenities:** 🎛 ⚿ A/C, cable TV w/movies. **Services:** 🚐 ⊿ ⊱ **Facilities:** fi 🔲 ⅙ **Rates:** $53–$60 S; $60 D. Extra person $5. Children under 18 stay free. Pking: Outdoor, free. Maj CC.

MODESTO
Map page M-2, D2

See also Oakdale

Hotels 🏨

≣≣≣ **Holiday Inn Modesto**, 1612 Sisk Rd, Modesto, CA 95350; tel 209/521-1612 or toll free 800/334-2030; fax 209/527-7666. Briggsmore exit off Calif 99; E to Sisk, then left. This well-maintained property boasts many features, most notably the Holidome, an indoor recreation center. A great place for families. **Rooms:** 186 rms and stes. CI 3pm/CO noon. Nonsmoking rms avail. Nicely furnished. Because of noise from Calif 99, ask for an interior room by the swimming pool. **Amenities:** 🎛 ⚿ ☎ A/C, satel TV. Refrigerator upon request. **Services:** ✗ 🚐 ⊿ ⊱ 🛎 Car-rental desk. **Facilities:** fi ᵗ🍴 🔲 ⅙ 1 rst, 2 bars (1 w/entertainment), games rm, sauna, whirlpool, washer/dryer.

Table tennis, billards, putting green. **Rates:** $85 S; $95 D; from $155 ste. Extra person $10. Children under 18 stay free. Spec packages avail. Pking: Outdoor, free. Maj CC.

▤▤▤ **Red Lion Hotel**, 1150 9th St, Modesto, CA 95354; tel 209/526-6000 or toll free 800/547-8010; fax 209/526-6096. Maze exit off Calif 99 S; go east. Central Modesto exit off Calif 99 N; left on 9th. A gorgeous hotel that is part of the city's convention center complex. Elegant lobby with marble floors, oak furnishings, and huge chandeliers. **Rooms:** 258 rms and stes. CI 3pm/CO 1pm. Express checkout avail. Nonsmoking rms avail. Oversized rooms; city views. **Amenities:** ▢ ☖ ▣ A/C, satel TV w/movies, shoe polisher. Some units w/terraces, some w/Jacuzzis. **Services:** ✗ ▨ ☎ ▨ ↵ ◁◊ **Facilities:** ▥ ▦ ▣ ▢ ☖ 2 rsts, 2 bars (1 w/entertainment), games rm, sauna, whirlpool. Lap pool; Club Max, a smartly styled nightclub with regular entertainment. **Rates:** $95–$139 S; $99–$155 D; from $199 ste. Extra person $15. Children under 18 stay free. Higher rates for spec evnts/hols. Spec packages avail. Pking: Indoor/outdoor, free. Maj CC.

Motels

▤▤▤ **Best Western Mallard's Inn**, 1720 Sisk Rd, Modesto, CA 95350; tel 209/577-3825 or toll free 800/528-1234; fax 209/577-1717. Briggsmore exit off Calif 99; E on Briggsmore; left on Sisk. Tastefully decorated motel, with traditional decor of dark wood and brick, accented by artwork focusing on mallard ducks. **Rooms:** 126 rms and stes. Exec-level rms avail. CI 3pm/CO noon. Nonsmoking rms avail. Rooms are clean and pretty. Honeymoon suite available. Ask for a room away from Calif 99. **Amenities:** ▢ ☖ ▣ A/C, cable TV w/movies. Some units w/Jacuzzis. Executive rooms come with refrigerator, cellular phone, and modem hook-up. **Services:** ✗ ☎ ▨ ↵ Complimentary *USA Today* Monday–Saturday. **Facilities:** ▥ ▣ ☖ 1 rst, whirlpool. Guest may use nearby fitness center for $5. Vintage Faire shopping mall is 1½ miles away. **Rates:** $70–$80 S; $75–$85 D; from $80 ste. Extra person $5. Children under 16 stay free. Spec packages avail. Pking: Outdoor, free. Maj CC.

▤▤ **Days Inn**, 1312 McHenry Ave, Modesto, CA 95350; tel 209/527-1010 or toll free 800/843-6633; fax 209/527-2033. Briggsmore exit off Calif 99; right on McHenry. Recently renovated. **Rooms:** 104 rms. CI noon/CO noon. Nonsmoking rms avail. Rooms are spacious and nicely appointed, and most overlook the pool. Accommodations for corporate travelers are separate from family travelers. **Amenities:** ▢ ☖ ▣ A/C, cable TV w/movies. Some units w/terraces. **Services:** ▨ ↵ ◁◊ Complimentary daily newspaper. **Facilities:** ▥ ▣ Whirlpool. Mexican restaurant on premises. Guests can use a nearby fitness center for $5. **Rates (CP):** $56 S; $60 D. Extra person $6. Children under 12 stay free. Spec packages avail. Pking: Outdoor, free. Maj CC.

▤▤▤ **Holiday Inn Express**, 4100 Salida Blvd, Modesto, CA 95358; tel 209/543-9000 or toll free 800/768-3500; fax 209/543-9500. Pelandale exit off Calif 99; W to Salida Blvd. New hotel with nice appointments and many of the features of much more expensive hotels. Easy access to Calif 99, but some freeway noise in rooms. **Rooms:** 65 rms. CI 2pm/CO 11am. Express checkout avail. Nonsmoking rms avail. 3 rooms available for guests with disabilities. **Amenities:** ▢ ☖ ▣ ☏ A/C, cable TV w/movies, refrig. **Services:** ▨ ↵ Free local phone calls. **Facilities:** ▥ ▦ ▣ ☖ Sauna, steam rm, whirlpool, washer/dryer. **Rates (CP):** $65–$85 S or D. Extra person $5. Children under 12 stay free. Higher rates for spec evnts/hols. Spec packages avail. Pking: Outdoor, free. Maj CC.

▤▤ **Ramada Inn–Modesto**, 2001 W Orangeburg Ave, Modesto, CA 95350; tel 209/521-9000 or toll free 800/228-2828; fax 209/521-6034. Briggsmore exit off Calif 99; right on Orangeburg. Spanish-style motel with easy freeway access; located 2 miles from Vintage Faire Shopping Mall. **Rooms:** 113 rms and stes. CI 3pm/CO noon. Express checkout avail. Nonsmoking rms avail. **Amenities:** ▢ ☖ ▣ A/C, cable TV w/movies, refrig, shoe polisher. Some units w/minibars. **Services:** ▨ Car-rental desk. **Facilities:** ▥ ▣ ☖ Whirlpool, washer/dryer. Cozy lounge area with fireplace and TV. Free privileges at nearby fitness center. **Rates (CP):** $62–$70 S; $67–$75 D; from $92 ste. Extra person $8. Spec packages avail. Pking: Outdoor, free. Maj CC.

▤ **Vagabond Inn**, 1525 McHenry Ave, Modesto, CA 95350; tel 209/521-6340 or toll free 800/522-1555; fax 209/575-2015. Briggsmore exit off Calif 99; E on Briggsmore, right on McHenry. Exterior and landscaping need renovation. **Rooms:** 99 rms and stes. CI 2pm/CO noon. Nonsmoking rms avail. Basic and slightly worn. New mattresses, carpeting, and more planned by new owner, Imperial Hotels. **Amenities:** ▢ ☖ ▣ A/C, cable TV w/movies. **Services:** ▨ ↵ ◁◊ Free local calls, free ironing. Complimentary incoming faxes and weekday newspapers. **Facilities:** ▥ ▣ ☖ **Rates (CP):** $48–$53 S; $58 D; from $60 ste. Extra person $5. Children under 18 stay free. Pking: Outdoor, free. Maj CC. 10th night free; corporate and senior discounts.

Restaurant ▦

Mallard's, in McHenry Village, 1700 McHenry Ave, Modesto; tel 209/522-3825. Briggsmore Ave exit off Calif 99; go east on Briggsmore to corner of McHenry Ave. **Californian.** A modern-day hunting lodge decorated with ducks, books, and rifles.

Comfortable, warm, and intimate. Mesquite wood is used in grilling poultry, meat, and seafood. A selection of pasta dishes is also offered. **FYI:** Reservations recommended. Children's menu. **Open:** Mon–Thurs 11am–9pm, Fri–Sat 11am–10pm, Sun 10am–9pm. Closed some hols. **Prices:** Main courses $6.95–$17.95. Maj CC. 🖤 ♿

Attractions 🎦

McHenry Museum, 1402 I St; tel 209/577-5366. Located one block southwest of the McHenry Mansion (see below), this museum deals with the history and development of the Modesto area. Exhibits include complete re-creations of a doctor's office and a general store; gold mining and firefighting equipment; and a collection of guns and cattle brands from Stanislaus County. Changing exhibit gallery with monthly presentations of pioneer artifacts or other historical subjects. Slide shows, movies; special events. **Open:** Tues–Sun noon–4pm. Closed some hols. Free.

McHenry Mansion, 15th and I Sts; tel 209/577-5341. Built in 1883 by Robert McHenry, this Victorian Italianate-style residence has a truncated hip roof with 6 chimneys and an octagonal cupola capped by an iron cresting and a weather vane. The interior features period decor typically found in Modesto homes of the era. **Open:** Tues–Thurs and Sun 1–4pm, Fri noon–3pm. Closed some hols. Free.

MONTECITO

Map page M-3, D1 (E of Santa Barbara)

Hotel 🏨

≡≡ **Miramar by the Sea Resort Hotel**, 1555 S Jameson Lane, Montecito, CA 93108 (Miramar Beach); tel 805/969-2203; fax 805/969-3163. 3 mi S of Santa Barbara. San Ysidro exit off US 101. This seaside resort has been attracting families and long-term winter guests for more than 80 years. The atmosphere is low-key and relaxed, but the decor somewhat out of date. **Rooms:** 146 rms, stes, and effic; 67 ctges/villas. CI 4pm/CO 1pm. Avoid rooms near the freeway, as they are noisy, and be prepared for train noise. **Amenities:** 🎬 Cable TV, refrig, stereo/tape player. No A/C. Some units w/terraces, some w/fireplaces. **Services:** ✗ 🍴 🛌 ⌐ Car-rental desk, masseur, babysitting. **Facilities:** 🏋 🚴 ⚓₂ 🏐 🛶 700 ♿ 2 rsts, 1 bar (w/entertainment), 1 beach (ocean), lifeguard, snorkeling, sauna, whirlpool, beauty salon, playground. A train car has been converted into a diner near the beach. **Rates:** HS May–Sept $75–$145 S or D; from $125 ste; from $185 effic; from $125 ctge/villa. Min stay HS. Lower rates off-season. Pking: Outdoor, free. Maj CC.

Resort

≡≡≡≡ **San Ysidro Ranch**, 900 San Ysidro Lane, Montecito, CA 93108; tel 805/969-5046 or toll free 800/368-6788; fax 805/565-1995. San Ysidro Rd exit off US 101; go north (inland), then right on Mountain Dr. 540 acres. One-of-a-kind property where Laurence Olivier and Vivien Leigh married, and John and Jacqueline Kennedy honeymooned. Feels like a ranch, with branding irons on the wall and threadbare-on-purpose orientals on the floor. **Rooms:** 44 ctges/villas. CI 3pm/CO noon. Set in cottages, each room is unique. Rose features 2 wood-burning fireplaces, while Magnolia 1 has a 4-poster bed. Redone baths in some rooms are an appealing blend of slick marble and old-fashioned tile. **Amenities:** 🎬 🔥 📺 🍷 Cable TV w/movies, refrig, VCR, shoe polisher, bathrobes. No A/C. All units w/mini-bars, all w/terraces, all w/fireplaces, some w/Jacuzzis. Upon arrival, guests find their name on a wooden sign on their cottage door. Kindling and logs are positioned in fireplaces. Pets have their own guest registry and amenities packages. **Services:** 🍴 VP 🍷 🛌 ⌐ 🐾 Twice-daily maid svce, car-rental desk, masseur, children's program, babysitting. Personalized pampering abounds. After tennis, for example, guests find bottles of chilled Evian waiting in their rooms. In-room massages can be arranged. **Facilities:** 🏋 🚴 ♨ 🎾 ⚓₂ 🏐 100 🖥 ♿ 3 rsts (see also "Restaurants" below), 1 bar (w/entertainment), games rm, lawn games, playground. The 19th-century Adobe Cottage is available for private parties of up to 12 people. Gardens are popular for weddings. Fitness center has an ocean view. **Rates:** HS June–Sept from $225 ctge/villa. Children under 18 stay free. Min stay wknds and spec evnts. Lower rates off-season. Spec packages avail. Pking: Outdoor, free. Maj CC. Romance and spa packages available.

Restaurant 🍽

♦ **The Stonehouse Restaurant**, in San Ysidro Ranch, 900 San Ysidro Lane, Montecito; tel 805/969-5046. San Ysidro Rd exit off US 101; go north (inland), then right on Mountain Dr. **Regional American.** Dining at a 100-year-old former citrus-packing house with thick sandstone walls, a sunny terrace, and ocean views. Chef Gerard Thompson is noted for his innovative regional American cuisine. **FYI:** Reservations recommended. Jazz. Children's menu. **Open:** Breakfast daily 8–11am; lunch daily 11:30am–2:30pm; dinner Sun–Thurs 6–9pm, Fri–Sat 6–10pm; brunch Sun 11:30am–2:30pm. **Prices:** Main courses $18.50–$22.50; PF dinner $37.50. Maj CC. 💛 🍴 🍾 VP

MONTEREY

Map page M-2, E2

See also **Carmel-by-the-Sea, Carmel Valley, Pacific Grove, Pebble Beach, Seaside**

Hotels 🛏

Bay Park Hotel, 1425 Munras Ave, Monterey, CA 93940; tel 408/649-1020 or toll free 800/338-3564; fax 408/373-4258. Off Calif 1 near Del Monte Shopping Center. Located next to a service station, functional, and fine for a pit stop. **Rooms:** 80 rms. CI 2pm/CO noon. Nonsmoking rms avail. **Amenities:** 🖥 💧 📶 Cable TV, refrig. No A/C. Some units w/terraces. **Services:** ✕ 🛄 🍸 🐦 Babysitting. **Facilities:** 🔥 👹 🖥 1 rst, 1 bar (w/entertainment), whirlpool. **Rates:** HS June 15–Sept $59–$129 S; $69–$129 D. Extra person $10. Children under 18 stay free. Min stay spec evnts. Lower rates off-season. Higher rates for spec evnts/hols. Pking: Outdoor, free. Maj CC.

Best Western Monterey Inn, 825 Abrego St, Monterey, CA 93940; tel 408/373-5345 or toll free 800/528-1234; fax 408/373-3246. Calif 156 W exit off Calif 1. Conveniently located, close to downtown and restaurants. **Rooms:** 80 rms and stes. CI 2pm/CO 11am. Nonsmoking rms avail. Very clean and nice. **Amenities:** 🖥 💧 🖥 Cable TV, refrig. No A/C. Some units w/terraces, some w/fireplaces. **Services:** 🍸 **Facilities:** 🔥 👹 🍸 Whirlpool. Small lending library. **Rates (CP):** HS June–Oct $83–$93 S; $88–$98 D; from $113 ste. Extra person $10. Min stay HS and spec evnts. Lower rates off-season. Higher rates for spec evnts/hols. Pking: Indoor/outdoor, free. Maj CC.

Best Western Victorian Inn, 487 Foam St, Monterey, CA 93940; tel 408/373-8000 or toll free 800/232-4141; fax 408/373-4815. Fisherman's Wharf exit off Calif 1; exit between Hoffman and McClellan. Wonderful gardens make this one of the prettiest properties in the area. The lobby features oriental rugs, Victorian-style sofas, and a fireplace. **Rooms:** 68 rms, stes, and effic. CI 4pm/CO noon. Nonsmoking rms avail. Beautifully decorated, furnished in wicker and natural fabrics. All rooms have marble fireplaces, and many have ocean views. **Amenities:** 🖥 💧 🖥 🍸 Cable TV, refrig, VCR, bathrobes. No A/C. All units w/minibars, some w/terraces, all w/fireplaces. **Services:** 🛄 🍸 Babysitting. Wine and cheese from 4–6pm. Tea and cookies in lobby. **Facilities:** 👹 Whirlpool. **Rates (CP):** HS June–Oct $99–$229 S or D; from $175 ste; from $99 effic. Extra person $10. Children under 13 stay free. Min stay HS and spec evnts. Lower rates off-season. Higher rates for spec evnts/hols. Spec packages avail. Pking: Indoor, free. Maj CC.

Casa Munras Garden Hotel, 700 Munras Ave, PO Box 1351, Monterey, CA 93942; tel 408/375-2411 or toll free 800/222-2558, 800/222-2446 in CA; fax 408/375-1365. Monterey/Munras Ave exit off Calif 1; Munras Ave N. This 1824 inn is an enduring symbol of hospitality. The location is deceptive; inside, the grounds are nice and well maintained, with lovely gardens around the pool. Popular with bus tours. **Rooms:** 151 rms and stes. CI 3pm/CO noon. Nonsmoking rms avail. **Amenities:** 🖥 💧 Cable TV. No A/C. 1 unit w/minibar, some w/terraces, some w/fireplaces. **Services:** 🛄 🍸 Babysitting. **Facilities:** 🔥 👹 👹 1 rst, 1 bar (w/entertainment). Library. **Rates:** HS June–Nov $79–$157 S; $89–$157 D; from $157 ste. Extra person $15. Children under 12 stay free. Min stay HS and spec evnts. Lower rates off-season. Higher rates for spec evnts/hols. Pking: Outdoor, free. Maj CC.

Doubletree Hotel at Fisherman's Wharf, 2 Portola Plaza, Monterey, CA 93940 (Downtown); tel 408/649-4511 or toll free 800/222-TREE; fax 408/649-4115. Del Monte exit off Calif 1. A well-maintained property with a pleasant atrium-style lobby in the heart of downtown Monterey. **Rooms:** 373 rms and stes. CI 3pm/CO noon. Express checkout avail. Nonsmoking rms avail. Nicely furnished rooms; some have views of the water. **Amenities:** 🖥 💧 Cable TV w/movies. No A/C. Some units w/terraces. **Services:** ✕ 🖥 🎥 🛄 🍸 Car-rental desk, babysitting. **Facilities:** 🔥 🚲 🔺 🏀 🏸 👹 🖥 👹 1 rst, 2 bars (1 w/entertainment), lawn games, whirlpool. Brasstree Lounge offers live entertainment several nights a week. Nintendo machines. **Rates:** HS July–Oct $125–$205 S; $145–$225 D; from $225 ste. Extra person $20. Children under 18 stay free. Min stay wknds and spec evnts. Lower rates off-season. Higher rates for spec evnts/hols. Spec packages avail. Pking: Indoor/outdoor, $8–$10. Maj CC.

Holiday Inn Resort, 1000 Aguajito Rd, Monterey, CA 93940; tel 408/373-6141 or toll free 800/234-5697; fax 408/655-8608. Pleasant property located in Monterey's 'sun belt'—usually sunny in summer, while surrounding areas are covered with fog. Gardeners take great pride in the landscaping. **Rooms:** 204 rms and stes. CI 4pm/CO 1pm. Nonsmoking rms avail. **Amenities:** 🖥 💧 🖥 A/C, satel TV w/movies. All units w/terraces. **Services:** ✕ 🛄 🍸 🐦 Car-rental desk. **Facilities:** 🔥 🎾 👹 👹 1 rst, 1 bar (w/entertainment), lawn games, sauna, whirlpool, washer/dryer. Monterey Rose offers early-bird dinners daily, entertainment on weekends. **Rates:** HS June 17–Aug $125–$215 S or D; from $325 ste. Extra person $15. Children under 18 stay free. Min stay HS, wknds, and spec evnts. Lower rates off-season. Higher rates for spec evnts/hols. Spec packages avail. Pking: Indoor/outdoor, free. Maj CC.

Hotel Pacific, 300 Pacific St, Monterey, CA 93940; tel 408/373-5700 or toll free 800/554-5542; fax 408/373-6921. Calif 1 to Fisherman's Wharf area. Designed like an adobe enclave and secluded from the bustle of downtown. Very attractive lobby, decorated in a southwestern motif, as is the rest of the hotel. Minimal grounds. Located near the Monterey Conference Center. **Rooms:** 105 rms and stes. CI 4pm/CO noon. Express checkout avail. Nonsmoking rms avail. Decorated in light tones of taupe in a southwestern style. **Amenities:** Cable TV, refrig, voice mail. No A/C. All units w/terraces, all w/fireplaces. **Services:** X Babysitting. Afternoon tea. **Facilities:** Whirlpool. **Rates (CP):** HS May–Oct $169–$229 S or D; from $299 ste. Extra person $10. Children under 12 stay free. Min stay wknds and spec evnts. Lower rates off-season. Higher rates for spec evnts/hols. Spec packages avail. Pking: Indoor/outdoor, free. Maj CC.

Monterey Bay Inn, 242 Cannery Row, Monterey, CA 93940; tel 408/373-6242 or toll free 800/424-6242; fax 408/373-7603. Del Monte exit off Calif 1. One of the best places on Cannery Row. **Rooms:** 47 rms. CI 4pm/CO noon. Nonsmoking rms avail. Spectacular ocean views. Rooms have bay windows and are tastefully decorated with bamboo shutters, wicker furniture, and upholstery in sunset hues. **Amenities:** Cable TV w/movies, refrig, VCR, bathrobes. No A/C. All units w/minibars, all w/terraces. **Services:** X Staff will arrange kayak rentals. **Facilities:** 1 beach (bay), spa, sauna, whirlpool. **Rates (CP):** HS June–Nov $129–$329 S or D. Extra person $10. Children under 12 stay free. Min stay HS and spec evnts. Lower rates off-season. Higher rates for spec evnts/hols. Spec packages avail. Pking: Indoor, free. Maj CC. Honeymoon and aquarium packages.

Monterey Hotel, 406 Alvarado St, Monterey, CA 93940 (Downtown); tel 408/375-3184 or toll free 800/727-0960; fax 408/373-2899. A 1904 downtown hotel renovated in 1988, with old Victorian charm. Convenient to many ethnic restaurants, Fisherman's Wharf, and historic attractions. **Rooms:** 45 rms and stes. CI 3pm/CO noon. Nonsmoking rms avail. **Amenities:** Cable TV. No A/C. Some units w/terraces, some w/fireplaces. **Services:** VP Masseur, babysitting. **Facilities:** **Rates (CP):** HS May 15–Aug from $175 ste. Extra person $10. Children under 13 stay free. Min stay spec evnts. Lower rates off-season. Spec packages avail. Pking: Outdoor, $9. Maj CC.

Monterey Marriott, 350 Calle Principal, Monterey, CA 93940 (Downtown); tel 408/649-4234 or toll free 800/228-9290; fax 408/375-4313. Del Monte/Pacific Grove exit off Calif 1 S; Aguajito exit off Calif 1 N. A clean, well-maintained hotel close to Monterey's many attractions. Ideal for meetings and conferences; adjacent to the Monterey Conference Center. **Rooms:** 341 rms and stes. CI 3pm/CO noon. Express checkout avail. Nonsmoking rms avail. **Amenities:** A/C, cable TV w/movies, refrig, stereo/tape player, voice mail. Some units w/terraces. **Services:** X VP Masseur, babysitting. **Facilities:** 3 rsts, 2 bars, spa, sauna, whirlpool, beauty salon. **Rates:** HS Apr–Oct $139–$169 S or D; from $250 ste. Extra person $15. Children under 18 stay free. Min stay spec evnts. Lower rates off-season. Higher rates for spec evnts/hols. Spec packages avail. Pking: Indoor/outdoor, $10. Maj CC.

Monterey Plaza Hotel, 400 Cannery Row, Monterey, CA 93940 (Cannery Row); tel 408/646-1700 or toll free 800/631-1339, 800/334-3999 in CA; fax 408/646-0285. Luxury hotel on Cannery Row has many rooms with lovely views of Monterey Bay. **Rooms:** 285 rms and stes. CI 4pm/CO noon. Express checkout avail. Nonsmoking rms avail. Rooms are large and comfortable. **Amenities:** Cable TV w/movies, refrig, bathrobes. No A/C. All units w/minibars, some w/terraces. **Services:** X VP Masseur, babysitting. Complimentary newspapers, morning coffee, and fresh fruit in lobby. **Facilities:** 1 rst, 1 bar, 1 beach (cove/inlet). **Rates:** HS June 15–Nov 15 $149–$199 S or D; from $349 ste. Extra person $20. Children under 12 stay free. Min stay spec evnts. Lower rates off-season. Higher rates for spec evnts/hols. Spec packages avail. Pking: Indoor/outdoor, $10. Maj CC.

Spindrift Inn, 652 Cannery Row, Monterey, CA 93940; tel 800/841-1879 or toll free 800/841-1879; fax 408/646-4532. This romantic beachfront inn has oriental carpets, tiled floors, distinctive antiques, and original art. The lobby, with its fireplace, conveys a lovely ambience. **Rooms:** 41 rms. CI 4pm/CO noon. Comfortable and clean; however, some are vulnerable to street noise. **Amenities:** Cable TV w/movies, refrig, VCR, bathrobes. No A/C. Some units w/minibars, some w/terraces, all w/fireplaces. **Services:** X VP Twice-daily maid svce. Afternoon wine and cheese. Continental breakfast can be delivered to guest rooms. **Facilities:** 1 bar, 1 beach (bay). **Rates (CP):** HS June–Oct $169–$389 S or D. Extra person $7. Min stay HS and spec evnts. Lower rates off-season. Higher rates for spec evnts/hols. Spec packages avail. Pking: Indoor, $6. Maj CC.

Way Station, 1200 Olmsted Rd, Monterey, CA 93940; tel 408/372-2945; fax 408/375-6267. Off Calif 68. The brown-shake buildings are not attractive, but the location is convenient to the airport. **Rooms:** 46 rms. CI 3pm/CO 11am. Large and clean, done in shades of brown and tan. **Amenities:** Cable TV. No A/C. Some units w/terraces, some w/fireplaces. **Services:** Car-rental desk, babysitting. **Facilities:** 1 rst, 1 bar, washer/dryer. **Rates (CP):** HS May 1–Oct 15 $69–$169 S or D. Min stay wknds and spec evnts. Lower rates off-season. Higher rates for spec evnts/hols. Pking: Outdoor, free. Maj CC.

Motels

≡≡≡ **Best Western De Anza Inn**, 2141 N Fremont St, Monterey, CA 93940; tel 408/646-8300 or toll free 800/858-8775; fax 408/646-8130. Calif 218 exit off Calif 1. Designed by a well-known architect, this is the best bet in this part of town. Quiet and secluded. **Rooms:** 43 rms and stes. CI 3pm/CO 11am. Nonsmoking rms avail. **Amenities:** 🛅 🐾 ⓩ Cable TV w/movies, refrig. No A/C. 1 unit w/terrace. **Services:** 🎿 🎩 Babysitting. **Facilities:** 🎣 💸 🐾 Whirlpool. **Rates:** HS May–Oct $55–$99 S; $60–$119 D; from $99 ste. Extra person $8. Children under 12 stay free. Min stay HS and spec evnts. Lower rates off-season. Higher rates for spec evnts/hols. Pking: Indoor, free. Maj CC.

≡≡ **Best Western Park Crest Motel**, 1100 Munras Ave, Monterey, CA 93940; tel 408/372-4576 or toll free 800/528-1236; fax 408/372-2317. Calif 156 W exit off Calif 1. Conveniently located near the heart of Monterey. Set amid flowers, pines, and palm trees. **Rooms:** 53 rms and stes. CI 2pm/CO 11am. Nonsmoking rms avail. **Amenities:** 🛅 🐾 ⓩ Cable TV w/movies. No A/C. **Services:** 🎩 **Facilities:** 🎣 💸 Whirlpool. **Rates (CP):** HS June–Oct $55–$99 S; $59–$149 D; from $75 ste. Extra person $6. Children under 12 stay free. Min stay spec evnts. Lower rates off-season. Higher rates for spec evnts/hols. Pking: Outdoor, free. Maj CC.

≡≡≡ **Colton Inn**, 707 Pacific St, Monterey, CA 93940; tel 408/649-6500 or toll free 800/848-7007; fax 408/373-6987. Calif 156 exit off Calif 1, to Munras Ave; left on El Dorado, right on Pacific St. A family-owned inn on the path of the Monterey historical walking tour, 2 blocks from downtown. Not elegant, but comfortable and well kept. **Rooms:** 50 rms, stes, and effic. CI 2pm/CO noon. Rooms are clean. **Amenities:** 🛅 🐾 ⓩ Cable TV w/movies, refrig, VCR, stereo/tape player. No A/C. Some units w/terraces, some w/fireplaces, some w/Jacuzzis. Microwave. **Services:** 🎿 🎩 Babysitting. Staff speaks Chinese and Spanish. Limo service. **Facilities:** 🎣 💸 Sauna. Large deck with barbecue facilities. **Rates:** HS Feb–Sept $59–$104 S or D; from $225 ste; from $125 effic. Extra person $10. Children under 17 stay free. Min stay HS, wknds, and spec evnts. Lower rates off-season. Higher rates for spec evnts/hols. Pking: Outdoor, free. Maj CC.

≡≡≡ **Mariposa Inn**, 1386 Munras Ave, Monterey, CA 93940; tel 408/649-1414 or toll free 800/824-2295; fax 408/649-5308. Munras Ave exit off Calif 1. Excellent location across

from the Del Monte shopping center; set back off the street for quiet and privacy. **Rooms:** 51 rms and stes. CI 3pm/CO noon. Nonsmoking rms avail. Tastefully decorated rooms. **Amenities:** 🛅 🐾 ⓩ Cable TV, refrig. No A/C. Some units w/terraces, some w/fireplaces, some w/Jacuzzis. **Services:** 🎩 Babysitting. **Facilities:** 🎣 💸 Whirlpool. Golf at nearby Rancho Canada or Laguna Seca golf clubs. **Rates (CP):** HS June 12–Sept 7 $68–$160 S or D; from $110 ste. Extra person $10. Children under 18 stay free. Min stay spec evnts. Lower rates off-season. Higher rates for spec evnts/hols. Spec packages avail. Pking: Outdoor, free. Maj CC. Golf and aquarium packages.

≡ **Motel 6**, 2124 N Fremont St, Monterey, CA 93940; tel 408/646-8585; fax 408/372-7429. Casaverde exit off Calif 1 S; Seaside/Fremont St exit off Calif 1 N. Basic economy hotel. Located close to the Monterey County Fairgrounds, it's almost always filled to capacity. Clean, convenient, safe. **Rooms:** 51 rms. CI 2pm/CO noon. Nonsmoking rms avail. **Amenities:** 🛅 Satel TV. No A/C. **Services:** 🎩 🎿 Friendly managers provide guests with information about Monterey Peninsula attractions. **Facilities:** 🎣 💸 **Rates:** HS May–Oct $45 S or D. Children under 17 stay free. Lower rates off-season. Pking: Outdoor, free. Maj CC.

≡≡ **Sand Dollar Inn**, 755 Abrego St, Monterey, CA 93940; tel 408/372-7551 or toll free 800/982-1986; fax 408/372-0916. Calif 68 W exit off Calif 1; right on Abrego. In the heart of the city, close to downtown and restaurants. **Rooms:** 63 rms and stes. CI 3pm/CO noon. Express checkout avail. Nonsmoking rms avail. Rooms are tasteful and clean. **Amenities:** 🛅 🐾 ⓩ A/C, cable TV w/movies, refrig. Some units w/terraces, some w/fireplaces. **Services:** 🎩 Babysitting. **Facilities:** 🎣 💸 1 rst, 1 bar (w/entertainment), sauna, whirlpool, washer/dryer. **Rates (CP):** HS June–Oct $64–$74 S; $74–$84 D; from $94 ste. Extra person $5. Children under 13 stay free. Min stay spec evnts. Lower rates off-season. Higher rates for spec evnts/hols. Pking: Outdoor, free. Maj CC.

Inn

≡≡≡≡ **Old Monterey Inn**, 500 Martin St, Monterey, CA 93940; tel 408/375-8284 or toll free 800/350-2344; fax 408/375-6730. Soledad/Munras exit off Calif 1 S; Munras Ave exit off Calif 1 N. Built in 1929, this Tudor-style half-timbered manse is set on 1¼ acres of parklike grounds with over 100 venerable trees. Throughout the house there are antiques and family heirlooms, as well as live orchids. Unsuitable for children under 12. **Rooms:** 9 rms and stes; 1 ctge/villa. CI 3pm/CO noon. No smoking. Each has its own personality. The Ashford Suite has a fireplace and a private sitting room. The Library has walls covered in books, and a private sun deck. **Amenities:** 🐾 🎩 Shoe polisher, bathrobes. No A/C, phone, or TV. Some units w/terraces, some w/fireplaces, 1 w/Jacuzzi. **Services:** 🚐 Twice-daily maid svce, masseur, afternoon tea and wine/sherry served. Full breakfast, in your room, the dining room, or the garden, might include a soufflé or berry-pear pancakes, plus fresh-baked scones and crumpets with homemade jam. Fruit and sherry available in the lounge round the clock. The owners will also lend you beach blankets and picnic baskets. **Facilities:** Guest lounge. Gardens are lovingly tended. Brick and stone paths wind to the rose garden, or to hammocks strung between the pines. **Rates (BB):** $170–$240 S or D; from $240 ste; from $240 ctge/villa. Extra person $50. Min stay wknds and spec evnts. Pking: Outdoor, free. Ltd CC.

Resort

≣≣≣ **Hyatt Regency Monterey**, 1 Old Golf Course Rd, Monterey, CA 93940; tel 408/372-1234 or toll free 800/824-2196; fax 408/375-9428. 23 acres. Adjacent to the Del Monte Golf Course. Well-maintained hotel. **Rooms:** 575 rms and stes. Exec-level rms avail. CI 3pm/CO noon. Express checkout avail. Nonsmoking rms avail. Large, comfortable, in shades of green and beige with modern furniture. Suite has sunken Roman bath and an iron and ironing board. All rooms have live plants. **Amenities:** 🛏 🔧 🖥 📞 Cable TV w/movies, refrig, voice mail, in-rm safe, shoe polisher. No A/C. Some units w/terraces, some w/fireplaces. **Services:** ✗ 🗝 🚐 ⚁ 🛏 🕊 Masseur, children's program, babysitting. Guests can order items from the pantry and have them delivered. **Facilities:** 🏂 🚲 ▶18 🎿 ⛴4 🏌 🏓 🎱 🖥 ❧ 2 rsts, 1 bar, lawn games, whirlpool, beauty salon, day-care ctr, playground. **Rates:** HS Feb–Oct $119–$170 S; $119–$195 D; from $275 ste. Extra person $25. Children under 18 stay free. Min stay spec evnts. Lower rates off-season. Spec packages avail. Pking: Indoor/outdoor, free. Maj CC.

Restaurants 🍴

Abalonetti Seafood Trattoria, 57 Fisherman's Wharf, Monterey; tel 408/373-1851. **Seafood.** Dining room features bay views, marble-topped tables, and hardwood floors. Menu offers a variety of well-prepared fresh fish dishes, including local calamari. "Marty's Special" has been a favorite entree for 40 years—it consists of fried calamari and eggplant in marinara sauce. There's also a wood-burning pizza oven. **FYI:** Reservations recommended. Children's menu. Beer and wine only. **Open:** Lunch daily 11am–4pm; dinner daily 4–10:30pm. **Prices:** Main courses $7.95–$18.95. Maj CC. 🖼 🖼 &

The Clock Garden Restaurant, 565 Abrego St, Monterey; tel 408/375-6100. **American.** Family-owned and -operated, this is a nice place for a leisurely meal: a bright, airy space with high beamed ceilings, a glassed atrium, and a large clock; there's also a charming patio. Specialties include barbecue ribs, veal, prime rib, and shrimp scampi, as well a daily fresh fish special. **FYI:** Reservations accepted. Jazz. **Open:** Lunch Mon–Sat 11am–3pm; dinner Sun–Thurs 5–9pm, Fri–Sat 5–10pm; brunch Sun 8am–2pm. **Prices:** Main courses $8.95–$16.95. Maj CC. ♥ 🍴 🖼 🚗

Cove Restaurant, 46 Fisherman's Wharf, Monterey; tel 408/373-6969. **Regional American/Seafood.** A good place for early risers to enjoy breakfast. Very casual restaurant with captain's chairs, vinyl tablecloths, and a view of the bay. The fish and chips is made with Monterey rock cod. Seafood entrees, steaks, pasta. **FYI:** Reservations recommended. **Open:** Breakfast daily 6:30–11:30am; lunch daily 11:30am–4:30pm; dinner daily 4:30–9:30pm. Closed some hols. **Prices:** Main courses $7.95–$15.95. Ltd CC. 🖼

★ **Domenico's**, 50 Fisherman's Wharf, Monterey; tel 408/372-3655. **Italian/Seafood.** Although the bar is noisy, the restaurant is quiet and tastefully decorated in blue and white, a color scheme that befits its harbor location. Much attention is paid to the presentation of such dishes as pasta Capri with tomatoes, shallots, olives, and baby shrimp; and angel-hair pasta with prawns. **FYI:** Reservations recommended. Children's menu. **Open:** Lunch Mon–Sat 11:30am–3pm, Sun 11am–3pm; dinner daily 4–10pm. **Prices:** Main courses $14.95–$29.95. Maj CC. 🖼

The Duck Club, 400 Cannery Row, Monterey; tel 408/646-1706. **Continental.** This brand-new addition to Cannery Row has an elegant atmosphere and beautiful ocean views. Among the specialties is Steinbeck duck, prepared in a wood-burning oven and topped with Valencia orange sauce. **FYI:** Reservations accepted. **Open:** Breakfast daily 6:30–10:30am; lunch daily 11:30am–2pm; dinner daily 6–10pm; brunch Sun 10:30am–2pm. **Prices:** Main courses $12.95–$24.50. Maj CC. 🖼 &

Mark Thomas' Outrigger, 700 Cannery Row, Monterey; tel 408/372-8543. **Seafood/Steak.** Spacious, attractive dining room with good views of Monterey Bay. A mecca for tourists, who can choose such dishes as king salmon or New York steak. The staff is very friendly. **FYI:** Reservations not accepted. Children's menu. **Open:** Lunch Mon–Fri noon–4pm, Sat–Sun 11:30am–4pm; dinner daily 4–10pm. **Prices:** Main courses $9.95–$35.95. Maj CC. 🖼 &

Monterey Joe's Ristorante, 2149 N Fremont, Monterey; tel 408/655-3355. **Italian.** Monterey Joe's is worth a drive across town, with a charming ambience, fine food, and an excellent wine list with nearly 100 choices. Lots of fresh fish, pasta, hearty soups, and pizza are offered. **FYI:** Reservations accepted. Children's menu. **Open:** Mon–Thurs 11am–10pm, Fri 11am–11pm, Sat 4–11pm, Sun 4–10pm. Closed some hols. **Prices:** Main courses $8.50–$16.95. Maj CC. &

♥ **Sardine Factory**, 701 Wave St, Monterey; tel 408/373-3775. **Californian.** Located in the former sardine processing district near Cannery Row. Plush, tasteful dining room is decorated with vintage photos of the cannery era, along with the works of local artists. Hallmarks of the menu are seafood Monterey and abalone bisque. Wine list with over 900 offerings. **FYI:** Reservations accepted. Children's menu. Jacket required. **Open:** Mon–Thurs 5–10:30pm, Fri–Sat 5–11pm, Sun 2–10pm. Closed Christmas week. **Prices:** Main courses $14.95–$39.95. Maj CC. ♥ ▲ ☁ ▼ VP

★ **The Whaler Steakhouse & Fresh Seafood Grill**, 635 Cass St, Monterey; tel 408/373-1933. **Steak.** A local favorite for 30 years. Dimly lit steak-house atmosphere with leather chairs. Features slow-roasted prime rib, steaks, and fresh seafood. **FYI:** Reservations recommended. Children's menu. **Open:** Lunch Tues–Fri 11:30am–2:30pm; dinner Tues–Thurs 5–9pm, Fri–Sat 5–10pm. **Prices:** Main courses $10.95–$17.95; PF dinner $10.95. Maj CC.

★ **Whaling Station Inn**, 763 Wave St, Monterey (Cannery Row); tel 408/373-3778. Between Prescott and Irving Aves. **New American.** Dark wood, Leroy Neiman lithographs, and almost century-old French posters add charm to this old-fashioned dinner house. Specials include steaks and seafood. **FYI:** Reservations recommended. Reservations accepted. Children's menu. **Open:** Daily 5pm–close. Closed some hols. **Prices:** Main courses $13.95–$39.95; PF dinner $27.50. Maj CC. ♥ ▲ VP &

Wharfside Restaurant and Lounge, 60 Fisherman's Wharf, Monterey; tel 408/375-3956. **Italian/Seafood.** Very casual restaurant overlooking Monterey Bay and marina. Decor's nothing special, but menu offers an array of fresh fish dishes, including cioppino and bouillabaisse; among various pasta dishes, homemade ravioli is a specialty. Desserts made fresh daily. **FYI:** Reservations recommended. Jazz. Children's menu. **Open:** Lunch daily 11am–4pm; dinner daily 4–10pm. Closed some hols. **Prices:** Main courses $6.95–$34.95. Maj CC. ▲ ▼ &

Attractions 📷

Cannery Row, on Monterey Bay between David and Drake Aves; tel 408/649-6690. Author John Steinbeck singlehandedly brought fame to Cannery Row when he immortalized it in his 1945 book of the same name. But by 1948, overfishing, changing currents, and pollution contributed to the disappearance of silver sardines from the waters off Monterey. The fishermen left, the canneries closed, and the Row fell into disrepair. But curious tourists, drawn by the author's *Cannery Row* and its sequel, *Sweet Thursday,* continued to visit the areas they had read about.

It didn't take long for entrepreneurs to take notice of the Row's location and international fame. The seaside strip's canneries and warehouses were renovated and converted; they now hold harbor restaurants, local artists' galleries, touristy hotels, and visitor-oriented gift shops. Many of the larger buildings have become self-contained mini-malls, containing myriad shops and eateries.

Fisherman's Wharf, 885 Abrego St. Lined with craft stores, gift shops, boating and fishing operations, and fish markets, the wharf remains perpetually busy year-round. But its primary attraction is its array of seafood restaurants, where hungry tourists can get anything from a simple cup of shrimp to a full sit-down meal. For details, phone 408/373-0600.

Maritime Museum of Monterey, 5 Custom House Plaza; tel 408/373-2469. Seven exhibit areas are housed in this facility located on the waterfront near Fisherman's Wharf. Serving as a beacon for the museum is a 2-story Fresnel lens, taken from the Lighthouse at Point Sur; it is illuminated and rotates on its original mechanism, just as it did at Point Sur in the 1890s. Other highlights include a 6-foot-long model of John Drake Sloat's ship, *Savannah;* rare, handcrafted sextants, chronometers, and other antique navigational instruments; a re-created sea captain's quarters; and comprehensive exhibits from the era of the Spanish conquistadores to Monterey's heyday as the sardine capital of the world in the 1930s and 40s. A 20-minute film chronicles Monterey's relationship with the sea.

Guided tours; research library with 4,000 volumes; gift shop. **Open:** Daily 10am–5pm; extended summer hours. Closed some hols. $$

Monterey Bay Aquarium, 886 Cannery Row; tel 408/648-4888. Opened in 1984, the Monterey Bay Aquarium quickly gained fame as one of the best exhibit aquariums in the world, and it is one of the largest as well. The facility sits on the border of one of the largest underwater canyons on earth—wider and deeper than even the Grand Canyon.

The museum's main exhibit is a 3-story, 335,000-gallon tank, which contains a towering kelp forest and hundreds of specimens of undersea life. Other "wet" exhibits re-create coastal streams, tidal pools, and other habitats found in Monterey Bay. A petting pool allows visitors to handle specimens such as bat rays and sea stars. Visitors also watch a live video feed continuously transmitted from a deep-sea research submarine below the surface of Monterey Bay. **Open:** Daily 10am–6pm (summer and hols open at 9:30am). $$$$

Dennis the Menace Playground, Pearl St, in the park at El Estero; tel 408/646-3866. Built in 1956 with the assistance of Hank Ketcham, creator of the Dennis the Menace comic strip, the park has undergone 3 renovations, the latest in 1988. Unique playground pieces include the Old No. 1285 steam engine for climbing, a Dennis the Menace Sculpture and Climbing Structure, the Giant Swing Ride, and the Maze. A bronze statue of Dennis himself watches over the children at play. **Open:** Daily 10am–dusk. Free.

MONTEREY HISTORIC AREA

Monterey State Historic Park. A 7-acre site preserving Monterey's cultural heritage, the park contains several old city buildings, which are preserved as historical monuments. Collectively, these structures comprise the Path of History, which includes buildings clustered around Fisherman's Wharf and the adjacent waterfront. Many of the path's best buildings are featured below; those without formal addresses have been listed with street references. Building hours and fees vary and are subject to change; call for the latest information (tel 408/649-7118) or visit the Orientation Center at 20 Custom House Plaza. Walking tours of the park begin at the center, and a Monterey history film is shown free of charge every 20 minutes.

Casa de Oro, Scott and Oliver Sts. Originally built as a warehouse, barracks, and hospital for American seamen who were left at the port under consular care, this 2-story adobe structure is called Casa de Oro (House of Gold) because miners supposedly stored their treasures in an iron safe here during the Gold Rush days. In 1849 the building was sold to Joseph Boston and Company and operated as a general store.

Today, Casa del Oro is once again a general store, operated by the Monterey History and Art Association. It is preserved as it was in the 19th century, stocked with and selling burlap sacks of coffee and beans, milk cans, old tools, fabrics, and more.

Casa Soberanes, 336 Pacific St. Often called the "House with the Blue Gate," this colonial-era adobe structure was built in the 1840s by the warden of the Custom House for his bride. The well-maintained interior is decorated with early New England furnishings and modern Mexican folk art.

Colton Hall, 522 Pacific St. Colton Hall was originally built as the town hall and public school. California's constitutional congress convened here in 1849 and penned the state constitution. Old Monterey Jail, its grim cell walls still marked by prisoners' scribblings, adjoins the property.

Monterey Custom House, 1 Custom House Plaza. Dating from about 1827, the Custom House, located just across from what is now the entrance to Fisherman's Wharf, is the oldest government building in California, although it served as such for only about 40 years. Until 1846, when Commodore John Drake Sloat raised the US flag here, the Custom House presided over Alta California's principal port. Under Mexican rule, customs duties were collected here; only after being inspected and taxed were ships permitted to trade on the California coast. The facility became obsolete in 1867, when San Francisco took over as California's primary port.

Larkin House, 510 Calle Principal. Built in 1835, this balconied 2-story adobe house was the home of Thomas Oliver Larkin, the US consul to Mexico from 1843–46. The house doubled as the consular office and is furnished with many fine antiques, including some original pieces. Next door is a house used by William Tecumseh Sherman, which now contains a museum depicting the roles of the 2 men in California history.

Pacific House, 10 Custom House Plaza. Built in 1847 for Thomas O Larkin, Pacific House was first used to house army offices and to store military supplies. Horses were corralled behind the building, which was also a popular spot for Sunday bull and bear fights. In later years, Pacific House has contained several small stores, a tavern, a courtroom, a newspaper office, a church—and a ballroom where a temperance society called the Dashaways held dances.

The first floor now houses a museum of California history. The second floor has an extensive collection of Native American artifacts, as well as a few Mexican-Indian and Inuit pieces.

Stevenson House, 530 Houston St. The original portion of this 2-story home dates to the 1830s, when it was the home of the first administrator of customs of Alta California. The owners made some additions and rented spare bedrooms to boarders, one of whom was Robert Louis Stevenson, who occupied a second-floor room during the autumn of 1879. While here, he wrote *The Old Pacific Capital,* an account of Monterey in the 1870s.

The building has been restored to its period look, and several rooms are devoted to Stevenson memorabilia.

MORRO BAY

Map page M-2, E2

Hotel 🏨

≣≣≣ **Embarcadero Inn**, 456 Embarcadero, Morro Bay, CA 93442; tel 805/772-2700 or toll free 800/292-ROCK; fax 805/

292-ROCK. Main St exit off Calif 1; turn right at Harbor, left at Embarcadero. Clean, contemporary inn with California nautical brass theme. **Rooms:** 32 rms and stes. CI 3pm/CO 11am. Nonsmoking rms avail. Attractive rooms with lovely views, decorated with photos of local fishermen and divers. **Amenities:** 📷 🛁 📺 Cable TV w/movies, refrig, VCR. No A/C. Some units w/minibars, some w/terraces, some w/fireplaces. **Services:** 🛎 **Facilities:** 🚶 Whirlpool. **Rates (CP):** HS Apr–Oct 15 $70–$115 S or D; from $170 ste. Extra person $10. Children under 12 stay free. Min stay wknds. Lower rates off-season. Pking: Indoor/outdoor, free. Maj CC.

Motels

📺📺📺 **Bay View Lodge**, 225 Harbor St, Morro Bay, CA 93442; tel 805/772-2771. Morro Bay Blvd exit off Calif 1. Older-style, well-kept motel 1 block from the waterfront. **Rooms:** 22 rms. CI 1:30pm/CO 11am. Nonsmoking rms avail. Rooms are nicely furnished in Queen Anne style, with ceiling fans and pretty quilts and pillows. **Amenities:** 📷 🛁 📺 Cable TV w/movies, refrig, VCR. No A/C. Some units w/fireplaces. **Services:** 🛎 **Facilities:** Whirlpool, day-care ctr, washer/dryer. Sundeck. **Rates (CP):** HS June–Sept $58–$72 S or D. Extra person $8. Min stay HS and spec evnts. Lower rates off-season. Pking: Outdoor, free. Maj CC.

📺📺📺 **Best Western San Marcos Motor Inn**, 250 Pacific St, Morro Bay, CA 93442; tel 805/772-2248 or toll free 800/772-7969; fax 805/772-6844. Morro Bay Blvd exit off Calif 1; left on Morro Ave to Pacific St. The lobby has a cheerful fireplace, and there's a 3-story atrium with fountain. **Rooms:** 32 rms. CI 3pm/CO noon. Nonsmoking rms avail. **Amenities:** 📷 🛁 📺 Cable TV w/movies, refrig, voice mail. No A/C. All units w/terraces. **Services:** 🛎 Evening wine and cheese; continental breakfast in lobby. **Facilities:** Whirlpool. **Rates (CP):** HS June 15–Sept 15 $62–$125 S or D. Extra person $5. Min stay wknds. Lower rates off-season. Higher rates for spec evnts/hols. Spec packages avail. Pking: Outdoor, free. Maj CC.

📺📺📺 **Blue Sail Inn**, 851 Market Ave, Morro Bay, CA 93442; tel 805/772-7132 or toll free 800/336-0707; fax 805/772-8406. Morro Bay Blvd exit off Calif 1; take to end, turn right. Attractive, clean property on a bluff overlooking the bay, with great views and easy walking access to the waterfront. **Rooms:** 48 rms and stes. CI 3pm/CO 11am. Nonsmoking rms avail. **Amenities:** 📷 🛁 📺 Cable TV w/movies, refrig. No A/C. Some units w/terraces, some w/fireplaces. **Services:** 🛎 **Facilities:** 🚶 Whirlpool. Outstanding hot tub/Jacuzzis in Cal-Japanese–style room. An ocean beach is a mile away. **Rates:** $65–$85 S or D; from $110 ste. Children under 18 stay free. Pking: Indoor/outdoor, free. Maj CC.

📺📺 **The Breakers**, 780 Market Ave, PO Box 110, Morro Bay, CA 93443; tel 805/772-7317 or toll free 800/932-8899. At Morro Bay Blvd. 1960s-style motel; dated but convenient to embarcadero/waterfront. **Rooms:** 25 rms. CI 2pm/CO noon. Nonsmoking rms avail. Great views from 3rd floor. Interiors dated. **Amenities:** 📷 🛁 📺 A/C, cable TV w/movies, refrig. Some units w/fireplaces. **Services:** 🛎 **Facilities:** 🛁 Whirlpool. **Rates:** HS May–Oct 15 $70–$96 S or D. Extra person $10. Min stay HS, wknds, and spec evnts. Lower rates off-season. Pking: Outdoor, free. Maj CC.

📺📺📺 **El Morro Lodge**, 1206 Main St, Morro Bay, CA 93442; tel 805/772-5633 or toll free 800/527-6782; fax 805/772-1404. Main St exit off Calif 1. A fun place, appointed with antiques in lobby and rooms. Good value. **Rooms:** 27 rms and stes. CI 2pm/CO 11am. Rooms have French provincial decor—an antique feel, but not stuffy. El Mirador Suite is very romantic. **Amenities:** 📷 🛁 📺 🍷 Cable TV w/movies, refrig, VCR. No A/C. Some units w/terraces, some w/fireplaces, some w/Jacuzzis. **Services:** 🛎 **Facilities:** 🚶 Whirlpool, washer/dryer. **Rates (CP):** HS June–Sept $60–$125 S or D; from $175 ste. Extra person $5. Children under 18 stay free. Min stay wknds. Lower rates off-season. Pking: Outdoor, free. Maj CC.

📺📺📺 **La Serena Inn**, 990 Morro Ave, Morro Bay, CA 93443; tel 805/772-5665 or toll free 800/248-1511; fax 805/772-5665. Main St exit off Calif 1 S; Morro Bay Blvd exit off Calif 1 N. Well kept. **Rooms:** 37 rms and stes. CI 1pm/CO 11am. Nonsmoking rms avail. Rooms are clean and nicely furnished, decorated with light pastels in southwestern style. Some have ocean views and balconies. **Amenities:** 📷 🛁 📺 A/C, cable TV w/movies, refrig. Some units w/terraces, some w/fireplaces. **Services:** 🛎 **Facilities:** 🛢 🚶 Sauna. Outside deck, outside showers, deck chairs with views. **Rates (CP):** HS Apr–Oct 15 $72–$89 S or D; from $110 ste. Extra person $5. Children under 9 stay free. Lower rates off-season. Pking: Indoor/outdoor, free. Maj CC.

📺📺 **Sundown Motel**, 640 Main St, Morro Bay, CA 93442; tel 805/772-7381 or toll free 800/696-6928. Morro Bay Blvd exit off Calif 1; 4 stop signs, turn left on Main. Small, bright, airy, clean motel. **Rooms:** 17 rms. CI noon/CO 11am. Nonsmoking rms avail. Quiet, with pleasant art. **Amenities:** 📷 📺 Cable TV w/movies. No A/C. Magic Fingers massage bed. Some rooms have refrigerators. **Services:** 🛎 **Facilities:** 🚶 **Rates:** HS June–Sept $42–$78 S or D. Extra person $5. Children under 12 stay free. Min stay spec evnts. Lower rates off-season. Pking: Outdoor, free. Maj CC.

📺📺 **The Villager**, 1098 Main St, Morro Bay, CA 93442; tel 805/772-1235 or toll free 800/444-0782. Morro Bay Blvd exit off Calif 1; turn right on Main St. Basic motel. Priced a bit high for what it delivers. **Rooms:** 22 rms. CI noon/CO 11am.

Nonsmoking rms avail. Carpets need replacing. **Amenities:** 🛅 📶 📺 Cable TV, refrig. No A/C. **Services:** 🛎 Ice available (25¢). **Facilities:** Whirlpool. **Rates:** HS June 10–Sept 10 $75–$95 S or D. Extra person $5. Min stay spec evnts. Lower rates off-season. Higher rates for spec evnts/hols. Pking: Outdoor, free. Maj CC.

Resort

📶📶📶 **The Inn at Morro Bay**, 60 State Park Rd, Morro Bay, CA 93442; tel 805/772-5651 or toll free 800/321-9566; fax 805/772-4779. 5 acres. The only lodging on the water in Morro Bay, this appealing property overlooks a marina and is adjacent to a state park. Gazing out the windows may bring sightings of blue heron or sea lions at play in the bay. The dining rooms offer spectacular views. **Rooms:** 96 rms. CI 4pm/CO noon. Nonsmoking rms avail. Rooms, furnished in country French style, are accented with lovely wallpaper and fabrics. **Amenities:** 🛅📺📶 Cable TV w/movies, refrig. No A/C. Some units w/terraces, some w/fireplaces, 1 w/Jacuzzi. Special amenities include soaps from Saks Fifth Avenue. **Services:** ✗📠🚗🖨🛎 Twice-daily maid svce, babysitting. **Facilities:** 🏋🚲🛶🎣🍸🏓 & 1 rst (*see also* "Restaurants" below), 1 bar (w/entertainment). Free use of bicycles for guests. Tennis, horseback riding, canoeing, and kayaking are nearby. Adjoining 18-hole public golf course. **Rates:** HS Apr–Oct $90–$210 S or D. Extra person $15. Children under 18 stay free. Min stay spec evnts. Lower rates off-season. Spec packages avail. Pking: Outdoor, free. Maj CC.

Restaurants 🍽

Brannigan's Reef, 781 Market Ave, Morro Bay; tel 805/772-7321. Morro Bay Blvd exit off Calif 1. **American.** Nautical atmosphere in an upgraded coffee shop with nice views and old photos on the wall. Dinner house/downstairs lounge offers views of Morro Bay. Seafood is the main attraction: tequila shrimp, shark, crab, lobster. **FYI:** Reservations recommended. Children's menu. **Open:** Lunch Sat 11:30am–3pm; dinner Sun–Thurs 4–9pm, Fri–Sat 4–10pm; brunch Sun 10am–2pm. **Prices:** Main courses $9.95–$34.95. Maj CC. 🍴🎭💟&

🍷 **The Inn at Morro Bay Dining Room**, 60 State Park Rd, Morro Bay; tel 805/772-5651. 1 mi S of downtown. Morro Bay Blvd exit off Calif 1. **New American/Californian/French.** A casual spot with outdoor deck for lunch. Fabulous views of Morro Rock. Excellent menu offers crispy crab risotto, seafood fricassee, cheese ravioli, and salmon tartare, plus a fixed-price tasting menu. **FYI:** Reservations recommended. Cabaret/jazz. **Open:** Breakfast Mon–Sat 7–11am, Sun 7–10am; lunch Mon–Sat 11:30am–2pm; dinner daily 5–9pm; brunch Sun 10am–2pm. **Prices:** Main courses $14.50–$21; PF dinner $28. Maj CC. 💟 🍴🍴💟

Attractions 🏛

Morro Bay State Park, State Park Rd; tel 805/772-7434. Among the various activities offered here are fishing, boating, camping, golfing on an 18-hole public course, and birdwatching. There is also a natural history museum located within the park (see below), perched on the cliffs overlooking the bay. **Open:** Daily dawn–dusk. $$$

Morro Bay State Park Museum of Natural History, State Park Rd; tel 805/772-2694. Located on White Point in Morro Bay State Park (see above), this museum contains exhibits covering various topics, including regional geology, flora and fauna, and the Chumash Indians. The Art Gallery shows original works portraying the many aspects of nature along the central coast; exhibits change periodically. The Discovery Center offers hands-on exploration of a variety of natural science subjects. **Open:** Daily 10am–5pm. Closed some hols. $

MOSS BEACH

Map page M-2, D1 (S of Pacifica)

Inn 🛏

📶📶📶📶 **Seal Cove Inn**, 221 Cypress Ave, Moss Beach, CA 94038; tel 415/728-7325; fax 415/728-4116. Gracious, beautifully furnished and maintained. Fresh flowers in public rooms. **Rooms:** 10 rms. CI 3pm/CO 11am. No smoking. Rooms are appointed with traditional English manor furnishings and paintings, including elegant bed and bath linens. **Amenities:** 🛅📺📶 TV w/movies, refrig, VCR. No A/C. All units w/terraces, all w/fireplaces, some w/Jacuzzis. Complimentary soft drinks, bottled water, and wine in rooms. **Services:** ✗🚗🖨🛎 Twice-daily maid svce, masseur, afternoon tea and wine/sherry served. Complimentary full breakfast and late-afternoon wine and refreshments; free movies for in-room viewing. Owner-managers will arrange for whale watching, fishing, golf, small meetings. Fax and copy machine available to guests. **Facilities:** 🖥 & 2 beaches within easy walking distance. **Rates (BB):** $150–$250 S or D. Extra person $25. Min stay spec evnts. Pking: Outdoor, free. Ltd CC.

Mountain View

Map page M-2, D2 (N of Santa Clara)

Hotel

≣≣≣ **Residence Inn by Marriott**, 1854 El Camino Real W, Mountain View, CA 94040; tel 415/940-1300 or toll free 800/331-3131; fax 415/969-4997. Shoreline/Rengstorff exit off US 101; go west on Rengstorff Ave to El Camino Real; turn right; ½ mi on right. Geared toward long-term stays by corporate clients or relocating families. **Rooms:** 112 effic. CI 2pm/CO noon. Express checkout avail. Nonsmoking rms avail. Apartments, 2 to 4 per building. Good soundproofing. All have separate entrance and full-size kitchen. Tub and toilet separate from sink. **Amenities:** 🛅 👁 ⊡ A/C, cable TV w/movies, refrig. All units w/terraces, some w/fireplaces. Many movies available with flexible scheduling. **Services:** ✗ ⊠ ⊲⊳ Car-rental desk, social director, children's program, babysitting. Continental breakfast and buffet in area off lobby; evening appetizers; Thursday barbecues. **Facilities:** 🔒 ●1 ⃞40 ⅙ Whirlpool, washer/dryer. Meeting room with audiovisual capabilities. Sports area with multipurpose tennis/volleyball court. Gazebos in garden area between buildings. **Rates (CP):** HS Feb–Oct from $139 effic. Children under 18 stay free. Lower rates off-season. Spec packages avail. Pking: Outdoor, free. Maj CC. Corporate rates available.

Motels

≣≣≣ **Best Western Inn**, 93 El Camino Real W, Mountain View, CA 94040; tel 415/967-6957 or toll free 800/445-7774; fax 415/967-4834. Rengstorff Ave exit off US 101; turn left on El Camino Real. Complete renovation of rooms in main building and expansion and upgrade of lobby near completion. **Rooms:** 58 rms, stes, and effic. Exec-level rms avail. CI 1pm/CO 11am. Express checkout avail. Nonsmoking rms avail. Second building has larger rooms updated with new carpeting and kitchenette. Smaller rooms have all new furnishings, seating area. **Amenities:** 🛅 👁 ⊡ ⃟ A/C, cable TV w/movies, refrig, VCR. Some units w/minibars, some w/Jacuzzis. All rooms have trouser presses, microwaves. **Services:** ⊠ ⊲⊳ Babysitting. **Facilities:** 🔒 ⃞ 💻 ⅙ 1 rst, 1 bar, whirlpool, washer/dryer. Full fitness center has new equipment. Adding solarium and bathroom for persons with disabilities. **Rates (CP):** HS June–Sept $65–$90 S or D; from $78 ste; from $73 effic. Children under 12 stay free. Lower rates off-season. Higher rates for spec evnts/hols. Spec packages avail. Pking: Outdoor, free. Maj CC.

≣≣ **Mountain View Inn**, 2300 W El Camino Real, Mountain View, CA 94040; tel 415/962-9912 or toll free 800/785-0005;

fax 415/962-9011. Rengstorff Ave exit off US 101. Attractive Cal-Mex-style building has teal-trimmed stucco exterior, wood-paneled Spanish-style doors, terra-cotta tile roof. **Rooms:** 71 rms, stes, and effic. CI 2pm/CO 11am. Express checkout avail. Nonsmoking rms avail. Satisfactory rooms. **Amenities:** 🛅 👁 ⊡ ⃟ A/C, cable TV w/movies, refrig, VCR. Some units w/Jacuzzis. **Services:** ⊠ ⊲⊳ Lackluster service. **Facilities:** 🔒 💻 ⃞30 ⅙ Sauna, steam rm, whirlpool, washer/dryer. **Rates (CP):** $55–$65 S; $65–$75 D; from $85 ste; from $65 effic. Extra person $10. Children under 14 stay free. Pking: Outdoor, free. Maj CC.

Restaurant 🍴

♥ **Chez TJ**, 938 Villa St, Mountain View; tel 415/964-7466. Moffett Blvd exit off US 101. **French.** Like going to a friend's house for dinner, if your friend happens to be a gourmet chef. This inviting restaurant welcomes diners with old-fashioned verandas, magnolia trees, and a restful dove-gray exterior. Inside are 4 dining areas in southwestern style. Prawns with cilantro, grilled salmon, roast pork loin, filet of beef. **FYI:** Reservations recommended. Beer and wine only. **Open:** Tues–Sat 5:30–8:30pm. Closed some hols. **Prices:** PF dinner $45–$57. Maj CC. ⃞⃟

Attraction 💼

NASA Ames Research Center; tel 415/604-6497. Located at Moffett Field, off US 101, the Ames Research Center is engaged in a variety of research tasks relating to space flight and exploration. The facility includes the world's most sophisticated wind tunnel complex and the most advanced supercomputing system.

Guided tours are conducted on weekdays and last 2 hours (2-week advance reservation required). Tour stops vary depending on research activities, but possible highlights include the world's largest wind tunnel, research aircraft, and flight simulation facilities. Gift shop. **Open:** Visitor center, Mon–Fri 8am–4:30pm. Tours by reservation only. Closed some hols. Free.

Mt Shasta

Map page M-2, A2

Motels

≣≣ **Mountain Air Lodge & Ski House**, 1121 S Mt Shasta Blvd, Mt Shasta, CA 96067; tel 916/926-3411. Lake St exit off I-5; E to Mt Shasta Blvd. Spectacularly large lobby looks like a combination ski lodge and lumber mill. Huge old trees shade property. **Rooms:** 38 rms and stes; 1 ctge/villa. CI 2pm/CO

11am. Nonsmoking rms avail. **Amenities:** 🛏 A/C, cable TV w/movies. **Services:** ♨ 📶 **Facilities:** Whirlpool. **Rates:** HS June–Oct/Dec–Mar $35 S; $46 D; from $85 ste; from $125 ctge/villa. Extra person $5. Lower rates off-season. Higher rates for spec evnts/hols. Pking: Outdoor, free. Maj CC.

≡ **Mt Shasta Swiss Holiday Lodge**, 2400 S Mt Shasta Blvd, PO Box 335, Mt Shasta, CA 96067; tel 916/926-2052. McCloud/Calif 89 exit off I-5; E of Hwy. No-frills lodging, close to skiing with a great view of the mountains. **Rooms:** 22 rms and stes. CI 2pm/CO 11am. Nonsmoking rms avail. **Amenities:** 🛏 A/C, cable TV w/movies. **Services:** ♨ **Facilities:** 🏋 🎿 📶 Whirlpool. **Rates:** HS Dec 16–Jan 1/May 25–Nov 1 $39–$41 S; $43–$59 D; from $90 ste. Extra person $4. Lower rates off-season. Pking: Outdoor, free. Maj CC. Special rates for seniors, business travelers.

Inn

≡≡≡ **Strawberry Valley Inn**, 1142 S Mt Shasta Blvd, Mt Shasta, CA 96067; tel 916/926-2052. Lake St exit off I-5; E to Mt Shasta Blvd. An obvious first choice for the discerning traveler. Inn has a great deal of charm without being cloying. **Rooms:** 25 rms, stes. CI 3pm/CO 11am. Rooms are beautifully designed, restored, and furnished. **Amenities:** 🛏 ⊘ 📶 Cable TV. No A/C. 1 unit w/fireplace. **Services:** ♨ Wine/sherry served. **Rates (CP):** HS June–Oct $50–$55 S or D; from $65 ste. Extra person $5. Children under 10 stay free. Lower rates off-season. Spec packages avail. Pking: Indoor/outdoor, free. Ltd CC.

Restaurant 🍽

★ **Lily's**, 1013 S Mt Shasta Blvd, Mt Shasta; tel 916/926-3372. Lake St exit off I-5. **New American.** This superb, informal restaurant, housed in a pretty garden cottage, serves the best food in Mount Shasta. The seasonal menu emphasizes California cuisine, with a touch of Mexico and the Pacific Rim. Rack of lamb is a specialty. A nice wine list, with a good selection by the glass. **FYI:** Reservations accepted. Children's menu. Beer and wine only. **Open:** HS June–Oct breakfast Mon–Fri 7–11am; lunch Mon–Fri 11am–3pm; dinner Mon–Fri 5–9:30pm, Sat–Sun 4–10:30pm; brunch Sat–Sun 7am–2pm. Reduced hours off-season. Closed Dec 25. **Prices:** Main courses $9.50–$14.95. Ltd CC. ♿

MUIR BEACH
Map page M-2, D1 (N of San Francisco)

Inn 🛏

≡≡≡ **The Pelican Inn**, 10 Pacific Way (Calif 1), Muir Beach, CA 94965; tel 415/383-6000. 15 mi NW of San Francisco. Stinson Beach exit off US 101; take Calif 1 toward Stinson Beach. The next best thing to a ticket on British Airways. Although the inn was built in 1979, it looks like the real thing, complete with half-timbered architecture, portraits of Anne Boleyn, and time-worn antiques. **Rooms:** 7 rms. CI 2pm/CO noon. Rooms might feature oriental rugs or antique 4-poster beds. Fresh flowers add color. **Amenities:** No A/C, phone, or TV. Some units w/terraces. **Services:** ✕ ♨ Wine/sherry served. **Facilities:** 🍽 1 rst (see also "Restaurants" below), 1 bar, guest lounge. Cozy sitting room with sofa, brick fireplace, and piano. Very good, very British restaurant and pub downstairs. Muir Beach is a short stroll away. **Rates (BB):** $140–$155 D. Pking: Outdoor, free. Ltd CC. Weekend reservations are at a premium—you have to book at least 6 months in advance.

Restaurant 🍽

★ **The Pelican Inn**, 10 Pacific Way (Calif 1), Muir Beach; tel 415/383-6000. 15 mi NW of San Francisco. Stinson Beach exit off US 101. Take Calif 1 toward Stinson Beach. **Pub.** A restaurant with an authentic British ambience, set in a Tudor-style inn with leaded windows. You can eat in the dining room at long, dark-wood tables; on the patio; or in the comfy pub. In addition to Anglo classics such as fish 'n' chips or cottage pie, daily specials might include sautéed trout or chicken with garlic. **FYI:** Reservations not accepted. Children's menu. Beer and wine only. **Open:** Lunch Tues–Fri 11:30am–3pm, Sat–Sun 11:30am–3:30pm; dinner Tues–Fri 6–9pm, Sat–Sun 5:30–9pm. Closed Dec 25. **Prices:** Main courses $7.95–$10.25. Ltd CC. ♥ ⛪ 🛄 ♿

MURPHYS
Map page M-2, D3

Hotel 🛏

≡≡≡ **Murphys Historic Hotel and Lodge**, 457 Main St, PO Box 329, Murphys, CA 95247; tel 209/728-3444 or toll free 800/532-7684; fax 209/728-1590. Extremely well-kept historic property dating to 1856. Visitors included Ulysses S Grant, Mark Twain, and highwayman Black Bart. The hotel has a noted restaurant plus a historic saloon bar popular with locals and tourists alike. **Rooms:** 29 rms and stes. CI 3pm/CO 11am. Nonsmoking rms avail. Original building maintains rooms with antiques and period decor; a modern unit on the ground floor offers motel-type rooms of high standard. **Amenities:** 🛅 A/C, cable TV. Some units w/terraces, some w/fireplaces. TVs and phones available only in modern units. All rooms air-conditioned except for "Historic Hotel" rooms. **Services:** 🛎 **Facilities:** 1 rst (*see also* "Restaurants" below), 1 bar. **Rates (CP):** $70–$80 S or D; from $75 ste. Extra person $6. Children under 12 stay free. Min stay spec evnts. Spec packages avail. Pking: Outdoor, free. Maj CC. A bargain.

Restaurant 🍴

⑤ Murphys Restaurant, in Murphys Historic Hotel and Lodge, 457 Main St, Murphys; tel 209/728-3444. **Continental/American.** Decorated with 19th-century furnishings, a burgundy carpet, and pink floral wallpaper. Lunch features 5 salads, various burgers, '49er chili, and prime-rib sandwiches; dinner choices include pastas, basil-garlic roasted chicken, rack of lamb, prime rib, and liver with caramelized onions. French nouvelle cuisine influences. **FYI:** Reservations recommended. **Open:** Breakfast daily 7am–3pm; lunch daily 11:30am–3pm; dinner daily 5–9:30pm. **Prices:** Main courses $7.95–$16.95. Maj CC. 🍷

MURRIETA

Map page M-3, E3 (N of Escondido)

Resort 🏖

🏊 **Murrieta Hot Springs Resort & Health Spa**, 39405 Murrieta Hot Springs Rd, Murrieta, CA 92563; tel 909/677-7451 or toll free 800/458-4393; fax 909/677-6261. 60 mi N of San Diego. Murietta Hot Springs Rd exit off I-15. 47 acres. This historic resort is centered on hot springs that bubble up from underground. Extensive spa facilities offset a somewhat shabby decor. Entire resort is nonsmoking. **Rooms:** 140 rms and stes. CI 2pm/CO noon. Rooms need renovation. **Amenities:** 🛅 A/C, satel TV. Some units w/terraces. **Services:** 🛎 Masseur. **Facilities:** 🛖 🎾 🏊12 🏌 🐎 🛝250 🚻 2 rsts, 2 bars (w/entertainment), spa, sauna, steam rm, whirlpool, beauty salon. Hot springs discovered in 1797 heat 3 very nice outdoor pools. **Rates:** $70–$100 S or D; from $100 ste. Extra person $5. Children under 13 stay free. Spec packages avail. Pking: Outdoor, free. Maj CC.

NAPA

Map page M-2, C2

See also Calistoga, Oakville, Rutherford, St Helena

Hotel 🏨

≣≣≣ **Inn at Napa Valley Crown Sterling Suites**, 1075 California Blvd, Napa, CA 94559; tel 707/253-9540 or toll free 800/433-4600; fax 707/253-9202. 1st St exit off Calif 29; go east; left on California Blvd. A property with a restful, inviting atmosphere and a very attractive courtyard. Excellent for business or family travelers. **Rooms:** 205 stes. CI 3pm/CO noon. Nonsmoking rms avail. All rooms are suites and have kitchenette, sofa bed, and table and chairs. **Amenities:** 🛅 🍷 📺 A/C, cable TV w/movies, refrig, voice mail. 1 unit w/fireplace. **Services:** ✗ 🗝 🧖 🛎 Babysitting. Full breakfast and evening wine tasting included. **Facilities:** 🛖 🚲 🛝220 🖥 🚻 1 rst, 1 bar (w/entertainment), lawn games, sauna, steam rm, whirlpool. **Rates (BB):** HS Apr–Oct from $134 ste. Extra person $15. Children under 13 stay free. Min stay HS. Lower rates off-season. Spec packages avail. Pking: Outdoor, free. Maj CC.

Motels

≣≣ **Best Western Inn**, 100 Soscol Ave, Napa, CA 94559; tel 707/257-1930 or toll free 800/528-1234; fax 707/255-0709. Calif 121 N exit off Calif 29. Comfortable motel in an unattractive location off the highway. **Rooms:** 68 rms and stes. CI 3pm/CO 11am. Nonsmoking rms avail. Spacious and pleasantly furnished. **Amenities:** 🛅 🍷 📺 🍴 A/C, cable TV w/movies. Some units w/minibars, some w/terraces. **Services:** 🧖 🛎 🔔 Babysitting. **Facilities:** 🛖 🛝50 🚻 1 rst, whirlpool. **Rates:** HS May–Nov 15 $65–$99 S; $89–$99 D; from $109 ste. Extra person $5. Children under 12 stay free. Min stay spec evnts. Lower rates off-season. Higher rates for spec evnts/hols. Spec packages avail. Pking: Outdoor, free. Maj CC. Hot-air balloon and Marine World/USA packages available.

≣ **Chablis Lodge**, 3360 Solano Ave, Napa, CA 94558; tel 707/257-1944 or toll free 800/443-3490; fax 707/226-6862. ½ mi N of downtown. Redwood Hwy W exit off Calif 29; S on Solano. No-frills motel; clean and comfortable. **Rooms:** 34 rms and effic. CI noon/CO noon. Nonsmoking rms avail. Some rooms have kitchenettes. **Amenities:** 🛅 🍷 📺 A/C, satel TV w/movies, refrig. All units w/minibars, some w/Jacuzzis. Wet bars. **Services:** 🛎 Babysitting. **Facilities:** 🛖 🛝10 🚻 Whirlpool. **Rates:** HS May 1–Nov 15 $64–$79 S or D; from $69 effic. Extra person $5.

Children under 16 stay free. Min stay HS and wknds. Lower rates off-season. Higher rates for spec evnts/hols. Pking: Outdoor, free. Maj CC.

▤▤ **The Chateau**, 4195 Solano Ave, Napa, CA 94558; tel 707/253-9300; fax 707/253-0906. 1 mi N of downtown. Wine Country Ave exit off Calif 29; left on Solano Ave. Attractive, comfortable lodgings on well-kept grounds. Convenient to Napa Valley vineyards. A good value. **Rooms:** 115 rms and stes. CI 3pm/CO noon. Express checkout avail. Nonsmoking rms avail. Clean, nicely furnished. **Amenities:** ☎ A/C, satel TV w/movies. Some units w/minibars, 1 w/terrace. Breakfast includes fresh breads, juices, applesauce, and other items. **Services:** ✗ ⌂ Babysitting. **Facilities:** ⌂ ⌷ ⅃ Whirlpool. **Rates (CP):** HS Apr–Oct $85–$95 S; $95–$105 D; from $140 ste. Extra person $10. Children under 13 stay free. Min stay wknds. Lower rates off-season. Pking: Outdoor, free. Maj CC.

▤ **Napa Valley Travelodge**, 853 Coombs St, Napa, CA 94559 (Downtown); tel 707/226-1871 or toll free 800/578-7878; fax 707/226-1707. 1st St exit off Calif 29; right on Coombs St. A satisfactory motel located in downtown Napa. **Rooms:** 45 rms. CI 3pm/CO noon. Nonsmoking rms avail. **Amenities:** ☎ ▣ A/C, TV w/movies. **Services:** ✗ **Facilities:** ⌂ **Rates:** HS May–Oct $65–$150 S or D. Extra person $10. Children under 17 stay free. Lower rates off-season. Higher rates for spec evnts/hols. Spec packages avail. Pking: Outdoor, free. Maj CC.

▤▤▤ **Sheraton Inn Napa Valley**, 3425 Solano Ave, Napa, CA 94558; tel 707/253-7433 or toll free 800/325-3535; fax 707/258-1320. Trancas exit off Calif 29; go west; turn right on Solano Ave. At gateway to Napa Valley, an excellent location for touring. **Rooms:** 191 rms and stes. CI 3pm/CO noon. Express checkout avail. Nonsmoking rms avail. Rooms, renovated within past year, are well-appointed, clean, and comfortable, with good security. **Amenities:** ☎ ⌷ A/C, cable TV w/movies. Some units w/minibars, some w/terraces. **Services:** ✗ ☞ ⊠ ⌂ ☍ Social director, masseur. Evening wine tasting in lobby. Concierge and assistance with local touring. **Facilities:** ⌂ ▦ ⌷ ⌷ 1 rst, 1 bar (w/entertainment), whirlpool. Attractive courtyard and pool; gift shop. **Rates:** HS June–Nov $159–$175 S or D; from $250 ste. Extra person $10. Children under 13 stay free. Min stay wknds. Lower rates off-season. Higher rates for spec evnts/hols. AP and MAP rates avail. Spec packages avail. Pking: Outdoor, free. Maj CC.

Inns

▤▤▤ **Beazley House**, 1910 1st St, Napa, CA 94559; tel 707/257-1649 or toll free 800/559-1649; fax 707/257-1518. 1st St exit off Calif 29; E on 2nd St; left on Warren. 115 acres. Built in

1902, this shingled manse opened as Napa's first B&B in 1981. Main house features French doors, lots of wood, stained-glass door and windows, as well as attractive gardens. Accommodations also in the Carriage House, nestled among greenery. **Rooms:** 11 rms and stes. CI 3:30pm/CO 11:30am. No smoking. Individually decorated with colorful fabrics and fine antiques. **Amenities:** ☎ ⌷ ▣ A/C. Some units w/terraces, some w/fireplaces, some w/Jacuzzis. **Services:** Afternoon tea and wine/sherry served. Breakfast of fresh-baked breads and fruits. **Facilities:** ⌷ Guest lounge. **Rates (BB):** $125–$140 D; from $160 ste. Extra person $25. Min stay wknds. Spec packages avail. Pking: Outdoor, free. Ltd CC. Wine Train and hot-air balloon packages available.

▤▤▤ **Churchill Manor Bed and Breakfast Inn**, 485 Brown St, Napa, CA 94559; tel 707/253-7733; fax 707/253-8836. 1st St exit off Calif 29; E on 2nd St, right on Coombs St, left on Elm. 1½ acres. Set amidst immaculate gardens, this enormous historic home was built in 1889 with details such as double doors set with bevelled glass. Comfortable public rooms downstairs are tastefully decorated with lots of antiques. Very popular for weddings. Unsuitable for children under 18. **Rooms:** 10 rms. CI 3pm/CO 11am. No smoking. Individually decorated with high-quality furnishings such as mirrored armoires and clawfoot tubs. **Amenities:** ☎ ⌷ A/C. Some units w/fireplaces, 1 w/Jacuzzi. **Services:** Masseur, afternoon tea and wine/sherry served. Cookies offered outdoors in the summer. **Facilities:** ⌷ ⌷ Games rm, guest lounge. Tandem bikes available. **Rates (BB):** HS May–Oct $75–$145 D. Extra person $15. Min stay wknds. Lower rates off-season. Spec packages avail. Pking: Outdoor, free. Ltd CC. Wine Train and hot-air ballooning packages available.

▤▤▤▤ **La Residence Country Inn**, 4066 St Helena Hwy, Napa, CA 94558; tel 707/253-0337; fax 707/253-0382. ½ mi N of Napa. 2 acres. Impressive inn located just off the highway, but in a quiet, secluded location. Property consists of an 1870 Greek revival manse and a newer annex styled after a French barn. **Rooms:** 20 rms and stes (2 w/shared bath). CI 2pm/CO 11am. No smoking. Comfortable rooms decorated with Laura Ashley prints, quality antiques, and fine linens. **Amenities:** ☎ ⌷ ⌷ A/C. Some units w/terraces, some w/fireplaces. Some rooms have CD players. **Services:** ⌂ Wine/sherry served. 3-course breakfast varies daily. Complimentary wine and cheese, fruit, and hors d'oeuvres in afternoon. **Facilities:** ⌷ ⌷ ⌷ Whirlpool, guest lounge. **Rates (BB):** HS May–Thanksgiving $90 D w/shared bath, $165 D w/private bath; from $200 ste. Extra person $20. Children under 2 stay free. Min stay wknds. Lower rates off-season. Spec packages avail. Pking: Outdoor, free. Ltd CC.

Resort

≣≣≣ **Silverado Country Club & Resort**, 1600 Atlas Peak Rd, Napa, CA 94558 (Silverado); tel 707/257-0200 or toll free 800/532-0500; fax 707/257-5400. Exit Trancas off Calif 29. Trancas exit off Calif 29; go east, then left on Atlas Peak Rd. 1,200 acres. Top golf and tennis facilities built around historic Napa estate. An 1870s mansion now houses the reception area and dining room. A grand entryway through white pillars and slate floors leads to a disappointing lobby. **Rooms:** 290 ctges/villas. CI 5pm/CO noon. Express checkout avail. Nonsmoking rms avail. In low white buildings with shingled roofs, accommodations are actually condos and private homes. Furnishings are done in a bland contemporary style. **Amenities:** 🛏️🗄️📱 📞 A/C, TV, voice mail. All units w/minibars, all w/terraces, some w/fireplaces. Since accommodations are individually owned, amenities vary. Some have cable TV with remote control. **Services:** 🍽️ 🗝️ VP 🚐 🖨️ 🛎️ Twice-daily maid svce, car-rental desk, masseur, babysitting. **Facilities:** 🏌️ 🚴 ▶︎36 📷 ●17 🎾 🏊 💻 ♿ 3 rsts, 3 bars (1 w/entertainment), lifeguard, whirlpool, washer/dryer. Home to the PGA Transamerica event, with 2 golf courses designed by Robert Trent Jones, Jr, as well as 2 putting greens and a driving range. With plexipaved courts and a pro shop, the tennis complex is northern California's largest. **Rates:** HS Mar 25–Nov 25 from $175 ctge/villa. Extra person $15. Children under 18 stay free. Lower rates off-season. Spec packages avail. Pkng: Indoor/outdoor, free. Maj CC. Excellent-value golf and tennis packages available.

Restaurants 🍴

♥★ **Bistro Don Giovanni**, 4110 St Helena Hwy (Calif 29), Napa; tel 707/224-3300. **Italian/Mediterranean.** The name honors Mozart's opera and plays upon the names of the restaurant's owners, Donna and Giovanni Scala. Stylish and airy with original art on the walls, it draws a smartly-dressed and animated crowd. Diners can start with one of the choices from the pizza oven, such as duck-sausage pizza. Several daily pastas including what may be the definitive linguine with clam sauce. Great desserts, too. **FYI:** Reservations recommended. **Open:** Sun–Thurs 11:30am–10pm, Fri–Sat 11:30am–11pm. Closed some hols. **Prices:** Main courses $8.50–$16.95. Maj CC. ♿

Napa Valley Wine Train, 1275 McKinstry St, Napa; tel 707/253-2111. **American.** A different perspective on the valley from glamorous turn-of-the-century burgundy-and-gold Pullman cars. Dine during a leisurely 3-hour, 36-mile round-trip from Napa to St Helena (you cannot disembark). Prix-fixe meals are overpriced and disappointing; you can save money by taking the deli car ($24 train fare). **FYI:** Reservations recommended. Dinner theater. Dress code. **Open:** HS June–Sept lunch Mon–Fri 11:30am–departure, Sat–Sun 12:30pm–departure; dinner Mon–Fri 6:30pm–departure, Sat–Sun 6pm–departure; brunch Sun 8:55am–departure. Reduced hours off-season. **Prices:** PF dinner $71.50. Maj CC. ♥ 🏞️

Pasta Prego, in Grapeyard Shopping Center, 3206 Jefferson St, Napa; tel 707/224-9011. Trancas St exit off Calif 29; drive east on Trancas, turn right onto Jefferson St. **Californian/Italian.** Casual, bistro-style decor with an open kitchen and a friendly atmosphere. A variety of pasta specialties are served, such as lemon-pepper spaghetti with seafood in white wine sauce, as well as grilled pork chops, chicken breast, fresh fish, and imaginative pizzas. A good value. **FYI:** Reservations recommended. Beer and wine only. **Open:** HS June–Sept lunch Mon–Sat 11:30am–2:30pm; dinner Mon–Sat 5–10pm, Sun 4–9:30pm. Reduced hours off-season. Closed some hols. **Prices:** Main courses $7.50–$15.95. Maj CC.

NEVADA CITY

Map page M-2, C2

Hotel 🏨

≣ **National Hotel**, 211 Broad St, Nevada City, CA 95959; tel 916/265-4551; fax 916/265-5259. Registered historical landmark dating back to the Gold Rush. The charming exterior is not matched by the deteriorating interior; renovation is planned. **Rooms:** 42 rms and stes. CI 2:30pm/CO noon. Nonsmoking rms avail. A mix of period antiques and kitsch and some 20th-century utilitarian furniture. Rooms are spacious with lofty ceilings, there's no historic feel. A 4-poster bed makes amends. **Amenities:** 🛏️ A/C, cable TV. Some units w/terraces, 1 w/fireplace. **Services:** ✕ Morning coffee in dining room. **Facilities:** 🏌️ 📷 ♿ 1 rst, 1 bar (w/entertainment). Pool open during summer months. **Rates:** $68 S or D; from $96 ste. Extra person $11. Children under 12 stay free. Min stay HS. Spec packages avail. Pkng: Outdoor, free. Maj CC. Lower prices on rooms with shared baths.

Motel

≣≣ **Northern Queen Inn**, 400 Railroad Ave, Nevada City, CA 95959; tel 916/265-5824; fax 916/265-3720. Basic motel in a wooded setting, surrounded by railroad trains and related memorabilia. Some cottages. **Rooms:** 70 rms, stes, and effic; 16 ctges/villas. CI 3pm/CO 11am. Nonsmoking rms avail. Clean chalets have loft and deck and full kitchen. Many rooms need rehab work. Cottages have kitchens. **Amenities:** 🛏️📱 A/C, cable TV, refrig, shoe polisher. Some units w/terraces, some w/fireplaces.

Picnic area and creek. **Services:** ⌐ Babysitting. **Facilities:** 🔗 🏊 ⟨ 1 rst, 1 bar, whirlpool. **Rates:** $50–$58 S; $55–$58 D; from $85 ste; from $83 effic; from $85 ctge/villa. Extra person $5. Children under 5 stay free. Min stay wknds. Pking: Outdoor, free. Maj CC.

Restaurant 🍴

Potager, 320 Broad St, Nevada City; tel 916/265-5697. Broad St exit off Calif 49/20. **Californian.** A classy yet casual restaurant with its own kitchen garden. Set in the woods, with high ceilings and private dining niches. Fresh ingredients go into dishes like seasonal grilled vegetables; other specialties are beef Wellington, scampi, and fettuccine ai quattro formaggi. Homemade desserts. Takeout available. **FYI:** Reservations recommended. Beer and wine only. **Open:** Dinner Tues–Thurs 6–9pm, Fri 6–9:30pm, Sat 5:30–9:30pm, Sun 5–9pm. Closed some hols; Jan 1–Jan 7. **Prices:** Main courses $9.95–$15.95. Maj CC. 🏰

Refreshment Stops 🥤

★ **Broad Street Books & Espresso Bar**, 426 Broad St, Nevada City; tel 916/265-4204. Broad St exit off Calif 49/20. **Coffeehouse.** Friendly, clean, and artistic. Books, new and used, provide the decor in a vintage home ambience. Offerings include pastries and sandwiches as well as gourmet teas and coffees, plus tortes, cheesecakes, and other desserts. **Open:** Daily 8am–8pm. Closed some hols. No CC. ☕

Dream Café, 316 Commercial St, Nevada City; tel 916/ 265-5282. 1 block N of Broad St. **Coffeehouse.** A tiny garden and excellent coffee are the main attractions at this traditional coffeehouse. The menu offers sandwiches and salads. **Open:** Mon–Fri 7am–6pm, Sat 7:30am–5:30pm, Sun 8am–5:30pm. Closed some hols. No CC.

Attraction 🏛

Nevada City Winery, 321 Spring St; tel 916/265-9463. Located in the Miners' Foundry Garage, this winery stands less than 2 blocks from the original site of its founding in the 1870s. Reopened in 1980, this producer of varietal wines offers daily tastings and guided tours by reservation. **Open:** Daily noon–5pm. Free.

NEWBURY PARK

Map page M-3, D2 (W of Thousand Oaks)

Attraction 🏛

Stagecoach Inn Museum Complex, 51 S Ventu Park Rd; tel 805/498-9441. Housed in this replica of an 1876 hotel, the Stagecoach Inn Museum contains exhibits and artifacts concerning the human and natural history of the region. Surrounding the museum is the Tri-Village, made up of replicas of a pioneer home, a Spanish-Mexican adobe, and a Chumash hut, representing 3 historic eras of the Conejo Valley. **Open:** Wed–Sun 1–4pm. $

NEWPORT BEACH

Map page M-3, D2 (NW of Laguna Beach)

Hotels 🏨

▤▤▤▤ **Four Seasons Hotel**, 690 Newport Center Dr, Newport Beach, CA 92660; tel 714/759-0808 or toll free 800/ 332-3442; fax 714/759-0568. The best luxury hotel in Newport Beach and Costa Mesa. Contemporary rendition of a grand hotel, with an impressive stone-paved driveway and a gracious marble lobby with views to the gardens and pools. **Rooms:** 285 rms and stes. CI 3pm/CO noon. Express checkout avail. Nonsmoking rms avail. Standard rooms are large, with an abundance of mirrors and counter space in the bathroom, plus a small TV. Executive suites provide a huge bathroom with separate dressing and vanity area done in 2 tones of beige marble. **Amenities:** 📺 🛁 🍽 A/C, cable TV w/movies, refrig, in-rm safe, bathrobes. All units w/minibars, all w/terraces. **Services:** 🍽 🛎 VP 🚗 ⌂ ⌐ 🐾 Twice-daily maid svce, car-rental desk, social director, masseur, babysitting. Complimentary shoeshine. **Facilities:** 🔗 🚲 ⛳ 🏊 🎾 🍸 💻 ⟨ 2 rsts (see also "Restaurants" below), 2 bars (1 w/entertainment), lifeguard, spa, sauna, whirlpool. In the workout room, each treadmill, Nordic Track, Stairmaster, etc., is accompanied by its own TV. Aerobics classes are also available. Complimentary cabanas available poolside. **Rates:** $205–$305 S; $235–$305 D; from $330 ste. Extra person $20. Children under 18 stay free. Spec packages avail. Pking: Indoor, $12.50. Maj CC. Golf, weekend, and honeymoon packages available.

▤▤▤ **Le Meridien Newport Beach**, 4500 MacArthur Blvd, Newport Beach, CA 92660; tel 714/476-2001 or toll free 800/ 543-4300; fax 714/476-0153. MacArthur Blvd exit off I-405; go south (toward ocean) 1½ mi. Although this 10-story structure resembles a modern-day pyramid, the accent is old-world

French. Divided into several different seating areas, the lobby feels intimate, not overblown. **Rooms:** 435 rms, stes, and effic. Exec-level rms avail. CI 3pm/CO noon. Express checkout avail. Nonsmoking rms avail. Hallway carpets, as well as rugs, bed-spreads, and fabrics in the rooms are worn, but are slated for replacement. Spacious accommodations with comfortable arm-chairs, lots of drawers, and plenty of counter space in the bathrooms. **Amenities:** 🛗 🛁 🍳 A/C, TV w/movies, refrig. Some units w/minibars, some w/terraces. Hairdryers and makeup mirrors are prehistoric. Many accommodations (including all suites) are outfitted with 36-inch TVs. **Services:** 🍽️ 🔑 VP 🚐 🛎️ 🛍️ Twice-daily maid svce, car-rental desk, social director, masseur, babysitting. **Facilities:** 🛗 🚲 🎿 🏊 🛎️ 600 🖥️ ♿ 3 rsts (*see also* "Restaurants" below), 2 bars (1 w/entertainment), lifeguard, spa, sauna, whirlpool. Good-size pool area is flanked by cabanas and potted palms. Exercise room features Nautilus machines. Half-court basketball court. **Rates:** $165 S or D; from $175 ste; from $800 effic. Extra person $20. Children under 18 stay free. Spec packages avail. Pking: Outdoor, free. Maj CC.

🏨🏨🏨 **Little Inn on the Bay**, 617 Lido Park Dr, Newport Beach, CA 92663 (Newport Peninsula); tel 714/673-8800 or toll free 800/438-4466; fax 714/673-8800. Newport Blvd exit off Calif 1; head toward Newport Beach; left on Via Lido; right on LaFayette; left on Lido Park Dr. A romantic inn where you can watch boats glide by in the picturesque harbor. Easy walk to shops and restaurants. **Rooms:** 30 rms and stes. CI 3pm/CO noon. Comfortably furnished with antiques. **Amenities:** 🛗 🛁 🍳 A/C, TV. Some units w/minibars, some w/terraces. Some bay-front suites have wet bars and, upon request, microwaves and refrigerators. **Services:** 🔑 🚐 🛍️ Masseur, babysitting. Complimentary newspapers. Massage available. Wine and cheese cruises on the bay can be arranged. **Facilities:** 🛗 **Rates (CP):** HS June–Aug $100–$125 S or D; from $125 ste. Lower rates off-season. Pking: Outdoor, free. Maj CC. Worth the price.

🏨🏨🏨🏨 **Newport Beach Marriott Hotel & Tennis Club**, 900 Newport Center Dr, Newport Beach, CA 92660; tel 714/640-4000 or toll free 800/228-9290; fax 714/640-5055. Newport Center exit off Calif 1; follow signs to Newport Beach. 23 acres. Well-located resort hotel in the center of Newport Beach, close to airport and major attractions. A 2-minute walk from Fashion Island, the area's best shopping center. Grounds have a pastoral feel. **Rooms:** 574 rms and stes. Exec-level rms avail. CI 4pm/CO noon. Express checkout avail. Nonsmoking rms avail. Most have bay, ocean, or golf course views, and are decorated in soothing pastels. **Amenities:** 🛗 🛁 📺 🍳 A/C, cable TV w/movies, stereo/tape player, voice mail. Some units w/terraces. State-of-the-art electronics. **Services:** ✕ 🔑 VP 🚐 🛍️ 🛎️ 🔔 Twice-daily maid svce, car-rental desk, masseur, babysitting. Tennis pro will arrange matches. **Facilities:** 🛗 🎿 📷 🛎️ 1K 🖥️ ♿ 1

rst, 1 bar (w/entertainment), spa, whirlpool, washer/dryer. Sushi bar in The View bar/nightclub has an all-you-can-eat buffet for $20 from 5–7pm. Tennis pro shop. **Rates:** HS June–Sept $109–$129 S; from $129 ste. Children under 18 stay free. Lower rates off-season. Higher rates for spec evnts/hols. Spec packages avail. Pking: Indoor/outdoor, free. Maj CC.

🏨🏨🏨 **Newport Beach Marriott Suites**, 500 Bayview Circle, Newport Beach, CA 92660 (Back Bay); tel 714/854-4500 or toll free 800/228-9290; fax 714/854-3937. Jamboree Rd exit off Calif 73; left on Bayview. Set high on a hill overlooking open meadows, with beautiful grounds that give a country-club feel. Located in a quiet business center, close to the airport. Good choice for business travelers. **Rooms:** 250 stes. Exec-level rms avail. CI 4pm/CO noon. Express checkout avail. Nonsmoking rms avail. Rooms are mini-suites with separate bedroom and sitting area, Murphy beds, sofa, and desk. **Amenities:** 🛗 🛁 🍳 A/C, cable TV w/movies, shoe polisher. All units w/terraces. **Services:** ✕ 🔑 🚐 🛍️ 🛎️ 🔔 Twice-daily maid svce, car-rental desk, babysitting. Efficient staff. **Facilities:** 🛗 🚲 🎿 🛎️ 500 ♿ 1 rst, 1 bar, 1 beach (ocean), lifeguard, sauna, whirlpool, washer/dryer. Relatively small lobby but a beautiful garden and pool area. Cozy bar with piano player. **Rates:** HS June–Sept from $118 ste. Lower rates off-season. Higher rates for spec evnts/hols. Spec packages avail. Pking: Outdoor, free. Maj CC.

🏨🏨🏨 **Portofino Beach Hotel**, 2306 W Oceanfront, Newport Beach, CA 92663; tel 714/673-7030; fax 714/723-4370. 32nd St exit off Calif 55 S; right at Wells Fargo Bank; left on Balboa St; right on 22nd St; right on Oceanfront. Cozy hotel close to shops and restaurants. **Rooms:** 15 rms; 9 ctges/villas. CI 3pm/CO noon. Nonsmoking rms avail. Each room is nicely decorated, some with brass or canopy beds. Many have ocean views. **Amenities:** 🛗 🛁 A/C, TV. Some units w/terraces, some w/fire-places, some w/Jacuzzis. **Services:** ✕ VP 🛍️ Twice-daily maid svce, car-rental desk, children's program, babysitting. Friendly, helpful staff. **Facilities:** 40 1 rst, 1 bar, 1 beach (ocean), lifeguard, washer/dryer. Elegant Italian restaurant with ocean view. **Rates (CP):** HS June–Oct $100–$250 S or D. Extra person $15. Children under 18 stay free. Lower rates off-season. Pking: Outdoor, free. Maj CC.

🏨🏨🏨 **Sheraton Newport Beach**, 4545 MacArthur Blvd, Newport Beach, CA 92660; tel 714/833-0570 or toll free 800/325-3535; fax 714/833-3927. 3 mi E of Newport Beach. MacArthur Blvd exit off I-405. Conveniently located near the major business center and 5 minutes from the airport, with easy access to freeways. Hotel occupies 2 buildings; public areas are large and comfortable. **Rooms:** 335 rms and stes. Exec-level rms avail. CI 3pm/CO 1pm. Express checkout avail. Nonsmoking rms avail. Rooms are clean and well kept. Major renovations to upgrade rooms and suites. **Amenities:** 🛏 🕿 ⌨ A/C, cable TV w/movies, stereo/tape player. Some units w/minibars, all w/terraces, 1 w/Jacuzzi. **Services:** ✗ ☎ 🚗 🗆 ⌐ Twice-daily maid svce, car-rental desk, babysitting. **Facilities:** 🉐 🅦2 🅦2 ⌐ 🗆 & 3 rsts, 1 bar, whirlpool. Basketball court. **Rates:** $79–$139 S or D; from $189 ste. Children under 12 stay free. Spec packages avail. Pking: Outdoor, free. Maj CC.

Inn

≣≣≣ **Doryman's Inn**, 2102 W Oceanfront, Newport Beach, CA 92633; tel 714/675-7300 or toll free 800/634-3303; fax 714/675-7300. Calif 55 S exit off I-405. Long on Americana and charm; located in a historical landmark, where fishermen brought their catch for over 100 years. Romance and elegance reign supreme. Close to the beach and shops. **Rooms:** 10 stes. CI 4pm/CO noon. Each room personally decorated by the owner, Victorian-era antiques. All have sunken marble tubs. Many have brass or canopy beds as well as ocean views. **Amenities:** 🛏 🕿 Cable TV. No A/C. Some units w/terraces, all w/fireplaces, some w/Jacuzzis. Microwave oven and coffee on each floor. **Services:** 🍽 🗆 ⌐ Twice-daily maid svce, masseur, babysitting, afternoon tea and wine/sherry served. Breakfast in your room consists of fresh pastries, eggs, fresh fruit, yogurt, cheese, and coffee or tea. **Facilities:** 🗆30 1 rst (*see also* "Restaurants" below), 1 bar (w/entertainment), 1 beach (ocean), lifeguard. One of the city's best restaurants on premises. Bicycle, rollerblade, and skateboard rentals nearby. **Rates (CP):** From $135 ste. Pking: Outdoor, free. Ltd CC.

Resort

≣≣≣ **Hyatt Newporter**, 1107 Jamboree Rd, Newport Beach, CA 92660; tel 714/729-1234 or toll free 800/233-1234; fax 714/644-1552. 50 mi S of Los Angeles. Jamboree Rd exit off Calif 73. 26 acres. A beautifully landscaped and well-maintained property located close to many area attractions. Family-oriented for vacation travelers, but a good choice for business travel too. **Rooms:** 410 rms and stes; 4 ctges/villas. Exec-level rms avail. CI 2pm/CO noon. Express checkout avail. Nonsmoking rms avail. Rooms have a fresh look. Decorated in cool pastel colors, whitewashed furniture, and wicker. **Amenities:** 🛏 🕿 A/C, cable TV w/movies, refrig. Some units w/minibars, some w/terraces, some w/Jacuzzis. All rooms have wet bars. **Services:** ✗ ☎ 🆅🅿 🚗 🗆 ⌐ Twice-daily maid svce, social director, children's program, babysitting. Jazz concerts offered in summer. **Facilities:** 🉐 🚲 ⛰ ⛳9 🖾 🅦20 🗄 🗆600 🖳 & 2 rsts, 2 bars (1 w/entertainment), lawn games, sauna, whirlpool, beauty salon, day-care ctr. **Rates (CP):** HS May–Sept $135–$164 S or D; from

$300 ste. Extra person $25. Children under 18 stay free. Lower rates off-season. Spec packages avail. Pking: Outdoor, free. Maj CC.

Restaurants 🍴

Antoine, in Le Meridien Hotel, 4500 MacArthur Blvd, Newport Beach; tel 714/476-2001. **French.** Very stylish, with gilt mirrors, impressionist-style art, fresh flowers, and candlelight. Look for creative flourishes in the classic French menu, with entrees such as steamed lobster with pasta, or veal chop in pomegranate sauce. For dessert, they're known for their soufflés. Ask about special winemaker dinners. **FYI:** Reservations recommended. Guitar. Jacket required. **Open:** Tues–Sat 6–9:30pm. **Prices:** Main courses $25–$34. Maj CC. 🆅🅿 &

The Arches, 3334 West Coast Hwy, Newport Beach; tel 714/645-7077. **American.** This place looks like a men's club. Gay '90s steak-house atmosphere is enhanced by dark wood paneling and lush, spacious leather booths. John Wayne loved the New York steak, potatoes, and salad; other house specialties include beef Wellington, chateaubriand, Maryland crab, and rack of lamb. **FYI:** Reservations recommended. **Open:** Lunch Mon–Fri 11am–3pm; dinner daily 4:30pm–1am. **Prices:** Main courses $16.95–$25.95. Maj CC. ♥ 🍺 🆅🅿 &

Ⓢ ✱ **Bistango**, in the Atrium Building, 19100 Von Karman Ave, Newport Beach; tel 714/752-5222. **Continental/Italian.** Delivering top value and consistently good food, this is a perfect spot for a business lunch. With high-tech European design, atrium, and marble bar, it's a favorite place in the area. Specialties are oriental chicken salad, pizza with grilled eggplant, pasta, and wood-fired chicken. **FYI:** Reservations recommended. Band. **Open:** Lunch Mon–Fri 11:30am–3pm; dinner Mon–Thurs 5–10:30pm, Fri–Sat 5–11:30pm, Sun 5–10:30pm. Closed some hols. **Prices:** Main courses $10.75–$20. Maj CC. ♥ 🍽 🆅🅿 &

The Cannery, 3010 Lafayette Ave, Newport Beach; tel 714/675-5777. Newport Blvd exit off Calif 55; follow Newport Blvd south and cross over Pacific Coast Hwy; turn left on 32nd St, then right on Lafayette. **American/Seafood.** A restaurant in a former cannery that appeals to tourists and locals alike. Decor is tasteful, with Victorian touches throughout, and some original machinery still in place. Menu items are primarily seafood and steak; house specialty is the Australian lobster tail. **FYI:** Reservations recommended. Blues/island music/jazz/rock. Children's menu. **Open:** Lunch Mon–Sat 11am–3pm; dinner Mon–Sat 5–10pm; brunch Sun 10am–2:30pm. Closed Dec 25. **Prices:** Main courses $15.50–$23.75. Maj CC. 🍺 🆅🅿 &

Marrakesh, 1100 West Coast Hwy, Newport Beach; tel 714/645-8384. **Moroccan.** An exotic place, with black-on-black interior in 2 connecting domed buildings. Dinners of 8 or 10 courses feature Moroccan renditions of lamb, chicken, rabbit, quail, duck, and seafood. **FYI:** Reservations recommended. Children's menu. Dress code. **Open:** Sun–Thurs 5–10pm, Fri–Sat 5–11pm. **Prices:** Main courses $18.50–$22.50. Maj CC. ♥ 📷 VP ఉ

Pascal, in Plaza Newport, 1000 Bristol St, Newport Beach; tel 714/752-0107. **French.** Country French decor with soft pinks and blues and lots of fresh flowers. The cuisine is classic French, featuring rabbit, rack of lamb, sea bass, free-range chicken, and lamb salad with apple dressing. Gourmet deli, Pascal Epicérie, across the way. Chef/owner also gives cooking lessons. **FYI:** Reservations recommended. **Open:** Lunch Mon–Fri 11:30am–2:30pm; dinner Mon–Fri 6–9:30pm, Sat 6–10pm. Closed some hols; Sept 15–30. **Prices:** Main courses $9.95–$22.50; PF dinner $40. Ltd CC. ♥ ఉ

The Pavilion, in Four Seasons Hotel, 690 Newport Center Dr, Newport Beach; tel 714/759-0808. Calif 73/Corona del Mar Fwy S off I-405 S. Jamboree Rd exit off I-405 N. **Californian/Mediterranean.** Classic elegance. Large windows overlook flower-filled gardens and patio, where there's outdoor dining much of the year. The menu melds flavors of California and the Mediterranean, with dishes such as pepper-crusted lamb with port wine, or grilled whitefish with shiitake mushrooms and gnocchi. **FYI:** Reservations recommended. Children's menu. Dress code. **Open:** Breakfast Mon–Fri 6:30–11am, Sat–Sun 6:30am–noon; lunch Mon–Fri 11am–2pm, Sat–Sun noon–2pm; dinner daily 6–11pm. **Prices:** Main courses $20–$25; PF dinner $29.50. Maj CC. VP ఉ

♣ **The Ritz**, in Fashion Island, 880 Newport Center Dr, Newport Beach; tel 714/720-1800. Jamboree Rd exit off I-405. **International.** One of the best restaurants in town; perfect for a special occasion. Elegantly decorated European-style dining room, where people dress up. Start with the famous carousel appetizer of house-cured gravlax, prawns, Dungeness crab, lobster, and pâté; then try the rack of lamb, pepper steak, or veal scaloppine with 3 types of mushrooms. **FYI:** Reservations recommended. Piano. Jacket required. **Open:** HS Dec lunch Mon–Fri 11:30am–3pm; dinner Mon–Thurs 6–10pm, Fri–Sat 5:30–11pm, Sun 5–10pm. Reduced hours off-season. Closed some hols. **Prices:** Main courses $18–$28. Maj CC. VP ఉ

★ **Sabatino**, in Cannery Village, 251 Shipyard Way Cabin D, Newport Beach (Balboa Peninsula); tel 714/723-0645. Newport Blvd exit off Calif 55. **Italian.** Tucked away in historic Cannery Village, a family-run trattoria popular with locals. Hand-painted murals of old Venice line the walls. Known for homemade Sicilian sausages, from a recipe dating back to 1864; fine fettuccine, linguine, veal saltimbocca, and lasagne also served. **FYI:** Reservations recommended. Dress code. Beer and wine only. **Open:** Breakfast daily 9am–1pm; lunch daily 11am–4pm; dinner daily 4–11pm; brunch Sun 8:30am–1pm. Closed Dec 25. **Prices:** Main courses $8.95–$17.95. Maj CC. ♥ 📷 📷

$ ★ **Tutto Mare**, in Newport Fashion Island, 545 Newport Center Dr, Newport Beach; tel 714/640-6333. **Italian.** One of the most attractive restaurants in town—great place for lunch or dinner. With marble floors, comfortable booths, and garden for dining. Pasta dishes are the favorites here, including fettuccine and spaghetti. They also serve a great veal chop and fine fried calamari. **FYI:** Reservations recommended. Jazz. **Open:** Mon–Thurs 11:30am–11pm, Fri–Sat 11:30am–midnight, Sun 11am–10pm. Closed Dec 25. **Prices:** Main courses $10–$20. Maj CC. ♥ 📷 ఉ

♣ **21 Ocean Front**, in Doryman's Inn, 2100 W Ocean Front, Newport Beach; tel 714/675-2566. Calif 55 exit off I-405. **Californian/Seafood.** Locals consider this a place for special occasions, with its beautiful setting in a historic Victorian-style inn and a spectacular ocean view. The house special is abalone ($48.50); abalone-lovers travel far and wide to get here. Other menu highlights include a wide variety of other fresh seafood. **FYI:** Reservations recommended. Piano. Dress code. **Open:** Daily 4pm–1am. Closed some hols. **Prices:** Main courses $15.95–$48.50. Maj CC. ♥ 📷 VP

What's Cooking, in Newport Hills Center Mall, 2632 San Miguel Dr, Newport Beach; tel 714/644-1820. McHarto Blvd exit off Calif 73. **Italian/Pizza.** Hidden away in a small strip mall, a cozy place with lackluster decor—but worth finding. Italian pizzas and pasta here are all made by grandma herself. Good food at reasonable prices. **FYI:** Reservations recommended. Singer. Children's menu. **Open:** Lunch daily 11am–2:30pm; dinner daily 5–10:30pm. **Prices:** Main courses $8–$16. Maj CC. 📷 🚗 ఉ

NORTH HOLLYWOOD

Map page M-3, D2 (Los Angeles)

Hotel 🏨

⬛⬛⬛ **Beverly Garland's Holiday Inn**, 4222 Vineland Ave, North Hollywood, CA 91602; tel 818/980-8000 or toll free 800/BEVERLY; fax 818/766-5230. In a lovely garden-like setting, with "church pews" under wide eaves so guests can sit in shade. **Rooms:** 258 rms and stes. CI 3pm/CO noon. Express checkout avail. Nonsmoking rms avail. Cool and comfortable, with decor of soft pastels and light wood. **Amenities:** 🛏🛁📺 A/C, cable TV w/movies, voice mail. All units w/terraces. TV in large armoire. **Services:** ✗🚐🧺🔔 Twice-daily maid svce, car-rental desk, children's program. Service is very attentive. **Facilities:** 🍴🏊 ⛳ 🎾 1 rst, 1 bar, sauna. Tennis courts have pro on duty 10 hours a day. **Rates:** $109 S; $119 D; from $175 ste. Extra person $10. Children under 18 stay free. Higher rates for spec evnts/ hols. Spec packages avail. Pking: Outdoor, free. Maj CC.

Inn

▀▀▀▀ **La Maida House**, 11159 La Maida St, North Hollywood, CA 91601; tel 818/769-3857. Megan Timothy, who was raised in central Africa, turned her 1920s Italianate villa into a B&B. Featured in international home-and-garden magazines, the inn is an oasis of serenity in the heart of North Hollywood. Unsuitable for children under 12. **Rooms:** 11 rms, stes, and effic. CI 4pm/CO 11am. No smoking. Each room is tastefully decorated with souvenirs from the innkeeper's world travels. The guest who stays in the "Giardino" room is given the memorable experience of taking care of the dozen multi-hued chickens and a small bunny that inhabit the backyard. **Amenities:** 🛏🛁📺 🍷 A/C, cable TV w/movies, refrig, bathrobes. All units w/minibars, 1 w/terrace, some w/fireplaces, some w/Jacuzzis. Fresh cut flowers in rooms. **Services:** 🍷 Wine/sherry served. Evening aperitifs; turn-down service. **Facilities:** 🍴 🎱 Guest lounge. Solarium. **Rates (CP):** $105–$165 D; from $160 ste; from $160 effic. Min stay. Pking: Outdoor, free. Ltd CC.

NORTH SHORE
Map page M-3, E3 (E of Oasis)

Attraction 💼

Salton Sea State Recreation Area, 100-225 State Park Rd; tel 619/393-3052. Located on Calif 111 at State Park Rd. One of the world's largest inland seas was accidentally created when a dike broke during the 1905 construction of the All-American Canal. The 360-square-mile basin is popular with boaters and fisher-men, who come to catch such ocean transplants as corvina, gulf croaker, and sargo. Swimming and waterskiing areas. Nature trails, interpretive programs; picnicking, camping. **Open:** Daily; phone for hours. $$

OAKDALE
Map page M-2, D2

Attraction 💼

Hershey Chocolate USA, Western Plant, 120 S Sierra Ave; tel 209/848-8126. Thirty-minute guided tours of this facility examine the chocolate-making process from cocoa bean to candy bar. The visitors center has exhibits and displays on the history of the company and of chocolate manufacture. Tours begin at the visitor center and are conducted from 8:30am–3pm. **Open:** Mon–Fri 8:30am–5pm. Closed some hols. Free.

OAKHURST
Map page M-2, D3 (S of Fish Camp)

Inn 🛏

▀▀▀▀ **Chateau du Sureau**, 48688 Victoria Lane, PO Box 577, Oakhurst, CA 93644; tel 209/683-6860; fax 209/ 683-0800. 2 blocks S of Oakhurst proper. A storybook castle with red-tile roof and a stone turret in a snoozy, Sierra foothills town 90 minutes from the valley floor of Yosemite. Little touches captivate the eye—a statue in a niche, the 17th-century tapestry by the stairway. Unsuitable for children under 12. **Rooms:** 9 rms. CI 2pm/CO noon. No smoking. Delightful rooms decked out with superb linens, antiques, and goosedown bedding. Geranium room offers a 4-poster bed and huge armoire, while Saffron room has an 1834 bedroom set of ebony inlaid with ivory. **Amenities:** 🛏 🍷 A/C, stereo/tape player, in-rm safe, bathrobes. All units w/terraces, all w/fireplaces. TV available upon request. Everything is top quality. Upon arrival, guests receive a bowl of fresh fruit. **Services:** ✗ 🆅🅿 🚐 🧺 Twice-daily maid svce, masseur, afternoon tea and wine/sherry served. Highly personalized service is lavished on guests. **Facilities:** 🍴 🏊 🎱 ⛱ 1 rst (see also "Restaurants" below), 1 bar, guest lounge. Serene pool surrounded by a white balustrade and colorful gardens. Small chapel is a perfect setting for weddings. **Rates (BB):** $260–$360 S or D. Min stay wknds and spec evnts. Spec packages avail. Pking: Outdoor, free. Ltd CC.

Restaurant 🍽

♣ **Erna's Elderberry House**, in Chateau du Sureau, 48688 Victoria Lane, Oakhurst; tel 209/683-6800. 2 blocks S of Oakhurst proper. **Californian/Continental.** A touch of southern France on Yosemite's outskirts. High-backed chairs and pewter chargers convey elegance. Fine cuisine features buttery, fresh-baked bread and a succulent pork tenderloin; desserts, such as poppy-seed cake or chocolate gâteau, are excellent. **FYI:** Reservations recommended. Dress code. **Open:** Lunch Wed–Fri 11:30am–1pm; dinner Wed–Mon 5:30–8:30pm; brunch Sun 11am–1pm. Closed first 3 weeks after New Year's. **Prices:** PF dinner $58. Maj CC. ♥ ≜

OAKLAND

Map page M-2, D2

See also Berkeley, Emeryville, Fremont, Hayward, Milpitas

Hotels 🏨

≣≣≣ **Clarion Suites Lake Merritt Hotel**, 1800 Madison St, Oakland, CA 94612 (Lake Merritt Business District); tel 510/832-2300 or toll free 800/933-HOTEL; fax 510/832-7150. A meticulously maintained 76-year-old, art deco Oakland landmark, located across the street from Lake Merritt. **Rooms:** 51 rms, stes, and effic. CI 3pm/CO 11am. Express checkout avail. Nonsmoking rms avail. Many units have lake views. Bathrooms are cramped, with free-standing sinks and no counter space. **Amenities:** 🛏 🗄 📺 Cable TV w/movies, refrig. No A/C. Some units w/minibars, 1 w/Jacuzzi. Air conditioning planned. **Services:** ✕ 🍷 VP 🚗 🛄 🛎 👐 Masseur, babysitting. Staff can customize suites to fit guest's needs. **Facilities:** 🛗₃₀₀ 🖥 1 rst, 1 bar, washer/dryer. Access to off-premises fitness center and health spa at a reduced rate, plus free transportation there. **Rates (CP):** $89–$159 S; $99–$169 D; from $119 ste; from $119 effic. Extra person $10. Children under 16 stay free. Spec packages avail. Pking: Indoor, $9. Maj CC.

≣≣ **Hampton Inn**, 8465 Enterprise Way, Oakland, CA 94621; tel 510/632-8900 or toll free 800/950-1191; fax 510/632-4713. Hegenberger Coliseum exit off I-880. Very neat and well-maintained property. Good location and excellent value for those transiting Oakland airport. **Rooms:** 149 rms. CI 2pm/CO noon. Nonsmoking rms avail. Closets are free-standing armoires and a bit small, but adequate for most travelers. All king rooms come with either a recliner chair or a fold-out couch. **Amenities:** 🛏 A/C, satel TV w/movies. A mini-fridge can be rented for $5 per day. **Services:** 🚗 🛄 🛎 Complimentary coffee in lobby at all times. Local and state guidebooks available for use at front desk. Free 24-hour shuttle service to Coliseum or rapid transit station. **Facilities:** 🛗₃₅ 🖥 Whirlpool. **Rates (CP):** $65–$69 S; $72–$76 D. Children under 18 stay free. Spec packages avail. Pking: Outdoor, free. Maj CC.

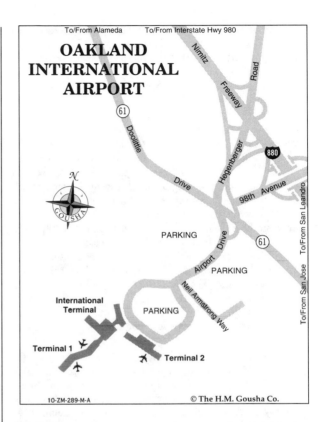

≣≣ **Holiday Inn Oakland**, 500 Hegenberger Rd, Oakland, CA 94621 (Oakland Int'l Airport); tel 510/562-5311 or toll free 800/HOLIDAY; fax 510/636-1539. 6½ mi S of Oakland. Hegenberger exit off I-880; entrance on Edes Ave. Close to airport and Oakland Coliseum. Excellent security and well-lit parking lot. **Rooms:** 290 rms and stes. Exec-level rms avail. CI 3pm/CO noon. Express checkout avail. Nonsmoking rms avail. **Amenities:** 🛏 🗄 A/C, cable TV w/movies. Some units w/minibars. **Services:** ✕ 🚗 🛄 🛎 Car-rental desk. Complimentary shuttle service to rapid transit station and Oakland Coliseum. **Facilities:** 🛗 🍽 🛗₂₅₀ 🖥 1 rst, 1 bar (w/entertainment), washer/dryer. **Rates:** $95 S; $105 D; from $129 ste. Extra person $10. Children under 12 stay free. Higher rates for spec evnts/hols. Spec packages avail. Pking: Outdoor, free. Maj CC.

≣≣≣ **Oakland Airport Hilton**, 1 Hegenberger Rd, Oakland, CA 94621 (Oakland Int'l Airport); tel 510/635-5000 or toll free 800/HILTONS; fax 510/635-5000. Hegenberger exit off I-880. Although this hotel ranks near the top of its rating group, the grounds need a bit of work and the service could be improved. **Rooms:** 362 rms and stes. Exec-level rms avail. CI 2pm/CO noon. Express checkout avail. Nonsmoking rms avail. **Amenities:** 🛏 🗄 A/C, cable TV w/movies. Some units w/minibars, some w/terraces. **Services:** ✗ 🚐 🗺 ↺ ↻ Car-rental desk. VCRs available for rent. **Facilities:** 🎣 🛢 600 ☐ & 2 rsts, 1 bar (w/entertainment), games rm, playground. **Rates:** $99–$139 S; $119–$159 D; from $299 ste. Extra person $20. Children under 18 stay free. Spec packages avail. Pking: Outdoor, free. Maj CC.

≣≣ **Parc Oakland Hotel**, 1001 Broadway, Oakland, CA 94607 (City Center); tel 510/451-4000 or toll free 800/338-1338; fax 510/839-0677. 12th/11th Sts exit off I-880; left on 11th St, 4 blocks. Adjacent to the Oakland Convention Center and within walking distance of many Oakland attractions, including Chinatown, City Center, restored Old Town, and Housewives Market. Next to Bay Area Rapid Transit station. **Rooms:** 488 rms and stes. Exec-level rms avail. CI 3pm/CO noon. Express checkout avail. Nonsmoking rms avail. **Amenities:** 🛢 & A/C, cable TV w/movies, shoe polisher. 1 unit w/Jacuzzi. **Services:** ✗ 🚐 🗺 ↻ Car-rental desk, babysitting. **Facilities:** 🎣 🛢 4K ☐ & 1 rst, 1 bar, whirlpool. **Rates:** HS June–Oct $105–$115 S or D; from $375 ste. Extra person $15. Children under 12 stay free. Lower rates off-season. Spec packages avail. Pking: Indoor/outdoor, $11. Maj CC.

≣≣ **Ramada Hotel**, 455 Hegenberger Rd, Oakland, CA 94621; tel 510/562-6100 or toll free 800/932-4550; fax 510/569-5681. 6½ mi S of downtown. Hegenberger exit off I-880. Property needs some improvements, especially to ground-floor bathrooms and landscaping. Close to the airport. **Rooms:** 342 rms and stes. Exec-level rms avail. CI 2pm/CO noon. Nonsmoking rms avail. **Amenities:** 🛢 A/C, satel TV w/movies. **Services:** ✗ 🚐 ↻ Twice-daily maid svce, car-rental desk. **Facilities:** 🎣 2.7K & 2 rsts, 1 bar (w/entertainment), washer/dryer. **Rates:** $99–$109 S or D; from $199 ste. Extra person $15. Children under 18 stay free. Higher rates for spec evnts/hols. Spec packages avail. Pking: Outdoor, free. Maj CC.

≣≣≣≣ **Waterfront Plaza Hotel**, 10 Washington St, Oakland, CA 94607 (Jack London Square); tel 510/836-3800 or toll free 800/729-3638; fax 510/832-6228. Built in 1990 in the heart of Jack London Square, just ½ block from the ferry to San Francisco. **Rooms:** 144 rms and stes. CI 3pm/CO noon. Nonsmoking rms avail. Beautifully furnished rooms; most have waterfront views. **Amenities:** 🛢 & 🖵 📞 A/C, cable TV w/movies, refrig, VCR, voice mail, in-rm safe. All units w/minibars, some w/terraces, some w/fireplaces, some w/Jacuzzis. **Services:** ✗ 🖿 VP 🗺 ↻ Twice-daily maid svce, babysitting. Free shuttle to downtown and rapid-transit station. **Facilities:** 🎣 🛢 200 ☐ & 1 rst, 1 bar (w/entertainment), sauna. **Rates:** $135–$145 S or D; from $165 ste. Extra person $10. Children under 16 stay free. Spec packages avail. Pking: Outdoor, $8. Maj CC.

Motels

≣≣ **Best Western Park Plaza Hotel**, 150 Hegenberger Rd, Oakland, CA 94621 (Oakland Int'l Airport); tel 510/635-5300 or toll free 800/635-5301; fax 510/635-9661. 6½ mi S of Oakland. Hegenberger Rd exit off I-880. Fairly standard airport hotel. **Rooms:** 187 rms and stes. CI 2pm/CO noon. Express checkout avail. Nonsmoking rms avail. **Amenities:** 🛢 & A/C, cable TV w/movies. All units w/terraces. Refrigerators in some rooms, with plans to add them to all rooms. **Services:** ✗ 🚐 🗺 ↻ Free transportation to BART station and Oakland Coliseum. Complimentary coffee and newspaper in lobby. **Facilities:** 🎣 🛢 70 2 rsts, 1 bar, sauna, whirlpool, washer/dryer. Walking distance to golf course. Jogging trail across the street. **Rates:** $89 S; $99 D; from $130 ste. Extra person $10. Children under 12 stay free. Higher rates for spec evnts/hols. Spec packages avail. Pking: Outdoor, free. Maj CC.

≣≣ **Best Western Thunderbird Inn**, 233 Broadway, Oakland, CA 94607 (Jack London Square); tel 510/452-4565 or toll free 800/633-5973; fax 510/452-4634. Fairly nice property once you get off the street. Good location, within walking distance of Chinatown and Jack London Square. **Rooms:** 100 rms and stes. CI 2pm/CO noon. Nonsmoking rms avail. Some rooms open onto landscaped area around pool; some are a little dark. **Amenities:** 🛢 & A/C, cable TV w/movies. Some units w/terraces. **Services:** 🗺 ↻ Free coffee service in an alcove on every floor. **Facilities:** 🎣 🛢 40 & Sauna. **Rates (CP):** $62–$80 S or D; from $140 ste. Extra person $5. Children under 12 stay free. Higher rates for spec evnts/hols. Spec packages avail. Pking: Indoor, free. Maj CC.

Resort

≣≣≣≣ **Claremont Resort, Spa & Tennis Club**, Ashby and Domingo Aves, Oakland, CA 94623 (Berkeley Hills); tel 510/843-3000 or toll free 800/551-7266; fax 510/848-6208. Claremont Ave exit off Calif 24 E; left on Claremont; right on Ashby. 22 acres. Landmark property reputed to be largest wooden structure in California. Beautiful landscaping in wooded hillside setting; large collection of Pacific Northwest art. **Rooms:** 239 rms and stes. CI 3pm/CO noon. Express checkout avail. Nonsmoking rms avail. Elegant, spacious rooms with good light and furnishings arranged for comfort. Most have views of San Francisco and bay. **Amenities:** 🛢 & 🖵 📞 A/C, cable TV w/movies, voice mail, bathrobes. 1 unit w/terrace. Irons and ironing boards in closets. **Services:** ✗ 🖿 VP 🚐 🗺 ↻ Twice-daily maid svce, car-rental desk, masseur, babysitting. **Facilities:** 🎣 🖢 🖳 🛢 550 ☐ & 3 rsts, 3 bars (1 w/entertainment), lifeguard, spa, sauna, steam rm, whirlpool, beauty salon. **Rates:** $159–$199 S; $179–$219 D; from $295 ste. Extra person $20. Children under 13 stay free. Higher rates for spec evnts/hols. AP and MAP rates avail. Spec packages avail. Pking: Outdoor, $8. Maj CC.

Restaurants 🍴

★ **Bay Wolf**, 3853 Piedmont Ave, Oakland; tel 510/655-6004. At Rio Vista. **Californian.** Housed in a converted Victorian house with a rustic wood exterior and polished wood interior, this homey restaurant features several intimate dining rooms and a covered terrace for outdoor dining. The California cuisine relies heavily on fresh local produce, fresh seafood, and grilled meats. **FYI:** Reservations accepted. Dress code. Beer and wine only. **Open:** Lunch Mon–Fri 11:30am–2pm; dinner Mon–Fri 6–9pm, Sat–Sun 5:30–9:30pm. Closed some hols. **Prices:** Main courses $12.25–$17. Ltd CC. ♥

Cafe de Bordeaux, 326 7th St, Oakland (Chinatown); tel 501/891-2338. **Continental/French.** Clean and tidy, though a little plain. Owned and operated by husband-and-wife team who are eager to help their customers. Specialties are continental and French dishes, such as steak au poivre vert, veal scaloppine marsala, scallop and shrimp vin blanc, prawn Provençale, and eggplant parmigiana. **FYI:** Reservations recommended. Children's menu. Dress code. Beer and wine only. **Open:** Mon–Fri 11:30am–9:30pm, Sat–Sun 2–9:30pm. **Prices:** Main courses $8.50–$17.50. Ltd CC. &

Gulf Coast Grill and Bar, 736 Washington St, Oakland; tel 510/836-3663. At 8th St. **Cajun.** Portions are so enormous here, it would take a hungry lumberjack to clean most plates. The narrow restaurant is decorated with polished wood, brick, tile, and large picture windows and has a distinct New Orleans flavor. Menu specialties include Cajun-style fish, jambalaya, baked oysters, and spicy sausages. **FYI:** Reservations accepted. Dress code. Beer and wine only. **Open:** Lunch Wed–Fri 11am–2:30pm; dinner Thurs–Sun 5–10pm; brunch Sun 11am–4pm. Closed some hols. **Prices:** Main courses $9.50–$18. Maj CC.

Jade Villa, 800 Broadway, Oakland; tel 510/839-1688. **Chinese.** Utilitarian, banquet-hall atmosphere with rows of tables and chairs. Large windows admit lots of light. Standard Chinese menu leans heavily toward seafood. A popular spot for social functions. **FYI:** Reservations accepted. Dress code. Beer and wine only. **Open:** Mon–Fri 9am–10pm, Sat–Sun 9am–10:30pm. **Prices:** Main courses $6.75–$18. Ltd CC. &

Kincaid's, in Jack London Square, 1 Franklin St, Oakland; tel 510/835-8600. On the waterfront. **American.** Polished wood floors, brass fixtures, and marble accents provide a turn-of-the-century elegance, and there's a superb view of the estuary. Diners may catch a glimpse of the former presidential yacht

Potomac cruising by. Grilled top-quality meats, plump fillets of fish, tender crab. **FYI:** Reservations accepted. Children's menu. Dress code. **Open:** Lunch Mon–Sat 11:15am–3pm; dinner Mon–Sat 5–10pm, Sun 4–9pm; brunch Sun 10:30am–3pm. Closed some hols. **Prices:** Main courses $10.95–$20.95. Maj CC.

★ **Mama's Royal Cafe**, 1012 Broadway, Oakland; tel 510/547-7600. **American.** This popular down-home cafe popular with locals boasts unique pagoda decorations left over from its days as a Chinese restaurant many years ago. With comfortable booths and a friendly staff, it serves up sandwiches, burgers, and superb breakfast fare. **FYI:** Reservations accepted. Beer and wine only. **Open:** Mon–Fri 7am–3pm, Sat–Sun 8am–3pm. Closed some hols. **Prices:** Lunch main courses $3–$9.25. No CC.

Nan Yang Rockridge, 6048 College Ave, Oakland; tel 510/655-3298. **Burmese.** Bright and modern Burmese restaurant shows off a European style. Tangy salads, flavorful soups, hearty curries. House specialties are ginger salad and green papaya salad. Also at: 301 8th St, Oakland (510/465-6924). **FYI:** Reservations accepted. Dress code. Beer and wine only. **Open:** Tues–Sat 11:30am–10pm, Sun noon–9pm. Closed some hols. **Prices:** Main courses $7.50–$14.95. Ltd CC.

★ **Oakland Grill**, 301 Franklin St, Oakland; tel 510/835-1176. 3 blocks from Jack London Square. **American.** A refined truck stop, this hole-in-the-wall is tucked into the corner of a warehouse in the railroad produce terminal. Diners can peer through picture windows at produce trucks delivering their cargoes, while dining on a forklift special, a juicy sirloin steak. **FYI:** Reservations accepted. Beer and wine only. **Open:** Mon–Fri 6am–9:30pm, Sat–Sun 8am–9:30pm. **Prices:** Main courses $7.50–$12.95. Maj CC.

Oliveto, 5655 College Ave, Oakland; tel 510/547-5356. **Italian.** A Tuscan dining experience. Sunny decor, exquisitely fresh food. The chefs change the menu regularly, offering the best of seasonal vegetables, fresh fish, and grilled and roasted meats. The serving staff can ably discuss daily specials, ingredients, and cooking styles. **FYI:** Reservations accepted. Dress code. Beer and wine only. **Open:** Lunch Mon–Fri 11:30am–2:30pm; dinner Mon–Sat 6–10pm, Sun 5:30–8:30pm. Closed some hols. **Prices:** Main courses $14–$16.50. Maj CC. &

Piemonte Ouest, 3909 Grand Ave, Oakland; tel 510/601-0500. **Italian.** Looks like a villa, featuring a courtyard filled with trees and flowers. And with heat lamps outdoors, it's nearly always pleasant to dine outside. Seasonal fresh fruits and vegetables are incorporated into many dishes; highlights include risotto, lamb sausage pizza, fresh pasta, and roasted chicken. **FYI:** Reservations accepted. Dress code. Beer and wine only. **Open:** Lunch

Fri 11:30am–2:30pm; dinner Tues–Thurs 5:30–9:30pm, Fri–Sat 5:30–10pm, Sun–Mon 5:30–9pm. Closed some hols. **Prices:** Main courses $9.75–$16.25. Maj CC. 🏛️ 🪣

★ **Rockridge Cafe**, 5492 College Ave, Oakland; tel 510/653-1567. **American.** A local favorite for great hamburgers. They also serve pizza, pasta, soups, and salads. Daily specials could include chili relleno, stir-fried chicken, or lamb stew. Fresh-baked pies. **FYI:** Reservations accepted. Beer and wine only. **Open:** Mon–Thurs 7:30am–10pm, Fri–Sat 7:30am–10:30pm, Sun 8am–10pm. Closed some hols. **Prices:** Main courses $4.50–$9.95. Ltd CC. &

★ **Thornhill Cafe**, 5761 Thornhill Dr, Oakland (Montclair); tel 510/339-0646. Thornhill exit off Calif 13. **French/Thai.** Light and airy, though a bit small. The Thai chef prepares French cuisine with an Asian flavor, as well as traditional Thai fish dishes. Poached and chilled salmon; grilled mahimahi with tamarind sauce; grilled soft-shelled crab with sea scallops in blackened butter; cassoulet of lamb, pork, sausage, and duck with white beans; beef bourguignon with pearl onions and mushrooms. **FYI:** Reservations recommended. Dress code. Beer and wine only. **Open:** Breakfast Tues–Fri 7–11am; lunch Tues–Fri 11:30am–3pm; dinner daily 5:30–10pm; brunch Sat–Sun 10:30am–3pm. Closed July 4. **Prices:** Main courses $10.95–$16.95. Maj CC. &

Ti Bacio, 5912 College Ave, Oakland; tel 510/428-1703. **Italian.** Etruscan-style villa with ancient design murals and vases, featuring health-conscious, low-fat Italian cooking. Many vegetarian dishes. **FYI:** Reservations accepted. Dress code. Beer and wine only. **Open:** Daily 4–10pm. Closed some hols. **Prices:** Main courses $11.95–$14.95. Ltd CC. &

★ **Yoshi's**, 6030 Claremont Ave, Oakland (Rockridge); tel 510/652-9200. **Japanese.** Modern Japanese decor. You can dine in the relaxing dining room, sit at the sushi bar, or listen to the jazz musicians at this pleasant neighborhood locale. **FYI:** Reservations accepted. Jazz. Dress code. **Open:** Daily 5:30–10pm. Closed some hols. **Prices:** Main courses $10–$15. Maj CC. &

Zza's, 552 Grand Ave, Oakland; tel 510/839-9124. At MacArthur Ave. **Italian.** Straight out of a Mediterranean village, with high ceilings and cool shade trees, offering pizza, pasta, and traditional Italian fare. A great place to bring kids, as tables are covered with butcher paper and jars of crayons to keep children amused. **FYI:** Reservations not accepted. Beer and wine only. **Open:** Sun–Tues 4:30–10pm, Wed–Thurs 11am–10pm, Fri 11am–11pm, Sat 4:30–11pm. Closed some hols. **Prices:** Main courses $7.50–$10.95. Ltd CC. 👥

Attractions 📷

Oakland Museum, 1000 Oak St; tel 510/238-3401. Actually 3 museums in 1, this facility has galleries dedicated to California history, culture, art, and environment and ecology. It includes works by California artists from Bierstadt to Diebenkorn; artifacts such as Pomo basketry and Country Joe McDonald's guitar; and re-creations of California habitats from the coast to the White Mountains. Also featured are rotating exhibits from the museum's various collections as well as traveling exhibits covering a wide range of topics. Guided tours available on request. Book and gift shop; cafe and snack bar. **Open:** Wed–Sat 10am–5pm, Sun noon–7pm. Closed some hols. $$

Jack London Square, Broadway and Embarcadero. The square, at the foot of Broadway on the waterfront, houses a complex of boutiques and eateries. In the center is the reconstructed rustic Yukon cabin in which London lived while prospecting in the Klondike during the Gold Rush of 1897. At 56 Jack London Square, at the foot of Webster St, is the First and Last Chance Saloon, where London did some of his writing (and much of his drinking); his corner remains much as he knew it. **Open:** Most restaurants and shops Mon–Sat 10am–9pm (some restaurants stay open later).

Greek Orthodox Church of the Ascension, 4700 Lincoln Ave; tel 510/531-3400. This beautiful and elaborate Byzantine-style church, built in 1960, features a copper-clad dome and an elaborate mosaic of the Ascension dominating the entrance to the nave. **Open:** Mon–Fri 9am–4pm. Closed some hols. Free.

Children's Fairyland, 1520 Lakeside Dr; tel 510/452-2259. Located on the north shore of Lake Merritt, Children's Fairyland is one of the most imaginative and skillful children's parks in the United States. Fables and fairy tales are brought to life through a clever mixture of live and mechanical characters in whimsical settings. Trained animal performances, puppet shows, and amusement park rides. **Open:** Summer, Wed–Sun 10am–4:30pm; fall–spring, Sat–Sun 10am–4:30pm. Closed some hols. $

Oakland Mormon Temple Visitors' Center, 4770 Lincoln Ave; tel 510/531-1475. Situated high in the Oakland hills, the Mormon temple offers a panoramic view from its terrace and gardens. Although the interior is not open to the public, visitors may browse the temple grounds. The Temple Visitors Center offers free guided tours that include a reproduction of Danish sculptor Bertel Thorvaldsen's *Christus* statue, special audiovisual presentations, and exhibits on Mormon faith and doctrine. Also on the grounds is the Family History Center, with resources for genealogical research. **Open:** Daily 9am–9pm. Free.

Oakland Zoo in Knowland Park, 9777 Golf Links Rd; tel 510/632-9525. Located within Knowland Park, this 100-acre zoo has 50 exhibits with 75 different species from around the world. An environmental education center is scheduled for completion sometime in 1995. Other features include the Skyride chairlift ride, a miniature train, and a carousel. Cafe, gift shop. **Open:** Park, daily 9am–5pm; zoo, daily 10am–4pm. Closed some hols. $$

Rotary Nature Center, 552 Bellevue, Lakeside Park; tel 510/238-3739. Located on the shores of Lake Merritt, the center offers seasonal displays of mammals, birds, and reptiles and has exhibits that cover topics like ecology and conservation. Lectures, nature walks, films, and other special programs. **Open:** Tues–Sun 10am–5pm, Mon noon–5pm. Free.

Oakland Coliseum Complex, Hegenberger Rd exit of I-880; tel 510/430-8020. From April to October, the Oakland Athletics play baseball in the Oakland Coliseum Stadium, which seats close to 50,000. The NBA's Golden State Warriors play basketball from November to April in the 15,025-seat Oakland Coliseum Arena. Tickets are available from the coliseum box office or by phone through BASS Ticketmaster (tel 510/762-2277). $$$$

OAKVILLE

Map page M-2, C2 (N of Napa)

Restaurant 🍴

♦ **Stars Oakville Cafe**, 7848 St Helena Hwy; PO Box 410, Oakville; tel 707/944-8905. E side of Calif 29. **French/Italian.** San Francisco super-chef Jeremiah Tower's new venture in wine country. In the large dining garden, diners sit under a green and white marquee, or amid olive trees. The food is very good to excellent; selections might include golden onion tart with fresh-picked salad greens, or pan-seared salmon with fresh corn, peas, potatoes, and beets. **FYI:** Reservations recommended. Beer and wine only. **Open:** Sun–Thurs 11:30am–9pm, Fri–Sat 11:30am–10pm. Closed Dec 25. **Prices:** Main courses $16.50–$19. Maj CC. 🍰 ♿

Refreshment Stop 🥤

★ **Oakville Grocery**, 7856 St Helena Hwy, Oakville; tel 707/944-8802. On Calif 29. **Deli.** A deli stocked with thousands of gourmet groceries from around the world—wild-mango chutney from Sri Lanka, Jamaican jerk spices, 16 varieties of olives, and a huge wine inventory. An ideal place to pick up a picnic, offering cheeses, pasta salads, sliced smoked tuna, and special sandwiches. **Open:** Daily 10am–6pm. Closed some hols. Maj CC.

Attraction 💼

Robert Mondavi Winery, 7801 St Helena Hwy (Calif 29); tel 707/259-9463. This is the ultimate high-tech Napa Valley winery, housed in a magnificent Mission-style facility. Almost every variable in the wine-making process is computer controlled. A free guided tour is followed by a tasting of selected current wines, which are sold by the glass. Reservations are recommended for the guided tour. **Open:** Daily 10am–5pm. Closed some hols. Free.

O'BRIEN

Map page M-2, B2 (N of Redding)

Attraction 💼

Lake Shasta Caverns; tel 916/238-2341 or toll free 800/795-CAVE. Located off Shasta Caverns Rd. Long a part of Wintu Indian folklore, these caverns were first explored by a white man in 1878. The name of J A Richardson and the date are still visible on the wall where he wrote them in carbon black on November 3. Filled with myriad multicolored columns, draperies, stalactites, stalagmites, and flowstone deposits, the cavern was made accessible to the general public in 1964. A tunnel was driven, and paved walkways, stairs, guardrails, and lighting were added, but the caverns were left in the most natural state possible.

The 2-hour tour begins with a scenic boat ride across Lake Shasta and a bus trip up the mountainside. More than 600 steps are traversed in the course of the tour, and the cave temperature remains a constant 58°F with 95% humidity. Tours depart hourly: Mem Day–Labor Day, daily 9am–5pm; Apr–late May and Sept, daily 9am–3pm; Oct–Mar, daily at 10am, noon, and 2pm. **Open:** Closed some hols. $$$$

OCEANSIDE

Map page M-3, E2

Motel 🏨

🏨🏨 **Best Western Marty's Valley Inn**, 3240 E Mission Ave, Oceanside, CA 92054; tel 619/757-7700 or toll free 800/747-3529; fax 619/439-3311. 35 mi N of San Diego. Mission Ave exit off I-5. Comfortable accommodations appealing to business travelers, who can use the conference center on site. **Rooms:** 111 rms and stes. Exec-level rms avail. CI noon/CO noon. Nonsmoking rms avail. **Amenities:** 🛁 A/C, satel TV w/movies. Some units w/terraces, 1 w/fireplace. **Services:** 🚗 🛎 Car-rental desk, babysitting. **Facilities:** 🏋 🏊 ♿ 1 rst, 1 bar (w/entertainment). **Rates (CP):** HS July–Sept 12 $59–$63 S; $63–$70 D; from $95 ste. Extra person $5. Children under 12 stay free. Lower rates off-season. Spec packages avail. Pking: Outdoor, free. Maj CC.

OJAI

Map page M-3, D1 (N of Ventura)

Motel 📧

≡ ≡ Best Western Casa Ojai, 1302 Ojai Ave, Ojai, CA 93023; tel 805/646-8175 or toll free 800/255-8175; fax 805/640-8247. Ojai/Calif 33 exit off US 101. A clean, well-maintained 2-story motel located on the outskirts of town. There's some traffic noise from Calif 150 during the daytime. **Rooms:** 45 rms and stes. CI 2pm/CO noon. Nonsmoking rms avail. Rooms are light and airy, with loveseat and chair, nice artwork, and brass reading lamps. **Amenities:** 🛋 🕹 🖲 A/C, cable TV. VCR in some rooms. **Services:** 🖓 **Facilities:** 🖼 ᶀ Whirlpool. Public golf course across street. **Rates (CP):** HS May–Sept $65–$100 S; $100–$125 D; from $135 ste. Extra person $5. Children under 12 stay free. Min stay spec evnts. Lower rates off-season. Spec packages avail. Pking: Outdoor, free. Maj CC. Golf package available.

Resort

≡ ≡ ≡ Ojai Valley Inn, Country Club Rd, Ojai, CA 93023; tel 805/646-5511 or toll free 800/422-6524; fax 805/646-7969. Exit 33 off US 101. 14 mi inland to Country Club Dr. 220 acres. Designed in 1923 by Wallace Neff and set on 220 peaceful acres in the Ojai Valley, the hacienda-style building features a lobby with high ceilings, polished tile floors, fireplace, oversized sofas, marble tables, original art, and fresh flowers. **Rooms:** 207 rms and stes; 3 ctges/villas. Exec-level rms avail. CI 4pm/CO noon. Nonsmoking rms avail. Rooms are very spacious and nicely appointed; each has views of the mountains, gardens, or golf course. Some bathrooms have marble countertops. **Amenities:** 🛋 🕹 🖲 🍽 A/C, cable TV w/movies, shoe polisher, bathrobes. All units w/minibars, all w/terraces, some w/fireplaces, some w/Jacuzzis. **Services:** 🍽 🖭 🚗 🖳 🖓 Twice-daily maid svce, social director, masseur, children's program, babysitting. **Facilities:** 🖼 ⛳ ▶₁₈ 🖼 🕹⁴ 🖼 🖳 💾 ⬛ ᶀ 2 rsts, 1 bar, lawn games, spa, sauna, steam rm, whirlpool, playground. 2 beautiful pools, including 60-foot lap pool. Horseback riding nearby; transportation provided. **Rates:** HS Mar–Nov $195–$345 S or D; from $345 ste; from $600 ctge/villa. Extra person $25. Children under 3 stay free. Min stay wknds. Lower rates off-season. Spec packages avail. Pking: Outdoor, free. Maj CC.

Restaurant 🍴

The Ranch House, South Lomita and Besa Rd, Ojai (Meiners Oaks); tel 805/646-2360. Tico Rd exit off Calif 33. **Continental/Vegetarian.** Tucked away in a beautiful garden setting. Dine outdoors next to meandering streams, lush foliage, and a bamboo forest while listening to classical music. Fresh herbs grown on site are used in the seasonal menu. Seafood, homemade soups, pasta; fresh-baked breads available to take home. Award-winning wine list. **FYI:** Reservations recommended. Children's menu. Beer and wine only. **Open:** HS May–Sept lunch Wed–Sat 11:30am–1:30pm; dinner Wed–Sat 6–8:30pm, Sun 1–7:30pm; brunch Sun 11am–1pm. Reduced hours off-season. Closed some hols. **Prices:** Main courses $19–$24. Maj CC. ♥ 🍰 ᶀ

OLEMA

Map page M-2, C1 (SW of Petaluma)

Inn 📧

≡ ≡ ≡ The Olema Inn, 10000 Sir Francis Drake Blvd, Olema, CA 94950; tel 415/663-9559 or toll free 800/532-9252; fax 415/453-9965. 40 mi NW of San Francisco. Sir Francis Drake Blvd exit off US 101; go west 30 mi to Olema. This 1876 inn has been updated with modern comforts, yet still maintains vintage charm. Located next to Point Reyes National Seashore, on a moderately trafficked road. **Rooms:** 6 rms. CI 2pm/CO 11am. No smoking. Pleasantly but not lavishly decorated, with a few antiques. Lined with white and Dresden-blue tiles, bathrooms offer paltry counter space; most have tubs with handheld showers. **Amenities:** No A/C, phone, or TV. **Services:** Afternoon tea and wine/sherry served. **Facilities:** 🖼 1 rst (see also "Restaurants" below), 1 bar (w/entertainment). Well-regarded restaurant. **Rates (CP):** $85–$105 D. Pking: Outdoor, free. Ltd CC.

Restaurant 🍴

The Olema Inn, 10000 Sir Francis Drake Blvd, Olema; tel 415/663-9559. 40 mi NW of San Francisco. Sir Francis Drake Blvd exit off US 101; 30 mi to Olema. **Californian/French.** A great place for Sunday brunch either before or after heading to nearby Point Reyes. Set in a charming wood-frame inn built in 1876, the restaurant is bright and airy, with large windows overlooking the garden and a dining terrace. Cuisine might include filet of beef with pinot noir sauce; or prawns Portuguese, accented with tomato, garlic, and fresh herbs. **FYI:** Reservations recommended. Guitar. Beer and wine only. **Open:** Lunch Mon–Sat noon–3pm; dinner daily 5–9:30pm; brunch Sun 11am–3pm. **Prices:** Main courses $14.50–$18.50. Ltd CC. 🍰 ᶀ

OLYMPIC VALLEY

Map page M-2, C3 (N of Tahoe City)

Hotel 🛏

≣≣≣ **Olympic Village Inn**, 1909 Chamonix Place, PO Box 2395, Olympic Valley, CA 96146; tel 916/581-6000 or toll free 800/845-5243. Take right at Squaw Valley entrance, go 2 mi. 4½ acres. Looks like a Tyrolean village of condominium suites in historic Squaw Valley. World's best athletes stayed here at the 1960 Olympic Games. **Rooms:** 90 stes and effic. CI 4pm/CO 11am. Express checkout avail. Nonsmoking rms avail. Clean, well-kept 1-bedroom suites with country French decor. Some kitchenettes. **Amenities:** 🛏 ◊ 🖻 Cable TV, refrig, VCR, stereo/tape player, bathrobes. No A/C. All units w/terraces, some w/fireplaces. **Services:** ⚿ 🐾 Social director, children's program, babysitting. **Facilities:** 🖻 🚲 🛶 🐾 🖼 🖫 ♿ Whirlpool, playground, washer/dryer. Nice lawn and play area. Luxurious patio near pool offers a comfortable place to relax. **Rates:** HS June–Sept 10/Dec–Mar 15 from $95 ste; from $135 effic. Min stay HS. Lower rates off-season. Pking: Outdoor, free. Maj CC.

Lodge

≣≣≣ **Squaw Valley Inn**, 1920 Squaw Valley Rd, PO Box 2407, Olympic Valley, CA 96146; tel 916/583-1576 or toll free 800/323-7666; fax 916/583-7619. 12 mi SW of Truckee. Squaw Valley exit off I-80; take Calif 89 S to Squaw Valley entrance, turn right. A 2-story wood-shingled structure within walking distance of the ski lifts. Decor is old English. **Rooms:** 60 rms and stes. CI 4pm/CO 11am. Nonsmoking rms avail. Renovated in 1992, the rooms have a British flair. **Amenities:** 🛏 ◊ 🖻 Cable TV, shoe polisher. No A/C. **Services:** ⚿ 🐾 Babysitting. **Facilities:** 🖻 🛶 🐾 🖼 🖫 🖳 1 rst, 1 bar, sauna. Basketball court; 2-level conference center. **Rates:** HS Dec–Apr $110–$185 S or D; from $300 ste. Extra person $15. Children under 12 stay free. Min stay HS. Lower rates off-season. Higher rates for spec evnts/hols. Spec packages avail. Pking: Outdoor, free. Maj CC.

Resort

≣≣≣≣ **Resort at Squaw Creek**, 400 Squaw Creek Rd, PO Box 3333, Olympic Valley, CA 96146; tel 916/583-6300 or toll free 800/583-6300; fax 916/581-6632. 10 mi S of Truckee. Squaw Valley exit off I-80. 636 acres. An upscale resort at 6,200 feet. Floor-to-ceiling windows in public areas showcase granite peaks of High Sierras. Busy with conventions, conferences, parties. **Rooms:** 405 rms and stes. Exec-level rms avail. CI 4pm/CO noon. Express checkout avail. Nonsmoking rms avail. Quality touches, such as granite vanity counters. **Amenities:** 🛏 ◊ 🖻 A/C, cable TV w/movies, refrig, voice mail, shoe polisher, bathrobes. All units w/minibars, some w/terraces, some w/fireplaces. **Services:** ✕ ⚿ 🆅🅿 🛶 🐾 Social director, masseur, children's program, babysitting. Almost seems to have more employees than customers. **Facilities:** 🖻 🚲 🏌18 🏊 🖼 🐾 🖫 ♨8 🎱 🖫950 🖳 ♿ 5 rsts, 3 bars (1 w/entertainment), lifeguard, games rm, lawn games, spa, sauna, whirlpool, beauty salon, day-care ctr. Championship golf course designed by Robert Trent Jones, Jr. Landscaped, spacious pools include rock wall water slide. Great patio, grand ballroom, and a variety of shops. **Rates:** HS Dec 20–Mar/June–Oct $250–$350 S or D; from $525 ste. Extra person $25. Children under 15 stay free. Min stay HS. Lower rates off-season. Spec packages avail. Pking: Outdoor, free. Maj CC. Special packages during the shoulder season.

Restaurant 🍴

♦ **Graham's**, 1650 Squaw Valley Rd, Olympic Valley (Squaw Valley); tel 916/581-0454. Squaw Valley exit off Calif 89; ½ mi east of Squaw Valley ski area, in the Christy Inn Lodge. **Californian/Mediterranean.** Open, airy, yet cozy, with a large stone fireplace. Big mountain-view windows add light. Romantic place for an après-ski drink and appetizer. Excellent food is a bit pricey for Tahoe, but worth a splurge. **FYI:** Reservations recommended. Children's menu. Dress code. Beer and wine only. **Open:** Daily 6–10pm. Closed Sept 15–Thanksgiving. **Prices:** Main courses $15–$22; PF dinner $22. Ltd CC. 🌐 🏔 🖢 ♿

Attractions 📷

Squaw Valley USA, Calif 89; tel 916/583-6985. This was the site of the 1960 Olympic Winter Games. Some 70% of Squaw's terrain is geared toward beginners and intermediates. There are 23 chairlifts and a 120-passenger cable car (see below). In summer, the area is opened to mountain bikers, and features many trails with varying levels of difficulty. **Open:** Mid-Nov–mid-May, daily. $$$$

Squaw Valley Cable Car; tel 916/583-6985. Located within Squaw Valley USA (see above), the cable car takes skiers, sightseers, and other recreational visitors 2,000 vertical feet to scenic High Camp. In addition to spectacular views of Lake Tahoe and the High Sierra, visitors can take part in a variety of activities, including ice skating, swimming, tennis, and mountain biking at the High Camp Bath and Tennis Club. **Open:** Daily 8am–4pm; summer and winter peak seasons, 8am–9pm. $$$$

ONTARIO

Map page M-3, D2 (E of Pomona)

Hotels 🏨

≡≡≡ **Doubletree Club Hotel**, 429 N Vineyard, Ontario, CA 91764 (Ontario Int'l Airport); tel 909/391-6411 or toll free 800/222-TREE; fax 909/391-2369. Vineyard Ave S exit off I-10. This shiny new hotel is near the airport, yet quiet. **Rooms:** 170 rms and stes. CI 3pm/CO 1pm. Express checkout avail. Nonsmoking rms avail. **Amenities:** 🔓 🗄 ☎ A/C, cable TV w/movies. **Services:** ✗ 🚐 🛄 🍴 Full breakfast included. 24-hour coffee service and complimentary morning newspaper; evening drinks and hors d'oeuvres. **Facilities:** 🏋 🛳 280 💻 ♿ 1 rst, 1 bar, whirlpool. Current periodicals in the Club Room, which is reminiscent of a private club. **Rates (BB):** $89 S or D. Extra person $10. Children under 12 stay free. Spec packages avail. Pking: Outdoor, free. Maj CC.

≡≡≡ **Holiday Inn Express**, 1818 E Holt Blvd, Ontario, CA 91761 (Ontario Int'l Airport); tel 909/988-8466 or toll free 800/760-4000; fax 909/986-5456. Vineyard S exit off I-10; ½ mi to Holt; right 1 block. Within walking distance of Ontario Airport. **Rooms:** 104 rms. CI noon/CO 11am. Nonsmoking rms avail. Nicely renovated rooms. **Amenities:** 🔓 🗄 A/C, satel TV w/movies. **Services:** 🚐 🛄 🍴 Car-rental desk. Complimentary breakfast and morning newspaper. **Facilities:** 🏋 130 💻 ♿ Whirlpool, washer/dryer. Business center has fax, copy machine, computers, and secretarial services. **Rates (CP):** $65 S or D. Extra person $6. Children under 12 stay free. Pking: Outdoor, free. Maj CC.

≡≡≡ **Ontario Airport Hilton**, 700 N Haven Ave, Ontario, CA 91764 (Ontario Int'l Airport); tel 909/980-0400 or toll free 800/645-1379; fax 909/941-6781. Haven Ave N exit off I-10. Splendid convention and conference hotel near the airport; a favorite of airline crews. **Rooms:** 308 rms and stes. Exec-level rms avail. CI 3pm/CO noon. Nonsmoking rms avail. **Amenities:** 🔓 🗄 🍴 A/C, cable TV w/movies, refrig, bathrobes. Some units w/terraces, some w/Jacuzzis. **Services:** 🍴 🚐 🛄 🍴 Twice-daily maid svce, car-rental desk. Secretarial services. **Facilities:** 🏋 🛳 600 💻 ♿ 2 rsts (see also "Restaurants" below), 1 bar (w/entertainment), whirlpool. Helicopter pad. **Rates:** $115–$135 S or D; from $150 ste. Extra person $15. Children under 18 stay free. Higher rates for spec evnts/hols. Spec packages avail. Pking: Outdoor, free. Maj CC.

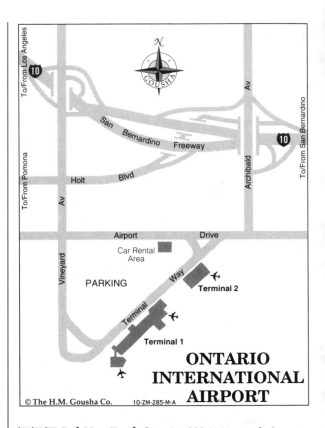

© The H.M. Gousha Co.   10-ZM-285-M-A

ONTARIO INTERNATIONAL AIRPORT

≡≡≡ **Red Lion Hotel–Ontario**, 222 N Vineyard, Ontario, CA 91764 (Ontario Int'l Airport); tel 909/983-0909 or toll free 800/547-8010; fax 909/983-8005. Vineyard Ave S exit off I-10; ¼ mi on left. Located close to the Ontario Airport, this hotel always bustles with conferences. At the entrance, the grand canopy looks like a Mexican pyramid. Lobby is enormous, and hospitality pervasive. **Rooms:** 340 rms and stes. Exec-level rms avail. CI 3pm/CO 1pm. Express checkout avail. Nonsmoking rms avail. **Amenities:** 🔓 🗄 ☎ 🍴 A/C, cable TV w/movies, refrig. Some units w/terraces, some w/Jacuzzis. **Services:** ✗ 🔑 🚐 🛄 🍴 🍴 Twice-daily maid svce. **Facilities:** 🏋 🛳 2K 💻 ♿ 2 rsts, 2 bars (1 w/entertainment), whirlpool, washer/dryer. Cappuccino cart in lobby until 10am. **Rates:** $104–$114 S or D; from $375 ste. Children under 18 stay free. Spec packages avail. Pking: Outdoor, free. Maj CC.

Motels

≡≡≡≡ **Country Side Suites**, 204 N Vineyard Ave, Ontario, CA 91764; tel 909/986-8550 or toll free 800/248-4661. Vineyard Ave S exit off I-10; 2 blocks S. The crown jewel of Country Side Inns, a southern California mini-chain, has gleaming marble, fine furnishings, French-style wallpaper, and marvelous staff. **Rooms:** 107 rms and stes. CI 2pm/CO noon. Nonsmoking rms avail. Large rooms. **Amenities:** 🔒 🐶 A/C, cable TV w/movies, refrig. Some units w/terraces, some w/Jacuzzis. **Services:** 🚐🛄🍴 Babysitting. Complimentary breakfast buffet and evening refreshments. Fresh fruit always available in the lobby. **Facilities:** 🛆 🏊 🐶 Whirlpool, washer/dryer. **Rates (BB):** $59–$110 S; $69–$120 D; from $100 ste. Extra person $10. Children under 12 stay free. Spec packages avail. Pking: Outdoor, free. Maj CC. Great value for the price.

📠📠 **Fairfield Inn by Marriott**, 3201 E Centrelake Dr, Ontario, CA 91761; tel 909/395-9300 or toll free 800/228-2800; fax 909/395-9300. Haven Ave S exit from I-10; right on Guasti Rd. This hotel, opened in 1990, provides great value for the money. Very quiet despite its highway location. **Rooms:** 117 rms. CI 3pm/CO noon. Nonsmoking rms avail. **Amenities:** 🔒🐶 A/C, cable TV w/movies. **Services:** 🚐🛄🍴 **Facilities:** 🛆 🏊 🐶 **Rates (CP):** HS Mar–May/Sept–Oct $38 S or D. Children under 18 stay free. Lower rates off-season. Spec packages avail. Pking: Outdoor, free. Maj CC.

📠📠 **Good Night Inn**, 1801 E G St, Ontario, CA 91764; tel 909/983-3604; fax 909/986-4724. Vineyard Ave S exit off I-10; go 1 block; turn right onto G St. Undergoing renovation under new ownership. **Rooms:** 186 rms. CI 2pm/CO 11am. Nonsmoking rms avail. **Amenities:** 🔒 🐶 A/C, satel TV w/movies, refrig. Some units w/terraces. **Services:** ✕ 🚐 🛄 🍴 🐕 Car-rental desk, babysitting. **Facilities:** 🛆 🏊 🖥 🐶 1 rst, 1 bar (w/entertainment), washer/dryer. **Rates:** $45 S; $50–$55 D. Extra person $5. Children under 18 stay free. Pking: Outdoor, free. Maj CC.

Restaurants 🍴

🍸 **Calla**, in the Ontario Airport Hilton, 700 N Haven Ave, Ontario; tel 909/980-0400. Haven Ave N exit off I-10. **Continental/French.** A beautiful room, with fine fabric–covered chairs, marvelously painted walls, Erté prints, and soft lighting. Chef Girard Seys, formerly of Maxim's in Paris, presents such dishes as rack of lamb with lavender herbs, braised veal chop stuffed with wild mushrooms wrapped in phyllo dough, and broiled salmon with fresh mango and curry mousseline. **FYI:** Reservations recommended. Piano. Children's menu. Jacket required. **Open:** Lunch Mon–Fri 11:30am–1:30pm; dinner Mon–Sat 6–10pm. Closed some hols. **Prices:** Main courses $21–$27.50. Maj CC. 💟 🐶

La Cheminée, 1133 W 6th St, Ontario; tel 909/983-7900. Mountain Ave exit off I-10. **Californian/French.** Diners are welcomed by comfortable sofas and chairs in front of a large

stone fireplace. The dining room, decorated with stained-glass panels and velvet-covered chairs, has an atmosphere of refined intimacy. Chef John Rose offers entrees such as pheasant sautéed with white wine and shallots, and chateaubriand with béarnaise sauce. **FYI:** Reservations recommended. Band. **Open:** Lunch Mon–Fri 11:30am–2:30pm; dinner Mon–Fri 5:30–9:30pm, Sat 6–10pm. Closed some hols. **Prices:** Main courses $13.50–$25. Maj CC. 💟 📧 🐶

★ **Rosa's**, 425 N Vineyard Ave, Ontario; tel 909/391-1971. **Italian.** Like a private villa set in the Italian countryside, this restaurant delights the eye with ceilings painted in a sky motif, faux marble columns, and mirrored doors separating several cozy dining rooms. Specialties include pasta from several regions of Italy, grilled and braised meats, seafood, and chicken. Vegetarian meals are also available. Good selection of cognacs and brandies. **FYI:** Reservations recommended. Piano/singer. Children's menu. **Open:** Lunch Mon–Fri 11:30am–4pm; dinner Mon–Fri 4–10pm, Sat 5–10pm, Sun 5–9pm. Closed some hols. **Prices:** Main courses $9.50–$24. Maj CC. 💟 🐶

Attraction 🏛

Museum of History and Art, Ontario, 225 S Euclid Ave; tel 909/983-3198. Housed in a handsome Mediterranean Revival building built in 1937 as Ontario's second city hall, this museum features exhibits on Ontario's rich heritage of agriculture, industry, and aviation. Temporary exhibits explore topics of local, regional, or national history. Art exhibits feature work by California artists Rex Brandt, and Emil Kosa, as well as local and regional talent. **Open:** Wed–Sun noon–4pm. Closed some hols. Free.

ORANGE

Map page M-3, D2 (E of Santa Ana)

Hotels 🏨

📠📠📠 **Doubletree Hotel**, 100 The City Dr, Orange, CA 92668; tel 714/634-4500 or toll free 800/222-TREE; fax 714/978-3839. 25 mi SE of Los Angeles. State College Blvd exit off I-5; turn right, then right on Chapman Ave. This lovely hotel, completely renovated in 1993, has pleasant gardens and public areas. Caters to the business traveler. Close to Disneyland and medical center. **Rooms:** 450 rms and stes. Exec-level rms avail. CI 3pm/CO noon. Express checkout avail. Nonsmoking rms avail. Rooms have nice furniture and drapes, comfortable chairs, attractive artwork. **Amenities:** 🔒 🐶 📧 A/C, cable TV w/movies, voice mail. Some units w/minibars, some w/Jacuzzis. **Services:**

X ▣ VP 🚐 ⛵ ⏎ Car-rental desk, babysitting. Shuttle service to Disneyland and convention center is accessible for guests with disabilities. **Facilities:** 🏊 🏋 🎱 💻 ♿ 2 rsts, 1 bar, whirlpool. Excellent meeting facilities. **Rates:** HS June–Aug $120 S; $130 D; from $250 ste. Extra person $10. Children under 18 stay free. Lower rates off-season. Spec packages avail. Pking: Outdoor, $4. Maj CC.

≣≣≣ **Hilton Suites**, 400 N State College Blvd, Orange, CA 92668; tel 714/938-1111 or toll free 800/HILTONS; fax 714/938-0930. 25 mi SE of Los Angeles. State College Blvd exit off I-5. An all-suites hotel located near the new Anaheim Arena, about a mile from Disneyland and the Anaheim Convention Center. All floors open out to a lovely atrium. **Rooms:** 230 stes. Exec-level rms avail. CI 3pm/CO noon. Express checkout avail. Nonsmoking rms avail. Large, bright, and airy, with nice furniture and linens. Comfortable couches and overstuffed chairs. **Amenities:** 📺 🅰 🖥 🍽 A/C, cable TV w/movies, refrig, VCR, voice mail, bathrobes. Some units w/terraces. Microwave. **Services:** X ▣ 🚐 ⛵ ⏎ 🍽 Car-rental desk, children's program, babysitting. Free videos. Complimentary shuttle to Disneyland is accessible for persons with disabilities. Complimentary full American breakfast and evening reception. **Facilities:** 🏊 🏋 🎱 💻 ♿ 1 rst, 1 bar, sauna, whirlpool. **Rates (BB):** HS June–Aug from $155 ste. Extra person $15. Children under 18 stay free. Lower rates off-season. Higher rates for spec evnts/hols. Spec packages avail. Pking: Outdoor, free. Maj CC.

≣≣≣ **Washington Suites Hotel**, 720 The City Dr S, Orange, CA 92668; tel 714/740-2700 or toll free 800/2SUITES; fax 714/971-1692. 25 mi SE of Los Angeles. City Drive exit off I-5; go south. Clean, well kept, and nicely designed, with spotless carpets and lots of brass. Good for families as well as corporate travelers. **Rooms:** 141 stes. CI 4pm/CO noon. Nonsmoking rms avail. Suites are very large, with upgraded furniture, clean, and well maintained. Full kitchen and separate bedroom area. Up to 3 rooms can interconnect. **Amenities:** 📺 🅰 🖥 A/C, cable TV w/movies, refrig, VCR. Some units w/Jacuzzis. **Services:** X 🚐 ⛵ ⏎ Car-rental desk, babysitting. Complimentary American breakfast in lounge or on patio, afternoon cocktail reception, shuttle to Disneyland and local businesses. No room service, but local restaurants deliver. **Facilities:** 🏊 🎱 💻 ♿ Games rm, whirlpool, beauty salon, day-care ctr, washer/dryer. Library is nice for meetings. **Rates (BB):** HS June–Aug from $140 ste. Extra person $15. Children under 18 stay free. Lower rates off-season. Spec packages avail. Pking: Outdoor, free. Maj CC.

Motel

≣≣ **Goodnite Inn**, 101 N State College Blvd, Orange, CA 92668; tel 714/634-9500 or toll free 800/544-6991; fax 714/

634-4751. 25 mi SE of Los Angeles. Chapman Ave S exit off I-5. Average property 2 miles from Disneyland and Convention Center. No lobby to speak of. **Rooms:** 143 rms and stes. CI 3pm/CO noon. Nonsmoking rms avail. Rooms are clean except for some grout problems in bathrooms. **Amenities:** 📺 🅰 🖥 A/C, cable TV w/movies. **Services:** 🚐 ⛵ ⏎ 🍽 Car-rental desk. Complimentary shuttle to Disneyland. **Facilities:** 🏊 🎱 ♿ 1 rst, 1 bar, whirlpool, washer/dryer. Nice pool ares; large parking lot for semi trucks. **Rates (CP):** HS June–Aug $34–$45 S or D; from $62 ste. Children under 12 stay free. Lower rates off-season. Higher rates for spec evnts/hols. Spec packages avail. Pking: Outdoor, free. Maj CC.

Restaurants 🍴

Cafe Francais, 1736 E Meats St, Orange; tel 714/998-6051. Lincoln exit off I-55. Located across from the Orange Mall. **French.** A quaint, lovely setting. Starters include French onion soup, escargot, and stuffed mushrooms. Then move on to the veal scaloppine, broiled salmon, Pacific red snapper, and duckling in raspberry sauce. **FYI:** Reservations recommended. Children's menu. Dress code. Beer and wine only. **Open:** Lunch Tues–Fri 11:30am–2pm; dinner Tues–Sat 5:30–10pm, Sun 5–9pm. Closed some hols. **Prices:** Main courses $14–$21. Maj CC. ♥

Caffe Piemonte, in the Thrifty Shopping Center, 1835 E Chapman Ave, Orange; tel 714/532-3296. **Italian.** Charming, comfortable, authentic. Menu specialties include antipasti; fresh fish of the day; pork loin with butter, sage, and garlic; and a wide variety of pasta with imaginative sauces. **FYI:** Reservations recommended. Dress code. Beer and wine only. **Open:** Lunch Tues–Fri noon–1:30pm; dinner Tues–Sun 5–9pm. Closed some hols. **Prices:** Main courses $8–$23. Maj CC.

OXNARD

Map page M-3, D1

See also Port Hueneme

Hotels 🏨

≣≣ **Casa Sirena Marina Resort**, 3605 Peninsula Rd, Oxnard, CA 93035; tel 805/985-6311 or toll free 800/228-6026; fax 805/985-4329. 5 mi W of downtown. Victoria Ave exit off US 101. Excellent waterfront location overlooking busy marina. Easy walk to Fisherman's Village shops and restaurants. **Rooms:** 275 rms and stes. CI 3pm/CO noon. Nonsmoking rms avail. North wing rooms are fine, but several are being renovated. **Amenities:** 📺 🖥 Cable TV w/movies, refrig. No A/C. Some units w/terraces, 1 w/Jacuzzi. **Services:** ✗ 🚐 ⊠ ⌐ Masseur. **Facilities:** 🎣 🏋 ❏ 🛳 500 ⅃ 2 rsts, 1 bar (w/entertainment), lifeguard, games rm, lawn games, snorkeling, spa, sauna, steam rm, whirlpool, beauty salon, playground. Lobster Trap restaurant very good. **Rates:** HS May–Oct $75–$90 S; $85–$100 D; from $125 ste. Extra person $10. Children under 12 stay free. Min stay spec evnts. Lower rates off-season. Spec packages avail. Pking: Outdoor, free. Maj CC.

≡≡≡ **Mandalay Beach Resort**, 2101 Mandalay Beach Rd, Oxnard, CA 93035; tel 805/984-2500 or toll free 800/582-3000; fax 805/984-8339. 6 mi W of downtown. Victoria Ave exit off US 101. Outstanding location right on the sand close to Channel Islands harbor. Elegant public areas and tasteful furnishings. **Rooms:** 249 stes. CI 4pm/CO noon. Express checkout avail. Nonsmoking rms avail. **Amenities:** 🛁 ⌕ 🔲 A/C, cable TV w/movies, refrig, voice mail. Some units w/terraces, some w/fireplaces, some w/Jacuzzis. Suites have wet bar and microwave, plus 2 full bathrooms. **Services:** ✗ 🗝 VP 🚐 ⊠ ⌐ Children's program, babysitting. Full breakfast; 2-hour complimentary bar service in the evenings. **Facilities:** 🎣 🚴 🏋 ❏ 865 ⅃ 1 rst, 1 bar (w/entertainment), 1 beach (ocean), board surfing, games rm, lawn games, whirlpool. **Rates (BB):** HS July–Labor Day from $159 ste. Extra person $15. Children under 12 stay free. Min stay HS and wknds. Lower rates off-season. Higher rates for spec evnts/hols. Spec packages avail. Pking: Indoor/outdoor, free. Maj CC.

≡≡ **Oxnard Hilton Inn**, 600 Esplanade Dr, Oxnard, CA 93030; tel 805/485-9666 or toll free 800/44-RELAX; fax 805/485-2061. Vineyard Ave exit off US 101. Decent location near a mall and the Financial Plaza complex. **Rooms:** 160 rms and stes. CI 3pm/CO noon. Express checkout avail. Nonsmoking rms avail. Comfortable yet unremarkable. **Amenities:** 🛁 ⌕ 🖢 A/C, cable TV, refrig, VCR. Some units w/terraces, 1 w/Jacuzzi. **Services:** ✗ 🚐 ⊠ ⌐ **Facilities:** 🎣 🏋 ❏ 600 ⅃ 1 rst, 1 bar (w/entertainment), whirlpool, beauty salon. **Rates:** $75–$100 S; $85–$110 D; from $150 ste. Extra person $10. Children under 12 stay free. Min stay spec evnts. Higher rates for spec evnts/hols. Spec packages avail. Pking: Outdoor, free. Maj CC.

≡≡≡ **Radisson Suite Hotel at River Ridge**, 2101 W Vineyard Ave, Oxnard, CA 93030; tel 805/988-0130 or toll free 800/333-3333; fax 805/583-2779. Vineyard Ave exit off US 101. A very nicely planned property. Lovely suites with full kitchen are good for family or long-term visits. **Rooms:** 250 stes. CI 3pm/CO noon. Express checkout avail. Nonsmoking rms avail. Four "green" suites for the environmentally conscious are very popular. **Amenities:** 🛁 ⌕ 🔲 A/C, cable TV w/movies, refrig. All units w/terraces, some w/fireplaces. **Services:** ✗ 🚐 ⊠ ⌐ Masseur. Complimentary home-style breakfast; welcome beverage coupon. **Facilities:** 🎣 ▶18 🏋 ❏ 🛳 600 ⅃ 1 rst, 1 bar (w/entertainment), spa, whirlpool, washer/dryer. **Rates (BB):** HS Mem Day–Labor Day from $85 ste. Extra person $10. Children under 18 stay free. Min stay spec evnts. Lower rates off-season. Higher rates for spec evnts/hols. Spec packages avail. Pking: Outdoor, free. Maj CC.

Attractions 💼

Gull Wings Children's Museum, 418 W Fourth St; tel 805/483-3005. Interactive museum with exhibits and special programs that encourage children to explore topics ranging from science to entertainment. **Open:** Wed–Fri and Sun 1–5pm, Sat 10am–5pm. Closed some hols. $

Maritime Museum at Channel Islands Harbor, 2731 S Victoria Ave; tel 805/984-6260. The region's maritime history is preserved with numerous artifacts and 36 models depicting the genealogy of sailing ships. The art collection includes works by leading American and European marine artists, dating from 1700 to the present. **Open:** Thurs–Mon 11am–5pm. Closed some hols. Free.

PACIFIC GROVE
Map page M-2, E1

Motels 🏨

≡≡ **Pacific Grove Motel**, Lighthouse Ave at Grove Acre, Pacific Grove, CA 93950; tel 408/372-3218 or toll free 800/858-8997. Pebble Beach/Pacific Grove exit off Calif 1. A clean, safe motel for the economy-minded traveler, within walking distance of downtown Pacific Grove and the ocean. Also close to the Asilomar Conference Center. Caters to scuba divers. **Rooms:** 30 rms. CI 1pm/CO 11am. **Amenities:** 🛁 ⌕ 🔲 Cable TV, refrig. No A/C. Some units w/terraces. **Services:** Babysitting. **Facilities:** 🎣 Whirlpool, playground. **Rates:** HS May–Sept $54–$94 S or D. Extra person $5. Min stay wknds. Lower rates off-season. Pking: Outdoor, free. Maj CC.

≡≡≡ **Rosedale Inn**, 775 Asilomar Blvd, Pacific Grove, CA 93950; tel 408/655-1000 or toll free 800/822-5606; fax 408/655-0691. Pebble Beach/Pacific Grove exit off Calif 1; follow Calif 68 W to Asilomar Blvd; turn right. A motel with a rustic feel. Located in a woodsy section of town near the Asilomar Conference Center and Asilomar State Beach. **Rooms:** 18 stes and effic. CI 2pm/CO 11am. Nonsmoking rms avail. Nothing really special, except for silk flower arrangements, microwaves, and popcorn in all rooms. Bathrooms feature Jacuzzis and TVs. **Amenities:** 🛁 ⌕ 🔲 🖢 Cable TV w/movies, refrig, VCR, shoe polisher. No A/C. Some units w/terraces, all w/fireplaces, all w/Jacuzzis. **Services:** 🛏 🖵 Masseur, babysitting. Free daily newspaper. **Facilities:** 🏊 ♿ **Rates (CP):** HS June–Sept from $115 ste; from $175 effic. Extra person $10. Children under 12 stay free. Min stay spec evnts. Lower rates off-season. Pking: Outdoor, free. Maj CC.

Inns

🏚🏚🏚 **Centrella Bed & Breakfast Inn**, 612 Central Ave, Pacific Grove, CA 93950 (Downtown); tel 408/372-3372 or toll free 800/233-3372; fax 408/372-2036. Pebble Beach/Pacific Grove exit off Calif 1. A charming inn built as a boarding house in 1889. Located downtown, near Pacific Grove Museum of Natural History and Lovers Point Park. Lovely landscaping and spacious parlor. **Rooms:** 21 rms and stes (2 w/shared bath); 5 ctges/villas. CI 2pm/CO 11am. No smoking. Cottages are cozy and secluded, with fireplaces. **Amenities:** 🔒 🕯 Cable TV. No A/C. Some units w/terraces, some w/fireplaces. **Services:** 🔑 🛏 🖵 Masseur, babysitting, afternoon tea and wine/sherry served. Self-serve breakfast. **Facilities:** ♿ Guest lounge w/TV. **Rates (BB):** HS May 16–Oct 15 $70–$90 S or D w/shared bath, $95–$125 S or D w/private bath; from $150 ste; from $175 ctge/villa. Extra person $15. Min stay wknds. Lower rates off-season. Spec packages avail. Pking: Outdoor, free. Ltd CC.

🏚🏚🏚 **Gosby House Inn**, 643 Lighthouse Ave, Pacific Grove, CA 93950 (Downtown); tel 408/375-1287. Pebble Beach/Pacific Grove exit off Calif 1. Located in the heart of the historic district, this delightful inn, more than 100 years old, reflects the town's Victorian heritage. **Rooms:** 22 rms and stes (2 w/shared bath); 2 ctges/villas. CI 2pm/CO noon. No smoking. **Amenities:** 🔒 🕯 Cable TV, bathrobes. No A/C. Some units w/terraces, some w/fireplaces, some w/Jacuzzis. Bottled water. **Services:** ✕ 🔑 🛏 🖵 Social director, afternoon tea and wine/sherry served. Country breakfast; freshly baked cookies. Turn-down service with chocolates and a rose. **Facilities:** 🚲 ♿ Guest lounge. **Rates (BB):** $100 S or D w/shared bath, $85–$150 S or D w/private bath; from $150 ste; from $150 ctge/villa. Extra person $15. Spec packages avail. Pking: Outdoor, free. Ltd CC. Honeymoon and other celebratory packages available.

🏚🏚🏚🏚 **Green Gables Inn**, 104 5th St, Pacific Grove, CA 93950; tel 408/375-2095; fax 408/375-5437. From Calif 1, go west on Calif 68. A lovely Victorian home, built in 1888, offering sweeping views of Monterey Bay's crashing surf and the Santa Cruz Mountains. Teddy bears can be found peeking out of bookcases, on beds, or next to the carousel horse in the living room. **Rooms:** 11 rms and stes (4 w/shared bath). CI 2pm/CO noon. No smoking. Beautifully appointed rooms are decorated with antiques. **Amenities:** 🔒 🕯 📻 🎧 Cable TV, bathrobes. No

A/C. Some units w/terraces, some w/fireplaces, 1 w/Jacuzzi. **Services:** ✕ 🔑 🛏 🖵 Afternoon tea and wine/sherry served. Cookies, soda, fruit, coffee, and tea always available. **Facilities:** Whirlpool, guest lounge. Small gift shop. The central area offers many places to sit and read, enjoy a fire in the fireplace, watch the ocean, or play a tune on the player piano. **Rates (BB):** $100–$135 D w/shared bath, $135–$160 D w/private bath; from $160 ste. Extra person $15. Children under 2 stay free. Spec packages avail. Pking: Outdoor, free. Ltd CC.

🏚🏚🏚🏚 **Martine Inn**, 255 Oceanview Blvd, Pacific Grove, CA 93950; tel 408/373-3388 or toll free 800/852-5588; fax 408/373-3896. Pebble Beach/Pacific Grove exit off Calif 1; take Calif 68 W to Forest Ave; turn right on Oceanview Blvd. Mediterranean-style property overlooking Monterey Bay is an antique lover's nirvana. Furnishings, china, and silverware reflect the turn-of-the-century ambience. **Rooms:** 19 rms and stes. CI 2pm/CO 11am. **Amenities:** 🔒 Refrig. No A/C or TV. Some units w/fireplaces. **Services:** ✕ 🔑 Masseur, babysitting, wine/sherry served. Complimentary full breakfast. **Facilities:** 🚲 🎱 🏊 ♿ Games rm, whirlpool, guest lounge w/TV. **Rates (BB):** $125–$230 S or D; from $280 ste. Extra person $35. Min stay wknds and spec evnts. Pking: Outdoor, free. Ltd CC.

🏚🏚🏚 **Pacific Gardens Inn**, 701 Asilomar Blvd, Pacific Grove, CA 93950; tel 408/646-9414 or toll free 800/262-1566 in CA. Pebble Beach/Pacific Grove exit off Calif 1; take Calif 68 W; turn right on Asilomar Blvd. Pleasant landscaping in a woodsy setting. Well located. **Rooms:** 28 rms and stes. CI 2pm/CO 11am. All suites have fully equipped kitchens. **Amenities:** 🔒 🕯 📺 Cable TV, refrig. No A/C. Some units w/terraces, some w/fireplaces. Popcorn machines in all rooms. **Services:** 🛏 🖵 🍴 Babysitting, afternoon tea and wine/sherry served. **Facilities:** 🏊 ♿ Guest lounge. **Rates (CP):** HS Mar–Oct $92–$115 S or D; from $120 ste. Children under 18 stay free. Lower rates off-season. Higher rates for spec evnts/hols. Pking: Outdoor, free. Ltd CC.

🏚🏚 **Pacific Grove Inn**, 581 Pine Ave, Pacific Grove, CA 93950; tel 408/375-2825. Calif 68 W exit off Calif 1. This inn, a Queen Anne–style structure with Colonial Revival detailing, is a National Historic Landmark. Built in 1905 for the family of Frank Buck, a prominent businessman and civic leader involved in the development of Pacific Grove. Unsuitable for children under 10. **Rooms:** 16 rms and stes. CI 2pm/CO noon. No smoking. Nicely furnished rooms are small but pretty. **Amenities:** 🔒 🕯 Cable TV. No A/C. Some units w/terraces, all w/fireplaces. **Services:** Babysitting. **Facilities:** Guest lounge. **Rates (BB):** HS July–Oct $90–$130 S or D; from $125 ste. Extra person $15–$20.

Children under 10 stay free. Min stay HS, wknds, and spec evnts. Lower rates off-season. Higher rates for spec evnts/hols. Pking: Outdoor, free. Ltd CC.

≋≋≋ **Quality Inn Pacific Grove**, 1111 Lighthouse Ave, Pacific Grove, CA 93950; tel 408/646-8885 or toll free 800/ 992-9060; fax 408/646-5976. Pacific Grove/Pebble Beach exit off Calif 1; take Calif 68 W to Forest Ave; turn left on Lighthouse Ave. Nicely maintained; 3 blocks from the ocean and the Pacific Grove Municipal Golf Links. **Rooms:** 50 rms, stes, and effic. CI 2pm/CO noon. **Amenities:** 🛏 🛁 📺 A/C, cable TV. Some units w/terraces, some w/fireplaces. Efficiencies have microwave. **Services:** ⌂ Babysitting, wine/sherry served. **Facilities:** 🏋 🏊 ₷ Sauna, whirlpool, guest lounge w/TV. **Rates (CP):** HS Mem Day–Oct $80–$160 S or D; from $180 ste; from $90 effic. Extra person $10. Children under 18 stay free. Min stay HS, wknds, and spec evnts. Lower rates off-season. Higher rates for spec evnts/hols. Pking: Outdoor, free. Ltd CC.

≋≋≋≋ **Seven Gables Inn**, 555 Ocean View Blvd, Pacific Grove, CA 93950; tel 408/372-4341. Pacific Grove/Pebble Beach exit off Calif 1; to Pacific Grove on Calif 68/Forest Ave; right on Ocean View Blvd. The ultimate Victorian B&B, set in a multigabled 1886 showplace with views of Monterey Bay and Lover's Point. Decorated with fabulous antiques, including Louis XV gilded tables. Unsuitable for children under 12. **Rooms:** 14 rms. CI 2:30pm/CO noon. No smoking. Each has an ocean view and unique decor. Victoria Room features a real Tiffany window as well as a pressed-tin ceiling, oak armoire, and lace-edged bed ruffle. In the Cypress Room, a sitting area in the bay window commands sweeping bay views. **Amenities:** No A/C, phone, or TV. **Services:** 🛎 Twice-daily maid svce, masseur, afternoon tea served. Lavish breakfast offerings include fresh-squeezed juice, varieties of fruit, egg dishes, plus hot pastries and muffins. Staff will help guests plan sightseeing excursions, picnics, etc. **Facilities:** Guest lounge w/TV. **Rates (BB):** HS June–Sept $105–$205 S or D. Min stay wknds. Lower rates off-season. Pking: Outdoor, free. Ltd CC.

Lodge

≋≋≋ **Lighthouse Lodge & Suites**, 1150 Lighthouse Ave, Pacific Grove, CA 93950; tel 408/655-2111 or toll free 800/ 858-1249; fax 408/655-4922. Pebble Beach/Pacific Grove exit off Calif 1; take Calif 68 W to Asilomar Blvd and turn right. The lodge and suites are in separate properties, both pleasant, in a wooded area close to the ocean and the Pacific Grove Golf Links. **Rooms:** 98 rms and stes; 1 ctge/villa. CI 4pm/CO 11am. Express checkout avail. Nonsmoking rms avail. Suites are more luxurious and upscale, and have kitchenettes and spa tubs. Some rooms overlook cemetery. **Amenities:** 🛏 📺 Cable TV. No A/C. Some

units w/minibars, some w/terraces, some w/fireplaces, some w/Jacuzzis. **Services:** ✕ 🕽 🖿 ⌂ 🛎 Twice-daily maid svce, children's program, babysitting. Accepts pets for an additional $10. **Facilities:** 🏋 🏊 ₷ Sauna, whirlpool. **Rates (BB):** HS June–Sept $89–$285 S; $99–$285 D; from $185 ste; from $325 ctge/villa. Extra person $10. Children under 16 stay free. Min stay wknds. Lower rates off-season. Higher rates for spec evnts/ hols. Spec packages avail. Pking: Indoor/outdoor, free. Maj CC.

Restaurants 🍴

Bagel Bakery, 1180C Forest Ave, Pacific Grove; tel 408/ 649-6272. **Deli.** Fresh bagels, baked daily without any oils, fats, or preservatives. The Pacific Grove outlet of this small chain is the oldest, smallest, and funkiest. A garnish of Monterey jack cheese, sprouts, and tomato is the local favorite. Also at: 539 Carmel Rancho Shopping Center, Carmel (408/625-5180); 201 Lighthouse Ave, Monterey (408/649-1714). **FYI:** Reservations not accepted. No liquor license. **Open:** Mon–Sat 7am–4:30pm, Sun 9am–2:30pm. Closed some hols. **Prices:** Lunch main courses $0.95–$3.55. No CC. 🍽 👬

★ **Central 159**, 529 Central Ave, Pacific Grove (Downtown); tel 408/655-4280. Entrance is on 15th St between Lighthouse and Central Aves. **New American.** Bistro-style restaurant serving creative cuisine. The owner/chef has won numerous local and national awards, including an award from the American Heart Association for a lime sorbet without sugar. Specialties: corn and sweet pepper chowder, grilled eggplant, fire-roasted duck in an oriental vinaigrette, Sonoma rabbit, fresh local seafood. Restaurant's market offers fresh salads, sandwiches, desserts, plus cookbooks and gourmet products. Picnic baskets upon request. **FYI:** Reservations accepted. Beer and wine only. **Open:** Mon–Sat 11am–9pm. Closed some hols. **Prices:** Main courses $8.50–$13. Maj CC. ♥ ₷

El Cocodrilo Rotisserie & Seafood Grill, 701 Lighthouse Ave, Pacific Grove; tel 408/655-3311. At Congress St. **Caribbean.** Bright, clean, fresh, and upbeat. Rain forest decor with artifacts and pottery from the tropical Americas. Specialties: Bahamian chowder, pasta paella, grilled snapper mardi gras, vegetarian plate, alligator nuggets El Dorado (from Florida farms), Jamaican curry crab cakes, Jamaican bread pudding with rum sauce, mango cheesecake. Imported raspberry beer and domestic beers from microbreweries available. **FYI:** Reservations recommended. Children's menu. Beer and wine only. **Open:** Wed–Mon 5–10pm. Closed some hols. **Prices:** Main courses $7.50–$13.95. Maj CC. 👬 ₷

★ **Fandango**, 223 17th St, Pacific Grove; tel 408/372-3456. Between Lighthouse and Laurel Aves. **Mediterranean.** A local favorite that has won many awards. Rustic wood beams, stucco walls, flowers on tables, fireplace, and outside patio create a warm atmosphere. Owner Pierre Bain is a 9th-generation restaurateur whose family owned the Grand Hotel Bain in southern France for 250 years. Mediterrean country-style dishes include paella, couscous Algerois, cassoulet, and cannelloni. Local fish. **FYI:** Reservations recommended. **Open:** Lunch daily 11am–3:30pm; dinner daily 5–9:30pm; brunch Sun 10am–2:30pm. **Prices:** Main courses $11.75–$14.95. Maj CC. ❤ ♿

⑤ **Fifi's Cafe & Bakery**, 1188 Forest Ave, Pacific Grove; tel 408/372-5325. **Californian/French.** Charming French cafe. Cafe-style decor with lace curtains and floral drapes. Specialties include roast leg of lamb, duck Seville or Grand Marnier, grilled sesame chicken salad. Superb French pastries. **FYI:** Reservations recommended. Beer and wine only. **Open:** Breakfast Mon–Fri 8–11am, Sat 8–11:45am; lunch Mon–Fri 11am–2:30pm, Sat noon–3pm; dinner Sun–Thurs 5–9pm, Fri–Sat 5–10pm; brunch Sun 9am–2:30pm. Closed some hols. **Prices:** Main courses $9.25–$13.75. Maj CC. ❤ ♿

⑤ **First Awakenings (formerly First Watch)**, in the American Tin Cannery Outlet Center, 125 Ocean View Blvd, Pacific Grove; tel 408/372-1125. **American.** The 2 young owners of this bright and airy breakfast spot worked their way up from dishwashers, busers, and waiters. The staff is happy to accommodate diners with just about any request or special order. Diners can enjoy a complimentary coffee while waiting. Omelettes and pancakes are specialties. **FYI:** Reservations accepted. Guitar. Children's menu. No liquor license. **Open:** Daily 7am–2:30pm. Closed some hols. **Prices:** Lunch main courses $1.95–$6.75. Maj CC. 👥 ♿

★ **The Fishwife at Asilomar Beach**, 1996 Sunset Dr, Pacific Grove; tel 408/375-7107. Sunset Dr exit off Calif 68 W. **Seafood.** Local favorite with good value. Casual atmosphere; marine-life decor. Specialties include Boston clam chowder, snapper Lafayette, calamari, and sea garden salad (mixed greens with grilled fish). **FYI:** Reservations recommended. Children's menu. Beer and wine only. **Open:** Lunch Wed–Mon 11am–4pm; dinner Wed–Mon 4–10pm; brunch Sun 10am–4pm. Closed some hols. **Prices:** Main courses $5.50–$11.75. Maj CC. 👥 ♿

Old Bath House Restaurant, 620 Ocean View Blvd, Pacific Grove; tel 408/375-5195. Pacific Grove/Pebble Beach exit off Calif 1. **Californian/Continental.** A venerable local favorite in a turn-of-the century bathhouse restored to Victorian elegance. Some tables have bay views. Specialties include local seafood, Australian lobster in puff pastry, wild boar sausage, and filet mignon. **FYI:** Reservations recommended. **Open:** Mon–Fri 5–10pm, Sat 4–10pm, Sun 3–10pm. **Prices:** Main courses $16.75–$32.50. Maj CC. ❤ 🍴 ❤

★ **Peppers MexiCali Cafe**, 170 Forest Ave, Pacific Grove; tel 408/373-6892. Between Lighthouse and Central Aves. **Californian/Mexican/Latin American.** Popular southwestern restaurant with lively atmosphere, butcher-block tables, and attractive art. Specialties include snapper Yucatan and other local fresh seafood, usually accompanied by black beans, tortillas, fresh salsas. Good selection of Monterey County and Central Coast wines. **FYI:** Reservations recommended. Beer and wine only. **Open:** Sun 4–10pm, Wed–Mon 11:30am–10pm. Closed some hols. **Prices:** Main courses $5.50–$10.95. Maj CC.

Taste Cafe & Bistro, 1199 Forest Ave, Pacific Grove; tel 408/655-0324. Pacific Grove/Pebble Beach exit off Calif 1. **Californian.** Very sophisticated little cafe with a rustic look. Dishes include grilled rabbit, fresh salmon on spinach leaves with herbs and vegetables in parchment paper, and many vegetarian selections. **FYI:** Reservations recommended. Reservations accepted. Children's menu. Beer and wine only. **Open:** Tues–Thurs 5–9pm, Fri–Sat 5–10pm, Sun 5–9pm. Closed some hols; between Christmas Eve and New Year's Eve. **Prices:** Main courses $9–$14. No CC. ♿

★ **Tillie Gort's**, 111 Central Ave, Pacific Grove; tel 408/373-0335. Pacific Grove/Pebble Beach exit off Calif 1. **Eclectic.** A local standby for 25 years, with an eclectic clientele drawn to the 1960s ambience. Food is mostly vegetarian, and servings are large. Veggie burger, quesadilla supreme, and "Jimmy's special" (steamed vegetables on grilled potatoes, topped with cheese) are among the offerings. **FYI:** Reservations accepted. Beer and wine only. **Open:** Mon–Fri 11am–10pm, Sat–Sun 8am–10pm. Closed Dec 25. **Prices:** Main courses $4.50–$8.50. Ltd CC. 👥

The Tinnery, 631 Ocean View Blvd, Pacific Grove; tel 408/646-1040. **Regional American.** Popular with tourists. Bright and airy restaurant with a panoramic view of Monterey Bay at Lover's Point. Specializing in fresh fish and steaks. **FYI:** Reservations recommended. Singer. Children's menu. **Open:** Breakfast daily 8–11am; lunch daily 11am–4pm; dinner daily 4–11pm; brunch Sun 8am–12pm. **Prices:** Main courses $7.99–$16.99. Maj CC. 🏔 👥 ❤ ♿

Toasties Cafe, 702 Lighthouse Ave, Pacific Grove; tel 408/373-7543. At Congress St. **American.** Flower boxes and ruffled curtains decorate the windows, while depictions of bunnies, cows, chickens, and other critters appear throughout this cozy, country-style restaurant. It's a local favorite, especially for breakfast. Specialties include huevos rancheros, corned beef hash, blintzes, and tortellini and eggs. **FYI:** Reservations not accepted. Children's menu. Beer and wine only. **Open:** Breakfast Mon–Sat 6am–3pm, Sun 7am–2pm; lunch daily 11am–3pm; dinner Tues–Sat 5–9pm. Closed some hols. **Prices:** Main courses $7.25–$10.95. Maj CC. 🚭 👥

Vito's Italian Restaurant, 1180 Forest Ave, Pacific Grove; tel 408/375-3070. Pacific Grove/Pebble Beach exit off Calif 1 to Calif 68 W; which becomes Forest Ave in Pacific Grove. **Italian.** Adorned with an enormous mural of the owner's home town near Palermo. Very Italian menu includes pastas, gnocchi, and tiramisù made on site. **FYI:** Reservations recommended. Reservations accepted. Beer and wine only. **Open:** Lunch daily 11:30am–2:30pm; dinner daily 5–10pm. Closed some hols. **Prices:** Main courses $9–$14.95. Maj CC.

Refreshment Stop

Rocky Coast Ice Cream Company, 708 Lighthouse Ave, Pacific Grove; tel 408/373-0587. **Hot dogs/Ice cream.** A folksy, friendly ice-cream parlor popular with all ages. Video and pinball games for kids. Offers 37 flavors of premium ice-cream, plus 6 nonfat frozen yogurt specials. Also, milkshakes, sundaes, soft drinks, candy, hot dogs, and bagel dogs. Good value. **Open:** HS Feb–Nov Sun noon–10pm, Mon–Sat 11am–10pm. Reduced hours off-season. Closed some hols. No CC.

Attraction

Pacific Grove Museum of Natural History, 165 Forest Ave; tel 408/648-3116. Considered one of the finest natural history museums of its size, this facility is fronted by a life-size sculpture of a gray whale. Exhibits inside deal mainly with local plants and wildlife, geology, and Native American culture. The **Native Plant Garden** features a number of rare and endangered species of the Monterey Peninsula. Traveling exhibitions, including those of the Smithsonian Institution, are also featured. Gift shop. **Open:** Tues–Sun and hols 10am–5pm. Closed some hols. Free.

PACIFIC PALISADES

Map page M-3, D2 (NW of Santa Monica)

Attraction

Will Rogers State Historic Park, 1501 Will Rogers State Park Rd; tel 310/454-8212. The 31-room ranch house and grounds of the "cracker-barrel philosopher" were willed to the state in 1944. Visitors may explore the grounds, including the former Rogers stables, and even watch polo matches (usually Saturday afternoons and Sunday mornings, weather permitting). Guided tours are given of the house, which is filled with original furnishings. A film on Will Rogers shown at the Visitor Center, where there is also a small gift shop. **Open:** Park, daily 8am–6pm, summer 8am–7pm. House, daily 10am–5pm. Closed some hols. $$

PAICINES

Map page M-2, D2 (E of Salinas)

Attraction

Pinnacles National Monument, 5000 Calif 146; tel 408/389-4485. Because of its distinctive geological features, Pinnacles was set aside as a national monument in 1908. What remains today are the eroded remnants of an ancient volcano, which formed at a point on the San Andreas Rift Zone. One portion of the volcano has remained at its point of origin; the other, moving at a rate of about 2 centimeters per year, has traveled 195 miles northwestward. The Pinnacles comprise the latter section. Hiking is the most popular activity; there are 11 marked trails of varying difficulty. Rock climbing, spelunking, and picnicking opportunities are also abundant. Camping is permitted only at the campsite at the west side of the monument. **Open:** Park, daily; visitor center, daily 9am–5pm. $$

PALMDALE

Map page M-3, D2

Hotel

Holiday Inn Palmdale/Lancaster, 38630 5th St W, Palmdale, CA 93551; tel 805/947-8055 or toll free 800/HOLIDAY; fax 805/947-9957. Palmdale Blvd exit off Calif 14. Attractive, quiet, fairly new hotel. Green marble in lobby. **Rooms:** 150 rms and stes. Exec-level rms avail. CI 6pm/CO noon. Express checkout avail. Nonsmoking rms avail. Little drawer and counter space. Excellent handicapped-accessible rooms, all adjoining, with flashing smoke alarms. 1 smoking floor. **Amenities:** A/C, cable TV w/movies. Some units w/terraces. **Services:** Breakfast buffet often included in rate. Complimentary happy hour 5–6pm Monday–Thursday in lounge. **Facilities:** 1 rst, 1 bar, games rm, whirlpool. **Rates (CP):** $70 S; $75 D; from $125 ste. Extra person $5. Children under 12 stay free. Spec packages avail. Pking: Outdoor, free. Maj CC.

PALM DESERT

Map page M-3, D3 (E of Palm Springs)

Hotel

Embassy Suites, 74-700 US 111, Palm Desert, CA 92260; tel 619/340-6600 or toll free 800/EMBASSY; fax 619/

340-9519. Spanish-style architecture, lush landscaping, 20 types of cactus and elaborate fountains greet guests to this all-suites hotel. **Rooms:** 198 stes. CI 3pm/CO noon. Nonsmoking rms avail. All suites have sleeper sofas. **Amenities:** 🏨 👜 📠 A/C, cable TV w/movies, refrig. All units w/minibars, some w/terraces. Wet bar. **Services:** ✗ 🛄 🍽 Children's program, babysitting. Complimentary cooked-to-order breakfast and evening cocktails. **Facilities:** 🛗 🏌 🍹 🛶 🛥 👟 1 rst, 1 bar (w/entertainment), games rm, lawn games, whirlpool, washer/dryer. Croquet lawn. **Rates:** HS Jan 15–Apr 30 from $164 ste. Extra person $15. Children under 12 stay free. Min stay wknds. Lower rates off-season. Higher rates for spec evnts/hols. Spec packages avail. Pking: Outdoor, free. Maj CC.

Motels

🚾🚾 **Casa Larrea Resort Motel**, 73-771 Larrea St, Palm Desert, CA 92260; tel 619/568-0311 or toll free 800/829-1556. Monterey Ave exit off I-10; to Calif 111, turn left to Portola Ave, right to Larrea St. Remodeling should be completed. Turquoise umbrellas and lawn furniture around the pool provide a striking contrast to the white stucco buildings. **Rooms:** 12 rms and stes. CI 2pm/CO noon. Individually decorated rooms all have private patios, landscaped with desert plants. **Amenities:** 🏨 👜 📠 A/C, cable TV, refrig. All units w/terraces. **Services:** 🍽 **Facilities:** 🛗 Whirlpool. **Rates (CP):** HS Nov 1–June 1 $54–$64 S or D; from $82 ste. Extra person $10. Min stay wknds and spec evnts. Lower rates off-season. Pking: Outdoor, free. Maj CC.

🚾🚾 **Deep Canyon Inn**, 74-470 Abronia Trail, Palm Desert, CA 92260; tel 619/346-8061 or toll free 800/253-0004; fax 619/341-9120. Designed around a pool and garden area, with large rooms and wonderful rattan furniture. Needs a bit of refurbishment. **Rooms:** 29 rms and stes; 2 ctges/villas. CI 2pm/CO noon. Nonsmoking rms avail. One attractive room has French doors that lead to patio. **Amenities:** 🏨 A/C, cable TV, refrig. All units w/terraces, 1 w/fireplace. **Services:** 🍽 🍹 Babysitting. **Facilities:** 🛗 👟 Whirlpool. **Rates (CP):** HS Jan–Apr $85–$95 S or D; from $150 ste; from $150 ctge/villa. Children under 12 stay free. Min stay HS. Lower rates off-season. Pking: Outdoor, free. Maj CC.

🚾🚾 **Desert Patch Inn**, 73-758 Shadow Mountain Dr, Palm Desert, CA 92260; tel 619/346-9161 or toll free 800/350-9758. 125 mi SE of Los Angeles. Monterey Ave exit off I-10. Well maintained, with lovely Mexican artifacts scattered throughout the grounds. Beautiful enclosed garden is a perfect spot for morning coffee. **Rooms:** 14 rms, stes, and effic. CI 2pm/CO noon. Comfortable. **Amenities:** 🏨 A/C, cable TV, refrig. Some units w/terraces, 1 w/fireplace. **Services:** 🚐 🍹 Complimentary continental breakfast. **Facilities:** 🛗 🛥 Lawn games,

whirlpool. Putting green, shuffleboard, croquet. **Rates (CP):** HS Oct–May $52 S or D; from $89 ste; from $70 effic. Extra person $15. Min stay HS, wknds, and spec evnts. Lower rates off-season. Pking: Outdoor, free. Maj CC.

🚾🚾 **Holiday Inn Express**, 74-675 Calif 111, Palm Desert, CA 92260; tel 619/340-4303 or toll free 800/HOLIDAY; fax 619/340-4303 ext 377. Convenient to Coachella Valley medical facilities and local shopping, this contemporary-style hotel features a 3-story atrium lobby. **Rooms:** 131 rms and stes. CI 3pm/CO noon. Express checkout avail. Nonsmoking rms avail. **Amenities:** 🏨 👜 📠 A/C, cable TV w/movies. All units w/terraces. Coffee in rooms. **Services:** 🛄 🍹 Babysitting. Complimentary breakfast bar. **Facilities:** 🛗 🍹1 🛥 👟 Games rm, lawn games, whirlpool, washer/dryer. **Rates (CP):** HS Feb–Mar $119–$139 S or D; from $145 ste. Extra person $10. Children under 18 stay free. Min stay wknds. Lower rates off-season. Pking: Outdoor, free. Maj CC.

🚾🚾🚾 **International Lodge of Palm Desert**, 74-380 El Camino, Palm Desert, CA 92260; tel 619/346-6161 or toll free 800/874-9338; fax 619/568-0563. Monterey Ave exit off I-10; Calif 111 S to Panorama Dr, E to El Camino. An exclusive enclave of individually decorated studio condominiums. **Rooms:** 50 effic. CI 2pm/CO noon. Nonsmoking rms avail. Full kitchens. **Amenities:** 🏨 👜 📠 A/C, cable TV w/movies, refrig. All units w/terraces. **Services:** 🚗 🛄 Car-rental desk. **Facilities:** 🛗 🛥 Whirlpool, washer/dryer. 2 Olympic-size swimming pools, with lovely views of mountains. **Rates:** HS Jan–Apr from $89 effic. Extra person $10. Children under 3 stay free. Min stay spec evnts. Lower rates off-season. Pking: Outdoor, free. Maj CC.

🚾🚾 **Vacation Inn Hotel**, 74-715 Calif 111, Palm Desert, CA 92260; tel 619/340-4441 or toll free 800/231-8675; fax 619/773-9413. The decor is casual southwest, and the location offers easy access to shops and restaurants. **Rooms:** 130 rms. CI 3pm/CO noon. Nonsmoking rms avail. **Amenities:** 🏨 📠 A/C, cable TV w/movies, refrig, in-rm safe. All units w/terraces. **Services:** 🛄 🍹 **Facilities:** 🛗 🍹2 🛥 👟 Lawn games, whirlpool, washer/dryer. **Rates (CP):** HS Jan 1–Apr 15 $82–$108 S or D. Children under 18 stay free. Min stay spec evnts. Lower rates off-season. Spec packages avail. Pking: Outdoor, free. Maj CC.

Resorts

🚾🚾🚾🚾 **Marriott's Desert Springs Spa & Resort**, 74-885 Country Club Dr, Palm Desert, CA 92260; tel 619/341-2211 or toll free 800/321-3112; fax 619/341-1872. Follow Bob Hope Dr south off I-10; left onto Country Club Dr. 400 acres. A sweeping palm-lined drive leads to the colorful gardens, tropical birds, and lakes, streams, and waterfalls at this resort. Unique indoor-outdoor lake; luxurious spa. **Rooms:** 895 rms and stes. CI 4pm/ CO noon. Express checkout avail. Nonsmoking rms avail. Rooms offer lots of luxuries. Views of the golf course and the San Jacinto Mountains. **Amenities:** 🛗 🖊 🍳 A/C, cable TV w/movies, in-rm safe, bathrobes. All units w/minibars, all w/terraces. **Services:** ✗ 🛏 VP 🖼 🎧 Twice-daily maid svce, car-rental desk, social director, masseur, children's program, babysitting. **Facilities:** 🖼 ▶₃₆ 🖼 🎱₁₃ 🏐 🏌️ 4K 💻 ♿ 5 rsts, 3 bars (2 w/entertainment), 1 beach (lake shore), lifeguard, games rm, lawn games, spa, sauna, steam rm, whirlpool, beauty salon. 2 golf courses, putting green. Lap pool and 2 hydrotherapy pools. Plans underway for more pools, indoor-outdoor restaurant, and children's playground. **Rates:** HS Jan 2–May 21 $250–$310 S or D; from $575 ste. Children under 18 stay free. Lower rates off-season. Spec packages avail. Pking: Indoor/outdoor, free. Maj CC.

≣≣≣ **Marriott's Desert Springs Villas**, 1091 Pinehurst Lane, Palm Desert, CA 92260; tel 619/779-1207 or toll free 800/ 331-3112; fax 619/779-1203. Monterey Ave exit off I-10. 3 acres. Well located, with luxurious grounds, near the extensive facilities of the Marriott Desert Springs Spa & Resort. **Rooms:** 236 ctges/villas. CI 4pm/CO 10am. Nonsmoking rms avail. Each villa is spacious and elegantly furnished; 1- and 2-bedroom villas feature full kitchen, washer/dryer, formal dining room, circular whirlpool, and gas fireplace. **Amenities:** 🛗 🖊 🍳 A/C, cable TV w/movies, refrig, VCR, voice mail, in-rm safe. All units w/ter- races, all w/fireplaces. **Services:** ✗ 🖼 🎧 Masseur, babysitting. **Facilities:** 🖼 ▶₃₆ 🖼 🎱₁₃ 🏐 🏌️ 4K 💻 ♿ 5 rsts, 3 bars (2 w/entertainment), 1 beach (lake shore), games rm, lawn games, spa, sauna, steam rm, whirlpool, beauty salon, washer/dryer. **Rates:** HS Jan 2–May 21 from $350 ctge/villa. Min stay spec evnts. Lower rates off-season. Pking: Outdoor, free. Maj CC.

≣≣ **Shadow Mountain Resort and Racquet Club**, 45-750 San Luis Rey Ave, Palm Desert, CA 92260; tel 619/346-6123 or toll free 800/472-3713; fax 619/346-6518. Monterey Ave exit off I-10. 24 acres. Located a short walk from the fashionable shops, galleries, and restaurants of El Paseo. **Rooms:** 101 rms, stes, and effic; 9 ctges/villas. CI 3pm/CO 11am. Express check- out avail. **Amenities:** 🛗 🍳 A/C, cable TV w/movies, refrig. All units w/terraces, some w/fireplaces. **Services:** 🖼 🎧 Children's program, babysitting. **Facilities:** 🖼 🚴 🎱₁₂ 🏐 🏌️ 400 ♿ 1 rst, 1 bar, lawn games, sauna, whirlpool, washer/dryer. Golf course nearby. **Rates:** HS Nov 24-27/Dec 23–Jan 1/Feb 18–Apr 16/ May 27–June 1 $124–$160 S or D; from $124 ste; from $193 effic; from $293 ctge/villa. Extra person $15. Children under 18 stay free. Min stay HS, wknds, and spec evnts. Lower rates off- season. Spec packages avail. Pking: Indoor/outdoor, free. Maj CC.

Restaurants 🍴

Andreino's, 73-098 Calif 111, Palm Desert; tel 619/773-3365. Bob Hope Dr exit off I-10. **Italian.** With knotty pine ceilings and large stone pillars. Signature dishes include fettuccine Andreino, with cream, butter, and fresh Parmesan, as well as other pasta dishes. If you're very hungry, try the Godfather's dinner— tenderloin of beef, spiedini, shrimp scampi, and veal picatta. **FYI:** Reservations recommended. Dress code. **Open:** HS Sept– July daily 5:30–midnight. Reduced hours off-season. Closed some hols. **Prices:** Main courses $12.95–$25.95. Maj CC. VP

A Touch of Mama's, 74-065 Calif 111, Palm Desert; tel 619/ 568-1315. Bob Hope Dr exit off I-10. **Italian.** Cozy atmosphere where fresh flowers complement the table settings of green glass plates with white china accents, while original oil paintings line the walls. Fresh-made pasta and sauces, veal marsala, osso buco, shrimp scampi, and eggplant Parmesan highlight the menu. **FYI:** Reservations accepted. Guitar. Dress code. **Open:** HS Oct–May daily 5–10:30pm. Reduced hours off-season. **Prices:** Main cour- ses $11.39–$23.95. Maj CC.

Cafe Milano, 73-375 El Paseo, Palm Desert; tel 619/776-1462. Monterey Ave exit off I-10. **Italian.** Overlooking El Paseo. Soft gray, rose, and mauve decor, with modern art on the walls. Italian specialties include risotto with porcini mushrooms, house-made gnocchi, angel-hair pasta with fresh tomatoes and basil, and salmon-stuffed ravioli with vodka and caviar sauce. Various fish, chicken, veal, and beef entrees also available. **FYI:** Reservations recommended. Piano. Dress code. **Open:** Lunch Fri–Sat 11:30am–2:30pm; dinner daily 5:30–11pm. Closed some hols. **Prices:** Main courses $12–$25.90. Maj CC.

Club 74, 73-061 El Paseo, Palm Desert; tel 619/568-2782. Monterey Ave exit off I-10. **French.** A magnificent entryway and carved staircase lead to dining rooms with oak paneling and landscape frescoes. Cuisine features dishes like veal medallions forestière, feuilleté au King Neptune, and poulet aux framboises. **FYI:** Reservations recommended. Piano. Dress code. **Open:** Lunch Mon–Sat 11:30am–2:30pm; dinner daily 5:30–10pm. Closed some hols; July. **Prices:** Main courses $17–$25. Maj CC. 🏔

Cuistot, 73-111 El Paseo, Palm Desert; tel 619/340-1000. Monterey Ave exit off I-10. **French.** A light and airy restaurant whose soft hues complement the contemporary setting. Special- ties include sautéed veal chops with wild mushrooms, roasted garlic, and thyme, and Chinese-style duck in a mango-ginger sauce. **FYI:** Reservations recommended. Dress code. **Open:** Lunch Tues–Sat 11:30am–2:30pm; dinner Tues–Sun 6–10pm. Closed some hols; Aug. **Prices:** Main courses $8.75–$13.95. Ltd CC. ♿

Le Paon, 45-640 Calif 74, Palm Desert; tel 619/568-3651. Monterey Ave exit off I-10 to Calif 74. **French.** Elegant ambience, with chandeliers, marble, granite, fireplaces, and upholstered Victorian chairs. French doors lead to the garden. Menu favorites include veal scaloppine, baked lobster tail, steak Diane (prepared tableside), rack of lamb, and veal calvados. **FYI:** Reservations recommended. Piano. Dress code. **Open:** HS mid-Sept–May Thurs–Sat 6–11pm, Sun–Wed 6–10pm. Reduced hours off-season. Closed Thanksgiving. **Prices:** Main courses $16.95–$48.95. Maj CC. 🌱 🍽 VP ♿

LG's Steakhouse, 74-225 Calif 111, Palm Desert; tel 619/779-9799. Monterey Ave exit off I-10 to Calif 111. **Steak.** Located in a neo-pueblo–style building that will be declared a National Historic Monument when it turns 50 in 1998. Prime corn-fed midwestern steaks are the specialty here, but you can also order rack of lamb, veal chops, pork chops, chicken, and fish. **FYI:** Reservations recommended. Dress code. **Open:** Sun–Thurs 5–10pm, Fri–Sat 5–10:30pm. **Prices:** Main courses $16.95–$44.50. Maj CC. VP

Mayo's on El Paseo, 73-990 El Paseo, Palm Desert; tel 619/346-2284. Monterey Ave exit off I-10. **Continental.** Burgundy-and-white china contrasts with gray walls, gray-and-black carpet, and a black piano bar. Cuisine is continental with an Italian flavor. Favorites include grilled veal chops, Lake Superior white fish with hollandaise, and other bistro-style dishes. **FYI:** Reservations recommended. Piano. Dress code. **Open:** Lunch Mon–Sat 11am–2:30pm; dinner Mon–Sun 5:30–10pm. Closed some hols. **Prices:** Main courses $12.95–$27.95. Maj CC.

Palomino Euro Bistro, 73-101 Calif 111, Palm Desert; tel 619/773-9091. Bob Hope Dr exit off I-10 to Calif 111. **Mediterranean.** The exhibition kitchen is only part of what contributes to the fun and energy of this restaurant. The ambience is decidedly elegant with Italian marble, dark veneer, hand-blown glass, and a 40-foot carved marble bar. Dishes include Pacific Northwest King salmon and original pastas. **FYI:** Reservations recommended. Dress code. **Open:** Lunch Mon–Sat 11am–2:30pm; dinner Sun–Thurs 5–10pm, Fri–Sat 5–11pm. Closed some hols. **Prices:** Main courses $8.95–$18.95. Maj CC. VP ♿

Ristorante Mamma Gina, 73-705 El Paseo, Palm Desert; tel 619/568-9898. Monterey exit off I-10 turn right on Calif 111 and right on El Paseo. **Tuscan.** Double oak doors open to a setting of oak and brass, mauve carpeting, and soft lights. Extensive menu includes veal, chicken, fresh fish, and homemade pasta. **FYI:** Reservations recommended. Piano. Dress code. **Open:** HS Oct–May lunch Mon–Sat 11:30am–2:30pm; dinner daily 5:15–10pm. Reduced hours off-season. Closed Dec 25; July 4th–Sept 4th. **Prices:** Main courses $13.90–$24.90. Maj CC. VP ♿

Ruth's Chris Steak House, 74-040 Calif 111, Palm Desert; tel 619/779-1998. Bob Hope Dr exit off I-10. **Steak.** Very sophisticated steak house, with rich, cherry-wood paneling, forest green carpeting, art deco wall sconces, and marble flooring. Specializes in corn-fed prime beef, including New York strip, rib-eye, filet mignon, and porterhouse steaks. **FYI:** Reservations recommended. Dress code. **Open:** Daily 5–10pm. Closed some hols. **Prices:** Main courses $16.50–$35.50. Maj CC. VP ♿

PALM SPRINGS
Map page M-3, D3

See also **Cathedral City, Desert Hot Springs, Idyllwild, Indian Wells, Indio, Joshua Tree National Park, La Quinta, Palm Desert, Pioneertown, Rancho Mirage, Twentynine Palms, Yucca Valley**

Hotels 🏨

🏨🏨🏨 **Courtyard by Marriott**, 1300 Tahquitz Way, Palm Springs, CA 92262; tel 619/322-6100 or toll free 800/321-2211; fax 619/322-6091. Calif 111 Business District (Palm Canyon Dr) to Tahquitz; turn left. Minutes away from downtown Palm Springs. Overlooks a central courtyard with a swimming pool and gazebo. **Rooms:** 149 rms and stes. CI 4pm/CO noon. Express checkout avail. Nonsmoking rms avail. Separate areas for work and relaxing. Most overlook pool area, which can be noisy. **Amenities:** 📺 ♨ A/C, cable TV w/movies, voice mail. Some units w/terraces. **Services:** 🚗 📋 🍴 Babysitting. **Facilities:** 🏋 🍽 🏊 ♿ 1 rst, 1 bar, whirlpool, washer/dryer. **Rates:** $39–$124 S or D; from $64 ste. Extra person $10. Children under 12 stay free. Min stay HS. Lower rates off-season. Pking: Outdoor, free. Maj CC.

🏨🏨🏨 **Holiday Inn–Palm Mountain Resort**, 155 S Belardo, Palm Springs, CA 92262; tel 619/325-1301 or toll free 800/622-9451; fax 619/323-8937. Calif 111 Business District (Palm Canyon Drive) to Tahquitz Canyon Way; turn right on Belardo. A blend of southwestern- and Mediterranean-style architecture. A good location at the foot of the San Jacinto Mountains makes this a very busy hotel. **Rooms:** 122 rms. CI 3pm/CO noon. Express checkout avail. Nonsmoking rms avail. **Amenities:** 📺 ♨ 🍴 A/C, cable TV w/movies, refrig. Some units w/terraces, some w/Jacuzzis. **Services:** ✕ 🚗 📋 🍴 Children's program, babysitting. **Facilities:** 🏋 🍽 1 rst, 2 bars, whirlpool. **Rates:** HS Jan 16–May $111–$141 S or D. Extra person $10. Children under 18 stay free. Min stay spec evnts. Lower rates off-season. Higher rates for spec evnts/hols. Spec packages avail. Pking: Outdoor, free. Maj CC.

▤▤▤▤ **Hyatt Regency Suites Palm Springs**, 285 N Palm Canyon Dr, Palm Springs, CA 92262; tel 619/322-9000 or toll free 800/233-1234; fax 619/322-6009. This luxurious all-suites hotel is situated in the heart of downtown, with views of the San Jacinto Mountains in the distance. **Rooms:** 192 stes. Exec-level rms avail. CI 3pm/CO noon. Express checkout avail. Nonsmoking rms avail. The 1- and 2-bedroom suites are beautifully appointed and have private balconies. **Amenities:** ☎ ⓠ ▤ ⌇ A/C, cable TV w/movies, refrig. All units w/minibars, all w/terraces, some w/Jacuzzis. Each suite features plants and jars filled with candy. **Services:** ⦿ ▤ VP ⛟ ☒ ⌇ ⥹ Twice-daily maid svce, car-rental desk, masseur, babysitting. **Facilities:** ⓕ ⌨ ▥ ㋵ 2 rsts, 2 bars (1 w/entertainment), lifeguard, whirlpool, beauty salon. Health club due to open. Golf and tennis available at the Rancho Mirage Country Club. **Rates:** HS Dec 28–May from $199 ste. Extra person $25. Children under 18 stay free. Min stay spec evnts. Lower rates off-season. Higher rates for spec evnts/hols. Spec packages avail. Pking: Indoor/outdoor, free. Ltd CC.

▤▤ **Las Brisas Resort Hotel—A Best Western Hotel**, 222 S Indian Canyon Ave, Palm Springs, CA 92262; tel 619/325-4372 or toll free 800/346-5714; fax 619/320-1371. Calif 111 exit off I-10, to Tahquitz Canyon Way; turn left on Indian Canyon Ave. 2.5 acres. Convenient to Palm Springs' most popular attractions; designed in a Mediterranean style. Property looks a bit fatigued. **Rooms:** 90 rms and stes. CI 3pm/CO noon. Nonsmoking rms avail. **Amenities:** ☎ ⓠ ▤ A/C, cable TV, refrig. Some units w/Jacuzzis. **Services:** ✕ ☒ ⌇ Car-rental desk, babysitting. **Facilities:** ⓕ ㋵ 1 rst, 2 bars, whirlpool, washer/dryer. **Rates (BB):** HS Feb–May $69–$113 S or D; from $69 ste. Extra person $10. Children under 17 stay free. Min stay wknds and spec evnts. Lower rates off-season. Higher rates for spec evnts/hols. Spec packages avail. Pking: Outdoor, free. Maj CC.

▤▤ **Ramada Hotel Resort**, 1800 E Palm Canyon Dr, Palm Springs, CA 92264; tel 619/323-1711 or toll free 800/245-6907; fax 619/322-1075. Located in the Smoke Tree area of Palm Springs, this hotel is designed around a garden and pool area. **Rooms:** 255 rms and stes. CI 3pm/CO noon. Nonsmoking rms avail. **Amenities:** ☎ ⓠ ▤ A/C, cable TV w/movies. All units w/terraces. **Services:** ✕ ⛟ ☒ ⌇ Car-rental desk, babysitting. **Facilities:** ⓕ ⌨ ▥ ㋵ 2 rsts, 1 bar (w/entertainment), games rm, sauna, whirlpool, washer/dryer. **Rates:** HS Feb–May $79–$119 S or D; from $85 ste. Extra person $15. Children under 18 stay free. Min stay HS, wknds, and spec evnts. Lower rates off-season. Spec packages avail. Pking: Outdoor, free. Maj CC.

▤▤▤ **Spa Hotel Resort & Mineral Springs**, 100 N Indian Canyon Way, Palm Springs, CA 92262; tel 619/325-1461 or toll free 800/854-1279; fax 619/325-3344. Calif 111 Business District (Palm Canyon Dr) to Tahquitz Canyon Way; turn left on Indian Canyon Way. 8 acres. Built on the site of an 1871 bathhouse of the Cabrilla Indians. The mineral-rich water flowing through the property is a constant 104°F. **Rooms:** 230 rms and stes. Exec-level rms avail. CI 4pm/CO 1pm. Express checkout avail. Nonsmoking rms avail. **Amenities:** ☎ ⓠ A/C, cable TV w/movies. All units w/minibars, some w/terraces, 1 w/Jacuzzi. **Services:** ✕ ▤ VP ⛟ ☒ ⌇ Car-rental desk, masseur, babysitting. **Facilities:** ⓕ ⌨ ▥ ㋵ 2 rsts, 2 bars (1 w/entertainment), lifeguard, spa, sauna, steam rm, whirlpool, beauty salon. **Rates:** HS Jan–May $105–$165 S or D; from $274 ste. Extra person $25. Children under 17 stay free. Lower rates off-season. Spec packages avail. Pking: Outdoor, free. Maj CC.

▤▤▤ **Wyndham Palm Springs Hotel**, 888 Tahquitz Canyon Way, Palm Springs, CA 92262; tel 619/322-6000 or toll free 800/872-4335, 800/346-7308 in CA; fax 619/322-5351. Calif 111 Business District (Palm Canyon Dr) to Tahquitz Canyon Way; turn left. A 60,000-square-foot courtyard, including a 5,000-square-foot oasis-style swimming pool (the largest in town) is surrounded by a Mediterranean-style hotel. Within walking distance of the business district, and connected to the convention center. **Rooms:** 409 rms and stes. CI 3pm/CO noon. Express checkout avail. Nonsmoking rms avail. **Amenities:** ☎ ⓠ ▤ A/C, cable TV w/movies, shoe polisher. Some units w/terraces. **Services:** ✕ ▤ VP ⛟ ☒ ⌇ Car-rental desk, masseur, babysitting. **Facilities:** ⓕ ⌨ ▥ ㋵ 2 rsts, 2 bars, games rm, spa, sauna, whirlpool, beauty salon. **Rates:** HS Jan–May $190–$240 S or D; from $179 ste. Extra person $15. Children under 18 stay free. Min stay spec evnts. Lower rates off-season. Spec packages avail. Pking: Outdoor, free. Maj CC.

Motels

▤▤ **Best Western Host Hotel**, 1633 S Palm Canyon Dr, Palm Springs, CA 92264; tel 619/325-9177 or toll free 800/222-4678; fax 619/325-9177. US 111 exit off I-10. Nestled against the San Jacinto Mountains, this secluded retreat offers the only hillside sundeck and pool in Palm Springs. **Rooms:** 72 rms and stes. CI 3pm/CO noon. Nonsmoking rms avail. **Amenities:** ☎ ⓠ A/C, cable TV w/movies, refrig. A good selection of reading material in each room. **Services:** ☒ ⌇ ⥹ Car-rental desk, babysitting. **Facilities:** ⓕ ▥ Whirlpool. **Rates (CP):** HS Dec 25–May $40–$118 S or D; from $100 ste. Extra person $6. Children under 12 stay free. Lower rates off-season. Spec packages avail. Pking: Outdoor, free. Maj CC.

▤▤ **El Rancho Lodge**, 1330 E Palm Canyon Dr, Palm Springs, CA 92264; tel 619/327-1339. Gene Autry Trail/Vista Chino exit off I-10. A classic California ranch-style motel with a warm and friendly atmosphere and several areas to relax after a swim.

Rooms: 19 rms, stes, and effic. CI 3pm/CO noon. **Amenities:** 🛅 🕹 🖭 A/C, cable TV, refrig. Some units w/terraces. **Services:** Car-rental desk, babysitting. **Facilities:** 🛅 Whirlpool, washer/ dryer. **Rates (CP):** HS Oct–May $61 S or D; from $131 ste; from $64 effic. Extra person $20. Min stay wknds. Lower rates off- season. Spec packages avail. Pking: Outdoor, free. Maj CC.

≡≡≡ **Four Seasons Apartment Hotel**, 290 San Jacinto Dr, Palm Springs, CA 92262; tel 619/325-6427. Calif 111 Business District (Palm Canyon Dr) to Baristo Rd; turn right on San Jacinto. A small apartment hotel set against the mountains in a quiet neighborhood within walking distance of downtown Palm Springs. **Rooms:** 11 rms, stes, and effic. CI 2pm/CO noon. Nonsmoking rms avail. Individually decorated suites are large and tastefully appointed. **Amenities:** 🛅 🕹 🖭 🍴 A/C, cable TV, refrig. Some units w/terraces, 1 w/fireplace. **Services:** 🕸 Baby- sitting. **Facilities:** 🛅 🕹 Whirlpool. Immaculately landscaped pool area. **Rates:** HS Feb–Mar $100 S or D; from $110 ste; from $120 effic. Extra person $15. Min stay wknds. Lower rates off- season. Pking: Outdoor, free. Ltd CC.

≡≡ **Golden Palm Villa**, 601 Grenfall Rd, Palm Springs, CA 92264; tel 619/327-1408 or toll free 800/833-5675; fax 619/ 327-7273. Ramon Rd exit off I-10. A comfortable motel geared toward senior citizens planning a relaxing getaway. **Rooms:** 14 rms. CI 1pm/CO 11am. Nonsmoking rms avail. **Amenities:** 🛅 🖭 A/C, cable TV, refrig. **Services:** 🚐 Car-rental desk. **Facilities:** 🛅 Lawn games, whirlpool, washer/dryer. **Rates:** HS Jan–May $60–$90 S or D. Lower rates off-season. Higher rates for spec evnts/hols. Pking: Outdoor, free. Maj CC.

≡ **Hampton Inn**, 2000 N Palm Canyon Dr, Palm Springs, CA 92262; tel 619/320-0555 or toll free 800/732-7755; fax 619/ 320-2261. Calif 111 exit off I-10. Within minutes of Palm Springs attractions. **Rooms:** 96 rms. CI 3pm/CO noon. Non- smoking rms avail. Contemporary-style decor. **Amenities:** 🛅 🕹 A/C, cable TV w/movies. **Services:** 🛅 🕸 Babysitting. **Facilities:** 🛅 🔲 🕹 Lawn games, whirlpool. 9-hole putting green. **Rates (CP):** HS Nov–Apr $69–$104 S or D. Extra person $5. Children under 18 stay free. Min stay spec evnts. Lower rates off-season. Higher rates for spec evnts/hols. Spec packages avail. Pking: Outdoor, free. Maj CC.

≡≡ **Quality Inn–Palm Springs**, 1269 E Palm Canyon Dr, Palm Springs, CA 92264; tel 619/323-2775 or toll free 800/ 472-4339; fax 619/323-4234. The parklike setting of this motel affords views of the San Jacinto and Santa Rosa mountains. **Rooms:** 144 rms and stes. CI 3pm/CO noon. Nonsmoking rms avail. **Amenities:** 🛅 🕹 🖭 A/C, cable TV w/movies. **Services:** 🚐 🕸 **Facilities:** 🛅 🔲 🕹 Whirlpool, washer/dryer. Barbecue

facilities available for groups. **Rates:** HS Dec 18–May $69–$119 S or D; from $129 ste. Extra person $5. Children under 19 stay free. Lower rates off-season. Pking: Outdoor, free. Maj CC.

≡≡≡ **Shilo Inn Palm Springs**, 1875 N Palm Canyon Dr, Palm Springs, CA 92262; tel 619/320-7676 or toll free 800/ 222-2244; fax 619/320-9543. 3 acres. A very well-maintained motel located just 1 mile from the heart of Palm Springs. **Rooms:** 124 rms and stes. CI 3pm/CO noon. Nonsmoking rms avail. Each room is mini-suite. **Amenities:** 🛅 🕹 🖭 A/C, cable TV, refrig. All units w/terraces. Microwaves. **Services:** 🚐 🛅 🕸 Fresh fruit and popcorn in lobby. **Facilities:** 🛅 🔲 🕹 Sauna, steam rm, whirlpool, washer/dryer. 2 courtyard swimming pools surrounded by well-manicured lawns and colorful gardens. **Rates (CP):** HS Jan–Mar $95–$155 S or D; from $95 ste. Extra person $12. Children under 12 stay free. Lower rates off-season. Higher rates for spec evnts/hols. Spec packages avail. Pking: Outdoor, free. Maj CC.

≡≡≡≡ **Sundance Villas**, 303 Cabrillo Rd, Palm Springs, CA 92262; tel 619/325-3888 or toll free 800/455-3888; fax 619/323-3029. 3.5 acres. Two- and 3-bedroom villas arranged duplex-style, with an enclosed garage, around a colorful garden and recreation area. **Rooms:** 19 ctges/villas. CI 3pm/CO 1pm. Express checkout avail. Nonsmoking rms avail. Spacious, lavish- ly appointed villas have private outdoor spas; most have pools as well. Separate dining area. **Amenities:** 🛅 🕹 🖭 A/C, cable TV w/movies, refrig, VCR, stereo/tape player. All units w/terraces, all w/fireplaces, all w/Jacuzzis. Guests are greeted with fruit and champagne and given orange juice and pastries for the following morning. There is a wet bar in each unit. **Services:** 🚐 🕸 Car- rental desk, babysitting. **Facilities:** 🛅 🔲 Sauna, washer/dryer. **Rates:** HS Dec 15–May from $295 ctge/villa. Extra person $25. Min stay wknds and spec evnts. Lower rates off-season. Pking: Indoor/outdoor, free. Maj CC.

≡≡ **Vagabond Inn**, 1699 S Palm Canyon Dr, Palm Springs, CA 92264; tel 619/325-7211 or toll free 800/522-1555; fax 619/322-9269. Set against the San Jacinto Mountains, this motel offers immaculate accommodations in a contemporary setting. **Rooms:** 120 rms and stes. CI 10am/CO noon. Nonsmoking rms avail. **Amenities:** 🛅 🕹 🖭 A/C, cable TV, voice mail. **Services:** 🕸 **Facilities:** 🛅 Sauna, whirlpool. **Rates:** HS Feb–Apr $64–$85 S; $68–$89 D; from $88 ste. Extra person $6. Children under 11 stay free. Min stay HS, wknds, and spec evnts. Lower rates off- season. Pking: Outdoor, free. Maj CC.

Inns

≡≡ **Casa Cody**, 175 S Cahuilla Rd, Palm Springs, CA 92262; tel 619/320-9346 or toll free 800/231-CODY; fax 619/

325-8610. Calif 111 Business District (Palm Canyon Dr) to Tahquitz Canyon Way, turn right on Cahuilla. A historic hotel originally conceived by a niece and nephew of Buffalo Bill Cody. Located a block off Palm Canyon Dr. Built in the Santa Fe style; not in top shape. **Rooms:** 17 rms and stes. CI 2pm/CO 11am. Room decor reflects the high desert theme of the architecture. **Amenities:** 🛏 🖭 A/C, cable TV, refrig. Some units w/terraces, some w/fireplaces. **Services:** ⤴ ⌘ **Facilities:** 🏊 ♿ Whirlpool. **Rates (CP):** HS Dec 22–Apr 29 $65–$105 S or D; from $125 ste. Extra person $10. Min stay HS, wknds, and spec evnts. Lower rates off-season. Spec packages avail. Pking: Outdoor, free. Ltd CC.

≣≣≣ **Estrella Inn at Palm Springs**, 415 S Belardo Rd, Palm Springs, CA 92262; tel 619/320-4117 or toll free 800/237-3687; fax 619/323-3303. 3 acres. A 1930s property restored and reopened in 1993 to rave reviews. Alluring tile-roofed Spanish-style inn with lush fruit trees, colorful flowers, towering palms, and a fountain courtyard. **Rooms:** 59 rms and stes; 15 ctges/villas. CI 3pm/CO noon. Oversize guest rooms, 2-bedroom suites, and individually decorated 1- and 2-bedroom bungalows. **Amenities:** 🛏 ♨ 🖭 A/C, cable TV, refrig. All units w/terraces, some w/fireplaces, some w/Jacuzzis. **Services:** ✕ 🚐 🖭 ⤴ ⌘ Car-rental desk, babysitting. **Facilities:** 🏊 🔟 Lawn games, whirlpool, washer/dryer, guest lounge. **Rates (CP):** HS Jan 15–Apr 15 $95–$130 S or D; from $125 ste; from $150 ctge/villa. Extra person $10. Children under 12 stay free. Min stay HS and wknds. Lower rates off-season. Higher rates for spec evnts/hols. Spec packages avail. Pking: Outdoor, free. Ltd CC.

≣≣≣ **Ingleside Inn**, 200 W Ramon Rd, Palm Springs, CA 92264; tel 619/325-0046 or toll free 800/772-6655 in the US, 800/258-6655 in Canada; fax 619/325-0710. Calif 111 exit off I-10; turn right on Ramon Rd. 2.5 acres. Created from a 1920s estate, this historic inn surrounded by high adobe walls is situated in the heart of Palm Springs. Unsuitable for children under 18. **Rooms:** 29 rms and stes. CI 2pm/CO noon. Each of the individually decorated rooms and mini-suites contain restored antiques; some have private steam baths and whirlpools. **Amenities:** 🛏 ♨ 🖭 A/C, cable TV, refrig. All units w/minibars, some w/terraces, some w/fireplaces. Refrigerators stocked with complimentary light snacks and cold drinks. **Services:** ✕ VP 🚐 🖭 ⤴ ⌘ Twice-daily maid svce, car-rental desk, babysitting. Complimentary daily newspaper and fruit basket. White limousine available for shopping expeditions. **Facilities:** 🏊 🔟 ♿ 1 rst (see also "Restaurants" below), 1 bar (w/entertainment), lawn games, whirlpool. **Rates (CP):** HS Oct–May $75–$205 D; from $235 ste. Extra person $20. Min stay wknds and spec evnts. Lower rates off-season. Spec packages avail. Pking: Outdoor, free. Ltd CC.

≣≣≣ **Korakia Pensione**, 257 S Patencio Rd, Palm Springs, CA 92262; tel 619/320-0708. Calif 111 exit off I-10. A pension in a 1920s Mediterranean-style villa that was once center for the literary and artistic community of old Palm Springs. Unsuitable for children under 15. **Rooms:** 10 rms and stes. CI 2pm/CO noon. Great rooms, with featherbeds and cotton sheets, antiques and handcrafted Mediterranean-style furniture. **Amenities:** 🛏 A/C, refrig. Some units w/terraces, some w/fireplaces. **Services:** ⌘ Babysitting. Expanded continental breakfast served in guest rooms or poolside. **Facilities:** 🏊 **Rates (CP):** HS Oct–June $79–$145 S or D; from $145 ste. Extra person $30. Min stay HS, wknds, and spec evnts. Lower rates off-season. Pking: Outdoor, free. Ltd CC. Closed: Aug.

≣≣≣ **Orchid Tree Inn**, 261 S Belardo Rd, Palm Springs, CA 92262; tel 619/325-2791 or toll free 800/733-3435; fax 619/325-3855. Calif 111 exit off I-10. 3.5 acres. With its tile-roofed Spanish-style bungalows, the inn evokes the charm and tranquility of Old Palm Springs. Sprawling grounds abound with colorful flowers and cacti. Unsuitable for children under 12. **Rooms:** 31 rms and stes; 9 ctges/villas. CI 2pm/CO noon. Individually decorated accommodations with unique furnishings, including ranch oak, wicker, and Craftsman pieces. **Amenities:** 🛏 ♨ A/C, cable TV. Some units w/terraces, some w/fireplaces, some w/Jacuzzis. **Services:** 🖭 Babysitting. **Facilities:** 🏊 🔟 Games rm, whirlpool, guest lounge w/TV. **Rates: Rates (CP):** HS Nov–May $80–$105 S or D; from $105 ste; from $105 ctge/villa. Extra person $15. Min stay HS and spec evnts. Lower rates off-season. Spec packages avail. Pking: Outdoor, free. Ltd CC.

≣≣≣ **Villa Royale**, 1620 Indian Trail, Palm Springs, CA 92264; tel 619/327-2314 or toll free 800/245-2314; fax 619/322-3794. Calif 111 S exit off I-80; follow Calif 111 S (Palm Canyon Dr). 3 acres. A European-style country inn, complete with cascading bougainvillea around quaint courtyards and paths that meander past fountains and shade trees. Unsuitable for children under 16. **Rooms:** 26 rms, stes, and effic; 7 ctges/villas. CI 2pm/CO noon. Each guest cottage is individually decorated with European antiques and custom-designed fabrics. Many have private spas. **Amenities:** 🛏 ♨ A/C, cable TV. Some units w/terraces, some w/fireplaces, some w/Jacuzzis. **Services:** ✕ 🖭 Car-rental desk, babysitting. Newspaper delivered to your door each morning. **Facilities:** 🏊 🔟 ♿ 1 rst (see also "Restaurants" below), 1 bar, whirlpool, guest lounge. Outdoor lounge area with fireplace and rattan chairs. **Rates (CP):** HS Oct–July 5 $75–$165 S or D; from $150 ste; from $99 effic; from $200 ctge/villa. Extra person $25. Min stay wknds and spec evnts. Lower rates off-season. Pking: Outdoor, free. Ltd CC.

Resorts

≡≡≡ **The Inn at the Racquet Club**, 2743 N Indian Canyon Dr, PO Box 1747, Palm Springs, CA 92262; tel 619/325-1281 or toll free 800/367-0946; fax 619/325-3429. 25 acres. An inn comprising cottages that were part of the original 1930s hotel, as well as condos and villas. **Rooms:** 54 rms, stes, and effic; 26 ctges/villas. CI 3pm/CO noon. Renovations planned and are much needed. **Amenities:** 🔒 🅰 A/C, cable TV, refrig. Some units w/terraces, some w/fireplaces. **Services:** 🚗 🖼 🍴 🛎 Car-rental desk, masseur. **Facilities:** 🏄 🚴 🎿 💬2 🏊10 💪 🎱800 🛁 1 bar, lawn games, spa, sauna, whirlpool. **Rates (CP):** HS Jan–May $79–$395 S or D; from $79 ste; from $89 effic; from $79 ctge/villa. Extra person $15. Children under 12 stay free. Min stay spec evnts. Lower rates off-season. Pking: Indoor/outdoor, free. Maj CC.

≡≡≡ **La Mancha Private Pool Villas & Court Club**, 444 Avenida Cabelleros, Palm Springs, CA 92262; tel 619/323-1773 or toll free 800/647-7482; fax 619/323-5928. Calif 111 exit off I-10; turn left on Avenida Cabelleros off Tahquitz Canyon Way. 20 acres. A private 20-acre villa-style resort with the atmosphere of a Mediterranean village. Except for a golf course, it has all the elements to make it a top-ranked property someday; however, some sprucing up is needed. **Rooms:** 54 ctges/villas. CI 2pm/CO 11am. Nonsmoking rms avail. Each 1-, 2-, and 3-bedroom villa is individually decorated. Some have their own private pools, spas, and tennis courts. **Amenities:** 🔒 🅰 📺 🍴 A/C, cable TV, refrig, voice mail, in-rm safe, bathrobes. All units w/terraces, some w/fireplaces, some w/Jacuzzis. Washer and dryer in each villa. **Services:** 🍴 🖼 🚗 🛎 🍴 Car-rental desk, masseur, babysitting. Fleet of 15 Chrysler LeBaron convertibles for rent. **Facilities:** 🏄 🚴 🎿 💬3 🏊 🛁 🎱200 1 rst, 1 bar, lawn games, sauna, whirlpool, washer/dryer. One main swimming pool and individual pools in 30 of the villas. 9-hole putting green. **Rates:** HS Dec 21–Apr 15 from $175 ctge/villa. Children under 18 stay free. Min stay wknds. Lower rates off-season. Spec packages avail. Pking: Indoor/outdoor, free. Maj CC.

≡≡≡ **Oasis Water Resort Villa Hotel**, 4190 E Palm Canyon Dr, Palm Springs, CA 92264; tel 619/328-1499 or toll free 800/247-4664; fax 619/328-8659. 27 acres. Resort combines villa living with a spacious water park and a 20,000-square-foot European health club. Excellent value. **Rooms:** 81 ctges/villas. CI 4pm/CO noon. 2-bedroom, 2-bath villas feature enclosed garages, private patios with barbecues, and full kitchens. **Amenities:** 🔒 📺 A/C, cable TV, refrig. All units w/terraces, 1 w/Jacuzzi. **Services:** 🚗 🍴 Car-rental desk, masseur, babysitting. **Facilities:** 🏄 🏊 🎱120 Lawn games, whirlpool, washer/dryer. 9 whirlpools. Nearby golf course. **Rates (CP):** HS Jan 22–May 28 from $269 ctge/villa. Children under 18 stay free. Min

stay wknds and spec evnts. Lower rates off-season. Higher rates for spec evnts/hols. Spec packages avail. Pking: Indoor, free. Maj CC.

≡≡≡ **Palm Springs Hilton Resort**, 400 E Tahquitz Canyon Way, Palm Springs, CA 92262; tel 619/320-6868 or toll free 800/522-6900 in the US, 800/527-8020 in Canada; fax 619/320-2126. Calif 111 Business District (Palm Canyon Dr) to Tahquitz Canyon Way; turn left. 10 acres. A 3-story contemporary building surrounding a courtyard and pool, 2 blocks from fashionable Palm Canyon Dr. **Rooms:** 245 rms and stes; 15 ctges/villas. CI 3pm/CO noon. Express checkout avail. Nonsmoking rms avail. A bit worn, but planned renovations will make a difference. **Amenities:** 🔒 🅰 🍴 A/C, cable TV w/movies, refrig. All units w/minibars, all w/terraces, some w/Jacuzzis. **Services:** ✗ 🖼 VP 🚗 🖼 🍴 🛎 Car-rental desk, masseur, children's program, babysitting. **Facilities:** 🏄 🏊 🛁 1 rst, 2 bars, games rm, sauna, beauty salon. Access to soon-to-open Caesers World Casino. **Rates:** HS Dec 28–May $195–$225 S or D; from $265 ste; from $195 ctge/villa. Extra person $20. Children under 18 stay free. Lower rates off-season. Spec packages avail. Pking: Outdoor, free. Maj CC.

≡≡≡ **Palm Springs Marquis Crowne Plaza Resort & Suites**, 150 S Indian Canyon Dr, Palm Springs, CA 92262; tel 619/322-2121 or toll free 800/223-1834, 800/223-1050 in CA; fax 619/322-4365. Calif 111 Business District (Palm Canyon Dr) to Baristo Rd; turn left to Indian Canyon Dr. 7 acres. Inspiring mountain range complements resort's contemporary architecture. Located in the center of Palm Springs. **Rooms:** 163 rms and stes; 101 ctges/villas. CI 4pm/CO noon. Express checkout avail. Nonsmoking rms avail. All guest rooms and suites recently renovated. Private balconies and patios provide gorgeous views of desert. **Amenities:** 🔒 🅰 📺 🍴 A/C, cable TV w/movies, in-rm safe. All units w/terraces, some w/fireplaces, some w/Jacuzzis. **Services:** ✗ 🖼 VP 🚗 🖼 🍴 Car-rental desk, social director, masseur, children's program, babysitting. **Facilities:** 🏄 🏊2 🛁 🎱2.1K 🛁 3 rsts, 3 bars, spa, whirlpool, beauty salon. Special signs for the blind included in elevators and at guest room entry doors. **Rates:** HS Jan–Apr $149 S or D; from $179 ste; from $179 ctge/villa. Extra person $15. Children under 16 stay free. Min stay spec evnts. Lower rates off-season. Spec packages avail. Pking: Indoor, $6. Maj CC.

≡≡≡ **Palm Springs Riviera Resort & Racquet Club**, 1600 N Indian Canyon Dr, Palm Springs, CA 92262; tel 619/327-8311 or toll free 800/444-8311; fax 619/327-4323. Calif 111 exit off I-10, to Vista Chino; turn left to Indian Canyon Dr. 24 acres. Located minutes from the heart of Palm Springs, this resort boasts the famous Bono Restaurant and Racquet Club. **Rooms:** 480 rms and stes. CI 3pm/CO noon. Express checkout avail. Nonsmoking rms avail. Plants in every room. **Amenities:** ⛖ ⎈ A/C, cable TV w/movies, refrig. All units w/terraces, some w/Jacuzzis. **Services:** ⎚○ ⎗ ⊻ℙ ⛨ ⛱ ⏎ ⎙ Car-rental desk, babysitting. **Facilities:** ⛩ ⛴ ⊛ ☒ ⛯ ⏁K ⎈ 1 rst (*see also* "Restaurants" below), 1 bar (w/entertainment), lifeguard, lawn games, whirlpool, beauty salon. Lighted 18-hole putting green and a stadium center tennis court. **Rates:** HS Nov 15–Mar 31 $119–$179 S or D; from $379 ste. Extra person $20. Children under 17 stay free. Lower rates off-season. Higher rates for spec evnts/hols. Spec packages avail. Pking: Outdoor, free. Maj CC.

Restaurants ⏍

Alfredo's Italian Gardens, 285 S Palm Canyon Dr, Palm Springs; tel 619/325-4060. **Italian.** Rich green decor adds to the garden ambience. Fettucine Alfredo, chicken piccata, shrimp scampi. Also American fare, like barbecued baby-back ribs. **FYI:** Reservations recommended. Dress code. **Open:** Lunch daily 11:30am–4pm; dinner daily 4–11pm. **Prices:** Main courses $6.95–$18.50. Maj CC. ⎈

★ **Billy Reed's**, 1800 N Palm Canyon Dr, Palm Springs; tel 619/325-1946. Calif 111 exit off I-10. **American.** With its Victorian decor and casual atmosphere, a perfect spot for family dining, offering yankee pot roast, broiled scallops, roast chicken, prime rib, and the fresh fish of the day. **FYI:** Reservations not accepted. Piano. Children's menu. Dress code. **Open:** Daily 7am–11pm. **Prices:** Main courses $8.95–$11.95. Maj CC. 🚹 ⚐ ⎈

Blue Coyote Grill, 445 N Palm Canyon Dr (Calif 111), Palm Springs; tel 619/327-1196. Calif 111 exit off I-10. **Mexican/ Southwestern.** Mexican tiled fountains and colorful gardens add to the pleasant ambience at this hacienda-style grill. Appealing courtyard with blue umbrellas, tiled bar, patio overlooking Palm Canyon Dr. Broiled twin tenderloin medallions of beef with Spanish cream sauce; rolled boneless chicken breast with jack cheese, red-corn tortillas, and cilantro. **FYI:** Reservations accepted. Children's menu. Dress code. **Open:** Lunch daily 11am–5pm; dinner Sun–Thurs 5–10pm, Fri–Sat 5–11pm. Closed some hols. **Prices:** Main courses $7.95–$18.95. Maj CC. 🍽 🚹 ⎈

Bono Restaurant & Racquet Club, in the Palm Springs Riviera Resort & Racquet Club, 1700 N Indian Canyon Dr, Palm Springs; tel 619/322-6200. Calif 111 exit off I-10. **Italian.** The ultramodern decor, with black-marble tabletops and crisp white tablecloths, provides a sleek but comfortable setting for this restaurant, named for Sonny Bono, who is often present to greet diners. It specializes in hearty Italian cuisine, with specialties that include lobster ravioli with vermouth and truffle sauce, and veal scaloppine with grilled portobello mushrooms. **FYI:** Reser-

vations recommended. Piano. Dress code. **Open:** Sun–Thurs 5–10pm, Fri–Sat 5–11pm. **Prices:** Main courses $12.50–$27. Maj CC. 🚹 🌄 ⚐ ⊻ℙ ⎈

Brew Meister's, 369 N Palm Canyon Dr, Palm Springs; tel 619/327-BREW. Calif 111 exit off I-10. **American.** Located in a renovated 1934 Spanish-style building, this brew pub and grill offers draft beer and a casual menu featuring burgers, sandwiches, and appetizers, as well as soups, salads, and entrees. **FYI:** Reservations not accepted. Guitar. Dress code. Beer and wine only. **Open:** Daily 11am–1:30am. **Prices:** Main courses $7.95–$13.95. Ltd CC. 🍽 ⎈

★ **Cedar Creek Inn**, 1555 S Palm Canyon Dr, Palm Springs; tel 619/325-7300. Ramon Rd exit off I-10. **American.** Inviting restaurant with an outdoor patio and 3 separate dining areas. Specialties include salmon poached in apple juice, and chicken breast stuffed with pesto cream cheese. Also at: 73-445 El Paseo, Palm Desert (619/340-1236); 384 Forest Ave, Laguna Beach (714/497-8696). **FYI:** Reservations accepted. Guitar/piano. Dress code. **Open:** Daily 11am–9pm. Closed some hols. **Prices:** Main courses $5.75–$17.95. Maj CC. 🍽 🚹 ⎈

★ **El Mirasol**, 140 E Palm Canyon Dr, Palm Springs; tel 619/323-0721. Calif 111 exit off I-10. **Mexican.** A favorite dining spot for families. Dining room is decorated with a desert landscape mural. Menu features regional cuisine of Mexico, including carne adobada, carnitas, chicken mole, and pork chile verde, as well as standard combination plates. Closed for lunch in summer. **FYI:** Reservations accepted. Dress code. **Open:** HS Sept–May lunch daily 11am–3pm; dinner daily 5–10pm. Reduced hours off-season. Closed some hols. **Prices:** Main courses $6.25–$10.75. Maj CC. 🚹

Europa Restaurant & Bar, in Villa Royale Inn, 1620 Indian Trail, Palm Springs; tel 619/327-2314. Ramon Rd exit off I-10. **Continental.** Terra-cotta stucco walls, European antiques, and old-world art define this restaurant, reminiscent of a European country inn. Specialty dishes of continental influence—one night it's Italian, another night it's French, Spanish, or Greek. **FYI:** Reservations recommended. Dress code. **Open:** Lunch Tues–Sun 11:30am–2pm; dinner Tues–Sun 5:30–10pm; brunch Sun 11:30am–2pm. Closed some hols; June–Oct. **Prices:** Main courses $12.95–$28; PF dinner $22–$28. Maj CC. ⚇ 🚹

Flower Drum, 424 S Indian Canyon Dr, Palm Springs; tel 619/323-3020. **Chinese.** A stream representing the Yangtze River threads its way through the center of the restaurant, complete with bridge and koi pond. Specializing in food inspired by the Hunan, Szechaun, Canton, Shanghai, and Peking regions of China, including tangerine beef, Kung Pao chicken, and shrimp blossom. Each evening, a traditional Chinese dance is performed along with other Chinese traditions. **FYI:** Reservations accepted. Dinner theater. Dress code. **Open:** Lunch daily 11:30am–3pm; dinner daily 4–10:30pm. Closed Thanksgiving. **Prices:** Main courses $7.95–$28. Maj CC. ◪

John Henry's Cafe, 1785 E Tahquitz Canyon Way, Palm Springs; tel 619/327-7667. Calif 111 exit off I-10. **Eclectic.** The main dining room overlooks an outdoor patio, which has potted and bedded flowers and a 3-tiered fountain. Eclectic menu includes grilled Lake Superior whitefish with lemon butter, roasted herb rack of lamb, and osso buco. **FYI:** Reservations recommended. Dress code. **Open:** HS Oct–May Mon–Sat 5–9:30pm. Reduced hours off-season. Closed some hols; June–Sept. **Prices:** Main courses $8.75–$13.50. Maj CC.

La Quinta Cliffhouse, 78-250 Calif 111, Palm Springs; tel 619/360-5991. Washington exit off I-10. **Regional American.** Dramatically perched halfway up a small mountain. Large picture windows look out on the surrounding mountains; dining terraces are carved into granite outcroppings. Menu favorites include aged filet mignon, marinated rack of lamb, and fresh fish. **FYI:** Reservations recommended. Guitar. Children's menu. Dress code. **Open:** HS Jan–Apr dinner daily 5–10pm; brunch Sun 10:30am–2pm. Reduced hours off-season. Closed Dec 25. **Prices:** Main courses $10.95–$21.95. Maj CC. ⬖ ▨ ◪ VP ⅋

Las Casuelas Terraza, 222 S Palm Canyon Dr, Palm Springs; tel 619/325-2794. Calif 111 exit off I-10. **Mexican.** Set in a hacienda-style building with dark wood interior and colorful Mexican accents. Specialties include carne asada, spicy pork, chicken and shrimp fajitas. Also at: 368 N Palm Canyon, Palm Springs (619/325-3213); 70-050 Calif 111, Rancho Mirage (619/328-8844); 73-703 Calif 111, Palm Desert (619/568-0011). **FYI:** Reservations recommended. Combo. Children's menu. Dress code. **Open:** Lunch Mon–Sat 11am–4pm, Sun 10am–4pm; dinner daily 4–10pm. Closed some hols. **Prices:** Main courses $5.95–$13.50. Maj CC. ⅋

♣ **Le Vallauris**, 385 W Tahquitz Canyon Way, Palm Springs; tel 619/325-5059. Calif 111 exit off I-10. **French.** Historic-landmark home decorated with tapestries and Louis XV furniture. Fireplaces dominate the main dining room, and doors open out onto a tree-lined patio. The daily menu highlights fresh and seasonal ingredients in such specialties as black ravioli with lobster bisque, roasted pork tenderloin, and Lake Superior whitefish with Dijon mustard mousseline. **FYI:** Reservations recommended. Piano. Dress code. **Open:** Lunch daily 11:30am–2:30pm; dinner daily 6–11pm; brunch Sun 11:30am–2:30pm. **Prices:** Main courses $19.40–$29. Maj CC. ◉ ▮ ⬖ ◪ VP

★ **Louise's Pantry**, 124 S Palm Canyon Dr, Palm Springs; tel 619/325-5124. Calif 111 exit off I-10. **American.** A diner-style restaurant in the heart of Palm Springs. It serves such all-American favorites as chicken and dumplings, roast turkey, and homemade cornbread, and is known for its cream pies. Also at: 44-491 Town Center Way, Palm Desert (619/346-1315). **FYI:** Reservations not accepted. Children's menu. Dress code. Beer and wine only. **Open:** HS Sept–May daily 7am–9pm. Reduced hours off-season. Closed Dec 25. **Prices:** Main courses $4.30–$9.95. No CC.

Lyons English Grille, 233 E Palm Canyon Dr, Palm Springs; tel 619/327-1551. Ramon Rd exit off I-10. **British.** Reminiscent of a 19th-century British inn, with dark woods, red leather, antiques, leaded-glass windows, and copper pots. Steak-and-kidney pie, prime rib, roast duckling. **FYI:** Reservations recommended. Piano/singer. Dress code. **Open:** HS Oct–May daily 4–10:30pm. Reduced hours off-season. Closed some hols; July–Sept. **Prices:** Main courses $12.95–$19.95. Maj CC. ▮ ◪ VP

Melvyn's, in the Ingleside Inn, 200 W Ramon Rd, Palm Springs; tel 619/325-2323. Calif 111 exit off I-10; turn right on Ramon Rd. **Continental.** Nestled in the gardens of the Ingleside Inn, this Renaissance-style restaurant features an intimate dining room as well as an enclosed patio. Continental menu includes veal Ingleside, steak au poivre, chicken topped with white shrimp and avocado. **FYI:** Reservations recommended. Piano. Dress code. **Open:** Lunch Mon–Fri 11:30am–3pm, Sat–Sun 9am–3pm; dinner daily 6–11pm; brunch Sat–Sun 9am–3pm. **Prices:** Main courses $13.95–$48.95. Maj CC. ◉ ▨ ▨ VP ⅋

★ **Nate's Delicatessen and Restaurant**, 100 S Indian Canyon Dr, Palm Springs; tel 619/325-3506. Calif 111 exit off I-10. **Deli.** A collection of framed caricatures (with Yiddish subtitles) line the walls of this New York–style delicatessen, where the bill of fare includes sandwiches, potato pancakes, cheese blintzes, corned beef and cabbage, and, of course, chicken soup. Also at: 72-281 Calif 111, Palm Desert (619/776-8400). **FYI:** Reservations accepted. Children's menu. Dress code. **Open:** Daily 8am–8pm. **Prices:** Main courses $10.95–$18.95. Maj CC. ◪ ⅋

Otani–A Garden Restaurant, 1000 Tahquitz Way, Palm Springs; tel 619/327-6700. Calif 111 exit off I-10. **Japanese.** A 40-foot peaked roof and a traditional Japanese garden create a distinctive atmosphere. Chefs present "food theater" in four separate areas: sushi bar, a teppanyaki table, tempura bar, and yakitori counter. There's also a regular dining room menu. **FYI:** Reservations recommended. Children's menu. Dress code. **Open:** Lunch Sun–Fri 11:30am–2pm; dinner daily 6:30–9:30pm; brunch Sun 11am–2:30pm. Closed some hols. **Prices:** Main courses $13.95–$24.95; PF dinner $18.50–$21.50. Maj CC. ◪ ⅋

Siamese Gourmet Restaurant, 4711 E Palm Canyon Dr, Palm Springs; tel 619/328-0057. Gene Autry Trail/Vista Chino exit off I-10. **Thai.** Cheerfully decorated with bamboo chairs and emerald green tablecloths. House specialties are chicken and beef curry, barbecued chicken, and clay-pot seafood combination. **FYI:** Reservations recommended. Dress code. Beer and wine only. **Open:** Lunch Mon–Sat 11:30am–2:30pm; dinner daily 5–10pm; brunch Sun 11am–2:30pm. Closed some hols. **Prices:** Main courses $7.95–$15.25. Maj CC.

Sorrentino's, 1032 N Palm Canyon Dr, Palm Springs; tel 619/325-2944. Calif 111 exit off I-10. **Continental.** For nearly 30 years the Sorrentino family has owned and operated this seafood house. Dining patio features a 25-foot pond. Specialties include live Maine lobster, clams, oysters, Dungeness crab cakes, and soft-shell crab; extensive menu also includes steak, veal, chicken, and pasta dishes. **FYI:** Reservations recommended. Piano. Children's menu. Dress code. **Open:** HS Sept–May daily 5–10pm. Reduced hours off-season. Closed Thanksgiving. **Prices:** Main courses $10.95–$23.95. Maj CC. VP

Attractions

Palm Springs Desert Museum, 101 Museum Dr; tel 619/325-7186. The triple focus of this museum is on art, natural science, and the performing arts. Galleries feature presentations from the museum's vast permanent collection, including classic American landscapes and Western art, as well as contemporary paintings and sculpture, with a particular focus on California. The natural science wing contains a variety of permanent exhibits, including interpretive dioramas of desert plant and animal life. The 450-seat **Annenberg Theater** hosts world-class dance, theater, and music performances. Sculpture gardens, museum store, cafe. **Open:** Sat–Thurs 10am–4pm, Fri 1–8pm. Closed some hols. Schedule may vary; call ahead. $$

Palm Springs Aerial Tramway, 1 Tramway Rd; tel 619/325-1391. The tram ascends 2½ miles up the slopes of Mt San Jacinto, traveling from the desert floor to cool alpine heights in less than 20 minutes; in winter the change is dramatic. At the top are a restaurant and cocktail lounge, a gift shop, a picnic area, and the starting points of numerous hiking trails, many dotted with camping areas. **Open:** Mon–Fri 10am–8pm, Sat–Sun 8am–8pm; open 1 hour later during Daylight Saving Time. $$$$

PALO ALTO

Map page M-2, D2

Hotels

Garden Court Hotel, 520 Cowper St, Palo Alto, CA 94301; tel 415/322-9000 or toll free 800/824-9028; fax 415/324-3609. 25 mi S of San Francisco. University Ave W exit off US 101. A charmer with a Mediterranean look in downtown Palo Alto. **Rooms:** 61 rms and stes. CI 2pm/CO noon. Express checkout avail. **Amenities:** A/C, cable TV w/movies, refrig, VCR, in-rm safe, bathrobes. All units w/minibars, all w/terraces, some w/fireplaces, some w/Jacuzzis. **Services:** VP Twice-daily maid svce, masseur, babysitting. Complimentary overnight shoe polishing. Four choices of newspaper. Complimentary shuttle within 5-mile radius. **Facilities:** 275 1 rst, 1 bar. Exercycle and rowing machine can be brought to room. Complimentary passes to a local spa. **Rates:** $175–$225 S or D; from $225 ste. Extra person $15. Children under 12 stay free. Pking: Indoor, $8.50. Maj CC.

Holiday Inn–Palo Alto–Stanford, 625 El Camino Real, Palo Alto, CA 94301; tel 415/328-2800 or toll free 800/HOLIDAY, 800/874-3516 in CA; fax 415/327-7362. 25 mi S of San Francisco. Embarcadeno Rd W exit off US 101. Popular for its location near downtown Palo Alto and Stanford University, and for its resortlike ambience. **Rooms:** 350 rms and stes. CI 3pm/CO noon. Express checkout avail. Nonsmoking rms avail. **Amenities:** A/C, cable TV w/movies, voice mail. Some units w/minibars, some w/terraces, some w/Jacuzzis. **Services:** Car-rental desk, babysitting. **Facilities:** 500 1 rst, 1 bar (w/entertainment), washer/dryer. **Rates (CP):** $131–$146 S; $141–$156 D; from $199 ste. Extra person $10. Children under 18 stay free. AP rates avail. Spec packages avail. Pking: Outdoor, free. Maj CC.

Hyatt Rickeys in Palo Alto, 4219 El Camino Real, Palo Alto, CA 94306; tel 415/493-8000 or toll free 800/233-1234; fax 415/424-0836. 30 mi S of San Francisco. San Antonio Rd S exit off US 101. This 50-year-old landmark hotel is still appealing, with its extensive grounds and popular restaurant. **Rooms:** 347 rms and stes. CI 3pm/CO noon. Express checkout avail. Nonsmoking rms avail. **Amenities:** A/C, cable TV w/movies, shoe polisher. Some units w/terraces, some w/fireplaces. **Services:** Car-rental desk, masseur, children's program, babysitting. Women may request an escort for walking the grounds at night. **Facilities:** 1450 1 rst, 1 bar (w/entertainment), lawn games, sauna, beauty salon.

Rates: $145–$170 S; $170–$195 D; from $230 ste. Extra person $25. Children under 18 stay free. AP rates avail. Spec packages avail. Pking: Outdoor, free. Maj CC.

≣≣ **Stanford Terrace Inn**, 531 Stanford Ave, Palo Alto, CA 94306; tel 415/857-0333 or toll free 800/729-0332; fax 415/857-0343. Embarcadero Rd exit off US 101; turn left on El Camino, right on Stanford. Overlooks the beautiful southern campus of Stanford University. **Rooms:** 79 rms and stes. CI 2pm/CO noon. Exceptionally large rooms and suites. All mini-suites have full kitchens including pots and pans. **Amenities:** 🛁 ⏳ 📱 A/C, cable TV w/movies, refrig. Some units w/terraces. **Services:** 🏖 🗨 Masseur, children's program, babysitting. **Facilities:** 🏋 🛏 Washer/dryer. **Rates (CP):** From $118 ste. Extra person $10. Children under 13 stay free. Pking: Outdoor, free. Ltd CC.

Motel

≣≣ **Creekside Inn Best Western**, 3400 El Camino Real, Palo Alto, CA 94306; tel 415/493-2411 or toll free 800/49-CREEK; fax 415/493-6789. 30 mi S of San Francisco. Oregon Expwy exit off US 101. Though located on a busy street, the motel has a pool and creek that give it a country feel. **Rooms:** 136 rms, stes, and effic. CI 3pm/CO noon. Express checkout avail. Nonsmoking rms avail. Suites have 2-burner stove and other kitchen amenities. **Amenities:** 🛁 ⏳ 📱 🗨 A/C, satel TV w/movies, refrig, VCR. All units w/terraces. Microwave in suites. **Services:** ✗ 🏖 🗨 Complimentary shuttle service within 10-mile radius. **Facilities:** 🏋 🍽 150 ⏳ 1 rst, 1 bar, sauna. Grocery store–deli and taco stand on premises. **Rates:** $80–$140 S or D; from $115 ste; from $115 effic. Extra person $3. Spec packages avail. Pking: Outdoor, free. Maj CC.

Inn

≣≣ **The Victorian on Lytton**, 555 Lytton Ave, Palo Alto, CA 94301; tel 415/322-8555; fax 415/322-7141. University Ave exit off US 101; right on Middlefield, left on Lytton. A cozy bed-and-breakfast located 1 block from charming downtown Palo Alto. **Rooms:** 10 rms. CI 3pm/CO 11am. No smoking. **Amenities:** 🛁 ⏳ A/C, TV. 1 unit w/fireplace. Evening sherry and bathrobes provided on request. **Services:** Afternoon tea served. **Facilities:** ⏳ Guest lounge. **Rates (CP):** $98–$200 D. Extra person $10. Spec packages avail. Pking: Outdoor, free. Ltd CC.

Restaurants 🍴

Fresco, 3398 El Camino Real, Palo Alto; tel 415/493-3470. Pagemill Rd exit off Calif 280; turn south on El Camino Real. **Californian/Pizza.** Family restaurant with black-and-white de-

cor and lots of plants. Counter for casual meals. Linguine with prawns or linguine primavera, pork chops, pizza, and calzone. **FYI:** Reservations not accepted. Children's menu. **Open:** Daily 6am–11pm. **Prices:** Main courses $8.20–$12. Maj CC. 🎴 ⏳

Scott's Seafood Grill & Bar, 2300 E Bayshore Rd, Palo Alto; tel 415/856-1046. Embarcadero E exit off US 101; turn right onto E Bayshore Rd. **Seafood.** Cape Cod looks, with Nautical photos, beamed ceilings, and wood wainscoting. Fireplace in lounge. Monterey Bay calamari, Boston clam chowder, petrale sole, and seafood sauté. Also, steak, chicken, pasta. **FYI:** Reservations recommended. Children's menu. **Open:** Lunch Mon–Fri 11:30am–5pm; dinner Sun–Mon 5–9pm, Tues–Sat 5–9:30pm. Closed Dec 25. **Prices:** Main courses $11.95–$25. Maj CC. 🍴 🎴 💟 ⏳

Attraction 🏛

Stanford Linear Accelerator Center, 2575 Sand Hill Rd; tel 415/926-2204. This facility, located 3 miles west of the main Stanford University campus, specializes in experimental and theoretical research in elementary particle physics. Built in the 1960s, the center's 2-mile-long linear electron acclerterator is used to create collisions of subatomic particles to study their effects and learn about the nature of matter. The accelerator generates electron beams with the highest energy available in the world, making it a valuable research tool for scientists from all over the world.

Public tours are conducted several times a week, by advance reservation only (phone for schedule). The 2-hour tour begins with an orientation and slide presentation and concludes with a guided bus tour of the 400-acre facility. The tour is not recommended for children under age 11. Free.

PASADENA

Map page M-3, D2

See also **San Marino**

Hotels 🛏

≣≣≣≣ **Doubletree Hotel Pasadena at Plaza las Fuentes**, 191 N Los Robles Ave, Pasadena, CA 91101; tel 818/792-2727 or toll free 800/222-TREE; fax 818/792-7669. Arroyo Pkwy exit off I-110. Gardens with fountains and exquisite tile work give this hotel a Spanish feel. Lovely public rooms. Located 2 blocks from shopping mall and convention center; 6 blocks from Old Town. **Rooms:** 350 rms and stes. Exec-level rms avail. CI 3pm/CO noon. Express checkout avail. Nonsmoking rms avail. Rooms aren't large but are attractively decorated. **Amenities:** 🛁 ⏳ A/C, cable TV w/movies. Some units w/terraces, some w/Jacuzzis. **Services:** 🍽️ 🔑 VP 🚐 🏖️ 🧺 Car-rental desk, babysitting. Excellent staff. **Facilities:** 🏋️ 🏌️ 600 💻 ♿ 1 rst, 2 bars (1 w/entertainment), spa, sauna, steam rm, whirlpool. Pool has spectacular view of the city hall dome. **Rates:** $140–$385 S; $155–$400 D; from $300 ste. Extra person $15. Children under 17 stay free. Min stay spec evnts. Higher rates for spec evnts/hols. Spec packages avail. Pking: Indoor, $4–$9. Maj CC.

≣≣≣ **Holiday Inn Pasadena**, 303 E Cordova St, Pasadena, CA 91105; tel 818/449-4000 or toll free 800/457-7940; fax 818/584-1390. Arroyo Pkwy exit off I-110. Adjacent to the convention center; great lobby filled with Chinese art. Close to Old Town and across from shopping mall. **Rooms:** 318 rms and stes. Exec-level rms avail. CI 4pm/CO noon. Express checkout avail. Nonsmoking rms avail. Newly decorated rooms are very large and airy; deluxe suites available. **Amenities:** 🏧 ♨️ 🍴 A/C, cable TV w/movies, refrig. Some units w/terraces. **Services:** ✕ 🚐 🏖️ 🧺 Car-rental desk, children's program. Happy hour. **Facilities:** 🏋️ 6 💻 400 ♿ 1 rst, 1 bar, washer/dryer. Ice-skating rink next door. **Rates:** $90–$100 S; $100–$110 D; from $115 ste. Extra person $12. Children under 19 stay free. Min stay spec evnts. Higher rates for spec evnts/hols. Spec packages avail. Pking: Indoor, $3.50–$5. Maj CC.

≣≣≣ **Pasadena Hilton**, 150 S Los Robles Ave, Pasadena, CA 91101; tel 818/577-1000 or toll free 800/HILTONS; fax 818/584-3148. Lake Ave exit off I-210; go south 3 blocks to Colorado; right 6 blocks to Los Robles. Well kept and pleasant; 2 blocks from the convention center. **Rooms:** 291 rms and stes. Exec-level rms avail. CI 3pm/CO 1pm. Express checkout avail. Nonsmoking rms avail. Rooms are nicely decorated and well maintained. **Amenities:** 🏧 ♨️ 📺 A/C, cable TV w/movies, refrig. All units w/minibars, some w/terraces. **Services:** ✕ 🚐 VP 🏖️ 🧺 Twice-daily maid svce, car-rental desk, social director, masseur, babysitting. **Facilities:** 🏋️ 🏌️ 900 💻 ♿ 1 rst, 1 bar, spa, beauty salon, washer/dryer. Meeting rooms feature great city views. Golf and tennis at nearby country club. **Rates:** $185 S or D; from $225 ste. Extra person $15. Children under 18 stay free. Min stay HS and spec evnts. Higher rates for spec evnts/hols. Spec packages avail. Pking: Indoor, $6. Maj CC.

≣≣≣≣ **Ritz-Carlton Huntington Hotel**, 1401 S Oak Knoll Ave, Pasadena, CA 91106; tel 818/568-3900 or toll free 800/241-3333; fax 818/568-3700. Take Calif 110 N to Arroyo Pkwy; right on California Blvd, right on Lake Ave. 23 acres. With red-tile roof and sand-beige stucco walls, this elegant hotel fits right into its crème-de-la-crème residential neighborhood. **Rooms:** 377 rms and stes; 6 ctges/villas. Exec-level rms avail. CI 3pm/CO noon. Express checkout avail. Nonsmoking rms avail. Recalls an English country house; dark furnishings plus comfort-

able armchair with ottoman. Marble baths are nicer in standard rooms than in suites. **Amenities:** 🏧 ♨️ 🍴 A/C, cable TV w/movies, refrig, in-rm safe, shoe polisher, bathrobes. All units w/minibars, some w/terraces, some w/Jacuzzis. **Services:** 🍽️ 🔑 VP 🚐 🏖️ 🧺 Twice-daily maid svce, car-rental desk, masseur, babysitting. **Facilities:** 🏋️ 🚲 🎾 🏌️ 800 💻 ♿ 2 rsts (see also "Restaurants" below), 2 bars (w/entertainment), lifeguard, games rm, lawn games, spa, sauna, steam rm, whirlpool, beauty salon. Tennis pro on staff. **Rates:** $160–$245 S or D; from $275 ste; from $350 ctge/villa. Extra person $25. Children under 18 stay free. Min stay spec evnts. Spec packages avail. Pking: Indoor/outdoor, $12. Maj CC.

Motels

≣≣ **Comfort Inn**, 2462 E Colorado Blvd, Pasadena, CA 91107; tel 818/405-0811 or toll free 800/221-2222; fax 818/796-0966. Sierra Madre exit off I-210. Nice hotel with easy access to area attractions. **Rooms:** 50 rms. CI 1pm/CO noon. Nonsmoking rms avail. Pleasantly decorated rooms. **Amenities:** 🏧 ♨️ 🍴 A/C, cable TV w/movies, refrig, VCR. Microwave. **Services:** 🏖️ 🧺 Babysitting. **Facilities:** 🏋️ 20 💻 ♿ Spa, sauna, whirlpool, washer/dryer. **Rates (CP):** $110 S or D. Extra person $5. Children under 18 stay free. Min stay spec evnts. Higher rates for spec evnts/hols. Pking: Outdoor, free. Maj CC.

≣≣≣ **Saga Motor Hotel**, 1633 E Colorado Blvd, Pasadena, CA 91106; tel 818/795-0431; fax 818/792-0559. Allen exit off I-210; go south 3 blocks to Colorado. Clean, well-cared for property with easy access to the freeway. Lobby has pleasant area in which to read, sip coffee, and gaze at the garden. **Rooms:** 70 rms and stes. CI noon/CO noon. Nonsmoking rms avail. Remodeled rooms are large and airy with a country atmosphere. **Amenities:** 🏧 ♨️ A/C, cable TV w/movies. 1 unit w/terrace. **Services:** 🔑 VP 🏖️ 🧺 **Facilities:** 🏋️ 30 **Rates:** $39–$59 S; $45–$69 D; from $58 ste. Extra person $7. Children under 16 stay free. Min stay spec evnts. Higher rates for spec evnts/hols. Spec packages avail. Pking: Outdoor, free. Maj CC. Call collect for reservations.

Restaurants 🍴

Ⓢ **Abiento**, 110 S Lake Ave, Pasadena; tel 818/449-4151. Lake St exit off I-210. **New American/Mediterranean.** This lovely, trattoria-style restaurant with ocher walls, garden plants, and lots of light is a lively place to dine, although it can be a bit noisy during happy hour. Menu specialties include the veal sausages with sweet onions, quail stuffed with risotto, and daily fresh fish specials. **FYI:** Reservations recommended. Children's menu.

Open: Mon–Fri 11am–10pm, Sat 8am–11pm, Sun 9am–3pm. Closed some hols. **Prices:** Main courses $7.95–$13.95. Maj CC. ♥ ☏ ⊞ ⅘

Bistro 45, 45 S Mentor Ave, Pasadena; tel 818/795-2478. Lake Ave exit off I-210. **Californian/French.** A charming bistro with several intimate rooms, lovely glassware, and huge floral arrangements. The French bistro fare includes roast leg of Colorado lamb, crispy duck, roast tenderloin of pork, and bouillabaisse. The restaurant has a nice feel to it. **FYI:** Reservations recommended. Dress code. **Open:** Lunch Tues–Fri 11:30am–2:30pm; dinner Tues–Thurs 6–10pm, Fri 6–11pm, Sat 5:30–11pm, Sun 5–9pm. Closed some hols. **Prices:** Main courses $15.50–$21.75. Maj CC. ♥ ☏ VP ⅘

The Cafe, in Ritz-Carlton Huntington Hotel, 1401 S Oak Knoll Ave, Pasadena; tel 818/568-3900. Follow Calif 110 N to Arroyo Pkwy; right on California Blvd; right on Lake Ave (which becomes Oak Knoll Ave). **Californian.** A 2-tiered dining room decorated in celadon and rose, with views of the dining patio and swimming pool. The big event is Sunday brunch ($38.50), with literally hundreds of selections—3 different pâtés, smoked fish, omelette and pasta stations, sushi, and a carvery. Cold selections are generally the best, desserts are tempting. Dancing on Friday and Saturday nights. **FYI:** Reservations accepted. Dancing/jazz. Children's menu. Dress code. **Open:** Breakfast Mon–Sat 6–11:30am; lunch Mon–Sat 11:30am–5pm; dinner Mon–Sun 5–10pm; brunch Sun 9:30am–3pm. **Prices:** Main courses $14–$21. Maj CC. ☏ VP ⅘

★ **The Chronicle**, 897 Granite Dr, Pasadena (South Lake); tel 818/792-1179. Lake St exit off I-210. **Eclectic.** Local favorite featuring lots of dark wood, brass rails, spittoons, and historic photographs. Specialties include steaks, shrimp scampi, grilled chicken, saddle of lamb, pasta, and salads. **FYI:** Reservations recommended. Dress code. **Open:** Lunch Mon–Sat 11:30am–2:30pm; dinner Sun–Thurs 5–9pm, Fri–Sat 5–10pm. Closed some hols. **Prices:** Main courses $12–$24. Maj CC. ♥ ☏ ⊞ ♥ VP ⅘

McCormick & Schmicks, in Las Fuentes Plaza, 111 N Los Robles, Pasadena; tel 818/405-0064. Lake St exit off I-210. **American.** Warm and inviting, with lots of dark wood and stained-glass windows. Open kitchen prepares Dungeness crab cakes in jalapeño hollandaise, shellfish stew, and crab in red wine broth. Special happy hour menu is a good value. **FYI:** Reservations recommended. Jazz/piano. Dress code. **Open:** Mon–Sat 11:30am–11pm, Sun 10:30am–10pm. **Prices:** Main courses $4.95–$19.95. Maj CC. ♥ ☏ ⌂ ⊞ VP ⅘

★ **Mi Piace**, 25 E Colorado Blvd, Pasadena (Old Town); tel 818/795-3131. Colorado Blvd exit off Calif 134. **Californian/**

Italian. This sleek and sophisticated restaurant boasts high ceilings, natural colors, and lots of light. One of the most popular places in town. The chef is formerly of Spago and expanded the menu to include risotto, smoked duck pizza, and a wide variety of pasta dishes. **FYI:** Reservations recommended. Dress code. Beer and wine only. **Open:** Lunch daily 11am–4pm; dinner Fri–Sat 4pm–1am, Sun–Thurs 4–11:30pm. Closed some hols. **Prices:** Main courses $6.95–$15.95. Maj CC. ☏ VP ⅘

$ **Old Town Restaurant & Bakery**, 166 W Colorado Blvd, Pasadena (Old Town); tel 818/792-7943. Colorado Blvd exit off Calif 134. **New American.** Part of Old Town's Tanner Market. Besides being a great baker, Amy Pressman offers chicken chorizo and eggs, homemade griddled corn tortillas, black beans, and vegetable quiche. Big mugs of cappuccino. **FYI:** Reservations not accepted. Children's menu. No liquor license. **Open:** HS June–Aug Sun–Thurs 7:30am–10pm, Fri–Sat 7:30am–midnight. Reduced hours off-season. Closed Dec 25. **Prices:** Main courses $4.95–$9.95. Maj CC. ▮ ☏ ⊞ VP ⅘

♣ **Parkway Grill**, 510 S Arroyo Pkwy, Pasadena; tel 818/795-1001. Arroyo Pkwy exit off I-110. **Regional American.** Housed in a beautiful old building with exposed brick walls, high ceilings with skylights, natural wood floors, and aqua accents, this place has great food and ambience. Adjacent to a lovely garden. Try the roasted pepper stuffed chicken and the wood-fired pizza. **FYI:** Reservations recommended. Piano. Dress code. **Open:** Lunch Mon–Fri 11:30am–2:30pm; dinner Mon–Thurs 5:30–10pm, Fri–Sat 5–11pm, Sun 5–10pm; brunch Sun 11am–2:30pm. Closed some hols. **Prices:** Main courses $12–$22.95. Maj CC. ♥ ▮ ⌂ VP

Pasadena Baking Company, 29 E Colorado Blvd, Pasadena (Old Town); tel 818/795-3131. Colorado Blvd exit off Calif 134. **Cafe/Bakery.** Simple cafe outfitted with gray tables, black chairs, and newspapers for patrons to read, known for fabulous coffee drinks. A great place for breakfast or after a movie. Featuring gigantic sandwiches and omelettes. **FYI:** Reservations accepted. Dress code. Beer and wine only. **Open:** Sun–Thurs 7am–11pm, Fri–Sat 8am–midnight. Closed some hols. **Prices:** Main courses $3.95–$9.95. Maj CC. ☏ VP ⅘

Roxxi, 1065 E Green St, Pasadena; tel 818/449-4519. Lake St exit off I-210; south on Lake St to Green. **Californian/Health/Spa.** A lively dining spot close to the Pasadena Playhouse and the Ambassador Auditorium. Colorful southwestern motif with art displays that change every 8 weeks. Grilled fish, duck ravioli, potstickers, roast chicken, and New York steak are just a few items on the eclectic menu. **FYI:** Reservations recommended. Beer and wine only. **Open:** HS Sept–May lunch Mon–Fri

11:30am–2:30pm; dinner Sun 4–9pm, Mon 5:30–9pm, Tues–Sat 5:30–10pm. Reduced hours off-season. Closed some hols. **Prices:** Main courses $11–$22. Maj CC. ♥ ♿

♥ **Shiro Restaurant**, 1505 Mission St, Pasadena; tel 818/799-4774. Fair Oaks exit off I-110; drive south 3 blocks to Mission St. **French/Japanese.** A very special place to dine, a quiet, peaceful ambience. The decor is minimalist and sophisticated. The signature dish is whole sizzling codfish in ponzu sauce. All dishes blend French and Japanese influences. **FYI:** Reservations recommended. Dress code. Beer and wine only. **Open:** Tues–Sat 6–10pm, Sun 5:45–9pm. Closed some hols; 3 weeks in Sept. **Prices:** Main courses $12.50–$19. Maj CC. ♥

Xiomara, 69 N Raymond Ave, Pasadena (Old Town); tel 818/796-2520. Fair Oaks exit off I-210. **French.** Subtle gray, black, and lots of mirrors give this place the feel of a sophisticated French bistro. Chef Patrick Healy is considered among the best chefs, and eating his daily specials will make you feel like you're in Paris. Try the terrine of duck with foie gras and the homemade sausages with mashed potatoes. **FYI:** Reservations recommended. **Open:** Lunch Mon–Fri 11:30am–2:30pm; dinner daily 5:30–10:30pm. Closed some hols. **Prices:** Main courses $17–$23; PF dinner $25. Maj CC. ♥ ▼ VP ♿

♥ **Yujean Kang**, 67 N Raymond Ave, Pasadena (Old Town); tel 818/585-0855. Fair Oaks exit off I-210. **Chinese.** Sophisticated, stylized Chinese cuisine. Yujean Kang is among the best Chinese chefs in the San Francisco and Los Angeles areas. The house specialty is "picture in the snow," which is chicken, smoked duck, black mushrooms, and a picture made of meringue. **FYI:** Reservations recommended. Dress code. Beer and wine only. **Open:** Lunch daily 11:30am–2:30pm; dinner Sun–Thurs 5–9:30pm, Fri–Sat 5–10pm. **Prices:** Main courses $8.95–$19.95. Maj CC. ♥ ⚑ VP ♿

Attractions 📷

Norton Simon Museum, 411 W Colorado Blvd; tel 818/449-6840. One of the most important art museums in California, Norton Simon has masterpieces from the Italian, Dutch, Spanish, Flemish, and French schools; also Impressionist paintings, tapestries, and 20th-century painting and sculpture. Includes works by Matisse, van Gogh, Rembrandt, and Picasso. There is also a superb collection of Southeast Asian and Indian sculpture. **Open:** Thurs–Sun noon–6pm. Closed some hols. $$

Pacific Asia Museum, 46 N Los Robles Ave; tel 818/449-2742. The arts and cultures of Pacific and Asian peoples are preserved and interpreted here. The Chinese Imperial Palace Courtyard-style building was built in 1925 by collector and art dealer Grace Nicholson, and was her home and sales showroom until her death in 1948. The traditional Chinese courtyard garden is one of only three in the United States.

Rotating exhibits from the museum's permanent collection are augmented by traveling exhibits. Special programs, lectures. Bookstore and gift shop. **Open:** Wed–Sun 10am–5pm. Closed some hols. $

Gamble House, 4 Westmoreland Place; tel 818/793-3334. The David B Gamble house, built in 1908 for David and Mary Gamble, of the Procter and Gamble Company, is the most complete and best-preserved example of the work of architects Charles Sumner Greene and Henry Mather Greene, who made a profound impact on the development of contemporary American architecture. Breaking sharply with the traditions of their time, Greene and Greene used nature as their guide rather than the dictates of popular historical styles. Extensive use of wood was inspired by the traditions of the Swiss and Japanese. Other features include wide terraces, open sleeping porches, and broad, overhanging eaves. In the true spirit of the Arts and Crafts Movement, the furniture, cabinetry, paneling, rugs, lighting, and landscaping were all custom-designed by the architects. In addition, every peg, oak wedge, downspout, air vent, and switchplate is a contributing part of the single design statement and harmonious living environment.

The University of Southern California School of Architecture administers the house and offers a 1 hour comprehensive guided tour. Bookstore, gift shop. **Open:** Thurs–Sun noon–3pm. Closed some hols. $$

Tournament House and Wrigley Gardens, 391 S Orange Grove Blvd; tel 818/449-4100. Chicago chewing gum magnate William Wrigley, Jr, purchased this house on Pasadena's historic "Millionaire's Row" in 1914. The next year, the Wrigleys acquired adjoining property and created what is now the breathtaking 4½-acre Wrigley Gardens.

Following Mrs Wrigley's death in 1958, family heirs presented the property to the city of Pasadena to serve as the permanent base of operations for the Tournament of Roses. Today the house serves as a working setting throughout the year for Tournament of Roses activities. The formal dining room is the only room furnished with original pieces; the Rose Bowl Room showcases a collection of memorabilia dating back to the first New Year's Day Game held in 1902; the Queen and Court Room features a display case with former Rose Queen and courts' crowns, tiaras, and jewelery dating back to the early 1900s; the Grand Marshals Room displays pictures of past Grand Marshals, including Walt Disney, Hank Aaron, and Bob Hope.

The gardens, featuring more than 1,500 varieties of roses, are continually augmented by growers throughout the nation. **Open:** Tours given Feb–late Aug, Thurs 2–4pm. Closed some hols. Free.

Kidspace Museum, 390 S El Molino Ave; tel 818/449-9144. A participatory museum aimed at kids aged 2–8, this facility allows children to learn through play, discovery, interaction, and creativity. Exhibits include KCBS Television Studio, Critter Caverns, Stargazer Planetarium, and Toddler Territory. Every December, the museum takes to the streets with the Rosebud Parade, a takeoff of the Pasadena Rose Parade. The event draws more than 400 children with decorated bicycles and wagons. **Open:** Summer, Tues–Fri 1–5pm, Sat–Sun 12:30–5pm; fall–spring, Wed 2–5pm, Sat–Sun 12:30–5pm. $$

Fenyes Mansion, 470 W Walnut St; tel 818/577-1660. Built in 1905, the Fenyes Mansion is representative of the cultured life on Pasadena's famed Orange Grove Ave, known as "Millionaire's Row" at the turn of the century. Today it has been restored to its original appearance, and its first floor houses the Pasadena Historical Society. Permanent and changing exhibits; research library and archives; museum store. Guided tours of the mansion are given. **Open:** Thurs–Sun 1–4pm. $$

PASO ROBLES

Map page M-3, C1 (N of Atascadero)

Motels 🛏

≣≣≣ **Best Western Black Oak Motor Lodge**, 1135 24th St, Paso Robles, CA 93446; tel 805/238-4740 or toll free 800/528-1234; fax 805/238-0726. 24th St exit off US 101; go west. An attractive, nicely landscaped, and well-maintained 2-story motel. **Rooms:** 110 rms and stes. CI 2pm/CO noon. Nonsmoking rms avail. Early American decor. Standard rooms have mahogany antique-style headboards, chairs, and a desk; country pine furniture in better rooms. **Amenities:** 🛏 🅰 🖭 A/C, cable TV, refrig. Some units w/Jacuzzis. Hairdryers in deluxe and super-deluxe rooms. Microwaves in super-deluxe kings and most suites. **Services:** �'' 🛄 🛎 **Facilities:** 🛗 ᕮ 1 rst, sauna, whirlpool, playground, washer/dryer. Coffee shop adjacent. Picnic tables, barbecue, and basketball hoop. **Rates:** HS May–Oct 14 $52–$68 S or D; from $61 ste. Extra person $6. Children under 5 stay free. Lower rates off-season. Pking: Outdoor, free. Maj CC.

≣≣ **Paso Robles Travelodge**, 2701 Spring St, Paso Robles, CA 93446; tel 805/238-0078 or toll free 800/578-7878. Spring St exit off US 101. A clean, cheerful, nicely landscaped property with brick exterior and bright blue doors. Large lawn with California oak trees. **Rooms:** 31 rms. CI 2pm/CO noon. Nonsmoking rms avail. **Amenities:** 🛏 🅰 🖭 A/C, cable TV w/movies, refrig. Some units w/terraces. **Services:** 🛄 🛎 🖂 **Facilities:** 🛗 Swing set; 2 picnic tables with umbrellas. **Rates:** HS May–Oct $38–$58 S; $48–$75 D. Extra person $5. Children under 17 stay free. Lower rates off-season. Higher rates for spec evnts/hols. Pking: Outdoor, free. Maj CC.

Restaurants 🍽

Black Oak Restaurant & Annie's Dinner House Saloon, 1535 24th St, Paso Robles; tel 805/238-6330. Paso Robles exit off US 101. **American.** A coffee shop and a saloon house sharing the same site. The coffee shop, with beamed ceiling, booths, and counter service, serves chicken pot pie, burgers, sandwiches, and salads. The saloon is candlelit, decorated with flowers and plants, and has a menu featuring prime rib, steaks, and seafood. **FYI:** Reservations accepted. Singer. Children's menu. **Open:** Daily 7am–10:30pm. **Prices:** Main courses $7.95–$10.95. Maj CC. 📷

Vine Street Grill, 512 13th St, Paso Robles; tel 805/238-7515. At Vine St. **Continental.** Located in a former Catholic church and surrounded by meandering grapevines. Dine in the bell tower or in the shadow of the beautiful stained-glass windows. The new owner and chef offer chicken, lobster, pasta, and cioppino on weekends. Mainly local wines. **FYI:** Reservations recommended. Band/piano/singer. Children's menu. Dress code. **Open:** Lunch Mon–Fri 11:30am–2:30pm; dinner Sun–Thurs 4:30–9pm, Fri–Sat 4:30–10pm; brunch Sun 10am–2pm. Closed some hols. **Prices:** Main courses $9.95–$22.95. Maj CC. 🍴🍽🖭ᕮ

Attraction 🏛

Helen Moe's Antique Doll Museum, US 101 and Wellsona Rd; tel 805/238-2740. Nearly 700 dolls comprise this collection, including antique, historical, and foreign pieces. A 400-year-old doll is on display, as are dioramas of an old-time schoolroom, a Christmas scene from 1907, a wedding of German dolls, and more. The gift shop sells toy and collectible dolls, doll supplies, and other items. **Open:** Mon–Sat 10am–5pm, Sun 1–5pm. Closed some hols. $

PEBBLE BEACH

Map page M-2, E2 (N of Carmel-by-the-Sea)

Resorts 🛏

≡ ≡ ≡ **Inn at Spanish Bay**, 17-Mile Dr, Pebble Beach, CA 93953; tel 408/647-7500 or toll free 800/654-9300; fax 415/624-6357. Pacific Grove/Pebble Beach exit off Calif 1. Surrounded by windswept sand dunes and facing an oft-tempestuous Pacific; a bagpipe player serenades late afternoons. Draws 75% group business. **Rooms:** 270 rms and stes. CI 4pm/CO noon. Express checkout avail. Nonsmoking rms avail. Rooms spacious enough to fit two comfortable armchairs by the (gas) fireplace. Counter space abounds in the bathrooms, done in beige marble with glass-enclosed showers. **Amenities:** 🛎 🛗 🍷 Cable TV w/movies, refrig, bathrobes. No A/C. All units w/minibars, some w/terraces, all w/fireplaces, some w/Jacuzzis. Every room comes with a garment steamer. **Services:** 🍽 🗝 💳 🚐 ⛱ 🛎 Twice-daily maid svce, car-rental desk, social director, masseur, children's program, babysitting. Concierge personally escorts arriving guests to their rooms. **Facilities:** 🚣 🚴 ▶81 🏊 🎿 ⚾6 🍴 500 💻 ♿ 3 rsts, 3 bars (1 w/entertainment), 1 beach (ocean), board surfing, spa, sauna, steam rm, whirlpool. Dunes and fairways intersperse the golf course. The fitness center rates a "10," with aerobics classes plus state-of-the art equipment. A 2-mile boardwalk circles the property. **Rates:** $245–$350 S or D; from $550 ste. Extra person $50. Children under 18 stay free. Min stay spec evnts. Spec packages avail. Pking: Outdoor, free. Maj CC. Golf and tennis packages available.

≡ ≡ ≡ ≡ **Lodge at Pebble Beach**, 17-Mile Dr, Pebble Beach, CA 93953; tel 408/624-3811 or toll free 800/654-9300; fax 408/625-8598. Pacific Grove/Pebble Beach exit off Calif 1. Among America's best resorts, in a choice setting on the brink of the Pacific Ocean within the private 5,000-plus-acre Del Monte Forest. **Rooms:** 161 rms and stes; 2 ctges/villas. CI 4pm/CO noon. Express checkout avail. Nonsmoking rms avail. Nearly all rooms have been redecorated and look stunning, with Empire-style furnishings plus unlikely flourishes. Baths are exquisite in taupe marble. **Amenities:** 🛎 🛗 🍷 Cable TV w/movies, refrig, VCR, in-rm safe, bathrobes. No A/C. All units w/minibars, all w/terraces, some w/fireplaces, some w/Jacuzzis. Most rooms offer wood-burning fireplaces. **Services:** 🍽 🗝 💳 🚐 ⛱ 🛎 ⛴ Twice-daily maid svce, car-rental desk, masseur, children's program, babysitting. Very helpful staff. Extensive junior summer program includes tennis clinics, swimming and sailing lessons, plus a day camp. **Facilities:** 🚣 🚴 ▶81 🏊 🎿 ⚾12 🍴 200 💻 ♿ 5 rsts (see also "Restaurants" below), 5 bars (2 w/entertainment), 1 beach (ocean), board surfing, spa, sauna, steam rm, whirlpool, beauty salon, playground. Fabled golf links

have been home to several US Open championships. Brand-new Beach & Tennis Club features 12 courts (2 clay), plus a 25-meter lap pool. Equestrian center is among the West's best. **Rates:** $295–$450 S or D; from $800 ste; from $1,800 ctge/villa. Extra person $50. Children under 18 stay free. Spec packages avail. Pking: Outdoor, free. Maj CC. Tennis and golf packages available.

Restaurant 🍴

🍷 **Club XIX**, in Lodge at Pebble Beach, 17-Mile Drive, Pebble Beach; tel 408/625-8519. Pacific Grove/Pebble Beach exit off Calif 1; follow signs to Pebble Beach. **French.** Spectacular outdoor dining on the Monterey Peninsula. Patio overlooks Carmel Bay; glass screens and heaters ensure comfort in any weather. Attractive indoor seating also available. Menu choices include duck breast with sun-dried cherry spinach, or chateaubriand for two. **FYI:** Reservations recommended. Dress code. **Open:** Lunch daily 11:30am–3:30pm; dinner daily 6:30–10:30pm. **Prices:** Main courses $19–$29.50. Maj CC. ❤ 🍽 🏞 💳 ♿

PETALUMA

Map page M-2, C1

Motels 🛏

≡ ≡ **Best Western Petaluma Inn**, 200 McDowell Blvd, Petaluma, CA 94954; tel 707/763-0994 or toll free 800/297-3846; fax 707/778-3111. E Washington St exit off US 101; go east; right on McDowell. Located just off the freeway, but well-soundproofed to minimize noise. **Rooms:** 75 rms and stes. Exec-level rms avail. CI 2pm/CO 11am. Nonsmoking rms avail. Large, basic rooms with new carpets. **Amenities:** 🛎 🛗 A/C, satel TV. Some units w/terraces. **Services:** ⛴ Free coffee and tea in lobby. **Facilities:** 🚣 10 ♿ Washer/dryer. **Rates:** HS Apr–Oct $76–$86 S or D; from $95 ste. Extra person $6. Children under 12 stay free. Lower rates off-season. Higher rates for spec evnts/hols. Pking: Outdoor, free. Maj CC.

≡ ≡ **Quality Inn Petaluma**, 5100 Montero Way, Petaluma, CA 94954; tel 707/664-1155 or toll free 800/221-2222. Redwood Hwy/Penngrove exit east off US 101. Clean property right off the freeway. **Rooms:** 110 rms and stes. CI 2:30pm/CO noon. Nonsmoking rms avail. Basic, comfortable rooms. **Amenities:** 🛎 🛗 A/C, satel TV w/movies, refrig, VCR. **Services:** ⛱ ⛴ ⛴ Masseur. Continental breakfast; movie rentals. **Facilities:** 🚣 25 ♿ Sauna, whirlpool, washer/dryer. **Rates (CP):** HS Apr–Oct $59–$114 S; $64–$119 D; from $105 ste. Extra person $5.

Children under 18 stay free. Min stay wknds and spec evnts. Lower rates off-season. Higher rates for spec evnts/hols. Spec packages avail. Pking: Outdoor, free. Maj CC.

Restaurants 🍽

Fino Cucina Italiana, 208 Petaluma Blvd N, Petaluma; tel 707/762-5966. Petaluma Blvd exit off US 101. **Italian.** Authentic Italian cuisines in a soothing environment, with modern decor and soft music. Menu highlights include angel hair pasta with clams, roast tenderloin of pork in grape sauce, and polenta with Gorgonzola and mushrooms. **FYI:** Reservations accepted. Beer and wine only. **Open:** Lunch Mon–Fri 11:30am–2pm; dinner Mon–Sat 5–9:30pm. Closed some hols. **Prices:** Main courses $11–$16. Maj CC. 💳

Steamer Gold Landing, 1 Water St, Petaluma (Steamer Landing); tel 707/763-6876. Washington St exit off US 101. **Californian/American.** Located in a historic building along the Petaluma River, with a huge outdoor dining deck and an enormous menu with something for everyone, from steaks and burgers to seafood, chicken, and omelettes. Local beers and wines and excellent desserts as well. Popular Sunday brunch. Weekend cabaret upstairs with country-western dancing and lessons. **FYI:** Reservations accepted. Country music/rock. Children's menu. **Open:** Mon–Sat 11:30am–10pm, Sun 10:30am–3pm. Closed some hols. **Prices:** Main courses $8–$17. Maj CC. 🍷 📷 💳

Attraction 💼

Petaluma Historical Library/Museum, 20 Fourth St; tel 707/778-4398. Constructed in 1903, with the help of $12,500 donated by Andrew Carnegie, the library features a beautiful stained-glass dome, one of the only free-standing domes in California. After its closure in 1976, the building reopened in 1978 as a research library and museum. Permanent and changing exhibits on the gallery and mezzanine floors depict Petaluma history from the early 1800s. **Open:** Mon and Thurs–Sat 10am–4pm, Sun 1–4pm. Closed some hols. Free.

PIONEERTOWN

Map page M-3, D3 (W of Twentynine Palms)

Restaurant 🍽

★ **Pappy & Harriet's**, Pioneertown Rd, Pioneertown; tel 619/365-5956. Calif 62 exit off I-10 to Twenty-Nine Palms Hwy; turn left on Pioneertown Road. **Barbecue/Tex-Mex.** Set in an old western movie location, this locally popular restaurant is an assemblage of rough-hewn boards, off-kilter beer signs, and license plates from around the country. Talk at the bar centers around racing new Harleys and '65 Mustangs. Portions are enormous—the iced tea comes in a mason jar and the hamburger measures as wide as a soup bowl. Country and western music on weekends. **FYI:** Reservations recommended. **Open:** Wed–Thurs 11am–11pm, Fri–Sat 11am–2pm, Sun 11am–11pm. Closed Dec 25. **Prices:** Main courses $6.95–$16.95. Maj CC. 💳

PISMO BEACH

Map page M-3, C1

Hotels 🏨

≡≡≡ **Best Western Shore Cliff Lodge**, 2555 Price St, Pismo Beach, CA 93449; tel 805/773-4671 or toll free 800/441-8885; fax 805/773-2341. 1½ mi N of Pismo Beach. Price St exit off US 101 S; Shell Beach Rd exit off US 101 N. Sprawling older-style motel set on a cliff with a stairway to the beach. Ocean-view lobby is furnished with wicker, plants, and ceiling fans. **Rooms:** 99 rms, stes, and effic. CI 3pm/CO 11am. Nonsmoking rms avail. Ocean views. **Amenities:** 🛁 ☕ 🅿 A/C, cable TV w/movies. All units w/terraces. **Services:** ✕ 🖼 🖐 Babysitting. **Facilities:** 🔧 🚲 📶 1 rst (see also "Restaurants" below), 1 bar (w/entertainment), 1 beach (cove/inlet), sauna, whirlpool. **Rates:** HS July–Aug $100–$130 S or D; from $195 ste; from $100 effic. Extra person $10. Children under 17 stay free. Min stay HS and spec evnts. Lower rates off-season. Higher rates for spec evnts/hols. Spec packages avail. Pking: Outdoor, free. Maj CC.

≡≡≡ **Quality Suites**, 651 Five Cities Dr, Pismo Beach, CA 93449; tel 805/773-3773 or toll free 800/982-SUITE; fax 805/773-5177. 4th St exit off US 101. Spanish/tropical-style hotel with a gorgeous lobby, paddle fans, a fountain, tilework, and an attractive library and lounge. **Rooms:** 133 stes. CI 2pm/CO noon. Nonsmoking rms avail. Nicely appointed suites with lots of drawer and counter space. 2 TVs per room. **Amenities:** 🛁 ☕ A/C, satel TV w/movies, refrig, VCR, stereo/tape player. Some units w/terraces. Complimentary full breakfast. Complimentary wine and beer 5:50–9:30pm. **Services:** 🖼 🖐 🍷 **Facilities:** 🔧 📶 ☕ 1 bar, whirlpool, washer/dryer. Very attractive breakfast room with European posters, and rattan furniture. Putting green. **Rates (BB):** From $69 ste. Extra person $6. Children under 19 stay free. Pking: Outdoor, free. Maj CC.

Motels

Edgewater Inn & Suites, 280 Wadsworth Ave, Pismo Beach, CA 93449; tel 805/773-4811; fax 805/773-4811. Wadsworth exit off Calif 1 N; Pismo Beach exit off Calif 1 S. Good for families; nice location close to beach. **Rooms:** 93 rms, stes, and effic. CI 3pm/CO 11am. Furnishings a little dated. **Amenities:** A/C, cable TV, refrig. Some units w/terraces, some w/Jacuzzis. **Services:** Continental breakfast in lobby or, in a rooftop room with ocean view. **Facilities:** 1 beach (ocean), whirlpool. **Rates (CP):** HS June–Sept $60–$85 S or D; from $85 ste; from $85 effic. Children under 18 stay free. Min stay spec evnts. Lower rates off-season. Spec packages avail. Pking: Outdoor, free. Maj CC.

Sea Crest Resort Motel, 2241 Price St, Pismo Beach, CA 93449; tel 805/773-4608 or toll free 800/782-8400. 1 mi N of Pismo. Price St exit off US 101. Set on cliffs above the beach, with stairs down to the sand. Rooms are nicer than the lobby. **Rooms:** 158 rms and stes. CI 4pm/CO noon. Nonsmoking rms avail. Handsomely appointed rooms. Dark-wood and French provincial furnishings. Some ocean views. **Amenities:** Satel TV w/movies, refrig. No A/C. All units w/terraces, some w/Jacuzzis. **Services:** Babysitting. **Facilities:** 1 beach (ocean), whirlpool, washer/dryer. Shuffleboard; picnic tables; barbecue grills. **Rates:** HS June–Aug $75–$95 S or D; from $105 ste. Extra person $10. Children under 12 stay free. Min stay wknds. Lower rates off-season. Pking: Outdoor, free. Maj CC.

Restaurants

★ **The Cliffs at Shell Beach**, 2757 Shell Beach Rd, Pismo Beach; tel 805/773-3555. **Californian.** Casual but attractive restaurant with French-country chairs, stained-glass windows, plants, fireplace, outdoor deck. Menu features shrimp scampi, coconut prawns, crab, lobster, steaks, prime rib. Pasta bar at lunch. **FYI:** Reservations recommended. **Open:** Breakfast Mon–Sat 7am–noon, Sun 7–9am; lunch Mon–Sat 11:30am–4pm; dinner Sun–Thurs 4–9:30pm, Fri–Sat 4–10pm; brunch Sun 9:30am–2pm. **Prices:** Main courses $9.95–$20.95; PF dinner $18.95–$26.95. Maj CC.

Shore Cliff Restaurant, in Best Western Shore Cliff Lodge, 2555 Price St, Pismo Beach; tel 805/773-4671. **Seafood/Steak.** Casual California-style cafe with plants, rattan furnishings, and picture windows overlooking the Pacific. Menu features cioppino, crab and steak, prime rib, Shore Cliff stuffed prawns. Nice for breakfast, with pancakes, eggs Benedict, and other dishes. **FYI:** Reservations recommended. Band/blues/country music/jazz. Children's menu. **Open:** Breakfast Mon–Sat 7–11:30am, Sun 7–10am; lunch Mon–Sat 11:30am–4pm, Sun 2–4pm; dinner Sun–Thurs 4–9pm, Fri–Sat 4–10pm; brunch Sun 10am–2pm. **Prices:** Main courses $9.95–$19.95. Maj CC.

PLACERVILLE

Map page M-2, C3

Hotel

Best Western Placerville Inn, 6850 Green Leaf Dr, Placerville, CA 95667; tel 916/622-9100 or toll free 800/854-9100; fax 916/622-9376. Missouri Flat exit off US 50. Good highway stopover in a safe, comfortable, and spacious country setting. A little noisy. **Rooms:** 105 rms and stes. CI 3pm/CO 11am. Nonsmoking rms avail. Poolside rooms have sliding glass doors, and are quieter. Most rooms on ground floor. **Amenities:** A/C, cable TV w/movies. Some units w/terraces, some w/fireplaces. **Services:** Some business services available at desk. **Facilities:** Whirlpool. No elevators. **Rates:** HS Apr–Oct $58 S; $64 D; from $135 ste. Extra person $6. Children under 12 stay free. Lower rates off-season. Spec packages avail. Pking: Outdoor, free. Maj CC.

Attractions

El Dorado County Historical Museum, 100 Placerville Dr; tel 916/621-5865. Exhibits in this museum focus mainly on the early days of the Gold Rush, when Placerville rivaled San Francisco in stature. Exhibits include an actual Concord Stagecoach, a re-created general store, an old Diamond & Caldor Shay steam engine, and water-driven Pelton wheels that powered early mines and mills. Guided tours available; bookshop. **Open:** Mar–Oct, Wed–Sat 10am–4pm, Sun noon–4pm or by appointment; Nov–Feb, Wed–Sun 10am–4pm. Closed some hols. Free.

Gold Bug Mine, Bedford Ave; tel 916/642-5232. Located in Hangtown's Gold Bug Park, the Gold Bug Mine was opened in 1888, near the site where the first placer was mined by Chileans in 1848, and continued to operate until World War II. On the eastern side of the famous Mother Lode vein, the municipally owned mine is open for self-guided tours (audio tape tours available), and allows visitors a peek at an exposed vein.

Also in the park is a restored gold stamp mill, with original machinery and exhibits of other mining equipment from the Gold Rush era. The park itself is undergoing development as a picnicking and hiking area. **Open:** May to mid-Sept, daily 10am–4pm; mid-Sept to Oct, Sat–Sun 10am–4pm. Closed some hols. $

PLEASANT HILL

Map page M-2, D2 (E of Richmond)

Hotel 🏨

≡≡≡ **Residence Inn by Marriott**, 700 Ellinwood Way, Pleasant Hill, CA 94523 (Ellinwood); tel 510/689-1010 or toll free 800/331-3131; fax 510/689-1098. Willow Pass Rd exit off I-680. Located in a residential area, this attractive complex resembles a townhouse development; walkways are lined with trees and flowering plants. **Rooms:** 126 stes and effic. Exec-level rms avail. CI 3pm/CO noon. Nonsmoking rms avail. Every unit is an apartment. All have kitchens with countertop dining, utensils, and dishes. Most living room sofas hide a bed. **Amenities:** 🛁 👤 📺 A/C, satel TV w/movies, refrig, voice mail. Some units w/fireplaces. **Services:** 📶 🍴 🐕 Children's program, babysitting. Complimentary wine, beer, and snacks in lobby 5 to 7pm weekdays; complimentary coffee 24 hours. VCR and movie rentals. **Facilities:** 🏊 🏋️ 🍴 🅿️ ♿ Whirlpool, washer/dryer. Barbecue grills. Outdoor "sport court" can be used for tennis, volleyball, basketball, and paddle tennis. **Rates (CP):** From $124 ste; from $124 effic. Children under 18 stay free. Spec packages avail. Pking: Outdoor, free. Maj CC.

PLEASANTON

Map page M-2, D2 (SE of Dublin)

Hotels 🏨

≡≡ **Courtyard by Marriott**, 5059 Hopyard Rd, Pleasanton, CA 94588 (Hacienda Business Park); tel 510/463-1414 or toll free 800/228-9290; fax 510/463-0113. Hopyard exit off I-580. A totally nonsmoking hotel oriented toward the business traveler. **Rooms:** 145 rms and stes. CI 3pm/CO 1pm. Express checkout avail. Nonsmoking rms avail. **Amenities:** 🛁 👤 A/C, cable TV w/movies, voice mail. Some units w/terraces. **Services:** 📶 🍴 Babysitting. **Facilities:** 🏊 🍴 🅿️ ♿ 1 rst, 1 bar, whirlpool, washer/dryer. Restaurants nearby. **Rates:** $54–$69 S or D; from $89 ste. Extra person $10. Children under 18 stay free. Higher rates for spec evnts/hols. Spec packages avail. Pking: Outdoor, free. Maj CC.

≡≡≡ **Doubletree Club Hotel**, 5990 Stoneridge Mall Rd, Pleasanton, CA 94588; tel 510/463-3330 or toll free 800/222-TREE; fax 510/463-3330 ext 644. Foothill exit off I-580; left on Dublin Canyon Rd; left on Stoneridge Mall Rd. Pleasant hotel with airy, cheerful lobby and ambience of a private home. Geared to business and weekend family travelers. Minimal landscaping.

Located across the street from a mall. **Rooms:** 173 rms and stes. CI 3pm/CO 1pm. Express checkout avail. Nonsmoking rms avail. **Amenities:** 🛁 👤 A/C, cable TV w/movies. Refrigerators and VCRs provided free upon request. **Services:** 📶 🍴 🐕 Babysitting. Complimentary 24-hour coffee and tea, with light night snacks 9–11pm. **Facilities:** 🏊 🍴 🅿️ ♿ 1 rst, 1 bar, sauna, whirlpool. **Rates (CP):** $89–$104 S; $99–$114 D; from $135 ste. Children under 18 stay free. Spec packages avail. Pking: Outdoor, free. Maj CC. Special weekend rates are available.

≡≡ **Holiday Inn Pleasanton Hotel**, 11950 Dublin Canyon Rd, Pleasanton, CA 94588-2818; tel 510/847-6000 or toll free 800/HOLIDAY; fax 510/463-2585. Foothill exit off I-580; right 1 block to Dublin Canyon Rd. Art deco decor makes this hotel more attractive than the usual Holiday Inn. Wooded hillside across the street. Opposite shopping mall. **Rooms:** 248 rms and stes. CI 3pm/CO noon. Nonsmoking rms avail. **Amenities:** 🛁 👤 📺 A/C, cable TV w/movies. 1 unit w/minibar. **Services:** 📶 🚗 📶 🍴 🐕 Babysitting. **Facilities:** 🏊 🍴 🅿️ ♿ 1 rst, 1 bar (w/entertainment), whirlpool, washer/dryer. **Rates:** $95 S; $105 D; from $125 ste. Extra person $10. Children under 18 stay free. Min stay HS, wknds, and spec evnts. Pking: Outdoor, free. Maj CC.

≡≡ **Pleasanton Hilton at the Club**, 7050 Johnson Dr, Pleasanton, CA 94588; tel 510/463-8000 or toll free 800/HILTONS; fax 510/463-3801. Hopyard exit off I-580, right on Owens Dr, right on Johnson; or Stoneridge Dr exit off I-680 E to Johnson Dr, left to hotel. Hotel is close to freeway but adequately soundproofed inside. Adjoins "Club Sport," which offers many amenities, including a driving range and putting green. **Rooms:** 294 rms and stes. Exec-level rms avail. CI 3pm/CO noon. Express checkout avail. Nonsmoking rms avail. **Amenities:** 🛁 👤 A/C, cable TV w/movies. Some units w/terraces, some w/fireplaces, 1 w/Jacuzzi. **Services:** 📶 📺 📶 🍴 🐕 Car-rental desk, masseur. **Facilities:** 🏊 🍴 🍴 🅿️ ♿ 1 rst, 1 bar (w/entertainment), racquetball, squash, spa, sauna, steam rm, whirlpool, beauty salon, day-care ctr. Day-care center available for fee, but parents must remain on hotel grounds. Heated lap pool. **Rates:** $144–$164 S; $154–$174 D; from $350 ste. Extra person $10. Children under 18 stay free. Spec packages avail. Pking: Outdoor, free. Maj CC.

≡≡≡ **Sheraton Inn Pleasanton**, 5115 Hopyard Rd, Pleasanton, CA 94588 (Hacienda Business Park); tel 510/460-8800 or toll free 800/325-3535; fax 510/847-9455. Hopyard exit off I-580. Attractive, well-kept property located in the Hacienda Business Park. **Rooms:** 214 rms and stes. Exec-level rms avail. CI 3pm/CO 1pm. Express checkout avail. Nonsmoking rms avail. **Amenities:** 🛁 👤 📺 🍴 A/C, cable TV w/movies, voice mail.

Some units w/terraces. Complimentary refrigerator available upon request. **Services:** ✗ ⌂ 🛎 Car-rental desk, babysitting. **Facilities:** 🏋 🍴 250 💻 ♿ 1 rst, 1 bar (w/entertainment), whirlpool. Outdoor swimming pool in park-like setting with pond and fountains. Jogging path nearby. **Rates:** $115–$135 S; $125–$145 D; from $250 ste. Extra person $10. Children under 18 stay free. Spec packages avail. Pking: Outdoor, free. Maj CC.

POINT ARENA

Map page M-2, C1 (N of Gualala)

Restaurant 🍴

★ **Pangaea**, 250 Main St, Point Arena; tel 707/882-3001. **Californian/Seafood.** A hot new restaurant on the Sonoma coast, presenting a warm Mediterranean terra-cotta decor with local art. Menu changes weekly, and all ingredients are organic. Try grilled rib-eye steak with coarse-grain mustard, pan-roasted salmon on a bed of braised leeks, grilled squash galette in pastry shell with roasted pepper sauce. Offers Mendocino County wines and microbrewery beers. **FYI:** Reservations recommended. Beer and wine only. **Open:** Wed–Sun 6–9pm. Closed some hols; late Dec–early Feb. **Prices:** Main courses $8–$18. Ltd CC. ♿

POINT REYES STATION

Map page M-2, C1 (S of Jenner)

See also Marshall

Restaurant 🍴

★ **Station House Cafe**, Main St (Calif 1), Point Reyes Station; tel 415/663-1515. **American/Californian.** A friendly, homey, neighborhood cafe with food good enough to get written up in *Gourmet* and *Bon Appétit*. The setting is high-tech country, with wainscoting to counterpoint exposed heating ducts; a lovely terrace is framed by climbing roses. Everything is tasty, from breakfast pancakes to dinner specials such as monkfish with green peppercorn sauce. **FYI:** Reservations recommended. Blues/jazz. Children's menu. **Open:** HS May–Oct Sun–Thurs 8am–9pm, Fri–Sat 8am–10pm. Reduced hours off-season. Closed some hols. **Prices:** Main courses $7–$17.50. Ltd CC. 🍽 ♿

POMONA

Map page M-3, D2

Hotels 🏨

▤▤▤ **Sheraton Suites Fairplex**, 600 W McKinley Ave, Pomona, CA 91768; tel 909/622-2220 or toll free 800/722-4055; fax 909/622-3577. White Ave N exit to McKinley off I-10; ½ mi N. Full-service, all-suites hotel with an elegant marble lobby, located adjacent to the Los Angeles County Fairgrounds. **Rooms:** 247 stes. Exec-level rms avail. CI 3pm/CO noon. Express checkout avail. Nonsmoking rms avail. **Amenities:** 🛁 🗄 🎣 A/C, cable TV w/movies, refrig, voice mail. Some units w/terraces. Microwave, 2 TVs. **Services:** ✗ 🚗 ⌂ 🛎 🦺 Complimentary cooked-to-order breakfast. **Facilities:** 🏋 🍴 800 💻 ♿ 1 rst, 1 bar, sauna, whirlpool, washer/dryer. 24-hour mini-mart. **Rates (BB):** HS Sept–Oct from $105 ste. Extra person $10. Children under 18 stay free. Lower rates off-season. Spec packages avail. Pking: Outdoor, free. Maj CC.

▤▤▤ **Shilo Inn Diamond Bar/Pomona**, 3200 Temple Ave, Pomona, CA 91768; tel 909/598-0073 or toll free 800/222-2244 in the US, 800/228-4489 in Canada; fax 909/594-5862. Temple Ave W exit off I-57. Across the street from the Shilo Inns–Hilltop Suites; less expensive, but run with the same cheerful professionalism. **Rooms:** 160 rms. CI 4pm/CO noon. Nonsmoking rms avail. **Amenities:** 🛁 🗄 🎣 A/C, cable TV w/movies, refrig. **Services:** ✗ 🚗 ⌂ 🛎 🦺 Babysitting. **Facilities:** 🏋 🍴 75 💻 ♿ 1 rst, 1 bar (w/entertainment), sauna, whirlpool, washer/dryer. **Rates (CP):** $75 S; $85 D. Extra person $12. Children under 12 stay free. Pking: Outdoor, free. Maj CC.

▤▤▤ **Shilo Inns–Hilltop Suites**, 3101 Temple Ave, Pomona, CA 91768; tel 909/598-7666 or toll free 800/222-2244 in the US, 800/228-4489 in Canada; fax 909/598-5654. Temple Ave W exit off I-57. Has most everything the business traveler might need. **Rooms:** 129 stes. Exec-level rms avail. CI 4pm/CO noon. Nonsmoking rms avail. **Amenities:** 🛁 🗄 🎣 A/C, cable TV w/movies, refrig, VCR. Rooms have microwaves, wet bars, 4 telephones with 2 lines, and 3 TVs. **Services:** ✗ 🚗 ⌂ 🛎 Babysitting. **Facilities:** 🏋 🍴 500 💻 ♿ 1 rst, 1 bar (w/entertainment), sauna, whirlpool, washer/dryer. **Rates (CP):** From $109 ste. Extra person $12. Children under 12 stay free. Spec packages avail. Pking: Outdoor, free. Maj CC.

Restaurant 🍴

★ **Rillo's Restaurant**, 510 E Foothill Blvd, Pomona; tel 909/621-4954. **Continental/Italian.** A beautifully designed southern California restaurant, with pale cream stucco walls, booths covered in finely pleated fabric, pink tablecloths, and large open umbrellas. A full range of northern and southern Italian specialties is served. Good wine list. **FYI:** Reservations recommended. Piano. Dress code. **Open:** Lunch Mon–Fri 11:30am–2:30pm; dinner Mon–Thurs 4:30–9:30pm, Fri–Sun 4:30–10:30pm. Closed some hols. **Prices:** Main courses $11.95–$19.95. Maj CC. ♥ ▼ &

PORT HUENEME

Map page M-3, D1 (SE of Oxnard)

Hotel

≡≡ **The Country Inn at Port Hueneme**, 350 E Hueneme Rd, Port Hueneme, CA 93041; tel 805/986-5353 or toll free 800/44-RELAX; fax 805/986-4399. 5 mi W of Oxnard. Ventura Rd exit off US 101. Nicest property in this navy town, near the base and the beach. Framed art and ceiling fans in hallways are appealing touches. **Rooms:** 135 rms and stes. CI 3pm/CO noon. Nonsmoking rms avail. Restful, homey rooms. **Amenities:** 🛏 ☖ ▣ ☕ A/C, cable TV, refrig, VCR. Some units w/fireplaces, some w/Jacuzzis. **Services:** ☒ ⊲ Babysitting. **Facilities:** ⓕ ﹐⁷⁵﹐ & Whirlpool, washer/dryer. **Rates (CP):** $85–$90 S; $95–$105 D; from $105 ste. Extra person $10. Children under 12 stay free. Min stay spec evnts. Higher rates for spec evnts/hols. Spec packages avail. Pking: Outdoor, free. Maj CC.

PRINCETON-BY-THE-SEA

Map page M-2, D1 (S of Pacifica)

Inn

≡≡≡ **Pillar Point Inn**, 380 Capistrano Rd, Princeton-by-the-Sea, CA 94018; tel 415/728-7377; fax 415/728-8345. 4 mi N of Half Moon Bay. Well located and in mint condition inside and out, with excellent furnishings. Unsuitable for children under 18. **Rooms:** 11 rms. CI 2pm/CO 11am. Attractive early American decor with new carpeting throughout. **Amenities:** 🛏 ☖ TV w/movies, refrig, VCR. No A/C. All units w/fireplaces. Large oaken refrigerators; 4 rooms have steam baths. **Services:** Afternoon tea and wine/sherry served. **Facilities:** 🍴 & Guest lounge. Large fitness center and 6 restaurants within walking

distance. Shore Bird restaurant next door. **Rates (BB):** $140–$160 S or D. Extra person $20. Min stay wknds. Pking: Outdoor, free. Ltd CC.

Restaurant ⅲ

★ **Shorebird Restaurant**, in Pillar Point Marina, 390 Capistrano Rd, Princeton-by-the-Sea; tel 415/728-5541. 4 mi N of Half Moon Bay. Capistrano Rd exit off Calif 1 (Cabrillo Hwy). **Seafood.** Largest and most popular restaurant in the area. Cape Cod theme with casement windows, wood-beamed ceiling, flowers. Every table has splendid view of harbor. Low noise level; unrushed, excellent service. Oyster bar. Offers seafood salads, local fresh fish, fish & chips, soup, smoked salmon with fettuccine, Maryland-style crab cakes, steamed clams. **FYI:** Reservations recommended. Children's menu. Dress code. **Open:** Lunch daily 11:30am–3pm; dinner daily 5:30–9pm. **Prices:** Main courses $8.95–$15.95. Maj CC. ▨ ▩ &

RANCHO CORDOVA

Map page M-2, C2 (NE of Sacramento)

Hotels

≡≡≡ **Courtyard by Marriott**, 10683 White Rock Rd, Rancho Cordova, CA 95670; tel 916/638-3800 or toll free 800/321-2211; fax 916/638-6776. 12 mi E of Sacramento. Zinfandel exit off US 50; S on Zinfandel to White Rock Rd. A comfortable, reasonably priced business hotel. Attractive gazebo and lobby. **Rooms:** 144 rms and stes. CI 3pm/CO 1pm. Express checkout avail. Nonsmoking rms avail. **Amenities:** 🛏 ☖ ▣ A/C, satel TV w/movies. Some units w/terraces. **Services:** ✕ ☒ ⊲ Coffee in lobby all day. Free newspaper delivery. **Facilities:** ⓕ ⛾ ﹐²⁵﹐ & 1 rst, 1 bar, whirlpool, washer/dryer. **Rates:** $75–$85 S or D; from $95 ste. Children under 18 stay free. Spec packages avail. Pking: Outdoor, free. Maj CC. Cheaper on weekends. Return clients receive membership in Courtyard Club.

≡≡ **Fairfield Inn by Marriott**, 10713 White Rock Rd, Rancho Cordova, CA 95670; tel 916/631-7500 or toll free 800/228-2800. 10 mi E of Sacramento. Zinfandel exit off US 50; south on Zinfandel; west on White Rock. Budget-range 3-year-old property on highway; adequate for single business travelers. **Rooms:** 117 rms. CI noon/CO noon. Nonsmoking rms avail. Too small for families, unless you book adjoining rooms. Some baths could use renovations. **Amenities:** 🛏 ☖ A/C, cable TV w/movies. **Services:** ☒ ⊲ Babysitting. Daily continental breakfast until 9am on lobby level. Coffee available 24 hours. Copy and fax in office may be used by guests. **Facilities:** ⓕ & **Rates**

(CP): HS Apr–Oct $42 S; $48–$51 D. Extra person $3. Children under 18 stay free. Lower rates off-season. Pking: Outdoor, free. Maj CC.

≣≣≣ **Holiday Inn Rancho Cordova**, 11131 Folsom Blvd, Rancho Cordova, CA 95670; tel 916/635-0666 or toll free 800/ HOLIDAY; fax 916/635-3297. 10 mi E of Sacramento. Sunrise Blvd exit off US 50; south on Sunrise; right on Folsom Blvd. Suburban hotel on a busy highway. Less crowded than other facilities that have business conventions. **Rooms:** 130 rms and stes. CI 3pm/CO noon. Express checkout avail. Nonsmoking rms avail. **Amenities:** 🛎 A/C, cable TV w/movies, refrig. Some units w/terraces. **Services:** ✕ ⟁ ⟳ **Facilities:** ⟦⟧ ⟦150⟧ ⟤ ⟁ 1 rst, 1 bar, whirlpool. **Rates:** HS Apr–Sept $69 S; $79 D; from $89 ste. Extra person $10. Children under 19 stay free. Lower rates off-season. Higher rates for spec evnts/hols. Spec packages avail. Pking: Outdoor, free. Maj CC. Kids under 12 eat free.

≣≣≣ **Quality Suites**, 11260 Point East Dr, Rancho Cordova, CA 95742; tel 916/638-4141 or toll free 800/444-1089; fax 916/638-4287. Sunrise Blvd exit off US 50; east on Folsom; left on Point East Dr. A newer property, laid out for comfortable family stays, with courtyard and off-highway setting. Offers more privacy than neighboring motels. **Rooms:** 127 stes. CI 3pm/CO noon. Nonsmoking rms avail. **Amenities:** 🛎⟁⟳ A/C, satel TV, refrig, VCR, stereo/tape player. Some units w/Jacuzzis. Poolside rooms have patios. **Services:** ✕ ⟁ ⟳ Complimentary full breakfast. **Facilities:** ⟦⟧ ⟤ ⟦60⟧ ⟁ 1 rst, 1 bar, whirlpool, washer/dryer. **Rates (MAP):** From $92 ste. Children under 16 stay free. Spec packages avail. Pking: Outdoor, free. Maj CC.

≣≣≣ **Sheraton Hotel Rancho Cordova**, 11211 Point East Dr, Rancho Cordova, CA 95742; tel 916/638-1100 or toll free 800/325-3535; fax 916/635-8356. Sunrise Blvd S exit off US 50; turn right on Sunrise Blvd; left on Folsom Blvd; left on Point East. Most services of any hotel on US 50 Business corridor. Fountains in lobby and pool mask highway noise somewhat. **Rooms:** 265 rms and stes. Exec-level rms avail. CI 4pm/CO noon. Express checkout avail. Nonsmoking rms avail. Nice vanity alcove with plugs and lights. Ask for "quiet" room. **Amenities:** 🛎⟁⟳⟳ A/C, cable TV w/movies, voice mail, shoe polisher. Refrigerators available upon request. **Services:** ✕ ⟳ ⟑ ⟁ ⟳ Car-rental desk, babysitting. Difficult to access. **Facilities:** ⟦⟧ ⟤ ⟦800⟧ ⟤ ⟁ 1 rst, 1 bar (w/entertainment), whirlpool. Current renovations will bring meeting capacity to 3,600. **Rates (MAP):** $79–$120 S; $99–$130 D; from $150 ste. Extra person $10. Children under 12 stay free. Spec packages avail. Pking: Outdoor, free. Maj CC. With 14-day advance reservation: $79 single, $89 double.

RANCHO CUCAMONGA
Map page M-3, D3 (W of San Bernardino)

Restaurants 🍴

★ **Magic Lamp Inn**, 8189 Foothill Blvd, Rancho Cucamonga; tel 909/981-8659. 1½ mi E of Euclid Ave. **American/Continental.** The real genie is the owner, who makes diners feel welcome here. Old-fashioned dining room has dark wood walls and leather chairs. Wonderful steak, seafood, and chicken dinners. More than 300 wines, including hard-to-find Italian vintages. **FYI:** Reservations recommended. Combo. Children's menu. Dress code. **Open:** Lunch daily 11:30am–2:30pm; dinner daily 5–10pm. Closed Dec 25. **Prices:** Main courses $9.95–$39.95. Maj CC. ⬛

Sycamore Inn, 8318 Foothill Blvd, Rancho Cucamonga; tel 909/982-1104. 1½ mi E of Euclid Ave. **American.** An inn since 1848; the present building dates from the 1920s. Large Victorian-style dining room with leather chairs, broad tables, chandeliers. Specialty is Black Angus beef, but pasta, other meat, seafood, and poultry are also served in large portions. Wine list has over 600 entries. **FYI:** Reservations recommended. Children's menu. **Open:** Lunch Mon–Fri 11:30am–2:30pm; dinner Mon–Thurs 5–10pm, Fri–Sat 5–11pm, Sun 3–10pm. Closed Dec 25. **Prices:** Main courses $12.95–$41.95. Maj CC. ⬛

Attraction 🗂

Casa de Rancho Cucamonga; tel 909/989-4970. Located at the corner of Hemlock and Vineyard Ave. Built in 1860 by Ohio brickmasons with bricks made from red clay on site, this was the home of John and Doña Merced Raines, who were prominent local citizens. The patio features a cistern with an open flume to carry water from springs through the kitchen, under the house, and into the orchard. **Open:** Wed–Sun 10am–4pm. Closed some hols. Free.

RANCHO MIRAGE
Map page M-3, D3 (E of Palm Springs)

Resorts 🛏

≣≣≣≣ **Marriott's Rancho Las Palmas Resort & Country Club**, 41-000 Bob Hope Dr, Rancho Mirage, CA 92270; tel 619/ 568-2727 or toll free 800/458-8786; fax 619/568-5845. Bob Hope Dr exit off I-10. 240 acres. Set amid lush fairways and landscaped lakes, this resort is reminiscent of a spacious early-

California-style hacienda. **Rooms:** 450 rms and stes. CI 4pm/CO noon. Express checkout avail. Nonsmoking rms avail. Comfortable guest rooms. **Amenities:** 🔒 ⚷ 🖭 A/C, cable TV w/movies. All units w/minibars, all w/terraces. **Services:** ✗ ☎ VP 🚐 ⛱ ⊃ ⊂ Car-rental desk, children's program, babysitting. Cactus Kids children's program. **Facilities:** ⛳ 🚲 ▶₂₇ 🎱₁₆ 🏊 🎾 1.4K ♿ 3 rsts, 2 bars, lifeguard, lawn games, whirlpool, beauty salon, playground, washer/dryer. **Rates:** HS Jan–Apr 15 $159–$240 S or D; from $275 ste. Extra person $10. Children under 14 stay free. Lower rates off-season. Spec packages avail. Pking: Outdoor, free. Maj CC.

≣≣≣≣ **Ritz-Carlton Rancho Mirage**, 68-900 Frank Sinatra Dr, Rancho Mirage, CA 92270; tel 619/321-8282 or toll free 800/241-3333; fax 619/321-6928. Bob Hope Dr exit off I-10. 25 acres. A desert resort on a spectacular mountain bluff. Sweeping views of the Coachella Valley and surrounding mountains. Wild bighorn sheep graze on the lawn. **Rooms:** 240 rms and stes. Exec-level rms avail. CI 3pm/CO noon. Nonsmoking rms avail. In the traditional Ritz-Carlton style. Accommodations decorated in tranquil yellows, blues, and purples that complement the desert palette. **Amenities:** 🔒 ⚷ 🍴 A/C, cable TV w/movies, refrig, bathrobes. All units w/minibars, all w/terraces. **Services:** 🍽 ☎ VP 🚐 ⛱ ⊃ Twice-daily maid svce, car-rental desk, social director, masseur, children's program, babysitting. **Facilities:** ⛳ 🏊 🎾 1.2K 🖥 ♿ 3 rsts (see also "Restaurants" below), 1 bar (w/entertainment), games rm, lawn games, spa, sauna, steam rm, whirlpool, day-care ctr, playground. Compact but well-equipped fitness center. Volleyball, basketball. **Rates:** HS Dec 27–May $260–$395 S or D; from $650 ste. Extra person $25. Children under 10 stay free. Lower rates off-season. Spec packages avail. Pking: Indoor, $12. Maj CC.

≣≣≣≣ **Westin Mission Hills Resort**, Dinah Shore Dr and Bob Hope Dr, Rancho Mirage, CA 92270; tel 619/770-2132 or toll free 800/999-8284; fax 619/321-2955. 360 acres. Designed to resemble a Moroccan palace, surrounded by pools, waterfalls, and lush gardens. Self-contained resort is an excellent choice for families. **Rooms:** 512 rms and stes. Exec-level rms avail. CI 4pm/CO noon. Express checkout avail. Nonsmoking rms avail. Rooms are a bit bland compared to the spectacular exteriors, but they do have lovely views of the mountains and golf course. **Amenities:** 🔒 ⚷ 🖭 🍴 A/C, cable TV w/movies, voice mail, in-rm safe, shoe polisher, bathrobes. All units w/minibars, all w/terraces, some w/Jacuzzis. **Services:** 🍽 ☎ VP ⛱ ⊃ ⊂ Twice-daily maid svce, car-rental desk, masseur, children's program, babysitting. Fully staffed activities center for children offers educational instruction about the flora, fauna, and history of the desert. **Facilities:** ⛳ 🚲 ▶₃₆ 🎾 🏊 🎾 3.8K 🖥 ♿ 2 rsts (see also "Restaurants" below), 3 bars (2 w/entertainment), lifeguard, games rm, lawn games, spa, steam rm, whirlpool,

beauty salon, day-care ctr, playground. Bicycle trails, competition running track, motocross, go-cart, and steeplechase dirt track. Excellent meeting facilities. **Rates:** HS Jan–May $239–$299 S or D; from $390 ste. Extra person $25. Children under 18 stay free. Min stay wknds. Lower rates off-season. Spec packages avail. Pking: Outdoor, free. Maj CC.

Restaurants 🍴

Bella Vista, in the Westin Mission Hills Resort, Dinah Shore and Bob Hope Drs, Rancho Mirage; tel 619/328-5955. Bob Hope Dr exit off I-10. **Californian.** The atrium dining room offers a light and cheery place to dine. Chef's specialties include grilled lamb chops; salmon fillet with oriental spices; and angel-hair pasta with shrimp, crayfish, and andouille sausage. **FYI:** Reservations accepted. Children's menu. Dress code. **Open:** Sun–Thurs 6:30am–3pm, Fri–Sat 6:30am–11pm. **Prices:** Main courses $12.50–$19.95. Maj CC. 🍴 🖭 VP ♿

The Club Grill, in the Ritz-Carlton Rancho Mirage, 68-900 Frank Sinatra Dr, Rancho Mirage; tel 619/321-8282. Bob Hope Dr exit off I-10. **Regional American.** Crystal chandeliers, unique floral arrangements, uphostered chairs, and fine china add to the sophisticated ambience. Roasted rack of lamb, herb fettuccine with scallops and shrimp, and roasted free-range chicken breast with herb glaze are all house specialties. **FYI:** Reservations recommended. Piano. Jacket required. **Open:** HS Oct–May Tues–Sat 6:30–11pm. Reduced hours off-season. Closed some hols; June–mid-Sept. **Prices:** Main courses $18.50–$32.50. Maj CC. VP ♿

Marconi's of San Francisco, 69-620 Calif 111, Rancho Mirage; tel 619/328-9000. Bob Hope Dr exit off I-10. **Seafood.** Pale green and soft salmon hues in a decor of pecan-stained wood and brass accents. The menu offers primarily seafood, such as cioppino, seafood paella, and petrale sole. **FYI:** Reservations recommended. Piano/singer. Dress code. **Open:** Tues–Sun 5–10pm. Closed some hols; July–mid-Sept. **Prices:** Main courses $10.95–$21.95. Maj CC. VP ♿

Touché, 42-250 Bob Hope Dr, Rancho Mirage; tel 619/773-1111. Bob Hope Dr exit off I-10. **Continental.** Private club-atmosphere, elaborate decor. Three rooms: an elegant dining room centered around a courtyard fountain, a nightclub with a plush living room, and a piano lounge for dining and dancing under a lighted dome. Serves lamb chops, shrimp scampi, chicken dishes. **FYI:** Reservations recommended. Piano/singer. Dress code. **Open:** Daily 6–11:30pm. **Prices:** Main courses $11.95–$21.95. Maj CC. VP ♿

Wally's Desert Turtle, 71-775 Calif 111, Rancho Mirage; tel 619/568-9321. **Continental.** The stunning decor features beveled-mirror ceilings, hand-painted murals, and Peruvian artifacts, complemented by crisp linen tablecloths and gleaming crystal. Menu highlights include roast duck, medallions of veal, and grilled scallops. Excellent continental cuisine and great ambience. **FYI:** Reservations recommended. Piano. Dress code. **Open:** Lunch Fri 11:30am–3pm; dinner daily 6–11pm. Closed some hols; June–Sept 10. **Prices:** Main courses $12–$30. Maj CC. 🐾 VP &

RANCHO PALOS VERDES

Map page M-3, D3 (E of Palm Springs)

Attraction 🏛

Wayfarers Chapel, 5755 Palos Verdes Dr S; tel 310/377-1650. The "glass church" was built by Lloyd Wright, the son of Frank Lloyd Wright. Constructed of glass, redwood, and native stone, it is a memorial to Emanuel Swedenborg, the 18th-century Swedish philosopher and theologian who claimed to have conversed with spirits and heavenly hosts in his visions. The chapel is often used for weddings; phone ahead. Free escorted tours are sometimes available. **Open:** Mon–Fri 9am–5pm, Sat 9am–1pm. Closed some hols. Free.

RANCHO SANTA FE

Map page M-3, E3 (NE of Del Mar)

Inn 🏨

≣ ≣ ≣ ≣ **Inn at Rancho Santa Fe**, 5951 Linea Del Cielo, PO Box 869, Rancho Santa Fe, CA 92067; tel 619/756-1131 or toll free 800/654-2928; fax 619/759-1604. Lomas Santa Fe exit off I-5. 22 acres. In a posh community, close to several golf courses. An elegant destination offering natural beauty and tranquility. **Rooms:** 9 rms; 81 ctges/villas. CI 3pm/CO noon. Secluded private cottages, many surrounded by lush foliage. **Amenities:** 🛏 🕭 🖃 A/C, TV, refrig. Some units w/minibars, all w/terraces, some w/fireplaces, some w/Jacuzzis. **Services:** ✕ 🛒 🖼 🛬 🖐 Twice-daily maid svce, car-rental desk, babysitting. The inn owns box seats at Del Mar Racetrack and some passes are available. **Facilities:** 🛗 🎾 🖥 🖾 2 rsts, 1 bar (w/entertainment), lawn games, washer/dryer, guest lounge. The inn also owns a cottage on Del Mar Beach where guests can shower and

dress. **Rates:** HS July–Aug $100–$180 S or D; from $260 ctge/villa. Children under 16 stay free. Min stay HS. Lower rates off-season. Spec packages avail. Pking: Outdoor, free. Ltd CC.

Resort

≣ ≣ ≣ ≣ **Rancho Valencia Resort**, 5921 Valencia Circle, PO Box 9126, Rancho Santa Fe, CA 92067; tel 619/756-1123 or toll free 800/548-3664; fax 619/756-0165. 40 acres. Low villas with red-tile roofs are interspersed with courtyards, archways, and grounds so lush you can pluck ripe oranges from trees. **Rooms:** 43 ctges/villas. CI 4pm/CO noon. Nonsmoking rms avail. Each casita resembles a private residence—some are as large as 1,200 square feet. Decorated in neutrals and earth tones, with tile floors and a Spanish-Colonial armoire, housing a 27-inch TV. Every suite features a walk-in closet, dressing room, and separate makeup vanity. **Amenities:** 🛏 🕭 🖃 🖢 A/C, cable TV w/movies, refrig, VCR, in-rm safe, bathrobes. All units w/minibars, all w/terraces, all w/fireplaces, 1 w/Jacuzzi. **Services:** 🔘 VP 🚗 🖾 🖐 Twice-daily maid svce, car-rental desk, masseur, babysitting. **Facilities:** 🛗 🚲 🖥 🍹18 🏓 🖾80 🖥 🖾 1 rst (*see also* "Restaurants" below), 1 bar (w/entertainment), lawn games, spa, sauna, whirlpool, washer/dryer. Palm trees, hibiscus hedges, and pots of flowers surround the beautiful pool, edged with painted tiles. This is also tennis heaven, with 18 courts and 6 pros on staff. There's a regulation-size croquet lawn. **Rates:** From $295 ctge/villa. Extra person $20. Children under 18 stay free. Min stay spec evnts. Spec packages avail. Pking: Outdoor, free. Maj CC. Tennis, golf, and spa packages available.

Restaurants 🍴

🌶 **Delicias**, 6106 Paseo Delicias, Rancho Santa Fe; tel 619/756-8000. Via de la Valle exit off I-5. **Californian.** Romantic, informal atmosphere, with chintz upholstered chairs and lots of windows; an open kitchen overlooks the dining room. Dishes include grilled salmon with red-onion marmalade and lemon-oregano sauce, and Chinese duck with ginger-and-pear sauce. **FYI:** Reservations recommended. Dress code. **Open:** Lunch Tues–Sun 11am–2:30pm; dinner Tues–Sun 6–10pm. Closed some hols. **Prices:** Main courses $15–$26. Maj CC. 🐾 &

The Dining Room, in Rancho Valencia Resort, 5921 Valencia Circle, Rancho Santa Fe; tel 619/756-1123. **Californian/Mediterranean.** A blend of Californian and Mediterranean elements. Spanish colonial–style art accents the airy, open dining room, with windows facing a terrace and rolling hills. The menu changes often; typical entrees are pan-roasted whitefish encrusted with whole-grain mustard, or grilled steak with roasted peppers and Maui onions. A dessert specialty is orange cake layered with orange custard and chocolate mousse. **FYI:** Reservations recommended. Guitar/jazz. Children's menu. **Open:** Daily 7am–10pm. **Prices:** Main courses $18.75–$26.25. Maj CC. ♥ ≝ 🔲 VP 𝄞

♣ **Mille Fleurs**, 6009 Paseo Delicias, Rancho Santa Fe; tel 619/756-3085. Via de la Valle exit off I-5. **Continental/French.** This restaurant has won countless accolades for its fine cuisine and the 800-item wine list. Decor is that of a French château, with a cozy fireplace and whitewashed walls. Starting with the freshest ingredients each day, the chef creates dishes such as loin of rabbit with morel sauce, medallions of venison with blueberry sauce, and sea bass in Pernod sauce. **FYI:** Reservations recommended. Piano. Dress code. **Open:** Lunch Mon–Fri 11:30am–2:30pm; dinner daily 6–10pm. Closed some hols. **Prices:** Main courses $23–$30. Maj CC. ♥ 🔲

Red Bluff

Map page M-2, B2

Motels 🏨

⊨⊨⊨ **Best Western Grand Manor Inn**, 90 Sale Lane, Red Bluff, CA 96080; tel 916/529-7060 or toll free 800/626-1900; fax 916/529-7077. Calif 36 E exit off I-5; right on Sale Lane. This property opened in 1994 and was designed and built like a grand manor. Great for business travelers and families who want high-quality lodging at a fair price. **Rooms:** 67 rms and stes. CI noon/CO 11am. Nonsmoking rms avail. Large, well-appointed rooms and suites. **Amenities:** 🛏 🕭 🔲 A/C, cable TV, refrig. Some units w/minibars, some w/terraces. **Services:** ⊖ **Facilities:** 🔲 🍴 🔟 𝄞 Whirlpool, washer/dryer. **Rates (CP):** $63–$69 S; $69–$73 D; from $69 ste. Extra person $6. Children under 12 stay free. Higher rates for spec evnts/hols. Pking: Outdoor, free. Maj CC.

⊨⊨ **Lamplighter Lodge**, 210 S Main St, Red Bluff, CA 96080; tel 916/527-1150 or toll free 800/521-4423; fax 916/527-5878. Attractive lodgings near old Victorian section of Red Bluff. **Rooms:** 51 rms and stes. CI 1pm/CO 11:30am. Nonsmoking rms avail. **Amenities:** 🛏 🕭 🔲 A/C, cable TV w/movies, refrig. **Services:** 🚐 ⊖ **Facilities:** 🔲 **Rates (CP):** $34–$38 S; $44–$48 D; from $65 ste. Extra person $4. Children under 12 stay free. Higher rates for spec evnts/hols. Pking: Outdoor, free. Maj CC.

⊨ **Super 8 Motel–Red Bluff**, 203 Antelope Blvd, Red Bluff, CA 96080; tel 916/527-8882 or toll free 800/800-8000; fax 916/527-5078. Calif 36 E exit off I-5; right on Antelope Blvd. Attractive motel. **Rooms:** 72 rms. CI 11am/CO 11am. Nonsmoking rms avail. **Amenities:** 🛏 🕭 A/C, satel TV. VCRs and videos for rent. **Services:** ⊖ 🖐 Babysitting. Fax service available. **Facilities:** 🔲 𝄞 **Rates (CP):** $36–$40 S; $42–$46 D. Extra person $6. Children under 12 stay free. Higher rates for spec evnts/hols. Pking: Outdoor, free. Maj CC.

Attraction 🖼

William B Ide Adobe State Park, 21659 Adobe Rd; tel 916/527-5927. William Brown Ide, a farmer from Illinois, became president of the Bear Flag Republic only 8 months after he and his family arrived in California in 1845. His presidency lasted only 26 days before the outbreak of the Mexican War led to American occupation of the region.

The present adobe is a restoration of a building built around 1852. Picnicking; pioneer crafts demonstrations in summer. **Open:** Daily 8am–dusk. Free.

Redding

Map page M-2, B2

Hotels 🏨

⊨⊨⊨ **Oxford Suites**, 1967 Hilltop Dr, Redding, CA 96002; tel 916/221-0100 or toll free 800/762-0133. Cypress Ave E exit off I-5; N on Hilltop Dr ¾ mi. Excellent lodging at a fair price for the discerning business and pleasure traveler. **Rooms:** 140 stes. CI 2pm/CO 1pm. Nonsmoking rms avail. Range from simple to grand suites. **Amenities:** 🛏 🕭 A/C, cable TV w/movies, refrig, VCR. Suites have microwave. **Services:** 🚐 🖾 ⊖ 🖐 Complimentary full breakfast and hosted evening reception with drinks and hors d'oeuvres. Fax and copying available. **Facilities:** 🔲 🔳 𝄞 Whirlpool, washer/dryer. **Rates (BB):** From $58 ste. Extra person $6. Children under 10 stay free. Pking: Outdoor, free. Maj CC. Discounts for qualified business travelers and government-agency personnel. Add 10% for pets.

⊨⊨ **Park Terrace Inn**, 1900 Hilltop Dr, Redding, CA 96002; tel 916/221-7500; fax 916/222-3008. Guests rooms under renovation. **Rooms:** 164 rms and stes. CI 3pm/CO noon. Nonsmoking rms avail. **Amenities:** 🛏 🕭 A/C, satel TV w/movies. Some units w/minibars. **Services:** ✕ 🚐 🖾 ⊖ 🖐 Babysitting. **Facilities:** 🔲 🍴 🔳 🖥 𝄞 1 rst, games rm, sauna, whirlpool, washer/dryer. **Rates:** HS June–Sept $65–$85 S; $75–$95 D; from $112 ste. Extra person $12. Children under 18 stay free. Lower rates off-season. Higher rates for spec evnts/hols. Spec packages avail. Pking: Outdoor, free. Maj CC.

⊨⊨⊨ **Red Lion Hotel Redding**, 1830 Hilltop Dr, Redding, CA 96002; tel 916/221-8700 or toll free 800/547-8010; fax 916/221-0324. Hilltop Dr exit off I-5. **Rooms:** 194 rms and stes.

CI 3pm/CO 1pm. Express checkout avail. Nonsmoking rms avail. **Amenities:** ☎ ♨ A/C, cable TV w/movies. Some units w/terraces. **Services:** ✗ 🚐 🗺 🍽 🛎 Car-rental desk, babysitting. Budget car rental in lobby. Shoeshine stand open during weekday business hours. Food served at poolside terrace by request. Guests receive personalized attention. **Facilities:** 🛗 🔟 🖥 ♿ 3 rsts (*see also* "Restaurants" below), 1 bar (w/entertainment), games rm, whirlpool. Use of fitness facilities off premises for $5 a day, with free transportation. **Rates:** HS June–Sept $85–$125 S; $100–$140 D; from $250 ste. Extra person $15. Children under 18 stay free. Lower rates off-season. Spec packages avail. Pking: Outdoor, free. Maj CC.

Motels

▤▤▤ Best Western Hilltop Inn, 2300 Hilltop Dr, Redding, CA 96002; tel 916/221-6100 or toll free 800/336-4880; fax 916/221-2867. Cypress Ave E exit off I-5; N on Hilltop Dr ¼ mi. A friendly, well-run place. **Rooms:** 115 rms and stes. CI 2pm/CO noon. Nonsmoking rms avail. **Amenities:** ☎ ♨ 🖥 🍷 A/C, cable TV w/movies, voice mail. 1 unit w/minibar. All king rooms have VCRs. All queen and king rooms have ironing boards and irons. **Services:** ✗ 🗺 🍽 Babysitting. **Facilities:** 🛗 🏊 ♿ 1 rst, 1 bar, whirlpool, washer/dryer. Restaurant open 11am–11pm. **Rates:** HS May–Sept $71–$78 S; $81–$88 D; from $150 ste. Extra person $10. Children under 12 stay free. Lower rates off-season. Higher rates for spec evnts/hols. Spec packages avail. Pking: Outdoor, free. Maj CC. Senior citizens receive a 10% discount.

▤▤ Colony Inn, 2731 Bechelli Lane, Redding, CA 96002; tel 916/223-1935 or toll free 800/354-5222; fax 916/223-1176. Cypress Ave exit off I-5; west 1 block to Bechelli. Very nice rooms at a budget price; however, it's close to the freeway, so you'll hear some traffic noise. **Rooms:** 75 rms. CI 1pm/CO 11am. Nonsmoking rms avail. **Amenities:** ☎ A/C, cable TV w/movies. **Services:** 🍽 **Facilities:** 🛗 ♿ **Rates (CP):** $34 S; $38–$42 D. Extra person $5. Children under 16 stay free. Pking: Outdoor, free. Maj CC.

▤▤ River Inn, 1835 Park Marina Dr, Redding, CA 96001; tel 916/241-9500 or toll free 800/995-4341; fax 916/241-5345. Cypress Ave exit off I-5; west 1 mi to Park Marina Dr. Host Larry Tappy works very hard to please his guests. **Rooms:** 79 rms. CI 2pm/CO 11am. Nonsmoking rms avail. Some units have riverfront views. **Amenities:** ☎ ♨ 🖥 A/C, cable TV w/movies, refrig. Some units w/terraces, 1 w/fireplace, some w/Jacuzzis. **Services:** 🍽 🛎 Anything you might have left at home is available at the front desk. **Facilities:** 🛗 ♿ 1 rst, 1 bar, sauna, whirlpool. A lake full of fish, with fishing poles available to guests and a barbecue for grilling their catch. **Rates:** HS June–Sept $50–$60 S; $60–$70 D; from $65 ste. Extra person $5. Children under 12 stay free. Lower rates off-season. Pking: Outdoor, free. Maj CC.

▤▤ Vagabond Inn, 536 E Cypress Ave, Redding, CA 96002; tel 916/223-1600 or toll free 800/522-1555; fax 916/221-4247. Cypress Ave W exit off I-5. Easy access to I-5. **Rooms:** 71 rms. CI 2pm/CO noon. Nonsmoking rms avail. **Amenities:** ☎ ♨ 🖥 A/C, cable TV w/movies. **Services:** 🍽 🛎 Free weekday newspaper, fresh fruit, coffee and tea, plus continental breakfast. **Facilities:** 🛗 ♿ **Rates (CP):** HS June–Oct $35–$60 S; $40–$65 D. Extra person $5. Children under 18 stay free. Lower rates off-season. Higher rates for spec evnts/hols. Pking: Outdoor, free. Maj CC.

Restaurant 🍴

★ **Misty's Dining Room**, in the Red Lion Hotel, 1830 Hilltop Dr, Redding; tel 916/221-8700. **New American.** Expansive space with high ceilings, many chandeliers. Muted pastel colors. Imaginative California grill food, flambé tableside dishes, specialty coffees. **FYI:** Reservations recommended. Band. Children's menu. **Open:** HS May–Dec dinner daily 5–10pm; brunch Sun 9am–2pm. Reduced hours off-season. **Prices:** Main courses $7.95–$14.95. Maj CC. ❤ ✉ ♿

Attractions 🏛

Shasta State Historic Park, Calif 299W; tel 916/243-8194. Located 6 miles west of Redding on Calif 299 are the remnants of Shasta City, once called the "Queen City" of California's northern mining territory. The Shasta County Courthuse has been restored to its 1861 appearance and now houses historical exhibits, artifacts, and historic paintings pertaining to the town and its era. A few other buildings still stand, but many are in ruins or gone altogether. Self-guided tour booklets are available that give a detailed account of the history of Shasta City and its historic structures. The visitor center, in a completely refurbished old building across from the Empire Hotel site, has interpretive displays and information. **Open:** Mar–Oct, Thurs–Mon 10am–5pm; Nov–Feb, Fri–Sun 10am–5pm. Closed some hols. $

Shasta Dam; tel 916/275-4463 or 275-1554. Located about 12 miles north of Redding via I-5, exit at Shasta Dam Blvd. Completed in 1945, this is one of the largest concrete structures ever built in the United States. The dam is 602 feet high, 883 feet thick at the bottom, 30 feet thick at the top, and 3,460 feet long; its spillway is the largest man-made waterfall in the world—487 feet (three times the height of Niagara Falls). The dam's power-plant contains 5 generators producing a combined total of 583,000 kW of electricity.

The visitor center has a 30-minute movie on the construction of the dam, displays, and guided tours of the dam and power-plant (schedule varies; phone ahead). Picnicking is permitted at the site, with views of the entire dam, Shasta Lake, and the snow-covered volcano, Mount Shasta, to the north. Shasta Lake, created by the dam, is the largest man-made reservoir in California. It is surrounded by the Whiskeytown-Shasta-Trinity National Recreation Area. **Open:** Visitor center: Mem Day–Labor Day, Mon–Fri 7:30am–5pm, Sat–Sun 8:30am–5pm; hours vary rest of the year. Closed some hols. Free.

Lassen Volcanic National Park; tel 916/595-4444. Located 44 miles east of Redding via Calif 44, this 165-square-mile national park reveals a history of violent volcanic activity. Lassen Peak (10,457 feet) is 1 of only 2 active volcanoes in the continental United States (the other is Mount St Helens in Washington), although it has been dormant since 1921. Today, peaceful coniferous forests, alpine meadows, and mountain lakes coexist with cinder cones, lava flows, boiling mud pots, and thermal springs. The summit affords a superb panoramic view of the surrounding area; access is via a 2- to 3-hour walk along a marked trail. There is also a scenic 30-mile drive between the park's southern entrance and Manzanita Lake (Lassen Park Rd).

Although the park is open year-round, heavy snowslides prevent access to Lassen Park Rd and certain areas of the park from late Oct–early June. There are 7 fully equipped camp-grounds (late May–late Sept). The visitor center on Manzanita Lake (northwest park entrance) is open in summer. For further information, contact the Superintendent, Lassen Volcanic National Park, PO Box 100, Mineral, CA 96063 (tel 916/595-4444). **Open:** Daily 24 hours. $$

REDLANDS

Map page M-3, D3

Attraction 🖼

San Bernardino County Museum, 2024 Orange Tree Lane; tel 909/798-8570. One of the largest museums in California, this facility exhibits collections in archaeology, history, geology, paleontology, biological sciences, and fine arts. Discovery Hall is a hands-on family learning center presenting specimens, arti-facts, and small animals. Traveling exhibitions in Elsie Munzig Exhibit Hall. Museum shop with souvenirs, collectibles, books. **Open:** Tues–Sun 9am–5pm. Closed some hols. $

REDONDO BEACH

Map page M-3, D2 (NW of Long Beach)

Hotels 🛏

≣≣ **Best Western Redondo Beach Inn**, 1850 S Pacific Coast Hwy, Redondo Beach, CA 90277; tel 310/540-3700 or toll free 800/528-1234; fax 310/540-3675. 1 mi NW of Torrance. I-110 S (Harbor Fwy) exit off I-405, to Pacific Coast Hwy; go west. A Mexican villa-style property with white stucco buildings and red-tiled roofs. **Rooms:** 108 rms and stes. CI 2pm/CO 11am. Express checkout avail. Nonsmoking rms avail. Colonial-style decor. Standard rooms are accessible via outdoor walkways; deluxe rooms open onto indoor corridors. Bathrooms are small. **Amenities:** 🛢 ⚮ A/C, satel TV w/movies, refrig. Some units w/terraces, 1 w/fireplace, 1 w/Jacuzzi. Deluxe rooms have refrigerators and sofas. **Services:** ✕ △ ⇦ Car-rental desk, babysitting. Food can be served poolside. **Facilities:** 🔓 ♂ ⛳ 40 ⚮ 1 rst, 1 bar, sauna, whirlpool. Small pool and sunning area. Complimentary bike use, tennis racquets, and tennis balls. **Rates:** HS June–Aug $59–$89 S or D; from $160 ste. Children under 18 stay free. Lower rates off-season. Higher rates for spec evnts/hols. Pking: Indoor/outdoor, free. Maj CC.

≣≣ **Best Western Sunrise Hotel–King Harbor**, 400 N Harbor Dr, Redondo Beach, CA 90277; tel 310/376-0746 or toll free 800/334-7384; fax 310/376-7384. Redondo Beach exit off I-405; exit east; right on Prairie; right on 190th; left on Harbor. Clean accommodations close to Hermosa and Redondo Beaches and across the street from King Harbor. **Rooms:** 111 rms and stes. CI 3pm/CO noon. Express checkout avail. Nonsmoking rms avail. Average in size and decor, rooms are a bit outdated but comfortable. Every room has live plants and some have views. **Amenities:** 🛢 ⚮ 🖥 A/C, cable TV w/movies, refrig, voice mail. **Services:** ✕ 🚗 △ ⇦ Car-rental desk. **Facilities:** 🔓 ♂ 175 ⚮ 1 rst, whirlpool, washer/dryer. **Rates:** $80–$90 S or D; from $125 ste. Children under 12 stay free. Min stay spec evnts. Pking: Outdoor, free. Maj CC.

≣≣≣ **Crowne Plaza Redondo Beach and Marina Hotel**, 300 N Harbor Dr, Redondo Beach, CA 90277; tel 310/318-8888 or toll free 800/368-9760; fax 310/376-1930. 2 mi S of Hermosa Beach. Redondo Beach exit off I-405. Oceanfront hotel has a large, newly renovated lobby with an aquarium for a centerpiece. So many amenities, facilities, and services that it feels like a resort. **Rooms:** 339 rms and stes. Exec-level rms avail. CI 3pm/CO noon. Express checkout avail. Nonsmoking rms avail. Large, with pastel color scheme and pine furnishings. Most have ocean views. **Amenities:** 🛢 ⚮ 🖥 🍷 A/C, cable TV w/movies, VCR, voice mail. All units w/minibars, all w/terraces. **Services:** 🍽

▤ 🚐 🖼 🛎 Car-rental desk, babysitting. Free shuttle to local malls. **Facilities:** 🛗 🍽 📶 🖥 ⚿ 1 rst (*see also* "Restaurants" below), 1 bar, games rm, spa, sauna, steam rm, whirlpool, beauty salon. Beauty parlor offers spa treatments. Free use of Gold's Gym next to hotel. **Rates:** $145 S; $160 D; from $275 ste. Extra person $10. Children under 19 stay free. Min stay spec evnts. Spec packages avail. Pking: Indoor, $8. Maj CC. Dive and spa packages available.

≣≣ **Palos Verdes Inn**, 1700 S Pacific Coast Hwy, Redondo Beach, CA 90277; tel 310/316-4211 or toll free 800/421-9241; fax 310/316-4863. Hawthorne Blvd exit off I-405; right on Pacific Coast Hwy. Located 3 blocks from the beach. Elegant lobby. **Rooms:** 110 rms and stes. CI 3pm/CO noon. Express checkout avail. Nonsmoking rms avail. Furnished in southwestern style with pine canopy beds. Rooms are small and bathrooms tiny, but closets are huge. **Amenities:** 🛁 ⚿ A/C, cable TV w/movies. Some units w/minibars, some w/terraces. Deluxe accommodations offer refrigerator, coffeemaker, and bar. Some balconies have ocean views. **Services:** ✗ ▤ 🚐 🖼 🛎 Car-rental desk, babysitting. Room service 7:30am–11pm from well-regarded restaurant. **Facilities:** 🛗 📶 ⚿ 1 rst (*see also* "Restaurants" below), 1 bar, whirlpool. Pool has half-acre sun deck with roof cover for bad weather. Free use of bicycles; passes to nearby health club. **Rates:** HS June–Sept $110–$120 S; $120–$130 D; from $225 ste. Children under 18 stay free. Lower rates off-season. Spec packages avail. Pking: Outdoor, free. Maj CC.

≣≣≣ **Portofino Hotel & Yacht Club**, 260 Portofino Way, Redondo Beach, CA 90277; tel 310/379-8481 or toll free 800/468-4292; fax 310/372-7329. 2 mi S of Hermosa Beach. Crenshaw Blvd exit off I-405 N; Inglewood Ave exit off I-405 S. Ideally located, nestled in a marina on a private peninsula between King Harbor and the Pacific Ocean. Classy, yet warm and very comfortable. Lobby has 3-story atrium and Mexican tile floors. **Rooms:** 165 rms and stes. CI 2pm/CO noon. Nonsmoking rms avail. Light and airy. Accommodations are whitewashed, with pine furnishings, desks, and couches in a southwestern style. All rooms have ocean or marina views from balconies. **Amenities:** 🛁 ⚿ 🎛 A/C, cable TV w/movies, refrig. All units w/minibars, all w/terraces, some w/Jacuzzis. **Services:** ✗ 🚐 🖼 🛎 Car-rental desk, babysitting. Free coffee, tea, and newspapers. **Facilities:** 🛗 ⛳ ⛵ 🍽 📶 ⚿ 2 rsts, 1 bar (w/entertainment), whirlpool. Free use of bikes. Rollerblades for rent. Sport fishing and boat charters available. **Rates:** HS July–Sept $133–$173 S or D; from $275 ste. Children under 12 stay free. Lower rates off-season. Spec packages avail. Pking: Outdoor, $5. Maj CC.

Restaurants 🍴

Chez Melange, in Palos Verdes Inn, 1700 S Pacific Coast Hwy, Redondo Beach; tel 310/540-1222. Rosecrans Ave exit off I-405. **Californian.** Upscale California bistro, complete with white tablecloths, a friendly staff, and a marble bar that features infused vodkas. The menu reflects American, Italian, French, and Oriental influences. There is roast turkey, bread pudding, mashed potatoes, and Cajun meatloaf as well as soy-seared albacore, crab-and-shrimp spring rolls with Thai sweet-and-sour sauce, pastas, and pizzas. Spa cuisine is also available, as are elegant breakfast dishes. **FYI:** Reservations recommended. **Open:** Breakfast Mon–Fri 7:30–11am; lunch Mon–Fri 11:30am–2:30pm; dinner daily 5–10pm; brunch Sat–Sun 7:30am–2:30pm. **Prices:** Main courses $10–$22. Maj CC. ⚿

Legends Restaurant & Sports Bar, in Crowne Plaza Redondo Beach and Marina Hotel, 300 N Harbor Dr, Redondo Beach; tel 310/374-7074. 2 mi S of Hermosa Beach. Redondo Beach exit off I-405. **American.** From the large mahogany bar with brass railings you can eye 30 TV monitors and original sports memorabilia while eating wings and both baby-back and pork ribs, as well as hamburgers, pastas, nachos, and salads, plus lighter fare such as turkey burgers and veggie burgers. All-you-can-eat Sunday brunch (7:30–11:30am). **FYI:** Reservations accepted. **Open:** Sun–Thurs 6pm–12:30am, Fri–Sat 6pm–1:30am. **Prices:** Main courses $6–$15. Maj CC. ⚿

REDWOOD CITY

Map page M-2, D2 (N of Palo Alto)

Hotel 🏨

≣≣≣≣ **Hotel Sofitel**, 223 Twin Dolphin Dr, Redwood City, CA 94065 (Redwood Shores); tel 415/508-7100 or toll free 800/SOFITEL; fax 415/598-0459. Marine World Pkwy exit off US 101; ½ mi to Twin Dolphin Dr; turn right; 1 mi on left. Impressive lobby with floral arrangements, fine furniture, good carpeting, marble floors, chandeliers. Faces lagoon. **Rooms:** 319 rms and stes. CI 3pm/CO noon. Express checkout avail. Nonsmoking rms avail. All rooms are concierge-level. Corner suites have great views. Thick towels, good lighting in bathrooms. **Amenities:** 🛁 ⚿ 🍷 A/C, cable TV w/movies, refrig, voice mail. All units w/minibars. **Services:** ✗ ▤ 🆅🅿 🚐 🖼 🛎 Twice-daily maid svce, car-rental desk, masseur, babysitting. Health spa provides European massages and facials, nail care. **Facilities:** 🛗 🏊 🍽 📶 ⚿ 2 rsts, 1 bar (w/entertainment), spa, sauna, beauty salon. Bake shop with French pastries. Attractive restaurants have views of lagoon and San Francisco Bay. **Rates:** $162–$185

S or D; from $198 ste. Extra person $20. Children under 12 stay free. Spec packages avail. Pking: Indoor/outdoor, free. Maj CC. Spa packages available.

Motel

≣ **Good Nite Inn**, 485 Veterans Blvd, Redwood City, CA 94063; tel 415/365-5500; fax 415/365-1119. W of US 101; N of Whipple Ave. Close to the highway on a busy street. **Rooms:** 126 rms. Exec-level rms avail. CI noon/CO noon. Nonsmoking rms avail. Rooms are clean with minimal charm. **Amenities:** 🛏 A/C, satel TV w/movies. All units w/terraces. **Services:** 🚗 🖼 🍴 🐾 **Facilities:** 🔟 🏊 Washer/dryer. **Rates:** $43–$53 S; $49–$59 D. Extra person $6. Children under 18 stay free. Spec packages avail. Pking: Outdoor, free. Maj CC.

Restaurant 🍴

Baccarat Room, in the Hotel Sofitel, 223 Twin Dolphin Dr, Redwood City; tel 415/598-9000. Ralston Ave exit off US 101; take Marine World Pkwy to Twin Dolphin Dr. **French.** Contemporary, elegant ambience, lagoon-front location. Baccarat crystal, etched-glass French doors. Rack of lamb, venison medallions, skinless chicken, pastas. **FYI:** Reservations recommended. Guitar/piano. **Open:** Lunch Mon–Fri 11:30am–2pm; dinner Mon–Thurs 6–10pm, Fri–Sat 6–10:30pm; brunch–Sun 10am–2pm. **Prices:** Main courses $18–$25; PF dinner $32. Maj CC. ♥ 🏔 🖼 ♿

RIVERSIDE

Map page M-3, D3

See also Redlands

Hotels 🛏

≣≣≣ **Holiday Inn Riverside**, 3400 Market St, Riverside, CA 92501; tel 909/784-8000 or toll free 800/HOLIDAY; fax 909/369-7127. A property with all the usual amenities for corporate travelers and families. Was undergoing renovation. **Rooms:** 286 rms and stes. CI 3pm/CO noon. Express checkout avail. Nonsmoking rms avail. **Amenities:** 🛏 🏊 🖥 A/C, cable TV w/movies. Some units w/terraces. **Services:** ✕ 🚗 🖼 🍴 🐾 Car-rental desk. **Facilities:** 🔟 🏋 🏊 ♿ 2 rsts, 1 bar, whirlpool. **Rates:** HS Oct–June $88–$145 S or D; from $236 ste. Extra person $10. Children under 18 stay free. Lower rates off-season. Spec packages avail. Pking: Indoor/outdoor, free. Maj CC.

≣≣≣≣ **Mission Inn**, 3649 7th St, Riverside, CA 92501; tel 909/784-0300 or toll free 800/843-7755; fax 909/683-1342.

This mission-style inn, a national historic monument, has hosted presidents, royalty, and countless celebrities. Unique blend of architectural styles and decorative details. **Rooms:** 236 rms and stes. CI 3pm/CO noon. Express checkout avail. Nonsmoking rms avail. Rooms are large but simply furnished. **Amenities:** 🛏 🏊 A/C, cable TV w/movies, refrig, voice mail. All units w/minibars, some w/terraces. **Services:** ✕ 🖼 🚗 🖼 🍴 Masseur. Guided tours are given of the property. **Facilities:** 🔟 🏋 🏊 🖥 ♿ 1 rst, 2 bars (1 w/entertainment), whirlpool. A museum, operated by the Mission Inn Foundation, displays a collection of artifacts from around the world. **Rates:** $85–$150 S or D; from $180 ste. Children under 18 stay free. Spec packages avail. Pking: Indoor, free. Maj CC.

Motels

≣≣ **Dynasty Suites**, 3735 Iowa Ave, Riverside, CA 92507; tel 909/369-8200; fax 909/369-2807. Management works hard to please the guests here; property opened in 1991. **Rooms:** 33 rms and stes. CI noon/CO noon. Nonsmoking rms avail. Large, well-appointed rooms. **Amenities:** 🛏 🏊 🍴 A/C, cable TV w/movies. Some units w/Jacuzzis. Microwave upon request. VCRs for rent come with a selection of tapes. Request a room that has a refrigerator. **Services:** 🍴 🐾 **Facilities:** 🔟 ♿ **Rates (CP):** $33 S; $35 D; from $80 ste. Extra person $5. Children under 5 stay free. Spec packages avail. Pking: Outdoor, free. Maj CC. First child stays free; each additional child costs $5.

≣≣ **Hampton Inn**, 1590 University Ave, Riverside, CA 92507; tel 909/683-6000 or toll free 800/HAMPTON; fax 909/782-8052. University exit off I-215; ½ mi W. Conveniently located close to downtown and the University of California at Riverside. **Rooms:** 116 rms. CI 3pm/CO 11am. Nonsmoking rms avail. **Amenities:** 🛏 🏊 A/C, cable TV w/movies. **Services:** 🍴 🐾 Car-rental desk. Generous continental breakfast served in lobby. **Facilities:** 🔟 🏋 ♿ **Rates (CP):** $52 S; $57 D. Extra person $5. Children under 18 stay free. Pking: Outdoor, free. Maj CC.

Restaurants 🍴

El Gato Gordo, 1360 University Ave, Riverside; tel 714/787-8212. University Ave exit off I-215. **Mexican.** Decorated with Mexican folk art and bright colors. Traditional plates of tacos, enchiladas, and burritos, as well as red snapper Veracruz, chili verde, and carnitas. **FYI:** Reservations accepted. Band. **Open:** Lunch Mon–Sat 11:30am–3pm; dinner Sun–Thurs 4–9pm, Fri–Sat 4–10pm; brunch Sun 10am–2pm. Closed some hols. **Prices:** Main courses $6.95–$10.65. Maj CC. ♿

Magnon Restaurant, 1630 Spruce St, Riverside; tel 909/781-8840. Spruce St exit off I-215. **Italian.** Soaring skylights, large windows, decorative pillars girded with grayish metallic tiles, open kitchen. Good pizzas, risotto, pasta, chicken, and fish. **FYI:** Reservations recommended. Combo. **Open:** Lunch Fri 11:30am–2:30pm; dinner Tues–Thurs 5:30–9:30pm, Fri–Sat 5:30–10:30pm. Closed some hols. **Prices:** Main courses $8.95–$17.95. Maj CC. 🖤 ♿

💲 ★ **Mario's Place**, 1725 Spruce St, Riverside; tel 909/684-7755. Spruce St exit off I-215. **Californian/French/Italian.** An exquisite blend of France and northern Italy, well worth a detour. The owners—the 3 Palagi brothers—clearly enjoy themselves. Food is beautifully prepared, and delicious. Grilled spiedini (skewer of lamb and radicchio with balsamic vinegar) is a house favorite. Pastas and risotto are also served. **FYI:** Reservations recommended. Band/combo/jazz/piano. Dress code. **Open:** Lunch Mon–Fri 11:30am–2:30pm; dinner Mon–Sat 5:30–10:30pm. Closed some hols. **Prices:** Main courses $11.50–$22. Maj CC. 🖤 ♿

★ **Riverside Brewing Company**, 3397 7th St, Riverside; tel 909/784-BREW. 7th St exit off Calif 91. **Pub.** A busy place popular for its handcrafted beers and ales. Food offerings include appetizers such as buffalo wings, beer-batter fried calamari, and deep-fried dill pickles. Soups, salads, sandwiches, pasta, and pizza are available, as is homemade root beer. **FYI:** Reservations accepted. Band. Children's menu. Beer and wine only. **Open:** Daily 11:30am–midnight. Closed Dec 25. **Prices:** Main courses $5.95–$13.95. Maj CC. 🖤 ♿

The Spanish Dining Room, in the Mission Inn, 3649 7th St, Riverside; tel 909/784-0300. 7th St exit off Calif 91. **Californian.** Coffered ceilings, glazed tiles, and a pretty patio suggest a very rich California mission. Chef Joe Cochran's outstanding creations include seared salmon with basil and spinach pesto, served with gold potatoes, fine green beans, and carrots; and penne with spicy sausage and opal basil. **FYI:** Reservations recommended. **Open:** Breakfast daily 6:30–10am; lunch Mon–Sat 11:30am–2pm; dinner daily 5:30–10pm; brunch Sun 10:30am–2pm. **Prices:** Main courses $11.50–$27. Maj CC. ♟ VP ♿

Refreshment Stop ☕

Java Books, in Mission Grove Shopping Plaza, 321 E Alessandro Ste 2A2, Riverside; tel 909/789-8684. **Coffeehouse.** A bookstore and coffee bar worth seeking out. A congenial atmosphere in which to read, chat, meditate, or just tune out. A wide variety of coffees is offered, along with the usual assortment of biscotti, and excellent coffee beans to take home. **Open:** Mon–Fri 6:30am–11pm, Sat 8am–11pm, Sun 8am–8pm. Closed some hols. Ltd CC. ♿

Attractions 🏛

Riverside Municipal Museum, 3720 Orange St; tel 909/782-5273. Exhibits depict local history, natural history, and Native American culture of the area. **Open:** Tues–Fri 9am–5pm, Sat–Sun 1–5pm. Closed some hols. Free.

UCR Botanical Garden, University Ave; tel 714/787-4650. Comprising nearly 40 scenic acres on the campus of the University of California, Riverside, the garden displays more than 3,000 plants from around the world. Highlights include the Cactus and Succulent Garden, Alder Canyon, Iris Garden, Rose Garden, Geodesic Lath Dome, and Subtropical Fruit Orchard. **Open:** Daily 8am–5pm. Closed some hols. Free.

March Field Museum, 16222 I-215; tel 909/655-2138. Housed in a new facility on the west side of the aerodrome at the intersection of I-215 and Van Buren Blvd, this museum depicts aviation history from 1918 to the present. Many refurbished historic aircraft are on display, including such famous models as the U-2 spy plane and the B-52 Stratofortress. Exhibits; gift shop. **Open:** Daily 10am–4pm. Closed some hols. Free.

ROHNERT PARK

Map page M-2, C1 (S of Santa Rosa)

Hotel 🏨

≡≡≡ **Red Lion Hotel**, 1 Red Lion Dr, Rohnert Park, CA 94928; tel 707/584-5466 or toll free 800/547-8010; fax 707/586-9726. Golf Course Dr exit off US 101; W on Commerce; right on Golf Course; left on Red Lion. Pleasant hotel on spacious grounds, close to a golf course and area attractions. Live evening piano music in the lobby. **Rooms:** 248 rms and stes. CI 3pm/CO noon. Nonsmoking rms avail. Large, clean rooms; the nicest overlook the pool. **Amenities:** 🛏 ♿ A/C, cable TV w/movies. Some units w/terraces. **Services:** ✕ ⊠ 🕭 Masseur, babysitting. **Facilities:** 🏋 🎳 🏊 ♿ 1 rst, 1 bar (w/entertainment), sauna, whirlpool. Espresso and wine bar in lobby; attractive pool area. **Rates:** HS June–Oct $105–$135 S; $120–$150 D; from $250 ste. Extra person $15. Children under 18 stay free. Lower rates off-season. Higher rates for spec evnts/hols. Spec packages avail. Pking: Outdoor, free. Maj CC. Special weekend packages.

RUTHERFORD

Map page M-2, C2 (N of Napa)

Hotel 🛏

▤▤▤▤ **Auberge du Soleil**, 180 Rutherford Hill Rd, Rutherford, CA 94573; tel 707/963-1211 or toll free 800/348-5406; fax 707/963-8764. Silverado Trail to Rutherford Hill Rd; go east about 1 mi. Ultra-chic, wine-country retreat amid olive groves in the Napa Valley foothills. Architecture recalls southern France, with sand-colored stucco walls and steep shingled roofs. Exquisite grounds with pergolas and fountains. **Rooms:** 2 rms; 48 ctges/villas. CI 3pm/CO noon. Nonsmoking rms avail. Countrified elegance, with tiled floors and very simple furnishings, accented by bright (maybe too bright) fuchsia and yellow fabrics. Top-of-the-line 1-bedroom suites are vast, with vaulted ceilings and a skylight over the tub. **Amenities:** 🔟 ⚿ 🖭 ⌖ A/C, cable TV w/movies, refrig, VCR, in-rm safe, shoe polisher, bathrobes. All units w/minibars, all w/terraces, some w/fireplaces, some w/Jacuzzis. Lots of special features—including slippers, a supply of candles, and bath salts placed by the tub. Spare roll of toilet paper even comes gift-wrapped. **Services:** 🍽 ⓋⓅ 🚗 🖾 Twice-daily maid svce, car-rental desk, masseur. Masseur can come to your room. **Facilities:** 🕃 🖾 ⬥3 🍴 🏊 ⅓ 1 rst (see also "Restaurants" below), 1 bar, sauna, steam rm, whirlpool, beauty salon. Edged by manicured oleander bushes, the pool deck faces the valley and the western mountains. Small workout room looks toward the hills. A ½-mile nature trail passes 50 sculptures. **Rates:** HS Aug–Nov $250–$275 S or D; from $325 ctge/villa. Extra person $40. Min stay wknds and spec evnts. Lower rates off-season. Spec packages avail. Pking: Outdoor, free. Maj CC.

Inn

▤▤▤ **Rancho Caymus**, 1140 Rutherford Rd, PO Box 78, Rutherford, CA 94573; tel 707/963-1777 or toll free 800/845-1777; fax 707/963-5387. Calif 128 exit off Calif 29. Distinctive hacienda-style property with outstanding furnishings. Spanish-style courtyard has a fountain and lovely gardens. **Rooms:** 26 stes. CI 3pm/CO noon. Rooms are individually decorated with handcrafted Latin American furniture and fabrics. Some have kitchenettes. Of special note are hand-hewn beams and doors, and hand-thrown stoneware basins. **Amenities:** 🔟 🖭 ⌖ A/C, TV, refrig. All units w/minibars, all w/terraces, some w/fireplaces, some w/Jacuzzis. Wet bar in all rooms. **Services:** Complimentary breakfast of homemade breads, granola, fresh fruit. **Facilities:** 🖾 ⅓ Outdoor terace has a fireplace; so does the breakfast room. **Rates:** HS Apr–Oct from $115 ste. Extra

person $15. Children under 13 stay free. Min stay wknds. Lower rates off-season. Spec packages avail. Pking: Outdoor, free. Ltd CC.

Restaurant 🍴

Auberge du Soleil, 180 Rutherford Hill Rd, Rutherford; tel 707/963-1211. Silverado Trail to Rutherford Hill Rd; E 1 mi. **Californian/French.** You'll savor the view from the deck at this elegant country French retreat above some of Napa Valley's most prized vineyards. The outdoor dining area has rough-hewn planking and sturdy wooden chairs. The food is competently prepared but overpriced; better to skip the restaurant and eat at the bar, which has the same vistas and a satisfactory menu at about half the price. **FYI:** Reservations recommended. **Open:** HS July–Aug breakfast daily 7–11am; dinner Mon–Fri 6–9:30pm, Sat–Sun 5:30–9:30pm. Reduced hours off-season. **Prices:** Main courses $25.50–$30. Maj CC. ♥ 🍷 🔲 🖾 ⓋⓅ ⅓

SACRAMENTO

Map page M-2, C2

See also Folsom, Rancho Cordova

Hotels 🛏

▤▤▤ **Beverly Garland Hotel**, 1780 Tribute Rd, Sacramento, CA 95815; tel 916/929-7900 or toll free 800/972-3976; fax 916/921-9147. Cal Expo Blvd exit off Business I-80. Location convenient to downtown and shopping district. Attractive lobby with lots of plants and a fireplace. **Rooms:** 205 rms and stes. CI 3pm/CO noon. Nonsmoking rms avail. New furnishings in some rooms. **Amenities:** 🔟 ⚿ A/C, cable TV w/movies. Some units w/minibars, all w/terraces. **Services:** ✗ 🚗 🖾 ⤵ ⬥ Babysitting. **Facilities:** 🕃 🖾 ⅓ 1 rst, 1 bar, whirlpool, washer/dryer. Access to nearby fitness facilities at Sacramento Court Club. **Rates:** $79–$99 S; $89–$109 D; from $95 ste. Children under 18 stay free. Spec packages avail. Pking: Outdoor, free. Maj CC.

▤▤ **Canterbury Inn**, 1900 Canterbury Inn Rd, Sacramento, CA 95815 (Woodlake); tel 916/927-0927 or toll free 800/932-3492; fax 916/641-8594. US 50 exit off Calif 160; left on Canterbury Rd. This older property is adequate for business stays. **Rooms:** 150 rms and stes. CI 4pm/CO noon. Nonsmoking rms avail. Basic. Some have courtyard view and a lot of light. **Amenities:** 🔟 ⚿ 🖭 ⌖ A/C, cable TV w/movies. Coffee in all rooms. **Services:** 🚗 🖾 ⤵ ⬥ 24-hour security. **Facilities:** 🕃 🖾 ⅓ 1 rst, 1 bar, whirlpool. Extra-large pool. Access to health club at nearby Radisson. **Rates (CP):** $55 S; $65 D; from $130 ste. Extra person $10. Children under 12 stay free. Min stay spec evnts. Spec packages avail. Pking: Outdoor, free. Maj CC.

≣≣≣ **Clarion Hotel Sacramento**, 700 16th St, Sacramento, CA 95814; tel 916/444-8000 or toll free 800/443-0880; fax 916/442-8129. 15th St exit off US 50/Business I-80. Shade trees provide a peaceful aura to this full-scale downtown hotel. Lots of ground-floor windows; views of gardens and pool area brighten the lobby and restaurant. **Rooms:** 239 rms and stes. Exec-level rms avail. CI 2pm/CO noon. Nonsmoking rms avail. Nicely appointed rooms, but carpet is slightly worn. **Amenities:** 🛏 🌐 🖪 A/C, satel TV w/movies. Some units w/terraces. **Services:** ✕ 🚗 🖼 🗘 🐾 Car-rental desk. Guests in executive-level rooms receive drink coupons and turndown service. **Facilities:** 🔓 ▥ 🛠 1 rst, 1 bar. All guests have access to Midtown Athletic Club. **Rates:** $79–$99 S; $89–$109 D; from $185 ste. Extra person $15. Children under 17 stay free. Min stay spec evnts. Spec packages avail. Pking: Outdoor, free. Maj CC.

≣≣≣ **Courtyard by Marriott**, 2101 River Plaza Dr, Sacramento, CA 95833 (South Natomas); tel 916/922-1120 or toll free 800/321-2211; fax 916/922-1872. Garden Hwy exit off I-5; right on Garden Hwy; right on Gateway Oaks; right on River Plaza Dr. The contemporary lobby is inviting, the cafe and lounge are rimmed with windows facing the garden. This spot attracts corporate travelers from nearby business parks and the airport. **Rooms:** 151 rms and stes. CI 3pm/CO 1pm. Express checkout avail. Nonsmoking rms avail. **Amenities:** 🛏 🌐 🖪 A/C, satel TV w/movies. Some units w/terraces. Extra-long cord on phones. Refrigerators available upon request. **Services:** ✕ 🚗 🖼 🗘 Babysitting. **Facilities:** 🔓 🛠 🔲 🛠 1 rst, 1 bar, whirlpool, washer/dryer. **Rates:** $85 S; $95 D; from $101 ste. Extra person $10. Children under 18 stay free. Min stay spec evnts. Higher rates for spec evnts/hols. Spec packages avail. Pking: Outdoor, free. Maj CC. Discount for repeat customers.

≣≣≣ **Delta King Hotel**, 1000 Front St, Sacramento, CA 95814; tel 916/444-5464 or toll free 800/825-5464; fax 916/444-5314. J St exit off I-5; follow signs to Old Sacramento. The region's most unusual property is a restored stern-wheel riverboat that traveled between San Francisco and Sacramento from 1927 and 1940. Today, it's docked on the bank of the Sacramento River at the edge of Old Town. **Rooms:** 44 rms and stes. CI 4pm/CO 11am. Small and well appointed. In keeping with the historic riverboat theme, the rooms have brass beds, pedestal sinks, and wood trim; some have clawfoot tubs. **Amenities:** 🛏 A/C, cable TV w/movies. **Services:** ✕ 🆅🅿 🖼 🗘 Personalized service, with evening turndown and valet parking. Expanded continental breakfast served. **Facilities:** 🔲 🛠 1 rst, 2 bars (w/entertainment). The Pilothouse Restaurant was voted Sacra-

mento's "best romantic dinner" and "best brunch" by readers of local newspapers. A theater is located on one of the lower decks. **Rates (CP):** $85–$125 S; $95–$135 D; from $200 ste. Extra person $10. Higher rates for spec evnts/hols. Spec packages avail. Pking: Outdoor, $6. Maj CC. Many weekend packages. Mid-week discount.

≣≣≣ **Governor's Inn**, 210 Richards Blvd, Sacramento, CA 95814 (Downtown); tel 916/448-7224 or toll free 800/999-6689; fax 916/448-7382. Richards Blvd exit off I-5. This small, new hotel is comfortable, and convenient to the downtown business district and capitol building. **Rooms:** 134 rms and stes. CI 3pm/CO 11am. Nonsmoking rms avail. Fairly large and well-appointed. **Amenities:** 🛏 🌐 🖪 A/C, cable TV w/movies. Some units w/terraces. **Services:** 🚗 🖼 🗘 Afternoon refreshments are served. **Facilities:** 🔓 🛠 🔲 🛠 Whirlpool. **Rates (CP):** $64–$84 S; $74–$94 D; from $114 ste. Extra person $10. Children under 12 stay free. Higher rates for spec evnts/hols. Pking: Outdoor, free. Maj CC.

≣≣≣ **Holiday Inn–Capitol Plaza**, 300 J St, Sacramento, CA 95814 (Downtown); tel 916/446-0100 or toll free 800/HOLIDAY. J St exit off I-5. A city property with the usual business amenities, adjacent to historic park and new shopping plaza. Renovations of public areas and guest corridors to be completed soon. **Rooms:** 368 rms and stes. Exec-level rms avail. CI 1pm/CO noon. Express checkout avail. Nonsmoking rms avail. **Amenities:** 🛏 🌐 A/C, cable TV w/movies. **Services:** ✕ 🔑 🖼 🗘 Car-rental desk, children's program. **Facilities:** 🔓 ▥ 🛠 2 rsts, 2 bars (1 w/entertainment), sauna. New outdoor cafe on plaza. Complimentary access to fitness club 1 block away. **Rates:** $88–$97 S; $98–$107 D; from $150 ste. Extra person $10. Children under 18 stay free. Min stay spec evnts. Higher rates for spec evnts/hols. Spec packages avail. Pking: Outdoor, free. Maj CC.

≣ **Host Airport Hotel**, 6945 Airport Blvd, Sacramento, CA 95837 (Metropolitan Airport); tel 916/922-8071 or toll free 800/228-9290; fax 916/929-8636. 10 mi N of Sacramento. Airport Blvd exit off I-5. Convenient to airport. Older property, surrounded by a parking lot, is showing its age. Renovation will upgrade lobby, restrooms, doors, locks, and fitness center. **Rooms:** 90 rms. CI 3pm/CO 1pm. Express checkout avail. Nonsmoking rms avail. **Amenities:** 🛏 🌐 A/C, cable TV, voice mail. **Services:** ✕ 🗘 **Facilities:** 🔓 🔲 🛠 Whirlpool. **Rates:** $72–$87 S; $97 D. Extra person $10. Children under 12 stay free. Spec packages avail. Pking: Outdoor, $5. Maj CC.

≣≣≣ **Howard Johnson Hotel**, 3343 Bradshaw Rd, Sacramento, CA 95827; tel 916/366-1266 or toll free 800/654-2000; fax 916/366-1266. Bradshaw Rd exit off US 50. Highway property with reasonable rates. **Rooms:** 124 rms and stes. Exec-level rms avail. CI 2pm/CO noon. Nonsmoking rms avail. Continental suite is large, with adjoining room. **Amenities:** 🔒 🐾 ⚏ A/C, cable TV w/movies. All units w/terraces. Wet bar in Continental suite. **Services:** ✗ 🖼 ⏚ ⬧ Executive floor has extras like newspaper and coffee. **Facilities:** 🛗 🕴 🔲 ⅄ 1 rst, 1 bar, whirlpool. Extra-large indoor-outdoor pool is open year-round. **Rates:** HS May–Sept $65–$70 S; $70–$75 D; from $120 ste. Extra person $5. Children under 18 stay free. Lower rates off-season. Spec packages avail. Pking: Outdoor, free. Maj CC.

≣≣≣≣ **Hyatt Regency Sacramento**, 1209 L St, Sacramento, CA 95814 (Downtown); tel 916/443-1234 or toll free 800/233-1234; fax 916/321-6699. 15th St exit off US 50/Business I-80. Left on 16th St; left on L St. Full-service urban hotel overlooking Capitol Park offers luxury amenities and extensive conference facilities in upscale surroundings. **Rooms:** 500 rms and stes. Exec-level rms avail. CI 3pm/CO noon. Express checkout avail. Nonsmoking rms avail. Counter space minimal in bathrooms. **Amenities:** 🔒 🐾 ⚏ A/C, cable TV w/movies, refrig, shoe polisher. All units w/minibars, some w/terraces, some w/Jacuzzis. **Services:** ✗ 🖙 🆅🅿 🚗 🖼 ⏚ Car-rental desk, babysitting. Poolside food and drink service; turn-down and twice-daily maid service available to many rooms. **Facilities:** 🛗 🕴 2.5K 🔲 ⅄ 2 rsts, 3 bars (2 w/entertainment), whirlpool. Pool heated year-round. **Rates:** $150 S; $175 D; from $195 ste. Extra person $25. Children under 18 stay free. Min stay spec evnts. Higher rates for spec evnts/hols. Spec packages avail. Pking: Indoor, $6. Maj CC.

≣≣≣ **Marriott Residence Suites**, 2410 W El Camino Ave, Sacramento, CA 95833 (South Natomas); tel 916/649-1300 or toll free 800/331-3131; fax 916/649-1395. W El Camino Ave exit off I-80. A home-away-from-home for families and business travelers. **Rooms:** 126 stes. CI 3pm/CO noon. Nonsmoking rms avail. 1- and 2-bedroom suites with full kitchen, 2 baths, and doors between living and sleeping areas. Some "green" offer filtered air and water and biodegradable products. **Amenities:** 🔒 🐾 ⚏ A/C, cable TV, refrig, VCR, voice mail. Some units w/fireplaces. **Services:** 🚗 🖼 ⏚ ⬧ Babysitting. Complimentary continental breakfast daily; hospitality hour Monday–Friday. Complimentary grocery shopping service and local area shuttle. **Facilities:** 🛗 🚲 🕴 40 ⅄ Whirlpool, washer/dryer. Sports court, gas grills. **Rates (CP):** From $99 ste. Children under 18 stay free. Spec packages avail. Pking: Outdoor, free. Maj CC. Reduced rates for stays of 7 nights or more.

≣≣≣≣ **Radisson Hotel Sacramento**, 500 Leisure Lane, Sacramento, CA 95815 (Woodlake); tel 916/922-2020 or toll free 800/333-3333; fax 916/649-9463. 15th St exit off US 80/US 50; L on Calif 160; 3½ mi N to Canterbury-Leisure exit. In a parklike setting adjacent to American River Pkwy, this hotel has 2 fountains, spacious grounds, and an amphitheater for concerts. **Rooms:** 314 rms and stes. Exec-level rms avail. CI 4pm/CO noon. Express checkout avail. Nonsmoking rms avail. Rooms recently renovated with modern furnishings. One large room overlooks the pool and lake. Executive suites have conference table in room. **Amenities:** 🔒 🐾 ⚏ A/C, cable TV w/movies, shoe polisher. Some units w/minibars, some w/terraces. **Services:** 🍽 🆅🅿 🚗 🖼 ⏚ ⬧ Car-rental desk, babysitting. Complimentary shuttle service to area attractions. **Facilities:** 🛗 🚲 🏋 🕴 5K 🔲 ⅄ 2 rsts, 1 bar (w/entertainment), games rm, whirlpool. Hiking trail. Outdoor pavilion for weddings and parties. Outdoor seating at bar. **Rates:** HS Mar–June/Aug–Nov $55–$130 S or D; from $130 ste. Extra person $10. Children under 18 stay free. Lower rates off-season. Spec packages avail. Pking: Outdoor, free. Maj CC.

≣≣≣ **Red Lion Hotel**, 2001 Point West Way, Sacramento, CA 95815 (Point West); tel 916/929-8855 or toll free 800/547-8010; fax 916/924-0719. Arden Way exit off Business I-80; right on Point West Way. Large, full-service hotel in busy suburban area adjacent to shopping and entertainment. Undergoing complete renovation, including room sprinklers and ADA-recommended upgrades for guests with disabilities. **Rooms:** 448 rms and stes. CI 3pm/CO noon. Express checkout avail. Nonsmoking rms avail. **Amenities:** 🔒 🐾 ⚏ A/C, cable TV w/movies, shoe polisher. Some units w/terraces, some w/Jacuzzis. **Services:** ✗ 🖙 🚗 🖼 ⏚ ⬧ Twice-daily maid svce, babysitting. **Facilities:** 🛗 🕴 1.4K ⅄ 2 rsts, 1 bar (w/entertainment), games rm, whirlpool, washer/dryer. Coffee shop with espresso-to-go bar. **Rates:** $104–$134 S; $119–$165 D; from $395 ste. Extra person $10. Children under 18 stay free. Spec packages avail. Pking: Outdoor, free. Maj CC.

≣≣≣ **Red Lion's Sacramento Inn**, 1401 Arden Way, Sacramento, CA 95815; tel 916/922-8041 or toll free 800/RED LION; fax 916/922-0386. Arden Way exit off Business I-80. All-purpose convention motel in a noisy but convenient location, with enough space that guests don't feel crowded. **Rooms:** 376 rms and stes. Exec-level rms avail. CI 3pm/CO 1pm. Express checkout avail. Nonsmoking rms avail. Adequate rooms, with older furnishings in good condition. Nice padded benches for luggage. **Amenities:** 🔒 🐾 A/C, satel TV w/movies, shoe polisher. Some units w/terraces, some w/Jacuzzis. **Services:** ✗ 🖙 🚗 🖼 ⏚ ⬧ Poolside food and beverage service. **Facilities:** 🛗 🕴 1.2K 🔲 ⅄ 1 rst, 1 bar (w/entertainment), washer/dryer. Putting green, extensive patio/lawn area. **Rates:** $89–$109 S; $104–$124 D; from $150 ste. Extra person $15. Children under 16 stay free. Min stay spec evnts. Spec packages avail. Pking: Outdoor, free. Maj CC.

≣≣≣ **Residence Inn by Marriott**, 1530 Howe Ave, Sacramento, CA 95825 (Point West); tel 916/920-9111 or toll free 800/333-3131; fax 916/921-5664. Howe Ave exit off US 50. A newer facility, and a good option for do-it-yourself travelers who prefers a cozy fireplace to a hotel bar. **Rooms:** 176 stes. CI 3pm/CO noon. Nonsmoking rms avail. Comfortable, large apartments. **Amenities:** 🛁 🅰 🖥 A/C, cable TV w/movies, refrig. Some units w/terraces, some w/fireplaces. **Services:** 🚐 ⬛ ⤶ **Facilities:** 🔧 🛢 🔥 Whirlpool, washer/dryer. **Rates (CP):** From $99 ste. Extra person $10. Children under 18 stay free. Spec packages avail. Pking: Outdoor, free. Maj CC. Discount for long stays.

≣≣≣ **Sacramento Hilton Inn**, 2200 Harvard St, Sacramento, CA 95815; tel 916/922-4700 or toll free 800/344-4321; fax 916/922-8418. Arden Way exit off Business I-80; west on Arden; right at Harvard. Urban hotel with business amenities in a suburban location. Public areas have festive atmosphere. **Rooms:** 330 rms and stes. Exec-level rms avail. CI 3pm/CO noon. Express checkout avail. Nonsmoking rms avail. **Amenities:** 🛁 🅰 A/C, cable TV w/movies, voice mail. Some units w/terraces, 1 w/fireplace, some w/Jacuzzis. Executive rooms on 11th and 12th floors include robes, irons, newspapers. **Services:** ✗ 🚐 ⬛ ⤶ 🖐 Car-rental desk, children's program, babysitting. Shuttle service to downtown attractions and nearby shopping. **Facilities:** 🔧 🏓 🆔 🔥 1 rst, 2 bars (w/entertainment), lifeguard, sauna, whirlpool. Sand volleyball court. Vacation Station program for kids offers board and video games, coloring books. **Rates:** $99–$129 S; $109–$139 D; from $250 ste. Extra person $15. Children under 18 stay free. Spec packages avail. Pking: Outdoor, free. Maj CC.

Motels

≣≣ **Best Western Ponderosa Inn**, 1100 H St, Sacramento, CA 95814 (Downtown); tel 916/441-1314 or toll free 800/528-1234; fax 916/441-5961. J St exit off I-5; left on 11th St. Downtown property convenient to the capitol, with a courtyard pool and a small, neatly furnished lobby. **Rooms:** 98 rms and stes. CI 3pm/CO noon. Nonsmoking rms avail. **Amenities:** 🛁 🅰 🍽 A/C, cable TV, voice mail. Some units w/terraces. VCR available for rent. **Services:** ✗ ⬛ ⤶ Babysitting. **Facilities:** 🔧 🔢 🔥 1 rst, 1 bar (w/entertainment). **Rates (CP):** $80–$100 S or D; from $130 ste. Extra person $8. Children under 12 stay free. Higher rates for spec evnts/hols. Spec packages avail. Pking: Outdoor. Maj CC.

SACRAMENTO METROPOLITAN AIRPORT

© The H.M. Gousha Co.   10-ZM-288-M-A

≣ **Coral Reef Lodge**, 2700 Fulton Ave, Sacramento, CA 95821; tel 916/483-6461 or toll free 800/995-6460; fax 916/488-2372. El Camino exit off Business I-80; left on Fulton Ave. Older property in a suburban setting, near shopping and business areas of North Sacramento. **Rooms:** 101 rms and stes. CI 3pm/CO 11am. Nonsmoking rms avail. Very basic rooms, with sliding-glass doors that may be a security risk. **Amenities:** 🛁 🖥 A/C, cable TV w/movies. Some units w/terraces. VCRs available at front desk. **Services:** ⤶ **Facilities:** 🔧 🔢 Washer/dryer. **Rates:** $40 S; $46 D; from $55 ste. Extra person $5. Children under 12 stay free. Spec packages avail. Pking: Outdoor, free. Maj CC.

≣≣ **Days Inn Discovery Park**, 350 Bercut Dr, Sacramento, CA 95814; tel 916/442-6971 or toll free 800/952-5516; fax 916/444-2809. Richards Blvd exit off I-5. Centrally located, but noisy. New management has hastened upgrade. **Rooms:** 100 rms and stes. Exec-level rms avail. CI 2pm/CO 11am. Nonsmoking rms avail. Some poolside rooms have newer furnishings and extra seating. **Amenities:** 🛁 🅰 🖥 A/C, cable TV w/movies. Some units w/terraces. Some poolside rooms have refrigerators and wet bars. New motel-wide phone system to include fax and modem hookups. **Services:** 🚐 ⬛ ⤶ 🖐 Computer and fax services for Business Club members. **Facilities:** 🔧 🔢 🔥

Whirlpool. Access to nearby fitness center. **Rates (CP):** $58–$68 S; $63–$78 D; from $75 ste. Extra person $5. Children under 18 stay free. Higher rates for spec evnts/hols. Spec packages avail. Pking: Outdoor, free. Maj CC. Special rates to Business Club members.

≣≣ **La Quinta Motor Inn–Sacramento North**, 4604 Madison Ave, Sacramento, CA 95841; tel 916/348-0900 or toll free 800/531-5900; fax 916/331-7160. Madison Ave exit off I-80. Modern furnishings, new exterior. Highway location. Self-serve approach keeps prices reasonable. **Rooms:** 127 rms and stes. CI open/CO noon. Express checkout avail. Nonsmoking rms avail. Executive king rooms have recliners. Rooms for guests with disabilities have parking at door and adjoining rooms for companions. **Amenities:** 🛋 🔥 A/C, satel TV w/movies. Coffeemaker and refrigerator in executive king rooms. Refrigerators and microwaves may be rented in other rooms. **Services:** 🖼 🛎 ✆ Car-rental desk. Coffee 24 hours. **Facilities:** 🏋 🟫 🔥 Washer/dryer. Use of nearby gym. **Rates (CP):** $45–$52 S; $50–$57 D; from $85 ste. Extra person $5. Children under 18 stay free. Higher rates for spec evnts/hols. Spec packages avail. Pking: Outdoor, free. Maj CC.

≣ **The Sacramento Vagabond Inn**, 909 Third St, Sacramento, CA 95814 (Old Sacramento); tel 916/446-1481 or toll free 800/522-1555. J St exit off I-5. Budget property located downtown, adjacent to historic park and the Chinese Cultural Center. **Rooms:** 107 rms. CI 3pm/CO noon. Express checkout avail. Nonsmoking rms avail. Rooms are pretty standard. Business club members get the best accommodations, equipped with remote-control TV, coffeemaker, and computer; available to nonmembers for an additional $5. **Amenities:** 🛋 🔥 🖥 A/C, cable TV w/movies, voice mail. Refrigerators available for $5 per day. **Services:** 🛎 🖼 ✆ 🛎 Shuttle service to local sights and train station. 24-hour coffee service. **Facilities:** 🏋 🟫 Restaurant next door. **Rates (CP):** HS Mar 31–Oct $60–$70 S; $65–$75 D. Extra person $5. Children under 18 stay free. Min stay spec evnts. Lower rates off-season. Higher rates for spec evnts/hols. Spec packages avail. Pking: Outdoor, free. Maj CC. Discounts available for frequent guests.

Inn

≣≣≣≣ **Sterling Hotel**, 1300 H St, Sacramento, CA 95814 (Downtown); tel 916/448-1300 or toll free 800/365-7660; fax 916/448-8066. J St exit off I-5; left at 13th St. An 1894 landmark converted into a personable inn, with Victorian touches. The overall feel here is businesslike. Popular with politicians visiting the nearby state capitol. **Rooms:** 12 rms. CI 3pm/CO 11am. No smoking. All rooms are different. Smaller rooms are nicer than larger ones, which look underfurnished. Furnishings might in-

clude 4-poster or sleigh beds, or Empire-design chairs. Bathrooms are tiled in marble. **Amenities:** 🛋 🔥 A/C, cable TV w/movies. 1 unit w/terrace, all w/Jacuzzis. **Services:** ✕ 🛎 🖼 ✆ Masseur. **Facilities:** 🟦 🖥 🔥 1 rst (see also "Restaurants" below), 1 bar. The lounge often functions as a meeting room, so guests can't use the space for relaxation. The glass conservatory is popular for weddings and special events. For $4, guests can use the health club 1 block away. **Rates:** $95–$225 S or D. Children under 18 stay free. Spec packages avail. Pking: Indoor, free. Ltd CC.

Restaurants 🍽

♣ **Biba**, 2801 Capitol Ave, Sacramento (Midtown); tel 916/455-BIBA. At 28th St. **Italian.** Located in an 1853 tavern building. Stylish and modern, with extensive use of glass, mirrors, and wood, as well as black lacquer chairs, white tablecloths, and fresh flowers on each table. Grilled lamb chops, breast of duck, homemade gnocchi, variety of pastas. Extensive wine list. **FYI:** Reservations recommended. Piano. **Open:** Lunch Mon–Fri 11:30am–2:30pm; dinner Mon–Thurs 5:30–9:30pm, Fri–Sat 5:30–10:30pm. Closed some hols. **Prices:** Main courses $17.75–$20. Maj CC. ❤ 🔥

California Fat's, in Old Sacramento State Historic Park, 1015 Front St, Sacramento; tel 916/441-7966. J St exit off I-5. **Eclectic.** The decor includes an in-house waterfall, granite-topped tables, and a neon Cadillac wall sculpture. The menu highlights wood-oven pizzas, clams, ahi tuna, ribs, chicken chow mein, lobster, and pasta. **FYI:** Reservations recommended. **Open:** Mon–Thurs 11am–11pm, Fri–Sat 11am–midnight, Sun 10:30am–10pm. Closed Dec 25. **Prices:** Main courses $7.75–$19.95. Maj CC. 🔟 ❤ 🔥

Capitol Grill, 2730 N St, Sacramento (Midtown); tel 916/736-0744. N St exit off Business I-80. **Californian/International.** The look is rustic with brick, brass, wood beams, and 1950s-era political memorabilia. Specialties are duck and shiitake potstickers for starters; entrees include lamb chops and many fresh fish dishes. Most sauces are freshly made. **FYI:** Reservations recommended. **Open:** Mon–Fri 11am–11pm, Sat 5–11pm, Sun 5–10pm. Closed some hols. **Prices:** Main courses $7.25–$18.50. Maj CC. VP 🔥

Chanterelle, in the Sterling Hotel, 1300 H St, Sacramento (Downtown); tel 916/442-0451. J St exit off I-5. Restaurant entrance is at 13th St. **Californian.** An elegant restaurant with classical music and some separate rooms for intimate dining. The cuisine is Californian with a twist: potato strudel with sun-dried tomatoes, stuffed pork chops served with lingonberry, and a changing lineup of game and fish specials. Small lounge upstairs.

FYI: Reservations recommended. **Open:** Breakfast Mon–Fri 7–9:30am; lunch Mon–Fri 11:30am–2pm; dinner daily 5:30–8:30pm; brunch Sun 8:30am–2pm. Closed some hols. **Prices:** Main courses $12.50–$19.50. Maj CC. ♥ 🍴 ♿

Chinois East/West, in University Plaza, 2232 Fair Oaks Blvd, Sacramento; tel 916/648-1961. Howe Ave exit off US 50. **Chinese.** Stylish, upscale ambience; art deco/Asian decor. Western ingredients are combined with Asian cooking techniques to produce items like "train wreck"—beef-and-tomato chow mein with pan-fried noodles; whole catfish with black bean sauce; sizzling lemongrass filet mignon; and Chinese duck pasta primavera. Dim sum selections include Peking ravioli and fried wonton puffs. **FYI:** Reservations accepted. **Open:** Mon–Sat 11am–10pm, Sun 4:30–9pm. Closed Dec 25. **Prices:** Main courses $6.99–$16.95. Maj CC. 🍽 ♿

Coral Reef, 2795 Fulton Ave, Sacramento; tel 916/483-5551. Marconi Ave on Fulton Ave exit off Business I-80. **American/Chinese.** The Pacific-islands decor—bamboo, ship's lanterns, and fish tanks—is set amid expanses of vinyl and Formica. This is a traditional Cantonese restaurant, although the menu also lists barbecued spare ribs, prime rib, and fresh lobster. **FYI:** Reservations recommended. Children's menu. Dress code. **Open:** Tues–Thurs 5–10pm, Fri–Sun 4–11pm. Closed some hols. **Prices:** Main courses $9.95–$17.95. Maj CC. 📧 ♿

David Berkley, in Pavilions Shopping Center, 515 Pavilions Lane, Sacramento; tel 916/929-4422. Howe Ave exit off US 50. **Californian/Deli.** Bustling gourmet deli/market/wine shop with upscale atmosphere, and choice of ethnic styles. Call ahead with your order, either to eat here or to go. Entrees not on the daily menu may be ordered with 3 days' notice. Features salads, soups, hot and cold sandwiches, pasta casseroles, lasagna béchamel or bolognese, osso buco, creamy chicken enchiladas, burritos, moussaka, seafood paella, corned beef hash, and more. **FYI:** Reservations not accepted. Beer and wine only. **Open:** Mon–Fri 10am–6:30pm, Sat 10am–6pm, Sun 11am–5pm. Closed some hols. **Prices:** Lunch main courses $3.99–$5.99. Ltd CC. 🍽 VP

♣ **The Firehouse**, in Old Sacramento State Historic Park, 1112 2nd St, Sacramento; tel 916/442-4772. J St exit off I-5; follow signs to Old Sacramento; enter at 2nd St or alley between 2nd and Front Sts. **Californian/Continental.** This 19th-century firehouse is a local tradition that's popular with tourists in Old Sacramento as well as politicians. The brass fire pole still exists, now in the bar. Scallop ravioli, swordfish wasabi, and roast duck are just a few of the dishes. Desserts include berries with Grand Marnier, and bourbon chocolate almond pie. **FYI:** Reservations

recommended. **Open:** Lunch Mon–Fri 11:30am–2:15pm; dinner Mon–Sat 5:30–10pm. Closed some hols. **Prices:** Main courses $15.50–$29. Maj CC. ♥ 🍴 🍽 ♿

⑤ **First Immigrant Café & Catering**, in Sacramento Antiques Mall, 855 57th St, Sacramento (East Sacramento); tel 916/452-3896. Between J and H Sts. **Californian.** Well regarded by locals, this cafeteria-style restaurant offers off-the-beaten-path dining in a homey atmosphere. Features sandwiches, such as smoked turkey with green chili mayonnaise, Caribbean pita with black beans; plus salads like tarragon chicken, Caribbean black bean. Minestrone daily, plus a second soup that is always fat free. Catering for parties. **FYI:** Reservations accepted. No liquor license. **Open:** Lunch Tues–Fri 11am–2pm. Closed some hols; Dec 25–Jan 1. **Prices:** Lunch main courses $3.95–$6.95. Ltd CC. 🍽 ♿

Fox and Goose Public House, 1001 R St, Sacramento (Downtown); tel 916/443-8825. 5th St exit off I-80. **British/Pub.** Breakfast and lunch served in a friendly, rustic British-style pub. Lunch menu: British pastries, rarebit, cheese board, salads, sandwiches, lemon curd tart. Breakfast: omelettes, waffles, sausage, kippers. Also vegetarian fare. **FYI:** Reservations not accepted. Blues/jazz. Beer and wine only. **Open:** Mon–Fri 7am–12:30am, Sat 9am–2am, Sun 9am–1pm. Closed some hols. **Prices:** Lunch main courses $3.60–$6.75. No CC. ♿

Fulton's Prime Rib, in Old Sacramento State Historic Park, 900 2nd St, Sacramento; tel 916/444-9641. J St exit off I-5. Follow signs to Old Sacramento parking. **Seafood/Steak.** Wood, brick, antiques, and a mounted deer's head lend a distinctive atmosphere to this dark but spacious dining room. There's also a brick patio with fountain. Specialties include prime rib, Mexican dishes, and seafood, as well as children's selections. **FYI:** Reservations recommended. Piano. **Open:** Lunch daily 11am–3pm; dinner Mon–Fri 5–10pm, Sat 5–11pm, Sun 4–10pm. Closed Dec 25. **Prices:** Main courses $7.95–$24.95. Maj CC. 🍴 🍽

★ **Greta's Cafe**, 1831 Capitol Ave, Sacramento (Midtown); tel 916/442-7382. **Eclectic.** A casual downtown coffeehouse with lots of windows, original artwork, and eclectic music. An on-site bakery dishes up light breakfasts. The menu includes sandwiches, pizzas, focaccia, and quiches, all nicely prepared. **FYI:** Reservations not accepted. No liquor license. **Open:** Mon 6:30am–5pm, Tues–Fri 6:30am–9pm, Sat–Sun 7:30am–9pm. Closed some hols. **Prices:** Main courses $3.75–$5.75. No CC. ♿

Jazzmen's Art of Pasta, in Old Sacramento State Historic Park, 1107 Firehouse Alley, Sacramento (Old Sacramento); tel 916/441-6726. J St exit off I-5. **Cajun/Italian.** A restaurant offering an outdoor bar and dining, plus musical accompaniment. Pastas come with a choice of sauces; also served are imperial crab lasagna and chicken Florentine. **FYI:** Reservations recommended. Jazz. **Open:** Sun–Thurs 11:30am–11pm, Fri–Sat 11:30am–2am. Closed Dec 25. **Prices:** Main courses $8.95–$14.95. Maj CC. ■ ☱ ㅂ

Lemon Grass Restaurant, 601 Munroe St, Sacramento; tel 916/486-4891. **Thai/Vietnamese.** Fun and fresh Vietnamese and Thai cuisine in an enjoyable setting. Such traditional favorites as Bangkok beef and lemongrass chicken share the menu with nouvelle creations like Thai burrito. Also at: 900 9th St, Sacramento (916/442-7991). **FYI:** Reservations accepted. **Open:** Lunch Mon–Fri 11:30am–2pm; dinner Mon–Thurs 5:30–9pm, Fri–Sat 5–10pm, Sun 5–9pm. Closed some hols. **Prices:** Main courses $8.95–$14.95. Maj CC. ☱ ㅂ

Mace's, in Pavilions Shopping Center, 501 Pavilion Lane, Sacramento; tel 916/922-0222. Howe Ave exit off US 50. **New American.** Elegant dining room with marble inlaid floors, plants, zebra skins, African artifacts, fans, and rattan furniture. Menu features many pastas, plus regional American fare such as pot pies and smoked chicken salad. Other offerings include roast duck with orange-ginger glaze, herb-roasted lamb. Hosts social events, with dancing at the bar or on the patio. **FYI:** Reservations accepted. Jazz. **Open:** Mon–Fri 11:30am–10:30pm, Sat 11:30am–11pm, Sun 10am–9pm. Closed some hols. **Prices:** Main courses $9.95–$19.95. Maj CC. ☱ VP ㅂ

Paragary's Bar and Oven, 1401 28th St, Sacramento (Midtown); tel 916/457-5737. J St exit off Business I-80 S or N St exit off Business I-80 N. **Californian/Italian.** A corner entrance leads to a nice long bar with small tables. There's also sidewalk dining. The menu lists chic pizza concoctions, lamb, T-bones, salmon, and various salads. A small barrier obstructs entry to restrooms for patrons with disabilities. **FYI:** Reservations accepted. **Open:** Mon–Fri 11:30am–2am, Sat–Sun 5pm–2am. Closed some hols. **Prices:** Main courses $7.50–$15.85. Maj CC. ☱ VP

✸ **Rubicon Brewing Company**, 2004 Capitol Ave, Sacramento; tel 916/448-7032. **Pub.** A gussied-up beer-brewing facility with big windows and spare furnishings. Menu lists onion soup, burgers, chef's salad, chicken fajitas, and other pub fare. Many microbrewed beers available. **FYI:** Reservations not accepted. Beer and wine only. **Open:** Mon–Thurs 11am–11pm, Fri 11am–12:30am, Sat 9am–12:30am, Sun 9am–10pm. Closed some hols. **Prices:** Main courses $2.75–$5.95. Maj CC. ㅂ

✸ **Tower Café**, 1518 Broadway, Sacramento (Tower District); tel 916/441-0222. **International/Vegetarian.** A hip crowd patronizes this cafe in a landmark building. Decorated with art from around the world. Menu features Malaysian chicken, ravioli, French-country entrees and crêpes, Thai shrimp salad,

and hamburgers. Over 60 different beers. **FYI:** Reservations accepted. Beer and wine only. **Open:** Sun–Thurs 7am–11pm, Fri–Sat 8am–1am. Closed some hols. **Prices:** Main courses $4.95–$11.95. Maj CC. ■ ☱ ㅂ

Woody's, in Riverbank Marina, 1379 Garden Hwy, Sacramento; tel 916/924-3434. Garden Hwy exit off I-5. **New American.** Accents of turquoise and wood plus both real and painted palm trees befit this riverside restaurant, where tropical drinks and beers are served under shady oaks. Appetizers are bar food items like cheese sticks and fried calamari. Menu includes burgers in various guises, as well as offbeat salads. **FYI:** Reservations recommended. Children's menu. **Open:** Mon–Thurs 11am–midnight, Fri–Sat 11–2am, Sun 9:30am–midnight. Closed some hols. **Prices:** Main courses $4.99–$7.49. Maj CC. ☱ ⛰ VP ㅂ

Attractions 📖

California State Capitol, 10th St, between N and L Sts; tel 916/324-0333. The dome-topped California state capitol, completed in 1874, is Sacramento's most distinctive landmark. Daily guided tours examine both the building's architecture and the workings of government. They are offered Mon–Fri 9am–4pm and Sat–Sun 10am–4pm, every hour on the hour. Pick up tickets at Room B-27 (in the north wing, basement level). **Open:** Daily 9am–5pm. Closed some hols. Free.

Governor's Mansion, 16th and I Sts; tel 916/323-3047. From 1903–1967, this Victorian-Gothic structure was the official residence of 13 governors of California. Hour-long guided tours are offered on the hour. **Open:** Daily 10am–4pm. $

Old Sacramento; tel 916/443-7815. Four square blocks at the "foot" of downtown Sacramento contain the greatest concentration of historical buildings in California. Free guided tours are offered in the spring, summer, and fall. Call 916/324-0040 for more information.

California State Railroad Museum, 111 1st St; tel 916/448-4466. More than 20 actual locomotives and rail cars are on display at this facility, along with a vast collection of artifacts that covers almost every aspect of the railroading industry. A film on the history of Western railroading is also shown. **Open:** Daily 10am–5pm. Closed some hols. $$

Discovery Museum, 101 I St; tel 916/264-7057. Officially known as the Sacramento Museum of History, Science and Technology, this museum was created by the merger of the Sacramento Museum of History and the Sacramento Science Center. Five galleries showcase permanent and traveling exhibits on a wide variety of science- and history-related topics. The

Learning Resource Center (formerly the Science Center) features the only planetarium in the region; it is located at 3615 Auburn Blvd. **Open:** Tues–Sun 10am–5pm. Closed some hols. $$

State Indian Museum, 2618 K St; tel 916/324-0971. Located on the same block as Sutter's Fort (see below), the Indian Museum reflects the culture and traditions of the Native Americans of California. Tribal elders helped select the objects and photographs on display, and many Native Americans donated personal items to the collection. Movies and slide shows are presented on weekends. **Open:** Daily 10am–5pm. Closed some hols. $

Sutter's Fort State Historic Park, 2701 L St; tel 916/445-4209. Swiss immigrant John Augustus Sutter established a settlement called "New Helvetia" in this area in 1839. With a small party of settlers and friendly local natives, Sutter built a fort of sun-dried adobe bricks on a small knoll near the confluence of the Sacramento and American Rivers.

An accurate reconstruction of the fort was begun in 1891, making this the nation's oldest reconstructed historic fort. In 1947, it became part of the California State Park System. Craft demonstrations and living history programs represent life at the fort as it was in the 1840s. The Trade Store stocks period items, including, toys, games, clothing, jewelery, and blankets. **Open:** Daily 10am–5pm. Closed some hols. $$

Crocker Art Museum, 216 O St; tel 916/264-5423. One of the oldest museums in the West, this museum also has one of the best collections of California art in the country. The Crocker Mansion Wing is modeled after the home of the museum's founder, Judge E B Crocker. It houses works by California artists from the 1960s to the present. Gift shop/bookstore. **Open:** Wed and Fri–Sun 10am–5pm, Thurs 10am–9pm. Closed some hols. $

Towe Ford Museum of Automotive History, 2200 Front St; tel 916/442-6802. One of the world's most comprehensive collections of antique Fords. About 170 vehicles represent nearly every Ford manufactured between 1903 and 1953, including a rare 1904 Model B touring car. Antique fire, mail, and commercial vehicles are also on display. Changing exhibits; special events. Gift shop. **Open:** Daily 10am–6pm. Closed some hols. $$

Blue Diamond Growers Video and Visitors Center, 1701 C St; tel 916/446-8409. This is the world's largest almond-packaging plant, with a visitor center and gift shop presenting a 25-minute video describing how almonds are processed from tree to table. Free samples offered. **Open:** Mon–Fri 10am–5pm, Sat 10am–4pm. Closed some hols. Free.

Waterworld USA, 1600 Exposition Blvd; tel 916/924-0556 or 924-3747. Large recreational water theme park featuring wave pool, river tube ride, wading pool, children's area, and 10 water slides. **Open:** Mem Day weekend–Labor Day, daily 10:30am. Closing hours vary. $$$$

Spirit of Sacramento **Historic Paddlewheeler**, 110 L St; tel 916/552-2933 or toll free 800/433-0263. One-hour narrated sightseeing trips aboard a 110-foot paddlewheeler built in 1942. Sold to actor John Wayne in 1954, the vessel appeared in his film *Blood Alley*. Also dining, cocktail, and murder mystery cruises (phone for details). **Open:** June–Aug, departures Wed–Sun 1:30 and 3pm; Apr–May and Sept–Oct, departures Fri–Sun 1:30 and 3pm. $$$$

ST HELENA

Map page M-2, C2 (N of Napa)

Hotel 🏨

≡≡≡ **Harvest Inn**, 1 Main St, St Helena, CA 94574; tel 707/963-9463 or toll free 800/950-8466; fax 707/963-4402. On Calif 29, just south of downtown St Helena. 22 acres. Quiet lodging among gardens and overlooking vineyards, yet within easy access of restaurants and touring. The English Tudor–style design is rather incongruous for this region. **Rooms:** 54 rms and stes; 15 ctges/villas. CI 3:30pm/CO 11am. Express checkout avail. Nonsmoking rms avail. Large, comfortable rooms with lots of extras, such as wet bars and separate vanities. **Amenities:** 📺 🔌 📲 🍷 A/C, cable TV w/movies, refrig. Some units w/terraces, some w/fireplaces, some w/Jacuzzis. **Services:** 🛎 👨 Masseur, babysitting. **Facilities:** 🛁 🏊 👥 1 bar (w/entertainment), whirlpool. **Rates (BB):** HS Apr 15–Oct $129–$189 S or D; from $200 ste; from $200 ctge/villa. Extra person $20. Min stay wknds. Lower rates off-season. Spec packages avail. Pking: Outdoor, free. Maj CC. Dinner, wine, and other packages available.

Motel

≡≡ **El Bonita Motel**, 195 Main St, St Helena, CA 94574; tel 707/963-3216 or toll free 800/541-3284; fax 707/963-8838. Excellent location in the heart of Napa Valley. Pleasant outdoor lounge and sunbathing area set in lush gardens. **Rooms:** 41 rms and stes. CI 2pm/CO 11:30am. Nonsmoking rms avail. Clean, attractive, spacious. **Amenities:** 📺 🔌 📲 A/C, satel TV, refrig, stereo/tape player. Some units w/terraces, some w/Jacuzzis. **Services:** 🛎 👨 Masseur. **Facilities:** 🛁 🏊 👥 Sauna, whirlpool.

Rates: HS June–Sept $75–$150 S; $82–$175 D; from $160 ste. Extra person $8. Min stay wknds. Lower rates off-season. Higher rates for spec evnts/hols. Pking: Outdoor, free. Maj CC.

Inns

☰☰ **Hotel St Helena**, 1309 Main St, St Helena, CA 94574; tel 707/963-4388; fax 707/965-5402. Hotel has Victorian decor and is loaded with antiques. **Rooms:** 18 rms and stes (4 w/shared bath). CI 3pm/CO noon. Rooms feature 4-poster beds, armoires, and clawfoot tubs. **Amenities:** ▥ A/C. 4 rooms have TV. **Services:** ⌂ ⬳ Wine/sherry served. **Facilities:** 1 bar, guest lounge w/TV. Wine bar. Upstairs solarium has a TV. **Rates (CP):** HS Feb 15–Nov 10 $110 S or D w/shared bath, $130–$160 S or D w/private bath; from $200 ste. Extra person $10. Children under 6 stay free. Min stay spec evnts. Lower rates off-season. Pking: Outdoor, free. Ltd CC.

☰☰☰ **Vineyard Country Inn**, 201 Main St, St Helena, CA 94574; tel 707/963-1000; fax 707/963-1794. Pleasant grounds with lovely gardens and walkways. **Rooms:** 21 stes. CI 3pm/CO 11am. Spacious 2-room units. **Amenities:** ▥ ⬟ A/C, cable TV, refrig. All units w/terraces, all w/fireplaces. All units have wet bar. **Services:** ⌂ Babysitting. Expanded continental breakfast offered. **Facilities:** ⬟ ⬟ ⬟ Whirlpool. **Rates:** HS May 15–Nov 14 from $165 ste. Extra person $10. Children under 5 stay free. Min stay wknds. Lower rates off-season. Pking: Outdoor, free. Ltd CC.

☰☰☰ **Wine Country Inn**, 1152 Lodi Lane, St Helena, CA 94574; tel 707/963-7077 or toll free 800/473-3463; fax 707/963-9018. 2 mi N of St Helena. Lodi Lane exit off Calif 29; go east. 10 acres. Comfortable and homelike. A tranquil country setting, with spectacular views of the hills from many rooms. **Rooms:** 24 rms. CI 2pm/CO noon. Individually decorated. **Amenities:** ▥ ⬟ A/C. Some units w/terraces, some w/fireplaces, some w/Jacuzzis. **Services:** Babysitting. **Facilities:** ⬟ ⬟ Whirlpool. Outdoor pool and spa enjoy fantastic hillside vistas. **Rates (BB):** HS Apr 15–Dec $96–$205 D. Extra person $20. Lower rates off-season. Pking: Outdoor, free. Ltd CC.

Lodge

☰ **White Sulphur Springs Resort & Spa**, 3100 White Sulphur Springs Rd, St Helena, CA 94574; tel 707/963-8588; fax 707/963-2890. 2 mi W of St Helena. Spring St exit off Calif 29; 2 mi W. Secluded, very basic but clean country lodge and spa. Founded in 1852 as California's first hot-springs resort, it has a beautiful setting amid redwoods, fir, and madrone. **Rooms:** 28 rms and effic; 9 ctges/villas. CI 3pm/CO 11am. Nonsmoking rms avail. 3 types of accommodations available. Creekside Cottages

are the largest, with some offering wood-burning stoves and kitchenettes. Lodgings also available in the inn and the Carriage House; several rooms share bath, and quarters are small. **Amenities:** No A/C, phone, or TV. Some units w/terraces. **Services:** ⌂ Masseur, babysitting. Full spa services include herbal wraps and volcanic-mud wraps. **Facilities:** ⬟ ⬟ ⬟ Lawn games, spa, whirlpool. Natural mineral pool. **Rates (BB):** $65 S or D; from $125 effic; from $100 ctge/villa. Extra person $15. Spec packages avail. Pking: Outdoor, free. Ltd CC. Group packages available.

Resort

☰☰☰☰ **Meadowood Resort Hotel**, 900 Meadowood Lane, St Helena, CA 94574; tel 707/963-3646 or toll free 800/458-8080; fax 707/963-3532. Silverado Trail to Howell Mt Rd; go east 500 ft; left on Meadowood Lane. 250 acres. Set in a lush, hidden valley. Feels like a residential estate, with wood-frame cottages tucked around the property. A private club as well as a hotel. **Rooms:** 85 ctges/villas. CI 3pm/CO noon. Express check-out avail. Nonsmoking rms avail. Cottages have white-trimmed windows, wainscoting, and peaked roofs. Huge decks are positioned for maximum privacy. Most accommodations have stone fireplaces. **Amenities:** ▥ ⬟ ▣ ⬟ A/C, cable TV w/movies, refrig, stereo/tape player, bathrobes. All units w/minibars, all w/terraces, some w/fireplaces. Complimentary wine tastings on Friday nights. **Services:** ✕ ⬟ ⬟ ⬟ ⌂ Twice-daily maid svce, car-rental desk, masseur, babysitting. **Facilities:** ⬟ ⬟ ⬟ ⬟ ⬟ ⬟ ⬟ ⬟ 2 rsts (see also "Restaurants" below), 2 bars, lifeguard, lawn games, spa, sauna, steam rm, whirlpool, playground. There are 2 regulation croquet lawns. The 3-mile hiking trail winds past madrone and redwoods. **Rates:** HS July–mid-Nov from $295 ctge/villa. Extra person $25. Children under 12 stay free. Min stay wknds and spec evnts. Lower rates off-season. Spec packages avail. Pking: Outdoor, free. Maj CC. Recreation (golf, tennis, croquet) and spa packages available.

Restaurants ▦

Brava Terrace, 3010 St Helena Hwy N, St Helena; tel 707/963-9300. **New American.** Casual and comfortable, featuring a large flagstone fireplace and an attractive outdoor courtyard with fountain and flowers. The menu offers risottos as pastas as well as roast chicken, cassoulet, and grilled pork tenderloin. **FYI:** Reservations recommended. **Open:** HS May–Oct daily noon–9pm. Reduced hours off-season. Closed some hols; ten days in Jan. **Prices:** Main courses $9.50–$16.95. Maj CC. ⬟ ⬟ ⬟

The Restaurant at Meadowood, in Meadowood Resort Hotel, 900 Meadowood Lane, St Helena; tel 707/963-3646. Silverado Trail to Howell Mt Rd; go east 500 ft; left on Meadowood Lane.

Californian/French. Tapestry-backed chairs, a high-beamed ceiling, and a white rosebud at every place setting. Cuisine is described as "Napa Valley Provençale." Main courses might include baked squab with caramelized endive, or crispy salmon with marinated tomatoes. Extensive 600-entry wine list. **FYI:** Reservations recommended. Jacket required. **Open:** Dinner Mon–Sun 6–10pm; brunch Sun 10:30am–2:30pm. **Prices:** Main courses $23–$26; PF dinner $37–$55. Maj CC. &

$ **Showley's at Miramonte**, in Miramonte Inn, 1327 Railroad Ave, St Helena; tel 707/963-1200. 1 block E of Main St between Hunt and Adams Sts. **Eclectic.** The feel of a historic country inn, complete with ceiling fans and original art; tables are decorated with seasonal fruits and vegetables. Patio dining in the shade of a huge tree. Eclectic cuisine includes Hawaiian albacore with plum salsa and polenta, shrimp brochettes with chicken sausage, fresh porcini and mango-corn salsa, and braised lamb shanks with garlic mashed potatoes. Great value. **FYI:** Reservations recommended. Jazz. Dress code. Beer and wine only. **Open:** Lunch Tues–Sun 11:30am–3pm; dinner Tues–Sun 6–9pm. Closed some hols; Dec 1–Dec 15. **Prices:** Main courses $15–$19. Maj CC.

Terra, 1345 Railroad Ave, St Helena; tel 707/963-8931. Adams St exit off Calif 29; go east to Railroad Ave and turn left. **Eclectic.** East meets West in the refined cuisine of Lissa Doumani (pastry chef) and her husband, Hiro Sone (chef), both alumni of Wolfgang Puck's kitchen at Spago. Located in a historic 1880 stone building, Terra manages to seem both avant-garde and countrified at the same time. The menu globetrots from a lamb and artichoke daube with polenta to a broiled, sake-marinated sea bass with shrimp dumplings. Desserts include a fine tiramisù. **FYI:** Reservations recommended. Dress code. Beer and wine only. **Open:** Sun–Mon 6–9:30pm, Wed–Thurs 6–9:30pm, Fri–Sat 6–10pm. Closed some hols; Jan 1–Jan 14. **Prices:** Main courses $13.50–$22. Ltd CC.

Tra Vigne Restaurant & Cantinetta, 1050 Charter Oak Ave, St Helena; tel 707/963-4444. E on Charter Oak Ave off Calif 29. **Italian/Mediterranean.** Food keeps getting better and better at this splendid restaurant. Design is "trattoria moderna," with 30-foot ceilings, vintage posters, and beaded lamps. In fine weather, try to snag a patio table. In addition to house-made breads and smoked meats, the changing menu might feature oak-roasted chicken, or pasta with seafood. The adjoining Cantinetta serves light Italian fare, plus breakfast on weekends. **FYI:** Reservations recommended. Dress code. **Open:** HS June–Sept daily 11:30am–10pm. Reduced hours off-season. Closed some hols. **Prices:** Main courses $12.50–$15.25. Ltd CC.

Trilogy, 1234 Main St, St Helena; tel 707/963-5507. **French.** Intimate dining room with ceiling fans, brass chandeliers, and original artwork. Prix-fixe menu changes daily. Among the specialties are grilled boneless quail and Asian green-tea-noodle salad with soy-sesame-ginger vinaigrette, pan-roasted port tenderloin with roasted garlic and rosemary jus, and roasted rack of lamb with toasted cumin and oven-dried tomatoes. **FYI:** Reservations recommended. Beer and wine only. **Open:** Lunch Tues–Fri noon–2pm; dinner Tues–Sun 6–9:30pm. Closed some hols; one week mid–Dec. **Prices:** Main courses $14.50–$20; PF dinner $32. Ltd CC.

Attractions

Silverado Museum, 1490 Library Lane; tel 707/963-3757. Devoted to the life and works of Robert Louis Stevenson, this museum contains more than 8,000 items, including original manuscripts, letters, photographs, and the desk Stevenson used in Samoa. The writer honeymooned here in 1880, at the abandoned Silverado Mine. **Open:** Tues–Sun noon-4pm. Closed some hols. Free.

Beringer Vineyards, 2000 Main St (Calif 29); tel 707/963-7115. The oldest continuously operating winery in the Napa Valley, Beringer Vineyards was founded in 1876. Tours cover various aspects of winemaking and include the hand-dug 19th-century cellaring tunnels that were part of the original winery; the Queen Anne Victorian–style Rhine House (1883); and the 1930s art deco Bottling Room. Free tastings are offered at the Rhine House and the Bottling Room. **Open:** Daily 9am–5pm. Closed some hols. Free.

SALINAS
Map page M-2, D2

Hotel

Ramada Inn, 808 N Main St, Salinas, CA 93906; tel 408/424-8661; fax 408/424-5628. N Main St exit off US 101. Too much asphalt here, but some care has gone into structure and design. Still, the property could use some upgrading. Convenient location near fairgrounds. **Rooms:** 163 rms and stes. CI 2pm/CO 2pm. Nonsmoking rms avail. Basic rooms are clean and done in browns. **Amenities:** A/C, cable TV. Some units w/terraces. **Services:** X **Facilities:** 1 rst, 1 bar (w/entertainment), whirlpool. **Rates:** $59–$98 S; $69–$98 D; from $79 ste. Extra person $5. Children under 18 stay free. Min stay spec evnts. Higher rates for spec evnts/hols. Pking: Outdoor, free. Maj CC.

Motels

≣ **Laurel Inn**, 801 W Laurel Dr, Salinas, CA 93906; tel 408/449-2474 or toll free 800/354-9831; fax 408/449-2476. Laurel exit off Calif 1. Close to the freeway, with minimal landscaping. **Rooms:** 146 rms and stes. CI noon/CO noon. Nonsmoking rms avail. Comfortable rooms. **Amenities:** 🛏 A/C, cable TV w/movies. 1 unit w/minibar, some w/terraces, some w/fireplaces. **Services:** 🖾 ↩ **Facilities:** 🔥 ⟨25⟩ ⅙ 1 rst, 1 bar, sauna, whirlpool. **Rates:** HS May–Sept $48–$85 S; $54–$90 D; from $72 ste. Extra person $6. Min stay wknds and spec evnts. Lower rates off-season. Higher rates for spec evnts/hols. Pking: Outdoor, free. Maj CC.

≣ **Vagabond Inn**, 131 Kern St, Salinas, CA 93906; tel 408/758-4693 or toll free 800/522-1555; fax 408/758-9835. Market St exit off US 101. Tidy and clean. **Rooms:** 70 rms. CI 2pm/CO noon. Nonsmoking rms avail. **Amenities:** 🛏 Cable TV. No A/C. Vagabond Club members get the best locations, rates, and amenities, including coffeemakers, fax outlets, and longer phone cords. Refrigerators available for fee. **Services:** ↩ ⟨⟩ Continental breakfast in lobby. **Facilities:** 🔥 ⅙ 1 rst, 1 bar. **Rates (CP):** HS Apr–Sept $45–$64 S; $64–$80 D. Extra person $5. Children under 18 stay free. Min stay spec evnts. Lower rates off-season. Higher rates for spec evnts/hols. Pking: Outdoor, free. Maj CC.

SAN BERNARDINO

Map page M-3, D3

Hotels 🏨

≣≣≣ **Radisson Hotel San Bernardino Convention Center**, 295 North E St, San Bernardino, CA 92401; tel 909/381-6181 or toll free 800/333-3333; fax 909/381-5288. 2nd St E exit off I-215; left on E St. The only full-service convention hotel in downtown San Bernardino; very modern building with a welcoming staff. Excellent service. **Rooms:** 231 rms and stes. Exec-level rms avail. CI 3pm/CO noon. Express checkout avail. Nonsmoking rms avail. **Amenities:** 🛏 ⟨⟩ 🖥 A/C, cable TV w/movies. Some units w/minibars. **Services:** ✕ 🆅🅿 🚗 🖾 ↩ Car-rental desk. **Facilities:** 🏋 ⟨1.5K⟩ 🖵 ⅙ 2 rsts (see also "Restaurants" below), 1 bar (w/entertainment), whirlpool. **Rates:** $65 S; $75 D; from $125 ste. Extra person $10. Children under 17 stay free. Spec packages avail. Pking: Indoor, free. Maj CC.

≣≣≣ **San Bernardino Hilton**, 285 E Hospitality Lane, San Bernardino, CA 92408; tel 909/889-0133 or toll free 800/HILTONS, 800/446-1065 in CA; fax 909/381-4299. Waterman Ave N exit off I-10; W on Hospitality Lane. A hotel with fine service and facilities suitable for business travelers and families. **Rooms:** 247 rms and stes. CI 3pm/CO noon. Express checkout avail. Nonsmoking rms avail. **Amenities:** 🛏 ⟨⟩ A/C, cable TV w/movies, refrig. **Services:** ✕ 🚗 🖾 ↩ Car-rental desk, babysitting. **Facilities:** 🔥 ⟨650⟩ ⅙ 1 rst, 1 bar, whirlpool. **Rates:** $85 S; $95 D; from $100 ste. Extra person $10. Children under 18 stay free. Spec packages avail. Pking: Outdoor, free. Maj CC.

Motels

≣ **E-Z 8 Motel**, 1750 S Waterman Ave, San Bernardino, CA 92408; tel 909/888-4827 or toll free 800/32-MOTEL ext 59. Waterman Ave exit off I-10. Generously sized rooms at very good rates. **Rooms:** 112 rms. CI 11am/CO 11am. Nonsmoking rms avail. **Amenities:** 🛏 A/C, cable TV w/movies. Refrigerators available for $3 per night. **Services:** ↩ ⟨⟩ **Facilities:** 🔥 ⅙ Games rm, whirlpool, washer/dryer. **Rates:** $27 S; $32 D. Extra person $5. Children under 13 stay free. Pking: Outdoor, free. Maj CC.

≣≣≣ **La Quinta Inn**, 205 E Hospitality Lane, San Bernardino, CA 92408; tel 909/888-7571 or toll free 800/531-5900; fax 909/884-3864. Waterman Ave N exit off I-10; W on Hospitality Lane. This chain is a favorite of business travelers. The southwestern architecture and friendly staff at this franchise will also appeal to families. **Rooms:** 151 rms. CI 3pm/CO noon. Nonsmoking rms avail. **Amenities:** 🛏 ⟨⟩ A/C, cable TV w/movies. Refrigerators and microwaves can be rented for $10 per night. **Services:** 🖾 ↩ ⟨⟩ Fax available. **Facilities:** 🔥 ⟨35⟩ ⅙ Free access to 2 nearby health clubs. Restaurants within walking distance. **Rates (CP):** $49 S; $54 D. Extra person $5. Children under 18 stay free. Spec packages avail. Pking: Outdoor, free. Maj CC.

≣≣≣ **Ramada Inn**, 2000 Ostrems Way, San Bernardino, CA 92407; tel 909/887-3001 or toll free 800/228-2828; fax 909/880-3792. University Pkwy W exit off I-215; left at Hallmark; right at Ostrems. This hotel, built in 1990 and located near Cal State–San Bernardino, is comfortable and well run by a highly professional staff. **Rooms:** 116 rms and stes. CI 3pm/CO noon. Express checkout avail. Nonsmoking rms avail. **Amenities:** 🛏 ⟨⟩ A/C, cable TV w/movies. Some units w/terraces. **Services:** ✕ 🚗 🖾 ↩ Car-rental desk. **Facilities:** 🔥 ⟨100⟩ ⅙ 1 rst, 1 bar (w/entertainment), whirlpool. **Rates (CP):** $59 S; $69 D; from $89 ste. Extra person $10. Children under 18 stay free. Spec packages avail. Pking: Indoor/outdoor, free. Maj CC.

≣ **Super 8 Lodge**, 294 E Hospitality Lane, San Bernardino, CA 92408; tel 909/381-1681 or toll free 800/800-8000; fax 909/888-5120. Waterman N exit off I-10; left at Hospitality Lane. Nicely run property with friendly, helpful staff. Many restaurants within walking distance. **Rooms:** 81 rms. CI 11am/CO 11am. Nonsmoking rms avail. **Amenities:** 🛏 A/C, cable TV w/movies. **Services:** 🖨 🍽 ⚓ **Facilities:** 🏋 ⛳ ♿ Whirlpool. **Rates (CP):** HS Apr–Sept $53 S; $57 D. Extra person $10. Children under 12 stay free. Lower rates off-season. Pking: Outdoor, free. Maj CC.

Restaurants 🍽

El Torito, 118 E Hospitality Lane, San Bernardino; tel 909/381-2316. **Mexican.** Nicely designed contemporary restaurant with a Mexican motif. Typical Mexican fare of tacos, enchiladas, fajitas, all attractively presented. Popular Sunday brunch. **FYI:** Reservations accepted. Children's menu. **Open:** Lunch Mon–Sat 11am–3pm; dinner Mon–Thurs 3–11pm, Fri–Sat 3pm–midnight, Sun 2–10pm; brunch Sun 9am–2pm. Closed some hols. **Prices:** Main courses $6.75–$11.95. Maj CC. 🚗 ♿

Spencer's Restaurant, in the Radisson Hotel, 295 North E St, San Bernardino (Downtown); tel 909/381-6181. 2nd St E exit off I-215. **American.** A nice, informal dining room of pastel colors with an art deco motif. Special menu items include baked salmon florentine, chicken Oscar, and filet mignon. **FYI:** Reservations accepted. Children's menu. **Open:** Daily 6:30am–11pm. **Prices:** Main courses $10.95–$17.95. Maj CC. 🅿 ♿

SAN BRUNO
Map page M-2, D2 (N of San Mateo)

Hotel 🛏

▦ ▦ ▦ **Courtyard by Marriott**, 1050 Bayhill Dr, San Bruno, CA 94066; tel 415/952-3333 or toll free 800/321-2211; fax 415/952-4707. A most welcoming lobby, with lots of natural light, is well furnished and very homey thanks to a fireplace. Courtyard garden has gazebo, lawn, and trees. **Rooms:** 147 rms and stes. CI 3pm/CO 1pm. Express checkout avail. Nonsmoking rms avail. Rooms are large and all have desks. **Amenities:** 🛏 🍷 A/C, cable TV w/movies, voice mail. Some units w/minibars, all w/terraces. Instant hot water for coffee and tea. **Services:** ✗ 🚐 🖨 🍽 Babysitting. **Facilities:** 🏋 🍴 🏊 ♿ 1 rst, 1 bar, whirlpool, washer/dryer. **Rates:** $95 S; $105 D; from $110 ste. Children under 18 stay free. Spec packages avail. Pking: Outdoor, free. Maj CC.

SAN CLEMENTE
Map page M-3, E2

Hotel 🛏

▦ ▦ **Quality Suites Hotel**, 2481 S El Camino Real, San Clemente, CA 92672; tel 714/366-1000 or toll free 800/772-3555; fax 714/366-1030. 45 mi N of San Diego, exit El Camino Real off I-5. El Camino Real exit off I-5; follow El Camino Real south; hotel ½ mi on left. Located near the ocean, the property has scenic views but is still convenient to the town of San Clemente. Suitable for families. **Rooms:** 66 stes. CI 2pm/CO noon. Express checkout avail. Nonsmoking rms avail. **Amenities:** 🛏 🍷 A/C, cable TV w/movies, refrig, VCR, stereo/tape player. All units w/minibars, some w/terraces, some w/Jacuzzis. Microwaves. **Services:** 🖨 Car-rental desk, babysitting. **Facilities:** 🏋 🍴 🏊 ♿ 1 bar, whirlpool. **Rates (BB):** HS June 15–Sept 15 from $79 ste. Extra person $10. Children under 7 stay free. Min stay spec evnts. Lower rates off-season. Spec packages avail. Pking: Indoor/outdoor, free. Maj CC.

Motel 🏨

▦ **San Clemente Beach Traveloge**, 2441 S El Camino Real, San Clemente, CA 92672; tel 714/498-5954 or toll free 800/843-1706; fax 714/498-6657. El Camino Rd exit off I-5; 90 south. Very plain older building, yet well maintained. **Rooms:** 23 rms and stes. CI 1pm/CO noon. Express checkout avail. Nonsmoking rms avail. Small, but bright and airy. **Amenities:** 🛏 🍷 🖨 A/C, cable TV w/movies, refrig. Some units w/terraces, some w/Jacuzzis. **Services:** 🚐 🍽 **Facilities:** ♿ **Rates:** HS May 15–Sept $49–$75 S; $59–$95 D; from $95 ste. Extra person $4. Children under 17 stay free. Lower rates off-season. Higher rates for spec evnts/hols. Pking: Indoor/outdoor, free. Maj CC.

SAN DIEGO
Map page M-3, E3

See also **Carlsbad, Chula Vista, Coronado, Del Mar, El Cajon, Escondido, Oceanside, Rancho Santa Fe, San Ysidro**

TOURIST INFORMATION

International Visitor Information Center First Ave at F St (tel 619/696-9371). Open Mon–Sat 8:30am–5pm, Sun 11am–5pm. Closed Thanksgiving, Dec 25, and Jan 1.

PUBLIC TRANSPORTATION

Metropolitan Transit System Buses Operate throughout greater San Diego area. Local fare $1.25, express fare $1.50–$2. "Day Tripper" unlimited use passes available; 1-day pass $4, 4-day pass $12. For information, call or visit the MTS's **Transit Store** at 449 Broadway, at 5th Ave (tel 619/233-3004). Open Mon–Sat 8:30am–5:30pm; telephone hours daily 5:30am–8:30pm.

San Diego Trolley Operates along C St from Kettner and Santa Fe stations. Runs every 15 minutes 5am–12:25am. Tickets purchased from machines at trolley stops; valid for 2 hours for travel in 1 direction only. For information call 619/233-3004 or 231-8549.

Hotels 🏨

⊟⊟⊟ **The Bay Club Hotel & Marina**, 2131 Shelter Island Dr, San Diego, CA 92106 (Shelter Island); tel 619/224-8888 or toll free 800/672-0800, 800/833-6565 in CA; fax 619/225-1604. 6 mi W of downtown. Rosecrans St exit off I-5. Set in the middle of Shelter Island. Cozy sitting area has leather sofas in front of a fireplace. The lobby is inviting with a large skylight and grand piano. **Rooms:** 105 rms and stes. CI 4pm/CO noon. Express checkout avail. Nonsmoking rms avail. Pristine furnishings in bright, airy rooms with beautiful marina and bay views.

Amenities: 🛏 A/C, cable TV, refrig. All units w/terraces. **Services:** ✕ ⊶ 🚘 🖼 🛎 Babysitting. Very helpful, eager staff. **Facilities:** 🏋 🚴 ⛰ 🏐 🏊 ᨑ 1 rst, 1 bar, whirlpool, washer/dryer. Restaurant overlooks the marina; so does the pool, which is surrounded by palm trees and lounge chairs. **Rates (BB):** $100–$140 S; $110–$150 D; from $185 ste. Extra person $10. Children under 12 stay free. Min stay spec evnts. Higher rates for spec evnts/hols. Spec packages avail. Pking: Indoor/outdoor, free. Maj CC.

⊟⊟ **Best Western Bayside Inn**, 555 W Ash St, San Diego, CA 92101 (Downtown); tel 619/233-7500 or toll free 800/341-1818; fax 619/239-8060. At Columbia St. Located in a quiet part of downtown, just a few blocks from the water. The lobby feels like a greenhouse, with lots of light and large windows. **Rooms:** 122 rms. CI 2pm/CO noon. Nonsmoking rms avail. Rooms are pleasant but not particularly inviting; each has a city or water view. **Amenities:** 🛏 🕙 A/C, cable TV w/movies. All units w/terraces. **Services:** ✕ 🚘 🖼 🛎 Babysitting. **Facilities:** 🏋 🏊 ᨑ 1 rst, 1 bar, whirlpool. The pool area needs renovation, and is surrounded by buildings, so it gets little sun. **Rates (CP):** HS July–Labor Day $80–$100 S; $86–$106 D. Extra person $6. Children under 12 stay free. Lower rates off-season. Spec packages avail. Pking: Indoor, free. Maj CC.

⊟⊟ **Best Western Hacienda Hotel**, 4041 Harney St, San Diego, CA 92110 (Old Town); tel 619/298-4707 or toll free 800/

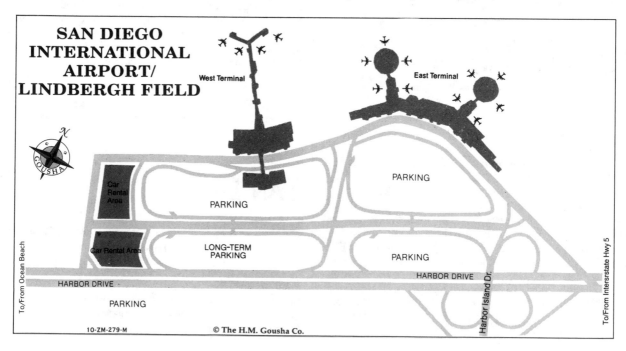

SAN DIEGO INTERNATIONAL AIRPORT/ LINDBERGH FIELD

West Terminal

East Terminal

N GOUSHA

Car Rental Area

Car Rental Area

PARKING

PARKING

PARKING

LONG-TERM PARKING

PARKING

HARBOR DRIVE

HARBOR DRIVE

PARKING

To/From Ocean Beach

Harbor Island Dr.

To/From Intersrstate Hwy 5

10-ZM-279-M

© The H.M. Gousha Co.

888-1991; fax 619/298-4707. 3 mi NW of downtown. Old Town Ave exit off I-5; take Old Town Ave to San Diego Ave, turn north to Harney St. Attractive, well-located hotel in the Spanish colonial style. Pleasant atmosphere with lots of plants, informal patios, Mexican tile roof. **Rooms:** 149 rms. CI 3pm/CO noon. Nonsmoking rms avail. Rooms have wooden shutters and bathrooms with quarry tile floors. **Amenities:** 🛏 ⚄ ▦ A/C, cable TV, refrig, VCR. Some units w/terraces. All rooms equipped with microwaves. **Services:** ✕ 🖛 🚗 🖾 ᗡ Car-rental desk, babysitting. Complimentary beer, wine, soft drinks, and margaritas Monday–Thursday, 6–7pm. **Facilities:** 🛅 🍴 ⟦125⟧ ⚄ 1 rst, 1 bar, whirlpool, washer/dryer. Mexican restaurant and cantina. **Rates:** HS July–Aug $109–$119 S or D. Extra person $10. Children under 16 stay free. Lower rates off-season. Spec packages avail. Pking: Indoor/outdoor, free. Maj CC. Good value.

🟰🟰🟰 **Best Western Hanalei Hotel**, 2270 Hotel Circle N, San Diego, CA 92108 (Hotel Circle); tel 619/297-1101 or toll free 800/882-0858; fax 619/297-6049. 4 mi N of downtown. Hotel Circle exit off I-8. Ignore the misleading, dated sign out front—the accommodations are more than adequate. **Rooms:** 416 rms and stes. CI 4pm/CO noon. Express checkout avail. Nonsmoking rms avail. Some rooms in an 87-story tower. **Amenities:** 🛏 ⚄ A/C, cable TV w/movies. All units w/terraces. **Services:** ✕ 🖾 ᗡ 🖑 Car-rental desk. Friday night poolside luaus. Room service 6:30am–10pm. **Facilities:** 🛅 ⟦500⟧ ⚄ 2 rsts, 1 bar (w/entertainment), whirlpool, washer/dryer. Island restaurant has tropical decor, including waterfalls and pools. **Rates:** $89–$99 S or D; from $250 ste. Extra person $10. Children under 18 stay free. Higher rates for spec evnts/hols. Pking: Outdoor, free. Maj CC.

🟰🟰🟰 **Bristol Court Hotel**, 1055 1st Ave, San Diego, CA 92101 (Downtown); tel 619/232-6141 or toll free 800/622-4477; fax 619/232-0118. On a quiet street downtown, this boutique hotel is most inviting, with exquisite decor and lots of natural light. Close to the convention center. An excellent value. **Rooms:** 102 rms and stes. Exec-level rms avail. CI 3pm/CO noon. Express checkout avail. Nonsmoking rms avail. Homey, comfortable rooms with fine appointments. **Amenities:** 🛏 ⚄ A/C, cable TV w/movies. **Services:** ✕ ⟦VP⟧ 🚗 🖾 ᗡ Babysitting. Very helpful staff. **Facilities:** 🍴 ⟦350⟧ 🖳 ⚄ 2 rsts, 1 bar. **Rates (CP):** HS Jan–Apr/June–Sept $129–$149 S or D; from $249 ste. Extra person $20. Children under 12 stay free. Lower rates off-season. Higher rates for spec evnts/hols. Pking: Indoor, $8. Maj CC.

🟰🟰🟰 **Capri by the Sea Rental Management**, 4767 Ocean Blvd, San Diego, CA 92109 (Pacific Beach); tel 619/483-6110 or toll free 800/248-5262; fax 619/483-9141. 9 mi NW of downtown. A 12-story property with attractive accommodations, located on the boardwalk. Very good value. **Rooms:** 140 effic. Exec-level rms avail. CI 4pm/CO 11am. Each 1- or 2-bedroom condo is individually owned and decorated. All are spacious and have kitchens. **Amenities:** 🛏 ⚄ ▦ Cable TV, refrig, VCR, stereo/tape player. No A/C. All units w/terraces, 1 w/fireplace, some w/Jacuzzis. **Services:** ᗡ Babysitting. Maid service available for an extra charge. Front desk is staffed from 9am–6pm. **Facilities:** 🛅 1 beach (ocean), lifeguard, board surfing, sauna, whirlpool, washer/dryer. Laundry room on every floor and a barbecue on rooftop deck. Swimming pool is two doors up the street. **Rates:** HS July–Sept from $165 effic. Extra person $10. Min stay. Lower rates off-season. Pking: Indoor/outdoor, free. Maj CC. Daily, weekly, and monthly rates offered.

🟰🟰🟰 **Clarion Hotel Bay View**, 660 K St, San Diego, CA 92101 (Downtown); tel 619/696-0234 or toll free 800/766-0234; fax 619/231-8199. Between 7th and 8th Aves. Guests can walk to the convention center, restaurants, and San Diego trolley. Public areas and rooms were recently renovated. **Rooms:** 312 rms and stes. CI 3pm/CO noon. Express checkout avail. Nonsmoking rms avail. **Amenities:** 🛏 ⚄ ▦ A/C, cable TV w/movies, in-rm safe. Some units w/minibars, all w/terraces. State-of-the-art phone system allows guests to get entertainment schedules, weather, horoscopes, and other information for the price of a local call. **Services:** ✕ 🖛 🚗 🖾 ᗡ Babysitting. **Facilities:** 🍴 ⟦750⟧ 🖳 ⚄ 1 rst, 1 bar (w/entertainment), games rm, sauna, whirlpool, washer/dryer. Functional facilities without a lot of appeal. Exception is the outdoor Jacuzzi on the rooftop. **Rates:** $99–$139 S or D; from $119 ste. Extra person $10. Children under 18 stay free. Spec packages avail. Pking: Indoor, $7. Maj CC.

🟰🟰🟰 **Courtyard by Marriott**, 9650 Scranton Rd, San Diego, CA 92121 (Mira Mesa); tel 619/558-9600 or toll free 800/321-2211; fax 619/558-4539. 15 mi N of downtown. Miramesa Blvd exit off I-805; E on Mira Mesa Blvd, left on Scranton Rd. Designed for business travelers, this hotel, located near several corporate offices, has a nice lounge area appropriate for meetings. **Rooms:** 149 rms and stes. Exec-level rms avail. CI 4pm/CO noon. Express checkout avail. Nonsmoking rms avail. Clean, modern rooms, with good work areas. **Amenities:** 🛏 ⚄ A/C, cable TV w/movies. Some units w/terraces. **Services:** ✕ 🚗 🖾 ᗡ Car-rental desk. **Facilities:** 🛅 🍴 ⟦50⟧ 🖳 ⚄ 1 rst, whirlpool, washer/dryer. **Rates:** HS July–Sept $74 S; $84 D; from $94 ste. Children under 15 stay free. Lower rates off-season. Spec packages avail. Pking: Outdoor, free. Maj CC.

🟰🟰🟰 **Doubletree Hotel at Horton Plaza**, 910 Broadway Circle, San Diego, CA 92101 (Downtown); tel 619/239-2200 or toll free 800/222-TREE; fax 619/239-3216. Located in a major downtown shopping area, close to restaurants, convention center, and harbor. Lobby boasts extensive marble, 2 staircases, and a crystal chandelier. **Rooms:** 450 rms and stes. Exec-level rms avail. CI 4pm/CO noon. Express checkout avail. Nonsmoking rms avail. Good soundproofing makes guests unaware of the activity outside. Rooms are very functional, decorated in pastel colors. **Amenities:** 🔒 ❄ 🔲 🍸 A/C, cable TV w/movies, refrig, voice mail, bathrobes. All units w/minibars, some w/terraces, some w/fireplaces, some w/Jacuzzis. **Services:** 🍽 📠 📺 🚗 🏊 🛎 Masseur, babysitting. **Facilities:** 🔣 🍴 🏋 🖳 ⛳ ⛄ 3 rsts, 2 bars, sauna, whirlpool. Extensive meeting facilities. Bar/lounge is a good gathering place, with comfortable overstuffed sofas. **Rates:** $119–$149 S; $129–$159 D; from $250 ste. Extra person $20. Children under 12 stay free. Higher rates for spec evnts/hols. Spec packages avail. Pking: Indoor, $8–$10. Maj CC.

� **Downtown Inn Hotel**, 660 G St, San Diego, CA 92101 (Downtown); or toll free 800/598-1810. Between 6th and 7th Aves. This somewhat austere property caters primarily to residential guests. Borders a questionable neighborhood. **Rooms:** 105 effic. CI 2pm/CO 1pm. Express checkout avail. Nonsmoking rms avail. **Amenities:** 🔒 ❄ Cable TV, refrig. No A/C. Additional charge for in-room telephones. **Services:** 🛎 **Facilities:** ⛄ Washer/dryer. **Rates:** HS June–Aug from $29 effic. Extra person $10. Lower rates off-season. Ltd CC.

🔣🔣🔣 **Embassy Suites San Diego Bay**, 601 Pacific Hwy, San Diego, CA 92101 (Downtown); tel 619/239-2400 or toll free 800/EMBASSY; fax 619/239-1520. Inviting lobby features an open atrium with lots of natural light and greenery. Location near the bay offers wonderful views. Close to Seaport Village and the convention center. **Rooms:** 337 stes. CI 4pm/CO noon. Express checkout avail. Nonsmoking rms avail. Suites are spacious with many amenities, but furnishings are not elaborate. **Amenities:** 🔒 ❄ 🔲 🍸 A/C, cable TV w/movies, refrig, voice mail. Some units w/terraces, some w/Jacuzzis. Microwave. **Services:** ✗ 📠 🚗 🏊 🛎 🚐 Twice-daily maid svce, car-rental desk, babysitting. Complimentary happy hour. **Facilities:** 🔣 🏋 ⛳ ⛄ 2 rsts, 1 bar, sauna, steam rm, beauty salon, washer/dryer. Sports bar. **Rates (BB):** HS Mem Day–Labor Day from $155 ste. Extra person $10. Children under 12 stay free. Lower rates off-season. Higher rates for spec evnts/hols. Spec packages avail. Pking: Indoor/outdoor, $3.50–$9. Maj CC.

🔣🔣🔣 **Gaslamp Plaza Suites**, 520 E St, San Diego, CA 92101 (Gaslamp Quarter); tel 619/232-9500 or toll free 800/443-8012; fax 619/238-9945. At 5th Ave. One of the first skyscrapers in San Diego, built in 1913 and designated a historic landmark. Marble walls and stairways, brass elevator doors, etched-glass window. Needs improved maintenance. **Rooms:** 50 rms and stes. CI 4pm/CO 11am. Renovation should be completed. **Amenities:** 🔒 🔲 A/C, cable TV, refrig, in-rm safe. All units

w/minibars, 1 w/Jacuzzi. **Services:** ✗ 📠 🚗 🏊 🛎 **Facilities:** ⛄ 1 rst, 1 bar (w/entertainment). The restaurant, Dakota's, is very popular. Roof terrace with deck chairs, and hot tub. **Rates (CP):** HS June 19–Sept 2 $69 S; $69–$99 D; from $109 ste. Extra person $10. Children under 10 stay free. Lower rates off-season. Spec packages avail. Maj CC.

🔣🔣 **Grosvenor Inn–Sports Arena**, 3145 Sports Arena Blvd, San Diego, CA 92110 (Sports Arena); tel 619/225-9999 or toll free 800/232-1212; fax 619/225-0958. 4 mi NW of downtown. Rosecrans exit off I-5 S; Pacific Coast Hwy exit off I-5 N. Located at a busy intersection across from the sports arena, at the Grosvenor Square, where you'll find shops and restaurants. **Rooms:** 206 rms and stes. CI 3pm/CO noon. Nonsmoking rms avail. Bright, contemporary rooms have lots of natural light, and are quiet despite the commercial setting. **Amenities:** 🔒 🔲 A/C, satel TV w/movies, refrig. Some units w/minibars, some w/terraces, 1 w/fireplace, some w/Jacuzzis. **Services:** ✗ 🚗 🏊 🛎 Car-rental desk. Continental breakfast buffet. **Facilities:** 🔣 🖳 ⛄ 3 rsts, 1 bar, whirlpool, beauty salon, washer/dryer. **Rates:** $68 S; $72 D; from $105 ste. Extra person $10. Children under 18 stay free. Min stay spec evnts. Spec packages avail. Pking: Outdoor, free. Maj CC.

🔣🔣🔣 **Holiday Inn Harbor View**, 1617 1st Ave, San Diego, CA 92101 (Downtown); tel 619/239-6171 or toll free 800/366-3164; fax 619/233-6228. On the edge of downtown next to a noisy freeway. Lobby offers a comfortable seating area. Short ride from shopping, restaurants, and the bay. **Rooms:** 202 rms. CI 3pm/CO noon. Nonsmoking rms avail. Rooms are comfortable but austere. Half have wonderful views of the city lights or the bay. **Amenities:** 🔒 ❄ 🔲 🍸 A/C, cable TV w/movies. Some units w/terraces. **Services:** ✗ 🚗 🏊 🛎 Twice-daily maid svce. **Facilities:** 🔣 🏋 🖳 ⛄ 1 rst, 1 bar, washer/dryer. Restaurant has spectacular views but poor ventilation. **Rates:** HS Mem Day–Labor Day $95–$115 S; $110–$130 D. Children under 18 stay free. Lower rates off-season. Higher rates for spec evnts/hols. Spec packages avail. Pking: Indoor/outdoor, free. Maj CC.

🔣🔣🔣 **Holiday Inn on the Bay**, 1355 N Harbor Dr, San Diego, CA 92101 (Downtown); tel 619/232-3861 or toll free 800/4BAY-SIDE; fax 619/232-4924. An excellent choice for families, this newly renovated property is the best value on the bay. **Rooms:** 600 rms and stes. CI 3pm/CO noon. Express checkout avail. Nonsmoking rms avail. Pleasing rooms with excellent views. **Amenities:** 🔒 ❄ 🍸 A/C, cable TV w/movies, voice mail. Some units w/minibars, all w/terraces. Irons in each room, direct telephone lines to restaurants, weather information, and the like. **Services:** ✗ 📠 🚗 🏊 🛎 🚐 Twice-daily maid svce, social director, children's program, babysitting. Concierge will arrange wide variety of water sports activities. **Facilities:** 🔣

🛐 1.4k ♿ 3 rsts, 2 bars, games rm, playground, washer/dryer. **Rates:** HS July–Aug $135–$165 S or D; from $250 ste. Extra person $10. Children under 18 stay free. Lower rates off-season. Spec packages avail. Pking: Indoor/outdoor, $10. Maj CC. Kids under 12 eat for free.

🏨🏨🏨 **Horton Grand Hotel**, 311 Island Ave, San Diego, CA 92101 (Gaslamp Quarter); tel 619/544-1886 or toll free 800/542-1886; fax 619/239-3823. At 3rd Ave. A visit to the past. Two turn-of-the-century hotels combined and rebuilt brick by brick. Courtyard is often the setting for weddings, room 309 is said to be home of a ghost, Roger. **Rooms:** 132 rms and stes. CI 3pm/CO noon. Express checkout avail. Nonsmoking rms avail. Every room uniquely furnished with antiques for a Victorian look, with fireplace and sitting area. Bathrooms boast pedestal sinks, all rooms have queen-size beds. **Amenities:** 🔟 ♧ A/C, cable TV w/movies. Some units w/terraces, all w/fireplaces. **Services:** ✗ VP 🚐 △ ♧ Twice-daily maid svce, babysitting. Afternoon tea in the lobby. Complimentary shoeshine. **Facilities:** 700 ♿ 1 rst, 1 bar (w/entertainment), washer/dryer. **Rates:** $109–$159 S or D; from $189 ste. Extra person $10. Children under 16 stay free. Spec packages avail. Pking: Indoor/outdoor, $8. Maj CC.

🏨🏨 **Hotel St James**, 830 6th Ave, San Diego, CA 92101 (Gaslamp Quarter); tel 619/234-0155 or toll free 800/221-2222; fax 619/235-9410. Between E and F Sts. On the fringe of the Gaslamp Quarter, close to restaurants, convention center, and harbor. Lobby is spacious but needs some attention. Property has a European feel, with 2 vintage elevators; roof terrace offers great views. **Rooms:** 99 rms, stes, and effic. CI 4pm/CO noon. Nonsmoking rms avail. Decor is a bit disappointing. **Amenities:** 🔟 ♧ 🔲 Cable TV w/movies, refrig. No A/C. Some units w/minibars, some w/Jacuzzis. **Services:** ✗ VP 🚐 △ ♧ Babysitting. **Facilities:** 12 1 rst, 1 bar (w/entertainment). **Rates:** HS June–Aug $69–$400 S or D; from $125 ste; from $125 effic. Extra person $5. Children under 12 stay free. Lower rates off-season. Higher rates for spec evnts/hols. Spec packages avail. Pking: Outdoor, $8. Maj CC.

🏨🏨🏨 **Humphrey's Half Moon Inn & Suites**, 2303 Shelter Island Dr, San Diego, CA 92106 (Shelter Island); tel 619/224-3411 or toll free 800/542-7400; fax 619/224-3478. 6 mi W of downtown. Rosecrans St exit off I-5. A good value for families. Hawaiian theme complete with thatched-roof entrance and staff dressed in island garb. Grounds boast palm trees, tropical flowers, waterfalls, and a pond with goldfish and ducks. A little worn around the edges. **Rooms:** 182 rms and stes. CI 4pm/CO noon. Hawaiian decor. Some rooms have views of the city or the bay. **Amenities:** 🔟♧🔲 ¶A/C, cable TV w/movies, refrig. Some units w/terraces. **Services:** ✗ 🚐 △ ♧ Babysitting. Compli-

mentary newspaper. **Facilities:** 🔟 🚲 250 ♿ 1 rst, 1 bar (w/entertainment), lawn games, whirlpool, washer/dryer. Stage for outdoor concerts featuring popular singers. Putting green, table tennis. **Rates:** HS Mid-June–Labor Day $79–$149 S; $89–$149 D; from $109 ste. Children under 18 stay free. Min stay spec evnts. Lower rates off-season. MAP rates avail. Spec packages avail. Pking: Outdoor, free. Maj CC.

🏨🏨🏨🏨 **Hyatt Regency San Diego**, 1 Market Place, San Diego, CA 92101 (Downtown); tel 619/232-1234 or toll free 800/233-1234; fax 619/233-6464. One of the foremost meeting and convention facilities in the city, the Hyatt features an impressive palm court inlaid with marble. Located conveniently near the Convention Center and the waterfront Seaport Village shopping and dining complex. Public areas can get crammed and noisy when a large group is in house. **Rooms:** 875 rms and stes. Exec-level rms avail. CI 3pm/CO noon. Express checkout avail. Nonsmoking rms avail. Rooms are attractively furnished in two-tone woods and floral bedspreads accented by a jaunty plaid ruffle. All have waterfront views. Tiled bathrooms provide great counter space, but are functional, not sexy. **Amenities:** 🔟 ♧ 🔲 ¶ A/C, cable TV w/movies, bathrobes. Some units w/minibars. Iron and ironing board in every room. Business Plan rooms have in-room fax. **Services:** 🍴 🔑 VP 🚐 △ ♧ Twice-daily maid svce, car-rental desk, masseur, children's program, babysitting. Concierge can set up boat rentals, fishing excursions, etc., from nearby docks. Business Plan rates include free buffet breakfast, free local and credit-card calls, plus workstation in hallway with copy machine. **Facilities:** 🔟 🏊4 🛐 3.8k 🖥 ♿ 2 rsts, 2 bars (w/entertainment), sauna, steam rm, whirlpool, beauty salon. Long lap pool has a deck with great bay views. Health club offers a variety of weight and cardio machines, but a skimpy aerobics area, although they do offer some classes. **Rates:** $149–$245 S; $175–$270 D; from $325 ste. Extra person $25. Children under 12 stay free. Spec packages avail. Pking: Indoor, $8–$11. Maj CC.

🏨🏨🏨 **Kings Inn**, 1333 Hotel Circle S, San Diego, CA 92108 (Hotel Circle); tel 619/297-2231 or toll free 800/78-KINGS; fax 619/296-5255. 4 mi N of downtown. Hotel Circle exit off I-8. Not much to look at from the outside, but a pleasant lobby and rooms. **Rooms:** 140 rms and stes. CI 3pm/CO noon. Express checkout avail. Nonsmoking rms avail. Rooms are attractive and clean. **Amenities:** 🔟 🔲 A/C, cable TV w/movies. Some units w/minibars, some w/terraces. **Services:** ✗ △ ♧ Car-rental desk. Front desk staff helps with tour bookings, etc. **Facilities:** 🔟 250 ♿ 2 rsts, 1 bar (w/entertainment), whirlpool. Entertainment in bar Thursday through Saturday nights. **Rates:** HS June–Sept $59–$89 S or D; from $100 ste. Lower rates off-season. Spec packages avail. Pking: Outdoor, free. Maj CC.

≡≡ **La Pensione Hotel**, 1700 India St, at Date St, San Diego, CA 92101 (Little Italy); tel 619/236-8000 or toll free 800/232-4685; fax 619/236-8088. ½ mi N of downtown. It does not offer a lot of amenities, but this property is very clean and comfortable; many guests stay for weeks at a time. **Rooms:** 80 rms. CI 3pm/CO 11am. Few frills. **Amenities:** 🛁 Cable TV, refrig. No A/C. Some units w/terraces. Microwave. **Services:** 🚐 Front desk staff is very helpful. **Facilities:** ⅘ 2 rsts, washer/dryer. Restaurants have the feel of Italian neighborhood cafes. **Rates:** $40–$60 S or D. Extra person $5. Spec packages avail. Pking: Indoor, free. Maj CC.

≡≡≡ **Pacific Terrace Inn**, 610 Diamond St, San Diego, CA 92109 (Pacific Beach); tel 619/581-3500 or toll free 800/344-3370; fax 619/274-3341. 9 mi NW of downtown. Grand-Garnet exit off I-5; right on Mission Blvd and left on Diamond St. Lovely boutique hotel has a pleasant ambience. Located right on the boardwalk along the beach, it's both quiet and private. **Rooms:** 73 rms, stes, and effic. CI 4pm/CO 11am. Charming, well-appointed rooms. **Amenities:** 🛁 🐾 🔲 🍽 A/C, cable TV, bathrobes. All units w/minibars, some w/terraces, some w/Jacuzzis. Some rooms have refrigerators, safes, spa tubs, and multiple telephones. Kitchens in 40 rooms. Thick towels. **Services:** 🗝 🛎 🚗 Car-rental desk, babysitting. Continental breakfast and afternoon snacks in lobby. Room service provided by local restaurants. **Facilities:** 🏖 🏄 🌊 ⅘ 1 beach (ocean), lifeguard, board surfing, whirlpool, washer/dryer. Lovely pool faces the ocean. Secure parking. **Rates (CP):** HS June–Sept $160–$200 S or D; from $270 ste; from $170 effic. Extra person $10. Min stay wknds. Lower rates off-season. Spec packages avail. Pking: Indoor/outdoor, free. Maj CC.

≡≡≡ **Pan Pacific Hotel**, 400 W Broadway, San Diego, CA 92101 (Downtown); tel 619/239-4500 or toll free 800/626-3988; fax 619/239-4527. In the Emerald-Shapery Center between State and Columbia Sts. This soaring signature on San Diego's skyline has been the filming location for several TV shows and movies. Glass elevators provide dynamite city views. **Rooms:** 436 rms and stes. CI 2pm/CO noon. Express checkout avail. Nonsmoking rms avail. **Amenities:** 🛁 🐾 🍽 A/C, cable TV w/movies, bathrobes. All units w/minibars, some w/terraces, some w/Jacuzzis. **Services:** ✕ 🗝 📺 🚐 🛎 🚗 Twice-daily maid svce, masseur, babysitting. **Facilities:** 🏋 🍽 🎱 🖥 ⅘ 2 rsts, 2 bars (w/entertainment), sauna, steam rm, whirlpool. Well-equipped health club has a wall of windows and a view of the city. Romeo Cucina serves very good Italian dishes. **Rates:** HS Sept–June $150–$170 S; $170–$190 D; from $300 ste. Extra person $15. Children under 18 stay free. Lower rates off-season. Spec packages avail. Pking: Indoor, $8. Maj CC.

≡≡ **Park Manor Suites**, 525 Spruce St, San Diego, CA 92103 (Hillcrest); tel 619/291-0999 or toll free 800/874-2649; fax 619/291-8844. At 5th Ave. 1½ mi N of downtown. A 1926 Italian Renaissance–style hotel opposite Balboa Park. Lobby has a European feel, with antiques, an oriental rug, and a baby grand piano. Rooftop bar offers great views. **Rooms:** 80 stes. CI 3pm/CO noon. Nonsmoking rms avail. Very spacious suites have kitchen area, living room, bedroom, and bath; modestly furnished, but well kept up. Bathrooms are very basic. **Amenities:** 🛁 🔲 Cable TV w/movies, refrig. No A/C. Some units w/terraces. **Services:** 🚐 🚗 🛎 Twice-daily maid svce, babysitting. Complimentary continental breakfast in rooftop bar. **Facilities:** 150 1 rst, 1 bar (w/entertainment), washer/dryer. **Rates (CP):** From $69 ste. Children under 12 stay free. Min stay spec evnts. Spec packages avail. Pking: Outdoor, free. Maj CC.

≡≡≡ **Ramada Hotel Old Town**, 2435 Jefferson St, San Diego, CA 92110 (Old Town); tel 619/260-8500 or toll free 800/255-3544; fax 619/297-2078. 3 mi NW of downtown. Old Town Ave exit off I-5; left on Jefferson. A Spanish-style property, near the center of Old Town. Lobby is decorated with Spanish artifacts and features a fireplace. **Rooms:** 151 rms and stes. Exec-level rms avail. CI 3pm/CO noon. Express checkout avail. Nonsmoking rms avail. Rooms have basic decor. Those facing the freeway can be very noisy. **Amenities:** 🛁 🐾 A/C, TV w/movies. Some units w/terraces, 1 w/Jacuzzi. **Services:** ✕ 🗝 🚐 🛎 🚗 Babysitting. Complimentary cocktails 5–7pm. **Facilities:** 🏋 🍽 630 ⅘ 1 rst, 1 bar, whirlpool, washer/dryer. The Gila House serves outstanding carne asada. **Rates (BB):** $129 S; $139 D; from $169 ste. Extra person $10. Children under 12 stay free. Min stay spec evnts. Higher rates for spec evnts/hols. Spec packages avail. Pking: Indoor/outdoor, free. Maj CC.

≡≡≡ **San Diego Marriott Hotel & Marina**, 333 W Harbor Dr, San Diego, CA 92101 (Downtown); or toll free 800/228-9290; fax 619/234-8678. Near the convention center on the bay. A 2-tower hotel complex ideally located on the bay next to the convention center. Beautiful pool area, landscaped with exotic plants and cascading waterfalls. Very busy lobby. **Rooms:** 1,355 rms and stes. Exec-level rms avail. CI 4pm/CO noon. Express checkout avail. Nonsmoking rms avail. A renovation of South Tower rooms has been completed; North Tower is undergoing one. **Amenities:** 🛁 🐾 🍽 A/C, cable TV w/movies, voice mail. Some units w/minibars, some w/terraces, some w/Jacuzzis. **Services:** 🍽 🗝 📺 🚐 🛎 🚗 🚗 Twice-daily maid svce, car-rental desk, masseur, children's program, babysitting. **Facilities:** 🏋 🚲 ⛳ 🏊 🍽 7K 🖥 ⅘ 6 rsts, 4 bars (2 w/entertainment), lifeguard, games rm, sauna, whirlpool, beauty salon, washer/dryer. **Rates:** $134–$200 S or D; from $350 ste. Children under 18 stay free. Spec packages avail. Pking: Indoor/outdoor, $8–$11. Maj CC.

≣≣≣ **Sheraton Harbor Island Hotel**, 1380 Harbor Island Dr, San Diego, CA 92113; tel 619/291-2900 or toll free 800/325-3535; fax 619/692-2337. 2 mi NW of downtown. ½ mi from the airport. On Harbor Island, overlooking the marina and close to shops and restaurants. Very convenient to the airport. **Rooms:** 1,048 rms and stes. Exec-level rms avail. CI 3pm/CO noon. Express checkout avail. Nonsmoking rms avail. Rooms are newly renovated. All have marble bathrooms and a downtown or marina view. **Amenities:** 🛅 🅰 ☎ A/C, cable TV w/movies, refrig, voice mail, bathrobes. All units w/minibars, all w/terraces, some w/Jacuzzis. Some rooms have hairdryers, robes, and safes. All have irons and ironing boards. **Services:** ⭕ ☎ 🆅🅿 🚗 🛅 🍽 Car-rental desk, masseur, children's program, babysitting. **Facilities:** 🛅 🚴 ⛱ 🏹 🎿 🐾² 🎣 ⛳ 🖼 💻 ᵹ 4 rsts, 3 bars (w/entertainment), games rm, lawn games, spa, sauna, whirlpool, beauty salon, washer/dryer. **Rates:** $180 S or D; from $275 ste. Extra person $10. Children under 17 stay free. Min stay spec evnts. Spec packages avail. Pking: Outdoor, $8–$11. Maj CC.

≣≣≣ **Town & Country Hotel**, 500 Hotel Circle N, San Diego, CA 92108 (Hotel Circle); tel 619/291-7131 or toll free 800/77-ATLAS; fax 619/291-3584. 4 mi N of downtown. Hotel Circle exit off I-8. Large property with lovely gardens. Caters primarily to conventions. **Rooms:** 1,000 rms and stes. CI 4pm/CO noon. Express checkout avail. Nonsmoking rms avail. Attractive decor with small bathrooms. Some rooms are in a 9-story tower; others are in low-rise buildings. **Amenities:** 🛅 🅰 A/C, cable TV w/movies. Some units w/terraces. **Services:** ✕ ☎ 🛅 🍽 Car-rental desk, babysitting. Hertz office on premises. **Facilities:** 🛅 🖼 ᵹ 4 rsts, 3 bars (w/entertainment), whirlpool, beauty salon, day-care ctr. **Rates:** $69–$89 S; $89–$99 D; from $200 ste. Extra person $10. Children under 18 stay free. Higher rates for spec evnts/hols. Spec packages avail. Pking: Indoor/outdoor, $5. Maj CC.

≣≣≣ **US Grant Hotel**, 326 Broadway, San Diego, CA 92101 (Downtown); tel 619/232-3121 or toll free 800/237-5029, 800/334-6957 in CA; fax 619/232-3626. Between 3rd and 4th Aves. This San Diego landmark welcomes guests with a warmth and civility that was once expected in the best hotels. **Rooms:** 280 rms and stes. Exec-level rms avail. CI 3pm/CO noon. Express checkout avail. Nonsmoking rms avail. Although not luxurious, rooms have an old-world charm. **Amenities:** 🛅 🅰 A/C, cable TV w/movies. Some units w/minibars, some w/terraces, some w/Jacuzzis. **Services:** ⭕ ☎ 🆅🅿 🚗 🛅 🍽 🍷 Car-rental desk, babysitting. **Facilities:** 🖼 💻 ᵹ 1 rst (see also "Restaurants" below), 1 bar (w/entertainment). Concierge will arrange

golf, tennis, and use of a nearby fitness club. The Grant Grill is a San Diego legend. **Rates:** HS Sept–May $135–$155 S; $155–$175 D; from $245 ste. Extra person $20. Children under 16 stay free. Lower rates off-season. Pking: Indoor/outdoor, $5–$10. Maj CC.

≣≣≣ **Vacation Inn**, 3900 Old Town Ave, San Diego, CA 92110 (Old Town); tel 619/299-7400 or toll free 800/451-9846; fax 619/299-1619. 3 mi NW of downtown. Old Town Ave exit off I-5. Hacienda-style hotel in Old Town has a European flair. Fountains, bougainvillea, and a spacious lobby with fireplace. Convenient to shopping, sightseeing, and many restaurants. **Rooms:** 125 rms and stes. CI 3pm/CO noon. Nonsmoking rms avail. French-country decor in pleasing color scheme. Very inviting and comfortable, but bathtub is small. **Amenities:** 🛅 🅰 ☎ A/C, cable TV w/movies, refrig. Some units w/terraces, 1 w/Jacuzzi. Microwave. **Services:** 🚗 🛅 🍽 Babysitting. Complimentary continental breakfast and afternoon refreshments. **Facilities:** 🛅 🖼 ᵹ Whirlpool, washer/dryer. **Rates (CP):** HS June–Aug $88–$107 S; $98–$117 D; from $116 ste. Extra person $10. Children under 17 stay free. Lower rates off-season. Spec packages avail. Pking: Indoor/outdoor, free. Maj CC.

≣≣≣≣ **Westgate Hotel**, 1055 2nd Ave, San Diego, CA 92101 (Downtown); tel 619/238-1818 or toll free 800/221-3802; fax 619/557-3737. Between Broadway and C St. With its Baccarat chandeliers, and original Louis XV concierge desk, this hotel looks as if it's been here for 100 years, although it actually opened in 1970. **Rooms:** 223 rms, stes, and effic. CI 2pm/CO noon. Express checkout avail. Nonsmoking rms avail. Each of the rooms is individually decorated. All feature foyers, plus charming touches. **Amenities:** 🛅 🅰 🍷 A/C, cable TV w/movies, refrig, shoe polisher, bathrobes. All units w/minibars. **Services:** ⭕ ☎ 🆅🅿 🚗 🛅 🍽 Twice-daily maid svce, car-rental desk, masseur, babysitting. Complimentary car service within the San Diego area. **Facilities:** 🖼 🖼 💻 ᵹ 3 rsts, 2 bars (w/entertainment), beauty salon. Piano bar is very popular on weekends, with repertoire ranging from opera to Top 40. **Rates:** $144–$164 S; $154–$174 D; from $295 ste; from $450 effic. Extra person $10. Children under 18 stay free. Spec packages avail. Pking: Indoor, $8. Maj CC.

Motels

≣≣ **Best Western Blue Sea Lodge**, 707 Pacific Beach Dr, San Diego, CA 92109 (Pacific Beach); tel 619/488-4700 or toll free 800/258-3732; fax 619/488-7276. 9 mi NW of downtown. Grand/Garnet exit off I-5; W on Grand Ave, S on Mission Blvd, W on Pacific Beach Dr. Located on the beachfront boardwalk, this property is due for renovation. Except for the entrance, it's an acceptable hotel. **Rooms:** 100 rms, stes, and effic. CI 3pm/

CO noon. Nonsmoking rms avail. Adequate. **Amenities:** 🛏 🐾 📻 A/C, cable TV, in-rm safe. All units w/terraces. **Services:** 🗺 🍴 Car-rental desk, babysitting. Complimentary breakfast buffet. Local restaurants will deliver. Front-desk staff helps arrange tours and rental cars. **Facilities:** 🏊 ♿ 🏖 ♿ 1 beach (ocean), board surfing, whirlpool, washer/dryer. **Rates (CP):** HS June–Sept $113–$128 S; $123–$153 D; from $190 ste; from $190 effic. Extra person $15. Children under 18 stay free. Min stay spec evnts. Lower rates off-season. Spec packages avail. Pking: Indoor/outdoor, free. Maj CC.

📶📶 **Crystal Pier Hotel**, 4500 Ocean Blvd at Garnet, San Diego, CA 92109 (Pacific Beach); tel 619/483-6983 or toll free 800/748-5894; fax 619/483-6811. 9 mi NW of downtown. Grand/Garnet exit off I-5; W on Garnet. This historic property (built in 1927) offers a rare opportunity to sleep over the water because of its pier location. Magnificent beach and water views. A major upgrade is in progress. **Rooms:** 26 effic. CI 1pm/CO 11am. Nonsmoking rms avail. New and remodeled units are of high caliber, but older ones look worn. Best units are upstairs. The further out on the pier, the quieter the lodging. **Amenities:** 🛏 🐾 📻 TV, refrig. No A/C. All units w/terraces. **Services:** ✕ 🍴 Car-rental desk. Adjacent Kono's Surf Club will deliver breakfast and lunch from 7am–2pm. **Facilities:** 🛶 🏖 ♿ 1 beach (ocean), lifeguard, board surfing. Bait, fishing poles, boogie boards, beach chairs, and umbrellas available. **Rates:** HS June–Sept from $140 effic. Min stay. Lower rates off-season. Higher rates for spec evnts/hols. Pking: Outdoor, free. Ltd CC.

📶📶 **Fabulous Inn–San Diego**, 2485 Hotel Circle Place, San Diego, CA 92108 (Hotel Circle); tel 619/291-7700 or toll free 800/647-1903; fax 619/297-6179. 4 mi N of downtown. Hotel Circle exit off I-8. Adequate lodging. Nice lobby and entranceway. **Rooms:** 175 rms and stes. CI 4pm/CO noon. Nonsmoking rms avail. **Amenities:** 🛏 🐾 A/C, cable TV. Some units w/terraces, some w/Jacuzzis. **Services:** 🚐 🗺 🍴 Car-rental desk. Airport transfers from 7am–10pm. **Facilities:** 🏊 🏀 ♿ Games rm, whirlpool, washer/dryer. **Rates:** HS June–Sept $56–$66 S; $60–$75 D; from $66 ste. Extra person $10. Children under 18 stay free. Min stay spec evnts. Lower rates off-season. Pking: Indoor/outdoor, free. Maj CC.

📶📶 **Hampton Inn**, 5434 Kearny Mesa Rd, San Diego, CA 92111 (Clairemont Mesa); tel 619/292-1482 or toll free 800/292-1482; fax 619/292-4410. 10 mi N of downtown. Clairemont Mesa Blvd exit off Calif 163; W on Clairemont Mesa Blvd; right on Kearny Mesa Rd. A 5-year-old property with spacious entry, comfortable lobby, and well-tended grounds. **Rooms:** 151 rms. Exec-level rms avail. CI 2pm/CO 11am. Nonsmoking rms avail. Nice rooms, most of which are nonsmoking. Some have kitchenettes. **Amenities:** 🛏 🐾 A/C, cable TV w/movies. Some

rooms have VCRs. **Services:** 🚐 🗺 🍴 Babysitting. Free grocery-shopping service available. **Facilities:** 🏊 📶 ♿ Washer/dryer. Nice pool, but some street noise and not much sun. **Rates (CP):** HS Mem Day–Labor Day $77 S; $83 D. Children under 18 stay free. Min stay spec evnts. Lower rates off-season. Spec packages avail. Pking: Outdoor, free. Maj CC.

📶📶 **Hotel Circle Inn & Suites**, 2201 Hotel Circle S, San Diego, CA 92108; tel 619/291-2711 or toll free 800/772-7711; fax 619/542-1227. 4 mi N of downtown. Hotel Circle exit off I-8. Good choice for families, particularly units with kitchens. **Rooms:** 197 rms and effic. CI 2pm/CO noon. Nonsmoking rms avail. Rooms are pleasant, bright, and clean. **Amenities:** 🛏 📻 A/C, satel TV w/movies. 1 unit w/minibar. **Services:** 🍴 Car-rental desk. Free coffee in lobby. **Facilities:** 🏊 1 rst, whirlpool, washer/dryer. **Rates:** HS Mem Day–Labor Day $59–$79 S or D; from $65 effic. Extra person $7. Min stay HS. Lower rates off-season. Higher rates for spec evnts/hols. Pking: Outdoor, free. Maj CC. Minimum stay for kitchen units in summer.

📶 **Motel 6**, 2424 Hotel Circle N, San Diego, CA 92108 (Hotel Circle); tel 619/296-1612; fax 619/543-9305. 4 mi N of downtown. Taylor St exit off I-8. Basic, clean rooms. **Rooms:** 202 rms. CI 3pm/CO noon. Nonsmoking rms avail. **Amenities:** 🛏 A/C, cable TV. Some units w/terraces. **Services:** 🍴 🐾 **Facilities:** 🏊 ♿ Washer/dryer. **Rates:** HS June–Sept $36 S; $40 D. Children under 18 stay free. Lower rates off-season. Pking: Outdoor, free. Maj CC.

📶📶 **Ocean Park Inn**, 710 Grand Ave, San Diego, CA 92109 (Pacific Beach); tel 619/483-5858 or toll free 800/231-7735; fax 619/274-0823. 9 mi NW of downtown. Grand/Garnet exit off I-5; W on Grand Ave. Attractive motor hotel built in 1992 on the boardwalk along the beach. Somewhat noisy. **Rooms:** 73 rms, stes, and effic. CI 2pm/CO 11am. Nonsmoking rms avail. Rooms are spacious, modern, and nicely coordinated. **Amenities:** 🛏 🐾 A/C, cable TV, refrig. All units w/terraces. **Services:** ✕ 🗺 🍴 Car-rental desk, babysitting. Front desk staff acts as concierge. Complimentary continental breakfast. **Facilities:** 🏊 🏖 ♿ 1 beach (ocean), lifeguard, board surfing, whirlpool, washer/dryer. Swimming pool overlooks the beach. **Rates (CP):** HS Mem Day–Sept 12 $85–$145 S or D; from $130 ste; from $170 effic. Extra person $10. Children under 12 stay free. Min stay wknds. Lower rates off-season. Spec packages avail. Pking: Indoor, free. Maj CC.

📶📶 **Padre Trail Inn**, 4200 Taylor St, San Diego, CA 92110 (Old Town); tel 619/297-3291 or toll free 800/255-9988; fax 619/692-2080. 3½ mi N of downtown. Taylor St off I-8; near intersection of I-5 and I-8. Typical 1950s-style motel, functional and clean but with few amenities. **Rooms:** 100 rms. CI noon/CO noon. **Amenities:** 🛏 🐾 A/C, satel TV. **Services:** ✕ 🍴 Babysitting. **Facilities:** ⛶ 🏊 ♿ 1 rst, 1 bar. Pleasant restaurant and bar have very reasonable prices. **Rates:** HS Mid-June–mid-Sept $44–$55 S; $49–$69 D. Extra person $5. Children under 18 stay free. Min stay spec evnts. Lower rates off-season. Higher rates for spec evnts/hols. Pking: Outdoor, free. Maj CC.

≣≣≣ Sommerset Suites Hotel, 606 Washington St, San Diego, CA 92103 (Hillcrest); tel 619/692-5200 or toll free 800/ 962-9665, 800/356-1787 in CA; fax 619/299-6065. 2½ mi N of downtown. Washington St exit off I-5; at 5th St. Located near 2 hospitals. No restaurant on site, but many within walking distance. **Rooms:** 80 effic. CI 2pm/CO noon. Nonsmoking rms avail. Very clean and attractive rooms. **Amenities:** 🛎 🅰 📺 A/C, cable TV w/movies, refrig, voice mail, in-rm safe. Some units w/terraces. All units have 2-line telephones and full kitchens. **Services:** 🚐 🖼 🐺 Car-rental desk, babysitting. Complimentary social hour with wine and beer 4–6pm. Free shuttle to zoo, shopping, and downtown. **Facilities:** ⛶ 🏊 ♿ Whirlpool, washer/dryer. Use of gas barbecues. **Rates (CP):** HS June–Sept from $120 effic. Extra person $10. Children under 12 stay free. Lower rates off-season. Pking: Indoor, free. Maj CC.

≣ Surf and Sand Motel, 4666 Mission Blvd, San Diego, CA 92109 (Pacific Beach); tel 619/483-7420 or toll free 800/ 800-8000; fax 619/237-9940. 9 mi NW of downtown. Grand-Garnet exit off I-5; W on Garnet, N on Mission Blvd. Modest motel ½ block from the beach, with a small but pleasant lobby. A bit noisy. **Rooms:** 25 rms, stes, and effic; 1 ctge/villa. CI noon/ CO 11am. Rooms are adequate in size but furnishings are old. There's a 3-bedroom, 2-bath house for rent adjacent to the motel. **Amenities:** 🛎 Cable TV, refrig. No A/C. 1 unit w/Jacuzzi. **Services:** 🚐 Car-rental desk. Free coffee in the lobby. **Facilities:** ⛶ **Rates:** HS June–Sept $54–$59 S or D; from $90 ste; from $59 effic. Min stay spec evnts. Lower rates off-season. Pking: Outdoor, free. Maj CC. Cottages/villas available by the week only, from $1200/wk.

≣ Surfer Motor Lodge, 711 Pacific Beach Dr, San Diego, CA 92109 (Pacific Beach); tel 619/483-7070 or toll free 800/ 787-3373; fax 619/274-1670. 9 mi NW of downtown. Grand-Garnet exit off I-5; W on Grand Ave; S on Mission Blvd; W on Pacific Beach Dr. Beachfront location is the biggest attraction of this 4-story hotel. **Rooms:** 52 rms and effic. CI 2pm/CO noon. **Amenities:** 🛎 TV, refrig. No A/C. Some units w/terraces. **Services:** 🐺 **Facilities:** ⛶ 🚴 🏖 1 beach (ocean), lifeguard, board surfing, washer/dryer. Pool faces the ocean. Excellent restaurant adjacent. **Rates:** HS June–Sept $77–$92 S or D; from $87 effic. Extra person $5. Lower rates off-season. Pking: Outdoor, free. Maj CC.

Resorts

≣≣≣ Bahia Resort Hotel, 998 W Mission Bay Dr, San Diego, CA 92109 (Mission Beach); tel 619/488-0551 or toll free 800/288-0770; fax 619/488-7055. 8 mi NW of downtown. Mission Bay Dr exit off I-8. 14 acres. A good place for families, well located on a peninsula on Mission Bay. Harbor seals live in a pond out front. **Rooms:** 325 rms, stes, and effic. CI 4pm/CO noon. Nonsmoking rms avail. **Amenities:** 🛎 🅰 A/C, cable TV w/movies, refrig. All units w/terraces. **Services:** ✕ 🖼 🐺 🐋 Car-rental desk, babysitting. Bellman will book tours and make recommendations. **Facilities:** ⛶ 🚴 ⛵ 🎿 🏊 ⚓ 🚤 ♿ 1 rst, 1 bar (w/entertainment), 1 beach (bay), lifeguard, whirlpool, playground. **Rates:** HS July–Aug $125–$155 S or D; from $225 ste; from $225 effic. Extra person $15. Children under 13 stay free. Min stay HS and wknds. Lower rates off-season. Pking: Outdoor, free. Maj CC.

≣≣≣ Carmel Highland Doubletree Golf & Tennis Resort, 14455 Peñasquitos Dr, San Diego, CA 92129; tel 619/ 672-9100 or toll free 800/622-9223; fax 619/672-9166. 25 mi N of downtown, exit off I-15. Carmel Mountain Rd exit off I-15; 1 block W of Carmel Mountain Rd. 130 acres. This resort has it all and presents it in a luxurious way. Caters to corporate travelers and business meetings as well as families. **Rooms:** 172 rms and stes. CI 3pm/CO noon. Nonsmoking rms avail. Rooms are fairly large, with comfortable furnishings. **Amenities:** 🛎 🅰 📺 🍶 A/C, cable TV w/movies, bathrobes. All units w/minibars, all w/terraces. **Services:** ✕ 🚐 🖼 🐺 🐋 Masseur, children's program, babysitting. Golf and tennis lessons available. **Facilities:** ⛶ 🚴 ⛳ 🎾 🎿 🏊 ♿ 2 rsts, 1 bar (w/entertainment), lifeguard, sauna, steam rm, whirlpool, day-care ctr, washer/dryer. **Rates:** $109–$159 S or D; from $129 ste. Extra person $10. Children under 16 stay free. Spec packages avail. Pking: Outdoor, free. Maj CC. Golf and tennis packages available.

≣≣≣ Catamaran Resort Hotel, 3999 Mission Blvd, San Diego, CA 92109 (Pacific Beach); tel 619/488-1081 or toll free 800/288-0770; fax 619/488-1619. 9 mi NW of downtown. Grand/Garnet exit off I-5; W on Grand, S on Mission Blvd. 8 acres. The landscaping is unusual, with plants from all over the world. Very attractive and well maintained. Lobby atrium has a waterfall, slate floor, and tropical foliage. **Rooms:** 312 rms, stes, and effic. CI 4pm/CO noon. Nonsmoking rms avail. Rooms in 13-story tower have views of Sail Bay, San Diego skyline, and Coronado Bridge. Rooms in the low-rise section have beach access. **Amenities:** 🛎 🅰 A/C, cable TV w/movies, refrig. All units w/terraces, 1 w/Jacuzzi. **Services:** ✕ 🍽 🆅🅿 🖼 🐺 🐋 Car-rental desk, babysitting. Room service 6am–1am. Lifeguard in summer only. **Facilities:** ⛶ 🚴 ⛵ 🎿 🏊 🚤 ♿ 1 rst (see also ''Restaurants'' below), 2 bars (w/entertainment), 1 beach (bay), lifeguard, lawn games, whirlpool. Beach volleyball, Award-winning restaurant. **Rates:** HS July–Aug $140–$195 S or D; from $265 ste; from $265 effic. Extra person $15. Children under 13 stay free. Min stay HS and wknds. Lower rates off-season. Spec packages avail. Pking: Indoor/outdoor, $5. Maj CC. Minimum stay on summer weekends.

≣≣≣ Handlery Hotel & Country Club, 950 Hotel Circle N, San Diego, CA 92108; tel 619/298-0511 or toll free 800/676-6567; fax 619/298-9793. 4 mi N of downtown. Hotel Circle exit off I-8. 225 acres. An older property, pleasant and very clean. **Rooms:** 217 rms and stes. CI 3pm/CO noon. Nonsmoking rms avail. **Amenities:** 🛗 ⚱ 🖭 A/C, cable TV w/movies. Some units w/terraces, 1 w/Jacuzzi. **Services:** ✕ 🛆 🚭 Car-rental desk, masseur. Room service 7am–10pm. Bellman will book tours. **Facilities:** 🛆 ▶27 🕳 🖳 350 🛆 3 rsts, 2 bars (1 w/entertainment), whirlpool, beauty salon, washer/dryer. Good golf and tennis facilities. No elevator. **Rates:** $75–$85 S; $85–$95 D; from $150 ste. Extra person $10. Children under 15 stay free. Min stay spec evnts. Spec packages avail. Pking: Outdoor, free. Maj CC.

≣≣≣ Hyatt Islandia, 1441 Quivira Rd, San Diego, CA 92109 (Mission Bay); tel 619/224-1234 or toll free 800/233-1234; fax 619/224-0348. 7 mi NW of downtown. West Mission Bay Dr exit off I-8. 7 acres. Nicely located on a marina in Mission Bay, with beautifully landscaped grounds. **Rooms:** 422 rms and stes. Exec-level rms avail. CI 4pm/CO noon. Express checkout avail. Nonsmoking rms avail. Rooms are located in low-rise units as well as an 18-story tower. **Amenities:** 🛗 ⚱ A/C, cable TV w/movies, voice mail. Some units w/minibars, all w/terraces, 1 w/fireplace. Refrigerators available on request. **Services:** ✕ 🛏 🛆 🚭 Car-rental desk, children's program, babysitting. Turn-down service on request. **Facilities:** 🛆 🚲 ⚠ 🔲 📷 🛆 🖳 500 🖳 🛆 2 rsts, 2 bars (1 w/entertainment), lawn games, whirlpool, washer/dryer. Boat rentals, and fishing and whale-watching expeditions, available at the marina. **Rates:** $109–$175 S or D; from $175 ste. Extra person $15. Children under 18 stay free. Min stay spec evnts. Spec packages avail. Pking: Indoor/outdoor, free. Maj CC.

≣≣≣ Rancho Bernardo Inn, 17550 Bernardo Oaks Dr, San Diego, CA 92128; tel 619/487-1611 or toll free 800/854-1065, 800/542-6096 in CA; fax 619/673-0311. 25 mi NE of downtown. Rancho Bernardo Rd exit E off I-15; left on Bernardo Oaks Dr. A relaxed resort with an emphasis on tennis and golf. Hacienda-style lobby is accented by beamed ceilings, adobe-textured walls, and wrought-iron fixtures. Five Italian-marble fountains beautify the grounds. **Rooms:** 287 rms and stes. CI 4pm/CO noon. Express checkout avail. Nonsmoking rms avail. Set in 2- to 3-story buildings around the property, rooms are

done in desert-tone fabrics and bleached woods. All accommodations have been recently refurbished. **Amenities:** 🛗 ⚱ A/C, cable TV, refrig, in-rm safe, shoe polisher. All units w/minibars, all w/terraces, some w/fireplaces, some w/Jacuzzis. Conspicuously lacking are amenities such as hairdryers and bathrobes (available on request). Room doors lack deadbolts and safety chains. **Services:** ✕ 🛏 VP 🚐 🛆 🚭 🍴 Twice-daily maid svce, car-rental desk, masseur, children's program, babysitting. Friendly staff gets a bit swamped when large meeting groups arrive or depart. Complimentary afternoon tea served in the cozy music room. **Facilities:** 🛆 🚲 ▶45 📷 ◈6 🔲 🖳 500 🖳 🛆 3 rsts, 2 bars (w/entertainment), lawn games, spa, sauna, steam rm, whirlpool. 108 holes of golf are within 30 minutes of the inn. On-site facilities include a pro shop plus Ken Blanchard's Golf University of San Diego. There's also an excellent Tennis College. **Rates:** $185–$215 S or D; from $230 ste. Children under 18 stay free. Spec packages avail. Pking: Outdoor, free. Maj CC. Tennis and golf packages available.

≣≣≣ San Diego Hilton Beach and Tennis Resort, 1775 E Mission Bay Dr, San Diego, CA 92109 (Mission Bay); tel 619/276-4010 or toll free 800/445-8667; fax 619/275-7992. 8 mi NW of downtown. From Tecolote Rd turn right onto E Mission Bay Dr. 18 acres. A major renovation is nearing completion. Pleasant decor. **Rooms:** 357 rms and stes. CI 3pm/CO noon. Express checkout avail. Nonsmoking rms avail. Spacious accommodations in an 8-story tower and 2-story buildings; 12 rooms for guests with disabilities. **Amenities:** 🛗 ⚱ 🖭 🍴 A/C, cable TV w/movies, refrig, voice mail. All units w/minibars, all w/terraces. Ceiling fan; iron and ironing board in room. **Services:** ✕ 🛏 🚐 🛆 🚭 🍴 Car-rental desk, masseur, children's program, babysitting. Scuba lessons available. **Facilities:** 🛆 🚲 ⚠ 🔲 📷 🔲 🛶 ▶ 🖳 700 🖳 🛆 3 rsts, 3 bars (1 w/entertainment), 1 beach (bay), lifeguard, games rm, sauna, whirlpool, beauty salon, playground, washer/dryer. **Rates:** HS July–Aug $150–$205 S; $170–$225 D; from $375 ste. Children under 13 stay free. Min stay spec evnts. Lower rates off-season. Spec packages avail. Pking: Outdoor, free. Maj CC.

≣≣ San Diego Princess Resort, 1404 W Vacation Rd, San Diego, CA 92109 (Mission Bay); tel 619/274-4630 or toll free 800/344-2626; fax 619/581-5929. 8 mi NW of downtown. Sea World Dr exit off I-5; Sea World Dr W to Ingraham St N; W on Vacation Rd. 44 acres. Bungalows are spread out on spacious grounds here; guests can park right next to their accommodations. **Rooms:** 462 ctges/villas. CI 4pm/CO noon. Express checkout avail. Nonsmoking rms avail. **Amenities:** 🛗 ⚱ A/C, cable TV w/movies, refrig. Some units w/minibars, some w/terraces. **Services:** ✕ 🛏 🛆 🚭 🍴 Car-rental desk, social director, masseur, children's program, babysitting. **Facilities:** 🛆 🚲 ⚠ 🔲 📷 🔲 🖳 120 🛆 3 rsts, 4 bars (2 w/entertainment), 1 beach (bay), lifeguard, games rm, lawn games, spa, sauna, steam rm, whirlpool, playground, washer/dryer. **Rates:** HS July–Aug from $165 ctge/villa. Extra person $20. Min stay spec evnts. Lower rates off-season. Higher rates for spec evnts/hols. Spec packages avail. Pking: Outdoor, free. Maj CC.

Restaurants 🍴

♥ **Anthony's Star of the Sea Room**, 1360 N Harbor Dr, San Diego (Downtown); tel 619/232-7408. At Ash St. **Seafood.** Old-world elegance, spacious tables, and a view of San Diego Bay. An intimate bar area features a crystal ship chandelier. Dishes include sole stuffed with lobster, shrimp, and crab; and marinated baked swordfish. Jackets are required (and provided if necessary). **FYI:** Reservations recommended. Jacket required. **Open:** Dinner daily 5:30–10:30pm. Closed some hols. **Prices:** Main courses $16.50–$32.50. Maj CC. ♥ ▲ ▼ VP &

★ **Athens Market**, 109 W F St, San Diego (Downtown); tel 619/234-1955. Between 1st and Front Sts. **Greek.** A gathering place for local television personalities. Tables topped with white linen surround the bar. The menu offers Greek specialties such as baked chicken with oregano, lemon, and olive oil, and moussaka. Belly dancers perform on weekends. **FYI:** Reservations recommended. Dancing. **Open:** Lunch daily 11:30am–4pm; dinner daily 4–11pm. Closed some hols. **Prices:** Main courses $9.95–$19.95. Maj CC. &

⑤ **The Atoll**, in the Catamaran Resort Hotel, 3999 Mission Blvd, San Diego (Pacific Beach); tel 619/488-1081. Garnet/Grand Aves exit off I-5. **Continental.** You may choose to dine indoors or outdoors at the Atoll. Inside is more sophisticated, with rattan chairs, crisp tablecloths, Villeroy and Boch china. Outside you'll find wrought-iron tables and chairs shaded by umbrellas and a dazzling view of Mission Bay. Lunch and dinner menus are extensive, from club sandwiches to sophisticated preparations of fresh ahi tuna, salmon, swordfish, and other seafood. Sunday brunch is very popular. Service is top-notch. **FYI:** Reservations recommended. Children's menu. Dress code. **Open:** HS June–Labor Day daily 6:30am–11pm. Reduced hours off-season. **Prices:** Main courses $6–$19. Maj CC. ⛴ ▲ VP &

Beach Boy's Cantina & Sports Grill, in Belmont Park, 3125 Ocean Front Walk, San Diego (South Mission Beach); tel 619/539-2697. W Mission Bay Dr exit off I-8. **Mexican.** Live entertainment, open-air seating, and a beachfront location are the big draws here. Fresh tortilla chips, soups, fajitas, and shrimp flamed with tequila are among the offerings. Happy hour daily 4–7pm. **FYI:** Reservations accepted. Band. Children's menu. **Open:** Daily 8am–10pm. Closed Dec 25. **Prices:** Main courses $5.95–$12.95. Maj CC. ▲ &

The Brigantine Seafood Grill, 2444 San Diego Ave, San Diego (Old Town); tel 619/298-9840. 3 mi N of downtown. Old Town Ave exit off I-5. **Californian/Seafood.** Nautical decor. The patio has a fireplace, while the indoor dining area is dark. Specialties are fresh swordfish and Pacific King Salmon served with caper-dill sauce. Also at: 2725 Shelter Island Dr, Pt Loma (619/224-2871); 1333 Orange Ave, Coronado (619/435-4166); 3263 Camino del Mar, Del Mar (619/481-1166). **FYI:** Reservations recommended. Children's menu. **Open:** HS Mem Day–Labor Day lunch Sun–Fri 11:30am–2:30pm, Sat 11:30am–3pm; dinner Sun–Thurs 5–10:30pm, Fri–Sat 5–11:30pm; brunch Sun 10:30am–3pm. Reduced hours off-season. Closed some hols. **Prices:** Main courses $7.95–$29.95. Maj CC. ▼ &

Café Lulu, 419 F St, San Diego (Gaslamp Quarter); tel 619/238-0114. Near entrance to Horton Plaza parking garage. **Coffeehouse.** One of the few places in town where you can dine in the wee hours. Avant-garde decor features metal sculpted tables and chairs, copper hanging lights, and a mosaic made of broken glass. Dozens of specialty coffee drinks are available, as well as breakfast fare, sandwiches, and salads. **FYI:** Reservations not accepted. Beer and wine only. **Open:** Mon–Thurs 9am–2am, Fri 9am–4am, Sat 10am–4am, Sun 10am–2am. **Prices:** Main courses $2.50–$5.75. No CC. &

Cafe Pacifica, 2414 San Diego Ave, San Diego (Old Town); tel 619/291-6666. 3 mi NW of downtown. Old Town Ave exit off I-5. **Seafood.** In the evening, a romantic hideaway with twinkling lights. Indoors, there are several intimate dining areas, and the outdoor patio is an excellent setting for lunch. The menu offers salmon and sweet-corn cakes, and ahi with shiitake mushrooms and ginger butter, among other specialties. **FYI:** Reservations recommended. Dress code. **Open:** Lunch Mon–Fri 11:30am–2pm; dinner Sun–Thurs 5:30–9:30pm, Fri–Sat 5:30–10pm. **Prices:** Main courses $14–$20. Maj CC. ♥ ▼ VP &

Casa De Bandini, in Bazaar Del Mundo, 2754 Juan St, San Diego (Old Town); tel 619/297-8211. 3 mi NW of downtown. Old Town Ave exit off I-5. **Mexican.** An authentic Mexican dining experience; busy during peak hours but worth the wait. Outdoor dining is under colorful umbrellas to music of strolling mariachis; the atmosphere is more formal inside. House specialties are tequila lime shrimp and the "taco feast." **FYI:** Reservations not accepted. Guitar. Dress code. **Open:** HS mid-June–Labor Day Mon–Thurs 11am–9:30pm, Fri–Sat 11am–10pm, Sun 10am–9:30pm. Reduced hours off-season. Closed some hols. **Prices:** Main courses $4.95–$14.50. Maj CC. ⛴ 🍴 &

Celadon, 3628 5th Ave, San Diego (Hillcrest); tel 619/295-8800. 2 mi N of downtown. Between Brookes and Pennsylvania Aves. **Thai.** Easy to spot on the west side of Fifth Ave, with its pink stucco exterior and heliotrope awning. Interior is very pretty in pink and green with Thai artifacts along the walls. Food is primarily Thai-style seafood, pork, beef, and chicken, including lemon-grass beef and the spicy coconut shrimp. **FYI:** Reservations accepted. Beer and wine only. **Open:** Lunch Mon–Fri 11:30am–2pm; dinner Mon–Sat 5–10pm. Closed some hols. **Prices:** Main courses $8.50–$14. Maj CC. 👍

Ⓢ **Century Cafe**, in Century Business College, 2665 5th Ave, San Diego (Hillcrest); tel 619/544-1555. 2 mi N of downtown. Between Nutmeg and Maple Sts. **Continental/American.** Meals here are prepared by culinary students at the college, so the menu varies. Decor includes ceiling fans and artificial plants. The food is better than the ambience. **FYI:** Reservations accepted. Beer and wine only. **Open:** Breakfast Mon–Fri 7–10am; lunch Mon–Fri 11am–2:30pm; dinner Mon–Fri 5–9pm. Closed some hols; mid Dec–early Jan. **Prices:** PF dinner $5.95. Ltd CC. 📺

Ⓢ **The Corvette Diner Bar & Grill**, 3946 5th Ave, San Diego (Hillcrest); tel 619/542-1476. 2½ mi N of downtown. Between Washington St and University Ave. **Diner.** An authentic 1950s diner with linoleum floors, booths, and soda fountain. A real Corvette hangs from the ceiling in the main dining room. Food includes meat loaf with mashed potatoes, chicken-fried steak, burgers, and shakes. Great for families. Good value. **FYI:** Reservations not accepted. Rock. Children's menu. **Open:** Sun–Thurs 11am–11pm, Fri–Sat 11am–midnight. Closed some hols. **Prices:** Main courses $4.50–$9.95. Maj CC. 📷 VP 👍

★ **Croce's**, 802 5th Ave, San Diego (Gaslamp Quarter); tel 619/233-4355. At F St. **Californian/Southwestern.** Operated by the wife of late singer Jim Croce, it has become a local favorite, renowned for fine food, jazz, and Jim Croce memorabilia. Black-and-white tiled floors and small tables give the place the feel of a cafe. The house specialty is the Alaskan halibut in avocado-lime mousseline. Ingrid Croce's (next door) serves American southwest cuisine and light entrees, and desserts are available at Upstairs at Croce's. Croce's Top Hat Bar & Grille serves up live jazz and rhythm and blues. **FYI:** Reservations not accepted. Jazz. **Open:** Breakfast daily 7:30am–noon; lunch Mon–Fri 11:30am–3pm, Sat 11:30am–4pm; dinner daily 4pm–midnight; brunch Sun 7:30am–noon. Closed Dec 25. **Prices:** Main courses $11.95–$21.95. Maj CC. VP 👍

★ **Dobson's Bar & Restaurant**, 956 Broadway Circle, San Diego (Downtown); tel 619/231-6771. ½ block S of Broadway, near Horton Plaza. **Californian/French.** Paul Dobson has really made a name for himself with this namesake restaurant, where framed photos of the city's movers and shakers line the walls. Dobson is often at the door greeting customers. The downstairs area is dominated by a handsome wooden bar adorned with brass nameplates of frequent customers. Upstairs, the decor is more intimate and formal. Specialties of the house include

mussel bisque, seafood stew, and veal sweetbreads. **FYI:** Reservations recommended. **Open:** Lunch Mon–Fri 11:30am–3pm; dinner Mon–Wed 5:30–10pm, Thurs–Sat 5:30–11pm. Closed some hols. **Prices:** Main courses $12–$28. Maj CC. VP 👍

★ **Filippi's Pizza Grotto**, 1747 India St, San Diego (Little Italy); tel 619/232-5095. ½ mi N of downtown. Between Date and Fir Sts. **Italian.** People line up to get a table at this bustling locale where everything smells authentic. Patrons enter through a store stacked high with Italian pasta and jars of olives. This is not trendy Italian food, but hearty fare like spaghetti and meatballs with lots of tomato sauce. Also at: 962 Garnet St, Pacific Beach (619/483-6222); 1747 India, San Diego (619/232-5094). **FYI:** Reservations not accepted. Beer and wine only. **Open:** Sun–Mon 9am–10pm, Tues–Thurs 9am–10:30pm, Fri–Sat 9am–11:30pm. Closed some hols. **Prices:** Main courses $4.60–$12.25. Maj CC. 📷

★ **Fio's Cucina Italiana**, 801 5th Ave, San Diego (Gaslamp Quarter); tel 619/234-3467. At F St. **Italian.** One of the top Italian restaurants in San Diego. Cream-colored walls provide an excellent backdrop for the brightly colored murals, while the upholstered chairs and booths are visually appealing and comfortable. An open kitchen and large picture windows provide plenty of entertainment. Try the breaded veal rolls and fried artichoke hearts. Extensive 175-item wine list emphasizes Italian, French, and California wines. **FYI:** Reservations recommended. Dress code. **Open:** Lunch Mon–Fri 11:30am–3pm; dinner Mon–Thurs 5–11pm, Fri–Sat 5pm–midnight, Sun 5–10pm. Closed some hols. **Prices:** Main courses $9.75–$17.95. Maj CC. VP 👍

Firehouse Beach Cafe, 722 Grand Ave, San Diego (Pacific Beach); tel 619/272-1999. 9 mi NW of downtown. Grand/Garnet Aves exit off I-5. **Cafe.** Located just a half-block from the beach, this restaurant has a light, sunny decor and ceiling fans that capture the sea breeze. Head to the upstairs deck and enjoy a beer, a burger, and the ocean view from one of the umbrella-shaded tables. Known for its hamburgers, but breakfast and weekend brunch are also very popular. **FYI:** Reservations accepted. Children's menu. **Open:** HS June–Sept Sun–Thurs 7am–10pm, Fri–Sat 7am–11pm. Reduced hours off-season. Closed some hols. **Prices:** Main courses $9.75–$11.95. Maj CC. 🍽 🏔 📷

The Fish Market/Top of the Market, 750 N Harbor Dr, San Diego (Downtown); tel 619/232-3474. **Seafood.** Upstairs, the Top of the Market offers elegant dining and panoramic views. Downstairs, the Fish Market features an oyster bar, windows facing the water, and an outdoor patio. Both serve ultrafresh fish and seafood, including delicacies such as Alaskan halibut, Catalina swordfish, and Chinook salmon. Also at: 640 Via de la Valle,

Del Mar (619/755-2277). **FYI:** Reservations not accepted. Children's menu. **Open:** Lunch daily 11am–4pm; dinner Sun–Thurs 4–9:30pm, Fri–Sat 4–10pm. Closed some hols. **Prices:** Main courses $8.65–$31.50. Maj CC. 🍷 🏞 🎦 VP &

⑤ Galaxy Grill, 522 Horton Plaza, San Diego (Downtown); tel 619/234-7211. **Diner.** Busy 1950s-style diner with simple Formica tables, vinyl booths, and an outdoor patio. Waitresses dressed in 1950s attire serve burgers and shakes. **FYI:** Reservations not accepted. Children's menu. Beer and wine only. **Open:** Mon–Thurs 11am–9pm, Fri–Sat 11am–10pm, Sun 11am–8pm. Closed some hols. **Prices:** Main courses $3.50–$6.50. Maj CC. 🎦 &

⑤ Grand Central Cafe, in YMCA bldg, 500 W Broadway, San Diego (Downtown); tel 619/234-CAFE. **American.** Standard coffee shop decor with tables and a counter. Classic American fare such as meat loaf, baked chicken, and chicken-fried steak. Pasta, sandwiches, and steaks also served. **FYI:** Reservations accepted. Beer and wine only. **Open:** Daily 7am–9pm. **Prices:** Main courses $5.50–$6.95. Maj CC. &

♣ Grant Grill, in US Grant Hotel, 326 Broadway, San Diego (Downtown); tel 619/239-6806. **Continental.** A men's club until 1972, when 3 unescorted women arrived and demanded to be seated. The place for power lunches for San Diego's business elite, offering a clubby atmosphere with leather booths, upholstered chairs, and oil paintings. A large wooden bar and a pool table complete the picture. Menu specialties include roast veal chop and turtle soup with a splash of sherry. **FYI:** Reservations recommended. Jazz/singer. Dress code. **Open:** Breakfast Mon–Fri 6:30–10:30am, Sat–Sun 6:30–11:30am; lunch Mon–Fri 11:30am–2pm; dinner Sun–Thurs 5:30–10pm, Fri–Sat 5:30–10:30pm; brunch Sat–Sun 11:30am–2pm. **Prices:** Main courses $13.25–$25.75. Maj CC. ♥ VP &

Kansas City Barbeque, 610 W Market St, San Diego (Downtown); tel 619/231-9680. **Barbecue.** An old-fashioned barbecue stand; scenes from *Top Gun* were filmed here. Walls are cluttered with license plates and naval airmens' hats; there's also an outdoor patio. Specialties are barbecued pork and beef ribs, and extra-large, flaky onion rings. **FYI:** Reservations not accepted. Beer and wine only. **Open:** Daily 11am–1am. **Prices:** Main courses $8.50–$38. Ltd CC.

Karl Strauss' Old Columbia Brewery & Grill, 1157 Columbia St, San Diego (Downtown); tel 619/234-BREW. **Californian/German.** A sprawling, enjoyable restaurant with a large bar and lots of wood and exposed brick. Among the specialties are the grilled Johnsonville sausage platter, beer-battered fish and chips, and beers brewed on the premises. **FYI:** Reservations recommended. Children's menu. Beer and wine only. **Open:**

Lunch daily 11:30am–4pm; dinner Mon–Wed 4–10pm, Thurs–Sat 4pm–midnight, Sun 4–10pm. Closed some hols. **Prices:** Main courses $6.95–$12.95. Ltd CC. &

⑤ Kung Food, 2949 5th Ave, San Diego (Hillcrest); tel 619/298-7302. 1½ mi N of downtown. Near Balboa Park. **Vegetarian.** San Diego's best-known vegetarian restaurant: no meat products, no bleached flours, no sugar, and lots of low-fat choices. Popular dishes include Greek spinach pie, tofu vegetable enchiladas, and fettuccine alfredo. Deli/gift shop next door sells vegetarian cookbooks, new age music, and take-out food. **FYI:** Reservations not accepted. Beer and wine only. **Open:** Mon–Fri 11:30am–10pm, Sat–Sun 8:30am–10pm. Closed some hols. **Prices:** Main courses $6.65–$9.55. Ltd CC. 🍷

La Gran Tapa, 611 B St, San Diego (Downtown); tel 619/234-8272. **Spanish.** Cafe-style chairs and small tables flanking a lively, dark wood bar. The draw here is the tapas (Spanish hors d'oeuvres), such as ajo al horno, baked whole heads of garlic with feta cheese. Also on the menu: empanadillas filled with chicken, cheese, and black beans, and paella with shrimp, octopus, clams, and mussels. **FYI:** Reservations recommended. Guitar. **Open:** Lunch daily 11am–3pm; dinner Mon–Tues 3–10pm, Wed 3–11pm, Thurs–Sat 3pm–midnight, Sun 2–10pm. Closed some hols. **Prices:** Main courses $9.50–$15.95. Maj CC. &

Liaison, 2202 4th Ave, San Diego; tel 619/234-5540. **French.** The ambience of a French-country inn, with exposed wood, stone, and copper pots and pans on display. Outdoor patio is a romantic spot to dine. Specials include rack of lamb and chateaubriand. **FYI:** Reservations accepted. Dress code. Beer and wine only. **Open:** Lunch Tues–Fri 11:30am–2pm; dinner Sun–Thurs 5–9:30pm, Fri–Sat 5–10:30pm. Closed some hols. **Prices:** PF dinner $17.50–$26.50. Maj CC. ♥ 🍷 &

Lino's Italian Restaurant, in Bazaar Del Mundo, 2754 Calhoun St, San Diego (Old Town); tel 619/299-7124. 3 mi NW of downtown. Old Town Area exit off I-5. **Italian.** A small, quaint restaurant. Color scheme is mostly red. There are several small dining rooms, as well as patio seating. Specialties include chicken with orange sauce, veal and scampi combination, and a number of pastas. **FYI:** Reservations recommended. Dress code. **Open:** HS Mem Day–Labor Day lunch daily 11am–5pm; dinner daily 5–10pm. Reduced hours off-season. Closed some hols. **Prices:** Main courses $6.95–$14.95. Maj CC. ♥ &

Marino's, 4475 Ingraham St, San Diego (Pacific Beach); tel 619/490-0168. Grand/Garnet exit off I-5. **Italian.** Family-owned and friendly. Decor features red tablecloths, ceiling fans, wood paneling, and large oil paintings depicting Italian scenes. Dishes include lasagna, manicotti, ravioli, pizza, eggplant Parmesan, and baked zucchini. Piano player on weekends. **FYI:** Reservations not accepted. Piano. Beer and wine only. **Open:** Tues–Thurs 4–10pm, Fri–Sat 4–11pm, Sun 4–10pm. Closed some hols. **Prices:** Main courses $8–$15.20. Ltd CC.

The Old Ox, 4474 Mission Blvd, San Diego (Pacific Beach); tel 619/275-3790. Grove/Garnet Aves exit off I-5. ½ block from beach at west end of Garnet Ave. **Californian.** Lots of greenery, exposed brick, and a glass ceiling give dining room the feel of a conservatory. Fresh fish is a good choice here, but there is also a selection of pastas, salads, and beef entrees on the dinner menu. Sunday brunch is also quite popular. There is a separate, slightly darker dining room for smokers. The bar draws a young crowd. **FYI:** Reservations accepted. Children's menu. **Open:** Lunch Mon–Fri 11am–2:30pm; dinner Sun–Thurs 5–10pm, Fri–Sat 5–11pm; brunch Sat–Sun 10am–2:30pm. Closed Dec 25. **Prices:** Main courses $10.95–$17.95. Maj CC. &

Ⓢ **The Old Spaghetti Factory**, 275 5th Ave, San Diego (Gaslamp Quarter); tel 619/233-4323. **Italian.** A family restaurant with a Victorian ambience. Decor features stained glass, Tiffany-style lamps, and a trolley car converted into a dining room. Menu lists homemade lasagna, spaghetti with 2 Greek cheeses, and Italian cream sodas for dessert. **FYI:** Reservations not accepted. Children's menu. **Open:** Lunch Mon–Thurs 11:30am–2pm; dinner Mon–Thurs 5–10pm, Fri 5–11pm, Sat noon–11pm, Sun noon–10pm. Closed some hols. **Prices:** Main courses $4.25–$8.10. Ltd CC. 🍴 &

Old Town Liquor & Deli, 2304 San Diego Ave, San Diego (Old Town); tel 619/291-4888. 3 mi NW of downtown. Old Town Ave exit off I-5. **Deli.** A deli and liquor store with seating at 2 plastic tables on a busy sidewalk. Good picnic spots nearby for take-out orders. Fare includes sandwiches (with pastrami and real turkey), shrimp salad on a croissant, and bagels and lox. **FYI:** Reservations not accepted. No liquor license. **Open:** Mon–Fri 7am–8:30pm, Sat 7am–6pm, Sun 8am–4:30pm. Closed some hols. **Prices:** Main courses $3.15–$4.25. Maj CC. 🚗

Ⓢ **Old Town Mexican Cafe**, 2489 San Diego Ave, San Diego (Old Town); tel 619/297-4330. 3 mi NW of downtown. Old Town Ave exit off I-5. **Mexican.** Nothing fancy, but perhaps the best Mexican restaurant in Old Town. Dark wood, booths, and Mexican artifacts set the tone. Fresh tortillas are made daily. The menu lists pork with tomato and beans, Mexican-style rotisserie pork ribs, and Old Town pollo (rotisserie chicken). **FYI:** Reservations not accepted. Children's menu. **Open:** Daily 7am–11pm. Closed some hols. **Prices:** Main courses $6.25–$11. Maj CC. &

Pacific Beach Bar & Grill, 860 Garnet Ave, San Diego (Pacific Beach); tel 619/2PB-GRILL. Grand/Garnet Aves exit off I-5. **Cafe.** An under-30 crowd flocks to this new restaurant and

sports bar for loud music and an extensive selection of beers, sandwiches, soft tacos, burgers, and pizza. Decor is nonexistent, unless you count the neon beer signs. Shorts, T-shirts, and in-line skates are the preferred attire; there are several television sets and 3 pool tables. **FYI:** Reservations not accepted. **Open:** Daily 11am–11pm. **Prices:** Main courses $3.75–$7.50. Maj CC.

Panda Inn, 506 Horton Plaza, San Diego (Downtown); tel 619/233-7800. Located on top floor. **Chinese.** Comfortable, upscale restaurant with black lacquered furnishings and a side room offering views of downtown and the bay. Specialties include sweet and pungent shrimp, and Kon Pao San Yan (sliced shrimp, chicken, and beef sautéed with green onion and peanuts in a spicy sauce). **FYI:** Reservations recommended. **Open:** Lunch daily 11am–3pm; dinner Sun–Thurs 3–10pm, Fri–Sat 3–11pm. Closed Thanksgiving. **Prices:** Main courses $7.75–$18.25. Maj CC. &

★ **Rainwater's on Kettner**, 1202 Kettner Blvd, San Diego (Downtown); tel 619/233-5757. Located at foot of B St near historic Sante Fe Depot. **American.** Known as the best place in San Diego for a "power lunch." Leather booths and cherrywood paneling make this look like a private club. Entrees include skillet steak flamed in brandy and topped with Stilton, salmon in parchment, and chicken breast with veal pan gravy and caramelized onions. **FYI:** Reservations recommended. Children's menu. Dress code. **Open:** Lunch Mon–Fri 11:30am–5pm; dinner Mon–Sat 5pm–midnight, Sun 5–11pm. Closed Dec 25. **Prices:** Main courses $14–$36; PF dinner $25. Maj CC. 🆅🅿 &

Rancho El Nopal, in Bazaar del Mundo, 2754 Calhoun St, San Diego (Old Town); tel 619/295-0584. 3 mi NW of downtown. Old Town Ave exit off I-5. **Mexican.** Authentic Mexican decor, with brightly colored tables and chairs. Food is somewhat lackluster, but prices are good and this is a fun place. **FYI:** Reservations recommended. Guitar. Children's menu. Dress code. **Open:** Daily 11am–10pm. Closed some hols. **Prices:** Main courses $4.50–$8.95. Maj CC. 🍴 &

Ⓢ **San Diego Chicken Pie Shop**, 2633 El Cajon Blvd, San Diego (North Park); tel 619/295-0156. 4 mi N of downtown. Washington St exit off Calif 63 or I-5. **American.** Oldest continuously operating restaurant in San Diego, reminiscent of a 1950s midwest diner. Specialty here is pot pie, filled with lots of chicken and turkey. Fast service and a great bargain. Popular cream pies and fruit pies are made here as well. **FYI:** Reservations not accepted. No liquor license. **Open:** Daily 10am–8pm. Closed some hols. **Prices:** Main courses $3.50–$6.75. No CC. 🍴 &

Saska's, 3768 Mission Blvd, San Diego (North Mission Beach); tel 619/488-5754. 9 mi NW of downtown. W Mission Bay Dr exit off I-8. **Seafood/Steak.** Inside, an English pub atmosphere, with lots of dark wood and red Leatherette booths; outside, the casual patio has a "beachy" feel. Specialties include steaks in various sizes and cuts, teriyaki chicken, and fresh fish specials. The bar is very popular with locals. **FYI:** Reservations accepted. **Open:** Mon–Thurs 11:30am–2am, Fri 11:30am–3am, Sat 9:30am–3am, Sun 9:30am–2am. Closed some hols. **Prices:** Main courses $6.95–$15.95. Maj CC. ♨ ⬛

Sfuzzi, 340 5th Ave, San Diego (Gaslamp Quarter); tel 619/231-2323. **Italian.** There's a patio outside, and European brick, wooden floors, and an inviting bar inside. Specialties include pastas, pizzas made in a wood-fired oven, and drinks like the frozen Sfuzzi—frozen peach puree and white wine. **FYI:** Reservations recommended. Dress code. **Open:** Lunch daily 11:30am–5:30pm; dinner Sun–Thurs 5:30–10pm, Fri–Sat 5:30–11pm; brunch Sun 11:30am–3pm. Closed some hols. **Prices:** Main courses $9.50–$19.95. Maj CC. ♨ &

⑤ **Taste of Thai**, 527 University Ave, San Diego (Hillcrest); tel 619/291-7525. 2½ mi N of downtown. Washington St exit off I-5; drive east on Washington to University Ave. **Thai/Vegetarian.** A very pleasant small restaurant with a small bar and an outdoor patio. Menu includes spicy duck—half a bird topped with curry paste—and vegetarian duck, served with peppers, peas, and bamboo shoots. **FYI:** Reservations recommended. Beer and wine only. **Open:** Lunch Mon–Sat 11:30am–3pm; dinner daily 5–11pm. Closed some hols. **Prices:** Main courses $5.95–$10.95. Maj CC. ♨ &

Refreshment Stops ☕

Extraordinary Desserts, 2929 5th Ave, San Diego (Hillcrest); tel 619/294-7001. 1½ mi N of downtown. Between Palm and Quince Sts. **Desserts.** A wonderful place, and one of the only dessert shops in town. Small wooden tables are topped with fresh flowers, set on a painted concrete floor. Everything is made fresh on the premises daily; Tahitian cheesecake and chocolate-macadamia torte are especially popular. Smoking allowed outside only. **Open:** Mon–Thurs 8:30am–11pm, Fri 8:30am–midnight, Sat 11am–midnight, Sun 2–11pm. Closed some hols. Ltd CC. &

Kensington Coffee Co, 4141 Adams Ave, San Diego (Kensington); tel 619/280-5153. 7 mi NE of downtown. Adams Ave exit off I-15; at Marlborough Dr. **Coffeehouse.** The wonderful scent of fresh-ground coffee pervades this cafe/restaurant with a black-and-white checkerboard floor and red and black chairs. Sip cappuccino or bite into great muffins, scones, pastries, and sandwiches. They also sell coffee beans, tea, mugs, teapots, and

greeting cards. Also at: 13479 Poway Rd, Poway (619/748-2887); 1106 1st St, Coronado (619/437-8506). **Open:** Daily 6am–11pm. Closed Dec 25. Maj CC.

Pannikin Coffee & Tea, 675 G St, San Diego (Gaslamp Quarter); tel 619/239-7891. At 7th St. **Coffeehouse.** Informal coffee house with colorful decor and comfortable seating. Coffee and tea paraphernalia is sold, as are specialty teas and coffees, including White Heat, a white-chocolate espresso drink, and pastries. Also at: 7467 Girard Ave, La Jolla (619/454-5463); 2670 Via de la Valle, Del Mar (619/481-8007). **Open:** Mon–Fri 8am–6pm, Sat–Sun 10am–5pm. Closed some hols. Maj CC. &

Attractions 💼

TOP ATTRACTIONS

Sea World, 1720 S Shores Rd (in Mission Bay); tel 619/226-3901. A 150-acre marine life entertainment park, Sea World is renowned for its performing dolphins, killer whales, and seals. At the 5,500-seat Shamu Stadium, visitors watch in awe as 4-ton black-and-white killer whales launch themselves into the air, and dolphins turn graceful midair somersaults and flips. But Sea World also offers numerous educational exhibits, shows, and rides that feature sharks, fish, otters, penguins, and even birds.

The newest attraction is **Mission: Bermuda Triangle,** a simulated deep-dive submarine ride that employs high-tech audio and video in conjunction with flight simulator technology to take riders on an undersea adventure. Other featured attractions and shows are **Shark Encounter,** where visitors walk through a transparent underwater tunnel that runs through the center of a 700,000-gallon habitat populated by 90 sharks of 13 different species; **Rocky Point Preserve,** where guests learn about bottlenose dolphins and Alaskan sea otters (survivors of the 1989 *Valdez* oil spill), who live in a natural rocky habitat; and **Wings of the World,** which showcases 50 feathered stars, including hawks, falcons, and macaws. There are numerous other aquariums, exhibits, and shows, plus a special play area reserved for children 37–61 inches tall. Several shops, snack bars, and restaurants. Guided 90-minute behind-the-scenes tours are offered daily (additional fee required). **Open:** Mid-June to early Sept, Sun–Thurs 9am–10pm, Fri–Sat 9am–11pm; Apr to mid-June and early Sept–Oct, daily 10am–6pm; Nov–Mar, daily 10am–5pm. $$$$

Seaport Village, W Harbor Dr and Kettner Blvd; tel 619/235-4014. A pleasant mix of 75 shops, seafood houses, and snack bars, Seaport Village also offers a quarter-mile bayside boardwalk and a colorful 1890 carousel with hand-carved horses. There is often free entertainment in the gazebo on weekend afternoons. (Some restaurants are open extended hours.) **Open:** Summer, daily 10am–10pm; fall–spring, daily 10am–9pm. Free.

Horton Plaza, Broadway and 4th Ave; tel 619/239-8180. Easily one of San Diego's most popular tourist attractions, this is much more than a shopping center. Patrons can shop, stroll, snack or dine, enjoy free entertainment, see a movie, and people-watch—all within a unique and colorful architectural framework. Stop by the information office on the lower level for a current schedule of events and entertainment. **Open:** Mon–Fri 10am–9pm, Sat 10am–6pm, Sun 11am–6pm; extended summer hours. Free.

Cabrillo National Monument; tel 619/557-5450. The 3rd most-visited national monument in the United States, Cabrillo National Monument is located at the tip of Point Loma, 10 miles west of I-8 on Calif 209 (Catalina Blvd). It commemorates the discovery of the western coast of North America by the explorer Juan Rodriguez Cabrillo in 1542. Cabrillo's statue dominates the tip of Point Loma, which also provides a vantage point for observing the migration of gray whales, who travel from the Arctic Ocean to Baja California between December and mid-March. A restored lighthouse (1855) allows a glimpse of what life was like here in the 19th century.

National Park Service rangers conduct walks at the monument (phone for details), and there are numerous tide pools to be explored. Films on Cabrillo, tide pools, and California gray whales are shown daily from 10am to 4pm, on the hour. **Open:** Sept–May, daily 9am–5:15pm; extended hours in summer. $$

MUSEUMS

San Diego Museum of Contemporary Art, 1001 Kettner Blvd; tel 619/234-1001. This museum focuses primarily on work produced since 1950. Its permanent collection includes works by Lichtenstein, Warhol, and others. Also traveling exhibitions. **Open:** Tues–Wed and Fri–Sun 11am–6pm, Thurs 11am–9pm. Closed some hols. $

Children's Museum of San Diego, 200 W Island Ave; tel 619/233-8792. Hands-on interactive exhibits, which are changed about every 6 months, explore the world from a kid's point of view. The Art Zone allows children to express their artistic impressions both in individual and group environments. **Open:** Tues–Sat 10am–4:30pm, Sun 11am–4:30pm. Closed some hols. $$

Maritime Museum, 1306 N Harbor Dr; tel 619/234-9153. This museum consists of a fine trio of ships: the full-rigged merchant ship *Star of India* (1863), whose impressive masts are an integral part of the San Diego cityscape; the steam-powered ferryboat *Berkeley* (1898), which worked around the clock carrying San

Franciscans to safety after the 1906 earthquake; and the sleek steam yacht *Medea* (1904), one of the few remaining such vessels in the world. **Open:** Daily 9am–8pm, to 9pm in summer. $$

Junípero Serra Museum, 2727 Presidio Dr; tel 619/297-3258. Perched on a hill above Old Town in Presidio Park (see below), this 1929 building stands near the site of the original Presidio of San Diego, the oldest European settlement on the west coast of the United States and Canada (ca. 1769–1835). Exhibits highlight the Spanish colonial and Mexican periods in San Diego's history, and include artifacts from excavations of the Presidio site; a collection of Spanish Renaissance furniture; and a room devoted to Majorca, Spain, birthplace of Father Serra, the founder of the Franciscan missions in California. The tower affords a view of Mission Valley, Mission Bay, and the Pacific Ocean, and features photographs documenting the development of the area over about 125 years. The bookstore has many books dealing with this period in history. **Open:** Tues–Sat 10am–4:30pm, Sun noon–4:30pm. Closed some hols. $

Firehouse Museum, 1572 Columbia St; tel 619/232-FIRE. Appropriately housed in San Diego's oldest firehouse, this museum features fire engines (including hand-drawn and horse-drawn models) and memorabilia of firemen from all over the world, such as antique alarms, fire hats, and foundry molds for fire hydrants. **Open:** Sat–Sun 10am–4pm. Closed some hols. Free.

HISTORICAL ATTRACTIONS

Mission Basilica San Diego de Alcala, 10818 San Diego Mission Rd; tel 619/281-8449. Established in 1769, this was the first link in a chain of 21 missions founded by Spanish missionary Padre Junípero Serra. The mission was moved to its present site in 1774; a few bricks remaining from the original mission can be seen in Presidio Park (see below) in Old Town. **Open:** Daily 9am–5pm; mass daily 7am and 5:30pm. Closed Dec 25. $

Presidio Park. Sometimes called the "Plymouth Rock of the Pacific," this was the site where Franciscan missionary Father Junípero Serra established the first in a chain of 21 Spanish missions in California. The mission was San Diego's only settlement from 1769 until the mid-1830s, when families began to move down the hill, establishing what is now known as Old Town. Only a few bricks remain of the original Presidio, which was relocated in 1774. The large cross in the park was made from floor tile taken from the Presidio ruins. The graceful **Junípero Serra Museum** (see above), with its 70-foot tower, sits atop a hill overlooking Old Town.

Old Town San Diego State Historic Park, 4002 Wallace St; tel 619/220-5243. The birthplace of San Diego—indeed, of

California itself—this park recaptures the aura of Mexican California, which existed here until the mid-1800s. Seven original buildings remain; the rest are reconstructions. Highlights include **La Casa de Estudillo** (1827), an original adobe house that depicts the lifestyle of a wealthy family during the Mexican era; the **Seeley Stables Museum,** which has a 17-minute slide show and 2 floors of wagons, buggies, stagecoaches, and other memorabilia; and the **San Diego *Union* Museum,** a restored original wood building (it was shipped around the Horn in 1850) that housed one of the first newspapers in the region. A free walking tour leaves daily from the Visitors Center at 2pm. **Open:** Visitors center, daily 10am–5pm; shops, daily 10am–8pm; restaurants, daily 10am–9pm. $

Gaslamp Quarter; tel 619/233-5227. In the heart of downtown San Diego, bounded by Broadway, Harbor Dr, and Fourth and Sixth Aves, these 16½ blocks contain outstanding Victorian-style commercial buildings built between the Civil War and World War I. Today an impressive number have been restored to their former grandeur, and their ground floors enlivened with restaurants, shops, and places to dance or listen to jazz.

Whaley House, 2482 San Diego Ave; tel 619/298-2482. This striking two-story brick house, the first in San Diego, was built in 1865 for Thomas Whaley and his family, and still contains many of their furnishings. Exhibits include a life mask of Abraham Lincoln (one of only 6 made); 2 bookcases given to President Grant on his inauguration; the spinet piano used in the film *Gone With the Wind;* and the concert piano that accompanied Jenny Lind on her final US tour.

The house is 1 of 2 in California with documented evidence of supernatural activity (spirits thought to reside here include those of Thomas Whaley and his wife, Anna), making the house a popular spot around Halloween. **Open:** Daily 10am–5pm; extended hours late Oct. $$

William Heath Davis House, 410 Island Ave; tel 619/ 233-5227 or 233-4692. Built in 1850, this is the oldest house in the Gaslamp Quarter. The ground floor is open to the public, as is the small park adjacent to the house. The top floor houses the Gaslamp Quarter Foundation, which has information on walking tours of the area. **Open:** Mon–Fri 11am–2pm, Sat 10am–1pm. Closed some hols. Free.

Villa Montezuma, 1925 K St; tel 619/239-2211. Built in 1887 for then internationally acclaimed musician and author Jesse Shepard, this opulent mansion has been painstakingly restored and furnished with period pieces by the San Diego Historical Society. Lush with Victoriana, the house was designed more as a place to entertain guests than a residence; the largest room in the house is the Music Room, where Shepard often entertained. The house features numerous stained-glass windows—some quite huge—which depict Mozart, Beethoven, Rubens, and St Cecilia (patron saint of musicians), among others. These windows accounted for more than a third of the mansion's construction cost. Guided tours last about 45 minutes. **Open:** Sat–Sun noon– 4:30pm. $

Heritage Park, 2455 Heritage Park Row; tel 619/565-5928. This small park is filled with original 19th-century houses moved here from other places and put to new uses, among them a bed-and-breakfast inn, a doll shop, and an antiques shop. The most recent addition is the small synagogue, placed near the entrance to the park in 1989. **Open:** Daily sunrise–sunset. Free.

Mormon Battalion Visitors Center, 2510 Juan St (Old Town); tel 619/298-3317. The longest infantry march in American history, made by a 500-member Mormon regiment from 1846– 1847, is commemorated at this facility. At the onset of the Mexican-American War, the men marched from Fort Leavenworth, Kansas, to San Diego—about 2,000 miles—but by the time they arrived the fighting had moved south. The only battle they fought was along the way—against a herd of wild bulls near Tucson. Exhibits include artifacts from the march, photographs, and a list of the men who made up the battalion; a diorama and a 15-minute slide show tell the story in detail. **Open:** Daily 9am– 9pm. Free.

BALBOA PARK

Visitor Center; tel 619/239-0512. Entrances at 6th Ave and Laurel St, and Park Blvd and Presidents Way. The center provides details on park facilities and the roughly 1,000 acres of walkways, gardens, historical buildings, and museums in the park. Free walking tours detail the ornate pavilion with the world's largest outdoor organ, a high-spouting fountain, a nationally acclaimed theater, and the world-famous zoo (see listings below). The center is open daily from 9am to 4pm; free organ concerts are given at the organ pavilion on Sunday at 2pm (and weekday evenings in summer); free tram transportation within the park is provided daily; ask at the Visitor Center for schedule. Free.

San Diego Zoo, Park Blvd and Zoo Place; tel 619/234-3153. This world-famous zoo, home to 3,200 animals, is set on 100 subtropical acres that double as a botanical garden. It is one of the few zoos outside Australia to have koalas, and features many rare and endangered species. Free aerial tram rides provide bird's-eye views of the park, and double-decker bus tours provide close-up glimpses of the animals and lively commentary by a park ranger. Tours cost $3 for adults, $2.50 for children, and last 40 minutes. Children's zoo, animal shows. Snack bars, restaurant. **Open:** Daily, from 9am; closing hour varies with season. $$$$

Museum of San Diego History, 1649 El Prado; tel 619/232-6203. Permanent and changing exhibits tell stories in words and photos about the city's (and the park's) colorful past. Free documentary videos are sometimes shown as well. The bookstore also sells Victorian-inspired items and dolls. **Open:** Wed–Sun 10am–4:30pm, second Tues of every month 10am–4:30pm. Closed some hols. $

San Diego Natural History Museum, 1788 El Prado; tel 619/232-3821. The primary focus of this museum is on its traveling exhibitions, which usually run for 3–5 months each. The permanent collection includes gems and minerals and exhibits on the desert, shore, and ocean ecology of the southwestern United States and Mexico. Phone ahead for details on exhibits, hours, and fees. **Open:** Daily, hours vary with exhibition. Closed some hols.

Museum of Man, 1350 El Prado; tel 619/239-2001. In a landmark building located just inside the park entrance at the Cabrillo Bridge, this museum is devoted to the peoples of North and South America. On display are life-size artists' models of a dozen varieties of Homo sapiens, from Cro-Magnon and Neanderthal to Peking Man, along with a replica of Lucy, the 3.5-million-year-old skeleton discovered in Ethiopia in 1974. Other permanent exhibits deal with ancient Egypt, the Maya, and the Kumeyaay Indians, who once inhabited the San Diego area. The museum also features traveling exhibits. **Open:** Daily 10am–4:30pm. Closed some hols. $$

San Diego Aerospace Museum, 2001 Pan American Way; tel 619/234-8291. The era of powered flight—from the Wright brothers to the Space Age—is chronicled in this museum. On display are more than 60 restored aircraft from all periods of aviation, including a replica of Lindbergh's *Spirit of St Louis,* an actual Japanese Zero from World War II, an SR-71 Blackbird spy plane, and replicas of American space capsules. A **Behind-the-Scenes Tour** is offered of the museum's aircraft restoration facilities, where visitors can observe at least 4 restoration projects in progress. **Open:** Mem Day–Labor Day, daily 9am–5pm; rest of the year, daily 10am–4pm. Closed some hols. $$

Reuben H Fleet Space Theater and Science Center, 1875 El Prado; tel 619/238-1233. The busiest museum in Balboa Park, the Science Center features 50 interactive exhibits, a Laserium, and an Omnimax theater with a 76-foot dome screen and shows almost hourly. Separate admission for each area. **Open:** Sun–Thurs 9:30am–9:30pm, Fri–Sat 9:30am–10:30pm. $$$

San Diego Museum of Art, 1450 El Prado; tel 619/232-7931. This renowned museum contains approximately 10,500 art objects, dating from Egyptian and pre-Columbian periods to the present. Its featured collections include works from the Italian Renaissance, the Dutch and Flemish schools, and the Spanish baroque period. An East Asian collection contains pieces from the neolithic Yang Shao culture of China; there's also a Japanese suit of armor (1578); and an acclaimed collection of Indian, Persian, and Turkish miniatures. You'll also find many noteworthy contemporary paintings and sculptures. Works are included by Renior, van Gogh, Picasso, and El Greco, among many others. Museum shop; sculpture garden cafe with outdoor seating. **Open:** Tues–Sun 10am–4:30pm. Closed some hols. $$$

Timken Museum of Art, 1500 El Prado; tel 619/239-5548. Called the "jewel of Balboa Park," this museum houses the Putnam Foundation's collection of European old masters, 19th-century American paintings, and an outstanding collection of Russian icons. **Open:** Tues–Sat 10am–4:30pm, Sun 1:30–4:30pm. Closed Sept and some hols. Free.

Museum of Photographic Arts, 1649 El Prado; tel 239-5262. One of the nation's finest photography museums, this facility offers changing exhibits of the works of master international photographers. About 6 shows are featured each year; emphasis is on both historical and contemporary work. The bookstore has an extensive selection. **Open:** Daily 10am–5pm. Closed some hols. $

San Diego Automotive Museum, 2080 Pan American Plaza; tel 619/231-2886. There are approximately 60 vehicles on display here at all times, from both the museum's large core selection and "featured attractions" on loan from collectors from all over the world. Displays change frequently, and cover a wide range of topics and all periods of automotive history. Comprehensive automobile resource center; gift shop with rare and unusual automobile-related items. **Open:** May–early Sept, daily 9am–5pm; rest of the year, daily 10am–4:30pm. Closed some hols. $$

Model Railroad Museum, in Casa de Balboa, 1649 El Prado; tel 619/696-0199. Perhaps the largest indoor model railroading museum in the United States, this 22,000-square-foot building houses 4 permanent operating scale-model railroads: the San Diego & Arizona, the Tehachapi Pass, the Cabrillo & Southwestern, and the Pacific Desert Lines. There is a working hands-on railroad layout for kids, along with several interactive exhibits on railroad history and model railroading. **Open:** Wed–Fri 11am–4pm, Sat–Sun 11am–5pm, first Tues of every month 11am–4pm. Closed some hols. $

Hall of Champions, 1649 El Prado; tel 619/234-2544. One of only a few multisport museums in the country, this facility encompasses more than 40 different sports. Highlights include a large selection of Ted Williams memorabilia, including the bat used to establish his record-breaking .406 batting average; a large Throroughbred racing exhibit with actual Preakness Stakes and Kentucky Derby trophies; and an extensive exhibit devoted to bass fishing. Interactive video exhibits; theater showing clips and features; gift shop. **Open:** Daily 10am–4:30pm. Closed some hols. $

House of Pacific Relations International Cottages (Balboa Park); tel 619/234-0739. This cluster of 1- and 2-room cottages offers a sample of the culture, traditions, and history of 31 national groups. Each cottage is decorated in the style of the nation it represents and offers samples of authentic food. **Open:** Sun 12:30–4:30pm and fourth Tues of month 12:30–3:30pm. Free.

Japanese Friendship Garden; tel 619/232-2780 or 232-2721 holidays. The gardens are located next to the Organ Pavilion in the park. Of the 11.5 acres designated for the garden, only an acre has been developed so far. A model inside the information center shows plans for future developments. The center is a Zen-style teahouse with shoji screens, a bonsai or ikebana display, and a garden through which a crooked path winds (evil spirits are throught to move in straight lines). Japanese festivals are celebrated here. **Open:** Tues and Fri–Sun 10am–3:45pm. $

Botanical Building and Lily Pond, El Prado; tel 619/234-8901. A collection of ivy, ferns, orchids, impatiens, begonias, and other plants sheltered beneath the iron framework of an old Santa Fe railroad station. The lily pond in front attracts sun worshipers and street entertainers. **Open:** Tues–Sun 10am–4:30pm. Free.

Spreckels Organ Pavilion; tel 619/239-0512. Given to the people of San Diego in 1914 by the brothers John D and Adolph Spreckels, the ornate, curved pavilion houses a magnificent organ with 4,445 individual pipes, which range in length from less than half an inch to more than 32 feet. Visitors may enjoy free hour-long concerts on Sunday at 2pm. There is seating for 2,400.

OTHER ATTRACTIONS

Coronado Bay Bridge. Four lanes wide and 2 miles long, this bridge linking downtown San Diego and Coronado was completed in 1969. Put out of business by its construction, commuter ferry services started up again in 1986, catering to tourists. Crossing the bridge you can see Mexico, the San Diego skyline, Coronado, the naval station, and San Diego Bay. The middle section of the bridge floats, so that in the event of its destruction ships would still have access to the harbor and the sea beyond. Toll charged when traveling from San Diego to Coronado only.

Old Town Trolley Tours, 2115 Kurtz St; tel 619/298-TOUR. A great way to see San Diego, this tour allows riders to get off at any

of the 9 stops along the route and reboard at their leisure (trolleys visit each stop about every half-hour). Stops include many of San Diego's major tourist spots. The length of one entire loop is about 1 hour. $$$$

Invader Cruises, 1066 N Harbor Dr; tel 619/234-8687 or toll free 800/445-4FUN. Daily tours of San Diego Bay on the *Invader,* an antique schooner built in 1905. Nightly dinner cruises; Sunday brunch cruises from 11am–1pm; also whale-watching trips.

Naval Ship Tours. At **Broadway Pier,** near the intersection of Broadway and Harbor Dr, visiting ships, including those of foreign navies, are usually open for tours on weekends (tel 619/532-1431). Visible from the pier are the aircraft carriers USS *Kitty Hawk* and USS *Constellation*. Both are based at **US Naval Air Station North Island,** and are usually made available for public tours on Saturday. Arrangements to visit these ships must be made 1 week in advance by calling 619/545-5669 (*Kitty Hawk*) or 619/545-2427 (*Constellation*).

San Diego Harbor Excursion, 1050 N Harbor Dr; tel 618/234-4111. At the foot of Broadway. Daily tours of the bay, plus dinner cruises and, in winter, whale-watching excursions.

PROFESSIONAL SPORTS

Jack Murphy Stadium, 9449 Friars Rd; tel 619/525-8282. The NFL's Chargers play here August to December (tel 619/283-4494). The National League Padres take the field for baseball from April to September (tel 619/280-2111).

SAN FRANCISCO

Map page M-2, D1

See also **Berkeley, Campbell, Corte Madera, Cupertino, Emeryville, Fremont, Hayward, Los Gatos, Menlo Park, Mill Valley, Milipitas, Millbrae, Mountain View, Oakland, Palo Alto, Redwood City, San Jose, San Mateo, San Rafael, Santa Clara, Saratoga, Sausalito, Sunnyvale, Tiburon, Union City**

TOURIST INFORMATION

San Francisco Visitor Information Center 900 Market St, on the lower level of Hallidie Plaza at Powell St (tel 415/391-2000); descend escalator at cable-car turnaround. Open Mon–Fri 9am–5:30pm, Sat 9am–3pm and Sun 10am–2pm. For recorded information about San Francisco events, call 415/391-2001.

Visitors Information Center of the Redwood Empire Association 785 Market St, 15th floor (tel 415/543-8334). Open Mon–Fri 9am–5pm. Free tour planning for San Francisco and areas north of the city available.

PUBLIC TRANSPORTATION

San Francisco Municipal Railway (MUNI) Cable Cars Three lines in operation approximately 6:30am–12:30am. The Powell-Hyde line travels from Powell and Market Sts to Victorian Square at Aquatic Park via Nob and Russian Hills. The Powell-Mason line travels from Powell and Market Sts to Bay St, 3 blocks from Fisherman's Wharf, via Nob Hill. The California Street line travels from the foot of Market St to Van Ness Ave via Chinatown and Nob Hill. Fare $2.

MUNI Buses Operate throughout all of San Francisco; service extends to Marin County and Oakland. Continuous service 6am–midnight, infrequent service thereafter. Buses usually travel down Market St or pass near Union Square. Fare $1 adults, 35¢ students and seniors.

MUNI Metro Streetcars Operate every 15 minutes Mon–Fri 5am–12:30am, Sat 6am–12:20am, Sun 8am–12:20am; more frequent service during rush hours. Five lines, J, K, L, M, and N, run underground downtown, on street in outer neighborhoods. Fare $1 adults, 35¢ students and seniors.

MUNI discount passes Allow unlimited travel on buses, Metro streetcars, and cable cars. Also allow free admission to 24 major attractions. One-day passport $6, 3 days $10, 7 days $15. For information on all Muni transportation services call 415/673-6864.

Bay Area Rapid Transit (BART) High-speed rail network connecting San Francisco with the East Bay, Oakland, Richmond, Concord, and Fremont. Operates every 15–20 minutes Mon–Fri 4am–midnight, Sat 6am–midnight, Sun 8am–midnight. Fare $0.80–$3. For information call 415/788-BART.

Hotels 🏨

Alexander Inn, 415 O'Farrell St, San Francisco, CA 94102 (Union Square); tel 415/928-6800 or toll free 800/843-8709; fax 415/928-3354. Dingy budget hotel in a convenient downtown location. **Rooms:** 60 rms. CI 2pm/CO 11am. Express checkout avail. Nonsmoking rms avail. Small and bare. **Amenities:** 🏋 ⚙ 📧 Cable TV, voice mail. No A/C. **Services:** ⌨ 🍴 🛎 **Rates (CP):** HS June–Oct $28–$72 S or D. Children under 18 stay free. Lower rates off-season. Maj CC.

ANA Hotel, 50 3rd St, San Francisco, CA 94103; tel 415/974-6400 or toll free 800/ANA-HOTELS; fax 415/495-6152. At Market St. A 36-story luxury hotel less than a block from the Center for the Arts and Moscone Center. **Rooms:** 667 rms and stes. CI 3pm/CO noon. Express checkout avail. Nonsmoking rms avail. Rooms, with a beautiful art deco decor, were renovated in 1993. For $10 extra, guests can stay in a "green" suite with environment-friendly recyclable products and water-saving shower head. **Amenities:** 🏋 ⚙ 📧 🍴 A/C, cable TV w/movies, voice mail, in-rm safe. All units w/minibars. **Services:** ✕ 🗝 🅅🄿 🚗 ⌨ 🛎 Car-rental desk, masseur, babysitting. **Facilities:** 🍴 🔟 🖥 ⚙ Upscale yet casual. Cafe 53 serves breakfast, lunch, and dinner. **Rates:** $180–$245 S; $205–$270 D; from $325 ste. Extra person $25. Children under 12 stay free. Spec packages avail. Pking: Indoor, $21. Maj CC.

Andrews Hotel, 624 Post St, San Francisco, CA 94109 (Downtown); tel 415/563-6877 or toll free 800/926-3739; fax 415/928-6919. At Taylor St. Built in 1905 as the Sultan Turkish Bath House. **Rooms:** 48 rms and stes. CI 3pm/CO noon. Nonsmoking rms avail. Slightly dingy rooms. **Amenities:** 🏋 ⚙ TV. No A/C. Some units w/minibars, some w/terraces. Coffee and tea served in lobby. Free wine at bar from 5:30–7pm. **Services:** ✕ 🗝 🅅🄿 🚗 ⌨ Babysitting. **Facilities:** 1 rst, 1 bar. **Rates (CP):** HS Aug–Oct $82–$119 S or D; from $119 ste. Extra person $10. Children under 12 stay free. Lower rates off-season. Spec packages avail. Pking: Outdoor, $13. Maj CC.

Atherton Hotel, 685 Ellis St, San Francisco, CA 94109 (Civic Center); tel 415/474-5720 or toll free 800/227-3608; fax 415/474-8256. At Larkin St. An offbeat hotel with a certain rustic charm; however, some might consider it dark and drab. **Rooms:** 74 rms. CI 2pm/CO noon. Rooms are very basic; those facing the street are noisy. **Amenities:** 🏋 Cable TV, in-rm safe. No A/C. **Services:** ✕ 🚗 ⌨ 🛎 Babysitting. **Facilities:** 🔟 1 rst, 1 bar. **Rates:** HS June–Nov $59–$79 S or D. Extra person $10. Children under 12 stay free. Lower rates off-season. Spec packages avail. Maj CC.

Beresford Arms, 701 Post St, San Francisco, CA 94109 (Union Square); tel 415/673-2600 or toll free 800/533-6533; fax 415/474-0449. At Jones St. Welcomes pets. San Diego Zoo trainers who stay here sometimes bring animals to rooms; they've been known to take monkeys to tea in the lobby. **Rooms:** 96 rms and stes. CI open/CO noon. Nonsmoking rms avail. 40 junior suites have wet bar or full kitchen. **Amenities:** 🏋 ⚙ 🍴 A/C, satel TV, refrig, VCR. All units w/minibars, some w/Jacuzzis. **Services:** 🅅🄿 🚗 ⌨ 🛎 Car-rental desk, babysitting. Complimentary afternoon tea and wine in the lobby. **Facilities:**

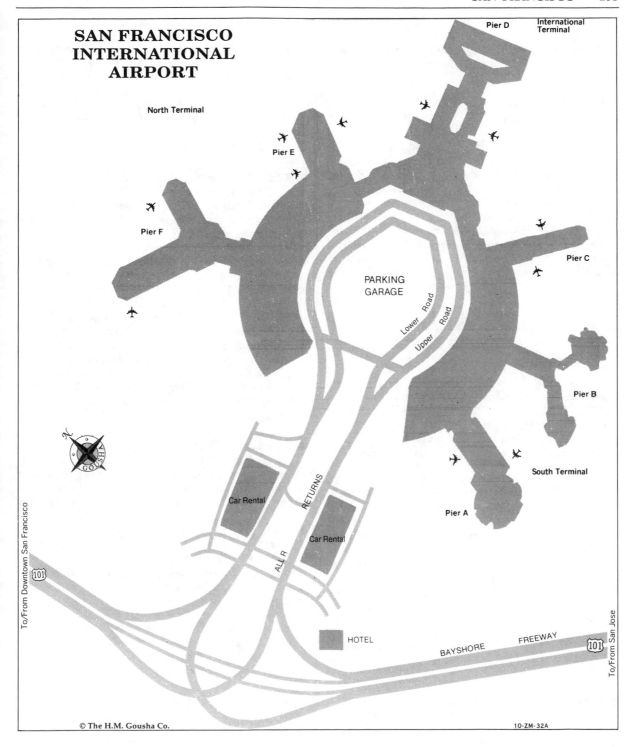

SAN FRANCISCO INTERNATIONAL AIRPORT

Pier D

International Terminal

North Terminal

Pier E

Pier F

PARKING GARAGE

Lower Road

Upper Road

Pier C

Pier B

South Terminal

Car Rental

RETURNS

ALL R

Car Rental

Pier A

To/From Downtown San Francisco

101

HOTEL

BAYSHORE FREEWAY

101

To/From San Jose

© The H.M. Gousha Co.

10-ZM-32A

[25] & **Rates (CP):** $79 S; $89 D; from $105 ste. Extra person $10. Children under 12 stay free. Pking: Indoor, $13–$15. Maj CC.

Best Western Americania, 121 7th St, San Francisco, CA 94103; tel 415/626-0200 or toll free 800/444-5816; fax 415/626-3974. Between Mission and Howard Sts. Average property in a Mediterranean style. **Rooms:** 143 rms and stes. CI 2pm/CO noon. Express checkout avail. Nonsmoking rms avail. Clean, comfortable rooms with charming decor. **Amenities:** 🛏 ⚴ 🖭 Cable TV w/movies, voice mail. No A/C. **Services:** ✕ 🚐 🖼 ⌂ Car-rental desk, babysitting. Free shuttle to shopping and business districts. Secretarial services and fax available. **Facilities:** 🏠 🖾 [50] & 1 rst, 1 bar, sauna, washer/dryer. **Rates:** HS Mem Day–Labor Day $69–$95 S; $74–$110 D; from $99 ste. Extra person $10. Children under 18 stay free. Lower rates off-season. Spec packages avail. Pking: Indoor/outdoor, free. Maj CC.

Best Western Canterbury Hotel, 750 Sutter St, San Francisco, CA 94109 (Union Square); tel 415/474-6464 or toll free 800/227-4788, 800/652-1614 in CA; fax 415/474-5856. At Taylor St. Conveniently located near Union Square. **Rooms:** 250 rms and stes. CI 1pm/CO noon. Nonsmoking rms avail. **Amenities:** 🛏 🖭 A/C, cable TV w/movies, refrig. Some units w/minibars, some w/terraces. Deluxe accommodations have refrigerators and coffeemakers. **Services:** ✕ 🖭 🖼 ⌂ Babysitting. **Facilities:** 🖾 [250] & 1 rst, 1 bar. **Rates:** HS May–Oct $95–$109 S; $99–$129 D; from $125 ste. Extra person $10. Children under 18 stay free. Lower rates off-season. Pking: Indoor, $12.50. Maj CC.

Best Western Carriage Inn, 140 7th St, San Francisco, CA 94013; tel 415/552-8600 or toll free 800/444-5817; fax 415/626-3974. Between Mission and Howard Sts. Lovely Victorian/colonial-style hotel. **Rooms:** 48 rms. CI 2pm/CO noon. Express checkout avail. Nonsmoking rms avail. Rooms are large. **Amenities:** 🛏 ⚴ 🖭 A/C, cable TV w/movies, voice mail. Some units w/fireplaces. Irons and ironing boards in rooms. Terry robes in suites. **Services:** ✕ 🚐 🖼 ⌂ Car-rental desk, children's program, babysitting. Continental breakfast and newspaper delivered to your room. **Facilities:** & Whirlpool. Use of pool at sister property, Best Western Americania. Laundry facilities. **Rates:** HS Apr–Oct $79–$109 S; $86–$116 D. Extra person $10. Children under 12 stay free. Spec packages avail. Pking: Indoor, free. Maj CC.

Brady Acres, 649 Jones St, San Francisco, CA 94102 (Union Square); tel 415/929-8033 or toll free 800/6-BRADY6; fax 415/441-8033. Between Post and Geary Sts. Small downtown hotel with reasonable rates. **Rooms:** 25 rms. CI noon/CO noon. Nonsmoking rms avail. Rooms are small but charming

with antique-style quilts, clawfoot tubs, and full kitchens. All recently redecorated. **Amenities:** 🛏 ⚴ 🖭 🖳 Cable TV, VCR, stereo/tape player. No A/C. All units w/minibars, all w/terraces. Microwaves, answering machines. **Services:** 🚐 ⌂ Free local calls. Personal, friendly staff. **Facilities:** Washer/dryer. **Rates:** HS May–Sept $50–$55 S; $60–$75 D. Extra person $10. Lower rates off-season. Spec packages avail. Pking: Indoor, $10. Ltd CC. Weekly rates.

Campton Place Hotel, 340 Stockton St, San Francisco, CA 94108 (Union Square); tel 415/781-5555 or toll free 800/426-3135; fax 415/955-5536. Between Sutter and Post Sts. This intimate jewel of a hotel just feels like a class act from the moment you enter the marble lobby. **Rooms:** 117 rms and stes. CI 3pm/CO 1pm. Nonsmoking rms avail. Beautifully decorated, rooms make a wonderful pied-à-terre in the city. Recently primed with new fabrics in soothing beige tones. Original art. **Amenities:** 🛏 ⚴ 🖳 A/C, cable TV w/movies, shoe polisher, bathrobes. All units w/minibars. Individual touches include thermometer for the bath. **Services:** 🖾 🖭 🖼 🚐 🖼 ⌂ 🖾 Twice-daily maid svce, car-rental desk, masseur, babysitting. On request, guests can have valet assistance with packing and unpacking. Complimentary shoe shine. **Facilities:** [12] 🖳 & 1 rst (see also "Restaurants" below), 1 bar. Rooftop garden with chairs and tables. Fitness center should be open. **Rates:** $195–$330 S or D; from $395 ste. Children under 12 stay free. Spec packages avail. Pking: Indoor, $19. Maj CC.

Carlton Hotel, 1075 Sutter St, San Francisco, CA 94109; tel 415/673-0242 or toll free 800/227-4496; fax 415/673-4904. Between Hyde and Larkin Sts. A young, enthusiastic staff runs this downtown hotel. A great lobby is decorated with antiques, Persian rugs, and flowers. Library has a fireplace and shelves of antique books. **Rooms:** 165 rms and stes. CI 3pm/CO 1pm. Nonsmoking rms avail. Some rooms are on the small side, but there's great attention to detail. Very clean; colonial furnishings. **Amenities:** 🛏 ⚴ 🖭 🖳 TV w/movies. No A/C. All units w/minibars. **Services:** ✕ 🖭 🚐 🖼 ⌂ Babysitting. Evening wine served 6–7pm, coffee and tea throughout the day. Complimentary limousine service to the Financial District; and shuttle service to various places. **Facilities:** [25] 1 rst. Oak Room Grille serves reasonably priced continental cuisine. **Rates:** HS Apr–Oct $114–$175 S or D; from $175 ste. Extra person $12. Children under 12 stay free. Lower rates off-season. Spec packages avail. Pking: Indoor, $8.50. Maj CC.

Cartwright Hotel, 524 Sutter St, San Francisco, CA 94102 (Downtown); tel 415/421-2865 or toll free 800/227-3844; fax 415/421-2865. At Powell St. Right off Union Square, with fine English furnishings, a small library, and a lovely breakfast room. **Rooms:** 114 rms and stes. CI 3pm/CO 1pm.

Nonsmoking rms avail. Rooms have average decor; not all have air conditioning. **Amenities:** 🛅 📶 Cable TV w/movies, bathrobes. No A/C. **Services:** ✗ 🚐 🖥 📞 Babysitting. Complimentary morning tea and coffee; afternoon tea and cookies. **Facilities:** 🏊20 **Rates:** HS June–Oct $99–$119 S; $109–$129 D; from $150 ste. Extra person $10. Lower rates off-season. Spec packages avail. Pking: Indoor, $13. Maj CC.

≣≣≣ **Cathedral Hill–A Quality Hotel**, 1101 Van Ness, San Francisco, CA 94109; tel 415/776-8200 or toll free 800/227-4730, 800/622-0855 in CA; fax 415/441-2841. At Geary St. A very functional hotel, but without much character. **Rooms:** 400 rms and stes. CI 3pm/CO noon. Nonsmoking rms avail. **Amenities:** 🛅 📶 A/C, cable TV w/movies. **Services:** ✗ 🚐 🖥 📞 Car-rental desk, babysitting. **Facilities:** 🍴 🏊UK 🚹 1 rst, 1 bar, beauty salon. Gift shop. **Rates:** HS Apr–Oct $140–$160 S or D; from $250 ste. Children under 18 stay free. Lower rates off-season. Higher rates for spec evnts/hols. Spec packages avail. Pking: Outdoor, $10. Maj CC.

≣≣ **Chancellor Hotel**, 433 Powell St, San Francisco, CA 94102 (Downtown); tel 415/362-2004 or toll free 800/428-4748; fax 415/362-1403. Between Sutter and Post Sts. Old San Francisco hotel with a genteel atmosphere; 1 block off Union Square. **Rooms:** 140 rms and stes. CI 3pm/CO noon. Nonsmoking rms avail. **Amenities:** 🛅 📶 Cable TV w/movies. No A/C. **Services:** ✗ 🚐 🖥 📞 Car-rental desk, babysitting. **Facilities:** 🍴24 1 rst, 1 bar. **Rates:** HS Apr–Oct $97 S; $114 D; from $165 ste. Extra person $20. Children under 18 stay free. Lower rates off-season. Spec packages avail. Pking: Indoor, $16. Maj CC.

≣≣≣ **Comfort Inn by the Bay**, 2775 Van Ness Ave, San Francisco, CA 94109; tel 415/928-5000 or toll free 800/223-5150; fax 415/441-3990. At Lombard St. From the upper floors, you can see San Francisco Bay. Near Ghirardelli Square. **Rooms:** 134 rms and stes. CI 2pm/CO noon. Nonsmoking rms avail. Standard, clean. **Amenities:** 🛅 📶 A/C, TV w/movies. **Services:** 🖥 📞 Car-rental desk, babysitting. Deluxe continental breakfast with many choices. **Facilities:** 🍴45 🚹 **Rates (CP):** HS July–Oct $79–$109 S or D; from $139 ste. Extra person $10. Children under 18 stay free. Lower rates off-season. Spec packages avail. Pking: Indoor/outdoor, $10. Maj CC.

≣≣ **Cornell Hotel**, 715 Bush St, San Francisco, CA 94108; tel 415/421-3154 or toll free 800/232-9698; fax 415/399-1442. At Powell St. European charm, with the feel of Paris. All receptionists are French. Charming flowers, beautiful antique elevators. Convenient location between Union Square and Nob Hill. **Rooms:** 58 rms and stes. CI 2pm/CO 11am. Nonsmoking rms avail. Ask for larger rooms in back of hotel. **Amenities:** 🛅 Cable TV. No A/C. **Services:** 🚐 📞 **Facilities:** 1 rst. Charming French-country restaurant "Jeanne d'Arc." **Rates (CP):** HS

May–Oct $60–$80 S; $70–$95 D; from $120 ste. Extra person $15. Lower rates off-season. MAP rates avail. Spec packages avail. Pking: Indoor, $10. Maj CC.

≣≣≣≣ **The Donatello**, 501 Post St, San Francisco, CA 94102 (Downtown); tel 415/441-7100 or toll free 800/227-3184; fax 415/885-8842. At Mason St. Elegant, with good-quality art on display, orchids everywhere, and classical music in lobby. **Rooms:** 94 rms and stes. Exec-level rms avail. CI 3pm/CO noon. Nonsmoking rms avail. Charming and appealing, with all-new furnishings; 5 rooms overlook garden. **Amenities:** 🛅 📶 A/C, cable TV w/movies, bathrobes. Some units w/terraces. VCRs available upon request. **Services:** ✗ 🖥 VP 🚐 🖥 📞 Car-rental desk, babysitting. **Facilities:** 🍴 🏊100 🖥 1 rst, 1 bar, spa. Club Donatello Lounge has a beautiful fireplace and terrace. Wonderful Grecian Jacuzzi is done in marble. Sunroom. Coffee bar. **Rates:** HS Aug–Oct $125–$225 S or D; from $175 ste. Children under 18 stay free. Lower rates off-season. Spec packages avail. Pking: Indoor, $16. Maj CC.

≣≣≣ **The Fairmont**, 950 Mason St, San Francisco, CA 94108 (Nob Hill); tel 415/772-5000 or toll free 800/527-4727; fax 415/772-5000. At California St. If the facade looks familiar, that's because The Fairmont served as the setting for the TV series *Hotel*. Larger-than-life touches include a florid lobby with marble columns, gold-leaf trim, and red carpeting. **Rooms:** 660 rms and stes. CI 3pm/CO 1pm. Express checkout avail. Nonsmoking rms avail. Accommodations in either the vintage 1907 main hotel or the 1960s-era tower. Some rooms have fantastic city and bay views. The Penthouse Suite, with a 50-person-capacity dining room, is one of the most expensive lodgings in the city—$6,000 per night. **Amenities:** 🛅 📶 A/C, satel TV w/movies, refrig, voice mail, shoe polisher, bathrobes. All units w/minibars, some w/terraces. **Services:** 🍴 🖥 VP 🚐 🖥 📞 📞 Twice-daily maid svce, car-rental desk, masseur, babysitting. Nightly turn-down service with chocolates. **Facilities:** 🍴 🏊1.5K 🖥 🚹 5 rsts, 4 bars (3 w/entertainment), spa, beauty salon. **Rates:** HS June–Oct $179–$299 S or D; from $450 ste. Extra person $30. Children under 18 stay free. Lower rates off-season. Spec packages avail. Pking: Indoor, $25. Maj CC.

≣ **Fitzgerald Hotel**, 620 Post St, San Francisco, CA 94109 (Downtown); tel 415/775-8100 or toll free 800/33-HOTEL; fax 415/775-1278. At Taylor St. Very basic, slightly shabby hotel. **Rooms:** 47 rms and stes. CI 3pm/CO noon. Nonsmoking rms avail. **Amenities:** 🛅 📶 Cable TV. No A/C. **Services:** 🖥 🚐 🖥 Babysitting. **Facilities:** 🚹 Nice breakfast room in lobby turns into a pub in evening. Use of pool and fitness center at Sheehan Hotel. **Rates (CP):** HS June–Oct $59–$89 S or D; from $105 ste. Extra person $10. Children under 12 stay free. Lower rates off-season. Spec packages avail. Maj CC. Theater package.

≣≣≣ **Four Seasons Clift San Francisco**, 495 Geary St, San Francisco, CA 94102 (Union Square); tel 415/775-4700 or toll free 800/332-3442; fax 415/776-9238. A city-by-the-bay stalwart, dating from the 1930s and still able to shrug off competition from newcomers. Located a few blocks from Union Square, but few rooms here, even on the 16th and 17th floors, can match the views from Nob Hill hotels. **Rooms:** 329 rms and stes. CI 3pm/CO 1pm. Express checkout avail. Nonsmoking rms avail. Decorated in classical style with Georgian reproduction furniture and Brunschwig fabrics. 12-foot ceilings. **Amenities:** 🛅 🐕 🍹 A/C, cable TV, refrig, bathrobes. All units w/minibars. Unusually generous and thoughtful amenities for kids—child-proofed sockets and faucets; kid-size bathrobes, tables, and chairs; baby shampoo; cookies and milk at turndown. **Services:** 🍽️ 🔑 VP 🖆 🍸 🐬 Twice-daily maid svce, children's program, babysitting. Noted for fine personal service. Complimentary limo to several downtown locations. Afternoon tea in lobby bar. Extra pizza menu for room service. Overnight laundry. **Facilities:** 🍸🗗 📮 2 rsts (*see also* "Restaurants" below), 2 bars (1 w/entertainment). Business center offers cellular phones and fax machines for rent. **Rates:** $215–$360 S or D; from $365 ste. Extra person $25. Children under 18 stay free. Spec packages avail. Pking: Indoor, $22. Maj CC.

≣≣≣≣ **Galleria Park Hotel**, 191 Sutter St, San Francisco, CA 94104 (Union Square/Financial District); tel 415/781-3060 or toll free 800/792-9639, 800/792-9855 in CA; fax 415/433-4409. At Kearny St. Elegant lobby decorated with flowers and a large fireplace. **Rooms:** 177 rms and stes. CI 3pm/CO noon. Express checkout avail. Nonsmoking rms avail. Clean and cheerful. **Amenities:** 🛅 🐕 A/C, cable TV w/movies. All units w/minibars, some w/fireplaces, 1 w/Jacuzzi. **Services:** ✗ 🔑 VP 🖆 🗗 🍸 Babysitting. **Facilities:** 🖼️ 🍸 🔲 🔓 2 rsts, 2 bars (w/entertainment). Rooftop jogging track. **Rates (CP):** HS Aug–Oct $149 S or D; from $185 ste. Extra person $15. Lower rates off-season. Higher rates for spec evnts/hols. Spec packages avail. Pking: Indoor, $16. Maj CC.

≣≣ **Golden Gate Hotel**, 775 Bush St, San Francisco, CA 94108 (Downtown); tel 415/392-3702 or toll free 800/835-1118; fax 415/392-6202. At Mason St. The feel of a European hotel. Beautiful antique elevator, historical photos in hallways. **Rooms:** 23 rms. CI 2pm/CO noon. Nonsmoking rms avail. Quaint decor. **Amenities:** 🛅 Cable TV. No A/C. **Services:** 🖆 🍸 Babysitting. Afternoon tea and cookies. **Rates (CP):** HS May–Oct $59–$89 S or D. Extra person $10. Children under 10 stay free. Lower rates off-season. Spec packages avail. Pking: Indoor, $14. Maj CC.

≣≣≣≣ **Grand Hyatt San Francisco on Union Square**, 345 Stockton St, San Francisco, CA 94108 (Union Square); tel 415/398-1234 or toll free 800/233-1234; fax 415/391-1780. Between Sutter and Post Sts. Sleek, 36-story hotel combines sophisticated decor with many amenities for the business traveler. Beautiful lobby accented by marble and oriental antiques. **Rooms:** 693 rms and stes. Exec-level rms avail. CI 3pm/CO noon. Express checkout avail. Nonsmoking rms avail. Smart and stylish. **Amenities:** 🛅 🐕 🍹 A/C, TV w/movies, refrig, voice mail. All units w/minibars, 1 w/Jacuzzi. Business Plan rooms ($15 extra to upgrade) feature a complete work station with a large desk, private fax machine, telephone with computer hook-up, enhanced lighting. Regency Club rooms offer perks like robes, coffeemakers, and bottled water. **Services:** ✗ 🔑 VP 🖆 🗗 🍸 Car-rental desk, social director, masseur, babysitting. **Facilities:** 🍸 🔲 📮 🔓 2 rsts, 1 bar (w/entertainment), spa, beauty salon, day-care ctr. Small but well-equipped health club. Club 36 bar features great views and live jazz Monday–Saturday. **Rates:** $169–$250 S; $169–$275 D; from $350 ste. Extra person $25. Children under 18 stay free. Spec packages avail. Pking: Outdoor, $20. Maj CC. Lower rates on weekends.

≣≣ **Grosvenor House**, 899 Pine St, San Francisco, CA 94108 (Nob Hill); tel 415/421-1899 or toll free 800/999-9189; fax 415/982-1946. At Mason St. A recently converted Nob Hill apartment building with many tenants still in residence. Lobby is a bit shabby but rooms are nice. **Rooms:** 200 rms and stes. CI open/CO noon. Nonsmoking rms avail. Clean, large suites with full kitchens and good city views. **Amenities:** 🛅 🐕 📶 Cable TV, refrig. No A/C. Some units w/terraces. Complimentary bottle of wine; microwave. **Services:** 🖆 🗗 🍸 🐬 Babysitting. Use of fax machine. **Facilities:** Washer/dryer. Use of nearby health club. **Rates (CP):** HS Apr–Oct $79–$99 S; $99–$149 D; from $119 ste. Children under 12 stay free. Min stay. Lower rates off-season. Spec packages avail. Pking: Indoor, $16. Maj CC.

≣≣ **Handlery Union Square Hotel**, 351 Geary St, San Francisco, CA 94102 (Downtown); tel 415/781-7800 or toll free 800/843-4343; fax 415/781-0269. At Powell St. Very clean. **Rooms:** 367 rms and stes. Exec-level rms avail. CI 2pm/CO noon. Express checkout avail. Nonsmoking rms avail. **Amenities:** 🛅 Cable TV w/movies, in-rm safe. No A/C. Some units w/minibars, some w/terraces. **Services:** ✗ 🔑 VP 🖆 🗗 🍸 Babysitting. Complimentary morning coffee and tea. **Facilities:** 🖼️ 🔲 🔓 1 rst, sauna, steam rm. One of the few heated outdoor pools in San Francisco. **Rates:** HS Mar–Oct $75–$85 S; $85–$95 D; from $150 ste. Extra person $10. Children under 14 stay free. Min stay spec evnts. Lower rates off-season. Spec packages avail. Pking: Indoor, $12.50. Maj CC.

≣≣≣ **Harbor Court Hotel**, 165 Steuart St, San Francisco, CA 94105 (Financial District); tel 415/882-1300 or toll free 800/346-0555; fax 415/882-1313. Between Mission and Howard Sts.

Elegant, comfortable 1907 landmark hotel with spectacular views of San Francisco Bay. Original vaulted ceilings, arches, and columns. Outstanding lobby/lounge. Near Financial District. **Rooms:** 131 rms and stes. CI 3pm/CO noon. Express checkout avail. Nonsmoking rms avail. Rooms done in soft pastels. Ask for bay views. **Amenities:** 🛏 ⏻ 🍷 Cable TV w/movies, refrig, voice mail, bathrobes. No A/C. All units w/minibars. **Services:** ✕ VP 🚐 🛄 ⏻ Car-rental desk, masseur, babysitting. Complimentary wine, coffee, tea. Free morning limo service to Financial District. **Facilities:** 🖥 ⓰ 1 rst (*see also* "Restaurants" below), 1 bar (w/entertainment). Good restaurant, lively bar. Free use of YMCA with pool and gym next door. **Rates:** HS Feb–Sept $150–$165 S or D; from $255 ste. Children under 18 stay free. Lower rates off-season. Spec packages avail. Pking: Indoor, $15. Maj CC.

≡≡ Holiday Inn–Civic Center, 50 8th St, San Francisco, CA 94103; tel 415/626-6103 or toll free 800/HOLIDAY; fax 415/552-0184. Between Market and Mission Sts. Somewhat run-down, but renovations are taking place. **Rooms:** 389 rms and stes. CI 2pm/CO noon. Nonsmoking rms avail. Renovated rooms are pleasant. **Amenities:** 🛏 ⓰ A/C, cable TV w/movies. All units w/terraces. **Services:** ✕ 🖚 🚐 🛄 ⏻ Car-rental desk, babysitting. **Facilities:** 🖥 250 ⓰ 1 rst, 1 bar, washer/dryer. **Rates:** HS May–Oct $95–$165 S or D; from $250 ste. Extra person $15. Children under 19 stay free. Lower rates off-season. Higher rates for spec evnts/hols. Spec packages avail. Pking: Indoor, free. Maj CC.

≡≡ Holiday Inn–Financial District, 750 Kearny St, San Francisco, CA 94108 (Chinatown); tel 415/433-6600 or toll free 800/424-8292; fax 415/765-7891. At Washington St. Book early if you want a bay view, available from the 12th floor up. In the heart of Chinatown, a good choice for visitors from Asia. **Rooms:** 566 rms and stes. CI 2pm/CO noon. Express checkout avail. Nonsmoking rms avail. Basic decor, smell of stale smoke in some rooms. **Amenities:** 🛏 ⓰ 🍷 A/C, cable TV w/movies, in-rm safe. Some units w/terraces. **Services:** ✕ 🚐 🛄 ⏻ Car-rental desk, babysitting. **Facilities:** 🖥 300 ⓰ 1 rst, 1 bar (w/entertainment), washer/dryer. Pool on roof. **Rates:** HS Apr–Oct $135–$165 S or D; from $250 ste. Extra person $15. Children under 19 stay free. Lower rates off-season. Higher rates for spec evnts/hols. Spec packages avail. Pking: Indoor, $7.50. Maj CC.

≡≡ Holiday Inn–Fisherman's Wharf, 900 Columbus Ave, San Francisco, CA 94133; tel 415/771-9000 or toll free 800/WHARF IT; fax 415/771-7006. Between North Point and Beach Sts. Good location near Fisherman's Wharf. **Rooms:** 585 rms and stes. Exec-level rms avail. CI 3pm/CO noon. Nonsmoking rms avail. Bathrooms are small. **Amenities:** 🛏 ⓰ A/C, cable TV w/movies, voice mail, in-rm safe. **Services:** ✕ 🖚 🚐 🛄 ⏻

Car-rental desk, children's program, babysitting. **Facilities:** 🖥 300 ⓰ 1 rst, 1 bar, washer/dryer. Charley's serves breakfast and a seafood buffet. Charley's Sports Pub features billiards, darts, and large-screen TV. **Rates:** HS June–Aug $120–$165 S or D; from $150 ste. Extra person $10. Children under 17 stay free. Lower rates off-season. Spec packages avail. Pking: Indoor/outdoor, $12. Maj CC.

≡≡ Holiday Inn–Golden Gateway, 1500 Van Ness Ave, San Francisco, CA 94109; tel 415/441-4000 or toll free 800/HOLIDAY; fax 415/441-8346. At Pine St. Good facilities for groups, but little ambience. **Rooms:** 500 rms and stes. CI 3pm/CO noon. Nonsmoking rms avail. Clean, but slightly old and dated. **Amenities:** 🛏 ⓰ A/C, cable TV w/movies. **Services:** ✕ 🛄 ⏻ Car-rental desk, babysitting. **Facilities:** 🖥 300 ⓰ 1 rst, 1 bar. **Rates:** HS Apr–Oct $115–$125 S; $130–$140 D; from $250 ste. Children under 18 stay free. Min stay spec evnts. Lower rates off-season. Spec packages avail. Pking: Indoor, $11. Maj CC.

≡≡≡ Holiday Inn–Union Square, 480 Sutter St, San Francisco, CA 94108 (Union Square); tel 415/398-8900 or toll free 800/243-1135; fax 415/989-8823. At Powell St. Pleasant, clean, efficient, but without personality. **Rooms:** 400 rms and stes. Exec-level rms avail. CI 3pm/CO noon. Express checkout avail. Nonsmoking rms avail. Newly remodeled and very neat rooms. **Amenities:** 🛏 ⓰ A/C, cable TV w/movies. Some units w/minibars, 1 w/Jacuzzi. **Services:** ✕ 🖚 VP 🚐 🛄 ⏻ Babysitting. **Facilities:** 🖳 50 🖥 ⓰ 1 rst, 1 bar (w/entertainment). **Rates:** HS May–Oct $145–$215 S; $165–$235 D; from $175 ste. Extra person $10–$20. Children under 19 stay free. Lower rates off-season. Higher rates for spec evnts/hols. MAP rates avail. Spec packages avail. Pking: Indoor, $18. Maj CC.

≡≡ Hotel Bedford, 761 Post St, San Francisco, CA 94109 (Union Square); tel 415/673-6040 or toll free 800/227-5642; fax 415/563-6739. At Jones St. Well-located hotel. **Rooms:** 144 rms and stes. CI 3pm/CO 11am. Nonsmoking rms avail. Some rooms have views all the way to the Golden Gate Bridge. **Amenities:** 🛏 ⓰ 🖳 Cable TV w/movies, refrig, VCR. No A/C. All units w/minibars. **Services:** ✕ VP 🚐 🛄 ⏻ Complimentary wine and cider in pub 5–7pm. **Facilities:** 60 1 rst, 1 bar. Canvas Cafe is fun and filled with art. **Rates:** HS July–Nov $109–$119 S or D; from $175 ste. Extra person $10. Children under 12 stay free. Min stay HS. Lower rates off-season. Higher rates for spec evnts/hols. Spec packages avail. Pking: Indoor, $15. Maj CC.

≡≡ Hotel Beresford, 635 Sutter St, San Francisco, CA 94102 (Union Square); tel 415/673-9900 or toll free 800/533-6533; fax 415/474-0449. At Mason St. Too brightly lit, and lacking personality. **Rooms:** 114 rms. CI noon/CO noon. Express checkout avail. Nonsmoking rms avail. **Amenities:** 🛏 ⓰ Cable

TV, refrig. No A/C. All units w/minibars, some w/terraces. **Services:** ✗ 🚐 🖼 💬 **Facilities:** 1 rst, 1 bar, washer/dryer. **Rates (CP):** HS June–Oct $67–$79 S; $85–$89 D. Extra person $10. Children under 8 stay free. Lower rates off-season. Spec packages avail. Pking: Indoor, free. Maj CC.

🏨 **Hotel Britton**, 112 7th St, San Francisco, CA 94103; tel 415/621-7001 or toll free 800/444-5819; fax 415/626-3974. Between Mission and Howard Sts. Very basic mid-scale accommodations. **Rooms:** 79 rms and stes. CI 2pm/CO noon. Express checkout avail. Nonsmoking rms avail. Rooms are simple, yet clean and comfortable. **Amenities:** 🖥 🕭 Cable TV w/movies, voice mail. No A/C. **Services:** ✗ 🚐 🖼 💬 Car-rental desk, babysitting. **Facilities:** 🕭 1 rst. Barbershop. Use of pool at nearby Best Western Americania and use of Jacuzzi at Best Western Carriage Inn. **Rates:** $52–$69 S; $59–$79 D; from $72 ste. Extra person $7. Children under 18 stay free. Spec packages avail. Pking: Indoor/outdoor, $6. Maj CC.

🏨🏨🏨 **Hotel David**, 480 Geary Blvd, San Francisco, CA 94102 (Downtown); or toll free 800/524-1888; fax 415/931-5442. Between Mason and Taylor Sts. The best deal downtown. Under the same ownership for 40 years, the hotel is across the street from the Curran Theater. Clean and modern. **Rooms:** 50 rms. CI 1pm/CO noon. Nonsmoking rms avail. Rooms are contemporary, and attractive. **Amenities:** 🖥 A/C, cable TV. **Services:** ✗ 🆅🅿 🚐 💬 Babysitting. Full breakfast. **Facilities:** 🕭 1 rst. Guests receive a 25% discount at deli next door. **Rates (BB):** HS June–Oct $69–$79 S; $89–$119 D. Extra person $20. Lower rates off-season. Spec packages avail. Pking: Indoor, free. Maj CC. Excellent value.

🏨🏨🏨 **Hotel Diva**, 440 Geary St, San Francisco, CA 94102 (Union Square); tel 415/885-0200 or toll free 800/553-1900; fax 415/346-6613. Between Mason and Taylor Sts. This hotel, done in an unusual, art deco–modern hybrid decor, has style and a good downtown location. **Rooms:** 108 rms and stes. CI 2pm/CO noon. Nonsmoking rms avail. **Amenities:** 🖥 🕭 Cable TV w/movies, VCR, in-rm safe. No A/C. All units w/minibars, 1 w/terrace. **Services:** ✗ 🆅🅿 🚐 🖼 💬 Babysitting. **Facilities:** 🍴 🏊 🖥 🕭 **Rates (CP):** HS June–Oct $109–$125 S or D; from $135 ste. Extra person $10. Children under 10 stay free. Lower rates off-season. Spec packages avail. Pking: Outdoor, $16. Maj CC.

🏨🏨🏨 **Hotel Griffon**, 155 Steuart St, San Francisco, CA 94105; tel 415/495-2100 or toll free 800/321-2201; fax 415/495-3522. Between Mission and Howard Sts. Elegant hotel in historic 1906 brick building. Good location on edge of Financial District near cable cars. Within walking distance of great restaurants, fun night life. One block to Sausalito ferry. **Rooms:** 62 rms and stes. CI 2pm/CO noon. Express checkout avail.

Nonsmoking rms avail. Small but cozy and well-appointed rooms. Ask for one with bay view. Most rooms have 1 king- or queen-size bed. **Amenities:** 🖥 🕭 Cable TV, refrig, bathrobes. No A/C. All units w/minibars, some w/terraces. **Services:** ✗ 🚐 🖼 💬 Masseur, babysitting. **Facilities:** 🍴 🖥 🕭 1 rst (*see also* "Restaurants" below), 1 bar. Fine restaurant. YMCA next door has gym and swimming pool. **Rates (CP):** $130–$160 S or D; from $225 ste. Children under 18 stay free. Spec packages avail. Pking: Indoor, $15. Maj CC.

🏨🏨🏨🏨 **Hotel Majestic**, 1500 Sutter St, San Francisco, CA 94109 (Lower Pacific Heights); tel 415/441-1100 or toll free 800/869-8966; fax 415/673-7331. Between Fillmore and Gough Sts. Historic hotel has a lovely lobby with antiques and orchids. **Rooms:** 57 rms and stes. CI 2pm/CO noon. Nonsmoking rms avail. Canopied beds laden with feather pillows. **Amenities:** 🖥 🕭 A/C, satel TV, refrig. Some units w/fireplaces. **Services:** ✗ 🆅🅿 🚐 🖼 💬 Masseur, babysitting. Morning limo to Financial District, afternoon sherry, complimentary newspaper. **Facilities:** 🍴 🕭 1 rst (*see also* "Restaurants" below), 1 bar (w/entertainment). **Rates (CP):** HS June–Oct $125–$160 S or D; from $250 ste. Extra person $15. Children under 12 stay free. Lower rates off-season. Spec packages avail. Pking: Indoor, $14. Maj CC.

🏨🏨🏨🏨 **Hotel Nikko San Francisco**, 222 Mason St, San Francisco, CA 94102 (Union Square); tel 415/394-1111 or toll free 800/NIKKO-US; fax 415/394-1106. Between Mason and O'Farrell Sts. Tranquil and elegant Japanese-style setting; lovely marble lobby with fountains. Near Union Square, close to shopping. **Rooms:** 521 rms and stes. Exec-level rms avail. CI 3pm/CO noon. Express checkout avail. Nonsmoking rms avail. Japanese decor with soft colors, large bathrooms. Many rooms have city views. **Amenities:** 🖥 🕭 🍹 A/C, cable TV w/movies, refrig, voice mail, bathrobes. All units w/minibars, some w/Jacuzzis. **Services:** 🍽 🔑 🆅🅿 🚐 🖼 💬 Twice-daily maid svce, car-rental desk, masseur, babysitting. **Facilities:** 🏋 🏊 🖥 🕭 1 rst, 1 bar, spa, sauna, steam rm, whirlpool, beauty salon. Spectacular pool and atrium, excellent fitness center with city views. **Rates:** HS June–Oct $185–$275 S; $215–$305 D; from $375 ste. Extra person $30. Children under 18 stay free. Lower rates off-season. Spec packages avail. Pking: Indoor, $23. Maj CC.

🏨🏨🏨 **Hotel Triton**, 342 Grant Ave, San Francisco, CA 94108 (Financial District); tel 415/394-0500 or toll free 800/433-6611; fax 415/394-0555. Between Sutter and Bush Sts. Hip, classy hotel on the edge of Chinatown. Dramatic decor: art deco lobby with gilded columns, local art in hallways. **Rooms:** 140 rms and stes. CI 3pm/CO noon. Nonsmoking rms avail. Eye-catching decor features unique deco furniture and paintings by local artists. **Amenities:** 🔟 🕭 A/C, cable TV w/movies, refrig. All units w/minibars, some w/Jacuzzis. **Services:** ✗ 🗝 VP 🖼 🍷 Masseur, babysitting. **Facilities:** 🛍 🔟 🕭 1 rst, 1 bar. Cafe and restaurant next door. **Rates:** HS June–Oct $99–$149 S or D; from $189 ste. Lower rates off-season. Spec packages avail. Pking: Indoor, $18. Maj CC.

🎵🎵 **Hotel Union Square**, 114 Powell St, San Francisco, CA 94102 (Downtown); tel 415/397-3000 or toll free 800/553-1900; fax 415/399-1874. Between O'Farrell and Ellis Sts. A basic hotel. **Rooms:** 131 rms and stes. CI 2pm/CO noon. Nonsmoking rms avail. Rooms a bit fatigued. **Amenities:** 🔟 🕭 Cable TV w/movies, refrig. No A/C. All units w/minibars, some w/terraces. **Services:** 🗝 🖨 🖼 🍷 Babysitting. **Facilities:** 🕭 **Rates (CP):** HS June–Oct $99–$129 S or D; from $129 ste. Extra person $10. Children under 10 stay free. Lower rates off-season. Spec packages avail. Pking: Indoor/outdoor, $16. Maj CC.

🎵🎵 **Hotel Vintage Court**, 650 Bush St, San Francisco, CA 94108; tel 415/392-4666 or toll free 800/654-1100; fax 415/433-4065. Located near Union Square, this hotel draws big tour groups and business clientele. Generally nice, but needs refurbishing. **Rooms:** 107 rms and stes. CI 3pm/CO noon. Nonsmoking rms avail. Large, but nondescript rooms. **Amenities:** 🔟 🕭 🖳 Cable TV w/movies, refrig. No A/C. All units w/minibars. **Services:** ✗ 🗝 🖨 🖼 🍷 Babysitting. Free weekday morning limo to Financial District. Complimentary afternoon wine. Coffee and tea available 24 hours. **Facilities:** 🔟 1 rst (see also "Restaurants" below), 1 bar. **Rates (CP):** HS June–Oct $119–$129 S or D; from $250 ste. Extra person $12. Children under 12 stay free. Lower rates off-season. Spec packages avail. Pking: Indoor, $15. Maj CC.

🎵🎵 **Howard Johnson Hotel–Fisherman's Wharf**, 580 Beach St, San Francisco, CA 94133; tel 415/775-3800 or toll free 800/645-9258; fax 415/441-7307. At Leavenworth St. Well located in the same building as the Anchorage Shopping Center. Minimal public space. **Rooms:** 128 rms and stes. CI 3pm/CO noon. Nonsmoking rms avail. **Amenities:** 🔟 🕭 A/C, cable TV w/movies. All units w/minibars, some w/terraces. **Services:** ✗ 🖨 🖼 🍷 **Facilities:** 🕭 1 rst, washer/dryer. Gray Line tour desk. Cafeteria-style Breakfast Nook restaurant is open 6:45–11am. **Rates:** HS July–Sept 5 $129 S; $139 D; from $140 ste. Extra person $10. Children under 18 stay free. Lower rates off-season. Spec packages avail. Pking: Indoor, $4.50. Maj CC.

🎵🎵🎵🎵 **Huntington Hotel**, 1075 California St, San Francisco, CA 94108 (Nob Hill); tel 415/474-5400 or toll free 800/227-4683, 800/652-1539 in CA; fax 415/474-6227. At Taylor St. Crowning Nob Hill, this family-run establishment feels like a sumptuous private club. The head housekeeper previously worked at Buckingham Palace. **Rooms:** 140 rms, stes, and effic. CI 3pm/CO noon. Since the building was originally designed for luxury apartments, no two accommodations are alike. Even standard rooms offer accents such as English hunting prints and chinoiserie. Suites are extremely elegant, with highboys and oriental screens. About 25% of the bathrooms gleam with opulent rose marble and chrome fixtures, but the remaining old white-tiled baths are decidedly frumpy. **Amenities:** 🔟 🕭 🖳 Cable TV, refrig, shoe polisher. No A/C. All units w/minibars, 1 w/Jacuzzi. **Services:** ✗ 🗝 VP 🖨 🖼 🍷 Twice-daily maid svce, car-rental desk, masseur, babysitting. Concierge has helped guests arrange everything from theater tickets to chartering a small plane with a tow banner to wish someone sailing on San Francisco Bay a happy birthday. **Facilities:** 🔟 🖳 1 rst, 1 bar (w/entertainment). Named for turn-of-the-century railroad magnates, the Big Four Restaurant and Bar is richly panelled in wood and hung with old railway prints and vintage photos of Nob Hill. **Rates:** $165–$215 S; $185–$250 D; from $315 ste; from $250 effic. Extra person $30. Children under 5 stay free. Spec packages avail. Pking: Indoor/outdoor, $16.50. Maj CC.

🎵🎵🎵 **Hyatt Fisherman's Wharf**, 555 N Point St, San Francisco, CA 94133; tel 415/563-1234 or toll free 800/750-4928; fax 415/563-2218. At Taylor St. Just 1 block from Fisherman's Wharf, this hotel has an elegant lobby with fireplace, fountain, and antiques. Good for families. **Rooms:** 319 rms and stes. CI 3pm/CO noon. Express checkout avail. Nonsmoking rms avail. Clean and comfortable. **Amenities:** 🔟 🕭 A/C, cable TV w/movies, voice mail, in-rm safe. Some units w/minibars, 1 w/Jacuzzi. Gold Passport rooms have hair dryer, coffeemaker; 20 rooms have fax machines. **Services:** ✗ 🗝 VP 🖨 🍷 Children's program, babysitting. **Facilities:** 🔟 🛍 🔟 🖳 🕭 Games rm, spa, sauna, steam rm, washer/dryer. **Rates:** HS May–Oct $160–$185 S or D; from $185 ste. Children under 18 stay free. Min stay wknds. Lower rates off-season. Spec packages avail. Pking: Indoor, $14. Maj CC.

🎵🎵🎵 **Hyatt Regency San Francisco**, 5 Embarcadero Center, San Francisco, CA 94111 (Embarcadero Center); tel 415/788-1234 or toll free 800/233-1234; fax 415/398-2567. End of Market St. Recently remodeled hotel in a great location near many excellent restaurants, California cable car line, Marin ferry terminal. Glassed-in cage elevators and atrium lobby. **Rooms:** 803 rms and stes. Exec-level rms avail. CI noon/CO noon. Express checkout avail. Nonsmoking rms avail. Standard decor. Ask for bay view. **Amenities:** 🔟 🕭 🖳 A/C, cable TV w/movies, refrig, voice mail. Some units w/terraces. **Services:** ✗ 🗝 VP 🖨 🖼 🍷 Twice-daily maid svce, car-rental desk, masseur, children's program, babysitting. For a fee, Camp Hyatt offers kids' activities 3–11pm. **Facilities:** 🛍 🔟 🖳 🕭 2 rsts, 2 bars (w/entertainment). **Rates:** $185–$230 S or D; from $250 ste. Children under 18 stay free. Spec packages avail. Pking: Indoor, $20. Maj CC.

≡≡≡ **Hyde Park Suites**, 2655 Hyde St, San Francisco, CA 94109 (Fisherman's Wharf); tel 415/771-0200 or toll free 800/ 227-3608; fax 415/346-8058. Between North Point and Lombard Sts. Located right along the cable car line, 1 block from Ghirardelli Square, this hotel offers views of Alcatraz and San Francisco Bay. There's also a lovely sundeck. **Rooms:** 24 stes. CI noon/CO noon. Nonsmoking rms avail. Rooms are all luxury suites; 3rd-floor rooms have Bay views. All have full kitchens. **Amenities:** 🛗 ⚱ 🎨 Cable TV, refrig, in-rm safe. No A/C. All units w/minibars, some w/terraces. All rooms have 2 TVs. **Services:** 🔑 ⓋⓅ 🖼 ⌕ Masseur, babysitting. Complimentary wine served in atrium; complimentary newspaper and limousine service; 24-hour concierge. **Facilities:** Washer/dryer. **Rates (CP):** HS Apr–Oct from $165 ste. Extra person $10. Children under 12 stay free. Lower rates off-season. Spec packages avail. Pking: Indoor, $12. Maj CC.

≡≡≡≡ **Inn at the Opera**, 333 Fulton St, San Francisco, CA 94102 (Civic Center); tel 415/863-8400 or toll free 800/ 325-2708; fax 415/861-0821. At Franklin St. A wonderful place from which to savor the magic of the nearby Opera House or Symphony Hall. It caters to visiting performers. **Rooms:** 48 rms and stes. CI 3pm/CO noon. Express checkout avail. Nonsmoking rms avail. Charming and elegant, with classic European furnishings and queen-size beds. **Amenities:** 🛗 ⚱ 🎨 Cable TV w/movies. No A/C. All units w/minibars. Terry-cloth bathrobes in rooms. **Services:** 🍽 🔑 ⓋⓅ 🚗 🖼 ⌕ Car-rental desk, babysitting. Gourmet continental breakfast. Secretarial service and other business services. **Facilities:** ⟐ 1 rst (*see also* "Restaurants" below), 1 bar (w/entertainment). **Rates (CP):** HS Sept–Oct $110–$155 S; $120–$165 D; from $165 ste. Extra person $10. Min stay spec evnts. Lower rates off-season. Spec packages avail. Pking: Outdoor, $16. Maj CC. Special "Performance Package" available.

≡≡≡ **Inn at Union Square**, 440 Post St, San Francisco, CA 94102 (Downtown); tel 415/397-3510 or toll free 800/AT-THE-INN; fax 415/989-0529. At Powell St. An intimate inn. Fragrant lobby has fresh flowers, candles over the fireplace mantel, and a garden view. Exclusively nonsmoking. **Rooms:** 30 rms and stes. CI 2pm/CO noon. All rooms individually decorated. **Amenities:** 🛗 ⚱ 🎨 Cable TV, shoe polisher, bathrobes. No A/C. Some units w/fireplaces, 1 w/Jacuzzi. **Services:** ✗ 🔑 ⓋⓅ 🚗 🖼 ⌕ Twice-daily maid svce, masseur, babysitting. Honor bar in hallway 2–10:30pm. Free evening wine and hors d'oeuvres. Complimentary newspapers. **Facilities:** 💻 ⟐ **Rates (CP):** HS May–Nov

$120–$180 S or D; from $170 ste. Extra person $15. Children under 4 stay free. Lower rates off-season. Pking: Indoor, $18. Maj CC.

≡≡≡ **Juliana Hotel**, 590 Bush St, San Francisco, CA 94108 (Downtown); tel 415/392-2540 or toll free 800/328-3880; fax 415/391-8447. At Sutter St. Pleasant, quiet hotel above Union Square. Pastel decor with flower arrangements and a warm, inviting lobby with fireplace. **Rooms:** 106 rms and stes. CI 2pm/ CO noon. Nonsmoking rms avail. **Amenities:** 🛗 ⚱ 🎨 A/C, cable TV w/movies, refrig. All units w/minibars. **Services:** ✗ 🚗 🖼 ⌕ Babysitting. Complimentary coffee and tea all day; afternoon wine. Free morning limo to financial district. **Facilities:** 🔟 ⟐ **Rates:** HS June–Oct $124–$134 S or D; from $140 ste. Extra person $10. Children under 18 stay free. Min stay HS. Lower rates off-season. Spec packages avail. Maj CC.

≡≡≡ **Kensington Park Hotel**, 450 Post St, San Francisco, CA 94102 (Downtown); tel 415/788-6400 or toll free 800/ 553-1900; fax 415/399-9484. At Powell St. Right off Union Square and the cable car line; rooms are basic but affordable. **Rooms:** 86 rms and stes. CI 2pm/CO noon. Nonsmoking rms avail. Queen Anne–style decor in rose and blue accents. **Amenities:** 🛗 ⚱ Cable TV. No A/C. 1 unit w/minibar, 1 w/fireplace, some w/Jacuzzis. **Services:** ✗ 🔑 ⓋⓅ 🚗 🖼 ⌕ Babysitting. Complimentary continental breakfast and afternoon sherry and cookies in lobby. **Facilities:** 🔟 ⟐ 1 bar. **Rates (CP):** HS Apr–Aug $115–$135 S or D; from $160 ste. Extra person $10. Children under 13 stay free. Min stay spec evnts. Lower rates off-season. Spec packages avail. Pking: Indoor, $16. Maj CC. Good midweek rates.

≡≡ **King George Hotel**, 334 Mason St, San Francisco, CA 94102 (Downtown); tel 415/781-5050 or toll free 800/ 288-6005; fax 415/391-6976. At Geary St. Built in 1914, this charming hotel is located near Union Square shops and restaurants. **Rooms:** 140 rms and stes. CI 3pm/CO noon. Standard decor. Request accommodations with 2 windows. **Amenities:** 🛗 Cable TV w/movies, in-rm safe. No A/C. **Services:** 🍽 🚗 🖼 ⌕ Car-rental desk, social director, masseur, babysitting. **Facilities:** 🔟 1 rst. Tea room. **Rates:** HS July–Oct $102 S; $112 D; from $196 ste. Extra person $10. Children under 12 stay free. Lower rates off-season. Spec packages avail. Pking: Indoor, $15.50. Maj CC. Special sweetheart packages.

≡≡ **Lombard Hotel**, 1015 Geary St, San Francisco, CA 94109 (Van Ness); tel 415/673-5232 or toll free 800/777-3210; fax 415/885-2802. At Polk St. A clean, charming old hotel on the edge of a slightly dubious neighborhood, San Francisco's Tenderloin district. **Rooms:** 101 rms. CI 2pm/CO noon. Nonsmoking rms avail. The airy rooms have louvered windows, big closets, and basic furniture. **Amenities:** 🛗 TV w/movies, refrig, in-rm safe. No A/C. Some units w/minibars. **Services:** ✗ VP 🛏 🗺 ⌧ Afternoon tea and sherry. Complimentary morning limousine service. **Facilities:** 🔲 Games rm. **Rates:** HS June–Aug $99 S or D. Extra person $10. Children under 12 stay free. Lower rates off-season. Spec packages avail. Pking: Indoor/outdoor, $10. Maj CC.

▤▤▤▤ Mandarin Oriental, San Francisco, 222 Sansome St, San Francisco, CA 94104 (Financial District); tel 415/885-0999 or toll free 800/622-0404. Between Pine and California Sts. The ultimate urban retreat—a skyscraper aerie which puts you on top of San Francisco. Because the hotel occupies floors 38 to 48 of the city's 3rd-largest building, every room has an incredible view. **Rooms:** 158 rms and stes. CI 3pm/CO noon. Express checkout avail. Nonsmoking rms avail. Layouts vary, but all are decorated with pale yellow walls and a whisper of the Orient in the throw pillows and art. Mandarin rooms feature a Jacuzzi tub next to floor-to-ceiling windows. **Amenities:** 🛏 🔥 🕏 A/C, cable TV w/movies, refrig, shoe polisher, bathrobes. All units w/minibars, some w/terraces. Features include clothes brushes, Thai slippers in bathroom, closets that light automatically, English toiletries. Marble baths are both stunning and well laid out. **Services:** ⦿ 🖙 VP 🛏 🗺 ⌧ Twice-daily maid svce, car-rental desk, masseur, babysitting. **Facilities:** 🔲 🖥 🕏 1 rst, 1 bar (w/entertainment). Full-service business center. Guest privileges at the Bay Club health club. **Rates:** $260–$395 S or D; from $575 ste. Extra person $45. Children under 12 stay free. Spec packages avail. Pking: Indoor, $20. Maj CC.

▤▤ Marina Inn Bed & Breakfast, 3110 Octavia St, San Francisco, CA 94123; tel 415/928-1000 or toll free 800/274-1420; fax 415/928-5909. At Lombard St. A small European-style hotel with a tiny lobby and not much public space. Parking in the neighborhood is very difficult. **Rooms:** 40 rms. CI 2pm/CO noon. Rooms are small, but clean and comfortable; each has a French window with a seating nook. **Amenities:** 🛏 Cable TV. No A/C. Guide to San Francisco in each room. **Services:** ⌧ Babysitting. Complimentary continental breakfast from 7 to 10am; evening sherry 4 to 6pm. **Facilities:** 🕏 Sitting room on the 2nd floor. **Rates:** $65–$85 S or D. Extra person $10. Children under 5 stay free. Maj CC.

▤▤▤▤ Mark Hopkins Inter-Continental San Francisco, 1 Nob Hill, San Francisco, CA 94108 (Nob Hill); tel 415/392-3434 or toll free 800/327-0200, 800/622-4455 in CA; fax 415/291-9020. At Mason St. San Francisco's grand hotel atop Nob Hill. Lobby has plenty of pizazz, with limestone floors, crystal chandeliers, potted palms, and bronze torchiers. All corridors and rooms recently refurbished. **Rooms:** 389 rms and stes. Exec-level rms avail. CI 3pm/CO 1pm. Express checkout avail. Nonsmoking rms avail. Many nice features, such as

comfortable armchairs and handsome burled armoires containing TV and minibar. Newly redone gray-and-white marble baths (in many accommodations) are beautiful, but counter space is very limited. **Amenities:** 🛏 🔥 A/C, cable TV w/movies, refrig, voice mail, shoe polisher, bathrobes. All units w/minibars, some w/terraces, 1 w/Jacuzzi. **Services:** ⦿ 🖙 VP 🛏 🗺 ⌧ Twice-daily maid svce, car-rental desk, masseur, babysitting. Guests on the executive floor receive complimentary continental breakfast, afternoon hors d'oeuvres, and access to a brew-it-yourself espresso bar. **Facilities:** 🔲 🔲 🖥 🕏 2 rsts, 3 bars (w/entertainment). Rooftop Top of the Mark bar has romantic views of the city through its wrap-around windows. **Rates:** $180–$275 S; $200–$305 D; from $375 ste. Extra person $20. Children under 18 stay free. Spec packages avail. Pking: Indoor, $23. Maj CC.

▤▤▤ Marriott at Fisherman's Wharf, 1250 Columbus Ave, San Francisco, CA 94133; tel 415/775-7555 or toll free 800/525-0956; fax 415/474-2099. Between Bay and North Point Sts. Clean and comfortable hotel offers nice public areas and friendly service. **Rooms:** 255 rms and stes. CI 3pm/CO noon. Express checkout avail. Nonsmoking rms avail. Recently renovated rooms have colonial furniture but small bathrooms. **Amenities:** 🛏 🔥 🕏 A/C, cable TV w/movies. All units w/minibars. Full-size iron and ironing board in each room. **Services:** ✗ 🖙 VP 🛏 🗺 ⌧ 🍴 Babysitting. Starbucks coffee and Pizza Hut pizza available through room service, as well as in lobby. **Facilities:** 🔲 🔲 🕏 1 rst, 1 bar, sauna. **Rates:** HS Apr–Oct $179–$189 S or D; from $205 ste. Lower rates off-season. Maj CC. "Two for breakfast" rate includes a breakfast buffet.

▤▤▤ Miyako Hotel, 1625 Post St, San Francisco, CA 94115; tel 415/392-8880 or toll free 800/533-4567; fax 415/921-0417. At Laguna St. A stay at this very classy hotel is a unique multicultural experience combining Japanese and Western styles and comforts. **Rooms:** 218 rms and stes. CI 2pm/CO 1pm. Express checkout avail. Nonsmoking rms avail. The 13 types of rooms include Japanese rooms with futons, shoji screens, and silk comforters, and "club" or western-style rooms. **Amenities:** 🛏 🔥 A/C, cable TV w/movies, refrig, voice mail, in-rm safe. All units w/minibars, some w/terraces, some w/Jacuzzis. Yukata (cotton kimono) robes in some rooms. **Services:** ✗ 🖙 VP 🗺 ⌧ Car-rental desk, masseur, babysitting. **Facilities:** 🔲 🕏 1 rst, 1 bar (w/entertainment). **Rates:** HS May–Sept $109–$160 S; $129–$179 D; from $189 ste. Children under 18 stay free. Lower rates off-season. Spec packages avail. Pking: Indoor/outdoor, $8.75–$15. Maj CC.

▤▤ Miyako Inn–Best Western, 1800 Sutter St, San Francisco, CA 94115; tel 415/921-4000 or toll free 800/528-1234; fax 415/923-1064. At Buchanan St. Located in Japantown, this hotel provides easy access to Union Square and Fisherman's Wharf.

Rooms: 125 rms and stes. CI 2pm/CO noon. Nonsmoking rms avail. Rooms are well appointed, spacious, and comfortable. Some have Japanese-style baths. **Amenities:** ☎ ⚲ A/C, cable TV. Some units w/terraces. **Services:** 🚐 ⬛ 🔌 Babysitting. **Facilities:** [150] ⚿ 1 bar. **Rates:** HS June–Oct $81 S; $91 D; from $158 ste. Extra person $10. Children under 18 stay free. Lower rates off-season. Spec packages avail. Pking: Indoor, $6. Maj CC. Families requiring more than 1 room pay the single rate for each additional room, regardless of the number of family members occupying it.

≣≣≣ **Monticello Inn**, 127 Ellis St, San Francisco, CA 94102 (Union Square); tel 415/392-8800 or toll free 800/669-7777; fax 415/398-2650. At Powell St. Charming colonial-style hotel in the heart of downtown. The comfortable and inviting lounge and lobby area has sofas and fireplace. **Rooms:** 91 rms and stes. CI 4pm/CO noon. Nonsmoking rms avail. Rooms are small but clean and attractively decorated with pink country floral designs. The 36 suites have larger rooms. **Amenities:** ☎ ⚲ A/C, cable TV w/movies, refrig. All units w/minibars, 1 w/fireplace, 1 w/Jacuzzi. **Services:** [VP] 🚐 ⬛ 🔌 Babysitting. Complimentary wine service is available in the evening; coffee and tea are always offered to guests in the lounge. **Facilities:** ⚿ A fine restaurant, Abiquiu, is on the premises. **Rates (CP):** HS June–Oct $120–$135 S or D; from $145 ste. Children under 12 stay free. Lower rates off-season. Spec packages avail. Pking: Indoor, $15–$25. Maj CC.

≣≣≣ **Nob Hill Lambourne**, 725 Pine St, San Francisco, CA 94108 (Nob Hill); tel 415/433-2287 or toll free 800/BRITINN; fax 415/433-0975. At Stockton St. A small, elegant hotel designed for the business traveler. **Rooms:** 20 rms and stes. CI 3pm/CO noon. Nonsmoking rms avail. Every room and suite is set up to function like an office. **Amenities:** ☎ ⚲ ▣ 🍷 Cable TV w/movies, refrig, VCR, stereo/tape player, voice mail, bathrobes. No A/C. All units w/minibars, some w/terraces. Computer, fax, voice mail. **Services:** ✗ [VP] 🚐 ⬛ 🔌 Masseur, babysitting. **Facilities:** 🏋 ▣ 💻 Spa. **Rates (CP):** HS June–Oct $125–$145 S or D; from $199 ste. Children under 18 stay free. Lower rates off-season. Spec packages avail. Pking: Indoor, $18. Maj CC. Spa packages available.

≣≣≣ **The Orchard**, 562 Sutter St, San Francisco, CA 94102 (Union Square); tel 415/433-4434 or toll free 800/433-4434; fax 415/433-3695. At Mason St. Good location just ½ block from the Powell St cable car. **Rooms:** 94 rms and stes. CI 2pm/CO noon. Nonsmoking rms avail. **Amenities:** ☎ 🍷 A/C, cable TV, refrig. All units w/minibars. **Services:** ✗ 🖙 🚐 ⬛ 🔌 Car-rental desk, babysitting. **Facilities:** 💻 ⚿ 1 rst, 1 bar. **Rates:** HS

April–Oct $110–$140 S or D; from $225 ste. Extra person $10. Children under 13 stay free. Lower rates off-season. AP and MAP rates avail. Spec packages avail. Pking: Indoor, $14. Maj CC.

≣ **Pacific Bay Inn**, 520 Jones St, San Francisco, CA 94102 (Union Square); tel 415/673-0234 or toll free 800/445-2631, 800/343-0880 in CA; fax 415/673-4781. Between Geary and O'Farrell Sts. A rather nondescript old hotel on the edge of the Tenderloin district. **Rooms:** 84 rms. CI 2pm/CO 11am. Nonsmoking rms avail. Some rooms have a faint odor of stale cigarette smoke. **Amenities:** ☎ ⚲ Cable TV. No A/C. **Services:** 🚐 ⬛ 🔌 **Facilities:** Good breakfast restaurant next door. **Rates:** HS April–Oct $55–$75 S or D. Extra person $10. Lower rates off-season. Higher rates for spec evnts/hols. Spec packages avail. Pking: Indoor, $12. Maj CC.

≣≣≣≣ **The Pan Pacific Hotel–San Francisco**, 500 Post St, San Francisco, CA 94102 (Union Square); tel 415/771-8600 or toll free 800/327-8585; fax 415/398-0267. At Mason St. Dramatic design from noted architect John Portman, with a 21-story skylit atrium, twin fireplaces in the lobby, glass elevators that rise like bubbles, and acres of marble. Celebrity guests have included Emma Thompson and Arnold Schwarzenegger. **Rooms:** 330 rms and stes. CI 3pm/CO open. Express checkout avail. Nonsmoking rms avail. Accommodations sparkle with contemporary flair and Asian touches like rosewood chairs; all upholsteries are to be updated. Portuguese marble lines the glamorous bathrooms, which come with lots of mirrors and chrome fixtures. **Amenities:** ☎ ⚲ 🍷 A/C, cable TV w/movies, refrig, in-rm safe, bathrobes. All units w/minibars, 1 w/terrace, 1 w/fireplace, some w/Jacuzzis. **Services:** [◯] 🖙 [VP] 🚐 ⬛ 🔌 🐕 Car-rental desk, masseur, babysitting. All rooms served by personal valets, who do everything from running errands to sewing buttons. Hotel can deliver a stair machine, treadmill, weights, or a Lifecycle right to your room—all complimentary. Complimentary limousine service by Rolls Royce within the downtown area. **Facilities:** [350] 💻 ⚿ 1 rst, 1 bar. **Rates:** $195–$295 S; $215–$315 D; from $335 ste. Children under 18 stay free. Spec packages avail. Pking: Indoor, $20. Maj CC.

≣≣≣ **Parc Fifty Five**, 55 Cyril Magnin St, San Francisco, CA 94012 (Union Square); tel 415/392-8000 or toll free 800/338-1338. At Market St. Urbane property conveniently located near Union Square. **Rooms:** 1,058 rms and stes. Exec-level rms avail. CI 3pm/CO noon. Express checkout avail. Nonsmoking rms avail. Rooms higher up have city views. **Amenities:** ☎ ⚲ 🍷 A/C, cable TV w/movies, in-rm safe, shoe polisher. Some units w/terraces, some w/Jacuzzis. **Services:** [◯] 🖙 [VP] 🚐 ⬛ 🔌 Twice-daily maid svce, car-rental desk, masseur, babysitting. Concierge-floor guests receive continental breakfast and evening hors d'oeuvres. **Facilities:** 🏋 [17K] 💻 ⚿ 2 rsts, 2 bars (w/entertainment). **Rates:** HS June–Aug $195 S or D; from $340 ste. Extra person $15. Children under 12 stay free. Lower rates off-season. MAP rates avail. Spec packages avail. Pking: Indoor, $22. Maj CC. Children under 12 eat free in the restaurant.

≡≡≡≡ **Park Hyatt San Francisco**, 333 Battery St, San Francisco, CA 94111 (Financial District); tel 415/392-1234 or toll free 800/233-1234; fax 415/421-2433. Modern 26-story structure designed primarily for business travelers, but with its proximity to Embarcadero Center's shops and waterfront, it attracts vacationers as well. Convenient driveway and porte cochere lead to attractive, uncluttered lobby paneled with Australian lacewood. Extensive collection of antiques and original artworks. **Rooms:** 360 rms and stes. CI 3pm/CO noon. Express checkout avail. Nonsmoking rms avail. Designed by people who've actually stayed in hotels. Some of the most comfortable, efficient rooms in the city; Park Rooms, with their multipurpose room dividers, are especially good. Angled architecture incorporates big windows, giving most rooms a sense of airiness and views of the city or bay. **Amenities:** 🛗 ⚷ 🍴 A/C, cable TV w/movies, refrig, voice mail, shoe polisher, bathrobes. All units w/minibars, some w/terraces, 1 w/fireplace, some w/Jacuzzis. Some suites have balconies just large enough for breakfast for 2. **Services:** 🍽 ☎ VP 🛆 🛍 Twice-daily maid svce, masseur, babysitting. 24-hour concierge. Mercedes-Benz for complimentary shuttling to business/shopping centers. Afternoon tea in lobby lounge. On-their-toes staffers make a point of getting guests' names right and somehow making the place seem intimate. **Facilities:** 250 🖥 ⚒ 1 rst (*see also* "Restaurants" below), 2 bars (1 w/entertainment). Library with leather armchairs, international newspapers, reference books, and chess. Elevated walkways to Embarcadero Center. Rowing machine and exercise bike rentals for in-room use. 3rd-floor, 150-seat Park Grill popular with executives. **Rates:** $240–$265 S; $265–$290 D; from $325 ste. Extra person $25. Children under 18 stay free. Min stay spec evnts. Spec packages avail. Pking: Indoor, $20. Maj CC.

≡≡≡ **Petite Auberge**, 863 Bush St, San Francisco, CA 94108 (Union Square); tel 415/928-6000; fax 415/775-5717. At Taylor St. Lots of teddy bears tucked everywhere in this charming inn/hotel. Breakfast room, garden terrace, and fireplace lounge all done like a cozy Victorian living room. **Rooms:** 26 rms and stes. CI 2pm/CO noon. Nonsmoking rms avail. **Amenities:** 🛗 ⚷ 🍴 Cable TV, bathrobes. No A/C. Some units w/minibars, some w/fireplaces. Guide books in each room. **Services:** ✗ ☎ VP ⚒ 🛆 🛍 Masseur, babysitting. Afternoon tea and cookies. Breakfast in bed for a fee. **Rates (BB):** HS May–Oct $110–$160 S or D; from $195 ste. Extra person $15. Children under 2 stay free. Lower rates off-season. Pking: Indoor, $17. Maj CC.

≡≡ **The Phoenix**, 601 Eddy St, San Francisco, CA 94109 (Civic Center); tel 415/776-1380 or toll free 800/CITY-INN; fax 415/885-3109. At Larkin St. This cheerful property has pastel-trimmed units surrounding a lovely pool. The pool area is surrounded by palm trees, a mural, and Caribbean-style artwork. Caters to a hip celebrity crowd. **Rooms:** 44 rms and stes. CI 2pm/CO noon. Express checkout avail. Rooms are funky; most have a view of the pool. There is little privacy, as floor-to-ceiling windows overlook walkways. **Amenities:** 🛗 ⚷ Cable TV. No A/C. Some units w/terraces. **Services:** ✗ ⚒ 🛆 🛍 🛎 Masseur, babysitting. **Facilities:** 🔲 60 🖥 1 rst (*see also* "Restaurants" below), 1 bar (w/entertainment). **Rates (CP):** HS June–Oct $89 S or D; from $139 ste. Extra person $10. Children under 12 stay free. Lower rates off-season. Spec packages avail. Pking: Outdoor, free. Maj CC.

≡≡ **Powell Hotel**, 28 Cyril Magnin St, San Francisco, CA 94102 (Union Square); tel 415/398-3200 or toll free 800/368-0700, 800/652-3399 in CA; fax 415/398-3654. At Powell St. Standard hotel near Union Square. Powell St cable car turn-around right in front. **Rooms:** 105 rms and stes. CI noon/CO noon. Nonsmoking rms avail. Wallpaper peeling off walls. **Amenities:** 🛗 TV. No A/C. **Services:** ✗ VP ⚒ 🛆 🛍 Babysitting. **Facilities:** 120 ⚒ 1 rst. Good restaurants within 1 block. **Rates:** HS June–Oct $65–$85 S; $75–$95 D; from $120 ste. Extra person $10. Children under 18 stay free. Lower rates off-season. Spec packages avail. Pking: Indoor, $16. Maj CC.

≡≡≡ **Prescott Hotel**, 545 Post St, San Francisco, CA 94102 (Union Square); tel 415/563-0303 or toll free 800/283-7322; fax 415/563-6831. Between Mason and Taylor Sts. Quietly elegant, offering good service. Displays of California Native American artifacts accent the lobby area. **Rooms:** 166 rms and stes. Exec-level rms avail. CI 3pm/CO noon. Nonsmoking rms avail. Rooms (on the small side) feature Empire-style furnishings, including a bow-front armoire and columned cherrywood headboard. **Amenities:** 🛗 ⚷ 🍴 A/C, cable TV w/movies, refrig, VCR, stereo/tape player, bathrobes. All units w/minibars, 1 w/fireplace, some w/Jacuzzis. **Services:** ✗ ☎ VP ⚒ 🛆 🛍 Twice-daily maid svce, car-rental desk, masseur, babysitting. Flanking a wonderful old-world fireplace, the "living room" lounge offers complimentary coffee and tea in the morning, wine and cheese in the afternoon. **Facilities:** 40 ⚒ 1 rst (*see also* "Restaurants" below), 1 bar. Use of nearby health club and pool for $12 fee. Superb downstairs restaurant, Postrio, provides room service. **Rates:** $185–$215 S or D; from $215 ste. Children under 18 stay free. Pking: Indoor, $18. Maj CC.

≡≡ **Queen Anne Hotel**, 1590 Sutter St, San Francisco, CA 94109 (Lower Pacific Heights); tel 415/441-2828 or toll free 800/227-3970; fax 415/775-5212. At Octavia St. Located on the outer edge of Pacific Heights, this elaborate Victorian also borders on the cute. **Rooms:** 49 rms and stes. CI 3pm/CO noon. Nonsmoking rms avail. Slightly shabby rooms, with old furniture and large but barren bathrooms. **Amenities:** 🛗 🕎 🏺 TV, refrig. No A/C. Some units w/fireplaces. **Services:** 🗝️ 🚐 ⚠️ ⟲ Car-rental desk, babysitting. Free afternoon tea and sherry in lobby; morning limo service; newspapers. **Facilities:** [65] 🚹 **Rates (CP):** HS May–Oct $99–$150 S or D; from $175 ste. Extra person $10. Children under 12 stay free. Lower rates off-season. Spec packages avail. Pking: Outdoor, $12. Maj CC.

≡≡≡ Ramada Hotel–Fisherman's Wharf, 590 Bay St, San Francisco, CA 94133; tel 415/885-4700 or toll free 800/228-8408; fax 415/771-8945. At Jones St. Average hotel with large rooms. **Rooms:** 232 rms and stes. CI 3pm/CO noon. Express checkout avail. Nonsmoking rms avail. Some of the largest rooms in Fisherman's Wharf, but bathrooms are small. **Amenities:** 🛗 🕎 🏺 A/C, cable TV w/movies. **Services:** ✕ 🚐 ⚠️ ⟲ Car-rental desk, babysitting. **Facilities:** [200] 🚹 1 rst, 1 bar. **Rates:** HS May–Oct $165–$214 S or D; from $250 ste. Children under 18 stay free. Min stay spec evnts. Lower rates off-season. Higher rates for spec evnts/hols. Spec packages avail. Pking: Indoor, $8. Maj CC.

≡≡≡ Ramada Hotel San Francisco, 1231 Market St, San Francisco, CA 94103; tel 415/626-8000 or toll free 800/227-4747; fax 415/861-1460. At 8th St. Very ornate and attractive, with beautiful architecture and sculpted ceilings. **Rooms:** 460 rms and stes. CI 3pm/CO noon. Express checkout avail. Nonsmoking rms avail. Clean, pleasant rooms are decorated in rose and teal, with large walk-in closets. **Amenities:** 🛗 🕎 🏺 A/C, TV w/movies, voice mail. **Services:** ✕ 🚐 ⚠️ ⟲ Car-rental desk, babysitting. **Facilities:** [200] 🚹 1 rst, 1 bar (w/entertainment), beauty salon, washer/dryer. **Rates:** HS May–Oct $79–$119 S or D; from $250 ste. Extra person $12. Children under 18 stay free. Lower rates off-season. Higher rates for spec evnts/hols. Spec packages avail. Pking: Indoor/outdoor, $8. Maj CC.

≡≡ The Raphael, 386 Geary St, San Francisco, CA 94102 (Union Square); tel 415/986-2000 or toll free 800/821-5343; fax 415/397-2447. Between Powell and Mason Sts. An attractive hotel with a friendly staff. **Rooms:** 153 rms and stes. CI open/CO 1pm. Express checkout avail. Nonsmoking rms avail. **Amenities:** 🛗 🕎 🏺 A/C, cable TV w/movies. **Services:** ✕ 🚐 ⚠️ ⟲ Babysitting. Complimentary coffee in lobby mornings. **Facilities:** [100] 1 bar. **Rates:** HS June–Oct $99–$124 S; $109–$134 D; from $145 ste. Extra person $10. Children under 10 stay free. Lower rates off-season. Spec packages avail. Pking: Indoor, $14.75. Maj CC.

≡≡ Richelieu Hotel, 1050 Van Ness Ave, San Francisco, CA 94109; tel 415/673-4711 or toll free 800/295-7424; fax 415/673-9362. Between O'Farrell and Geary Sts. Old San Francisco charmer with newly decorated lobby, French windows, and skylights. Limited facilities. Renovations planned. **Rooms:** 150 rms and stes. CI 3pm/CO noon. Nonsmoking rms avail. Rooms are small, especially bathrooms. Decor outdated. **Amenities:** 🛗 🕎 🏺 Cable TV w/movies, refrig, in-rm safe. No A/C. All units w/minibars, 1 w/Jacuzzi. **Services:** 🗝️ ⚠️ ⟲ Twice-daily maid svce, car-rental desk, babysitting. Afternoon tea. **Facilities:** 🍴 [75] 🚹 **Rates:** HS Apr–Oct $89 S; $99 D; from $125 ste. Children under 5 stay free. Min stay spec evnts. Lower rates off-season. Spec packages avail. Pking: Outdoor, $10. Maj CC.

≡≡≡≡ The Ritz-Carlton San Francisco, 600 Stockton St, San Francisco, CA 94108 (Nob Hill); tel 415/296-7465 or toll free 800/241-3333; fax 415/291-8559. At California St. Grand, turn-of-the-century, Federal Reserve–style landmark converted to hotel in 1991, with palatial furnishings (Bohemian crystal chandeliers, silk wall-coverings) and museum-caliber artworks. Located on 8 floors around a U-shaped central courtyard with flowerbeds and a white-umbrellaed cafe that reminds some visitors of the Hotel Bristol in Paris. **Rooms:** 336 rms and stes. Exec-level rms avail. CI 3pm/CO noon. Express checkout avail. Nonsmoking rms avail. Impeccably furnished with period furniture; sumptuous Italian marble bathrooms. Some rooms offer skyline or harbor views. **Amenities:** 🛗 🕎 🏺 A/C, cable TV w/movies, refrig, in-rm safe, shoe polisher, bathrobes. All units w/minibars, 1 w/terrace, 1 w/Jacuzzi. Suites have VCRs. **Services:** 🍽️ 🗝️ VP ⚠️ ⟲ Twice-daily maid svce, car-rental desk, masseur, babysitting. 24-hour concierge. Afternoon tea in elegant lounge. Room service massage. Complimentary town cars to several downtown locations. Cellular phones for rent. **Facilities:** 🔥 🍴 [600] 🚹 2 rsts (see also "Restaurants" below), 3 bars (2 w/entertainment), lifeguard, spa, sauna, steam rm, whirlpool. 8,000-square-foot fitness center has one of the city's few indoor lap pools. **Rates:** $225–$345 S or D; from $400 ste. Spec packages avail. Pking: Indoor, $25. Maj CC. Rates vary by floor and view rather than size. (For a real bargain, room 312 at $265 is hard to beat.)

≡≡≡ San Francisco Hilton, 333 O'Farrell St, San Francisco, CA 94142 (Union Square); tel 415/771-1400 or toll free 800/HILTONS; fax 415/771-6807. At Mason St. A mammoth hotel near Union Square. **Rooms:** 1,914 rms and stes. Exec-level rms avail. CI 2pm/CO noon. Express checkout avail. Nonsmoking rms avail. Standard rooms with great views. **Amenities:** 🛗 🕎 A/C, cable TV w/movies, refrig, voice mail. All units w/minibars, some w/terraces, some w/fireplaces. **Services:** ✕ 🗝️ VP 🚐 ⚠️ ⟲ 🍷 Car-rental desk, masseur, children's program, babysitting. **Facilities:** 🔥 🍴 [13K] 🖥️ 🚹 5 rsts, 2 bars (w/entertainment), sauna, steam rm, whirlpool, beauty salon. Outdoor pool is well protected from wind. Rooftop restaurant on 46th floor. **Rates:** HS June–Oct $175–$240 S; $200–$265 D; from $450 ste. Extra person $25. Children under 18 stay free. Lower rates off-season. Spec packages avail. Pking: Indoor, $22. Maj CC.

San Francisco Marriott, 55 4th St, San Francisco, CA 94103; tel 415/896-1600 or toll free 800/228-9290; fax 415/777-2799. At Mission St. Splashy hotel with beautiful public spaces. Excellent for conventions and families, with a central location across from Moscone Center. **Rooms:** 1,498 rms and stes. Exec-level rms avail. CI 4pm/CO 1pm. Express checkout avail. Nonsmoking rms avail. Many suites have views of the city. Some rooms have kitchens. **Amenities:** A/C, cable TV w/movies, voice mail, in-rm safe. All units w/minibars, some w/terraces, some w/Jacuzzis. Some suites have wet bars. **Services:** Car-rental desk, masseur, babysitting. Use of computers, fax machines, secretarial services, and multilingual business center. **Facilities:** 2 rsts, 2 bars, lifeguard, sauna, steam rm, whirlpool. Health club with largest indoor pool in the city. Shops. Rooftop lounge. **Rates:** HS Apr–Oct $185–$215 S or D; from $225 ste. Extra person $10. Children under 18 stay free. Lower rates off-season. Higher rates for spec evnts/hols. Spec packages avail. Pking: Indoor/outdoor, $24. Maj CC.

Savoy Hotel, 580 Geary St, San Francisco, CA 94102 (Downtown); tel 415/441-2700 or toll free 800/227-4223; fax 415/441-2700 ext 297. Between Jones and Powell Sts. Old-time San Francisco atmosphere in lobby. **Rooms:** 83 rms and stes. CI 3pm/CO noon. Nonsmoking rms avail. Beds have feather pillows. **Amenities:** Cable TV, refrig. No A/C. All units w/minibars, some w/Jacuzzis. **Services:** Babysitting. Free overnight shoeshine. Complimentary afternoon tea, cookies, sherry. **Facilities:** 1 rst, 1 bar. **Rates (CP):** HS June–Oct $99–$119 S or D; from $149 ste. Extra person $10. Children under 10 stay free. Lower rates off-season. Spec packages avail. Pking: Outdoor, $16. Maj CC. Package deal includes room, parking, dinner, and breakfast for 2.

Shannon Court Hotel, 550 Geary St, San Francisco, CA 94102 (Downtown); tel 415/775-5000 or toll free 800/228-8830; fax 415/775-9388. Between Taylor and Jones Sts. Classic San Francisco decor. **Rooms:** 173 rms, stes. Exec-level rms avail. CI 2pm/CO noon. Nonsmoking rms avail. Very large and clean. **Amenities:** Satel TV w/movies, refrig, shoe polisher. No A/C. Some units w/terraces, 1 w/fireplace. **Services:** Babysitting. **Facilities:** 1 rst, 1 bar. Great cafe downstairs: City of Paris. **Rates (CP):** HS May–Oct

$110 S; $120 D; from $200 ste. Extra person $10. Children under 12 stay free. Lower rates off-season. Spec packages avail. Pking: Outdoor, $13. Maj CC.

The Sheehan, 620 Sutter St, San Francisco, CA 94102 (Union Square); tel 415/775-6500 or toll free 800/848-1529; fax 415/775-3271. At Mason St. Worn-looking hotel has one of the largest indoor lap pools in San Francisco. **Rooms:** 68 rms. CI 3pm/CO 11am. Nonsmoking rms avail. **Amenities:** Cable TV. No A/C. **Services:** Babysitting. **Facilities:** 1 rst, 1 bar, lifeguard, beauty salon. **Rates (CP):** HS June–Nov $50–$70 S; $60–$99 D. Extra person $10. Children under 13 stay free. Lower rates off-season. Pking: Outdoor, $12. Maj CC.

Sheraton at Fishermans' Wharf, 2500 Mason St, San Francisco, CA 94133; tel 415/362-5500 or toll free 800/325-3535; fax 415/956-5275. At Beach St. This hotel, scheduled to undergo a major renovation, has an attractive lobby ideal for groups. **Rooms:** 524 rms and stes. Exec-level rms avail. CI 3pm/CO noon. Express checkout avail. Nonsmoking rms avail. **Amenities:** A/C, cable TV w/movies, voice mail. **Services:** Car-rental desk, children's program, babysitting. **Facilities:** 1 rst, 1 bar (w/entertainment), beauty salon. Use of 24-hour Nautilus center across the street ($3 per day). American Express travel agency, Hertz rental car office, and travel and tour desk on site. **Rates:** HS May 26–Oct 26 $115–$149 S or D; from $149 ste. Children under 17 stay free. Min stay wknds. Lower rates off-season. Spec packages avail. Pking: Indoor, $12. Maj CC.

Sheraton Palace Hotel, 2 New Montgomery St, San Francisco, CA 94105; tel 415/392-8600 or toll free 800/325-3538; fax 415/243-4120. At Market St. After a $150 million renovation (completed in 1991), this vintage 1909 classic rules again as one of the top hotels of San Francisco. The crown jewel is the Garden Court, with its crystal chandeliers, gilt-topped columns, and iridescent-glass ceiling. **Rooms:** 550 rms and stes. CI 3pm/CO noon. Express checkout avail. Nonsmoking rms avail. Accented by high ceilings, accommodations are well-appointed with English-style furnishings. **Amenities:** A/C, cable TV w/movies, voice mail, in-rm safe, bathrobes. All units w/minibars, some w/fireplaces, some w/Jacuzzis. Guests can stock their minibars as they wish with items ordered from room service. **Services:** Twice-daily maid svce, car-rental desk, masseur, babysitting. **Facilities:** 3 rsts, 2 bars (w/entertainment), lifeguard, spa, sauna, steam rm, whirlpool. Health club features a glass-ceilinged swimming pool from which parts of the skyline can be seen. In addition, pool is accessible for guests with disabilities, with a ladder and special chair. Popular Pied Piper Bar is adorned with a splendid mural by Maxfield Parrish. **Rates:** $255–$305 S or D; from $500 ste. Extra person $20. Children under 18 stay free. Higher rates for spec evnts/hols. Spec packages avail. Pking: Indoor, Maj CC.

▤▤▤ **Sir Francis Drake**, 450 Powell St, San Francisco, CA 94102 (Downtown); tel 415/392-7755 or toll free 800/227-5480; fax 415/677-9341. Between Post and Sutter Sts. Grand hotel in the old San Francisco style; built in 1928, but recently refurbished. Located on the cable-car line, 1 block from Union Square. **Rooms:** 417 rms and stes. CI 3pm/CO noon. Nonsmoking rms avail. **Amenities:** ▣ ▢ A/C, cable TV w/movies. Some units w/minibars. **Services:** ✗ ▬ 𝖵𝖯 ▦ ▨ ♫ ◁ Car-rental desk, babysitting. **Facilities:** ▤ ▦ ▢ ▤ 2 rsts, 2 bars (1 w/entertainment). **Rates:** HS July–Aug $140–$180 S or D; from $180 ste. Extra person $20. Children under 12 stay free. Lower rates off-season. Spec packages avail. Pking: Indoor, $23. Maj CC.

▤▤ **Stanyan Park Hotel**, 750 Stanyan St, San Francisco, CA 94117; tel 415/751-1000; fax 415/668-5454. At Waller St. Small Victorian-style hotel built in 1904 and listed on the National Register of Historic Places. Right across from Golden Gate Park and close to museums, jogging trails, and other area attractions. **Rooms:** 36 rms, stes, and effic. CI 3pm/CO noon. Rooms are individually decorated and colonial in decor. A little worn, but clean and comfortable. **Amenities:** ▣ ▢ ▤ TV. No A/C. **Services:** ▨ ♫ Babysitting. Complimentary afternoon tea and cookies. **Facilities:** ▤ **Rates:** $78–$96 S or D; from $120 ste; from $120 effic. Extra person $20. Children under 3 stay free. Maj CC.

▤▤▤▤ **Stouffer Stanford Court Hotel**, 905 California St, San Francisco, CA 94108 (Nob Hill); tel 415/989-3500 or toll free 800/468-3571; fax 415/391-0513. Handsome Nob Hill architecture; rooms on 7 floors situated around central courtyard with landscaped roof. Spacious lobby with antiques, wood paneling, and domed roof with Tiffany-style decorative glass. **Rooms:** 400 rms and stes. CI 3pm/CO noon. Express checkout avail. Nonsmoking rms avail. Some rooms above 4th floor have harbor views and double-glazed windows that block out clanging of trolleys, but many regulars prefer rooms at the rear, above the courtyard. Some rooms are a bit cramped and skimpily furnished. **Amenities:** ▣ ▢ ▤ A/C, cable TV w/movies, bathrobes. 1 unit w/fireplace, 1 w/Jacuzzi. Heated towel racks and mini-TVs in bathrooms. No closet doors, no desks (other than pullout shelves in the TV armoires) in most rooms. **Services:** ▮◎▮ ▬ 𝖵𝖯 ▨ ♫ Twice-daily maid svce, car-rental desk, babysitting. Complimentary pot of coffee and newspaper placed outside door to back up wake-up call. Overnight laundry service. Complimentary limousine to business, shopping, and theater districts.

Facilities: ▣ ▢ ▤ 1 rst (*see also* "Restaurants" below), 2 bars (1 w/entertainment). Fourno's Ovens Restaurant is noted for its open rotisserie/kitchen and 20,000-bottle wine cellar. **Rates:** $205–$260 S; $235–$290 D; from $295 ste. Extra person $30. Children under 18 stay free. Spec packages avail. Pking: Indoor, $22. Maj CC. Rates vary by floor and view.

▤▤▤ **Tuscan Inn at Fisherman's Wharf**, 425 Northpoint St, San Francisco, CA 94133; tel 415/561-1100 or toll free 800/648-4626; fax 415/561-1199. At Mason St. A European-style inn with beautiful public areas. **Rooms:** 221 rms and stes. CI 3pm/CO noon. Express checkout avail. Nonsmoking rms avail. Rooms are bright, comfortable, and clean. **Amenities:** ▣ ▢ ▤ ▤ A/C, cable TV w/movies, voice mail. All units w/minibars, 1 w/fireplace. **Services:** ✗ ▬ 𝖵𝖯 ▦ ▨ ♫ Car-rental desk, babysitting. Complimentary morning coffee, tea, and biscotti; limo to the Financial District; wine served by the fireplace every evening. **Facilities:** ▤ ▤ 1 rst, 1 bar. Cafe Pescatore, an Italian trattoria, serves breakfast, lunch, and dinner. **Rates:** HS June–Oct $138–$198 S or D; from $198 ste. Extra person $20. Children under 18 stay free. Lower rates off-season. Higher rates for spec evnts/hols. Spec packages avail. Pking: Indoor/outdoor, $13. Maj CC.

▤▤ **Vagabond Inn**, 2550 Van Ness Ave, San Francisco, CA 94109; tel 415/776-7500; fax 415/776-5689. Between Union and Filbert Sts. Well-located just 2 blocks from cable car, 6 blocks from Fisherman's Wharf. **Rooms:** 132 rms, stes, and effic. CI 3pm/CO noon. Nonsmoking rms avail. Clean and comfortable. **Amenities:** ▣ ▢ ▤ Cable TV w/movies, shoe polisher. No A/C. **Services:** ▦ ▨ ♫ Free continental breakfast, newspaper, and local phone calls. **Facilities:** ▤ ▤ ▤ 1 rst, 1 bar. 24-hour restaurant and lounge. **Rates:** HS May 15–Sept 15 $99 S; $109 D; from $125 ste; from $150 effic. Extra person $10. Children under 18 stay free. Lower rates off-season. Spec packages avail. Pking: Outdoor, free. Maj CC.

▤▤▤ **Villa Florence**, 225 Powell St, San Francisco, CA 94102 (Downtown); tel 415/397-7700 or toll free 800/553-4411; fax 415/397-1006. Between Geary and O'Farrell Sts. Excellent Union Square location. **Rooms:** 180 rms and stes. CI 3pm/CO noon. Nonsmoking rms avail. Rooms are clean and spacious, but plain. **Amenities:** ▣ ▢ ▤ ▤ Cable TV w/movies, refrig. No A/C. All units w/minibars. Ironing board in each room. **Services:** ✗ ▦ ▨ ♫ Babysitting. **Facilities:** ▤ ▤ 1 rst, 1 bar. **Rates:** HS June–Oct $139–$149 S or D; from $159 ste. Extra person $15. Children under 10 stay free. Lower rates off-season. AP and MAP rates avail. Spec packages avail. Pking: Indoor, $17. Maj CC.

▤▤▤ **Warwick Regis Hotel**, 490 Geary St, San Francisco, CA 94102 (Downtown); tel 415/928-7900 or toll free 800/

827-3447; fax 415/441-8788. At Taylor St. Somewhat generic but pleasant hotel with a grand, attractive lobby. Right off Union Square. **Rooms:** 80 rms and stes. CI 3pm/CO 1pm. Express checkout avail. Nonsmoking rms avail. Rooms are small but comfortable. **Amenities:** 🛏 🔊 Cable TV w/movies, bathrobes. No A/C. All units w/minibars, some w/terraces, some w/fireplaces. **Services:** 🍴 VP 🚐 🖼 🔧 Twice-daily maid svce, masseur, babysitting. Complimentary continental breakfast, newspaper. Overnight shoeshine. **Facilities:** 120 💻 🔧 1 rst, 1 bar (w/entertainment). Elegant restaurant and bar. **Rates (CP):** HS June–Oct $95–$175 S or D; from $145 ste. Extra person $10. Children under 12 stay free. Lower rates off-season. Higher rates for spec evnts/hols. Spec packages avail. Pking: Indoor, $18. Maj CC.

≡≡≡ Westin St Francis, 335 Powell St, San Francisco, CA 94102 (Union Square); tel 415/397-7000 or toll free 800/228-3000; fax 415/774-0124. Between Post and Geary Sts. Classic San Francisco hotel—one of the grande dames of the city. Very elegant with charming Compass Rose tea room. **Rooms:** 1,200 rms and stes. CI 3pm/CO 1pm. Express checkout avail. Nonsmoking rms avail. **Amenities:** 🛏 🔊 A/C, cable TV w/movies, refrig, voice mail, in-rm safe, shoe polisher. All units w/minibars, some w/terraces, some w/fireplaces, some w/Jacuzzis. Kids Club features a bag of fun presents. Kids' room-service menu available. **Services:** 🍴 📞 VP 🚐 🖼 🔧 ✈ Twice-daily maid svce, car-rental desk, masseur, babysitting. Japanese-language service desk. **Facilities:** 🏋 🏊 💻 🔧 5 rsts, 5 bars (1 w/entertainment), beauty salon. **Rates:** $150–$245 S; $180–$274 D; from $300 ste. Extra person $35. Children under 18 stay free. Min stay spec evnts. Spec packages avail. Pking: Indoor, $23. Maj CC.

≡≡≡ The York Hotel, 940 Sutter St, San Francisco, CA 94109 (Downtown); tel 415/885-6800 or toll free 800/808-YORK; fax 415/885-2115. Between Hyde and Leavenworth Sts. Elegant lobby with extensive marble, ceiling fans, and plush sofas. A hip hotel with character, a favorite of many actors. Scenes for *Vertigo* were filmed here. **Rooms:** 96 rms and stes. CI 3pm/CO noon. Nonsmoking rms avail. Clean, modern rooms with pleasant decor, large closets, window seats, and sitting areas. **Amenities:** 🛏 🔊 🖥 Cable TV w/movies, refrig, in-rm safe. No A/C. All units w/minibars. **Services:** ✗ VP 🚐 🖼 🔧 Nightly hospitality hour. Limousine service available to Fisherman's Wharf and Union Square. **Facilities:** 🏋 50 1 bar (w/entertainment). The elegant Plush Room cabaret features top San Francisco performers. **Rates (CP):** HS Apr–Sept $95–$110 S or D; from $175 ste. Extra person $10. Lower rates off-season. Spec packages avail. Pking: Indoor, $12. Maj CC. Some packages include tickets to Plush Room performances. Senior discounts and corporate rates available.

Motel

≡≡ Cow Hollow Motor Inn & Suites, 2190 Lombard St, San Francisco, CA 94123; tel 415/921-5800; fax 415/922-8515. At Steiner St. Clean, well-managed, upscale motor inn with complete access for guests with disabilities. **Rooms:** 129 rms and stes. CI 3pm/CO noon. Nonsmoking rms avail. Suites are a great bargain, with Persian-style rugs, full kitchen, and living and dining area. Standard rooms are attractively arranged. **Amenities:** 🛏 🖥 A/C, cable TV. Some units w/fireplaces. **Services:** 🚐 🖼 🔧 Babysitting. **Facilities:** 40 🔧 1 rst. Use of nearby health club for $5. **Rates:** $73–$86 S; $78–$85 D; from $175 ste. Extra person $7. Children under 5 stay free. Pking: Indoor, free. Maj CC.

Inns

≡≡ Adelaide Inn, 5 Isadora Duncan, San Francisco, CA 94102 (Union Square); tel 415/441-2261; fax 415/441-0161. Off Taylor St between Geary and Post Sts. A European-style pensione featuring shared bath, located in a quiet alley near Union Square. **Rooms:** 18 rms (all w/shared bath). CI 9am–1pm/CO 1pm. Rooms are bare and sparse. **Amenities:** Cable TV. No A/C or phone. **Services:** Babysitting. **Facilities:** Guest lounge w/TV. Cozy breakfast room. No elevator. **Rates (CP):** HS June–Sept $32–$48 S or D w/shared bath. Extra person $6. Children under 9 stay free. Lower rates off-season. Ltd CC.

≡≡ Archbishops Mansion, 1000 Fulton St, San Francisco, CA 94117; tel 415/563-7872 or toll free 800/543-5820; fax 415/885-3193. Alamo Square Park; across from Steiner St. Built in 1904 for the Catholic archbishop of California, this Victorian mansion is now a B&B. Although it needs renovation, it provides special and romantic accommodations. **Rooms:** 15 rms and stes. CI 3pm/CO 11am. No smoking. Spacious rooms are individually decorated. **Amenities:** 🛏 🔊 Cable TV. No A/C. 1 unit w/minibar, some w/fireplaces, some w/Jacuzzis. Generous complimentary continental breakfast. Wine served 5:30 to 7:30pm. **Services:** 📞 🖼 🔧 Masseur, wine/sherry served. **Facilities:** 50 Guest lounge. **Rates (CP):** HS June–Nov $115–$189 D; from $205 ste. Extra person $20. Min stay wknds. Lower rates off-season. Spec packages avail. Pking: Outdoor, free. Ltd CC.

≡≡≡ Bed & Breakfast Inn, 4 Charlton Court, San Francisco, CA 94123; tel 415/921-9784. Private drive off Union between Laguna and Buchanan Sts. Popular inn set in 3 century-old Victorians on a charming mews. Book 6 to 9 weeks in advance to guarantee a specific room. An exceptional value. Unsuitable for children under 15. **Rooms:** 11 rms and stes (4 w/shared bath); 3 ctges/villas. CI 3pm/CO noon. Each room is uniquely decorated with family furniture and antiques. Garden Suite accommodates up to 4 people; Celebration Suite is very romantic. **Amenities:** 🏧 💧 Cable TV. No A/C. 1 unit w/terrace, 1 w/fireplace, 1 w/Jacuzzi. **Services:** Wine/sherry served. Sherry service at all times. **Rates (CP):** $70–$90 D w/shared bath, $115–$140 D w/private bath; from $115 ste; from $190 ctge/villa. Ltd CC. Garden Suite is 1,300 square feet for $250 per night.

≣≣≣ **The Mansions**, 2220 Sacramento St, San Francisco, CA 94115; tel 415/929-9444 or toll free 800/826-9398; fax 415/567-9391. Between Laguna and Buchanan Sts. A stay here is a unique experience. The 1887 Victorian and adjacent 1903 Greek revival mansions are crammed with eclectic antiques and adorned with stained glass. **Rooms:** 21 rms and stes. CI 2pm/CO noon. Charming, individually decorated rooms with antique furnishings. **Amenities:** 🏧 No A/C or TV. Some units w/terraces, some w/fireplaces, 1 w/Jacuzzi. **Services:** ✗ 🍴 🛍️ 🛎️ ⟐ Afternoon tea and wine/sherry served. Breakfast in bed; nightly piano concert performed by the resident ghost. **Facilities:** [15] 1 rst, guest lounge w/TV. Sitting room, library, and dining room with gourmet cuisine. **Rates:** $129–$159 S or D; from $189 ste. Extra person $18. Children under 18 stay free. Pking: Indoor/outdoor, $10. Ltd CC.

≣≣ **Red Victorian Bed & Breakfast Inn**, 1665 Haight St, San Francisco, CA 94117; tel 415/864-1978. Between Cole and Belvedere Sts. This place has been here since 1904, and withstood the big earthquake. Located in the heart of the Haight district near Golden Gate Park. **Rooms:** 18 rms and stes (14 w/shared bath). CI 3pm/CO 11am. No smoking. Rooms are worn. **Amenities:** 🏧 💧 No A/C or TV. **Services:** 🚐 **Facilities:** Meditation room. **Rates (CP):** $38–$55 D w/shared bath; from $100 ste. Extra person $15. Min stay wknds and spec evnts. Ltd CC.

🔱 **The Sherman House**, 2160 Green St, San Francisco, CA 94123 (Pacific Heights); tel 415/563-3600 or toll free 800/424-5777; fax 415/563-1882. 1 acre. Luxurious city inn, opened in 1984, housed in a restored 1876 mansion that once hosted tenor Enrico Caruso and pianist Ignace Paderewski. It's expensive, but regular guests are willing to pay for the exquisite style and seclusion—and a garden in the city. Located in the fashionable Pacific Heights district, close to many of San Francisco's major sights. **Rooms:** 14 rms and stes; 1 ctge/villa. CI 2pm/CO noon. Most rooms and suites are in the main house; some are compact, some spacious. A few rooms are in a carriage house in the lovely, peaceful garden. Every room is individually decorated with antiques and refined wall decorations. **Amenities:** 🏧 💧 🍴 Cable TV, stereo/tape player, bathrobes. No A/C. Some units w/terraces, all w/fireplaces, some w/Jacuzzis. All bathrooms have TVs, some have whirlpools or Roman tubs. 3 phones and radio/cassette players in every room. No air conditioning, but not

needed most of the year. Personalized stationery. Fresh orchids from the garden greenhouse. **Services:** 🍽️ ✗ 🆅🅿 🛍️ 🛎️ ⟐ Twice-daily maid svce, babysitting. Room butlers rather than bellmen and waiters (1 for every 2 rooms). 24-hour Butler's Menu. In-room meals served on Lenox china, course by course, if requested. Guest directory lists direct line to chef, for guests who'd like to plan meals in advance. Afternoon tea served in antique-filled lounge. **Facilities:** [60] 1 rst, guest lounge. 12-table dining room for exclusive use of guests. **Rates:** $175–$350 D; from $575 ste; from $1,200 ctge/villa. Children under 18 stay free. Pking: Indoor, $8. Ltd CC.

≣≣ **Victorian Inn on the Park**, 301 Lyon St, San Francisco, CA 94117; tel 415/931-1830 or toll free 800/435-1967. This inn has a casual atmosphere but could be cleaner and more professionally run. **Rooms:** 12 rms and stes. CI 2pm/CO noon. Individually decorated rooms with some antiques. **Amenities:** 🏧 No A/C or TV. 1 unit w/terrace, some w/fireplaces. **Services:** 🔑 Babysitting, afternoon tea and wine/sherry served. Fresh baked goods for breakfast. **Facilities:** [12] Guest lounge w/TV. **Rates (CP):** $99–$159 D w/shared bath; from $159 ste. Extra person $20. Children under 10 stay free. Min stay wknds. Spec packages avail. Pking: Outdoor, $9. Ltd CC.

≣≣≣ **Washington Square Inn**, 1660 Stockton St, San Francisco, CA 94133 (North Beach); tel 415/981-4220 or toll free 800/388-0220; fax 415/397-7242. At Filbert St. Small, elegant inn close to shops and restaurants in North Beach and within walking distance of Chinatown and Fisherman's Wharf. **Rooms:** 15 rms (5 w/shared bath). CI 2pm/CO noon. No smoking. Immaculate, quiet rooms, some with shared bath. **Amenities:** 🏧 💧 TV, shoe polisher, bathrobes. No A/C. **Services:** 🔑 🆅🅿 🚐 🛍️ ⟐ Twice-daily maid svce, masseur, babysitting, afternoon tea and wine/sherry served. **Facilities:** Guest lounge. **Rates (CP):** HS May–Nov $85–$95 S or D w/shared bath, $95–$180 S or D w/private bath. Extra person $15. Children under 4 stay free. Lower rates off-season. Pking: Indoor, $17. Maj CC.

≣≣≣ **White Swan Inn**, 845 Bush St, San Francisco, CA 94108 (Union Square); tel 415/775-1755; fax 415/775-5717. At Taylor St. The charm of a small European inn; complete with a beautiful library and fireplace. **Rooms:** 26 rms and stes. CI 2pm/CO noon. No smoking. Very charming. **Amenities:** 🏧 🍴 Cable TV, refrig, bathrobes. No A/C. All units w/minibars, all w/fireplaces. **Services:** ✗ 🔑 🆅🅿 🚐 🛍️ ⟐ Masseur, babysitting, afternoon tea and wine/sherry served. Complimentary newspapers delivered to room. **Facilities:** [30] Guest lounge. Cozy breakfast area and garden patio. **Rates (BB):** HS May–Oct

$145–$160 S or D; from $195 ste. Extra person $15. Children under 2 stay free. Lower rates off-season. Pking: Indoor, $17. Maj CC.

Restaurants 🍴

Abiquiu, 129 Ellis St, San Francisco (Union Square); tel 415/392-5500. **Southwestern.** Newly opened restaurant presents eclectic menu in an artistic setting with wood and brass accents, large black-and-white photos of New Mexico, and stunning red floral arrangements. Southwestern and Asian dishes include Maine lobster "Gallegos Ranch style" with pinto beans, corn brioche stuffing, and lime butter; and Chinese-style air-dried duck with juniper berry sauce. Varieties of caviar. **FYI:** Reservations recommended. **Open:** Daily 11:30am–11pm. Closed Dec 25. **Prices:** Main courses $11–$20. Maj CC. 🆅🅿 &

Acquerello, 1722 Sacramento St, San Francisco; tel 415/567-5432. Between Polk St and Van Ness Ave. **Italian.** *Acquerello* means watercolors, and this pretty restaurant highlights watercolor paintings from local artists on its high-gloss walls in what used to be a chapel. The menu changes frequently and offers carefully crafted classic Italian dishes such as gnocchi, veal with oyster mushrooms, marinated pork loin, and braised sturgeon. **FYI:** Reservations recommended. Beer and wine only. **Open:** Tues–Sat 5:30–10:30pm. Closed some hols. **Prices:** Main courses $18–$22. Maj CC.

Act IV, in the Inn at the Opera, 333 Fulton St, San Francisco (Civic Center); tel 415/553-8100. Off Franklin St behind Opera. **Californian/Continental.** Located just behind the Opera House, this is a good place to rub shoulders with ballet stars, opera divas, and other performers, as well as a very romantic spot for dining before or after the theater. The dinner menu might include smoked sturgeon on a bed of wild rice, or rack of lamb with eggplant flan. The fine continental buffet breakfast includes French cheese, smoked meats, and pastries. **FYI:** Reservations recommended. Piano. **Open:** Breakfast daily 7–10am; lunch Mon–Fri 11:30am–2pm; dinner Sun–Thurs 5–9pm, Fri–Sat 5–10:30pm; brunch Sun 11:30am–2pm. **Prices:** Main courses $19–$25. Maj CC. ♥ 🖼 🆅🅿 &

Aioli, 469 Bush St, San Francisco (Financial District); tel 415/249-0900. At Grant Ave. **Mediterranean.** Modern, with wrought-iron fixtures and terra cotta walls. This warm, comfortable restaurant connects to a bookstore and coffeehouse, Cafe de la Presse. Game dishes, such as wild-boar ravioli, rabbit stew, and bison carpaccio, highlight the menu. Good selection of other meat and seafood dishes also available, including the namesake seafood aioli (steamed fish and shellfish in a garlic broth). **FYI:**

Reservations recommended. Jazz. **Open:** Daily 11am–10pm. Closed some hols. **Prices:** Main courses $11.50–$17.50. Maj CC. ✅ &

♣ **Alain Rondelli**, 126 Clement St, San Francisco; tel 415/387-0408. Between 2nd and 3rd Sts. **French.** The decor and food are decidedly French, with a copper bar, frescoed walls, tiled floors, and country French chairs. The chef has his own style of cuisine based on contemporary French cooking, featuring lamb, lobster, salmon, and veal on the frequently changing menu. A 6-course tasting menu is available for $45. **FYI:** Reservations recommended. **Open:** Tues–Thurs 5:30–10pm, Fri–Sat 5:30–10:30pm. Closed Dec 25. **Prices:** Main courses $16–$24; PF dinner $45. Ltd CC. ♥

♣ **Aqua**, 252 California St, San Francisco (Financial District); tel 415/956-9662. At Sansome St. **Seafood.** One of San Francisco's most stylish and popular places, decorated with huge floral arrangements, large upholstered chairs, floor-to-ceiling mirrors, a long bar, and high ceilings. It's known for elaborate presentations of seafood, including steamed lobster, Hawaiian swordfish, halibut, and sea scallops. They offer several 5- and 6-course tasting menus, including vegetarian, ranging from $45–$65. **FYI:** Reservations recommended. **Open:** Lunch Mon–Fri 11:30am–2:30pm; dinner Mon–Thurs 5:30–10:30pm, Fri–Sat 5:30–11pm. Closed some hols. **Prices:** Main courses $25–$65; PF dinner $55–$65. Maj CC. &

A Sabella's, 2766 Taylor St, San Francisco (Wharf); tel 415/771-6775. At Jefferson St. **Seafood.** Classy and elegant, this is a San Francisco institution. Fresh crab, daily seafood specials, and an award-winning wine list make this a popular spot. On weekends, there's a murder mystery dinner in a separate dining room. Piano music nightly. **FYI:** Reservations recommended. Piano. Dress code. **Open:** Daily 11am–10:30pm. Closed Dec 25. **Prices:** Main courses $20–$30. Maj CC. &

Bistro Roti, in the Hotel Griffon, 155 Steuart St, San Francisco (SoMa); tel 415/495-6500. Between Mission and Howard Sts. **French.** Rich woods, leather, and brass create warm supper-club atmosphere at this eatery located near remodeled Embarcadero waterfront. Wood-burning fire on chilly days. In addition to the oyster bar, it offers seafood, spit-roasted meats, fragrant chicken, filet mignon au poivre, salad Provençale. Superior wine list, quality beers on tap. **FYI:** Reservations recommended. **Open:** Mon–Thurs 11:30am–10pm, Fri 11:30am–11pm, Sat 5:30–11pm, Sun 5:30–10pm. Closed some hols. **Prices:** Main courses $11–$17. Maj CC. 🆅🅿 &

Bix, 56 Gold St, San Francisco (Jackson Square); tel 415/433-6300. **American.** This restaurant, in historic gold rush–era building hidden away down an alley, has the ambience of an old supper club. An art deco mural, a mahogany bar, and jazz music set the scene for enjoying such specialties as chicken hash and grilled pork chop. Fine wines are served by the glass. **FYI:** Reservations recommended. Piano. **Open:** Mon–Thurs 11:30am–11pm, Fri 11:30am–midnight, Sat 5:30pm–midnight, Sun 6–10pm. Closed some hols. **Prices:** Main courses $13–$26. Maj CC. ♥ ♨ VP

Bizou, 598 4th St, San Francisco; tel 415/543-2222. At Brannan St. **French/Italian.** With mustard-colored walls, warm recessed lighting, and soft jazz music, this place glows like a fireplace at night. It's chic and elegant. Feast on oysters, lasagna, duck breast, braised baked salmon, quail, and other imaginative fare. **FYI:** Reservations recommended. **Open:** Lunch Mon–Fri 11:30am–2:30pm; dinner Mon–Thurs 8:30–10pm, Fri–Sat 8:30–10:30pm. Closed some hols. **Prices:** Main courses $10–$17. Maj CC. &

Boulevard, 1 Mission St, San Francisco; tel 415/543-6084. At Steuart St. **New American.** Exquisite food and a stylish decor reminiscent of a turn-of-the-century Parisian bistro have combined to make this one of the hottest restaurants in town. With decor by Pat Kuleto and food by superchef Nancy Oakes, plus spectacular views of the Bay Bridge, this place has it all, including chicken cooked in a wood-fired oven, roasted salmon, spit-roasted pork loin, and what some call the best desserts in the city. Jazz saxophonist not too loud. **FYI:** Reservations recommended. **Open:** Lunch Mon–Fri 11:30am–2:15pm; dinner daily 5:30–10pm. Closed some hols. **Prices:** Main courses $15.95–$19.75. Maj CC. ♨ VP &

★ **Brandy Ho's Hunan Food**, 217 Columbus Ave, San Francisco (North Beach); tel 415/788-7527. **Chinese.** Very popular; a good place for spicy food. Smoked duck and smoked ham made on premises. Lunch specials for $5. Also at: 450 Broadway, San Francisco (415/362-6268). **FYI:** Reservations recommended. Beer and wine only. **Open:** Daily 11:30am–11pm. Closed some hols. **Prices:** Main courses $6–$20. Maj CC.

⑤ ★ **Cafe Macaroni**, 59 Columbus Ave, San Francisco (North Beach); tel 415/956-9737. **Italian.** Cozy, chef-owned cafe, one of the most popular Italian restaurants in San Francisco. Exceptional antipasti are displayed in a case. Gnocchi with gorgonzola, pork medallions with fennel-seed sauce. **FYI:** Reservations recommended. Beer and wine only. **Open:** Lunch Mon–Fri 11:30am–2:30pm; dinner Mon–Sat 5:30–10pm. Closed some hols. **Prices:** Main courses $7–$14. No CC.

Cafe Majestic, in Hotel Majestic, 1500 Sutter St, San Francisco; tel 415/776-6400. **Eclectic.** Upscale ambience, fine cuisine. Romantic Edwardian decor with graceful columns and hues of apricot and sea-foam green. Appetizers include corn fritter with

prawns, shiitake mushrooms, and aioli. The roster of entrees features sautéed sea scallops with lemon grass and curry, grilled veal chop with blue cheese and port. Great eggs Benedict for brunch. **FYI:** Reservations recommended. Jazz/piano. **Open:** Lunch Tues–Fri 11:30am–2pm; dinner daily 5:30–9:30pm; brunch Sat–Sun 10am–2pm. Closed some hols. **Prices:** Main courses $14–$24. Maj CC. ♥ VP &

Café Marimba, 2317 Chestnut St, San Francisco; tel 415/776-1506. Between Scott and Divisadero Sts. **Mexican.** A colorful and very hip restaurant with palm trees out in front and original art inside. The menu lists 3 kinds of tamales, as well as various tacos and enchiladas, grilled meats, and seafood. There are 22 different tequilas, and great specialty drinks. **FYI:** Reservations not accepted. Guitar. **Open:** Mon 5:30–11pm, Tues–Thurs 11:30am–11pm, Fri 11:30am–midnight, Sat 10:30am–midnight. Closed some hols. **Prices:** Main courses $6–$12. Ltd CC. &

Cafe Mozart, 708 Bush St, San Francisco (Union Square); tel 415/391-8480. At Powell St. **Californian/French/Italian.** Cozy, intimate, romantic setting with candles and flowers. Watch the chef cook in the display kitchen at the center of the restaurant. Organic produce is used. Try chateaubriand with wild mushrooms. **FYI:** Reservations recommended. Beer and wine only. **Open:** HS June–Sept Tues–Sun 5:30–10:30pm. Reduced hours off-season. **Prices:** Main courses $11–$22. Maj CC. ♥ ▣

Cafe Tiramisu, 28 Belden St, San Francisco (Financial District); tel 415/421-7044. Between Bush and Pine Sts. **Italian.** Italian trattoria located down a charming alley. Attractive frescoes in golden tones. Braised lamb shanks with rosemary sauce, sea bass, salmon cannelloni. **FYI:** Reservations recommended. **Open:** Lunch Mon–Sat 11am–3pm; dinner Mon–Sat 5–10:30pm. Closed some hols. **Prices:** Main courses $8–$19. Maj CC.

⑤ **Caffe Freddy's**, 901 Columbus Ave, San Francisco (North Beach); tel 415/922-0151. Between Lombard and Chestnut Sts. **Italian.** Fun place to eat in the heart of North Beach. Hip, artsy trattoria ambience. Offering micro-brewed beers, local wines, and wholesome Italian specialties including caesar salad, eggplant, polenta, pizza, pasta, and calzone. **FYI:** Reservations accepted. Beer and wine only. **Open:** Mon–Fri 10am–10pm, Sat–Sun 9am–10pm. **Prices:** Main courses $5–$9; PF dinner $8–$15. Ltd CC.

★ **Caffe Sport**, 574 Green St, San Francisco (North Beach); tel 415/981-1251. At Columbus Ave. **Italian.** Everyone sits at crowded family-style tables in this restaurant that has become a North Beach institution. The decor, a riot of color, was created by the chef/owner, who keeps an easel in the kitchen, awaiting moments of sudden inspiration. Specializes in hearty Sicilian fare—cioppino with lots of garlic, and seafood and pasta dishes. **FYI:** Reservations recommended. Beer and wine only. **Open:** Lunch Tues–Thurs noon–2pm, Fri–Sat noon–2:30pm; dinner Tues–Thurs 5–10pm, Fri–Sat 6:30–10:30pm. Closed some hols. **Prices:** Main courses $15–$26. No CC. ▮

Campton Place, in Campton Place Hotel, 340 Stockton St, San Francisco (Union Square); tel 415/781-5155. Between Sutter and Post Sts. **New American.** Consistently regarded as one of the city's top restaurants. Conveys classic elegance with etched glass, potted palms, and empire-style chairs. The contemporary American menu contrasts tastes and textures, with offerings like sautéed squab with foie gras and saffron pappardelle, or grilled lamb chops with fava beans and couscous. Wine list has a lot of depth and includes moderately priced California and Oregon selections. The business lunch special is a great deal at $19.50. **FYI:** Reservations recommended. Children's menu. Jacket required. **Open:** Breakfast Mon–Fri 7–11am, Sat–Sun 8–11:30am; lunch Mon–Fri 11:30am–2:30pm, Sat–Sun noon–2:30pm; dinner Sun–Thurs 5:30–10pm, Fri–Sat 5:30–10:30pm. **Prices:** Main courses $22.50–$30. Maj CC. ♥ VP

Casa Aguila, 1240 Noriega Ave, San Francisco (Sunset); tel 415/661-5593. Between 19th and 20th Aves. **Mexican.** Red tablecloths, piñatas, and kitschy Mexican trinkets lend lots of character. Offerings include seafood, chicken, and steaks with a Mexican flavor. **FYI:** Reservations not accepted. Beer and wine only. **Open:** Lunch daily 10:30am–3:30pm; dinner daily 4:30–10pm. Closed some hols. **Prices:** Main courses $10–$25. Maj CC.

Cha Cha Cha, 1805 Haight St, San Francisco (Haight-Ashbury); tel 415/386-5758. At Shrader St. **Caribbean.** With a Caribbean island flavor, it's casual, festive, and fun, decorated with marble tables, island-style patterned tablecloths and palm trees. The food is lively, including baked Yucatan chicken, fried plantains with black beans, steamed mussels, and shrimp in Cajun spices. There's also a tapas bar and weekend brunch. But service can be noticeably poor. **FYI:** Reservations not accepted. Beer and wine only. **Open:** Lunch Mon–Fri 11:30am–3pm; dinner Sun–Thurs 5–11pm, Fri–Sat 5–11:30pm; brunch Sat–Sun 10am–4pm. Closed some hols. **Prices:** Main courses $4–$8. No CC.

★ **China Moon**, 639 Post St, San Francisco (Downtown); tel 415/775-4789. Between Jones and Taylor Sts. **Californian/Chinese.** A 1930s-style, art deco coffee shop redecorated with a modern Asian flavor. Inventive Chinese cuisine includes black-mushroom steamed trout, noodle pillows topped with spicy beef ribbons, pickled salmon, and crispy spring rolls with curried

chicken. **FYI:** Reservations recommended. Beer and wine only. **Open:** Daily 5:30–10pm. Closed some hols. **Prices:** Main courses $15–$18. Maj CC. ♿

Ciao, 230 Jackson St, San Francisco (Jackson Square); tel 415/892-9500. At Front St. **Italian.** Slick, modern Italian bistro offering good Italian cuisine. The chef prepares daily fish and pasta specials, as well as 3 kinds of carpaccio, lobster ravioli, and sausage stewed with peppers and polenta. The wine list favors California wines but also includes a good selection of Italian reds. **FYI:** Reservations recommended. **Open:** Sun 4–10:30pm, Mon–Thurs 11:30am–11pm, Fri–Sat 11:30am–midnight. Closed some hols. **Prices:** Main courses $9–$16. Maj CC. VP ♿

Circolo Restaurant & Champagneria, in Crocker Galleria, 161 Sutter St, San Francisco (Financial District); tel 415/362-0404. At Kearny St. **Mediterranean.** Elegant setting with marble floors, upholstered chairs, flowers at each table and large windows overlooking Sutter St. Specializes in domestic and imported champagnes, homemade pastas, mixed grills, and herbed rice. **FYI:** Reservations recommended. Jazz/piano. **Open:** Lunch Mon–Sat 11am–3:30pm; dinner Mon–Sat 5–10pm. Closed some hols. **Prices:** Main courses $10–$17. Maj CC. ♿

♣ **Cypress Club**, 500 Jackson St, San Francisco (Downtown); tel 415/296-8555. At Columbus Ave. **New American.** Very busy, very in. Copper banquettes and tile floors give the look of a 1920s New York supper club. Specializes in simple, elegant food like king salmon wrapped in pancetta, and beef sirloin with bread pudding. **FYI:** Reservations recommended. **Open:** Mon–Thurs 4:30–10pm, Fri–Sat 4:30–11pm. Closed some hols. **Prices:** Main courses $21–$25. Maj CC. VP ♿

⑤ **David's**, 480 Geary St, San Francisco (Union Square); tel 415/771-1600. Between Mason and Taylor Sts. **Deli.** Basic diner/deli with counter seating. Lox and bagels, stuffed cabbage, goulash, corned beef hash. **FYI:** Reservations not accepted. Beer and wine only. **Open:** Mon–Fri 7am–midnight, Sat–Sun 8am–midnight. **Prices:** Main courses $7–$17; PF dinner $17. Maj CC.

The Dining Room, in the Ritz-Carlton San Francisco, 600 Stockton St, San Francisco (Nob Hill); tel 415/296-7465. **Californian/French.** Classically sumptuous, this restaurant woos diners with elegant details such as Rosenthal china and the Ritz-Carlton's signature cobalt-blue glasses from Schlottweisel. Chef Gary Danko offers creative dishes like rack of lamb cloaked in pistachio crust, or seared sturgeon with fennel, peas, and mint. However, service can be befuddled and disorganized. The bar offers the largest selection of single-malt scotches in the country.

FYI: Reservations recommended. Harp. Children's menu. Dress code. **Open:** Mon–Sat 6–9:30pm. Closed July 4. **Prices:** PF dinner $36–$57. Maj CC. ● VP &

Doidge's, 2217 Union St, San Francisco (Pacific Heights); tel 415/921-2149. **New American.** An upscale breakfast joint with comfortable old-fashioned appeal. Rare lithographs of Paris line the dining room's white walls. Menu favorites include pancakes topped with fresh berries, Doidge's homemade granola, and shrimp creole Benedict. Reservations necessary on weekends. Serves wine only. **FYI:** Reservations recommended. **Open:** Sat–Sun 8am–2:45pm, Mon–Fri 8am–1:45pm. Closed Dec 25. **Prices:** Lunch main courses $7–$10. Ltd CC.

★ **Ebisu**, 1283 9th Ave, San Francisco; tel 415/566-1770. Between Irving St and Lincoln Way. **Japanese.** Very popular with the locals—a small place with Asian decor, fresh flowers, and a sushi bar. Specialties include tempura, teriyaki, sukiyaki, and fried oysters. Prix-fixe sushi bar and Japanese beers are available. **FYI:** Reservations not accepted. Beer and wine only. **Open:** Lunch Mon–Fri 11:30am–2pm; dinner Mon–Wed 5–10pm, Thurs–Sat 5pm–midnight. Closed some hols. **Prices:** Main courses $8–$14. Maj CC.

♣ **Elka**, in Japan Center, 1611 Post St, San Francisco (Japantown); tel 415/922-7788. **French/Japanese.** Award-winning restaurant from well-known chef Elka Gilmore. Stunning decor with ocher and red walls framing hand-blown glass fixtures, metal sculptures, and a 20-foot mural. Cuisine blends French cooking techniques with Japanese ingredients, featuring fresh seafood and locally grown organic vegetables. Piano music on weekend evenings. **FYI:** Reservations recommended. Piano. **Open:** Breakfast daily 6:30–11am; lunch daily 11:30am–2pm; dinner Sun–Thurs 5:30–10pm, Fri–Sat 5:30–10:30pm. **Prices:** Main courses $19–$25. Maj CC. &

★ **Ernie's**, 847 Montgomery St, San Francisco; tel 415/397-5969. At Jackson St. **New American.** One of the finest restaurants in the city, it offers an elegant Victorian setting with rich fabrics, large floral arrangements, plush carpets, and high-back chairs. The gorgeous bar features antique stained glass. The menu changes according to the season, but may feature roast rack of lamb, grilled lobster brochettes, and terrine of rabbit and is complemented by an extensive, award-winning wine list. **FYI:** Reservations recommended. Jacket required. **Open:** Mon–Sat 6–10pm. Closed some hols. **Prices:** Main courses $24–$26; PF dinner $66. Maj CC. ▆ VP

$ **The Family Inn Coffee Shop**, 505 Jones St, San Francisco (Union Square); tel 415/771-5995. Between O'Farrell and Geary Sts. **American.** Family-style operation has little ambience and only a counter and 1 table. But good, wholesome inexpensive food, including meat loaf, hamburger steak, roast chicken, and spaghetti. **FYI:** Reservations not accepted. No liquor license. **Open:** Tues–Fri 7am–6pm, Sat 7am–4:30pm. Closed some hols. **Prices:** Lunch main courses $4–$6. No CC.

Fino, in The Andrews Hotel, 624 Post St, San Francisco (Union Square); tel 415/928-2080. Between Taylor and Jones Sts. **Italian.** Cozy ambience, intimate dining near the fireplace. Fish and shellfish specialties may include scallops and prawns pomodoro over angel-hair pasta. **FYI:** Reservations recommended. **Open:** Tues–Sat 5:30–10:30pm, Sun–Mon 5:30–9:30pm. Closed Dec 25. **Prices:** Main courses $11–$15. Maj CC. ● ▣ ▼ VP

Fleur De Lys, 777 Sutter St, San Francisco (Nob Hill); tel 415/673-7779. Between Taylor and Jones Sts. **French/Mediterranean.** One of San Francisco's most elegant restaurants, with superb cuisine from acclaimed chef Hubert Keller. Decor suggests an immense garden tent set in the French countryside. Menu choices might include roasted quail and fresh foie gras, or seared ahi tuna on creamed spinach. Over 300 wines offered. **FYI:** Reservations recommended. Jacket required. **Open:** Mon–Thurs 6–10pm, Fri–Sat 5:30–10:30pm. Closed some hols; June 23–July 7. **Prices:** Main courses $26–$32. Maj CC. ● VP &

Flying Saucer, 1000 Guerrero St, San Francisco (Mission District); tel 415/641-9955. At 22nd Ave. **Eclectic.** Literally part of San Francisco—marble on tables and wood paneling were rescued from demolished buildings. Other pieces include a 19th-century church lamp and an art deco frieze from the 1920s. The chef's "world beat cuisine" highlights fresh fish and seafood prepared with spices and techniques from France, Morocco, Japan, Thailand, and Egypt. **FYI:** Reservations recommended. Beer and wine only. **Open:** Tues–Sat 5:30–10pm. Closed 2 weeks in July. **Prices:** Main courses $15–$24. No CC. &

Fog City Diner, 1300 Battery St, San Francisco (Telegraph Hill); tel 415/982-2000. At Embarcadero. **Diner.** Imagine a 1950s-style diner gone upscale and you have the picture of Fog City Diner, where you can dine in great style on excellent meat loaf with mashed potatoes, pork chops, and pot roast. You can also find imaginative seafood specials, including red curry mussel stew. Homemade breads. **FYI:** Reservations recommended. **Open:** Sun–Thurs 11:30am–11pm, Fri–Sat 11:30am–midnight. Closed Dec 25. **Prices:** Main courses $12–$14. Ltd CC. ▦

★ **Fournou's Ovens**, in Stouffer Stanford Court Hotel, 905 California St, San Francisco (Nob Hill); tel 415/989-1910. **Continental.** Multilevel rooms and alcoves face a 54-square-foot roasting oven or the large, open, tiled kitchen and spit. There's a conservatory room alongside the street. Best for dinner, with specialties that include Dungeness crab cakes;

ricotta gnocchi with organic vegetables; rib of veal with rosemary; planked salmon with vegetable succotash; and rack of lamb with ratatouille. 20,000-bottle wine cellar. **FYI:** Reservations recommended. **Open:** Breakfast daily 6:30–11:30am; lunch daily 11:30am–2:30pm; dinner daily 5:30–10pm. **Prices:** Main courses $16.50–$29.50. Maj CC. ♥ VP ♿

★ **Fringale**, 570 Fourth St, San Francisco (SoMa); tel 415/543-0573. Between Bryand and Brannan Sts. **French/Basque.** One of the finest French bistros in the city, it has a comfortable atmosphere, like a European country cafe. The intimate dining room boasts blond woods and a curved, oxidized copper bar, along with changing displays of art. Tables are cozy and close together but the food is superb, including duck confit, pork tenderloin, and mussels with garlic. Great food at very reasonable prices. **FYI:** Reservations recommended. **Open:** Lunch Mon–Fri 11:30am–3pm; dinner Mon–Sat 5:30–10:30pm. Closed some hols. **Prices:** Main courses $10–$15. Maj CC. ♿

Garibaldi's on Presidio, 347 Presidio Ave, San Francisco; tel 415/563-8841. Between Clay and Sacramento Sts. **Italian.** With decor that is simple and comfortable, it appeals to locals, who also like its good, fresh food, including Mediterranean lamb tenderloin, daily pasta specials, risotto, and excellent hamburgers with caramelized onions. **FYI:** Reservations recommended. **Open:** Lunch Mon–Fri 11:30am–2:30pm; dinner Sun–Thurs 5:30–10pm, Fri–Sat 5:30–10:30pm; brunch Sun 10:30am–2pm. Closed some hols. **Prices:** Main courses $14–$18. Maj CC.

Gaylord's, in Ghiradelli Square, 900 N Point St, San Francisco; tel 415/771-8822. **Indian.** One of the prettiest restaurants in the city. The elegant, dazzling dining room looks out to Alcatraz and the bay. Northern Indian specialties include spicy curries, aromatic vegetarian dishes, tandoori chicken, and Indian breads. **FYI:** Reservations recommended. **Open:** Lunch Mon–Sat 11:45am–1:45pm; dinner daily 5–11pm; brunch Sun 11:45am–2:45pm. Closed some hols. **Prices:** Main courses $12–$20; PF dinner $22–$28.75. Maj CC.

Gordon Biersch Brewery Restaurant, 2 Harrison St, San Francisco (SoMa); tel 415/243-8246. On Embarcadero across from Bay Bridge. **Californian.** In this former coffee roastery overlooking the Bay Bridge, you can choose from 3 different beers brewed on the premises. The large and lively bar area features a great view of the brewery. Upstairs, the restaurant serves a globetrotting and beer-friendly menu, ranging from baby-back ribs with garlic fries to linguine with chicken and butternut squash. The 3rd Saturday of each month features a Brewer's Lunch ($25), including a brewery tour, tastings, and meal. **FYI:** Reservations recommended. Beer and wine only. **Open:** Sun–Thurs 11am–10pm, Fri–Sat 11am–10:30pm. Closed Dec 25. **Prices:** Main courses $12–$16. Maj CC. ♿

Greens at Fort Mason, in Fort Mason Center, Buchanan St and Marina Blvd, San Francisco (Marina); tel 415/771-6222. **Vegetarian.** This cavernous restaurant (a former warehouse) run by the San Francisco Zen Center offers spectacular bay views. Menus change weekly, but all feature organic, seasonal produce grown at the Zen Center's Green Gulch Farms in Marin County. Tomato, white bean, and sorrel soup; linguine with onion confit, goat cheese, and walnuts. Fresh breads from its Tassajara Bakery. **FYI:** Reservations recommended. Beer and wine only. **Open:** Lunch Tues–Thurs 11:30am–2pm, Fri–Sat 11:30am–2:30pm; dinner Mon–Thurs 5:30–9:30pm, Fri–Sat 6–9:30pm; brunch Sun 10am–2pm. **Prices:** Main courses $10–$12. Ltd CC. ▄▄ ♿

Hamburger Mary's, 1582 Folsom St, San Francisco (SoMa); tel 415/626-5767. At 12th St. **New American.** Hamburger joint serves up hamburgers, vegetarian specials, chili, and homemade desserts. Bar with 13 varieties of beer. **FYI:** Reservations accepted. **Open:** Tues–Thurs 11:30am–1am, Fri–Sat 10am–2am, Sun 10am–1am. Closed some hols. **Prices:** Main courses $5–$10. Maj CC. ♿

Harbor Village, 4 Embarcadero Center (lobby level), Sacramento St, San Francisco; tel 415/781-8833. At Market St. **Chinese.** Spacious, high-ceilinged restaurant with back room overlooking plaza and Ferry Building. Excellent dim sum, served at lunch only. Good classic Chinese food, with specials such as abalone and shark fin soup. **FYI:** Reservations recommended. **Open:** Lunch Mon–Fri 11am–2:30pm, Sat 10:30am–2:30pm, Sun 10am–2:30pm; dinner daily 5:30–9:30pm. **Prices:** Main courses $9–$24. Maj CC.

Hard Rock Cafe, 1699 Van Ness Ave, San Francisco (near Nob Hill); tel 415/885-1699. At Sacramento St. **New American.** Elaborately decorated with movie and rock-and-roll memorabilia, this is a popular spot for tourists. Steaks, hamburgers, salads, sandwiches, big selection of desserts. Music is loud. **FYI:** Reservations not accepted. **Open:** Sun–Thurs 11am–11:30pm, Fri–Sat 11am–12:30pm. **Prices:** Main courses $6–$13. Maj CC. VP ♿

Harris', 2100 Van Ness Ave, San Francisco (near Chinatown); tel 415/673-1888. At Pacific Ave. **Steak.** A sophisticated steak house with leather booths and dark, wood-paneled walls. The corn-fed midwestern beef is dry-aged 21 days on the premises and then mesquite-grilled. Lamb, chicken, prime rib, and seafood are also served. **FYI:** Reservations recommended. Jazz. Dress code. **Open:** Mon–Fri 6–9:30pm, Sat–Sun 5–9:30pm. Closed some hols. **Prices:** Main courses $18–$24.50. Maj CC. VP ♿

★ **Harry Denton's Bar & Grill**, in the Harbor Court Hotel, 161 Steuart St, San Francisco (SoMa); tel 415/882-1333. **New**

American. Lively ambience in a turn-of-the-century saloon atmosphere accented by rich colors and fabrics. Menu lists pot roast, hamburgers, fresh fish, crab cakes, and similar brasserie-style dishes. **FYI:** Reservations recommended. Dancing/jazz/piano. **Open:** Breakfast Mon–Fri 7–10am; lunch Mon–Fri 11:30am–3pm; dinner daily 5:30pm–midnight; brunch Sat–Sun 8am–3pm. Closed some hols. **Prices:** Main courses $8–$16; PF dinner $32. Maj CC. VP &

Hayes Street Grill, 320 Hayes St, San Francisco; tel 415/863-5545. Between Franklin and Gough Sts. **Seafood.** This upscale fish house, near the Opera House and Davies Symphony Hall, features walls lined with pictures of opera, ballet, and symphony stars. Salmon, halibut, yellowfin tuna, scallops, and swordfish are often featured. Also, steaks and seafood salads, and an extensive wine list. **FYI:** Reservations recommended. Beer and wine only. **Open:** Lunch Mon–Fri 11am–2pm; dinner Mon–Thurs 5–9:30pm, Fri 5–10:30pm, Sat 6–10:30pm, Sun 5–8:30pm. Closed some hols. **Prices:** Main courses $13–$24. Ltd CC. &

Helmand, 430 Broadway, San Francisco (North Beach); tel 415/362-0641. At Kearny St. **Afghani.** Afghan meals served in a handsome, romantic dining room with soft lighting, white linen tablecloths, and fine service. The food is fresh and exotic and the prices are reasonable. Lamb dishes are particularly good. **FYI:** Reservations accepted. **Open:** Lunch Mon–Fri 11:30am–2:30pm; dinner Mon–Thurs 6–11pm, Fri–Sun 6–10pm. **Prices:** Main courses $8–$14. Maj CC.

⑤★ House of Nanking, 919 Kearny St, San Francisco (Chinatown); tel 415/421-1429. At Columbus Ave. **Chinese.** A very popular, inexpensive basic Chinatown diner, crowded at all hours. With only a few tables and a counter, there is often a wait. The menu tends toward typical Chinese fare like moo-shu pork and Hunan beef, with such notable exceptions as prawns with Tsing Tao beer sauce. Owner Peter Fang is happy to order for you. **FYI:** Reservations not accepted. No liquor license. **Open:** Mon–Fri 11am–10pm, Sat noon–10pm, Sun 4–10pm. Closed some hols. **Prices:** Main courses $3.50–$8. No CC.

House of Prime Rib, 1906 Van Ness Ave, San Francisco (Financial District); tel 415/885-4605. Between Washington and Jackson Sts. **Steak.** Despite a curved bar, leather stools, a lovely lounge with fireplace, and soft lighting, the best decoration here is the aroma of prime rib cooking. Steaks and roasts are carved tableside. **FYI:** Reservations recommended. Children's menu. **Open:** Daily 5–10pm. **Prices:** Main courses $18.75–$22.25. Maj CC. ▮ ▣ VP

Hunan Restaurant, 924 Sansome St, San Francisco (Financial District); tel 415/956-7727. At Broadway. **Hunan Chinese.** A fun, casual place serving some of the spiciest Hunan food in the city. The neon-lit dining room is a bit bare, but the bar is quite attractive. Specialties include ginger beef, garlic chicken, and kung pao shrimp. **FYI:** Reservations accepted. **Open:** Daily 11:30am–9:30pm. **Prices:** Main courses $6–$14. Maj CC. &

★ Hyde Street Bistro, 1521 Hyde St, San Francisco (Russian Hill); tel 415/441-7778. Between Pacific Ave and Jackson St. **Italian/Austrian.** A small bistro favored by locals, decorated in wood and brass. The frequently changing menu may offer ravioli with chicken and wild mushrooms, Wiener schnitzel with potato pancakes, grilled halibut, and other German-Italian specialties. **FYI:** Reservations not accepted. Beer and wine only. **Open:** Daily 5:30–10:30pm. Closed some hols. **Prices:** Main courses $9–$15. Maj CC. VP &

Il Fornaio, 1265 Battery St, San Francisco (Telegraph Hill); tel 415/986-0100. At Greenwich St. **Italian.** Part of a successful California-based group. Decorated with a long marble bar, dome windows, tile floors, and gold-toned walls. Fresh pastas, rotisserie items. Also at: 223 Corte Madera Town Center, Corte Madera (415/927-4400); Garden Court Hotel, 520 Cowper St, Palo Alto (415/853-3888). **FYI:** Reservations recommended. **Open:** Mon–Thurs 7am–11pm, Fri 7am–midnight, Sat 9am–midnight, Sun 9am–11pm. Closed some hols. **Prices:** Main courses $8–$18. Maj CC. VP &

Indian Oven, 233 Fillmore St, San Francisco; tel 415/626-1628. At Haight St. **Indian.** Stylish and modern, with an open kitchen and glass bar. Diners can listen to classical Indian music while they dine on tandoori chicken, Indian curries, and other regional dishes. Parking is scarce. Be alert when walking to and from your car. **FYI:** Reservations accepted. Beer and wine only. **Open:** Daily 5:30–10pm. Closed some hols. **Prices:** Main courses $7.95–$16.95. Maj CC. ♥

Izzy's Steak & Chophouse, 3345 Steiner St, San Francisco; tel 415/563-0487. Between Lombard and Chestnut Sts. **Steak.** A dark bar and dining room that lack character. Casual but expensive for a steak house. **FYI:** Reservations accepted. **Open:** Mon–Sat 5–11:30pm, Sun 5–10pm. Closed some hols. **Prices:** Main courses $15–$20. Maj CC.

Jack's, 615 Sacramento St, San Francisco (Financial District); tel 415/986-9854. Between Montgomery and Kearny Sts. **American.** Landmark restaurant first opened in 1864 by the father of the current owner, who was born in 1903 and is still at the restaurant nearly everyday. The turn-of-the-century furnishings are still intact, with white tablecloths and bentwood chairs. The long, narrow dining room serves up coq au vin and double French lamb chops, among other classics. Private banquet rooms for 4–65 people. **FYI:** Reservations accepted. **Open:** Mon–Fri 11:30am–9:30pm, Sat 5–9:30pm. Closed some hols. **Prices:** Main courses $7–$17. Maj CC. ■ &

(S) ✹ **J & J Restaurant**, 615 Jackson St, San Francisco (Chinatown); tel 415/981-7308. Between Grant Ave and Kearny St. **Chinese.** Real Cantonese food and dim sum. Clientele is mostly Chinese-speaking, but several on staff speak English. Serves one of the best dim sum selections in the city, including delectable shrimp dumplings in near-transparent skins. Most spectacular entree is the baked lobster with vermicelli and garlic sauce. (Hint—pick up one of the take out menus up front, then point to your selection.) **FYI:** Reservations accepted. No liquor license. **Open:** Lunch daily 9am–2pm; dinner daily 5:30–10pm. **Prices:** Main courses $6–$12. Maj CC.

John's Grill, 63 Ellis St, San Francisco (Union Square); tel 415/966-DASH. At Powell St. **American.** Dashiell Hammett used to eat here and mentions this place in his novels—a lunch favorite for Sam Spade in *The Maltese Falcon.* Classic San Francisco decor with photos of the famous and prints from *The Maltese Falcon* movie. Menu features Dungeness crab cocktail, lamb chops with baked potato and sliced tomatoes, sole stuffed with bay shrimp. **FYI:** Reservations recommended. **Open:** Mon–Sat 11am–10pm, Sun 5–10pm. **Prices:** Main courses $13.95–$24.95. Maj CC. ■

Julie's Supper Club and Lounge, 1123 Folsan St, San Francisco (SoMa); tel 415/861-0707. Between 7th and 8th Sts. **New American/Eclectic.** Fun is the theme at this hip restaurant, popular before and after attending clubs and theater in the SoMa area. Wacky decor includes the aquarium-style Marlin Room. Entrees might include grilled mahimahi with spicy long beans and sesame-ginger noodles, or grilled brochette of lamb with roasted eggplant. Several pasta selections, too. On the weekend, a very lively rhythm-and-blues band encourages dancing in the aisles. **FYI:** Reservations accepted. Blues. **Open:** Mon–Wed 5:30–10:30pm, Thurs 5:30–11pm, Fri–Sat 5:30–11:30pm. Closed some hols. **Prices:** Main courses $8–$15. Maj CC. &

Kabuto Sushi, 5116 Geary Blvd, San Francisco (Richmond); tel 415/752-5652. Between 15th and 16th Aves. **Japanese.** This restaurant lacks ambience, but its sushi is very popular; tempura and teriyaki are also served. **FYI:** Reservations accepted. Beer and wine only. **Open:** Tues–Sat 5:30–11pm, Sun 5:30–10pm. Closed some hols. **Prices:** Main courses $15–$20. Ltd CC.

Khan Toke Thai House, 5937 Geary Blvd, San Francisco (Richmond); tel 415/668-6654. Between 23rd and 24th Aves. **Thai.** A beautiful place. Elaborate, authentic Thai decor features carved wood furniture and imported wood carvings. Specialties include chicken coconut soup, duck salad, Thai crab, and a

seafood curry. **FYI:** Reservations accepted. Beer and wine only. **Open:** Daily 5pm–10am. Closed some hols. **Prices:** Main courses $4.95–$10.50. Maj CC. &

✹ **Kuleto's**, in Villa Florence, 221 Powell St, San Francisco (Downtown); tel 415/397-7720. Between Geary and O'Farrell Sts. **Italian.** Popular, with a lively, attractive bar and separate espresso bar. Offers northern Italian cuisine using fresh local produce. Specialties include fish grilled over hardwoods; breast of chicken stuffed with herbed ricotta in roasted-pepper butter sauce; marinated grilled prawns with Belgian endive, orange, and red pepper salad; and roast duck with grappa-soaked cherries, braised cabbage, and black pepper polenta. **FYI:** Reservations recommended. **Open:** Daily 7am–11pm. **Prices:** Main courses $8–$17. Maj CC. [▲] [VP] &

La Quiche, 550 Taylor St, San Francisco (Union Square); tel 415/441-2711. **French.** Looks like a French country inn, with pink decor, cafe chairs, and much artwork. Known for classic French cuisine at reasonable prices, but a new chef has just taken over, so only time will tell if the same high standards will continue. Offers French specialties such as crêpes and beef bourguignon. Feels like you're in France because everyone here speaks French. **FYI:** Reservations accepted. Beer and wine only. **Open:** Lunch Mon–Fri 11:30am–2:30pm; dinner Mon–Sat 5:30–10pm. Closed some hols. **Prices:** Main courses $8–$14. Maj CC. ♥

Le Central, 453 Bush St, San Francisco (Financial District); tel 415/391-2233. At Kearny St. **French.** A casually elegant restaurant that resembles a French bistro, where all the patrons seem to know each other. Good bar menu: oysters, escargot, pâté. Also, roast chicken with thin crispy french fries, cassoulet, and excellent crab cakes in beurre blanc. **FYI:** Reservations recommended. **Open:** Mon–Sat 11:30am–10:30pm. Closed some hols. **Prices:** Main courses $12–$20. Maj CC.

Little City, 673 Union St, San Francisco (North Beach); tel 415/434-2900. On Washington Square. **Italian.** Elegant Italian bar and restaurant. Great wines by the glass and wonderful appetizers to go with them. Specialties include baked brie and roasted garlic appetizer, wild mushroom ravioli, and grilled ahi tuna with caper sauce. **FYI:** Reservations recommended. **Open:** Daily 11:30am–2am. Closed some hols. **Prices:** Main courses $8–$15. Maj CC. &

✹ **LuLu's**, 816 Folsom St, San Francisco (SoMa); tel 415/495-5775. Between 4th and 5th Sts. **Californian/Italian.** Located in the trendy SoMa enclave, this restaurant has been a great success since it opened in 1993. The vast room recalls an old-fashioned airplane hangar, with food served on colorful, hand-painted earthenware. The kitchen has a huge wood-burning oven for preparing items like roasted chicken and pork loin with fennel and garlic. Wonderful pizzas, too, including lamb sausage, eggplant, and peppers. **FYI:** Reservations recommended. **Open:** Lunch Mon–Sat 11:30am–3pm; dinner Mon–Thurs 5:30–10:30pm, Fri–Sat 5:30–11:30pm. Closed some hols. **Prices:** Main courses $9–$14. Maj CC. &

The Mandarin, in Ghirardelli Square, 900 N Point St, San Francisco; tel 415/673-8812. **Chinese.** With views of San Francisco Bay as a backdrop, the Mandarin is tastefully decorated with intricate tile floors, silk fabric walls, oriental lithographs, ornate flower arrangements, and wooden sculptures. The opulent surroundings match the food, which includes elaborate northern Chinese dishes of beef, lamb, chicken, and Peking duck. The wine list is exceptional. **FYI:** Reservations recommended. **Open:** Daily 11:30am–11pm. Closed some hols. **Prices:** Main courses $8–$16; PF dinner $16–$38. Maj CC. ▲

Marnee Thai, 2225 Irving St, San Francisco (Sunset); tel 415/665-9500. Between 23rd and 24th Aves. **Thai.** A neighborhood restaurant serving authentic cuisine in a simple atmosphere. Thai curries, green-papaya salad, and prawn and calamari dishes are specialties. Chef will modify seasonings at diner's request. **FYI:** Reservations accepted. Beer and wine only. **Open:** Wed–Mon 11:30am–10pm. **Prices:** Main courses $6.50–$11. Maj CC.

Marrakech, 419 O'Farrell St, San Francisco (Union Square); tel 415/776-6717. Between Jones and Taylor Sts. **Moroccan.** Like a visit to Morocco. There's a fountain out front, and inside Persian rugs cover the banquettes. The exotic menu features b'stilla (boneless chicken pastry), lamb with honey and almonds, rabbit, and chicken with lemon. **FYI:** Reservations accepted. **Open:** Daily 6–10pm. Closed some hols. **Prices:** Main courses $14–$23. Maj CC.

Masa's, in Hotel Vintage Court, 648 Bush St, San Francisco (Union Square); tel 415/989-7154. Between Powell and Stockton Sts. **New American/French.** Brilliant classic cuisine from chef Julian Serrano. The dining room is low key and designed to focus all attention on the food. Guests select either a 4-course menu du jour or a 7-course menu degustation, which might include fillet of black bass sautéed with saffron sauce, or medallions of fallow deer. **FYI:** Reservations recommended. Dress code. **Open:** Tues–Sat 6–9:30. Closed some hols. **Prices:** PF dinner $68–$75. Maj CC. 🆅🅿

The Metro Bar and Restaurant, 3600 16th St, San Francisco; tel 415/703-9750. **Hunan Chinese.** Exotic decor with funky color scheme, and gold Indonesian camel and horse statues accenting a black circular bar. Hunan specialties include Kung Pao chicken, sizzling scallops with black mushrooms, Mongolian

lamb, and Szechuan bean-curd pork. **FYI:** Reservations not accepted. Sing along. **Open:** Daily 5:30–11pm. **Prices:** Main courses $6–$11. Ltd CC.

Miss Pearl's Jam House, in the Phoenix Hotel, 601 Eddy St, San Francisco (Civic Center); tel 415/775-5267. Between Polk and Larkin Sts. **Caribbean.** With palm trees lining the windows and a canoe dangling over the bar, this restaurant feels like a tropical hideaway. The Caribbean-style cooking features favorites such as coconut prawns in beer-batter, roast pork loin adobo, and jerk chicken. Reggae and steel bands play on weekends. **FYI:** Reservations recommended. Dancing/island music. **Open:** Dinner Tues–Sun 6:30–10pm; brunch Sun 11:30am–2:30pm. Closed some hols. **Prices:** Main courses $8–$15. Maj CC. 🆅🅿 &

★ **Moose's**, 1652 Stockton St, San Francisco (North Beach); tel 415/989-7800. At Filbert St. **Californian/Mediterranean.** Always lively and packed, and popular with media and sports figures. An airy setting with masculine decor. Menu changes daily; dishes include grilled dry-aged New York strip steak with artichoke–smoked Gouda gratin, as well as terrific pastas and pizzas. **FYI:** Reservations recommended. Jazz. **Open:** Lunch Mon–Sat 11:30am–2:30pm; dinner Mon–Thurs 5:30–10pm, Fri–Sat 5:30–11pm; brunch Sun 10:30am–3pm. Closed Dec 25. **Prices:** Main courses $9–$24. Maj CC. 🆅🅿 &

★ **North Beach Restaurant**, 1512 Stockton St, San Francisco (North Beach); tel 415/392-1587. At Columbus Ave. **Northern Italian.** Classic peasant dishes of Tuscany served by Italian-speaking waiters. Full dinners include antipasto, green salad, soup, salad, pasta with prosciutto sauce, and a choice of entree. The *Wine Spectator* named the wine cellar one of the 100 best in the United States. **FYI:** Reservations recommended. **Open:** Daily 11:30am–11:45pm. Closed some hols. **Prices:** Main courses $10–$27; PF dinner $22.95. Maj CC. ❤ 🆅🅿 &

North India Restaurant, 3131 Webster St, San Francisco; tel 415/931-1556. **Indian.** Attractively decorated with art, wood sculptures, chandeliers, and plants, this restaurant serves authentic Indian cuisine. Offers fixed-price, 3-course business lunch. Menu features curries, tandoori items, vegetarian dishes, and salads. Try lamb cooked with saffron, cardamom, and almonds; or jumbo prawns in a light curry sauce. **FYI:** Reservations accepted. Beer and wine only. **Open:** Lunch Mon–Fri 11:30am–2:30pm; dinner Mon–Sat 5–10:30pm, Sun 5–10pm. Closed some hols. **Prices:** Main courses $10–$20. Maj CC. 🚗 &

Ocean Restaurant, 726 Clement St, San Francisco; tel 415/668-8896. At 6th Ave. **Chinese.** One of the more nicely decorated Chinese restaurants in the city. Seafood is the specialty, especially the rock cod over cooked lettuce and shrimp with sweet walnuts. There is also a selection of Cantonese beef, pork, and vegetable dishes. Portions are generous. **FYI:** Reservations accepted. Beer and wine only. **Open:** Lunch daily 11:30am–3pm; dinner daily 4:30–9:30pm. Closed some hols. **Prices:** Main courses $6–$15; PF dinner $15–$26. Ltd CC.

Olive's Gourmet Pizza, 3249 Scott St, San Francisco; tel 415/567-4488. Between Chestnut and Lombard Sts. **Pizza.** Cute and simple California pizza kitchen offering crayons and paper at tables and alternative rock music. Menu includes gourmet pizza, such as Blue Toscano with mozzarella, Gorgonzola, salami, and fresh tomatoes. Also offers calzone and pasta. **FYI:** Reservations not accepted. Beer and wine only. **Open:** Sun–Thurs 11:30am–10:30pm, Fri–Sat 11:30am–11:30pm. Closed Dec 25. **Prices:** Main courses $8–$12. No CC.

♥ **One Market**, 1 Market St, San Francisco; tel 415/777-5577. Off Embarcadero Plaza. **New American.** Run by Bradley Ogden, one of America's leading chefs, One Market is surrounded by 20-foot-tall windows facing the ferry building. Although huge, the space is not cavernous. Burnished woods and wine-tone upholsteries provide a Jazz Age feel. Smoked and wood-roasted items are the trademark here—grilled salmon with corn-souffle spoonbread, or oak-grilled double pork chops. The "Chef's Table" in the kitchen can be reserved for dining in the middle of the action. **FYI:** Reservations recommended. Piano. **Open:** Lunch Mon–Fri 11:30am–2pm; dinner Sun 5–9pm, Mon–Thurs 5:30am–9:30pm, Fri–Sat 5–10pm; brunch Sun 10am–2pm. Closed some hols. **Prices:** Main courses $18–$25. Maj CC. VP &

Pacific Cafe, 7000 Geary Blvd, San Francisco; tel 415/387-7091. At 34th Ave. **Seafood.** Wooden booths help to create a comfortable setting in this restaurant, popular with the locals. Specialties include fresh abalone, Dungeness crab cakes, grilled tuna, halibut, and sturgeon with capers and mushrooms, a favorite dish from old San Francisco fish houses. **FYI:** Reservations not accepted. Beer and wine only. **Open:** Daily 5–10pm. Closed some hols. **Prices:** Main courses $12–$16. Maj CC. &

Pacific Heights Bar & Grill, 2001 Fillmore St, San Francisco; tel 415/567-3337. At Pine St. **Eclectic.** Casual yet elegant neighborhood restaurant with an oyster bar up front and a huge main bar with tables where drinks or a full meal can be enjoyed. Appetizers may include baked brie with jalapeño grape salsa and roasted garlic. Among entree specialties are fresh fish; pasta; grilled meat; and steamed, blackened, or baked fish. **FYI:** Reservations recommended. **Open:** Lunch Wed–Sun 11:30am–4pm; dinner Mon–Thurs 5:30–9:30pm, Fri–Sat 4–10:30pm, Sun 4–9:30pm. Closed some hols. **Prices:** Main courses $8.95–$16.95. Maj CC. &

Pane e Vino, 3011 Steiner St, San Francisco (Pacific Heights); tel 415/346-2111. At Union St. **Italian.** Charming Italian restaurant with terra-cotta floors, wall sconces, sponge-painted walls, and a wood-burning stove in the dining room. Featuring fresh pasta, braised rabbit, and whole roasted fish. **FYI:** Reservations recommended. Beer and wine only. **Open:** Lunch Mon–Sat 11:30am–2:30pm; dinner Sun–Thurs 5–10pm, Fri–Sat 5–10:30pm. Closed some hols. **Prices:** Main courses $7.50–$17.95. Ltd CC.

♥ **Park Grill**, in the Park Hyatt Hotel, 333 Battery St, San Francisco (Embarcadero Center); tel 415/392-1234. **Californian.** Club-like setting on the 2nd floor, with windows that look out to the Embarcadero Center; particularly popular with business people at lunchtime because of its widely spaced tables, low sound level, and efficient service. Specialties include Sonoma greens with tapenade croutons; roasted monkfish; and sautéed free-range chicken with morels and porcini mushrooms. **FYI:** Reservations recommended. Piano. Children's menu. **Open:** Breakfast daily 6:30–11am; lunch daily 11:30am–5:30pm; dinner daily 5:30–10:30pm; brunch Sun 10am–2:30pm. **Prices:** Main courses $14–$25. Maj CC. VP &

Pauline's Pizza Pie, 260 Valencia St, San Francisco; tel 415/552-2050. **Pizza.** Decorated with art from an upstairs gallery, the pleasant dining room offers gourmet pizza with special toppings, such as sautéed leeks and double-smoked ham. Salads and toppings are made from locally grown organic ingredients, and there's an extensive wine list. **FYI:** Reservations not accepted. Band. Beer and wine only. **Open:** Tues–Sat 5–10pm. Closed some hols; Christmas week. **Prices:** Main courses $10–$20. Ltd CC. 🚗

The Pork Store Cafe, 1451 Haight St, San Francisco (Haight-Ashbury); tel 415/864-6981. Between Ashbury St and Masonic Ave. **Cafe.** Very casual, friendly cafe. Specials include pork chops, pancakes, huevos rancheros, burgers, and sandwiches at breakfast and lunch. **FYI:** Reservations not accepted. Beer and wine only. **Open:** Mon–Fri 7am–3pm, Sat–Sun 8am–4pm. **Prices:** Lunch main courses $2.95–$6.75. Ltd CC.

♥ **Postrio**, in the Prescott Hotel, 545 Post St, San Francisco (Union Square); tel 415/776-7825. Between Mason and Taylor Sts. **Californian/Mediterranean/Asian.** When chefs visit from out of town, they always check what's new at Postrio, with its triumvirate of celebrity chefs: Wolfgang Puck, and Anne and David Gingrass. Stylishly contemporary, the dining room has an inlaid marble floor up front, stunning light fixtures, and original art by Rauschenberg and others. The daily menu might carry grilled sea scallops with red-curry lobster sauce or roasted leg of Sonoma lamb. Extensive wine list. **FYI:** Reservations recommended. **Open:** Breakfast Mon–Fri 7–10am; lunch Mon–Fri

11:30am–2pm; dinner daily 5:30–10pm; brunch Sat–Sun 9am–2pm. Closed some hols. **Prices:** Main courses $19–$25. Maj CC. VP &

Pot Sticker, 150 Waverly Place, San Francisco (Chinatown); tel 415/397-9985. **Chinese.** Set in an alley in Chinatown. Spicy Hunan and Cantonese dishes include lemon chicken, braised bean curd, and sizzling rice soup. **FYI:** Reservations accepted. Beer and wine only. **Open:** Daily 11:30am–9:45pm. Closed Dec 25. **Prices:** Main courses $6.25–$14.95; PF dinner $8–$10. Maj CC. &

Prego, 2000 Union St, San Francisco; tel 415/563-3305. At Buchanan St. **Italian.** The woodburning pizza oven is open to view here, and there's a circular granite bar with brass railings. Sidewalk dining is available. Specialties are pizza with homemade sausage, pastas, and grilled meats. **FYI:** Reservations recommended. **Open:** Daily 11:30am–midnight. Closed some hols. **Prices:** Main courses $7–$18. Maj CC. &

♦ **Redwood Room**, in the Four Seasons Clift, 495 Geary St, San Francisco (Union Square); tel 415/775-4700. **Californian.** Moderately priced, innovative lunches and light after-theater dinners are served in one of the most beautiful rooms in California. Walls are covered with wood from a single 2,000-year-old redwood and accented with art deco motifs and reproductions of Gustav Klimt paintings. Dinner is served in the adjoining **French Room,** a very elegant, château-like salon lit by chandeliers. Chef Martin Frost's cuisine highlights fresh California produce. Examples include baby spinach leaves with sundried tomato crostini and grilled gulf prawns, and grilled and marinated vegetable club sandwich on sourdough toast with roast eggplant spread. **FYI:** Reservations recommended. Children's menu. **Open:** Daily noon–3pm. **Prices:** Lunch main courses $12.50–$14.75. Maj CC. ● ▮ VP &

♦ **Regina Chichi Beignet**, 101 Cyril Magnia, San Francisco (Union Square); tel 415/421-4254. **French/Southern.** New restaurant from noted chef Regina Charbonneau, located downstairs in cavernlike room and patronized by theater/music people. Southern-accented menu features delicious biscuits, shrimp remoulade, salt-and-peppercorn oysters with caviar, game hen with garlic, and grilled catfish with crawfish étoufée. **FYI:** Reservations recommended. Jazz/piano. **Open:** Tues–Thurs 5:30pm–midnight, Fri–Sat 5:30pm–1am, Sun 5:30–9:30pm. Closed some hols. **Prices:** Main courses $13–$20. Maj CC. ● VP

Ristorante Ecco, 101 South Park, San Francisco (SoMa); tel 415/495-3291. **Italian.** From the tile floors to the beautiful flower arrangements, "casual chic" best describes the spare yet elegant atmosphere. Choose from a wide array of antipasti,

pasta, pizzas, chicken, fish, and meats, including a San Francisco classic: cacciucco, a seafood stew bursting with mussels, prawns, scallops, and assorted fish served with garlic bruschetta. Nice selection of Italian desserts. **FYI:** Reservations recommended. **Open:** Lunch Mon–Fri 11:30am–2:30pm; dinner Mon–Sat 5:30–10pm. Closed some hols. **Prices:** Main courses $10–$16. Maj CC. &

Salmagundi, 442 Geary St, San Francisco (Downtown); tel 415/441-0894. **Salad/Sandwiches.** Convenient for pre-theater supper. Cafeteria-style eatery offers light fare—sandwiches, salads, soups, and desserts. Bring your bowl back for an extra ladle of the same soup, or sample another for free. **FYI:** Reservations not accepted. Beer and wine only. **Open:** Tues–Sat 11am–11pm, Sun–Mon 11am–9pm. Closed some hols. **Prices:** Main courses $3.50–$6. Maj CC. ●

★ **Sam's Grill and Seafood Restaurant**, 374 Bush St, San Francisco (Financial District); tel 415/421-0594. **Seafood.** A San Francisco landmark—a dark, somber, business lunch spot. Seafood is fresh and consistently good. Specialties are crab Louie, sautéed shellfish, and oyster stew. **FYI:** Reservations not accepted. **Open:** Mon–Fri 11am–8:30pm. Closed some hols. **Prices:** Main courses $8–$17. Maj CC. ▮

Ⓢ **Sam Wo**, 813 Washington St, San Francisco (Chinatown); tel 415/982-0596. Between Grant Ave and Stockton St. **Chinese.** One of the oldest restaurants in the heart of Chinatown. Two floors of dining offering roast pork rice noodles, soups, chow mein, eggrolls, and the like. Very good value. **FYI:** Reservations not accepted. No liquor license. **Open:** Mon–Sat 11am–3am, Sun 11am–9:30pm. **Prices:** Main courses $2–$6. No CC. ▮

Sanppo, 1702 Post St, San Francisco (Japantown); tel 415/346-3486. At Buchanan St. **Japanese.** Popular Japantown eatery. Has the decor of a Japanese country inn, with lots of plants. Sushi, sashimi, tempura. **FYI:** Reservations recommended. Beer and wine only. **Open:** Tues–Sat 11:45am–10pm, Sun 3–10pm. Closed some hols. **Prices:** Main courses $8–$16. Ltd CC.

Savoy Brasserie, in Savoy Hotel, 580 Geary Blvd, San Francisco (Downtown); tel 415/474-8686. Between Jones and Taylor. **Californian/French/Seafood.** Wonderful old Parisian bistro atmosphere with marble floors. Shellfish bar in back. **FYI:** Reservations recommended. **Open:** Tues–Sun 5:30–10pm. **Prices:** Main courses $9–$18. Maj CC. ▮ VP &

★ **Scott's Seafood Grill & Bar**, 3 Embarcadero Center, San Francisco (Financial District); tel 415/981-0622. **Seafood.** Good basic seafood restaurant located close to the Financial District. Glass walls overlook strolling area on top of Embaracadero Plaza.

Seafood dishes: pan-seared seafood sautéed with roasted garlic mashed potatoes, local sand dabs with caper butter, smoked salmon carpaccio. **FYI:** Reservations recommended. **Open:** Sun–Thurs 11am–10pm, Fri–Sat 11am–11pm. Closed some hols. **Prices:** Main courses $9–$27. Maj CC. &

Sears Fine Foods, 439 Powell St, San Francisco (Downtown); tel 415/986-1160. Between Sutter and Post Sts. **American/ Diner.** Popular, it's a basic San Francisco shopper's cafeteria. Serves hamburgers, omelettes, Swedish meatballs, little pancakes. **FYI:** Reservations recommended. No liquor license. **Open:** Wed–Sun 6:30am–3:30pm. Closed some hols. **Prices:** Lunch main courses $6–$9. No CC. &

♣ **The Sherman House**, in the Sherman House Hotel, 2160 Green St, San Francisco (Pacific Heights); tel 415/563-3600. Between Webster and Fillmore Sts. **French.** Small, romantic restaurant at one of San Francisco's most chic hotels. Lovely bay views and gorgeous flower arrangements. Food is cooked to order, and the menu changes daily, with choices such as crisp salad with baby greens, honey-and-lavender roasted squab with rice pilau, or herb-crusted cod. **FYI:** Reservations recommended. Piano. Jacket required. Beer and wine only. **Open:** Breakfast daily 7–10:30am; lunch Mon–Sat 11:30am–2pm; dinner daily 5:30–9:30pm; brunch Sun 10am–2pm. **Prices:** Main courses $26–$28; PF dinner $65. Maj CC. ⊗ 🍴 📷 VP

South Park Cafe, 108 South Park Ave, San Francisco (SoMa); tel 415/495-7275. **French/Bistro.** Feels like a Parisian bistro, with crisp, white tablecloths, fresh flowers on each table, and elegant bistro fare, located on a quiet tree-lined street far from the noise of the city. Roast rabbit, grilled salmon, vegetable couscous, chocolate madeleines, almond biscotti. **FYI:** Reservations recommended. **Open:** Mon–Fri 7:30am–10:30pm, Sat 6–10pm. Closed some hols. **Prices:** Main courses $10–$17. Maj CC. &

Splendido, 4 Embarcadero Center, San Francisco (Financial District); tel 415/986-3222. **Italian/Mediterranean.** Popular Mediterranean trattoria with charming ambience. Stone domed ceiling evokes ancient Etruscan style, and 200-year-old olive wood doors come from Spain. Marble tables in bar area; other tables overlook square and Ferry Building. Grilled swordfish, sautéed quail with wild rice and vinaigrette, hearty breads, pizza, desserts. **FYI:** Reservations recommended. **Open:** Lunch Mon–Sat 11:30am–2:30pm; dinner daily 5:30–9:30pm. Closed some hols. **Prices:** Main courses $10–$22. Maj CC. &

♣ **Square One**, 190 Pacific Ave, San Francisco (Downtown); tel 415/788-1110. At Front St. **Italian/Mediterranean.** Consistently rated one of the top restaurants in town, the large, elegant dining room is contemporary and casual, offering fine Mediterranean-influenced cuisine from star chef Joyce Goldstein. The

daily menu may include lamb chops in a Moroccan marinade, linguine with prawns and scallops, or roast pork in a sherry cream. Vegetarian dishes available. Overlooks Jackson Square. **FYI:** Reservations recommended. **Open:** Lunch Mon–Fri 11:30am–2:30pm; dinner Mon–Thurs 5:30–10pm, Fri–Sat 5:30–10:30pm, Sun 5–9:30pm. Closed Dec 25. **Prices:** Main courses $12–$25. Maj CC. VP &

♣ **Stars**, 150 Redwood Alley, San Francisco (Civic Center); tel 415/861-7827. Between McAllister St and Golden Gate Ave. **New American/Californian.** One of San Francisco's top restaurants, Stars is known for consistently good food and a happening atmosphere, thanks to chef/owner Jeremiah Tower. It features the longest bar in the city and an open kitchen. The menu changes daily to take advantage of fresh seasonal ingredients; choices include grilled yellowtail jack in roasted-tomato sauce, and grilled lamb with red-pepper salad. Fruit pies and other desserts come from the restaurant's bakery. **FYI:** Reservations recommended. Piano. **Open:** Lunch Mon–Fri 11:30am–2:30pm; dinner daily 5:30–10:30pm. Closed some hols. **Prices:** Main courses $20–$29. Maj CC. VP &

★ **Stars Cafe**, 500 Van Ness Ave, San Francisco (Civic Center); tel 415/861-4344. **New American.** Not just "son of Stars," this is a terrific restaurant in its own right. French bistro atmosphere features mirrored columns, cafe chairs, and slate floors. The menu presents superchef Jeremiah Towers' innovative cuisine at reasonable prices—under $15 for entrees. In addition to specials such as saffron risotto with mussels, or wood-roasted chicken, is one of the best hamburgers in town. **FYI:** Reservations accepted. **Open:** Daily 11:30am–10pm. **Prices:** Main courses $7–$14. Maj CC. &

The Stinking Rose, 325 Columbus Ave, San Francisco (North Beach); tel 415/781-ROSE. At Broadway. **Italian.** Garlic, garlic everywhere, and so much to eat. From chicken with 40 cloves of garlic to bagna calda (roasted garlic in olive oil and butter with a hint of anchovy for dipping bread), this folksy restaurant specializes in garlic, otherwise known as the stinking rose. The decor is heavy with garlic braids, and there's even a gift shop full of garlicky offerings. It's no surprise that the restaurant's motto is "We season our garlic with food." **FYI:** Reservations recommended. **Open:** Sun–Thurs 11am–11pm, Fri–Sat 11am–midnight. Closed some hols. **Prices:** Main courses $7–$18. Maj CC. &

★ **Swan Oyster Depot**, 1517 Polk St, San Francisco (near Nob Hill); tel 415/673-1101. Between Sacramento and California Sts. **Seafood.** A classic San Francisco seafood bar, in operation since 1912 and oozing with character. No table seating; diners are served at an old-fashioned marble bar. Crab, shrimp, prawns, oysters, and clams are all served with sourdough bread. **FYI:**

Reservations not accepted. Beer and wine only. **Open:** Mon–Sat 8am–5:30pm. Closed some hols. **Prices:** Lunch main courses $2–$20. No CC. 🍷 🚙 ♿

Tadich Grill, 240 California St, San Francisco (Financial District); tel 415/391-1849. At Sansome St. **Seafood.** A San Francisco institution dating back to the gold rush; part of the city's colorful history. Known for simply prepared fresh seafood, hearty clam chowder, and crusty sourdough bread. Daily fish specials include petrale sole, poached salmon, swordfish steak, and Dungeness crab salad. **FYI:** Reservations not accepted. **Open:** Mon–Fri 11am–9pm, Sat 11:30am–9pm. Closed some hols. **Prices:** Main courses $12–$16. No CC. 🍷

♥ **The Terrace**, in the Ritz-Carlton San Francisco, 600 Stockton St, San Francisco (Nob Hill); tel 415/296-7465. Between California and Pine Sts. **Mediterranean.** On a sunny day, you can't beat this outdoor courtyard terrace surrounded by roses and next to a tinkling fountain. Inside, a more formal dining area offers Provençale-style chairs and crystal chandeliers. The Mediterranean cuisine emphasizes seasonal ingredients. Sunday Jazz Brunch, a local favorite, includes 3 choices of caviar and items from a made-to-order sushi cart. **FYI:** Reservations recommended. Jazz/piano. Children's menu. Dress code. **Open:** Daily 6:30am–10:30pm. **Prices:** Main courses $16–$21. Maj CC. 🍱 🎟 ♿

Thai Stick, 698 Post St, San Francisco (Downtown); tel 415/928-7730. At Jones St. **Thai.** One of the best Thai restaurants downtown, this spacious restaurant has floor-to-ceiling windows and is decorated in soothing, soft pastels. Try the Thai-style crêpes with shrimp, roast duck in red curry and coconut milk, and the charbroiled pork with sweet garlic sauce. **FYI:** Reservations accepted. Beer and wine only. **Open:** Lunch Mon–Fri 11am–3pm, Sat–Sun 11am–5pm; dinner Sun–Thurs 5–10pm, Fri–Sat 5–11pm. Closed some hols. **Prices:** Main courses $7–$12. Maj CC.

★ **This Is It**, 430 Geary Blvd, San Francisco (Union Square); tel 415/749-0201. At Mason St. **Middle Eastern.** Modern, clean family-run restaurant offering authentic Middle Eastern cuisine. Good value. **FYI:** Reservations not accepted. No liquor license. **Open:** Daily 10am–11pm. Closed Dec 25. **Prices:** Main courses $5–$14. Ltd CC.

Tommaso's, 1042 Kearny St, San Francisco (North Beach); tel 415/398-9696. At Broadway. **Italian.** One of San Francisco's favorite pizzerias. Small and intimate, decorated with murals. The pizza is made in a wood-fired oven. **FYI:** Reservations not accepted. Beer and wine only. **Open:** Tues–Sat 5–10:45pm, Sun 4–9:45pm. Closed Dec 25; Dec 18–Jan 8. **Prices:** Main courses $8–$20. Ltd CC.

⑤ **Tommy's Joynt**, 1109 Geary St, San Francisco (near Japantown); tel 415/775-4216. At Van Ness Ave. **German.** This San Francisco institution is known for its garish outdoor mural, hearty food, and low prices. Buffalo chili, oxtail sauté, meats carved to order. Dozens of imported beers. If you're really hungry, this is a great value. **FYI:** Reservations not accepted. **Open:** Daily 11am–2am. Closed some hols. **Prices:** Main courses $4–$6. No CC. 🍷

♥ **Tommy Toy's Chinoise**, 655 Montgomery St, San Francisco (Downtown); tel 415/397-4888. **Chinese/French.** The most refined Chinese restaurant in San Francisco. Tables are decorated with fine crystal and flowers. Cuisine combines Chinese, French, and California influences; menu offers lobster pot stickers, sea scallops, smoked duck with plum sauce, and wok-charred prawns in spices. **FYI:** Reservations recommended. **Open:** Lunch Mon–Fri 11:30am–3pm; dinner Mon–Sat 6–10pm, Sun 6–9:30pm. Closed some hols. **Prices:** Main courses $14–$19; PF dinner $48. Maj CC. 🎟 ♿

Vivande Porta Via, 2125 Fillmore St, San Francisco (Pacific Heights); tel 415/346-4430. At California St. **Italian.** An expensive trattoria attached to a specialty shop that sells Italian foods and products. Restaurant has tables and a marble counter for diners. Menu includes pastas, frittatas, and deli cold plates, as well as daily specials, soup, dessert, and Italian wines. **FYI:** Reservations not accepted. Beer and wine only. **Open:** Daily 11:30am–10pm. Closed some hols. **Prices:** Main courses $11–$17. Maj CC.

Wing Lum Cafe, 1150 Polk St, San Francisco; tel 415/771-6888. Between Sutter and Post Sts. **Chinese.** Extensive menu includes such classics as Kung Pao prawns, crispy duck, Mongolian beef, moo-shu pork, and hot and spicy eggplant. Lunch specials are inexpensive. **FYI:** Reservations not accepted. Beer and wine only. **Open:** Mon–Sat 11am–10pm, Sun 4–10pm. **Prices:** Main courses $6–$7; PF dinner $7.95–$8.95. Maj CC. 🚙 ▣

★ **Yank Sing**, 49 Stevenson St, San Francisco (Financial District); tel 415/541-4949. Off 1st St. **Chinese.** Casually elegant, modern Chinese dining, with floor-to-ceiling windows, etched glass, and mahogany pillars. Renowned for their dim sum—carts of appetizers roll by and you choose the ones you want. Try the steamed shrimp dumplings, pot stickers, scallops in rice balls, and barbecued pork buns. **FYI:** Reservations recommended. **Open:** Mon–Fri 11am–3pm. Closed some hols. **Prices:** Lunch main courses $2.50–$6. Maj CC. ♿

Ya Ya, 1220 9th Ave, San Francisco (Sunset); tel 415/566-6966. At Lincoln Way. **Californian/Middle Eastern.** Middle Eastern cuisine meets Californian in this small, popular restaurant.

Incredible decor of blue tiles, columns, and murals of Mesopotamia. Among the specialties are dolmas, seafood biriani, vegetarian ravioli, and bourak—ground beef in phyllo dough. **FYI:** Reservations accepted. Beer and wine only. **Open:** Lunch Tues–Fri 11:30am–2pm; dinner Tues–Sun 5:30–9:30pm. Closed some hols. **Prices:** Main courses $12.50–$26. Maj CC. &

Zona Rosa, 1797 Haight St, San Francisco (Haight-Ashbury); tel 415/668-7717. At Schrader St. **Mexican.** Brightly colored Formica tables, Mexican stone sculptures, and loud salsa aptly describe this taquería, serving burritos, tacos, and fajitas. **FYI:** Reservations not accepted. No liquor license. **Open:** Daily 11am–10:30pm. Closed some hols. **Prices:** Main courses $2.25–$5. No CC.

★ **Zuni Cafe**, 1658 Market St, San Francisco (Civic Center); tel 415/552-2522. Between Franklin and Gough Sts. **Mediterranean.** With a southwestern motif, featuring a tiled facade, glazed terra-cotta floors, a copper bar, and as the centerpiece a grand piano with a huge vase of flowers. The food is extremely good and reasonably priced, leaning to French and Italian specialties, including wood-fired pizza, roast chicken, house-cured pork chops, and grilled yellowfin tuna. **FYI:** Reservations recommended. Piano. **Open:** Tues–Sat 7:30am–midnight, Sun 7:30am–11pm. Closed some hols. **Prices:** Main courses $10–$18. Maj CC. &

Refreshment Stop 🍵

★ **Mario's Bohemian Cigar Store**, 566 Columbus Ave, San Francisco (North Beach); tel 415/362-0536. At Union St. **Cafe/Italian.** Neighborhood bar and cafe with historic flavor, small and always packed: a good spot to meet local artists, musicians, and eccentrics. Sandwiches on focaccia bread, homemade meatball sandwiches, and ricotta cheesecake are specialties. **Open:** Daily 11am–midnight. Closed some hols. No CC.

Attractions 🖼

TOP ATTRACTIONS

Alcatraz Island; tel 415/546-2628 or 556-0560. In 1934 the United States inaugurated what would quickly become the most famous maximum-security prison in the world: the federal penitentiary on Alcatraz Island. During the heyday of organized crime, several notorious mobsters did time on "the Rock," as it came to be called. These included such legendary figures as John Dillinger, Al Capone, "Pretty Boy" Floyd, and "Machine Gun" Kelly. Located only a mile from shore, Alcatraz was nonetheless considered escape-proof because it was surrounded by the bone-chilling waters of San Francisco Bay, with currents powerful enough to defeat even the strongest swimmer. Potential escapees

often drowned in the attempt, although no bodies were ever recovered after a jailbreak by 3 inmates in 1962. The prison was finally shut down in 1963.

Today a trip to Alcatraz Island is among San Francisco's top tourist attractions. National Park Service rangers conduct tours of the island that cover a wide range of topics. Visitors may also take an audio tour of the prison cell house and view a slide show. The **Red and White Fleet** makes trips several times daily; ferries depart from Pier 41 by Fisherman's Wharf approximately every 30 minutes. Advance reservations highly recommended. **Open:** Winter, daily 9:30am–2:45pm; extended hours in summer. Closed some hols. $$$

Golden Gate Bridge; tel 415/921-5858. Probably the most beautiful, and certainly the most frequently photographed, bridge in the world, the mile-long Golden Gate Bridge towers a maximum of 746 feet above the waters of San Francisco Bay, connecting San Francisco with southern Marin County. If traveling by car ($3 toll, payable southbound), park in the lot at the foot of the bridge (on the city side; when approaching the bridge drive slowly, stay in the right-hand lane, and exit into the lot at the base of the bridge) and make the crossing by foot. Millions of pedestrians walk across the bridge each year, but be prepared; it's often windy, cold, and the bridge vibrates. **Open:** Daily. Closed during foggy periods. $

Cable Cars; tel 415/673-6864. Designated official historic landmarks by the National Park Service in 1964, these rolling symbols continuously cross the city like mobile museum pieces. The world's only surviving system of cable cars, it underwent a $60 million renovation in 1982. The two types of cable cars in use hold, respectively, a maximum of 90 and 100 passengers and the limits are rigidly enforced. **Open:** Daily. $

Fisherman's Wharf. Originally called Meigg's Wharf, this bustling strip of waterfront, located at the foot of Taylor St, got its present name from the generations of fishermen who used to base their boats here. Upon landing at the wharf, fishermen would sell their catch fresh off the boat to homemakers and restauranteurs.

The area is now a festive marketplace pulsing with shoppers, diners, people-watchers, and street performers. There are no fishermen to be found, but there are scores of seafood restaurants and stalls, as well as dozens of stores, selling everything from original art to cans of "San Francisco Fog," and innumerable street hawkers and tourist traps. Cruises to Alcatraz Island and around the bay also leave from this area. **Open:** Wharf, daily 24 hours; most area shops, daily 11am–8pm (later during summer); most restaurants, Sun–Thurs 10am–midnight, Fri–Sat 10am–2am.

Ghirardelli Square, 900 North Point St; tel 415/775-5500. Located at Polk and Larkin Sts, the Ghirardelli complex is best known as the former chocolate and spice factory of Domingo Ghirardelli. Saved from demolition in 1962, it is now a 10-level mall with more than 50 shops and 20 eateries in all price ranges. A free map and mall guide is available at the information booth located in the center courtyard. On the plaza level is the Ghirardelli soda fountain, where small amounts of chocolate are still made and are available for purchase. **Open:** Shops, Mem Day–Labor Day, Mon–Sat 10am–9pm, Sun 10am–6pm; fall–spring, Mon–Thurs 10am–7pm, Fri–Sat 10am–9pm, Sun 10am–6pm. Restaurant hours vary. Free.

Pier 39; tel 415/981-7437 (recorded info). Located on the waterfront at Embarcadero and Beach St. This $54-million, 4.5-acre waterfront complex is the busiest of San Francisco's tourist-oriented bayside malls. Constructed on an abandoned cargo pier a few blocks east of Fisherman's Wharf, it is ostensibly a re-creation of a turn-of-the-century street scene, with more than 100 shops, 10 restaurants, a double-decked Venetian carousel, an arcade, and an assortment of street entertainers. A pair of marinas, housing the Blue and Gold bay sightseeing fleet, flank the pier. In recent years, a colony of about 600 California sea lions has taken up residence on the adjacent floating docks. They can usually be seen from Aug–June; a free interpretive program about the colony is usually given on weekends (call for details). **Open:** Shops, daily 10:30am–8:30pm; restaurants, daily 11:30am–11:30pm; bars, daily until 2am. Free.

The Cannery, 2801 Leavenworth St; tel 415/771-3112. Built in 1894 as a Del Monte company fruit-canning plant, this structure was redeveloped in 1963 as a vaguely Florentine shopping, eating, and entertainment complex. There are about a dozen eateries and more than 50 shops, and in the courtyard, amid a grove of century-old olive trees, are vendors' stalls and sidewalk cafes. The Museum of the City of San Francisco is located on the third floor. **Open:** Winter, Mon–Sat 10am–6pm, Sun 11am–6pm; summer and hols, Mon–Sat 10am–9pm, Sun 11am–9pm. Free.

Lombard Street. Between Hyde and Leavenworth Sts. Known as the "crookedest street in the world," Lombard Street makes 9 hairpin turns in the space of about a block, meandering down an extremely steep hillside dotted with expensive homes and rich flower gardens. The short stretch is one way, downhill only, and is sometimes choked with tourists. The hill can be negotiated on foot, either up or down, via staircases (without curves) on either side of the street.

USS Pampanito, Pier 45, Fisherman's Wharf; tel 415/441-5819. This battle-scarred World War II fleet submarine saw plenty of action in the Pacific. Now completely restored, the Pampanito's compartments are all open for visitors to explore. A taped guided audio tour is included with the admission fee. **Open:** Late May–Oct, daily 9am–8pm; Nov–late May, Sun–Thurs 9am–6pm, Fri–Sat 9am–8pm. $$

Mission Dolores, 16th and Dolores Sts; tel 415/621-8203. Surrounded by a 4-foot-thick adobe wall, Mission Dolores is the oldest structure in the city. It was founded as the sixth of the California missions by Friar Francisco Palou in 1776. Its interior is a curious mixture of native construction methods and Spanish-colonial style. **Open:** Daily 9am–4pm; Good Fri 10am–noon. Closed some hols. $

Coit Tower, 1 Telegraph Hill; tel 415/362-0808. Located atop Telegraph Hill, just east of North Beach, the 210-foot stone tower offers magnificent 360-degree views of San Francisco. Inside the base are some colorful murals entitled *Life in California, 1934*. Commissioned by the Public Works of Art project, under Franklin D Roosevelt's New Deal program, the restored frescoes are a curious blend of art and politics. **Open:** Summer, daily 10am–7pm; fall–spring, daily 10am–6pm. $

Fort Point National Historic Site; tel 415/556-2857. Located under the southern portion of the Golden Gate Bridge in the Presidio, Fort Point was completed in 1861. Although troops from the fort were used to guard the Golden Gate during the Civil War and World War II, no battle ever occurred at the fort. During construction of the Golden Gate Bridge (1933–37), the fort served as construction center of operations.

Designated a National Historic Site in 1970, Fort Point offers guided, self-guided, and audio cassette walking tours; a 17-minute movie covering the history of Fort Point from 1776 to World War II; and demonstrations of Civil War–era cannon loading and firing. Small museum at the visitor center. **Open:** Wed–Sun 10am–5pm. Closed some hols. Free.

Presidio of San Francisco, Lombard and Lyon Sts; tel 415/556-3111 or 556-1874. Once the headquarters for the US 6th Army, the Presidio is now part of the Golden Gate National Recreation Area. It offers 15,000 acres of extremely hilly, wooded parkland, popular with hikers and cyclists. **Open:** Daily 24 hours. Free.

San Francisco Zoological Gardens and Children's Zoo, Sloat Blvd and 45th Ave; tel 415/753-7080 or 753-7083 (recorded info). Among America's highest-rated animal parks, the zoo covers more than 65 acres and is home to more than 1,000 animals living in realistically landscaped enclosures. Major features are the Primate Discovery Center, known for its many rare and endangered species; Koala Crossing, patterned after an Australian outback station; Gorilla World, one of the world's largest great ape exhibits; Wolf World, exhibiting the sophisticated social behavior of the North American timber wolf; Lion House, home of Prince Charles, a rare white tiger; and Musk Ox Meadow, a 2.5-acre habitat for a herd of rare white-fronted musk oxen brought from Alaska. The **Children's Zoo,** adjacent to the main park, allows visitors to get close to a variety of baby animals. A free, informal walking tour of the zoo leaves from Koala Crossing at 12:30 and 2:30pm on weekends. The Zebra Zephyr train tour takes visitors on a 20-minute "safari" daily (in winter, only on weekends). The tour is $2 for adults, $1 for children 15 and under. **Open:** Main zoo, daily 10am–5pm; children's zoo, daily 11am–4pm. $$$

San Francisco Experience, Pier 39; tel 415/982-7394 or 982-7550 (recorded info). Located on the waterfront at Embarcadero and Beach St. Two centuries of the city's history have been condensed into a 28-minute multimedia show, supplemented by special effects that include a San Francisco "fog" that actually rolls in. Presented on a 70- by 30-foot screen, the show is fast-paced, informative, and highly entertaining. **Open:** Jan–Mar, shows daily (every half hour) 10am–8:30pm; Apr–Dec, shows daily (every half hour) 10am–9:30pm. $$$

San Francisco–Oakland Bay Bridge. Although less visually appealing than the nearby Golden Gate, the Bay Bridge is spectacular as a feat of structural engineering. With a total length of 8¼ miles, it is one of the world's longest steel bridges, but is actually made up of a superbly dovetailed series of spans. The upper deck carries 5 lanes of traffic westbound, the lower, 5 lanes eastbound. Drive across the bridge (the toll is $1, paid westbound), or catch a bus at the Transbay Terminal (Mission St at First St) and ride to downtown Oakland.

MUSEUMS

San Francisco Museum of Modern Art, 151 Third St; tel 415/357-4000. *(The museum should be reopened at this new site, between Mission and Howard Sts, by press time.)* Opened in 1935, SFMOMA was the first museum on the West Coast devoted solely to 20th-century art, and one of the first to recognize photography as a serious art form. Its new home, a 225,000-square-foot building, is the second-largest single structure in the United States devoted to modern art. The permanent collection contains more than 4,000 paintings, sculptures, and works on paper, as well as objects related to architecture and the media arts. There are more than 8,000 photographs by such notables as Ansel Adams, Alfred Stieglitz, and Edward Weston. Temporary exhibits cover a broad range of styles and media. Guided tours are offered daily (phone for schedule). Bookstore; cafeteria. **Open:** Tues–Wed and Fri–Sun 11am–6pm, Thurs 11am–9pm. Closed some hols. $$$

San Francisco Maritime National Historical Park and Museum, Foot of Polk St (at Beach St); tel 415/556-3002. This museum is a treasure trove of sailing, whaling, and fishing lore. Exhibits include intricate ship models, scrimshaw, and photographs, including an 1851 shot of hundreds of abandoned ships that were deserted *en masse,* their crews having succumbed to "gold fever." Two blocks east of the museum building are the Historic Ships at Hyde Street Pier, several museum-operated historic vessels that are now moored and open to the public. They include the *Balclutha,* one of the last surviving square-riggers and the handsomest vessel in San Francisco Bay; the *Eureka,* the last of the 50 paddle-wheeled ferries that plied the waters of San Francisco Bay; the West Coast lumber schooner *C.A. Thayer;* and the *Hercules,* a huge 1907 oceangoing steam tug. **Open:** Daily 10am–5pm. Closed some hols. Free.

M H de Young Memorial Museum; tel 415/750-3600, or 863-3330 (recorded info). One of the city's oldest museums, the de Young is located on the Music Concourse in Golden Gate Park, near 10th Ave and Fulton St. It houses a hodgepodge of art that spans continents and centuries, but it is best known for its American art, which has pieces dating from colonial times to the 20th century. There is an important textile collection as well, with primary emphasis on rugs from central Asia and the Near East. Traveling exhibitions are equally eclectic, ranging from ancient rugs to great Dutch paintings. Docent tours are offered daily; phone for times. Admission includes the Asian Art Museum (see below). (Admission fee may be higher for special exhibitions; no admission fee is charged on the first Wednesday and first Saturday morning of each month.) **Open:** Wed–Sun 10am–5pm. Closed some hols. $$

California Academy of Sciences; tel 415/221-5100 or 750-7145 (recorded info). Located on the Music Concourse of Golden Gate Park, this group of related exhibitions (all part of the Natural History Museum) includes: the **Steinhart Aquarium,** with some 14,000 specimens of fish, marine mammals, amphibians, reptiles, and penguins, and a living coral reef that is the largest display of its kind in the country; the **Morrison Planetarium,** with its 65-foot dome, presenting 4 major exhibits each year (phone for schedule; shows not recommended for preschoolers); the "Wild California" exhibit, featuring a 14,000-gallon aquarium and a seabird rookery; and "Life Through Time," a massive exhibit that ushers visitors through 3.5 billion years of earth history and evolution. **Open:** Labor Day–July 4, daily 10am–5pm; July 4–Labor Day, daily 10am–7pm; first Wed of every month, 10am–8:45pm. $$$

Asian Art Museum; tel 415/668-8921. Located near 10th Ave and Fulton St in Golden Gate Park, this museum contains an array of art and artifacts from 40 countries, especially from

China, including sculptures, paintings, bronzes, ceramics, jades, and decorative objects. Also exhibits from Pakistan, India, Tibet, Japan, and Southeast Asia, including the oldest known dated Chinese Buddha. Guided tours dauly; phone for hours. Admission includes M H de Young Memorial Museum (see above). **Open:** Wed–Sun 10am–5pm. $$

Cable Car Museum, 1201 Mason St; tel 415/474-1887. Preserved here is the history of the only surviving operational cable car system in the world. Antique cars, including one of Andrew Halladie's first Clay St cars from 1873, are on display, along with historic photographs and memorabilia, a scale model collection, and a video illustrating the operation of the cable car system. An underground viewing room lets visitors witness the operation of the cable winding machinery. At the museum shop visitors can buy cable and track sections, conductor bells, models, and more. **Open:** Apr–Oct, daily 10am–6pm; Nov–Mar, daily 10am–5pm. Closed some hols. Free.

Old Mint, 5th and Mission Sts; tel 415/744-6830. First opened in 1874, the Old Mint is one of the finest examples of Federal classical revival architecture in the West. Left intact and standing virtually alone after the devastating 1906 earthquake, the Mint was the only financial institution able to open for business and took over responsibility for the city's monetary affairs.

The restored building is now a museum, featuring the offices of the superintendent, director, and treasurer, all redecorated in 19th-century style; the gold vault; an authentic re-creation of a miner's cabin; and several exhibits, including a display of US national medals, a stampmill for crushing ore, and an 1869 coin press equipped with a trigger to let visitors strike their own bronze souvenir medal. Numismatic sales room on first floor. **Open:** Mon–Fri 10am–4pm. Closed some hols. Free.

Ansel Adams Center for Photography, 250 4th St; tel 415/495-7000. The center features 5 galleries of changing exhibits of photography in all its forms, ranging from 19th-century works to installations that incorporate sound, sculpture, and video. Guided tours available. Free admission first Tues of the month. **Open:** Tues–Sun 11am–5pm, first Thurs of month 11am–8pm. Closed some hols. $$

Exploratorium, 3601 Lyon St; tel 415/563-7337 or 561-0360 (recorded info). This fun, hands-on science fair is a participatory venture, with more than 650 permanent exhibits that explore everything from color theory to Einstein's Theory of Relativity. Housed in the only building left standing from the Panama-Pacific Exposition of 1915, which celebrated the opening of the Panama Canal. **Open:** Mem Day–Labor Day, Mon–Tues and Thurs–Sun 10am–5pm, Wed 10am–9:30pm; rest of the year, Tues and Thurs–Sun 10am–5pm, Wed 10am–9:30pm. Closed some hols. $$$

Wells Fargo History Museum, 420 Montgomery St; tel 415/396-2619. This history museum, at the bank's head office, houses hundreds of genuine relics from the company's early history during the Gold Rush era. A genuine Concord stagecoach stands in the window of the main room. Other exhibits include telegraph equipment, gold nuggets and coins, western Pony Express stamps, and mementos of such infamous figures as "Black Bart," the verse-writing humorist who single-handedly robbed 27 stages. **Open:** Mon–Fri 9am–5pm. Closed some hols. Free.

Treasure Island Museum, 410 Palm Ave; tel 415/395-5067. Located on Treasure Island, 2 miles E of San Francisco via the Bay Bridge, this museum contains exhibits covering a wide range of topics, including the history of Yerba Buena Island, the Bay Bridge, the famous *China Clipper* seaplanes of the 1930s, and the Golden Gate International Exposition of 1939–40, for which Treasure Island was constructed. **Open:** Daily 10am–3:30pm. Closed some hols. Free.

Guinness Museum of World Records, 235 Jefferson St; tel 415/771-9890. Kids will enjoy this large collection of exhibits, which deal with a variety of worldwide superlatives, from the world's fattest man to the world's smallest camera. Participatory exhibits let visitors try to break records of their own. **Open:** Summer, Sun–Thurs 10am–11pm, Fri–Sat 10am–midnight; spring–fall, Sun–Thurs 11am–10pm, Fri–Sat 10am–midnight. Closed some hols. $$$

Ripley's Believe It Or Not! Museum, 175 Jefferson St; tel 415/771-6188. A bizarre collection of oddities collected by Robert L Ripley in the course of his world travels; includes a one-third-scale model of a cable car built from matchsticks and a dinosaur made of chrome car bumpers. **Open:** June 15–Labor Day, daily 9am–11pm; early Sept–June 14, Sun–Thurs 10am–10pm, Fri–Sat 10am–midnight. $$$

Wax Museum, 145 Jefferson St; tel 415/202-0400. Features more than 200 lifelike figures, mostly devoted to modern-day celebrities such as pop star Michael Jackson. Other tableau themes include Royalty, Great Humanitarians, Feared Leaders, and Chamber of Horrors. **Open:** Daily 9am–10pm; extended hours in summer and on holidays. $$$

OTHER ATTRACTIONS

Alamo Square Historic District. San Francisco's plethora of beautiful Victorian homes is one of the city's greatest assets. Most of the 14,000 extant structures are private residences dating from the second half of the 19th century. The small area bordered by Divisadero St on the west, Golden Gate Ave on the north, Webster St on the east, and Fell St on the south has one of the city's greatest concentrations of these "Painted Ladies." Almost uniformly tall and narrow, these houses were built *en masse*, in developments, and many share common walls. Having little to do with the Victorian style of architecture, they are called Victorian only because they were built during the reign of Queen Victoria.

Haas–Lilienthal House, 2007 Franklin St; tel 415/441-3004 (recorded info). One of the city's many gingerbread Victorians, this 1886 structure features all the architectural frills of the period, and is fully furnished with contemporary pieces. One-hour guided tours are given 2 days a week. **Open:** Wed noon–4pm, Sun 11am–5pm. $$

Octagon House, 2645 Gough St; tel 415/441-7512. This unusual, 8-sided, cupola-topped house (1861) contains furniture, silverware, American pewter, and even some historical documents from the Colonial and Federal periods. Maintained by the National Society of Colonial Dames of America. **Open:** 2nd Sun and 2nd and 4th Thurs of each month, noon–3pm. Closed Jan and hols. Free.

Transamerica Pyramid, 600 Montgomery St; tel 415/983-4100. This 48-story wedge, capped by a 212-foot spire, is the tallest and most distinctive building in the San Francisco skyline. It was completed in 1972.

Bank of America World Headquarters, 555 California St. This carnelian marble-covered building dates from 1969. Its 52 stories are topped by a panoramic restaurant and bar, the Carnelian Room. The focal point of the building's formal plaza is an abstract black granite sculpture known locally as the "Banker's Heart."

Japan Center, Post and Buchanan Sts; tel 415/922-6776. This is an immense, Asian-oriented shopping mall located in San Francisco's revitalized Japantown, about a mile west of Union Square. Dozens of shops feature everything from cameras and radios to pearls and silk kimonos. The mall's centerpiece is a 5-tiered Peace Pagoda designed by Japanese architect Yoshiro Taniguchi. The renowned **Kabuki Hot Spring,** 1750 Geary Blvd (tel 922-6000), is the center's most famous tenant. Japantown, or Nihonmachi, San Francisco's Japanese quarter, occupies four square blocks directly north of the Japan Center. **Open:** Mon–Fri 10am–10pm, Sat–Sun 9am–10pm.

Bay Area Rapid Transit (BART), 800 Madison St; tel 415/788-BART or 510/465-BART in Oakland. One of the world's most famous commuter systems, BART's 71 miles of rail link 8 San Francisco stations with Daly City to the south and 25 stations in the East Bay. BART runs under the bay using one of the world's longest underwater tunnels. The people who run BART think so highly of their trains and stations that they sell a $2.60 "Excursion Ticket," which allows visitors, in effect, to "sightsee" the BART system (phone for details). **Open:** Daily, 24 hours. $

Fort Mason, Bay and Franklin Sts. This former military installation and headquarters for the Pacific Fleet during World War II is now a park. Fort Mason Center is a complex of buildings housing theaters, galleries, and various arts programs. Hundreds of activities are held here each month, including concerts and fairs on the adjacent piers.

Aquatic Park. Located at the foot of Hyde St, adjacent to Ghirardelli Square, this green lawn and protected marina were built in 1937 as a project of the federal Works Progress Administration.

Haunted Gold Mine, 113 Jefferson St; tel 415/202-0440. All the elements of a traditional fun house—mazes, a hall of mirrors, wind tunnels, and animated ghouls—comprise this haunted house. Even young children will probably not find it too scary. **Open:** Daily 9am–10pm; extended hours in summer and on hols. $$

Garden Court, Sheraton Palace Hotel, 2 New Montgomery St; tel 415/392-8600. This spectacular enclosed courtyard is topped by a lofty, iridescent glass roof supported by 16 Doric columns. Rebuilt in 1909 after the Great Earthquake, the elegant court has been painstakingly restored, with marble floors, crystal chandeliers, and a leaded-glass ceiling. The hotel, situated between Market and Third Sts, reopened in 1991. **Open:** Daily 24 hours. Free.

Candlestick Park, Giants Dr and Gilman Ave. Located about 8 miles south of downtown on US 101. From April–October the National League Giants play their home baseball games at the park (tel 415/467-8000). The NFL's 49ers play from late August–September (tel 415/468-2249). Tickets available at the park or by phone through BASS Ticketmaster (510/762-2277).

SAN FRANCISCO INTERNATIONAL AIRPORT

See Burlingame, Millbrae, San Francisco, South San Francisco

SAN GABRIEL

Map page M-3, D2 (E of Los Angeles)

Attraction 🖼

Mission San Gabriel Archangel, 537 W Mission Dr; tel 818/282-5191. The mission compound encompasses an aqueduct, a cemetery, a winery, a tannery, a mission church, and a famous set of bells. The most notable contents of the museum are Native American paintings depicting the Stations of the Cross, painted on sailcloth with paints made from crushing the petals of desert flowers. **Open:** Daily 9am–4pm. $

SAN JOSE

Map page M-2, D2

Hotels 🖼

≣≣≣ Courtyard by Marriott, 1727 Technology Dr, San Jose, CA 95110 (San Jose Int'l Airport); tel 408/441-6111 or toll free 800/321-2211; fax 408/441-8039. N 1st St exit off US 101; left on Technology Dr. Great location near San Jose International Airport and Silicon Valley, yet not noisy. A very nice lobby area, a lot of natural light, and a pleasant restaurant for breakfast. **Rooms:** 151 rms and stes. CI 3pm/CO 1pm. Express checkout avail. Nonsmoking rms avail. **Amenities:** 🛅 🗄 📲 A/C, cable TV w/movies, voice mail. Some units w/terraces. **Services:** ✕ 🚐 🖂 ⊄ **Facilities:** 🔁 🏋 🎱 ⅙ 1 rst, 1 bar, whirlpool, washer/dryer. **Rates:** $95 S; $105 D; from $108 ste. Children under 12 stay free. Spec packages avail. Pking: Outdoor, free. Maj CC. Corporate rates available.

≣≣≣≣ Fairmont Hotel, 170 Market St, San Jose, CA 95113 (Downtown); tel 408/998-1900; fax 408/287-1648. Guadalupe Pkwy (Calif 87) exit off I-280. Opened in 1987, the Fairmont recalls the glamour of grand hotels, with crystal chandeliers, 3-foot-thick columns, and what seems like acres of marble in the lobby. **Rooms:** 544 rms and stes. CI 3pm/CO noon. Express checkout avail. Nonsmoking rms avail. European-style furnishings. Bathrooms, lined in Italian marble, have ample counter space. Lanai accommodations have private terraces right beside the pool area. **Amenities:** 🛅 🗄 🍷 A/C, cable TV w/movies, refrig, voice mail, shoe polisher, bathrobes. All units w/minibars, some w/terraces, some w/fireplaces, some w/Jacuzzis. Small TV and scale in the bathroom, oversize towels, electric shoe polisher. **Services:** |◎| 🗝 📼 🚐 🖂 ⊄ Twice-daily maid svce, car-rental desk, masseur, babysitting. **Facilities:** 🔁 🏋 🖳 ⅙ 4 rsts, 5 bars (1 w/entertainment), spa, sauna, steam rm,

beauty salon. Swimming pool is bordered by palm trees. Extremely well-equipped health club offers Nautilus machines, Stairmasters, massage rooms, extensive locker facilities. **Rates:** $135–$195 S or D; from $400 ste. Extra person $25. Children under 18 stay free. Higher rates for spec evnts/hols. Spec packages avail. Pking: Indoor, $9.75. Maj CC. Rates lower on weekends.

≣≣≣ Holiday Inn–Park Center Plaza, 282 Almaden Blvd at San Carlos, San Jose, CA 95113 (Downtown); tel 408/998-0400 or toll free 800/HOLIDAY; fax 408/289-9081. Guadalupe Pkwy exit off US 101. Lobby clean, but uninspired. Uninviting entrance. **Rooms:** 231 rms and stes. CI 2pm/CO noon. Express checkout avail. Nonsmoking rms avail. **Amenities:** 🛅 🗄 A/C, cable TV, voice mail. **Services:** ✕ 🚐 🖂 ⊄ ⊄ Twice-daily maid svce, car-rental desk. **Facilities:** 🔁 🏋 🖳 ⅙ 1 rst, 1 bar (w/entertainment). **Rates:** $101 S or D; from $201 ste. Extra person $10. Children under 21 stay free. Spec packages avail. Pking: Indoor/outdoor, free. Maj CC. Special deals for business travelers.

≣≣≣ Holiday Inn Silicon Valley, 399 Silicon Valley Blvd, San Jose, CA 95138; tel 408/972-7800 or toll free 800/HOLIDAY; fax 408/972-0157. Bernal exit off US 101; turn left on Silicon Valley Blvd. A 5-year-old hotel in a Spanish-style building with high-ceilings and a huge atrium lobby. Set in the southernmost part of San Jose. **Rooms:** 147 rms and stes. CI 3pm/CO noon. Nonsmoking rms avail. Rooms are standard but attractively decorated. **Amenities:** 🛅 🗄 🍷 A/C, cable TV w/movies. Some units w/terraces. **Services:** ✕ 🚐 🖂 ⊄ Car-rental desk. Complimentary newspapers. **Facilities:** 🔁 🏋 🖳 ⅙ 1 rst, 1 bar (w/entertainment), whirlpool. **Rates:** $79–$89 S or D; from $89 ste. Extra person $10. Children under 12 stay free. Spec packages avail. Pking: Outdoor, free. Maj CC.

≣≣≣ Homewood Suites, 10 W Trimble Rd, San Jose, CA 95131; tel 408/428-9900 or toll free 800/CALL-HOME; fax 408/428-0222. **Rooms:** 140 stes. CI 3pm/CO noon. Express checkout avail. Nonsmoking rms avail. Suites have ceiling fans in bedroom, iron and ironing boards. Some 2-bedroom suites available. **Amenities:** 🛅 🗄 📲 A/C, satel TV w/movies, refrig, VCR, voice mail. All units w/minibars, some w/terraces, some w/fireplaces. **Services:** 🗝 🚐 🖂 ⊄ ⊄ Twice-daily maid svce, car-rental desk, babysitting. Complimentary breakfast, grocery shopping service, free coffee and popcorn. Free shuttle within 5 miles. **Facilities:** 🔁 🏋 🎱 🖳 ⅙ Whirlpool, washer/dryer. Volleyball and basketball courts; convenience store on premises. **Rates (BB):** From $129 ste. Children under 18 stay free. Higher rates for spec evnts/hols. Spec packages avail. Pking: Outdoor, free. Maj CC.

≣≣≣≣**Hotel De Anza**, 233 W Santa Clara St, San Jose, CA 95113 (Downtown); tel 408/286-1000 or toll free 800/843-3700; fax 408/286-0500. Park Ave exit off 87. A refurbished historic hotel in the heart of downtown San Jose. Very special accommodations, particularly for business travelers. **Rooms:** 101 rms and stes. CI 3pm/CO noon. Express checkout avail. Nonsmoking rms avail. High-ceilinged rooms are elegantly outfitted with art deco–style furniture, original artwork, crown moldings, and inlaid wooden cabinets. Padded benches at the foot of each bed. **Amenities:** 🛗 🕎 A/C, cable TV w/movies, refrig, VCR, voice mail, bathrobes. Some units w/minibars, some w/terraces, 1 w/fireplace, some w/Jacuzzis. VCRs, minibars, television and telephone in bathroom. Multiple-line desk phone with dedicated fax line in each room. Fax machines and computers available. **Services:** ✗ 🗝 VP 🚗 🛅 🛎 Twice-daily maid svce, car-rental desk, babysitting. Complimentary "Raid Our Pantry" buffet 10pm–5am daily. Full secretarial service available. **Facilities:** 🍴 75 🖥 2 rsts, 1 bar (w/entertainment), washer/dryer. Palm Court Terrace, an entertainment patio and garden, is available for parties and receptions. Meeting rooms are beautiful. **Rates:** $120–$140 S or D; from $250 ste. Children under 12 stay free. Spec packages avail. Pking: Indoor, $3–$5. Maj CC.

≣≣≣≣**Hotel Sainte Claire**, 302 S Market St, San Jose, CA 95113 (Downtown); tel 408/295-2000 or toll free 800/824-6835. Elegant old-fashioned lobby with fine furnishings and classical music. Beautiful beamed and stenciled ceiling, potted palms, and fireplace give an old-world feel. **Rooms:** 170 rms and stes. CI 3pm/CO noon. Express checkout avail. Nonsmoking rms avail. Fine furnishings, original artwork, coordinated upholstery and linens. High, old-fashioned beds. **Amenities:** 🛗 🕎 🖥 A/C, cable TV w/movies, refrig, voice mail, in-rm safe, shoe polisher. All units w/minibars, some w/fireplaces, some w/Jacuzzis. **Services:** 🍽 🗝 VP 🚗 🛅 🛎 Twice-daily maid svce, car-rental desk, babysitting. **Facilities:** 🍴 250 🖥 🕎 1 rst, 1 bar (w/entertainment). **Rates:** $95–$105 S; $135–$155 D; from $165 ste. Extra person $15. Children under 12 stay free. Spec packages avail. Pking: Indoor, $8. Maj CC.

Hyatt San Jose at San Jose Airport, 1740 N 1st St, San Jose, CA 95112 (San Jose Int'l Airport); tel 408/993-1234 or toll free 800/233-1234; fax 408/453-0259. Blooming flowers and manicured gardens make the grounds very attractive. Unrated. **Rooms:** 474 rms and stes. Exec-level rms avail. CI 3pm/CO noon. Express checkout avail. Nonsmoking rms avail. Rooms are a bit small. **Amenities:** 🛗 🕎 🖥 A/C, cable TV w/movies. Some

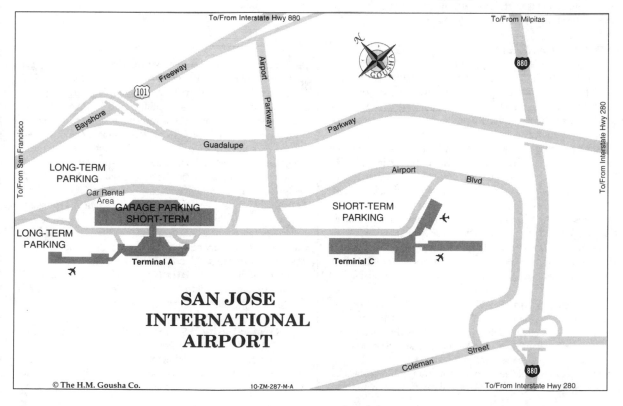

SAN JOSE INTERNATIONAL AIRPORT

© The H.M. Gousha Co.   10-ZM-287-M-A

units w/minibars, some w/terraces, 1 w/Jacuzzi. **Services:** ✗ 🗝 🚗 🖼 🛎 Twice-daily maid svce, car-rental desk, masseur, babysitting. **Facilities:** 🎏 🏋 🛎 🎱 💻 ♿ 3 rsts, 1 bar, games rm, whirlpool, beauty salon. New fitness center and business center. **Rates:** $105–$129 S; $130–$154 D; from $149 ste. Extra person $25. Children under 18 stay free. Spec packages avail. Pking: Outdoor, free. Maj CC.

≣≣≣ **Le Baron Hotel**, 1350 N 1st St, San Jose, CA 95112; tel 408/453-6200 or toll free 800/662-9896; fax 408/437-9558. This hotel is being upgraded to meet Best Western standards. An ornate but tacky spiral staircase leads to lounge area, decorated with commercial artwork and fake plants. **Rooms:** 327 rms and stes. Exec-level rms avail. CI 3pm/CO noon. Nonsmoking rms avail. Suites are dramatic and sumptuous, but rooms are not. **Amenities:** 🛏 🍸 🗣 A/C, cable TV w/movies, voice mail. Some units w/minibars, some w/Jacuzzis. **Services:** ✗ 🗝 🚗 🖼 🛎 🔔 Car-rental desk, children's program, babysitting. **Facilities:** 🎏 🛎 🎱 💻 ♿ 2 rsts, 3 bars (1 w/entertainment), washer/dryer. Small pool area, visible from lobby, is edged by potentially slippery deck. Pretty 9th-floor restaurant has garden theme, with lattices and floral draperies. **Rates:** HS July–Oct $75–$95 S or D; from $125 ste. Extra person $10. Children under 18 stay free. Lower rates off-season. Higher rates for spec evnts/hols. Spec packages avail. Pking: Outdoor, free. Maj CC.

≣≣≣ **Radisson Plaza Hotel**, 1471 N 4th St, San Jose, CA 95112; tel 408/452-0200 or toll free 800/333-3333; fax 408/452-0736. N 1st St exit off US 101; right on 1st St, left on Gish Rd, left on N 4th St. Lovely styling with wood paneling, European furnishings, and tasteful crystal chandeliers. Close to the airport and civic center. **Rooms:** 185 rms and stes. Exec-level rms avail. CI 3pm/CO noon. Express checkout avail. Nonsmoking rms avail. Rooms are individually decorated and quite lovely, with nice fabrics and artwork. **Amenities:** 🛏 🍸 🗣 A/C, cable TV w/movies, voice mail. All units w/minibars, some w/terraces, some w/Jacuzzis. **Services:** ✗ 🗝 🚗 🖼 🛎 Car-rental desk, babysitting. Shuttle to shopping and restaurants. **Facilities:** 🎏 🛎 🏊 ♿ 1 rst, 1 bar, whirlpool. Beautiful, antique-filled restaurant. Use of San Jose Athletic Club for $6. **Rates:** HS Jan–Oct $89 S; $109 D; from $125 ste. Extra person $11. Children under 12 stay free. Lower rates off-season. Higher rates for spec evnts/hols. Pking: Indoor/outdoor, free. Maj CC.

≣≣≣ **Red Lion Hotel**, 2050 Gateway Place, San Jose, CA 95110; tel 408/453-4000 or toll free 800/547-8010; fax 408/437-2899. The lobby is slightly gaudy, with marble-tiled floors, plastic-paneled chandeliers, and lots of brass and glass. **Rooms:** 505 rms and stes. Exec-level rms avail. CI 3pm/CO 1pm. Express checkout avail. Nonsmoking rms avail. Suites are tasteful and spacious, with beautiful lighting, full bar area, lots of mirrors,

and a luxurious bathroom. **Amenities:** 🛏 🍸 🗣 A/C, cable TV w/movies. All units w/terraces, some w/Jacuzzis. **Services:** ✗ 🗝 🆅🅿 🚗 🖼 🔔 Car-rental desk, babysitting. **Facilities:** 🎏 🏋 🛎 🍸 ♿ 2 rsts, 2 bars (1 w/entertainment), sauna, whirlpool, beauty salon, washer/dryer. **Rates:** $125–$147 S; $135–$157 D; from $225 ste. Extra person $15. Children under 18 stay free. Spec packages avail. Pking: Outdoor, free. Maj CC.

≣≣≣ **San Jose Hilton and Towers**, 300 Almaden Blvd, San Jose, CA 95110 (Downtown); tel 408/287-2100 or toll free 800/HILTONS; fax 408/947-4488. Vine/Almaden exit off I-280; left on Almaden Blvd. In the heart of the business district, with a light-rail station just outside hotel entrance. Well-appointed lobby with nice artwork. **Rooms:** 355 rms and stes. Exec-level rms avail. CI 4pm/CO 1pm. Express checkout avail. Nonsmoking rms avail. **Amenities:** 🛏 🍸 🗣 A/C, cable TV w/movies, voice mail. Some units w/minibars. **Services:** ✗ 🗝 🆅🅿 🚗 🖼 🛎 🔔 Car-rental desk, babysitting. Business services available. **Facilities:** 🎏 🛎 🏊 ♿ 1 rst, 1 bar, lifeguard, whirlpool, washer/dryer. Very small outside pool on 3rd-floor deck. Guests have access to San Jose Athletic Club facilities. **Rates:** $125–$155 S; $145–$175 D; from $250 ste. Extra person $20. Children under 18 stay free. Spec packages avail. Pking: Indoor, $5–$9. Maj CC.

Motels

≣≣≣ **Best Western Gateway Inn**, 2585 Seaboard Ave, San Jose, CA 95131; tel 408/435-8800 or toll free 800/437-8855; fax 408/435-8879. Trimble Rd exit off US 101; right on Seaboard Ave. Elegant high ceilings, faux marble, and nice European-style furniture accent the lobby, along with floor-to-ceiling windows and crystal chandeliers. **Rooms:** 146 rms. Exec-level rms avail. CI 2pm/CO noon. Express checkout avail. Nonsmoking rms avail. Rooms are nicely appointed, in spite of fluorescent lighting. Most rooms are nonsmoking. **Amenities:** 🛏 🍸 🗣 A/C, satel TV w/movies, refrig. **Services:** 🚗 🖼 🛎 🔔 Twice-daily maid svce, car-rental desk, children's program, babysitting. Complimentary breakfast buffet in the lobby. Free coffee, tea, and cookies in the afternoon. Free local telephone calls. Free shuttle service within a 5-mile radius. **Facilities:** 🎏 🛎 🏊 ♿ Sauna, whirlpool. Complimentary use of nearby California Athletic Club. **Rates (CP):** HS June–Aug $62 S; $67 D. Extra person $5. Children under 18 stay free. Lower rates off-season. Spec packages avail. Pking: Outdoor, free. Maj CC.

≣≣ **Comfort Inn**, 1215 S 1st St, San Jose, CA 95110; tel 408/280-5300 or toll free 800/221-2222. Almaden/Vine exit off I-280. Sparsely decorated lobby off a busy street near a shabby neighborhood. **Rooms:** 57 rms and effic. CI 2pm/CO 11am. Nonsmoking rms avail. Good soundproofing and lots of extras.

Amenities: ▨ ▨ ▨ ▨ A/C, cable TV w/movies, refrig, VCR. All units w/minibars, some w/Jacuzzis. **Services:** ▨ ▨ **Facilities:** ▨ **Rates (CP):** $45–$50 S; $55–$65 D; from $55 effic. Children under 18 stay free. Higher rates for spec evnts/hols. Pking: Outdoor, free. Maj CC.

Restaurants ▨

El Maghreb, 145 W Santa Clara St, San Jose; tel 408/294-2243. Guadalupe Pkwy exit off Calif 280. **Moroccan.** Exotic, romantic Moroccan atmosphere. Sit on low cushions or banquettes covered in jewel-toned velvet. Moorish mosaics, oriental carpets, desert murals cover the walls. Offers several multicourse dinners, which include 3 Moroccan salads, bastella (flaky pastry filled with chicken), couscous with vegetables, an entree, and more, all to be eaten with your fingers. **FYI:** Reservations recommended. Beer and wine only. **Open:** Mon–Sat 6–10pm. Closed some hols. **Prices:** PF dinner $14.95–$21.95. Maj CC. ▨

Emile's, 545 S 2nd St, San Jose; tel 408/289-1960. Guadalupe Pkwy exit off US 101. **French.** A South Bay institution since 1972, established by Swiss-born Emile Mooser, who has a wall full of the many awards garnered by his restaurant. The main dining room features a large, metal ceiling sculpture that allows dimmed lighting for romantic ambience. In addition to fresh fish and game, the menu offers grilled veal medallion with polenta croutons and rosemary-tomato jus lie, and prawns and scallops in light curry sauce in a flaky pastry shell. **FYI:** Reservations recommended. **Open:** Lunch Fri 11:30am–2pm; dinner Tues–Sat 6–10pm. Closed some hols. **Prices:** Main courses $14–$28. Maj CC. ▨ ▨ ▨

★ **Eulipia**, 374 S 1st St, San Jose; tel 408/280-6161. Vine/Almaden exit off I-280. **Eclectic.** Artistically conceived restaurant with purple-and-bright-yellow walls, a black-and-white diamond floor, and a raised wood platform. Offers fixed-price dinners showcasing ethnic cuisine, such as west African, Brazilian, Thai, Italian, traditional and contemporary Mexican, plus southwestern and American. Try chicken breast with brie and roasted garlic sauce, or roasted marinated pork loin with apricot. **FYI:** Reservations recommended. **Open:** Lunch Tues–Fri 11:30am–1:30pm; dinner Tues–Thurs 5:30–9pm, Fri–Sat 5–10pm, Sun 4:30–9pm. Closed some hols. **Prices:** Main courses $9.95–$18.50; PF dinner $23.50. Maj CC. ▨

Gervais, in the Park Naglee Plaza, 1798 Park Ave, San Jose; tel 408/275-8631. Calif 880 N exit off Calif 280. **French.** Warm country French dining spot makes guests feel welcome with its blue-and-white-tiled entry and frosted glass dividers. Entrees include homemade bouillabaisse, grilled fillet of lamb with fresh thyme and artichokes, grilled tournedos of white veal with sautéed shrimp in white wine. Chocolate, Grand Marnier, royal, and framboise soufflés. **FYI:** Reservations recommended. **Open:** Lunch Tues–Fri 11:30am–2pm; dinner Tues–Sat 5:30–10pm. Closed some hols. **Prices:** Main courses $10.95–$25. Maj CC. ▨

Le Papillon, 410 Saratoga Ave, San Jose; tel 408/296-3730. Saratoga Ave exit off Calif 280. **French.** Cranberry upholstered dining chairs contrast nicely with white wainscoting, gray rough-plastered walls, and gray tile. The chef augments the regular menu with low-fat and low-cholesterol options on request, including grilled fish or chicken with sun-dried tomato. Entrees come with soup and salad. **FYI:** Reservations recommended. **Open:** Lunch Mon–Fri 11:30am–2:30pm; dinner Mon–Sat 5–10pm, Sun 5–9pm. Closed some hols. **Prices:** Main courses $22–$26. Maj CC.

Les Saisons, in the Fairmont Hotel, 170 S Market St, San Jose; tel 408/998-3950. Guadalupe Pkwy exit off US 101. **Continental/French.** Very posh restaurant hung with gold-framed paintings depicting the 4 seasons. A baby grand piano separates the dining room from the bar. Roasted Maine lobster with herbs; angel-hair pasta and vanilla sauce; fresh Santa Barbara abalone with tomatoes, capers, and herb sauce; herb-roasted double lamb chops; seared Moroccan spiced sea bass. **FYI:** Reservations recommended. Piano. Jacket required. **Open:** Daily 5:30–10:30pm. **Prices:** Main courses $22–$42. Maj CC. ▨ ▨ ▨

Louisiana Territory, in The Pavilion, 150 S 1st St, San Jose; tel 408/281-1000. Vine/Almaden exit off I-280. **Cajun/Creole.** Living up to its name, Louisiana Territory has New Orleans Mardi Gras and Jazz murals by Taylor Blackwell lining the entrance stairway. Diners wear handfuls of beads to get in the mood to enjoy the strolling jazz musicians who enter around 7pm. Entrees include grilled chicken breast with béarnaise sauce over a slice of Canadian bacon with a sherry-mushroom demi-glaze, blackened fish, shrimp creole or étouffée, shellfish bordelaise, eggplant with spicy bread stuffing, and pasta with sausage and shrimp. **FYI:** Reservations recommended. Combo/jazz. **Open:** Lunch daily 11am–4pm; dinner daily 4–10pm. Closed some hols. **Prices:** Main courses $13–$18.50. Maj CC. ▨

Palermo Ristorante Italiano, 394 S 2nd St, San Jose; tel 408/297-0607. Guadalupe Pkwy exit off US 101. **Italian/Pizza.** Diners enter from a stone-paved street and are greeted by a full-size replica of a plumed horse pulling a cart. Serve yourself from another wagon offering antipasto selections, or order other appetizers, such as eggplant parmigiana. The menu offers 16 pastas, including bow-tie pasta with sausage sauce. Also, veal stuffed with cheese, ham, and salami, and rotisserie chicken. **FYI:** Reservations recommended. **Open:** Mon–Fri 11:30am–9:30pm, Sat–Sun 4–9:30pm. Closed some hols. **Prices:** Main courses $8–$15.50. Maj CC. ▨ ▨ ▨ ▨ ▨

Paolo's, in the River Park Plaza, 333 W San Carlos St, San Jose; tel 408/294-2558. Vine/Almaden exit off Calif 280. **Italian.** Features modern art on loan from a local gallery as well as views of the greenery of River Park. Organically raised produce and naturally raised meats, poultry, and game are used when possible. Try veal prosciutto or one of the pastas, such as ravioli with duck in cream sauce dusted with pistachios and orange zest. **FYI:** Reservations recommended. **Open:** Lunch Mon–Fri 11am–2:30pm; dinner Mon–Sat 5:30–10pm. Closed some hols. **Prices:** Main courses $9.25–$19; PF dinner $32.50. Maj CC. 🖼 🕭

Teske's Germania, 255 N 1st St, San Jose; tel 408/292-0291. **German.** Come for the great German food and unusual decor. The 2 dining rooms—the brick-and-wood Bavarian Room and the Victorian Room—are in 2 different 19th-century buildings. Favorite dishes include sauerbraten (marinated beef) with home-made noodles and Wiener schnitzel (breaded veal cutlet) with potato salad. Generously portioned dinners come with soup, salad, entree, dessert. **FYI:** Reservations recommended. Children's menu. **Open:** Lunch Mon–Fri 11am–2pm; dinner Mon–Sat 5–9:30pm. Closed some hols. **Prices:** Main courses $12.50–$22.95. Maj CC. 🍽 🎦

Attractions 🏛

Winchester Mystery House, 525 S Winchester Blvd; tel 408/247-2101. Begun in 1884, this house is the legacy of Sarah L Winchester, widow of the son of the famous rifle magnate. After the deaths of her husband and baby daughter, Mrs Winchester became convinced that continuous building would appease the spirits of those killed with Winchester repeaters. Construction went on at the house 24 hours a day, 7 days a week, for 38 years until her death in 1922. The red-roofed, stylized Victorian mansion contains 160 rooms and sprawls across a half-dozen acres. Doors that open onto blank walls, stairs that lead no-where, and a window set into the floor are among the many unusual elements designed to confound the demons that the heiress believed were plaguing her.

Several rooms have been restored and furnished with period pieces. The hour-long tour visits 110 of the rooms, after which visitors can take a self-guided tour of the manicured gardens and visit the Winchester Historic Firearms and Antique Products Museum, which displays not only firearms, but also such items as knives, roller skates, tools, and flashlights manufactured by the Winchester company in the early 1900s. **Open:** Summer, daily 9am–8pm; fall–spring, Mon–Fri 9am–4:30pm, Sat–Sun 9am–5pm. $$$$

San Jose Museum of Art, 110 S Market St; tel 408/294-2787. Traveling exhibitions of international art are presented here.

Guided tours are available. Free admission on the first Thurs of each month. **Open:** Tues–Sun 10am–5pm, Thurs 10am–8pm. Closed some hols. $$

Egyptian Museum and Planetarium, in Rosicrucian Park, Park and Naglee Aves; tel 408/947-3636. Set amid beautiful gardens and buildings inspired by ancient Egyptian temples, and housed in a building patterned after the Temple of Amon at Karnak. The Egyptian Museum and Planetarium houses the largest collection of ancient Egyptian, Babylonian, Assyrian, and Sumerian arti-facts on exhibit on the west coast, including textiles, statuary, and art.

Highlights include an exhibit of everyday household items of the ancient Egyptians; a large collection of mummies that includes several cats, crocodiles, and a baboon, as well as humans; and guided tours through a full-size reproduction of an Egyptian nobleman's tomb (ca 2100 BC). The planetarium presents several star shows that emphasize both the scientific and cultural aspects of astronomy, which was very important to the people of ancient Egypt. Opened in 1936, this was one of the first planetariums in the United States. **Open:** Daily 9am–5pm; planetarium hours vary (call for exact show times). $$$

Happy Hollow Park and Zoo, 1300 Senter Rd; tel 408/295-8383 or 277-3000. Located in downtown San Jose's Kelley Park, Happy Hollow is a 12-acre family entertainment attraction featuring amusement rides, themed play areas, puppet theater, and picnic groves. The zoo displays 50 species of domestic, exotic, and endangered animals and features a hands-on contact area. Snack bars, gift shop. **Open:** May–Oct, Mon–Sat 10am–5pm, Sun 11am–6pm; Nov–Apr, daily 10am–5pm. Closed Dec 25. $$

Alum Rock Park, 16240 Alum Rock Ave (Calif 130); tel 408/259-5477. Located within the Alum Rock Canyon in the foothills of the Diablo Range, this park offers 700 acres of natural beauty with opportunities for hiking, horseback riding, bicycling along several miles of trails, picnicking, and more. Between 1890 and 1932 the park was a nationally recognized health spa, with 27 mineral springs. Today its emphasis is as a natural preserve; rangers give interpretive talks, and the visitor center, located in the mid-canyon area, has exhibits and services. **Open:** Park, daily 8am–½ hour before sunset. Free.

Lick Observatory, Mt Hamilton Rd; tel 408/274-5061. Owned and operated by the University of California at Santa Cruz, this working observatory, about an hour's drive from San Jose, offers exhibits and guided lectures to the public. Features a 120-inch reflecting telescope (appointment required) and a 36-inch tele-scope. Nighttime observation programs in summer; phone for schedule. **Open:** Daily 10am–5pm; guides available from 12:30pm. Closed some hols. Free.

SAN JUAN BAUTISTA

Map page M-2, D2 (W of Hollister)

Attraction 📧

San Juan Bautista State Historic Park, 2nd and Washington Sts; tel 408/623-4881. Located within the park is **Mission San Juan Bautista,** founded in 1797, the 15th established by the Franciscan order. Construction of the mission church, the largest of its kind in California, was begun in 1803, and despite damage from numerous earthquakes, it has been in continuous use since 1812. At one time more than 1,000 Indians lived and worked at the mission, and more than 4,300 are buried in the old cemetery beside the northeast wall of the church. Parts of the mission can be toured and there are artifacts on display, but the buildings still belong to the Catholic Church and are technically not a part of the park. Today, the grounds are best known to movie buffs as the setting for some of the scariest scenes in Alfred Hitchcock's *Vertigo.*

Facing the plaza is the **Plaza Hotel** (1858), restored to its original appearance, during the days when San Juan was an important stop on the stage route between Northern and Southern California. Its debut in January 1859 was widely advertised and the hotel quickly became famous for its fine food and drink.

Nearby is the **Plaza Stable** (1861), built to handle the influx of stagecoach and wagon traffic that characterized San Juan's busiest years. Restored to its 1870s appearance, it now houses an assortment of wagons and carriages, harnesses, and other related items. Behind it is the blacksmith's shop, displaying many tools used by the wagonwright.

Other buildings around the plaza include the **Plaza Hall,** site of many grand balls, public meetings, and traveling shows; the **Castro House,** an adobe building once owned by surivors of the Donner Party; and a short section of the original El Camino Real, the highway that connected all of the California missions and later served as a major stage and wagon road. **Open:** Daily 10am–4:30pm. Closed some hols. $

SAN JUAN CAPISTRANO

Map page M-3, E2

Motel 📧

≋≋ **Best Western Capistrano Inn**, 27174 Ortega Hwy, San Juan Capistrano, CA 92675; tel 714/493-5661 or toll free 800/441-9438; fax 714/661-8293. Calif 74 exit off I-5. Quiet location on a picturesque highway. Facility is clean and ade-

quate. **Rooms:** 108 rms and effic. CI open/CO noon. Nonsmoking rms avail. Some rooms have kitchenettes. **Amenities:** 📧 ₰ 📧 A/C, satel TV. 1 unit w/terrace. Some rooms have microwaves. **Services:** ⊂⊃ ⊲⊳ Complimentary full breakfast and happy hour are available weekdays. **Facilities:** 📧 ₷ Whirlpool. **Rates (BB):** HS Mar–Sept $64–$75 S; $64–$75 D; from $70 effic. Extra person $6. Children under 13 stay free. Lower rates off-season. Pking: Outdoor, free. Maj CC.

Attraction 📧

Mission San Juan Capistrano; tel 714/248-2049. Located just west of I-5 Ortega Hwy exit. The 7th and most famous of California's missions, Mission San Juan was founded in 1776 by the Spanish Franciscan Friar Junípero Serra. The famous swallows of Capistrano depart traditionally on St Johns Day (Oct 23). They return to the mission on St Joseph's Day (Mar 19), having migrated some 6,000 miles from their native Argentina.

Self-guided tours of the mission include the Serra Chapel (1777), the oldest standing church in California; the Great Stone Church (1797), which collapsed in an 1812 earthquake; the padres' living quarters; Native American displays; and the North Corridor, where swallows' nests are visible at the western end of the building.

Living History Days are held the last Sat of every month (Feb–Nov). Mission Visitor's Center; gift shop. **Open:** Daily 8:30am–5pm. Closed some hols. $$

SAN LUIS OBISPO

Map page M-3, C1

Hotels 📧

≋≋≋ **Holiday Inn Express**, 1800 Monterey St, San Luis Obispo, CA 93401; tel 805/544-8600 or toll free 800/822-8601; fax 805/541-4698. 1 mi N of downtown San Luis Obispo. Monterey St exit off US 101 S; Grand Ave exit off US 101 N. Clean, well-maintained terra-cotta building. **Rooms:** 100 rms and stes. CI 3pm/CO noon. Express checkout avail. Nonsmoking rms avail. Attractive rooms with new decor in rich jewel colors; turquoise carpets. **Amenities:** 📧 ₰ 📧 A/C, cable TV w/movies. 1 unit w/minibar. **Services:** 📧 △ ⊂⊃ **Facilities:** 📧 📧 ₷ Whirlpool. **Rates (CP):** HS May–Sept $80 S; $90 D; from $130 ste. Extra person $10. Children under 12 stay free. Min stay spec evnts. Lower rates off-season. Higher rates for spec evnts/hols. Pking: Outdoor, free. Maj CC.

≋≋≋ **Madonna Inn**, 100 Madonna Rd, San Luis Obispo, CA 93405; tel 805/543-3000 or toll free 800/543-9666; fax 805/

543-1800. Madonna Rd exit off US 101. A long-time roadside attraction, visible from US 101. It's one of a kind, great fun, and has reasonable rates. **Rooms:** 109 rms and stes. CI 4pm/CO noon. Each room displays a different theme. The "Caveman" has a rock shower and leopard-print bedspread. The 2-story "Pick and Shovel" has a huge living room, red vinyl couch, fireplace, banistered staircase, and pick-and-shovel lamp. **Amenities:** 🛏 ☎ A/C, cable TV. Some units w/terraces, some w/fireplaces. **Services:** 🚐 🛎 **Facilities:** 500 2 rsts (*see also* "Restaurants" below), 1 bar. Gift shop, bakery, coffee shop/soda fountain, and fine dining room. **Rates:** HS Mem Day–Labor Day $72–$170 S or D; from $130 ste. Extra person $6–$12. Children under 18 stay free. Lower rates off-season. Pking: Outdoor, free. Ltd CC.

≡≡ **Pacific Suites Hotel & Conference Center**, 333 Madonna Rd, San Luis Obispo, CA 93405 (Central Coast Mall); tel 805/549-0800 or toll free 800/864-6000; fax 805/543-5273. 1 mi S of downtown. Madonna Rd exit off US 101, left on Madonna Rd. Located in a shopping mall, this building has an attractive pastel atrium lobby with lots of light, air, and plants. **Rooms:** 195 stes. CI 3pm/CO noon. Express checkout avail. Nonsmoking rms avail. Rooms facing the interior courtyard seem dark. Contemporary decor in variations of beige. **Amenities:** 🛏 ☎ 📺 A/C, cable TV w/movies, refrig, voice mail. All units w/minibars, all w/terraces, some w/Jacuzzis. **Services:** ✗ 🚐 🛎 🛎 Car-rental desk. Free cocktails. **Facilities:** 🔦 🏋 350 ⅙ 1 rst, 1 bar, whirlpool, washer/dryer. **Rates (BB):** HS May–Sept from $129 ste. Extra person $10. Children under 12 stay free. Lower rates off-season. Higher rates for spec evnts/hols. Spec packages avail. Pking: Outdoor, free. Maj CC.

≡≡≡ **Quality Suites**, 1631 Monterey St, San Luis Obispo, CA 93401; tel 805/541-5001 or toll free 800/221-2222; fax 805/546-9475. ¼ mi N of downtown. Monterey St exit off US 101. Nice, quiet, parklike setting, with lovely lobby and handsomely furnished library. **Rooms:** 138 stes. CI 2pm/CO noon. Express checkout avail. Nonsmoking rms avail. Big suites are nicely furnished, some with sofas, queen-size beds, and a desk. **Amenities:** 🛏 ☎ A/C, cable TV, refrig, VCR, stereo/tape player. Some units w/terraces. **Services:** 🚐 🛎 🛎 Complimentary cooked-to-order breakfast. **Facilities:** 🔦 30 ⅙ 1 bar, whirlpool, washer/dryer. Gift shop. **Rates (BB):** HS Mar–Oct from $125 ste. Extra person $10. Children under 18 stay free. Min stay spec evnts. Lower rates off-season. Higher rates for spec evnts/hols. Spec packages avail. Pking: Outdoor, free. Maj CC.

Motels

≡≡ **Howard Johnson Lodge**, 1585 Calle Joaquin, San Luis Obispo, CA 93405; tel 805/544-5300 or toll free 800/654-2000;

fax 805/541-2823. 4 mi S of downtown. Los Osos Valley Rd exit off US 101. Convenient to the highway, but some rooms have nice views of the trees. **Rooms:** 64 rms. CI 2pm/CO 11am. Nonsmoking rms avail. Rooms are basic and need updating. **Amenities:** 🛏 ☎ A/C, cable TV w/movies. All units w/terraces. **Services:** 🛎 🛎 🛎 Children's program. **Facilities:** 🔦 ⅙ 1 rst, 1 bar, washer/dryer. **Rates:** HS May–Oct $39–$69 S or D. Children under 18 stay free. Lower rates off-season. Pking: Outdoor, free. Maj CC. Good value.

≡≡ **Lamplighter Inn**, 1604 Monterey St, San Luis Obispo, CA 93401; tel 805/547-7777 or toll free 800/547-7787; fax 805/547-7787. ½ mi N of downtown. Monterey St exit off US 101. Cheerful, clean, well-kept 2-story motel. **Rooms:** 42 rms, stes, and effic. CI 3pm/CO 11am. Express checkout avail. Nonsmoking rms avail. A bit outdated, but comfortable. Rooms with up to 4 beds available. **Amenities:** 🛏 📺 A/C, cable TV, refrig, voice mail. Some units w/terraces, 1 w/fireplace. Microwave oven. **Services:** 🛎 **Facilities:** 🔦 30 Whirlpool, washer/dryer. **Rates (CP):** HS Aug $59–$79 S; $69–$89 D; from $89 ste; from $89 effic. Extra person $3–$5. Children under 8 stay free. Min stay spec evnts. Lower rates off-season. Higher rates for spec evnts/hols. Pking: Outdoor, free. Maj CC.

≡≡ **Motel 6**, 1433 Calle Joaquin, San Luis Obispo, CA 93401; tel 805/549-9595; fax 805/544-2826. 1 mi S of downtown. Los Osos exit off US 101, head west. Standard motel that offers cleanliness, easy highway access, and good value. **Rooms:** 87 rms. CI 3pm/CO noon. Nonsmoking rms avail. Clean, with fresh white paint and new bedspreads. Some rooms for deaf and hard of hearing guests. **Amenities:** 🛏 A/C, satel TV w/movies. **Services:** 🛎 🛎 Free local calls; no hotel charge on long distance. **Facilities:** 🔦 ⅙ **Rates:** HS May 26–Aug $32 S; $36 D. Extra person $4. Children under 17 stay free. Lower rates off-season. Pking: Outdoor, free. Maj CC.

≡≡ **Olive Tree Inn Best Western**, 1000 Olive St, San Luis Obispo, CA 93405 (Downtown); tel 805/544-2800 or toll free 800/777-5847. Calif 1/Morro Bay exit off US 101 N; Santa Rosa St exit off US 101 S. Standard 2-story motel; near the freeway, but quiet. **Rooms:** 38 rms and stes. CI 2pm/CO 11am. Nonsmoking rms avail. Spartan rooms with basic motel furnishings. Some rooms have lovely porches overlooking a creek. 6 suites have kitchen facilities. **Amenities:** 🛏 ☎ Cable TV. No A/C. Some units w/terraces, 1 w/fireplace. **Services:** 🛎 🛎 🛎 **Facilities:** 🔦 ⅙ 1 rst, sauna, washer/dryer. **Rates:** HS June–Sept 15 $65–$92 S; $75–$92 D; from $85 ste. Extra person $4. Min stay spec evnts. Lower rates off-season. Higher rates for spec evnts/hols. Pking: Outdoor, free. Maj CC.

≡≡ **San Luis Obispo Travelodge**, 1825 Monterey St, San Luis Obispo, CA 93401; tel 805/543-5110 or toll free 800/

255-3050; fax 805/543-3406. Monterey exit off US 101. Clean motel-style property on motel row, close to restaurants. **Rooms:** 39 rms. CI noon/CO 11am. Nonsmoking rms avail. Rooms in back offer nice views of the mountains. **Amenities:** 🔒 🎞 A/C, cable TV w/movies. **Services:** 🍽 🛍 **Facilities:** 🎣 ⅋ **Rates:** HS mid-June–mid-Sept $48–$99 S or D. Extra person $7. Children under 17 stay free. Lower rates off-season. Higher rates for spec evnts/hols. Pking: Outdoor, free. Maj CC.

Inn

📰📰📰 **Garden Street Inn**, 1212 Garden St, San Luis Obispo, CA 93401 (Downtown); tel 805/545-9802. Marsh exit off US 101; 5 blocks to Garden, turn right. A stunning example of Italianate/Queen Anne Victorian architecture, built in 1887 with high ceilings and a grand staircase. Unsuitable for children under 16. **Rooms:** 13 rms and stes. CI 3pm/CO 11am. No smoking. Charming rooms have antiques, sinks with washstands, a dressing table, and high ceilings. **Amenities:** A/C, stereo/tape player, bathrobes. No phone or TV. Some units w/terraces, some w/fireplaces, some w/Jacuzzis. **Services:** ✗ 🛍 Twice-daily maid svce, wine/sherry served. Lovely breakfasts, plus evening wine and cheese. **Facilities:** ⬜10 ⅋ Guest lounge. Living room with piano. **Rates (BB):** $90–$120 S or D; from $140 ste. Min stay spec evnts. Pking: Indoor/outdoor, free. Ltd CC.

Restaurants 🍽

Apple Farm Restaurant, 2015 Monterey St, San Luis Obispo; tel 805/544-6100. Monterey St exit off US 101. **American.** A popular country-style family restaurant decked out in oak furniture and Tiffany lamps. Cuisine includes apple sausage, eggs, and biscuits for breakfast; sandwiches, salads, and pot pie for lunch; roast turkey, prime rib, and pan-fried trout for dinner. **FYI:** Reservations recommended. Children's menu. Beer and wine only. **Open:** Breakfast Mon–Fri 7–11:30am, Sat–Sun 7am–noon; lunch Mon–Fri 11:30am–5pm, Sat–Sun noon–5pm; dinner Mon–Sat 5–10pm, Sun 4–10pm. **Prices:** Main courses $9.95–$14.95. Maj CC. 🍷 🖼 ♥ ⅋

★ **Gold Rush Dining Room**, in the Madonna Inn, 100 Madonna Rd, San Luis Obispo; tel 805/543-3000. Madonna Rd exit off Calif 1. **American.** A coastal California landmark for decades. Dining and dancing in the Gold Rush Dining Room is an event. The ambience is romantic in an overdone way. Nearly everything is pink and gold, with lots of hearts and flowers and chandeliers. The cuisine emphasizes steaks and prime rib as well as seafood dishes, including lobster, salmon, and abalone. Homemade desserts from the pastry shop. **FYI:** Reservations accepted. Combo/dancing. Children's menu. **Open:** Daily 5:30–10pm. **Prices:** Main courses $15.95–$22.95. Ltd CC. ♥ 🍷 🖼

SAN LUIS REY
Map page M-3, E2 (E of Oceanside)

Attraction 💼

Mission San Luis Rey de Francia, 4050 Mission Ave; tel 916/757-3651. Founded in 1798, the largest of California's 21 missions was the 18th to be established. For a time, the mission church was the largest structure in California. Visitors may take a self-guided tour of the small museum, whose exhibits include a large collection of 18th- and 19th-century vestments; the old Indian cemetery; and the first pepper tree planted in California (1830). **Open:** Mon–Sat 10am–4:30pm, Sun noon–4:30pm. $

SAN MARINO
Map page M-3, D2 (N of Los Angeles)

See also Pasadena

Attractions 💼

Huntington Library, Art Collections, and Botanical Gardens, 1151 Oxford Rd; tel 818/405-2100 or 405-2141. The 207-acre estate of pioneer industrialist Henry E Huntington has become an educational and cultural center for scholars, art devotees, and the general public. The house is now an art gallery that contains paintings, tapestries, furniture, and other decorative arts, mainly of English and French origin and dating from the 18th century. The most celebrated painting here is Thomas Gainsborough's *Blue Boy*.

The adjacent **Virginia Steele Scott Gallery for American Art** houses a variety of paintings from 1720–1930, which are hung in chronological order. The **Library Exhibition Hall** displays numerous American and English first editions, manuscripts, and letters, including Benjamin Franklin's handwritten manuscript for his *Autobiography*. The **Botanical Gardens** are studded with rare shrubs, trees, and 17th-century statuary from Padua; also a Japanese Garden, Desert Garden, Camellia Garden, and Zen Garden. **Open:** Tues–Fri 1–4:30pm, Sat–Sun 10:30am–4:30pm. $$

El Molino Viejo, 1120 Old Mill Rd; tel 818/449-5450. El Molino Viejo ('the Old Mill") was the first water-powered grist mill in southern California, built around 1816 by Native American labor under the supervision of the Franciscan Padres at Mission San Gabriel. After its secularization in 1833, the building was used primarily as a residence. Restored in 1928, the mill is now the southern headquarters of the California Historical Society. Changing art and photographic exhibits on 2nd floor. **Open:** Tues–Sun 1–4pm. Closed some hols. Free.

SAN MATEO

Map page M-2, D2

Hotels 🏨

≣≣≣ **Dunfey Hotel**, 1770 S Amphlett Blvd, San Mateo, CA 94402; tel 415/573-7661 or toll free 800/843-6664; fax 415/573-0533. Delaware exit off Calif 92. Reminiscent of a Tudor-style castle, this place is popular with tour groups, conventions, and business travelers. **Rooms:** 280 rms and stes. CI 3pm/CO noon. Express checkout avail. Nonsmoking rms avail. Rooms have a variety of floor plans. **Amenities:** 🛁 🕭 🍴 A/C, cable TV w/movies. Some units w/terraces. **Services:** ✗ 🚗 🖼 🛏 🧹 Car-rental desk, babysitting. **Facilities:** 🏋 🍴 🕭 1 rst, 3 bars (1 w/entertainment), washer/dryer. Large lawn area for picnics. **Rates (CP):** $130 S or D; from $180 ste. Extra person $10. Children under 12 stay free. Spec packages avail. Pking: Outdoor, free. Maj CC.

≣≣≣ **Residence Inn by Marriott**, 2000 Winward Way, San Mateo, CA 94404; tel 415/574-4700 or toll free 800/331-3131; fax 415/572-9084. Mariners Island Blvd exit off Calif 92. More like apartments than a hotel, this property, made up of detached units, is set up to accommodate stays longer than 1 night. Quiet, considering proximity to freeway. **Rooms:** 159 effic. CI 3pm/CO noon. Nonsmoking rms avail. Full kitchen in each unit. Good furnishings. **Amenities:** 🛁 🕭 🖵 A/C, cable TV w/movies, refrig, voice mail. All units w/minibars, some w/terraces, some w/fireplaces. **Services:** ✗ 🚗 🖼 🛏 🧹 Car-rental desk, babysitting. Price includes generous continental breakfast and free hors d'oeuvres 5–7pm. Grocery shopping and delivery service. **Facilities:** 🏋 🏊 🍴 🕭 🕭 Spa, whirlpool, playground, washer/dryer. **Rates (CP):** HS Apr–Nov from $132 effic. Children under 18 stay free. Lower rates off-season. Spec packages avail. Pking: Outdoor, free. Maj CC. Higher rates for 1-night occupancies; rates decrease with longer stays.

≣≣≣ **Villa Quality Hotel**, 4000 S El Camino Real, San Mateo, CA 94403; tel 415/341-0966 or toll free 800/341-2345; fax 415/573-0164. Hillside Blvd exit off US 101 to El Camino Real; turn left. The decor is slightly dated, but this family-run hotel has a nice ambience and a caring staff. **Rooms:** 286 rms and stes. CI 3pm/CO 1pm. Express checkout avail. Nonsmoking rms avail. Half the rooms are nonsmoking. **Amenities:** 🛁 🕭 🖵 A/C, cable TV. Some units w/terraces. **Services:** 🍴 🖂 🅥🅟 🚗 🖼 🛏 🧹 Car-rental desk, masseur, babysitting. **Facilities:** 🏋

🔊 🚐 🖵 🕭 1 rst, 1 bar (w/entertainment), beauty salon. 24-hour coffee shop. 24-hour full-service Kinko's copy shop across the street. **Rates (CP):** $99–$149 S; $107–$157 D; from $119 ste. Extra person $8. Children under 18 stay free. Higher rates for spec evnts/hols. Pking: Indoor/outdoor, free. Maj CC.

Restaurant 🍴

231 Ellsworth, 231 S Ellsworth Ave, San Mateo; tel 415/347-7231. 3rd Ave W exit off US 101; pass 5 lights and turn right on Ellsworth. **French.** Understatement and attention to detail are hallmarks of this award-winning, contemporary French restaurant. Teal and peach southwestern decor and modern art create a romantic ambience at night. Fresh seafood is a favorite. The owner grows his own mushrooms, which crop up in risotto and other dishes. Specialties include scallops with fennel and tomato confit. Also, grilled bass, braised duck, veal sweetbreads. **FYI:** Reservations recommended. Beer and wine only. **Open:** Lunch Mon–Fri 11:30am–2pm; dinner Mon–Sat 5:30–9:30pm. Closed some hols. **Prices:** Main courses $17–$20; PF dinner $29.50. Maj CC. ♥ 🕭

Attraction 🏛

Coyote Point Museum, 1651 Coyote Point Dr; tel 415/342-7755. Located in a scenic bayside park, this museum seeks to foster an appreciation and understanding of the natural world and humankind's place in it. Displays in Environmental Hall feature realistic wildlife habitats, including baylands, coastal area, and a redwood forest, with mammals, birds, and reptiles native to the San Francisco Bay area. Walk-through aviary; working beehive; computerized displays. **Open:** Tues–Sat 10am–5pm, Sun noon–5pm. Closed some hols. $$$

SAN PEDRO

Map page M-3, D2 (W of Long Beach)

Hotels 🏨

≣≣ **Best Western Sunrise Hotel at Ports O'Call**, 525 S Harbor Blvd, San Pedro, CA 90731; tel 310/548-1080 or toll free 800/356-9609; fax 310/519-0380. Harbor Blvd exit off I-110. Somewhat dated, basic hotel. Not noisy, but a steady flow of traffic outside. **Rooms:** 150 rms and stes. CI 2pm/CO noon. Nonsmoking rms avail. Rooms are dark and drab, and need updating. **Amenities:** 🛁 🕭 🖵 🍴 A/C, cable TV w/movies, refrig. Some units w/terraces. **Services:** 🧹 Twice-daily maid svce, babysitting. **Facilities:** [符][150] & Whirlpool, washer/dryer. **Rates (BB):** $58 S; $66 D; from $99 ste. Children under 12 stay free. Spec packages avail. Pking: Outdoor, free. Maj CC.

≣≣≣ **Doubletree Hotel–Los Angeles World Port**, 2800 Via Cabrillo Marina, San Pedro, CA 90731; tel 310/514-3344 or toll free 800/559-5888; fax 310/514-8945. Harbor Blvd exit off I-110 S. Located right next to the marina. **Rooms:** 226 rms and stes. Exec-level rms avail. CI 3pm/CO 1pm. Express checkout avail. Nonsmoking rms avail. Rooms are spacious, clean, and attractive. **Amenities:** [符] & A/C, cable TV w/movies, shoe polisher. 1 unit w/minibar, some w/terraces. **Services:** ✗ ⬛ ⤸ Babysitting. **Facilities:** [符] ⌀ △ ⬛ ⬛ ▶ ⬛ [750] & 2 rsts, 2 bars (w/entertainment), sauna, whirlpool, beauty salon. **Rates (CP):** $129–$144 S or D; from $225 ste. Extra person $10. Children under 18 stay free. Higher rates for spec evnts/hols. Spec packages avail. Pking: Outdoor, free. Maj CC.

≣≣≣ **Sheraton Los Angeles Harbor Hotel**, 601 S Palos Verdes St, San Pedro, CA 90731; tel 310/519-8200 or toll free 800/HOTEL18; fax 310/519-8421. Harbor Blvd exit off I-110; go south at 6th St. Looks a bit industrial on the outside but is charming and comfortable within. **Rooms:** 244 rms and stes. Exec-level rms avail. CI 3pm/CO noon. Nonsmoking rms avail. Clean and comfortable rooms are decorated in rose pastel tones. **Amenities:** [符] & ⬛ A/C, cable TV w/movies. Some units w/terraces. **Services:** ▣ ⬛ VP ⬛ ⤸ Car-rental desk, babysitting. **Facilities:** [符] ⬛ ⬛ & 1 rst (see also "Restaurants" below), 1 bar (w/entertainment), spa, sauna, steam rm, whirlpool, washer/dryer. **Rates:** $95 S or D; from $145 ste. Extra person $10. Children under 17 stay free. Higher rates for spec evnts/hols. Spec packages avail. Pking: Indoor/outdoor, $1–$5. Maj CC.

Motel

≣ **Vagabond Inn–San Pedro**, 215 S Gaffey St, San Pedro, CA 90731; tel 310/831-8911 or toll free 800/522-1555; fax 310/831-2649. Gaffey St exit off I-110. Clean, but could use improved maintenance and better soundproofing of rooms. **Rooms:** 72 rms. CI noon/CO noon. Express checkout avail. Nonsmoking rms avail. **Amenities:** [符] & ⬛ A/C, cable TV w/movies, refrig. **Services:** ⤸ ⬛ Room service from Denny's restaurant next door. **Facilities:** [符] **Rates (CP):** $45–$55 S; $50–$70 D. Extra person $5. Children under 18 stay free. Higher rates for spec evnts/hols. Spec packages avail. Pking: Outdoor, free. Maj CC. 10th night free.

Restaurants [¶]

Madeo Ristorante–San Pedro, 295 Whales Walk, San Pedro; tel 310/831-1199. Harbor Blvd exit off I-110. **Italian.** A little sterile-looking, but good for a business lunch. Menu items include fish of the day, roast veal, a large selection of pasta, and salads. Antipasti table at lunch. **FYI:** Reservations recommended. Piano. Dress code. **Open:** Lunch Mon–Fri 11:30am–2pm; dinner daily 5–10pm. Closed some hols. **Prices:** Main courses $9.95–$19.95. Maj CC. ▣ &

Meridian 1050, 1050 Nagoya Way, San Pedro; tel 310/514-1050. Harbor Blvd exit off I-110. **Californian/Continental.** This place has a classy feel, with an art deco design in black, white, and gray with yellow accents, fresh flowers, and lovely view of the harbor. Daily seafood specials, wide selection of fresh salads. Banquet facilities can seat as many as 280 people. **FYI:** Reservations recommended. Jazz/piano. Children's menu. Dress code. **Open:** Lunch Mon–Fri 11am–2:30pm; dinner Mon–Sat 5:30–10pm, Sun 5–10pm; brunch Sun 10:30am–2pm. Closed some hols. **Prices:** Main courses $8.50–$21.95. Maj CC. ⬛ ⬛ ⬛ &

Moonraker, in Sheraton Los Angeles Harbor Hotel, 601 S Palos Verdes St, San Pedro; tel 310/519-8200. Harbor Blvd exit off I-110. **Continental.** Festive family restaurant with pastel colors and an Asian theme. The menu is truly eclectic, offering Italian, Chinese, and American dishes. **FYI:** Reservations accepted. **Open:** Breakfast daily 6–10:30am; lunch daily 11:30am–2pm; dinner daily 5–10pm. **Prices:** Main courses $4.95–$13.95. Maj CC. VP &

SAN RAFAEL

Map page M-2, D1

Hotels [▣]

≣≣≣ **Embassy Suites**, 101 McInnis Pkwy, San Rafael, CA 94903 (Civic Center); tel 415/499-9222 or toll free 800/EMBASSY in the US, 800/458-5848 in Canada; fax 415/499-9268. 3 mi N of San Rafael. N San Pedro Rd exit off US 101 N; Freitas Pkwy exit off US 101 S. **Rooms:** 235 stes. CI 3pm/CO 1pm. Express checkout avail. Nonsmoking rms avail. **Amenities:** [符] & ⬛ ⬛ A/C, cable TV w/movies, refrig, VCR. All units w/minibars. **Services:** ✗ ⬛ ⬛ ⬛ ⤸ Car-rental desk, masseur, babysitting. **Facilities:** [符] ⬛ [160] ⬛ 1 rst, 1 bar, sauna, steam rm, whirlpool, beauty salon, washer/dryer. **Rates (BB):** From $150 ste. Extra person $15. Children under 12 stay free. Spec packages avail. Pking: Outdoor, free. Maj CC.

≣≣≣ **Holiday Inn Marin–San Rafael**, 1010 Northgate Dr, San Rafael, CA 94903; tel 415/479-8800 or toll free 800/231-2911; fax 415/479-6739. Terra Linda/Freitas Pkwy exit off US 101; go west. Located close to the highway and across from the Northgate mall, this is a pleasant full-service hotel. **Rooms:** 223 rms, stes, and effic. Exec-level rms avail. CI 2pm/CO noon. Nonsmoking rms avail. Many rooms have recently been refurbished. For the best deal and nicest accommodations, choose the concierge floor. **Amenities:** 🛏 🕭 A/C, cable TV w/movies. Some units w/minibars. **Services:** ✕ 🖿 🚗 🖾 🗗 🕭 Twice-daily maid svce, car-rental desk. Concierge-room guests get continental breakfast, afternoon drinks. **Facilities:** 🔁 🕭 🔟 🕭 1 rst, 1 bar, whirlpool, beauty salon, washer/dryer. Garden courtyard is popular for weddings. In addition to the small workout room, guests have privileges at a nearby Y. **Rates:** HS May–Sept $89–$120 S; $99–$140 D; from $125 ste; from $225 effic. Extra person $10. Children under 18 stay free. Min stay HS and wknds. Lower rates off-season. Spec packages avail. Pking: Outdoor, free. Maj CC.

Motel

≣≣ **Villa Inn**, 1600 Lincoln Ave, San Rafael, CA 94901; tel 415/456-4975 or toll free 800/424-4777; fax 415/456-1520. Lincoln Ave exit off US 101 S; Central San Rafael exit off US 101 N. Family-run for 23 years, this motel is maintained with pride. Pleasant lobby with floral-print sofa and a good selection of sightseeing brochures. **Rooms:** 60 rms and effic. CI noon/CO noon. Nonsmoking rms avail. Floral bedspreads paired with newish carpeting. **Amenities:** 🛏 A/C, cable TV, refrig. **Services:** ✕ 🗗 🕭 Twice-daily maid svce. **Facilities:** 🔁 🔟 🕭 1 rst, 1 bar, whirlpool, washer/dryer. Big glass-topped pool with Jacuzzi open from April to October. Extremely pleasant Cafe Villa serves huge family-style portions of Basque dishes, very reasonably priced. **Rates (CP):** HS May–Sept $64–$67 S; $69–$76 D; from $72 effic. Extra person $5. Children under 18 stay free. Lower rates off-season. Higher rates for spec evnts/hols. Pking: Outdoor, free. Maj CC.

SAN RAMON

Map page M-2, D2 (E of San Francisco)

Hotels 🛏

≣≣≣ **Residence Inn by Marriott**, 1071 Market Place, San Ramon, CA 94583; tel 510/277-9292 or toll free 800/331-3131; fax 510/277-0687. Bollinger Canyon Rd exit off I-680. Attractive, fairly new, townhouse-like complex located in suburban business park. **Rooms:** 106 stes. Exec-level rms avail. CI 3pm/

CO noon. Nonsmoking rms avail. All units have fully equipped kitchens. Most have sofas that convert into beds. **Amenities:** 🛏 🕭 🖾 A/C, cable TV w/movies, refrig, voice mail. Some units w/fireplaces. VCR rentals available. **Services:** ✕ 🖾 🗗 🕭 Grocery shopping service. Complimentary wine, beer, and snacks served Monday–Friday 5–7pm; Complimentary barbecue Wednesday nights during summer. **Facilities:** 🔁 🕭 🖾 🕭 Whirlpool, washer/dryer. Local gym accessible for a fee. Basketball court and sport court for tennis, volleyball, and paddle tennis. Board games available for kids. **Rates (CP):** HS June–Labor Day from $124 ste. Children under 18 stay free. Lower rates off-season. Spec packages avail. Pking: Outdoor, free. Maj CC.

≣≣≣ **San Ramon Marriott**, 2600 Bishop Dr, San Ramon, CA 94583; tel 510/867-9200 or toll free 800/228-9290; fax 510/830-9326. Bollinger Canyon Rd exit off I-680; go east, then left on Sunset Dr, left on Bishop Dr. Spacious, comfortable hotel in business-park district. Large lawn in back has a patio with tables and chairs. **Rooms:** 368 rms and stes. CI 3pm/CO noon. Express checkout avail. Nonsmoking rms avail. **Amenities:** 🛏 🕭 A/C, cable TV w/movies, voice mail. Some units w/minibars, some w/terraces. All rooms have irons and ironing boards. Suites have coffeemakers and complete audio systems. **Services:** ✕ 🖿 🅅🅿 🖾 🗗 🕭 Babysitting. Free valet parking for guests with disabilities. **Facilities:** 🔁 🕭 🔟 🖥 🕭 1 rst, 1 bar, lifeguard, spa, sauna, whirlpool, washer/dryer. **Rates:** $129 S or D; from $300 ste. Children under 18 stay free. Spec packages avail. Pking: Outdoor, free. Maj CC. Special weekend rates.

SAN SIMEON

Map page M-2, E2

See also **Cambria**

Motels 🛏

≣≣ **Best Western Green Tree Inn**, 9450 Castillo Dr, San Simeon, CA 93452; tel 805/927-4691 or toll free 800/992-9240, 800/231-6461 in CA; fax 805/927-1473. Standard 2-story motel. **Rooms:** 117 rms and stes. CI 3pm/CO noon. Nonsmoking rms avail. **Amenities:** 🛏 🕭 🖾 A/C, cable TV. Some units w/terraces, 1 w/fireplace. **Services:** 🗗 Continental breakfast in atrium lobby with pool. **Facilities:** 🔁 🖾 🔟 🕭 Games rm, whirlpool, washer/dryer. **Rates (CP):** HS June–Sept $39–$95 S or D; from $175 ste. Extra person $10. Children under 17 stay free. Min stay spec evnts. Lower rates off-season. Higher rates for spec evnts/hols. Spec packages avail. Pking: Outdoor, free. Maj CC. Hearst Castle ticket packages available.

≡≡≡ **Cavalier Oceanfront Resort**, 9415 Hearst Dr, San Simeon, CA 93452 (San Simeon); tel 805/927-4688 or toll free 800/826-8168; fax 805/927-0497. 38 mi N of San Luis Obispo. Hearst Dr exit off Calif 1. A great location, on the beach near Hearst Castle, with terrific ocean views. A good value. **Rooms:** 90 rms. CI 4pm/CO noon. Express checkout avail. Nonsmoking rms avail. Rooms are all oversized, very clean, and have ocean views and fireplaces. **Amenities:** 🛏 🍴 Cable TV w/movies, refrig, VCR, voice mail. No A/C. All units w/minibars, some w/terraces, some w/fireplaces. Wet bar. **Services:** ✗ ⏲ ☞ Babysitting. **Facilities:** 🏋 🚲 ⛱ 🅿 2 rsts, 1 bar, 1 beach (ocean), whirlpool, washer/dryer. Video store, gift shop, Italian restaurant. **Rates:** HS May 27–Sept 4 $71–$125 S or D. Extra person $6. Min stay wknds. Lower rates off-season. Spec packages avail. Pking: Outdoor, free. Maj CC.

Attraction 💼

Hearst Castle, Calif 1; tel toll free 800/444-4445. William Randolph Hearst left an astounding monument to wealth on a hill called La Cuesta Encantada (The Enchanted Hill). The mansion, which was donated to the state by the Hearst family in 1958, is now administered by the California Department of Parks and Recreation as the Hearst–San Simeon State Historical Monument.

The focal point of today's estate is the incredible **Casa Grande,** a sprawling mansion with more than 100 rooms filled with priceless art and antiques: Flemish tapestries, 15th-century Gothic fireplaces, intricately carved 16th-century Spanish and 18th-century Italian ceilings, a 16th-century Florentine bedstead, Renaissance paintings, and innumerable other treasures. The Doge's Suite was reserved for the house's most important guests, among them Winston Churchill and Calvin Coolidge. The library contains over 5,000 volumes, including many rare editions, as well as one of the world's greatest collections of Greek vases.

There are also 2 swimming pools: a Byzantine-inspired indoor pool with intricate mosaic work surrounded by replicas, in Carrara marble, of the most famous statues of antiquity; and the Greco-Roman Neptune outdoor pool, flanked by Etruscan-style marble colonnades and surrounded by more Carrara statuary, considered one of the mansion's most memorable features.

The mansion can be visited only by **guided tour**. Four separate tours are offered on a daily basis, each lasting almost 2 hours. They include some of the gardens as well as the outdoor and indoor pools. Tours cover about 1½ miles and include between 150 and 300 steps (visitors confined to wheelchairs can make special arrangements by calling 805/927-2020). Tour I, recommended for the first-time visitor, includes the gardens, a guest house, and the ground floor of the main house—including the movie theater where Hearst home movies are shown. Tours are conducted daily, beginning at 8:20am, and continuing every 20 minutes until 3pm. $$$$

SANTA ANA

Map page M-3, D2

Hotels 🏨

≡≡ **Courtyard by Marriott**, 3002 S Harbor Blvd, Santa Ana, CA 92704; tel 714/545-1001 or toll free 800/321-2211; fax 714/545-8439. Harbor Blvd N exit off I-405. Basic, clean, and in a convenient location, but not quite up to similar Marriott properties' level. **Rooms:** 145 rms and stes. CI 3pm/CO 1pm. Express checkout avail. Nonsmoking rms avail. Standard, with basic furnishings. **Amenities:** 🛏 🔅 ▣ A/C, cable TV w/movies. Some units w/terraces. **Services:** ⏷ ⏲ Car-rental desk. **Facilities:** 🏋 ⛱ 📶 ⛄ 1 rst, 1 bar, whirlpool, washer/dryer. **Rates:** HS June–Sept $54–$62 S or D; from $77 ste. Lower rates off-season. Pking: Outdoor, free. Maj CC.

≡≡≡ **Radisson Suite Hotel–Santa Ana**, 2720 Hotel Terrace Dr, Santa Ana, CA 92705; tel 714/556-3838 or toll free 800/333-3333; fax 714/241-1008. Dyer exit off Calif 55. Good for business travelers visiting nearby executive parks. **Rooms:** 122 stes. CI 3pm/CO noon. Express checkout avail. Nonsmoking rms avail. **Amenities:** 🛏 🔅 ▣ A/C, cable TV w/movies, refrig. **Services:** ✗ ▣ 🚗 ⏷ ⏲ Babysitting. **Facilities:** 🏋 ⛱ 📶 ⛄ 1 bar, whirlpool. **Rates (BB):** HS June–Aug from $95 ste. Extra person $10. Children under 17 stay free. Lower rates off-season. Spec packages avail. Pking: Outdoor, free. Maj CC.

Motel

≡ **Santa Ana Inn**, 2600 N Main St, Santa Ana, CA 92701; tel 714/836-5141; fax 714/543-0841. Main St exit off Calif 22. Acceptable lodgings. **Rooms:** 118 rms and stes. CI 3pm/CO 11am. Nonsmoking rms avail. Rooms need some upgrades but are comfortable. **Amenities:** 🛏 🔅 A/C, cable TV. **Services:** ⏲ **Facilities:** 🏋 📶 ⛄ Whirlpool. **Rates:** $42 S; from $60 ste. Extra person $6. Children under 18 stay free. Pking: Outdoor, free. Maj CC.

Restaurants 🍴

✦ **Antonello**, in South Coast Village Shopping Center, 1611 Sunflower, Santa Ana; tel 714/751-7153. Bristol St N exit off I-405. **Italian.** Intimate and romantic Mediterranean decor designed to create the feeling of walking through the streets of

Italy. A classical Italian menu with lots of veal, pasta, and fish. **FYI:** Reservations recommended. **Open:** Lunch Mon–Fri 11:30am–2pm; dinner Mon–Thurs 5:45–10pm, Fri–Sat 5:45–11pm. Closed some hols. **Prices:** Main courses $12–$28. Maj CC. ♥ 🍴 🍽 🎴 📺 [VP] &

Favori, 3502 W 1st St, Santa Ana; tel 714/531-6838. Harbor Blvd exit off I-405. **French/Vietnamese.** Country French decor with lots of fresh flowers. Menu offers a full range of French entrees along with a wide selection of Vietnamese dishes. **FYI:** Reservations recommended. Beer and wine only. **Open:** Daily 11am–10pm. Closed some hols. **Prices:** Main courses $6.95–$9.95. Ltd CC.

Gustaf Anders, in South Coast Plaza Village shopping center, 1651 Sunflower Ave, Santa Ana; tel 714/668-1737. **Californian/Scandinavian.** Located in a quiet shopping plaza, this restaurant has a pleasant ambience and an excellent reputation. Eclectic blend of California and Scandinavian fare includes gravlax with dill mustard sauce, smoked salmon and black caviar sandwich on pumpernickel, polenta sandwich with grilled vegetables and sun-dried tomato sauce, and braised lamb shanks with white-bean puree. Excellent wine selection. **FYI:** Reservations recommended. **Open:** Lunch Mon–Sat 11:30am–2pm; dinner daily 5:30–10:30pm. Closed some hols. **Prices:** Main courses $45–$50. Maj CC. &

★ **Planet Hollywood**, 1641 W Sunflower, Santa Ana; tel 714/434-7827. Bristol St N exit off I-405; turn left on Sunflower. **American.** Action-packed restaurant with an illuminated wall-size map of Hollywood in black and white and a re-creation of the city skyline. Basic American fare features pizzas, hamburgers, sandwiches, salads, and pastas. Good for children. **FYI:** Reservations not accepted. **Open:** HS July–Sept daily 11:30am–1am. Reduced hours off-season. Closed some hols. **Prices:** Main courses $4.95–$16.95. Maj CC. 📷 [VP] &

Topaz Cafe, in Bowers Museum, 2002 N Main, Santa Ana; tel 714/835-2002. Exit 17 off I-5 N. At 20th St. **Eclectic.** Museum-quality artifacts lend a dramatic touch to the decor. Unique menu changes daily and features a variety of grilled chicken, meat, and fish dishes. One Friday each month, cafe offers an evening of Native American cuisine and live Native American entertainment. **FYI:** Reservations recommended. Children's menu. **Open:** Lunch Tues–Sat 11:30am–3pm; dinner Thurs 5–8pm; brunch Sun 10am–3pm. Closed Dec 25. **Prices:** Main courses $9–$14. Maj CC. 🍴 &

SANTA BARBARA
Map page M-3, D1

See also **Goleta, Montecito, Summerland**

Hotels 🏨

▤▤▤▤ **El Encanto Hotel & Garden Villas**, 1900 Lasuen Rd, Santa Barbara, CA 93103 (the Riviera); tel 805/687-5000 or toll free 800/223-5652; fax 805/687-3903. 1 mi W of downtown. Mission St exit off US 101. Romantic hotel set among lush, tropical grounds on a hillside overlooking Santa Barbara and the Pacific. Well-appointed, quiet, and serene. **Rooms:** 45 rms and stes; 39 ctges/villas. CI 3pm/CO noon. Nonsmoking rms avail. Rooms are charmingly decorated with bleached wood and brightly painted country-style furnishings. **Amenities:** 🖥 👁 Cable TV w/movies, refrig, bathrobes. No A/C. All units w/minibars, all w/terraces, some w/fireplaces. English lavender soaps and shampoos. **Services:** ✕ ☞ [VP] 🛆 🕬 Twice-daily maid svce, masseur, babysitting. **Facilities:** 🛍 🍸1 200 1 rst, 1 bar (w/entertainment), washer/dryer. Restaurant offers outdoor dining and great views. **Rates:** HS June–Sept $140–$220 S or D; from $280 ste; from $660 ctge/villa. Children under 2 stay free. Min stay HS, wknds, and spec evnts. Lower rates off-season. Spec packages avail. Pking: Outdoor, free. Maj CC.

▤▤▤ **Fess Parker's Red Lion Resort**, 633 E Cabrillo Blvd, Santa Barbara, CA 93103; tel 805/564-4333 or toll free 800/879-2929; fax 805/962-8198. Milpas exit off US 101 S; Cabrillo Blvd exit off US 101 N. Large, convention/event-oriented hotel located across from the ocean. Nice views. **Rooms:** 360 rms and stes. CI 4pm/CO noon. Express checkout avail. Nonsmoking rms avail. Rooms are oversized, with oak furnishings. **Amenities:** 🖥 👁 🍸A/C, cable TV w/movies. All units w/minibars, all w/terraces, some w/fireplaces, some w/Jacuzzis. **Services:** ✕ ☞ [VP] 🚗 🛆 🕬 🕬 Car-rental desk, masseur, babysitting. **Facilities:** 🛍 🚲 🏖 🏊 🎱 1K & 2 rsts, 1 bar (w/entertainment), games rm, spa, sauna, whirlpool, beauty salon, washer/dryer. Great jazz combo performs in lounge. Shuffleboard, basketball, and putting green available. **Rates:** HS Mem Day–Labor Day $189–$289 S or D; from $395 ste. Extra person $15. Children under 18 stay free. Min stay spec evnts. Lower rates off-season. Spec packages avail. Pking: Outdoor, free. Maj CC.

▤▤▤ **Montecito Inn**, 1295 Coast Village Rd, Santa Barbara, CA 93108 (Montecito); tel 805/969-7854 or toll free 800/843-2017; fax 805/969-0623. 3 mi S of downtown. Olive Mill Rd exit off US 101; head inland; left on Coast Village Rd. Built in 1928 by Charlie Chaplin, this European-style hotel is elegant but not stuffy, with a fireplace in the marble lobby. Caters to corporate clientele and couples. **Rooms:** 60 rms and stes. CI 3pm/CO noon. Nonsmoking rms avail. Rooms are wallpapered in mauve, blue, and purple with French provincial armoires and nightstands. Also fresh flowers and ceiling fans, and hand-painted tiles in bathrooms. Rooms for guests with disabilitites should be completed. **Amenities:** 🏖 🍷 Cable TV w/movies, refrig, VCR. No A/C. Some units w/fireplaces, some w/Jacuzzis. Most rooms have VCRs and refrigerators. **Services:** ✗ VP 🖅 🔁 Twice-daily maid svce, masseur, babysitting. Complimentary continental breakfast. Complete library of Charlie Chaplin films available for use on VCRs. **Facilities:** 🛖 🚲 ⛳ 📷 1 rst, sauna, whirlpool. Walking distance to beach, shops, and restaurants. The excellent Montecito Cafe is on premises. **Rates (CP):** $150–$195 S or D; from $205 ste. Extra person $15. Children under 18 stay free. Min stay wknds and spec evnts. Pking: Indoor/outdoor, free. Maj CC.

≣≣≣ **Radisson Hotel Santa Barbara**, 1111 E Cabrillo Blvd, Santa Barbara, CA 93103 (East Beach); tel 805/963-0744 or toll free 800/333-3333; fax 805/962-0985. Cabrillo exit off US 101. Sprawling full-service hotel across from the beach; caters to families and conventions. **Rooms:** 174 rms, stes, and effic. CI 3pm/CO noon. Express checkout avail. Nonsmoking rms avail. Rooms have simple Old West/Spanish decor; great views from the 2nd floor. **Amenities:** 🏖 🍷 A/C, cable TV w/movies, refrig, VCR, voice mail, shoe polisher. All units w/minibars, some w/terraces. **Services:** ✗ ⚷ 🚐 🖅 🔁 Children's program, babysitting. **Facilities:** 🛖 🚲 ⛳ 📷 🖥 ♿ 1 rst, 1 bar (w/entertainment), washer/dryer. **Rates:** HS June–Oct $179–$219 S or D; from $350 ste. Extra person $20. Children under 18 stay free. Min stay HS and wknds. Lower rates off-season. Spec packages avail. Pking: Indoor/outdoor, free. Maj CC. Efficiencies available by the month only, for $1,550 to $2,600/month.

≣≣≣ **Santa Barbara Inn**, 901 E Cabrillo Blvd, Santa Barbara, CA 93103 (East Beach); tel 805/966-2285 or toll free 800/231-0431; fax 805/966-6584. Recently refurbished beachside hotel; great for families. **Rooms:** 71 rms, stes, and effic. CI 3pm/CO noon. Nonsmoking rms avail. Bright, airy rooms with exceptional views. **Amenities:** 🏖 🍷 📺 Cable TV, refrig. No A/C. Some units w/minibars, all w/terraces. **Services:** ✗ VP 🖅 🔁 Twice-daily maid svce, babysitting. **Facilities:** 🛖 📷 🖥 ♿ 1 rst, 1 bar (w/entertainment), whirlpool. **Rates:** HS Apr–Oct $149–$189 S or D; from $250 ste; from $149 effic. Min stay HS and wknds. Lower rates off-season. Spec packages avail. Pking: Indoor/outdoor, $2. Maj CC.

≣≣≣ **The Upham**, 1404 De La Vina St, Santa Barbara, CA 93101; tel 805/962-0058 or toll free 800/727-0876; fax 805/

963-2825. Arrellaga St exit off US 101 N; Mission St exit off US 101 S. Operated as a hotel since 1871. A stay at this property, with its wicker-filled sun porch, fireplace, and lovely gardens, is like a step back in time. **Rooms:** 49 rms and stes. CI 3pm/CO noon. Nonsmoking rms avail. Furnished in lovely antiques, with fresh flowers. Downstairs rooms have very high ceilings. **Amenities:** 🏖 🍷 Cable TV. No A/C. 1 unit w/minibar, some w/terraces, some w/fireplaces, 1 w/Jacuzzi. **Services:** ✗ 🖅 🔁 Babysitting. Complimentary continental breakfast; afternoon wine and cheese; milk and cookies after 8pm. **Facilities:** 🍽 1 rst. Lovely gazebo in the garden. Restaurant has indoor and outdoor dining. Use of Santa Barbara Athletic Club at a minimum charge. **Rates (CP):** HS July–Aug $110–$180 S or D; from $180 ste. Extra person $10. Children under 12 stay free. Min stay wknds and spec evnts. Lower rates off-season. Pking: Outdoor, free. Maj CC.

Motels

≣≣≣ **Best Western Encina Lodge**, 2220 Bath St, Santa Barbara, CA 93105; tel 805/682-7277 or toll free 800/526-2282; fax 805/563-9319. Mission St exit off US 101; follow Mission north, turn left on Bath St. A comfortable and friendly property convenient to local hospitals. **Rooms:** 121 rms, stes, and effic. CI 3pm/CO noon. Express checkout avail. Nonsmoking rms avail. Very nice, private, relaxing rooms with high beamed ceilings and bright colors. **Amenities:** 🏖 🍷 📺 🍶 A/C, cable TV w/movies, refrig, in-rm safe. Some units w/terraces. Fruit, coffee, and candy in room. **Services:** ✗ 🚐 🖅 🔁 Babysitting. Continental breakfast delivered to rooms. Masseur and twice-daily maid service upon request. TDD offered for deaf and hard of hearing guests. **Facilities:** 🛖 ♿ 1 rst, 1 bar (w/entertainment), sauna, whirlpool, beauty salon, washer/dryer. Fichera's restaurant serves continental cuisine and is popular with locals. **Rates:** HS May–Sept $112 S; $118 D; from $126 ste; from $136 effic. Extra person $6. Children under 3 stay free. Min stay HS and wknds. Lower rates off-season. Spec packages avail. Pking: Indoor/outdoor, free. Maj CC.

≣≣≣ **Best Western Pepper Tree Inn**, 3850 State St, Santa Barbara, CA 93105; tel 805/687-5511 or toll free 800/338-0030; fax 805/682-2410. State St exit off US 101. This property underwent a full renovation in 1994. Spanish-style architecture with 2 fountains, and palm trees bordering the grounds. **Rooms:** 150 rms and stes. CI 3pm/CO noon. Nonsmoking rms avail. New furnishings. **Amenities:** 🏖 🍷 📺 🍶 A/C, cable TV w/movies, refrig, in-rm safe. Some units w/terraces. All rooms come with baskets of fresh fruit and candy. **Services:** ✗ ⚷ 🚐 🖅 🔁 Car-rental desk, masseur, babysitting. **Facilities:** 🛖 ⛳ 📷 1 rst, 1 bar, sauna, whirlpool, beauty salon, washer/dryer. Well-equipped fitness room. Free admission to YMCA ½ block away. **Rates:** HS May–Sept $114 S; $120 D; from $130 ste. Extra person $6. Children under 5 stay free. Min stay HS and wknds. Lower rates off-season. Pking: Outdoor, free. Maj CC.

≣≣≣ **Cathedral Oaks Lodge**, 4770 Calle Real, Santa Barbara, CA 93110; tel 805/944-3511 or toll free 800/228-4581 in CA; fax 805/964-0075. 3 mi N of downtown. A lagoon with ducks, carp, waterfall, lily pads, and palm trees makes the pool and courtyard areas very attractive. **Rooms:** 126 rms and stes. Exec-level rms avail. CI 3pm/CO noon. Nonsmoking rms avail. **Amenities:** 🛋 🕭 🕿 A/C, cable TV w/movies, shoe polisher. All units w/terraces. **Services:** 🚐 🛆 ⌂ Babysitting. European-style breakfast is served poolside or in the Valley Room. Free local calls. **Facilities:** 🛁 🏊 ⅃ Whirlpool, washer/dryer. Four golf courses nearby. **Rates (BB):** HS May–Sept $75–$85 S; $85–$95 D; from $120 ste. Extra person $10. Children under 12 stay free. Min stay spec evnts. Lower rates off-season. Higher rates for spec evnts/hols. Pking: Outdoor, free. Maj CC.

≣≣≣ **Franciscan Inn**, 109 Bath St, Santa Barbara, CA 93101 (West Beach); tel 805/963-8845; fax 805/564-3295. This family-run property, located just 1 block from the beach, is very well maintained and nicely decorated. **Rooms:** 53 rms, stes, and effic. CI 3pm/CO noon. Nonsmoking rms avail. 18 different styles of rooms, each attractively decorated in a country motif accented with fresh flowers. **Amenities:** 🛋 🕭 Cable TV w/movies, refrig. No A/C. Some units w/terraces, 1 w/fireplace. **Services:** 🛆 ⌂ Free local telephone calls and morning newspaper. Continental breakfast included. Complimentary coffee and cookies in the afternoon. Trolley will pick up guests for tours. **Facilities:** 🛁 🏊 Whirlpool, washer/dryer. **Rates (CP):** HS May 15–Oct 15 $70–$85 S; $85–$95 D; from $99 ste; from $99 effic. Extra person $8. Children under 5 stay free. Lower rates off-season. Spec packages avail. Pking: Outdoor, free. Maj CC.

≣≣≣ **Harbor View Inn**, 28 W Cabrillo Blvd, Santa Barbara, CA 93101; tel 805/963-0780 or toll free 800/755-0222; fax 805/963-7967. Castillo St exit off US 101; W on Castillo toward ocean; left on Cabrillo. Best location in town, with Beach and Stearns wharf across the street. Major renovation, currently in progress, will enhance an already beautiful property. **Rooms:** 64 rms. CI 3pm/CO noon. Nonsmoking rms avail. Fresh flowers in all rooms. **Amenities:** 🛋 🕭 Cable TV w/movies, refrig. No A/C. Some units w/minibars, some w/terraces. Some rooms air-conditioned. **Services:** 🍽 🛆 ⌂ Babysitting. Continental breakfast in restaurant. Wine and cheese 5 to 7pm on patio facing beach. **Facilities:** 🛁 🚴 🏊 🏊 1 rst, whirlpool. Skate rentals. Boat rentals nearby. **Rates (CP):** HS May–Sept $85–$215 S or D. Extra person $15. Children under 5 stay free. Min stay HS, wknds, and spec evnts. Lower rates off-season. Spec packages avail. Pking: Outdoor, free. Maj CC.

≣≣ **Motel 6**, 3505 State St, Santa Barbara, CA 93105; tel 805/687-5400. Las Positas exit off US 101; turn left onto State St; go north ¼ mi. Although not near the beach, this motel provides safe, clean, comfortable rooms for families at a reasonable rate. Many foreigners stay here. **Rooms:** 60 rms. CI 2pm/CO noon. Nonsmoking rms avail. The rooms are bright, cheery, and very clean. They were recently renovated, and look brand-new. **Amenities:** 🛋 A/C, cable TV w/movies. **Services:** ⌂ 🐾 Very security-conscious staff. **Facilities:** 🛁 🏊 Pool is large, inviting, and extremely clean, but has no vegetation around it. **Rates:** HS May 26–Oct 25 $46 S or D. Children under 17 stay free. Lower rates off-season. Pking: Outdoor, free. Maj CC.

≣ **Mountain View Inn**, 3955 De La Vina St, Santa Barbara, CA 93105; tel 805/687-6636; fax 805/569-6809. Las Positas exit off US 101; go right on State St. Good view of the mountains in a quiet location. Homey lobby almost has the feel of a B&B. Adequate accommodation for a reasonable price. **Rooms:** 34 rms. CI 2pm/CO noon. Nonsmoking rms avail. Somewhat small rooms are not outstanding but not shabby either. Some are outdated but are being remodeled. **Amenities:** 🛋 A/C, cable TV w/movies, refrig. **Services:** ⌂ **Facilities:** 🛁 **Rates (CP):** HS May–Sept $55–$83 S or D. Extra person $5. Children under 5 stay free. Min stay wknds. Lower rates off-season. Spec packages avail. Pking: Outdoor, free. Maj CC.

≣≣ **Ocean Palms Hotel**, 232 W Cabrillo Blvd, Santa Barbara, CA 93101; tel 805/966-9133 or toll free 800/350-2326; fax 805/965-7882. Spanish-style building with red-tile roof, painted tiles, and charming archways, located across from the beach. Nice cottages for families. **Rooms:** 32 rms and effic; 5 ctges/villas. CI 3pm/CO noon. Nonsmoking rms avail. **Amenities:** 🛋 🕭 🕿 Satel TV w/movies. No A/C. Some units w/terraces, some w/fireplaces. **Services:** 🛆 ⌂ 🐾 Masseur, babysitting. **Facilities:** 🛁 🏊 Lawn games, whirlpool. Pool has a sundeck. Restaurants, harbor, and pier nearby. **Rates (CP):** HS July–Oct 15 $85–$175 S or D; from $110 effic; from $150 ctge/villa. Extra person $10. Children under 10 stay free. Min stay HS, wknds, and spec evnts. Lower rates off-season. Spec packages avail. Pking: Outdoor, free. Maj CC.

≣≣≣ **Pacifica Suites**, 5490 Hollister Ave, Santa Barbara, CA 93111; tel 805/683-6722 or toll free 800/338-6722; fax 805/683-4121. Patterson exit off US 101; turn toward ocean, to Hollister. Quiet, rural resort-style motel styled after an 1880 restored Victorian mansion on the property. **Rooms:** 75 stes. CI 3pm/CO noon. Express checkout avail. Nonsmoking rms avail. **Amenities:** 🛋 🕭 🕿 🖥 A/C, cable TV w/movies, refrig, VCR, stereo/tape player. All units w/terraces. **Services:** 🚐 🛆 ⌂ 🐾 Babysitting. Free happy hour. **Facilities:** 🛁 🚴 🏊 🏊 1 rst, 1 bar, spa, whirlpool, playground. **Rates (BB):** From $109 ste.

Extra person $10. Children under 18 stay free. Min stay HS and wknds. Higher rates for spec evnts/hols. Spec packages avail. Pking: Outdoor, free. Maj CC.

≡≡ **Sandman Inn**, 3714 State St, Santa Barbara, CA 93105; tel 805/687-2468 or toll free 800/350-8174; fax 805/687-6581. 3 mi N of downtown. State St exit off US 101. This property is on a busy street across from a shopping mall, but it extends far back off the street and has a homey feel. **Rooms:** 113 rms, stes, and effic. CI 3pm/CO noon. Nonsmoking rms avail. Rooms are a bit cramped but clean. **Amenities:** 🛏 A/C, cable TV w/movies. Some units w/terraces. **Services:** ⌂ Babysitting. **Facilities:** 🛋 🖺 ⅙ 1 rst, 1 bar, whirlpool, washer/dryer. Free passes to YMCA ½ block away. **Rates (CP):** HS Mem Day–Labor Day $71–$114 S; $81–$124 D; from $71 ste; from $91 effic. Extra person $10. Children under 18 stay free. Min stay HS and wknds. Lower rates off-season. Pking: Outdoor, free. Maj CC.

≡≡ **Tropicana Inn**, 223 Castillo St, Santa Barbara, CA 93101 (West Beach); tel 805/966-2219 or toll free 800/468-1988; fax 805/962-9428. Castillo St exit off US 101. A clean property close to the beach and good for long stays; 100% nonsmoking. **Rooms:** 31 rms and stes. CI 3pm/CO noon. Rooms have large immaculate kitchens with French country decor; 3rd-floor rooms have nice mountain views. **Amenities:** 🛏 ⅛ Cable TV, refrig. No A/C. **Services:** 🖺 ⌂ Babysitting. Continental breakfast served in lobby. **Facilities:** 🛋 🖺 ⅙ Whirlpool. Tennis courts in park next door. **Rates (CP):** HS May 27–Sept 4 $92–$112 S or D; from $112 ste. Extra person $5. Children under 3 stay free. Min stay HS, wknds, and spec evnts. Lower rates off-season. Spec packages avail. Pking: Outdoor, free. Maj CC.

Inns

≡≡≡ **The Cheshire Cat**, 36 W Valerio St, Santa Barbara, CA 93101; tel 805/569-1610; fax 805/682-1876. Cozy Victorian-era bed-and-breakfast filled with antiques. Very well kept. **Rooms:** 14 rms and stes. CI 3pm/CO noon. No smoking. Rooms are individually decorated with cheerful chintz fabrics and wallpaper, fresh flowers, and original art. **Amenities:** 🛏 No A/C. Some units w/minibars, some w/terraces, some w/fireplaces, some w/Jacuzzis. English soaps, herbal shampoo, chocolates, and liqueurs. Not all rooms have TV. **Services:** Afternoon tea and wine/sherry served. Continental breakfast weekdays and full breakfast buffet on weekends. Tea and cookies in the afternoon. **Facilities:** 🚴 🖺 Whirlpool, guest lounge w/TV. Gazebo. **Rates (BB):** HS June–Oct $119–$139 S or D; from $169 ste. Extra person $25. Min stay wknds. Lower rates off-season. Spec packages avail. Pking: Outdoor, free. Ltd CC.

≡≡≡ **Glenborough Bed & Breakfast Inn**, 1327 Bath St, Santa Barbara, CA 93101 (Downtown); tel 805/966-0589 or toll free 800/962-0589; fax 805/564-2369. This antiques-filled B&B combines 3 houses—the 1906 Craftsman-style main house, the Victorian cottage, and the California classic white house—in a residential neighborhood a few blocks from downtown. Unsuitable for children under 12. **Rooms:** 11 rms and stes (6 w/shared bath). CI 3pm/CO 11am. No smoking. Decors range from art nouveau to nautical; rooms are furnished with real and reproduction antiques. **Amenities:** 🛏 ⅛ Bathrobes. No A/C or TV. Some units w/terraces, some w/fireplaces. **Services:** Twice-daily maid svce, masseur, babysitting, afternoon tea served. Full breakfast served in guest rooms, parlor, or garden. **Facilities:** Lawn games, whirlpool, guest lounge. Private time can be reserved in the open-air Jacuzzi in the rear garden. **Rates (BB):** HS Aug–Oct $70–$90 S or D w/shared bath, $110–$125 S or D w/private bath; from $145 ste. Extra person $25. Min stay wknds and spec evnts. Lower rates off-season. Spec packages avail. Pking: Outdoor, free. Ltd CC.

≡≡≡≡ **Simpson House Inn**, 121 E Arrellaga, Santa Barbara, CA 93101; tel 805/963-7067 or toll free 800/676-1280; fax 805/564-4811. Garden St exit off US 101. 1 acre. A very special B&B in a quiet neighborhood, with a lovely garden and beautifully decorated public rooms. A historic landmark, built in 1874. **Rooms:** 13 rms and stes; 3 ctges/villas. CI 3pm/CO 11am. No smoking. Very beautiful rooms with antiques, nice wallpaper, and clawfoot tubs. Carriage-house rooms are especially attractive. **Amenities:** 🛏 ⅛ 🍷 A/C, TV w/movies, VCR, stereo/tape player, bathrobes. Some units w/minibars, some w/terraces, some w/fireplaces, some w/Jacuzzis. Collection of more than 100 videos. **Services:** ✗ 🖺 Masseur, afternoon tea and wine/sherry served. Breakfast delivered to room. **Facilities:** 🚴 Lawn games, guest lounge. Gorgeous grounds with fountains. **Rates (BB):** $105–$245 S or D; from $245 ste; from $245 ctge/villa. Extra person $25. Children under 3 stay free. Min stay wknds. Spec packages avail. Pking: Outdoor, free. Ltd CC.

Resort

≡≡≡≡ **Four Seasons Biltmore**, 1260 Channel Dr, Santa Barbara, CA 93108; tel 805/969-2261 or toll free 800/332-3442; fax 805/969-4682. Olive Mill Rd exit off US 101; go south (toward ocean). 20 acres. A classic, opened in 1927, with red tile roof and stucco walls. Splendid lobby has coffered ceilings, terra-cotta floors, and handpainted tiles. All this, plus acres of gardens and the deep blue Pacific across the way. **Rooms:** 234 rms and stes. CI 3pm/CO noon. Express checkout avail. Nonsmoking rms avail. Rooms are tastefully decorated in soft earth tones. Ceiling fans keep things cool and airy. White marble bathrooms are extremely well laid out. **Amenities:** 🛏 ⅛

Cable TV w/movies, refrig, VCR, in-rm safe, shoe polisher, bathrobes. No A/C. All units w/minibars, some w/terraces, some w/fireplaces. **Services:** ▯▯ ▯▯ VP ▯▯ ▯▯ ▯▯ ▯▯ Twice-daily maid svce, car-rental desk, masseur, children's program, baby-sitting. Complimentary shoeshine service. In-room spa treatments available. **Facilities:** ▯ ▯ ▯ ▯ ▯ 350 ▯ ▯ 3 rsts, 2 bars (1 w/entertainment), 1 beach (ocean), lawn games, spa, sauna, steam rm, whirlpool, beauty salon. The beachside art deco Coral Casino is the social center of Santa Barbara. Stunning 50-meter pool, and a new workout room well equipped with exercise bikes, treadmill, and more. **Rates:** HS June–Sept $199–$370 S or D; from $450 ste. Extra person $30. Children under 18 stay free. Min stay wknds. Lower rates off-season. Spec packages avail. Pking: Outdoor, free. Maj CC. Tennis, golf, spa, and other packages available. Midweek "Paradise" packages are extremely well priced, offering 2 nights' accommodation plus breakfast for $495 per couple.

Restaurants ▯▯▯

Andersen's Danish Bakery and Restaurant, 1106 State St, Santa Barbara (Downtown); tel 805/962-5085. **Danish.** Sunny and social place, good for watching the activity on State St. Scandinavian blue-and-white tiles, umbrella-covered tables outdoors. The menu changes daily, featuring specialties like smoked salmon, goulash, schnitzel, fresh fish, as well as baked goods. Mini-smorgasbord for 2. Good Morning breakfast is a best-seller. **FYI:** Reservations not accepted. Beer and wine only. **Open:** Wed–Mon 8am–6pm. Closed some hols. **Prices:** Lunch main courses $3.95–$9.95. No CC. ▯ ▯

Arnoldi's Cafe, 600 Olive St, Santa Barbara; tel 805/962-5394. 5 blocks E of State St. **Italian/Steak.** Housed in an old stone building, this homey Italian restaurant features wooden booths, red-and-white-checkered tablecloths, and a jukebox. Basic Italian fare, as well as chicken, steak, and lamb chops. **FYI:** Reservations accepted. **Open:** Thurs–Tues 5–11pm. Closed some hols. **Prices:** Main courses $8.95–$14.95. No CC. ▯ ▯

Brophy Brothers Clam Bar & Restaurant, Yacht Basin and Marina, Santa Barbara; tel 805/966-4418. Castillo St exit off US 101. **Seafood.** A great place with an atmosphere as authentic as it gets. The patio overlooks the harbor; inside, there are wooden floors, low ceilings, and big windows. The simple menu includes the expected clams, mussels, ceviche, seafood salads, and fried fish. Daily specials depend on the catch. **FYI:** Reservations not accepted. **Open:** Daily 11am–10pm. Closed some hols. **Prices:** Main courses $5.95–$15.95. Maj CC. ▯ ▯

♣ Casa de Sevilla, 428 Chapala St, Santa Barbara; tel 805/966-4370. 2 blocks W of State St. **Seafood/Steak.** One of the first bars opened after Prohibition, it has been popular with generations of Santa Barbarans. Reminiscent of a private club, with a fireplace and old fiesta and bullfight posters. The menu runs to seafood with a California twist, offering ceviche and chili rellenos for starters, a variety of seafood specials, and barbecued meats. **FYI:** Reservations recommended. Jacket required. **Open:** Lunch Tues–Sat noon–2pm; dinner Tues–Sat 6–10pm. Closed some hols. **Prices:** Main courses $12–$25; PF dinner $22. Maj CC. ▯ ▯ ▯ ▯

★ Cold Spring Tavern, 5995 Stagecoach Rd, Santa Barbara; tel 805/967-0066. 12 mi NW of downtown. Off Calif 154, right on Stagecoach Rd 1 mi. **Californian.** One of the best hideaway hangouts in California. A 126-year-old stagecoach stop is the setting for the restaurant, which serves steak, fish, pastas, and game dishes. The log-cabin tavern offers a lighter bar menu. Live music Wednesday through Sunday. **FYI:** Reservations accepted. Blues/country music/jazz. **Open:** Breakfast Sat–Sun 8–11am; lunch Mon–Sun 11am–3pm; dinner Sun–Thurs 5–9pm, Fri–Sat 5–10pm. Closed Dec 25. **Prices:** PF dinner $8.50–$22. Ltd CC. ▯ ▯

★ Joe's Cafe, 536 State St, Santa Barbara (Downtown); tel 805/966-4638. **American.** A Santa Barbara classic; traditional family restaurant with red-and-white-checkered tablecloths and wooden booths. The walls are lined with historic black-and-white photos of Santa Barbara. The menu is basic steak, spaghetti, liver and onions, and burgers. **FYI:** Reservations accepted. **Open:** Mon–Thurs 11am–11:30pm, Fri–Sat 11am–12:30pm, Sun 4–11:30pm. Closed Dec 25. **Prices:** Main courses $9.25–$18.25. Maj CC. ▯ ▯ ▯

★ La Super-Rica Taqueria, 622 N Milpas St, Santa Barbara; tel 805/963-4940. Milpas St exit off US 101. **Mexican.** One of Santa Barbara's most popular spots. Seating is at wooden tables on a canvas-canopied patio. Authentic and delicious food offerings come with homemade tortillas and salsa: fare includes quesadillas and tacos of charbroiled steak, and pork with onions and chiles. Daily specials are available. Portions are small. **FYI:** Reservations not accepted. Beer and wine only. **Open:** Sun–Thurs 11am–9:30pm, Fri–Sat 11am–10pm. Closed some hols. **Prices:** Main courses $3–$8. No CC. ▯ ▯ ▯

Mousse Odile, 18 E Cota St, Santa Barbara; tel 805/962-5393. 1 block E of State St. **French.** One of the best French restaurants in Santa Barbara. Light and airy by day, romantic by night, with a high ceiling, lots of plants, and a peaceful patio for outside dining. Offers omelettes, quiches, and finely prepared seafood, veal, and filet mignon. Specialties include osso buco and couscous with lamb. **FYI:** Reservations accepted. **Open:** Breakfast Mon–Sat 8–11:30am; lunch Mon–Sat 11:30am–2:30pm; dinner Mon–Sat 5:30–9pm. Closed some hols. **Prices:** Main courses $8.95–$16.25. Maj CC. ♥ ≙ ☕

Oysters, in Victoria Court, 9 W Victoria St, Santa Barbara; tel 805/962-9888. 1 block W of State St. **Californian/Seafood.** Simply decorated, with a pleasant patio surrounded by lush trees. The specialty is oysters, which come fried, grilled, as shooters, or on the half shell. The menu also offers fresh fish, pasta, chicken, and a selection of salads with gourmet greens. **FYI:** Reservations accepted. **Open:** Lunch Tues–Sat 11:30am–2:30pm; dinner Tues–Sun 5–11pm; brunch Sun 9:30–11:30am. Closed some hols. **Prices:** Main courses $10.95–$19.95. Maj CC. ♥ ≙ ☕

★ **Palace Cafe**, 8 E Cota St, Santa Barbara; tel 805/966-3133. 1 block E of State St. **Cajun/Caribbean/Creole.** With high ceilings, wood floors, and murals, this is a fun and flamboyant hot spot. The exotic fare includes Caribbean and Cajun/Creole specialties like crawfish étoufée, blackened redfish, Cajun popcorn, gumbo, and barbecued shrimp. Tables are stocked with 4 kinds of fresh-baked muffins. On weekends, a saxophonist serenades the crowds waiting to enter. **FYI:** Reservations accepted. **Open:** Sun–Thurs 5:30–10pm, Fri–Sat 5:30–11pm. Closed Dec 25. **Prices:** Main courses $11.75–$18.75. Maj CC. ☕

Paradise Cafe, 702 Anacapa St, Santa Barbara; tel 805/962-4416. 1 block E of State St. **New American.** Housed in a historic building in Santa Barbara, with an umbrella-filled patio and 2 comfortable indoor dining rooms graced with palm trees. Variety of fresh seafood, burgers, pasta, and fresh salads, as well as entrees from the oak grill. **FYI:** Reservations accepted. **Open:** Mon–Sat 11am–11pm, Sun 8:30am–11pm. Closed some hols. **Prices:** Main courses $5.95–$16.95. Maj CC. ▮ ≙

Piatti's Ristorante, 516 San Ysidro Rd, Santa Barbara (Montecito); tel 805/969-7520. San Ysidro exit off US 101. **Italian.** A serene restaurant with soft murals, wood and leather chairs, and classical music. An outdoor patio overlooks a beautiful creek. Extensive selection of antipasti, salads, pizzas, pastas, grilled vegetables, seafood, and chicken. Some dishes have a California twist, like the homemade cannelloni stuffed with chicken, artichokes, ricotta, and sage. **FYI:** Reservations accepted. **Open:** Sun–Thurs 11:30am–10pm, Fri–Sat 11:30am–11pm. Closed Dec 25. **Prices:** Main courses $7.95–$16.95. Maj CC. ♥ ≙ ☕

Presidio Cafe, 812 Anacapa St, Santa Barbara; tel 805/962-3740. 1 block E of State St. **New American.** Located across the street from historic El Paseo, this place is clean and fresh, with a stone-tiled patio. A fountain adds a peaceful air. The menu is simple, with breakfasts of pancakes, eggs, and tofu scrambles, as well as seafood crepes, lox, and bagels. The lunch menu

includes sandwiches on fresh-baked breads, New Zealand lamb, and rigatoni. **FYI:** Reservations accepted. Beer and wine only. **Open:** Mon–Sat 7am–3pm, Sun 8am–3pm. **Prices:** Lunch main courses $6–$11. Ltd CC. ♥ ≙ ☕

Woody's, 229 W Montecito St, Santa Barbara; tel 805/963-9326. Castillo St exit off US 101. **Barbecue/Pizza.** Funky western cantina known for its ribs. The wild decor of this lively hangout includes sawdust on the floor, license plates on the walls, and an eclectic assortment of lanterns, moose heads, flags, stoplights, and even a bathtub. Pizza, burgers, tacos, ribs. Diners order from a counter and serve themselves from the salad bar and drink dispenser. **FYI:** Reservations accepted. Band. Children's menu. **Open:** Sun–Thurs 11am–midnight, Fri–Sat 11am–1am. Closed some hols. **Prices:** Main courses $5.95–$13.95. Maj CC. 📟 🚗 ☕

Your Place, 22A N Milpas St, Santa Barbara; tel 805/966-5151. Milpas St exit off US 101. **Thai.** Among the myriad Thai restaurants in Santa Barbara, this one is consistently well received. Colorful umbrellas hang from the ceiling, and golden peacocks adorn the walls. The seafood platter is a combination of shrimp, fish, crab claws, scallops, water chestnuts, cashews, and ginger. Pad Thai, fried noodles, is a favorite. **FYI:** Reservations accepted. Beer and wine only. **Open:** Tues–Thurs 11am–10pm, Fri–Sat 11am–11pm, Sun 11am–10pm. Closed Dec 25. **Prices:** Main courses $5.25–$12.95. Maj CC. ☕

Zia Cafe, 532 State St, Santa Barbara (Downtown); tel 805/962-5391. **New Mexican.** One of the only restaurants in Southern California offering authentic Santa Fe products, this southwestern restaurant is cozy and attractive, with a copper bar and classic Santa Fe style. Whether you prefer spicy green or mild red chili sauce, you'll find them both served with enchiladas, blue corn tacos, chili rellenos, tamales, and burritos. **FYI:** Reservations recommended. Children's menu. **Open:** HS June–Oct breakfast Sat–Sun 9am–2pm; lunch daily 11am–3pm; dinner daily 3–11pm. Reduced hours off-season. Closed some hols. **Prices:** Main courses $5.95–$9.95. Ltd CC. ≙ ☕

Attractions 💼

Santa Barbara Mission, Mission and Laguna Sts; tel 805/682-4173 or 682-4175. Its twin bell towers and graceful beauty have earned this mission the title "Queen of the Missions." The tenth of the 21 California Spanish missions, it was established in 1786 and is still used as a local parish. Displayed in its museum are a typical early missionary's bedroom; 18th- and 19th-century furnishings; paintings and sculptures from Mexico; period kitchen utensils; and Native American tools, crafts, and artifacts. **Open:** Daily 9am–5pm. $

Santa Barbara County Courthouse, 1100 Anacapa St; tel 805/962-6464. Occupying a full city block and set in a lush tropical garden, this building incorporates elements of Spanish-Moorish design, with towers and a turret, brilliant Tunisian tilework, and intricately stenciled ceilings. Historic murals by Dan Sayre Groesbeck depict memorable episodes in Santa Barbara history; a 10x13-foot Groesbeck painting on plaster that inspired the mural hangs outside the Mural Room. An elevator takes visitors to an observation deck on the roof of the clock tower for a view of the ocean, the mountains, and the red terra-cotta tile roofs of the city. A free guided tour is offered Wednesday and Friday at 10:30am, and Monday through Saturday at 2pm. **Open:** Mon–Fri 8:30am–5pm; Sat–Sun and hols 8:30am–4:30pm. Free.

Santa Barbara Historical Museum, 136 E de la Guerra St; tel 805/966-1601. This charming adobe complex contains one of the finest collections of regional history in California. Exhibits of local lore feature such art and artifacts as saddles and antique toys; late 19th-century paintings of California missions by Edwin Deakin; a 16th-century carved Spanish coffer from Majorca, Spain; and a collection of objects from the Chinese community that once flourished here, highlighted by a carved Tong shrine from the turn of the century. Also on display are early letters, antique dolls, a late 19th-century period costume collection, and assorted memorabilia; the Gledhill Library has extensive holdings of books, maps, photographs, and manuscripts. Free guided tour every Wednesday, Saturday, and Sunday at 1:30pm.

Adjacent to the museum are two 19th-century adobes surrounding a tree-shaded courtyard. **Casa Covarrubias** was constructed on this site in 1817. The adjoining **Historic Adobe** was built in 1836 and was later moved to this location. **Open:** Tues–Sat 10am–5pm, Sun noon–5pm. Closed some hols. Free.

Santa Barbara Museum of Art, 1130 State St; tel 805/963-4364. Featured collections of this museum include Greek and Roman sculpture; works from the Italian Renaissance and Flemish schools; European impressionist paintings, including works by Monet; works by such early 20th-century European modernists as Chagall, Picasso, and Kandinsky; and a variety of American and Asian art. The photography collection boasts more than 1,500 items.

Most of the museum's 14,000-plus works are exhibited on a rotating basis. Temporary shows are also presented. Free guided tours are given Tuesday–Sunday at 1pm; focus tours given selected Wednesday and Saturday at noon. **Open:** Tues–Wed and Fri–Sat 11am–5pm, Thurs 11am–9pm, Sun noon–5pm. Closed some hols. $$

Santa Barbara Museum of Natural History, 2559 Puesta del Sol Rd; tel 805/682-4711. Outside this museum visitors will encounter a 72-foot blue whale skeleton, 1 of only 2 on display in the country. Exhibits inside focus on the display, study, and interpretation of Pacific Coast natural history: flora, fauna, and prehistoric life. Local Native American history and culture are illustrated, with exhibits on basketry, textiles, and a full-size replica of a Chumash canoe. Other exhibits include the Nature Art Gallery, Geology and Fossil Hall, and a planetarium presenting star shows on weekends. Traveling exhibits are also featured. **Open:** Mon–Sat 9am–5pm, Sun and hols 10am–5pm. Closed some hols. $$

Fernald Mansion and Trussell–Winchester Adobe, 414 W Montecito St; tel 805/966-1601. The Fernald Mansion (1862) is a fine example of Victorian architecture. The 14-room Queen Anne–style residence of Judge Charles Fernald, it features intricately carved exterior woodwork and is beuatifully furnished within. Next door is the Trussell–Winchester Adobe, built in 1854. An adobe structure with wood siding, its design is known as "Yankee Adobe," a typical hybrid of Mexican and American architectural periods. Its furnishings include some pieces that are a century old. **Open:** Sun 2–4pm. Closed some hols. Free.

Moreton Bay Fig Tree, Chapala and Montecito Sts. Famous for its size, this massive specimen casts a noontime shadow big enough to accommodate an estimated 10,000 people. Planted in 1877, it is thought to be the largest of its kind in the United States.

Stearns Wharf, end of State St; tel 805/963-2633. In addition to a small collection of shops, attractions, and restaurants, the city's 1872-vintage pier offers terrific views of the city and good dropline fishing. The Dolphin Fountain at the foot of the wharf was created by Bud Bottoms for the city's 1982 bicentennial (copies are located in Puerto Vallarta, Mexico; Toba, Japan; and Yalta, Ukraine).

Santa Barbara Zoological Gardens, 500 Niños Dr; tel 805/962-5339 or 962-6310 (recorded info). This small zoo has more than 500 animals in open, naturalistic settings. Beautiful botanic displays augment the exhibits. There's also a children's Discovery Area; a miniature train ride; and a small carousel. Gift shop; snack bar. Picnic area with grills. **Open:** June–Aug, daily 9am–6pm; Sept–May, daily 10am–5pm. $$

Santa Barbara Botanic Garden, 1212 Mission Canyon Rd; tel 805/682-4726. More than 60 acres of native trees, shrubs, cactii, and wildflowers can be seen at the garden, and there are more than 5 miles of trails. Free guided tours are offered daily at 2pm, with additional tours on Thursday, Saturday, and Sunday at 10:30am. **Open:** Daily 8am–sunset. $

SANTA CLARA

Map page M-2, D2

Hotels 🛏

≣≣≣ Biltmore Hotel & Suites, 2151 Laurelwood Rd, Santa Clara, CA 95054; tel 408/988-8411 or toll free 800/255-9925; fax 408/988-0225. Montague Expressway exit off US 101. **Rooms:** 262 rms and stes. CI 3pm/CO noon. Express checkout avail. Nonsmoking rms avail. **Amenities:** 📷 ⚙ 🕾 A/C, cable TV w/movies. Some units w/minibars. **Services:** ✗ 🚐 🛄 ⇩ Car-rental desk. **Facilities:** 🏠 🏋 350 ᕪ 1 rst, 2 bars, whirlpool. **Rates (BB):** $99–$119 S; $109–$129 D; from $119 ste. Extra person $10. Children under 18 stay free. Spec packages avail. Pking: Outdoor, free. Maj CC.

≣≣≣ Embassy Suites, 2885 Lakeside Dr, Santa Clara, CA 95054; tel 408/496-6400 or toll free 800/EMBASSY; fax 408/988-7529. Great American Pkwy exit off US 101 onto Bowers; turn right on Augustine Dr, right on Lakeside Dr. Atrium-style lobby with bar and restaurant adjacent. Glass elevators afford lovely views. **Rooms:** 257 stes. CI 3pm/CO 1pm. Express checkout avail. Nonsmoking rms avail. Wood furniture, good lighting, attractive bedside lamps. **Amenities:** 📷 ⚙ 🕾 A/C, satel TV w/movies, refrig, voice mail, bathrobes. **Services:** ✗ 🚐 🛄 ⇩ Car-rental desk. Complimentary full breakfast. **Facilities:** 🏠 🏋 100 ᕪ 1 rst, 1 bar, sauna, whirlpool, washer/dryer. Very pleasant indoor pool with overhead windows and plants. **Rates (BB):** From $159 ste. Extra person $15. Children under 13 stay free. Spec packages avail. Pking: Outdoor, free. Maj CC.

≣≣ Mariani's Inn, 2500 El Camino Real, Santa Clara, CA 95051; tel 408/243-1431 or toll free 800/553-8666; fax 408/243-5745. Motel-like property has basic accommodations and a popular restaurant. **Rooms:** 134 rms, stes, and effic. CI 2pm/CO 11am. Nonsmoking rms avail. **Amenities:** 📷 ⚙ 🕾 A/C, cable TV w/movies, refrig, shoe polisher. Fresh flowers in guest rooms. **Services:** ✗ 🖾 🚐 🛄 ⇩ 🕭 Babysitting. Complimentary breakfast is served in the restaurant. **Facilities:** 🏠 225 ᕪ 1 rst, 1 bar (w/entertainment), whirlpool, washer/dryer. Barbecue pit. **Rates (CP):** $48–$70 S; $55–$78 D; from $59 ste; from $59 effic. Extra person $8. Children under 12 stay free. Spec packages avail. Pking: Outdoor, free. Maj CC.

≣≣≣ Quality Suites, 3100 Lakeside Dr, Santa Clara, CA 95054; tel 408/748-9800 or toll free 800/345-1554; fax 408/748-1476. Great America/Bowers exit off US 101; go south on Bowers; turn right on Augustine, right on Lakeside. Subtle art deco furnishings adorn the lobby, which has dark cherry woods and a high ceiling and is flanked by an overhanging balcony. The

raised lounge area outside is done in "library" style with fake plants, brass, glass stairs, and some fluorescent wall sconces. **Rooms:** 220 stes. Exec-level rms avail. CI 4pm/CO noon. Express checkout avail. Nonsmoking rms avail. Decor is dark, done in mostly blues and mauves. Both living and bed areas have windows for light and armoires for closet space. VIP rooms are accessible via special key and have many amenities. **Amenities:** 📷 ⚙ 🕾 A/C, cable TV w/movies, refrig, VCR, stereo/tape player. All units w/minibars. One large unit has a microwave. **Services:** VP 🚐 🛄 ⇩ Full cooked-to-order breakfast included. Complimentary cocktails. **Facilities:** 🏠 🏋 85 🖵 ᕪ 1 bar, whirlpool, washer/dryer. **Rates (BB):** HS Apr–May from $119 ste. Extra person $10. Children under 3 stay free. Lower rates off-season. Spec packages avail. Pking: Indoor/outdoor, free. Maj CC.

≣≣≣≣ Santa Clara Marriott, 2700 Mission College Blvd, Santa Clara, CA 95054; tel 408/988-1500 or toll free 800/228-9290; fax 408/727-4353. Great America Pkwy exit off US 101; turn right. Provides elegance and good service. Highly rated by conventioneers. **Rooms:** 754 rms and stes. Exec-level rms avail. CI 3pm/CO 11am. Express checkout avail. Nonsmoking rms avail. **Amenities:** 📷 ⚙ A/C, cable TV w/movies, voice mail. Some units w/minibars, all w/terraces. Interactive network on TV provides services and information to guests. **Services:** ✗ 🖾 VP 🚐 🛄 ⇩ 🕭 Car-rental desk, babysitting. Complimentary trolley to Great America (late March–October). **Facilities:** 🏠 🏊 🏋 1.5K 3 rsts, 2 bars (1 w/entertainment), games rm, whirlpool, washer/dryer. **Rates:** $129 S; $144 D; from $400 ste. Children under 18 stay free. MAP rates avail. Spec packages avail. Pking: Indoor/outdoor, free. Maj CC.

≣≣≣ Westin Santa Clara, 5101 Great America Pkwy, Santa Clara, CA 95054; tel 408/986-0700 or toll free 800/228-3000; fax 408/980-3990. Great America Pkwy exit off US 101; turn right. Adjacent to Santa Clara Convention Center, this is also convenient for the leisure traveler visiting Great America. Close to the Santa Clara Golf and Tennis Club, too. No smoking in public areas, only inside designated guest rooms. **Rooms:** 500 rms and stes. Exec-level rms avail. CI 3pm/CO noon. Express checkout avail. Nonsmoking rms avail. **Amenities:** 📷 ⚙ A/C, cable TV w/movies, voice mail. Some units w/minibars, some w/terraces, 1 w/Jacuzzi. **Services:** 🍴 🖾 VP 🚐 🛄 ⇩ 🕭 Children's program, babysitting. **Facilities:** 🏠 🏋 125 🖵 ᕪ 2 rsts, 1 bar (w/entertainment), spa, whirlpool. Fitness Room has Lifecycles, free weights, treadmill, bicycles. **Rates:** $159 S; $169 D; from $159 ste. Extra person $10. Children under 18 stay free. Spec packages avail. Pking: Indoor/outdoor, free. Maj CC.

≣≣≣ Woodcrest Hotel, 5415 Stevens Creek Blvd, Santa Clara, CA 95051; tel 408/446-9636 or toll free 800/862-8282; fax 408/446-9739. Lawrence Expwy exit off I-280; left on

Stevens Creek Blvd. **Rooms:** 60 rms and stes. CI 3pm/CO noon. Nonsmoking rms avail. Courtyard rooms are especially quiet. **Amenities:** 🛎 🕐 🖵 📞 A/C, cable TV w/movies, VCR, shoe polisher, bathrobes. Some units w/fireplaces, 1 w/Jacuzzi. Light dinner and snacks kept in the refrigerator. **Services:** 🛌 🛒 Babysitting. Free videos. **Facilities:** 🗓 🕭 1 bar. **Rates (CP):** $114 S; $129 D; from $124 ste. Extra person $15. Children under 12 stay free. Spec packages avail. Pking: Outdoor, free. Maj CC. Rates go down substantially on weekends.

Motels

🏨 **Days Inn Santa Clara**, 4200 Great America Pkwy, Santa Clara, CA 95054; tel 408/980-1525 or toll free 800/329-7466; fax 408/988-0976. Great America Pkwy exit off US 101; go right. Outside doesn't look promising, but interior is very nice, with old-world style lobby. High-ceilinged atrium has sky painting and huge flower arrangements. **Rooms:** 168 rms. CI 3pm/CO noon. Pleasing, with warm pastels and lots of light. **Amenities:** 🛎 A/C, TV w/movies. **Services:** ✗ 🚐 🛌 🛒 **Facilities:** 🗓 🕭 1 rst, whirlpool. Nicely landscaped pool area. Ballroom available. Meeting rooms open onto garden. **Rates:** HS June–Aug $79 S or D. Children under 12 stay free. Lower rates off-season. AP rates avail. Spec packages avail. Pking: Outdoor, free. Maj CC. Great America packages available when theme park is open.

🏨 **Santa Clara Travelodge**, 3477 El Camino Real, Santa Clara, CA 95051; tel 408/984-3364 or toll free 800/578-7878; fax 408/244-5561. Lawrence Expwy S exit off US 101; left on El Camino Real. On busy El Camino Real, basic accommodations for a reasonable price. **Rooms:** 43 rms. CI noon/CO noon. Nonsmoking rms avail. The closer to El Camino, the less quiet the room. **Amenities:** 🛎 🖵 A/C, cable TV, refrig. **Services:** 🛒 **Facilities:** 🗓 🕭 Whirlpool. Small pool needs resurfacing. **Rates:** HS May 15–Aug 15 $42 S; $48–$52 D. Extra person $5. Children under 18 stay free. Lower rates off-season. Spec packages avail. Pking: Outdoor, free. Maj CC.

🏨 **Santa Clara Vagabond Inn**, 3580 El Camino Real, Santa Clara, CA 95051; tel 408/241-0771 or toll free 800/522-1555; fax 408/247-3386. From US 101 take Lawrence Expwy S; left on El Camino Real. Spacious grounds. Rooms in need of major refurbishing. **Rooms:** 70 rms and stes. Exec-level rms avail. CI noon/CO noon. Nonsmoking rms avail. **Amenities:** 🛎 🕐 A/C, cable TV w/movies, shoe polisher. Modem jack available. **Services:** ✗ 🛌 🛒 🍴 Complimentary continental breakfast, weekday newspapers, coffee, tea, popcorn in lobby. Discount tickets to local attractions. **Facilities:** 🗓 🕭 1 rst, washer/dryer. **Rates (CP):** $39–$49 S; $49–$55 D; from $65 ste. Extra person $5. Children under 18 stay free. Spec packages avail. Pking: Outdoor, free. Maj CC. Vagabond Business Club, for a member-

ship fee of $15, offers upgraded rooms, discount coupons, complimentary in-room coffee and tea, free local phone calls, modem jack, free spouse stays, and 10th night free.

Restaurant 🍽

Alexander's, in the Marriott Hotel, 2700 Mission College Blvd, Santa Clara; tel 408/988-4300. Great America Pkwy exit off US 101; turn right on Mission College Blvd. **Californian.** This California bistro sports a crisp decor with coordinated artwork and a minimalist Japanese garden. A red rose in a silver bud vase on each table adds romantic ambience. Entrees include roasted free-range chicken breast with pancetta, sun-dried tomato stuffing, creamy polenta, and port wine glaze; grilled swordfish with sautéed Swiss chard and mustard-thyme vinaigrette; artichoke linguine with smoked chicken. **FYI:** Reservations recommended. **Open:** Lunch Mon–Fri 11:30am–2pm; dinner Mon–Sat 6–10pm. Closed some hols. **Prices:** Main courses $12.95–$21.95. Maj CC. 🌐 VP 🕭

Attractions 🧳

De Saisset Museum, 500 El Camino Real, Santa Clara University; tel 408/554-4528. The repository of an extensive California history collection, which focuses primarily on the period of Native American habitation and the Mission Period. Changing art exhibitions throughout the year. **Open:** Tues–Sun 11am–4pm. Closed some hols. Free.

Mission Santa Clara de Asis, 500 El Camino Real; tel 408/554-4023. This mission, the first outpost of Spanish civilization in the Santa Clara Valley, was founded in 1777. The original mission gardens surround the present church building, the sixth, built in 1927. A replica of the third mission church, it was built after the fifth church burned in 1926. Olive trees and grinding stones in the gardens date from the early mission period. **Open:** Daily 7am–7pm; Sun Mass at 10am. Free.

Paramount's Great America, 2401 Agnew Rd; tel 408/988-1800. Located 3 miles north via US 101, this 100-acre park combines amusement park and Hollywood movie–based entertainment. It offers more than 100 attractions, including 6 rollercoasters, numerous other thrill rides, an IMAX movie theater, 4 stage shows, a double-decker carousel, and the *Days of Thunder* motion simulator ride. Characters from Hanna-Barbera cartoons and such Paramount features as Star Trek are on hand to greet visitors. Children's play area, restaurants, snack shops. **Open:** Late May–Labor Day, Sun–Fri 10am–9pm, Sat–Sun 10am–11pm; rest of the year, schedule varies. Phone ahead to confirm hours. $$$$

SANTA CRUZ

Map page M-2, D2

See also Aptos, Capitola-by-the-Sea

Hotel

Dream Inn, 175 W Cliff Dr, Santa Cruz, CA 95060; tel 408/426-4330 or toll free 800/622-3838; fax 408/426-4015. Bay St exit off Calif 1/71. This aging property is wearing out. Carpeting in the hall and in some rooms is soiled. **Rooms:** 164 rms and stes. CI 4pm/CO noon. Express checkout avail. Nonsmoking rms avail. **Amenities:** A/C, satel TV w/movies, refrig, VCR, voice mail. All units w/terraces. TVs are equipped for the deaf and hard of hearing. **Services:** Facilities: 2 rsts, 1 bar, 1 beach (ocean), games rm, sauna, whirlpool. **Rates:** HS Mem Day–Labor Day $139–$249 S or D; from $195 ste. Extra person $10. Children under 18 stay free. Min stay wknds. Lower rates off-season. Higher rates for spec evnts/hols. Spec packages avail. Pking: Outdoor, free. Maj CC.

Motels

Holiday Inn, 611 Ocean St, Santa Cruz, CA 95060; tel 408/426-7100 or toll free 800/465-4329, 800/241-1555 in CA; fax 408/429-1044. Calif 1 S becomes Mission St; right on Ocean St. An older property that is now just acceptable in general appearance and upkeep. Unrated. **Rooms:** 167 rms. CI 4pm/CO noon. Nonsmoking rms avail. No twins. **Amenities:** A/C, cable TV w/movies, VCR. Some units w/terraces. **Services:** Babysitting. **Facilities:** 1 rst, 1 bar, 1 beach (ocean). **Rates:** HS Apr–Sept $89–$125 S or D. Extra person $10. Children under 19 stay free. Lower rates off-season. Spec packages avail. Pking: Outdoor, free. Maj CC.

The Inn at Pasatiempo, 555 Calif 17, Santa Cruz, CA 95060; tel 408/423-5000; fax 408/426-1737. Pasatiempo Dr exit off Calif 17; go west. Located in an upscale neighborhood and beside an 18-hole golf course. Beautifully kept grounds. **Rooms:** 54 rms and stes. CI 3pm/CO noon. Nonsmoking rms avail. Excellent accommodations, tastefully furnished, larger-than-average motor-inn rooms. **Amenities:** Cable TV, refrig. No A/C. Some units w/minibars, some w/fireplaces, some w/Jacuzzis. Suites have bathrobes. **Services:** Babysitting. **Facilities:** 1 rst, 1 bar (w/entertainment). Golf available with advance reservations at $95 per person. **Rates (CP):** HS Mem Day–Labor Day $99 S or D; from $175 ste. Extra person $10. Lower rates off-season. Higher rates for spec evnts/hols. Pking: Outdoor, free. Maj CC.

Mission Inn, 2250 Mission St, Santa Cruz, CA 95060; tel 408/425-5455 or toll free 800/995-0289; fax 408/457-0861. Calif 1 S becomes Mission St. Located on the main road into town, near several retail establishments. Not in the best neighborhood. Unrated. **Rooms:** 53 rms and stes. CI 4pm/CO noon. Nonsmoking rms avail. **Amenities:** TV w/movies, refrig, VCR, stereo/tape player. No A/C. 1 unit w/Jacuzzi. **Services:** Free coffee in lobby. **Facilities:** Whirlpool, washer/dryer. **Rates:** HS May–Sept $65–$75 S or D; from $95 ste. Extra person $10. Children under 18 stay free. Min stay wknds. Lower rates off-season. Pking: Outdoor, free. Maj CC. Discount for seniors and children under 16.

Ocean Pacific Inn, 120 Washington, Santa Cruz, CA 95060; tel 408/457-1234 or toll free 800/995-0289; fax 408/457-0861. Boardwalk exit off Calif 1. Located 2 blocks from the ocean. **Rooms:** 57 rms and stes. CI 4pm/CO noon. Nonsmoking rms avail. Larger than average. Mini-suites very attractive. **Amenities:** Cable TV w/movies, VCR. No A/C. Some units w/minibars, some w/Jacuzzis. **Services:** **Facilities:** Sauna, whirlpool. **Rates (CP):** HS Mem Day–Labor Day $105 S or D; from $159 ste. Extra person $10. Children under 16 stay free. Lower rates off-season. Pking: Outdoor, free. Maj CC.

Inn

Babbling Brook Inn, 1025 Laurel St, Santa Cruz, CA 95060; tel 408/427-2437 or toll free 800/866-1131; fax 408/427-2437. Laurel St exit off Calif 1; 1½ blocks downhill toward ocean. The largest inn in Santa Cruz, a secluded property with waterfalls, a creek, and a gazebo amid gardens, pines, and redwoods. Near the beach, wharf, boardwalk, shops, tennis courts, running paths, and historic homes. **Rooms:** 12 rms. CI 3pm/CO noon. No smoking. Country French decor. Most rooms have outside entrance. **Amenities:** Cable TV. No A/C. Some units w/terraces, some w/fireplaces, some w/Jacuzzis. **Services:** Afternoon tea and wine/sherry served. Country breakfast, afternoon wine and cheese and homemade cookies. **Facilities:** Guest lounge. **Rates (BB):** $85–$150 S or D. Extra person $21.50. Min stay wknds. Pking: Outdoor, free. Ltd CC.

Resort

The Chaminade at Santa Cruz, 1 Chaminade Lane, PO Box 2788, Santa Cruz, CA 95065; tel 408/475-5600 or toll free 800/283-6569; fax 408/476-4798. Soquel Dr exit off Calif 1. 280 acres. Primarily an executive conference facility, Chaminade welcomes individual travelers as well. The retreat offers many distractions, but is perfect for relaxation. **Rooms:** 152 rms and stes. CI 4pm/CO noon. Nonsmoking rms avail. In 11 buildings, rooms in various configurations—some with two vanity areas and work space. **Amenities:** 🖥 🛁 A/C, cable TV w/movies. Some units w/terraces, some w/Jacuzzis. **Services:** ✗ ☎ 🆚 🚗 🛟 ↩ Car-rental desk, babysitting. **Facilities:** 🏬 ⛱ 🍽 📶 💻 ♿ 2 rsts, 1 bar (w/entertainment), games rm, spa, sauna, whirlpool. Indoor basketball, 3 Jacuzzis, volleyball and badminton court, and nature trails. **Rates:** $125–$145 S or D; from $175 ste. Extra person $35. Children under 5 stay free. Spec packages avail. Pking: Outdoor, free. Maj CC.

Restaurants ⏐⏐⏐

✱ **Gilbert's**, 15 Municipal Wharf, Santa Cruz; tel 408/423-5200. Boardwalk exit off Calif 1. **Seafood/Pasta.** With ocean views like this, no decor is necessary. It's a pleasant, open room with quick service. Seafood is the main event; but a number of pasta dishes as well as steaks and chicken are also served. **FYI:** Reservations recommended. Children's menu. Dress code. **Open: Prices:** Main courses $7.95–$14.95. Maj CC. 🏔 🎛 🚗 ♿

✱ **Miramar**, in the Municipal Pier on the Boardwalk of Santa Cruz, 45 Municipal Wharf, Santa Cruz (Waterfront); tel 408/423-4441. Boardwalk exit off Calif 1. **Seafood.** Tables are placed so everyone has a view of the ocean. A good selection of local seafood includes salmon, sole, red snapper, and the calamari for which this area is famous. **FYI:** Reservations recommended. Piano. Dress code. **Open:** HS June–Aug lunch Tues–Sun 11am–4pm; dinner daily 4–9:30pm. Reduced hours off-season. Closed Thanksgiving. **Prices:** Main courses $10.95–$21.95. Maj CC. 🏔 🎛 🚗 ♿

♥ **The Sunset Dining Room**, in the Chaminade at Santa Cruz, 1 Chaminade Lane, Santa Cruz (Heavy Forest–Rolling Hills); tel 408/475-5600. Paul Sweet Rd exit off Calif 1. **Eclectic.** Elegant furnishings with lovely views of the hills and the ocean, particularly from the patio. Nightly buffets include the Wednesday-night northern Italian spread, with Parmesan-baked chicken, ratatouille, tortellini, and sea bass, as well as desserts. Champagne brunch on Sunday, and on Sunday night, a California regional buffet. **FYI:** Reservations recommended. Jacket required. **Open:** Breakfast daily 7–9:30am; lunch daily noon–2pm; dinner daily 6–9pm; brunch Sun 9am–2pm. **Prices:** Main courses $17–$20. Maj CC. ♥ 🍺 🏔 🚗 🆚 ♿

Attractions 🖼

Santa Cruz City Museum of Natural History, 1305 E Cliff Dr; tel 408/429-3773. Overlooking Seabright Beach between the Boardwalk and the Small Craft Harbor, the museum offers collections, exhibits, and educational programs focusing on the natural and cultural history of the northern Monterey Bay area. Some highlights are exhibits of prehistoric animal life, with a fossilized 20,000-year-old mastodon skull; a life-size model of a California gray whale; a tidepool exhibit with living specimens; and exhibits on the culture of the Ohlone Indians. Tours available. **Open:** Tues–Fri 10am–5pm, Sat–Sun 1–5pm. Closed some hols. Free.

University of California, Santa Cruz Arboretum; tel 408/427-9798. Located on the southern edge of the UCSC campus. Renowned for its unique collections, the arboretum contains 8,000 plants, with noteworthy collections from Australia and South Africa, and an exceptionally complete New Zealand garden. There are also large exhibits of native and drought-tolerant California plants. Book and gift shop; library. **Open:** Daily 9am–5pm. Closed some hols. Free.

Joseph M Long Marine Laboratory, 100 Shaffer Rd; tel 408/459-4308. Located past the end of Delaware St, near Natural Bridges State Beach (see below). This University of California marine research facility offers guided tours that cover the aquarium and such exhibits as a model of the Monterey Bay submarine canyon, fossils, an 85-foot blue whale skeleton, and a touch tank. Changing exhibits, spanning a variety of topics, are also visited. Gift and book shop. **Open:** Tues–Sun 1–4pm. Closed some hols. Free.

Natural Bridges State Beach, 2531 West Cliff Dr; tel 408/423-4609 or 688-3241. Although a fascinating array of wildlife can be found within this park's 65 acres, the most notable is the annual population of 100,000 Monarch butterflies, who migrate to the park each winter. The park's eucalyptus grove, planted by early settlers, provides the Monarchs with a safe wintering place until spring. A trail runs through the middle of the Monarch Natural Preserve (October–March; guided tours on weekends).

Another trail winds through the meadows and down to the Moore Creek wetlands, and tidepools are accessible during low-tide periods (tours available). The visitor center has trail maps, exhibits, and a book and gift shop. Beach activities are also popular in the park; picnic tables with grills are available beneath the eucalyptus trees around the main parking lot. **Open:** Daily dawn–dusk; Visitor Center, daily 10am–4pm. $$$

SANTA MARIA

Map page M-3, C1

Hotels 🏨

🏨🏨 **Ramada Suites**, 2050 N Preisker Lane, Santa Maria, CA 93454; tel 805/928-6000 or toll free 800/2-RAMADA; fax 805/

928-0356. Broadway exit off US 101. New Spanish-style stucco hotel. Spacious, plant-filled lobby has hand-painted murals and ceiling fans. Furnishings and carpeting seem a bit worn around the edges. **Rooms:** 210 stes. CI 4pm/CO noon. Express check-out avail. Nonsmoking rms avail. Very large rooms have blond furniture, beige carpet, and kitchen with stove and eating counter. **Amenities:** 🛏 🦮 🎣 A/C, cable TV w/movies, refrig. Wet bar. **Services:** 🍴 🛍 🍸 🐕 **Facilities:** 🏊 🎾 🦽 1 rst, 1 bar (w/entertainment), whirlpool, washer/dryer. **Rates:** HS June–Oct from $58 ste. Extra person $10. Children under 18 stay free. Min stay wknds. Lower rates off-season. MAP rates avail. Spec packages avail. Pking: Outdoor, free. Maj CC.

🏨🏨 **Santa Maria Airport Hilton**, 3455 Skyway Dr, Santa Maria, CA 93455 (Santa Maria Airport); tel 805/928-8000 or toll free 800/HILTONS; fax 805/928-5251. Betteravia exit off US 101; go west and follow signs to airport. Modern 4-story hotel near south end of town. Lobby opens onto central atrium with sunken seating area, glass elevators, water sculpture, and garden cafe. **Rooms:** 190 rms and stes. Exec-level rms avail. CI 3pm/CO noon. Nonsmoking rms avail. Interior rooms face atrium and are quite dark. Some rooms have view of airstrip. **Amenities:** 🛏 🦮 A/C, cable TV w/movies, refrig. Some units w/terraces. **Services:** ✗ 🚐 🛍 🍸 Car-rental desk, babysitting. **Facilities:** 🏊 🎾 🦽 1 rst, 3 bars (w/entertainment), games rm, whirlpool. Nightclub with dancing. YMCA pass available. **Rates:** $54–$84 S or D; from $74 ste. Children under 18 stay free. Spec packages avail. Pking: Outdoor, free. Maj CC.

🏨🏨🏨 **Santa Maria Inn**, 801 S Broadway, Santa Maria, CA 93454; tel 805/928-7777 or toll free 800/462-4276; fax 805/928-5690. Historic inn, now in 2 buildings, has a lovely, oak-paneled lobby filled with antiques. Grounds feature a beautiful brick patio with wrought-iron tables, a fountain, and an award-winning rose garden. **Rooms:** 166 rms and stes. CI 3pm/CO noon. Nonsmoking rms avail. Antique-style furnishings. Rooms in original building are smaller than newer ones. Zaca Mesa suite has hand-painted tile fireplace; bridal suite has canopy bed. **Amenities:** 🛏 🦮 🎣 🍷 A/C, satel TV w/movies, refrig, VCR. Some units w/minibars, some w/terraces, some w/fireplaces, some w/Jacuzzis. **Services:** ✗ 🚐 🛍 🍸 Masseur. **Facilities:** 🏊 🍸 300 🦽 2 rsts (see also "Restaurants" below), 3 bars (1 w/entertainment), sauna, steam rm, whirlpool, beauty salon. Wine cellar with wine bar; gallery with ice cream parlor, shops. Putting green, Ping-Pong. **Rates:** HS May–Oct $84–$125 S; $94–$135 D; from $150 ste. Extra person $10. Children under 12 stay free. Lower rates off-season. Spec packages avail. Pking: Indoor/outdoor, free. Maj CC.

Motel

🏩 **Howard Johnson Lodge**, 210 S Nicholson Ave, Santa Maria, CA 93454; tel 805/922-5891 or toll free 800/654-2000; fax 805/928-9222. E Main St exit off US 101; head E 1 block to S Nicholson, turn right. Apart from the pleasant grounds with abundant trees, this is a typical Howard Johnson. Caters to families. **Rooms:** 62 rms. CI 3pm/CO noon. Nonsmoking rms avail. Large rooms with pastel tropical decor, light wood furnishings. **Amenities:** 🛏 🦮 A/C, cable TV w/movies, refrig. All units w/terraces. **Services:** 🛍 🍸 🐕 Children's program, babysitting. **Facilities:** 🏊 40 🦽 Whirlpool, playground, washer/dryer. Children's pool. **Rates:** HS June–Sept $55 S; $65 D. Extra person $10. Children under 18 stay free. Lower rates off-season. Pking: Outdoor, free. Maj CC.

Restaurant 🍴

★ **Santa Maria Inn Restaurant**, 801 S Broadway, Santa Maria; tel 805/928-7777. **Regional American.** Old building with English decor, antique fireplace in lobby, garden room, and English pub. Specialty is Santa Maria–style barbecue: top sirloin, pork chops, tri-tip, chicken, or baby back pork ribs cooked over Santa Maria Valley red oak wood. Prime rib and a number of vegetarian dishes are also served. Friday happy hour includes complimentary barbecue. **FYI:** Reservations recommended. Combo. Children's menu. **Open:** Breakfast daily 6–11am; lunch daily 11am–2pm; dinner daily 5–9pm; brunch Sun 11am–1pm. **Prices:** Main courses $9.45–$17.45. Maj CC. 🍷 🎉 💳 🦽

Attraction 🖼

Santa Maria Valley Historical Society and Museum, 616 S Broadway; tel 805/922-3130. Exhibits arranged in chronological order begin with the Chumash Indian culture and progress through the Mission, Rancho, and Pioneer periods. Children's Corner has exhibits appealing to younger visitors. Includes pictures, artifacts, and memorabilia from each period. **Open:** Tues–Sat noon–5pm. Closed major hols. Free.

SANTA MONICA

Map page M-3, D2

Hotels 🏨

🏨🏨🏨 **Holiday Inn Bay View Plaza**, 530 Pico Blvd, Santa Monica, CA 90405; tel 310/399-9344 or toll free 800/HOLIDAY; fax 310/399-2504 or 3322. At 6th St, W of Lincoln. Well located 4 blocks from Santa Monica's beach. It is a serviceable hotel catering to tour groups, with no frills. Modern, high-ceilinged lobby is austere and uninviting. **Rooms:** 309 rms and stes. CI 4pm/CO noon. Nonsmoking rms avail. Most rooms have ocean views. **Amenities:** 📺 💧 🗣 A/C, cable TV w/movies, voice mail. Some units w/minibars, all w/terraces, some w/Jacuzzis. **Services:** ✗ 🔑 VP 🚌 🛍 🛎 Car-rental desk, babysitting. Desk clerks speak English, Spanish, French, and Japanese. **Facilities:** 🏊 🛥 500 🖥 ♿ 2 rsts, 1 bar (w/entertainment), whirlpool, beauty salon, washer/dryer. **Rates:** $103–$123 S; $113–$133 D; from $250 ste. Extra person $10. Children under 17 stay free. Higher rates for spec evnts/hols. Spec packages avail. Pking: Indoor, free. Maj CC.

≣≣≣ Loews Santa Monica Beach Hotel, 1700 Ocean Ave, Santa Monica, CA 90401; tel 310/458-6700 or toll free 800/23-LOEWS; fax 310/458-0020. A grand hotel by the sea, with an art deco facade and 5-story glass atrium. Hotel gets a high rating, but carpets in rooms and meeting areas are worn, and corridor alcoves are used as small meeting spaces. **Rooms:** 347 rms and stes. CI 3pm/CO noon. Express checkout avail. Nonsmoking rms avail. Done in sunset-hued pastels with marble-topped dressers, most rooms are comfortable, but lacking in polish. Ocean Premier rooms ($425) feature big terraces accented by planters facing the Pacific. **Amenities:** 📺 💧 🗣 A/C, cable TV w/movies, refrig, voice mail, bathrobes. All units w/minibars, some w/terraces. All accommodations come with a scale, plus iron and ironing board; some feature private fax machines. **Services:** 🍽 🔑 VP 🚌 🛍 🛎 🚗 Twice-daily maid svce, car-rental desk, masseur, children's program, babysitting. "Star" service promises to respond to guest needs quickly. **Facilities:** 🏊 🚴 🏋 🛥 900 🖥 ♿ 2 rsts, 2 bars (1 w/entertainment), 1 beach (ocean), lifeguard, spa, sauna, steam rm, whirlpool, beauty salon, day-care ctr, playground. Topped by a glass dome, the pool has a dynamite ocean view. Free weights and exercise machines are also located here. For serious workouts, the on-premises Jackson Sousa facility offers, among other things, weight and cardiovascular equipment and aerobics classes ($8 fee). **Rates:** HS June–Sept $255–$415 S; $275–$425 D; from $305 ste. Extra person $20. Children under 12 stay free. Lower rates off-season. Spec packages avail. Pking: Indoor, $13.20–$15.40. Maj CC.

≣≣ Oceana Suites Hotel, 849 Ocean Ave, Santa Monica, CA 90403; tel 310/393-0486 or toll free 800/777-0758. At Montana. An apartment-style hotel very popular with families; excellent location in a residential neighborhood across from Pacific Palisades, with an ocean view. Remodelling should be completed. **Rooms:** 60 effic. CI 3pm/CO 11am. 1- and 2-bedroom apartments. Rooms are clean, but furniture is old. **Amenities:** 📺 🗣 Cable TV, refrig, VCR. No A/C. All units w/terraces. **Services:** 🛍 🛎 Babysitting. Small continental

breakfast; newspaper; coffee in lobby at all times. **Facilities:** 🏊 🛥 Washer/dryer. **Rates:** HS Apr 9–Oct 25 from $99 effic. Lower rates off-season. Higher rates for spec evnts/hols. Spec packages avail. Pking: Indoor, free. Maj CC.

≣≣ Pacific Shore Hotel, 1819 Ocean Ave, Santa Monica, CA 90401; tel 310/451-8711 or toll free 800/622-8711; fax 310/394-6657. At Pico Blvd. A basic, nondescript hotel with unexceptional rooms; however, located right across from the Santa Monica beach. **Rooms:** 168 rms. CI 3pm/CO noon. Nonsmoking rms avail. **Amenities:** 📺 💧 🗣 🗣 A/C, cable TV w/movies, voice mail, in-rm safe, shoe polisher. 1 unit w/fireplace, 1 w/Jacuzzi. Some units have refrigerators. **Services:** ✗ 🔑 🛍 🛎 Car-rental desk, babysitting. **Facilities:** 🏊 🛥 40 1 rst, 1 bar, sauna, whirlpool, washer/dryer. **Rates:** HS May–Sept $115–$125 S; $125–$135 D. Extra person $15. Children under 12 stay free. Lower rates off-season. Spec packages avail. Pking: Outdoor, free. Maj CC.

≣≣≣ Radisson-Huntley Hotel, 1111 2nd St, Santa Monica, CA 90403; tel 310/394-5454 or toll free 800/333-3333; fax 310/458-9776. This 17-story hotel, the tallest in Santa Monica, features an outdoor elevator. An old building with a small art deco lobby. Close to Santa Monica beach. **Rooms:** 213 rms and stes. CI 3pm/CO noon. Express checkout avail. Nonsmoking rms avail. Small rooms and baths. **Amenities:** 📺 💧 A/C, cable TV w/movies, voice mail. **Services:** ✗ 🔑 VP 🛍 🛎 Car-rental desk, babysitting. **Facilities:** 100 ♿ 1 rst, 1 bar, beauty salon. Toppers serves mainly Mexican food, sports a south-of-the-border decor, and offers a wonderful view on 3 sides. **Rates:** $135 S; $145 D; from $160 ste. Extra person $10. Children under 17 stay free. Spec packages avail. Pking: Indoor, $5.50. Maj CC.

≣≣≣≣ Sheraton Miramar Hotel, 101 Wilshire Blvd, Santa Monica, CA 90401; tel 310/576-7777 or toll free 800/325-3535; fax 310/458-7912. Great location, right across from Santa Monica Beach. Gorgeously landscaped with old Moreton fig tree in courtyard, beautiful flowers, and sub-tropical shrubs. There are 3 facilities: an older brick building, a newer tower, and a luxury bungalow complex. **Rooms:** 272 rms and stes; 31 ctges/villas. Exec-level rms avail. CI 3pm/CO noon. Nonsmoking rms avail. Small bathrooms, except in new bungalows. **Amenities:** 📺 💧 🗣 🗣 A/C, cable TV w/movies, refrig, voice mail, in-rm safe, bathrobes. All units w/minibars, all w/terraces. Iron and ironing board in every room. **Services:** 🍽 🔑 VP 🛍 🛎 Car-rental desk, babysitting. **Facilities:** 🏊 1K ♿ 1 rst, 1 bar, beauty salon. American Airlines office in building. New fitness center, luxury dining room, and health spa scheduled to open. **Rates:** $195–

$275 S or D; from $275 ste; from $275 ctge/villa. Extra person $20. Children under 17 stay free. AP rates avail. Spec packages avail. Pking: Indoor/outdoor, $11. Maj CC.

≣≣≣≣ **Shutters on the Beach**, 1 Pico Blvd, Santa Monica, CA 90405; tel 310/458-0030 or toll free 800/334-9000; fax 415/458-4589. This hotel, located right on Santa Monica's magnificent strand, looks like an overgrown Cape Cod cottage, with grey clapboard, fishscale shingles, and jaunty gray-and-white awnings. **Rooms:** 198 rms and stes. CI 3pm/CO noon. Express checkout avail. Nonsmoking rms avail. Rooms are as fresh as a sea breeze, with crisp white-linen duvets pinstriped in blue. Marble bathroom. Ocean views. **Amenities:** 🛢 🛁 🍳 A/C, cable TV w/movies, refrig, VCR, voice mail, in-rm safe, shoe polisher, bathrobes. All units w/minibars, all w/terraces, some w/fireplaces, some w/Jacuzzis. Winning features include a water-proof Walkman and toy rubber whale by the tub. Showers have three heads. 27-inch TV with VCR. **Services:** 🍽 ☎ VP 🚗 🖂 ⤸ Twice-daily maid svce, car-rental desk, social director, masseur, babysitting. **Facilities:** 🏋 🚲 🛥 👯 🖳 �👸 2 rsts, 2 bars (w/entertainment), 1 beach (ocean), lifeguard, spa, sauna, steam rm, whirlpool. Equipped with free weights and a fleet of Lifecycles and other machines, the workout room (no charge for guests) is spacious and paired with attractive locker facilities. The beautiful pool is located in the courtyard and is surrounded by flowers. **Rates:** HS June–Oct $250–$350 S or D; from $475 ste. Extra person $25. Children under 12 stay free. Lower rates off-season. Spec packages avail. Pking: Indoor, $15. Maj CC.

Inn

≣≣≣ **Channel Road Inn**, 219 W Channel Rd, Santa Monica, CA 90402; tel 310/459-1920; fax 310/454-9920. ½ block E of Pacific Coast Hwy. Everything an inn should be. This 3-story blue building, ½ block from the beach, features a homey parlor with fireplace, oak floors, Chinese rugs, and lovely English furniture. **Rooms:** 14 rms and stes. CI 3pm/CO noon. No smoking. Each room is uniquely and lovingly decorated. **Amenities:** 🛢 🛁 Cable TV w/movies, refrig, VCR, bathrobes. No A/C. Some units w/terraces. **Services:** ✗ ☎ 🖂 ⤸ Babysitting, afternoon tea and wine/sherry served. Gracious staff. Complimentary full breakfast. Fresh lemonade. **Facilities:** 🚲 👸 Games rm, whirlpool, washer/dryer, guest lounge w/TV. Free use of bicycles. **Rates (BB):** $95–$180 D; from $175 ste. Pking: Outdoor, free. Ltd CC.

Restaurants 🍴

⭐ **Border Grill**, 1445 4th St, Santa Monica; tel 310/451-1655. **Mexican.** After-work meeting place popular with singles. Festive decor includes Mexican cartoon figures covering high walls, and bare tables with tall, colored candles. Loud rock music can drown out conversation. Specialties include grilled cactus salad, green corn tamales, chicken al carbón, border vegetarian grill. Excellent margaritas. **FYI:** Reservations recommended. Children's menu. **Open:** Dinner Mon–Thurs 5:30–10pm, Fri–Sat 5:30–11pm, Sun 5–10pm. Closed some hols. **Prices:** Main courses $9.50–$15.50. Maj CC. 🚗 VP 👸

Cafe Athens, 1000 Wilshire Blvd, Santa Monica; tel 310/395-1000. **Greek.** Spacious Greek restaurant decorated in blue and white, with posters of Greece on the walls. Moussaka and souvlaki. Also, fixed-price 15-course Greek feast. **FYI:** Reservations recommended. Combo/dancing. **Open:** Tues–Thurs 11:30am–4pm, Fri 11:30am–midnight, Sat 4pm–12:30am, Sun 4–11pm. **Prices:** Main courses $11.95–$19.50; PF dinner $21.95. Maj CC. 👥 VP

⭐ **Camelions**, 246 26th St, Santa Monica; tel 310/395-0746. **Californian/French.** Resembles an Italian country villa, with red brick exterior and several dining rooms with fireplaces, all on a rambling property. Patronized by Brentwood and Santa Monica gentry, the restaurant serves trendy French-California dishes: crostini of foie gras, red lentil cakes with smoked salmon and arugula, Lake Superior whitefish and fried spinach, lemon tart, crème brûlée. **FYI:** Reservations recommended. **Open:** Lunch Tues–Sun 11:30am–2:30pm; dinner Tues–Sun 6–10pm. Closed some hols. **Prices:** Main courses $11–$22. Maj CC. ⚅ ☂ 🖼 👸

Carrots, 2834 Santa Monica Blvd, Santa Monica; tel 310/453-6505. **Californian/French.** Fine California-French cuisine from the former chef at Wolfgang Puck's Chinois on Main. Located in a strip mall, but the interior is chic, with minimalist gray and green decor and an open kitchen. Specialties include sautéed foie gras, crab cakes in port wine sauce, sautéed John Dory in mushroom cream sauce, and grilled lamb chops with cucumber vinaigrette. Reserve well in advance. **FYI:** Reservations recommended. Beer and wine only. **Open:** Tues–Sun 6–10:30pm. Closed some hols. **Prices:** Main courses $15.75–$20.75. Maj CC. 👸

⚘ **Chinois on Main**, 2709 Main St, Santa Monica; tel 310/392-9025. **French/Asian.** From superchef Wolfgang Puck, a trendy restaurant with bright lacquered tables and chic decor. Signature dishes are sizzling catfish, Szechuan beef, and Shanghai lobster. **FYI:** Reservations recommended. **Open:** Lunch Wed–Fri 11:30am–2pm; dinner Mon–Sat 6:30–10:30pm, Sun 5:30–10pm. Closed some hols. **Prices:** Main courses $18–$29. Maj CC. VP 👸

Il Forno, in the Ocean Park Place Shopping Center, 2901 Ocean Park Blvd, Santa Monica; tel 310/450-1241. **Italian.** Features trattoria decor, with pink tablecloths, a granite bar, and a large, open kitchen, located across the street from bluffs overlooking the ocean. Menu specialties include pizza, pasta, veal scaloppine, lemon chicken, and curried scampi. **FYI:** Reservations recommended. **Open:** Lunch Mon–Sat 11:30am–3pm; dinner Mon–Thurs 5:30–11pm, Fri–Sat 5:30–11:30pm. Closed some hols. **Prices:** Main courses $8.95–$15.95. Maj CC. 🍰 &

★ **Knoll's Black Forest Inn**, 2454 Wilshire Blvd, Santa Monica; tel 310/395-2212. **Continental/German.** The jovial owner has cooked here for 35 years and decorated it like a country inn. Great for family celebrations. With many repeat customers, it's regarded as a treasure in Santa Monica. German specialties include venison, goose, veal with chanterelles, and pork with red cabbage. Big selection of German beers. **FYI:** Reservations recommended. **Open:** Lunch Tues–Sun 11:30am–2:30pm; dinner Tues–Sun 5–10pm. Closed some hols. **Prices:** Main courses $11.95–$20. Maj CC. 🌑 🍰 📶 VP &

♥ **Michael's**, 1147 3rd St, Santa Monica; tel 310/451-0843. **French.** Celebrities come to be seen and to enjoy the sensational cooking of Michael McCarty, a pioneer of California-French cuisine since the '70s. Located in an updated 1930s house with salmon stucco, the pink-walled dining room contains a valuable contemporary art collection. A magnificent dining patio is under canvas awnings. Chicken and goat-cheese salad, duck breast with peppercorn cognac sauce, steak with french fries. **FYI:** Reservations recommended. **Open:** Lunch Tues–Fri noon–2pm; dinner Tues–Sat 6:30–10pm. Closed some hols. **Prices:** Main courses $18–$29.75. Maj CC. 🌑 🍰 VP &

Ocean Ave Seafood, 1401 Ocean Ave, Santa Monica; tel 310/394-5669. **Seafood.** Very popular restaurant with an affluent, older crowd and local business types. Holds over 200 people in spaces broken up for privacy. Its long, semi-outdoor dining room offers a view of Ocean Blvd, the Palisades, and the ocean. Oyster bar features many varieties. Specialties include chilled and steamed shellfish, Maine lobster, pasta, chicken, steak, plus an award-winning cioppino. **FYI:** Reservations recommended. Children's menu. **Open:** Lunch Mon–Fri 11:30am–3pm, Sat–Sun noon–3pm; dinner Mon–Sat 5:30–10pm, Sun 5–10pm; brunch Sun 11:30am–3pm. Closed some hols. **Prices:** Main courses $12–$20. Maj CC. 🍰 🏞 📶 VP &

Opus, in the Water Garden, 2425 W Olympic Blvd, Santa Monica; tel 310/829-2112. **Californian/Seafood.** Gorgeous setting in a glass-and-steel business complex, this is an "in" place for lunch among power brokers. Floor-to-ceiling windows overlook a lake, lawns, and palms. Airy, contemporary dining room paneled in pear wood. Although steaks and roasts appear on the menu, this is principally a seafood restaurant, with dishes like sturgeon with fennel and leek confit, and sautéed John Dory with artichoke hearts. **FYI:** Reservations recommended. **Open:**

Lunch Mon–Fri noon–3pm; dinner Mon–Sat 6–10pm. Closed some hols. **Prices:** Main courses $9.95–$19.95; PF dinner $24.95. Maj CC. 🌑 🍰 🏞 VP &

Rockenwagner, in Edgemar Museum and Shopping Complex, 2435 Main St, Santa Monica; tel 310/399-6504. **Californian/German.** An "in" place on Main St, Santa Monica's restaurant row, next door to a contemporary art museum. The decor features bizarre artistic touches, fountains, and walls of glass. The food includes Maine lobster, crab soufflé, and lamb. Also serves excellent weekend brunch. A long bakery counter lines 1 side of the restaurant, where you can pick up fresh baked goods to take home. **FYI:** Reservations recommended. **Open:** Lunch Tues–Fri 11:30am–2:30pm; dinner Mon–Fri 6–10pm, Sat–Sun 5:30–10pm; brunch Sat–Sun 9am–2:30pm. Closed July 4. **Prices:** Main courses $18–$28. Ltd CC. 🌑 📶 VP &

⑤ **Sabor, Too!**, 3221 Pico Blvd, Santa Monica; tel 310/829-3781. **Cajun/Californian/South American.** Urbanized flavors of the southern United States and south of the border, including South America. The setting is that of a Latin American town square. Specialties include Yucatán chicken-lime soup, buttermilk coxinha puffs filled with chicken and goat cheese, and chile rellenos with cascabel chiles. Novel desserts. Also at: 2538 Hyperion Ave, Silverlake (213/660-0886). **FYI:** Reservations recommended. Beer and wine only. **Open:** Lunch Mon–Fri 11:30am–2:30pm; dinner daily 5:30–10pm. Closed some hols. **Prices:** Main courses $8.50–$17.95. Maj CC. VP

Schatzi on Main, 3110 Main St, Santa Monica; tel 310/399-4800. **New American/Austrian.** California-style decor with light wood furnishings, used-brick floors, plants, well-spaced tables and booths. Owners Maria Shriver and Arnold Schwarzenegger often stop by for breakfast. Eclectic menu includes 3-cheese pizza, Chinese chicken salad. **FYI:** Reservations recommended. **Open:** Mon–Thurs 8am–10pm, Fri 8am–11pm, Sat 9am–11pm, Sun 9am–10pm. Closed some hols. **Prices:** Main courses $8–$23. Maj CC. 🍰 📶 VP &

♥ **Valentino**, 3115 Pico Blvd, Santa Monica; tel 310/829-4313. **Italian.** One of the best Italian restaurants in Los Angeles. It has attracted a clientele of Hollywood celebrities and business diners for 24 years. Elegant but welcoming, decor is ultra-sophisticated, with silver and gold lacquered walls. Although the menu changes constantly, you'll find specialties such as northern Italian risottos, osso buco, pastas, and veal chops. Known for its excellent, well-priced, encyclopedic wine list. **FYI:** Reservations recommended. **Open:** Lunch Fri 11:30am–2pm; dinner Mon–Sat 5:30–10:30pm. Closed some hols. **Prices:** Main courses $17.50–$25. Maj CC. 🌑 VP &

Refreshment Stop ☕

Benita's Frites, 1433 3rd St Promenade, Santa Monica; tel 310/458-2889. **French fries.** Located in the food court along the promenade, the only item served is french fries, accompanied by various types of salsa. But some say they're the best fries in town. **Open:** Daily 10am–9pm. No CC. 🍴 ♿

Attractions 🏛

Museum of Flying, 2772 Donald Douglas Loop N; tel 310/392-8822. One of the largest collections of planes on the West Coast is on display here, housed in a dramatic steel-and-glass structure at the site where Douglas Aircraft was founded in 1922. Approximately 40 aircraft, maintained in flight-ready condition, are on display at all times, along with numerous metal and wooden production models of concept planes, and a collection of model aircraft from World War I to the present. Exhibits, video kiosks, children's interactive area, theater showing classic aviation films. Museum store. **Open:** Tues–Sun 10am–5pm. Closed some hols. $$$

California Heritage Museum, 2612 Main St; tel 310/392-8537. Housed in a historic landmark building built in 1894, the Heritage Museum has been open to the public since 1980. It features rotating exhibits of regional history and local artwork by internationally respected artists. Concerts, lectures, and workshops are also presented. Gift shop. **Open:** Wed–Sat 11am–4pm, Sun noon–4pm. Closed hols. $

SANTA ROSA

Map page M-2, C1

Hotels 🏨

Doubletree Hotel, 3555 Round Barn Blvd, Santa Rosa, CA 95403; tel 707/523-7555 or toll free 800/528-0444; fax 707/545-2807. From US 101, take Old Redwood Hwy north to Mendocino Ave exit; left on Fountain Grove; left on Round Barn. Set on a hill overlooking the city; caters to a mostly corporate clientele. **Rooms:** 247 rms and stes. CI 3pm/CO noon. Express checkout avail. Nonsmoking rms avail. Rooms are cozy and comfortable, with views of the pool. **Amenities:** 🛏🕯📺 🍷 A/C, cable TV w/movies, refrig, bathrobes. Some units w/minibars, some w/terraces. **Services:** ✕ 🛎 🖨 🍷 🛍 Masseur. **Facilities:** 🏊🏋 ⟨350⟩ ♿ 2 rsts, 1 bar, whirlpool. Lap pool. Golf and country club nearby. **Rates:** HS June–Oct $129–$159 S or D; from $179 ste. Extra person $10. Children under 18 stay free. Lower rates off-season. Higher rates for spec evnts/hols. Spec packages avail. Pking: Outdoor, free. Maj CC.

Flamingo Resort Hotel, 2777 4th St, Santa Rosa, CA 95405; tel 707/545-8530 or toll free 800/848-8300; fax 707/528-1404. 7 acres. Family-run hotel with extensive grounds and spa facilities. **Rooms:** 136 rms and stes. CI 3pm/CO 11am. Nonsmoking rms avail. Rooms are large and recently redecorated; those overlooking the pool are nicest. **Amenities:** 🛏🕯📺 A/C, cable TV w/movies, refrig. Some units w/terraces, some w/Jacuzzis. **Services:** ✕ 🛎 🖨 🍷 Masseur. **Facilities:** 🏊🎾🏋 ⟨5⟩ 🎳 ⟨600⟩ ♿ 1 rst, 1 bar (w/entertainment), lawn games, spa, sauna, steam rm, whirlpool, beauty salon, playground. Shuffleboard, table tennis. **Rates:** HS Apr–Oct $76–$146 S or D; from $146 ste. Extra person $11. Children under 12 stay free. Lower rates off-season. Spec packages avail. Pking: Outdoor, free. Maj CC.

Fountain Grove Inn, 101 Fountaingrove Pkwy, Santa Rosa, CA 94503; tel 707/578-6101 or toll free 800/222-6101. Mendocino Ave/Old Redwood Hwy exit off US 101; continue east 10 mi. Business-oriented hotel in a beautiful oak and stone structure with a huge wood-sculpted horse in the lobby. Decor suggests a fine wine cellar. **Rooms:** 84 rms and stes. CI 3pm/CO noon. Nonsmoking rms avail. Rooms are spacious and classy, with nice furnishings and a separate work space for business travelers. **Amenities:** 🛏🕯🍷 A/C, cable TV w/movies, refrig, shoe polisher. Some units w/Jacuzzis. **Services:** ✕ 🖨 🍷 Masseur. Complimentary coffee and tea, evening appetizers. **Facilities:** 🏊 ⟨65⟩ 🖥 ♿ 1 rst, 1 bar, sauna, steam rm, whirlpool. Restaurant has the largest wine list in the area. Use of nearby health club. Golf nearby. **Rates (CP):** HS Apr–Nov $99–$119 S or D; from $135 ste. Extra person $10. Children under 12 stay free. Min stay spec evnts. Lower rates off-season. Spec packages avail. Pking: Outdoor, free. Maj CC.

Los Robles Lodge, 925 Edwards Ave, Santa Rosa, CA 94501; tel 707/545-6330 or toll free 800/255-6330; fax 707/575-5826. Right off highway; traffic noise can be a problem. **Rooms:** 106 rms. CI 4pm/CO noon. Nonsmoking rms avail. Rooms are plain but pleasant; some have a pool view. Executive suites are more luxurious. **Amenities:** 🛏🕯📺 A/C, cable TV w/movies, refrig. Some units w/terraces, some w/Jacuzzis. **Services:** ✕ 🛎 🖨 🍷 🛍 Babysitting. Discount of 10% in nearby restaurants. **Facilities:** 🏊 ⟨45⟩ ♿ 1 rst, 1 bar, sauna, whirlpool, washer/dryer. **Rates:** $75–$90 S; $80–$95 D. Extra person $5. Children under 12 stay free. Spec packages avail. Pking: Outdoor, free. Maj CC.

Vintners Inn, 4350 Barnes Rd, Santa Rosa, CA 95403; tel 707/575-7350 or toll free 800/421-2584; fax 707/575-1426. River Rd W exit off US 101; go west on River Rd 1 block; left on Barnes. Completely surrounded by mature vineyards in a lovely quiet location. The hacienda-style hotel has red-tiled roofs and many little walkways between the 2-story buildings. Adjacent to John Ash, an excellent restaurant. **Rooms:** 44 rms and stes. CI 3pm/CO noon. Huge rooms. Upstairs accommodations have vaulted ceilings. All have oak or pine furnishings, vineyard views, and country-French decor. **Amenities:** 🛏 🐱 A/C, cable TV w/movies, refrig. Some units w/terraces, some w/fireplaces, some w/Jacuzzis. **Services:** ✗ 🔑 🖾 ⚲ Masseur, babysitting. Hearty breakfast, with homemade Belgian waffles, served in a charming breakfast room. Informational videos for touring Sonoma County available. **Facilities:** ⟦40⟧ ⚲ 1 rst (*see also* "Restaurants" below), 1 bar. **Rates (CP):** HS Apr–Nov $118–$168 S or D; from $155 ste. Extra person $10. Min stay HS and wknds. Lower rates off-season. Higher rates for spec evnts/hols. Spec packages avail. Pking: Outdoor, free. Maj CC.

Restaurants 🍴

Cafe Lolo, 620 5th St, Santa Rosa (Downtown); tel 707/576-7822. Downtown Santa Rosa exit off US 101. **Californian.** Small, chef-owned restaurant downtown featuring fine cuisine in a cool and airy space. Willow branches wrapped in silk adorn the windows. Try the whole roasted fish, grilled veal chop, or marinated seafood salad. **FYI:** Reservations recommended. Beer and wine only. **Open:** Lunch Mon–Fri 11:30am–2pm; dinner Mon–Sat 5:30–9:30pm. Closed some hols. **Prices:** Main courses $7.95–$16.95. Ltd CC. ⚲

Fonseca's, 117 4th St, Santa Rosa (Old Town); tel 707/576-0131. Downtown Santa Rosa exit off US 101. **Mexican.** Classic, cozy Mexican restaurant decorated with piñatas and bullfighting posters. A good place to feast on green chili, tacos, burritos, and quesadillas. **FYI:** Reservations accepted. Guitar. Children's menu. Beer and wine only. **Open:** Mon–Thurs 10am–9pm, Fri–Sat 9am–10pm, Sun 9am–9pm. Closed some hols. **Prices:** Main courses $6–$12. Maj CC.

Gary Chu's, 611 5th St, Santa Rosa (Downtown); tel 707/526-5840. Downtown Santa Rosa exit of US 101. **Chinese.** Many locals consider this place to have the best Chinese cuisine in Sonoma County. Elegant setting with large fish tanks. Try the walnut prawns, sesame-pineapple chicken, four-season lamb, or moo shu pork. **FYI:** Reservations accepted. Beer and wine only. **Open:** Daily 11:30am–9:30pm. Closed some hols. **Prices:** Main courses $6–$11; PF dinner $10–$12. Maj CC. ⚲

♦ **John Ash & Co**, 4330 Barnes Rd, Santa Rosa; tel 707/527-7687. River Rd W exit off US 101. **Californian.** John Ash, who moved his popular restaurant here from an eastside location, keeps drawing both new and longtime fans. Adjacent to Vintners Inn (*see* "Hotels" above), the restaurant has outdoor dining with views of lawns and vineyards. Soft pinks and terra cotta dominate the color scheme of the high-ceilinged main room, in which oversized paintings are hung. Known for its inventive use of local products, the restaurant has a changing menu that may include Dungeness crab cakes, braised rabbit, smoked lamb, local cheeses, and salads. **FYI:** Reservations recommended. **Open:** Lunch Tues–Sat 11:30am–5:30pm, Sun 2–5:30pm; dinner Tues–Sun 5:30–9:30pm; brunch Sun 10:30am–2pm. Closed Dec 25. **Prices:** Main courses $13–$30. Maj CC. ⚱ ⚲

La Gare French Restaurant, 208 Wilson St, Santa Rosa; tel 707/528-4355. Downtown Santa Rosa exit off US 101; turn left on 3rd St, then right on Wilson St. **French.** Large, old brick building spruced up with lace curtains, fine goblets, and nice furnishings to create a French bistro atmosphere. Dishes include baked salmon fillet, medallions of beef in tarragon sauce, braised duck, and sole amandine. Excellent service. **FYI:** Reservations accepted. Beer and wine only. **Open:** Tues–Thurs 5:30–10pm, Fri–Sat 5–10pm, Sun 5–9pm. Closed some hols. **Prices:** Main courses $10–$15. Maj CC. ⚲

★ **Lisa Hemenway's**, in Montgomery Village Shopping Center, 714 Village Court, Santa Rosa; tel 707/526-5111. **Eclectic.** Lots of windows, beautiful gardens, and many flower arrangements inside make for a restaurant that is casually elegant, with an Asian/Mediterranean flair. The eclectic menu includes appetizers such as a tapas platter with almonds, cheese, and grilled vegetables, and entrees like filet mignon with crisp onion rings in a pesto sauce, as well as various seafood specialties that have won this restaurant numerous awards. There is also an oyster bar and a take out café nearby. **FYI:** Reservations recommended. **Open:** Lunch Mon–Sat 11:30am–2:30pm; dinner Mon–Sat 5:30–9:30pm, Sun 5–9pm; brunch Sun 10am–2pm. Closed Dec 25. **Prices:** Main courses $13–$19. Ltd CC. ⚱ ⚲

♦ **The Mixx**, 135 4th St, Santa Rosa (Railroad Square); tel 707/573-1344. **New American.** A family-run American bistro with an art deco look, lovely glass chandeliers, and an oak bar. Extensive seasonal menu offers fresh fish and pasta, grilled prawns, leg of venison, and much more. Many heart-healthy dishes. Fresh-baked pastries. Extensive wine list. **FYI:** Reservations recommended. Beer and wine only. **Open:** Lunch Mon–Fri 11:30am–2pm; dinner Mon–Thurs 5:30–9:30pm, Fri–Sat 5:30pm–midnight. Closed some hols. **Prices:** Main courses $11–$19. Maj CC. ⚲

Omelette Express, 112 4th St, Santa Rosa (Railroad Square); tel 707/525-1690. **Diner.** This breakfast and lunch place in old town delivers satisfying food, including sandwiches, burgers, bagels, over 50 omelettes, and espresso. **FYI:** Reservations not accepted. Beer and wine only. **Open:** Mon–Fri 6:30am–3pm, Sat–Sun 7am–4pm. Closed some hols. **Prices:** Lunch main courses $5–$7. Ltd CC. ♿

Siena, 1229 N Dutton Ave, Santa Rosa; tel 707/578-9421. College Ave exit off US 101. **Italian.** A large, Tuscan-inspired trattoria, with strands of garlic and sausages hanging from the ceiling, a wood-burning pizza oven, and terra-cotta walls. Hearty food includes grilled eggplant pizza, grilled prawns wrapped in pancetta, salmon with fennel, and chicken scaloppine. **FYI:** Reservations recommended. Beer and wine only. **Open:** Lunch Mon–Fri 11:30am–2pm; dinner daily 5:30–9pm; brunch Sun 10am–2pm. Closed some hols. **Prices:** Main courses $9–$16. Ltd CC. ♿

Attractions 🗂

Sonoma County Museum, 425 7th St; tel 707/579-1500. Housed in the 1909 Old Post Office and Federal Building, this museum focuses on regional art and history. The museum's permanent collections include fine 19th-century California landscape paintings, with works by renowned artist Thomas Hill, and works by Sonoma County artisans and craftsmen such as Harry Dixon and Elwin Millerick. Changing exhibits are also featured, and there are special events throughout the year. **Open:** Wed–Sun 11am–4pm. Closed some hols. $

Luther Burbank Home and Gardens, Santa Rosa and Sonoma Aves; tel 707/524-5445. Luther Burbank (1849–1926) was a famed horticulturist whose plant breeding experiments produced approximately 800 varieties of plants and 200 varieties of fruits, vegetables, nuts, grains, and flowers during his lifetime. He lived in Santa Rosa for 50 years, and the 1.6-acre garden that remains today served as his outdoor laboratory.

Dedicated in 1960, the central garden was redesigned as a memorial park. A 50-foot outdoor display describes Burbank's life and work, and includes information on the history of the property. The park is filled with numerous specimens of fruit trees, cacti, roses, and many others that were the result of Burbank's experiments.

The gardens surround Burbank's modified Greek Revival home, which is accessible only by guided tour. The Greenhouse contains changing exhibits and a replica of Burbank's office containing many of his tools; and the Carriage House houses museum exhibits, a gift shop, and the tour registration desk. **Open:** Gardens, daily dawn–dusk; home tours, Apr–Oct, Wed–Sun, 10am–3:30pm. Closed some hols. $

De Loach Vineyards, 1791 Olivet Rd; tel 707/526-9111. This winery encompasses more than 300 acres in the Russian River Valley. Tours are given by appointment, and visitors may sample wines and picnic at an area adjoining the vineyard. **Open:** Daily 10am–4:30pm. Closed some hols. Free.

San Ysidro
Map page M-3, E3 (E of Imperial Beach)

Motel 🛏

▤▤ **International Motor Inn**, 190 E Calle Primera, San Ysidro, CA 92173; tel 619/428-4486; fax 619/428-3618. 18 mi S of San Diego. San Ysidro exit off I-5. Many guests here are patients at cancer clinics in Mexico. Landscaping is meticulous and grounds are pleasant. Close to factory outlets, fast-food restaurants. **Rooms:** 100 rms and effic. CI 11am/CO 11am. Nonsmoking rms avail. Rooms available with kitchenettes, including toaster oven, cooktop, refrigerator, and dishes. **Amenities:** 🛏 🐾 📺 A/C, cable TV w/movies, refrig. **Services:** ✕ 🛎 🖨 🗞 🐾 Babysitting. Free shuttle to many local spots. **Facilities:** 🛗 ♿ Whirlpool, washer/dryer. Adjoins RV park. **Rates:** $32–$38 S; $36–$42 D; from $37 effic. Extra person $3. Pking: Outdoor, free. Maj CC.

Saratoga
Map page M-2, D2 (S of Santa Clara)

Inn 🛏

▤▤▤▤ **The Inn at Saratoga**, 20645 4th St, Saratoga, CA 95070; tel 408/867-5020 or toll free 800/543-5020; fax 408/741-0981. 12 mi NW of San Jose. The most elegant inn in the Saratoga–Los Gatos area, with a helpful staff and homey touches. **Rooms:** 45 rms and stes. CI 3pm/CO noon. **Amenities:** 🛏 🐾 🗞 A/C, cable TV w/movies, refrig, stereo/tape player, shoe polisher, bathrobes. All units w/minibars, all w/terraces, some w/Jacuzzis. Some rooms have VCRs. **Services:** ✕ 🛎 🖨 🐾 Babysitting, wine/sherry served. Breakfast (3 kinds of pastries) served in lobby or in guest's room. **Facilities:** 🖼 ♿ Guest lounge. Pleasant patio overlooking a creek. No restaurant on premises, but many within walking distance. **Rates (CP):** HS Apr–Oct $145–$245 D; from $390 ste. Extra person $15. Children under 18 stay free. Lower rates off-season. Spec packages avail. Pking: Outdoor, free. Ltd CC.

Restaurants 🍴

♦ **La Mère Michelle**, 14467 Big Basin Way, Saratoga; tel 408/867-5272. Calif 9 exit off I-280; turn right onto Big Basin Way. **Continental/French.** Family-owned restaurant decorated with flourishes from Italy, Sweden, and Eastern Europe. Start with pâté or French onion soup, before moving on to fish, white veal with lemon and capers, Wiener schnitzel, curried boneless breast of chicken, or seafood in Mornay sauce. **FYI:** Reservations recommended. **Open:** Lunch Tues–Sun 11:30am–2pm; dinner Tues–Thurs 6–9:30pm, Fri–Sat 6–10pm, Sun 5:30–9pm; brunch Sat 11:30am–2pm, Sun 10:30am–2pm. Closed some hols. **Prices:** Main courses $16.50–$23.50; PF dinner $30. Maj CC. ❤ 🍽 &

Le Mouton Noir, 14560 Big Basin Way, Saratoga; tel 408/867-7017. Calif 9 exit off Calif 280. **French.** Le Mouton Noir (the black sheep) is divided into several intimate dining rooms, each with a French country motif. A stained-glass window features the namesake sheep out among the vineyards. Appetizers include gnocchi with smoked goose, and escargot with garlic and mushrooms. Main courses include sweetbreads, filet mignon with foie gras, and the house specialty duck. **FYI:** Reservations recommended. Beer and wine only. **Open:** Lunch Tues–Sat 11:30am–2pm; dinner Mon–Sat 6–9:30pm, Sun 5–9pm. Closed some hols. **Prices:** Main courses $17–$25. Maj CC. ❤ 🍽 📷 &

Attraction 🏛

Hakone Gardens, 21000 Big Basin Way; tel 408/741-4994. Four gardens make up this tranquil 15-acre park: the Hill and Pond Garden, created in the style of 17th-century Japan; the Tea Garden, an enclosed garden where tea services are held in season; the Zen Garden, a dry garden intended for viewing only; and the *Kizuna-En,* a bamboo garden respresenting the relationship between Saratoga and its sister city, Muko-shi, Japan.

The Upper House and Lower House were built by the original owners of the property, who also constructed the original gardens in the 1910s. The Cultural Exchange Center is an authentic reproduction of a 19th-century Kyoto tea merchant's house and shop, assembled in Japan and raised on a prepared site.

Guided tours on weekends Apr–Sept; Tea Service weekend afternoons Apr–Sept. Gift shop open Mar–Sept. Parking fee charged. **Open:** Mon–Fri 10am–5pm, Sat–Sun 11am–5pm. Closed some hols. Free.

SAUSALITO
Map page M-2, D1 (S of San Rafael)

Hotel 🛏

▤▤ **Alta Mira Hotel**, 125 Bulkley Ave, PO Box 706, Sausalito, CA 94966; tel 415/332-1350; fax 415/331-3862. From Bridgeway, take Princess to Bulkley. Rambling, pink-painted building nestled in the foothills. Town is just a short walk away. Atmosphere decidedly funky, with worn carpets and tiny, dated bathrooms. Still, a Sausalito tradition. **Rooms:** 15 rms and stes; 13 ctges/villas. CI 2pm/CO noon. Nonsmoking rms avail. No two rooms are alike. Some have Victorian furnishings. The cottages, formerly private homes, are spacious and tranquil, although furnishings are old and nondescript. **Amenities:** 🏠 Cable TV. No A/C. Some units w/terraces, some w/fireplaces. **Services:** ✕ 🗝 VP 🚗 ⛱ ↪ Car-rental desk, social director, masseur, babysitting. **Facilities:** 🍴 1 rst, 1 bar (w/entertainment). The bar and outdoor terrace are the spot for sunset cocktails, with dazzling city views. Garden area with towering redwoods popular for weddings. **Rates:** HS May–Oct $70–$170 S or D; from $105 ste; from $105 ctge/villa. Extra person $10. Children under 6 stay free. Min stay wknds. Lower rates off-season. Pking: Outdoor, free. Maj CC.

Inn

▤▤▤▤ **Casa Madrona Hotel**, 801 Bridgeway, Sausalito, CA 94965 (Downtown); tel 415/332-0502 or toll free 800/288-0502; fax 415/332-2537. A small, deluxe hotel with the feel of a charming B&B, in the heart of Sausalito. **Rooms:** 29 rms and stes; 5 ctges/villas. CI 3pm/CO noon. All rooms are different, many decorated with antiques. Many offer spectacular views of the bay and San Francisco. Accommodations in the New Casa are the most elegant, with touches like stenciled woodwork and designer fabrics. "Old House" rooms offer the charms of a vintage 1885 structure. **Amenities:** 🏠 ♨ Cable TV, refrig, shoe polisher, bathrobes. No A/C. All units w/minibars, some w/terraces, some w/fireplaces. **Services:** ✕ 🗝 VP 🚗 ⛱ ↪ Twice-daily maid svce, car-rental desk, masseur, babysitting, wine/sherry served. Complimentary wine and cheese served in the Victorian-style parlor each afternoon. **Facilities:** 🍴 🖥 & 1 rst (*see also* "Restaurants" below), 1 bar (w/entertainment), whirlpool, guest lounge w/TV. **Rates (BB):** $105–$185 S or D; from $225 ste; from $145 ctge/villa. Children under 18 stay free. Min stay wknds. Spec packages avail. Pking: Outdoor, $5. Ltd CC. Warm Winter Whim package (Dec–Apr) offers a midweek rate of $185, including room and dinner for 2.

Restaurants 🍽️

Casa Madrona Restaurant, 801 Bridgeway, Sausalito (Downtown); tel 415/331-5888. **Pacific Rim.** Pacific Rim cuisine has hit California like a tidal wave—and one of the most deft practitioners is chef Nicholas Boer. His best dishes meld and contrast tastes and textures, such as Dungeness crab cakes with sesame and Thai chile, or guava-macadamia-crusted rack of lamb. Meanwhile, floor-to-ceiling windows offer spectacular views of the bay, with a roof that rolls back for al fresco dining. Wine list is excellent and reasonably priced. Save room for the signature dessert, white-chocolate "nachos." **FYI:** Reservations recommended. Piano. Beer and wine only. **Open:** Breakfast daily 7:30–9:30am; lunch Mon–Fri 11:30am–2:30pm; dinner daily 6–10pm; brunch Sun 10am–2:30pm. **Prices:** Main courses $11–$19.50. Maj CC. ♥ ▲ VP

⑤ **Guernica**, 2009 Bridgeway, Sausalito (Downtown); tel 415/332-1512. Sausalito exit off US 101. **French/Basque.** A good place to sample hearty French-Basque cuisine at very reasonable prices in a setting resembling a simple, European-style dining hall. You can start off with steamed clams or artichoke bottoms in hollandaise sauce, then move on to entrees such as paella Valenciana, rack of lamb, or the fresh catch of the day. **FYI:** Reservations recommended. Beer and wine only. **Open:** Sun–Thurs 5–10:30pm, Fri–Sat 5–11pm. Closed Dec 25. **Prices:** Main courses $9.50–$15. Maj CC. ▣

North Sea Village, 300 Turney St, Sausalito (Downtown); tel 415/331-3300. Sausalito exit off US 101; 2 mi N on Bridgeway. **Chinese.** A real Hong Kong–style seafood restaurant, stylishly decorated in elegant peach and green tones. It's especially packed for dim sum lunches on the weekend, with offerings such as steamed shrimp balls, pork buns, and stuffed crab claws. **FYI:** Reservations accepted. Beer and wine only. **Open:** Mon–Fri 11am–10pm, Sat–Sun 10am–10pm. **Prices:** Main courses $7–$15. Maj CC. ♿

Scoma's, 588 Bridgeway, Sausalito (Downtown); tel 415/332-9551. Sausalito exit off US 101; 1 mi N on Bridgeway. **Italian/Seafood.** Fabulous sailboats lie at anchor in San Francisco Bay, right off the restaurant's pier location. Inside, the decor is nautical-Victorian, with cane chairs, beveled mirrors, and lots of windows. Fresh fish selections vary daily, with up to 8 choices—perhaps including Dungeness crab or petrale sole. Other favorites include cioppino (seafood stew) and pasta dishes. **FYI:** Reservations recommended. Children's menu. Dress code. **Open:** Thurs–Mon 11:30am–9:30pm, Tues–Wed 5:30–9:30pm. Closed some hols; Christmas week. **Prices:** Main courses $14–$18. Maj CC. ▲ VP ♿

The Spinnaker, 100 Spinnaker Dr, Sausalito (Downtown); tel 415/332-1500. **Seafood.** A top choice for both views and ultra-fresh seafood. The atmosphere is elegant and sopisticated, with rattan chairs, crisp white linens, and panoramic views of San Francisco through floor-to-ceiling windows. Selections might include local Dungeness crab cakes, halibut, or caldo de mariscos, a seafood stew spiked with roasted chiles and cilantro. Pasta, meat, and poultry dishes are offered as well. **FYI:** Reservations recommended. Children's menu. **Open:** Daily 11am–11pm. Closed some hols. **Prices:** Main courses $12–$19. Maj CC. ▲ VP

⑤ **The Stuffed Croissant, Etc**, 43 Caledonia St, Sausalito; tel 415/332-7103. Between Pine and Johnson. **Eclectic.** A tiny hole-in-the-wall, with seating at the counter only. Nonetheless, a local favorite for breakfast, with a terrific espresso bar and fresh-baked muffins and scones. Employees contribute their own ethnic specialties—Indian samosas, Italian pizzas, Mexican enchiladas. The Indian lunch special, which is served all day and might consist of a huge helping of curried chicken, vegetables, rice, and yogurt, is just $5.50. **FYI:** Reservations not accepted. No liquor license. **Open:** Mon–Sat 6am–10pm, Sun 7am–9pm. Closed Dec 25. **Prices:** Main courses $2.75–$5.50. No CC. ♿

Venice Gourmet Delicatessen, 625 Bridgeway, Sausalito (Downtown); tel 415/332-3544. **Deli.** A deli and gourmet kitchenware store with a wide variety of copperware, condiments, and wine. Its broad selection of sandwiches and salads make it a perfect place to buy a picnic lunch. Try the roasted turkey or the Greek salad, which is accompanied by sourdough bread. **FYI:** Reservations not accepted. Beer and wine only. **Open:** Daily 9am–7pm. Closed some hols. **Prices:** Lunch main courses $2.95–$4.95. Maj CC. VP ♿

Attraction 💼

Bay Model Visitors Center, 2100 Bridgeway; tel 415/332-3871. Built and maintained by the US Army Corps of Engineers, this 1½-acre model of San Francisco's bay and delta allows engineers to simulate changes in the bay's water flow and study their effects. The model reproduces (in scale) the rise and fall of tides, the flows and currents of water, the mixing of fresh and salt water, and indicates trends in sediment movement. There is a 10-minute orientation video, and a taped audio tour is available in several languages. The model is most interesting to watch when it is in operation; phone ahead. **Open:** Winter, Tues–Sat 9am–4pm; summer, Tues–Fri 9am–4pm, Sat–Sun and hols 10am–6pm. Closed some hols. Free.

SEAL BEACH

Map page M-3, D2 (E of Long Beach)

Inn 🏨

■■■■ **Seal Beach Inn & Gardens**, 212 5th St, Seal Beach, CA 90740; tel 310/493-2416 or toll free 800/HIDE-AWAY; fax 310/799-0483. 5 mi S of Long Beach. Seal Beach Blvd exit off I-405; SW on Seal Beach, right on Pacific Coast Hwy, left on 5th St. Beautiful property surrounded by lush gardens, accented by antique ironwork. Just 300 yards from the beach. Unsuitable for children under 7. **Rooms:** 23 rms, stes, and effic. CI 4pm/CO 11am. No smoking. Each room is individually decorated and named for a flower. All suites have kitchens and are decorated with antiques and collectibles. **Amenities:** 🛁 🔥 TV, refrig, bathrobes. No A/C. Some units w/terraces, some w/fireplaces, some w/Jacuzzis. A/C in penthouse suite. **Services:** ✕ 🚗 🖼 Twice-daily maid svce, car-rental desk, afternoon tea and wine/sherry served. Desk offers information on lake and watersport equipment rentals. **Facilities:** 🏠 🔲 ᒼ Guest lounge. Parlor games in lounge, business center 3 blocks away. **Rates (BB):** HS June–Sept $95–$185 S or D; from $155 ste; from $155 effic. Extra person $10. Lower rates off-season. AP and MAP rates avail. Spec packages avail. Pking: Outdoor, free. Ltd CC.

SEA RANCH

Map page M-2, F1 (S of Gualala)

Lodge 🏨

■■■ **Sea Ranch Lodge**, 60 Sea Walk Dr, PO Box 44, Sea Ranch, CA 95497; tel 707/785-2371 or toll free 800/732-7262; fax 707/785-2243. With a secluded 10-mile stretch of private beach, Sea Ranch Lodge is famous for the way its architecture melds with the stunning coastal setting. A good place to watch for whales and unwind. **Rooms:** 20 rms. CI 2pm/CO noon. Nonsmoking rms avail. All rooms are comfortable with ocean views. **Amenities:** 🔥 No A/C, phone, or TV. All units w/terraces, some w/fireplaces, some w/Jacuzzis. Some rooms have hot tubs. Board games available. **Services:** ᒼ **Facilities:** 🏠 🔲 ▶₉ ⛳ 🖼 🔲 ᒼ 1 rst, 1 bar, 1 beach (ocean), sauna, whirlpool. Beautiful golf course above the ocean. **Rates:** $125–$180 S or D. Extra person $15. Min stay wknds. Spec packages avail. Pking: Outdoor, free. Maj CC. Midweek packages with 2-night minimum stay.

SEASIDE

Map page M-2, D2 (N of Pacific Grove)

Restaurant 🍴

★ **Fishwife Seafood Deli & Cafe**, 789 Trinity Ave, Seaside; tel 408/394-2027. At Fremont St. **Cajun/Seafood.** Eat in or take out at this popular cafe. Decor is clean and simple. Catfish and Cajun snapper sandwiches are among the specials, along with a sea garden salad and various pastas, soups, and desserts. **FYI:** Reservations not accepted. Children's menu. Beer and wine only. **Open:** Fri–Sat 11am–9:30pm, Mon–Thurs 11am–9pm. Closed some hols. **Prices:** Main courses $6.25–$11.95. Maj CC. 🚤 🖼 ᒼ

SELMA

Map page M-3, B1

Motel 🏨

■■ **Best Western John Jay Inn**, 2799 Floral Ave, Selma, CA 93662; tel 209/891-0300 or toll free 800/528-1234; fax 209/891-1538. Floral Ave exit off Calif 99; go east. A modern hotel (built in 1992). Some noise near the pool but rooms are well soundproofed. Close to shopping and restaurants. **Rooms:** 57 rms and stes. CI open/CO 11am. Nonsmoking rms avail. Pleasantly decorated. Request a room away from the highway. **Amenities:** 🛁 🔥 A/C, cable TV w/movies, shoe polisher. Some units w/minibars, some w/terraces, some w/fireplaces. Refrigerators available on request. **Services:** 🖼 ᒼ **Facilities:** 🏠 🔲 🔲 ᒼ Sauna, steam rm, whirlpool, washer/dryer. **Rates (CP):** $45 S; $50–$55 D; from $65 ste. Extra person $5. Children under 12 stay free. Spec packages avail. Pking: Outdoor, free. Maj CC.

SEQUOIA AND KINGS CANYON NATIONAL PARKS

Map page M-2, D4

For accommodations, see **Cedar Grove, Giant Forest, Grant Grove, Three Rivers**

Domain of the giant trees, Sequoia National Park is, after Yellowstone, the oldest national park in the United States.

Created in 1890 to safeguard the redwood forests on the slopes of the Sierra Nevada, the park boasts magnificent scenery that embraces granite and mountain crests, canyons, mountain lakes, and dense forests. The adjoining Kings Canyon National Park was established in 1940, and the 2 parks are now administered as a unit. Nearby are the giant peaks of Mount Whitney, tallest in the lower 48 states (14,495 feet), Split Mountain (14,054 feet), and Mount Goethe (13,274 feet).

Named for Sequoyah, the Cherokee scholar and inventor of the Cherokee alphabet, sequoias have been known to grow as tall as 295 feet, with a circumference at the base of 100 feet or more. Their bark, 2 feet thick, is resistant to both fire and insects. The largest redwood now standing in the park, the **General Sherman Tree,** is more than 275 feet tall, and its estimated age of 2,500 years makes it among the very oldest living things on earth.

In spite of the huge area they cover, the parks have only 75 miles of surfaced roads. Points off these roads are reached only by horseback or on foot. There are, however, 900 miles of walking trails. Visitor centers providing park information, exhibits, and programs are located at Grant, Foothills, and Lodgepole. Camping (some sites open year-round); fishing. For further information, contact the Superintendent, Sequoia and Kings Canyon National Parks, Three Rivers, CA 93271 (tel 209/565-3134 or 565-3341).

SEQUOIA NATIONAL FOREST

Map page M-2, E4

Motel

Stony Creek Lodge, Generals Hwy, Sequoia National Forest, CA 93262; tel 209/561-3314. Stony Creek Village exit off Generals Hwy. Nicest motel rooms in the park. No landscaping. Many forests and other attractions are close by. Mailing address: Guest Services, PO Box 789, Three Rivers, CA 93271. **Rooms:** 11 rms. CI 4pm/CO 11am. Nonsmoking rms avail. Comfortable, clean. **Amenities:** No A/C, phone, or TV. **Services:** Park tours available all day. **Facilities:** 1 rst, washer/dryer. Nearby trout fishing creek. Also hiking trails, picnic areas. **Rates:** HS May 25–Labor Day $78 S or D. Extra person $6.50. Children under 13 stay free. Lower rates off-season. Pking: Outdoor, free. Ltd CC.

SHELL BEACH

Map page M-3, C1 (N of Pismo Beach)

Hotels

The Cliffs at Shell Beach–Oceanfront Resort Hotel, 2757 Shell Beach Rd, Shell Beach, CA 93449; tel 805/773-5000 or toll free 800/826-7827; fax 805/773-0764. Spyglass Rd exit off US 101 N; Shell Beach exit off US 101 S. 4 acres. For elegance and romantic ambience, this is the best hotel in the area. Designed like a ship. Expensive, but worth it. **Rooms:** 165 rms and stes. CI 3pm/CO noon. Nonsmoking rms avail. Suites are luxurious and have ocean views. **Amenities:** A/C, cable TV w/movies, refrig, voice mail, shoe polisher. All units w/terraces, some w/Jacuzzis. Upscale in-room amenities, such as Crabtree and Evelyn soaps and shampoos. **Services:** Masseur, babysitting. **Facilities:** 1 rst, 1 bar (w/entertainment), 1 beach (cove/inlet), spa, sauna, steam rm, whirlpool, washer/dryer. Great pool-size Jacuzzi. **Rates:** HS May–Oct $115–$165 S or D; from $215 ste. Extra person $10. Children under 12 stay free. Min stay HS and wknds. Lower rates off-season. Spec packages avail. Pking: Outdoor, free. Maj CC.

Spyglass Inn, 2705 Spyglass Dr, Shell Beach, CA 93449; tel 805/773-4855 or toll free 800/824-2612; fax 805/773-5298. Spyglass Dr exit off US 101. Attractive gray Cape Cod–style buildings. Lobby has wood floors and beamed ceilings. **Rooms:** 82 rms and stes. CI 3pm/CO noon. Nonsmoking rms avail. Large rooms with attractive bedspreads and prints. **Amenities:** Cable TV w/movies, VCR. No A/C. Some units w/terraces. Ceiling fans. **Services:** **Facilities:** 1 rst, 1 bar (w/entertainment), whirlpool. Miniature golf, shuffleboard. **Rates (BB):** HS June–Aug $96–$125 S or D; from $125 ste. Extra person $6. Children under 12 stay free. Min stay HS and wknds. Lower rates off-season. Pking: Outdoor, free. Maj CC.

SHERMAN OAKS

Map page M-3, D2 (N of Santa Monica)

Hotel

Carriage Inn, 5525 Sepulveda Blvd, Sherman Oaks, CA 91411; tel 818/787-2300 or toll free 800/772-8527; fax 818/782-9373. This 30-year-old property is well maintained, despite a deteriorating neighborhood. **Rooms:** 183 rms and stes. CI 3pm/CO noon. Express checkout avail. Nonsmoking rms avail.

Decor of dark wood with forest-green carpeting makes the small rooms seem even smaller. **Amenities:** 📞 🛁 📺 A/C, cable TV w/movies, refrig. **Services:** ✗ 🚐 🗻 🍽 Twice-daily maid svce, car-rental desk. **Facilities:** 🏊 🍴 2 rsts, 1 bar (w/entertainment), whirlpool. Bar has a band on weekends. **Rates:** $79–$99 S or D; from $150 ste. Children under 18 stay free. Spec packages avail. Pking: Outdoor, free. Maj CC.

SIMI VALLEY

Map page M-3, D2 (N of Thousand Oaks)

Hotels 🏨

📶📶 **Clarion Hotel Simi Valley**, 1775 Madera Rd, Simi Valley, CA 93065; tel 805/584-6300 or toll free 800/221-2222; fax 805/527-9969. 45 mi NW of Los Angeles. Madera Rd exit off Calif 118. Needed renovations are scheduled soon. Excellent location for visiting the Reagan Library. **Rooms:** 120 rms and stes. CI 3pm/CO 11am. Express checkout avail. Nonsmoking rms avail. **Amenities:** 📞 🛁 📺 A/C, cable TV w/movies. Some units w/terraces, some w/fireplaces, some w/Jacuzzis. **Services:** ✗ 🚐 🗻 🍽 Children's program, babysitting. Complimentary continental breakfast and evening cocktails. **Facilities:** 🏊 🍴 💻 & 1 rst, 1 bar, whirlpool, washer/dryer. **Rates (CP):** $70–$90 S or D; from $125 ste. Extra person $10. Children under 17 stay free. Min stay spec evnts. Spec packages avail. Pking: Outdoor, free. Maj CC.

📶📶 **Radisson Hotel–Simi Valley**, 999 Enchanted Way, Simi Valley, CA 93065; tel 805/583-2000 or toll free 800/333-3333; fax 805/583-2779. 1st St exit off Calif 118. Under new ownership; rooms and public spaces are being renovated. Easy access to Reagan Library. **Rooms:** 195 rms and stes. CI 3pm/CO noon. Express checkout avail. Nonsmoking rms avail. Worn but clean. **Amenities:** 📞 🛁 📺 A/C, cable TV w/movies, refrig. Some units w/terraces, 1 w/Jacuzzi. **Services:** ✗ 🚐 🗻 🍽 🍷 Twice-daily maid svce. Complimentary cocktail parties weekdays. **Facilities:** 🏊 🏋 🍴 💻 & 1 rst, 2 bars (1 w/entertainment), whirlpool. **Rates:** $99 S; $109 D; from $139 ste. Extra person $10. Children under 17 stay free. Min stay spec evnts. Spec packages avail. Pking: Outdoor, free. Maj CC.

SOLVANG

Map page M-3, D1

See also **Los Olivos**

Motel 🏨

📶📶📶 **Solvang Royal Scandinavian Inn**, 400 Alisal Rd, PO Box 30, Solvang, CA 93464; tel 805/688-8000 or toll free 800/624-5572; fax 805/688-0761. This quiet property on the edge of town exudes serenity and relaxation. **Rooms:** 133 rms and stes. CI 4pm/CO 11am. Express checkout avail. Nonsmoking rms avail. Poolside rooms have beautiful views; very clean, with Scandinavian decor. **Amenities:** 📞 🛁 🍽 A/C, satel TV w/movies, stereo/tape player. Some units w/terraces. Refrigerators available. **Services:** ✗ 🚐 🗻 🍽 Masseur, babysitting. Coffee and newspapers in lobby. **Facilities:** 🏊 🍴 💻 & 1 rst, 1 bar (w/entertainment), whirlpool, day-care ctr. Outstanding pool area with gazebo, tables and chairs, and a basket of towels for guests. **Rates:** HS June–Sept $95–$135 S or D; from $145 ste. Extra person $10. Children under 17 stay free. Lower rates off-season. Spec packages avail. Pking: Outdoor, free. Maj CC.

Attraction 🎭

Mission Santa Ines, 1760 Mission Dr; tel 805/688-4815. Founded in 1804, this restored mission was the 19th in California's 21-mission series. After a series of restorations, the most recent in 1988, the mission looks much as it must have shortly after it was founded. The church, chapel, and grounds are open to the public, as is the museum, which houses early Native American and European mission artifacts. **Open:** Summer, Mon–Fri 9:30am–5pm, Sun noon–5pm; fall–spring, Mon–Sat 9:30am–4:30pm, Sun noon–4:30pm. Free.

SONOMA

Map page M-2, C2

See also **Glen Ellen, Kenwood, Santa Rosa**

Hotels 🏨

📶📶📶 **Best Western Sonoma Valley Inn**, 550 2nd St W, Sonoma, CA 95476 (Downtown); tel 707/938-9200 or toll free 800/334-5784; fax 707/938-0935. Lovely hotel with nice grounds. **Rooms:** 75 rms. CI 3pm/CO noon. Nonsmoking rms avail. Rooms are comfortable and have photographs of Sonoma Valley on the walls. Poolside patio rooms that open onto the garden and pool are nicest. **Amenities:** 📞 🛁 📺 🍽 A/C, cable TV w/movies, refrig. Some units w/terraces, some w/fireplaces, some w/Jacuzzis. **Services:** ☒ ⏻ ⏦ Babysitting. Continental breakfast delivered to your room. Friday night wine tasting in summer. **Facilities:** 🛗 ⑤⑩ ♿ Whirlpool, washer/dryer. Lovely pool area. **Rates (CP):** HS May–Oct $135–$149 S or D. Extra person $10. Children under 12 stay free. Min stay wknds and spec evnts. Lower rates off-season. Spec packages avail. Pking: Outdoor, free. Maj CC. Many special activity packages.

≣≣≣ **El Dorado Hotel**, 405 1st St W, Sonoma, CA 95476; tel 707/996-3030 or toll free 800/289-3031; fax 707/996-3148. Nice hotel right on the plaza with a wonderful restaurant, Piatti, downstairs. **Rooms:** 27 rms. CI 4pm/CO 1pm. Rooms decorated in soothing peach tones, with attractive furnishings and down comforters. Some have French doors. **Amenities:** 🛗 Cable TV. No A/C. All units w/terraces. Complimentary bottle of wine. **Services:** ☒ ⏻ Attentive staff. **Facilities:** 🛗 ⑤⑩ ♿ 1 rst (see also "Restaurants" below), 1 bar. **Rates (CP):** HS May–Oct $105–$145 S or D. Extra person $25. Min stay wknds. Lower rates off-season. Spec packages avail. Pking: Outdoor, free. Maj CC.

≣≣≣ **Sonoma Hotel**, 110 W Spain St, Sonoma, CA 95476; tel 707/996-2996 or toll free 800/468-6016; fax 707/996-7014. Unique old hotel furnished with antiques; they feel of an 1880s European inn. **Rooms:** 17 rms and stes. CI 2pm/CO noon. Nonsmoking rms avail. Well-appointed rooms have lots of antiques, including clawfoot tubs in rooms with private baths. **Amenities:** No A/C, phone, or TV. Some units w/terraces, some w/fireplaces. **Facilities:** 1 rst (see also "Restaurants" below), 1 bar, washer/dryer. **Rates (CP):** HS May–Oct $75–$115 S or D; from $120 ste. Lower rates off-season. Pking: Outdoor, free. Maj CC.

Resort

≣≣≣ **Sonoma Mission Inn & Spa**, 18140 Calif 12, PO Box 1447, Sonoma, CA 94576; tel 707/938-9000 or toll free 800/862-4945; fax 707/996-5358. 3 mi NW of Sonoma. At Boyes Blvd. 8 acres. Designed like an overgrown mission with pink walls and a red-tile roof, the resort is surrounded by emerald lawns and ancient oaks and sequoias. It is one of only 3 luxury resorts in the country to use its own natural mineral waters in treatments. **Rooms:** 170 rms and stes. CI 4pm/CO noon. Express checkout avail. Nonsmoking rms avail. Accommodations available in either the historic 1920s inn (charming but very small) or newer wings with spacious "wine country" rooms. Many of the latter have been redone with down quilts and antiqued armoires, lending a residential feel (but the concrete corridors they are in have the allure of a high school locker room). **Amenities:** 🛗 ♨ 🖥 A/C, cable TV w/movies, refrig, VCR.

All units w/minibars, some w/terraces, some w/fireplaces. Bathroom toiletries include products from the Inn's own line. **Services:** ✗ ☎ 🆅🅿 🚗 ☒ ⏻ Twice-daily maid svce, car-rental desk, masseur, babysitting. **Facilities:** 🛗 🚴 🏊 🎾 ⑮⓪ 🖥 ♿ 2 rsts (see also "Restaurants" below), 3 bars (1 w/entertainment), spa, sauna, steam rm, whirlpool, beauty salon. The spa is the largest and most complete in northern California, with 40 treatment rooms featuring an array of services, from a 2-hour "revitalizer" pick-me-up to stress-management techniques. Superb aerobics program. **Rates:** HS May–Oct $135–$375 S or D; from $375 ste. Extra person $40. Children under 18 stay free. Min stay wknds. Lower rates off-season. Spec packages avail. Pking: Outdoor, free. Maj CC. Spa packages available.

Restaurants 🍴

★ **Babette's**, 464 1st St, Sonoma; tel 707/939-8921. **Californian/French.** Nestled in a cobblestoned courtyard off Sonoma Plaza, this romantic restaurant serves modern French cuisine that emphasizes local organic products. The wine bar has a Paris-in-the-1920s feel. The menu offers local salmon, oven-roasted shiitake mushrooms, carrot and fennel soup, and roasted quail. **FYI:** Reservations recommended. Guitar. Beer and wine only. **Open:** Wed–Sat 6–10pm, Sun 5–9pm. Closed some hols. **Prices:** Main courses $13–$18. Ltd CC. ♥ ♿

Bistro Lunel, in Sonoma Hotel, 110 W Spain St, Sonoma; tel 707/996-2996. **Californian/French.** New restaurant has a real bistro feel. Decor evokes a rustic Gold Rush–style parlor inside; there's a lovely outdoor dining area too. Menu specialties are leg of lamb, goat cheese ravioli, and roast game hen. **FYI:** Reservations recommended. **Open:** Mon 11:30am–12:30am, Sat–Sun 11am–4pm. Closed some hols. **Prices:** Main courses $9–$16. Maj CC. ▮ ⛱ ♿

Depot 1870 Restaurant, 241 1st St W, Sonoma; tel 707/938-2980. **Italian.** Located in a onetime hotel for 19th-century train passengers. Ambience is charming, with a dining room overlooking the garden. Well-known chef prepares classic Italian food, including carpaccio, caesar salad, linguine, and veal parmigiana. **FYI:** Reservations accepted. **Open:** Lunch Wed–Fri 11:30am–2pm; dinner Wed–Sun 5–10pm. Closed some hols. **Prices:** Main courses $8–$16. Maj CC. ▮ ⛱ ♿

★ **East Side Oyster Bar & Grill**, 133 E Napa St, Sonoma; tel 707/939-1266. 1 block E of Sonoma Plaza. **Eclectic.** Among the Bay Area's most innovative cooking—creative without being quirky. Chef Charles Saunders (formerly of Sonoma Mission Inn) combines cuisines effortlessly, pairing sea-sweet oysters with tomatillo salsa, or accompanying Sonoma lamb with chick—pea mash, grilled eggplant, and red-onion confit. In addition to the

1930s-style restaurant up front, there's an outdoor brick patio. Service is well-meaning if somewhat bewildered. **FYI:** Reservations recommended. Beer and wine only. **Open:** Lunch daily 11am–2:30pm; dinner daily 5:30–10pm; brunch Sun 11:30am–2:30pm. Closed some hols. **Prices:** Main courses $12.50–$15.75. Maj CC. ♦ ♥

Feed Store Cafe and Bakery, 529 1st St W, Sonoma; tel 707/938-2122. **American/Cafe.** Country farm kitchen atmosphere in a former feed store with an award-winning bakery; pleasant garden patio with duck pond. Scrumptious homemade pastries, baked breads, chicken sandwiches, and vegetarian club sandwich. **FYI:** Reservations not accepted. Beer and wine only. **Open:** Mon–Fri 6am–5:30pm, Sat–Sun 7am–5:30pm. Closed some hols. **Prices:** Lunch main courses $5–$8. Ltd CC. ♦

The Grille, in Sonoma Mission Inn & Spa, 18140 Calif 12, Sonoma; tel 707/938-9000. At Boyes Blvd and Calif 12; turn west on Boyes Blvd. **Californian.** Impressionistic paintings of flowers plus oversize magnums and imperials of the valley's finest wines set the mood at this restaurant serving wine-country cuisine. The menu uses many Sonoma products—local lettuces, aged cheeses, Dungeness crab, and duck. Several "spa cuisine" dishes as well, with offerings such as grilled Sonoma lamb with roasted garlic and tomato-zucchini gratin weighing in at less than 300 calories. The wine list features over 200 Sonoma and Napa labels. **FYI:** Reservations recommended. Dress code. **Open:** Lunch daily 11:30am–2:30pm; dinner daily 6:30–9:30pm; brunch Sun 10am–2pm. **Prices:** Main courses $16–$22; PF dinner $35–$49. Maj CC. VP ♦

La Casa, 121 E Spain St, Sonoma; tel 707/996-3406. **Mexican.** Serving traditional Mexican specialties for the past 20 years. Atmosphere is festive, with lots of flowers, bright colors, and ceiling fans. Try the ceviche, black-bean soup, fajitas, or snapper Veracruz. **FYI:** Reservations accepted. Children's menu. **Open:** Mon–Thurs 11:30am–9pm, Fri–Sun 11:30am–10pm. Closed some hols. **Prices:** Main courses $6–$10. Maj CC. ♦ ♦

Murphy's Irish Pub, 464 1st St E, Sonoma; tel 707/935-0660. **Pub.** A good place to relax, right off the plaza. Traditional Irish pub, with 8 beers on tap and standard pub grub at good prices. Live music three nights a week. **FYI:** Reservations not accepted. Guitar. Beer and wine only. **Open:** Daily 11am–11pm. Closed Dec 25. **Prices:** Main courses $5–$7. No CC. ♦ ▥ ♦

Old Swiss Hotel, in the Swiss Hotel, 18 W Spain St, Sonoma; tel 707/938-2884. **Italian.** Set in a landmark 1848 adobe structure; it's been a hotel since 1909, and the decor has been lovingly restored. Great patio dining next to a fireplace. Menu specialties include baby spinach and artichoke salad, pan-roasted halibut, braised beef ribs, and risotto with rock shrimp.

FYI: Reservations accepted. **Open:** Lunch Mon–Fri 11:30am–2:30pm; dinner Mon–Fri 5–9pm, Sat–Sun 5–10pm. **Prices:** Main courses $9–$15. Ltd CC. ▮ ♦ ▦ ♦

Piatti, in the El Dorado Hotel, 405 1st St W, Sonoma; tel 707/996-2351. **Italian.** Known as the best Italian restaurant in Sonoma. Decor features Tuscan-influenced tile floors, an open kitchen, and lovely murals of food on the walls. Outdoor dining area is draped in wisteria. Try the clams, calamari, calzone, angel hair pasta, and roasted chicken. **FYI:** Reservations recommended. **Open:** Daily 11:30am–10pm. Closed some hols. **Prices:** Main courses $8–$17. Maj CC. ♦ ♦

Refreshment Stop ⊽

★ **Angelo's Wine Country Deli**, 23400 Arnold Dr (Calif 121), Sonoma (Schellville); tel 707/938-3688. On Calif 121 just north of Sonoma Valley Airport/Schellville. **Deli.** A great place to pick up goodies for a wine-country picnic. You can't miss it—there's a near-life-size model cow perched over the doorway. What you see inside—18 varieties of sausages, garlicky salsas, smoked meats—is the single-handed work of Angelo Ibleto. "I can't find anybody else who'll put love in the food," he explains. **Open:** Sun–Thurs 9am–6pm, Fri–Sat 9am–7pm. Closed some hols. No CC.

Attractions ▦

Sebastiani Vineyards Winery, 389 4th St E; tel 707/938-5532 or toll free 800/888-5532. Tours here highlight the winery's original turn-of-the-century crusher and press, as well as the largest collection of oak-barrel carvings in the world. Tastings include some of the vineyards 95 award-winning vintages. Picnic area. **Open:** Daily 10am–5pm. Free.

Buena Vista Winery, 18000 Old Winery Rd; tel 707/938-1266. A state historic landmark, the winery was founded in 1857 by Colonel Agoston Haraszthy, a Hungarian count. Haraszthy brought hundreds of grape varieties back from Europe, which became the foundation stock for the California wine industry. A self-guided tour includes historical displays, photographs, and an art gallery. Tasting room, cellars, wooded picnic area. **Open:** Daily 10am–5pm.

Sonoma Cattle Company; tel 707/996-8566. Located in Jack London State Historic Park (see above), this operation offers guided tours on horseback over various trails (the same ones that Jack London once followed), which wind through redwood stands, eucalyptus groves, and vineyards. Some trails ascend to the top of Mount Sonoma for a magnificent view of the countryside. **Open:** Daily, by appointment only. $$$$

Jack London State Historic Park, 2400 London Ranch Rd; tel 707/938-5216. About 8 miles north of Sonoma via Calif 12, the 800-acre park includes the "House of Happy Walls," built in 1919 by London's wife, Charmian, which now houses a considerable collection of objects and memorabilia from the author's life. London's cottage has recently been restored and is open to visitors on weekends. Trails lead up to the site of Wolf House, the Londons' mansion, which burned down in 1913, and to their gravesite; maps available. A free golf cart service is offered to elderly and visitors with disabilities who may have trouble negotiating the trails. **Open:** Park: winter, daily 10am–5pm; summer, daily 10am–7pm. Museum: daily 10am–5pm; closed some hols. $$

SONORA

Map page M-3, A1

Motels 🏨

Aladdin Motor Inn, 14260 Mono Way, Sonora, CA 95370; tel 209/533-4971 or toll free 800/696-3969 in CA; fax 209/532-1522. Mono Ave exit off Calif 108. Pleasant facility on country highway. Limits pets to certain rooms. **Rooms:** 62 rms, stes, and effic. Exec-level rms avail. CI 2pm/CO noon. Express checkout avail. Nonsmoking rms avail. **Amenities:** 🛅 🅰 📺 A/C, cable TV w/movies, refrig. VCR rental. **Services:** ✗ 🆚 📠 ➴ 🛎 Babysitting. Complimentary full breakfast at on-premises restaurant. Guests may use fax and copier in office. Hotel kit available for the deaf and hard of hearing. **Facilities:** 🛆 ⚿ 1 rst, whirlpool, washer/dryer. **Rates (MAP):** HS May–Oct $59 S; $64 D; from $85 ste; from $85 effic. Extra person $8. Children under 6 stay free. Min stay spec evnts. Lower rates off-season. Spec packages avail. Pking: Outdoor, free. Maj CC.

Best Western Sonora Oaks, 19551 Hess Ave, Sonora, CA 95370; tel 209/533-4400 or toll free 800/532-1944; fax 209/532-1964. Nice hotel on rural highway. Oak grove on back property. **Rooms:** 72 rms and stes. CI 1pm/CO 11am. Nonsmoking rms avail. Poolside rooms available. **Amenities:** 🛅 🅰 📺 A/C, cable TV w/movies. Some units w/terraces. **Services:** ➴ 🔑 📠 ➴ Offers ADA kit for deaf and hard of hearing guests. **Facilities:** 🛆 🎱 ⚿ 1 rst, 1 bar (w/entertainment), whirlpool. New meeting room under construction will accommodate 300 when completed. **Rates:** $62–$85 S; $67–$90 D; from $115 ste. Extra person $5. Children under 12 stay free. Spec packages avail. Pking: Outdoor, free. Maj CC. Ski and resort packages available.

Miners Motel, 18740 Calif 108, PO Box 1, Sonora, CA 95370; tel 209/532-7850 or toll free 800/446-1333, 800/

451-4176 in CA; fax 209/532-6401. A modest, older property. **Rooms:** 18 rms. CI 1pm/CO 11am. Nonsmoking rms avail. **Amenities:** 🛅 📺 A/C, cable TV w/movies, refrig. **Services:** ➴ **Facilities:** 🛆 Playground. Barbecue pit, basketball court. **Rates:** HS May 10–Oct 15 $40–$75 S or D. Children under 18 stay free. Min stay spec evnts. Lower rates off-season. Spec packages avail. Pking: Outdoor, free. Maj CC. Low off-season rate.

Restaurants 🍽️

Gagliardi's at La Torre, 39 N Washington St, Sonora; tel 209/532-0565. **Italian.** Victorian restaurant located in a historic building, decorated with floral carpet in pink and plum hues. Complete dinners with soup, salad, fresh vegetable, and dessert, including prime rib, pepper steak, homemade cannelloni and daily seafood specials. **FYI:** Reservations accepted. Children's menu. **Open:** Lunch Mon–Fri 11:30am–2:30pm; dinner Mon–Sat 4:30–10pm, Sun 3:30–9pm. Closed some hols. **Prices:** Main courses $9.50–$15.95. Ltd CC. ⚿

Good Heavens, A Restaurant, 49 N Washington St, Sonora; tel 209/532-3663. **Eclectic.** Restaurant with homey feel, decorated with old photos, prints, and paintings. A nice stop for lunch, the only meal served. Menu changes daily and features quiche, crepes, and desserts including homemade jams. **FYI:** Reservations recommended. Beer and wine only. **Open:** Tues–Sun 11am–2:30pm. Closed some hols. **Prices:** Lunch main courses $5.95–$8.95. No CC.

SOUTH LAKE TAHOE

Map page M-2, C3

Hotels 🏨

Embassy Suites Resort Lake Tahoe, 4130 Lake Tahoe Blvd, South Lake Tahoe, CA 96150; tel 916/544-5400 or toll free 800/EMBASSY; fax 916/544-4900. Large lobby with water wheel in atrium. **Rooms:** 400 stes. CI 3pm/CO noon. Express checkout avail. Nonsmoking rms avail. Living area is spacious. Excellent-quality furnishings. **Amenities:** 🛅 🅰 📺 🎮 A/C, cable TV w/movies, refrig, VCR, voice mail, shoe polisher, bathrobes. All units w/minibars, some w/terraces. Microwave in each suite. **Services:** ✗ 🔑 🆚 🚐 📠 ➴ Car-rental desk, babysitting. Complimentary cooked-to-order breakfast. Complimentary cocktails or beverages 4:30–6:30pm. **Facilities:** 🛆 🚴 🏊 🎱 ⚿ 🎱 ⚿ 2 rsts, 1 bar (w/entertainment), sauna, whirlpool, washer/dryer. Ski rental on premises. **Rates (MAP):** HS mid-June–mid-Sept/Feb–mid-Apr from $129 ste. Extra person $25. Children under 13 stay free. Min stay wknds and spec evnts. Lower rates off-season. Higher rates for spec evnts/hols. Spec packages avail. Pking: Indoor, free. Maj CC.

≣≣≣ **Flamingo Lodge**, 3961 Lake Tahoe Blvd, South Lake Tahoe, CA 96150; tel 916/544-5288 or toll free 800/544-5288; fax 916/544-5333. Exceptionally clean hotel. **Rooms:** 90 rms and stes. CI 2pm/CO noon. Nonsmoking rms avail. Each attractive room has a 2-burner stove and small sink and counter. **Amenities:** 🛏 🖥 A/C, cable TV, refrig. Some units w/minibars, some w/fireplaces, 1 w/Jacuzzi. **Services:** 🖨 **Facilities:** 🏋 Sauna, whirlpool, washer/dryer. **Rates:** HS June 24–Sept 10 $49–$87 S; $54–$92 D; from $82 ste. Extra person $10. Children under 18 stay free. Min stay wknds and spec evnts. Lower rates off-season. Spec packages avail. Pking: Outdoor, free. Maj CC.

≣≣ **Sierra-Cal Lodge**, 3838 Lake Tahoe Blvd, South Lake Tahoe, CA 96150; tel 916/541-5400 or toll free 800/245-6343; fax 916/541-7170. Within walking distance of the beaches. Fireplace in lobby provides welcome warmth on winter days. **Rooms:** 121 rms and stes. CI 2pm/CO 11am. Nonsmoking rms avail. Rooms are color-coordinated, but not especially attractive. Some have views of Heavenly Valley ski area. **Amenities:** 🛏 🖥 A/C, cable TV. **Services:** 🖺 🖨 🖐 Ski shuttle from lodge to 5 major ski areas; 24-hour shuttle to casinos. **Facilities:** 🏋 🛝 🏊 🔢 Whirlpool. **Rates:** HS Ski season/June–Aug $58–$68 S or D; from $78 ste. Extra person $10. Children under 10 stay free. Min stay spec evnts. Lower rates off-season. Higher rates for spec evnts/hols. Spec packages avail. Pking: Outdoor, free. Maj CC.

Motels

≣≣≣ **Best Western Station House Inn**, 901 Park Ave, South Lake Tahoe, CA 96150; tel 916/542-1101 or toll free 800/ 822-5953; fax 916/542-1714. Quiet, with views of the mountains. A rock wall surrounds an attractive pool area and the lobby is extremely appealing. **Rooms:** 100 rms and stes; 2 ctges/villas. CI 3pm/CO noon. Nonsmoking rms avail. Rooms have coordinated bedspreads and draperies in subtle shades; good furniture. **Amenities:** 🛏 🖥 A/C, cable TV. Some units w/terraces, 1 w/fireplace, some w/Jacuzzis. Chalets have refrigerators. **Services:** 🖺 🖨 Babysitting. Complimentary American breakfast, October–May. **Facilities:** 🏋 🔢 🖥 1 rst, 1 bar, whirlpool. Complimentary passes to nearby beach. **Rates:** HS June–Oct $98–$108 S; $108–$118 D; from $125 ste; from $175 ctge/villa. Extra person $10. Children under 12 stay free. Min stay wknds and spec evnts. Lower rates off-season. Higher rates for spec evnts/hols. Spec packages avail. Pking: Outdoor, free. Maj CC.

≣≣≣ **Best Western Timber Cove Lodge**, 3411 Lake Tahoe Blvd, South Lake Tahoe, CA 96150; tel 916/541-6722 or toll free 800/972-8558; fax 916/541-7959. One of the best deals in the South Lake Tahoe area. **Rooms:** 262 rms and stes. CI 3pm/CO noon. Express checkout avail. Nonsmoking rms avail. Rooms are plain but well kept. **Amenities:** 🛏 🖥 A/C, cable TV w/movies. Some units w/terraces. **Services:** ✕ 🗝 🖺 🖨 Babysitting. **Facilities:** 🏋 🚲 ⛰ 🛝 🖥 🏋 🏊 🔢 1 rst, 1 bar, 1 beach (lake shore), whirlpool, washer/dryer. Swimming pool area has great views of lake. Attractive restaurant has outdoor dining with views of lake and pool. Wedding chapel on premises. Reception room under construction. **Rates:** HS June 24–Sept 24 $49 S; $59 D; from $105 ste. Extra person $10. Children under 12 stay free. Min stay wknds and spec evnts. Lower rates off-season. Spec packages avail. Pking: Outdoor, free. Maj CC.

≣≣ **Casino Area Travelodge**, 4003 Lake Tahoe Blvd, PO Box 6500, South Lake Tahoe, CA 95729; tel 916/541-5000 or toll free 800/578-7878; fax 916/544-6910. Adequate rooms. Easy walking distance to casinos. **Rooms:** 66 rms. CI 1pm/CO noon. Express checkout avail. Nonsmoking rms avail. **Amenities:** 🛏 🖥 A/C, cable TV. **Services:** 🖨 Babysitting. **Facilities:** 🏋 Restaurants, markets, shopping centers are nearby. **Rates:** $39–$103 S or D. Extra person $5. Children under 18 stay free. Pking: Outdoor, free. Maj CC.

≣≣≣ **Forest Inn Suites**, 1101 Park Ave, PO Box 4300, South Lake Tahoe, CA 96157; tel 916/541-6655; fax 916/544-3135. Beautiful forest setting. Renovating wedding chapel, lobby, meeting rooms, hallways, continental breakfast room. **Rooms:** 124 rms and stes. CI 3pm/CO 11am. Nonsmoking rms avail. Suites have dining areas, living rooms, kitchens, and a large amount of closet space. Each bedroom has a bath. Tasteful decorations. **Amenities:** 🛏 A/C, cable TV w/movies, refrig. Some units w/terraces. VCRs available for a fee. **Services:** 🖨 Babysitting. **Facilities:** 🏋 🚲 🛝 🖥 🖥 Games rm, spa, sauna, steam rm, whirlpool, playground, washer/dryer. 9 golf putting greens and driving cage. Volleyball. **Rates:** HS May 21–Sept 15 $86 S; from $109 ste. Extra person $10. Children under 2 stay free. Min stay wknds and spec evnts. Lower rates off-season. Spec packages avail. Pking: Outdoor, free. Maj CC.

≣≣ **Holiday Lodge**, 4095 Laurel Ave, PO Box 4007, South Lake Tahoe, CA 95729; tel 916/544-4101 or toll free 800/ 654-4095, 800/544-4095 in CA; fax 916/542-4932. A comfortable hotel. **Rooms:** 163 rms and stes; 2 ctges/villas. CI 3pm/CO 11am. Nonsmoking rms avail. **Amenities:** 🛏 A/C, cable TV. Some units w/terraces, some w/fireplaces. **Services:** 🖨 Babysitting. **Facilities:** 🏋 🛝 🖥 Sauna, whirlpool, washer/dryer. **Rates:** HS June 15–Sept 15 $65–$75 S; $70–$90 D; from $82 ste; from $145 ctge/villa. Extra person $5. Min stay HS, wknds, and spec evnts. Lower rates off-season. Higher rates for spec evnts/hols. Spec packages avail. Pking: Outdoor, free. Maj CC.

≣≣≣ **Inn by the Lake**, 3300 Lake Tahoe Blvd, South Lake Tahoe, CA 96150; tel 916/542-0330 or toll free 800/877-1466; fax 916/541-6596. One of the nicer properties at South Lake Tahoe, tastefully decorated throughout. Attractive landscaping with flowers and trees. Interior renovation in progress. **Rooms:** 99 rms, stes, and effic. CI 3pm/CO noon. Express checkout avail. Nonsmoking rms avail. King bedrooms have lake views. **Amenities:** 🛏 🍷 📺 🖥 A/C, cable TV w/movies, refrig, VCR. Some units w/minibars, all w/terraces, some w/Jacuzzis. VCR available upon request. **Services:** 🚐 🛎 🛜 Babysitting. Complimentary continental breakfast. Video rental in library. **Facilities:** 🏔 🏋 🛥 🏊50 ♿ 1 rst, sauna, whirlpool, washer/dryer. Closed-circuit TV security in all hallways. Bicycle and ski storage adjacent to lobby. **Rates (CP):** HS July–Aug/Christmas $84–$148 S or D; from $165 ste; from $275 effic. Children under 18 stay free. Min stay wknds and spec evnts. Lower rates off-season. Higher rates for spec evnts/hols. Spec packages avail. Pking: Outdoor, free. Maj CC.

≣≣≣ **Lakeland Village**, 3535 Lake Tahoe Blvd, PO Box 1356, South Lake Tahoe, CA 96156; tel 916/544-1685 or toll free 800/822-5969; fax 916/544-0193. Lovely wooded setting. **Rooms:** 212 rms, stes, and effic. CI 3pm/CO 11am. Express checkout avail. Attractively decorated units, including beachfront condos. Lodge loft rooms have bedrooms with wash basin, closet, and end tables in loft, kitchen and living area below. **Amenities:** 🛏 📺 A/C, cable TV, refrig. All units w/terraces, all w/fireplaces. **Services:** 🔑 🚐 🛜 🛎 Social director, babysitting. **Facilities:** 🏔 🏔 🏋 🛥 ⛵2 🚲 🍴 🏊220 1 beach (lake shore), games rm, sauna, whirlpool, playground, washer/dryer. Beautiful pool with umbrellas and landscaped grounds. **Rates:** HS Dec 17–Jan 2 $85–$95 S or D; from $125 ste; from $140 effic. Min stay HS and spec evnts. Lower rates off-season. Higher rates for spec evnts/hols. Spec packages avail. Pking: Indoor, free. Maj CC.

≣≣ **South Tahoe Travelodge**, 3489 Lake Tahoe Blvd, PO Box 70512, South Lake Tahoe, CA 96156; tel 916/544-5266 or toll free 800/255-3050; fax 916/544-6985. Centrally located. Front desk staff not particularly friendly or helpful. **Rooms:** 59 rms. CI 1pm/CO noon. Nonsmoking rms avail. **Amenities:** 🛏 🍷 📺 A/C, cable TV. Some units w/terraces. **Services:** 🚐 🛎 Free shuttle to casinos and ski areas. **Facilities:** 🏔 🏋 🛥 **Rates:** HS June–Sept $73–$103 S or D. Extra person $5. Children under 16 stay free. Min stay spec evnts. Lower rates off-season. Higher rates for spec evnts/hols. Spec packages avail. Pking: Outdoor, free. Maj CC. Special rates for senior citizens.

≣≣≣ **Tahoe Beach & Ski Club**, 3601 Lake Tahoe Blvd, PO Box 1267, South Lake Tahoe, CA 95705; tel 916/541-6200 or toll free 800/822-5962. Very attractive condo units. **Rooms:** 131 rms and effic. CI 3pm/CO 11am. Well-equipped tiled kitchen area. Balconies off both bedroom and living area. Rooms are tastefully furnished. **Amenities:** 🛏 🍷 📺 A/C, cable TV, refrig. Some units w/minibars, all w/terraces, some w/Jacuzzis. 2 TVs. **Services:** 🛎 Babysitting. **Facilities:** 🏔 🏋 🛥 1 rst, 1 beach (lake shore), sauna, whirlpool, washer/dryer. **Rates:** HS June 15–Sept 15/Feb–Mar $105 S or D; from $145 effic. Extra person $15. Children under 6 stay free. Min stay wknds and spec evnts. Lower rates off-season. Spec packages avail. Pking: Outdoor, free. Maj CC.

≣≣ **Tahoe Chalet Inn**, 3860 Lake Tahoe Blvd, South Lake Tahoe, CA 96150; tel 916/544-3311 or toll free 800/821-2656; fax 916/544-4069. Beach is a short walk from hotel. **Rooms:** 67 rms, stes, and effic. CI 3pm/CO 11am. Nonsmoking rms avail. Rooms are small but not cramped. Attractive color coordination. Standard rooms are pleasant; luxury rooms lavishly decorated. **Amenities:** 🛏 A/C, cable TV w/movies. Some units w/fireplaces, some w/Jacuzzis. Amenities vary according to the room. **Services:** 🚐 🛎 **Facilities:** 🏔 🏋 🛥 🎱 Games rm, spa, sauna, washer/dryer. **Rates:** HS June 15–Labor Day/Dec 22–Apr 1 $52–$128 S or D; from $98 ste; from $92 effic. Children under 18 stay free. Min stay wknds and spec evnts. Lower rates off-season. Higher rates for spec evnts/hols. Spec packages avail. Pking: Outdoor, free. Maj CC.

Resort

≣≣≣ **Richardson's Resort**, Calif 89 and Jameson Beach Rd, PO Box 9028, South Lake Tahoe, CA 96158; tel 916/541-1801 or toll free 800/544-1801; fax 916/541-2793. 80 acres. Pleasant lobby with pine paneling, a large stone fireplace, and comfortable furniture. Huge pine trees all around. Great beach. **Rooms:** 36 rms and effic; 39 ctges/villas. CI 2pm/CO 10am. Nonsmoking rms avail. Cabins, inn rooms near the beach, and lodge rooms are tastefully decorated with a rustic theme. **Amenities:** 🛏 🍷 📺 Refrig. No A/C or TV. Some units w/terraces, some w/fireplaces. Cabins have kitchens. **Services:** 🛎 Babysitting. **Facilities:** 🚣 🏔 🏔 🏋 🛥 🍴 🏊50 1 rst (see also "Restaurants" below), 1 bar (w/entertainment), 1 beach (lake shore), games rm, playground, washer/dryer. Ice cream shop, cappuccino cafe/bakery, deli on premises. A variety of sports facilities is available on the beach. **Rates:** HS June–Oct $39–$89 S or D; from $70 effic; from $79 ctge/villa. Children under 12 stay free. Min stay HS. Lower rates off-season. Spec packages avail. Pking: Outdoor, free. Maj CC. 7-night minimum for efficiencies July and August.

Restaurant 🍴

★ **The Beacon**, in Richardson's Resort, Calif 89 at Jameson Beach Rd, South Lake Tahoe; tel 916/541-0630. Jameson Beach Rd exit off Calif 89. **American/Italian.** Gray, blue, and white color scheme; seascapes on the walls. Fresh vegetables and San Francisco sourdough bread accompany entrees, which range from fresh lake trout to scampi Italiano. Chicken Tallac, stuffed with spinach, is named for the mountain peak visible in the mirror behind the bar. **FYI:** Reservations recommended. Guitar/island music/rock. **Open:** HS June–Sept 10 lunch daily 11:30am–3pm; dinner daily 5–10pm; brunch Sat–Sun 10:30am–3pm. Reduced hours off-season. Closed Dec 25. **Prices:** Main courses $8.95–$20.95. Maj CC. ▣ ⅙

SOUTH SAN FRANCISCO

Map page M-2, D2 (N of San Mateo)

Hotels 🛏

≣ **Best Western Grosvenor Hotel**, 380 S Airport Blvd, South San Francisco, CA 94080 (San Francisco Int'l Airport); tel 415/873-3200 or toll free 800/722-7141; fax 415/589-3495. 10 mi S of San Francisco. S Airport Blvd exit off US 101. Standard hotel needs sprucing up. Location is noisy because of highway traffic. **Rooms:** 203 rms, stes, and effic. CI 3pm/CO noon. Nonsmoking rms avail. **Amenities:** 📷 🛁 📺 A/C, cable TV w/movies. Some units w/Jacuzzis. **Services:** ✕ 🚗 🛁 ↻ Babysitting. **Facilities:** 🔒 ⟦350⟧ ⅙ 1 rst, 1 bar. **Rates (CP):** HS May–Sept $72–$89 S; $77–$94 D; from $125 ste. Extra person $8. Children under 12 stay free. Lower rates off-season. Spec packages avail. Pking: Outdoor, free. Maj CC.

≣≣≣ **Comfort Suites**, 121 E Grand Ave, South San Francisco, CA 94080; tel 415/589-7766 or toll free 800/221-2222; fax 415/588-2231. Grand Ave exit off US 101; go east. Charming 2-story lobby decorated with Mexican tiles, potted plants, archways, and a fireplace. Popular with long-term guests. Site is near freeways and rather noisy. **Rooms:** 165 stes. CI 3pm/CO noon. Nonsmoking rms avail. Soundproofing and sealed windows cut down on outside noise. Rooms feature a sitting area separated from sleeping area by a half-wall. **Amenities:** 📷 🛁 📺 A/C, satel TV w/movies, refrig, VCR. All units w/minibars. **Services:** 🚗 🛁 ↻ Expanded continental breakfast. Twice-monthly tastings of Napa Valley wines. Complimentary soup bar from 5 to 7pm. **Facilities:** ⟦30⟧ ⅙ Whirlpool, washer/dryer. Fitness club

passes provided. **Rates (CP):** From $118 ste. Extra person $10. Children under 18 stay free. Spec packages avail. Pking: Outdoor, free. Maj CC. Park-and-fly packages available.

≣≣≣ **Crown Sterling Suites**, 250 Gateway Blvd, South San Francisco, CA 94080 (San Francisco Int'l Airport); tel 415/589-3400 or toll free 800/433-4600; fax 415/876-0305. Grand Ave exit off US 101; left on Gateway Blvd. A lovely place. The beautiful lobby has murals, a babbling brook, and a koi pond. **Rooms:** 313 stes. Exec-level rms avail. CI 3pm/CO 11am. Nonsmoking rms avail. Rooms are large, with fine furniture. Corner units are executive suites with large floor-to-ceiling windows. **Amenities:** 📷 🛁 📺 A/C, cable TV w/movies, refrig, voice mail. All units w/minibars. Laptop computers available. **Services:** ✕ 🚗 🛁 ↻ Car-rental desk, babysitting. Cheerful staff. **Facilities:** 🔒 ⟦400⟧ ⅙ 1 rst, 1 bar, sauna, whirlpool, washer/dryer. Beautiful indoor pool. **Rates:** From $129 ste. Extra person $10. Children under 12 stay free. Higher rates for spec evnts/hols. Pking: Outdoor, free. Maj CC.

≣≣≣ **Holiday Inn North**, 275 S Airport Blvd, South San Francisco, CA 94080 (San Francisco Int'l Airport); tel 415/873-3550 or toll free 800/HOLIDAY; fax 415/873-4524. Airport Blvd exit off US 101. Nice-looking hotel in an industrial area with buzzing electrical towers overhead. Close to the airport and convention center. **Rooms:** 221 rms and stes. Exec-level rms avail. CI 3pm/CO noon. Express checkout avail. Nonsmoking rms avail. Large, newly refurbished rooms. **Amenities:** 📷 🛁 📺 A/C, cable TV w/movies, voice mail. All units w/minibars. **Services:** ✕ 🚗 🛁 ↻ Car-rental desk, babysitting. Continental breakfast. **Facilities:** ⟦350⟧ ⅙ 1 rst, 1 bar, sauna, whirlpool. Fitness center has a tanning bed. **Rates (CP):** $108–$130 S or D; from $260 ste. Extra person $10. Children under 19 stay free. Spec packages avail. Pking: Outdoor, free. Maj CC.

≣≣ **Holiday Inn San Francisco International Airport North**, 275 S Airport Blvd, South San Francisco, CA 94080 (San Francisco Int'l Airport); tel 415/873-3550 or toll free 800/HOLIDAY; fax 415/873-4524. 10 mi S of San Francisco. S Airport Blvd exit off US 101. Located in a fairly industrial area by a busy highway, and within earshot of airport noise. Comfortable, pleasant rooms. **Rooms:** 224 rms and stes. CI 3pm/CO noon. Express checkout avail. Nonsmoking rms avail. **Amenities:** 📷 🛁 📺 A/C, cable TV w/movies, refrig, voice mail, bathrobes. All units w/minibars. **Services:** ✕ 🔌 🚗 🛁 ↻ Twice-daily maid svce, children's program, babysitting. **Facilities:** ⟦350⟧ ⅙ 1 rst, 1 bar, spa. **Rates (CP):** HS Feb–Oct $85–$118 S or D; from $260 ste. Extra person $10. Children under 12 stay free. Lower rates off-season. Higher rates for spec evnts/hols. Spec packages avail. Pking: Outdoor, free. Maj CC.

≝ **Ramada Inn San Francisco International Airport North**, 245 S Airport Blvd, South San Francisco, CA 94080 (San Francisco Int'l Airport); tel 415/589-7200 or toll free 800/452-3456; fax 415/588-5007. 10 mi S of San Francisco. S Airport Blvd exit off US 101. Motel units are being upgraded to hotel standards. Extensive lobby, central garden. **Rooms:** 323 rms and stes. CI 3pm/CO noon. Express checkout avail. Nonsmoking rms avail. **Amenities:** 🛏 🖥 🍴 A/C, cable TV w/movies. **Services:** ✗ 🚐 🖼 🍽 🍷 Car-rental desk, babysitting. **Facilities:** 🛗 💺 ⅙ 1 rst, 1 bar, beauty salon, washer/dryer. **Rates (CP):** $59–$85 S; $69–$99 D; from $200 ste. Extra person $8. Children under 18 stay free. Higher rates for spec evnts/hols. Spec packages avail. Pking: Outdoor, free. Maj CC.

≝≝≝ **San Francisco Airport Hilton**, San Francisco International Airport, PO Box 8355, South San Francisco, CA 94128; tel 415/589-0770 or toll free 800/HILTONS; fax 415/589-4696. San Francisco Int'l Airport exit off US 101. Closest hotel to the airport. **Rooms:** 527 rms and stes. CI 3pm/CO noon. Express checkout avail. Nonsmoking rms avail. **Amenities:** 🛏 🖥 A/C, cable TV w/movies, voice mail. All units w/minibars, some w/terraces. **Services:** ✗ 🅅🅟 🚐 🖼 🍽 🍷 Babysitting. **Facilities:** 🛗 🏊 🚲 🖥 ⅙ 2 rsts, 1 bar (w/entertainment), sauna, whirlpool. **Rates (CP):** $145–$165 S; $165–$185 D. Extra person $20. Children under 12 stay free. Higher rates for spec evnts/hols. AP and MAP rates avail. Spec packages avail. Pking: Outdoor, $5–$10. Maj CC.

Motels

≝≝ **La Quinta Inn**, 20 Airport Blvd, South San Francisco, CA 94080; tel 415/583-2223 or toll free 800/531-5900; fax 415/589-6770. 10 mi S of San Francisco. S Airport Blvd exit off US 101. Located in an industrial neighborhood with a busy freeway nearby—but close to Candlestick Park, and reasonably priced. **Rooms:** 174 rms. CI 3pm/CO noon. Nonsmoking rms avail. **Amenities:** 🛏 🖥 A/C, satel TV w/movies. Some units w/terraces. **Services:** 🚐 🖼 🍽 🍷 Masseur. **Facilities:** 🛗 🏊 💺 ⅙ Whirlpool, washer/dryer. **Rates (CP):** HS Mem Day–Labor Day $58–$68 S; $68–$78 D. Extra person $10. Children under 18 stay free. Lower rates off-season. Pking: Outdoor, free. Maj CC.

≝ **San Francisco Airport North Travelodge**, 326 S Airport Blvd, South San Francisco, CA 94086 (San Francisco Int'l Airport); tel 415/583-9600 or toll free 800/578-7878; fax 415/873-9392. S Airport Blvd exit off US 101. A well-maintained basic motel that offers lots of amenities to guests. **Rooms:** 197 rms and stes. CI noon/CO 1pm. Nonsmoking rms avail. **Amenities:** 🛏 🖥 A/C, cable TV w/movies, voice mail. Available for guests with disabilities are decoders for TVs, alarm clocks that shake the pillow, special telephone aids. **Services:** 🔌 🚐 🖼 🍷

Car-rental desk. **Facilities:** 🛗 💺 1 rst. **Rates:** $63–$73 S; $70–$80 D; from $78 ste. Extra person $7. Children under 18 stay free. Spec packages avail. Pking: Outdoor, free. Maj CC.

STOCKTON

Map page M-2, D2

Hotels 🏨

≝≝≝ **Holiday Inn Stockton**, 111 E March Lane, Stockton, CA 95207; tel 209/474-3301 or toll free 800/633-3737; fax 209/474-7612. March Lane exit off I-5; E 2½ mi to El Dorado Rd. Guests enjoy a fresh look and consistent high quality regardless of room type. **Rooms:** 194 rms and stes. CI 3pm/CO noon. Express checkout avail. Nonsmoking rms avail. Rooms vary in size. Some poolside accommodations. **Amenities:** 🛏 🖥 A/C, satel TV w/movies, refrig, voice mail. Some units w/terraces, some w/Jacuzzis. New TVs. VCRs available on request. **Services:** ✗ 🖼 🍷 🍽 Complimentary coffee 6–9am. **Facilities:** 🛗 💺 🖥 ⅙ 1 rst, 1 bar, games rm, whirlpool. Passes available to off-site fitness facilities. **Rates:** $69 S or D; from $150 ste. Extra person $10. Children under 18 stay free. Spec packages avail. Pking: Outdoor, free. Maj CC.

≝≝≝ **Stockton Hilton**, 2323 Grand Canal Blvd, Stockton, CA 95207; tel 209/957-9090 or toll free 800/444-9094; fax 209/473-8908. March Lane exit off I-5. Rooms are on street level, overlooking pool or Grand Canal. **Rooms:** 198 rms and stes. CI 3pm/CO 11am. Express checkout avail. Nonsmoking rms avail. Some rooms have double vanities in bath area. Desk with drawer serves as main table. Half of rooms are nonsmoking. **Amenities:** 🛏 🖥 A/C, cable TV w/movies, shoe polisher. Some units w/terraces. **Services:** ✗ 🖼 🍷 Babysitting. Twenty-four hour security. **Facilities:** 🛗 💺 ⅙ 2 rsts, 1 bar, whirlpool. Renovation will add new meeting space. Free use of health club across street. **Rates:** $85–$109 S; $97–$121 D; from $210 ste. Extra person $12. Children under 18 stay free. Spec packages avail. Pking: Outdoor, free. Maj CC.

Motels

≝ **Best Western Stockton Inn**, 4219 E Waterloo Rd, Stockton, CA 95206; tel 209/931-3131 or toll free 800/528-1234; fax 209/931-0423. Waterloo E exit off Calif 99. Older highway property suitable for an overnight if you can get the discount rate. Wheelchair access virtually unavailable. **Rooms:** 141 rms and stes. CI 3pm/CO noon. Nonsmoking rms avail. Some adjoining rooms available. **Amenities:** 🛏 A/C, satel TV w/movies. **Services:** 🖼 🍷 Fax and copy service. Security guard

5pm–6am. **Facilities:** 🔲 🔲 1 rst, 1 bar, whirlpool. Free access to racquet club 4 miles away. **Rates:** HS Apr–July $62–$80 S; $80–$98 D; from $135 ste. Extra person $8. Children under 12 stay free. Lower rates off-season. Spec packages avail. Pking: Outdoor, free. Maj CC.

≡ **Days Inn**, 33 N Center St, Stockton, CA 95202; tel 209/948-6151 or toll free 800/DAYS-INN; fax 209/948-1220. Downtown exit off Calif 4; left at Weber, left at Center. Near port of Stockton. Renovations in progress. **Rooms:** 97 rms. CI 2pm/CO 11am. Nonsmoking rms avail. About half have been redecorated to upgrade flooring and furnishings. **Amenities:** 🔲 🔲 A/C, satel TV. VCRs and mobile remotes available from office. **Services:** Night security guard on duty. Coffee and doughnuts in lobby each morning. **Facilities:** 🔲 🔲 🔲 **Rates (CP):** HS Apr–Sept $42–$50 S; $45–$55 D. Extra person $5. Lower rates off-season. Spec packages avail. Pking: Outdoor, free. Maj CC.

≡≡ **La Quinta Motor Inn**, 2710 W March Lane, Stockton, CA 95219; tel 209/952-7800 or toll free 800/531-5900; fax 209/472-0732. March Lane exit off I-5; W on March Lane. Renovation of the motel's public areas to be completed soon. New carpets, drapes, and bedspreads were also to be installed. **Rooms:** 153 rms and stes. Exec-level rms avail. CI 3pm/CO noon. Nonsmoking rms avail. **Amenities:** 🔲 🔲 A/C, cable TV w/movies. Executive rooms have recliner, full-length mirror, refrigerator, and computer jack. **Services:** 🔲 🔲 🔲 Security staff on duty 11pm–6am. **Facilities:** 🔲 🔲 🔲 Washer/dryer. Free access to health club at Quail Lakes. **Rates (CP):** $53–$68 S; $58–$73 D; from $75 ste. Extra person $8. Children under 16 stay free. Pking: Outdoor, free. Maj CC.

Attraction 🔲

Pixie Woods, Mount Diablo Rd at Occidental; tel 209/937-8220 or 466-9890. Located in Louis Park, at the west end of Mount Diablo Rd, Pixie Woods features amusement rides, attractions, Mother Goose characters, train and ferryboat rides, and a puppet show theater. Built in 1954, this playland includes a small lagoon with islands containing a Japanese Garden and a pirates' enclave. **Open:** June–late Sept, Wed–Fri and hols 11am–5pm, Sat–Sun 11am–6pm; late Sept–Oct and Feb–May, weekends and hols noon–5pm. $$

STUDIO CITY
Map page M-3, D2 (W of Glendale)

Hotel 🔲

≡≡≡ **Sportsmen's Lodge Hotel**, 12825 Ventura Blvd, Studio City, CA 91604; tel 818/769-4700 or toll free 800/821-1625 in CA, 800/821-8511 in the US, 800/341-6363 in Canada; fax 213/877-3898. Coldwater Canyon Ave exit off US 101. Unique 32-year-old hotel on park-like grounds with meandering streams, populated by white and black swans, peacocks, and ducks. Lovely, peaceful, and quiet despite location on busy Ventura Blvd. Hotel attracts a celebrity crowd. **Rooms:** 200 rms and stes. CI 3pm/CO noon. Nonsmoking rms avail. Rooms nicely decorated in country pine. **Amenities:** 🔲 🔲 A/C, cable TV w/movies, voice mail. All units w/terraces. Kit for the deaf and hard of hearing available that lights up phone when it rings. **Services:** 🔲 🔲 🔲 🔲 Car-rental desk, babysitting. **Facilities:** 🔲 🔲 🔲 🔲 3 rsts, 2 bars (1 w/entertainment), whirlpool, beauty salon. Huge lap-size pool. Great shops and restaurants are within walking distance on Ventura Blvd. **Rates:** $85–$120 S or D; from $155 ste. Extra person $10. Children under 18 stay free. Spec packages avail. Pking: Outdoor, free. Maj CC.

Restaurants 🔲

★ **Art's Deli**, 12224 Ventura Blvd, Studio City; tel 818/762-1221. **Deli/Jewish.** A fixture in the San Fernando Valley for many years, it was closed because of a fire following the 1994 earthquake, but reopened in fall 1994. A showbiz crowd hangs out here, although there's nothing elegant or ritzy. Well-known for corned beef and pastrami sandwiches. **FYI:** Reservations not accepted. Beer and wine only. **Open:** Mon–Thurs 6am–11pm, Fri–Sat 6am–midnight, Sun 6am–10pm. Closed some hols. **Prices:** Main courses $7.95–$11.95. Maj CC. 🔲 🔲

♣ **The Bistro Garden at Coldwater**, 12950 Ventura Blvd, Studio City; tel 818/501-0202. **Californian/Continental.** One of the most romantic restaurants in the San Fernando Valley. Open, airy, gardenlike decor, with twinkling lights on the trees. Spectacular 30-foot ceiling. Popular with stars and studio moguls. Famous for tuna tartare, which is lightly tossed with ginger and avocado. For dessert, try the crème caramel or the profiteroles, light and airy and drizzled with chocolate. **FYI:** Reservations recommended. Piano. **Open:** Lunch Mon–Fri 11:30am–3pm; dinner Mon–Thurs 5:30–10:30pm, Fri–Sat 5:30–11:30pm, Sun 5:30–10:30pm. Closed some hols. **Prices:** Main courses $15.75–$29.75. Maj CC. 🔲 🔲 🔲

Il Mito, 11801 Ventura Blvd, Studio City; tel 818/762-1818. **Italian.** A wonderfully rustic restaurant in a charming 50-year-old building. Patrons seated in the main area can communicate with the chef as he works in a display kitchen. Specialties include grilled fish of the day and a roast duck in wild blueberry sauce. **FYI:** Reservations accepted. **Open:** Lunch Mon–Sat 11am–2:30pm; dinner Mon–Sat 6–10:30pm, Sun 6–10pm. Closed some hols. **Prices:** Main courses $14.50–$19.25. Maj CC. 🍴 VP

🍷 **Pinot Bistro**, 12969 Ventura Blvd, Studio City; tel 818/990-0500. **French.** Clubby bistro atmosphere with dark wood paneling, leather banquettes, and fireplace. Especially popular are the low-calorie "spa offerings," though beef steak with french fries is also served. **FYI:** Reservations recommended. **Open:** Lunch Mon–Fri 11:30am–2pm; dinner Mon–Fri 6–10pm, Sat 5:30–10:30pm, Sun 5:30–9pm. Closed some hols. **Prices:** Main courses $16–$19. Maj CC. VP &

$ **Poquito Mas**, 3701 Cahuenga Blvd W, Studio City; tel 818/760-TACO. **Mexican.** A world-famous taco stand in a strip mall near Universal Studios that attracts clientele ranging from stars to pool cleaners. Try the giant tostadas with meat, shrimp tacos San Felipe with fresh cilantro wrapped in corn tortillas, or chicken tostada in a flour tortilla shell. Choice of sauces, from mild to dragon's breath. **FYI:** Reservations not accepted. No liquor license. **Open:** Sun–Thurs 10am–midnight, Fri–Sat 10am–1am. Closed some hols. **Prices:** Main courses $2.95–$4.75. No CC. 🍰

SUISUN CITY
Map page M-2, C2 (S of Fairfield)

Hotel 🏨

🏨🏨 **Hampton Inn**, 4441 Central Place, Suisun City, CA 94585; tel 707/864-1446 or toll free 800/531-0202; fax 707/864-4288. Suisun Valley Rd exit off I-80; right on overpass; left on Central. Clean and well maintained. Adequate for business or highway accommodations. **Rooms:** 57 rms and stes. CI 2pm/CO noon. Nonsmoking rms avail. Travelers with disabilities should ask ahead for assistance; 2 accessible rooms are near parking. **Amenities:** 🎛️ 🧊 📞 A/C, satel TV w/movies, refrig. Some units w/Jacuzzis. **Services:** ✕ 🚗 🍸 **Facilities:** 🔥 💪 30 & 1 rst, 1 bar, washer/dryer. Breakfast room with TV and newspapers. Complimentary access to Body Image Gym. **Rates (CP):** HS Mem Day–Labor Day $55–$65 S; $65–$75 D; from $110 ste. Extra person $10. Children under 18 stay free. Lower rates off-season. Pking: Outdoor, free. Maj CC.

Attraction

Western Railway Museum, 5848 Calif 12; tel 707/374-2978 or toll free 800/290-2313. More than 100 vintage railroad cars and engines are held in the collection of this museum, including such nostalgic examples as an 1887 New York "el" car, a plush observation car from Utah, and articulated trains that ran on the San Francisco Bay Bridge in the 1940s and 50s. Vehicles are in various stages of restoration, and many are in operating condition. Visitors are invited to ride along a 1¼-mile rail line traversing the museum grounds aboard electric streetcars, interurbans, and occasional diesel trains (Mar–Apr only). The bookstore is one of the largest dealing exclusively with railroads. **Open:** July 4–Labor Day, Wed–Sun 11am–5pm; rest of the year, Sat–Sun 11am–5pm. Closed some hols. $$

SUMMERLAND
Map page M-3, D1 (E of Santa Barbara)

Inn 🏨

🏨🏨🏨 **Inn on Summer Hill**, 2520 Lillie Ave, Summerland, CA 93067; tel 805/969-9998 or toll free 800/845-5566; fax 805/969-9998. 6 mi S of Santa Barbara. Summerland exit off US 101. This very decorated, California craftsman-style inn opened in 1989. Unsuitable for children under 10. **Rooms:** 16 rms and stes. CI 3pm/CO 11am. No smoking. All rooms have ocean views. Decorated with pine furniture, canopied beds, print linens, and original artwork. **Amenities:** 🎛️ 🧊 📞 📺 A/C, cable TV w/movies, refrig, VCR, stereo/tape player, bathrobes. All units w/terraces, all w/fireplaces, all w/Jacuzzis. **Services:** ✕ 🔑 🛎️ Twice-daily maid svce, masseur, afternoon tea and wine/sherry served. Complimentary breakfast (may include eggs benedict, walnut waffles, fresh scones); gourmet dessert in the evening. Staff will arrange theater tickets and dinner reservations. **Facilities:** 12 & Whirlpool, guest lounge. Charming English country-style dining room. **Rates (BB):** $160–$195 D; from $225 ste. Extra person $20. Children under 2 stay free. Min stay wknds and spec evnts. Spec packages avail. Pking: Outdoor, free. Ltd CC. Lower midweek rates available.

SUNNYVALE
Map page M-2, D2 (N of Santa Clara)

Hotels 🏨

🏨🏨 **Ambassador Inn of Sunnyvale**, 910 E Fremont Ave, Sunnyvale, CA 94087; tel 408/738-0500 or toll free 800/

538-1600, 800/672-1444 in CA; fax 408/245-4167. 10 mi N of San Jose. Wolfe Rd exit off I-280 N; right on Wolfe to Fremont. Particularly suitable for long-term guests who plan to cook in their rooms. **Rooms:** 204 rms and stes. CI 3pm/CO noon. Nonsmoking rms avail. **Amenities:** 🛏 🕗 ▣ 🖥 A/C, cable TV w/movies, refrig. Some units w/Jacuzzis. **Services:** 🖾 🛎 **Facilities:** 🛗 🎱 Games rm, whirlpool, washer/dryer. Complimentary passes to 24-hour Nautilus fitness facility. **Rates (CP):** $62–$72 S; $70–$80 D; from $105 ste. Extra person $8. Children under 12 stay free. Higher rates for spec evnts/hols. Spec packages avail. Pking: Outdoor, free. Maj CC. Rates lower on weekends.

Quality Inn–Sunnyvale, 1280 Persian Dr, Sunnyvale, CA 94089; tel 408/744-0660 or toll free 800/433-9933; fax 408/744-0660 ext 136. Lawrence Expwy exit off Calif 237; right on Persian Dr. Simple but nice lobby. Unrated. **Rooms:** 72 rms. CI noon/CO noon. Nonsmoking rms avail. **Amenities:** 🛏 🕗 A/C, cable TV, refrig. Some units w/terraces. **Services:** 🚐 🖾 🛎 Continental breakfast. **Facilities:** 🛗 🎱 🕭 **Rates (CP):** $68–$73 S or D. Extra person $5. Children under 18 stay free. Pking: Outdoor, free. Maj CC.

≣≣≣ Radisson Haus Inn, 1085 E El Camino Real, Sunnyvale, CA 94087; tel 408/247-0800 or toll free 800/333-3333; fax 408/984-7120. 7 mi N of San Jose. Lawrence Expwy off I-280; left on El Camino Real. Lots of nice touches at this hotel include spacious rooms, soft water, and a restaurant for guests only. **Rooms:** 136 rms and stes. CI 2pm/CO noon. Nonsmoking rms avail. Rooms facing inward, overlooking the lobby, are quiet. **Amenities:** 🛏 🕗 ▣ A/C, cable TV w/movies. All units w/minibars, all w/terraces, some w/Jacuzzis. **Services:** ✕ 🍴 🚐 🖾 🛎 Car-rental desk, babysitting. Complimentary evening cocktails and hors d'oeuvres Monday through Thursday. Special aids available for guests with disabilities. **Facilities:** 🛗 🎱 🏓 ▣ 🖳 🕭 1 rst, 1 bar, whirlpool. Huge mezzanine with big-screen TV. **Rates (CP):** HS Oct–Dec/Jan–June $59–$115 S; $69–$125 D; from $79 ste. Extra person $10. Children under 18 stay free. Lower rates off-season. Spec packages avail. Pking: Indoor/outdoor, free. Maj CC.

≣≣≣ Residence Inn by Marriott Silicon Valley 2, 1080 Stewart Dr, Sunnyvale, CA 94086; tel 408/720-1000 or toll free 800/331-3131; fax 408/720-8749. Nice hotel with a friendly staff. **Rooms:** 247 stes. CI 1pm/CO noon. Nonsmoking rms avail. Suites have a homey feel, some with French doors to separate living and sleeping area. Complete kitchens in every suite. **Amenities:** 🛏 🕗 ▣ A/C, satel TV w/movies, refrig, voice mail. All units w/minibars, all w/terraces, some w/fireplaces. Microwave. **Services:** ✕ 🚐 🖾 🛎 🐾 Car-rental desk, babysitting. Complimentary newspapers in lobby, grocery shopping

service. **Facilities:** 🛗 🏊 🕭 Whirlpool, washer/dryer. Outdoor barbecue grills. Complimentary use of nearby fitness center. Will soon be adding a business service center. **Rates:** $123–$159 S or D. Higher rates for spec evnts/hols. Spec packages avail. Pking: Outdoor, free. Maj CC.

≣≣≣ Sheraton Inn Sunnyvale, 1100 N Mathilda Ave, Sunnyvale, CA 94089; tel 408/745-6000 or toll free 800/836-8686; fax 408/743-8276. Matilda Expwy exit off Calif 237. With terra-cotta tiled floors, tropical plants, and peach and green decor, this place has the feel of a vacation resort in a tropical locale. Extensive grounds, with lagoon. **Rooms:** 174 rms and stes. Exec-level rms avail. CI 3pm/CO 1pm. Express checkout avail. Nonsmoking rms avail. Newly refurbished rooms have flowered upholstery and drapes, rattan furniture. Sunny, bright, and inviting. **Amenities:** 🛏 🕗 ▣ A/C, cable TV w/movies, voice mail. Some units w/terraces. **Services:** ✕ 🚐 🖾 🛎 Car-rental desk, babysitting. Full breakfasts, complimentary coffee. Shuttle to Great America theme park and fitness center. **Facilities:** 🛗 🏓 ▣ 🕭 1 rst, 2 bars, whirlpool. Close to shopping and fitness center. **Rates (BB):** $115–$135 S; $125–$145 D; from $230 ste. Extra person $10. Children under 17 stay free. Spec packages avail. Pking: Outdoor, free. Maj CC.

≣≣≣ Sunnyvale Hilton, 1250 Lakeside Dr, Sunnyvale, CA 94086; tel 408/738-4888 or toll free 800/543-3322; fax 408/737-7147. Lawrence Expwy S exit off US 101; left on Oakmead, left on Lakeside Dr. Reminiscent of a California mission, with adobe walls and southwestern decor. Complete with landscaped walkways and a lagoon. Close to business park. **Rooms:** 372 rms and stes. CI 2pm/CO noon. Express checkout avail. Nonsmoking rms avail. Rooms are large with high ceilings. **Amenities:** 🛏 🕗 A/C, cable TV w/movies, voice mail. Some units w/minibars, some w/terraces, some w/Jacuzzis. Executive rooms have make-up mirrors, irons, and ironing boards. **Services:** ✕ 🚐 🖾 🛎 Car-rental desk, children's program, babysitting. **Facilities:** 🛗 🏊 ▣ 🕭 2 rsts, 1 bar, 1 beach (cove/inlet), sauna, whirlpool. Ballroom with floor-to-ceiling windows and spectacular water views. Complimentary passes to California Athletic Club nearby. **Rates:** $89–$150 S; $104–$165 D; from $195 ste. Extra person $15. Children under 18 stay free. Spec packages avail. Pking: Outdoor, free. Maj CC. Family packages available.

≣≣≣ Woodfin Suites, 635 E El Camino Real, Sunnyvale, CA 94087; tel 408/738-1700 or toll free 800/237-8811; fax 408/738-0840. 10 mi N of San Jose. Fair Oaks S exit off US 101; left on El Camino. Suites have the residential appearance of condominium units. **Rooms:** 88 stes. CI 4pm/CO noon. Nonsmoking rms avail. Very conducive for long-term stay, with living room, bedroom, and kitchen. **Amenities:** 🛏 🕗 ▣ A/C, satel TV w/movies, refrig, VCR. Some units w/fireplaces. **Services:** 🚐

⊠ ♫ ⋘ Complimentary lemonade, orange juice, newspapers, plus cappuccino machine in lobby. Social hour Monday–Thursday 5–6:30pm. Hot American breakfast served buffet-style. **Facilities:** ⌂ ⌨ ⌖ Whirlpool, washer/dryer. Gift shop sells frozen dinners, ice cream, and other edibles. Stores, restaurants within walking distance. **Rates (BB):** $139–$152 S or D. Extra person $5. Children under 18 stay free. Higher rates for spec evnts/hols. Spec packages avail. Pking: Outdoor, free. Maj CC. Lower on weekends.

≣≣≣ **Wyndham Garden Hotel**, 1300 Chesapeake Terrace, Sunnyvale, CA 94089; tel 408/747-0999 or toll free 800/822-4200; fax 408/745-0759. Lawrence Expwy exit off US 101; left on Maffett Park Dr, left into business park and Chesapeake Terrace. Located in a business park surrounded by fountains, picnic tables, and a basketball court. Ideal for the business traveler, with nice landscaping and a lovely lobby. **Rooms:** 180 rms and stes. CI 3pm/CO noon. Express checkout avail. Nonsmoking rms avail. Appealing rooms with pleasant lighting and decor, including mirrored walls. Some rooms have king-size beds and large desks. **Amenities:** ⌂ ⌖ ⌘ ⋐ A/C, cable TV w/movies, stereo/tape player, voice mail. Some units w/minibars. Some rooms have wet bars. Oversized down pillows available. **Services:** ✕ ⌸ ⊠ ♫ Full breakfast included. Complete business services, including secretarial services and fax machine at front desk. **Facilities:** ⌂ ⌘ ⌷ ⌖ 1 rst, 1 bar, whirlpool, washer/dryer. Indoor whirlpool spa is being renovated. **Rates (BB):** $99 S; $109 D; from $109 ste. Extra person $10. Children under 18 stay free. Spec packages avail. Pking: Outdoor, free. Maj CC.

Motels

≣≣ **Ramada Inn**, 1217 Wildwood Ave, Sunnyvale, CA 94089; tel 408/245-5330 or toll free 800/888-3899; fax 408/732-2628. Lawrence Expwy N exit off US 101; quick right on Wildwood. A bright hotel with high ceilings and skylights, decorated in aqua and mauve. Friendly and charming. **Rooms:** 176 rms and stes. CI 2pm/CO noon. Express checkout avail. Nonsmoking rms avail. Most rooms face the pool/lawn area with palm trees; others face the parking lot. **Amenities:** ⌂ ⌖ ⌘ ⋐ A/C, cable TV w/movies. **Services:** ✕ ⌸ ⊠ ♫ Car-rental desk. **Facilities:** ⌂ ⌷ ⌖ 2 rsts, 1 bar, whirlpool, washer/dryer. **Rates:** $99 S; $104 D; from $160 ste. Spec packages avail. Pking: Outdoor, free. Maj CC.

≣≣≣ **Sundowner Inn**, 504 Ross Dr, Sunnyvale, CA 94089; tel 408/734-9900 or toll free 800/223-9901; fax 408/747-0580. Matilda Ave S exit off Calif 237, turn right at Ross Dr. An older property, this motel has a large grassy plot perfect for kids. Security is light, but doesn't seem to be a problem. **Rooms:** 105

rms and stes. CI 3pm/CO noon. Nonsmoking rms avail. Plain but spotless. **Amenities:** ⌂ ⌖ ⌘ ⋐ A/C, cable TV w/movies, refrig, VCR, voice mail. All units w/minibars. Microwave and refrigerator for an additional 50 cents per day. Mobile TV remote available with $20 deposit. **Services:** ✕ ⌸ ⊠ ♫ Babysitting. Free local phone calls. Books, games, and movies in lobby. **Facilities:** ⌂ ⌘ ⌷ ⌷ ⌖ Sauna, washer/dryer. Complimentary use of mountain bikes. **Rates (BB):** $99 S; $109 D; from $99 ste. Extra person $10. Higher rates for spec evnts/hols. Spec packages avail. Pking: Outdoor, free. Maj CC.

Restaurant 🍴

Lion & Compass, in the Fair Oaks Business Park, 1023 N Fair Oaks Ave, Sunnyvale; tel 408/745-1260. Fair Oaks exit off US 101. **New American.** Tropical main dining room has palms, wicker chairs, and street-lamp lighting and is light and spacious; 3 smaller rooms are available for private parties. An electronic ticker tape runs during lunch. Among several creative appetizers are salmon smoked 3 ways and house-made pâtés. Entrees range from potato-leek cake to ahi tuna and roasted chicken breast with Saint Andre cheese and sun-dried tomato couscous. **FYI:** Reservations recommended. **Open:** Lunch Mon–Fri 11:30am–2pm; dinner Mon–Fri 5:30–9:30pm, Sat 5:30–9pm. Closed some hols. **Prices:** Main courses $10.95–$18.95. Maj CC. ⌹ ⌖

SUSANVILLE

Map page M-2, B3

Motel 🏨

≣≣ **Best Western Trailside Inn**, 2785 Main St, PO Box 759, Susanville, CA 96130; tel 916/257-4123 or toll free 800/528-1234; fax 916/257-2665. A good rest stop before and after recreational activities in northern California's Sierra Nevada area. **Rooms:** 90 rms and stes. CI noon/CO 11am. Nonsmoking rms avail. **Amenities:** ⌂ ⌖ A/C, cable TV w/movies, refrig. Some units w/Jacuzzis. **Services:** ♫ ⋘ **Facilities:** ⌂ ⌷ 1 rst. Restaurant is open 24 hours. **Rates (CP):** HS Apr–Oct $48–$54 S or D; from $78 ste. Extra person $5. Lower rates off-season. Pking: Outdoor, free. Maj CC. A golf package includes golfing at Emerson Lake Golf Course, accommodations, breakfast, and dinner.

Attractions 📷

Bizz Johnson Trail; tel 916/257-0456. Begins at Susanville Depot Trailhead, Richmond Rd. Following an old branch line of the Southern Pacific Railroad, this 25.4-mile trail winds from

Susanville to Mason Station, traversing the rugged Susan River Canyon. Built in 1914 to service the newly founded logging community of **Westwood,** the rail line hauled logs, lumber, passengers, and supplies for over 40 years. Gradually, its use declined, and the last trains operated along the line in 1958. Legally abandoned in 1978, the line was converted to its present state as a scenic trail. Hikers, cyclists, equestrians, cross-country skiiers, as well as railroad history buffs now enjoy the trail, which is surfaced with aggregate material and has a maximum 3% grade.

At Mason Station, the trail follows existing roads an additional 4½ miles to Westwood, where a railroad station kiosk has interpretive displays on the history of this region's railroading and logging era. A 25-foot carved redwood statue of Paul Bunyan stands nearby. **Open:** Daily 8am–dusk. Free.

Eagle Lake; tel 916/257-2151. The remnant of a large prehistoric lake, Eagle Lake covers 26,000 acres, about 15 miles north of town via County Hwy A1, within Lassen National Forest. Gallatin Beach, at the south end of the lake, has a marina and facilities for swimming and water sports. There are 5 campgrounds, some available on a first-come, first-serve basis, and many can accommodate RVs. Campgrounds are generally open mid-May–mid-September, depending on weather conditions. For detailed information contact the Forest Supervisor, USDA-Lassen National Forest, 55 S Sacramento St, Susanville, CA 96130. **Open:** Daily sunrise–sunset. Free.

SUTTER CREEK

Map page M-2, C2

Hotel 🛏

≣≣ **Aparicio's Hotel**, 271 Hanford St, PO Box 1839, Sutter Creek, CA 95685; tel 209/267-9177; fax 209/267-5303. Off Calif 49. New roadside hotel offering modern conveniences for Gold Country tourists. **Rooms:** 52 rms and stes. CI 3pm/CO 11am. Nonsmoking rms avail. A few nice touches, including mini-blinds and attractive light fixtures. One suite has a small seating area. **Amenities:** 🛏 A/C, cable TV. **Services:** 🚗 Coffee in lobby. **Facilities:** 🎱 👤 1 rst, 1 bar, games rm, sauna. Restaurant not always open. **Rates:** $45–$150 S or D; from $150 ste. Extra person $8. Min stay spec evnts. Spec packages avail. Pking: Outdoor, free. Maj CC.

Inn

≣≣≣ **Sutter Creek Inn**, 75 Main St, PO Box 385, Sutter Creek, CA 95685; tel 209/267-5606. 1 acre. An intimate country inn. Owner/operator Jane Way provides the personable ambience that makes one feel at home. Wonderfully situated within a few minutes' walk of attractions and restaurants. **Rooms:** 18 rms; 4 ctges/villas. CI 2:30pm/CO 11am. No smoking. Spacious and quiet accommodations, some with canopied beds. **Amenities:** A/C. No phone or TV. Some units w/fireplaces. The lawn has lounge chairs. **Services:** Afternoon tea and wine/sherry served. **Facilities:** 🖭 Washer/dryer, guest lounge w/TV. **Rates (BB):** $50–$97 S or D; from $115 ste; from $88 ctge/villa. Extra person $25. Min stay wknds. Higher rates for spec evnts/hols. Pking: Outdoor, free. Ltd CC.

Restaurant 🍴

Ron & Nancy's Palace Restaurant & Saloon, 76 Main St, Sutter Creek; tel 209/267-1355. **New American/Italian.** An old-time saloon renovated in contemporary woods with 19th-century furnishings, lace tablecloths, and candlelight. Entrees include linguine with clam sauce, veal scaloppine, chicken marsala, and a choice of steaks and seafood. Large portions and fast, cheerful service. **FYI:** Reservations accepted. Children's menu. **Open:** Lunch daily 11:30am–3pm; dinner daily 5–9pm. **Prices:** Main courses $5.95–$11.95. Maj CC. ♥ 🎖

TAHOE CITY

Map page M-2, C3

Hotel 🛏

≣≣≣ **Sunnyside Lodge**, 1850 W Lake Blvd, PO Box 5969, Tahoe City, CA 96145; tel 916/583-7200. 2 mi S of Tahoe City. Excellent lakeside location with a marina atmosphere. Log architecture. Always bustling. **Rooms:** 23 rms and stes. CI 2pm/CO noon. Nonsmoking rms avail. All rooms have a view, or a partial view. Decor is very tasteful and airy in a country style. **Amenities:** 🛏 👤 Cable TV, shoe polisher. No A/C. All units w/terraces, some w/fireplaces. **Services:** ✕ 🖭 🕪 **Facilities:** △ 🖭 🏊 🗻 🗲 🖭 👤 1 rst (see also "Restaurants" below), 1 bar (w/entertainment), 1 beach (lake shore). **Rates (CP):** HS June–Oct/Dec–Mar $75–$125 S or D; from $125 ste. Min stay HS. Lower rates off-season. Spec packages avail. Pking: Outdoor, free. Maj CC.

Motel

≣≣ **Travelodge**, 455 N Lake Blvd, PO Box 84, Tahoe City, CA 96145; tel 916/583-3766 or toll free 800/578-7878; fax 916/583-8045. Truckee/Calif 89 exit off I-80. All the technical amenities of a good roadside motel, with lake and golf course views and a central location in the Tahoe area. Ample parking. **Rooms:** 47 rms. CI 3pm/CO 11am. Nonsmoking rms avail. Clean, simple. Bathrooms have been retiled. All beds are Beautyrest. Security system. **Amenities:** 🛁 🐶 🖭 📺 Cable TV w/movies. No A/C. Ski racks inside rooms. Massage shower head. **Services:** 🐾 Guests receive a 10% discount at many restaurants around the lake. **Facilities:** 🔗 🚶 📺 📅 Sauna, whirlpool. **Rates:** HS Dec–Mar/July–Aug $47–$115 S or D. Extra person $5–$15. Children under 16 stay free. Min stay HS. Lower rates off-season. Higher rates for spec evnts/hols. Pking: Outdoor, free. Maj CC.

Inn

🏔🏔🏔 **Cottage Inn at Lake Tahoe**, 1690 W Lake Blvd, PO Box 66, Tahoe City, CA 96145; tel 916/581-4073 or toll free 800/581-4073; fax 916/581-0226. 2 mi S of Tahoe City. Squaw Valley exit off I-80; on Tahoe's west shore. 2 acres. Nestled in the trees on the shores of Lake Tahoe, this is a great Old Tahoe-style lodge with cozy knotty-pine cottages and lots of privacy. Unsuitable for children under 12. **Rooms:** 14 rms and stes; 6 ctges/villas. CI 3pm/CO 11am. No smoking. Each cottage is individually decorated, with new furnishings throughout and top-quality accessories. Kitchen available. A cultivated "rustic" decor. **Amenities:** 🐶 Cable TV w/movies, bathrobes. No A/C or phone. 1 unit w/minibar, some w/terraces, all w/fireplaces, 1 w/Jacuzzi. **Services:** Masseur, afternoon tea and wine/sherry served. Full breakfast. **Facilities:** 🚶 📺 💻 1 beach (lake shore), sauna, guest lounge. **Rates (BB):** HS Dec–Feb/June–Aug $100–$135 S or D; from $140 ste. Extra person $15. Min stay HS. Lower rates off-season. Higher rates for spec evnts/hols. Spec packages avail. Pking: Outdoor, free. Ltd CC.

Lodge

🏔🏔 **River Ranch**, Calif 89 and Alpine Meadows Rd, PO Box 197, Tahoe City, CA 96145; tel 916/583-4264; fax 916/583-7237. 10 mi S of Truckee. Squaw Valley exit off I-80. Closest lodging to Alpine Meadows ski area. Needs renovation. Back of property has splendid outside seating overlooking Truckee River. Near bike path that runs from Tahoe City to Squaw Valley. **Rooms:** 19 rms. CI 3pm/CO 11am. Nonsmoking rms avail. Antique furniture and good-size bathrooms. A little worn. **Amenities:** 🛁 🐶 Cable TV, stereo/tape player. No A/C. Some units w/terraces. **Facilities:** 🚶 📺 1 rst, 1 bar (w/entertainment). Frequent entertainment. Fine bar with friendly atmosphere. **Rates (CP):** HS July–Sept/Dec–Apr $30–$110 S or D. Extra person $15. Children under 6 stay free. Min stay HS. Lower rates off-season. Higher rates for spec evnts/hols. Pking: Outdoor, free. Maj CC.

Resort

🏔🏔🏔 **Granlibakken Resort & Conference Center**, Granlibakken Rd, PO Box 6329, Tahoe City, CA 96145; tel 916/583-4242 or toll free 800/543-3221; fax 916/583-7641. 1 mi S of Tahoe City. 74 acres. A secluded, condominium-style resort with classic "Old Tahoe" ambience and a summer-camp atmosphere. The ski hill was the site of the Olympic trials for the 1952 Winter Games. Quiet and relaxing. **Rooms:** 76 rms, stes, and effic. CI 4pm/CO 11am. Nonsmoking rms avail. All are condo-style. **Amenities:** 🛁 🐶 Cable TV, refrig, VCR. No A/C. Some units w/minibars, all w/terraces, some w/fireplaces. **Services:** 🗝 🐾 Social director, babysitting. **Facilities:** 🔗 🎱 🎿 🚶 📺 🏊6 🎯 Sauna, whirlpool, washer/dryer. Multiple trails for hiking, mountain biking, and cross-country skiing. **Rates (BB):** HS Dec 24–Jan 2 $80–$95 S or D; from $115 ste; from $175 effic. Children under 2 stay free. Min stay wknds and spec evnts. Lower rates off-season. Spec packages avail. Pking: Outdoor, free. Maj CC.

Restaurants 🍽

⑤ **Burger Spa**, 126 W Lake Blvd, Tahoe City; tel 916/583-4111. 13 mi S of Truckee. Squaw Valley/Tahoe City exit off I-80. **Burgers.** A small establishment near the touristy Fanny Bridge, located in an A-frame building with limited seating. Burgers, chicken, and fries are good values. **FYI:** Reservations not accepted. Children's menu. Beer and wine only. **Open:** HS June–Sept/Dec–Feb daily 11am–8pm. Reduced hours off-season. Closed some hols. **Prices:** Lunch main courses $2.95–$5.50. No CC. 🍺

★ **The Galley Cafe**, in Roundhouse Mall, 700 N Lake Blvd, Tahoe City; tel 916/581-3305. Squaw Valley exit off I-80. **New American.** A comfortable restaurant located upstairs in a mall next to a marina. Decorated to resemble a ship's galley. Fresh meat and produce, with lots of vegetarian options, make this a good place for families. **FYI:** Reservations accepted. Children's menu. Beer and wine only. **Open:** HS Dec–Sept Mon–Fri 11am–3pm, Sat–Sun 9am–3:30pm. Reduced hours off-season. Closed some hols. **Prices:** Lunch main courses $3.95–$7.50. Ltd CC. 🏔 🏕

Sunnyside Restaurant, in Sunnyside Lodge, 1850 W Lake Blvd, Tahoe City; tel 916/583-7200. Tahoe City/Squaw Valley exit off I-80. **Seafood/Steak.** The large dining room has high ceilings and hardwood floors; an outside patio faces Lake Tahoe. Specialties at breakfast, lunch, and dinner utilize fresh produce and lots of seafood. Prices are a bit high; you're paying for the views. **FYI:** Reservations accepted. Guitar/singer. Children's menu. **Open:** HS July–Aug breakfast Mon–Sat 10am–2:30pm;

lunch Mon–Sat 10am–2:30pm; dinner daily 5:30–10pm; brunch Sun 9:30am–2:30pm. Reduced hours off-season. **Prices:** Main courses $11.95–$18.95. Maj CC. 🍴 🏞 ⚹

Tahoe House, 625 W Lake Blvd, Tahoe City; tel 916/583-1377. Squaw Valley exit off I-80. **Californian/Swiss.** The spacious main dining room seems appealing for family dining; the wine cellar room, for private parties or larger groups, is lined with wooden wine racks. The menu is strong on "heart smart" options: lean meats, fat-free breads, and cholesterol-free oils. Herbs and much produce are grown on the site. **FYI:** Reservations recommended. Children's menu. Dress code. **Open:** Daily 5–10pm. **Prices:** Main courses $6.95–$17.95. Maj CC. 🅰

Wolfdale's, 640 N Lake Blvd, Tahoe City; tel 916/583-5700. 13 mi S of Truckee. Tahoe City or Squaw Valley exit off I-80. **Eclectic.** Tastefully decorated with a Thai theme and specially designed ceramic dinnerware. Long oak bar edged with tile. Eclectic cuisine, with unique entrees such as Thai seafood stew or crusted roast rack of lamb. A bit expensive—you're paying for ambience and unusual food. **FYI:** Reservations recommended. Dress code. **Open:** HS July–Aug daily 5:30–10pm. Reduced hours off-season. Closed Thanksgiving. **Prices:** Main courses $14–$20. Ltd CC. ❤ 🏞 ⚹

Refreshment Stop ☕

★ **Café O'Lake**, 550 N Lake Blvd, Tahoe City; tel 916/581-5104. Tahoe City exit off Calif 89. **Cafe.** The top choice of all Tahoe's sit-down cafes. Decor is country European; outdoor picnic table has a lake view. Offerings include house-baked breads, freshly roasted coffee, creative salads, and eccentric desserts. **Open:** Daily 7am–7pm. Closed Dec 25. Maj CC. 🍴 🏞 ⚹

Attractions 📷

Gatekeeper's Log Cabin Museum, 130 W Lake Blvd; tel 916/583-1762. Now that the floodgates are operated from an office tower in Reno, the rustic old gatekeeper's house has been made into a museum operated by the North Lake Tahoe Historical Society. Restored to its original state, the log cabin contains artifacts from its past, as well as Native American baskets and clothing, and mementos from Lake Tahoe's history. **Open:** May–Sept, daily 11am–5pm. Closed some hols. Free.

North Tahoe Cruises, 850 North Lake Blvd; tel 916/583-0141. Two-hour cruises of Emerald Bay and the northwestern shore of Lake Tahoe. June–September, departures daily at 11am, 1:30 and 3:30pm; sunset cocktail cruises mid-June to mid-September, daily at 6pm. Schedule varies. $$$$

Tahoe State Recreation Area; tel 916/583-3074. A 13-acre park is off Calif 28, near the east end of Tahoe City. Offers direct access to the lake shoreline and a pier. Swimming, fishing. Campsite available; picnicking. **Open:** Late May–Sept, daily 8am–8pm; Oct–late May, hours may vary. $$

D L Bliss State Park, Calif 89; tel 916/525-7277. One of lake Tahoe's finest and most popular beaches is found here. There are several trails, one along the lakeshore and another leading to Balancing Rock. **Open:** Mid-June–mid-Sept, daily 8am–11pm. $$

Emerald Bay State Park/Vikingsholm, Calif 89; tel 916/541-3030 (summer only). Approximately 600 acres at the southern boundary of D L Bliss State Park (see above), this park was created around a nucleus of land donated to the state in 1953 by Placerville lumberman Harvey West. It includes facilities to accommodate campers, hikers, boaters, picnickers, and anglers. There are also fine panoramic views of Lake Tahoe and Eagle Falls.

Vikingsholm (1929) was built for Mrs Lora J Knight of Santa Barbara and Chicago, inspired by a Norse fortress from around 800 AD. Considered the finest example of Scandinavian architecture in the Western Hemisphre, the building employed many of the construction methods and materials of ancient Scandinavia. It features a sod roof with living grass like those sometimes used in Scandinavia to feed livestock during the winter. Many of the furnishings are exact duplicates of historic pieces found in Norway and Sweden. Mrs Knight also had guesthouses built and created a teahouse on Fannette Island. She spent her summers here until her death in 1945.

Guided tours can be taken for a nominal fee from July–Labor Day. A steep 1-mile trail leads down from the parking lot at the Emerald Bay Overlook. **Open:** Mid-June–mid-Sept, daily 8am–11pm. $$

TAHOE VISTA

Map page M-2, C3 (S of Truckee)

Motel 🏨

🛏 **Tatami Cottage Resort**, 7449 N Lake Blvd, PO Box 18, Tahoe Vista, CA 96148; tel 916/546-3523. 1 mi W of Kings Beach. 2 acres. Near all lake activities and points of interest. Very rustic, no frills. **Rooms:** 18 ctges/villas. CI 2pm/CO 11am. Some units have kitchen facilities; 3 oriental-theme cottages have futon bedding. **Amenities:** 📺 Cable TV, refrig. No A/C or phone. All units w/terraces, some w/fireplaces. **Services:** 🛎 🐕 Babysitting. **Facilities:** 🎿 🏖 1 beach (lake shore). **Rates:** HS June 15–Sept 15/Nov 24–Apr from $69 effic; from $59 ctge/villa. Children under 12 stay free. Min stay spec evnts. Lower rates off-season. Higher rates for spec evnts/hols. Pking: Outdoor, free. Maj CC.

Lodge

≣≣ **Cedar Glen Lodge**, 6589 N Lake Blvd, PO Box 188, Tahoe Vista, CA 96148; tel 916/546-4281 or toll free 800/341-8000, 800/500-8246 in CA; fax 916/546-2250. 1½ mi W of Kings Beach. 1½ acres. Clean, well-kept cottages form a horseshoe around the pool. Hotel/lodge in rear area. Across the street from the beach. **Rooms:** 14 rms and stes; 17 ctges/villas. CI 2pm/CO 11am. Nonsmoking rms avail. Rustic appearance and furnishings. **Amenities:** 🛋 🐾 ▣ 🍸 Cable TV, refrig, shoe polisher. No A/C. All units w/terraces, 1 w/fireplace. **Services:** ⟲ Children's program, babysitting. **Facilities:** 🔗 🏋 🎬 Games rm, sauna, whirlpool, day-care ctr, playground, washer/dryer. **Rates (CP):** HS June–Sept $39–$90 S or D; from $39 ste; from $46 ctge/villa. Extra person $5. Min stay HS. Lower rates off-season. Higher rates for spec evnts/hols. Spec packages avail. Pking: Outdoor, free. Maj CC.

Resort

≣≣ **The Mourelato's Lakeshore Resort**, 6834 N Lake Blvd, PO Box 77, Tahoe Vista, CA 96148; tel 916/583-5334 or toll free 800/2-RELAX-U; fax 916/546-2744. 1 mi W of Kings Beach. 3 acres. Two buildings on the shore of Lake Tahoe. Landscaping needs work. New wing recommended exclusively. **Rooms:** 32 rms, stes, and effic. CI 2pm/CO 11am. Nonsmoking rms avail. Rooms in new wing are tastefully decorated. **Amenities:** 🛋 🐾 ▣ Cable TV, refrig. No A/C. Some units w/terraces. **Services:** ⟲ Babysitting. **Facilities:** 🏋 🎬 🔗 1 beach (lake shore), playground. **Rates:** HS June–Sept $75–$130 S or D; from $75 ste; from $105 effic. Extra person $6. Children under 1 stay free. Min stay HS. Lower rates off-season. Higher rates for spec evnts/hols. Spec packages avail. Pking: Outdoor, free. Maj CC.

TEHACHAPI

Map page M-3, C2

Hotel 📠

≣≣ **Tehachapi Summit Travelodge**, 500 Steuber Rd, PO Box 140, Tehachapi, CA 93581; tel 805/823-8000 or toll free 800/578-7878; fax 805/823-8006. Monolith exit off Calif 58 E; Tehachapi Blvd exit off Calif 58 W. A bright, cheerful property right off the freeway, owned and operated by the person who

built it. **Rooms:** 81 rms, stes, and effic. CI 3pm/CO 11am. Nonsmoking rms avail. Spacious and clean, with tile floors in bathrooms and natural wood on counters. **Amenities:** 🛋 ▣ A/C, cable TV. Some units w/minibars, some w/terraces, 1 w/fireplace, 1 w/Jacuzzi. **Services:** ⟲ 🍽 **Facilities:** 🔗 🏊 🔗 1 rst (see also "Restaurants" below), 1 bar, whirlpool. **Rates:** $49–$52 S; $56–$59 D; from $61 ste; from $61 effic. Extra person $7. Children under 18 stay free. Spec packages avail. Pking: Outdoor, free. Maj CC.

Resort

≣≣≣ **Sky Mountain Resort**, 18100 Lucaya Way, Tehachapi, CA 93561; tel 805/822-5581; fax 805/822-4055. Calif 202 exit off Calif 58. 4,600 acres. Clean, peaceful spot with invigorating mountain air. About 15 miles to Tehachapi old town. **Rooms:** 63 rms and stes; 21 ctges/villas. CI 3pm/CO noon. Nonsmoking rms avail. Rooms are tastefully decorated. Some have large canopy bed and big seating area with sofa and view of canyon. **Amenities:** 🛋 🐾 ▣ A/C, cable TV. Some units w/terraces, some w/fireplaces. **Services:** 🚐 ⟲ 🍽 Twice-daily maid svce, social director, masseur, children's program, babysitting. **Facilities:** 🔗 🚴 🏊 🏌 ⛳ 🎬 🎱 🏊 🔗 2 rsts, 2 bars (1 w/entertainment), lifeguard, games rm, spa, sauna, steam rm, whirlpool, day-care ctr, playground, washer/dryer. Putting green. **Rates:** HS Apr–Nov $75–$130 D; from $130 ste; from $155 ctge/villa. Children under 18 stay free. Min stay wknds. Lower rates off-season. Spec packages avail. Pking: Outdoor, free. Maj CC.

Restaurant 🍴

The Summit Dining Hall & Saloon, in the Tehachapi Summit Travelodge, 480 Steuber Rd, Tehachapi; tel 805/823-1000. **Steak.** Western-style rustic, with natural woods and a large stone fireplace in the corner, stuffed animal heads, and cowboy mural. Steaks are hand-cut and aged on the premises and have a smoky oak flavor from the open-fire grill. Chicken tortilla soup is brought to each table. Weak wine list, but 53 beers from around the world are available. **FYI:** Reservations accepted. Children's menu. **Open:** Breakfast daily 5:30–11am; lunch daily 11am–9pm; dinner daily 5–9pm. **Prices:** Main courses $7.50–$21.95. Maj CC. 🎥 🔗

TEMECULA

Map page M-3, E3 (N of Escondido)

Hotel 🛏

≣≣≣ **Embassy Suites–Temecula**, 29345 Rancho California Rd, Temecula, CA 92591; tel 909/676-5656 or toll free 800/416-6116; fax 909/699-3928. Rancho California Rd exit off I-15. Conveniently located near I-15, hotel has contemporary styling and pleasant accommodations. **Rooms:** 136 rms and stes. CI 4pm/CO noon. Express checkout avail. Nonsmoking rms avail. Extra-large rooms. **Amenities:** 🛏 ♨ 🖥 🍷 A/C, satel TV w/movies, refrig, VCR, voice mail. Microwave, 2 TVs. **Services:** ✗ 🖼 🎎 Babysitting. Complimentary evening beverages. **Facilities:** 🔟 🏊 🍸 ⅗ 1 rst, 1 bar, whirlpool, washer/dryer. **Rates (BB):** $79–$89 S or D; from $99 ste. Extra person $10. Children under 12 stay free. Min stay spec evnts. Higher rates for spec evnts/hols. Spec packages avail. Pking: Outdoor, free. Maj CC.

Resort

≣≣≣ **Temecula Creek Inn**, 44501 Rainbow Canyon Rd, PO Box 129, Temecula, CA 92592; or toll free 800/962-7335; fax 909/676-3422. Calif 79 exit off I-15; right on Pala Rd, right on Rainbow Canyon Rd. 305 acres. A paradise for golfers, and well located for those interested in nearby wineries. Very good value. **Rooms:** 80 rms and stes. CI 3pm/CO noon. Nonsmoking rms avail. Spacious and comfortable rooms; some have golf-course views. **Amenities:** 🛏 ♨ 🖥 🍷 A/C, cable TV, refrig, in-rm safe. All units w/minibars, some w/terraces. Each room has a coffee grinder and beans. Suites have bathrobes. **Services:** ✗ 🖼 🎎 🐾 Babysitting. Free daily newspapers. Children's golf camp in August. **Facilities:** 🔟 ▶₂₇ 🏊 🍸₂ 🍽 ⅗ 2 rsts (see also "Restaurants" below), 1 bar (w/entertainment), lawn games, whirlpool. Top-rated golf course. **Rates:** $115–$125 S or D; from $135 ste. Extra person $20. Children under 16 stay free. Min stay wknds. Spec packages avail. Pking: Outdoor, free. Maj CC. Golf and wine-country packages available.

Restaurants 🍴

Baily Wine Country Cafe, in Town Center Shopping Center, 27644 Ynez Rd, Temecula; tel 909/676-9567. Rancho California Rd exit off I-15. **Californian/Continental.** Contemporary decor. An outdoor seating area borders a shopping center parking lot. Lunch menu includes warm Thai beef salad, grilled chicken, and salads and pastas. At dinner, there are ravioli, scampi, New York pepper steak, and duck salad. Large selection of local wines. **FYI:** Reservations recommended. Beer and wine only. **Open:** Lunch Mon–Fri 11:30am–3pm, Sat–Sun 11:30am–5pm; dinner Mon–Thurs 5–9pm, Fri–Sat 5–9:30pm, Sun 5–9pm. Closed some hols. **Prices:** Main courses $9.50–$19.50. Maj CC. ⅗

★ **Café Champagne**, in Thornton Winery, 32575 Rancho California Rd, Temecula; tel 909/699-0088. 53 mi N of San Diego. Rancho California Rd exit off I-15; 3½ mi E. **Californian.** Patio dining beneath a pergola, and indoor dining in a bright airy space with floral fabrics and brass chandeliers. All desserts and breads are prepared daily on site. **FYI:** Reservations recommended. Jazz. **Open:** Lunch daily 11am–4:30pm; dinner daily 4:30–9pm; brunch Sun 10am–4:30pm. Closed some hols. **Prices:** Main courses $12.95–$20.95. Maj CC. 🍽 🏔 ⅗

Temet Grill, in the Temecula Creek Inn, Rainbow Canyon Rd, Temecula; tel 909/694-1000. Calif 79 S exit off I-15; right on Pala Rd; right on Rainbow Canyon Rd. **Southwestern.** Overlooking a golf course, with floor-to-ceiling windows, and southwestern Native American artifacts in glass cases hung on the walls. Menu focuses on southwestern preparations, such as lamb osso buco and veal chops with sun-dried tomato and chipotle demiglaze. **FYI:** Reservations recommended. Piano. Dress code. **Open:** Breakfast Mon–Fri 6:30–11am, Sat–Sun 6–11am; lunch Mon–Sat 11am–2:30pm; dinner daily 5–10pm; brunch Sun 10am–2:30pm. **Prices:** Main courses $15.50–$19.50. Maj CC. 🏔 🍷 ⅗

Attraction 🧳

Old Town Temecula Museum, 41950 Main St; tel 909/676-0021. A chronicle of daily life in the early days of Temecula, this museum contains many artifacts, especially household items of the type used by early settlers; also exhibits about local Native Americans, dioramas, small gift shop. Walking tour maps of the town and wine country maps available. **Open:** Wed–Sun 11am–4pm. Closed some hols. Free.

THOUSAND OAKS

Map page M-3, D2

See also Newbury Park, Westlake Village

Hotels 🛏

≣≣ **Holiday Inn Thousand Oaks**, 495 N Ventu Park Rd, Thousand Oaks, CA 91320; tel 805/498-6733 or toll free 800/866-5012; fax 805/498-9789. 30 mi N of Los Angeles. Ventu Park Rd exit off US 101. Traditional 2-story 70s-era Holiday Inn with easy freeway access. **Rooms:** 154 rms, stes, and effic. CI 2pm/CO noon. Express checkout avail. Nonsmoking rms avail. Scheduled for refurbishing. **Amenities:** 📺 ☕ 🍽 A/C, cable TV. **Services:** ✕ 🚐 🔲 ↩ Car-rental desk, babysitting. **Facilities:** 🏊 🍽 ⅙ 1 rst, 1 bar (w/entertainment), whirlpool, washer/dryer. **Rates:** HS Mem Day–Labor Day $69–$99 S or D; from $79 ste; from $95 effic. Extra person $10. Children under 12 stay free. Lower rates off-season. Higher rates for spec evnts/hols. Spec packages avail. Pking: Outdoor, free. Maj CC.

📧 **Thousand Oaks Inn**, 75 W Thousand Oaks Blvd, Thousand Oaks, CA 91360; tel 805/497-3701; fax 805/497-1875. Moorpark Rd exit off US 101. Good location off US 101 with easy access to shopping. **Rooms:** 107 rms and stes. CI 3pm/CO noon. Express checkout avail. Nonsmoking rms avail. Rooms that are newly refurbished are acceptable. **Amenities:** 📺 A/C, cable TV w/movies. **Services:** 🔲 ↩ Complimentary continental breakfast served poolside. **Facilities:** 🏊 🍽 ⅙ 1 rst, whirlpool, washer/dryer. **Rates (CP):** $59–$69 S or D; from $129 ste. Children under 18 stay free. Pking: Outdoor, free. Maj CC.

THREE RIVERS

Map page M-2, E3 (E of Visalia)

Motel 🛏

📧📧 **Best Western Holiday Lodge**, 40105 Sierra Dr, PO Box 129, Three Rivers, CA 93271; tel 209/561-4119 or toll free 800/528-1234; fax 209/561-3527. This motel is just 10 minutes from the entrance to Sequoia and Kings Canyon National Parks, and only 100 yards from the Kaweah River. The new 10-room unit, which opened in 1994, has lovely, large rooms. The older portion of this motel is less appealing. **Rooms:** 54 rms and stes. CI 1pm/CO 11am. Nonsmoking rms avail. 20 rooms have river views and private balconies. There are 2 rooms for guests with disabilities. **Amenities:** 📺 ☕ 🔲 🍽 A/C, cable TV w/movies, refrig. Some units w/terraces, some w/fireplaces. TDDs for deaf and hard of hearing guests. **Services:** ↩ 🐕 **Facilities:** 🏊 △ 📧 🎿 🏊 🎣 ⅙ Whirlpool, playground. Fishing on the Kaweah River. Boating and fishing on Lake Kaweah, 1 mile away. **Rates (CP):** HS May–Sept $55–$75 S; $57–$75 D; from $76 ste. Extra person $4. Lower rates off-season. Pking: Outdoor, free. Maj CC.

TIBURON

Map page M-2, D1 (S of San Rafael)

Motel 🛏

📧📧 **Tiburon Lodge & Conference Center**, 1651 Tiburon Blvd, Tiburon, CA 94920; tel 415/435-3133 or toll free 800/762-7770, 800/TIBURON in CA; fax 415/435-2451. Tiburon Blvd exit off US 101; 4½ mi E. A cut above a standard motel, with a marble lobby and Jacuzzis in some rooms, though the overall ambience is a little offbeat. Near center of Tiburon as well as the ferry to San Francisco and Angel Island. **Rooms:** 102 rms and effic. CI 3pm/CO noon. Nonsmoking rms avail. Top-floor accommodations, dubbed "Winchester" rooms, all have cathedral ceilings. Top-of-the-line "Spa Royal" rooms have motifs such as "Venetian Cave" or "Purple Harem." **Amenities:** 📺 ☕ A/C, satel TV, refrig. Some units w/minibars, some w/terraces, some w/Jacuzzis. **Services:** ✕ 🚐 ↩ 🐕 Car-rental desk. **Facilities:** 🏊 🖥 🔲 ⅙ 1 rst. **Rates:** HS July–Sept $65–$250 S; $80–$250 D; from $120 effic. Extra person $10. Children under 12 stay free. Lower rates off-season. Higher rates for spec evnts/hols. Spec packages avail. Pking: Indoor/outdoor, free. Maj CC.

Restaurants 🍴

Guaymas Restaurante, 5 Main St, Tiburon; tel 415/435-6300. **Mexican.** A winner for its creative Mexican cuisine and its views; sailing yachts are moored just a few feet away from tables on the outdoor decks. The fiesta-inspired decor includes paper flags, rough-hewn wooden chairs, and a big adobe hearth in the corner. On the menu, you'll find unusual Mexican regional dishes, such as shrimp sautéed with chipotle sauce or roasted duck in pumpkin seed sauce. Tortillas are made fresh on the premises. Very popular for happy hour. **FYI:** Reservations recommended. **Open:** Mon–Thurs 11:30am–10pm, Fri–Sat 11:30am–11pm, Sun 10:30am–10pm. Closed some hols. **Prices:** Main courses $10–$18. Maj CC. 🍷 🏞 ⅙

Sam's Anchor Cafe, 27 Main St, Tiburon; tel 415/435-4527. **Californian/American.** The best outdoor deck in Tiburon, offering a view of the San Francisco skyline behind masts of sailboats from the Corinthian Yacht Club. The menu features everything from burgers and sandwiches to fresh fish and steaks, with specials such as smoked chicken cappellini or broiled sturgeon. **FYI:** Reservations accepted. Children's menu. **Open:** Sun–Thurs 11am–10:30pm, Fri–Sat 11am–11pm. Closed Dec 25. **Prices:** Main courses $10–$15. Maj CC. 🍷 🏞

Sweden House Bakery-Cafe, 35 Main St, Tiburon; tel 415/435-9767. **Cafe/Scandinavian.** A little bit of Scandinavia on the shores of San Francisco Bay. Perfect for breakfast or a light lunch. A small deck overlooks the water. Serves breakfast omelettes and open-faced sandwiches, as well as desserts. After 3pm (4pm on weekends), only dessert is served. **FYI:** Reservations not accepted. Beer and wine only. **Open:** HS May–Nov Mon–Fri 8am–6pm, Sat–Sun 8am–7pm. Reduced hours off-season. Closed Dec 25. **Prices:** Lunch main courses $6–$8. Ltd CC. 🍴

TRINIDAD

Map page M-2, A1

Motel 🏨

Bishop Pine Lodge, 1481 Patricks Point Dr, Trinidad, CA 95570; tel 707/677-3314. Seawood exit off US 101 S; Trinidad exit off US 101 N. Like a Swiss alpine lodge near the sea—the best of both worlds. Hospitality is quiet and unobtrusive. **Rooms:** 13 ctges/villas. CI 2pm/CO 11am. Accommodations in individual wooden cottages, some with kitchen. **Amenities:** 🛁 📞 Cable TV w/movies, refrig, in-rm safe. No A/C. All units w/terraces, some w/Jacuzzis. **Services:** 🐕 ⤵ Pets must be kept on leashes. **Facilities:** Whirlpool, playground. **Rates:** HS Oct 15–Mar from $60 ctge/villa. Extra person $8. Lower rates off-season. Pking: Outdoor, free. Maj CC.

Attraction 🎭

Little River State Beach; tel 707/677-3570 or 445-6547. Located 4 miles south of Trinidad off US 101. This park's 112 acres of undeveloped expanses of flat sand and low dunes are located on the south side of Little River. **Open:** Daily 24 hours. Free.

TRUCKEE

Map page M-2, C3

Hotel 🏨

Best Western–Truckee Tahoe Inn, 11331 Calif 267, Truckee, CA 96161; tel 916/587-4525 or toll free 800/528-1234, 800/824-6385 in CA; fax 916/587-8173. 1 mi S of Truckee. Downtown Truckee exit off I-80; take Calif 267 over railroad tracks. Clean and well kept. Good security. **Rooms:** 100 rms and stes. CI 2pm/CO 11am. Express checkout avail. Nonsmoking rms avail. **Amenities:** 🛁 📞 A/C, satel TV w/movies. 1 unit w/minibar. **Services:** ⤵ Babysitting.

Fishing poles and other sporting equipment may be borrowed from front desk. **Facilities:** 🛁 ⛷ 📺 🍳 💯 🖥 ♿ Sauna, whirlpool, playground, washer/dryer. **Rates (CP):** HS June 15–Aug/Jan–Apr $64–$78 S or D; from $83 ste. Extra person $7. Children under 13 stay free. Lower rates off-season. Higher rates for spec evnts/hols. Spec packages avail. Pking: Outdoor, free.

Inn

The Truckee Hotel, 10007 Bridge St, PO Box 884, Truckee, CA 96160; tel 916/587-4444 or toll free 800/659-6921; fax 916/587-1599. Victorian hotel, built in 1873, has the feel of a bed-and-breakfast. Much charm and historical elegance. Parlor has high-backed, cushioned chairs. **Rooms:** 37 rms (29 w/shared bath). CI 4pm/CO 11am. No smoking. American- and European-style rooms. European rooms share bath. All have antique decor, comforters, radiators. Plenty of light. **Amenities:** 👞 Shoe polisher. No A/C, phone, or TV. Some units w/terraces. **Services:** ⤵ Babysitting, afternoon tea served. **Facilities:** ⛷ 📺 📺 1 rst, 1 bar (w/entertainment), guest lounge. Retail gift shop with southwestern souvenirs and variety of wines. Excellent bar and restaurant. **Rates (BB):** HS Nov–Apr $80–$115 S w/shared bath, $95–$130 S w/private bath. Extra person $10. Lower rates off-season. Spec packages avail. Pking: Outdoor, free. Ltd CC.

Resort

Northstar-at-Tahoe-Resort, , PO Box 2499, Truckee, CA 96160; tel 916/562-1010 or toll free 800/466-6784; fax 916/562-2215. 6 mi S of Truckee. Downtown Truckee exit off I-80; right on Northstar Dr. 600 acres. A self-contained resort community. All facilities in excellent condition. Great resort for families. **Rooms:** 250 rms, stes, and effic. CI 5pm/CO 11am. Express checkout avail. Nonsmoking rms avail. Condos and homes are located 1 mile from the main area and facilities. All condos are clean and well furnished. **Amenities:** 🛁 📞 📺 Cable TV, refrig, VCR, stereo/tape player. No A/C. All units w/terraces, all w/fireplaces. **Services:** ⤵ Social director, children's program, babysitting. Superb management. **Facilities:** 🏌 🚴 ⛳18 🎿 🎾 ⛷ 📺 ♿10 🍳 💯200 🖥 ♿ 6 rsts, 5 bars (2 w/entertainment), lifeguard, games rm, lawn games, sauna, whirlpool, daycare ctr, playground, washer/dryer. **Rates:** $99 S or D; from $125 ste; from $125 effic. Min stay spec evnts. Higher rates for spec evnts/hols. Spec packages avail. Pking: Indoor/outdoor, free. Maj CC.

Restaurants 🍴

The Left Bank, 10098 Commercial Row, Truckee; tel 916/587-4694. Downtown Truckee exit off I-80. **French/Seafood.**

Once an elegant setting, it's now a little worn around the edges, but the food is still very good. Nightly specials of fresh fish, pasta, and some game dishes. Owner sometimes closes on a whim, so call ahead. **FYI:** Reservations recommended. Dress code. **Open:** Lunch Wed–Mon 11:30am–3pm; dinner Wed–Mon 5:30–9:30pm. **Prices:** Main courses $13.50–$17.95. Maj CC. ● ▬

✱ **Squeeze In**, 10060 Commercial Row, Truckee; tel 916/587-9814. Downtown Truckee exit off I-80. **American.** A Truckee tradition for breakfast. Historic Truckee memorabilia hangs from the rafters and clutters the shelves. Lots of skylights. Its omelettes—57 outrageous combinations—are all named after local characters. Also offers a variety of creative sandwiches. Great service. **FYI:** Reservations not accepted. Children's menu. Beer and wine only. **Open:** Daily 7am–2pm. Closed Dec 25. **Prices:** Lunch main courses $5.25–$6. No CC. ▬ ▬ ઙ

✱ **Truckee Trattoria**, in Safeway shopping center, 11310-1 Donner Pass Rd, Truckee (Gateway); tel 916/582-1266. Squaw Valley exit off I-80; N 1 mi. **Californian/Italian.** Only true attempt at Italian cuisine in Truckee. Small and intimate; tasteful decor with black-and-white tile, track lighting, sculpture. The light fare includes pastas and seafood. Menu changes monthly. **FYI:** Reservations recommended. Beer and wine only. **Open:** Wed–Sat 11:30am–9pm. Closed Thanksgiving; May 15–25/Nov 1–14. **Prices:** Main courses $5.75–$8.25. Ltd CC. ઙ

Zena's, in C B White house, 10292 Donner Pass Rd, Truckee; tel 916/587-1771. Downtown Truckee exit off I-80. **Eclectic.** Located in historic Victorian dating to 1873. Eclectic menu. **FYI:** Reservations not accepted. Country music/guitar/jazz/sing along. Children's menu. Beer and wine only. **Open:** Daily 7am–2pm. **Prices:** Lunch main courses $5.95–$6.95. Maj CC. ▬ ▬ ઙ

Attraction 🗔

Donner Memorial State Park, 12593 Donner Pass Rd; tel 916/582-7892. Located just west of town off I-80. The winter of 1846–47 proved to be one of the most severe ever to hit the Sierrra, which was unfortunate for the 81 members of the Donner Party, who became trapped in this mountain pass by early blizzards. Many members froze or starved to death; only 48 people survived, most of them by eating the remains of their deceased companions.

The park's 350 acres offer swimming, camping, picnicking, and cross-country skiing and snowshoeing in winter; naturalist programs in summer. The Emigrant Trail Museum has exhibits on the Donner Party, local wildlife, and Native American history and culture. **Open:** Daily dawn–dusk; museum, daily 10am–4pm. Closed some hols. $$

TWENTYNINE PALMS

Map page M-3, D3

Motel 🛏

▬▬ **Best Western Gardens Motel**, 71-487 Twentynine Palms Hwy, Twentynine Palms, CA 92277; tel 619/367-9141 or toll free 800/528-1234; fax 619/367-2584. Calif 62 exit off I-10. Located minutes from Joshua Tree National Monument. This motel is distinguished by its white-roofed modified Spanish architecture. Trees, gardens, and patches of lawn give it the atmosphere of an oasis. Needs better maintenance. **Rooms:** 84 rms and stes. CI 2pm/CO noon. Nonsmoking rms avail. **Amenities:** 🛖 A/C, cable TV. Some units w/Jacuzzis. **Services:** ⤵ **Facilities:** 🏊 ઙ Whirlpool. **Rates (CP):** $60 S; $64 D; from $100 ste. Extra person $8. Children under 12 stay free. Pking: Outdoor, free. Maj CC.

Inn

▬ **Circle C Lodge**, 6340 El Rey Ave, Twentynine Palms, CA 92277; tel 619/367-7615 or toll free 800/545-9696; fax 619/361-0247. Calif 62 exit off I-10; turn left on El Rey Ave off Twentynine Palms Hwy. Bed-and-breakfast situated within sight of Joshua Tree National Monument. **Rooms:** 11 rms. CI 3pm/CO 11am. Rooms are large, but somewhat dark. **Amenities:** 🛖 ▣ A/C, cable TV w/movies, refrig, VCR. **Facilities:** 🏊 Whirlpool, guest lounge. **Rates (CP):** $80–$95 S or D. Extra person $35. Min stay wknds. Pking: Outdoor, free. Ltd CC.

UKIAH

Map page M-2, C1

Motels 🛏

▬▬▬ **Discovery Inn**, 1340 N State St, Ukiah, CA 95482; tel 707/462-8873; fax 707/462-1249. N State St exit off US 101; turn left at State St. The best of the motel offerings in this area. Rooms at the back of the complex are quieter. **Rooms:** 154 rms and stes. CI 2pm/CO noon. Nonsmoking rms avail. Pleasant, nice decor, clean. All furnishings are new. **Amenities:** 🛖 ▣ ▣ A/C, cable TV w/movies, refrig, shoe polisher. Some units w/terraces, 1 w/Jacuzzi. **Services:** ⤵ Coffee available in lobby. **Facilities:** 🏊 ▣ ▣ ઙ Spa, sauna, whirlpool, washer/dryer. Bowling alley across the street. **Rates:** HS May–Sept $50–$60 S; $56–$65 D; from $65 ste. Extra person $5. Children under 12 stay free. Lower rates off-season. Pking: Outdoor, free. Maj CC.

≣≣**Western Travelers Motel**, 693 S Orchard Ave, Ukiah, CA 95482; tel 707/468-9167 or toll free 800/794-3551; fax 707/468-8268. Perkins exit off US 101; E on Perkins; left on Orchard. Adequate motel. Located right off the freeway, so it can be somewhat noisy. **Rooms:** 55 rms. CI 2pm/CO 11am. Nonsmoking rms avail. **Amenities:** 🖴 A/C, cable TV. **Services:** 🕭 **Facilities:** 🛋 🕭 **Rates:** $36–$44 S; $44–$56 D. Extra person $5. Children under 12 stay free. Pking: Outdoor, free. Maj CC.

Resort

≣≣≣**Vichy Springs Resort**, 2605 Vichy Springs Rd, Ukiah, CA 95482 (Vichy Springs); tel 707/462-9515; fax 707/462-9516. 4 mi E of Ukiah. Vichy Springs Rd exit off US 101; follow state historic landmark signs. 700 acres. A hot-springs bed-and-breakfast resort in the countryside. Resort has the only warm, naturally carbonated mineral baths in North America, called the "Champagne Baths." The redwood hotel was built in the 1860s. **Rooms:** 12 rms; 2 ctges/villas. CI 3pm/CO noon. Express checkout avail. Nonsmoking rms avail. 2 cabins and 12 rooms are cozy and sweet. **Amenities:** 🖴 🕭 A/C. All units w/terraces, all w/fireplaces. Some rooms have refrigerators. **Services:** ✕ 🚐 🖾 Masseur, babysitting. Massage, facials, and reflexology can be arranged. **Facilities:** 🛋 🏋 🎱 Lawn games, whirlpool, washer/dryer. Olympic-size pool, mineral baths, and hot tub, plus 4,000 acres for hiking, mountain biking, and bird watching. **Rates (BB):** HS May–Oct $85 S; $125 D; from $150 ctge/villa. Extra person $25. Children under 1 stay free. Lower rates off-season. Spec packages avail. Pking: Outdoor, free. Maj CC.

Restaurant 🍽

Thai Cafe, 801 N State St, Ukiah; tel 707/462-0238. Perkin St exit off US 101. **Thai.** Believe it or not, there's a fine Thai restaurant in Ukiah—in a former brothel, no less—and it's one of the best places to eat in town. The room is attractive, with golden-hued walls, high ceilings, white-oak chairs, and crisp white linens. On the menu you'll find choices like Thai barbecue chicken, garlic-pepper pork, green-curry prawns, and a whole page of vegetarian selections. **FYI:** Reservations accepted. Beer and wine only. **Open:** Mon–Fri 11am–9pm, Sat noon–9:30pm. Closed some hols. **Prices:** Main courses $6.95–$8.95. Ltd CC. 🚢 🗹 🕭

Attractions 🏛

Grace Hudson Museum and Sun House, 431 S Main St; tel 707/462-3370. This art, history, and anthropology museum focuses on the works of painter Grace Hudson and her ethnologist husband, Dr John W Hudson, as well as other regional artists. Permanent and changing exhibits study the native Pomo-an-speaking people, the white settlement of Mendocino County, and numerous examples of the works of both Hudsons.

The Hudsons built their Craftsman home, the **Sun House,** in 1911. Most of the property is preserved today, and the 6-room house is decorated with items from their eclectic collection. **Open:** Museum: Wed–Sat 10am–4:30pm, Sun noon–4:30pm. Sun House: Wed–Sun noon–3pm. Closed some hols. Free.

Parducci Wine Cellars, 501 Parducci Rd; tel 707/462-WINE. Adolph Parducci founded this family winemaking operation in 1931, and produced one of the first varietal bottlings of a California Zinfandel in 1944. Still operated by the Parducci family, the winery offers tours daily, on the hour 10am–3pm, weather permitting. **Open:** Daily 9am–5pm. Closed some hols. Free.

UNION CITY

Map page M-2, D2 (W of Fremont)

Hotel 🛄

≣≣ **Holiday Inn Union City**, 32083 Alvarado-Niles Rd, Union City, CA 94587; tel 510/489-2200 or toll free 800/HOLIDAY; fax 510/489-7642. Alvarado-Niles Rd exit off I-880. A finer Holiday Inn than most, in spite of the fact that hallways are dreary and could use some attention. Well located. **Rooms:** 262 rms and stes. Exec-level rms avail. CI 3pm/CO noon. Express checkout avail. Nonsmoking rms avail. Rooms are clean. **Amenities:** 🖴 🕾 A/C, cable TV w/movies, bathrobes. **Services:** ✕ 🚐 🖾 🕭 Children's program. **Facilities:** 🛋 🚲 🏋 🏊 🛳 🎱 💻 🕭 2 rsts, 1 bar (w/entertainment), games rm, racquetball, sauna, whirlpool, washer/dryer. Exceptionally large pool. **Rates:** $85–$95 S or D; from $125 ste. Extra person $10. Children under 18 stay free. Spec packages avail. Pking: Indoor/outdoor, free. Maj CC. Children accompanied by parents stay and eat free.

UNIVERSAL CITY

Map page M-3, D2 (SW of Glendale)

Hotels 🛄

≣≣≣≣ **Sheraton Universal**, 333 Universal Terrace Pkwy, Universal City, CA 91608; tel 818/980-1212 or toll free 800/325-3535; fax 818/985-4980. Located on the Universal Studios lot. This hotel just underwent a major renovation and emerged a truly lovely property. Not far from Hollywood, but totally peaceful and quiet. **Rooms:** 441 rms and stes. Exec-level rms avail. CI 3pm/CO noon. Express checkout avail. Nonsmoking rms avail. Fabulous views from rooms on the upper floors. **Amenities:** 🔐 🛁 ⚏ A/C, cable TV w/movies, voice mail, in-rm safe. All units w/minibars, some w/terraces. **Services:** ✗ ☎ 🆅🅿 ⚏ 🛎 Car-rental desk, babysitting. Pleasant, accommodating staff that deals equally well with children and celebrities. **Facilities:** 🏊 💪 🔟3K 👤 1 rst, 1 bar (w/entertainment), games rm, whirlpool. Fabulous pool. **Rates:** $155–$195 S; $175–$215 D; from $205 ste. Extra person $20. Children under 18 stay free. Spec packages avail. Pking: Indoor, $9.50–$12.50. Maj CC.

≣≣≣≣ **Universal City Hilton**, 555 Universal Terrace Pkwy, Universal City, CA 91608; tel 818/506-2500 or toll free 800/727-7110; fax 818/509-2058. One of the most upscale properties in the San Fernando Valley, with spectacular views of CityWalk and the Universal and Burbank Studios. **Rooms:** 446 rms and stes. Exec-level rms avail. CI 3pm/CO noon. Express checkout avail. Nonsmoking rms avail. The rooms are thoughtfully planned with unusual angles. **Amenities:** 🔐 💪 🍴 A/C, cable TV w/movies, voice mail, in-rm safe, bathrobes. Some units w/minibars, some w/terraces. Lots of special toiletries. Beds are triple-sheeted. **Services:** ⦿ ☎ 🆅🅿 🚐 ⚏ 🛎 Twice-daily maid svce, car-rental desk, babysitting. **Facilities:** 🏊 💪 🔟2K 👤 1 rst, 1 bar (w/entertainment), spa, sauna, steam rm, whirlpool, beauty salon. Huge meeting rooms, gigantic ballroom. **Rates:** $145–$200 S or D; from $250 ste. Children under 18 stay free. Spec packages avail. Pking: Indoor, $9–$12. Maj CC.

Attraction 📷

Universal Studios Hollywood, 100 Universal City Plaza; tel 818/777-3750. Accessible via Hollywood Freeway (US 101), Lankersham Blvd exit. Universal began offering behind-the-scenes tours to the public in 1964. These days the tour has taken on an amusement park–like character, and attracts more than 5 million tourists a year. Visitors board a tram for a one-hour guided tour of the studio's 420 acres, passing stars' dressing rooms, backlot sets, and numerous departments involved in film and TV production. The tour encounters several staged "disasters" along the way, from an earthquake and flash flood to a shark attack and a laser battle with deadly robots.

After the ride, visitors can seek out the numerous rides, shows, and other attractions at the **Studio Center** and the **Entertainment Center,** including the popular *ET Adventure* ride, *Back to the Future*—The Ride, and *Backdraft* Live. **Open:** Daily 9am–7pm (hours may vary); extended hours summer and hol periods. $$$$

VALLEJO
Map page M-2, C2

Motels 🏨

≣≣ **Holiday Inn–Marine World Africa USA**, 1000 Fairgrounds Dr, Vallejo, CA 94589; tel 707/644-1200 or toll free 800/465-4329; fax 707/643-7011. Fairgrounds Dr exit off I-80. Good location near Marine World Africa USA. Excellent facility for families. **Rooms:** 167 rms and stes. Exec-level rms avail. CI 2pm/CO noon. Express checkout avail. Nonsmoking rms avail. No-frills; in fact, somewhat drab. **Amenities:** 🔐 💪 A/C, cable TV w/movies. Executive-floor rooms have refrigerators, microwaves, and in-room coffee. **Services:** ✗ 🚗 ⚏ 🛎 🐕 Children's program. Morning newspapers in executive-floor rooms. **Facilities:** 🏊 🔟20 👤 1 rst, 1 bar (w/entertainment), sauna, whirlpool, washer/dryer. Fun sports bar. Guests have use of a Nautilus fitness center 1 mile away. **Rates:** HS Mem Day–Labor Day $68–$110 S or D; from $150 ste. Extra person $5. Children under 19 stay free. Lower rates off-season. Higher rates for spec evnts/hols. Spec packages avail. Pking: Outdoor, free. Maj CC. Good value. Marine World packages and Wine Country packages available as well as Kids Getaway Weekend.

≣≣ **Royal Bay Inn**, 44 Admiral Callaghan Lane, Vallejo, CA 94590; tel 707/643-1061 or toll free 800/643-8887; fax 707/643-4719. Tennessee St exit off I-80. Located on a very busy street. Very basic motel, but clean. **Rooms:** 78 rms and stes. CI 1pm/CO 11am. Nonsmoking rms avail. **Amenities:** 🔐 A/C, cable TV. Some units w/terraces. **Services:** ✗ 🛎 🐕 **Facilities:** 🏊 🔟55 👤 1 rst, washer/dryer. **Rates:** HS Mem Day–mid-Sept $30–$41 S; $44–$55 D; from $55 ste. Extra person $5. Children under 13 stay free. Lower rates off-season. Pking: Outdoor, free. Maj CC.

Restaurant 🍴

El Nopal, 406 Virginia St, Vallejo; tel 707/557-0456. **Mexican.** Wooden furniture, tiled floors, and walls lined with Mexican calendars. Standard menu of tacos, burritos, and enchiladas, but better than most. Close to Marine World Africa USA. **FYI:** Reservations accepted. **Open:** Mon–Sat 11am–8pm. Closed some hols. **Prices:** Main courses $6.10–$8.35. Ltd CC. 💳

Attractions 📷

Marine World Africa USA, Marine World Pkwy; tel 707/643-6722 (recorded info) or 644-4000. Located at the intersection of I-80 and Calif 37. A one-of-a-kind wildlife park, Marine

World Africa USA is devoted to educating the public about mankind's relationship with animals of the sea, land, and air. Eight shows feature performing seals, killer whales, chimps, lions, exotic birds, and others. Still more animals are featured in their own innovative habitats.

More than 15 participatory exhibits include **Shark Experience,** a 300,000-gallon habitat for tropical sharks and fish where visitors ride a moving walkway through a clear acrylic tunnel, completely surrounded by waters filled with 15 species of sharks and 100 species of tropical fish. **Dinosaurs! A Prehistoric Adventure** features 22 robotic dinosaurs in a Jurassic-period forest, numerous interactive exhibits, and a re-created archeological dig site where kids work together to uncover a 40-foot-long Apatosaurus skeleton. Also Butterfly World, Seal Cove, Giraffe Feeding Dock, Reptile Discovery, Animal Nursery, and Gentle Jungle.

Animals are sometimes brought out to stroll through the park with their trainer and interact with visitors. There are a few public picnic sites with grills; several restaurants and gift shops. Overnight RV accommodations available. **Open:** Mem Day–Labor Day, daily 9:30am–6:30pm; rest of year, Wed–Sun 9:30am–5:30pm. $$$$

Vallejo Naval and Historical Museum, 734 Marin St; tel 707/643-0077. Located in the old City Hall building, this museum contains 5 galleries dealing with the history of the region and of the Navy Yard at Mare Island. Purchased in 1853, Mare Island became the site of the first navy yard on the west coast. From 1859–1970 Mare Island built more than 500 ships for the US Navy. Retired Navy and US Marine personnel make up a significant portion of Vallejo's present population.

Exhibits include selections from the museum's permanent collection, local private collections, traveling exhibitions, and borrowed artifacts from the extensive collection at Mare Island. Library, bookstore, and gift shop. **Open:** Tues–Sat 10am–4:30pm. Closed some hols. $

VAN NUYS
Map page M-3, D2 (NW of Glendale)

Hotel 🛏

Airtel Plaza Hotel, 7277 Valjean Ave, Van Nuys, CA 91406; tel 818/997-7676 or toll free 800/2AIRTEL; fax 818/785-8864. A business hotel with attractive grounds and fountains. Fly your private plane to one of the hotel's tie-downs and walk right into the lobby. Although this hotel is adjacent to Van Nuys Airport, the busiest private airport in the world, there's no noise inside. **Rooms:** 268 rms and stes. CI 3pm/CO noon.

Express checkout avail. Nonsmoking rms avail. **Amenities:** 🛏 🕻 🍷A/C, cable TV w/movies, shoe polisher. Some units w/terraces, some w/Jacuzzis. **Services:** ✗ 🖛 △ ← ↩ Car-rental desk, babysitting. No van service to LAX, but hotel will pick up incoming guests for free at Midpoint Terminal. **Facilities:** 🚶 ⛳ 🏊 ⅋ 2 rsts, 1 bar (w/entertainment), whirlpool. **Rates (BB):** $99 S; $109 D; from $135 ste. Extra person $10. Children under 18 stay free. Spec packages avail. Pking: Outdoor, free. Maj CC.

Restaurant 🍽

★ **Dr Hogly Wogly's Tyler Texas Bar-Be-Que**, 8136 N Sepulveda Blvd, Van Nuys; tel 818/780-6701. **Barbecue.** No-nonsense service and food, and the best aromas this side of Texas. An Asian element is exemplified by huge bouquets of fresh flowers. This place is famous for barbecued spare ribs, beef, and pork—and for the bread. **FYI:** Reservations not accepted. Beer and wine only. **Open:** Daily 11:30am–10pm. Closed some hols. **Prices:** Main courses $9.95–$17.95. Ltd CC. 🖼 ⅋

Attraction 🎫

Japanese Garden, 6100 Woodley Ave; tel 818/756-8166. Located at LA's Donald C Tillman Water Reclamation Plant, this is an authentic, 6½-acre Japanese garden displayed in 3 distinct styles: a Zen Garden of symbolic stone arrangements and gravel; a wet strolling garden; and a tea garden. **Open:** Tours Tues, Thurs, and Sat by appointment. Free.

VENICE
Map page M-3, D2 (S of Santa Monica)

Hotel 🛏

Marina Pacific Hotel & Suites, 1697 Pacific Ave, Venice, CA 90291; tel 310/452-1111 or toll free 800/421-8151; fax 310/452-5479. 5 mi N of Los Angeles Int'l Airport. Pacific Ave exit off Santa Monica Fwy. A small, modest hotel with barebones lobby; surprisingly well cared for. Overlooks the famous Venice Beach boardwalk. **Rooms:** 90 rms, stes, and effic. CI noon/CO noon. Rooms are simple, and many have an ocean view. 1- and 2-bedroom suites with kitchens available. **Amenities:** 🛏 🕻 A/C, cable TV w/movies, refrig. Some units w/terraces. **Services:** ✗ △ ↩ **Facilities:** 🏊 1 rst, washer/dryer. **Rates:** HS June–Sept $90–$125 S; $95–$125 D; from $135 ste; from $145 effic. Extra person $10. Children under 12 stay free. Lower rates off-season. Pking: Indoor, free. Maj CC.

Restaurants 🍴

Sidewalk Café, 8 Horizon Ave, Venice; tel 310/399-5547. **American.** A front-row seat for the action on the Venice boardwalk. A local favorite for breakfast and lunch, offering omelettes, pizza, pasta, burgers, and salads. Very casual attire. **FYI:** Reservations not accepted. Band/singer. **Open:** Daily 8am–midnight. Closed Dec 25. **Prices:** Main courses $5.25–$9.95. Maj CC. 🍴 🖼 &

West Beach Cafe, 60 N Venice Blvd, Venice; tel 310/823-5396. **Californian.** Simple bistro serving breast of chicken Mediterranean, Chilean sea bass, grilled salmon on potato pancakes, lemon soufflé. Good wine list. **FYI:** Reservations recommended. **Open:** Lunch Sat–Sun 11:30am–2:45pm; dinner daily 6pm–midnight; brunch Sat–Sun 10am–2:45pm. Closed some hols. **Prices:** Main courses $15–$22. Maj CC. 🍴 VP

Attraction 🧳

Venice Beach. One of the LA area's greatest cultural treasures, Venice Beach today is a sort of "Coney Island West," a carnival of humanity populated by skaters, hipsters, and posers of every age and shape. People-watching is the major pastime here.

VENTURA

Map page M-3, D1

Hotels 🏨

≣≣ The Country Inn of Ventura, 298 Chestnut St, Ventura, CA 93001; tel 805/653-1434 or toll free 800/44-RELAX; fax 805/648-7126. Calif St exit off US 101 N; Main St exit off US 101 S. Country-style B&B hotel has nice decor, but it's next to noisy freeway. **Rooms:** 120 rms, stes, and effic. CI 3pm/CO noon. Nonsmoking rms avail. Some rooms have canopied beds; all are tastefully decorated with country prints, dried flowers, and wingback chairs. **Amenities:** 🛢 🗗 A/C, cable TV w/movies, refrig, VCR. All units w/minibars, some w/terraces, some w/fireplaces, some w/Jacuzzis. Microwave. **Services:** 🛆 🗗 Complimentary full breakfast and evening happy hour. **Facilities:** 🗗 🅿 & 1 bar, whirlpool, washer/dryer. **Rates (BB):** HS Mem Day–Labor Day $99–$109 S or D; from $104 ste; from $159 effic. Extra person $10. Children under 11 stay free. Lower rates off-season. Spec packages avail. Pking: Indoor, free. Pking: Outdoor, free. Maj CC.

≣≣≣ Doubletree Hotel at Ventura, 2055 Harbor Blvd, Ventura, CA 93001; tel 805/643-6000 or toll free 800/222-TREE; fax 805/643-7137. 1 mi W of downtown. Seaward Ave exit off US 101. A convention-oriented hotel, 1 block from the ocean, also suitable for families and vacationers. Atrium lobby with fountains, wicker, and flora. **Rooms:** 285 rms and stes. CI 3pm/CO noon. Express checkout avail. Nonsmoking rms avail. Spacious, clean rooms have oak furnishing and signed original prints. **Amenities:** 🛢 🗗 A/C, satel TV. 1 unit w/minibar, 1 w/Jacuzzi. **Services:** ✕ 🚐 🛆 🗗 **Facilities:** 🗗 🖈 🖂 & 1 rst, 2 bars (1 w/entertainment), lifeguard, sauna, whirlpool. Work of local artists is on sale in the Gallery restaurant, open for breakfast, lunch, and dinner. **Rates:** HS Mem Day–Labor Day $119–$129 S or D; from $175 ste. Extra person $10. Lower rates off-season. Higher rates for spec evnts/hols. Spec packages avail. Pking: Outdoor, free. Maj CC.

≣≣≣ Holiday Inn Ventura Beach Resort, 450 E Harbor Blvd, Ventura, CA 93001; tel 805/648-7731 or toll free 800/842-0800; fax 805/653-6202. California St exit off US 101 N; Seaward exit off US 101 S. A beachfront high-rise that caters to groups but is also good for families and leisure travelers. **Rooms:** 260 rms and stes. CI 4pm/CO noon. Nonsmoking rms avail. Attractive rooms with country-style decor. **Amenities:** 🛢 🗗 A/C, cable TV w/movies. All units w/terraces. **Services:** ✕ 🛆 🗗 **Facilities:** 🗗 🚲 🖈 🖂 & 2 rsts, 2 bars (w/entertainment), 1 beach (ocean), lifeguard, board surfing, games rm, washer/dryer. Attractively landscaped pool overlooks the pier and the Pacific. Rooftop lounge serves Sunday brunch. **Rates:** HS June–Sept $79–$99 S or D; from $120 ste. Extra person $10. Children under 18 stay free. Min stay HS and wknds. Lower rates off-season. Spec packages avail. Pking: Indoor/outdoor, free. Maj CC.

≣≣≣ Pierpont Inn, 550 Sanjon Rd, Ventura, CA 93001; tel 805/653-6144 or toll free 800/285-INNS; fax 805/641-1501. 1 mi N of downtown Ventura. Sanjon exit off US 101 N; Seaward Ave exit off US 101 S. 6 acres. Landmark 1908 inn, owned by the same family for more than 65 years. The cozy lobby is distinguished by a California craftsman-style lattice entrance, 2-sided fireplace, and great views. **Rooms:** 69 rms and stes; 2 ctges/villas. CI 3pm/CO noon. Nonsmoking rms avail. Cottages have timbered ceilings, brick fireplaces, and stenciling. Other rooms are attractively decorated with dark wood repro-antique furnishings and colorful prints, but are marred by highway noise. **Amenities:** 🛢 🗗 🖵 Cable TV w/movies. No A/C. 1 unit w/minibar, some w/terraces, some w/fireplaces. **Services:** ✕ 🛆 🗗 Masseur. **Facilities:** 🗗 🎾 🖈 🖂 & 1 rst, 1 bar (w/entertainment), lawn games, racquetball, spa, sauna, steam rm, whirlpool. Lawn with garden chairs. Indoor-outdoor dining with lovely ocean views. Guest privileges at the Pierpont Racquet Club. **Rates (CP):** HS Mar–Oct $79–$89 S or D; from $119 ste;

from $129 ctge/villa. Extra person $10. Children under 12 stay free. Lower rates off-season. Spec packages avail. Pking: Outdoor, free. Maj CC.

Motel

≣≣≣ **La Quinta Motor Inn**, 5818 Valentine Rd, Ventura, CA 93003; tel 805/658-6200 or toll free 800/531-5900; fax 805/642-2840. Victoria St exit off US 101; go west. A clean whitebrick motel with a very attractive lobby, but a horrible smell outside from nearby mushroom cannery. **Rooms:** 142 rms and stes. CI 3pm/CO noon. Nonsmoking rms avail. Rooms are simple, practical, decorated in earth tones with southwestern-style bleached wood furniture. **Amenities:** 🛋 🗄 A/C, satel TV w/movies. **Services:** 🛎 🛜 Complimentary continental breakfast. **Facilities:** 🗄 🗄 🗄 Whirlpool. Driving net, putting green. **Rates (CP):** HS June–Sept 15 $57 S; $62 D; from $77 ste. Extra person $5. Children under 18 stay free. Lower rates off-season. Pking: Outdoor, free. Maj CC.

Inn

≣≣≣ **Bella Maggiore Inn**, 67 S California St, Ventura, CA 93001; tel 805/652-0277 or toll free 800/523-8479. Italian-inspired B&B with a spacious comfortable lobby distinguished by antiques, a fireplace, and a grand piano. Downtown location within walking distance of shops and restaurants. **Rooms:** 24 rms, stes. CI 3pm/CO noon. Large high-ceilinged rooms with ceiling fans are well appointed, with a hand-painted design over the bed and fresh flowers. **Amenities:** 🛋 🗄 Satel TV w/movies, refrig. Some units w/minibars, some w/terraces, some w/fireplaces, some w/Jacuzzis. Hand-made chocolate truffles. **Services:** ✗ 🛜 Babysitting, wine/sherry served. Complimentary breakfast and late-afternoon refreshments. **Facilities:** 🗄 🗄 1 rst, guest lounge. **Rates (BB):** $50–$150 S or D; from $135 ste. Extra person $10. Children under 12 stay free. Spec packages avail. Pking: Outdoor, free. Ltd CC.

Resort

≣≣≣ **Colony Harbortown Marina Resort**, 1050 Schooner Dr, Ventura, CA 93001 (Ventura Harbor); tel 805/658-1212 or toll free 800/777-1700; fax 805/658-6347. 2 mi S of downtown Ventura. Seaward exit off US 101; follow Harbor Blvd to Harbortown. 17 acres. Designed by the Frank Lloyd Wright Foundation with fossilized stone throughout, this is the only hotel on the Ventura Marina. **Rooms:** 152 rms, stes, and effic. CI 4pm/CO noon. Nonsmoking rms avail. Bright and airy rooms are decorated in spring colors and bleached wood furniture. Some have harbor views. **Amenities:** 🛋 🗄 🗄 Cable TV w/movies. No A/C. Some units w/fireplaces. **Services:** ✗ 🚐 🗄 🛜 Children's

program, babysitting. **Facilities:** 🗄 🚲 🏊 🗄 🗄 1 rst, 2 bars (1 w/entertainment), whirlpool. Restaurant on the marina. The bar, popular amoung locals, sponsors Tropical Nights, with salsa dance lessons or country dancing. **Rates:** HS May–Aug $79–$89 S or D; from $145 ste; from $79 effic. Extra person $10. Children under 11 stay free. Min stay spec evnts. Lower rates off-season. AP and MAP rates avail. Spec packages avail. Pking: Outdoor, free. Maj CC.

Attractions 🧳

Ventura County Museum of History and Art, 100 E Main St; tel 805/653-0323. The museum's permanent collection of Ventura County historical artifacts is on display in the Huntsinger Gallery; art and other exhibits are housed in the Hoffman Gallery. The Smith Gallery contains George Stuart Historical Figures, relating to famous (and infamous) persons in world history. An outdoor exhibit features an extensive collection of horsedrawn farm implements. Library and archives; museum store. **Open:** Tues–Sun 10am–5pm. Closed some hols. $

Albinger Archaeological Museum, 113 E Main St; tel 805/648-5823. In 1973 the buildings that stood on this site were demolished as part of an urban redevelopment project. Archeological testing suggested the existence of cultural remains beneath the soil, leading to an intensive archeological investigation that uncovered more than 30,000 artifacts in 1974 and 1975. The property was withdrawn from the redevelopment project and designated as the Ventura Mission Historic District in 1975. In 1980 the Albinger Archaeological Museum opened to the public, displaying 3,500 years of regional history.

Within the museum are many artifacts discovered at the site, including bone whistles, milling stones, crucifixes, bottles, and pottery. Artifacts date as far back as 1600 BC, to a race of prehistoric people who came to the Ventura area seasonally over a period of 1,500 years. Also represented are Chumash Indians (1500–1834), the Spanish (1782–1822), the Mexicans (1822–1847), the Americans (1847–present), and the Chinese (1905–1920s). Outside the building are a number of archeological features, including the foundations of the "lost mission church," an ancient earth oven, and the mission water filtration building. **Open:** June–Aug, Wed–Sun 10am–4pm; Sept–May, Wed–Fri 10am–2pm, Sat–Sun 10am–4pm. Closed some hols. Free.

Mission San Buenaventura, 225 E Main St; tel 805/643-4318. This mission was the 9th and last to be founded by Padre Junípero Serra, the moving force behind California's 21 missions. The second mission church, begun in 1792, is still used for masses in Spanish and English. Self-guided tours include the church, museum, and the mission grounds. Gift shop. **Open:** Grounds, daily dawn–dusk; museum and gift shop, Mon–Sat 10am–5pm, Sun 10am–4pm. Closed some hols. Free.

VICTORVILLE

Map page M-3, D3

Motel ⊟

≣≣ **Days Inn Suites**, 14865 Bear Valley Rd, Victorville, CA 92345; tel 619/948-0600 or toll free 800/325-2525; fax 619/956-8645. Exit Bear Valley Rd E exit off I-15. The exterior of this hotel has the look and feel of Santa Fe. Inside it's very modern. Great value. **Rooms:** 29 rms and stes. CI 12:30pm/CO 11am. Nonsmoking rms avail. **Amenities:** ☎ A/C, cable TV w/movies, refrig. Some units w/Jacuzzis. **Services:** ⊠ ⌂ ◁ **Facilities:** ⛲ ⒖ ⅙ Whirlpool, playground, washer/dryer. **Rates (CP):** HS June–Sept $39–$55 S; $45–$65 D; from $39 ste. Extra person $6. Children under 18 stay free. Lower rates off-season. Higher rates for spec evnts/hols. Pking: Outdoor, free. Maj CC.

Restaurants ⑪

Chateau Chang, in Park Centre Shopping Center, 15425 Anacapa Rd, Victorville; tel 619/241-3040. Palmdale Rd exit off I-15. **Chinese/French.** Art deco–style restaurant with burgundy-and-black interior, mirrors, and elevated dining room. The chef melds French and Chinese influences to create unusual and interesting dishes. **FYI:** Reservations recommended. Piano. **Open:** Lunch Mon–Sat 11:30am–2:30pm; dinner Mon–Thurs 5–9:30pm, Fri–Sat 5–10:30pm. Closed some hols. **Prices:** Main courses $10.95–$27.95. Maj CC. ⅙

Marie Callender Restaurant, 12180 Mariposa Rd, Victorville; tel 619/241-6973. Bear Valley Rd E exit off I-15; immediate left on Mariposa Rd. **American.** The quintessential American restaurant, wholesome, bright, and clean. Friendly staff serves such classics as meat loaf, fried chicken, pot roast, and barbecued ribs. There are 35 different kinds of pie. **FYI:** Reservations not accepted. Children's menu. **Open:** Mon–Thurs 6am–10pm, Fri–Sat 6:30am–11pm, Sun 8am–10pm. Closed Dec 25. **Prices:** Main courses $7.95–$10.95. Maj CC. ⚎ ⅙

Richie's Real American Diner, 7th St at Palmdale Rd, Victorville; tel 619/955-1113. **Diner.** With just enough chrome to evoke the 1950s, this classic American diner offers traditional breakfast fare as well as burgers and fries, milk shakes and sundaes, meat loaf and chicken pot pie. **FYI:** Reservations not accepted. Children's menu. Beer and wine only. **Open:** HS June–Sept breakfast daily 6am–1pm; lunch daily 10am–4pm;

dinner Sun–Thurs 4–10pm, Fri–Sat 4–11pm. Reduced hours off-season. Closed Dec 25. **Prices:** Main courses $3.45–$6.95. Maj CC. ⅙

Attraction ▣

Roy Rogers–Dale Evans Museum, 15650 Seneca Rd; tel 619/243-4547. On display are items from the personal and professional lives of the famous couple. Highlights include the Rose Parade Saddle, many hunting trophies, and a gun collection. **Open:** Daily 9am–5pm. Closed some hols. $$

VISALIA

Map page M-2, E3

Hotels ⊟

≣≣≣ **Holiday Inn Plaza Park**, 9000 W Airport Dr, Visalia, CA 93277 (Municipal Airport); tel 209/651-5000 or toll free 800/348-8877, 800/821-1127 in CA; fax 209/651-5014. Calif 983 exit off Calif 99. Nice family hotel near a city park; showplace lobby. **Rooms:** 258 rms and stes. CI 3pm/CO noon. Nonsmoking rms avail. Recently refurbished rooms are attractive and comfortable. **Amenities:** ☎ ⓐ ▣ A/C, cable TV w/movies. **Services:** ⦿ ☎ ⊠ ⌂ ◁ Car-rental desk, babysitting. **Facilities:** ⒡ ⛲ ⒤ⓚ ⅙ 1 rst, 1 bar (w/entertainment), games rm, sauna, whirlpool, washer/dryer. Dancing in the lounge. Mini–convention center. **Rates:** HS Mid-Apr–mid-Sept $79–$109 S; $89–$109 D; from $99 ste. Extra person $10. Children under 17 stay free. Min stay spec evnts. Lower rates off-season. Higher rates for spec evnts/hols. Spec packages avail. Pking: Outdoor, free. Maj CC.

≣≣≣ **Radisson Hotel Visalia**, 300 S Court, Visalia, CA 93291 (Downtown); tel 209/636-1111 or toll free 800/333-3333, 800/734-3144 in CA; fax 209/636-8224. Exit 198E off I-99. This lovely 4-year-old hotel is part of the Visalia Convention Center complex and is within walking distance of historic downtown Visalia. A 35-minute drive from Sequoia National Park, fishing, and other recreation. **Rooms:** 201 rms and stes. Exec-level rms avail. CI 3pm/CO noon. Express checkout avail. Nonsmoking rms avail. Elegantly furnished in art deco style. Several ecologically sensitive "green" suites available. **Amenities:** ☎ ⓐ A/C, satel TV w/movies, refrig, VCR, shoe polisher. All units w/minibars, some w/terraces, 1 w/Jacuzzi. **Services:** ✕ ⌸ ☎ ⊠ ⌂ Car-rental desk, babysitting. **Facilities:** ⒡ ⛲ ⒧⒮⒪ ⅙ 1 rst, 1 bar, whirlpool. **Rates:** $90–

$100 S; $100–$110 D; from $200 ste. Extra person $10. Children under 13 stay free. Min stay HS. Higher rates for spec evnts/hols. Spec packages avail. Pking: Outdoor, free. Maj CC.

Motels

≡≡ Best Western Visalia Inn, 623 W Main St, Visalia, CA 93277; tel 209/732-4561 or toll free 800/528-1234; fax 209/738-0562. Mooney Blvd exit off Calif 198. Older motel in downtown area. Exterior is plain. **Rooms:** 40 rms. CI 2pm/CO 11am. Nonsmoking rms avail. Well kept and nicely decorated. **Amenities:** 📺 🛁 📞 🗞 A/C, cable TV w/movies, refrig. **Services:** 🖐 📞 **Facilities:** 🗄 **Rates (CP):** $54–$60 S; $64–$72 D. Extra person $4. Higher rates for spec evnts/hols. Pking: Outdoor, free. Maj CC.

≡≡ Lamp Liter Inn, 3300 W Mineral King Ave, Visalia, CA 93291; tel 209/732-4511 or toll free 800/662-6692; fax 209/732-1840. County Center St exit off Calif 99. Quiet, landscaped setting. **Rooms:** 100 rms and stes; 4 ctges/villas. Exec-level rms avail. CI 3pm/CO noon. Express checkout avail. Nonsmoking rms avail. **Amenities:** 📺 🛁 A/C, cable TV w/movies, shoe polisher. Some units w/fireplaces. **Services:** ✕ 📞 📠 🖐 **Facilities:** 🗄 🏊 🛁 2 rsts, 1 bar (w/entertainment). **Rates:** $50–$90 S or D; from $72 ste; from $92 ctge/villa. Extra person $10. Children under 18 stay free. Higher rates for spec evnts/hols. Spec packages avail. Pking: Outdoor, free. Maj CC.

Restaurants 🍴

The Depot Restaurant, 207 E Oak St, Visalia; tel 209/732-8611. Central Visalia exit off Calif 198 E; go 3 lights and turn left on Court, then right on Oak. **Californian.** 1890s styling with high-backed banquettes and tables in building constructed in 1897 and remodeled in 1971. Decor a bit worn. Specialties include black pepper steak à la gitano, Yucatan prawns in red jalapeño sauce, sautéed prawn scampi. **FYI:** Reservations recommended. Children's menu. **Open:** Lunch Mon–Sat 11am–2:30pm; dinner Mon–Sat 5–10pm. Closed some hols. **Prices:** Main courses $10.95–$19.95. Maj CC. 🔳 🛁

Michael's on Main, 123 W Main St, Visalia; tel 209/635-2686. Calif 63 N exit off Calif 198; left on Center, left on Locust, right on Main. **Mediterranean.** Intimate restaurant in the historic part of Visalia. Chicken, fish, steak, lamb, and pasta, with many items prepared on the grill. Award-winning cioppino. **FYI:** Reservations recommended. Jazz/piano. **Open:** Lunch Mon–Fri 11am–3:30pm; dinner Mon–Sat 5–11pm, Sun 5–10pm. Closed Dec 25. **Prices:** Main courses $12–$30. Maj CC.

♦ **The Vintage Press**, 216 N Willis St, Visalia; tel 209/733-3033. Central Visalia exit off Calif 198 E. **Californian.** Visalia's most famous restaurant, set in an art nouveau Victorian house with garden dining available. Menu features seafood and local specialties such as antelope and venison. Pastries and breads baked on premises. **FYI:** Reservations recommended. Children's menu. Dress code. **Open:** Lunch Mon–Sat 11:30am–2pm; dinner Mon–Thurs 6–10:30pm, Fri–Sat 6–11pm. Closed Dec 25. **Prices:** Main courses $11.95–$34.95. Maj CC. 🛁

WALNUT CREEK

Map page M-2, D2 (N of Oakland)

Hotels 🏨

≡≡≡ Embassy Suites Hotel, 1345 Treat Blvd, Walnut Creek, CA 94596; tel 510/934-2500 or toll free 800/EMBASSY; fax 510/256-7233. Treat Blvd exit off I-680. Relatively new property with lovely 8-story atrium. Across the street from rapid transit station. **Rooms:** 249 stes. CI 3pm/CO 1pm. Express checkout avail. Nonsmoking rms avail. **Amenities:** 📺 🛁 📞 🗞 A/C, cable TV w/movies, refrig, voice mail. 1 unit w/minibar, 1 w/Jacuzzi. All suites have microwave and wet bars. TV in living room and bedroom. **Services:** ✕ 📞 📠 🖐 🔔 Children's program. Manager's reception 5:30–7:30pm daily, with complimentary hors d'oeuvres and alcoholic and non-alcoholic beverages. Complimentary van service to points within a 5-mile radius. **Facilities:** 🗄 🏋 🛏 🛁 1 rst, 1 bar, sauna, whirlpool, washer/dryer. Free pass to large gym just 1 block away. **Rates (BB):** From $135 ste. Extra person $15. Children under 12 stay free. Spec packages avail. Pking: Indoor, free. Maj CC.

≡≡ Holiday Inn Walnut Creek, 2730 N Main St, Walnut Creek, CA 94596; tel 510/932-3332 or toll free 800/HOLIDAY; fax 510/256-7672. Main St exit off I-680. The small lobby opens to a bar area, where patrons are allowed to smoke. **Rooms:** 147 rms and stes. CI 2pm/CO noon. Express checkout avail. Nonsmoking rms avail. Starting to show some wear, but renovations are in progress. **Amenities:** 📺 🛁 📞 🗞 A/C, cable TV w/movies. Some units w/minibars. **Services:** ✕ 📞 📠 🖐 Pick-up service for pets at nearby pet hotel. Complimentary shuttle to rapid transit station, stores, and business offices, and to nearby fitness center, which guests can use for a fee. **Facilities:** 🗄 🏊 🖥 🛁 1 rst, 1 bar, whirlpool. **Rates:** $77–$100 S or D; from $120 ste. Children under 12 stay free. Spec packages avail. Pking: Indoor/outdoor, free. Maj CC.

Restaurant 🍽️

Spiedini, 101 Ygnacio Valley Rd, Walnut Creek; tel 510/939-2100. **Italian.** Spacious dining room with roomy booths and lots of marble, providing a sleek, Italian look. Fine dishes include several pizzas, fresh pasta, and anything grilled on the huge rotisserie. A beautiful restaurant with professional staff and food to match. **FYI:** Reservations accepted. Dress code. **Open:** Mon–Fri 11:30am–10:30pm, Sat 4:30–10:30pm, Sun 4:30–10pm. Closed some hols. **Prices:** Main courses $7.95–$16.95. Maj CC. 🍱 VP ♿

Attraction 📷

Lindsay Museum, 1931 1st Ave; tel 510/935-1978. The purpose of this natural history museum is to educate the public, especially children, about caring for the environment and living with nature. It is also one of the nation's oldest and largest wildlife rehabilitation centers. Exhibits include more than 40 species of live, non-releasable animals, including hawks, owls, raccoons, and rattlesnakes.

In the Exhibit Hall are 2 large areas where visitors watch the daily feeding, bathing, and exercising of display animals; also displays of natural history objects, aquariums, and an insectarium. A small theater continually shows nature films.

A separate "Especially for Children" room introduces children to "the wildlife in their own backyard," and includes a Petting Circle for interaction with animals. A pet library allows local children to "borrow" hamsters, rabbits, and guinea pigs, for a week at a time. Bookstore and gift shop. **Open:** Sept–June, Wed–Sun 1–5pm; July–Aug, Wed–Sun 11am–5pm. Closed some hols. $

WEED

Map page M-2, A2

See also **Dunsmuir, Mt Shasta**

Motel 🛏️

🈁🈁 **Sis-Q-Inn Motel**, 1825 Shastina Dr, Weed, CA 96094; tel 916/938-4194; fax 916/938-2569. South Weed exit off I-5. Spectacular views of Mt Shasta from many rooms. Many repeat customers. **Rooms:** 22 rms and stes. CI 1pm/CO 11am. Nonsmoking rms avail. **Amenities:** 🔋 ♨ A/C, cable TV. **Services:** ⊃ Facilities: Whirlpool. **Rates (CP):** $36–$41 S; $44–$50 D; from $55 ste. Extra person $5. Pking: Outdoor, free. Maj CC.

WEST HOLLYWOOD

Map page M-3, D2 (Los Angeles)

Hotels 🛏️

🈁🈁🈁🈁 **Bel Age Hotel**, 1020 N San Vincente Blvd, West Hollywood, CA 90069; tel 310/854-1111 or toll free 800/424-4443; fax 310/289-2763. A European-style hotel with period furniture in the lobby and a $5 million art collection displayed throughout the hotel, even in the rooms. **Rooms:** 188 stes. Exec-level rms avail. CI 3pm/CO noon. Express checkout avail. Nonsmoking rms avail. Huge, well-furnished rooms. **Amenities:** 🔋 ♨ 🍴 A/C, cable TV w/movies, refrig, voice mail. All units w/minibars, all w/terraces. **Services:** ⦿ 🗝 VP 🚗 ⊿ ⊃ 🔔 Twice-daily maid svce, car-rental desk, masseur, babysitting. **Facilities:** 🔲 🍴 375 2 rsts (*see also* "Restaurants" below), 2 bars, spa, whirlpool, beauty salon. Rooftop swimming pool with great view. **Rates:** From $175 ste. Extra person $25. Children under 12 stay free. Spec packages avail. Pking: Indoor, $16. Maj CC.

🈁🈁🈁 **Hyatt on Sunset**, 8401 Sunset Blvd, West Hollywood, CA 90069; tel 213/656-1234 or toll free 800/223-1234; fax 213/650-4469. Located just west of the Chateau Marmont, on very busy Sunset Blvd, and just east of major entertainment area. **Rooms:** 262 rms and stes. Exec-level rms avail. CI 3pm/CO noon. Express checkout avail. Nonsmoking rms avail. Large rooms furnished in contemporary style. Penthouse 41 is elegant and loaded with features. **Amenities:** 🔋 ♨ 🍴 A/C, cable TV w/movies, refrig, voice mail, in-rm safe. Some units w/terraces. **Services:** ✕ 🗝 VP 🚗 ⊿ ⊃ Twice-daily maid svce, babysitting. Good security—elevator requires a suite key in order to gain access to each floor. **Facilities:** 🔲 700 🖥️ ♿ 1 rst, 1 bar, games rm, spa, sauna. **Rates:** HS June–Sept $125–$142 S; $152–$168 D; from $189 ste. Extra person $25. Children under 18 stay free. Lower rates off-season. Spec packages avail. Pking: Indoor, $7–$10. Maj CC.

🈁🈁🈁 **Mondrian Hotel De Grande Classe**, 8440 Sunset Blvd, West Hollywood, CA 90069; tel 213/650-8999 or toll free 800/525-8029; fax 213/650-5215. Draws a professional clientele. Also appeals to art lovers, with 2,000 paintings and sculptures by various artists, changed periodically. **Rooms:** 224 stes and effic. CI 3pm/CO noon. Nonsmoking rms avail. Rooms well protected from noise of busy street. Good views of LA on south side of building. Art deco–style furniture. **Amenities:** 🔋 ♨ 🍴 A/C, cable TV w/movies, refrig, VCR. All units w/minibars, some w/terraces. **Services:** ⦿ 🗝 VP 🚗 ⊿ ⊃ 🔔 Twice-daily maid svce, car-rental desk, masseur, babysitting. **Facilities:** 🔲 🍴 120 🖥️ 1 rst, 2 bars (1 w/entertainment), spa, sauna, steam rm, whirlpool. Business facilities modest: 2 computers, no fax or modems. **Rates:** HS Sept–May from $160 ste; from $185 effic. Children under 17 stay free. Lower rates off-season. Spec packages avail. Pking: Indoor, $5–$14. Maj CC.

≡≡≡≡**Sunset Marquis Hotel & Villas**, 1200 N Alta Loma Rd, West Hollywood, CA 90069; tel 310/657-1333 or toll free 800/858-9758; fax 310/652-5300. A bucolic setting complete with rolling lawns, waterfalls, and fish ponds. Ambience is relaxed, rather than glitzy; draws a celebrity clientele ranging from Bruce Springsteen to Julio Iglesias. If you love rock 'n' roll, this place is great. **Rooms:** 106 stes and effic; 12 ctges/villas. Exec-level rms avail. CI 3pm/CO 1pm. Express checkout avail. Nonsmoking rms avail. Accommodations in a born-again apartment building, or in more lavish villas. Furnishings have understated 1940s styling. Closet space in the main building is dazzling. **Amenities:** 🛏 ⚷ ☎ A/C, cable TV w/movies, refrig, VCR, voice mail, in-rm safe, bathrobes. All units w/terraces, some w/fireplaces, some w/Jacuzzis. 4 suites with baby grand pianos. **Services:** 🍴 🔑 VP 🚗 🖂 ↻ Twice-daily maid svce, car-rental desk, masseur, babysitting. Personalized attention is lavished on guests. **Facilities:** 🏠 ⛳ 🎰 🖥 ♿ 2 rsts, 1 bar, games rm, spa, sauna, steam rm, whirlpool, playground. There's a new 48-track recording studio on premises. **Rates:** From $215 ste; from $215 effic; from $450 ctge/villa. Extra person $35. Children under 18 stay free. Spec packages avail. Pking: Indoor, free. Maj CC.

Restaurants 🍽

★ **Astro Burgers**, 7475 Santa Monica Blvd, West Hollywood; tel 213/874-8041. 8 mi mi N of Los Angeles. Santa Monica Blvd W exit off US 101. **Burgers.** This spanking clean, '50s-style fast-service restaurant lined with vintage movie star posters attracts a celebrity clientele. Owned by the 2nd-generation Andrianos family, the diner features an enormous Greek-influenced menu. Specialties include marinated, charbroiled chicken breast sandwiches, Mexican breakfast fare, and hefty cheeseburgers served with giant onion rings or fried zucchini sticks. **FYI:** Reservations not accepted. Children's menu. No liquor license. **Open:** Sun–Thurs 7am–2am, Fri–Sat 7am–3:30am. Closed some hols. **Prices:** Main courses $4–$6.50. No CC. ☎ 🎱 🍴 ♿

Babylon, 616 N Robertson Blvd, West Hollywood; tel 310/289-9743. **Mediterranean.** Middle-eastern themed, with a small patio and baroque touches. Small corner restaurant jumps with celebrity crowds until the wee hours on a high-energy, engaging side street packed with nightclubs and boutiques. The menu features a Mediterranean vegetarian sampler with grape leaves, hummus, tabbouleh, baba ghanouj, and falafel. Entrees include seared rare ahi pepper steak, fillet of salmon on polenta,

paella, and fusilli with smoked chicken. **FYI:** Reservations recommended. Blues/jazz. **Open:** Mon–Thurs 7–11pm, Fri–Sat 7pm–midnight. Closed Dec 25. **Prices:** Main courses $13–$18. Maj CC. ☎ VP ♿

🍷 **Diaghilev**, in Bel Age Hotel, 1020 N San Vicente Blvd, West Hollywood; tel 310/854-1111. **French/Russian.** Original art from Diaghilev's own collection frame the dining room of this elegant Old World hotel. French-Russian-style dining is presided over by a veteran maitre d' as Russian balalaika music entertains guests. The menu continues the theme, with egg shells filled with whipped eggs, chives, and fine caviar; venison shashlik; borscht; leg of duck with honey calvados; and other exotica. **FYI:** Reservations recommended. Piano. **Open:** Tues–Sat 6:30–10:30pm. Closed some hols. **Prices:** Main courses $15–$28. Maj CC. ❤ VP ♿

House of Blues, 8430 Sunset Blvd, West Hollywood; tel 213/650-0476. **Eclectic.** Celebrates American music and racial unity as only Tennessee-bred Isaac Tigret (of Hard Rock Cafe design fame) imagines it. Gaily colored African-American art covers every inch of this massive 3-story center, which includes a family-style restaurant, theater, and gallery. The chef adds international dishes to the basic southern soul-food menu featuring favorites like gumbo, dirty rice, chicken-fried steak, and jambalaya. **FYI:** Reservations recommended. Blues/country music/jazz/rock. **Open:** Daily 11:30am–midnight. Closed Dec 25. **Prices:** Main courses $9.50–$17.95. Maj CC. 🍴 VP ♿

★ **Hugo's**, 8401 Santa Monica Blvd, West Hollywood; tel 213/654-3993. **Californian/Italian.** A favorite, especially among young entertainment industry moguls who gather for power breakfasts of chilaquiles and pumpkin pancakes. The fare leans toward health food (there's even a juice bar), but with a definite southwestern bent. Lunch and dinner menus include a variety of pastas, pizzas, sandwiches, and salads. **FYI:** Reservations accepted. Beer and wine only. **Open:** Daily 7:30am–10:30pm. Closed some hols. **Prices:** Main courses $7–$10. Maj CC. ♿

Le Petit Bistro, 631 N La Cienega Blvd, West Hollywood; tel 310/289-9797. **French/Moroccan.** Moroccan-French owner Robert Lochkar took the best of his experience at the legendary Le St Germain bistro, retaining the salmon walls and huge mirrors and paintings, and updated it with inexpensive dishes and informal seating. Shrimp picante, escargots, cured Norwegian salmon, and eggplant tart with tomato sauce are specialties. **FYI:** Reservations recommended. **Open:** Lunch daily 11:30am–2:30pm; dinner daily 5:30pm–midnight. Closed some hols. **Prices:** Main courses $8–$13. Maj CC. ♿

Nowhere Cafe, 8009 Beverly Blvd, West Hollywood; tel 213/655-8895. **Health/Spa.** Next door to Nowhere Health Food

Market, this sparkling-white cafe features bleached wood floors and changing contemporary art. Chef Romero Herrera's dairy- and sugar-free menu includes both popular and original salads, meatless entrees, and poultry and seafood dishes. Examples are Tuscan-bean griddle cakes with grilled eggplant, and turkey burgers. Some desserts are chocolate mocha toffee mousse and individual deep-dish fruit pies. **FYI:** Reservations recommended. Beer and wine only. **Open:** Lunch daily noon–2:30pm; dinner Sun–Thurs 6–10pm, Fri–Sat 6–10:30pm; brunch Sun 11:30am–3pm. Closed some hols. **Prices:** Main courses $4–$12; PF dinner $25. Maj CC.

♣ **The Palm Restaurant**, 9001 Santa Monica Blvd, West Hollywood; tel 310/550-8811. **American.** This New York–style steak house is known as "the commissary" for show business agents and entertainers. A wall mural has caricatures of celebrity customers. Food is average but pricey. Huge side orders of hash browns and french-fried onions. **FYI:** Reservations accepted. **Open:** Mon–Fri noon–10:30pm, Sat 5–10:30pm, Sun 5–9:30pm. Closed some hols. **Prices:** Main courses $15–$28. Maj CC.

♣ **Spago**, 8795 Sunset Blvd, West Hollywood (Sunset Strip); tel 310/652-4025. **New American/Californian.** A celebrity clientele, prime vantage point overlooking Sunset Strip, and superstar chef Wolfgang Puck all helped put Spago on the map. Famed for designer pizzas from its wood-burning oven, with such toppings as duck sausage, grilled garlic chicken, and sautéed foie gras with sweet and sour plum sauce. **FYI:** Reservations recommended. **Open:** Dinner Mon–Fri 6pm–midnight, Sat–Sun 5:30–11pm. Closed some hols. **Prices:** Main courses $18–$28. Ltd CC.

Tail O the Pup, 329 N San Vicente Blvd, West Hollywood; tel 310/652-4517. **Burgers/Hot dogs.** A family-owned, themed hot dog stand that has been a Hollywood tradition for 3 generations. The parking lot is used for tented parties. Six types of hot dogs, including the Baseball Special, Manhattan, Mexican Olé, Boston Celtic, Red Eye, and the Extreme, with all the trimmings. **FYI:** Reservations not accepted. No liquor license. **Open:** Daily 5am–5:30pm. Closed some hols. **Prices:** Main courses $2.17–$2.75. No CC.

Tommy Tang, 7473 Melrose Ave, West Hollywood; tel 213/651-1810. **Thai/Sushi Bar.** Tommy Tang's breezy, animated, celebrity-filled restaurant helped to make Melrose Ave internationally known. Sophisticated white walls, high ceilings, and a Spanish patio planted with trees and ivy. Progressive Thai cuisine features Tommy Duck, with honey-ginger sauce, Thai black bean soup, wild mushroom risotto with basil, and spicy mint noodles. Sushi bar. **FYI:** Reservations recommended. Beer and wine only.

Open: Mon–Thurs 11:30am–10:30pm, Fri–Sat 11:30am–midnight, Sun 10:30am–1pm. Closed some hols. **Prices:** Main courses $9–$16.95. Maj CC.

ⓢ **Trocadero**, 8280 Sunset Blvd, West Hollywood; tel 213/656-7161. **New American.** Small, art deco dining room, dedicated to the famous '30s club of the same name. Dishes often incorporate unusual fresh fruits and vegetables. Wine suggestions are made at each course. Specialties include butternut squash soup with potatoes and Louisiana chicken. **FYI:** Reservations recommended. Beer and wine only. **Open:** Lunch Mon–Fri 11:30am–2:30pm; dinner daily 6:30pm–1:30am. Closed some hols. **Prices:** Main courses $9–$15. Maj CC.

WESTLAKE VILLAGE
Map page M-3, D2 (S of Thousand Oaks)

Restaurant 🍴

★ **Ritrovo**, in Von's Pavillion–North Ranch, 1125 Lindero Canyon Rd, Westlake Village; tel 818/889-0191. Lindero exit off US 101. **Italian.** A trendy new restaurant in an upscale neighborhood, with a modern, open kitchen and an antipasto bar. Specialties are wood-fired pizza, and fish dishes in various preparations. Dessert features tiramisù. Service can be slow. **FYI:** Reservations accepted. Piano. **Open:** Lunch Mon–Sat 11:30am–2:30pm; dinner Mon–Thurs 5:30–10:30pm, Fri–Sat 5:30–11pm, Sun 5:30–10pm. Closed some hols. **Prices:** Main courses $10.95–$20.75. Maj CC.

WEST LOS ANGELES
Map page M-3, D2 (Los Angeles)

Restaurants 🍴

★ **The Apple Pan**, 10801 W Pico Blvd, West Los Angeles; tel 310/475-3585. **Burgers.** A little white shack with Formica counter and stools—and a favorite of locals for 47 years. The limited menu includes steak, burgers, and apple and pecan pie. **FYI:** Reservations not accepted. No liquor license. **Open:** Tues–Thurs 11am–midnight, Fri–Sat 11am–1am. Closed some hols. **Prices:** Main courses $3–$4.90. No CC.

ⓢ **Café Niel**, 2117 Sawtelle Ave, West Los Angeles; tel 310/477-3359. **French.** A storefront in a strip mall, this eatery serves fine food in a chic, sparse setting. Decor consists of contemporary art on white walls. Try grilled rare tuna, crusty salmon, pork tenderloin, or pepper steak. **FYI:** Reservations recommended. Beer and wine only. **Open:** Lunch Mon–Sat 11:30am–2:30pm; dinner Mon–Thurs 5:30–9pm, Fri–Sat 5:30–10pm, Sun 5:30–9pm. Closed some hols. **Prices:** Main courses $13.95–$17.95. Maj CC. ♥ 🛏 ♿

WILLITS

Map page M-2, B1

Motels 🛏

▬▬ **Baechtel Creek Inn**, 101 Gregory Lane, Willits, CA 95490; tel 707/459-9063 or toll free 800/459-9911; fax 707/459-1522. The best place to stay in Willits. **Rooms:** 46 rms. CI 2pm/CO 11am. Nonsmoking rms avail. Standard, but clean and pleasant. **Amenities:** 🛁 ⚲ A/C, cable TV. **Services:** ⌐ Babysitting. **Facilities:** 🛗 [50] ♿ Sauna. **Rates (CP):** $69–$159 S or D. Extra person $5. Children under 5 stay free. Min stay spec evnts. Spec packages avail. Pking: Outdoor, free. Maj CC.

▬ **Pepperwood Motel**, 452 S Main St, Willits, CA 95490; tel 707/459-2231. Willits exit off US 101. Decent motel. **Rooms:** 21 rms. CI 11am/CO 11am. Nonsmoking rms avail. Ask for a room in back by the creek. **Amenities:** 🛁 A/C, cable TV. **Services:** ⌐ **Facilities:** 🛗 **Rates:** HS June–Sept $32 S; $35 D. Children under 12 stay free. Lower rates off-season. Pking: Outdoor, free. Maj CC.

Restaurant 🍴

⑤ ★ **Tsunami**, 50 S Main St, Willits; tel 707/459-4750. **Japanese/Seafood.** A fine restaurant where the owner, a local fisherman, catches much of what is served. Decor reminiscent of a Japanese country inn, with simple clean lines and a sunny patio. Unique blend of Japanese and international cuisine includes grilled ahi tuna, tasty tempura, chicken yakitori. Free-range chicken, brown rice, and whole grain breads for the health-conscious. Homemade desserts. **FYI:** Reservations recommended. Beer and wine only. **Open:** Mon–Sat 9:30am–8:30pm, Sun 4:30–9pm. Closed some hols. **Prices:** Main courses $8–$15. No CC. 🛏

WILLOWS

Map page M-2, B2

Motels 🛏

▬▬▬ **Best Western Golden Pheasant Inn**, 249 N Humboldt Ave, Willows, CA 95988; tel 916/934-4603 or toll free 800/338-1387; fax 916/934-4275. Willows/Elk Creek/Glenn Rd exit off I-5. Pleasant location near Glenn County Sacramento Bird Refuge. **Rooms:** 104 rms and stes. CI noon/CO noon. Nonsmoking rms avail. **Amenities:** 🛁 ⚲ A/C, cable TV w/movies, refrig, VCR. Some units w/terraces, some w/fireplaces, some w/Jacuzzis. Refrigerators installed upon request. **Services:** ✗ 🚗 ⌐ ⌐ Kennel for pets. **Facilities:** 🛗 [30] 1 rst, 1 bar, washer/dryer. **Rates (CP):** HS June–Sept $49–$55 S; $55–$67 D; from $75 ste. Extra person $4. Children under 12 stay free. Lower rates off-season. Pking: Outdoor, free. Maj CC.

▬ **Cross Roads West Inn**, 452 N Humboldt Ave, Willows, CA 95988; tel 916/934-7026 or toll free 800/814-6301. Willows–Elk Creek–Glenn Rd exit off I-5. Clean, simple lodging. **Rooms:** 41 rms. CI 11am/CO 11am. Nonsmoking rms avail. **Amenities:** 🛁 A/C, cable TV. **Services:** ⌐ **Facilities:** 🛗 **Rates:** HS Mar–Dec $28–$35 S; $38–$44 D. Extra person $6. Children under 5 stay free. Lower rates off-season. Pking: Outdoor, free. Maj CC. Guests 62 and over get 5% off.

Attraction

Sacramento National Wildlife Refuge; tel 916/934-2801. Located just south of Willows via Calif 99 W, this refuge is part of the Sacramento National Wildlife Refuge Complex, which also includes the Colusa, Delevan, and Sutter refuges, totaling about 23,000 acres of northern California uplands and wetlands. The region is an important wintering area for the millions of migrating waterfowl who travel along the Pacific Flyway.

Over 300 species of birds and mammals, both resident and migratory, inhabit the refuges at various times throughout the year. Trails and auto tour routes provide opportunities for wildlife observation. Hunting is permitted Oct–Jan (contact the California Dept of Fish and Game for current dates, regulations, and other information). **Open:** Daily sunrise–sunset. Free.

WOODLAND HILLS

Map page M-3, D2 (N of Santa Monica)

Hotels 🏨

≡≡≡ Holiday Inn Woodland Hills, 21101 Ventura Blvd, Woodland Hills, CA 91364; tel 818/883-6110 or toll free 800/HOLIDAY; fax 818/340-6550. Desoto exit off US 101; right on Ventura Blvd. An older property, toward the low end of the quality scale for this chain. Close to shops and stores. **Rooms:** 126 rms. Exec-level rms avail. CI 3pm/CO noon. Nonsmoking rms avail. **Amenities:** 🛁 🔥 📺 🍽 A/C, cable TV w/movies. **Services:** ✕ 🛎 🚗 Car-rental desk, children's program, babysitting. **Facilities:** 🏊 ⛳ 🏋 ⛓ 1 rst, 1 bar, playground, washer/dryer. **Rates (BB):** $69–$92 S or D. Extra person $8. Children under 17 stay free. Higher rates for spec evnts/hols. Spec packages avail. Pking: Outdoor, free. Maj CC.

≡≡≡ Warner Center Hilton & Towers, 6360 Canoga Ave, Woodland Hills, CA 91367; tel 818/595-1000 or toll free 800/922-2400; fax 818/595-1090. A perfect business hotel. No landscaping except for trees, but in keeping with the surrounding Warner business center. One of the best hotels in the area. **Rooms:** 318 rms and stes. Exec-level rms avail. CI 3pm/CO noon. Express checkout avail. Nonsmoking rms avail. Sufficiently large for business travelers, with adequate desks and lighting. **Amenities:** 🛁 🔥 A/C, cable TV w/movies, stereo/tape player, voice mail. All units w/minibars, some w/terraces, some w/Jacuzzis. **Services:** ✕ 🍴 🅥🅟 🛎 🚗 🛍 Twice-daily maid svce, car-rental desk, babysitting. Secretarial, notary, and fax services on premises. **Facilities:** 🏊 ⛳ 🏋 ⛓ 1 rst, 2 bars, spa, whirlpool. The attractive Trillium Health Club next door is available to guests for a small charge. **Rates:** $100–$130 S or D; from $650 ste. Children under 18 stay free. Pking: Indoor/outdoor, free. Maj CC.

Motel

≡≡ Best Western Aku Aku Motor Inn, 21830 Ventura Blvd, Woodland Hills, CA 91364; tel 818/340-1000 or toll free 800/528-1234; fax 818/340-1020. A typical, low-budget motel with a nicely done lobby. **Rooms:** 69 rms and effic. CI 2pm/CO 11am. Nonsmoking rms avail. Adequate, with blackout drapes and soundproofing to keep out the noise of Ventura Blvd. **Amenities:** 🛁 A/C, satel TV w/movies, refrig. Some units w/terraces. **Services:** 🛎 🚗 Twice-daily maid svce. Coffee available all day. Complimentary continental breakfast. **Facilities:** 🏊 ⛓ Whirlpool. No elevator to 2nd floor. **Rates (CP):** $49–$54 S; $53–$63 D; from $62 effic. Extra person $5. Children under 12 stay free. Pking: Outdoor, free. Maj CC.

Restaurants 🍽

La Paz, 21040 Victory Blvd, Woodland Hills; tel 818/883-4761. **Mexican/Seafood.** Despite an inauspicious location in a strip mall, nonexistent decor, and a lack of windows, the food in this family-run restaurant is excellent. Patrons praise Maria's paella Ole!—a treasure hunt of lobster, shrimp, clams, and crab legs. Other items are octopus enchiladas and shrimp tacos plus conch and abalone appetizers. **FYI:** Reservations recommended. **Open:** Sun–Thurs 11am–9pm, Fri–Sat 11am–10pm. Closed some hols. **Prices:** Main courses $9.95–$19.95. Ltd CC. 🍴 ⛓

Milano's Italian Kitchen, 21550 Oxnard St, Woodland Hills; tel 818/340-8400. **Northern Italian.** A bright, airy eatery with crisp, modern decor. Attracts a big lunch crowd with well-priced food and a pleasant, low-key atmosphere. Features items cooked over a wood fire, such as pizza, grilled mushrooms, Italian sausage, and barbecued chicken. Also at: 525 North Brand St, Glendale (818/244-1150); 1056 Westwood Blvd, Los Angeles (310/443-5401). **FYI:** Reservations accepted. **Open:** Mon–Thurs 11am–10pm, Fri–Sat 11am–11pm, Sun 3–10pm. Closed some hols. **Prices:** Main courses $5.95–$9.95. Maj CC. 🍽 🍴 ⛓

★ The Seashell Restaurant, 19723 Ventura Blvd, Woodland Hills; tel 818/884-6500. **Continental/Seafood.** Skylights give this place the feel of a patio. Upholstered booths and carved wood chairs afford an old-fashioned ambience. Specialties include Maryland crab cakes, poached fresh salmon, and seafood ravioli. **FYI:** Reservations recommended. **Open:** Lunch Mon–Fri 11:30am–2pm; dinner Mon–Sat 5:30–10pm, Sun 5:30–9:30pm. Closed some hols. **Prices:** Main courses $16.50–$28.50. Maj CC. ♥ ⛓

YERMO

Map page M-3, D3

Attraction 💼

Calico Ghost Town, Ghost Town Rd; tel 619/254-2122. In its heyday, the town of Calico boasted 22 saloons, a population of about 4,000, and the richest silver strike in California history. The Silver King Mine was found by 2 prospectors in 1881. Soon thereafter, hundreds of miners arrived and the new town was founded. In a little over a decade, $86 million in silver ore and $9 million in borax had been removed from the area. When silver prices declined in 1896, most of the miners moved on to more lucrative diggings.

In 1950 the site was purchased by the Knott family and completely restored. It is now operated by San Bernardino

County. Mine tour; railroad excursion; playhouse. Camping area nearby. **Open:** Daily 7am–dusk, shops and attractions 9am–5pm. Closed Dec 25. $$

YOSEMITE NATIONAL PARK

Map page M-2, D3

See also **El Portal, Fish Camp**

Hotels 🏨

The Ahwahnee, Yosemite Valley, Yosemite National Park, CA 95389; tel 209/252-4848. Built in 1927, a larger-than-life castle embellished with massive pillars and polished sugarpine rafters and fireplaces tall enough to stand in. The stony facade has all the flinty grandeur of Mt Rushmore. Unrated. **Rooms:** 99 rms and stes; 25 ctges/villas. CI 5pm/CO noon. Nonsmoking rms avail. Hotel rooms have been recently refurbished. Try to reserve one of the cottages, which cost the same as rooms in the main hotel but are more spacious. **Amenities:** 🛅 🍸 📺 A/C, satel TV, refrig. Some units w/fireplaces, 1 w/Jacuzzi. **Services:** ✕ 🔑 🛅 🛎 Babysitting. **Facilities:** 🛅 🛅 🛅 1 rst, 1 bar (w/entertainment). "Badger Pups" ski program for kids in the winter. **Rates:** HS Apr–Oct $201–$208 S or D; from $400 ste. Children under 12 stay free. Lower rates off-season. Pking: Outdoor, free. Maj CC.

Wawona Hotel, Calif 41, Yosemite National Park, CA 95389; tel 209/252-4848. 20 mi N of Oakhurst. Built in 1879, the Victorian-style main building brims with offbeat charm. Overlooking lawns, a fountain thick with lily pads, and a 9-hole golf course, the 2-story, white-frame buildings are surrounded by porches furnished with wicker chairs. **Rooms:** 104 rms. CI 4pm/CO 11am. Nonsmoking rms avail. 54 rooms have shared bath. Cramped and old—disappointing compared with the public space. Many accommodations have claw-foot bathtubs and lack showers. **Amenities:** No A/C, phone, or TV. **Services:** 🛎 Babysitting. **Facilities:** 🛅 🛅 🛅 🛅 🛅 🛅 🛅 2 rsts, 1 bar (w/entertainment), lawn games. Golf shop, hiking nearby. **Rates:** HS Apr–Oct $63–$86 S or D. Extra person $10. Children under 12 stay free. Lower rates off-season. Spec packages avail. Pking: Outdoor, free. Ltd CC. Open weekends only in the off-season.

Lodges

Curry Village, Yosemite Valley, Yosemite National Park, CA 95389; tel 209/252-4848. Nestled in the trees on the valley floor; simple and quaint. **Rooms:** 600 rms. CI 2pm/CO 11am. Nonsmoking rms avail. Very basic accommodations—cabins (many with bath) and tent cabins. Separate central showerhouse facilities available. There is also a limited number of hotel rooms with private bath, including one suite. **Amenities:** No A/C, phone, or TV. **Services:** 🛎 Children's program. **Facilities:** 🛅 🚲 🏊 🏊 🛅 3 rsts, 1 bar, lifeguard. Raft rentals next door. **Rates:** HS Apr–Oct $35–$77 S or D. Extra person $10. Children under 12 stay free. Lower rates off-season. Spec packages avail. Pking: Outdoor, free. Maj CC.

Tuolumne Meadows Lodge, Tioga Pass Rd, Yosemite National Park, CA 95389; tel 209/252-4848. 30 mi W of Lee Vining. 60 mi E of Yosemite Valley on Calif 120. A jump-off point for High Sierra vacations. Tent cabins are very basic, but you get a bed and access to a hot shower. **Rooms:** 69 ctges/villas. CI 3pm/CO 11am. No electricity, only candles and wood stoves. Minimal furniture. Hot shower in public bathhouse. **Amenities:** No A/C, phone, or TV. **Facilities:** 🏊 🏊 🛅 1 rst. **Rates:** HS Mem Day–Labor Day from $39 ctge/villa. Extra person $6. Lower rates off-season. Pking: Outdoor, free. Ltd CC. Accommodations often book up a year in advance.

Yosemite Lodge, Calif 41/140, Yosemite National Park, CA 95389; tel 209/252-4848. Top advantage is the location—right in the heart of the valley across from Yosemite Falls. The wood-frame lodge is basic but appealing, with a comfortable, family feel. The best accommodations for the money on the valley floor. **Rooms:** 496 rms. CI 2pm/CO 11am. Nonsmoking rms avail. Motel-type rooms or cabins; some share bath or use separate central bathhouse. **Amenities:** 🛅 No A/C or TV. **Services:** 🛎 Friendly staff. **Facilities:** 🛅 🚲 🛅 🏊 🏊 🛅 3 rsts, 1 bar, lifeguard, day-care ctr, washer/dryer. Huge outdoor swimming pool. Rafts available for rent. **Rates:** HS Apr–Oct $50–$90 S or D. Children under 12 stay free. Lower rates off-season. Pking: Outdoor, free. Maj CC.

Attractions 🎒

Yosemite National Park. Typically described as breathtaking, spectacular, and awe-inspiring, the Yosemite Valley evolved when glaciers moved through the canyon, which had been created by the Merced River during repeated geological rises of the Sierras. When these glaciers began to melt, the moraine (accumulated earth and stones deposited by a glacier) dammed part of the Merced River to form Lake Yosemite in the new valley. Eventually, sediment filled the lake, thus accounting for the flat floor of Yosemite Valley. The same process, but on a much smaller scale, is even now occuring with Mirror Lake at the base of Half Dome.

The Native American Ahwahneechees had been living in the valley for several thousand years before they first encountered Europeans in the middle of the 19th century. Members of the Joseph Reddeford Walker party were probably the first "foreigners" to see Yosemite Valley when they crossed from the east side of the Sierras in 1833. Later intrusions resulted in indiscriminate abuses of the environment. To forestall any commercial exploitation of the valley, President Abraham Lincoln granted Yosemite Valley and the Mariposa Grove of giant sequoias to California as a public trust. Federal legislation created Yosemite National Park in 1890.

Today, Yosemite Valley is, as it has been for thousands of years, a glacier-carved canyon with sheer walls of granite rising thousands of feet from the valley floor. It remains a sensual blend of open meadows, wildflowers, and woodlands with ponderosa pine, incense cedar, and Douglas fir. All kinds of wildlife, from monarch butterflies and 223 species of birds to black bears and mule deer flourish in this protected environment.

A wide variety of sports and recreational activities are available at the park. Some of these include: **bicycling** on the many trails geared to cyclists or **horseback riding** on 30 miles of bridle trails in the valley. Bikes can be rented at Yosemite Lodge and Curry Village; stable facilities are located near Curry Village (summer only).

Hikers can traverse over 700 miles of trails that cover a diverse terrain marked by jagged mountains and rolling meadows. A wilderness permit is required for backcountry trails; these are available at any of the 5 permit stations in the park or by writing to the Wilderness Office, PO Box 577, Yosemite National Park, CA 95389.

With vertical granite walls surrounding two-thirds of the valley, Yosemite is considered by experts to be one of the finest **climbing** areas in the world. The Yosemite Mountaineering School at Curry Village has classes for beginning, intermediate, and advanced climbers.

Camping at Yosemite is available at 300 year-round sites scattered over 17 different campgrounds. From June–Sept 15 camping permits are limited to 7 days in the valley and 14 days in the rest of the park; during the rest of the year permits are granted for up to 30 days. Many of the campgrounds are located in the 7 square miles that make up Yosemite Valley, the area's primary focal point. Some of the park's most famous features are nearby, including Yosemite Falls, Mirror Lake, Half Dome, and El Capitan.

For more information, contact Visitor Information (209/372-0200 or 372-0265), Yosemite National Park, PO Box 577, Yosemite National Park, CA 95389.

Yosemite Visitor Center. In addition to informative audiovisual programs and other exhibits relating to park history and activities, the Visitor Center can recommend tours of Yosemite's 216 miles of paved roads and point visitors toward such scenic points as the sequoia groves, granite summits, and waterfall bases. Dozens of daily activities may include lectures on photography, a ranger-led fireside discussion on bears, a guided luncheon hike to a waterfall, a geological history tour, or a puppet show with an environmental theme. There are fewer activities in the off-season. **Open:** Apr–May, daily 9am–6pm; June–Aug, daily 8am–8pm; Sept–Oct, daily 8am–6pm; Nov–Mar, daily 9am–5pm.

Tuolumne Meadows. At an elevation of 8,600 feet, Tuolumne Meadows is the largest alpine meadow in the High Sierras and a gateway to the High Country. Closed in winter, it's 55 miles from the valley by way of highly scenic Big Oak Flat and Tioga Roads. A walk through this natural alpine garden makes a delightful day's excursion. In summer the park operates a large campground here, with a full-scale naturalist program.

Happy Isles Nature Center. This nature center is another gateway to the High Country, with trailheads for the John Muir Trail and for Vernal and Nevada falls (the Mist Trail). Accessible by shuttle bus, the center can provide information about hiking to Nevada Falls and Mirror Lake.

Mariposa Grove. The largest of Yosemite's 3 groves of giant sequoias, Mariposa Grove has hundreds of trees, more than 200 of which measure 10 feet or more in diameter. Among them is the **Grizzly Giant,** more than 34 feet in diameter at its base and 209 feet tall. Private vehicles can drive to the entrance of the grove, beyond which visitors may hike or board a free shuttle bus. Not to be confused with the town of Mariposa, the grove is 35 miles south of the valley.

Glacier Point. Offering a sweeping 180-degree panorama of the High Sierras and a breathtaking view from 3,200 feet above the valley, Glacier Point looks out over Nevada and Vernal falls, the Merced River, and the snow-covered Sierra peaks of Yosemite's backcountry. The approach from the Badger Pass intersection (closed in winter) winds through verdant red-fir and pine forest and meadow. Many fine trails lead back down to the valley floor.

Badger Pass Ski Area. Badger Pass Ski Area, located 23 miles outside the valley, opened in 1935, making it the oldest ski resort in California. The terrain is mostly geared to intermediate-level skiiers, with about 35% of the trails marked for beginners and 15% for experts. Instructors offer beginner and refresher lessons, as well as lessons for children. Facilities include a triple chairlift, 3 double chairlifts, and a rope tow for beginners. The slopes are open November to Easter (weather permitting).

Yosemite also encompasses 90 miles of **cross-country ski-ing trails,** 22 miles of which are machine-groomed track, set several times weekly from Badger Pass to Glacier Point. Skiiers can stay overnight at the Glacier Point Ski Hut or at the Ostrander Lake Ski Hut. For further information contact Badger Pass Ski Area, Yosemite National Park, CA 95389 (tel 209/372-1330 or call the Badger Pass Snow Phone, 209/372-1338).

YOUNTVILLE

Map page M-2, C2 (N of Napa)

Hotels 🖼

≣≣≣ **Napa Valley Lodge**, 2230 Madison St, Yountville, CA 94599; tel 707/944-2468 or toll free 800/368-2468; fax 707/944-9362. Yountville exit off Calif 29; go east, then left on Washington St. **Rooms:** 55 rms and stes. CI 3pm/CO noon. Nonsmoking rms avail. Spacious and comfortable. **Amenities:** 🛋 🐾 🖵 🍴 A/C, cable TV w/movies, refrig, voice mail. All units w/minibars, all w/terraces, some w/fireplaces. **Services:** 🔑 🚐 🛎 🕭 Car-rental desk, masseur, babysitting. Afternoon tea, plus wine tasting in the evening. **Facilities:** 🚶 ⛳ 🎱 🖵 & Sauna, whirlpool. Park across the street has a children's playground. **Rates (BB):** HS May–Nov $132–$152 S or D; from $155 ste. Extra person $10. Children under 12 stay free. Min stay HS and wknds. Lower rates off-season. Higher rates for spec evnts/hols. Spec packages avail. Pking: Outdoor, free. Maj CC. Golf and Romance packages available.

≣≣≣ **Vintage Inn**, 6541 Washington St, Yountville, CA 94599; tel 707/944-1112 or toll free 800/9-VALLEY, 800/351-1133 in CA; fax 707/944-1617. Yountville exit off Calif 29; go east, then left on Washington St. Hotel services are offered in an inn-like setting, with attractive gardens and separate units. Located within walking distance of shops and restaurants. Excellent for small business groups. **Rooms:** 80 rms and stes; 4 ctges/villas. CI 4pm/CO noon. Nonsmoking rms avail. Spacious, well-maintained rooms have quality furniture. **Amenities:** 🛋 🐾 🖵 🍴 A/C, cable TV w/movies, refrig, voice mail, bathrobes. All units w/terraces, all w/fireplaces, all w/Jacuzzis. **Services:** ✕ 🔑 🚐 🕭 🕭 Twice-daily maid svce, babysitting. Expanded continental breakfast included in rate. Limo service for touring available. **Facilities:** 🚶 🚲 🍴2 🎱 & 1 rst, 1 bar, whirlpool. 60-foot lap pool. **Rates (BB):** HS Apr–Sept $124–$174 S; $134–$184 D; from $184 ste; from $174 ctge/villa. Extra person $25. Min stay HS and wknds. Lower rates off-season. Spec packages avail. Pking: Outdoor, free. Maj CC.

Restaurants 🍴

★ **The Diner**, 6476 Washington St, Yountville; tel 707/944-2626. Yountville exit off Calif 29; E to Washington St. **Mexican/American.** An authentic diner in what was once the town's Greyhound bus depot, complete with the original counter. Crowds flock in for the hefty portions of comfort food. Features freshly baked breads and homemade desserts. In addition to great breakfasts, they offer burgers, roast chicken, and Mexican specialties such as quesadillas and carne barbacoa. **FYI:** Reservations not accepted. Children's menu. Beer and wine only. **Open:** Breakfast Tues–Sun 8am–3pm; lunch Tues–Sun 11am–3pm; dinner Tues–Sun 5:30–9pm. Closed some hols; Dec 15–25. **Prices:** Main courses $7.95–$12.50. No CC. 🎦 💟 &

♦ **Domaine Chandon**, in Domaine Chandon Winery, California Dr, Yountville; tel 707/944-2892. Yountville exit off Calif 29; enter property on west side of highway. **Californian/French.** Open, light, and airy, with large windows looking out to gardens and the vineyards beyond. Known for elegant dining, with selections such as venison tournedos, grilled salmon wrapped in pancetta, and roast rack of lamb with goat-cheese potato gratin. Outdoor terrace is open for lunch in nice weather. **FYI:** Reservations recommended. Jacket required. Beer and wine only. **Open:** HS May–Nov lunch daily 11:30am–2:30pm; dinner Wed–Sun 6–9:30pm. Reduced hours off-season. Closed some hols; 1st 2 weeks in Jan. **Prices:** Main courses $24–$28. Maj CC. 💟 🚹 &

♦ **French Laundry**, 6640 Washington St, Yountville; tel 707/944-2380. Yountville exit off Calif 29; at corner of Washington and Creek Sts. **New American/French.** Acclaimed chef/owner Thomas Keller is now at one of the valley's most romantic restaurants—a stone structure bowered in flowers and surrounded by brick walkways. His menus reinterpret classic cooking, balancing flavors and textures in dishes such as pan-sautéed California squab and breast of veal with glazed garlic. **FYI:** Reservations recommended. Beer and wine only. **Open:** Tues–Sun 5:30–10pm. Closed some hols. **Prices:** PF dinner $38–$46. Maj CC. 💟

★ **Mustards Grill**, 7399 St Helena Hwy, Yountville; tel 707/944-2424. **New American.** Terrific food at extremely reasonable prices in a lively California-style bistro accented by black-and-white marble floors, brown wainscoting, and appealing original art. Choices might include yellowtail jack with Dijon crème fraîche, or grilled Mongolian pork chop with mashed potatoes. The wine list is spectacular, and moderately priced. **FYI:** Reservations recommended. Children's menu. **Open:** Daily 11:30am–10pm. Closed some hols. **Prices:** Main courses $10.95–$15.90. Ltd CC. &

Piatti, 6480 Washington St, Yountville; tel 707/944-2070. Yountville exit off Calif 29; E to Washington St. **Californian/ Italian.** This comfortable, country-style restaurant has French doors opening onto a flower-filled courtyard. Herbed olive oil on the tables, rustic wood chairs, and stucco walls painted with food-related designs establish a Mediterranean mood. Open kitchen with wood-burning stove. Ravioli filled with veal and truffles, homemade Italian sausages, imaginative pizzas. **FYI:** Reservations recommended. Children's menu. **Open:** HS June–Nov Sun–Thurs 11:30am–10pm, Fri–Sat 11:30am–11pm. Reduced hours off-season. Closed some hols. **Prices:** Main courses $7.95–$16.95. Maj CC. 🌑 🍽 ♿

Attraction 💼

Domaine Chandon, California Dr; tel 707/944-2280. Free guided tours illustrate the making of sparkling wines. A small gallery in the visitor center houses artifacts depicting the history of champagne. The restaurant here (*see also* "Restaurants" above) is one of the finest in the valley. Wines are sold by the bottle or glass, and are accompanied by hors d'oeuvres. **Open:** Nov–Apr, Wed–Sun 11am–6pm; May–Oct, daily 11am–5pm. Free.

YREKA

Map page M-2, A2

Motels 🛏

📶📶 **Klamath Motor Lodge**, 1111 S Main St, Yreka, CA 96097; tel 916/842-2751. Central Yreka exit off I-5; ¾ mi S. Family-run business since 1962. Many repeat customers. **Rooms:** 28 rms and stes. CI 2pm/CO 11am. Nonsmoking rms avail. **Amenities:** 📶 🛁 📺 A/C, cable TV w/movies, refrig. **Services:** 🍴 **Facilities:** 🏋 **Rates:** HS June–Sept $36–$38 S; $40–$44 D; from $60 ste. Extra person $3. Lower rates off-season. Pking: Outdoor, free. Maj CC.

📶 **Thunderbird Lodge**, 526 S Main St, Yreka, CA 96097; tel 916/842-4404 or toll free 800/554-4339; fax 916/842-4404. Central Yreka exit from I-5; ¼ mi S. Property has been upgraded by new owners. **Rooms:** 44 rms. CI 11:30am/CO 11:30am. Nonsmoking rms avail. **Amenities:** 📶 📺 A/C, cable TV w/movies. **Services:** 🚐 🖨 🍴 🧺 Babysitting. **Facilities:** 🏋 **Rates:** HS June–Sept $32–$37 S; $35–$41 D. Extra person $3. Lower rates off-season. Pking: Outdoor, free. Maj CC.

Attractions 💼

Siskiyou County Museum, 910 S Main St; tel 916/842-3836. Exhibits in this museum interpret the history of Siskiyou County from prehistoric times, through the Gold Rush era, and into the present. Topics include local Native American cultures, fur trapping, mining, settlement, lumbering, agriculture, and 20th-century themes. The research library contains extensive collections of photographs, manuscripts, newspapers, and other material available for public use. Gift shop.

On the grounds is a 2½-acre **Outdoor Museum,** open in summer only, which includes a pioneer cabin, miner's cabin, blacksmith's shop, a church, and an operating general store. **Open:** Tues–Sat 9am–5pm. Closed some hols. $

Yreka Western Railroad, 300 E Miner St; tel 916/842-4146. The Blue Goose Excursion train departs from Yreka Depot on a 3-hour tour through the scenic Shasta Valley. The 100-year-old historic short line railroad crosses the Shasta River, provides scenic views of 14,162-foot Mount Shasta, and crosses through cattle ranch lands first established in the 1850s. The train makes a 1-hour stop at the historic cattle town of Montague, where riders may disembark and explore the town before making the return trip to Yreka. **Open:** Mid-June–Labor Day, Wed–Sun; May–mid-June and Sept–Oct, Sat–Sun. Departures at 10am. $$$

YUCCA VALLEY

Map page M-3, D3 (N of Palm Springs)

Inn 🛏

📶📶 **Oasis of Eden Inn & Suites**, 56377 Twentynine Palms Hwy, Yucca Valley, CA 92284; tel 619/365-6321; fax 619/365-9592. Calif 62 exit off I-10. Property features a small garden and hand-painted murals outdoors. **Rooms:** 40 rms, stes, and effic. CI 2pm/CO 11am. Guests can stay in one of the theme accommodations, including the Orient, Ancient Rome, the Deep South, Art Deco, and Russia rooms. **Amenities:** 📶 A/C, cable TV w/movies, shoe polisher. Some units w/terraces, some w/Jacuzzis. **Services:** 🍴 🧺 Babysitting. **Facilities:** 🏋 ♿ Whirlpool, guest lounge. **Rates (CP):** HS Feb–June $45–$65 S or D; from $70 ste; from $72 effic. Extra person $5. Lower rates off-season. Higher rates for spec evnts/hols. Spec packages avail. Pking: Outdoor, free. Ltd CC.

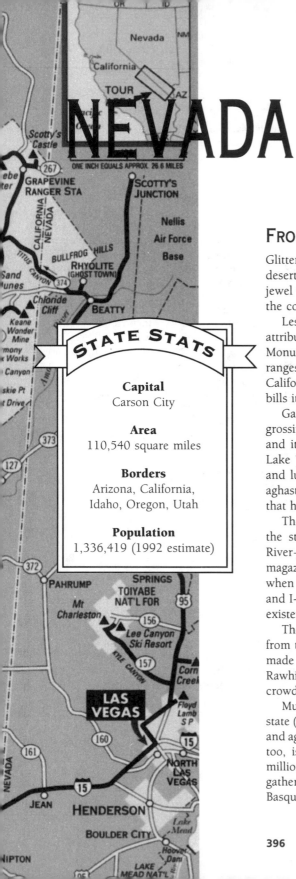

NEVADA

FROM LADY LUCK TO MOTHER NATURE

Glittering hotel casinos and hauntingly beautiful ghost towns, parched deserts strewn with bleached bones, and Lake Tahoe, a lonely mountain jewel whose azure waters are turned to gold by the setting sun. These are the contrasting images of an appealing state that begs discovery.

Less celebrated in guidebooks than California, Nevada shares many attributes with its larger neighbor. Lake Tahoe and Death Valley National Monument straddle their common border, while California's mountain ranges create the rain shadow that dictates Nevada's dry climate. And Californians are irresistibly drawn to Las Vegas and Reno, the town that bills itself "The Biggest Little City in the World."

Gambling is Nevada's biggest attraction and its biggest industry, grossing over $1 billion a year. The 2 main nerve centers for this activity and its accompanying distractions are Las Vegas–Laughlin and Reno–Lake Tahoe: dizzying kaleidoscopes of neon lights, dazzling marquees, and luxury hotels. The Mormons who first settled Las Vegas would be aghast at the bare-skinned cabaret acts and perpetual-motion gambling that has been going on since Nevada legalized gaming in 1931.

The tinsel trimmings of Las Vegas, Reno, Lake Tahoe, and Laughlin—the state's fastest growing resort area on the banks of the Colorado River—have almost eclipsed another Nevada. Nev 50, designated by *Life* magazine as the "loneliest road in America," provides a sense of the days when covered wagons battled their way across the sun-baked region; it, and I-80–US 40, gives access to rugged canyons and ghost towns whose existence can hardly be imagined from the road.

Though hundreds of 19th-century mining towns have all but vanished from the Nevada landscape, America's nostalgia for things historical has made those that remain—such as Rhyolite, Goldfield, Hamilton, and Rawhide—regular stops for caravans of tourists. When winter returns the crowds drift away, leaving the ghostly towns to their few inhabitants.

Much about Nevada belies its sere, stark image. America's 7th-largest state (but 47th in population) even produces wines in the Pahrump Valley, and agriculture flourishes where irrigation has been introduced. Ranching, too, is a mainstay of the economy—sheep and cattle graze some 60 million acres. The annual National Basque Festival, the West's largest gathering of Basque-Americans, attests to the enduring influence of the Basque shepherds who settled the rangelands during the last century.

396

At the western edge of the state, the shoulders of the Sierra Nevada are clad in emerald forest and in winter by a thick pelt of snow—a far cry from the furnace deserts of southeast Nevada. Glassy blue Lake Tahoe has no difficulty living up to its reputation as a skier's paradise. In the spring the snow melts and Tahoe becomes a perfect place for boating, hiking, mountain biking, windsurfing, and merely relaxing. Carson City, the gingerbread-trimmed state capital in the lee of the Sierra Nevada, also provides myriad opportunities for year-round entertainment.

A BRIEF HISTORY

THE NEW FRONTIER The Nevada region was *terra incognita*—unknown land—to all but the Paiute, Washoe, and Shoshone Indians until well into the 19th century. Only a Spanish priest, Father Francisco Garces, and a handful of brave adventurers and fur traders had entered this forbidding territory during its term as a Spanish, then Mexican possession. Explorer John Fremont, whose expeditions in 1843 and 1845 were led by legendary scout Kit Carson, made the first official report of the region, which was then under the Mexican flag. The report came out in 1848, the same year the Treaty of Guadalupe Hidalgo made Nevada a US possession.

The first permanent non-Indian settlement—Genoa, a Mormon trading post in the Carson Valley—was established in 1850. In 1855, the Mormons also established a mission fort at a lonesome outpost known as "the meadows"—Las Vegas. However, the Mormon influence was short-lived: In 1857, when relations with the federal government grew strained, Brigham Young, head of the Mormon church, pulled his followers back to Salt Lake City.

Hardy pioneers were already passing through Nevada in growing numbers en route to the California gold fields. Today I-80–US 40 marks the route they traveled through a bleak landscape of mountains and deserts along the 500-mile California Trail.

BOOM OR BUST In 1850 gold was discovered along the Carson River—the first hint that Nevada was itself a mineral-rich state. Just how rich did not become apparent until 1859 and the discovery of the Comstock Lode, one of the most fabulous finds in history. The strike spawned Nevada's first mining boom, a human migration that nearly rivaled the California Gold Rush. The Comstock produced $1 billion worth of silver and gold, enriching the US Treasury during the Civil War and giving Nevada territorial status in March 1861. Nevada became the Union's 36th state on October 31, 1864.

Mining towns sprouted overnight, including Virginia City, which briefly bloomed as the West's 2nd-largest city. Samuel Clemens, who worked as a miner before finding his fortune as a writer with the pen name Mark Twain, wrote that it "was no place for a Presbyterian and I did not remain one very long."

A decade later, bust followed boom. Then in the 1870s, a second boom—the "Big Bonanza"—made millionaires who added grandiose mansions to the scene. Reno and Carson City are still studded with the stately Victorian homes of mining tycoons.

When the boom ended in the 1880s, Nevada's population dwindled. At the turn of the century, another gold and silver mining strike provided a third lease on life before it, too, collapsed.

> ### ≈§ *Fun Facts* ﴾
>
> • *Las Vegas—"sin city"—has more churches per capita than any other city.*
>
> • *Northern Nevada's Highway 50, which runs from Ely in the east to Fernley in the west, was chosen as the "Loneliest Road in America" by* Life *magazine.*
>
> • *Nevada is the driest of the 50 states, measuring an average of only 9 inches of rainfall annually.*
>
> • *There is enough water in Lake Tahoe to cover the state of California at a depth of 35.5 centimeters.*
>
> • *The stage in the Ziegfeld Room in Reno is reportedly the largest in the world—176 feet long. It has 3 main elevators, each capable of raising 1,200 show girls; 2 turntables that measure almost 63 feet in circumference; and 800 spotlights.*

DRIVING DISTANCES:

Reno

30 miles N of Carson City
58 miles NE of South Lake Tahoe, CA
158 miles NE of Sacramento, CA
227 miles NE of San Francisco, CA
289 miles SW of Elko
445 miles NW of Las Vegas
473 miles NW of Los Angeles, CA
554 miles SW of Ogden, UT

Las Vegas

228 miles NW of San Bernardino, CA
241 miles NW of Flagstaff, AZ
265 miles NE of Los Angeles, CA
400 miles SW of Wendover, UT
445 miles SE of Reno
447 miles SE of Carson City
469 miles SE of Elko
577 miles SE of San Francisco, CA

Elko

108 miles W of Wendover, UT
289 miles NE of Reno
308 miles NE of Carson City
336 miles NE of South Lake Tahoe, CA
423 miles NE of Sacramento, CA
469 miles NW of Las Vegas
545 miles NE of San Francisco, CA
569 miles NE of Barstow, CA

THE RICHEST STRIKE OF ALL   To even out the boom-and-bust cycle, irrigation channels were laid and farms established in the larger northern valleys. And the state legalized gambling (and liberalized divorce and marriage laws) in 1931 to net part of the resulting purse. Today almost 40 percent of the state's revenues are derived from tax revenues on gambling, and the challenge for visitors seems often to be in avoiding the ever-present lures of Lady Luck.

A CLOSER LOOK
Geography

Nevada lies in the bowl of the arid **Great Basin.** It is penned in to the west by California's evergreen-forest-ed Sierra Nevada, which rise to 13,143 feet at **Boundary Peak** just inside the Nevada border; and to the east by the wrinkled old **Wasatch Range,** which runs north-to-south through Idaho and Utah. In the southeastern part of the state, parched valleys drop to only 490 feet above sea level near the **Colorado River,** where the Hoover Dam lies wedged into the Nevada–Arizona state line.

Most of the state's other rivers would elsewhere be called streams, for much of the tortured landscape receives as little as 3 inches of rain a year. These meager rivers flow inward, where their precious waters are impounded by dams; in the northeast, they escape north and eventually link up with the mighty **Snake River.**

Lakes are few and far between. Surpassing them all is man-made **Lake Mead,** formed by the **Hoover Dam** in Nevada's southeast corner. Other natural lakes are scattered like turquoise gemstones throughout the northwest corner, where juniper and piñon trees clothe the land. Pungent sagebrush covers much of the rest of the state—the ubiquitous plant even adorns the state flag.

To the south, a corner of **Death Valley National Monument** extends into Nevada. The parched deserts of the southland are corrugated with range upon range of desert mountains in hues of rose, gray, and purple. From their peaks it is possible to see for a hundred miles in every direction without any signs of habitation. Below, in the valleys, conditions are so arid that camels were used in the 1860s to carry salt. Today, the only movement you are likely to see is that of deer and wild mustangs roaming the impassable bluffs.

Climate

Nevada's climate varies widely from north to south: average temperatures vary from 70°F in the south to 45° in the north. (On the fringes of Death Valley, temperatures can climb to 120° in summer; in the Sierra Nevada, they can drop to 40° below zero in winter, when the cooling altitudes of northeast Nevada may also be tinted with snow.) Everywhere rain is sparse. At an elevation of 2,174 feet, Las Vegas has comfortably cool nights, even after the hottest days. While summer temperatures in Las Vegas can soar to over 100°, the average winter temperature is only 48°.

In the deserts, dust storms can blow up suddenly. If

AVERAGE MONTHLY TEMPERATURES (°F) & INCHES OF RAINFALL			
	Las Vegas	**Reno**	**Elko**
Jan	45/0.5	33/1.1	23.4/11.3
Feb	51/0.5	38/1.0	29.6/7.4
Mar	56/0.4	43/0.7	36.5/6.6
Apr	64/0.2	49/0.4	44.1/3.4
May	74/0.3	56/0.7	52.7/1.7
June	85/0.1	65/0.5	60.9/0.7
July	91/0.4	72/0.3	69.8/0.4
Aug	89/0.5	70/0.3	67.1/0.4
Sept	80/0.3	60/0.4	57.6/0.4
Oct	68/0.2	51/0.4	46.9/0.7
Nov	55/0.4	40/0.9	35.2/0.8
Dec	46/0.4	33/1.0	25.7/1.1

driving, pull over and let the tempest pass. Be cautious, too, of flash floods triggered by sudden torrential rain.

What to Pack

In summer, hot weather dictates cool cottons throughout the state, though a warm sweater or jacket will be required for nights at higher elevations. In winter, bring warm clothing—even the southern deserts can be surprisingly cool. You may safely forgo raingear.

Casual clothes are fine in most casinos. A large percentage of visitors to Las Vegas and Reno favor sports jackets and cocktail dresses at night.

Tourist Information

The Nevada Commission on Tourism publishes *Nevada,* a bimonthly tourism magazine. For subscriptions ($14.95 per year) contact Nevada Magazines Subscriptions, PO Box 1942, Marion, OH 43305 (tel toll free 800/669-1002). For information on events, accommodations, and attractions statewide, contact the NevadaCommission on Tourism, Capitol Complex, NV 89710 (tel 702/687-3636).

A catalog and price list of maps can be obtained by writing to the Nevada Department of Transportation, Map Section, Rm. 206, 1263 S Stewart St, Carson City, NV 89712.

For information on Las Vegas, contact the Las Vegas Convention and Visitors Authority, 3150 Paradise, Las Vegas, NV 89109 (tel 702/892-0711). The Reno-Sparks Convention and Visitors Authority, 4590 S

Virginia St, Reno, NV 89502 (tel 702/827-7600) and the Carson City Convention and Visitors Bureau, 1900 S Carson St, Carson City, NV 89701 (tel 702/687-7410) can provide information on the Reno-Tahoe area.

Driving Rules & Regulations

Minimum age for drivers is 16. Unless otherwise noted, the speed limit on Nevada highways is 55 mph and 65 mph on rural interstate freeways.

Laws against drunk driving are strictly enforced. Note that it is illegal to carry an open container of alcohol in your car.

Use of seat belts is mandatory for all passengers, and children under 5 years or under 40 pounds must be secured in an approved child safety seat. Motorcyclists must wear a helmet. Auto insurance is mandatory.

Right turns are allowed after stops at a red light.

For road conditions, call 702/793-1313 (northern Nevada) or 702/486-3116 (Las Vegas). Listen for flash-flood advisories on your car radio. Motorists are advised to inquire locally about road conditions before traveling on unpaved roads. Check water and fluid levels; temperatures can be extreme and service stations in some areas are few and far between.

Renting a Car

In addition to local car rental companies, all of the major car rental firms have offices in Reno, Carson City, and Las Vegas. Minimum-age requirements range from 19 to 25. Collision damage waiver (CDW) protection is sold separately (check with your credit card or insurance company to see if you are already covered).

- **Alamo** (tel toll free 800/327-9633)
- **Avis** (tel 800/331-1212)
- **Budget** (tel 800/527-0700)
- **Dollar** (tel 800/421-6878)
- **Hertz** (tel 800/654-3131)
- **National** (tel 800/328-4567)
- **Thrifty** (tel 800/367-2277)

Essentials

Area Code: The area code for Nevada is 702.

Emergencies: Call 911 from anywhere in the state for emergency police, fire, and ambulance services.

Liquor Laws: Alcoholic beverages may be purchased by anyone 21 years or older with proof of age.

Gambling: Gambling is limited to adults 21 or over.

Smoking: While Nevada has not enacted strict regulations as California has, the state does prohibit smoking in public buildings and requires most restaurants and certain businesses to have nonsmoking areas.

Taxes: Nevada's statewide sales tax is 6.75%. Some cities and counties impose an additional tax of 0.25 to 0.50%.

Time Zone: Nevada is in the Pacific time zone (GMT minus 8 hours), 3 hours behind New York. Daylight savings time is observed.

BEST OF THE STATE

What to See & Do

NATIONAL & STATE PARKS Nevada has 24 state parks, 3 federally protected areas, plus 2 national forests: Toiyabe and Humboldt, both with 2.5 million acres. One of the most intriguing options is **Death Valley National Monument,** perhaps America's most eerie wasteland. It's reached via Beatty or Pahrump, and visitors can explore many fascinating scenic locations, including the Ubehebe Crater and Furnace Creek ranch. Formed 150 million years ago, **Valley of Fire State Park,** 15 miles southwest of Overton, has been sculpted by wind and rain into spectacular domes, spirals, beehives, and other unusual formations. **Berlin-Ichthyosaur State Park,** on the western slopes of the Shoshone Mountains, 23 miles east of Gabbs, yields the fossils of huge fish dinosaurs. Berlin is also a ghost town. And to see the world's oldest and largest groves of ancient bristlecone pines, a glacier, Lehman Caves, and magnificent Wheeler Peak (13,163 feet), go to the 77,100-acre **Great Basin National Park,** near Ely and the Utah border.

NATURAL WONDERS Pyramid Lake, one of the premier sights in Nevada, is a vast prehistoric lake that once covered much of northwestern Nevada. Its receding level has revealed wonderfully old formations of porous tufa rock, which rise above the surface of the lake's deep-blue water. In Great Basin National Park, **Lehman Caves** proffer labyrinthine corridors and colorful monuments: stalactites, stalagmites, and helictites. Just 20 minutes west of Las Vegas, **Red Rock Canyon** displays a natural "art gallery" with its amazing arches, natural bridges, and massive sculptures of colored rock strata.

WILDLIFE There's everything from deer, elk, and waterfowl to mustangs seen at full gallop with their shaggy manes and tails streaming. Many lakes are winter breeding grounds for migratory waterfowl; **Anaho Island,** in Pyramid Lake, a federal bird sanctuary popular with white pelicans, is worth more than a flying visit. **Desert National Wildlife Range,** near Las Vegas, protects a large colony of desert bighorn sheep.

FAMILY FAVORITES Boomtown's Family Funland, located west of Reno, features a high-tech motion theater, miniature golf course, and carousel. **Wet 'n Wild,** a water theme park on the Las Vegas Strip, is lots of fun and a good place to beat the heat; it features a variety of water slides, pools, and rides. For the world's only indoor double-loop roller coaster, head to **Grand Slam Canyon** in Las Vegas, a 5-acre amusement park offering water thrills, animated dinosaurs, and more. The Las Vegas **MGM Grand Hotel and Theme Park,** the world's largest resort, boasts 33 acres of rides and attractions. For a change of pace, kids may want to explore the **Lied Discovery Children's Museum,** which is designed for hands-on learning about science, art, and other subjects.

MUSEUMS The **Nevada State Museum,** housed in the former US Mint in Carson City, offers a look into the Silver State's rich past. Visitors can see the machinery that stamped $50 million in silver and gold coins as well as a life-size ghost town, a replica of an underground mine, and Indian artifacts. Also in Carson City, the **Nevada State Railway Museum** has two beautifully restored steam locomotives as well as other railroad equipment. The **Western Folklife Center** in Elko features exhibits of cowboy gear, western and Native American folk art, and demonstrations of old-fashioned folk dances. Fascinating in the extreme is the **Guinness World of Records Museum,** in Las Vegas, with 3-dimensional displays of superlatives from around the globe. The **Liberace Museum,** also in Las Vegas, exhibits the expensive cars, elaborate gemstone capes, candelabras, and other memorabilia that helped make the pianist/entertainer a legend. And over 200 antique, classic, and special-interest vehicles, including Adolf Hitler's 1939 Mercedes-Benz and President Eisenhower's 1952 Imperial, are on view at the **Imperial Palace Auto Collection** in Las Vegas.

HISTORICAL BUILDINGS & SITES The **Nevada State Capitol** in Carson City, built in 1870 of native sandstone, has hallways of Alaskan marble and polished-wood wall panels. One of the most famous silver boomtowns in America—**Virginia City**—offers museums, mine tours, a cemetery, and restored shops and saloons. Strolling its streets, it is easy to imagine days when lucky miners ate caviar and drank French champagne. **Eureka,** the most picturesque of Nevada's 19th-century mining towns and also its best preserved, has fine brick-and-stone Victorian buildings highlighted by the still-used Eureka County Courthouse, which has a pressed-tin ceiling, original wainscoting, and chandeliers. West of Ely, the **Ward Charcoal Ovens Historic State Monument** lets you peer into 30-foot-tall beehive-shaped ovens that in the 1870s and 1880s turned piñon logs into fuel. The **Old Las Vegas Mormon Fort,** part of the original 1855 Mormon settlement, is the oldest standing Anglo-American structure in Nevada. Today a ghost town, **Rhyolite State Historical Park** was a thriving mining town in the first decade of the 20th century; the photogenic ruins of once-substantial buildings make the town worth a visit. Also of interest is the refurbished **Bowers Mansion,** 20 miles south of Reno, built in 1864 by the first Comstock Lode millionaire.

PARKS & GARDENS The **Ethel M Chocolate Factory and Cactus Garden,** at Henderson, boasts one of the most complete collections of western cactus plants in the country, while the **Wilbur D May Arboretum and Botanical Garden,** in Reno, has theme gardens displaying native and ornamental plants.

ARCHITECTURE The **Hoover Dam** has an elevator that whisks you down 528 feet to the dam's concrete innards for a guided tour of one of the world's great engineering marvels. And the tallest observation tower in America is the **Stratosphere Tower** in Las Vegas.

Events/Festivals

- **Chrysler Celebrity Ski Classic,** Heavenly Ski Resort. January. Call 702/586-7000 for information.
- **Best in the Desert Grand Prix Motorcycle Race,** Mesquite. Late January. Call 702/346-5295.
- **Las Vegas International Marathon,** Las Vegas. February. Call 702/731-2115.
- **Hoover Dam Square Dance Weekend,** Boulder City. March. Call 702/293-4918.
- **Airfest,** Las Vegas. March. Call 702/434-4122.
- **Rhyolite Living History Festival,** Beatty. March. Call 702/553-2424.
- **Mesquite Days Invitational Rodeo,** Aravada Ranch Rodeo Grounds. May. Call 702/346-5295.
- **Silver State Square and Round Dance Festival,** Reno. May. Call 702/322-0027.
- **Senior Pro Rodeo,** Winnemucca. May. Call 702/623-2225.
- **Silver State Classic Car Show,** Pioche. May. Call 702/962-5544.
- **Desert Oasis Bluegrass Festival,** Fallon. May. Call 702/423-2544.
- **National Basque Festival,** Winnemucca. June. Call 702/623-5071.
- **Cowboy Music Gathering,** Elko. June. Call 702/738-7135.
- **Best in the Desert Motorcycle Race,** Ely. June. Call 702/289-8877.
- **Sports Cars and All That Jazz,** Reno. July. Call 702/786-3030.
- **Nevada State Fair,** Reno. August. Call 702/688-5767.
- **Las Vegas Jaycees State Fair,** Las Vegas. September. Call 702/457-8832.

- **Great Reno Balloon Race,** Reno. September. Call 702/829-2810.
- **Virginia City International Camel Race,** Virginia City. September. Call 702/847-0311.
- **National Championship Air Races,** Reno. September. Call 702/972-6663.
- **Numanga Indian Days Celebration,** Reno-Sparks Indian Colony. September. Call 702/329-2936.
- **Art in the Park,** Boulder City. October. Call 702/293-2034.
- **Las Vegas Balloon Classic,** Las Vegas. October. Call 702/434-0848.
- **Nevada Day Celebration and Parade,** Carson City. October. Call 702/882-2600.
- **Nellis Air Force Base Open House,** Las Vegas. November. Call 702/652-2750.
- **Owyhee Reservation Indian Day Pow Wow,** November. Call 702/757-3211.
- **National Finals Rodeo,** Las Vegas. December. Call 702/731-2115.
- **Parade of Lights,** Boulder City. December. Call 702/293-2034.

For a free copy of the *Nevada Events Guide,* contact the Nevada Commission on Tourism, Capitol Complex, Carson City, NV 89710 (tel 800/NEVADA-8).

Spectator Sports

BASEBALL The **Las Vegas Stars,** an affiliate of the San Diego Padres in the Class AAA Pacific Coast League, play home games at Cashman Field (tel 702/386-7200) in North Las Vegas. The **Reno Silver Sox,** a Class A farm team of the Oakland A's in the California League, play ball at Moana Stadium (tel 702/825-0678).

BASKETBALL The **Runnin' Rebels** of the **University of Nevada–Las Vegas** (UNLV), a frequent Top 25 team in college polls, play their NCAA home games at the 18,500-seat Thomas & Mack Center (tel 702/739-3761) in Las Vegas.

BOXING Professional boxing matches, including championship bouts, are held throughout the year at several venues in Las Vegas, among them Bally's 5,000-seat Goldwyn Events Center (tel 702/739-4111); Caesar's Palace (tel 702/731-7110 or toll free 800/634-6698); and the Hilton Center at the Las Vegas Hilton (tel 702/732-5755 or 800/222-5361). Also, the Mirage (tel 702/791-7111 or 800/627-6667) features championship boxing matches several times a year, as does the Riviera (tel 702/734-5110 or 800/634-6753). The Sahara (tel 702/737-2111) hosts occasional ESPN-televised matches.

FOOTBALL The **UNLV Rebels** of college football take to the gridiron at the Sam Boyd Silver Bowl (tel 702/739-3900) on the UNLV campus; this is also the stadium where the Las Vegas Football Bowl is held each December.

RODEO The **Reno Rodeo,** held each June at the Livestock Events Center (tel 702/329-3877) in Reno, is considered one of the top 10 rodeos in the country and includes such standard events as steer wrestling and calf-roping. The Thomas & Mack Arena in Las Vegas (tel 702/731-2115) hosts the world championship of rodeo, the **National Finals Rodeo,** in early December. The 15 top money winners in the country compete in bull-riding, saddle-bronco riding, and other events for almost $3 million in prize money.

Activities A to Z

What Nevada lacks in spectator sports it more than makes up for in participatory sports and activities at all times of year. Lake Mead National Recreation Area and Mt Charleston serve Las Vegas, and Lake Tahoe serves the Reno–Carson City area for those eager for the outdoor life.

BICYCLING Nevada is mountain-biking territory *par excellence.* The annual One Awesome Tour: Bike Ride Across Nevada (OAT-BRAN) is held in late September. For information contact TGFT Productions, Box 5123, Stateline, NV 89449 (tel 702/588-9658). For information on bicycling in general, contact the Nevada Department of Transportation, 1263 S Stewart St, Carson City, NV 89712.

BOATING Water may be a scarce commodity in Nevada, but fun afloat can be had at both **Lake Tahoe** and the **Lake Mead National Recreation Area.** The latter—a 247-square-mile reservoir—extends upriver 110 miles from Hoover Dam and has 6 marinas. Zephyr Cove Marina (tel 702/588-3833) has boat rentals at Lake Tahoe.

CAMPING   Most state parks have camping facilities year-round, though many are difficult to access in winter. If camping in remote areas, carry adequate drinking water. For information contact the Nevada Division of State Parks, Capitol Complex, Carson City, NV 89710 (tel 702/687-4370 or 687-4384).

DOG-SLED RIDES   A unique way to explore the mountain wilderness in winter. Try Husky Express (tel 702/782-3047).

FISHING   Bass, Mackinaw trout, crappie, whitefish, walleye, and catfish are among the species that attract anglers to lakes and reservoirs in northern Nevada. **Cave Lake State Park,** near Ely, is recommended for brown trout. In the Lake Tahoe area, call O'Malley's Fishing Charters at 702/588-4102.

Fishing permits ($45.50 annually) can be obtained from the Nevada Department of Wildlife, State Headquarters, 1100 Valley Rd, Reno, NV 89512 (tel 702/688-1500). Note: You will need a tribal permit to fish on Indian reservations.

GOLF   Dozens of lush golf courses defy the state's image as an arid wasteland. Las Vegas has no fewer than 16 courses, including 4 municipal courses—Angel Park, Desert Rose, Las Vegas Golf Course, and North Las Vegas Golf Course. The Reno–Tahoe–Carson City area has over 20 courses to choose from, including the Edgewood Tahoe Golf Course (tel 702/588-3566) and Incline Village Championship Golf Course (tel 702/832-1144). There's even a public course in Death Valley—Furnace Creek Golf Course (tel 702/786-2301).

GUIDED TOURS   In addition to Las Vegas city tours, sightseeing tours are offered from Las Vegas to the Grand Canyon, Hoover Dam, Lake Mead, Red Rock Canyon, and Valley of Fire State Park. Day trips are also available to Death Valley, Mt Charleston, and Laughlin. Contact the Nevada Commission on Tourism (see "Tourist Information," above) for a listing of recommended tour operators. There is also a **Fiesta Queen River Cruise,** departing Laughlin, which relives the nostalgic era when steamboats plied the Colorado River.

HIKING   Luring hikers around the Lake Tahoe ridgetop and the upper elevations of the Carson Range is the

Tahoe Rim Trail—a 150-mile system of hiking and equestrian trails. For information contact Nevada Lake Tahoe State Park (tel 702/831-0494). The 5-mile-long **River Mountain Hiking Trail,** built in 1935 by the Civilian Conservation Corps, offers breathtaking views of Lake Mead and Las Vegas valley.

For a free map of trails, contact the Nevada Division of State Parks, Capitol Complex, Carson City, NV 89710.

HORSEBACK RIDING   Nevada is cowboy country. The Mt Charleston area is popular for horseback trips out of Las Vegas. Zephyr Cove Stables (tel 702/588-5664) can arrange trips at Lake Tahoe.

PACK TRIPS   Elko Guide Service (tel 702/779-2336) offers pack trips into the Ruby Mountains.

SCUBA DIVING   Yes, this desert state has scuba diving, at Lake Tahoe. Contact The Diving Edge, PO Box 2978, Lake Tahoe, NV 89449 (tel 702/588-5262).

SKIING   The Reno–Lake Tahoe region offers the largest concentration of ski areas in the country. For brochures, contact Ski Lake Tahoe, PO Box 1654, Zephyr Cove, NV 89449 (tel 702/588-8598). The following are the state's most popular ski areas:

- **Diamond Peak,** 2 miles southeast of Incline Village, is a favorite family resort with 20 acres of glade skiing for advanced skiers. It also features 10 cross-country trails.
- **Heavenly,** 2 miles southeast of the town of South Lake Tahoe, has 24 lifts, the world's largest snowmaking system, and over 85 runs, including Tahoe's longest—almost 6 miles.
- **Mt Rose,** 2 miles east of Incline Village, has the highest base elevation in the area, with 41 runs on 900 acres.

You can also ski in Kyle and Lee Canyons (tel 702/646-0793) in the southeast corner of Nevada, good for both downhill and cross-country skiing.

SNOWMOBILING   Explore the High Sierra by taking a guided tour or doing your own thing. Call Zephyr Cove Snowmobile Center at 702/588-3833.

TENNIS   Most resort hotels have private tennis courts. For a list of municipal courts, refer to the

"Government" pages of the local telephone directory.

WHITE-WATER RAFTING   One-day explorations of the Black Canyon of the Colorado River set off from below Hoover Dam; contact Black Canyon River Raft Tours at 702/293-3776. The Truckee River Rafting Center (tel 916/583-7238) offers "bucking bronco" rides on the Truckee River, at Tahoe City.

SCENIC DRIVING TOUR

DEATH VALLEY THROUGH CENTRAL NEVADA

Start: Las Vegas
Finish: Death Valley
Distance: 144 miles
Time: 1–2 days
Highlights: Death Valley National Monument, Scotty's Castle, ghost towns, Tule Springs, Corn Creek

Simply stated, Death Valley is the most famous desert in the United States. Set between the lofty Black and Panamint mountain ranges, it is known for its exquisite but merciless terrain. A region of vast expanse (the national monument portion is equal to the combined area of Connecticut and Rhode Island) and plentiful plant life (over 900 plant species subsist here, 22 of them indigenous to the area), Death Valley holds a magician's bag of tricks and surprises. It is a giant geology lab of salt beds, sand dunes, and badlands, and an 11,000-foot mountain peak. Its multi-tiered hills contain layers that are windows to the history of the earth. One level holds Indian arrowheads, another Ice Age fish, and beneath these deposits lies 600-million-year-old Precambrian rock.

Death Valley received its name in 1849 when a party of pioneers from Salt Lake City, intent on following a shortcut to the California gold fields, crossed the wasteland, barely escaping with their lives. Later, prospectors worked the territory, discovering rich borax deposits during the 1880s and providing the region with a cottage industry.

Due to the extreme summer temperatures (average July highs of 116°F!), travel to the valley is not recommended in summer months. The best time to see the park is from October through April. In late February and March (average highs of 73°, dropping to a cool 46° average at night) the desert comes alive with spring blossoms such as Death Valley sage and Panamint daisies.

The drive to Death Valley from the neon glow of Las Vegas takes slightly more than 2 hours, and will take you through some of southern Nevada's most scenic and historic treasures. From the Las Vegas Strip, take US 15 north to the downtown area, then exit onto US 95 northbound. Continue for 14 miles until you reach:

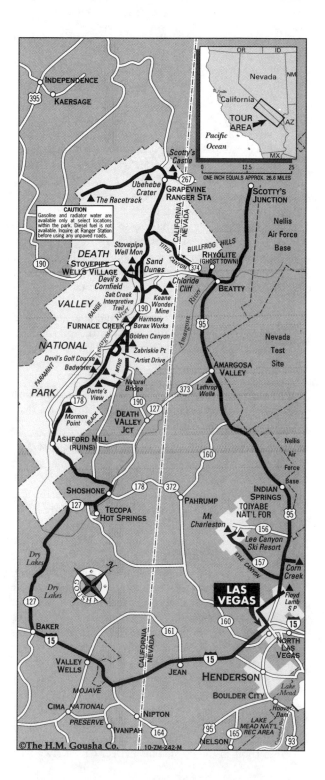

1. **Tule Springs,** also known as Floyd Lamb State Park (tel 702/486-5413), a haven for anglers, birders, picnickers, and hikers. You can feed the ducks on the large and small lakes connected by a stream, stroll around the trimmed lawns on sidewalks, or set up your picnic on one of the many tables. Birders will appreciate the variety of waterfowl that pass through on spring and fall migrations, including ruddy ducks, pintails, white-faced scaup, cinnamon and green-winged teal, and Canadian, snow, and Ross's geese. Imported peacocks also wander the grounds.

Tule Springs is named for the large reed-like plants indigenous to the area. Photographers will find inspiration in the pastoral setting and the buildings of the old **Tule Springs Ranch,** a former dude ranch; horse stables, tack rooms, a wooden water tower, and a barn all remain standing. Fossils have been discovered at a site 5 miles southeast of the park, marking the presence of several extinct animals—the ground sloth, mammoth, prehistoric horse, and American camel, as well as the giant condor.

Return to US 95 and drive north for 3½ miles, then make a left turn onto Kyle Canyon Rd (Nev 157), which will take you to:

2. **Mount Charleston,** an alpine wilderness area that evolves with the colors and climates of 4 seasons while the desert floor bakes below. Only 30 minutes from Las Vegas, Mount Charleston and the surrounding **Toiyabe National Forest** are popular destinations for hiking, backpacking, picnicking, overnight camping, and skiing during the winter months. Notice the change in vegetation as the elevation increases. Approaching the mountains you'll see Joshua trees, yucca, and creosote bush that have adapted well to the 120° summer temperatures and scant rainfall. As you reach the 5,000-foot elevation, piñon pine and junipers take over the landscape, along with scatterings of sagebrush, rabbitbrush, and scarlet trumpeter. You probably won't see them from the road, but deer and elk move into this region as the winter snows deepen at higher elevations.

The pine stands grow larger as you progress up the mountain, and at about this point you'll see a turnoff to the right. This is Deer Creek Hwy (Nev 158), leading into the **Lee Canyon Ski Resort** (tel 702/646-0008) area. You'll also see the **Mount Charleston Hotel** (tel 702/872-5500), one of the only overnight accommodations on the mountain, with a weathered wood exterior, open-beam rafters, ponderosa pine pillars, and an open-pit fireplace. The hotel has a dining room, a gift shop, a cocktail lounge, and a slot machine arcade.

The paved road ends at roughly 7,500 feet, but you can see the bristlecone pine forests at elevations of 9,000 feet and higher. The cabins and rustic homes perched on sites carved out of Kyle Canyon walls have become a colony for nearly 200 Las Vegans who commute into the city. Stop at the **Ranger Station** (tel 702/331-6444) for maps and information on the area.

☕

REFRESHMENT STOP

At the end of the short gravel road near the Ranger Station is the **Mount Charleston Lodge** (tel 702/386-6899), a very popular restaurant and bar with sweeping canyon views, a circular fireplace, and an excellent menu of game bird entrees, and a charming antique shop next-door.

Backtrack down Kyle Canyon Rd until you reach US 95, turn left, and continue northbound for 7 miles until you reach a well-graded gravel road that will take you to:

3. **Corn Creek,** a former working ranch and stagecoach stop just ¼ mile off the highway. It is now a field station for the vast Desert National Wildlife Range and a special sanctuary of the once endangered Nelson's desert bighorn sheep. This small, rugged oasis is a marvelous site for birdwatching. On the edge of the California flyway, it attracts an astonishing variety of birdlife from hummingbirds to hawks. The natural springs of Corn Creek have formed upper and lower ponds connected by a gurgling brook. You can walk under the huge cottonwoods, mesquite, willows, fruit trees, cattails, and tules clustered around the waterways.

There's also a small picnic area with tables, canopies, grills, restrooms, and water. A walk beyond the ponds takes you to mesquite-filled arroyos where you may unearth arrowheads left behind by the ancient Native American tribes.

Return to US 95 and continue north. The open desert to the right is the Nellis Air Force Base bombing and gunnery range, with the Desert Range mountains in the distance. The highway turns westward and continues for 8 miles to:

4. **Indian Springs,** which was originally a ranch owned by a small group of Native Americans. It was later used as a train stop on the run between Las Vegas and Tonopah. Indian Springs has 2 gas stations, convenience stores, and a truck stop; it is also a checkpoint into the Air Force's gunnery range.

Continue along US 95 for about 15 miles and you'll pass by the:

5. **Nevada Test Site,** which is identified by a historical marker to the right of the highway. It was here during the 1950s and early 1960s that the Atomic Energy Commission detonated more than 200 nuclear devices.

Do not take the town of Mercury exit because visitors are not allowed into the area. Instead, stay on US 95 and drive for an additional 22 miles to the Lathrop Wells rest area, where you'll find restrooms, tables, garbage cans, and free overnight trailer parking. Continue for another 18 miles to the small mining town of:

6. **Beatty,** which sits in a fairly green valley, watered by the underground Amargosa River, and surrounded by the crumbly, whitewashed Bullfrog Mountains slopes. Beatty blossomed into a town in 1904 when gold was discovered in the Bullfrog hills, but by 1910 the gold ran out and miners left. Beatty survived, however, thanks mainly to the railroad and the routing of US 95 through the town. Most recently a new gold-processing plant west of town has jump-started the local economy. Today the town sports 4 hotels, a library, several restaurants, and cocktail lounges.

From Beatty, drive 4 miles west on Nev 374, past the modern carbon-cynanide gold mill. Turn right at the sign and go up the hill to:

7. **Rhyolite,** one of Nevada's most picturesque ghost towns, which was spawned by a major gold strike in the neighboring Bullfrog Mountains in 1904. By 1906 it had a population of more than 10,000 people. In its heyday, the town had 10 hotels, an opera house, a 2-story school, 56 saloons, and a 2-story railroad station which still stands. You can see the skeletons of stone and brick buildings, with horseshoes, steamer trunks, and other rubble strewn over the surrounding hillsides. The most famous of the ruins is the **bottle house,** built in 1906 from 10,000 purple, brown, and turquoise beer and whiskey bottles. Another photogenic relic is the crumbling remains of the 3-story Cook building, which was once a bank and post office.

Return to Nev 374, turn right, and drive for 2 miles to the sign, turn right and prepare for a thrilling ride through:

8. **Titus Canyon,** a colorful gorge split by a winding, 24-mile road through the Grapevine Mountains. About 3 miles into the canyon, you'll pass a marker indicating you've entered **Death Valley National Monument.** The one-way road is extremely narrow in places, with sheer rock walls shooting skyward for several hundred feet. Halfway through the canyon, it widens to expose an old Indian campground and Klare Spring. Nearby are petroglyphs attributed to people of the Ice Age, who inscribed them more than 20,000 years ago.

You'll encounter 2-way traffic as you approach the mouth of Titus Canyon. At the base of the canyon, turn right on Calif 190 and drive 21 miles to the very end of Death Valley National Monument, bear right on Nev 267 for 2 miles, where you'll find the strangest feature in the entire park—a place called:

9. **Scotty's Castle.** Though Scotty never owned it, it seems that one Walter ''Death Valley Scotty'' Scott, a former trick rider in Buffalo Bill's Wild West Show, once convinced a Chicago millionaire, Albert Johnson, to invest in a nonexistent gold mine. Johnson traveled west to see the mine, discovered that the dry desert clime helped his fragile health, forgave Scotty, and decided during the 1920s to build a mansion in the sand. The result was a $2 million, 18-room Moorish castle, a

wonderfully ornate affair with wrought-iron detailing, Spanish tile, expensive tapestry, leather drapery, European antiques, a large moat, and 3 towers. Scotty, the greatest storyteller in Death Valley history, told everyone it was his castle. Hence the name.

Return to the paved road and backtrack along Nev 267 for 8 miles until you reach the moonlike terrain that surrounds:

10. **Ubehebe Crater.** A half-mile in diameter and reaching a depth of 500 feet, this magnificent natural landmark was created by a single volcanic explosion. The force of the volcanic steam scattered debris over a 6-square-mile area and blew the crater walls so clean that one side retains its original sedimentary colors. Whether the crater dates back 10,000 years or is only a few hundred years old has been debated by geologists.

From the crater a winding gravel road leads 27 miles to:

11. **The Racetrack,** a 2-mile mud playa, set at the bottom of a dry lake, which is oval-shaped like a racecourse. An outcropping at the north end of the valley is dubbed The Grandstand. The racers, oddly enough, are rocks, ranging in size from pebbles to 600-pound boulders. Pushed by heavy winds across the mud-slick surface, they leave long, faint tracks that reveal the distances they have raced, up to 500 feet in some cases.

Retrace your route back to Calif 190 and head south for 24 miles, over which you'll descend from 3,000 feet to sea level, until you reach a sign along the highway that marks a lookout area where faint wagon-wheel tracks, made many years ago, can be seen. Further along the highway rests the old:

12. **Stovepipe Well Monument,** from which the nearby village derived its name. Used by prospectors crossing Death Valley, the well was fitted with a tall stovepipe so travelers could see it even when sand blanketed the area. Although the well is now dry, a stone and bronze monument commemorates the site.

Take the unpaved road south from the monument for 1 mile to the:

13. **Sand Dunes,** which are 80-feet high in some places and cover an area of 14 square miles. They are made up of sand that blew in from nearby mountains, mostly from the cottonwood ranges to the west and northwest, and support numerous plant species, including creosote bushes, mesquite, and pickleweed. Coyotes hunt prey in the sandhills, such as kit fox, lizards, and kangaroo rats.

Continue south on the unpaved road for 2 miles, then turn right on the paved highway, Calif 190, and drive the 3 miles to:

14. **Devil's Cornfield,** a conglomeration of arrowweed bushes that are growing in clumps because of sand deflation and erosion. Stalks of the plants were once used by Indians for arrow shafts. The strange sight looks like a field of eerie haystacks.

Just 4 miles south of the Cornfield is one of Death Valley's 2 villages:

15. **Stovepipe Wells Village,** Calif 190 (tel 619/786-2387), where you'll find a motel, restaurant, store, gas station, and campground. It was here at **Burned Wagons Point** (historic marker) that a desperate party of '49ers killed their oxen and dried the meat by burning their wagons.

☕

REFRESHMENT STOP

A good spot for a bite is the **Stovepipe Wells Village motel's restaurant,** which is embellished with Native American rugs and paintings of the Old West. The cuisine matches the ambience, an all-American menu featuring fried chicken, rainbow trout, steak, veal, and cod. You can quench your thirst at the **Badwater Saloon,** which features a jukebox and a dance floor.

Backtrack to Calif 190 S, turn right and drive 5 miles to the:

16. **Salt Creek Interpretive Trail.** Six times saltier than the ocean, Salt Creek enters the salt pan at about 200 feet below sea level and has waterfalls,

and even fish. The pupfish are descendants of fish that lived in ancient Lake Manly, perhaps 15,000 years ago. They are 1 to 3 inches long, swim in schools most of the time, and can be seen during the spring and summer months.

Continue south on Calif 190 for 2 miles to the Beatty Cutoff, turn left, and drive 7 miles to:

17. **Keane Wonder Mine,** a productive gold mine from 1908 to 1916. Still on the property are the remnants of a mill, dilapidated houses, and a tram.

A couple of miles north of the mine are the remains of:

18. **Chloride Cliff,** one of Death Valley's oldest developments. The site was a silver mining camp from 1873 to 1883, then again as late as 1916. In its heyday, the camp consisted of a blacksmith shop, an assay office, a cookhouse, a bunkhouse, and a few other buildings. Today only a few wooden structures and the mill foundation remain.

Return to Calif 190 and drive south 7 miles to the once prosperous:

19. **Harmony Borax Works,** which is now crumbling adobe walls, old boilers, and vats. Built in 1882 by a wealthy San Francisco businessman, the plant used Chinese labor to scrape the borate crust off the valley floor. Production ended in 1888 when borate was found in the Mojave Desert, close to the Santa Fe Railroad. Important as a cleaning agent, the white crystal eventually became the region's most valuable mineral.

Just a mile south of the Borax Works is Death Valley's only major center of civilization:

20. **Furnace Creek,** a welcome oasis consisting of a gas station, a campground, restaurants, and 2 hotels. You'll also find the **Death Valley National Monument Visitor Center** (tel 619/786-2331), which houses a museum recreating the history of Native Americans and early prospectors. Most of the accommodations and dining facilities are located here. **Furnace Creek Ranch** (tel toll free 800/528-6367), a 124-unit resort with cabins and standard rooms, sprawls across several acres and features 3 restaurants, a saloon, a general store, and a swimming pool. The poshest lodging in

Death Valley is **Furnace Creek Inn** (tel 619/786-2361), a 70-room hotel set on a hillside overlooking the valley. This Spanish-Moorish-style building, built of stone and adobe, is surrounded by flowering gardens and palm trees. There are 2 restaurants, tennis courts, and a spring-fed swimming pool; guest rooms are quite comfortably furnished and most have fireplaces.

A few hundred feet south of the Visitor Center is the:

21. **Borax Museum,** which features the oldest house in Death Valley, a sturdy 1883 structure built by a borax miner. Among the displays is a collection of borates and precious metals, old photographs of the 20-mule teams, Native American baskets, dated arrowheads, mining tools, and historical papers. Outside, there's a wonderful collection of stagecoaches, wagons, and old locomotive, and a contraption once used to extract gold deposits from rock.

Drive south for a mile past the junction of Calif 178 and proceed for 3 miles to:

22. **Zabriskie Point.** In the east, amber-colored hills roll like waves toward the horizon. To the west lies spectacular badlands, burnished by blown sand to fierce reds and soft pastels. These mustard-colored hills are dry mud, lake-bed sediments deposited between 2 and 12 million years ago, then uplifted to their present height. During the early morning and late afternoon, the place is suffused with color. Just to the east of the Point is a channel that divides Furnace Creek Wash and Gowers Gulch. The US Park Service cut the channel to divert the flow of the wash into the gulch to prevent flash-flooding at the Furnace Creek settlement. However, considerable erosion has resulted, especially at the gulch's mouth.

For a view from above it all, drive south on Calif 190 for 36 miles and climb to:

23. **Dante's View,** a 5,475-foot perch on the crest of the Black Mountains, with a 360° vista. From this advantageous position, the salt flats and trapped pools of Death Valley resemble a bleak watercolor. Though the Panamint Mountains wall off the western horizon, a steep ½-mile trail (up the knoll north of the parking lot) leads to a point where you

can gaze beyond them to the snow-thatched Sierra Nevada. Here in a single glance you can see Badwater and Mt Whitney, the lowest and highest points in the continental United States.

Backtrack down the mountain and retrace your route along Calif 190 until you reach Calif 178, then turn left and drive for 2 miles to:

24. **Golden Canyon,** where erosion has chiseled chasms into the bright yellow walls of the narrow gorge. Hike the ¾-mile trail here and you arrive in a natural amphitheater, named for the iridescent quality of the canyon walls. Once the bottom of an ancient lake, the area is now virtually devoid of life.

About 8 miles south of Golden Canyon, take the turn-off through:

25. **Artist Drive,** a 9-mile loop through the Black Mountains' multicolored badlands, and one of southern California's most magnificent roads. The hills all around are splashed with color—soft pastels, striking reds, creamy browns—and rise to sharp cliffs. Along the loop you'll see **Artists Palette,** where the hills are colored so vividly they seem to pulsate. All this beauty results from oxidation: Chloride deposits create the green hues, manganese oxides form the blacks, and the reds, yellows, and oranges are shades of iron oxide. These contrasting colors are most spectacular during late afternoon.

Continuing south for 7 miles on the paved highway brings you to the:

26. **Devil's Golf Course.** This flat expanse is a huge salt trap, complete with salt towers, pinnacles, and brine pools. The sodium chloride here is 95% pure, comparable to table salt, and the salt deposits are 3 to 5 feet thick. They were formed by a small lake that evaporated 2,000 years ago. The 2-to 3-foot-tall salt towers, which resemble inverted golf tees, are cracked by expansion, and you can sometimes hear the creaking and cracking on hot days.

Two miles south of the Golf Course, you'll discover the:

27. **Natural Bridge,** a 50-foot-high arch that was carved by torrents of water that cascaded down from the mountains. Behind the bridge, you can still see the lip of what was once an ancient waterfall. The formations along the canyon walls were left by evaporating water and resemble dripping wax.

Drive south 3 miles and you'll find the place you've been reading about since 3rd-grade geography:

28. **Badwater,** the lowest point in the western hemisphere at 282 feet below sea level. It could also be the hottest spot on earth; ground temperatures can exceed 200 degrees. Take a stroll out onto the salt flats and you'll find that the crystals are joined into a white carpet extending for miles. Despite the inhospitable environment, the pool here supports water snails, bronze water beetles, and other invertebrates. Salt grass, pickleweed, and desert holly also endure here. Evaporation from the pool is heavy, but it contains water throughout the year. Out on the flats you can gaze west at 11,049-foot **Telescope Peak** across the valley. Then be sure to glance back at the cliff to the west of the road; high in the rocks above you, a lone sign marks Sea Level.

The main highway continues south 12 miles across the salt flats to:

29. **Mormon Point.** As you traverse this expanse, notice how the Black Mountains to the east turn from dark colors to reddish hues as gray Precambrian rocks give way to younger volcanic and sedimentary deposits.

Drive south 26 miles along Calif 178 to the ruins of:

30. **Ashford Mill,** once a 50-ton gold mill that was built during World War I when gold mining enjoyed a comeback. The concrete skeletons of several buildings are all that remain of that early dream. About a 2-mile hike west of the mill is a vista point that overlooks **Shoreline Butte,** a curving hill marked by a succession of horizontal lines that represent the ancient shorelines of Lake Manly, which covered the valley to a depth of 600 feet and stretched for 90 miles. Formed perhaps 75,000 years ago, the lake dried up about 10,000 years ago.

Calif 178 turns eastward as you head 12 miles

to the southern entrance of the park, then another 15 miles to the junction of Calif 127. Turn right (south) and drive 18 miles to a side road that leads to:

31. **Tecopa Hot Springs,** a series of rich mineral baths once used by Paiute Indians. Today this natural resource has been transformed into a bizarre tourist attraction. A white mineral patina covers the ground everywhere. Water sits in stagnant pools. Wherever you look—backgrounded by rugged, stark, glorious mountains—there are trailers, painted white like the earth and equipped with satellite dishes. The species that inhabits these tin domiciles is on permanent vacation.

A fitting ending to dusty Death Valley lies along the southern gateway to this hauntingly beautiful destination. Here, stretching south along Calif 127 to the town of Baker, is a chain of:

32. **Dry Lakes.** Once part of Lake Mojave, an ancient body of water which drained over 3,500 square miles, they are now flat expanses baked white in the sun. **Silver Dry Lake,** which appears to the west 4 miles outside Baker, is part of an area inhabited by Native Americans over 10,000 years ago. To the east rise the **Silurian Hills,** backdropped by the Kingston Range. If there is a snow-domed mountain in the far distance, it's probably 11,918-foot **Charleston Peak,** 60 miles away in Nevada. Those pretty white hills with the soft curves are the **Dumont Dunes,** 30 miles north of Baker.

To return to Las Vegas, continue south on Calif 127 to the junction with US 15, turn left (north), and drive the 82 miles back to Las Vegas.

BOULDER CITY

Map page M-4, E4

Motels 🛏️

▤▤ **Best Western Lighthouse Inn**, 110 Ville Dr, Boulder City, NV 89005; tel 702/293-6444 or toll free 800/528-1234; fax 702/293-6547. Hacienda-style building with red-tile roof, pink stucco walls, and palm trees. Situated on a knoll with views of Lake Mead in the distance. **Rooms:** 70 rms. CI 3pm/CO noon. Nonsmoking rms avail. Modern furnishings decorated in southwestern-style prints and colors. **Amenities:** 🛎️ 🎛️ A/C, cable TV w/movies. **Services:** 🍴 **Facilities:** 🏋️ Whirlpool, washer/dryer. **Rates (CP):** HS May 16–Sept 15 $62–$82 S or D. Extra person $10. Children under 12 stay free. Lower rates off-season. Higher rates for spec evnts/hols. Pking: Outdoor, free. Maj CC.

▤▤ **Nevada Inn**, 1009 Nevada Hwy, Boulder City, NV 89005; tel 702/293-2044 or toll free 800/638-8890; fax 702/293-0023. Basic motel. **Rooms:** 55 rms, stes, and effic. CI Open/CO noon. Nonsmoking rms avail. Rooms are a bit outdated and beginning to show wear. **Amenities:** 🛎️ 🎛️ A/C, cable TV, refrig. Some units w/terraces, some w/Jacuzzis. **Services:** 🍴 🍷 **Facilities:** 🏋️ Whirlpool, washer/dryer. Pool surrounded by sundeck. Parking for boats and RVs. **Rates:** $45–$55 S or D; from $55 ste; from $65 effic. Extra person $5. Children under 18 stay free. Pking: Outdoor, free. Maj CC.

▤▤ **Super 8 Motel**, 704 Nevada Hwy, Boulder City, NV 89005; tel 702/294-8888 or toll free 800/800-8000; fax 702/293-4344. Well-kept motel. **Rooms:** 138 rms and stes. CI 3pm/CO noon. Nonsmoking rms avail. Rooms have older furniture but are clean. Honeymoon suite has circular bed and mirror. **Amenities:** 🛎️ 🎛️ A/C, cable TV, refrig. Some units w/terraces, some w/Jacuzzis. Suites have whirlpools. **Services:** 🍴 🍷 **Facilities:** 🏋️ 🍽️ 1 rst, 1 bar, games rm, whirlpool, washer/dryer. Sundeck outside pool house. **Rates:** $40–$44 S or D; from $80 ste. Children under 18 stay free. Higher rates for spec evnts/hols. Spec packages avail. Pking: Outdoor, free. Maj CC.

Attractions 🧳

Lake Mead National Recreation Area, 601 Nevada Hwy; tel 702/293-8906. Formed by the damming of the Colorado River, Lake Mead is one of the region's top recreation destinations. More than 8 million people visit the lake annually to boat, ski, fish, swim, and camp. The 2,300-mile area surrounds both Lake Mead and Lake Mohave, which extends from Hoover Dam downstream to Davis Dam.

There are a number of developed areas on both the Nevada and the Arizona sides of the lake, offering accommodations, boat facilities and rentals, and campgrounds. These include Boulder Beach and Echo Bay on the Nevada side and Temple Bar on the Arizona side. On nearby Lake Mohave, Katherine Landing, just outside Bullhead City, AZ, provides all amenities.

Black Canyon, between Hoover Dam and Lake Mohave, is one of the last undammed stretches of the Colorado River and is part of the recreation area. It is still possible to canoe or raft down this section of river, and along the way there are rapids and several side canyons worth exploring. Several tour-boat operators in the area offer a variety of guided boat tours of the Lake Mead area, including Black Canyon.

The **Alan Bible Visitor Center,** 4 miles northeast of Boulder City on US 93 at Nev 166 (tel 702/293-8906), can provide information on all area activities and services. For more information contact the Superintendent, Lake Mead National Recreation Area, 601 Nevada Hwy, Boulder City, NV 89005-2426. **Open:** Daily 24 hours. Free.

Hoover Dam, US 93; tel 702/293-8367. Located about 8 miles east of Boulder City on US 93. Constructed between 1931 and 1935, this was the was the first major dam on the Colorado River. By providing the huge amounts of electricity and water needed by Arizona and California, the Hoover Dam project helped trigger the phenomenal growth experienced in this region during this century.

At 726 feet from bedrock to the roadway along its top, it is the highest concrete dam in the Western Hemisphere. The 110-mile-long **Lake Mead** (see above), which was created by the dam, is the largest human-made reservoir in the United States. Bureau of Reclamation guides conduct tours through Hoover Dam daily. An exhibit housing a model of a generating unit and a topographical model of the Colorado River Basin is also open to the public. **Open:** June–Aug, daily 9am–7pm; Sept–May, daily 9am–4pm. Closed Dec 25. $

CARSON CITY

Map page M-4, C1

Hotels 🛏️

▤▤ **Best Western Carson Station Casino/Hotel**, 900 S Carson St, Carson City, NV 89701; tel 702/883-0900 or toll free 800/528-1234; fax 702/882-7569. Casino/hotel with newly remodeled rooms and suites. **Rooms:** 92 rms and stes. CI 3pm/CO noon. Nonsmoking rms avail. **Amenities:** 🛎️ 🍸 A/C, cable TV. Some units w/minibars, all w/terraces. **Services:** 🆅🅿️ 🧺 🍴 **Facilities:** 🍽️ 🛗 2 rsts, 2 bars (1 w/entertainment). Casino;

Sports Book lounge, where guests can wager on all major sporting events. Cabaret with nightly live entertainment. **Rates:** HS Apr–Oct $45–$65 S or D; from $85 ste. Extra person $5. Children under 12 stay free. Min stay wknds and spec evnts. Lower rates off-season. Higher rates for spec evnts/hols. Spec packages avail. Pking: Outdoor, free. Maj CC.

≝≝≝ **Hardman House Inn**, 917 N Carson St, Carson City, NV 89701; tel 702/882-7744 or toll free 800/626-1793; fax 702/887-0321. Renovation near completion; furniture, wallpaper, bedspreads, and draperies in the guest rooms are being replaced. **Rooms:** 62 rms and stes. CI noon/CO noon. Express checkout avail. Nonsmoking rms avail. **Amenities:** 🛁 A/C, cable TV. Some units w/terraces. Refrigerators and microwaves available for $6 per day. **Services:** 🛆 ⏱ Complimentary coffee in the lobby. **Rates:** HS May 15–Oct 15 $42–$50 S; $46–$55 D; from $70 ste. Extra person $6–$15. Children under 3 stay free. Min stay spec evnts. Lower rates off-season. Higher rates for spec evnts/hols. Pking: Indoor/outdoor, free. Maj CC.

Motels

≝≝ **Best Western Trailside Inn**, 1300 N Carson St, Carson City, NV 89707; tel 702/883-7300 or toll free 800/626-1900; fax 702/883-7300. Delightful lobby, handsome exteriors, pleasing rooms—perhaps the most attractive property in Carson City. **Rooms:** 67 rms. CI 2pm/CO 11am. Nonsmoking rms avail. Charming bedrooms in navy blue, gray, and rose prints make up for lack of bath decor. **Amenities:** 🛁 🔲 A/C, cable TV, refrig. **Services:** ⏱ ⏰ **Facilities:** 🔲 ⚃ Pool, next to highway, is noisy. **Rates:** HS June–Sept $52–$76 S or D. Extra person $6. Children under 12 stay free. Min stay wknds. Lower rates off-season. Higher rates for spec evnts/hols. Pking: Outdoor, free. Maj CC.

≝ **Round House Inn**, 1400 N Carson St, Carson City, NV 89701; tel 702/882-3446. **Rooms:** 39 rms and stes. CI 11am/CO 11am. Nonsmoking rms avail. Attempts have been made to coordinate furnishings, but beds and chests of drawers are of poor quality. **Amenities:** 🛁 🔲 A/C, cable TV, refrig. **Services:** ⏱ ⏰ **Facilities:** 🔲 The pool is located next to the highway and noisy. **Rates:** HS May 15–Sept 15 $45–$50 S; $50–$60 D; from $60 ste. Extra person $4. Children under 16 stay free. Lower rates off-season. Pking: Outdoor, free. Maj CC.

Restaurant 🍴

♥ **Adele's Restaurant & Bar**, 1112 N Carson St, Carson City; tel 702/882-3353. **Continental/Seafood.** Located in an 1875 Victorian house with mansard roof. Victorian decor throughout—heavy lace tablecloths, lace-trimmed napkins, and stained-glass windows. An eclectic menu features traditional dishes with contemporary variations, such as barbecued Cajun prawns, goose liver pâté, carpaccio, blackened salmon, or swordfish. **FYI:** Reservations recommended. Jazz. Dress code. **Open:** Lunch Mon–Fri 11am–4:30pm, Sat 11:30am–2:30pm; dinner Mon–Sat 5–10pm. Closed some hols; Jan 2–15. **Prices:** Main courses $16–$34. Maj CC. ♥ 🍷

Attractions 💼

Nevada State Museum, 600 N Carson St; tel 702/687-4810. Among the exhibits and displays featured here are the nation's largest exhibited Imperial mammoth skeleton; coins and other artifacts from the former US Mint in Carson City; a diorama of the Lost City pueblo; and a reconstructed Great Basin Indian Camp. The Earth Science Gallery explores Nevada's geological history and includes a walk-through Devonian Sea diorama. **Open:** Daily 8:30am–4:30pm. Closed some hols. $

Nevada State Railroad Museum, 2180 S Carson St (at the Capitol Complex); tel 702/687-6953. Considered one of the finest regional railroad museums in the country, this facility houses more than 25 pieces of rolling stock, including 5 steam locomotives and several restored coaches and freight cars. Also diplayed are historical artifacts, a depot, a dispatcher's office, an engine house, and machine and blacksmith shops. Most of the equipment is from the Virginia & Truckee Railroad, the richest and most famous short line in the annals of 19th-century railroading. Guided tours are available.

Highlights of the summer season include the regular weekend operation of a 65-year-old rail bus, special events, and the operation of historic railroad equipment. **Open:** Wed–Sun 8:30am–4:30pm. Closed some hols. $

CRYSTAL BAY

Map page M-4, C3 (S of Truckee)

Lodge 🖥

≝≝ **Cal-Neva Lodge**, 2 Stateline Rd, PO Box 368, Crystal Bay, NV 89402; tel 702/832-4000 or toll free 800/CAL-NEVA; fax 702/831-9007. 3 mi W of Incline. Cal-Neva exit off Nev 28. 14 acres. A diverse, somewhat bizarre place. Heavily promotes its past association with Frank Sinatra and the Rat Pack and draws a diverse crowd of gamblers and young newlyweds. Offers ongoing entertainment, from school plays to cabaret. **Rooms:** 180 rms and stes; 23 ctges/villas. CI 3pm/CO noon. Express checkout avail. Nonsmoking rms avail. Rooms are spacious and done in a country-French style. Every room and suite has a view of Lake

Tahoe. Separate cabins and honeymoon cottages available. **Amenities:** 🛏 ⚃ 📠 A/C, cable TV w/movies. Some units w/terraces, some w/fireplaces, 1 w/Jacuzzi. **Services:** ✕ 🔑 VP 📺 🍴 Masseur, babysitting. **Facilities:** 🛗 🏊 🎣 🎾 2 💪 360 ♿ 1 rst, 1 bar, games rm, spa, sauna, steam rm, whirlpool, beauty salon. 3 wedding chapels, outdoor tents for receptions or meetings, small casino, show room/bar/lounge. Round bar is a classic—decorated with Washoe Indian memorabilia, leather couches, high beamed ceiling. **Rates:** HS May 27–Sept 30 $89–$139 S or D; from $189 ste; from $89 ctge/villa. Extra person $10. Children under 11 stay free. Min stay HS. Lower rates off-season. Higher rates for spec evnts/hols. Spec packages avail. Pking: Outdoor, free. Maj CC.

ELKO

Map page M-4, A3

Hotels 🏨

▤▤ **Holiday Inn**, 3015 Idaho St, Elko, NV 89801; tel 702/738-8425 or toll free 800/465-4329; fax 702/753-7906. Exit 303 off I-80. There's a new wing here, with rooms equal to any in town. **Rooms:** 170 rms. CI 4pm/CO noon. Nonsmoking rms avail. New rooms far superior to old ones. Bathrooms have two basins, one outside bathroom door. **Amenities:** 🛏 ⚃ A/C, cable TV. Some rooms have refrigerators, microwaves. **Services:** ✕ 🚗 📺 🍴 🛎 **Facilities:** 🛗 💪 200 ♿ 1 rst, 1 bar (w/entertainment), games rm, whirlpool, washer/dryer. **Rates:** HS May–Sept $59–$69 S or D. Extra person $10. Children under 18 stay free. Lower rates off-season. Higher rates for spec evnts/hols. Spec packages avail. Pking: Outdoor, free. Maj CC.

▤▤▤ **Red Lion Inn & Casino**, 2065 Idaho St, Elko, NV 89801; tel 702/738-2111 or toll free 800/545-0044; fax 702/753-9859. Nice property. Casino is one of town's largest. **Rooms:** 223 rms and stes. CI 4pm/CO noon. Express checkout avail. Nonsmoking rms avail. Suites are huge. Furniture is attractive and high quality. **Amenities:** 🛏 ⚃ 📠 A/C, satel TV w/movies. Some units w/minibars, some w/terraces, some w/Jacuzzis. **Services:** 🚗 📺 🍴 🛎 **Facilities:** 🛗 250 ♿ 2 rsts, 3 bars (1 w/entertainment), games rm, beauty salon. **Rates:** $64–$95 S; $74–$95 D; from $94 ste. Extra person $10. Children under 16 stay free. Higher rates for spec evnts/hols. Pking: Outdoor, free. Maj CC.

Motels

▤▤ **Best Western AmeriTel Inn Express**, 837 Idaho St, Elko, NV 89801; tel 702/738-7261 or toll free 800/600-6001; fax 702/738-0118. Exit 301 off I-80. Located near downtown and convention center. Pleasant atmosphere. **Rooms:** 49 rms and stes. CI 1pm/CO 11am. Nonsmoking rms avail. **Amenities:** 🛏 ⚃ A/C, cable TV, refrig. Microwave. **Services:** 🚗 📺 🍴 **Facilities:** 🛗 **Rates:** HS Apr–Sept 1 $54 S; $59 D; from $59 ste. Extra person $5. Children under 12 stay free. Min stay spec evnts. Lower rates off-season. Higher rates for spec evnts/hols. Pking: Outdoor, free. Maj CC.

▤▤▤ **Best Western AmeriTel Inn–Elko**, 1930 Idaho St, Elko, NV 89801; tel 702/738-8787 or toll free 800/600-6001; fax 702/753-7910. Exit 303 off I-80. A very inviting spot. **Rooms:** 110 rms, stes, and effic. CI open/CO 11am. Nonsmoking rms avail. Rooms are fresh and cheerful looking. **Amenities:** 🛏 ⚃ A/C, cable TV, refrig. **Services:** 🚗 📺 🍴 🛎 **Facilities:** 🛗 💪 Fast-food restaurants nearby. **Rates (CP):** HS May 15–Oct 15 $60 S; $65 D; from $104 ste; from $104 effic. Extra person $5. Children under 15 stay free. Lower rates off-season. Spec packages avail. Pking: Outdoor, free. Ltd CC.

▤▤▤ **Shilo Inn**, 2401 Mountain City Hwy, Elko, NV 89801; tel 702/738-5522 or toll free 800/222-2244; fax 702/738-6247. Exit 301 off I-80. Inviting property. Indoor pool a major plus in hot climate. **Rooms:** 70 stes. CI 2pm/CO noon. Nonsmoking rms avail. Rooms have 2 large closets, 1 small. Also 2-burner stove, dishwasher, loveseat, and table and 3 chairs. **Amenities:** 🛏 ⚃ 🍴 A/C, cable TV w/movies, refrig. All units w/minibars. Microwave. VCR and movies available for rent. **Services:** 🚗 📺 🍴 🛎 Complimentary continental breakfast, popcorn, *USA Today*. **Facilities:** 🛗 💪 75 ♿ Sauna, steam rm, whirlpool, washer/dryer. **Rates:** HS Mem Day–Labor Day from $72 ste. Extra person $10. Children under 12 stay free. Lower rates off-season. Higher rates for spec evnts/hols. Pking: Outdoor, free. Maj CC.

Restaurant 🍴

Nevada Dinner House, 351 Silver St, Elko; tel 702/738-8485. **American/Basque.** A mural of the Pyrénées backs the bar, and various Basque items, such as bota bags, provide decoration. Family-style dinners include spaghetti, T-bone steak, grilled lamb chops, and fried shrimp. **FYI:** Reservations recommended. Dress code. **Open:** Tues–Sat 5–10pm, Sun 5–9pm. Closed some hols. **Prices:** Main courses $13.95–$17.95. Maj CC. ■

ELY

Map page M-4, B4

Attractions 📷

Cave Lake State Recreation Area, Nev 486; tel 702/728-4467 (District Office). Located at an elevation of 7,300 feet in the Schell Creek Range, 8 miles south of Ely via US 93, then 7 miles east on Success Summit Rd (Nev 486). The park covers 1,240 acres and has a 32-acre reservoir, providing excellent trout fishing, boating, and swimming. Also hiking, picnicking, and camping; cross-country skiing, ice skating, and ice fishing in winter. Information kiosks are located throughout the park. Interpretive programs. **Open:** Daily 24 hours. Free.

Nevada Northern Railway Museum, Ave A at 11th St E (in East Ely); tel 702/289-2085. The Nevada Northern Railway Depot, built in 1906, was in continuous use until the railway was shut down in 1983. The depot itself is maintained just as it was when it was in operation, making it one of the best-preserved shortline railroad depots in the United States. Guided tours (45–60 min) take in the entire depot. Excursions aboard an original turn-of-the-century steam passenger train are offered on weekends (additional fee; phone for schedule). **Open:** Mem Day–Labor Day, tours daily at 9 and 11am, 1:30 and 3:30pm; by appointment rest of year. $

FALLON

Map page M-4, B2

Motels 📷

Best Western Bonanza Inn & Casino, 855 W Williams Ave, Fallon, NV 89406; tel 702/423-6031 or toll free 800/528-1234; fax 702/423-6283. With a small casino and restaurant, easily accessible from the highway. **Rooms:** 75 rms and stes. CI 6pm/CO noon. Nonsmoking rms avail. Pleasant and tastefully furnished. The hallways are dingy. **Amenities:** 📷 A/C, cable TV w/movies. **Services:** ⟲ ⟲ **Facilities:** 📷 📷 📷 1 rst, 1 bar, games rm. Enclosed pool is located in the parking lot, so there's noise from the highway. **Rates:** HS May–Sept $50 S; $55 D; from $65 ste. Extra person $7. Children under 12 stay free. Lower rates off-season. Pking: Outdoor, free. Maj CC.

Comfort Inn, 1830 W Williams Ave, Fallon, NV 89406; tel 702/423-5554 or toll free 800/221-2222; fax 702/423-0663. **Rooms:** 49 rms and stes. Exec-level rms avail. CI 2pm/CO noon. Nonsmoking rms avail. Rooms are tasteful but blandly decorated in quiet colors. **Amenities:** 📷 📷 A/C, cable TV. Some units w/Jacuzzis. Refrigerators available upon request. **Services:** ⟲ Complimentary breakfast in sunny area of the lobby. VCR and movie rentals available. **Facilities:** 📷 Whirlpool. **Rates:** $46–$52 S; $52–$75 D; from $61 ste. Extra person $5. Children under 18 stay free. Higher rates for spec evnts/hols. Pking: Outdoor, free. Maj CC.

Econo Lodge, 70 E Williams Ave, Fallon, NV 89406; tel 702/423-2194 or toll free 800/553-2666; fax 702/423-7187. A clean property undergoing renovation. **Rooms:** 30 rms and stes. CI 6:30am/CO 11am. Nonsmoking rms avail. Pleasant, cheerful decor, with furniture of modest quality. Bathrooms could be better, and are slated for renovation. **Amenities:** 📷 📷 A/C, cable TV w/movies, refrig. Microwave and refrigerator available at no charge. **Services:** 📷 ⟲ Free continental breakfast. Fax and copy services available. **Facilities:** 📷 **Rates:** HS May 15–Oct 15 $40–$45 S; $43–$55 D; from $50 ste. Extra person $5. Children under 18 stay free. Lower rates off-season. Higher rates for spec evnts/hols. Pking: Outdoor, free. Maj CC.

Restaurant 🍴

$ Prospector Room, in Nugget Casino, 70 Maine St, Fallon; tel 702/423-3111. **American.** A bright, cheerful cafe with a reputation for good food. Part of a fast-dying breed of Nevada small-town casino cafes. Western decor, traditional fare: BLTs, calf's liver, banana cream pie. **FYI:** Reservations accepted. Children's menu. **Open:** Sun–Thurs 6am–10pm, Fri–Sat 6am–2pm. **Prices:** Main courses $4.99–$11.99. Maj CC. 📷 📷

Attraction 📷

Lahontan State Recreation Area, 16799 Lahontan Dam; tel 702/867-3500 or 577-2226. Located 18 miles west of Fallon via US 50, this 30,000-acre area includes Lahontan Reservoir, which has 69 miles of shoreline, is 17 miles long, and covers 10,000 surface acres when full. Fishing, boating, and waterskiing are popular activities. Camping and picnicking are also available; interpretive programs. **Open:** Daily 24 hours. $

GARDNERVILLE

Map page M-4, C1

Motels 📷

Topay Lodge & Casino, 1979 Hwy 395 S, PO Box 187, Gardnerville, NV 89410; tel 702/266-3338 or toll free 800/962-0732. This hotel overlooking Topaz Lake caters to water-skiers and fishing enthusiasts. Down-home, friendly casino. **Rooms:** 59 rms. CI 2pm/CO 11am. Rooms are nicely decorated; some have views of the lake. **Amenities:** ☎ A/C, cable TV w/movies. **Services:** ⬤ **Facilities:** 🛗△◻♨♦⬤ 1 rst, 2 bars (1 w/entertainment), games rm. **Rates:** $39–$53 S or D. Extra person $2. Children under 5 stay free. Pking: Outdoor, free. Maj CC.

≡ **Westerner Motel**, 1353 US 395, PO Box 335, Gardnerville, NV 89410; tel 702/782-3602. **Rooms:** 25 rms. CI 1pm/CO 11am. Nonsmoking rms avail. **Amenities:** ☎ A/C, cable TV. **Services:** ⬤ ⬤ **Facilities:** 🛗 **Rates:** HS Apr–Oct $30–$43 S or D. Extra person $3–$5. Children under 1 stay free. Min stay HS, wknds, and spec evnts. Lower rates off-season. Higher rates for spec evnts/hols. Pking: Outdoor, free. Maj CC.

GOODSPRINGS

Map page M-4, E3 (SW of Las Vegas)

Attraction 🛍

Goodsprings Ghost Town. Located 35 miles southwest of Las Vegas on I-15 S and west on Nev 161. Goodsprings, founded in the 1860s, was once the biggest town in Nevada, a thriving metropolis built around nearby silver and lead mines with a population of 2,000. In the years following World War I, mining days ended and the population began to decline; by 1967 the population had dwindled to 62. The once-famous Goodsprings Hotel burned to the ground, and one of the town's last remaining businesses, a general store, was torn down. Today this authentic ghost town is an eerie relic of Nevada's boom-to-bust mining era.

The heart of the town is the **Pioneer Saloon** (tel 702/874-9362), which from its weathered exterior does not look operative. It has, however, been a going concern since 1913. The only complete decorative-metal building left standing in the United States, the saloon has pressed-tin walls (interior and exterior) and ceiling. Many of the fixtures and furnishings are original. The saloon is open daily 10am–midnight.

GREAT BASIN NATIONAL PARK

Map page M-4, C4

Established in 1986, this 77,100-acre national park boasts an exceptionally wide range of plant and animal habitats: from the Pinion–Juniper Life Zone, characterized by jackrabbits, scrub-jays, and sagebrush, to the frigid Alpine Life Zone at higher elevations.

The **Visitor Center** (tel 702/234-7331) is located 5 miles east on Nev 488, in the town of Baker, NV, and is open daily 8am–5pm. The center has displays describing the Great Basin's flora and fauna, geological development, and history. The Great Basin was named by explorer John C Frémont because its rivers and streams flowed inland, soaking into the earth, evaporating, or forming lakes with no outlet to the sea.

Within the park is **Lehman Caves,** formerly Lehman Caves National Monument. Discovered in 1885, these caves are among the most highly decorated limestone solution caverns in the United States. Guided tours (90 minutes) depart from the Visitor Center and follow a half-mile trail through chambers with names like the Gothic Palace, the Cypress Swamp, and the Grand Palace. Cave temperature is always 50°F; those under age 16 must be accompanied by an adult.

The 12-mile **Wheeler Peak Scenic Drive** begins east of the Visitor Center and ends at a campground and trailhead 10,000 feet up the northern flank of Wheeler Peak. A variety of marked hiking trails begins at this point, including a trail to the glacier at the base of Wheeler Peak and one to the summit of Wheeler Peak (13,063 ft). Three campgrounds are located along the scenic drive, and a fourth is located south of the Visitor Center.

Lexington Arch, near the southeast border of the park, is another highlight, a natural limestone arch more than 6 stories high. To reach the arch, an unpaved road leads to a 1-mile trail.

For more information write to the Superintendent, Great Basin National Park, Baker, NV 89311.

HENDERSON

Map page M-4, E4

Motel 🛏

≡≡ **Best Western Lake Mead Motel**, 85 W Lake Mead Dr, Henderson, NV 89015; tel 702/564-1712 or toll free 800/528-1234; fax 702/564-7642. 13 mi S of Las Vegas. Lake Mead Dr exit off Boulder Hwy. Popular with truckers and RVers because of the huge parking lot; noise from tractor-trailers can be annoying. **Rooms:** 58 rms. CI 3pm/CO 11am. Nonsmoking rms avail. Modern furnishings include upgraded carpets, drapes, and brass wall lamps. Earth-tone colors predominate. **Amenities:** ☎ 🖥 A/C, cable TV. **Services:** 🛆 **Facilities:** 🛗 Washer/dryer. **Rates:** $43–$55 S; $48–$60 D. Extra person $5. Children under 12 stay free. Pking: Outdoor, free. Maj CC.

Attractions 📷

Clark County Heritage Museum, 1830 S Boulder Hwy; tel 702/455-7955. A museum illustrating the history of southern Nevada, this facility offers both indoor and outdoor exhibits. Inside is a permanent exhibit in the form of a time line that starts with a prehistoric Nevada dire wolf display and extends to the 20th-century development of casinos and the gaming industry; there are also several changing exhibitions. Outdoor exhibits include an authentic ghost town; the original 1931 Boulder City train depot and a collection of authentic railroad rolling stock; and Heritage Street, with 6 restored historic buildings that have been relocated here, restored, and opened for tours. **Open:** Daily 9am–4:30pm. Closed Dec 25. $

Kidd Marshmallow Factory, 8203 Gibson Rd; tel 702/564-5400. Kidd and Co has been a family-owned and -operated business since the late 1800s. Today it distributes more than 150 brands of marshmallow products throughout North America. Self-guided tours visit the marshmallow-making process from start to finish. Free samples; gift shop. **Open:** Daily 9am–4:30pm. Closed some hols. Free.

INCLINE VILLAGE

Map page M-4, C1 (NW of Carson City)

Resort 🏨

Hyatt Regency Lake Tahoe, Country Club Dr at Lake Shore, PO Box 3239, Incline Village, NV 89450-3239; tel 702/832-1234 or toll free 800/233-1234; fax 702/831-7508. 30 mi SW of Reno. 28 acres. Near the lakefront, this mid-rise hotel has a medium-size casino, where lots of activity seems crammed into a small space. Unrated. **Rooms:** 434 rms and stes; 24 ctges/villas. Exec-level rms avail. CI 3pm/CO 11am. Express checkout avail. Nonsmoking rms avail. Fairly standard. **Amenities:** 🕿 ♨ 📻 A/C, cable TV w/movies, voice mail, in-rm safe. All units w/minibars, some w/terraces, some w/fireplaces. **Services:** |O| ◘ 🚐 🛎 ♨ Car-rental desk, social director, masseur, children's program, babysitting. **Facilities:** 🗗 🏌 🛝 🚴 ⛳ 🏊 ⛵ 🚣 🏓 🖼 🖳 🏋 3 rsts, 3 bars (w/entertainment), 1 beach (lake shore), games rm, spa, sauna, steam rm, whirlpool, day-care ctr, playground. Cafe/restaurant with an all-you-can-eat buffet. **Rates:** HS June 20–Sept 4 $169–$239 S or D; from $299 ste; from $424 ctge/villa. Extra person $25. Children under 18 stay free. Lower rates off-season. Higher rates for spec evnts/hols. Spec packages avail. Pking: Outdoor, free. Maj CC.

Attractions 📷

Ponderosa Ranch and Western Theme Park, 100 Ponderosa Ranch Rd; tel 702/831-0691. Located just off Nev 28. Many visitors will probably recognize this movie-set ranch as the location for the hit TV series *Bonanza*. Many show-oriented exhibits include dozens of props and the original 1959 Cartwright Ranch House. Activities include pony rides, staged gunfights, hayrides, a petting farm, and a blacksmith's shop. From Memorial Day–Labor Day a hayride breakfast is offered from 8–9:30am. **Open:** Mid-Apr–Oct, daily 9:30am–5pm. $$$

Lake Tahoe Nevada State Park, 2005 Nev 28; tel 702/831-0494. Comprising approximately 14,000 acres along the eastern shore of Lake Tahoe, this park is comprised of 5 areas: **Sand Harbor,** the most popular, has sandy beaches, swimming, picnicking, boat launching, and a visitors center; **Spooner Lake,** offers hiking, fishing, and mountain biking; **Cave Rock** is popular for boating and fishing; **Memorial Point** and **Hidden Beach** offer more secluded access to the shores of Lake Tahoe. The majority of the park is backcountry in the mountains east of the lake. Two primitive campsites and portions of the Tahoe Rim Trail are located in the Spooner Lake area. **Open:** Daily 24 hours. $$

LAS VEGAS

Map page M-4, E3

See also **Boulder City, Goodsprings, Henderson**

TOURIST INFORMATION

Las Vegas Convention and Visitors Authority 3150 Paradise Rd, in the Las Vegas Convention Center (tel 702/892-7550 or toll free 800/332-5333). Open daily 8am–6pm.

Las Vegas Chamber of Commerce 711 E Desert Inn Rd (tel 702/735-1616). Open Mon–Fri 8am–5pm.

PUBLIC TRANSPORTATION

Citizens Area Transit (CAT) Buses Operate 5:30am–1:30am to residential neighborhoods and 24 hours along the strip. Fare $1 for residential routes, $1.50 along the strip; 50¢ for seniors and students on all routes, children under 5 free. Exact fare required. For information call 702/228-7433, or visit the Downtown Transportation Center, at corner of Casino Center Blvd and Stuart Ave, Mon–Fri 6am–9:45pm, Sat–Sun 6am–5:45pm. Monthly passes, tokens, and information available.

Las Vegas Strip Trolley Operates every 20–30 minutes 9:30am–1:30am. Travels between the Hacienda Hotel and Las Vegas Hilton, stopping at all major hotels along the strip. Fare $1.10; exact change required. For information call 702/382-1404.

Hotels 🏨

≡≡≡ **Alexis Park Resort Las Vegas**, 375 E Harmon Ave, Las Vegas, NV 89109; tel 702/796-3300 or toll free 800/453-8000; fax 702/796-0766. Turn east on Harmon Ave off Las Vegas Blvd. 20 acres. Remains one of the finest places off the strip. **Rooms:** 500 rms and stes. CI 2pm/CO 11am. Express checkout avail. Nonsmoking rms avail. Huge rooms resemble cottages and villas, many with 2 levels. Deluxe rooms available. **Amenities:** 🏠 📺 A/C, cable TV w/movies, refrig. Some units w/minibars, some w/terraces, some w/fireplaces, some w/Jacuzzis. **Services:** ⊙ 🔑 VP 📠 ↵ 🛎 Social director, masseur, children's program, babysitting. **Facilities:** 🏋 🏊 ⛳ 🎱 ♿ 1 rst, 1 bar (w/entertainment), lifeguard, spa, sauna, steam rm, whirlpool, washer/dryer. Putting green. **Rates:** $109–$200 S or D; from $225 ste. Extra person $15. Children under 12 stay free. Higher rates for spec evnts/hols. Spec packages avail. Pking: Outdoor, free. Maj CC.

≡≡≡ **Algiers Hotel**, 2845 Las Vegas Blvd S, Las Vegas, NV 89109; tel 702/735-3311 or toll free 800/732-3361; fax 702/792-1212. One of the best deals on the strip. Small, centrally located hotel offers guests a comfortable, friendly stay without the hustle of newer establishments. **Rooms:** 105 rms and stes. CI noon/CO noon. A more "homey" feel than most Las Vegas accommodations. Soundproofing is so good you might forget you're in town. **Amenities:** 🏠 A/C, cable TV w/movies. Extra blankets and pillows upon request. **Services:** 📠 ↵ Car-rental desk, babysitting. **Facilities:** 🏋 ♿ 1 rst, 1 bar. On-site wedding chapel and several attached stores. Reasonably priced restaurant has great specials. **Rates:** $40–$60 S or D; from $60 ste. Extra person $5. Children under 12 stay free. Min stay spec evnts. Pking: Outdoor, free. Maj CC.

≡≡≡≡ **Bally's Las Vegas**, 3645 Las Vegas Blvd S, Las Vegas, NV 89109; tel 702/739-4111 or toll free 800/634-3434. On the strip. This hotel has large, bright, comfortable rooms which may be the best in Las Vegas. A renovation project nearing completion will make Bally's even better. **Rooms:** 2,814 rms and stes. Exec-level rms avail. CI 3pm/CO 11am. Express checkout avail. Nonsmoking rms avail. Renovations in late 1993 created "new" rooms with faux marble and large windows. **Amenities:** 🏠 A/C, cable TV w/movies, voice mail. Some units w/Jacuzzis. **Services:** ⊙ VP 📠 ↵ Car-rental desk, masseur, babysitting. Can arrange excursions to Hoover Dam and the

Grand Canyon. **Facilities:** 🏋 🏊5 🏊 ⛳ 4.5K ♿ 7 rsts, 5 bars (1 w/entertainment), lifeguard, games rm, spa, whirlpool, beauty salon. New $2 million health spa. **Rates:** $89–$189 S or D; from $250 ste. Extra person $15. Children under 17 stay free. Higher rates for spec evnts/hols. Spec packages avail. Pking: Indoor/outdoor, free. Maj CC. Higher than most Las Vegas hotels, but worth it.

≡≡≡ **Barbary Coast Hotel & Casino**, 3595 Las Vegas Blvd S, Las Vegas, NV 89109; tel 702/737-7111 or toll free 800/634-6755. On the strip. A small casino with an adjacent hotel. Unimpressive exterior, but decor inside rooms and casino is rich with Victorian touches and stained-glass windows. The casino and corridors are being refurbished. **Rooms:** 200 rms and stes. CI 2pm/CO noon. Express checkout avail. Nonsmoking rms avail. Rooms are surprisingly luxurious. Currently undergoing renovations. **Amenities:** 🏠 A/C, cable TV w/movies. Some units w/Jacuzzis. **Services:** ⊙ VP 📠 Car-rental desk. Free shuttle to Gold Coast. **Facilities:** ♿ 2 rsts, 2 bars. **Rates:** HS June–Nov $40–$175 S or D; from $125 ste. Extra person $5. Children under 12 stay free. Min stay spec evnts. Lower rates off-season. Higher rates for spec evnts/hols. Spec packages avail. Pking: Indoor/outdoor, free. Maj CC.

≡≡≡≡ **Caesars Palace**, 3570 Las Vegas Blvd S, Las Vegas, NV 89109; tel 702/731-7110 or toll free 800/634-6001; fax 702/731-7331. On the strip. 85 acres. Still considered among the best in Las Vegas. One of the largest hotels on the strip, catering to stars, high rollers, and other top clientele. **Rooms:** 1,500 rms and stes; 14 ctges/villas. Exec-level rms avail. CI 3pm/CO noon. Nonsmoking rms avail. Well-maintained accommodations include some of the largest standard rooms on the strip, and are currently being upgraded. Many have Roman tubs. **Amenities:** 🏠 🅰 📞 A/C, cable TV w/movies, voice mail, in-rm safe. Some units w/minibars, some w/Jacuzzis. **Services:** ⊙ 🔑 VP 📠 ↵ Car-rental desk, masseur, babysitting. **Facilities:** 🏋 🏊5 ⛳ 4K ♿ 6 rsts (see also "Restaurants" below), 6 bars (3 w/entertainment), lifeguard, games rm, racquetball, spa, sauna, steam rm, whirlpool, beauty salon. **Rates:** $95–$225 S or D; from $270 ste. Extra person $15. Higher rates for spec evnts/hols. Spec packages avail. Pking: Indoor/outdoor, free. Maj CC.

≡≡≡ **California Hotel/Casino & RV Park**, 12 Ogden Ave, PO Box 630, Las Vegas, NV 89101 (Downtown); tel 702/385-1222 or toll free 800/634-6255; fax 702/388-2660. Aloha theme is popular with visitors from Hawaii. **Rooms:** 650 rms and stes. CI 2pm/CO noon. Express checkout avail. Nonsmoking rms avail. Rooms have southwestern decor, in muted turquoise and mauve. **Amenities:** 🏠 A/C, cable TV w/movies, in-rm safe. Some units w/minibars. **Services:** ✗ VP 🚌 📠 ↵ 🛎 Car-rental desk, babysitting. Friendly, receptive staff. **Facilities:** 🏋 575 ♿ 4 rsts,

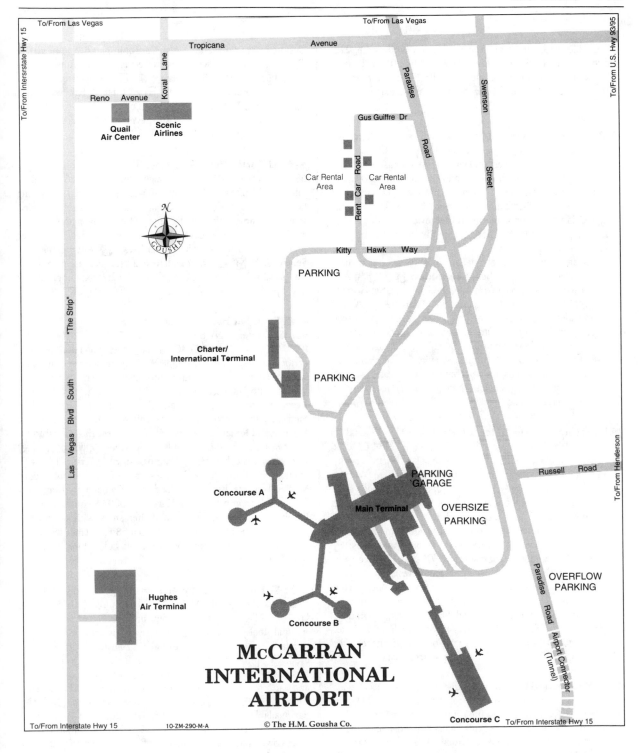

To/From Las Vegas

To/From Las Vegas

Tropicana Avenue

Koval Lane

Paradise Road

Swenson Street

To/From Interstate Hwy 15

To/From U.S. Hwy 93/95

Reno Avenue

Quail Air Center

Scenic Airlines

Gus Guiffre Dr

Car Rental Area

Rent Car Road

Car Rental Area

N GOUSHA

Kitty Hawk Way

PARKING

"The Strip"

Charter/ International Terminal

PARKING

Russell Road

To/From Henderson

PARKING GARAGE

Las Vegas Blvd South

Concourse A

Main Terminal

OVERSIZE PARKING

OVERFLOW PARKING

Hughes Air Terminal

Concourse B

Paradise Road

Airport Connector (Tunnel)

McCARRAN INTERNATIONAL AIRPORT

Concourse C

To/From Interstate Hwy 15

10-ZM-290-M-A

© The H.M. Gousha Co.

To/From Interstate Hwy 15

3 bars, lifeguard, games rm. Hawaiian shop, candy store; 222-space RV park across the street. **Rates:** $40–$60 S or D; from $75 ste. Extra person $5. Children under 12 stay free. Higher rates for spec evnts/hols. Spec packages avail. Pking: Indoor, free. Maj CC.

≣≣≣ **Carriage House**, 105 E Harmon Ave, Las Vegas, NV 89109; tel 702/798-1020 or toll free 800/777-1700; fax 702/798-1020 ext 112. Turn east on Harmon Ave off Las Vegas Blvd. Although rooms are available for nightly rental, most accommodations here are used by time-share customers. Located right next to the MGM theme park. **Rooms:** 154 rms and effic. CI 3pm/CO 11am. Nonsmoking rms avail. Provided you don't mind the rates, these rooms are among the best in the middle range of hotels. All are suites and resemble mini-apartments. Despite some wear, rooms are nicely decorated and well-maintained. Deluxe suites have full kitchens. **Amenities:** 🛏 🛁 📺 🍽 A/C, cable TV w/movies, refrig, in-rm safe, shoe polisher. **Services:** ✕ 🚐 🖾 ↵ Children's program, babysitting. **Facilities:** 🛐 🍸 🏊 1 rst (*see also* "Restaurants" below), 1 bar (w/entertainment), whirlpool, washer/dryer. Outdoor pool and sundeck, laundry facilities on each floor, rooftop restaurant and lounge. **Rates:** $95–$245 S; $125–$345 D; from $125 effic. Children under 18 stay free. Min stay wknds and spec evnts. Higher rates for spec evnts/hols. Spec packages avail. Pking: Outdoor, free. Maj CC. Family package available.

≣≣≣ **Circus Circus Hotel & Casino**, 2880 Las Vegas Blvd S, PO Box 14967, Las Vegas, NV 89114; tel 702/734-0410 or toll free 800/444-CIRCUS. On the strip. The original family theme hotel in Las Vegas; a circus carnival atmosphere. With its sloping stairways and hilly walkways, some may think it's a bit rundown, but it makes up with attractions. A great place to take kids. **Rooms:** 2,800 rms and stes. CI 2pm/CO noon. Express checkout avail. Nonsmoking rms avail. Rooms are basic and comfortable and decorated in primary colors. **Amenities:** 🛏 A/C, cable TV w/movies. **Services:** ✕ 🆅🅿 🚐 ↵ Twice-daily maid svce, car-rental desk, babysitting. **Facilities:** 🛐 ⅚ 6 rsts, 3 bars (2 w/entertainment), lifeguard, games rm, whirlpool, beauty salon, playground. Carnival midway with games and circus acts. Making additions, including Grand Slam Canyon, an indoor theme park. **Rates:** HS June–Aug $38–$55 D; from $55 ste. Children under 18 stay free. Lower rates off-season. Higher rates for spec evnts/hols. Pking: Indoor/outdoor, free. Maj CC.

≣≣≣ **Courtyard by Marriott**, 3275 Paradise Rd, Las Vegas, NV 89109; tel 702/791-3600 or toll free 800/321-2211; fax 702/796-7981. E Sahara exit off I-15; turn south on Paradise Rd. Typical of low-end Marriotts, this caters primarily to business travelers attending conventions. **Rooms:** 149 rms and stes. CI 4pm/CO 1pm. Express checkout avail. Nonsmoking rms avail.

Despite recent renovations, rooms are unimpressive. **Amenities:** 🛏 🛁 A/C, cable TV w/movies, voice mail. Some units w/minibars, all w/terraces. **Services:** ✕ 🚐 🖾 ↵ Car-rental desk, babysitting. **Facilities:** 🛐 🖳 🔟 ⅚ 1 rst, 1 bar, whirlpool, washer/dryer. **Rates:** $78–$88 S or D; from $100 ste. Children under 12 stay free. Min stay spec evnts. Higher rates for spec evnts/hols. Pking: Outdoor, free. Maj CC.

≣≣ **El Cortez Hotel & Casino**, 600 E Fremont St, PO Box 680, Las Vegas, NV 89101 (Downtown); tel 702/385-5200 or toll free 800/634-6703; fax 702/385-1554. This busy, sprawling hotel has the city's oldest casino. Caters to budget-minded seniors. **Rooms:** 308 rms. CI 2pm/CO noon. Nonsmoking rms avail. Garden rooms have 1950s-style furnishings, but tower rooms are more modern. **Amenities:** 🛏 A/C, cable TV. **Services:** ✕ 🆅🅿 ↵ 🍽 **Facilities:** 2 rsts, 3 bars, games rm. **Rates:** $23–$40 S or D. Extra person $3. Children under 12 stay free. Spec packages avail. Pking: Indoor, free. Maj CC.

≣≣ **Excalibur Hotel/Casino**, 3850 Las Vegas Blvd S, PO Box 96778, Las Vegas, NV 89109; tel 702/597-7777 or toll free 800/937-7777; fax 702/597-7040. On the strip. A hotel designed as a cartoon fantasy Camelot, complete with multicolored spires and turrets. There's a drawbridge entry over a moat. A mecca for families with children. **Rooms:** 4,032 rms and stes. CI 3pm/CO 11am. Express checkout avail. Nonsmoking rms avail. Bold medieval theme, with dark wood furniture, colorful red and pink accents, and Renaissance artwork. **Amenities:** 🛏 A/C, cable TV w/movies. Some units w/minibars. **Services:** ✕ 🆅🅿 🚐 🖾 ↵ Car-rental desk, babysitting. **Facilities:** 🛐 ⅚ 7 rsts, 4 bars (1 w/entertainment), lifeguard, games rm, whirlpool, beauty salon. Medieval village has shops, food, and Camelot midway with games and street performers. Huge, 100,000-square-foot casino. Knights on horseback perform dinner show with Merlin the magician. **Rates:** $44–$79 S or D; from $85 ste. Children under 12 stay free. Higher rates for spec evnts/hols. Pking: Outdoor, free. Maj CC.

≣≣≣ **Fairfield Inn by Marriott**, 3850 Paradise Rd, Las Vegas, NV 89109; tel 702/791-0899 or toll free 800/228-2800; fax 702/791-0899. 1 mi S of Convention Center. The inn has a tranquil lobby and sitting room with overstuffed chairs, a fireplace, and a television. **Rooms:** 129 rms. Exec-level rms avail. CI 3pm/CO noon. Express checkout avail. Nonsmoking rms avail. Modern and tasteful decor with hardwood furniture and earth tones. Furnished with desks for the business traveler. **Amenities:** 🛏 🛁 A/C, cable TV w/movies. **Services:** 🚐 🖾 ↵ Fax available. **Facilities:** 🛐 🔙 ⅚ Whirlpool. **Rates (CP):** HS Jan–June/Sept–Nov $49–$65 S or D. Children under 18 stay free. Lower rates off-season. Higher rates for spec evnts/hols. Spec packages avail. Pking: Outdoor, free. Maj CC.

≡≡ **Fitzgeralds Casino/Hotel**, 301 E Fremont St, Las Vegas, NV 89101 (Downtown); tel 702/388-2400 or toll free 800/274-5825; fax 702/388-2181. Nevada's tallest building, at 34 stories, decorated with an Irish theme. Shamrocks, leprechauns, and 4-leaf clovers adorn the public areas. **Rooms:** 654 rms. CI 2pm/CO noon. Express checkout avail. Nonsmoking rms avail. Corner rooms have excellent views. **Amenities:** 🛏 A/C, cable TV w/movies. Some units w/Jacuzzis. **Services:** 🍽 📺 🚗 🛅 🍸 🛎 Car-rental desk. **Facilities:** ♿ 2 rsts, 2 bars, games rm. **Rates:** $38–$70 S or D. Extra person $10. Children under 12 stay free. Higher rates for spec evnts/hols. Spec packages avail. Pking: Indoor, free. Maj CC.

≡≡ **Flamingo Hilton Las Vegas**, 3555 Las Vegas Blvd S, Las Vegas, NV 89109; tel 702/733-3111 or toll free 800/732-2111; fax 702/733-3353. On the strip. The casino is the main attraction here. The hotel razed the original garden rooms to make way for a new tower. **Rooms:** 3,100 rms and stes. CI 2pm/CO noon. Express checkout avail. Nonsmoking rms avail. Most rooms are decorated in blue and green with a tropical motif. **Amenities:** 🛏 🐾 A/C, cable TV w/movies, in-rm safe. Some units w/minibars, some w/terraces, some w/Jacuzzis. **Services:** 🍽 📺 🚗 🛅 🍸 🛎 Car-rental desk, masseur, babysitting. **Facilities:** 🎱 🏊 🎾 💪 🏋 🎰 ♿ 9 rsts, 4 bars (1 w/entertainment), lifeguard, games rm, spa, sauna, steam rm, whirlpool, beauty salon. Large pool with palm trees, fountains, and sundeck. Huge casino and show room. **Rates:** $65–$115 S or D; from $200 ste. Extra person $16. Children under 18 stay free. Higher rates for spec evnts/hols. Spec packages avail. Pking: Indoor, free. Maj CC.

≡≡ **Four Queens Hotel & Casino**, 202 E Fremont St, PO Box 370, Las Vegas, NV 89101 (Downtown); tel 702/385-4011 or toll free 800/634-6045; fax 702/387-5122. The lobby suggests the New Orleans French Quarter, with a carved wood registration desk, brass trim, and chandeliers. **Rooms:** 720 rms and stes. CI 1pm/CO noon. Express checkout avail. Nonsmoking rms avail. Rooms have early American furnishings and brocade wallpaper, and some have 4-poster beds. **Amenities:** 🛏 🐾 A/C, cable TV w/movies. Some units w/minibars. **Services:** 🍽 📺 🚗 🛅 🍸 🛎 Car-rental desk. **Facilities:** 🎰 ♿ 3 rsts, 3 bars (1 w/entertainment), games rm. 60,000-square-foot casino. French Quarter Lounge presents jazz on Monday nights. **Rates:** $47–$57 S or D; from $85 ste. Extra person $8. Children under 12 stay free. Higher rates for spec evnts/hols. Spec packages avail. Pking: Indoor, free. Maj CC.

≡≡≡ **Golden Nugget Hotel & Casino**, 129 E Fremont St, PO Box 2016, Las Vegas, NV 89101 (Downtown); tel 702/385-7111 or toll free 800/634-3454; fax 702/386-8362. Clearly the jewel of downtown, with lots of white marble and gold everywhere. The lobby features lovely gold-leaf chandeliers, white marble floors, and red oriental rugs. **Rooms:** 1,907 rms and stes. Exec-level rms avail. CI 2pm/CO noon. Express checkout avail. Nonsmoking rms avail. Rooms are among the most luxurious in town, with cream-colored carpets, rattan accents, and a tropical feel. **Amenities:** 🛏 🐾 A/C, cable TV w/movies. Some units w/minibars, some w/terraces, some w/Jacuzzis. **Services:** 🍽 📺 🚗 🛅 🛎 Car-rental desk, masseur, babysitting. Golf privileges at nearby Mirage Country Club. **Facilities:** 🎱 🏋 ♿ 4 rsts, 4 bars (1 w/entertainment), lifeguard, games rm, spa, sauna, whirlpool, beauty salon. Gift and apparel shops. Extensive health club has a tanning salon. **Rates:** $58–$110 S or D; from $210 ste. Extra person $20. Children under 12 stay free. Higher rates for spec evnts/hols. Spec packages avail. Pking: Indoor, free. Maj CC.

≡≡ **Hacienda Hotel Casino**, 3950 Las Vegas Blvd S, PO Box 98506, Las Vegas, NV 89119; tel 702/739-8911 or toll free 800/634-6713; fax 702/798-8289. Spanish-theme hotel with red tile, adobe arches, and colorful art in the lobby. Remote location away from the strip. **Rooms:** 1,140 rms and stes. CI 3pm/CO 11am. Express checkout avail. Nonsmoking rms avail. Tower rooms are more modern and nicer, but garden rooms offer better access to pool area. **Amenities:** 🛏 📺 A/C, cable TV w/movies. Some units w/minibars, some w/terraces. **Services:** ✕ 📺 🚗 🛅 🛎 Car-rental desk, babysitting. Friendly, helpful staff. **Facilities:** 🎱 🎾 🎰 ♿ 3 rsts, 2 bars (1 w/entertainment), lifeguard, games rm, beauty salon. Pool surrounded by lush landscaping, casino, wedding chapel, and show room. **Rates:** $28–$88 S or D; from $125 ste. Extra person $10. Children under 12 stay free. Higher rates for spec evnts/hols. Spec packages avail. Pking: Indoor/outdoor, free. Maj CC.

≡≡ **Harrah's Casino Hotel Las Vegas**, 3475 Las Vegas Blvd S, Las Vegas, NV 89109; tel 702/369-5000 or toll free 800/634-6765; fax 702/369-4147. On the strip. Main building resembles an old Mississippi River paddlewheeler. **Rooms:** 1,700 rms and stes. CI 2pm/CO noon. Express checkout avail. Nonsmoking rms avail. Spacious, modern rooms decorated in pastel colors. **Amenities:** 🛏 🐾 A/C, cable TV w/movies. Some units w/minibars, some w/terraces. **Services:** 🍽 📺 🚗 🛅 🛎 Car-rental desk, masseur, babysitting. **Facilities:** 🎱 🏋 🎰 🖥 ♿ 6 rsts, 5 bars (1 w/entertainment), lifeguard, games rm, spa, sauna, steam rm, whirlpool, beauty salon, washer/dryer. Sports bar, wedding chapel. **Rates:** $55–$90 S or D; from $75 ste. Extra person $10. Children under 12 stay free. Higher rates for spec evnts/hols. Spec packages avail. Pking: Indoor, free. Maj CC.

≡≡≡ **Holiday Inn**, 325 E Flamingo Rd, Las Vegas, NV 89109; tel 702/732-9100 or toll free 800/732-7889; fax 702/731-9784. ½ mi E of the strip. Set back from busy Flamingo Rd, with public areas facing away from the street. The comfortable lobby has an indoor fountain and a parlor area decorated with overstuffed furniture and a fireplace. **Rooms:** 150 rms and stes. CI 2pm/CO noon. Nonsmoking rms avail. Modern, with tasteful furnishings and a cool pastel palette. All have sitting areas with couch and recliner. **Amenities:** 🏨 ⚙ 🔲 🍽 A/C, cable TV w/movies, refrig. Some units w/minibars, some w/terraces. **Services:** 🚐 🍴 **Facilities:** 🔲 🏌 250 ♿ 1 rst, 1 bar, whirlpool. **Rates:** $69–$129 S or D; from $149 ste. Extra person $15. Children under 18 stay free. Higher rates for spec evnts/hols. Spec packages avail. Pking: Outdoor, free. Maj CC.

Holiday Inn Boardwalk Hotel & Casino, 3750 Las Vegas Blvd S, Las Vegas, NV 89109; tel 702/735-1167 or toll free 800/635-4581; fax 702/739-8125. On the strip. Recently purchased by Holiday Inn; major renovations are underway. Unrated. **Rooms:** 203 rms. Exec-level rms avail. CI 3pm/CO noon. Nonsmoking rms avail. The renovated rooms have attractive, new furnishings and pastel color schemes. **Amenities:** 🏨 ⚙ A/C, cable TV. 1 unit w/minibar, 1 w/Jacuzzi. **Services:** ✕ 🖐 🖼 🍴 Car-rental desk, babysitting. **Facilities:** 🔲 20 ♿ 2 rsts, 1 bar, games rm, washer/dryer. **Rates:** $65–$125 S or D. Extra person $10. Children under 12 stay free. Min stay spec evnts. Higher rates for spec evnts/hols. Pking: Outdoor, free. Maj CC.

Imperial Palace Hotel & Casino, 3535 Las Vegas Blvd S, Las Vegas, NV 89109; tel 702/731-3311 or toll free 800/634-6441; fax 702/735-8578. On the strip. A 5-story tower behind a small, blue, pagoda facade. Asian-theme hotel is popular with tour groups. **Rooms:** 2,700 rms and stes. CI 3pm/CO noon. Express checkout avail. Nonsmoking rms avail. Far East decor continues in rooms with Japanese art and rattan and bamboo furnishings. **Amenities:** 🏨 A/C, cable TV w/movies. Some units w/minibars, some w/terraces, some w/Jacuzzis. **Services:** 🍽 VP 🚐 🖼 🍴 Car-rental desk, babysitting. **Facilities:** 🔲 🏌 1.6K 🖥 ♿ 9 rsts, 6 bars (1 w/entertainment), lifeguard, games rm, whirlpool, beauty salon. Shops; show room; collection of nearly 800 antique and classic automobiles. **Rates:** $55–$95 S or D; from $150 ste. Extra person $12. Children under 12 stay free. Higher rates for spec evnts/hols. Spec packages avail. Pking: Indoor, free. Maj CC.

Jackie Gaughan's Plaza Hotel/Casino, 1 Main St, Las Vegas, NV 89101 (Downtown); tel 702/386-2110 or toll free 800/634-6575; fax 702/382-8281. Registration desk is almost lost in the chaos of the very glitzy casino. Quiet area on mezzanine level has restaurants and meeting rooms. Amtrak and Greyhound depots next door. **Rooms:** 1,037 rms and stes. CI 2pm/CO noon. Express checkout avail. Nonsmoking rms avail. Rooms are bright, airy, and spacious, with light wood furniture and pastel decor. **Amenities:** 🏨 A/C, cable TV w/movies. Some

units w/minibars, some w/Jacuzzis. **Services:** 🍽 VP 🚐 🖼 🍴 🐕 Car-rental desk, babysitting. **Facilities:** 🔲 🏌 🏊 300 ♿ 3 rsts, 3 bars (1 w/entertainment), lifeguard, games rm, beauty salon. Wedding chapel, show room. **Rates:** $40–$80 S or D; from $90 ste. Extra person $8. Children under 12 stay free. Higher rates for spec evnts/hols. Spec packages avail. Pking: Indoor/outdoor, free. Maj CC.

Lady Luck Casino/Hotel, 206 N 3rd St, PO Box 1060, Las Vegas, NV 89101 (Downtown); tel 702/477-3000 or toll free 800/523-9582; fax 702/477-3002. A bustling hotel that caters to groups. Good value. **Rooms:** 791 rms and stes. CI 3pm/CO noon. Express checkout avail. Nonsmoking rms avail. Junior suites have large windows, sitting areas. **Amenities:** 🏨 ⚙ A/C, cable TV w/movies, refrig. Some units w/minibars, some w/Jacuzzis. All junior suites have Jacuzzis. **Services:** 🍽 VP 🚐 🖼 🍴 🐕 Car-rental desk. **Facilities:** 🔲 ♿ 4 rsts, 2 bars, lifeguard, games rm. Show room. **Rates:** $39–$60 S or D; from $90 ste. Extra person $8. Children under 12 stay free. Higher rates for spec evnts/hols. Pking: Indoor, free. Maj CC.

Las Vegas Club Hotel & Casino, 18 E Fremont St, PO Box 1719, Las Vegas, NV 89101 (Downtown); tel 702/385-1664 or toll free 800/634-6532; fax 702/387-6071. One of downtown's best-kept secrets, with a quiet lobby and friendly atmosphere. **Rooms:** 224 rms and stes. CI 2pm/CO noon. Express checkout avail. Nonsmoking rms avail. Rooms are tastefully decorated in southwestern motifs, with rattan and light wood furniture. **Amenities:** 🏨 A/C, cable TV w/movies, in-rm safe. Some units w/minibars, some w/terraces. **Services:** 🍽 VP 🚐 🖼 🍴 **Facilities:** ♿ 2 rsts, 2 bars. Coffee shop. **Rates:** $40–$50 S or D; from $80 ste. Extra person $8. Children under 12 stay free. Higher rates for spec evnts/hols. Spec packages avail. Pking: Indoor, free. Maj CC.

Las Vegas Hilton, 3000 Paradise Rd, PO Box 93147, Las Vegas, NV 89109 (Convention Center); tel 702/732-5111 or toll free 800/732-7117; fax 702/732-5834. 2 blocks east of Las Vegas Blvd. Far from the clamor of the strip, on nice manicured grounds with the feel of a resort. Lobby glitters with crystal chandeliers, marble floors, brass fixtures. **Rooms:** 3,174 rms and stes. Exec-level rms avail. CI 2pm/CO noon. Express checkout avail. Nonsmoking rms avail. Spacious, bright rooms with light wood furniture, sofa, and dressing area; decorated in muted pastels. Many have view of city skyline or nearby country club. **Amenities:** 🏨 ⚙ A/C, cable TV w/movies, voice mail, in-rm safe. Some units w/minibars, some w/terraces, some w/fireplaces, some w/Jacuzzis. **Services:** 🍽 🖐 VP 🚐 🖼 🍴 Car-rental desk, masseur, children's program, babysitting. Youth hostel for children of guests. **Facilities:** 🔲 🏌 🏊 🏌 10K 🖥 ♿ 12 rsts, 6 bars (1 w/entertainment), lifeguard, games rm, spa, sauna, steam rm, whirlpool, beauty salon, day-care ctr. Elegant casino with rich wood and crystal chandeliers; shopping arcade; theatrical events. **Rates:** $79–$249 S or D; from $300 ste. Extra person $20. Children under 12 stay free. Higher rates for spec evnts/hols. Spec packages avail. Pking: Indoor/outdoor, free. Maj CC.

Luxor Hotel/Casino, 3900 Las Vegas Blvd S, PO Box 98640, Las Vegas, NV 89119; tel 702/262-4000 or toll free 800/288-1000; fax 702/262-4809. On the strip. New Egyptian-theme hotel built as a 30-story pyramid, with a huge interior atrium encircled by a canal, 3 levels of public areas, and a 10-story sphinx. **Rooms:** 2,526 rms and stes. CI 2pm/CO 11am. Express checkout avail. Nonsmoking rms avail. Rooms are well-appointed; wood furniture has Egyptian carvings. Sloping windows afford a view of the city, and door opens into the atrium. **Amenities:** A/C, cable TV w/movies, voice mail. Some units w/minibars, some w/Jacuzzis. **Services:** Car-rental desk, babysitting. **Facilities:** 7 rsts, 3 bars (1 w/entertainment), lifeguard, games rm, beauty salon. Movie theaters, virtual-reality arcade, show rooms. Barges ferry passengers from lobby to elevators. A monorail runs to the Excalibur Hotel next door. **Rates:** $59–$99 S or D; from $150 ste. Extra person $10. Children under 12 stay free. Higher rates for spec evnts/hols. Pking: Indoor/outdoor, free. Maj CC.

Maxim Hotel/Casino, 160 E Flamingo Rd, Las Vegas, NV 89109; tel 702/731-4300 or toll free 800/634-6987; fax 702/735-3252. 1 block E of the strip. Convenient to Caesar's, the Mirage, and several other casinos. There is no real lobby, just a registration desk near the casino. **Rooms:** 800 rms and stes. CI 2pm/CO noon. Express checkout avail. Nonsmoking rms avail. Nondescript, with earth-toned carpeting, floral print upholstery, and dark wood furniture. **Amenities:** A/C, cable TV w/movies. Some units w/minibars, some w/terraces, some w/Jacuzzis. **Services:** Car-rental desk. **Facilities:** 4 rsts, 2 bars (1 w/entertainment), lifeguard, games rm, whirlpool, beauty salon. Casino and a showroom with comedy-club theme. **Rates:** $44–$69 S or D; from $125 ste. Extra person $8. Children under 12 stay free. Higher rates for spec evnts/hols. Spec packages avail. Pking: Indoor/outdoor, free. Maj CC.

MGM Grand Hotel, 3799 Las Vegas Blvd S, PO Box 77711, Las Vegas, NV 89109; tel 702/891-1111 or toll free 800/929-1111; fax 702/891-1112. On the strip. World's largest hotel. A huge emerald-green monolith with a gold stucco lion at the entrance and a *Wizard of Oz* theme inside. **Rooms:** 5,005 rms and stes. CI 2pm/CO noon. Express checkout avail. Nonsmoking rms avail. Rooms have emerald-green carpet, gold moldings, red poppy-patterned bedspreads, and stills from the *Wizard of Oz*. **Amenities:** A/C, cable TV w/movies, voice

mail. Some units w/minibars, some w/terraces, some w/Jacuzzis. **Services:** Car-rental desk, children's program, babysitting. **Facilities:** 8 rsts, 4 bars (2 w/entertainment), lifeguard, games rm, spa, sauna, steam rm, whirlpool, beauty salon, day-care ctr. Theme park with Hollywood motif; 2 show rooms; 170,000-square-foot casino. **Rates:** $69–$119 S or D; from $99 ste. Extra person $10. Children under 12 stay free. Higher rates for spec evnts/hols. Spec packages avail. Pking: Indoor/outdoor, free. Maj CC.

The Mirage, 3400 Las Vegas Blvd S, PO Box 98544, Las Vegas, NV 89109; tel 702/791-7111 or toll free 800/627-6667; fax 702/791-7446. On the strip. South Seas–theme hotel with lush landscaping, man-made volcano, waterfalls, and lagoon. Tropical rainforest in atrium. **Rooms:** 3,049 rms and stes. Exec-level rms avail. CI 2pm/CO noon. Express checkout avail. Nonsmoking rms avail. Tropical motif with parrot colors; white wood and rattan furnishings. **Amenities:** A/C, cable TV w/movies, voice mail. Some units w/minibars, some w/terraces, some w/Jacuzzis. **Services:** Car-rental desk, masseur, babysitting. **Facilities:** 12 rsts, 4 bars (1 w/entertainment), lifeguard, games rm, spa, sauna, steam rm, whirlpool, beauty salon. Dolphin habitat, show room, shops. Golf privileges at nearby country club. **Rates:** $79–$350 S or D; from $450 ste. Extra person $30. Children under 12 stay free. Higher rates for spec evnts/hols. Pking: Indoor/outdoor, free. Maj CC.

Residence Inn by Marriott, 3225 Paradise Rd, Las Vegas, NV 89109; tel 702/796-9300 or toll free 800/331-3131; fax 702/796-9562. Across the street from Las Vegas Convention Center. Condominium-like units are located in garden buildings spread over beautifully landscaped grounds. The lobby area, the Hearth Room, has a fireplace, Scandinavian furnishings, and books as well as a TV set. **Rooms:** 195 effic. CI 2pm/CO noon. Nonsmoking rms avail. All have well-equipped kitchens. Studios have sitting areas and a fireplace; penthouse has 2 bedrooms and 2 baths. **Amenities:** A/C, cable TV w/movies, refrig, VCR. Some units w/terraces, some w/fireplaces. **Services:** Car-rental desk. Continental breakfast served in the lobby. A barbecue on Wednesdays and a hospitality hour with beverages and snacks on weeknights. Staff will deliver groceries and fireplace logs for a fee. Guests can order from nearby restaurants from in-room menus. **Facilities:** Racquetball, whirlpool, washer/dryer. Sports court for basketball, volleyball, and racquetball. **Rates (CP):** From $85 effic. Extra person $10. Children under 18 stay free. Pking: Outdoor, free. Maj CC.

Rio Suite Hotel & Casino, 3700 W Flamingo Rd, PO Box 14160, Las Vegas, NV 89103; tel 702/252-7777 or toll free 800/888-1818; fax 702/252-7791. ½ mi W of the strip. Calypso-theme hotel features brass parrots in the lobby, nautilus shells on the ceiling, and colorful carpeting that suggests confetti and streamers. Neon ribbons wind through the public areas, and the hotel's marquee is a massive neon geyser. **Rooms:** 861 stes. CI 2pm/CO noon. Express checkout avail. Nonsmoking rms avail. Suites have sitting areas with sofas, chaise lounges, and smoked glass coffee tables. Tropical prints abound. **Amenities:** 🛏 📺 A/C, cable TV w/movies, refrig, in-rm safe. Some units w/minibars. **Services:** 🍽 VP 🚗 🖨 🛎 Car-rental desk, masseur, babysitting. Free shuttle to Harrah's on the strip. **Facilities:** 🛎 🍴 🏋 🏊 6 rsts, 5 bars (1 w/entertainment), lifeguard, games rm, whirlpool, beauty salon. Lushly landscaped pool area has waterfall, palm trees, and a sandy beach. Carnival-themed casinos. Dinner show, "Conga!," is reminiscent of the nearly extinct dinner shows of the '60s. **Rates:** From $85 ste. Extra person $15. Children under 12 stay free. Higher rates for spec evnts/hols. Pking: Indoor/outdoor, free. Maj CC.

■■■ **Riviera Hotel**, 2901 Las Vegas Blvd S, PO Box 14520, Las Vegas, NV 89109; tel 702/734-5110 or toll free 800/634-3414; fax 702/794-9451. On the strip. Opened in the 1950s, this classic Las Vegas hotel is home to one of the largest casinos in the world. **Rooms:** 2,100 rms and stes. CI 2pm/CO noon. Express checkout avail. Nonsmoking rms avail. Rooms are larger than average, with older furnishings, yet clean and well-kept. **Amenities:** 🛏 🍴 A/C, cable TV w/movies, in-rm safe. Some units w/minibars, some w/terraces, some w/fireplaces, some w/Jacuzzis. **Services:** 🍽 🔑 VP 🚗 🖨 🛎 🐕 Car-rental desk, masseur, babysitting. **Facilities:** 🛎 🎾 🍴 15K 🖥 ♿ 4 rsts, 5 bars (1 w/entertainment), lifeguard, games rm, spa, sauna, steam rm, whirlpool, beauty salon. Several shops. **Rates:** $59–$95 S or D; from $115 ste. Extra person $12. Children under 14 stay free. Higher rates for spec evnts/hols. Spec packages avail. Pking: Indoor/outdoor, free. Maj CC.

■■ **Sahara Hotel & Casino**, 2535 Las Vegas Blvd S, PO Box 98503, Las Vegas, NV 89109; tel 702/737-2111 or toll free 800/634-6666; fax 702/735-5921. On the strip. A traditional hotel; long walks from rooms to the casino or restaurant. **Rooms:** 2,100 rms and stes. CI 3pm/CO noon. Express checkout avail. Nonsmoking rms avail. Garden rooms near the pool feature dark wood decor; roomier quarters are in the newer Alexandria wing. **Amenities:** 🛏 A/C, cable TV w/movies. Some units w/minibars, some w/terraces, some w/Jacuzzis. **Services:** 🍽 VP 🚗 🖨 🛎 Car-rental desk, babysitting. **Facilities:** 🛎 5.3K ♿ 7 rsts, 3 bars (1 w/entertainment), lifeguard, games rm, whirlpool, beauty salon. Show room, lovely pool area with palm trees and thatched huts. **Rates:** $55–$95 S or D; from $165 ste. Extra person $10. Children under 14 stay free. Higher rates for spec evnts/hols. Spec packages avail. Pking: Indoor/outdoor, free. Maj CC.

■■ **Sam Boyd's Fremont Hotel & Casino**, 200 E Fremont St, PO Box 940, Las Vegas, NV 89101 (Downtown); tel 702/385-3232 or toll free 800/634-6460; fax 702/385-6209. Caters to visitors from Hawaii, with a tropical island motif. **Rooms:** 452 rms and stes. CI 2pm/CO noon. Express checkout avail. Nonsmoking rms avail. Modern rooms with teal carpet, striped wallpaper, and floral drapes. **Amenities:** 🛏 A/C, cable TV w/movies, in-rm safe. Some units w/minibars. **Services:** ✗ VP 🚗 🖨 🛎 🐕 Babysitting. **Facilities:** 350 ♿ 5 rsts, 5 bars, games rm. Use of pool at California Hotel. **Rates:** $25–$60 S or D; from $50 ste. Extra person $8. Children under 12 stay free. Higher rates for spec evnts/hols. Spec packages avail. Pking: Indoor, free. Maj CC.

■■ **Sands Hotel Casino**, 3355 Las Vegas Blvd S, Las Vegas, NV 89109; tel 702/733-5000 or toll free 800/634-6901; fax 702/733-5624. On the strip. Distinctive 18-story tower is a landmark, though the once-classy casino is now very commercialized and noisy. **Rooms:** 715 rms and stes. CI 3pm/CO noon. Express checkout avail. Nonsmoking rms avail. Tower rooms are tastefully done in soft pastels, with armoires and makeup tables. **Amenities:** 🛏 ♿ A/C, cable TV w/movies. Some units w/minibars, some w/terraces. **Services:** 🍽 VP 🚗 🖨 🛎 Car-rental desk, masseur, babysitting. **Facilities:** 🛎 🍴 25K ♿ 3 rsts, 3 bars (1 w/entertainment), lifeguard, games rm, spa, sauna, steam rm, whirlpool, beauty salon. Landscaped pool area, 9-hole putting green, show room. **Rates:** $65–$185 S or D; from $150 ste. Extra person $10. Children under 12 stay free. Higher rates for spec evnts/hols. Spec packages avail. Pking: Indoor/outdoor, free. Maj CC.

■■■ **Sheraton Desert Inn Resort & Casino**, 3145 Las Vegas Blvd S, Las Vegas, NV 89109; tel 702/733-4444 or toll free 800/634-6906; fax 702/733-4437. On the strip. Among the nicest hotels on the strip, with 6 towers and garden-style rooms. **Rooms:** 821 rms and stes. CI 3pm/CO noon. Express checkout avail. Nonsmoking rms avail. Rooms are well appointed; some have chaise lounges, armoires, and English country furnishings. **Amenities:** 🛏 A/C, cable TV w/movies, in-rm safe. Some units w/minibars, some w/terraces. **Services:** 🍽 🔑 VP 🚗 🖨 🛎 🐕 Car-rental desk, masseur, babysitting. **Facilities:** 🛎 ⛳18 🎾 ♿5 🎾 🍴 1.9K 🖥 ♿ 5 rsts, 3 bars (1 w/entertainment), lifeguard, games rm, spa, sauna, whirlpool, beauty salon. Championship-quality golf course; show room; city's largest spa. **Rates:** HS Dec 29–May/Sept 2–Nov 19 $145–$205 S or D; from $250 ste. Extra person $25. Lower rates off-season. Higher rates for spec evnts/hols. Pking: Indoor/outdoor, free. Maj CC.

■■ **Showboat Hotel Casino & Bowling Center**, 2800 Fremont St, Las Vegas, NV 89104; tel 702/385-9123 or toll free 800/626-2800; fax 702/385-9163. 8 mi E of dowtown Las

Vegas. A Vegas landmark since 1953, this riverboat-theme hotel is a mecca for low-rollers and locals who flock to the bowling alley and the city's largest bingo hall. Bright registration area has plantation murals, flower boxes, plants, and chandeliers. **Rooms:** 500 rms and stes. CI 2pm/CO noon. Nonsmoking rms avail. Newer tower rooms decorated with dark wood furniture and earth tones. Older garden rooms (by the pool) are less luxurious but still comfortable. **Amenities:** 🛏 A/C, cable TV w/movies. Some units w/terraces. **Services:** 🍽 VP 🚃 ⊠ ⏚ ⏚ Car-rental desk, babysitting. On-site day care center. **Facilities:** 🏊 1.6K 4 rsts, 6 bars (1 w/entertainment), lifeguard, games rm, beauty salon, day-care ctr. 106-lane bowling alley and 24-hour bingo hall. Casino is brightly lit and large enough to give gamblers plenty of elbow room. **Rates:** $26–$85 S or D; from $90 ste. Extra person $10. Children under 12 stay free. Higher rates for spec evnts/hols. Pking: Indoor/outdoor, free. Maj CC.

≣≣≣ **Stardust Resort & Casino**, 3000 Las Vegas Blvd S, Las Vegas, NV 89109; tel 702/732-6111 or toll free 800/634-6757; fax 702/732-6257. On the strip. Newly expanded and renovated hotel, with tasteful public areas spread out on rambling grounds. **Rooms:** 2,400 rms and stes. CI 2pm/CO noon. Express checkout avail. Nonsmoking rms avail. Nicest rooms are in the 32-story tower built in 1990. Older rooms are larger; motel units are available at the rear of the property. **Amenities:** 🛏 🕯 A/C, cable TV w/movies, in-rm safe. Some units w/minibars, some w/terraces. **Services:** 🍽 VP 🚃 ⊠ ⏚ ⏚ Car-rental desk, babysitting. **Facilities:** 🏊 🍴 2K 🖥 ⅙ 6 rsts (see also "Restaurants" below), 4 bars (1 w/entertainment), lifeguard, games rm, spa, whirlpool, beauty salon. Show room. **Rates:** $49–$119 S or D; from $150 ste. Extra person $10. Children under 12 stay free. Higher rates for spec evnts/hols. Spec packages avail. Pking: Indoor/outdoor, free. Maj CC.

≣≣≣ **Treasure Island at the Mirage**, 3300 Las Vegas Boulevard S, PO Box 7711, Las Vegas, NV 89109; tel 702/894-7111 or toll free 800/627-6667; fax 702/894-7788. On the strip. Pirate-theme hotel with buccaneer village, treasure chests, and a mock sea battle in a strip-side lagoon several times daily. **Rooms:** 2,900 rms and stes. CI 2pm/CO noon. Express checkout avail. Nonsmoking rms avail. Bright and airy rooms with light carpeting, whitewashed wood furniture, brass fixtures, and nautical paintings. **Amenities:** 🛏 A/C, cable TV w/movies. Some units w/minibars, some w/terraces, some w/Jacuzzis. **Services:** 🍽 📠 VP 🚃 ⊠ ⏚ ⏚ Car-rental desk, babysitting. **Facilities:** 🏊 1K ⅙ 4 rsts, 2 bars (1 w/entertainment), lifeguard, games rm, spa, sauna, steam rm, whirlpool, beauty salon. 2 wedding chapels, show room. Golf privileges at nearby Mirage Country Club. **Rates:** $49–$259 S or D; from $100 ste. Extra person $25. Children under 12 stay free. Higher rates for spec evnts/hols. Pking: Indoor/outdoor, free. Maj CC.

≣≣ **Tropicana Resort and Casino**, 3801 Las Vegas Blvd S, PO Box 97777, Las Vegas, NV 89109; tel 702/739-2222 or toll free 800/634-4000; fax 702/739-2448. On the strip. Popular with tour groups, and always busy. Tropical-island decor with rainforest landscaping, waterfalls, tiki torches, and thatched huts. **Rooms:** 1,908 rms and stes. CI 2pm/CO noon. Express checkout avail. Nonsmoking rms avail. Tropical motif in rooms, with rattan and bamboo furnishings. **Amenities:** 🛏 🕯 A/C, cable TV w/movies, in-rm safe. Some units w/minibars, some w/terraces. **Services:** 🍽 VP 🚃 ⊠ ⏚ ⏚ Car-rental desk, masseur, babysitting. **Facilities:** 🏊 🍴 7.8K 🖥 ⅙ 6 rsts, 4 bars (2 w/entertainment), lifeguard, games rm, spa, sauna, steam rm, whirlpool, beauty salon. Pool area is a 5-acre waterpark with lagoons, waterslide, and spa. Shopping arcade, show room. **Rates:** $59–$149 S or D; from $85 ste. Extra person $15. Children under 12 stay free. Higher rates for spec evnts/hols. Spec packages avail. Pking: Indoor/outdoor, free. Maj CC.

≣≣ **Westward-Ho Hotel/Casino**, 2900 Las Vegas Blvd S, Las Vegas, NV 89109; tel 702/731-2900 or toll free 800/634-6803. On the strip. Sprawling motel-style property with guest parking outside each room. Public areas face the strip. **Rooms:** 800 rms and stes. CI 2pm/CO noon. Nonsmoking rms avail. Motel-quality furnishings, clean but hardly elegant. Suites are popular with families. **Amenities:** 🛏 A/C, cable TV. Some units w/terraces. **Services:** 🚃 ⊠ **Facilities:** 🏊 3 rsts, 2 bars (1 w/entertainment). **Rates:** $40–$51 S or D; from $77 ste. Extra person $10. Children under 18 stay free. Higher rates for spec evnts/hols. Pking: Outdoor, free. Ltd CC.

Motels

≣≣ **Center Strip Inn**, 3688 Las Vegas Blvd S, Las Vegas, NV 89109; tel 702/739-6066 or toll free 800/777-7737; fax 702/736-2521. On the strip. The newest building here has all the amenities the Vegas visitor looks for, and more. **Rooms:** 148 rms and stes. CI 2pm/CO noon. Express checkout avail. Nonsmoking rms avail. Standard accommodations are not special, but the deluxe rooms really are, with steam rooms and new furnishings. **Amenities:** 🛏 🕯 A/C, cable TV w/movies, refrig, VCR, in-rm safe. **Services:** ⊠ ⏚ Car-rental desk. **Facilities:** 🏊 40 Washer/dryer. **Rates:** $30–$150 S; $40–$150 D; from $68 ste. Extra person $5–$10. Higher rates for spec evnts/hols. Spec packages avail. Pking: Outdoor, free. Maj CC.

≣≣≣ **Days Inn Center Strip**, 3265 Las Vegas Blvd S, Las Vegas, NV 89109; tel 702/735-5102 or toll free 800/828-8032; fax 702/735-0168. On the strip. Undergoing renovation. Across from Treasure Island, with its showy pirate-ship battle out front. **Rooms:** 126 rms and stes. CI 3pm/CO 11am. Nonsmoking rms avail. Ask for one of the newly renovated rooms. **Amenities:** 🛏

A/C, cable TV w/movies, refrig. Some units w/minibars, some w/terraces. **Services:** 🚐 🛎 🚗 Car-rental desk, babysitting. Coffee available in lobby. Complimentary daily copy of *USA Today*. **Facilities:** 🛗 Washer/dryer. **Rates:** $42–$95 S; $47–$105 D; from $65 ste. Extra person $5. Children under 12 stay free. Higher rates for spec evnts/hols. Pking: Outdoor, free. Maj CC.

≣≣≣ Days Inn Downtown, 707 E Fremont St, Las Vegas, NV 89101; tel 702/388-1400 or toll free 800/325-3244; fax 702/388-9622. The largest Days Inn in the region, and a perfect motel for budget travelers who still want decent lodging. Recently upgraded. **Rooms:** 146 rms and stes. CI 2pm/CO noon. Nonsmoking rms avail. Just-renovated rooms are large and quiet. **Amenities:** 🛗 A/C, cable TV w/movies. VCRs on request. **Services:** ✕ 🛎 Children's program, babysitting. **Facilities:** 🛗 ♿ 1 rst, games rm. The pool is well cared for and recently got a new canopy. **Rates:** $32–$100 S or D; from $80 ste. Extra person $10. Children under 12 stay free. Higher rates for spec evnts/hols. Spec packages avail. Pking: Outdoor, free. Maj CC.

≣≣≣ La Quinta Motor Inn, 3782 Las Vegas Blvd S, Las Vegas, NV 89109; tel 702/739-7457 or toll free 800/531-5900; fax 702/736-1129. Located well away from the strip, this Spanish-style property has a red-tile roof, stucco exterior, and palm tree landscaping. The homey lobby features rattan furniture, a fireplace, throw rugs, and ficus trees. **Rooms:** 114 rms. CI 2pm/CO noon. Express checkout avail. Nonsmoking rms avail. Spacious rooms feature warm colors, wood desks and furniture, a recliner and ottoman, and art on the walls. **Amenities:** 🛗 ♿ A/C, cable TV w/movies. Some units w/terraces. **Services:** 🚐 🛎 🚗 Car-rental desk. **Facilities:** 🛗 ♿ Whirlpool. **Rates (CP):** $58–$68 S or D. Extra person $5. Children under 18 stay free. Higher rates for spec evnts/hols. Pking: Outdoor, free. Maj CC.

≣≣ Motel 6, 195 E Tropicana Ave, Las Vegas, NV 89109; tel 702/798-0728; fax 702/798-5657. 3 blocks E of the strip. Two-story, U-shaped building wrapped around a pool. Located directly across the street from the MGM Grand, this motel is always packed with families with children. **Rooms:** 880 rms. CI 4pm/CO 11am. Express checkout avail. Nonsmoking rms avail. Clean and simple. Floral print spreads, pressed-wood furniture. **Amenities:** 🛗 A/C, cable TV. **Services:** 🛎 🚗 Tour desk. **Facilities:** 🛗 Lifeguard, games rm, washer/dryer. Motel gift shop is a mini-mart with soft drinks, sandwiches, etc. **Rates:** $27–$40 S; $33–$46 D. Extra person $3. Children under 17 stay free. Pking: Outdoor, free. Maj CC.

≣≣ Rodeway Inn, 3786 Las Vegas Blvd S, Las Vegas, NV 89109; tel 702/736-1434 or toll free 800/350-1132; fax 702/736-6058. On the strip. Located near Excalibur, MGM Grand, and Luxor. **Rooms:** 97 rms and stes. CI 2pm/CO noon.

Nonsmoking rms avail. Rooms located well off the boulevard. Modern furnishings, with glass top tables, light wood furniture, and floral bedspreads. **Amenities:** 🛗 A/C, cable TV w/movies. Some units w/terraces. **Services:** 🛎 🚗 Car-rental desk, babysitting. Show and tour tickets available through front desk. **Facilities:** 🛗 ♿ **Rates:** $49–$89 S or D; from $150 ste. Extra person $10. Children under 18 stay free. Higher rates for spec evnts/hols. Pking: Outdoor, free. Maj CC.

Restaurants 🍴

⭐ **Alpine Village Inn**, 3003 Paradise Rd, Las Vegas; tel 702/734-6888. E Sahara exit off I-15. **German.** Alpine villa atmosphere, with pewter dinnerware and silverware. Daily specials may include Schweinehaxen and various preparations of pork shank and sausage. Upstairs is for fine German dining; downstairs is a rathskeller with a simple and less expensive menu. **FYI:** Reservations recommended. Sing along. Children's menu. **Open:** Daily 5am–11pm. **Prices:** Main courses $12–$24. Maj CC. 🆅🅿 ♿

Andre's, 401 S 6th St, Las Vegas (Downtown); tel 702/385-5016. Charleston Ave exit off I-15. **French.** Considered one of the top French restaurants in Las Vegas. Four dining rooms are named for French cities; 2 rooms can accommodate small groups up to 10 people. Known for its 800-label wine cellar. The signature dish is rack of lamb. **FYI:** Reservations recommended. **Open:** Daily 6–10pm. Closed some hols. **Prices:** Main courses $19–$34. Maj CC. ❤ 🆅🅿 ♿

🍷 **Bacchanal**, in Caesars Palace, 3570 Las Vegas Blvd S, Las Vegas; tel 702/734-7110. **Continental.** One of Caesars Palace's most renowned restaurants, with Roman-style vases and statues, vines that cover everything, and a fountain in the center. On the menu are continental and seasonal dishes. **FYI:** Reservations recommended. Dancing/dinner theater. Jacket required. **Open:** Tues–Sat 6–9pm. **Prices:** PF dinner $65. Maj CC. 🆅🅿 ♿

Camelot, in the Excalibur Hotel, 3850 Las Vegas Blvd S, Las Vegas; tel 702/597-7777. E Tropicana Ave exit off I-15. **Continental/American.** Part elegant English countryside, with forest-like murals and plants, part English castle, with mock fireplace and armaments as decorations. Tables are large and service is exceptional. Specialties include veal piccata (chef's favorite) and rack of lamb black knight. Excellent desserts. Reasonably priced. May close early on slow nights. **FYI:** Reservations recommended. **Open:** Sun–Thurs 6–10pm, Fri–Sat 5–11pm. **Prices:** Main courses $10–$20. Maj CC. 🆅🅿 ♿

Chili's Grill & Bar, 2590 S Maryland Pkwy, Las Vegas; tel 702/733-6462. **Burgers/Tex-Mex.** Family-oriented restaurant with Tex-Mex decor. Specialties include onion blossom appetizer and chicken salads. **FYI:** Reservations not accepted. Children's menu. **Open:** Mon–Thurs 11am–11pm, Fri–Sat 10am–11pm, Sun 11am–10pm. Closed some hols. **Prices:** Main courses $5–$10. Maj CC. 🎦 &

★ **Chin's**, in Fashion Show Mall, 3200 Las Vegas Blvd S, Las Vegas; tel 702/733-8899. E Spring Mountain exit off I-15. **Chinese.** Simple in layout, the decor is beautiful, with white china and white table linen. Spacious dining room is lit by soft ceiling lights. Known for original creations like strawberry chicken and pepper orange roughy. Food prepared on jet burner creating intense heat that seals juices. **FYI:** Reservations recommended. Piano. **Open:** Thurs–Sat 11:30am–9:30pm. Closed some hols. **Prices:** Main courses $8–$24. Maj CC. 🆅 &

Dragon Court, in MGM Grand Hotel Casino & Theme Park, 3799 Las Vegas Blvd S, Las Vegas; tel 702/891-7380. E Tropicana exit off I-15. **Chinese.** The dazzling decor tries to recall ancient China, re-creating the appearance of a Chinese emperor's court, with small trees, lanterns, tapestries, and tents to divide dining areas. Specialties of the house include Peking duck carved tableside and sizzling spicy scallops. Special cooking method prevents food from being greasy. **FYI:** Reservations recommended. **Open:** Daily 5–11pm. **Prices:** Main courses $9.75–$40. Maj CC. 🍷 🆅 &

The Famous Pacific Fish Company, 3925 Paradise Rd, Las Vegas; tel 702/796-9676. E Sahara exit off I-15. **Seafood.** Decorated with cargo nets, oars, rope ladders, and even boats. Fresh fish are flown in Monday to Saturday; among the best dishes are chile ragotti, Santa Fe pasta, and stuffed swordfish. **FYI:** Reservations recommended. Children's menu. **Open:** Mon–Thurs 11am–10pm, Fri–Sat 11am–11pm, Sun 4–10pm. Closed Dec 25. **Prices:** Main courses $12–$42.95. Maj CC. 🗸&

Ⓢ **Gandhi India's Cuisine**, 4080 Paradise, Las Vegas; tel 702/734-0094. Flamingo exit off I-15. **Indian.** An appealing place decorated with tapestries and murals. Tandoor oven cooking is a specialty here; a good introduction is the South Indian thali platter. For dessert, there's kulfi, saffron-flavored ice cream with mango. Indian beers are available. **FYI:** Reservations accepted. **Open:** Lunch daily 11am–2:30pm; dinner daily 5–11pm. **Prices:** PF dinner $12.75. Maj CC. &

★ **Ginza**, 1000 E Sahara Ave, Las Vegas; tel 702/732-3080. E Sahara exit off I-15. **Japanese.** What this restaurant lacks in appearance, it makes up for with the food. Lovely paper lanterns and Japanese vases provide charm. Most patrons come for the sushi bar, but menu items including shabu-shabu, tempura, and yosenabe, a Japanese bouillabaisse, are also good. **FYI:** Reservations accepted. **Open:** Tues–Sun 5pm–1am. Closed Dec 25. **Prices:** Main courses $14–$17.50. Maj CC. &

★ **Kiéfer's atop the Carriage House**, 105 E Harmon Ave, Las Vegas; tel 702/739-8000. E Tropicana exit off I-15. **New American.** Decorated in pink, red, and off-white, with wicker chairs and comfortable booths. The place is famous for its caesar salad. A local favorite is orange roughy with crabmeat, asparagus, and béarnaise sauce; veal piccata is also recommended. **FYI:** Reservations recommended. Piano. Children's menu. Dress code. **Open:** Breakfast Mon–Sat 7:30–10am, Sun 7:30am–noon; dinner Sun–Thurs 5–11pm, Fri–Sat 5pm–midnight. **Prices:** Main courses $15–$20. Maj CC. 🍷 📷 🆅 &

La Piazza Food Court, in Caesars Palace, 3750 Las Vegas Blvd, Las Vegas; tel 702/731-7110. **Eclectic.** A cross between a cafeteria and a food court, with modern, clean decor. Menus appear above each food station. Chinese stir-fry, Mexican tacos, pizzas, and other dishes are available. There is often live entertainment in the common dining area. **FYI:** Reservations not accepted. Band. **Open:** Daily 24 hrs. **Prices:** Main courses $5.50–$8. Maj CC. 🎦 🆅 &

♣ **Le Montrachet**, in the Las Vegas Hilton, 3000 Paradise Rd, Las Vegas; tel 702/732-5111. E Sahara exit off I-95. **French.** A quiet place away from the casino, this round room is lavishly elegant with red mohair booths, pastoral scenes on the walls, and a huge glass chandelier. The seasonal menu features grilled Dover sole and grilled double-cut lamb chops. For dessert, there's almond ice cream in a chocolate cup. **FYI:** Reservations recommended. Jacket required. **Open:** HS May–Sept Wed–Mon 6–10:30pm. Reduced hours off-season. Closed some hols. **Prices:** Main courses $18–$28. Maj CC. 🍷 🆅

Margarita Grille, in the Las Vegas Hilton, 3000 Paradise Rd, Las Vegas; tel 702/732-5111. E Sahara exit off I-95. **Mexican.** Decor features piñatas and dark woods. The small tables are decorated with festive colors and woven place mats. A chips and salsa cart offers 9 salsas, from mild to super hot. Most items on menu are standard, but Filipino fare is also available. Smaller portions for children upon request. **FYI:** Reservations recommended. **Open:** Daily 5–11pm. **Prices:** Main courses $7.95–$10.95. Maj CC. 🎦 🆅

The Monte Carlo Room, in the Sheraton Desert Inn, 3145 Las Vegas Blvd S, Las Vegas; tel 702/733-4444. E Spring Mountain exit off I-15. **French.** Overlooking the hotel's pool and courtyard. Murals, plants, and a plush atmosphere. The 3 signature dishes here are shrimp flambé, grilled tuna with dill sauce, and stuffed baby veal chop with Gruyère and ginger. Kitchen will make special dishes on request. **FYI:** Reservations recommended. Jacket required. **Open:** Thurs–Mon 6–11pm. **Prices:** Main courses $26–$54. Maj CC. 🍷 📷 🆅 &

Pamplemousse, 400 E Sahara Ave, Las Vegas; tel 702/733-2066. 3 blocks E of the strip. **Continental/French.** An intimate French dining room with a step-down wine cellar and a solarium alcove. Typical entrees are rack of lamb, fresh Norwegian salmon, steaks, and lobsters. A specialty is roast Wisconsin duckling with cranberry sauce, cream of garlic sauce, or green peppercorns. **FYI:** Reservations recommended. Dress code. **Open:** Tues–Sun 6–11:30pm. **Prices:** Main courses $19–$35. Maj CC. ♥ VP &

♥ **Rosewood Grille and Lobster House**, 3339 Las Vegas Blvd S, Las Vegas; tel 702/792-5965. Spring Mountain exit off I-15. **Seafood.** A local favorite, adorned in rosewood, with original art and a single red rose on each table. This place is known for serving the largest lobsters on the strip—up to 17 pounds! They also carry excellent steaks and chateaubriand, and offer one of the most extensive wine lists in town. **FYI:** Reservations recommended. Dress code. **Open:** Daily 4:30–11:30pm. Closed Thanksgiving. **Prices:** Main courses $17.50–$28.50. Maj CC. &

Sacred Sea Room, in the Luxor Hotel and Casino, 3900 Las Vegas Blvd S, Las Vegas; tel 702/262-4000. E Tropicana Ave exit off I-15. **Seafood.** Overlooking the casino, a stunning restaurant decorated in Egyptian motifs, with murals depicting the Nile River. Wonderful food, including stuffed prawns, and entrees baked in parchment with wine and herbs. There's always a meat and chicken entree on the menu. Expect excellent service. **FYI:** Reservations recommended. Dress code. **Open:** Daily 5–11pm. **Prices:** Main courses $7.95–$25. Maj CC. VP &

Stefano's, in the Golden Nugget, 129 E Fremont St, Las Vegas (Downtown); tel 702/385-7111. Casino Center exit off I-515. **Italian.** A good-times atmosphere, complete with singing waiters. Latticework, plants, and Italianate murals create the feeling of outdoor dining indoors. Known for the osso buco; also offering cioppino and fresh pastries. **FYI:** Reservations recommended. Sing along. **Open:** Sun–Thurs 5:30–11pm, Fri–Sat 6–11pm. **Prices:** Main courses $10–$28. Maj CC. VP &

Tony Roma's–A Place for Ribs, in the Stardust Resort & Casino, 3000 Las Vegas Blvd S, Las Vegas; tel 702/732-6111. **Barbecue.** Choose from baby-back ribs basted with honey-molasses or tangy Cajun-style sauce, barbecued chicken, and assorted combination plates. **FYI:** Reservations recommended. Dress code. **Open:** Sun–Thurs 5–11pm, Fri–Sat 5pm–midnight. **Prices:** Main courses $6.95–$19.95. Maj CC. VP &

Attractions 📷

Las Vegas Natural History Museum, 900 Las Vegas Blvd N; tel 702/384-3466. This museum features animated model dinosaurs, a marine life exhibit in a 3,000-gallon tank, and other wildlife displays. The Discovery Room features hands-on exhibits for children. Gift shop. **Open:** Daily 9am–4pm. $$

Las Vegas Art Museum, 3333 W Washington Ave; tel 702/647-4300. Currently housed in one of the original buildings of historic Twin Lakes Ranch in beautiful Lorenzi Park, this museum features a permanent collection with works by such noted artists as Alexander Calder and Pablo Picasso, along with several traveling exhibitions per year. Collector's auction gallery, museum store. **Open:** Mon–Sat 10am–3pm, Sun noon–3pm. Closed some hols. Free.

Lied Discovery Children's Museum, 833 Las Vegas Blvd N; tel 702/382-KIDS. More than 100 hands-on exhibits demonstrate the wonders of art, science, and the humanities. Exhibits include Toddler Tower, Gyrochair, Musical Pathway, and KKID radio. **Open:** Tues and Thurs–Sat 10am–5pm, Wed 10am–7pm, Sun noon–5pm. $$

Liberace Museum, 1775 E Tropicana Ave; tel 702/798-5595. Devoted to the career memorabilia of "Mr. Showmanship," 3 exhibit areas display Liberace's spectacular cars, costumes, jewelry, photographs and much more. Some highlights are Liberace's mirror-tiled Rolls-Royce Phantom V (one of seven made), his famed candelabras, antique and custom-made pianos, and the world's largest rhinestone (50.6 lbs). **Open:** Mon–Sat 10am–5pm, Sun 1–5pm. Closed some hols. $$$

Imperial Palace Auto Collection, 3535 Las Vegas Blvd S; tel 702/794-3311 or toll free 800/634-6441. Located on the 5th floor of the Imperial Palace Hotel, this museum displays, on a rotating basis, approximately 750 antique, classic, and special-interest vehicles, including one of the world's largest collections of Model J Dusenbergs. There are also cars belonging to world leaders and celebrities. **Open:** Daily 9:30am–11:30pm. $$$

Guinness World of Records Museum, 2780 Las Vegas Blvd S; tel 702/792-3766. Displays, life-size replicas, and interactive exhibits bring the famous *Guinness Book of World Records* to 3-dimensional life. Topics include the human world, with the world's tallest, shortest, heaviest, and other superlative people; natural wonders; sports and entertainment. **Open:** Daily 9am–8pm. $$

Bethany's Celebrity Doll Museum, 1775 E Tropicana Ave; tel 702/798-3036. A museum devoted to celebrity dolls, this attraction features a large number of stage and screen luminaries, from Redd Foxx and Captain Kangaroo to the Beatles and Grace Kelly. Fictional characters are also included, such as Barbie, the entire cast of *Gone with the Wind,* and the characters of *Alice in Wonderland.* **Open:** Mon–Sat 10am–5pm, Sun 1–5pm. Closed some hols. $

MGM Grand Adventures, 3799 Las Vegas Blvd S; tel 702/891-7979. A full-scale, 33-acre theme park which can only be accessed by passing through the MGM Grand Hotel and Casino. The park features 6 rides, 3 theatres, and 8 themed areas. Each theme area has rides and shows, as well as shopping and dining establishments.

Popular attractions at the park include the Lightning Bolt roller coaster located in the New York Street section. The high-tech ride is completely indoors and simulates high-speed space travel with meteor showers and a black hole. The Backlot River Tour in Asian Village is a boat ride with special effects usually seen in movie productions such as fog, rain, earthquakes, and gunfire from an attack helicopter. One of the most popular rides at the park is Grand Canyon Rapids, a 5-minute whitewater raft ride that virtually assures a visitor receiving a complete drenching. Other attractions at the park are an audience participation movie, a stunt show, and an interactive film about the creation of cartoons.

A new system being implemented at the park assures a guest will never have to wait longer than 45 minutes in line for a ride. The system works by limiting the number of guests allowed into the park on a given day and will work on a reservation network; visitors are advised to call in advance to assure entrance on a specific day. **Open:** Daily 10am–10pm. $$$$

Grand Slam Canyon, 2880 Las Vegas Blvd; tel 702/794-3939. Situated directly behind the main hotel and casino of Circus Circus. Architecturally compelling, the entire 5-acre park is built 2 stories high atop the casino's parking structure, and is totally enclosed by a glass dome. The dome allows light in, blocks ultraviolet rays, and keeps the park air conditioned and climate-controlled 365 days a year.

As its name implies, the park is designed to resemble a classic Western desert canyon. From top to bottom, hand-painted artificial rock is sculpted into caverns, pinnacles, steep cliffs, and buttes. A stream runs through the stark landscape, cascading over a 90-foot falls into a rippling blue-green pool. Embellishing the scene are several life-sized animatronic dinosaurs, a re-creation of an archeological dig, a fossil wall, and a replica of a Pueblo Indian cliff dwelling.

Grand Slam Canyon's premier attractions are the Canyon Blaster, the only indoor, double-loop, corkscrew roller coaster in the United States; and the Rim Runner, a 3½-minute water flume ride. Secondary attractions include Twist & Shout, a 45-foot-high, dry corkscrew slide in a dark tube; and Hot Shots, a game where participants duel with harmless laser guns in a convoluted

cavelike setting. One ride on each of the attractions is covered in the cost of admission. **Open:** Sun–Thurs 10am–5pm, Fri–Sat 10am–midnight. $

Wet 'n' Wild, 2601 Las Vegas Blvd S; tel 702/734-0088. Located on the strip just south of Sahara Ave, this 26-acre water theme park features water slides, flumes, inner-tube rides, and a half-million-gallon wave pool, plus a children's area. Picnicking, concessions. **Open:** Daily, hours vary. $$$$

Scandia Family Fun Center, 2900 Sirius Ave; tel 702/364-0070. Entrance on Rancho Dr, between Sahara Ave and Spring Mountain Rd. This family amusement center offers three 18-hole miniature golf courses, a video arcade, go-carts, bumper boats, and batting cages. (Fee charged for each activity.) **Open:** Sept–early June, Sun–Thurs 10am–11pm, Fri–Sat 10am–midnight; mid-June–Aug, Sun–Thurs 10am–midnight, Fri–Sat 10am–1am. Free.

Dolphin Habitat, Mirage Hotel, 3400 Las Vegas Blvd S; tel 702/791-7111. Designed to educate the public about marine mammals and provide a healthy, nurturing environment for 6 Atlantic bottlenose dolphins, the Dolphin Exhibit is a 1.5-million-gallon pool with above- and below-ground viewing areas. The 15-minute tour includes a video of a resident dolphin (Duchess) giving birth (to Squirt) underwater.

Also at the Mirage are a royal white tiger habitat and a 53-foot, 20,000-gallon simulated coral reef aquarium behind the registration desk. **Open:** Mon–Fri 11am–7pm, Sat–Sun and hols 9am–7pm. $

Ethel M Chocolates, 2 Cactus Garden Dr; tel 702/458-8864. A tourist attraction drawing 18,000 visitors a day, this ultramodern factory is located 6 miles from the Las Vegas strip, in the Green Valley Business Park. Self-guided tours allow visitors to see the candy-making process from a glass-enclosed viewing aisle; all equipment is labeled to aid visitor comprehension. Video presentations are shown along the way.

Also on the premises is a 2½-acre garden displaying 350 species of rare and exotic cacti. Signs are provided to facilitate self-guided tours. **Open:** Daily 8:30am–7pm. Closed Dec 25. Free.

Floyd Lamb State Park, 9200 Tule Springs Rd; tel 702/486-5413. Located 10 miles north of downtown Las Vegas, off US 95. Originally known as Tule Springs, this park was an early watering stop for Native Americans. It later became a privately owned working ranch, as well as a guest/dude ranch where guests could wait out the 6-week residency requirement to obtain a quick divorce. In addition to the historic Tule Springs

Ranch area, the park offers fishing and picnicking opportunities and a walking/bicycle path that winds through the park. **Open:** Daily. $$

Bonnie Springs Ranch/Old Nevada; tel 702/875-4400. Located about 24 miles west of Las Vegas on Nev 159, Old Nevada is a microcosm of a mid-1800s western Nevada town, its main street lined with weathered-wood buildings fronted by covered verandas. Live bands and melodramas are presented in the saloon; also featured are stunt shoot-outs, a wax museum, an Old Movie House, mine tours, stagecoach rides, and horseback riding. Small zoo; aviary; shops and restaurants; Trading Post museum and gift shop. **Open:** May–Oct, daily 10:30am–6pm; Nov–Apr, daily 10:30am–5pm. $$$

LAUGHLIN

Map page M-4, E4

Hotels 🛏

🛏🛏 Don Laughlin's Riverside Resort Hotel & Casino, 1650 Casino Dr, PO Box 500, Laughlin, NV 89029; tel 702/298-2535 or toll free 800/227-3849; fax 702/298-2614. The original Laughlin hotel and casino, built by the city's founder; one of the busiest places in town. **Rooms:** 660 rms and stes. CI 2pm/CO 11am. Nonsmoking rms avail. Garden rooms are showing wear, but rooms in the tower are modern. **Amenities:** 🛏 A/C, cable TV w/movies. Some units w/minibars, some w/terraces. **Services:** 🍴 🆚 🚗 ⛵ ↩ Car-rental desk, babysitting. **Facilities:** 🏋 600 ⚐ 4 rsts, 4 bars (2 w/entertainment), lifeguard, games rm, beauty salon. Collection of antique slot machines and casino memorabilia; 3 movie theaters; country music dance hall. RV park next door. **Rates:** $25–$69 S or D; from $120 ste. Extra person $10. Children under 12 stay free. Higher rates for spec evnts/hols. Pking: Indoor/outdoor, free. Maj CC.

🛏🛏 Edgewater Hotel Casino, 2020 S Casino Dr, PO Box 30707, Laughlin, NV 89028; tel 702/298-2453 or toll free 800/677-4837; fax 702/298-5606. Turn right on Casino Dr off Nev 163. Frosty white 26-story tower has the most river-view rooms in town. Native American art and decor. **Rooms:** 1,450 rms and stes. CI 2pm/CO noon. Nonsmoking rms avail. Bright and spacious, all rooms are new or newly redecorated with southwestern motif. Great views. **Amenities:** 🛏 A/C, cable TV w/movies. Some units w/minibars, some w/terraces. **Services:** 🍴 🆚 🚗 ⛵ ↩ Car-rental desk, babysitting. Free shuttle across the Colorado River. **Facilities:** 🏋 ⚐ 4 rsts, 3 bars (1 w/entertainment), lifeguard, games rm, whirlpool, beauty salon.

Picnic area. **Rates:** $28–$57 S or D; from $95 ste. Children under 12 stay free. Higher rates for spec evnts/hols. Pking: Indoor/outdoor, free. Maj CC. Lower midweek rates.

🛏🛏🛏 Flamingo Hilton Laughlin, 1900 S Casino Dr, PO Box 30630, Laughlin, NV 89029; tel 702/298-5111 or toll free 800/352-6464; fax 702/298-5042. Turn right on Casino Dr off Nev 163. The hotel's shiny pink towers are separated by a beautifully landscaped garden overlooking the river. Inside, ribbons of pink neon wind through the casino and restaurants. **Rooms:** 2,000 rms and stes. CI 3pm/CO 11am. Express checkout avail. Nonsmoking rms avail. Walls of windows provide spectacular views of the Colorado River and surrounding mountains. **Amenities:** 🛏 📺 A/C, cable TV w/movies. Some units w/minibars. **Services:** 🍴 🔑 🆚 🚗 ⛵ ↩ ◁ Car-rental desk, babysitting. **Facilities:** 🏋 🎾 ⚐ 4 rsts, 3 bars (1 w/entertainment), lifeguard, games rm, beauty salon. Video arcade and midway for children; show room. **Rates:** $25–$80 S or D; from $200 ste. Extra person $14. Children under 12 stay free. Higher rates for spec evnts/hols. Spec packages avail. Pking: Indoor/outdoor, free. Maj CC.

🛏🛏🛏 Harrah's Casino Hotel Laughlin, 2900 S Casino Dr, PO Box 33000, Laughlin, NV 89029; tel 702/298-4600 or toll free 800/477-8700; fax 702/298-3023. Turn right on Casino Dr off Nev 163. Hotel features 3 high-rise towers in a small isolated canyon. **Rooms:** 1,658 rms and stes. CI 2pm/CO noon. Express checkout avail. Nonsmoking rms avail. Rooms have views of Colorado River and surrounding mountains. Dark wood furniture with colorful southwestern upholstery and bedspreads. **Amenities:** 🛏 A/C, cable TV w/movies. Some units w/minibars. **Services:** 🍴 🆚 ⛵ ↩ ◁ Car-rental desk, children's program, babysitting. **Facilities:** △ 🎾 ⚐ 5 rsts, 4 bars (1 w/entertainment), 1 beach (cove/inlet), lifeguard, games rm, spa, beauty salon. Soft sand beach is the only one along Casino Row. **Rates:** $25–$90 S or D; from $125 ste. Extra person $12. Children under 12 stay free. Higher rates for spec evnts/hols. Pking: Indoor/outdoor, free. Maj CC.

LOVELOCK

Map page M-4, B2

Attraction 🧳

Rye Patch State Recreation Area; tel 702/538-7321. Located 22 miles east of Lovelock off I-80. Consisting of a 200,000-acre reservoir surrounded by 27,000 acres of land, this recreation area is popular for fishing, swimming, boating, and waterskiing. Camping facilities are available. **Open:** Daily. $

MINDEN

Map page M-4, C1 (S of Carson City)

Hotel 🛏

≣≣≣ **Carson Valley Inn**, 1627 Hwy 395, Minden, NV 89423; tel 702/782-9711 or toll free 800/321-6983; fax 702/782-7472. A much better property than one might expect. **Rooms:** 157 rms and stes. CI 3pm/CO noon. Express checkout avail. Nonsmoking rms avail. Color photos by Nevadan Linda Dufferena are superior to the art in most comparable accommodations. Wallpaper and bedspreads add charm. **Amenities:** 🛏 🕭 A/C, cable TV, voice mail. Some units w/minibars, 1 w/terrace, some w/Jacuzzis. Refrigerators in suites; in other rooms for additional charge. **Services:** 🆅🅿 🖂 🗗 Babysitting. **Facilities:** 🏊 ፊ 2 rsts, 3 bars (1 w/entertainment), games rm, whirlpool, washer/dryer. Casino on 1st floor. Outdoor whirlpool and deck have fabulous views of the Sierra Nevada Mountains. **Rates:** HS Apr–Oct $39–$79 S or D; from $99 ste. Extra person $6. Children under 12 stay free. Min stay spec evnts. Lower rates off-season. Higher rates for spec evnts/hols. Spec packages avail. Pking: Outdoor, free. Maj CC.

PANACA

Map page M-4, C4

Attraction 💼

Cathedral Gorge State Park; tel 702/728-4467. Unusual erosion patterns have created the dramatic cliffs and spires that give this scenic park its name. The grayish-tan formations are bentonite-like clay deposits from a prehistoric lake bed. The 1,600-acre park attracts campers, picnickers, and hikers, as well as photographers. Today trails and roadways take visitors to several points of interest, including Miller Point; the site is located above the canyon and provides great views of the park. There is a 16-unit campground and shaded areas for picnics. Water is not available from November to April. **Open:** Daily. $

RENO

Map page M-4, B1

See also **Carson City, Incline Village, Sparks**

Hotels 🛏

≣≣≣ **Best Western Airport Plaza Hotel**, 1981 Terminal Way, Reno, NV 89502 (Reno Cannon Int'l Airport); tel 702/348-6370 or toll free 800/648-3525; fax 702/348-9722. Plumb-Villanova exit off US 395. Very upbeat ambience with exceptional landscaping for this area. **Rooms:** 270 rms and stes. CI 3pm/CO noon. Nonsmoking rms avail. Attractive as any rooms in Reno. Double-pane glass in windows. Grab-bar in bathroom not adequate for guests with disabilities. Plans to add wheelchair-accessible showers. **Amenities:** 🛏 🕭 A/C, cable TV w/movies, refrig. Some units w/fireplaces. Bottled water in every room. Refrigerators in suites and deluxe rooms (and available for rent if room doesn't have one). **Services:** ✕ 🚐 🖂 🗗 Car-rental desk, babysitting. **Facilities:** 🔼 ⛱ 🍴 💻 ፊ 1 rst, 1 bar, games rm, sauna, whirlpool. Small casino adjoins lobby. **Rates:** HS May–Sept $64–$96 S; $68–$105 D; from $125 ste. Extra person $10. Children under 12 stay free. Min stay spec evnts. Lower rates off-season. Higher rates for spec evnts/hols. Spec packages avail. Pking: Outdoor, free. Maj CC.

≣≣ **Circus Circus Hotel/Casino**, 500 N Sierra, Reno, NV 89503; tel 702/329-0711 or toll free 800/648-5010; fax 702/329-0599. Rooms are surprisingly good. Although the casino is loaded with security guards, women might not feel secure in the halls at night. **Rooms:** 1,625 rms and stes. CI 3pm/CO noon. Nonsmoking rms avail. **Amenities:** 🛏 A/C, cable TV w/movies. **Services:** ✕ 🆅🅿 🚐 🖂 🗗 Car-rental desk, babysitting. **Facilities:** 🔼 ፊ 3 rsts, 5 bars (1 w/entertainment), games rm. **Rates:** HS Dec 25–Jan 1/Apr–Oct $22–$52 S or D; from $37 ste. Extra person $6. Children under 12 stay free. Min stay wknds. Lower rates off-season. Higher rates for spec evnts/hols. Spec packages avail. Pking: Indoor/outdoor, free. Maj CC. Mini-suites at $15 above current rack rate are a great buy.

≣≣≣ **Comstock Hotel & Casino**, 200 W 2nd St, Reno, NV 89501 (Downtown); tel 702/329-1880 or toll free 800/648-4866; fax 702/348-0539. Quiet location 2 blocks from Reno's main street. Old West theme. Popular for small conventions and groups. **Rooms:** 310 rms and stes. CI 3pm/CO 11am. Nonsmoking rms avail. Rooms are attractive, with an old-fashioned look. Guest room doors have electronic locks. In process of meeting ADA requirements for guests with disabilities. **Amenities:** 🛏 A/C, satel TV w/movies. Some units w/Jacuzzis. **Services:** ✕ 🆅🅿 🚐 🗗 Car-rental desk, babysitting. **Facilities:**

🏠 🛁 🔲 ♿ 3 rsts, 3 bars, games rm, spa, sauna, whirlpool, beauty salon. **Rates:** HS Feb 15–Nov 15 $49–$125 S or D; from $140 ste. Extra person $5. Lower rates off-season. Higher rates for spec evnts/hols. Spec packages avail. Pking: Indoor/outdoor, free. Maj CC.

To/From Mill Creek Road

RENO-CANNON INTERNATIONAL AIRPORT

Pilot Way

International Charter Commuter Building

N GOUSHA

North Concourse

Sky Way

PARKING

Terminal Building

Terminal Way

E Plumb La

To/From Downtown Reno

South Concourse

Car Rental Areas

Aviation St

© The H.M. Gousha Co.   10-ZM-286-M-A

≣≣≣ **Eldorado Hotel & Casino**, 345 N Virginia St, Reno, NV 89501 (Downtown); tel 702/786-5700 or toll free 800/648-5966; fax 702/322-7124. Breaking ground for additional expansion. **Rooms:** 800 rms and stes. CI 3pm/CO noon. Express checkout avail. Nonsmoking rms avail. **Amenities:** 📺 ♨ A/C, cable TV w/movies. Some units w/minibars, some w/Jacuzzis. Bath seats for guests with disabilities available; also extra grab bars/stands. **Services:** 🍽 ➤ 🚐 ⛵ ↵ Car-rental desk, babysitting. **Facilities:** 🏠 🔲 💻 ♿ 8 rsts, 8 bars (2 w/entertainment), games rm, whirlpool. **Rates:** HS Apr 29–Sept 19 $59–$110 S or D; from $119 ste. Extra person $6. Children under 12 stay free. Min stay wknds. Lower rates off-season. Higher rates for spec evnts/hols. Spec packages avail. Pking: Indoor/outdoor, free. Maj CC.

≣≣ **Fitzgerald's Casino-Hotel**, 255 N Virginia St, Reno, NV 89501 (Downtown); tel 702/785-3300 or toll free 800/648-5022; fax 702/786-7180. Located in the heart of Reno's casino row. Big casino on main floor. No lobby. **Rooms:** 352 rms and stes. CI 3pm/CO noon. Express checkout avail. Inexpensive furnishings. Color-coordinated, but not attractive. Renovation of rooms in progress. **Amenities:** 📺 A/C, satel TV w/movies. **Services:** ✗ 💳 🚐 ⛵ Car-rental desk. **Facilities:** ♿ 2 rsts, 3 bars (1 w/entertainment), games rm. **Rates:** HS Mem day–Oct $98–$104 S or D; from $78 ste. Extra person $8. Children under 12 stay free. Min stay wknds and spec evnts. Lower rates off-season. Higher rates for spec evnts/hols. Spec packages avail. Pking: Indoor/outdoor, free. Maj CC.

≣≣ **Flamingo Hilton Reno**, 255 N Sierra St, PO Box 1291, Reno, NV 89501 (Downtown); tel 702/322-1111 or toll free 800/648-4882; fax 702/785-7057. A good location, just 1 block from Virginia St. Although it earns its 2-flag rating, the hallways and carpets could be better. **Rooms:** 604 rms and stes. CI 3pm/CO 11am. Express checkout avail. Nonsmoking rms avail. The south-facing rooms on the upper floors have panoramic views. Those on the north side, overlooking the railroad tracks, are noisier. Guest rooms are decorated in reds and pinks, and are not very attractive. **Amenities:** 📺 ♨ A/C, cable TV w/movies. Some units w/minibars, some w/Jacuzzis. **Services:** 🍽 💳 🚐 ⛵ ↵ Car-rental desk, masseur, babysitting. **Facilities:** 🛁 🔲 ♿ 6 rsts, 2 bars (w/entertainment), games rm, beauty salon. **Rates:** HS Mem Day–Sept $59–$219 S or D; from $150 ste. Extra person $15. Children under 18 stay free. Lower rates off-season. Higher rates for spec evnts/hols. Spec packages avail. Pking: Indoor/outdoor, free. Maj CC.

≣≣≣ **Harrah's Casino Hotel Reno**, 219 N Center St, PO Box 10, Reno, NV 89504 (Downtown); tel 702/786-3232 or toll free 800/427-7247; fax 702/788-3274. Located right in the center of Reno's gambling action, Harrah's has the reputation of being a well-run property. Guests must pass through casino to reach the hotel lobby. **Rooms:** 565 rms and stes. CI 3pm/CO noon. Express checkout avail. Nonsmoking rms avail. Well-appointed rooms. **Amenities:** 📺 ♨ A/C, satel TV w/movies. Some units w/minibars, some w/terraces. **Services:** 🍽 ➤ 🚐 ⛵ ↵ ⬧ Twice-daily maid svce, car-rental desk, masseur. **Facilities:** 🏠 🛁 🔲 ♿ 4 rsts, 5 bars (1 w/entertainment), lifeguard, games rm, spa, beauty salon. Dozens of restaurants are within walking distance. **Rates:** $79–$130 S or D; from $229 ste. Extra person $10. Children under 15 stay free. Min stay HS, wknds, and spec evnts. Higher rates for spec evnts/hols. Spec packages avail. Pking: Indoor/outdoor, free. Maj CC.

≣≣ **Holiday Hotel Casino**, 111 Mill St, Reno, NV 89501 (Downtown); tel 702/329-0411 or toll free 800/648-5431; fax 702/322-4944. Good location on the river, within easy walking distance of downtown casinos. Quiet, older property, off the main track. **Rooms:** 193 rms and stes. CI 3pm/CO noon. Nonsmoking rms avail. Rooms are modestly furnished, but not unpleasant. Best are with balconies overlooking river. **Amenities:** ▥ A/C, TV. Some units w/minibars, some w/terraces. **Services:** ▥ ▥ ▥ ▥ ▥ ▥ Twice-daily maid svce, car-rental desk, babysitting. **Facilities:** ▥ ▥ 1 rst, 2 bars (1 w/entertainment). **Rates:** HS Aug–Nov $32–$125 S or D; from $75 ste. Extra person $8. Children under 18 stay free. Min stay wknds. Lower rates off-season. Higher rates for spec evnts/hols. Spec packages avail. Pking: Outdoor, free. Maj CC.

▤▤▤ **Holiday Inn Downtown**, 1000 E 6th St, Reno, NV 89512; tel 702/786-5151 or toll free 800/648-4877; fax 702/786-2447. 18 miles E of downtown. Medium-size casino through lobby. Not advisable to walk after dark in this neighborhood. **Rooms:** 286 rms and stes. CI 2pm/CO noon. Express checkout avail. Nonsmoking rms avail. Tastefully decorated, with good housekeeping services. Rooms accessible for the disabled have added features, such as visual smoke detectors. **Amenities:** ▥ ▥ ▥ A/C, cable TV w/movies. Some units w/minibars. Excellent security. **Services:** ✗ ▥ ▥ ▥ ▥ Car-rental desk, babysitting. **Facilities:** ▥ ▥ ▥ 1 rst, 1 bar. **Rates:** HS Mar–Oct $55–$99 S or D; from $125 ste. Extra person $5. Children under 18 stay free. Min stay HS and wknds. Lower rates off-season. Higher rates for spec evnts/hols. MAP rates avail. Spec packages avail. Pking: Outdoor, free. Maj CC. Continental breakfast available in some packages.

▤▤▤ **Peppermill Hotel Casino**, 2707 S Virginia St, Reno, NV 89502; tel 702/826-2121 or toll free 800/648-6992; fax 702/826-5205. **Rooms:** 632 rms and stes. CI 3pm/CO noon. Express checkout avail. Nonsmoking rms avail. Tower rooms have king-size beds and sofas. **Amenities:** ▥ ▥ A/C, cable TV w/movies. All units w/minibars, some w/Jacuzzis. **Services:** ▥ ▥ ▥ ▥ ▥ Car-rental desk, masseur, babysitting. **Facilities:** ▥ ▥ ▥ 4 rsts, 7 bars (1 w/entertainment), games rm, sauna, whirlpool, beauty salon. **Rates:** HS July–Sept $54–$99 S or D; from $200 ste. Children under 18 stay free. Min stay wknds. Lower rates off-season. Higher rates for spec evnts/hols. Spec packages avail. Pking: Outdoor, free. Maj CC. Up to 4 people can stay in one room at no extra charge.

▤▤ **Pioneer Inn**, 221 S Virginia St, Reno, NV 89501 (Downtown); tel 702/324-7777 or toll free 800/648-5468 in the US, 800/879-8879 in Canada; fax 702/323-5434. A few blocks from the main casino district. Caters to group tours. **Rooms:** 252 rms and stes. CI 2pm/CO noon. Nonsmoking rms avail. Inexpensive furnishings, but colors are pleasing. **Amenities:** ▥ A/C, cable TV w/movies. Some units w/minibars, some w/Jacuzzis. **Services:** ▥ ▥ **Facilities:** ▥ ▥ ▥ 3 rsts, 3 bars. Restaurant on premises has a local following. **Rates:** HS Sept–Oct $39–$65

S or D; from $125 ste. Extra person $6. Min stay wknds. Lower rates off-season. Higher rates for spec evnts/hols. Pking: Indoor/outdoor, free. Maj CC.

▤▤▤ **Reno Hilton**, 2500 E 2nd St, Reno, NV 89595; tel 702/789-2000 or toll free 800/648-5080; fax 702/789-1678. Exit 66 off US 395. Huge casino. Arcade downstairs with about 50 upscale shops. **Rooms:** 2,001 rms and stes. CI 2pm/CO noon. Express checkout avail. Nonsmoking rms avail. **Amenities:** ▥ ▥ A/C, cable TV w/movies, voice mail. Some units w/minibars. **Services:** ▥ ▥ ▥ ▥ ▥ Car-rental desk, masseur, babysitting. Turn-down service in VIP accommodations. **Facilities:** ▥ ▥ ▥ ▥ ▥ ▥ 5 rsts, 6 bars (1 w/entertainment), lifeguard, games rm, spa, sauna, steam rm, whirlpool, beauty salon. At Aqua Driving Range, drive golf balls over water onto man-made islands. Outdoor and indoor tennis. **Rates:** HS Mem Day–Sept $69–$119 S or D; from $130 ste. Extra person $15. Children under 12 stay free. Lower rates off-season. Higher rates for spec evnts/hols. Spec packages avail. Pking: Outdoor, free. Maj CC.

▤▤▤ **The Sands Regency Hotel Casino**, 345 N Arlington Ave, Reno, NV 89501 (Downtown); tel 702/348-2200 or toll free 800/648-3553; fax 702/348-2226. One of the few larger properties that are locally owned. **Rooms:** 938 rms and stes. CI 3pm/CO noon. Express checkout avail. Nonsmoking rms avail. Well maintained. Good views from upper floors. Quality varies greatly from room to room. **Amenities:** ▥ A/C, satel TV w/movies. Some units w/minibars, some w/terraces, 1 w/fireplace, some w/Jacuzzis. **Services:** ✗ ▥ ▥ ▥ Car-rental desk, masseur, babysitting. **Facilities:** ▥ ▥ ▥ ▥ 8 rsts, 5 bars, lifeguard, games rm, spa, whirlpool, beauty salon. Large casino. **Rates:** $29–$195 S or D; from $95 ste. Extra person $7. Children under 12 stay free. Min stay wknds and spec evnts. Higher rates for spec evnts/hols. Spec packages avail. Pking: Indoor/outdoor, free. Maj CC.

▤▤ **Truckee River Lodge**, 501 W 1st St, Reno, NV 89503; tel 702/786-8888 or toll free 800/635-8950. 5 blocks W of S Virginia St. Nontraditional hotel—a place for grown-ups who used to go to hostels. Nonsmoking throughout. Somewhat worn. **Rooms:** 213 rms and stes; 1 ctge/villa. CI 3pm/CO noon. Nonsmoking rms avail. 2-burner stove in each room. Some rooms have lovely views of river. Vertical blinds shut out light. Some baths have large vanity areas. **Amenities:** ▥ ▥ ▥ A/C, cable TV, refrig. Microwave. **Services:** ▥ ▥ ▥ ▥ Car-rental desk, babysitting. **Facilities:** ▥ ▥ ▥ ▥ ▥ 1 rst, washer/dryer. Washers/dryers on every floor. **Rates:** HS May–Sept $31–$85 S; $40–$90 D; from $80 ste. Extra person $10. Children under 3 stay free. Lower rates off-season. Higher rates for spec evnts/hols. Spec packages avail. Pking: Indoor/outdoor, free. Maj CC.

Motels

≣≣≣ **Best Western Continental Lodge**, 1885 S Virginia St, Reno, NV 89502; tel 702/329-1001 or toll free 800/626-1900; fax 702/324-5402. Virginia St exit off I-80. An oasis of quiet near one of Reno's busiest corners, this hotel combines charm with handsomely appointed rooms. A major shopping mall and 2 smaller ones are nearby. Inviting courtyard and pool setting. **Rooms:** 103 rms. CI 2pm/CO 11am. Nonsmoking rms avail. Quality furniture, pleasing color coordination. **Amenities:** 📺 ⚗ 📷 A/C, cable TV w/movies, refrig. All units w/terraces. **Services:** 🚗 Car-rental desk. **Facilities:** 🔥 🔲 🕭 1 rst, 1 bar (w/entertainment). **Rates:** HS Apr–Sept $48–$100 S; $53–$100 D. Extra person $5. Children under 12 stay free. Min stay HS, wknds, and spec evnts. Lower rates off-season. Higher rates for spec evnts/hols. Pking: Outdoor, free. Maj CC.

≣≣≣ **Best Western Daniel's Motor Lodge**, 375 N Sierra St, Reno, NV 89501 (Downtown); tel 702/329-1359 or toll free 800/528-1234; fax 702/329-2508. At 4th St. Rooms attractive despite plain exterior. Ongoing renovation. **Rooms:** 89 rms and stes. CI 2pm/CO 11:30am. Express checkout avail. Nonsmoking rms avail. Tasteful, traditionally furnished rooms. **Amenities:** 📺 A/C, cable TV. Some units w/terraces. **Services:** 🚐 🛎 🚗 Car-rental desk, babysitting. Complimentary continental breakfast in coffee room. **Rates (CP):** HS Apr–Oct $55–$95 S; $60–$101 D; from $50 ste. Extra person $7. Children under 12 stay free. Lower rates off-season. Higher rates for spec evnts/hols. Spec packages avail. Pking: Outdoor, free. Maj CC. In low season, rates go down to $35 single, $45 double.

≣ **Holiday Inn Convention Center**, 5851 S Virginia St, Reno, NV 89502 (Downtown); tel 702/826-2940; fax 702/826-3835. 9 mi S of convention center. Attractive, spacious lobby is the nicest feature of this property. **Rooms:** 153 rms and stes. CI 2pm/CO noon. Express checkout avail. Nonsmoking rms avail. Not tastefully decorated, but chests and headboards are of good quality. **Amenities:** 📺 ⚗ 📷 A/C, cable TV w/movies. **Services:** ✕ 🚐 🛎 🚗 🍴 **Facilities:** 🔥 🔲 🕭 1 rst, 1 bar (w/entertainment), whirlpool. **Rates:** HS Mem Day–Sept $55–$65 S or D; from $95 ste. Extra person $5. Children under 12 stay free. Lower rates off-season. Higher rates for spec evnts/hols. Pking: Outdoor, free. Maj CC.

≣≣ **La Quinta Inn**, 400 Market St, Reno, NV 89502 (Reno Cannon Int'l Airport); tel 702/348-6100 or toll free 800/531-5900; fax 702/348-8794. Exit 65A off US 395. Easy highway access. Renovation of lobby and exterior underway. **Rooms:** 130 rms and stes. CI 3pm/CO noon. Express checkout avail. Nonsmoking rms avail. Recently renovated, rooms are clean and modest. **Amenities:** 📺 ⚗ A/C, cable TV w/movies. **Services:** 🚐 🛎 🚗 🍴 Car-rental desk. **Facilities:** 🔥 🕭 **Rates:** $49–$64 S; $57–$72 D; from $100 ste. Extra person $8. Children under 16 stay free. Higher rates for spec evnts/hols. Pking: Outdoor, free. Maj CC.

≣ **Vagabond Inn Inc**, 3131 S Virginia St, Reno, NV 89502; tel 702/825-7134 or toll free 800/522-1555; fax 702/825-3096. US 395 S exit off I-80. Located near many diversions, including a gym, a multiplex theater, a bowling alley, and restaurants. **Rooms:** 129 rms. CI 2pm/CO noon. Nonsmoking rms avail. Connecting family suites have a king-bedded room. One room has 4 bunk beds. Most rooms show signs of heavy use. **Amenities:** 📺 ⚗ A/C, cable TV w/movies. Some units w/terraces. Corporate rooms come with coffeemakers and extended phone cords. Refrigerators available at extra charge. **Services:** ✕ 🚐 🚗 🍴 **Facilities:** 🔥 🔲 **Rates:** HS May–Oct $40–$85 S; $50–$85 D. Extra person $5. Children under 18 stay free. Min stay spec evnts. Lower rates off-season. Higher rates for spec evnts/hols. Spec packages avail. Pking: Outdoor, free. Maj CC.

Restaurants 🍽

Bavarian World, 595 Valley Rd, Reno; tel 702/323-7646. **German/American.** Lives up to its name with murals of alpine scenes, wrought-iron railings, and German-style decorations. Menu offers all the traditional German favorites (in huge portions), with a wide selection of continental beers. Adjoining delicatessen features everything from imported chocolate bars to German tapes and newspapers. Entertainment from accordian players, dancers, or other German performers on Friday and Saturday nights. **FYI:** Reservations recommended. Band/dancing. Dress code. **Open:** Lunch Mon–Sat 11am–4pm; dinner Mon–Sat 4–9pm. Closed some hols. **Prices:** Main courses $12.95–$19.95. Ltd CC. 🕭

Cheese Board & Wine Seller, 247 California Ave, Reno; tel 702/323-3115. 2 blocks W of Virginia St. **International.** White tablecloths, black chairs, and original art give this restaurant a crisp, sophisticated look. Crayons and glass next to flowers on each table and a big sheet of paper at each table encourage doodlers. Frittatas, quiches, and various pastas appear daily on the chalkboard. **FYI:** Reservations not accepted. Dress code. Beer and wine only. **Open:** Mon–Fri 8am–5:30pm, Sat 10am–4pm. Closed some hols. **Prices:** Lunch main courses $3.75–$6.75. Ltd CC. 🕭

★ **Josef's Vienna Konditorei & Bakery**, in Moana West Center, 933 W Moana Lane, Reno; tel 702/825-0451. **Cafe.** Knotty pine beams, ceiling fans, and big windows give a light, open feeling. Not fancy, but pleasant. Bakery turns out Viennese pastries, and there is a small sidewalk cafe. Sandwiches come with potato salad and a dessert. **FYI:** Reservations not accepted.

Beer and wine only. **Open:** Breakfast Mon–Fri 7am–3pm, Sat 8am–3pm, Sun 8am–1pm; lunch Mon–Sat 11am–3pm. Closed some hols. **Prices:** Lunch main courses $4–$7. Ltd CC. 🍰 🖼️ &

La Piñata, 1575 Vassar St, Reno; tel 702/323-3210. **Mexican.** Whitewashed walls, decorative tiles, colonial-style tables and chairs, piñatas, Mexican art. Five separate dining areas plus courtyard with flower beds. Traditional Mexican fare at reasonable prices. **FYI:** Reservations recommended. Dress code. **Open:** Daily 11am–10pm. Closed Dec 25. **Prices:** Main courses $3.50–$12.95. Maj CC. &

Marie's Petit Bistro, 1470 S Virginia St, Reno; tel 702/329-9899. **French/Italian/Southwestern.** Delightful French flavor, with black-and-white-checkered upholstered furniture, charcoal brick walls, high ceilings, and elaborate light fixtures. Eclectic fare with a number of salads featured at lunch. More imaginative than most Reno restaurants. **FYI:** Reservations recommended. **Open:** Lunch Mon–Fri 11am–2pm; dinner Mon–Sat 5:30–10pm. Closed some hols. **Prices:** Main courses $13.75–$17.50. Maj CC. ♥ &

★ **Palais de Jade**, in Moana West Center, 960 W Moana Lane, Reno; tel 702/827-5233. **Chinese.** A storefront cafe popular with locals, with a sophisticated decor. Cantonese, Mandarin, Hunan, and Szechuan specialties range from Jade salad to Kung Pao chicken to Szechuan-style eggplant with meat sauce. **FYI:** Reservations accepted. **Open:** Lunch Tues–Sun 11am–3pm; dinner Tues–Sun 3–10pm. Closed some hols. **Prices:** Main courses $6.50–$16.50; PF dinner $10.95–$14.95. Maj CC. &

Pimparel's La Table Française Restaurant, 3065 W 4th St, Reno; tel 702/323-3200. 1½ mi W of Virginia St. **French.** Gourmet cuisine from Yves Pimparel, formerly assistant chef at La Tour d'Argent in Paris. Elegant decor features country French antiques, paintings, fringed lamps and draperies. Each table is adorned by spectacular flower arrangements and exquisite china. Serving French classics like steak au poivre and duck á l'orange. **FYI:** Reservations recommended. Dress code. **Open:** Wed–Thurs 6:30–8:30pm, Fri–Sat 6:30–9:30pm. Closed some hols. **Prices:** Main courses $15.95–$22. Maj CC. ♥ &

★ **Rapscallion**, 1555 S Wells, Reno; tel 702/323-1211. **Eclectic.** Used brick and wood exterior with brick walled patio for warm weather dining. Handsome back bar has fireplace and juke box. Menu follows latest culinary trends; seafood is the specialty. **FYI:** Reservations accepted. **Open:** Lunch Mon–Fri 11:30am–5pm; dinner Sun–Thurs 5–10pm, Fri–Sat 5–10:30pm; brunch Sun 10am–2pm. Closed some hols. **Prices:** Main courses $12.95–$18.95. Maj CC. 🍰 &

Attractions 💼

Nevada Historical Society Museum, 1650 N Virginia St; tel 702/688-1190. Displays on the prehistory and modern history of Nevada. Beautiful collection of Native American artifacts; mementos of the West. **Open:** Mon–Sat 10am–5pm. Closed some hols. Free.

Pyramid Lake. The last vestige of the prehistoric inland sea known as Lake Lahontan, Pyramid Lake is 36 miles northeast of Reno via I-80 and Nev 447. The lake is strangely beautiful, surrounded by bald and barren mountains. In 1844, General John C Frémont, the first white American to explore the region, christened it Pyramid Lake because of the conical shape of several islands of porous volcanic rock that protrude from its center. The largest, Anahoe Island, serves as a sanctuary for a colony of 10,000 white pelicans.

Pyramid Lake is famous for its rainbow and cutthroat trout, which can weigh up to 50 lbs, as well as for the curious *cui-ui* fish, a surviving prehistoric species that can only be found here. Fishing permits are issued at the offices of the Native American reservation at Sutcliffe, Pyramid Lake Indian Tribal Enterprises (tel 702/673-6335). The northern part of the lake, with its strange lunar landscapes, is sacred ground to the Paiute people and off-limits to tourists.

SPARKS

Map page M-4, B1

Hotels 🛏️

🛏️ **Best Western McCarran House**, 55 E Nugget Ave, Sparks, NV 89431; tel 702/358-6900 or toll free 800/548-5798; fax 702/359-6065. Exit 19 off I-80. Very good upkeep in public areas. **Rooms:** 220 rms and stes. CI 2pm/CO noon. Nonsmoking rms avail. Rooms good in quality and appearance, but bathrooms poor. Highway noise; back rooms quiet except when trains pass. **Amenities:** 🗄️ 🗄️ A/C, satel TV. All units w/terraces. **Services:** 🚗 🗄️ 🍴 **Facilities:** 🗄️ 🗄️ & 1 rst, 1 bar, games rm. **Rates:** HS July–Oct $30–$85 S or D; from $95 ste. Extra person $10. Children under 12 stay free. Min stay wknds. Lower rates off-season. Higher rates for spec evnts/hols. Spec packages avail. Pking: Outdoor, free. Maj CC.

🛏️🛏️🛏️ **John Ascuaga's Nugget Hotel**, 1100 Nugget Ave, Sparks, NV 89431; tel 702/356-3300 or toll free 800/648-1177; fax 702/356-4198. 5 mi E of Reno, exit 18 off I-80. Well-run establishment. **Rooms:** 615 rms and stes. CI 3pm/CO 11am. Express checkout avail. Nonsmoking rms avail. Highway noise in front-facing rooms; the back is quieter. Quality of rooms varies considerably. **Amenities:** 🛁 ⏰ A/C, cable TV, bathrobes. Some units w/minibars. Club-level rooms come with hairdryers and color TV in bathroom. **Services:** 🍽 🔑 VP 🚐 🛄 ⤸ Car-rental desk, masseur. Club-level guests get twice-daily maid service. **Facilities:** 🏊 🏋 ⚓ 🖥 ⅋ 8 rsts, 4 bars (2 w/entertainment), games rm, spa, whirlpool, beauty salon. Big casino. **Rates:** HS Mem Day–Sept $59–$89 S or D; from $175 ste. Extra person $10. Children under 11 stay free. Lower rates off-season. Higher rates for spec evnts/hols. Spec packages avail. Pking: Indoor/outdoor, free. Maj CC.

STATELINE

Map page M-4, C1

Hotels 🏨

■■■ **Caesars Tahoe**, 55 US 50, PO Box 5800, Stateline, NV 89449; tel 702/588-3515 or toll free 800/648-3353; fax 702/586-2056. Large casino hotel with no lobby. The elevators are quite a distance along an inclined hallway, past shops. **Rooms:** 440 rms and stes. Exec-level rms avail. CI 3pm/CO noon. Express checkout avail. Nonsmoking rms avail. Rooms are well maintained but not very stylish. **Amenities:** 🛁 🖭 A/C, cable TV w/movies, voice mail. Some units w/minibars, some w/terraces, some w/fireplaces, some w/Jacuzzis. **Services:** 🍽 VP 🚐 🛄 ⤸ Car-rental desk, social director, masseur, babysitting. **Facilities:** 🏊 🏋 ⚓ ⛵ 🏋 🔲 🖥 ⅋ 6 rsts, 3 bars (1 w/entertainment), lifeguard, games rm, racquetball, spa, sauna, steam rm, whirlpool, beauty salon. Shopping arcade. Planet Hollywood restaurant. **Rates:** HS May–Aug $110–$175 S or D; from $300 ste. Extra person $10. Children under 18 stay free. Lower rates off-season. Higher rates for spec evnts/hols. Spec packages avail. Pking: Outdoor, free. Maj CC.

■■■■ **Harrah's Casino Hotel Lake Tahoe**, US 50, PO Box 8, Stateline, NV 89504; tel 702/588-6611 or toll free 800/648-3773; fax 702/586-6630. Views of Lake Tahoe from all but 10 rooms. Spent $4 million on renovations in 1994. **Rooms:** 534 rms and stes. Exec-level rms avail. CI 4pm/CO noon. Nonsmoking rms avail. Every room has 2 bathrooms. Superior decor, excellent-quality furniture. Walk-in closet is huge, with clothes hamper. **Amenities:** 🛁 ⏰ 🍷 A/C, cable TV w/movies, bathrobes. All units w/minibars. Phone and TV in bathrooms. **Services:** 🍽 🔑 VP 🚐 🛄 ⤸ ⤹ Twice-daily maid svce, masseur, babysitting. **Facilities:** 🏊 🏋 🏊 7 rsts (see also "Restaurants" below), 8 bars (4 w/entertainment), games rm, spa, whirlpool, beauty salon, day-care ctr. Two of the restaurants are first-rate. **Rates:** HS June 15–Sept 15 $119–$219 S or D;

from $159 ste. Extra person $20. Children under 16 stay free. Min stay HS, wknds, and spec evnts. Lower rates off-season. Spec packages avail. Pking: Indoor/outdoor, free. Maj CC.

■■■■ **Harvey's Resort Hotel & Casino**, US 50, PO Box 128, Stateline, NV 89449; tel 702/588-2411 or toll free 800/648-3361; fax 702/588-6643. This is as close to elegant as a casino hotel gets. Except for the casino, nothing about Harvey's is flashy. The rooms and halls are understated and conservatively decorated. **Rooms:** 740 rms and stes. CI 3:30pm/CO noon. Express checkout avail. Nonsmoking rms avail. The rooms in the new tower are the best, but those in the older part of the property are also very nice. A well-equipped room for guests with disabilities is available. **Amenities:** 🛁 ⏰ A/C, cable TV w/movies. Some units w/minibars, some w/terraces. **Services:** 🍽 🔑 VP 🚐 🛄 ⤸ Car-rental desk, masseur, children's program, babysitting. **Facilities:** 🏊 🏋 🏊 8 rsts (see also "Restaurants" below), 9 bars (1 w/entertainment), games rm, spa, sauna, steam rm, whirlpool, beauty salon. Two of the finest restaurants in Lake Tahoe. **Rates:** HS July–Labor Day $95–$180 S or D; from $179 ste. Extra person $20. Children under 18 stay free. Min stay wknds. Lower rates off-season. Spec packages avail. Pking: Indoor/outdoor, free. Maj CC.

Restaurants 🍴

Friday's Station, in Harrah's Casino Hotel Lake Tahoe, US 50, Stateline; tel 702/588-6611. **New American/Steak.** Floor-to-ceiling windows offer panoramic views of Lake Tahoe from almost every table. Dramatic carved wood columns. Hearty southwest mixed grill; lamb marinated in mango chutney, wine, garlic, and spices. **FYI:** Reservations recommended. Dress code. **Open:** Daily 5–10pm. **Prices:** Main courses $19.75–$37.95. Maj CC. 🖼 VP ⅋

Llewellyn's, in Harvey's Resort Hotel & Casino, US 50, Stateline; tel 702/588-2411. **International.** Spectacular view of Lake Tahoe. Blue, taupe, and rust color scheme, flower arrangements, and upholstered chairs create an elegant ambience. Menu offers imaginative dishes like squab wrapped with puff pastry and stuffed with braised cabbage. Prices are low considering the quality of food and presentation. Dinner dancing Wednesday nights off-season. **FYI:** Reservations recommended. Dancing/piano. Dress code. **Open:** HS July–Sept lunch Wed–Sat 11:30am–2:30pm; dinner Sun–Fri 6–9:30pm, Sat 5–10pm; brunch Sun 10am–2pm. Reduced hours off-season. **Prices:** Main courses $16.75–$26.75. Maj CC. 🖼 VP ⅋

Sage Room, in Harvey's Resort Hotel & Casino, US 50, Stateline; tel 702/588-2411. **American/Steak.** Dark paneling, western art prints, and western-style light fixtures create a men's-club atmosphere. Tableside service is a hallmark; steak Diane, rack of lamb, and steak Gilroy are among the favorite dishes. **FYI:** Reservations recommended. Dress code. **Open:** Mon–Fri 6–10pm, Sat–Sun 5:30–10pm. Closed week after Thanksgiving. **Prices:** Main courses $18–$24. Maj CC. ▮ VP

♥ **The Summit**, in Harrah's Casino Hotel Lake Tahoe, US 50, Stateline; tel 702/588-6611. **New American/Eclectic.** Sophisticated town-house ambience with good art and upholstered chairs, turquoise table linen, fine china, beautiful crystal. All 3 dining rooms have view of Lake Tahoe. Herbed brioche accompanies each meal. Features live Maine lobster Thermidor, prime beef Wellington with truffle-Madeira sauce, phyllo-wrapped chicken breast with a sweet onion confit, venison loin with melted brie. **FYI:** Reservations recommended. Piano. Dress code. **Open:** Wed–Thurs 5:30–10pm, Fri–Sat 5:30–11pm, Sun 5:30–10pm. Closed 2nd week in Dec. **Prices:** Main courses $26–$32; PF dinner $50–$70. Maj CC. ▨ VP &

TONOPAH

Map page M-4, C2

Hotel 🛏

≣≣ **Station House**, 1100 Erie Main St, Tonopah, NV 89049; tel 702/482-9777; fax 702/482-8762. Air Force Rd exit off US 95; E of hwy. Railroad station–style architecture with rustic pine paneling and furniture in public areas. **Rooms:** 75 rms and stes. CI 2pm/CO 11am. Nonsmoking rms avail. Motel-style rooms, clean but showing signs of age. **Amenities:** 🛅 🖳 A/C, cable TV w/movies. Some units w/minibars. **Services:** ⏚ Car-rental desk. **Facilities:** 🏊 & 1 rst, 2 bars (1 w/entertainment). Casino with slots and live table games. Downstairs sports bar has wide-screen TV. Whistle Stop restaurant serves generous portions of "downhome" favorites. Adjoining RV park has grocery and bakery. **Rates:** $33–$45 S; $36–$48 D; from $60 ste. Extra person $3. Higher rates for spec evnts/hols. Spec packages avail. Pking: Outdoor, free. Maj CC.

Motels

≣≣ **Best Western Hi-Desert Inn**, 328 S Main St, PO Box 351, Tonopah, NV 89049; tel 702/482-3511 or toll free 800/ 528-1234; fax 702/482-3300. ¼ mi W of jct US 95/US 6. Well-kept, U-shaped building with fieldstone walls and a shake roof. **Rooms:** 62 rms. CI 3pm/CO 11am. Nonsmoking rms avail. Rooms are modern, with standard motel decor. **Amenities:** 🛅 🖳 A/C, cable TV w/movies. **Services:** ⏚ ⏛ **Facilities:** 🏊 & Whirlpool, washer/dryer. **Rates (CP):** HS Mar–Oct $42–$52 S;

$52–$62 D. Extra person $6. Children under 12 stay free. Lower rates off-season. Higher rates for spec evnts/hols. Pking: Outdoor, free. Maj CC.

≣≣ **Jim Butler Motel**, 100 S Main St, PO Box 1352, Tonopah, NV 89049; tel 702/482-3577 or toll free 800/635-9455; fax 702/482-5240. West side of town, at Brougher St. Western-style, wood-frame building with creaky wood stairs, weathered banisters, and a 2nd-floor veranda that encircles the motel. One can walk next door to the city's only landmark, the 5-story turn-of-the-century Mizpah Hotel. **Rooms:** 25 rms. CI 3pm/CO noon. Nonsmoking rms avail. Despite the motel's age, rooms are clean, if compact, with modern furnishings. **Amenities:** 🛅 A/C, cable TV. **Rates:** $29–$39 S or D. Extra person $5. Children under 12 stay free. Pking: Outdoor, free. Maj CC.

Attraction 📷

Central Nevada Museum, Logan Field Rd; tel 702/482-9676. On display here are exhibits on the history of central Nevada, including Native American and settlement periods, railroading, and mining; also natural history of the area. On the grounds are pieces of heavy mining equipment, stamp mill, blacksmith shop, miner's cabin, and others. **Open:** May–Sept, daily 11am–5pm; Oct–Apr, Tues–Sat noon–5pm. Closed some hols. Free.

VALLEY OF FIRE STATE PARK

Map page M-4, D4

Located 60 miles NE of Las Vegas at exit 75 off I-15, the 39,900-acre Valley of Fire derives its name from the brilliant sandstone formations which were created 150 million years ago by a great shifting of sand and continue to be shaped by the geologic processes of wind and water erosion. Billions of years ago these rocks were under hundreds of feet of ocean. When this ocean floor began to rise some 200 million years ago, the receding waters left behind a muddy terrain that eventually gave way to a great sandy desert. Oxidation of iron in the sands and mud turned the rocks the many hues of red, pink, russet, lavender, and white that can be seen today. Logs of ancient forests washed down from far away highlands and became petrified fossils which can be seen along 2 interpretive trails.

Some of the most notable formations in the park have been named for the shapes they vaguely resemble or evoke—a duck, an elephant, 7 sisters, domes, beehives, and so on. Native American petroglyphs, some dating back 3,000 years, have been etched into the rock walls and boulders. They can be observed along self-guided trails. Petroglyphs at Atlatl Rock and Petroglyph Canyon are the most easily accessible.

The **Visitor Center** is on Nev 169, 6 miles west of North Shore Rd (open daily 8:30am–4:30pm; tel 702/397-2088). Exhibits here explain the origin and geologic history of the colorful sandstone formations, describe the ancient peoples who carved their rock art on canyon walls, and identify indigenous plants and wildlife. Hiking, picnicking, and camping information may be obtained here from park rangers.

WINNEMUCCA

Map page M-4, A2

Motels 🛏

≣≣≣ **Gold Country Inn**, 921 W Winnemucca Blvd, Winnemucca, NV 89445; tel 702/623-6999 or toll free 800/346-5306; fax 702/623-9190. Exit 76 off I-80. Nicest, newest property in town. Unusually attractive lobby with high ceiling. **Rooms:** 71 rms, stes, and effic. CI 1pm/CO noon. Nonsmoking rms avail. **Amenities:** 🛋 🕭 A/C, cable TV. **Services:** 🚐 ⌂ ⌂ ⌂ **Facilities:** ⌂ & Whirlpool. **Rates:** HS May–Oct $60–$70 S; $70–$80 D; from $80 ste; from $70 effic. Extra person $10. Children under 12 stay free. Lower rates off-season. Higher rates for spec evnts/hols. Spec packages avail. Pking: Outdoor, free. Maj CC.

≣≣ **Pyrenees Motel**, 714 W Winnemucca Blvd, PO Box 3591, Winnemucca, NV 89446; tel 702/623-1116; fax 702/623-9022. Exit 76 off I-80 E; exit 78 off I-80 W. Within walking distance of downtown and several restaurants, this is a reasonable place for travelers on a budget. **Rooms:** 46 rms. CI 11am/CO 11am. Nonsmoking rms avail. **Amenities:** 🛋 A/C, cable TV. Refrigerators and microwaves in 15 rooms. **Facilities:** & Washer/dryer. **Rates:** HS Apr–Sept $40 S; $45 D. Extra person $5. Children under 15 stay free. Lower rates off-season. Spec packages avail. Pking: Outdoor, free. Maj CC.

≣≣≣ **Red Lion Inn**, 741 W Winnemucca Blvd, Winnemucca, NV 89445; tel 702/623-2565 or toll free 800/633-6435; fax 702/623-5702. Winnemucca exit off I-80; left onto Winnemucca Blvd. Walking distance from downtown. Nicest casino in Winnemucca. **Rooms:** 107 rms and stes. CI 4pm/CO noon. Express checkout avail. Nonsmoking rms avail. Rooms and baths nicely decorated; quality furnishings. **Amenities:** 🛋 🕭 🕭 A/C, cable TV. 1 unit w/minibar, some w/terraces, 1 w/Jacuzzi. **Services:** 🚐 ⌂ ⌂ ⌂ **Facilities:** ⌂ & 1 rst, 1 bar, games rm, whirlpool. Pool shared with adjacent inn, could get crowded in hot weather. **Rates:** HS May–Oct $60–$70 S; $70–$80 D; from

$80 ste. Extra person $10. Children under 12 stay free. Lower rates off-season. Spec packages avail. Pking: Outdoor, free. Maj CC.

≣≣ **Thunderbird Motel**, 511 W Winnemucca Blvd, Winnemucca, NV 89445; tel 702/623-3661; fax 702/623-4234. Exit 76 off I-80 E; exit 78 off I-80 W. Good location near downtown and restaurants. Very clean, well maintained. **Rooms:** 40 rms. CI 4pm/CO noon. Nonsmoking rms avail. Attractively decorated. **Amenities:** 🛋 🕭 A/C, cable TV. **Services:** 🚐 ⌂ ⌂ ⌂ **Facilities:** ⌂ **Rates:** HS May–Oct $40–$65 S or D. Extra person $10. Children under 12 stay free. Lower rates off-season. Spec packages avail. Pking: Outdoor, free. Maj CC.

Restaurant 🍽

★ **The Martin Hotel**, Railroad and Melarkey Sts, Winnemucca; tel 702/623-3197. **Basque.** Food is served boardinghouse-style in this popular Basque restaurant. The decor and view of the railroad tracks are hardly the attractions here; rather, it's the hearty meals. Dinners consist of a choice of steak, lamb, or shrimp; 2 side dishes, such as tongue stew, tripe, or chorizo; rice; soup; salad; crusty hunks of bread; beans; red wine; and dessert, usually bread pudding. **FYI:** Reservations not accepted. Children's menu. **Open:** HS spring–fall lunch Mon–Fri 11am–2pm; dinner daily 5–9:30pm. Reduced hours off-season. Closed some hols. **Prices:** PF dinner $15.90. Ltd CC. &

INDEX

THE ROAD GUIDE FOR TODAY'S TRAVELER.

SAVE $4 OFF
GENERAL ADMISSION

Present coupon at Front Gate before bill is totalled. Not valid with any other discounts or special offers. Limit 6 guests per coupon. Photocopies not accepted. Operating hours and general admission prices subject to change without notice.

COUPON VALID THRU 12/31/95

BUSCH GARDENS
TAMPA BAY, FLORIDA

PLU# 3175c/23176a An Anheuser-Busch Theme Park

SAVE $4 OFF
GENERAL ADMISSION

Present coupon at Front Gate before bill is totalled. Not valid with any other discounts or special offers. Limit 6 guests per coupon. Photocopies not accepted. Operating hours and general admission prices subject to change without notice.

COUPON VALID 3/31/95 THRU 10/29/95

ADVENTURE ISLAND
TAMPA'S WATER PARK

PLU# 3175c/23176a An Anheuser-Busch Theme Park

Limit six guests per certificate. Not valid with other discounts or on purchase of multi-park/multi-visit passes or tickets. Present certificate at Front Gate before bill is totaled. Redeemable only at time of ticket purchase. Photocopies not accepted. Certificate has no cash value. Operating hours and general admission price subject to change without notice. Valid through 3/31/95 only.

Sea World
Orlando, Florida
Anheuser-Busch Theme Parks.

Make Contact With Another World®

©1994 Sea World of Florida, Inc.   PLU# 4556/4555

Discount valid for up to 6 people through 12/31/95.
Coupon has no cash value and is not valid with any other offers.
Offer subject to change without notice. Parking fee not included.
©1994 Universal Studios Florida. All Rights Reserved.

6101944075662

Name _____

Address _____

City _____ State _____ Zip _____

Phone (____)_____

Name _____

Address _____

City _____ State _____ Zip _____

Phone (____)_____

Name _____

Address _____

City _____ State _____ Zip _____

Phone (____)_____

Name _____

Address _____

City _____ State _____ Zip _____

Phone (____)_____

THE ROAD GUIDE FOR TODAY'S TRAVELER.

STAY WITH US & SAVE!

10%

Ramada Limiteds, Inns, Hotels, Resorts and Plaza Hotels offer you the value and accommodations you expect . . . And so much more!

- Over 750 convenient locations
- Children under 18 always stay free
- Non-smoking and handicap rooms available

For reservations call 1-800-228-2828

10%

1-800-4-CHOICE
(1-800-424-6423)

Advance reservations through 1-800-4-CHOICE required. Based on availability at participating hotels and cannot be used in conjunction with any other discount.

TERMS AND CONDITIONS

Offer valid on an Intermediate (Group C) through a Full Size 4-Door (Group E) car for a 5-day minimum rental. Coupon must be surrendered at time of rental; one per rental. May not be used in conjunction with any other coupon, promotion or offer. Coupon valid at Avis corporate and participating licensee locations in the continental U.S. Offer not available during holiday and other blackout periods. Offer may not be available on all rates at all times. **An advance reservation is required.** Cars subject to availability. Taxes, local government surcharges and optional items, such as LDW, additional driver fee and refueling, are extra. Renter must meet Avis age, driver and credit requirements. Minimum age is 25 but may vary by location. Offer expires December 31, 1995.

Rental Sales Agent Instructions
At Checkout: • in CPN, enter MUFA527. • Complete this information:
RA#_____ Rental Location_____
• Attach to COUPON tape.

© 1995 Wizard Co., Inc. 1/95 DTPS/

AVIS®
We try harder.

DAYS INN®
The Best Value Under The Sun.™

- **Available at participating properties.**
- **This coupon cannot be combined with any other special discount offer.**
- **Limit one coupon per room, per stay.**
- **Expires December 31, 1996.**

1-800-DAYS INN

Terms and Conditions

Advance reservations are required and blackout periods may apply. Present this certificate at time of rental or, for Gold rentals, at time of return, and receive $10 off Hertz Leisure Weekly rates at participating locations in the U.S. This certificate has no cash value, must be surrendered and may not be used with any other rate, discount or promotion. Standard rental qualifications, rental period and return restrictions must be met or offer is void. Weekly rentals require a minimum rental period of five days, including a Saturday night. Minimum rental age is 25. Taxes and optional items, such as refueling, are not included and are not subject to discount. All cars are subject to availability at time of rental. Certificate expires 12/31/95.

Hertz rents Fords and other fine cars.

HERE ARE SOME OF THE DETAILS YOU SHOULD KNOW:

Just mention promotion code TCB/MCBC087 when you reserve a compact through luxury size car and receive $20 off your weekly rental. Five-day minimum rental necessary to qualify for discount. This offer is valid at participating budget locations through 3/3/96 and is subject to vehicle availability. Car must be returned to renting location, except in some metro areas where inter-area drop-offs are permitted. Local rental and age requirements apply. Discount applies to time and mileage only and is not available in conjunction with any other discount, promotional offer, CorpRate™, government, or tour/wholesale rate. Refueling services, taxes and optional items are extra. Additional driver, under-age driver and other surcharges are extra. Blackout dates may apply.

Terms and Conditions

- Offer includes 10% discount off all time and mileage charges on Cruise America or Cruise Canada vehicles only.
- Offer not available in conjunction with other discount offers or promotional rates.
- Excludes other rental charges, deposits, sales tax, and fuels.
- Normal rental conditions and customer qualification procedures apply.
- Members must reserve vehicles through Central Reservations only, at least one week in advance of pick up and mention **Frommer's America on Wheels** at time of reservation.

For reservations: 1-800-327-7799 - US and Canada

Rental Rates and Conditions

This offer is subject to availability and may not be used in conjunction with any other certificate or promotion. Offers apply only to economy through intermediate size car. Blackout periods may apply. This coupon has no cash value, and must be surrendered at time of rental. Coupon valid at all participating locations in the U.S. Taxes, fuel, LDW/CDW, under age and additional driver fees are extra. Some additional charges may apply.

FROMMER'S AMERICA ON Wheels

THE ROAD GUIDE FOR TODAY'S AMERICA FROM THE FIRST NAME IN TRAVEL

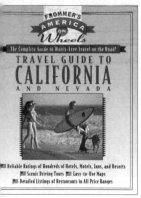

ISBN:0-02-860146-7

ISBN:0-02-860144-0

ISBN:0-02-860145-9

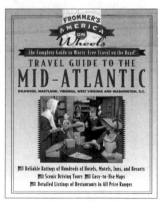

ISBN:0-02-860143-2

New titles coming in 1996

Northeast (includes Maine, Vermont, New Hampshire, Connecticut, Rhode Island, New York, and Massachusetts)

Northwest & North Central (includes Oregon, Washington, Idaho, Montana, Wyoming, North Dakota, South Dakota, Nebraska, Iowa)

Great Lakes (includes Michigan, Wisconsin, Illinois, Indiana, Ohio, Minnesota)

Southeast (includes South Carolina, North Carolina, Kentucky, Tennessee, Mississippi, Georgia, Alabama)

South Central (includes Louisiana, Arkansas, Oklahoma, Texas, Missouri)

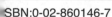

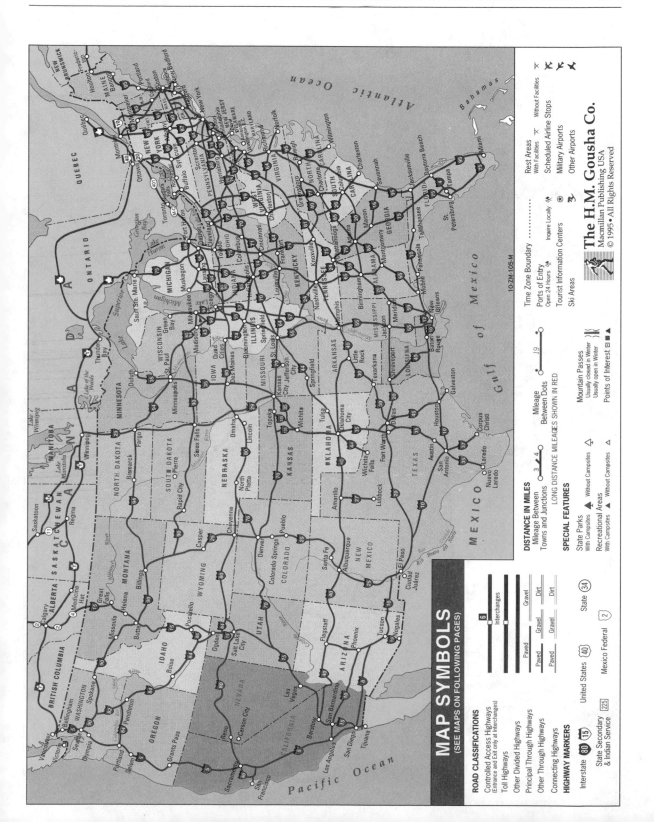

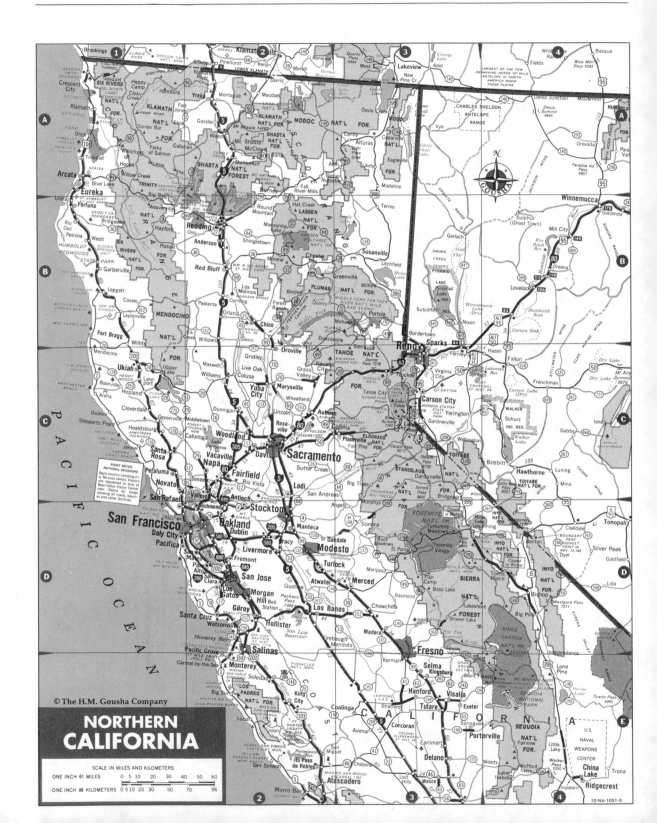

© The H.M. Gousha Company

NORTHERN CALIFORNIA

SCALE IN MILES AND KILOMETERS
ONE INCH 61 MILES   0 5 10   20   30   40   50   60
ONE INCH 98 KILOMETERS 0 510 20 30   50   70   96

10-NA-1051-S

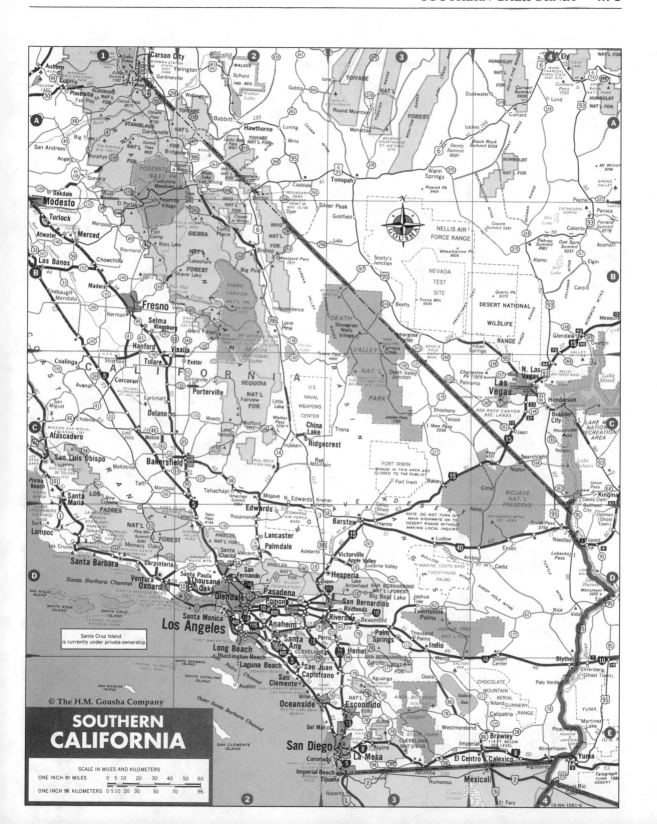

SOUTHERN
CALIFORNIA

© The H.M. Gousha Company

SCALE IN MILES AND KILOMETERS

ONE INCH 61 MILES   0 5 10   20   30   40   50   60

ONE INCH 98 KILOMETERS   0 5 10   20   30   50   70   96

10-NA-1051-S

Santa Cruz Island
is currently under private ownership

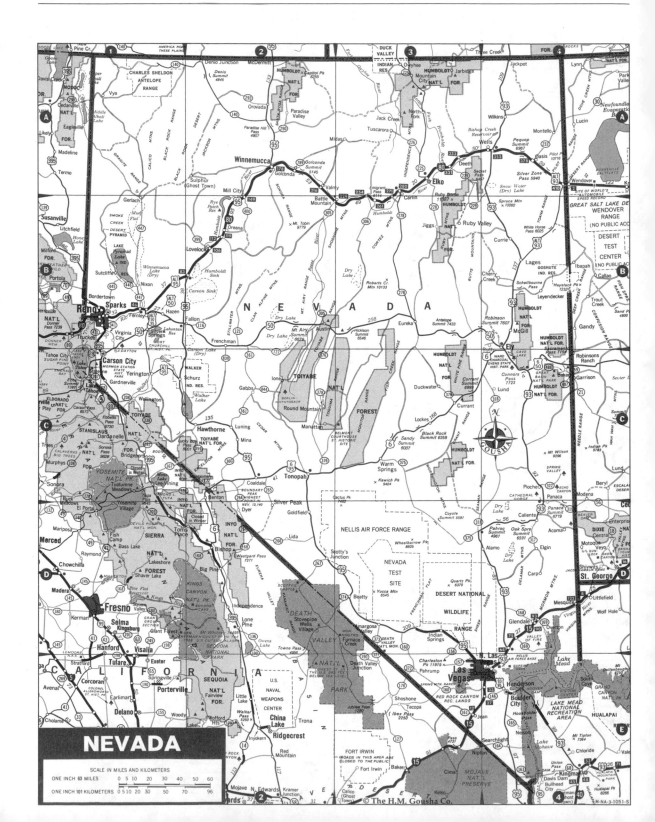

NEVADA

SCALE IN MILES AND KILOMETERS

ONE INCH 63 MILES   0 5 10   20   30   40   50   60

ONE INCH 101 KILOMETERS   0 5 10 20 30   50   70   96

© The H.M. Gousha Co.

M-NA-3-1051-S

CALIFORNIA

CITIES AND TOWNS

State Pop. (1990) 29,760,021
State Area 158,693

• County Seat

Each city within this index is followed by a page number in bold, followed by the map location key.

- Adelanto 8,517 **M-3**,D3
- Adin **M-2**,A3
- Aguanga **M-3**,E3
- Alpine **M-3**,E3
- Alturas • 3,231 **M-2**,A3
- Amboy **M-3**,D4
- Anaheim 266,406 **M-3**,D2
- Anderson 8,299 **M-2**,B2
- Angels 2,409 **M-2**,D3
- Antioch 62,195 **M-2**,D2
- Appley Valley 46,079 **M-3**,D3
- Arcata 15,197 **M-2**,A1
- Atascadero 23,138 **M-3**,C1
- Atwater 22,282 **M-2**,D2
- Auburn • 10,592 **M-2**,C2
- Avalon 2,918 **M-3**,E2
- Avenal 9,770 **M-3**,C1
- Baker **M-3**,C3
- Bakersfield • 174,820 **M-3**,C2
- Barstow 21,472 **M-3**,D3
- Bartel **M-2**,A2
- Bass Lake **M-2**,D3
- Beaumont 9,685 **M-3**,D3
- Belden **M-2**,B2
- Bell Station **M-2**,D2
- Benton **M-3**,A2
- Bieber **M-2**,A2
- Big Bar **M-2**,B1
- Big Bear Lake 5,351 **M-3**,D3
- Big Pine **M-3**,B2
- Big Sur **M-2**,E3
- Big Trees **M-3**,A1
- Bishop **M-3**,B2
- Blue Lake **M-2**,A1
- Blythe 8,428 **M-3**,E4
- Boonville **M-2**,C1
- Brawley 18,923 **M-3**,E4
- Bridgeport • **M-3**,A2
- Bridgeville **M-2**,B1
- Buck Meadows **M-2**,D3
- Burney **M-2**,A2
- Cadiz **M-3**,D4
- Cahuilla **M-3**,E3
- Calexico 18,633 **M-3**,E4
- Calico (Ghost Town) **M-3**,D3
- Calistoga 4,468 **M-2**,C1
- Callahan **M-2**,A2
- Calpatria **M-3**,E4
- Canby **M-2**,A3
- Carmel-by-the-Sea 4,239 **M-2**,F2
- Carpintera 13,747 **M-3**,D1
- Cedarville **M-2**,A3
- Chester **M-2**,B2
- Chico 40,079 **M-2**,B2
- China Lake **M-3**,C2
- Cholame **M-3**,C1
- Chowchilla 5,930 **M-3**,B1
- Cima **M-3**,C4
- Clear Creek **M-2**,A1
- Cloverdale 4,924 **M-2**,C1
- Coalinga 8,212 **M-2**,E3
- Coloma **M-2**,C3
- Colusa • 4,934 **M-2**,C2
- Corcoran 13,364 **M-2**,E3
- Corning 5,870 **M-2**,B2
- Coronado 26,540 **M-3**,E3
- Covelo **M-2**,B1
- Crescent City • 4,380 **M-2**,A1
- Daly City 92,311 **M-2**,D1
- Dardanelle **M-3**,A1
- Davis 46,209 **M-2**,C2
- Davis Creek **M-2**,A3
- Death Valley Junction **M-3**,C3
- Delano 22,762 **M-3**,C1
- Del Mar 4,860 **M-3**,E3
- Desert Center **M-3**,D4
- Dorris 892 **M-2**,A2
- Downieville • **M-2**,B3
- Dublin 23,229 **M-2**,D2
- Dunnigan **M-2**,C2
- Dunsmuir 2,129 **M-2**,A2
- Eagleville **M-2**,A3
- Earlimart **M-3**,C1
- Earp **M-3**,D4
- Edwards **M-3**,D2
- El Centro • 31,384 **M-3**,E4
- Elk Creek **M-2**,B2
- El Monte 106,209 **M-3**,D2
- El Paso de Robles 18,583 **M-2**,E2
- El Portal **M-2**,D3
- Escondido 108,635 **M-3**,E3
- Essex **M-3**,D4
- Etna 835 **M-2**,A1
- Eureka • 27,025 **M-2**,A1
- Exeter 7,276 **M-3**,C2
- Fairfield • 77,211 **M-2**,C2
- Fair Play **M-2**,C3
- Fairview **M-3**,C2
- Fall River Mills **M-2**,A2
- Firebaugh 4,429 **M-2**,D2
- Fish Camp **M-3**,B1
- Forest Ranch **M-2**,B2
- Forks of Salmon **M-2**,A1
- Fort Bragg 6,078 **M-2**,B1
- Fort Irwin **M-3**,C3
- Fort Jones 639 **M-2**,A2
- Fortuna 8,788 **M-2**,B1
- Fremont 173,339 **M-2**,D2
- Fresno • 354,202 **M-2**,D3
- Furnace Creek **M-3**,B3
- Garberville **M-2**,B1
- Gasquet **M-2**,A1
- Gazelle **M-2**,A2
- Geyersville **M-2**,C1
- Giant Forest **M-3**,B2
- Gilroy 31,487 **M-2**,D2
- Glendale 180,038 **M-3**,D2
- Glenn **M-2**,B2
- Grass Valley 9,048 **M-2**,C2
- Greenville **M-2**,B3
- Gridley 4,631 **M-2**,C2
- Gualala **M-2**,C1
- Gustine 3,931 **M-2**,D2
- Hamburg **M-2**,A1
- Hanford • 30,897 **M-3**,B1
- Happy Camp **M-2**,A1
- Hat Creek **M-2**,B2
- Hayfork **M-2**,B1
- Healdsburg 9,469 **M-2**,C1
- Hemet 36,094 **M-3**,D3
- Hesperia 50,418 **M-3**,D3
- Hollister • 19,212 **M-2**,D2
- Hoopa **M-2**,A1
- Hopland **M-2**,C1
- Huntington Beach 181,519 **M-3**,D2
- Imperial 4,113 **M-3**,E4
- Imperial Beach 26,512 **M-3**,E3
- Independence • **M-3**,B2
- Indio 36,793 **M-3**,D3
- Inyokern **M-3**,C2
- Jacumba **M-3**,E3
- Jenner **M-2**,C1
- Jolon **M-2**,E2
- Joshua Tree **M-3**,D3
- Julian **M-3**,E3
- Kelso **M-3**,D4
- Kerman 5,448 **M-2**,E3
- King City 7,634 **M-2**,E2
- Kingsburg 7,205 **M-2**,E3
- Klamath **M-2**,A1
- Klamath River **M-2**,A2
- Kramer Junction **M-3**,D2
- Laguna Beach 23,170 **M-3**,E2
- Lake Arrowhead **M-3**,D3
- Lake Isabella **M-3**,C2
- Lakeport • 4,390 **M-2**,C1
- Lakeshore **M-3**,B2
- La Mesa 52,931 **M-3**,E3
- Lancaster 97,291 **M-3**,D2
- Las Cruces **M-3**,D1
- Laxtonville **M-2**,B1
- Lebec **M-3**,D2
- Lee Vining **M-3**,A2
- Leggett **M-2**,B1
- Likely **M-2**,A3
- Lincoln 7,248 **M-2**,C2
- Litchfield **M-2**,B3
- Little Lake **M-3**,C2
- Live Oak 4,320 **M-2**,C2
- Livermore 56,741 **M-2**,D2
- Lodi 51,874 **M-2**,C2
- Loleta **M-2**,B1
- Lompoc 37,649 **M-3**,D1
- Lone Pine **M-3**,B2
- Long Beach 429,433 **M-3**,D2
- Los Angeles • 3,485,398 **M-3**,D2
- Los Banos 14,519 **M-2**,D2
- Los Gatos 27,357 **M-2**,D2
- Los Molinos **M-2**,B2
- Lost Hills **M-3**,C1
- Lucerne Valley **M-3**,D3
- Lucia **M-2**,E2
- Ludlow **M-3**,D3
- Macdoel **M-2**,A2
- Madeline **M-2**,A3
- Madera • 29,281 **M-2**,D3
- Manteca 40,773 **M-2**,D2
- Manzanita Lake **M-2**,B2
- Maricopa 1,193 **M-3**,C1
- Mariposa • **M-2**,D3
- Marysville • 12,324 **M-2**,C2
- Maxwell **M-2**,C2
- McKittrick **M-3**,C1
- McCloud **M-2**,A2
- Mecca **M-3**,E3
- Meiners Oaks **M-3**,D1
- Mendocino **M-2**,C1
- Mendota 6,821 **M-2**,D3
- Merced • 56,216 **M-2**,D3
- Middleton **M-2**,C1
- Milford **M-2**,B3
- Miller **M-3**,E2
- Mineral **M-2**,B2
- Modesto • 164,730 **M-2**,D2
- Mohawk **M-2**,B3
- Mojave **M-3**,C2
- Montague 1,415 **M-2**,A2
- Monterey 31,954 **M-2**,E2
- Morgan Hill 23,928 **M-2**,D2
- Morro Bay 9,664 **M-2**,E2
- Mount Shasta 3,460 **M-2**,A2
- Murphys **M-2**,D3
- Napa • 61,842 **M-2**,C2
- Needles 5,191 **M-3**,D4
- Nevada City • 2,855 **M-2**,C2
- New Cuyama **M-3**,C1
- Niland **M-3**,E4
- Nipton **M-3**,C4
- North Edwards **M-3**,C2
- Novato 47,585 **M-2**,C1
- Nubieber **M-2**,A2
- Oakdale 11,961 **M-2**,D2
- Oakland • 372,242 **M-2**,D2
- Oasis **M-3**,E3
- Oceanside 128,398 **M-3**,E2
- Ono **M-2**,B2
- Orick **M-2**,A1
- Orland 5,052 **M-2**,B2
- Oroville • 11,960 **M-2**,C2
- Oxnard 142,216 **M-3**,D1
- Pacifica 37,670 **M-2**,D1
- Pacific Grove 16,117 **M-2**,E2
- Palmdale 68,842 **M-3**,D2
- Palm Springs 40,181 **M-3**,D3
- Palo Alto 55,900 **M-2**,D2
- Paloverde **M-3**,E4
- Pasadena 131,591 **M-3**,D2
- Paskenta **M-2**,B2
- Perris 21,460 **M-3**,D3
- Petaluma 43,184 **M-2**,C1
- Petrolia **M-2**,B1
- Picacho **M-3**,E4
- Pismo Beach 7,669 **M-3**,C1
- Placerville • 8,355 **M-2**,C3
- Platina **M-2**,B1
- Pomona 131,723 **M-3**,D2
- Point Arena 407 **M-2**,C1
- Porterville 29,563 **M-2**,E4
- Portola 2,193 **M-2**,B3
- Quincy • **M-2**,B2
- Raymond **M-2**,D3
- Red Bluff • 12,363 **M-2**,B2
- Redding • 66,462 **M-2**,B2
- Redlands 60,394 **M-3**,D3
- Red Mountain **M-3**,C2
- Rice **M-3**,D4
- Richmond 87,425 **M-2**,D2
- Ridgecrest 27,725 **M-3**,C2
- Rio Dell 3,012 **M-2**,B1
- Rio Vista 3,316 **M-2**,C2
- Riverside • 226,505 **M-3**,D3
- Rosamond **M-3**,D2
- Roseville 44,685 **M-2**,C2
- Round Mnt **M-2**,B2
- Sacramento • 369,365 **M-2**,C2
- Salinas • 108,777 **M-2**,D2
- San Andreas • **M-2**,C2
- San Bernardino • 164,164 **M-3**,D3
- San Clemente 41,100 **M-3**,E2
- San Diego • 1,110,549 **M-3**,E3
- San Fernando 22,580 **M-3**,D2
- San Francisco • 723,959 **M-2**,D1
- San Jose • 782,248 **M-2**,D2
- San Juan Capistrano 26,183 **M-3**,E2
- San Luis Obispo • 41,958 **M-3**,C1
- San Mateo 85,486 **M-2**,D2
- San Miguel **M-2**,E2
- San Rafael • 48,404 **M-2**,D1
- San Simeon **M-2**,E2
- Santa Ana • 293,742 **M-3**,D2
- Santa Barbara • 85,571 **M-3**,D1
- Santa Clara 93,613 **M-2**,D2
- Santa Clarita 110,642 **M-3**,D2
- Santa Cruz • 49,040 **M-2**,D2
- Santa Maria 61,284 **M-3**,C1
- Santa Monica 86,905 **M-3**,D2
- Santa Paula 25,062 **M-3**,D2
- Santa Rosa • 113,313 **M-2**,C1
- Selma 14,757 **M-3**,B1
- Shaver Lake **M-3**,B1
- Shingletown **M-2**,B2
- Shoshone **M-3**,C3
- Sierraville **M-2**,C3
- Soledad 7,146 **M-2**,E2
- Solvang 4,741 **M-3**,D1
- Somes Bar **M-2**,A1
- Sonoma 8,121 **M-2**,C2
- Sonora • 4,153 **M-3**,A1
- South Lake Tahoe 21,586 **M-2**,C3
- Springville **M-3**,C2
- Squaw Valley **M-2**,D3
- Stewarts Point **M-2**,C1
- Stockton • 210,943 **M-2**,D2
- Stovepipe Wells Village **M-3**,B3
- Stratford **M-3**,C1
- Surf **M-3**,D1
- Susanville • 7,279 **M-2**,B3
- Sutter Creek 1,835 **M-2**,C2
- Taft 5,902 **M-3**,C1
- Tahoe City **M-2**,C3
- Tecopa **M-3**,C3
- Tehachapi 5,791 **M-3**,C2
- Termo **M-2**,B3
- Thousand Oaks 104,352 **M-3**,D2
- Thousand Palms **M-3**,D3
- Toms Place **M-3**,B2
- Tracy 33,558 **M-2**,D2
- Trinidad 362 **M-2**,A1
- Trona **M-3**,C3
- Truckee **M-2**,C3
- Tulare 33,249 **M-3**,C1
- Tulelake 1,010 **M-2**,A2
- Tuolumne Meadows **M-3**,A1
- Turlock 42,198 **M-3**,B1
- Twentynine Palms 11,821 **M-3**,D3
- Ukiah • 14,599 **M-2**,C1
- Upper Lake **M-2**,C1
- Vacaville 71,479 **M-2**,C2
- Vallejo 109,199 **M-2**,C2
- Ventura • **M-3**,D1
- Victorville 40,674 **M-3**,D3
- Vidal **M-3**,D4
- Vincent **M-3**,D2
- Visalia • 75,636 **M-2**,E3
- Wasco 12,412 **M-3**,C1
- Watsonville 31,099 **M-2**,D2
- Weaverville • **M-2**,B1
- Weed 3,062 **M-2**,A2
- Weitchpec **M-2**,A1
- Weott **M-2**,B1
- Westmoreland 1,380 **M-3**,E4
- Wheatland 1,631 **M-2**,C2
- Williams 2,297 **M-2**,C2
- Willits 5,027 **M-2**,B1
- Willow Creek **M-2**,A1
- Willows • 5,988 **M-2**,B2
- Winterhaven **M-3**,E4
- Wofford Hghts. **M-3**,C2
- Woodland • 39,802 **M-2**,C2
- Woody **M-3**,C2
- Yermo **M-3**,D3
- Yosemite Village **M-3**,B1
- Yreka • 6,948 **M-2**,A2
- Yuba City • 27,437 **M-2**,C2

NEVADA

CITIES AND TOWNS

State Pop. (1990) 1,201,833
State Area 110,540

• County Seat

Each city within this index is followed by a page number in bold, followed by the map location key.

- Acoma **M-4**,D4
- Alamo **M-4**,D4
- Amargosa Valley **M-4**,D3
- Austin **M-4**,B2
- Baker **M-4**,C4
- Battle Mountain • **M-4**,B3
- Beatty **M-4**,D3
- Bordertown **M-4**,B1
- Boulder City 12,567 **M-4**,E4
- Caliente 1,111 **M-4**,D4
- Carlin 2,220 **M-4**,A3
- Carp **M-4**,D4
- Carson City • 40,443 **M-4**,C1
- Cherry Creek **M-4**,B4
- Coaldale **M-4**,C2
- Currant **M-4**,C3
- Currie **M-4**,B4
- Deeth **M-4**,A3
- Denio Junction **M-4**,A2
- Duckwater **M-4**,C3
- Dyer **M-4**,D2
- Elgin **M-4**,D4
- Elko • 14,736 **M-4**,A3
- Ely • 4,756 **M-4**,B4
- Eureka • **M-4**,B3
- Fallon • 6,438 **M-4**,B2
- Fernley **M-4**,B1
- Frenchman **M-4**,B2
- Gabbs 667 **M-4**,C2
- Gardnerville **M-4**,C1
- Gerlach **M-4**,B1
- Glendale **M-4**,D4
- Golconda **M-4**,A2
- Goldfield • **M-4**,D2
- Hawthorne • **M-4**,C2
- Hazen **M-4**,B1
- Henderson 64,942 **M-4**,E4
- Indian Springs **M-4**,D3
- Ione **M-4**,C2
- Jack Creek **M-4**,A3
- Jackpot **M-4**,A4
- Jarbidge **M-4**,A3
- Jean **M-4**,E3
- Jiggs **M-4**,B3
- Lages **M-4**,B4
- Las Vegas • 258,295 **M-4**,E3
- Leyendecker **M-4**,B4
- Lida **M-4**,D2
- Lovelock • 2,069 **M-4**,B2
- Lund **M-4**,C4
- Luning **M-4**,C2
- Manattan **M-4**,C2
- McDermitt **M-4**,A2
- McGill **M-4**,B4
- Mesquite 1,871 **M-4**,D4
- Midas **M-4**,A3
- Mill City **M-4**,A2
- Mina **M-4**,C2
- Montello **M-4**,A4
- Mountain City **M-4**,A3
- Nelson **M-4**,E4
- Nixon **M-4**,B1
- North Fork **M-4**,A3
- North Las Vegas 47,707 **M-4**,E4
- Oasis **M-4**,A4
- Oreana **M-4**,B2
- Orovada **M-4**,A2
- Overton **M-4**,D4
- Owyhee **M-4**,A3
- Pahrump **M-4**,E3
- Panaca **M-4**,C4
- Paradise Valley **M-4**,A2
- Pioche • **M-4**,C4
- Reno • 133,850 **M-4**,B1
- Round Mountain **M-4**,C2
- Ruby Valley **M-4**,B3
- Ruth **M-4**,B4
- Scotty's Junction **M-4**,D2
- Searchlight **M-4**,E4
- Silver Peak **M-4**,D2
- Silver Springs **M-4**,B1
- Sparks 53,367 **M-4**,B1
- Stateline **M-4**,C1
- Sulphur (Ghost Town) **M-4**,A2
- Sutcliffe **M-4**,B1
- Tonopah • **M-4**,C2
- Tuscarora **M-4**,A3
- Valmy **M-4**,A2
- Virginia City • **M-4**,B1
- Vya **M-4**,A1
- Warm Springs **M-4**,C3
- Wellington **M-4**,C1
- Wells 1,256 **M-4**,A4
- Wilkins **M-4**,A4
- Winnemucca • 6,134 **M-4**,A2
- Yerington 2,367 **M-4**,C1

NA-1051-S-XA

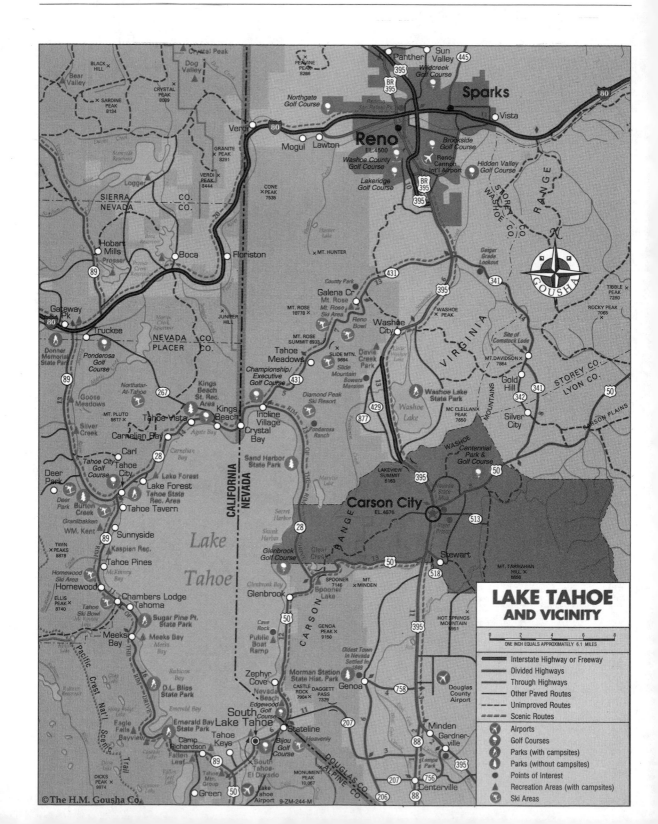

LAKE TAHOE AND VICINITY

ONE INCH EQUALS APPROXIMATELY 6.1 MILES

Interstate Highway or Freeway	
Divided Highways	
Through Highways	
Other Paved Routes	
Unimproved Routes	
Scenic Routes	
Airports	
Golf Courses	
Parks (with campsites)	
Parks (without campsites)	
Points of Interest	
Recreation Areas (with campsites)	
Ski Areas	

©The H.M. Gousha Co.

9-ZM-244-M

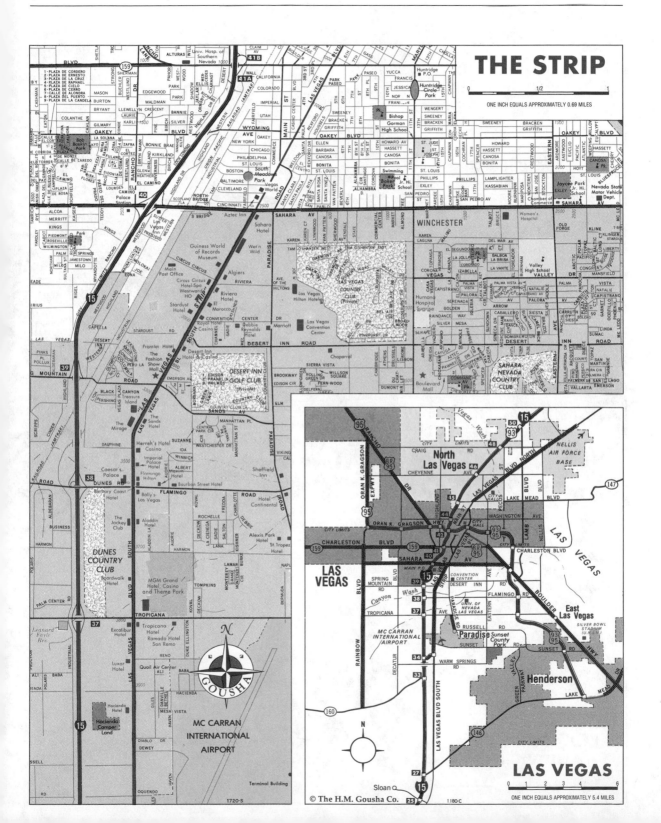

THE STRIP

0   1/2   1
ONE INCH EQUALS APPROXIMATELY 0.69 MILES

LAS VEGAS

0 1 2 3 4 5 6
ONE INCH EQUALS APPROXIMATELY 5.4 MILES

© The H.M. Gousha Co.

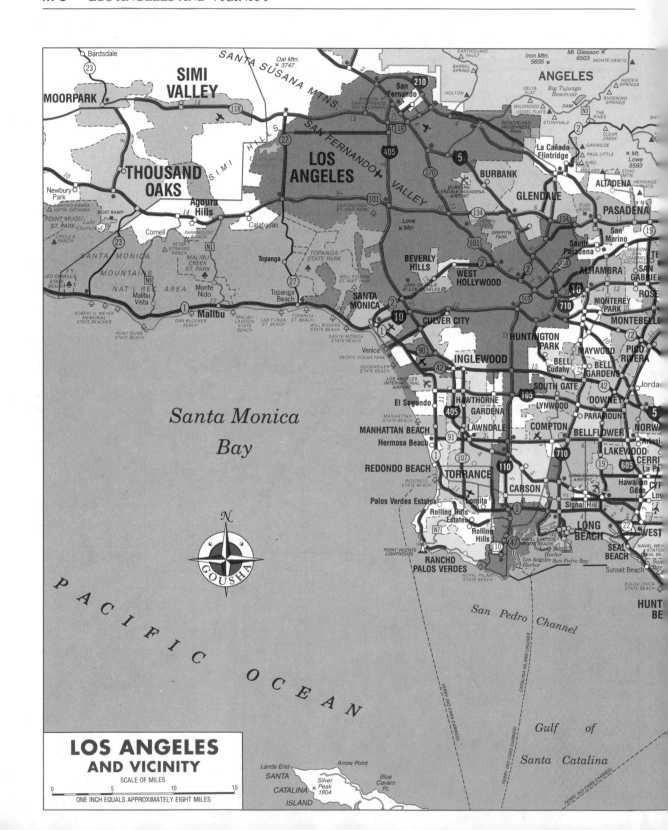

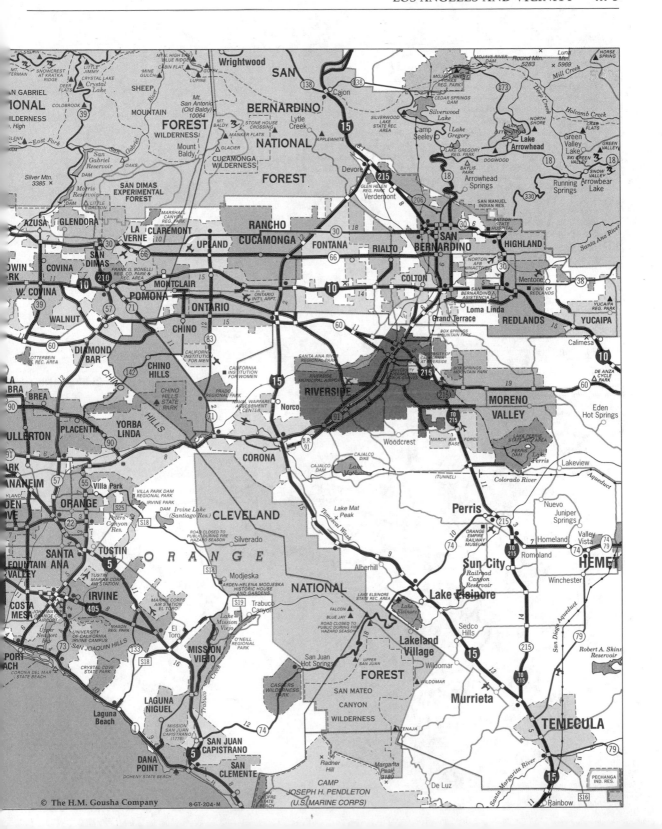

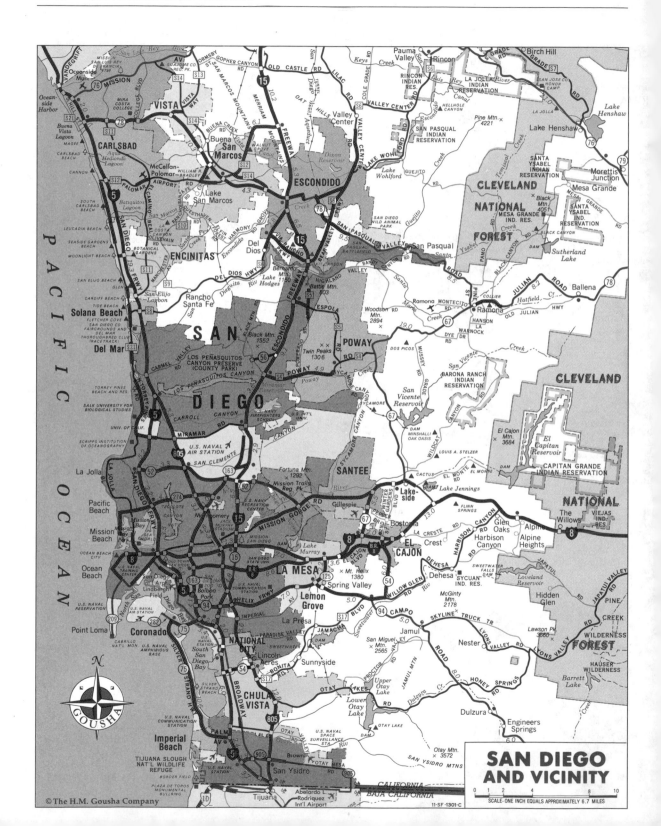

SAN DIEGO
AND VICINITY

0 1 2   4   8   10

SCALE-ONE INCH EQUALS APPROXIMATELY 6.7 MILES

© The H.M. Gousha Company

11-SF-1301-C

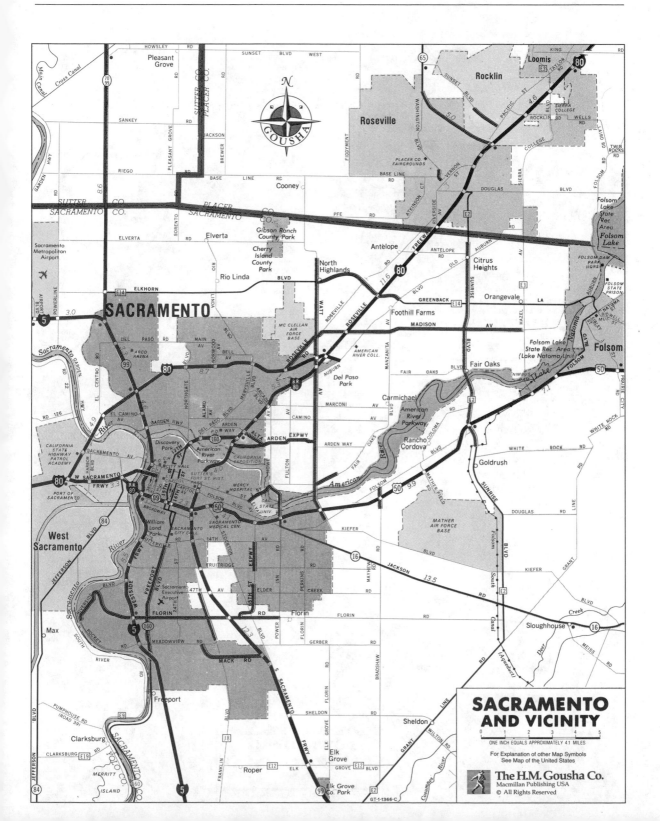

SACRAMENTO
AND VICINITY

0 1 2 3 4 5
ONE INCH EQUALS APPROXIMATELY 4.1 MILES

For Explanation of other Map Symbols
See Map of the United States

The H.M. Gousha Co.
Macmillan Publishing USA
© All Rights Reserved

GT-1-1366-C

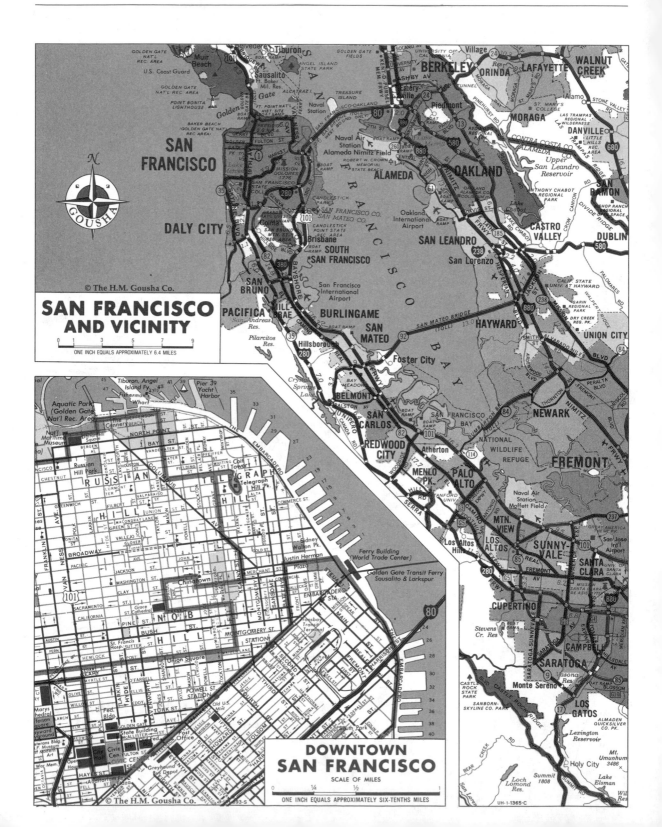

SAN FRANCISCO AND VICINITY

© The H.M. Gousha Co.

0 1 3 5 7 9

ONE INCH EQUALS APPROXIMATELY 6.4 MILES

DOWNTOWN SAN FRANCISCO

SCALE OF MILES

0   ¼   ½   1

ONE INCH EQUALS APPROXIMATELY SIX-TENTHS MILES

© The H.M. Gousha Co.

UH-1-1365-C

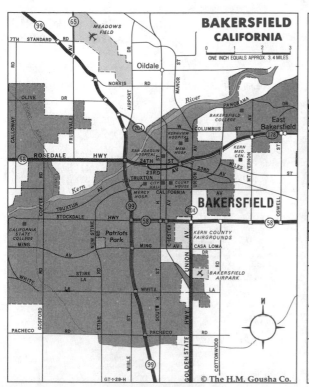

BAKERSFIELD
CALIFORNIA

ONE INCH EQUALS APPROX. 3.4 MILES

© The H.M. Gousha Co.

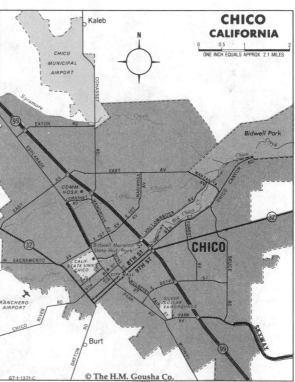

CHICO
CALIFORNIA

ONE INCH EQUALS APPROX. 2.1 MILES

© The H.M. Gousha Co.

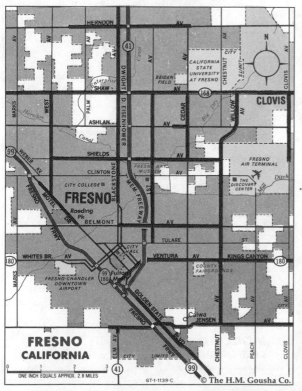

FRESNO
CALIFORNIA

ONE INCH EQUALS APPROX. 2.8 MILES

© The H.M. Gousha Co.

KINGS CANYON
AND SEQUOIA
NATIONAL PARKS
CALIFORNIA

ONE INCH EQUALS APPROX. 19.0 MILES

© The H.M. Gousha Co.

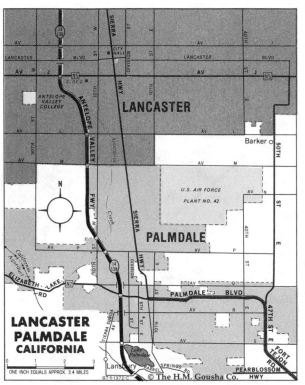

LANCASTER PALMDALE CALIFORNIA

ONE INCH EQUALS APPROX. 3.4 MILES

© The H.M. Gousha Co.

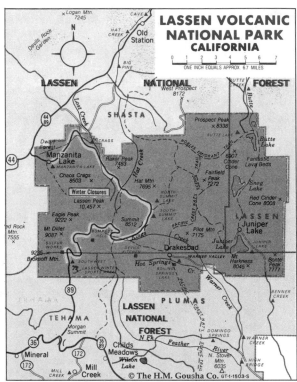

LASSEN VOLCANIC NATIONAL PARK CALIFORNIA

ONE INCH EQUALS APPROX. 6.7 MILES

© The H.M. Gousha Co.

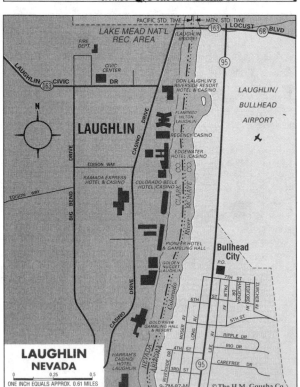

LAUGHLIN NEVADA

ONE INCH EQUALS APPROX. 0.61 MILES

© The H.M. Gousha Co.

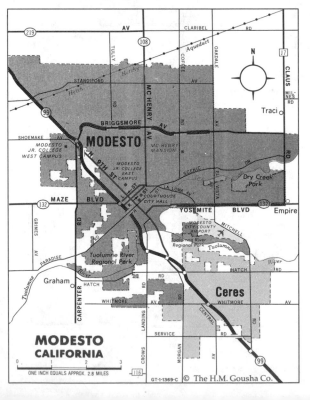

MODESTO CALIFORNIA

ONE INCH EQUALS APPROX. 2.8 MILES

© The H.M. Gousha Co.

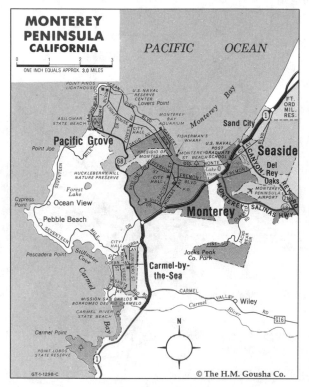

MONTEREY PENINSULA CALIFORNIA

ONE INCH EQUALS APPROX. 3.0 MILES

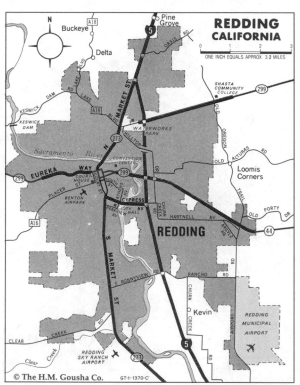

REDDING CALIFORNIA

ONE INCH EQUALS APPROX. 3.2 MILES

© The H.M. Gousha Co.

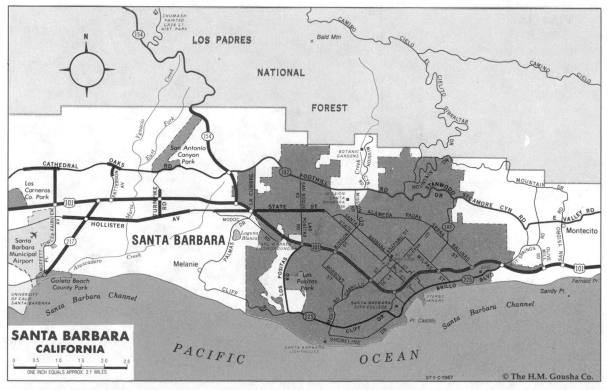

SANTA BARBARA CALIFORNIA

ONE INCH EQUALS APPROX. 2.1 MILES

© The H.M. Gousha Co.

SAN LUIS OBISPO
CALIFORNIA

ONE INCH EQUALS APPROX. 2.2 MILES

GT-1-1368-C   © The H.M. Gousha Co.

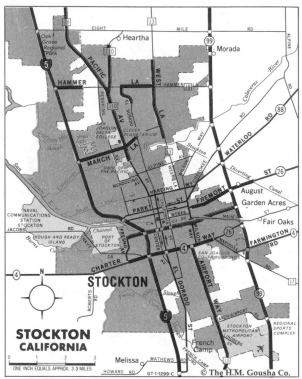

STOCKTON
CALIFORNIA

ONE INCH EQUALS APPROX. 3.3 MILES

GT-1-1299-C   © The H.M. Gousha Co.

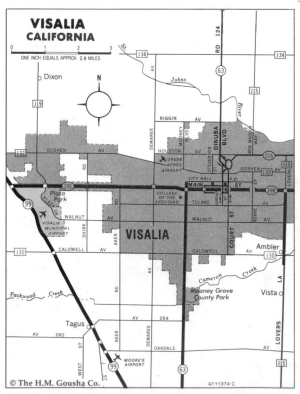

VISALIA
CALIFORNIA

ONE INCH EQUALS APPROX. 2.9 MILES

© The H.M. Gousha Co.   GT-1-1374-C

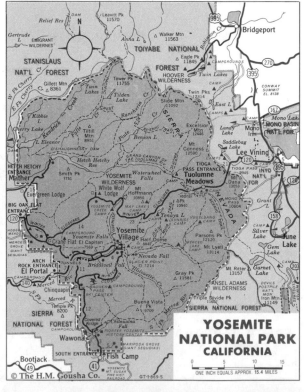

**YOSEMITE
NATIONAL PARK**
CALIFORNIA

ONE INCH EQUALS APPROX. 15.4 MILES

© The H.M. Gousha Co.   GT-1-869-S